# Psychological Testing and Assessment

*An Introduction to Tests and Measurement*

## EIGHTH EDITION

**Ronald Jay Cohen**
RJ COHEN CONSULTING

**Mark E. Swerdlik**
ILLINOIS STATE UNIVERSITY

**Edward D. Sturman**
STATE UNIVERSITY OF NEW YORK—PLATTSBURGH

**ONLINE LEARNING CENTER**
www.mhhe.com/cohentesting8

*Connect Learn Succeed*™

PSYCHOLOGICAL TESTING AND ASSESSMENT:
AN INTRODUCTION TO TESTS AND MEASUREMENT, EIGHTH EDITION

1  2  3  4  5  6  7  8  9  0  QDB/QDB  1  0  9  8  7  6  5  4  3  2

ISBN: 978-0-07-131827-3
MHID: 0-07-131827-5

www.mhhe.com

*This book is dedicated with love to the memory of Edith and Harold Cohen.*

# Contents

## PART II  *The Science of Psychological Measurement*

## 5   Reliability   145

PART **III**   *The Assessment of Intelligence*

# PART V  *Testing and Assessment in Action*

# Preface

In the late 1970s, when work first began on our introductory measurement text, there were only a few textbooks available on the subject of measurement in psychology. All of these books provided students with a basic grounding in psychometrics, but in our opinion none of them did a very satisfactory job of it. More specifically, these books all had a variety of shortcomings that really needed to addressed.

## Problems with the Available Measurement Textbooks

From our perspective, the available measurement textbooks had many problems:

- *Reading those books was a challenge.* The books seemed to us to be written for instructors to teach from. By contrast, we believed that such books should be written for students to learn from.

- *The authors of competing books had little or no actual experience in test administration and test interpretation.* The writing in the existing books was academic enough. However, the writing betrayed a total lack of any "hands-on," working knowledge of the subject matter. One might read the entire text, cover to cover, and never find a shred of evidence that the writer had ever administered a psychological test, personally interpreted findings from a test, or dealt face-to-face with an assessee (or any other interested party).

- *Coverage of certain key subject areas was nonexistent.* Today it's commonplace to cover topics such as legal/ethical issues in assessment, forensic assessment, neuropsychological assessment, and psychological assessment in business. But back in those days, any coverage of these topics in the existing measurement books was the exception rather than the rule. Cohen et al. pioneered such coverage, and Cohen et al. continued to lead the way in standard-setting coverage in other areas such as culture-related issues in assessment. As late as the previous (seventh) edition of our text, we introduced a chapter on the subject of test utility—this at a time when most other competing textbooks did not even list the terms *utility* or *test utility* in their subject index.

- *The other books contained way too much description of tests.* Granted, a book on the subject of testing must contain a description of some tests. However, back then, portions of existing texts were as replete with descriptions of tests as *Tests in Print*.

- *The art program in those books did not adequately support what was written.* What passed for an art program in the books that existed at the time was some number-intensive graphs and tables, as well as some photos of test materials. Photos seemed to be inserted more to break up text than to complement it. By contrast, we believed that supplemental art could be effectively used to reinforce learning. More specifically, it could be used to stimulate the reader's imagination and help solidify meaningful visual associations to the text.

- *Coverage of the heritage and history of the assessment enterprise was scant.* In the books that existed prior to the publication of our own, little or no effort was made to convey a sense of how all of the facts being presented fit within the grand scheme or context of the subject matter. Tests of intelligence were presented with little or no discussion of what was meant by *intelligence*. Tests of personality were presented with little or no discussion of what was meant by *personality*. By contrast, we would make an effort to place such material not only in a historical context, but in a logical context. Our appreciation for the importance of history and context is emphasized by the fact that the first feature readers are greeted by as they open our book—as well as the last feature they may see before closing it—is a listing of noteworthy historical landmarks set within the front and back covers of our book.

- *Books existing at the time made implicit assumptions—not true in all cases—about the level of preparation students had coming in to a measurement course.* All of the measurement textbooks that came before Cohen et al. were written based on the assumption that every student taking the course was up to speed on all of the statistical concepts that would be necessary to build on learning about psychometrics. In theory, at least, there was no reason not to assume this; statistics was a prerequisite to taking testing. In practice, a different picture emerged. It was simply not the case that all students were adequately and equally prepared to begin learning statistics-based measurement concepts. Our remedy for this problem was to include a "Statistics Refresher" chapter early on, just prior to building on students' statistics-based knowledge.

## Our Vision for a New Generation of Students

We envisioned something better for students who would be using our book, and for the succeeding generations of students. At a minimum, our book would impart a sound grounding in basic psychometrics, as well as all that was minimally necessary for students to achieve a clear conceptual understanding of the assessment enterprise. We would strive to present material in meaningful—even familiar, when possible—contexts. This meant that an unprecedented effort would be made to "breathe life" into all of the numbers, equations, models, and other statistics-related material. Features like *Everyday Psychometrics* and *Close-Ups* helped in this objective, as did subsequent pedagogical aids such as *Meet an Assessment Professional*. Further, we envisioned:

- *a book that students could read easily and learn from.* Not only would our book be one that was easy for instructors to teach from, it would be one that students could read (dare we say even *enjoy* reading?). We attempted to accomplish this most challenging goal by working hard to make the content and the writing as engaging as possible. We introduced concepts and terminology in an orderly way, building on subject matter already presented. Throughout, we tried to maintain a level of writing that was scholarly, engaging, and easily managed by most students.

- *a book that would convey to students the "feel" of actually working with tools of assessment.* It was important to us that this textbook convey something of the "hands-on feel" of actually using psychological tests. In contrast to many of the people writing textbooks about testing and assessment when our book was first published—and still true today—our authorship team has a great deal of experience in administering, scoring, and interpreting tests in clinical, counseling, school, research, and business-related contexts. We felt that students could profit from our sharing of this experience. In recent editions, this vision has also been supported by introducing students to other "real life" test users in each chapter's *Meet an Assessment Professional* feature.

- **a book that would provide students with a working overview of relevant legal and ethical issues in psychological testing and assessment.** Students taking an overview course in measurement should have a solid grounding in legal/ethical issues pertinent to the assessment enterprise. Accordingly, discussion of legal/ethical issues, which sets a context for all that follows, was placed early on in the book (Chapter 2), rather than at the end of the book (where it was, and still is, in the organization of some competing textbooks).

- **a book that would provide students with an overview of areas where tools of assessment are employed.** A clear need existed for coverage of various applied areas of test use (such as neuropsychological and forensic applications), and this type of material broke new ground in our first edition, and has continued to evolve with changes in applications of assessment ever since.

- **a book that contained meaningful and useful illustrations.** Our view is and has been that illustrations need to supplement learning, strengthen associations, entertain, and help "humanize" the material being presented.

## More About This Book's Heritage

Our book was originally published by a small, independent publisher. To give the reader an idea of how small that publisher was, the company had a sales force of about five people (which included the president of the company and the acquisitions editor who acquired the book). By comparison, the existing books were published by publishers with sales forces of over 100 dedicated sales people. The "marketing" of the first edition of our book consisted of the publisher buying a list of instructors who taught a measurement course and then sending out a sample copy of the book to everyone on that list.

It did not take a huge marketing campaign on the part of this small publisher to make this book a hit among instructors and their students. One after another, in one unsolicited letter after another, instructors voiced appreciation for our perspective on the discipline, our organization of topics, our selection of subject matter to be covered, and our lucid presentation of the material. By the time we began work on the second edition, our textbook was the one that was being emulated by all of the others. It still is.

Today, coverage of many of the topics we first deemed to be essential in a measurement text is now "standard" in measurement textbooks. We assure you that such material—a statistics refresher, coverage of behavioral assessment, coverage of legal and ethical issues, and so on—were by no means standard when the first edition of our book was published.

## The Organization of This Book and Related Variables

Textbook authors—past as well as present—are confronted with many choices, especially regarding variables related to presentation of the material, such as *organization* of topic areas, *content* selected, *art* used to supplement the text, *pedagogical tools* to reinforce learning, and the *writing style* or *voice* used to "speak to" readers. We believe these variables are all critically important vis-à-vis how much students ultimately take away from the textbook they are assigned. Let's briefly consider each of these areas and the choices that textbook authors have to make with respect to them.

## Organization

From the first edition of our book forward, we have organized the information to be presented into five major sections. We have no illusions that this organization will reach the iconic status of another "big five," but this organization has been proven to work well for both students and instructors alike. Part I, *An Overview*, contains two chapters that do just that. Chapter 1 provides a comprehensive overview of the field, including some important definitional issues, a general description of tools of assessment, and related important information couched as answers to questions regarding the *who, what, why, how,* and *where* of the enterprise.

The foundation for the material to come continues to be laid in the second chapter of the overview, which deals with historical, cultural, and legal/ethical issues. The material presented in Chapter 2 clearly sets a context for everything that will follow. To relegate such material to the back of the book (as a kind of elective topic, much like the way that legal/ethical issues are treated in some books), or to ignore presentation of such material altogether (as most other books have done with regard to cultural issues in assessment), is, in our estimation, a grave error. "Back page infrequency" (to borrow an MMPI-2 term) is too often the norm, and relegation of this critically important information to the back pages of a textbook too often translates to a potential shortchanging of students with regard to key cultural, historical, and legal/ethical information.

Part II, *The Science of Psychological Measurement*, contains Chapters 3 through 8. These six chapters were designed to build—logically and sequentially—on the student's knowledge of psychometric principles. Part II begins with a chapter reviewing basic statistical principles and ends with a chapter on test construction. In between, there is extensive discussion of assumptions inherent in the enterprise, the elements of good test construction, as well as the concepts of norms, correlation, inference, reliability, and validity. In Chapter 7, entitled, "Utility," readers will find information they need to know about this important concept, including the many factors that can affect a test's utility. The Chapter 7 *Close-Up* provides a step-by-step, informative illustration of a hypothetical utility analysis. Students will come away from this chapter with a working knowledge of not only what utility is, but how an index of utility is derived.

Let's note here that topics such as utility and utility analysis can get extremely complicated. However, we have never shied away from the presentation of complicated subject matter. For example, we were the first introductory textbook to present detailed information related to factor analysis. As more commercial publishers and other test users have adopted the use of item response theory (IRT) in test construction, our coverage of IRT has kept pace. As more test reviews have begun to evaluate tests not only in terms of variables such as reliability and validity but in terms of *utility*, we saw a need for the inclusion of a chapter on that topic. By the way, we could find no comparable coverage—nor any reference at all, for that matter, to *utility* or *test utility*—in any competing textbook at the time we decided to devote a chapter to that subject.

Of course, no matter how "difficult" the concepts we present are, we never for a moment lose sight of the appropriate level of presentation, or who the students are who have been assigned our text. This book is designed for students taking a first course in psychological testing and assessment. Our objective in presenting material on methods such as IRT and utility analysis is simply to acquaint the introductory student with these techniques. The depth of the presentation in these and other areas has always been guided and informed by extensive reviews from a geographically diverse sampling of instructors who teach measurement courses. For users of this textbook, what currently tends to be required is a conceptual understanding of commonly used IRT methods. We believe our presentation of this material effectively conveys such an understanding. Moreover, it does so without unnecessarily burdening students with level-inappropriate formulas and calculations.

Part III of this book, *The Assessment of Intelligence*, contains three chapters, two that deal with the concept of intelligence and tests of intelligence, and a third chapter that deals more generally with school-related assessments. Readers will find that Chapter 11 presents a most informative, updated discussion of the response to intervention (RtI) approach to diagnosing learning abilities.

Part IV, *The Assessment of Personality*, contains two chapters, which respectively overview how personality assessments are conducted, and the various methods used.

Part V, *Testing and Assessment in Action*, is designed to convey to students a sense of how tests and other tools of assessment are actually used in clinical, counseling, business, and other settings. Instructors who teach from Chapter 15 (Neuropsychological Assessment) will be pleased to find updated material on *f*MRI as a tool of assessment.

On occasion we have recognized the need to reorganize material. If such reorganization better serves the interest of a logical presentation of material, we will implement it without hesitation. In this edition, for example, instructors who have used previous editions will notice that the coverage of correlation, formerly in Chapter 4, has been moved to Chapter 3. This change in the organization of material was prompted by a persuasive suggestion made by an instructor who teaches an undergraduate measurement course.

## Content

In addition to a logical organization that sequentially builds on student learning, we view *content* selection as another key element of our appeal. The multifaceted nature and complexity of the discipline affords textbook authors wide latitude in terms of what material to elaborate on, what material to ignore, and what material to highlight, exemplify, or illustrate. We take full advantage of the wide range of choices available and include not only what students *must* know, but what students (and instructors) might *like* to know as well. As such, we pepper the text with sometimes unexpected, intriguing facts and perspectives. Our objective here has always been to enhance the memorability of the material, while enriching students' appreciation for it.

So, for example, in the context of discussing projective techniques, students are introduced to one (surprising) pioneer in projective testing, B. F. Skinner (yes, *that* B. F. Skinner!). In Chapter 12, students are privy to an "inside look" at the detention center at Guantanamo Bay, Cuba, through the eyes of a consulting psychologist. In the *Close-Up* in Chapter 2, we introduce students to the fascinating but controversial life and times of Henry Herbert Goddard. How many of us knew (or could ever imagine) that the first coach of the University of Southern California (USC) football team was none other than H. H. Goddard?

And speaking of *Close-Ups*—the pedagogical tool employed in each chapter since the first edition to focus-in and supplement knowledge on a particular assessment-related topic—we believe that students will find a wealth of useful information in the wide array of topics covered in our eighth-edition *Close-Ups*. For example, the *Close-Up* in Chapter 1 tackles the growing controversy regarding the issue of third-party presence during test administration. The Chapter 5 *Close-Up* introduces students to item response theory (IRT). In Chapter 12, the *Close-Up* presents timely material on measures of acculturation.

## The Art Program

Complementing a judicious selection of manuscript content is an equally thoughtful (and thought-provoking) selection of illustrations. See, for example, the series of photos used to illustrate a computer-assisted method of quantifying back stress (Chapter 1), the turn-of-the-century photo of the immigrants being tested at Ellis Island (Chapter 2), and the dramatic photo capturing hockey violence in the context of discussion of the trait of aggression and a questionnaire designed to measure that trait (Chapter 12). In the world of textbooks, such photos may not seem very revolutionary. And maybe they are not. However, in the world of *measurement* textbooks, our innovative art program was indeed revolutionary (and by all accounts, still is). In some instances, figures have been used to pay homage to some very well-known (as well as some not-so-well-known) contributors to the field (such as L. L. Thurstone and Lev Vygotsky), as well as more contemporary psychologists (such as John L. Holland and John E. Exner) who have recently left us.

## Pedagogical Tools

The objective of incorporating timely, relevant, and intriguing illustrations of assessment-related material is furthered by several *pedagogical tools* built into the text. We have already made reference to our strategic use of *Close-Ups*. Another pedagogical tool we innovated seven editions ago is *Everyday Psychometrics*. In each chapter of the book, relevant, practical, and "everyday" examples of the material being discussed are highlighted in an *Everyday Psychometrics* box. For example, in the *Everyday Psychometrics* presented in Chapter 1 ("Everyday Accommodations"), students will be introduced to accommodations made in the testing of persons with handicapping conditions. In Chapter 4, the *Everyday Psychometrics* feature ("Putting Tests to the Test") equips students with a working overview of the variables they need to be thinking about when reading about a test and evaluating how satisfactory the test really is for a particular purpose. In Chapter 5, the subject of the *Everyday Psychometrics* is the reliability of the instrumentation used by law enforcement authorities to measure alcoholic intoxication.

A pedagogical tool called *Meet an Assessment Professional* was introduced in the previous (seventh) edition. This feature provides a forum through which everyday users of psychological tests from various fields can share insights, experiences, and advice with students. The result is that in each chapter of our book, students are introduced to a different test user and provided with an intriguing glimpse of their professional life—this in the form of an excerpt from their *Meet and Assessment Professional (MAP)* essay. *MAP* essays in their entirety are presented on our companion instructional website: www.mcgrawhill.com/cohentesting8, which, by the way, also contains a wealth of other course-enhancing, assessment-related information for students.

Beyond introducing students to accomplished test users who are earning a living doing assessment-related work, each *MAP* essay serves to underscore the practical value of learning about psychological tests. For example, in Chapter 4, students will meet a team of test users, Drs. Steve Julius and Howard Atlas, who have pressed psychometric knowledge into the service of professional sports. They provide a unique and fascinating account of how application of their knowledge of was used to improve the on-court of achievement of the Chicago Bulls. New to this edition are *MAP* essays from Stephen Finn, the well-known proponent of therapeutic assessment (Chapter 1);

Nathaniel Mohatt, a valued contributor in the area of cultural issues in assessment (Chapter 2); Benoît Verdon, a French clinical psychologist (Chapter 3); Eliane Hack, a working school psychologist (Chapter 11); Anthony Bram, an independent practitioner who is also a clinical instructor at Harvard Medical School (Chapter 13); Joel Goldberg, an independent practitioner who is Director of Clinical Training at York University's Department of Psychology (Chapter 14); Jeanne Ryan, a practicing neuropsychologist who is Clinical Director at the Neuropsychology Clinic at State University of New York at Plattsburgh (Chapter 15); and Chris Gee, a corporate psychologist who is Director of Research Services at the Self Management Group (Chapter 16).

There are other pedagogical tools that readers (as well as other textbook authors) may take for granted—but we do not. Consider, in this context, the various tables and figures found in every chapter. In addition to their more traditional use, we view tables as space-saving devices in which a lot of information may be presented. For example, in the first chapter alone, tables are used to provide succinct but meaningful comparisons between *testing* and *assessment*, the *pros* and *cons* of computer-assisted psychological assessment, and the *pros* and *cons* of using various sources of information about tests.

*Critical thinking* may be defined as "the active employment of judgment capabilities and evaluative skills in the thought process" (Cohen, 1994, p. 12). *Generative thinking* may be defined as "the goal-oriented intellectual production of new or creative ideas" (Cohen, 1994, p. 13). The exercise of both of these processes, we believe, helps optimize one's chances for success in the academic world as well as in more applied pursuits. In the early editions of this textbook, questions designed to stimulate critical and generative thinking were raised "the old-fashioned way." That is, they were right in the text, and usually part of a paragraph. Acting on the advice of reviewers, we made this special feature of our writing even more special in the sixth edition of this book; we raised these critical thinking questions in the margins with a *Just Think* heading. Perhaps with some encouragement from their instructors, motivated students will, in fact, give thoughtful consideration to these (critical and generative thought-provoking) *Just Think* questions.

In addition to critical thinking and generative thinking questions called out in the text, other pedagogical aids in this book include original cartoons created by the authors, original illustrations created by the authors (including the model of memory in Chapter 15), and original acronyms created by the authors.[1] Each chapter ends with a *Self-Assessment* feature that students may use to test themselves with respect to key terms and concepts presented in the text. By the way, many of the same terms listed in the *Self-Assessment* exercise are used as the response keyed correct in the corresponding crossword puzzles presented for student distribution in this text's companion website.

## Writing Style

What type of *writing style* or author *voice* works best with students being introduced to the field of psychological testing and assessment? Instructors familiar with the many measurement books that have come (and gone) may agree with us that the "voice" of too many authors in this area might best be characterized as humorless and academic to

---

1. By the way, our use of the French word for black (*noir*) as an acronym for levels of measurement (nominal, ordinal, interval, and ratio) now appears in other textbooks. So if, as they say, "imitation is the sincerest form of flattery," we'll use this occasion to express our gratitude to fellow textbook authors for paying us their highest compliments.

the point of arrogance or pomposity. Students do not tend to respond well to textbooks written in such styles, and their eagerness and willingness to spend study time with these authors (and even their satisfaction with the course as a whole) may easily suffer as a consequence.

In a writing style that could be characterized as somewhat informal and—to the extent possible, given the medium and particular subject being covered—"conversational," we have made every effort to convey the material to be presented as clearly as humanly possible. In practice, this means:

- keeping the vocabulary of the presentation appropriate (without ever "dumbing-down" or trivializing the material);
- presenting so-called difficult material in step-by-step fashion where appropriate, and always preparing students for its presentation by placing it in an understandable context;
- italicizing the first use of a key word or phrase and then bolding it when a formal definition is given;
- providing a relatively large glossary of terms to which students can refer;
- supplementing material where appropriate with visual aids, tables, or other illustrations.
- incorporating timely, relevant, and intriguing illustrations of assessment-related material in the text as well as in the online materials.

In addition, we have interspersed some elements of humor in various forms (original cartoons, illustrations, and vignettes) throughout the text. The judicious use of humor to engage and maintain student interest is something of a novelty among measurement textbooks. Where else would one turn for pedagogy that employs an example involving a bimodal distribution of test scores from a new trade school called *The Home Study School of Elvis Presley Impersonators*? As readers learn about face validity, they discover why it "gets no respect" and how it has been characterized as "the Rodney Dangerfield of psychometric variables." Numerous other illustrations could be cited here. But let's reserve those smiles as a pleasant surprise when readers happen to come upon them.

Also in the interest of engaging and maintaining student interest, we do not hesitate to draw on popular culture for examples. *The X-Factor, Iron Chef, The Apprentice, South Park,* and *Survivor* are television shows that many students watch, and a surprise reference to one of them to illustrate an assessment-related point can pair pleasant feelings of recognition with learning—perhaps more solidly involving students in the material. In the course of learning how to write a good matching-type item, for example, students are challenged to identify what actors Pierce Brosnan, Sean Connery, Daniel Craig, Timothy Dalton, George Lazenby, David Niven, and Roger Moore all have in common.

## *"Humanization" of Material*

Perhaps our treatment of the discipline—and how radically different that treatment is from other textbooks on the subject—is best characterized by our dedicated and persistent efforts to *humanize* the presentation. While other authors in this discipline impress us as blindly intent on viewing the field as Greek letters to be understood and formulas to be memorized, we view an introduction to the field to be about *people* as much as anything else. Students are more motivated to learn this material when they can place it in a human context. Many psychology students simply do not respond well to endless presentations of psychometric concepts and formulas. In our opinion, to *not* bring a human face to the field of psychological testing and assessment, is to risk perpetuating all of those unpleasant (and now unfair) rumors about the course that first began circulating long before the time that the senior author himself was an undergraduate.

Our effort to humanize the material is evident in the various ways we have tried to bring a face (if not a helping voice) to the material. The inclusion of *Meet an Assessment Professional* (much like the *Test Developer Profiles* in past editions) is a means toward that end, as it quite literally "brings a face" to the enterprise. Our inclusion of interesting biographical facts on historical figures in assessment is also representative of efforts to humanize the material. Consider in this context the photo and brief biographical statement of MMPI-2 senior author James Butcher in Chapter 12 (p. 428). Whether through such images of historical personages or by other means, our objective has been made to truly involve students via intriguing, real-life illustrations of the material being discussed. See, for example:

- the discussion of life-or-death psychological assessment and the ethical issues involved (pp. 69–71)
- the intriguing hypotheses that have been advanced regarding the relationship between categorical cutoffs and human emotion (p. 8)
- the candid "confessions" of a behavior rater in the *Everyday Psychometrics* feature in Chapter 12 (pp. 477–478)
- the research that has been conducted linking life outcomes and personality to evaluations of college yearbook photos (p. 485)
- the discussion of the utility of tests to measure aggressiveness (p. 395) and dangerousness (pp. 513–514)
- the material on the use of tests by the military to select pilots and NASA to select astronauts (pp. 585–587)

We believe that assessment is, after all, a uniquely human, problem-solving enterprise in which data from a variety of tools (tests among them) is gathered, skillfully assimilated, and professionally interpreted. The process of assessment may be distinguished from, and contrasted with, the administration of tests. The latter process, otherwise known as *testing*, is one that may result simply in a test score; it can be, and often is, relatively mechanistic and devoid of any problem-solving efforts. In a bygone era, no distinction was made between the terms *testing* and *assessment*. Consequently, textbooks might be titled *Psychological Testing* even if, in substance, these books were actually much broader in scope (dealing with the use of various tools of assessment and the application of measurement principles). Today, to equate *testing* with *assessment* seems to us to be anachronistic. Moreover, such an equation confuses a problem-solving process that requires professional skill, knowledge of measurement theory, and knowledge of applicable legal, ethical, and cultural issues, with a process more akin to summing the number of responses keyed correct on an answer sheet.

So how has our "humanization" of the material in this discipline been received by some of its more "hard core" and "old school" practitioners? Very well, thank you—at least from all that we have heard, and the dozens of reviews that we have read over the years. What stands out prominently in my own mind was the reaction of one particular psychometrician whom I happened to meet at an APA convention not long after the first edition of this text was published. Lee J. Cronbach was quite animated as he shared with me his delight with the book, and how refreshingly different he thought that it was from anything comparable that had been published. I was so grateful to Lee for his encouragement, and felt so uplifted by that meeting, that I subsequently requested a photo from Lee for use in the second edition. The photo he sent was indeed published in the second edition of this book—this despite the fact that at that time, Lee had a measurement book that could be viewed as a direct competitor to ours. Regardless, I felt it was important not only to acknowledge Lee's esteemed place in measurement history, but to express my sincere gratitude in this way for his kind words and for what I perceived as his most valued "seal of approval."

## What Has Changed: New to This Edition

Of course, this eighth edition of *Psychological Testing and Assessment* has been thoroughly updated. It contains updated discussions of any instruments highlighted, as well as updated information about new test-related legislation, judicial decisions, and administrative regulations. Additionally, new and updated coverage is also presented on a wide variety of assessment-related topics, a small sampling of which would include the presentation of new material on: the new, fifth edition of the *Diagnostic and Statistical Manual of Mental Disorders (DSM-V)*; new neuropsychological tools such as the *f*MRI; response to intervention (RtI) as a measure for learning disabilities; Robert Sternberg's concept of *successful intelligence*; Maria Kozhevnikov's concept of *visual-object intelligence*; a new measure for evaluating the internal consistency of a test called the *average proportional distance* (developed by our own Eddy Sturman); historical information on assessment in ancient Egypt; conditions that might prompt a neuropsychological evaluation; and the utility of the nominal distinction between *objective* versus *projective* assessment.

We have expanded our discussions of the Flynn effect, the MMPI-2, the timeline followback (TLFB) method in behavioral assessment, competency to stand trial, systematic versus random error in measurement, test validation strategies, classical test theory as contrasted to item response theory, nature versus nurture as factors in measured intelligence, and the purpose of educational assessment within the context of current legislation. In addition, instructors who have used previous editions will find many more "Just Thinks" to engage students, as well as more glossary terms (and corresponding "Self-Assessment" terms) added as pedagogical tools.

## What Has Not Changed

We have written at length about how this book was conceived, and how it has changed over time. What has *not* changed and what will not change is our dedicated resolve to provide a leading-edge, much-emulated-but-never-duplicated, measurement textbook that

- "speaks to" students with an author voice that humanizes the discipline, making it all the more understandable;
- introduces students to the assessment enterprise and overviews the wide range of instruments and procedures they may encounter;
- familiarizes students with the reasoning behind the construction of tests and the rationale of various approaches to assessment;
- leaves students with a sense of what constitutes the appropriate uses of tests and the various legal and ethical issues involved;
- leaves students with a sense of what constitutes the appropriate and inappropriate uses of tests;

- compels students to think critically, generatively, and actively about issues related to testing and assessment; and,
- provides instructors with a text that has timely, new elements in each edition, and a classroom-proven package of ancillaries (including a new eighth-edition *Instructor's Manual*, complete with a new and revised *Test Item Bank*), as well as intriguing supplementary material posted for students at our online learning center, www.mhhe.com/cohentesting8.

It took about 12 years from initial conception of this book to the publication of our first edition. History (in the form of user reviews) records that, for the most part, we "got it right." Consequently, we're not about to stop "getting it right" now.

## Meet the Authors

New to this edition is Edward Sturman, Ph.D., an Associate Professor of Psychology at the State University of New York, Plattsburgh. Dr. Sturman is the co-coordinator of the Psychology program at the Queensbury branch campus, where he has taught many courses, including a seminar in Psychological Assessment. Dr. Sturman has developed several psychological tests, including the Mood Disorders Insight Scale (MDIS) and the Involuntary Subordination Questionnaire (ISQ), which have been linked to the course and outcome of mood disorders. He has also conducted research into the assessment of competency and developed a new method to evaluate the reliability of tests. His research findings have been published in well-regarded psychological journals and presented at major psychological conferences. Prior to his current teaching position, Dr. Sturman worked at the Self-Management Group as a consultant investigating the link between personality and performance in competitive environments, including sales and management positions at large corporations. His current research is primarily focused on the vulnerability of various personality styles to mental disorder as well as the evolutionary underpinnings of mental disorder. Dr. Sturman thanks his students, and in particular, Michelle Mann-Saumier, Kylie McKeighan, Joyalina David, Jeff Merrigan, and Jennifer Burch Dean for their work on his contribution to this book.

Mark E. Swerdlik, Ph.D., ABPP, is Professor of Psychology at Illinois State University, where he has taught the undergraduate psychological measurement course, conducted professional seminars addressing legal/ethical issues in assessment, and supervised practicum students in assessment. He has served as an editorial board member of several journals, written test reviews for several journals, reviewed test-scoring software for a major test publisher, and served as a reviewer for the *Mental Measurements Yearbook*. In various professional capacities, he has participated in the standardization of many psychological tests, including, for example, the WISC-R, the WISC-III, the Kaufman Assessment Battery for Children (K-ABC), the Stanford-Binet IV, the Peabody Picture Vocabulary Test (PPVT), the Kaufman Test of Educational Achievement, the Vineland Adaptive Behavior Scale, the Psychological Processing Checklist (PPC), and the Psychological Processing Checklist-Revised (PPC-R). As a licensed clinical psychologist, a nationally certified school psychologist, independent practitioner, and consultant, Dr. Swerdlik administers and interprets psychological tests, and conducts seminars to train fellow professionals in proper test administration, scoring, and interpretation procedures. He has also served as a program evaluator for many programs, a partial listing of which would include the Heart of Illinois Low Incidence Association (HILA), the Autism/Pervasive Developmental Delays Training and Technical Assistance Project, and the Illinois National Guard Statewide Reintegration Program for Combat Veterans (for veterans who served in Iraq and Afghanistan, from 2006 to the present).

Ronald Jay Cohen, Ph.D., ABPP, is a Diplomate of the American Board of Professional Psychology in Clinical Psychology, and a Diplomate of the American Board of Assessment Psychology (ABAP). He is a New York State licensed psychologist, and a "scientist-practitioner" and "scholar-professional" in the finest traditions of each of those terms. During a long and gratifying professional career in which he has published numerous journal articles and books, Dr. Cohen has had the privilege of personally working alongside some of the luminaries in the field of psychological assessment, including David Wechsler (while Cohen was a clinical psychology intern at Bellevue Psychiatric Hospital in New York City) and Doug Bray (while working as an assessor for AT&T in its Management Progress Study). After serving his clinical psychology internship at Bellevue, Dr. Cohen was appointed Senior Psychologist there, and his clinical duties entailed not only psychological assessment but the supervision and training of others in this enterprise. Subsequently, as an independent practitioner in the New York City area, Dr. Cohen taught various courses at local universities on an adjunct basis, including undergraduate and graduate courses in psychological assessment. Asked by a colleague to conduct a qualitative research study for an advertising agency, Dr. Cohen would quickly become a sought-after qualitative research consultant with a client list of major companies and organizations—among them Paramount Pictures, Columbia Pictures, NBC Television, the Campbell Soup Company, Educational Testing Service, and the College Board. Dr. Cohen's approach to qualitative research, referred to by him as *dimensional qualitative research*, has been emulated and written about by qualitative researchers around the world. Working as a consultant to one major company that wanted to learn more about its corporate culture, Dr. Cohen developed the Discussion of Organizational Culture (a qualitative research instrument discussed in Chapter 16). It was Dr. Cohen's work in the area of qualitative assessment that led him to found the scholarly journal *Psychology & Marketing*, which in 2012 celebrated some 30 years of consecutive publishing with Dr. Cohen as editor-in-chief.

## Thanks

The authors have been focused and diligent in their efforts to bring you a leading-edge measurement textbook that involves students in the subject matter and imparts a wealth of academic and applied information essential to understanding psychological testing and assessment. Of course, there are a number of people who must be thanked for helping to make this eighth edition the exciting and fresh revision that it is. Professor Jennifer Kisamore of the University of Oklahoma wrote the early drafts of the chapter on test utility as well as early drafts of the corresponding chapter in the instructor's manual for the previous edition of this book. Dr. Bryce Reeve of the National Institutes of Health wrote the *Meet an Assessment Professional* essay for Chapter 5. We were so intrigued by his recounting of his "real life" use of item response theory (IRT) that we asked him to expand his contribution in the form of the *Close-Up* that is also presented in that chapter. Let's take this opportunity to thank each and every one of the 17 professionals who wrote intriguing, often inspiring, *Meet an Assessment Professional* essays, one for each chapter in this book.[2] Thanks are also due Susan Cohen, the senior author's wife,

---

2. There are 16 chapters in the book but 17 *Meet an Assessment Professional* contributors. How did this happen? Two sports psychologists to the Chicago Bulls who collaborated on their essay for Chapter 4 "came as a team."

who helped in the creation of the chapter-by-chapter crossword puzzles presented on this text's companion website, and Ramya Thirumavalavan for her skillful production editing. Thanks also to all of the reviewers who supplied helpful input:

Wendy Dunn, *Coe College*

Jameson Hirsch, *East Tennessee State University*

Sharon Rae Jenkins, *University of North Texas*

Jeff Maney, *Midwestern University*

Kerry Schwanz, *Coastal Carolina University*

Noam Shpancer, *Otterbein College*

Brian Carey Sims, *North Carolina A&T State University*

Randi Smith, *Metropolitan State College of Denver*

Of course, the present authorship team has sole responsibility for all material in this eighth edition, and we take complete responsibility for any possible errors that may have somehow found their way in to it.

## And on a Personal Note . . .

I think back to the time when we were just wrapping up work on the sixth edition of this book. At that time, I received the unexpected and most painful news that my mother had suffered a massive and fatal stroke. It is impossible to express the sense of sadness and loss experienced by myself, my brother, and my sister, as well as the countless other people who knew this gentle, loving, and much-loved person. To this day, we continue to miss her counsel, her sense of humor, and just knowing that she's there for us. We continue to miss her genuine exhilaration, which in turn exhilarated us, and the image of her welcoming, outstretched arms whenever we came to visit. Her children were her life, and the memory of her smiling face, making each of us feel so special, survives as a private source of peace and comfort for us all. She always kept a copy of this book proudly displayed on her coffee table, and I am very sorry that a copy of more recent editions did not make it to that most special place. My dedication of this book is one small way I can meaningfully acknowledge her contribution, as well as that of my beloved, deceased father, to my personal growth. As in the sixth edition, I am using my parents' wedding photo in the dedication. They were so good together in life. And so there Mom is, reunited with Dad. Now, that is something that would make her very happy.

As the reader might imagine, given the depth and breadth of the material covered in this textbook, it requires great diligence and effort to create and periodically re-create an instructional tool such as this that is timely, informative, and readable. Thank you, again, to all of the people who have helped through the years. Of course, I could not do it myself were it not for the fact that even through eight editions, this truly Herculean undertaking remains a labor of love.

*Ronald Jay Cohen, Ph.D., ABPP*
*Diplomate, American Board of Professional Psychology (Clinical)*
*Diplomate, American Board of Assessment Psychology*

# 1

# Psychological Testing and Assessment

All fields of human endeavor use measurement in some form, and each field has its own set of measuring tools and measuring units. For example, if you're recently engaged or thinking about becoming engaged, you may have learned about a unit of measure called the carat. If you've been shopping for a computer, you may have learned something about a unit of measurement called a byte. As a student of psychological measurement, you need a working familiarity with some of the commonly used units of measure in psychology as well as knowledge of some of the many measuring tools employed. In the pages that follow, you will gain that knowledge as well as an acquaintance with the history of measurement in psychology and an understanding of its theoretical basis.

## Testing and Assessment

The roots of contemporary psychological testing and assessment can be found in early twentieth-century France. In 1905, Alfred Binet and a colleague published a test designed to help place Paris schoolchildren in appropriate classes. Binet's test would have consequences well beyond the Paris school district. Within a decade an English-language version of Binet's test was prepared for use in schools in the United States. When the United States declared war on Germany and entered World War I in 1917, the military needed a way to screen large numbers of recruits quickly for intellectual and emotional problems. Psychological testing provided this methodology. During World War II the military would depend even more on psychological tests to screen recruits for service. Following the war, more and more tests purporting to measure an ever-widening array of psychological variables were developed and used. There were tests to measure not only intelligence but also personality, brain functioning, performance at work, and many other aspects of psychological and social functioning.

### Psychological Testing and Assessment Defined

The world's receptivity to Binet's test in the early twentieth century spawned not only more tests but more test developers, more test publishers, more test users, and the emergence of what, logically enough, has become known as a testing enterprise. "Testing" was the term used to refer to everything from the administration of a test (as in "Testing in progress") to the interpretation of a test score ("The testing indicated that . . ."). During World War I the term "testing" aptly described the group screening of thousands of military recruits. We suspect that it was then that the term gained a powerful foothold in the vocabulary of professionals and laypeople. The use of "testing" to denote everything from test administration to test interpretation can be found in postwar textbooks (such as Chapman, 1921; Hull, 1922; Spearman, 1927) as well as in various test-related writings for decades thereafter. However, by World War II a semantic distinction between testing and a more inclusive term, "assessment," began to emerge.

During World War II the U.S. Office of Strategic Services (OSS), a predecessor to today's Central Intelligence Agency (CIA), used a variety of procedures and measurement tools—psychological tests among them—in selecting military personnel for highly specialized positions involving espionage, intelligence gathering, and the like. For example, one of the tools employed was a very uncomfortable, group-on-one interview technique to evaluate how well candidates might respond to Gestapo-like interrogation. With a light harshly pointed at their face, interviewees would have to draw on their own creativity, persuasive abilities, and other resources to satisfactorily defend and explain a given scenario to a group of increasingly hostile interviewers. Candidates might have to explain why they were in a particular building that was off-limits to them, and doing something that they were not authorized to do, such as looking at or removing classified files. Candidates were evaluated on a number of variables, such as their ability to maintain noncontradictory responses. Today, such an assessment method, or any assessment method that has potential for harming the persons being assessed, would be likely to raise serious ethical concerns.

As summarized in *Assessment of Men* (OSS Assessment Staff, 1948) and elsewhere (Murray & MacKinnon, 1946), the assessment data generated were subjected to thoughtful integration and evaluation by highly trained assessment center staff. The OSS model—using an innovative variety of evaluative tools along with data from the evaluations of highly trained assessors—would later inspire what is now referred to as the assessment center approach to personnel evaluation (Bray, 1982).

Military, clinical, educational, and business settings are but a few of the many contexts that entail behavioral observation and active integration by assessors of test scores and other data. In such situations, the term *assessment* may be preferable to *testing*. In contrast to testing, assessment acknowledges that tests are only one type of tool used by professional assessors (along with other tools, such as the interview), and that the value of a test, or of any other tool of assessment, is intimately linked to the knowledge, skill, and experience of the assessor.

The semantic distinction between psychological testing and psychological assessment is blurred in everyday conversation. Somewhat surprisingly, the distinction between the two terms still remains blurred in some published "psychological testing" textbooks. Yet the distinction is important. Society at large is best served by a clear definition of and differentiation between these two terms as well as related terms such as *psychological test user* and *psychological assessor*. Clear distinctions between such terms may also help avoid the turf wars now brewing between psychology professionals and members of other professions seeking to use various psychological tests. In many psychological evaluation contexts, conducting an assessment requires greater education, training, and skill than simply administering a test.

We define **psychological assessment** as the gathering and integration of psychology-related data for the purpose of making a psychological evaluation that is accomplished through the use of tools such as tests, interviews, case studies, behavioral observation, and specially designed apparatuses and measurement procedures. We define **psychological testing** as the process of measuring psychology-related variables by means of devices or procedures designed to obtain a sample of behavior. Some of the differences between these two processes are presented in Table 1–1.[1]

**JUST THINK . . .**

Describe a situation in which testing is more appropriate than assessment. By contrast, describe a situation in which assessment is more appropriate than testing.

**Table 1–1**
**Testing in Contrast to Assessment**

*In contrast to the process of administering, scoring, and interpreting psychological tests (psychological testing), psychological assessment may be conceived as a problem-solving process that can take many different forms. How psychological assessment proceeds depends on many factors, not the least of which is the reason for assessing. Different tools of evaluation—psychological tests among them—might be marshaled in the process of assessment, depending on the particular objectives, people, and circumstances involved as well as on other variables unique to the particular situation.*

*Admittedly, the line between what constitutes testing and what constitutes assessment is not always as clear as we might like it to be. However, by acknowledging that such ambiguity exists, we can work to sharpen our definition and use of these terms. It seems useful to distinguish the differences between testing and assessment in terms of the objective, process, and outcome of an evaluation and also in terms of the role and skill of the evaluator. Keep in mind that, although these are useful distinctions to consider, exceptions can always be found.*

| Testing | Assessment |
|---|---|
| *Objective* | |
| Typically, to obtain some gauge, usually numerical in nature, with regard to an ability or attribute. | Typically, to answer a referral question, solve a problem, or arrive at a decision through the use of tools of evaluation. |
| *Process* | |
| Testing may be individual or group in nature. After test administration, the tester will typically add up "the number of correct answers or the number of certain types of responses . . . with little if any regard for the how or mechanics of such content" (Maloney & Ward, 1976, p. 39). | Assessment is typically individualized. In contrast to testing, assessment more typically focuses on how an individual processes rather than simply the results of that processing. |
| *Role of Evaluator* | |
| The tester is not key to the process; practically speaking, one tester may be substituted for another tester without appreciably affecting the evaluation. | The assessor is key to the process of selecting tests and/or other tools of evaluation as well as in drawing conclusions from the entire evaluation. |
| *Skill of Evaluator* | |
| Testing typically requires technician-like skills in terms of administering and scoring a test as well as in interpreting a test result. | Assessment typically requires an educated selection of tools of evaluation, skill in evaluation, and thoughtful organization and integration of data. |
| *Outcome* | |
| Typically, testing yields a test score or series of test scores. | Typically, assessment entails a logical problem-solving approach that brings to bear many sources of data designed to shed light on a referral question. |

---

1. Especially when discussing general principles related to the creation of measurement procedures, as well as the creation, manipulation, or interpretation of data generated from such procedures, the word *test* (as well as related terms, such as *test score*) may be used in the broadest and most generic sense; that is, "test" may be used in shorthand fashion to apply to almost any procedure that entails measurement (including, for example, situational performance measures). Accordingly, when we speak of "test development" in Chapter 8, many of the principles set forth will apply to the development of other measurements that are not, strictly speaking, "tests" (such as situational performance measures, as well as other tools of assessment). Having said that, let's reemphasize that a real and meaningful distinction exists between the terms *psychological testing* and *psychological assessment,* and that effort should continually be made not to confuse the meaning of these two terms.

**The process of assessment**   In general, the process of assessment begins with a referral for assessment from a source such as a teacher, school psychologist, counselor, judge, clinician, or corporate human resources specialist. Typically one or more referral questions are put to the assessor about the assessee. Some examples of referral questions are: "Can this child function in a regular classroom?," "Is this defendant competent to stand trial?," and "How well can this employee be expected to perform if promoted to an executive position?"

The assessor may meet with the assessee or others before the formal assessment in order to clarify aspects of the reason for referral. The assessor prepares for the assessment by selecting the tools of assessment to be used. For example, if the assessment occurs in a corporate or military setting and the referral question concerns the assessee's leadership ability, the assessor may wish to employ a measure (or two) of leadership. Typically the assessor's own past experience, education, and training play a key role in the specific tests or other tools to be employed in the assessment. Sometimes an institution in which the assessment is taking place has prescribed guidelines for which instruments can and cannot be used. In most every assessment situation, particularly situations that are relatively novel to the assessor, the tool selection process may be informed by some research in preparation for the assessment. For example, in the assessment of leadership, the tool selection procedure might be informed by publications dealing with behavioral studies of leadership (Derue et al., 2011) psychological studies of leaders (Kouzes & Posner, 2007), cultural issues in leadership (Byrne & Bradley, 2007), or whatever aspect of leadership the assessment will be focused on (e.g., Carnevale et al., 2011; Elliott, 2011; Kalshoven et al., 2011).

**JUST THINK . . .**

What qualities makes a good leader? How might these qualities be measured?

Subsequent to the selection of the instruments or procedures to be employed, the formal assessment will begin. After the assessment, the assessor writes a report of the findings that is designed to answer the referral question. More feedback sessions with the assessee and/or interested third parties (such as the assessee's parents and the referring professional) may also be scheduled.

Different assessors may approach the assessment task in different ways. Some assessors approach the assessment with minimal input from assessees themselves. Other assessors view the process of assessment as more of a collaboration between the assessor and the assessee. For example, in one approach to assessment, referred to (logically enough) as **collaborative psychological assessment,** the assessor and assessee may work as "partners" from initial contact through final feedback (Finello, 2011; Fischer, 1978, 2004, 2006). One variety of collaborative assessment includes an element of therapy as part of the process. Stephen Finn and his colleagues (Finn, 2003, 2011; Finn & Martin, 1997; Finn & Tonsager, 2002) have described a collaborative approach to assessment called **therapeutic psychological assessment.** Here, therapeutic self-discovery and new understandings are encouraged throughout the assessment process. Learn more about this approach, and "say hello" to Dr. Stephen Finn himself, in this chapter's *Meet an Assessment Professional.* This feature was designed to help readers acquire a firsthand acquaintance with "real life" test use. In each chapter of this book, you will be introduced to a different test user, and a unique perspective on the assessment enterprise. All assessment professionals featured were asked to write an essay sharing their own thoughts and experiences. A brief excerpt of each essay is presented in each chapter, and the complete version of each essay is available online at *www.mhhe.com/cohentesting8.*

Another approach to assessment that seems to have picked up momentum in recent years, most notably in educational settings, is referred to as *dynamic assessment*

## Meet Dr. Stephen Finn

In Therapeutic Assessment, we use a variety of psychological instruments including tests of cognitive functioning (e.g., the WAIS-IV), self-report tests of personality and symptomatology (e.g., the MMPI-2-RF), and performance-based personality tests (e.g., the Rorschach). We select the tests we use based on our initial session with a client. In that meeting, we help clients formulate personalized "assessment questions" they wish to have answered, such as "Why do I have such a difficult time making eye contact?" or "Why have I never been able to have an intimate relationship?" We then select tests that will help address the clients' questions as well as those questions given to us by any referring professionals. For example, with the questions just mentioned, we might propose that a client take the MMPI-2-RF and the Rorschach, because our experience is that the combination of a self-report and performance-based personality test is helpful in helping us understand these types of issues. In our initial session, we would also collect comprehensive background information about the concerns reflected in the client's questions. For example, we would ask about when it is most difficult or easiest for the client to make eye contact, when this problem began, and what the client already has tried to address this problem. We would also ask about previous attempts to have intimate relationships.

We believe that at their best, psychological tests serve as "empathy magnifiers"—helping us to get "in our clients' shoes" and understand puzzles, quandaries, or stuck points in their lives that they have not been able to address in other ways. We administer tests in a standardized fashion early in our assessments, and find that the information they provide yields very useful hypotheses about why clients have the problems they do. Often, through our tests, we are able to help people understand puzzling, even self-destructive or off-putting behaviors that other mental health professionals have not been able to understand or ameliorate. And we consciously use tests to identify people's strengths as well as their struggles.

We involve clients as collaborators and "co-experimenters" during our testing sessions. For example, with the client mentioned above, we might discuss actual MMPI-2 items suggesting

**Stephen Finn, Ph.D., Founder, Center for Therapeutic Assessment, Austin, Texas.**

that the client felt worthless and ashamed. Or we might ask the client to think with us about the following Rorschach responses: "A bat that is flying with terribly damaged wings—I don't know how it's continuing to fly" and "A mangy dog—the kind no one would ever take home from the animal shelter." We might even ask the client to experiment in session with making more eye contact with the assessor, and to pay attention to what he or she feels. All of these interactions might lead to discussions about the client's feeling inadequate and ashamed, how such feelings came to be, and how this is all related to the client's assessment questions about making eye contact and having intimate relationships.

At the end of the assessment, we would show and talk to the client about the actual test scores, and we would discuss "next steps" the client could take to address the problems in living that were the focus of the assessment. Often a therapeutic assessment is a good entry into further psychological treatment . . .

*Read more of what Dr. Finn had to say—his complete essay—at www.mhhe.com/cohentesting8.*

(Poehner & van Compernolle, 2011). The term *dynamic* may suggest that a psychodynamic or psychoanalytic approach to assessment is being applied. However, that is not the case. As used in the present context, *dynamic* is used to describe the interactive, changing, or varying nature of the assessment. In general, **dynamic assessment** refers to an interactive approach to psychological assessment that usually follows a model of (1) evaluation, (2) intervention of some sort, and (3) evaluation. Dynamic assessment is most typically employed in educational settings, although it may be employed in correctional, corporate, neuropsychological, clinical, and most any other setting as well.

Intervention between evaluations, sometimes even between individual questions posed or tasks given, might take many different forms, depending upon the purpose of the dynamic assessment (Haywood & Lidz, 2007). For example, an assessor may intervene in the course of an evaluation of an assessee's abilities with increasingly more explicit feedback or hints. The purpose of the intervention may be to provide assistance with mastering the task at hand. Progress in mastering the same or similar tasks is then measured. In essence, dynamic assessment provides a means for evaluating how the assessee processes or benefits from some type of intervention (feedback, hints, instruction, therapy, and so forth) during the course of evaluation. In some educational contexts, dynamic assessment may be viewed as a way of measuring not just learning but "learning potential," or "learning how to learn" skills. Computers are one tool used to help meet the objectives of dynamic assessment (Wang, 2011). There are others . . .

## The Tools of Psychological Assessment

### The Test

A **test** may be defined simply as a measuring device or procedure. When the word *test* is prefaced with a modifier, it refers to a device or procedure designed to measure a variable related to that modifier. Consider, for example, the term *medical test*, which refers to a device or procedure designed to measure some variable related to the practice of medicine (including a wide range of tools and procedures, such as X-rays, blood tests, and testing of reflexes). In a like manner, the term **psychological test** refers to a device or procedure designed to measure variables related to psychology (for example, intelligence, personality, aptitude, interests, attitudes, or values). Whereas a medical test might involve analysis of a sample of blood, tissue, or the like, a psychological test almost always involves analysis of a sample of behavior. The behavior sample could range from responses to a pencil-and-paper questionnaire, to oral responses to questions related to the performance of some task. The behavior sample could be elicited by the stimulus of the test itself, or it could be naturally occurring behavior (observed by the assessor in real time as it occurs, or recorded).

Psychological tests and other tools of assessment may differ with respect to a number of variables, such as content, format, administration procedures, scoring and interpretation procedures, and technical quality. The *content* (subject matter) of the test will, of course, vary with the focus of the particular test. But even two psychological tests purporting to measure the same thing—for example, personality—may differ widely in item content. This is so because two test developers might have entirely different views regarding what is important in measuring "personality"; different test developers employ different definitions of "personality." Additionally, different test developers come to the test development process with different theoretical orientations. For example, items on a psychoanalytically oriented personality test may have little resemblance to those on a behaviorally oriented personality test, yet both are personality tests. A psychoanalytically oriented personality test might be chosen for use by a psychoanalytically oriented assessor, and an existentially oriented personality test might be chosen for use by an existentially oriented assessor.

The term **format** pertains to the form, plan, structure, arrangement, and layout of test items as well as to related considerations such as time limits. *Format* is also used to refer to the form in which a test is administered: computerized, pencil-and-paper, or some other form. When making specific reference to a computerized test, the format may also involve the form of the software: PC- or Mac-compatible. The term *format* is not confined to tests. *Format* is also used to denote the form or structure of other evaluative tools and processes, such as the guidelines for creating a portfolio work sample.

**JUST THINK . . .**

Imagine you wanted to develop a test for a personality trait you termed "goth." How would you define this trait? What kinds of items would you include in the test? Why would you include those kinds of items?

Tests differ in their *administration procedures*. Some tests, particularly those designed for administration on a one-to-one basis, may require an active and knowledgeable test administrator. The test administration may involve demonstration of various kinds of tasks demanded of the assessee, as well as trained observation of an assessee's performance. Alternatively, some tests, particularly those designed for administration to groups, may not even require the test administrator to be present while the testtakers independently complete the required tasks.

Tests differ in their *scoring and interpretation procedures*. To better understand how and why, let's define *score* and *scoring*. Sports enthusiasts are no strangers to these terms. For them, these terms refer to the number of points accumulated by competitors and the process of accumulating those points. In testing and assessment, we may formally define **score** as a code or summary statement, usually but not necessarily numerical in nature, that reflects an evaluation of performance on a test, task, interview, or some other sample of behavior. **Scoring** is the process of assigning such evaluative codes or statements to performance on tests, tasks, interviews, or other behavior samples. In the world of psychological assessment, many different types of scores exist. Some scores result from the simple summing of responses (such as the summing of correct/incorrect or agree/disagree responses), and some scores are derived from more elaborate procedures.

Scores themselves can be described and categorized in many different ways. For example, one type of score is the *cut score*. A **cut score** (also referred to as a *cutoff score* or simply a *cutoff*) is a reference point, usually numerical, derived by judgment and used to divide a set of data into two or more classifications. Some action will be taken or some inference will be made on the basis of these classifications. Cut scores on tests, usually in combination with other data, are used in schools in many contexts. For example, they may be used in grading, and in making decisions about the class or program to which children will be assigned. Cut scores are used by employers as aids to decision making about personnel hiring, placement, and advancement. State agencies use cut scores as aids in licensing decisions. There are probably more than a dozen different methods that can be used to formally derive cut scores (Dwyer, 1996). If you're curious about what some of those different methods are, stay tuned; we cover that in an upcoming chapter.

Sometimes no formal method is used to arrive at a cut score. Some teachers use an informal "eyeball" method to proclaim, for example, that a score of 65 or more on a test means "pass" and a score of 64 or below means "fail." Whether formally or informally derived, cut scores typically take into account, at least to some degree, the values of those who set them. Consider, for example, two teachers who teach the same course at the same college. One teacher might set a cut score for passing the course that is significantly higher (and more difficult for students to attain) than the other teacher. There is also another side to the human equation as it relates to cut scores, one that is seldom written about in measurement texts. This phenomenon concerns the emotional consequences of "not making the cut" and "just making the cut" (see Figure 1–1).

Tests differ widely in terms of their guidelines for scoring and interpretation. Some tests are self-scored by the testtakers themselves, others are scored by computer, and others require scoring by trained examiners. Some tests, such as most tests of intelligence, come with test manuals that are explicit not only about scoring criteria but also about the nature of the interpretations that can be made from the scores. Other tests, such as the Rorschach Inkblot Test, are sold with no manual at all. The (presumably qualified) purchaser buys the stimulus materials and then selects and uses one of many available guides for administration, scoring, and interpretation.

**Figure 1–1**
**Emotion Engendered by Categorical Cutoffs**

*People who just make some categorical cutoff may feel better about their accomplishment than those who make the cutoff by a substantial margin. But those who just miss the cutoff may feel worse than those who miss it by a substantial margin. Evidence consistent with this view was presented in research with Olympic athletes (Medvec et al., 1995; Medvec & Savitsky, 1997). Bronze medalists were—somewhat paradoxically—happier with the outcome than silver medalists. Bronze medalists might say to themselves "At least I won a medal" and be happy about it. By contrast, silver medalists might feel frustrated that they tried for the gold and missed winning it.*

Tests differ with respect to their **psychometric soundness** or technical quality. Synonymous with the antiquated term *psychometry*, **psychometrics** may be defined as the science of psychological measurement. Variants of these words include the adjective *psychometric* (which refers to measurement that is psychological in nature) and the nouns **psychometrist** and **psychometrician** (both terms referring to a professional who uses, analyzes, and interprets psychological test data). One speaks of the psychometric soundness of a test when referring to how consistently and how accurately a psychological test measures what it purports to measure. Assessment professionals also speak of the psychometric *utility* of a particular test or assessment method. In this context, **utility** refers to the usefulness or practical value that a test or other tool of assessment has for a particular purpose. These concepts are elaborated on in subsequent chapters. Now, returning to our discussion of tools of assessment, meet one well-known tool that, as they say, "needs no introduction."

**JUST THINK . . .**

How might one test of intelligence have more utility than another test of intelligence in the same school setting?

## The Interview

In everyday conversation, the word *interview* conjures images of face-to-face talk. But the interview as a tool of psychological assessment typically involves more than talk. If the interview is conducted face-to-face, then the interviewer is probably taking note of not only the content of what is said but also the way it is being said. More specifically, the interviewer is taking note of both verbal and nonverbal behavior. Nonverbal behavior may include the interviewee's "body language," movements, and facial expressions in response to the interviewer, the extent of eye contact, apparent willingness to cooperate, and general reaction to the demands of the interview. The interviewer may also take note of the way the interviewee is dressed. Here, variables such as neat versus sloppy, and appropriate versus inappropriate, may be noted.

Because of a potential wealth of nonverbal information to be gained, interviews are ideally conducted face-to-face. However, face-to-face contact is not always possible and interviews may be conducted in other formats. In an interview conducted by telephone, for example, the interviewer may still be able to gain information beyond the responses to questions by being sensitive to variables such as changes in the interviewee's voice pitch or the extent to which particular questions precipitate long pauses or signs of emotion in response. Of course, interviews need not involve verbalized speech, as when they are conducted in sign language. Interviews may also be conducted by various electronic means, as would be the case with online interviews, e-mail interviews, and interviews conducted by means of text messaging. In its broadest sense, then, we can define an **interview** as a method of gathering information through direct communication involving reciprocal exchange.

**JUST THINK . . .**

What type of interview situation would you envision as ideal for being carried out entirely through the medium of text messaging?

Interviews differ with regard to many variables, such as their purpose, length, and nature. Interviews may be used by psychologists in various specialty areas to help make diagnostic, treatment, selection, or other decisions. So, for example, school psychologists may use an interview to help make a decision about the appropriateness of various educational interventions or class placements. A court-appointed psychologist may use an interview to help guide the court in determining whether a defendant was insane at the time of a commission of a crime. A specialist in head injury may use an interview to help shed light on questions related to the extent of damage to the brain that was caused by the injury. A psychologist studying consumer behavior may use an interview to learn about the market for various products and services, as well as how best to advertise and promote them.

An interview may be used to help professionals in human resources to make more informed recommendations about the hiring, firing, and advancement of personnel. In some instances, what is called a **panel interview** (also referred to as a *board interview*) is employed. Here, more than one interviewer participates in the assessment. A presumed advantage of this personnel assessment technique is that any idiosyncratic biases of a lone interviewer will be minimized (Dipboye, 1992). A disadvantage of the panel interview relates to its utility; the cost of using multiple interviewers may not be justified (Dixon et al., 2002).

The popularity of the interview as a method of gathering information extends far beyond psychology. Just try to think of one day when you were not exposed to an interview on television, radio, or the Internet! Regardless of the medium through which it is conducted, an interview is a reciprocal affair in that the interviewee reacts to the interviewer and the interviewer reacts to the interviewee. The quality, if not the quantity, of useful information produced by an interview depends in no small part on the skills of the interviewer. Interviewers differ in many ways: their pacing of interviews, their rapport with interviewees, and their ability to convey genuineness, empathy, and humor. Keeping these differences firmly in mind, consider Figure 1–2. How might the distinctive personality attributes of these two celebrities affect responses of interviewees? Which of these two interviewers do you think is better at interviewing? Why?

**JUST THINK . . .**

What types of interviewing skills must the host of a talk show possess to be considered an effective interviewer? Do these skills differ from those needed by a professional in the field of psychological assessment? If so, how?

## The Portfolio

Students and professionals in many different fields of endeavor ranging from art to architecture keep files of their work products. These work products—whether retained on paper, canvas, film, video, audio, or some other medium—constitute what is called a **portfolio.** As samples of one's ability and accomplishment, a portfolio may be used as a tool of evaluation. Employers of commercial artists, for example, will make hiring decisions based, in part, on the impressiveness of an applicant's portfolio of sample drawings. As another example, consider the employers of on-air radio talent. They, too, will make hiring decisions that are based partly upon their judgments of audio samples of the candidate's previous work.

The appeal of portfolio assessment as a tool of evaluation extends to many other fields, including education. Some have argued, for example, that the best evaluation of a student's writing skills can be accomplished not by the administration of a test, but by asking the student to compile a selection of writing samples. Also in the field of education, portfolio assessment has been employed as a tool in the hiring of instructors. An instructor's portfolio may consist of various documents such as lesson plans, published writings, and visual aids

**JUST THINK . . .**

If you were to prepare a portfolio representing "who you are" in terms of your educational career, your hobbies, and your values, what would you include in your portfolio?

**Figure 1–2**
**On Interviewing and Being Interviewed**

*Different interviewers have different styles of interviewing. How would you characterize the interview style of Jay Leno as compared to that of Nancy Grace?*

developed expressly for teaching certain subjects. All of these materials can be extremely useful to those who must make hiring decisions.

## Case History Data

**Case history data** refers to records, transcripts, and other accounts in written, pictorial, or other form that preserve archival information, official and informal accounts, and other data and items relevant to an assessee. Case history data may include files or excerpts from files maintained at institutions and agencies such as schools, hospitals, employers, religious institutions, and criminal justice agencies. Other examples of case history data are letters and written correspondence, photos and family albums, newspaper and magazine clippings, and home videos, movies, and audiotapes. Work samples, artwork, doodlings, and accounts and pictures pertaining to interests and hobbies are yet other examples.

Case history data is a useful tool in a wide variety of assessment contexts. In a clinical evaluation, for example, case history data can shed light on an individual's past and current adjustment as well as on the events and circumstances that may have contributed to any changes in adjustment. Case history data can be of critical value in neuropsychological evaluations, where it often provides information about neuropsychological functioning prior to the occurrence of a trauma or other event that results in a deficit. School psychologists rely on case history data for insight into a student's current academic or behavioral standing. Case history data is also useful in making judgments concerning future class placements.

**Figure 1–3**
**Case Study of the "Groupthink" Phenomenon**

*According to* Victims of Groupthink, *a classic work by social psychologist Irving Janis (1972), decisions made by committee or groups may, in some cases, not be as sound as decisions made by individuals. This phenomenon, referred to as* **groupthink,** *arises as a result of the varied forces that may drive the decision-makers to reach a consensus (such as the motivation to compromise and to minimize conflicting views). Although such forces may result in agreement, they do not necessarily result in the optimal course of action. This issue of* Life *dated May 10, 1963, chronicled a failed invasion of Castro's Cuba at a southern inlet of that island called the Bay of Pigs. The "miscalculation" referred to on the cover of the magazine was, according to Janis, a case study of groupthink.*

The assembly of case history data, as well as related data, into an illustrative account is referred to by terms such as *case study* or *case history.* We may formally define a **case study** (or **case history**) as a report or illustrative account concerning a person or an event that was compiled on the basis of case history data. A case study might, for example, shed light on how one individual's personality and a particular set of environmental conditions combined to produce a successful world leader. A case study of an individual who attempted to assassinate a high-ranking political figure could shed light on what types of individuals and conditions might lead to similar attempts in the future. Work on a social psychological phenomenon referred to as *groupthink* contains rich case history material on collective decision making that did not always result in the best decisions (Janis, 1972; see Figure 1–3).

**JUST THINK . . .**

What are the pros and cons of using case history data as a tool of assessment?

## Behavioral Observation

If you want to know how someone behaves in a particular situation, observe his or her behavior in that situation. Such "down-home" wisdom underlies at least one approach to evaluation. **Behavioral observation,** as it is employed by assessment professionals, may be defined as monitoring the actions of others or oneself by visual or electronic means while recording quantitative and/or qualitative information regarding those actions. Behavioral observation is often used as a diagnostic aid in various settings such as inpatient facilities, behavioral research laboratories, and classrooms. Behavioral observation may be used for purposes of selection or placement in corporate or organizational settings. In such instances, behavioral observation may be used as an aid in identifying personnel who best demonstrate the abilities required to perform a particular task or job. Sometimes researchers venture outside of the confines of clinics, classrooms, workplaces, and research laboratories in order to observe behavior of humans in a natural setting—that is, the setting in which the behavior would typically be expected to occur. This variety of behavioral observation is referred to as **naturalistic observation.** So, for example, to study the socializing behavior of autistic children with same-age peers, one research team opted for natural settings rather than a controlled, laboratory environment (Bellini et al., 2007).

Behavioral observation as an aid to designing therapeutic intervention has proven to be extremely useful in institutional settings such as schools, hospitals, prisons, and group homes. Using published or self-constructed lists of targeted behaviors, staff can observe firsthand the behavior of individuals and design interventions accordingly. In a school situation, for example, naturalistic observation on the playground of a culturally different child suspected of having linguistic problems might reveal that the child does have English language skills but is unwilling—for reasons of shyness, cultural upbringing, or whatever—to demonstrate those abilities to adults.

**JUST THINK . . .**

What are the pros and cons of naturalistic observation as tools of assessment?

In practice, behavioral observation, and especially naturalistic observation, tends to be used most frequently by researchers in settings such as classrooms, clinics, prisons, and other types of facilities where observers have ready access to assessees. For private practitioners, it is typically not practical or economically feasible to spend hours out of the consulting room observing clients as they go about their daily lives. Still, there are some mental health professionals, such as those in the field of assisted living, who find great value in behavioral observation of patients outside of their institutional environment. For them, it may be necessary to accompany a patient outside of the institution's walls to learn if that patient is capable of independently performing activities of daily living. In this context, a tool of assessment that relies heavily on behavioral observation, such as the Test of Grocery Shopping Skills (see Figure 1–4), may be extremely useful.

**Figure 1–4**
**Price (and Judgment) Check in Aisle 5**

*Designed primarily for use with persons with psychiatric disorders, the context-based Test of Grocery Shopping Skills (Hamera & Brown, 2000) may be very useful in evaluating a skill necessary for independent living.*

## Role-Play Tests

**Role play** may be defined as acting an improvised or partially improvised part in a simulated situation. A **role-play test** is a tool of assessment wherein assessees are directed to act as if they were in a particular situation. Assessees may then be evaluated with regard to their expressed thoughts, behaviors, abilities, and other variables. (Note that *role play* is hyphenated when used as an adjective or a verb but not as a noun.)

Role play is useful in evaluating various skills. So, for example, grocery shopping skills (Figure 1–4) could conceivably be evaluated through role play. Depending upon how the task is set up, an actual trip to the supermarket could or could not be required. Of course, role play may not be as useful as "the real thing" in all situations. Still, role play is used quite extensively, especially in situations where it is too time-consuming, too expensive, or simply too inconvenient to assess in a real situation. So, for example, astronauts in training may be required to role-play many situations "as if" in outer space. Such "as if" scenarios for training purposes result in truly "astronomical" savings.

**JUST THINK . . .**

What are the pros and cons of role play as a tool of assessment? In your opinion, what type of presenting problem would be ideal for assessment by role play?

Individuals being evaluated in a corporate, industrial, organizational, or military context for managerial or leadership ability may routinely be placed in role-play situations. They may be asked, for example, to mediate a hypothetical dispute between personnel at a work site. The format of the role play could range from "live scenarios" with live actors, or computer-generated simulations. Outcome measures for such an assessment might include ratings related to various aspects of the individual's ability to resolve the conflict, such as effectiveness of approach, quality of resolution, and number of minutes to resolution.

Role play as a tool of assessment may be used in various clinical contexts. For example, it is routinely employed in many interventions with substance abusers. Clinicians may attempt to obtain a baseline measure of abuse, cravings, or coping skills by administering a role-play test prior to therapeutic intervention. The same test is then administered again subsequent to completion of treatment. Role play can thus be used as both a tool of assessment and a measure of outcome.

## Computers as Tools

We have already made reference to the role computers play in contemporary assessment in the context of generating simulations. They may also help in the measurement of variables that in the past were quite difficult to quantify (see Figure 1–5). But perhaps the more obvious role as a tool of assessment is their role in test administration, scoring, and interpretation.

As test administrators, computers do much more than replace the "equipment" that was so widely used in the past (a number 2 pencil). Computers can serve as test administrators (online or off) and as highly efficient test scorers. Within seconds they can derive not only test scores but patterns of test scores. Scoring may be done on-site (**local processing**) or conducted at some central location (**central processing**). If processing occurs at a central location, test-related data may be sent to and returned from this central facility by means of phone lines (**teleprocessing**), mail, or courier. Whether processed locally or centrally, an account of a testtaker's performance can range from a mere listing of a score or scores (a **simple scoring report**) to the more detailed **extended scoring report,** which includes statistical analyses of the testtaker's performance. A step up from

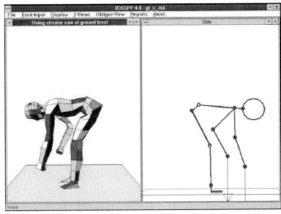

**Figure 1–5**
**A Method of Quantifying Back Stress**

*The innovative application of computer technology has facilitated the measurement of traits or abilities by techniques that could not be measured by more traditional methods. One such assessment methodology marries video and computer technology to obtain a continuous assessment of back stress (Mirka et al., 2000). An image (in this case, of a person sawing) is captured with a video camera and then converted into a computer-measurable representation.*

scoring reports is the **interpretive report,** which is distinguished by its inclusion of numerical or narrative interpretive statements in the report. Some interpretive reports contain relatively little interpretation and simply call attention to certain high, low, or unusual scores that need to be focused on. At the high end of interpretive reports is what is sometimes referred to as a **consultative report.** This type of report, usually written in language appropriate for communication between assessment professionals, may provide expert opinion concerning analysis of the data. Yet another type of computerized scoring report is designed to integrate data from sources other than the test itself into the interpretive report. Such an **integrative report** will employ previously collected data (such as medication records or behavioral observation data) into the test report.

The acronym **CAPA** refers to the term *computer assisted psychological assessment.* By the way, here the word *assisted* typically refers to the assistance computers provide to the test user, not the testtaker. Another acronym you may come across is **CAT,** this for *computer adaptive testing.* The *adaptive* in this term is a reference to the computer's ability to tailor the test to the testtaker's ability or test-taking pattern. So, for example, on a computerized test of academic abilities, the computer might be programmed to switch from testing math skills to English skills after three consecutive failures on math items.

**JUST THINK . . .**

Describe a test that would be ideal for computer administration. Then describe a test that would not be ideal for computer administration.

CAPA opened a world of possibilities for test developers, enabling them to create psychometrically sound tests using mathematical procedures and calculations so complicated that they may have taken weeks or months to use in a bygone era. It opened a new world to test users, enabling the construction of tailor-made tests with built-in scoring and interpretive capabilities previously unheard of. For many test users, CAPA was a great advance over the past, when they had to personally administer tests and possibly even place the responses in some other form prior to analysis (such as by manually using a scoring template or other device). And even after doing all of that, they would then begin the often laborious tasks of scoring and interpreting the resulting data. Still, every rose has its thorns; some of the pros and cons of CAPA are summarized in Table 1–2.

In recent years, the prospect of assessment via the Internet seems to have gained favor with clinicians, researchers, and other test users (Bartram & Hambleton, 2006; Bersoff et al., 2012; Terzis & Economides, 2011). Published studies have employed the Internet as a medium for risk assessment for Alzheimer's disease (Brandt & Rogerson, 2011), alcohol and drug abuse (Sinadinovic et al., 2011), even Internet addiction (Young, 2011). Online

**Table 1–2**
**CAPA: Some Pros and Cons**

| Pros | Cons |
| --- | --- |
| CAPA saves professional time in test administration, scoring, and interpretation. | Professionals must still spend significant time reading software and hardware documentation and even ancillary books on the test and its interpretation. |
| CAPA results in minimal scoring errors resulting from human error or lapses of attention or judgment. | With CAPA, the possibility of software or hardware error is ever present, from difficult-to-pinpoint sources such as software glitches or hardware malfunction. |
| CAPA ensures standardized test administration to all testtakers with little, if any, variation in test administration procedures. | CAPA leaves those testtakers at a disadvantage who are unable to employ familiar test-taking strategies (previewing test, skipping questions, going back to previous question, etc.). |
| CAPA yields standardized interpretation of findings due to elimination of unreliability traceable to differing points of view in professional judgment. | CAPA's standardized interpretation of findings based on a set, unitary perspective may not be optimal; interpretation could profit from alternative viewpoints. |
| Computers' capacity to combine data according to rules is more accurate than that of humans. | Computers lack the flexibility of humans to recognize the exception to a rule in the context of the "big picture." |
| Nonprofessional assistants can be used in the test administration process, and the test can typically be administered to groups of testtakers in one sitting. | Use of nonprofessionals leaves diminished, if any, opportunity for the professional to observe the assessee's test-taking behavior and note any unusual extra-test conditions that may have affected responses. |
| Professional groups such as APA develop guidelines and standards for use of CAPA products. | Profit-driven nonprofessionals may also create and distribute tests with little regard for professional guidelines and standards. |
| Paper-and-pencil tests may be converted to CAPA products with consequential advantages, such as a shorter time between the administration of the test and its scoring and interpretation. | The use of paper-and-pencil tests that have been converted for computer administration raises questions about the equivalence of the original test and its converted form. |
| Security of CAPA products can be maintained not only by traditional means (such as locked filing cabinets) but by high-tech electronic products (such as firewalls). | Security of CAPA products can be breached by computer hackers, and integrity of data can be altered or destroyed by untoward events such as introduction of computer viruses. |
| Computers can automatically tailor test content and length based on responses of testtakers. | Not all testtakers take the same test or have the same test-taking experience. |

methodologies have been used to assess interests (Tracey, 2010 ), problem-solving skills (Mayotte, 2010), and personality traits (Migliore, 2011), among other attributes and conditions.

The APA Committee on Psychological Tests and Assessment was convened to consider the pros and cons of computer-assisted assessment, and assessment using the Internet (Naglieri et al., 2004). Among the advantages over paper-and-pencil tests cited were (1) test administrators have greater access to potential test users because of the global reach of the Internet, (2) scoring and interpretation of test data tend to be quicker than for paper-and-pencil tests, (3) costs associated with Internet testing tend to be lower than costs associated with paper-and-pencil tests, and (4) the Internet facilitates the testing of otherwise isolated populations, as well as people with disabilities for whom getting to a test center might prove a hardship. We might add that Internet testing tends to be "greener," as it may conserve paper, shipping materials, and so forth. Further, there is probably less chance for scoring errors with Internet-based tests as compared to paper-and-pencil tests.

Although Internet testing appears to have many advantages, it is not without potential pitfalls, problems, and issues. One basic issue has to do with what Naglieri et al. (2008) termed "test-client integrity." In part this refers to the verification of the identity of the testtaker when a test is administered online. It also refers, in more general terms, to the sometimes varying interests of the testtaker versus that of the test administrator. Depending upon the conditions of the administration, testtakers may have unrestricted access to notes, other Internet resources, and other aids in test-taking—this despite the guidelines for the test administration. At least with regard to achievement tests, there is some evidence that unproctored Internet testing leads to "score inflation" as compared to more traditionally administered tests (Carstairs & Myors, 2009).

A related aspect of test-client integrity has to do with the procedure in place to ensure that the security of the Internet-administered test is not compromised. What will prevent other testtakers from previewing past—or even advance—copies of the test?

Naglieri et al. (2008) reminded their readers of the distinction between testing and assessment, and the importance of recognizing that Internet testing is just that—*testing*, not assessment. As such, Internet test users should be aware of all of the possible limitations of the source of the test scores.

**JUST THINK . . .**

What cautions should Internet test users keep in mind regarding the source of their test data?

## Other Tools

The next time you have occasion to play a DVD, take a moment to consider the role that video can play in assessment. In fact, specially created videos are widely used in training and evaluation contexts. For example, corporate personnel may be asked to respond to a variety of video-presented incidents of sexual harassment in the workplace. Police personnel may be asked how they would respond to various types of emergencies, which are presented either as reenactments or as video recordings of actual occurrences. Psychotherapists may be asked to respond with a diagnosis and a treatment plan for each of several clients presented to them on videotape. The list of video's potential applications to assessment is endless.

In addition to video, many other commonplace items that you may not readily associate with psychological assessment may be pressed into service for just that purpose. For example, psychologists may use many of the tools traditionally associated with medical health, such as thermometers to measure body temperature and gauges to measure blood pressure. Biofeedback equipment is sometimes used to obtain measures of bodily reactions (such as muscular tension) to various sorts of stimuli. And then there are some less common instruments, such as the penile plethysmograph. This

**JUST THINK . . .**

When is assessment using video a better approach than using a paper-and-pencil test? What are the pitfalls, if any, to using video in assessment?

instrument, designed to measure male sexual arousal, may be helpful in the diagnosis and treatment of sexual predators. Impaired ability to identify odors is common in many disorders in which there is central nervous system involvement, and simple tests of smell may be administered to help determine if such impairment is present. In general, there has been no shortage of innovation on the part of psychologists in devising measurement tools, or adapting existing tools, for use in psychological assessment.

To this point, our introduction has focused on some basic definitions, as well as a look at some of the "tools of the (assessment) trade." We now raise some fundamental questions regarding the who, what, why, how, and where of testing and assessment.

## Who, What, Why, How, and Where?

Who are the parties in the assessment enterprise? In what types of settings are assessments conducted? Why is assessment conducted? How are assessments conducted? Where does one go for authoritative information about tests? Think about the answer to each of these important questions before reading on. Then check your own ideas against those that follow.

### Who Are the Parties?

Parties in the assessment enterprise include developers and publishers of tests, users of tests, and people who are evaluated by means of tests. Additionally, we may consider society at large as a party to the assessment enterprise.

**The test developer** Test developers and publishers create tests or other methods of assessment. The American Psychological Association (APA) has estimated that more than 20,000 new psychological tests are developed each year. Among these new tests are some that were created for a specific research study, some that were created in the hope that they would be published, and some that represent refinements or modifications of existing tests. Test creators bring a wide array of backgrounds and interests to the test development process.[2]

Test developers and publishers appreciate the significant impact that test results can have on people's lives. Accordingly, a number of professional organizations have published standards of ethical behavior that specifically address aspects of responsible test development and use. Perhaps the most detailed document addressing such issues is one jointly written by the American Educational Research Association, the American Psychological Association, and the National Council on Measurement in Education (NCME). Referred to by many psychologists simply as "the Standards," *Standards for Educational and Psychological Testing* covers issues related to test construction and evaluation, test administration and use, and special applications of tests, such as special considerations

---

2. For an intriguing glimpse at biographical information on a sampling of test developers, navigate to the "Test Developer Profiles" section of our website: *www.mhhe.com/cohentesting8*.

when testing linguistic minorities. Initially published in 1954, revisions of the *Standards* were published in 1966, 1974, 1985, and 1999. The *Standards* is an indispensable reference work not only for test developers but for test users as well.

**The test user**  Psychological tests and assessment methodologies are used by a wide range of professionals, including clinicians, counselors, school psychologists, human resources personnel, consumer psychologists, experimental psychologists, and social psychologists. However, the question of who is qualified to use psychological tests has generated a great deal of debate.

The *Standards* and other published guidelines from specialty professional organizations have had much to say in terms of identifying just who is a qualified test user and who should have access to (and be permitted to purchase) psychological tests and related tools of psychological assessment. Still, controversy exists about which professionals with what type of training should have access to which tests. Members of various professions, with little or no psychological training, have sought the right to obtain and use psychological tests. In many countries, no ethical or legal regulation of psychological test use exists (Leach & Oakland, 2007).

So who are (or should be) test users? Should occupational therapists, for example, be allowed to administer psychological tests? What about employers and human resources executives with no formal training in psychology? And what about the issue of third parties in the room when the assessment is taking place? This latter question is the subject of this chapter's *Close-Up* discussion.

**JUST THINK . . .**

In addition to psychologists, who should be permitted access to, as well as the privilege of using, psychological tests?

So far, we've listed a number of controversial *Who?* questions that knowledgeable assessment professionals still debate. Fortunately, there is at least one *Who?* question about which there is very little debate: the one regarding who the testtaker or assessee is.

**The testtaker**  We have all been testtakers. However, we have not all approached tests in the same way. On the day a test is to be administered, testtakers may vary with respect to numerous variables, including these:

- The amount of test anxiety they are experiencing and the degree to which that test anxiety might significantly affect their test results
- The extent to which they understand and agree with the rationale for the assessment
- Their capacity and willingness to cooperate with the examiner or to comprehend written test instructions
- The amount of physical pain or emotional distress they are experiencing
- The amount of physical discomfort brought on by not having had enough to eat, having had too much to eat, or other physical conditions
- The extent to which they are alert and wide awake as opposed to nodding off
- The extent to which they are predisposed to agree or disagree when presented with stimulus statements
- The extent to which they have received prior coaching
- The importance they may attribute to portraying themselves in a good (or bad) light
- The extent to which they are, for lack of a better term, "lucky" and can "beat the odds" on a multiple-choice achievement test (even though they may not have learned the subject matter).

## Should Observers Be Parties to the Assessment Process?

The assessor and the assessee are two parties in any assessment. The third party in an assessment may be an observer who is there for any number of reasons. The third-party observer may be a supervisor of the assessor, a friend or relative of the assessee, a representative of the institution in which the assessment is being conducted, a translator, an attorney, or someone else. But do third parties have a legitimate place in the room during an assessment for any reason? According to Robert J. McCaffrey (2007), the answer to this question is clear and unambiguous: "No, third parties should not be allowed to be present during an assessment."

McCaffrey and others cite research to support the view that a social influence process takes place through the mere presence of a third party (Gavett & McCaffrey, 2007; Vanderhoff et al., 2011; Yantz & McCaffrey, 2005, 2009). This social influence may be sufficient to affect the assessee's performance, particularly on tasks involving memory, attention, and other cognitive functions (Gavett et al., 2005). The observing third party does not even have to be physically present to affect an assessee's performance—observation by means of a video camera, a one-way mirror, or similar device may also affect an assessee's performance (Constantinou et al., 2005).

The social influence effect that occurs has been referred to in the testing and assessment literature as **social facilitation,** probably because the presence of third parties was initially associated with increments in performance (Aiello & Douthitt, 2001). However, in light of additional research suggesting that an audience may also have the effect of inhibiting performance, a more inclusive term—such as *social facilitation and inhibition*—would probably be more accurate (McCaffrey et al., 2005).

Proponents of third-party access to psychological assessment argue that it is necessary for purposes such as clinical training; there is no substitute for having a supervisor right there, in the room, to correct any test administration errors that an assessor-in-training might make during the course of an assessment. Other arguments in favor of third-party access may cite the need for translators or for an attorney to ensure that

an assessee's rights are respected. Some state statutes specifically provide for the presence of third-party observers under certain conditions, although most states still have not addressed this issue by either legislation or judicial action (Duff & Fisher, 2005). One polling of a small sample ($n = 27$) of forensic experts concluded that a majority ($n = 14$) was in favor of allowing third-party observers; the remaining respondents were either against it or unclassifiable as favoring either position (Witt, 2003).

Advocates of the strict enforcement of a policy that prohibits third-party observers during psychological assessment argue that alternatives to such observation either exist or must be developed. For example, instead of allowing supervisors in the room during an assessment, better training procedures—including greater reliance on role play prior to actual test administrations—should be instituted. McCaffrey (2005) has cautioned that certain assessment data gathered in the presence of a third-party observer may be deemed unreliable in a court of law and thus inadmissible. He further advised that any time there is a third party to an assessment, that fact should be clearly noted on the assessment report along with the possible consequences of the third party's presence.

In the broad sense in which we are using the term "testtaker," anyone who is the subject of an assessment or an evaluation can be a testtaker or an assessee. As amazing as it sounds, this means that even a deceased individual can be considered an assessee. True, this is the exception to the rule, but there is such a thing as a *psychological autopsy.*

A **psychological autopsy** may be defined as a reconstruction of a deceased individual's psychological profile on the basis of archival records, artifacts, and interviews previously conducted with the deceased assessee or people who knew him or her. For example, using psychological autopsies, Townsend (2007) explored the question of whether suicide terrorists were indeed suicidal from a classical psychological perspective. She concluded that they were not. Other researchers have provided fascinating postmortem psychological evaluations of people from various walks of life in many different cultures (Bhatia et al., 2006; Chan et al., 2007; Dattilio, 2006; Fortune et al., 2007; Foster, 2011; Giner et al., 2007; Goldstein et al., 2008; Heller et al., 2007; McGirr et al., 2007; Owens et al., 2008; Palacio et al., 2007; Phillips et al., 2007; Pouliot & DeLeo, 2006; Sanchez, 2006; Thoresen et al., 2006; Vento et al., 2011; Zonda, 2006).

> **JUST THINK . . .**
>
> What recently deceased public figure would you like to see a psychological autopsy done on? Why? What results might you expect?

### Society at large

> The uniqueness of individuals is one of the most fundamental characteristic facts of life. . . . At all periods of human history men have observed and described differences between individuals. . . . But educators, politicians, and administrators have felt a need for some way of organizing or systematizing the many-faceted complexity of individual differences. (Tyler, 1965, p. 3)

The societal need for "organizing" and "systematizing" has historically manifested itself in such varied questions as "Who is a witch?," "Who is schizophrenic?," and "Who is qualified?" The specific questions asked have shifted with societal concerns. The methods used to determine the answers have varied throughout history as a function of factors such as intellectual sophistication and religious preoccupation. Proponents of palmistry, podoscopy, astrology, and phrenology, among other pursuits, have argued that the best means of understanding and predicting human behavior was through the study of the palms of the hands, the feet, the stars, bumps on the head, tea leaves, and so on. Unlike such pursuits, the assessment enterprise has roots in science. Through systematic and replicable means that can produce compelling evidence, the assessment enterprise responds to what Tyler (1965, p. 3) described as society's demand for "some way of organizing or systematizing the many-faceted complexity of individual differences."

Society at large exerts its influence as a party to the assessment enterprise in many ways. As society evolves and as the need to measure different psychological variables emerges, test developers respond by devising new tests. Through elected representatives to the legislature, laws are enacted that govern aspects of test development, test administration, and test interpretation. Similarly, by means of court decisions, society at large exerts its influence on various aspects of the testing and assessment enterprise.

**Other parties**   Beyond the four primary parties we have focused on here, let's briefly make note of others who may participate in varied ways in the testing and assessment enterprise. Organizations, companies, and governmental agencies sponsor the development of tests for various reasons, such as to certify personnel. Companies and services offer test-scoring or interpretation services. In some cases these companies and services are simply extensions of test publishers, and in other cases they are independent. There are people whose sole responsibility is the marketing and sales of tests. Sometimes these people are employed by the test publisher; sometimes they are not. There are academicians who review tests and evaluate their psychometric soundness. All of these people, as well as many others, are parties to a greater or lesser extent in the assessment enterprise.

Having introduced you to some of the parties involved in the *Who?* of psychological testing and assessment, let's move on to tackle some of the *What?* and *Why?* questions.

## *In What Types of Settings Are Assessments Conducted, and Why?*

**Educational settings**    You are probably no stranger to the many types of tests administered in the classroom. As mandated by law, tests are administered early in school life to help identify children who may have special needs. In addition to school ability tests, another type of test commonly given in schools is an **achievement test,** which evaluates accomplishment or the degree of learning that has taken place. Some of the achievement tests you have taken in school were constructed by your teacher. Other achievement tests were constructed for more widespread use by educators working with measurement professionals. In the latter category, acronyms such as SAT and GRE may ring a bell.

You know from your own experience that a **diagnosis** may be defined as a description or conclusion reached on the basis of evidence and opinion. Typically this conclusion is reached through a process of distinguishing the nature of something and ruling out alternative conclusions. Similarly, the term **diagnostic test** refers to a tool of assessment used to help narrow down and identify areas of deficit to be targeted for intervention. In educational settings, diagnostic tests of reading, mathematics, and other academic subjects may be administered to assess the need for educational intervention as well as to establish or rule out eligibility for special education programs.

Schoolchildren receive grades on their report cards that are not based on any formal assessment. For example, the grade next to "Works and plays well with others" is probably based more on the teacher's *informal evaluation* in the classroom than on scores on any published measure of social interaction. We may define **informal evaluation** as a typically nonsystematic assessment that leads to the formation of an opinion or attitude.

**JUST THINK . . .**

What tools of assessment could be used to address a student's reading ability?

Informal evaluation is, of course, not limited to educational settings; it is very much a part of everyday life. In fact, many of the tools of evaluation we have discussed in the context of educational settings (such as achievement tests, diagnostic tests, and informal evaluations) are also administered in various other settings. And some of the types of tests we discuss in the context of the settings described next are also administered in educational settings. So please keep in mind that the tools of evaluation and measurement techniques that we discuss in one context may well be used in other contexts. Our objective at this early stage in our survey of the field is simply to introduce a sampling (not a comprehensive list) of the types of tests used in different settings.

**Clinical settings**    Tests and many other tools of assessment are widely used in clinical settings such as public, private, and military hospitals, inpatient and outpatient clinics, private-practice consulting rooms, schools, and other institutions. These tools are used to help screen for or diagnose behavior problems. What types of situations might prompt the employment of such tools? Here's a small sample.

- A private psychotherapy client wishes to be evaluated to see if the assessment can provide any nonobvious clues regarding his maladjustment.

- A school psychologist clinically evaluates a child experiencing learning difficulties to determine what factors are primarily responsible for it.

- A psychotherapy researcher uses assessment procedures to determine if a particular method of psychotherapy is effective in treating a particular problem.

- A psychologist-consultant retained by an insurance company is called on to give an opinion as to the reality of a client's psychological problems; is the client really experiencing such problems or just malingering?

- A court-appointed psychologist is asked to give an opinion as to a defendant's competency to stand trial.

- A prison psychologist is called on to give an opinion regarding the extent of a convicted violent prisoner's rehabilitation.

The tests employed in clinical settings may be intelligence tests, personality tests, neuropsychological tests, or other specialized instruments, depending on the presenting or suspected problem area. The hallmark of testing in clinical settings is that the test or measurement technique is employed with only one individual at a time. Group testing is used primarily for screening—that is, identifying those individuals who require further diagnostic evaluation.

> **JUST THINK . . .**
>
> What kinds of issues do psychologists have to consider when assessing prisoners in contrast to assessing workplace managers?

**Counseling settings**   Assessment in a counseling context may occur in environments as diverse as schools, prisons, and governmental or privately owned institutions. Regardless of the particular tools used, the ultimate objective of many such assessments is the improvement of the assessee in terms of adjustment, productivity, or some related variable. Measures of social and academic skills and measures of personality, interest, attitudes, and values are among the many types of tests that a counselor might administer to a client. Referral questions to be answered range from "How can this child better focus on tasks?" to "For what career is the client best suited?" to "What activities are recommended for retirement?" Having mentioned retirement, let's hasten to introduce another type of setting in which psychological tests are used extensively.

**Geriatric settings**   In the United States, more than 12 million adults are currently in the age range of 75 to 84; this is about 16 times more people in this age range than there were in 1900. Four million adults in the United States are currently 85 years old or older, which is a 33-fold increase in the number of people of that age since 1900. People in the United States are living longer, and the population as a whole is getting older.

Older Americans may live at home, in special housing designed for independent living, in housing designed for assisted living, or in long-term care facilities such as hospitals and hospices. Wherever older individuals reside, they may at some point require psychological assessment to evaluate cognitive, psychological, adaptive, or other functioning. At issue in many such assessments is the extent to which assessees are enjoying as good a *quality of life* as possible. The definition of quality of life has varied as a function of perspective in different studies. In some research, for example, quality of life is defined from the perspective of an observer; in other research it is defined from the perspective of assessees themselves and refers to an individual's own self-report regarding lifestyle-related variables. However defined, what is typically assessed in **quality of life** evaluations are variables related to perceived stress, loneliness, sources of satisfaction, personal values, quality of living conditions, and quality of friendships and other social support.

Generally speaking, from a clinical perspective, the assessment of older adults is more likely to include screening for cognitive decline and *dementia* than the assessment of younger adults (Gallo & Bogner, 2006; Gallo & Wittink, 2006). **Dementia** is a loss of cognitive functioning (which may affect memory, thinking, reasoning, psychomotor speed, attention, and related abilities, as well as personality) that occurs as the result of damage to or loss of brain cells. Perhaps the best known of the many forms of dementia that exist is Alzheimer's disease. The road to diagnosis by the clinician is complicated by the fact that severe depression in the elderly can contribute to cognitive functioning that mimics dementia, a condition referred to as **pseudodementia** (Madden et al., 1952). It is also true that the majority of individuals suffering from dementia exhibit depressive symptoms (Strober & Arnett, 2009). Clinicians rely on a variety of different tools of assessment to make a diagnosis of dementia or pseudodementia.

**JUST THINK . . .**

Tests are used in geriatric, counseling, and other settings to help improve quality of life. But are there some aspects of quality of life that a psychological test just can't measure?

**Business and military settings** In business, as in the military, various tools of assessment are used in sundry ways, perhaps most notably in decision making about the careers of personnel. A wide range of achievement, aptitude, interest, motivational, and other tests may be employed in the decision to hire as well as in related decisions regarding promotions, transfer, job satisfaction, and eligibility for further training. For a prospective air traffic controller, successful performance on a test of sustained attention to detail may be one requirement of employment. For promotion to the rank of officer in the military, successful performance on a series of leadership tasks may be essential.

Another application of psychological tests involves the engineering and design of products and environments. Engineering psychologists employ a variety of existing and specially devised tests in research designed to help people at home, in the workplace, and in the military. Products ranging from home computers to office furniture to jet cockpit control panels benefit from the work of such research efforts.

Using tests, interviews, and other tools of assessment, psychologists who specialize in the marketing and sale of products are involved in taking the pulse of consumers. They help corporations predict the public's receptivity to a new product, a new brand, or a new advertising or marketing campaign. Psychologists working in the area of marketing help "diagnose" what is wrong (and right) about brands, products, and campaigns. On the basis of such assessments, these psychologists might make recommendations regarding how new brands and products can be made appealing to consumers, and when it is time for older brands and products to be retired or revitalized.

**JUST THINK . . .**

Assume the role of a consumer psychologist. What ad campaign do you find particularly effective in terms of pushing consumer "buy" buttons? What ad campaign do you find particularly ineffective in this regard? Why?

**Governmental and organizational credentialing** One of the many applications of measurement is in governmental licensing, certification, or general credentialing of professionals. Before they are legally entitled to practice medicine, physicians must pass an examination. Law school graduates cannot present themselves to the public as attorneys until they pass their state's bar examination. Psychologists, too, must pass an examination before adopting the official title "psychologist."

Members of some professions have formed organizations with requirements for membership that go beyond those of licensing or certification. For example, physicians can take further specialized training and a specialty examination to earn the distinction of being "board certified" in a particular area of medicine. Psychologists specializing in certain areas may be evaluated for a diploma from the American Board of Professional Psychology (ABPP) to recognize excellence in the practice of psychology. Another organization, the American Board of Assessment Psychology (ABAP), awards its diploma on the basis of an examination to test users, test developers, and others who have distinguished themselves in the field of testing and assessment.

**Academic research settings** Conducting any sort of research typically entails measurement of some kind, and any academician who ever hopes to publish research should ideally have a sound knowledge of measurement principles and tools of assessment. To emphasize this simple fact of research life, consider Table 1–3. It contains a (very) random sampling of some recently published studies, with information concerning the research question asked and the tools of assessment used to research the answer to that question.

**Table 1–3**
**Tools of Assessment Used in a (Random) Sample of Research Studies**

| The Research Question | Tool(s) of Assessment Employed |
|---|---|
| *What is the role of inspiration in the writing process?* (Thrash et al., 2010) | (1) Specially constructed questionnaires such as one probing the occurrence of creative ideas and inspiration during the prior week, scored on a scale from 1 (never) to 7 (very often); (2) a four-page paper written by the study participants; and (3) various paper-and-pencil tests, including part of a published test called the Inspiration Scale. |
| *How well do childhood peer relationship and behavioral measures predict young adult communication behavior on social networking websites?* (Mikami et al., 2010) | (1) Peer nominations; (2) behavioral observation and rating of peer interaction; (3) all or part of published tests; and (4) number of friends on *My Space* or *Facebook* websites of participants rated for number of friends and friends' posts, as well as related information, such as photo of self (rated for appropriateness), and written description of self (rated for perceived aggression, hostility, or negativity). |
| *Are pigeons smarter than mathematicians?* (Herbranson & Schroeder, 2010) | For pigeons, the measurement device used was three operant chambers containing three pecking keys and a feeder through which birds could gain access to food. Each of these units was interfaced to a computer that controlled experimental events, recorded data, and calculated statistics. For humans, the measurement device was a 15-inch flat-panel monitor equipped with an infrared touch frame that allowed participants to respond to stimulus items by touching the screen. This device was interfaced to a computer that controlled experimental events, recorded data, and calculated statistics. |
| *What can we learn about novice teen drivers' behavior crash risk by observing them driving?* (Lee, Simons-Morton, et al., 2011) | Analysis of data from electronic data acquisition system installed in the vehicles of newly licensed, 16-year-old drivers. The system consisted of cameras, sensors and a computer with removable hard drive. |
| **How can evaluation of teachers' portfolios contribute to effective teacher education?** (Fox et al., 2011) | Qualitative evaluation of teacher portfolio data. |
| *What can be learned from observation of the deliberations of a simulated jury with regard to the presentation of certain types of evidence?* (Finkelstein & Bastounis, 2010) | Behavioral observation of responses of simulated juries to experimental manipulations. |
| *How do children held back in first grade compare to their counterparts who are promoted to second grade with regard to long- and short-term psychosocial outcomes?* (Wu et al., 2010) | (1) Case history data obtained from the school including academic achievement records; (2) various published and specially derived paper-and-pencil tests; and (3) peer assessments of social behavior. |

*(continued)*

**Table 1–3**
*(continued)*

| The Research Question | Tool(s) of Assessment Employed |
|---|---|
| *In patients with multiple sclerosis, what is the relation between their self-reported cognitive fatigue and their performance on a response-time measure?* (Bruce et al., 2010) | A number of tests, administered either orally, by computer, or paper-and-pencil, including all or part of (1) the Computerized Assessment of Response Bias, (2) the Test of Everyday Attention, and (3) the Fatigue Impact Scale. |
| *Does one's level of hypnotizability predict response to suggestions designed to lessen the experience of pain?* (Milling et al., 2010) | (1) Carleton University Responsiveness to Suggestion Scale (a measure of hypnotizability); (2) an apparatus used to induce measurable finger pressure pain; and (3) the measurement of pain intensity by means of an 11-point scale. |
| *As compared to non-Hispanic Caucasians, do Hispanic Caucasians report more severe posttraumatic stress disorder (PTSD) symptoms?* (Marshall et al., 2009) | (1) Interview to verify ethnicity of participants; and (2) Posttraumatic Stress Disorder Checklist (used to measure PTSD symptom severity). |
| *Is group cognitive-behavior therapy for smoking cessation effective with African American smokers?* (Webb et al., 2010) | (1) Smoking history questionnaire; (2) measure of readiness to quit smoking; (3) Fagerstrom Test for Nicotine Dependence; and (4) instrument to measure breath carbon monoxide. |
| *How can death row inmates' last statements be categorized?* (Gerhart et al., 2010) | Case study of public records published by the State of Texas. |
| *How valid is a virtual role-play procedure to assess women's responses to sexual threat?* (Jouriles et al., 2011) | Observed responses of female subjects in face-to-face role play, or virtual role play, involving a sexually threatening situation. |
| *How can we better understand emotional aspects of the coach–athlete relationship?* (Huguet & Philippe, 2011) | Case study analysis of four interviews with an athlete, including analysis of past relationships with coaches. |
| **Can the potential for violence of an ideological group be assessed by studying the group's website?** (Angie et al., 2011) | Evaluation of material posted on the online message boards for the purpose of assessing processes particular to ideological group membership. |
| **How can we better understand wartime stress and its role in soldiers' post-traumatic stress syndrome?** (Lee, Goudarzi, et al., 2011) | In-theater, online assessment system to record and evaluate various aspects of soldiers' experience of wartime stress. |

**Other settings**  Many different kinds of measurement procedures find application in a wide variety of settings. For example, the courts rely on psychological test data and related expert testimony as one source of information to help answer important questions such as "Is this defendant competent to stand trial?" and "Did this defendant know right from wrong at the time the criminal act was committed?"

> **JUST THINK . . .**
>
> What is a research question that you think needs to be addressed? What tools of assessment would be used in a study to address that question?

Measurement may play an important part in program evaluation, whether it is a large-scale government program or a small-scale, privately funded one. Is the program working? How can the program be improved? Are funds being spent in the areas where they ought to be spent? How sound is the theory on which the program is based? These are the types of general questions that tests and measurement procedures used in program evaluation are designed to answer.

Tools of assessment can be found in use in research and practice in every specialty area within psychology. For example, consider **health psychology,** a discipline that focuses on understanding the role of psychological variables in the onset, course, treatment, and prevention of illness, disease, and disability (Cohen, 1994). Health psychologists are involved in teaching, research, or direct-service activities designed to promote good health. Individual interviews, surveys, and paper-and-pencil tests are some of the tools that may be employed to help assess current status with regard to some disease or condition, gauge treatment progress, and evaluate outcome of intervention.

One general line of research in health psychology focuses on aspects of personality, behavior, or lifestyle as they relate to physical health. The methodology employed may entail reporting on measurable respondent variables as they change in response to some intervention, such as education, therapy, counseling, change in diet, or change in habits. Measurement tools may be used to compare one naturally occurring group of research subjects to another such group (such as smokers compared to nonsmokers) with regard to some other health-related variable (such as longevity). Many of the questions raised in health-related research have real, life-and-death consequences. All of these important questions, like the questions raised in other areas of psychology, require that sound techniques of evaluation be employed.

## How Are Assessments Conducted?

If a need exists to measure a particular variable, a way to measure that variable will be devised. As Figure 1–6 just begins to illustrate, the ways in which measurements can be taken are limited only by imagination. Keep in mind that this figure illustrates only a small sample of the many methods used in psychological testing and assessment. The photos are not designed to illustrate the most typical kinds of assessment procedures. Rather, their purpose is to call attention to the wide range of measuring tools that have been created for varied uses.

Responsible test users have obligations before, during, and after a test or any measurement procedure is administered. For purposes of illustration, consider the administration of a paper-and-pencil test. Before the test, ethical guidelines dictate that when test users have discretion with regard to the tests administered, they should select and use only the test or tests that are most appropriate for the individual being tested. Before a test is administered, the test should be stored in a way that reasonably ensures that its specific contents will not be made known to the testtaker in advance. Another obligation of the test user before the test's administration is to ensure that a prepared and suitably trained person administers the test properly.

The test administrator (or examiner) must be familiar with the test materials and procedures and must have at the test site all the materials needed to properly administer the test. Materials needed might include a stopwatch, a supply of pencils, and a sufficient number of test *protocols.* By the way, in everyday, non-test-related conversation, *protocol* refers to diplomatic etiquette. A less common use of the word is a synonym for the first copy or rough draft of a treaty or other official document before its ratification. With reference to testing and assessment, **protocol** typically refers to the form or sheet or booklet on which a testtaker's responses are entered. The term may also be used to refer to a description of a set of test- or assessment-related procedures, as in the sentence "The examiner dutifully followed the complete protocol for the stress interview."

Test users have the responsibility of ensuring that the room in which the test will be conducted is suitable and conducive to the testing. To the extent possible, distracting conditions such as excessive noise, heat, cold, interruptions, glaring sunlight, crowding, inadequate ventilation, and so forth should be avoided. Of course, creating an ideal testing environment is not always something every examiner can do (see Figure 1–7).

During test administration, and especially in one-on-one or small-group testing, *rapport* between the examiner and the examinee can be critically important. In this context, **rapport** may be defined as a working relationship between the examiner and the examinee. Such a working relationship can sometimes be achieved with a few words of small talk when examiner and examinee are introduced. If appropriate, some words about the nature of the test and why it is important for examinees to do their best may also be helpful. In other instances—for example, with a frightened child—the achievement of

At least since the beginning of the nineteenth century, military units throughout the world have relied on psychological and other tests for personnel selection, program validation, and related reasons (Hartmann et al., 2003). In some cultures where military service is highly valued, students take preparatory courses with hopes of being accepted into elite military units. This is the case in Israel, where rigorous training such as that pictured here prepares high-school students for physical and related tests that only 1 in 60 military recruits will pass.

Evidence suggests that some people with eating disorders may actually have a self-perception disorder; that is, they see themselves as heavier than they really are (Thompson & Smolak, 2001). J. Kevin Thompson and his associates devised the adjustable light-beam apparatus to measure body image distortion. Assessees adjust four beams of light to indicate what they believe is the width of their cheeks, waist, hips, and thighs. A measure of accuracy of these estimates is then obtained.

Herman Witkin and his associates (Witkin & Goodenough, 1977) studied personality-related variables in some innovative ways. For example, they identified field (or context) dependent and field independent people by means of this specially constructed tilting room–tilting chair device. Assessees were asked questions designed to evaluate their dependence on or independence of visual cues.

**Figure 1–6**
**The Wide World of Measurement**

*Pictures such as these sample items from the Meier Art Judgment Test might be used to evaluate people's aesthetic perception. Which of these two renderings do you find more aesthetically pleasing? The difference between the two pictures involves the positioning of the objects on the shelf.*

*Impairment of certain sensory functions can indicate neurological deficit. For purposes of diagnosis, as well as measuring progress in remediation, the neurodevelopment training ball can be useful in evaluating one's sense of balance.*

*The Stresseraser is a handheld and self-administered biofeedback device designed to facilitate change in bodily relaxation. Vagus nerve functioning is monitored from the pulse of the index finger and fed back to the user through images on a screen. Users may then alter breathing and mental focus to affect sympathetic-parasympathetic functioning in order to obtain therapeutic benefits. The unit has the advantage of portability; it can be used to facilitate relaxation in a variety of settings.*

**Figure 1–7**
**Less-Than-Optimal Testing Conditions**

*In 1917, new Army recruits sat on the floor as they were administered the first group tests of intelligence—not ideal testing conditions by current standards.*

rapport might involve more elaborate techniques such as engaging the child in play or some other activity until the child has acclimated to the examiner and the surroundings. It is important that attempts to establish rapport with the testtaker not compromise any rules of the test administration instructions.

After a test administration, test users have many obligations as well. These obligations range from safeguarding the test protocols to conveying the test results in a clearly understandable fashion. If third parties were present during testing or if anything else that might be considered out of the ordinary happened during testing, it is the test user's responsibility to make a note of such events on the report of the testing. Test scorers have obligations as well. For example, if a test is to be scored by people, scoring needs to conform to pre-established scoring criteria. Test users who have responsibility for interpreting scores or other test results have an obligation to do so in accordance with established procedures and ethical guidelines.

**JUST THINK . . .**

What unforeseen incidents could conceivably occur during a test session? Should such incidents be noted on the report of that session?

**Assessment of people with disabilities** People with disabilities are assessed for exactly the same reasons people with no disabilities are assessed: to obtain employment, to earn a professional credential, to be screened for psychopathology, and so forth. A number of laws have been enacted that affect the conditions under which tests are administered to people with disabling conditions. For example, one law mandates the development and implementation of "alternate assessment" programs for children who, as a result of a disability, could not otherwise participate in state- and district-wide assessments. Defining exactly what "alternate assessment" meant was left to the individual states or their local school districts. These authorities define who requires alternate assessment, how such assessments are to be conducted, and how meaningful inferences are to be drawn from the assessment data.

In general, alternate assessment is typically accomplished by means of some *accommodation* made to the assessee. The verb *to accommodate* may be defined as "to adapt, adjust, or make suitable." In the context of psychological testing and assessment, **accommodation** may be defined as the adaptation of a test, procedure, or situation, or the substitution of one test for another, to make the assessment more suitable for an assessee with exceptional needs.

At first blush, the process of accommodating students, employees, or other testtakers with special needs might seem straightforward. For example, the individual who has difficulty reading the small print of a particular test may be accommodated with a large-print version of the same test or with a specially lit test environment. A student with a hearing impairment may be administered the test in sign language. An individual with ADHD might have an extended evaluation time, with frequent breaks during periods of evaluation. Although this may all seem simple at first, it can actually become quite complicated.

Consider, for example, the case of a student with a visual impairment who is scheduled to be given a written, multiple-choice test. There are several possible alternate procedures for test administration. For example, the test could be translated into Braille and administered in that form, or the test could be administered by means of audiotape. However, some students may do better with a Braille administration and others with audiotape. Students with superior short-term attention and memory skills for auditory stimuli would seem to have an advantage with the audiotaped administration. Students with superior haptic (sense of touch) and perceptual-motor skills might have an advantage with the Braille administration. And so, even in this relatively simple example, it can be readily appreciated that a testtaker's performance (and score) on a test may be affected by the manner of the alternate administration of the test. This reality of alternate assessment raises important questions about how equivalent such methods really are. Indeed, because the alternate procedures have been individually tailored, there is seldom compelling research to support equivalence. Governmental guidelines for alternate assessment will evolve to include ways of translating measurement procedures from one format to another. Other guidelines may suggest substituting one assessment tool for another. Currently there are many ways to accommodate people with disabilities in an assessment situation (see this chapter's *Everyday Psychometrics*), and many different definitions of *alternate assessment*. For the record, we offer our own, general definition of that elusive term. **Alternate assessment** is *an evaluative or diagnostic procedure or process that varies from the usual, customary, or standardized way a measurement is derived, either by virtue of some special accommodation made to the assessee or by means of alternative methods designed to measure the same variable(s).*

Having considered some of the *who, what, how,* and *why* of assessment, let's now consider sources for more information with regard to all aspects of the assessment enterprise.

> **JUST THINK . . .**
>
> Are there some types of assessments for which no alternate assessment procedure should be developed?

## Everyday Accommodations

It has been estimated that as many as one in seven Americans has a disability that interferes with activities of daily living. In recent years society has acknowledged more than ever before the special needs of citizens challenged by physical and/or mental disabilities. The effects of this ever-increasing acknowledgment are visibly evident: special access ramps alongside flights of stairs, captioned television programming for the hearing-impaired, and large-print newspapers, books, and magazines for the visually impaired. In general, there has been a trend toward altering environments to make individuals with handicapping conditions feel less challenged.

Depending on the nature of a testtaker's disability and other factors, modifications—referred to as accommodations—may need to be made in a psychological test (or measurement procedure) in order for an evaluation to proceed. Accommodation may take many different forms. One general type of accommodation involves the form of the test as presented to the testtaker, as when a written test is set in larger type for presentation to a visually impaired testtaker. Another general type of accommodation concerns the way responses to the test are obtained. For example, a speech-impaired individual might be allowed to write out responses in an examination that would otherwise be administered orally. Students with learning disabilities may be accommodated by being permitted to read test questions aloud (Fuchs et al., 2000).

Modification of the physical environment in which a test is conducted is yet another general type of accommodation. For example, a test that is usually group-administered at a central location may on occasion be administered individually to a disabled person in his or her home. Modifications of the interpersonal environment in which a test is conducted is another possibility (see Figure 1).

Which of many different types of accommodation should be employed? An answer to this question is typically approached by consideration of at least four variables:

1. the capabilities of the assessee;
2. the purpose of the assessment;
3. the meaning attached to test scores; and
4. the capabilities of the assessor.

**Figure 1**
**Modification of the Interpersonal Environment**

*An individual testtaker who requires the aid of a helper or working dog may require the presence of a third party (or animal) if a particular test is to be administered. In some cases, because of the nature of the testtaker's disability and the demands of a particular test, a more suitable test might have to be substituted for the test usually given if a meaningful evaluation is to be conducted.*

### The Capabilities of the Assessee

Which of several alternate means of assessment is best tailored to the needs and capabilities of the assessee? Case history data, records of prior assessments, and interviews with friends, family, teachers, and others who know the assessee all can provide a wealth of useful information concerning which of several alternate means of assessment is most suitable.

### The Purpose of the Assessment

Accommodation is appropriate under some circumstances and inappropriate under others. In general one looks to the purpose of the assessment and the consequences of the accommodation in order to judge the appropriateness of modifying a test to accommodate a person with a disability. For example, modifying a written driving test—or a road test—so a blind person could be tested for a driver's license is clearly inappropriate. For their own as well as the public's safety, the blind are prohibited from driving automobiles. On the other hand, changing the form of most other written tests so that a blind person could take them is another matter entirely. In general, accommodation is simply a way of being true to a social policy that promotes and guarantees equal opportunity and treatment for all citizens.

### The Meaning Attached to Test Scores

What happens to the meaning of a score on a test when that test has not been administered in the manner that it was designed to be? More often than not, when test administration instructions are modified (some would say "compromised"), the meaning of scores on that test becomes questionable at best. Test users are left to their own devices in interpreting such data. Professional judgment, expertise, and, quite frankly, guesswork can all enter into the process of drawing inferences from scores on modified tests. Of course, a precise record of just how a test was modified for accommodation purposes should be made on the test report.

### The Capabilities of the Assessor

Although most persons charged with the responsibility of assessment would like to think that they can administer an assessment professionally to almost anyone, this is actually not the case. It is important to acknowledge that some assessors may experience a level of discomfort in the presence of people with particular disabilities, and this discomfort may affect their evaluation. It is also important to acknowledge that some assessors may require additional training prior to conducting certain assessments, including supervised experience with members of certain populations. Alternatively, the assessor may refer such assessment assignments to another assessor who has had more training and experience with members of a particular population.

A burgeoning scholarly literature has focused on various aspects of accommodation, including issues related to general policies (Burns, 1998; Nehring, 2007; Shriner, 2000; Simpson et al., 1999), method of test administration (Calhoon et al., 2000; Danford & Steinfeld, 1999), score comparability (Elliott et al., 2001; Johnson, 2000; Pomplun & Omar, 2000, 2001), documentation (Schulte et al., 2000), and the motivation of testtakers to request accommodation (Baldridge & Veiga, 2006). Before a decision about accommodation is made for any individual testtaker, due consideration must be given to issues regarding the meaning of scores derived from modified instruments and the validity of the inferences that can be made from the data derived.

## *Where to Go for Authoritative Information: Reference Sources*

Many reference sources exist for learning more about published tests and assessment-related issues. These sources vary with respect to detail. Some merely provide descriptions of tests, others provide detailed information on technical aspects, and still others provide critical reviews complete with discussion of the pros and cons of usage.

**Test catalogues** Perhaps one of the most readily accessible sources of information is a catalogue distributed by the publisher of the test. Because most test publishers make available catalogues of their offerings, this source of test information can be tapped by a simple telephone call, e-mail, or note. As you might expect, however, publishers' catalogues usually contain only a brief description of the test and seldom contain the kind of detailed technical information that a prospective user might require. Moreover, the catalogue's objective is to sell the test. For this reason, highly critical reviews of a test are seldom, if ever, found in a publisher's test catalogue.

**Test manuals**   Detailed information concerning the development of a particular test and technical information relating to it should be found in the test manual, which usually can be purchased from the test publisher. However, for security purposes the test publisher will typically require documentation of professional training before filling an order for a test manual. The chances are good that your university maintains a collection of popular test manuals, perhaps in the library or counseling center. If the test manual you seek is not available there, ask your instructor how best to obtain a reference copy. In surveying the various test manuals, you are likely to see that they vary not only in the details of how the tests were developed and deemed psychometrically sound but also in the candor with which they describe their own test's limitations.

**Reference volumes**   The Buros Institute of Mental Measurements provides "one-stop shopping" for a great deal of test-related information. The initial version of what would evolve into the *Mental Measurements Yearbook* was compiled by Oscar Buros (Figure 1–8) in 1933. At this writing, the latest edition of this authoritative compilation of test reviews is the *18th Annual Mental Measurements Yearbook,* published in 2010 (though the 19th cannot be far behind). The Buros Institute also distributes *Tests in Print,* which lists all commercially available English-language tests in print. This volume, which is also updated periodically, provides detailed information for each test listed, including test publisher, test author, test purpose, intended test population, and test administration time.

**Journal articles**   Articles in current journals may contain reviews of the test, updated or independent studies of its psychometric soundness, or examples of how the instrument was used in either research or an applied context. Such articles may appear in a

**Figure 1–8**
**Oscar Krisen Buros (1906–1978)**

*Buros is best remembered as the creator of the* Mental Measurements Yearbook (MMY), *a kind of* Consumer Reports *for tests and a much-needed source of "psychometric policing" (Peterson, 1997, p. 718). His work lives on at* The Buros Institute of Mental Measurements, *located at the University of Nebraska in Lincoln. In addition to the* MMY, *which is updated periodically, the institute publishes a variety of other test-related materials.*

wide array of behavioral science journals, such as *Psychological Bulletin, Psychological Review, Professional Psychology: Research and Practice, Journal of Personality and Social Psychology, Psychology & Marketing, Psychology in the Schools, School Psychology Quarterly,* and *School Psychology Review.* There are also journals that focus more specifically on matters related to testing and assessment. For example, take a look at journals such as the *Journal of Psychoeducational Assessment, Psychological Assessment, Educational and Psychological Measurement, Applied Measurement in Education,* and the *Journal of Personality Assessment.* Journals such as *Psychology, Public Policy, and Law* and *Law and Human Behavior* frequently contain highly informative articles on legal and ethical issues and controversies as they relate to psychological testing and assessment. Journals such as *Computers & Education, Computers in Human Behavior,* and *Cyberpsychology, Behavior, and Social Networking* frequently contain insightful articles on computer and Internet-related measurement.

**Online databases**    One of the most widely used bibliographic databases for test-related publications is that maintained by the Educational Resources Information Center (ERIC). Funded by the U.S. Department of Education and operated out of the University of Maryland, the ERIC website at *www.eric.ed.gov* contains a wealth of resources and news about tests, testing, and assessment. There are abstracts of articles, original articles, and links to other useful websites. ERIC strives to provide balanced information concerning educational assessment and to provide resources that encourage responsible test use.

The American Psychological Association (APA) maintains a number of databases useful in locating psychology-related information in journal articles, book chapters, and doctoral dissertations. PsycINFO is a database of abstracts dating back to 1887. ClinPSYC is a database derived from PsycINFO that focuses on abstracts of a clinical nature. PsycSCAN: Psychopharmacology contains abstracts of articles concerning psychopharmacology. PsycARTICLES is a database of full-length articles dating back to 1894. Health and Psychosocial Instruments (HAPI) contains a listing of measures created or modified for specific research studies but not commercially available; it is available at many college libraries through BRS Information Technologies and also on CD-ROM (updated twice a year). PsycLAW is a free database, available to everyone, that contains discussions of selected topics involving psychology and law. It can be accessed at *www.apa.org/psyclaw.* For more information on any of these databases, visit APA's website at *www.apa.org.*

The world's largest private measurement institution is Educational Testing Service (ETS). This company, based in Princeton, New Jersey, maintains a staff of some 2,500 people, including about 1,000 measurement professionals and education specialists. These are the folks who bring you the Scholastic Aptitude Test (SAT) and the Graduate Record Exam (GRE), among many other tests. Descriptions of these and the many other tests developed by this company can be found at their website, *www.ets.org.*

**Other sources**    Your school library contains a number of other sources that may be used to acquire information about tests and test-related topics. For example, two sources for exploring the world of unpublished tests and measures are the *Directory of Unpublished Experimental Mental Measures* (Goldman & Mitchell, 2007) and Tests in Microfiche, administered by ETS. Some pros and cons of the various sources of information we have listed are summarized in Table 1–4.

**Table 1–4**
**Sources of Information About Tests: Some Pros and Cons**

| Information Source | Pros | Cons |
|---|---|---|
| Test catalogue available from the publisher of the test as well as affiliated distributors of the test | Contains general description of test, including what it is designed to do and who it is designed to be used with. Readily available to most anyone who requests a catalogue. | Primarily designed to sell the test to test users and seldom contains any critical reviews. Information not detailed enough for basing a decision to use the test. |
| Test manual | Usually the most detailed source available for information regarding the standardization sample and test administration instructions. May also contain useful information regarding the theory the test is based on, if that is the case. Typically contains at least some information regarding psychometric soundness of the test. | Details regarding the test's psychometric soundness are usually self-serving and written on the basis of studies conducted by the test author and/or test publisher. A test manual itself may be difficult for students to obtain, as its distribution may be restricted to qualified professionals. |
| Reference volumes such as the *Mental Measurements Yearbook,* available in bound book form or online | Much like *Consumer Reports* for tests, contain descriptions and critical reviews of a test written by third parties who presumably have nothing to gain or lose by praising or criticizing the instrument, its standardization sample, and its psychometric soundness. | Few disadvantages if reviewer is genuinely trying to be objective and is knowledgeable, but as with any review, can provide a misleading picture if this is not the case. Also, for very detailed accounts of the standardization sample and related matters, it is best to consult the test manual itself. |
| Journal articles | Up-to-date source of reviews and studies of psychometric soundness. Can provide practical examples of how an instrument is used in research or applied contexts. | As with reference volumes, reviews are valuable to the extent that they are informed and, as far as possible, unbiased. Reader should research as many articles as possible when attempting to learn how the instrument is actually used; any one article alone may provide an atypical picture. |
| Online databases | Widely known and respected online databases such as the ERIC database are virtual "gold mines" of useful information containing varying amounts of detail. Although some legitimate psychological tests may be available for self-administration and scoring online, the vast majority are not. | Consumer beware! Some sites masquerading as databases for psychological tests are designed more to entertain or to sell something than to inform. These sites frequently offer tests you can take online. As you learn more about tests, you will probably become more critical of the value of these self-administered and self-scored "psychological tests." |

Many university libraries also provide access to online databases, such as PsycINFO, and electronic journals. Most scientific papers can be downloaded straight to one's computer using such an online service. This is an extremely valuable resource to students, as non-subscribers to such databases may be charged hefty access fees for such access.

Armed with a wealth of background information about tests and other tools of assessment, we'll explore historical, cultural, and legal/ethical aspects of the assessment enterprise in the following chapter.

## Self-Assessment

Test your understanding of elements of this chapter by seeing if you can explain each of the following terms, expressions, and abbreviations:

| | | |
|---|---|---|
| accommodation | CAPA | central processing |
| achievement test | case history | collaborative psychological |
| alternate assessment | case history data | assessment |
| behavioral observation | case study | consultative report |

cut score
dementia
diagnosis
diagnostic test
dynamic assessment
extended scoring report
format
groupthink
health psychology
informal evaluation
integrative report
interpretive report
interview
local processing
naturalistic observation
panel interview

portfolio
protocol
pseudodementia
psychological assessment
psychological autopsy
psychological test
psychological testing
psychometrician
psychometrics
psychometric soundness
psychometrist
quality of life
rapport
role play
role-play test
score

scoring
scoring report
simple scoring report
social facilitation
teleprocessing
test
test catalogue
test developer
test manual
testtaker
test user
therapeutic psychological
    assessment
third parties in psychological
    assessment
utility

# 2

# Historical, Cultural, and Legal/Ethical Considerations

**W**e continue our broad overview of the field of psychological testing and assessment with a look backward, the better to appreciate the historical context of the enterprise. We also present "food for thought" regarding cultural and legal/ethical matters. Consider this "food" only as an appetizer; material on historical, cultural, and legal/ethical considerations is interwoven where appropriate throughout this book.

## A Historical Perspective

### Antiquity to the Nineteenth Century

It is believed that tests and testing programs first came into being in China as early as 2200 B.C.E. (DuBois, 1966, 1970). Testing was instituted as a means of selecting who, of many applicants, would obtain government jobs. In a culture with a long tradition of one's social position being determined solely by the family into which one was born, the fact that one could improve one's lot in life by scoring high on an examination was a significant step forward. In reality, passing the examinations required knowledge that usually came from either long hours of study or work with a tutor. Given those facts of life, it was likely that only the land-owning gentry could afford to have their children spend the time necessary to prepare for the tests. Still, tales emerged of some people who were able to vastly improve their lot in life by passing the state-sponsored examinations. Testtakers' excitement when "the roll was released" (see Figure 2–1) has a modern day parallel in university hallways around the world; just listen to high-scorers' cheers or other expressions of self-satisfaction when grades on an important examination are posted.

What were applicants for jobs in ancient China tested on? As might be expected, the content of the examination changed over time and with the cultural expectations of the day—as well as with the values of the ruling dynasty. In general, the tests examined proficiency in subjects like music, archery, horsemanship, writing, and arithmetic, as well as agriculture, geography, civil law, and military strategy. Knowledge of and skill in the rites and ceremonies of public and social life were also evaluated. During the Song (or Sung) dynasty, which ran from 960 to 1279 C.E., tests emphasized knowledge of classical literature. Testtakers who demonstrated their command of the classics were

**Figure 2–1**
**Releasing the Roll**

*For a period of about 3,000 years, forms of proficiency testing existed in China. Some time after taking a test, men—the tests were open only to men, with the exception of a brief period in the 1800s—gathered to see who passed when the results were posted on a wall. (Sound familiar?) This posting of test results was referred to as "releasing the roll."*

perceived as having acquired the wisdom of the past and were therefore entitled to a government position. During some dynasties, testing was virtually suspended and government positions were given to family members or friends, or simply sold.

In dynasties with state-sponsored examinations for official positions (referred to as *imperial examination*), the privileges of making the grade varied. During some periods, those who passed the examination were entitled not only to a government job but also to wear special garb; this entitled them to be accorded special courtesies by anyone they happened to meet. In some dynasties, passing the examinations could result in exemption from taxes. Passing the examination might even exempt one from government-sponsored interrogation by torture if the individual was suspected of committing a crime. Clearly, it paid to do well on these difficult examinations.

> **JUST THINK . . .**
>
> What parallels in terms of privileges and benefits can you draw between doing well on examinations in ancient China and doing well on modern-day civil service examinations?

We know from historical records such as the Edwin Smyth Papyrus, a document that dates back to 1600 B.C.E., that ancient Egyptian physicians had a developing knowledge of human anatomy, as well as budding expertise in medical and surgical procedures. However, psychological assessment (in the broadest sense of that term), as well as counseling and psychotherapy, were probably more the province of the priest than the physician. Egyptian priests were trained in much more than religion. They typically had knowledge of the healing arts, philosophy, architecture, math, and astronomy (Erman, 1971; White, 1963; Wilson, 1951). They were called upon to answer questions related to the meaning of dreams, as well as many other questions related to life—and the afterlife. The Ebers papyrus (1550 B.C.E.), another ancient Egyptian document, listed incantations used in efforts to ward off demons presumed to wreak havoc with one's physical and mental health.

Also intriguing from a historical perspective are ancient Greco-Roman writings indicative of attempts to categorize people in terms of personality types. Such categorizations typically included reference to an overabundance or deficiency in some bodily fluid (such as blood or phlegm) as a factor believed to influence personality. During the Middle Ages, a question of critical importance was "Who is in league with the Devil?" and various measurement procedures were devised to address this question.

**JUST THINK . . .**

Among the most critical "diagnostic" questions during the Middle Ages was "Who is in league with the Devil?" What is one of the most critical diagnostic questions today?

It would not be until the Renaissance that psychological assessment in the modern sense began to emerge. By the eighteenth century, Christian von Wolff (1732, 1734) had anticipated psychology as a science and psychological measurement as a specialty within that science.

In 1859, the book *On the Origin of Species by Means of Natural Selection* by Charles Darwin (1809–1882) was published. In this important, far-reaching work, Darwin argued that chance variation in species would be selected or rejected by nature according to adaptivity and survival value. He further argued that humans had descended from the ape as a result of such chance genetic variations. This revolutionary notion aroused interest, admiration, and a good deal of enmity. The enmity came primarily from religious individuals who interpreted Darwin's ideas as an affront to the biblical account of creation in Genesis. Still, the notion of an evolutionary link between human beings and animals conferred a new scientific respectability on experimentation with animals. It also raised questions about how animals and humans compare with respect to states of consciousness—questions that would beg for answers in laboratories of future behavioral scientists.[1]

History records that it was Darwin who spurred scientific interest in individual differences. Darwin (1859) wrote:

> The many slight differences which appear in the offspring from the same parents . . . may be called individual differences. . . . These individual differences are of the highest importance . . . [for they] afford materials for natural selection to act on. (p. 125)

Indeed, Darwin's writing on individual differences kindled interest in research on heredity by his half cousin, Francis Galton. In the course of his efforts to explore and quantify individual differences between people, Galton became an extremely influential contributor to the field of measurement (Forrest, 1974). Galton (1869) aspired to classify people "according to their natural gifts" (p. 1) and to ascertain their "deviation from an average" (p. 11). Along the way, Galton would be credited with devising or contributing to the development of many contemporary tools of psychological assessment, including questionnaires, rating scales, and self-report inventories.

Galton's initial work on heredity was done with sweet peas, in part because there tended to be fewer variations among the peas in a single pod. In this work Galton pioneered the use of a statistical concept central to psychological experimentation and

---

1. The influence of Darwin's thinking is also apparent in the theory of personality formulated by Sigmund Freud. In this context, Freud's notion of the primary importance of instinctual sexual and aggressive urges can be better understood.

testing: the coefficient of correlation. Although Karl Pearson (1857–1936) developed the product-moment correlation technique, its roots can be traced directly to the work of Galton (Magnello & Spies, 1984). From heredity in peas, Galton's interest turned to heredity in humans and various ways of measuring aspects of people and their abilities.

At an exhibition in London in 1884, Galton displayed his Anthropometric Laboratory, where for a few pence you could be measured on variables such as height (standing), height (sitting), arm span, weight, breathing capacity, strength of pull, strength of squeeze, swiftness of blow, keenness of sight, memory of form, discrimination of color, and steadiness of hand. Through his own efforts and his urging of educational institutions to keep anthropometric records on their students, Galton excited widespread interest in the measurement of psychology-related variables.

Assessment was also an important activity at the first experimental psychology laboratory, founded at the University of Leipzig in Germany by Wilhelm Max Wundt (1832–1920), a medical doctor whose title at the university was professor of philosophy. Wundt and his students tried to formulate a general description of human abilities with respect to variables such as reaction time, perception, and attention span. In contrast to Galton, Wundt focused on how people were similar, not different. In fact, Wundt viewed individual differences as a frustrating source of error in experimentation, and he attempted to control all extraneous variables in an effort to reduce error to a minimum. As we will see, such attempts are fairly routine in contemporary assessment. The objective is to ensure that any observed differences in performance are indeed due to differences between the people being measured and not to any extraneous variables. Manuals for the administration of many tests provide explicit instructions designed to hold constant or "standardize" the conditions under which the test is administered. This is so that any differences in scores on the test are due to differences in the testtakers rather than to differences in the conditions under which the test is administered. In Chapter 4 we will elaborate on the meaning of terms such as *standardized* and *standardization* as applied to tests.

> **JUST THINK . . .**
>
> Which orientation in assessment research appeals to you more, the Galtonian orientation (researching how individuals differ) or the Wundtian (researching how individuals are the same)? Why? Do you think researchers arrive at similar conclusions despite these two contrasting orientations?

In spite of the prevailing research focus on people's similarities, one of Wundt's students at Leipzig, an American named James McKeen Cattell (Figure 2–2), completed a doctoral dissertation that dealt with individual differences—specifically, individual differences in reaction time. After receiving his doctoral degree from Leipzig, Cattell returned to the United States, teaching at Bryn Mawr and then at the University of Pennsylvania, before leaving for Europe to teach at Cambridge. At Cambridge, Cattell came in contact with Galton, whom he later described as "the greatest man I have known" (Roback, 1961, p. 96).

Inspired by his interaction with Galton, Cattell returned to the University of Pennsylvania in 1888 and coined the term *mental test* in an 1890 publication. Boring (1950, p. 283) noted that "Cattell more than any other person was in this fashion responsible for getting mental testing underway in America, and it is plain that his motivation was similar to Galton's and that he was influenced, or at least reinforced, by Galton." Cattell went on to become professor and chair of the psychology department at Columbia University. Over the next 26 years, he not only trained many psychologists but also founded a number of publications (such as the *Psychological Review, Science,* and *American Men of Science*). In 1921, Cattell was instrumental in founding the Psychological Corporation, which named 20 of the country's leading psychologists as its directors.

**Figure 2–2**
**The Cattells—James McKeen and Psyche**

*The psychologist who coined the term* mental test, *James McKeen Cattell (1860–1944), has often been mistakenly credited (along with another psychologist, Raymond B. Cattell, no relation) with the authorship of a measure of infant intelligence called the Cattell Infant Intelligence Scale (CIIS). Actually, it was Psyche (1893–1989), the third of seven children of Cattell and his wife, Josephine Owen, who created the CIIS. From 1919 through 1921, Psyche assisted her famous father in statistical analyses for the third edition of* American Men of Science. *In 1927, she earned a doctor of education degree at Harvard. In 1931 she adopted a son, becoming one of the first unmarried women to do so (Sokal, 1991). Later in the decade she adopted a daughter. Her book* The Measurement of Intelligence in Infants and Young Children, *published in 1940, introduced the CIIS. Later in her career she would write a child-rearing guide,* Raising Children with Love and Limits. *This book refuted the permissiveness advocated by authorities such as Benjamin Spock.*

The goal of the corporation was the "advancement of psychology and the promotion of the useful applications of psychology."[2]

Other students of Wundt at Leipzig included Charles Spearman, Victor Henri, Emil Kraepelin, E. B. Titchener, G. Stanley Hall, and Lightner Witmer. Spearman is credited with originating the concept of test reliability as well as building the mathematical framework for the statistical technique of factor analysis. Victor Henri is the Frenchman who would collaborate with Alfred Binet on papers suggesting how mental tests could be used to measure higher mental processes (for example, Binet & Henri, 1895a, 1895b, 1895c). Psychiatrist Emil Kraepelin was an early experimenter with the word association technique as a formal test (Kraepelin, 1892, 1895). Lightner Witmer received his Ph.D. from Leipzig and went on to succeed Cattell as director of the psychology laboratory at the University of Pennsylvania. Witmer has been cited as the "little-known founder of clinical psychology" (McReynolds, 1987), owing at least in part to his being challenged to treat a "chronic bad speller" in March of 1896 (Brotemarkle, 1947). Later that year Witmer founded the first psychological clinic in the United States at the University of

---

2. Today, many of the products and services of what was once known as the Psychological Corporation have been absorbed under the "PsychCorp" brand of a corporate parent, Pearson Assessment, Inc.

Pennsylvania. In 1907 Witmer founded the journal *Psychological Clinic*. The first article in that journal was entitled "Clinical Psychology" (Witmer, 1907).

## The Twentieth Century

Much of the nineteenth-century testing that could be described as psychological in nature involved the measurement of sensory abilities, reaction time, and the like. Generally the public was fascinated by such testing. However, there was no widespread belief that testing for variables such as reaction time had any applied value. But all of that would change in the early 1900s with the birth of the first formal tests of intelligence. These were tests that were useful for reasons readily understandable to anyone who had school-age children. Public receptivity to psychological tests would shift from mild curiosity to outright enthusiasm as more and more instruments that purportedly quantified mental ability were introduced. Soon there would be tests to measure sundry mental characteristics such as personality, interests, attitudes, values, and widely varied mental abilities. It all began with a single test designed for use with young Paris pupils.

**The measurement of intelligence**   As early as 1895, Alfred Binet (1857–1911) and his colleague Victor Henri published several articles in which they argued for the measurement of abilities such as memory and social comprehension. Ten years later, Binet and collaborator Theodore Simon published a 30-item "measuring scale of intelligence" designed to help identify mentally retarded Paris schoolchildren (Binet & Simon, 1905). The Binet test would subsequently go through many revisions and translations—and, in the process, launch both the intelligence testing movement and the clinical testing movement. Before long, psychological tests were being used with regularity in such diverse settings as schools, hospitals, clinics, courts, reformatories, and prisons (Pintner, 1931).

> **JUST THINK . . .**
>
> In the early 1900s, the Binet test was being used worldwide for various purposes far beyond identifying exceptional Paris schoolchildren. What were some of the other uses of the test? How appropriate do you think it was to use this test for these other purposes?

In 1939 David Wechsler, a clinical psychologist at Bellevue Hospital in New York City, introduced a test designed to measure adult intelligence. For Wechsler, intelligence was "the aggregate or global capacity of the individual to act purposefully, to think rationally, and to deal effectively with his environment" (Wechsler, 1939, p. 3). Originally christened the Wechsler-Bellevue Intelligence Scale, the test was subsequently revised and renamed the Wechsler Adult Intelligence Scale (WAIS). The WAIS has been revised several times since then, and versions of Wechsler's test have been published that extend the age range of testtakers from early childhood through senior adulthood. These tests will be discussed in greater detail in the chapters that deal with the assessment of intelligence.

> **JUST THINK . . .**
>
> Should the definition of *intelligence* change as one moves from infancy through childhood, adolescence, adulthood, and senior adulthood?

A natural outgrowth of the individually administered intelligence test devised by Binet was the *group* intelligence test. Group intelligence tests came into being in the United States in response to the military's need for an efficient method of screening the intellectual ability of World War I recruits. This same need again became urgent as the United States prepared for entry into World War II. Psychologists would again be called upon by the government service to develop group tests, administer them to recruits, and interpret the test data.

After the war, psychologists returning from military service brought back a wealth of applied testing skills that would be useful in civilian as well as governmental applications. Psychological tests were increasingly used in diverse settings, including large corporations and private organizations. New tests were being developed at a brisk pace to measure various abilities and interests as well as personality.

**The measurement of personality**    Public receptivity to tests of intellectual ability spurred the development of many other types of tests (Garrett & Schneck, 1933; Pintner, 1931). Only eight years after the publication of Binet's scale, the field of psychology was being criticized for being too test oriented (Sylvester, 1913). By the late 1930s, approximately 4,000 different psychological tests were in print (Buros, 1938), and "clinical psychology" was synonymous with "mental testing" (Institute for Juvenile Research, 1937; Tulchin, 1939).

World War I had brought with it not only the need to screen the intellectual functioning of recruits but also the need to screen for recruits' general adjustment. A governmental Committee on Emotional Fitness chaired by psychologist Robert S. Woodworth was assigned the task of developing a measure of adjustment and emotional stability that could be administered quickly and efficiently to groups of recruits. The committee developed several experimental versions of what were, in essence, paper-and-pencil psychiatric interviews. To disguise the true purpose of one such test, the questionnaire was labeled as a "Personal Data Sheet." Draftees and volunteers were asked to indicate *yes* or *no* to a series of questions that probed for the existence of various kinds of psychopathology. For example, one of the test questions was "Are you troubled with the idea that people are watching you on the street?"

The Personal Data Sheet developed by Woodworth and his colleagues never went beyond the experimental stages, for the treaty of peace rendered the development of this and other tests less urgent. After the war, Woodworth developed a personality test for civilian use that was based on the Personal Data Sheet. He called it the Woodworth Psychoneurotic Inventory. This instrument was the first widely used measure of personality. In general, **self-report** refers to a process whereby assessees themselves supply assessment-related information by responding to questions, keeping a diary, or self-monitoring thoughts or behaviors.

Personality tests that employ self-report methodologies have both advantages and disadvantages. On the face of it, respondents are arguably the best-qualified people to provide answers about themselves. However, there are also compelling arguments *against* respondents supplying such information. For example, respondents may have poor insight into themselves. People might honestly believe some things about themselves that in reality are not true. And regardless of the quality of their insight, some respondents are unwilling to reveal anything about themselves that is very personal or that could put them in a negative light. Given these shortcomings of the self-report method of personality assessment, there was a need for alternative types of personality tests.

Various methods were developed to provide measures of personality that did not rely on self-report. One such method or approach to personality assessment came to be described as *projective* in nature. A **projective test** is one in which an individual is assumed to "project" onto some ambiguous stimulus his or her own unique needs, fears, hopes, and motivation. The ambiguous stimulus might be an inkblot, a drawing, a photograph, or something else. Perhaps the best known of all projective tests is the Rorschach, a series of inkblots developed by the Swiss psychiatrist Hermann Rorschach.

**JUST THINK . . .**

Describe an ideal situation for obtaining personality-related information by means of self-report. In what type of situation might it be inadvisable to rely solely on an assessee's self-report?

The use of pictures as projective stimuli was popularized in the late 1930s by Henry A. Murray, Christiana D. Morgan, and their colleagues at the Harvard Psychological Clinic.

When pictures or photos are used as projective stimuli, respondents are typically asked to tell a story about the picture they are shown. The stories told are then analyzed in terms of what needs and motivations the respondents may be projecting onto the ambiguous pictures. Projective and many other types of instruments used in personality assessment will be discussed in Chapter 13.

**JUST THINK . . .**

What potential problems do you think might attend the use of projective methods to assess personality?

**The academic and applied traditions**   Like the development of its parent field, psychology, the development of psychological measurement can be traced along two distinct threads: the academic and the applied. In the tradition of Galton, Wundt, and other scholars, researchers at universities throughout the world use the tools of assessment to help advance knowledge and understanding of human and animal behavior. Yet there is also an applied tradition, one that dates at least back to ancient China and the examinations developed there to help select applicants for various positions on the basis of merit. Today society relies on the tools of psychological assessment to help answer important questions. Who is best for this job? What class should this child be placed in? Who is competent to stand trial? Tests and other tools of assessment, when used in a competent manner, can help provide answers.

Today perhaps more than ever before, there is a great appreciation for the role of culture in the human experience. So, whether in academic or applied settings, assessment professionals recognize the need for cultural sensitivity in the development and use of the tools of psychological assessment. In what follows, we briefly overview some of the issues that such cultural sensitivity entails.

# Culture and Assessment

**Culture** may be defined as "the socially transmitted behavior patterns, beliefs, and products of work of a particular population, community, or group of people" (Cohen, 1994, p. 5). As taught to us by parents, peers, and societal institutions such as schools, culture prescribes many behaviors and ways of thinking. Spoken language, attitudes toward elders, and techniques of child rearing are but a few critical manifestations of culture. Culture teaches specific rituals to be performed at birth, marriage, death, and other momentous occasions. Culture imparts much about what is to be valued or prized as well as what is to be rejected or despised. Culture teaches a point of view about what it means to be born of one or another gender, race, or ethnic background. Culture teaches us something about what we can expect from other people and what we can expect from ourselves. Indeed, the influence of culture on an individual's thoughts and behavior may be a great deal stronger than most of us would acknowledge at first blush.

Professionals involved in the assessment enterprise have shown increasing sensitivity to the role of culture in many different aspects of measurement. This sensitivity is manifested in greater consideration of cultural issues with respect to every aspect of test development and use, including decision making on the basis of test data. Unfortunately, it was not always that way.

**JUST THINK . . .**

Can you think of one way in which you are a product of your culture? How about one way this fact might come through on a psychological test?

## Evolving Interest in Culture-Related Issues

Soon after Alfred Binet introduced intelligence testing in France, the U.S. Public Health Service began using such tests to measure the intelligence of people seeking to immigrate to the United States (Figure 2–3). Henry H. Goddard, who had been highly instrumental in getting Binet's test adopted for use in various settings in the United States, was the chief researcher assigned to the project. Early on, Goddard raised questions about how meaningful such tests are when used with people from various cultural and language backgrounds. Goddard (1913) used interpreters in test administration, employed a bilingual psychologist, and administered mental tests to selected immigrants who appeared mentally retarded to trained observers. Although seemingly sensitive to cultural issues in assessment, Goddard's legacy with regard to such sensitivity is, at best, controversial. Goddard found most immigrants from various nationalities to be mentally deficient when tested. In one widely quoted report, 35 Jews, 22 Hungarians, 50 Italians, and 45 Russians were selected for testing among the masses of immigrants being processed for entry into the United States at Ellis Island. Reporting on his findings in a paper entitled "Mental Tests and the Immigrant," Goddard (1917) concluded that, in this sample, 83% of the Jews, 80% of the Hungarians, 79% of the Italians, and 87% of the Russians were feebleminded. Although Goddard had written extensively on the genetic

**Figure 2–3**
**Psychological Testing at Ellis Island**

*Immigrants coming to America via Ellis Island were greeted not only by the Statue of Liberty but also by immigration officials ready to evaluate them with respect to physical, mental, and other variables. Here, a block design test, one measure of intelligence, is administered to a would-be American. Immigrants who failed physical, mental, or other tests were returned to their country of origin at the expense of the shipping company that had brought them. Critics would later charge that at least some of the immigrants who had fared poorly on mental tests were sent away from our shores not because they were actually mentally deficient but simply because they did not understand English well enough to follow instructions. Critics also questioned the criteria on which these immigrants from many lands were being evaluated.*

nature of mental deficiency, it is to his credit that he did not summarily conclude that these test findings were the result of hereditary. Rather, Goddard (1917) wondered aloud whether the findings were due to "hereditary defect" or "apparent defect due to deprivation" (p. 243). In reality, the findings were largely the result of using a translated Binet test that overestimated mental deficiency in native English-speaking populations, let alone immigrant populations (Terman, 1916).

**JUST THINK . . .**

From a cultural perspective, what are the pros and cons of testing the intelligence of potential immigrants?

Goddard's research, although leaving much to be desired methodologically, fueled the fires of an ongoing nature–nurture debate about what intelligence tests actually measure. On one side were those who viewed intelligence test results as indicative of some underlying native ability. On the other side were those who viewed such data as indicative of the extent to which knowledge and skills had been acquired. More details about the highly influential Henry Goddard and his most controversial career are presented in this chapter's *Close-Up.*

If language and culture did indeed have an effect on mental ability test scores, then how could a more unconfounded or "pure" measure of intelligence be obtained? One way that early test developers attempted to deal with the impact of language and culture on tests of mental ability was, in essence, to "isolate" the cultural variable. So-called **culture-specific tests,** or tests designed for use with people from one culture but not from another, soon began to appear on the scene. Representative of the culture-specific approach to test development were early versions of some of the best-known tests of intelligence. For example, the 1937 revision of the Stanford-Binet Intelligence Scale, which enjoyed widespread use until it was revised in 1960, included no minority children in the research that went into its formulation. Similarly, the Wechsler-Bellevue Intelligence Scale, forerunner of a widely used measure of adult intelligence, contained no minority members in the samples of testtakers used in its development. Although "a large number" of Blacks had, in fact, been tested (Wechsler, 1944), that data had been omitted from the final test manual because the test developers "did not feel that norms derived by mixing the populations could be interpreted without special provisos and reservations." Hence, Wechsler (1944) stated at the outset that the Wechsler-Bellevue norms could not be used for "the colored populations of the United States." In like fashion, the inaugural edition of the Wechsler Intelligence Scale for Children (WISC), first published in 1949 and not revised until 1974, contained no minority children in its development.

**JUST THINK . . .**

Try your hand at creating one culture-specific test item on any subject. Testtakers from what culture would probably succeed in responding correctly to the item? Testtakers from what culture would not?

Even though many published tests were purposely designed to be culture-specific, it soon became apparent that the tests were being administered—improperly—to people from different cultures. Perhaps not surprisingly, testtakers from minority cultures tended to score lower as a group than people from the group for whom the test was developed. Illustrative of the type of problems encountered by test users was this item from the 1949 WISC: "If your mother sends you to the store for a loaf of bread and there is none, what do you do?" Many Hispanic children were routinely sent to the store for tortillas and so were not familiar with the phrase "loaf of bread."

Today test developers typically take many steps to ensure that a major test developed for national use is indeed suitable for such use. Those steps might involve administering a preliminary version of the test to a tryout sample of testtakers from various cultural backgrounds, particularly from those whose members are likely to be administered the final version of the test. Examiners who administer the test may

## The Controversial Career of Henry Herbert Goddard

Born to a devout Quaker family in Maine, Henry Herbert Goddard (1866–1957) was the fifth and youngest child born to farmer Henry Clay Goddard and Sarah Winslow Goddard. The elder Goddard was gored by a bull and succumbed to the injuries he sustained when young Henry was 9. Sarah would subsequently marry a missionary, and she and her new husband would travel the United States and abroad preaching. Young Henry attended boarding school at Oak Grove Seminary in Maine and the Friends School in Providence, Rhode Island. After earning his bachelor's degree from Haverford College, a Quaker-founded school just outside of Philadelphia, he set off to California to visit an older sister. While there he accepted a temporary teaching post at the University of Southern California (USC) that included coaching the school's football team. And so it came to pass that, among Herbert H. Goddard's many lifelong achievements, he could list the distinction of being USC's first football coach (along with a co-coach; see Pierson, 1974).

Goddard returned to Haverford in 1889 to earn a master's degree in mathematics and then took a position as a teacher, principal, and prayer service conductor at a small Quaker school in Ohio. In August of that year he married Emma Florence Robbins; the couple never had children. Goddard enrolled to study psychology at Clark University and by 1899 had earned a doctorate under G. Stanley Hall. Goddard's doctoral dissertation, a blending of his interests in faith and science, was entitled, "The Effects of Mind on Body as Evidenced in Faith Cures."

Goddard became a professor at the State Normal School in West Chester, Pennsylvania, a teacher's college, where he cultivated an interest in the growing child-welfare movement. As a result of his interest in studying children, Goddard had occasion to meet Edward Johnstone, the superintendent of the New Jersey Home for Feeble-Minded Children in Vineland, New Jersey. In 1902 Goddard and Johnstone, along with educator Earl Barnes, founded a "Feebleminded Club," which—despite its misleading name by current standards—served as an interdisciplinary forum for the exchange of ideas regarding special education. By 1906 Goddard felt frustrated in his teaching position. His friend Johnstone created the position of Director of Psychological Research at the Vineland facility and so Goddard moved to New Jersey.

In 1908, with a newfound interest in the study of "feeblemindedness" (mental deficiency), Goddard toured psychology laboratories in Europe. It is a matter of historical interest that on this tour he did *not* visit Binet at the Sorbonne in Paris. Rather, it happened that a Belgian psychologist (Ovide Decroly) informed Goddard of Binet's work and gave him a copy of the Binet-Simon Scale. Few people at the time could appreciate just how momentous the Decroly–Goddard meeting would be nor how influential Goddard would become in terms of launching the testing movement. Returning to New Jersey, Goddard oversaw the translation of Binet's test and distributed thousands of copies of it to professionals working in various settings. Before long, Binet's test would be used in schools, hospitals, and clinics to help make diagnostic and treatment decisions. The military would use the test, as well as other newly created intelligence tests, to screen recruits. Courts would even begin to mandate the use of intelligence tests to aid in making determinations as to the intelligence of criminal defendants. Such uses of psychological tests were very "cutting edge" at the time.

At the Vineland facility, Goddard found that Binet's test appeared to work very well in terms of quantifying degrees of mental deficiency. Goddard devised a system of classifying assessees by their performance on the test, coining the term *moron* and using other such terms that today are out of favor and not in use. Goddard fervently believed that one's placement on the test was revealing in terms of many facets of one's life. He believed intelligence tests held the key to answers to questions about everything from what job one should be working at to what activities could make one happy. Further, Goddard came to associate low intelligence with many of the day's most urgent social problems, ranging from crime to unemployment to poverty. According to him, addressing the problem of low intelligence was a prerequisite to addressing prevailing social problems.

Although previously disposed to believing that mental deficiency was primarily the result of environmental factors, Goddard's perspective was radically modified by exposure to the views of biologist Charles Davenport. Davenport was a strong believer that heredity played a role in mental deficiency and was a staunch advocate of **eugenics,** the science of improving the qualities of a breed (in this case, humans) through intervention with factors related to heredity. Davenport collaborated with Goddard in collecting hereditary information on children at the Vineland school. At Davenport's urgings, the research included a component whereby a "eugenic field worker," trained to identify mentally deficient individuals, would be sent out to research the mental capabilities of relatives of the residents of the Vineland facility.

The data Goddard and Davenport collected was used to argue the case that mental deficiency was caused by a recessive gene and could be inherited, much like eye color is inherited. Consequently, Goddard believed that—in the interest of the greater good of society at large—mentally deficient individuals should be segregated or institutionalized (at places such as Vineland) and not be permitted to reproduce. By publicly advocating this view, Goddard, along with Edward Johnstone, "transformed their obscure little institution in rural New Jersey into a center of international influence—a model school famous for its advocacy of special education, scientific research, and social reform" (Zenderland, 1998, p. 233).

Goddard traced the lineage of one of his students at the Vineland school back five generations in his first (and most famous) book, *The Kallikak Family: A Study in the Heredity of Feeble-Mindedness* (1912). In this book Goddard sought to prove how the hereditary "menace of feeble-mindedness" manifested itself in one New Jersey family. "Kallikak" was the fictional surname given to the Vineland student, Deborah, whose previous generations of relatives were from distinctly "good" (from the Greek *kalos*) or "bad" (from the Greek *kakos*)

genetic inheritance. The book traced the family lineages resulting from the legitimate and illegitimate unions of a Revolutionary War soldier given the pseudonym "Martin Kallikak." Martin had fathered children both with a mentally defective waitress and with the woman he married— the latter being a socially prominent and reportedly normal (intellectually) Quaker. Goddard determined that feeblemindedness ran in the line of descendants from the illegitimate tryst with the waitress. Deborah Kallikak was simply the latest descendant in that line of descendants to manifest that trait. By contrast, the line of descendants from Martin and his wife contained primarily fine citizens. But how did Goddard come to this conclusion?

One thing Goddard did *not* do was administer the Binet to all of the descendants on both the "good" and the "bad" sides of Martin Kallikak's lineage over the course of some 100 years. Instead Goddard employed a crude case study approach ranging from analysis of official records and documents (which tended to be scarce) to reports of neighbors (later characterized by critics as unreliable gossip). Conclusions regarding the feeblemindedness of descendants were likely to be linked to any evidence of alcoholism, delinquency, truancy, criminality, prostitution, illegitimacy, or economic dependence. Some of Martin Kallikak's descendants, alive at the time the research was being conducted, were classified as feebleminded solely on the basis of their physical appearance. Goddard (1912) wrote, for example:

> The girl of twelve should have been at school, according to the law, but when one saw her face, one realized that it made no difference. She was pretty, with olive complexion and dark, languid eyes, but there was no mind there. (pp. 72–73)

Although well received by the public, the lack of sophistication in the book's research methodology was a cause for concern for many professionals. In particular, psychiatrist Abraham Myerson (1925) attacked the Kallikak study, and the eugenics movement in general, as pseudoscience (see also Trent, 2001). Myerson reanalyzed data from studies purporting to support the idea that various physical and mental conditions could be inherited, and he criticized those studies on statistical grounds. He especially criticized Goddard for making sweeping and unfounded generalizations from questionable data. Goddard's book became an increasing cause for concern because it was used (along with related writings on the menace of feeblemindedness) to support radical arguments in favor of eugenics, forced sterilization, restricted immigration, and other social causes. Goddard classified many people as feebleminded based on undesirable social status,

*(continued)*

# The Controversial Career of Henry Herbert Goddard *(continued)*

illegitimacy, or "sinful" activity. This fact has left some scholars wondering how much Goddard's own religious upbringing—along with biblical teachings linking children's problems with parents' sins—may have been inappropriately emphasized in what was supposed to be strictly scientific writing.

After 12 years at Vineland, Goddard left under conditions that have been the subject of some speculation (Wehmeyer & Smith, 2006). From 1918 through 1922, Goddard was director of the Ohio Bureau of Juvenile Research. From 1922 until his retirement in 1938, Goddard was a psychology professor at the Ohio State University. In 1947 Goddard moved to Santa Barbara, California, where he lived until his death at the age of 90. His remains were cremated and interred at the Vineland school, along with those of his wife, who had predeceased him in 1936.

Goddard's accomplishments were many. It was largely through his efforts that state mandates requiring special education services first became law. These laws worked to the benefit of many mentally deficient as well as many gifted students. Goddard's introduction of Binet's test to American society attracted other researchers, such as Lewis Terman, to see what they could do in terms of improving the test for various applications. Goddard's writings certainly had a momentous heuristic impact on the nature–nurture question. His books and papers stimulated many others to research and write, if only to disprove Goddard's conclusions. Goddard advocated for court acceptance of intelligence test data into evidence and for the limitation of criminal responsibility in the case of mentally defective defendants, especially with respect to capital crimes. He personally contributed his time to military screening efforts during World War I. Of more dubious distinction, of course, was the Ellis Island intelligence testing program he set up to screen immigrants. Although ostensibly well intentioned, this effort resulted in the misclassification and consequential repatriation of countless would-be citizens.

Despite an impressive list of career accomplishments, the light of history has not shone favorably on Henry Goddard. Goddard's (1912) recommendation for segregation of the mentally deficient and his calls for their

sterilization tend to be viewed as, at best, misguided. The low esteem in which Goddard is generally held today is perhaps compounded by the fact that Goddard's work has traditionally been held in very *high* esteem by some groups with radically offensive views, such as the Nazi party. During the late 1930s and early 1940s, more than 40,000 people were euthanized by Nazi physicians simply because they were deemed mentally deficient. This action preceded the horrific and systematic mass murder of more than 6 million innocent civilians by the Nazi military. The alleged "genetic defect" of most of these victims was that they were Jewish. Clearly, eugenicist propaganda fed to the German public was being used by the Nazi party for political means. The purported goal was to "purify German blood" by limiting or totally eliminating the ability of people from various groups to reproduce.

It is not a matter of controversy that Goddard used ill-advised research methods to derive many of his conclusions; he himself acknowledged this sad fact in later life. At the very least Goddard could be criticized for being too easily influenced by the (bad) ideas of others, for being somewhat naive in terms of how his writings were being used, and for not being up to the task of executing methodologically sound research. Goddard focused on the nature side of the nature–nurture controversy not because he was an ardent eugenicist at heart but rather because the nature side of the coin was where researchers at the time all tended to focus. Responding to a critic some years later, Goddard (letter to Nicolas Pastore dated April 3, 1948, quoted in J. D. Smith, 1985) wrote, in part, that he had "no inclination to deemphasize environment . . . [but] in those days environment was not being considered."

The conclusion of Leila Zenderland's relatively sympathetic biography of Goddard leaves one with the impression that he was basically a decent and likable man who was a product of his times. He harbored neither evil intentions nor right-wing prejudices. For her, a review of the life of Henry Herbert Goddard should serve as a warning not to reflexively jump to the conclusion that "bad science is usually the product of bad motives or, more broadly, bad character" (1998, p. 358).

be asked to describe their impressions with regard to various aspects of testtakers' responses. For example, subjective impressions regarding testtakers' reactions to the test materials or opinions regarding the clarity of instructions will be noted. All of the accumulated test scores from the tryout sample will be analyzed to determine if any individual item seems to be biased with regard to race, gender, or culture. In addition, a panel of independent reviewers may be asked to go through the test items and screen them for possible bias. A revised version of the test may then be administered to a large sample of testtakers that is representative of key variables of the latest U.S. Census data (such as age, gender, ethnic background, and socioeconomic status). Information from this large-scale test administration will also be used to root out any identifiable sources of bias. More details regarding the contemporary process of test development will be presented in Chapter 8.

## Some Issues Regarding Culture and Assessment

Communication between assessor and assessee is a most basic part of assessment. Assessors must be sensitive to any differences between the language or dialect familiar to assessees and the language in which the assessment is conducted. Assessors must also be sensitive to the degree to which assessees have been exposed to the dominant culture and the extent to which they have made a conscious choice to become assimilated. Next, we briefly consider assessment-related issues of communication, both verbal and nonverbal, in a cultural context.

**Verbal communication**   Language, the means by which information is communicated, is a key yet sometimes overlooked variable in the assessment process. Most obviously, the examiner and the examinee must speak the same language. This is necessary not only for the assessment to proceed but also for the assessor's conclusions regarding the assessment to be reasonably accurate. If a test is in written form and includes written instructions, then the testtaker must be able to read and comprehend what is written. When the language in which the assessment is conducted is not the assessee's primary language, he or she may not fully comprehend the instructions or the test items. The danger of such misunderstanding may increase as infrequently used vocabulary or unusual idioms are employed in the assessment. All of the foregoing presumes that the assessee is making a sincere and well-intentioned effort to respond to the demands of the assessment. Although this is frequently presumed, it is not always the case. In some instances, assessees may purposely attempt to use a language deficit to frustrate evaluation efforts (Stephens, 1992).

When an assessment is conducted with the aid of a translator, different types of problems may emerge. Depending upon the translator's skill and professionalism, subtle nuances of meaning may be lost in translation, or unintentional hints to the correct or more desirable response may be conveyed. Whether translated "live" by a translator or in writing, translated items may be either easier or more difficult than the original. Some vocabulary words may change meaning or have dual meanings when translated.

Interpreters may have limited understanding of mental health issues. In turn, an assessor may have little experience in working with a translator. So in some cases, where possible, it may be desirable to have some pre-training for interpreters on the relevant issues, and some pre-training for assessors on working with translators (Searight & Searight, 2009).

> **JUST THINK . . .**
>
> What might an assessor do to make sure that a prospective assessee's competence in the language a test is written in is sufficient to administer the test to that assessee?

In interviews or other situations in which an evaluation is made on the basis of an oral exchange between two parties, a trained examiner may detect through verbal or nonverbal means that the examinee's grasp of a language or a dialect is too deficient to proceed. A trained examiner might not be able to detect this when the test is in written form. In the case of written tests, it is clearly essential that the examinee be able to read and comprehend what is written. Otherwise the evaluation may be more about language or dialect competency than whatever the test purports to measure. Even when examiner and examinee speak the same language, miscommunication and consequential effects on test results may result owing to differences in dialect (Wolfram, 1971).

In the assessment of an individual whose proficiency in the English language is limited or nonexistent, some basic questions may need to be raised: What level of proficiency in English must the testtaker have, and does the testtaker have that proficiency? Can a meaningful assessment take place through a trained interpreter? Can an alternative and more appropriate assessment procedure be devised to meet the objectives of the assessment? In addition to linguistic barriers, the contents of tests from a particular culture are typically laden with items and material—some obvious, some very subtle—that draw heavily from that culture. Test performance may, at least in part, reflect not only whatever variables the test purports to measure but also one additional variable: the degree to which the testtaker has assimilated the culture.

**Nonverbal communication and behavior**   Humans communicate not only through verbal means but also through nonverbal means. Facial expressions, finger and hand signs, and shifts in one's position in space may all convey messages. Of course, the messages conveyed by such body language may be different from culture to culture. In American culture, for example, one who fails to look another person in the eye when speaking may be viewed as deceitful or having something to hide. However, in other cultures, failure to make eye contact when speaking may be a sign of respect.

If you have ever gone on or conducted a job interview, you may have developed a firsthand appreciation of the value of nonverbal communication in an evaluative setting. Interviewees who show enthusiasm and interest have the edge over interviewees who appear to be drowsy or bored. In clinical settings, an experienced evaluator may develop hypotheses to be tested from the nonverbal behavior of the interviewee. For example, a person who is slouching, moving slowly, and exhibiting a sad facial expression may be depressed. Then again, such an individual may be experiencing physical discomfort from any number of sources, such as a muscle spasm or an arthritis attack. It remains for the assessor to determine which hypothesis best accounts for the observed behavior.

Certain theories and systems in the mental health field go beyond more traditional interpretations of body language. For example, in **psychoanalysis,** a theory of personality and psychological treatment developed by Sigmund Freud, symbolic significance is assigned to many nonverbal acts. From a psychoanalytic perspective, an interviewee's fidgeting with a wedding band during an interview may be interpreted as a message regarding an unstable marriage. As evidenced by his thoughts on "the first chance actions" of a patient during a therapy session, Sigmund Freud believed he could tell much about motivation from nonverbal behavior:

> The first . . . chance actions of the patient . . . will betray one of the governing complexes of the neurosis. . . . A young girl . . . hurriedly pulls the hem of her skirt over her exposed ankle; she has betrayed the kernel of what analysis will discover later; her narcissistic pride in her bodily beauty and her tendencies to exhibitionism. (Freud, 1913/1959, p. 359)

This quote from Freud is also useful in illustrating the influence of culture on diagnostic and therapeutic views. Freud lived in Victorian Vienna. In that time and in that place, sex was not a subject for public discussion. In many ways Freud's views regarding a sexual basis for various thoughts and behaviors were a product of the sexually repressed culture in which he lived.

An example of a nonverbal behavior in which people differ is the speed at which they characteristically move to complete tasks. The overall pace of life in one geographic area, for example, may tend to be faster than in another. In a similar vein, differences in pace of life across cultures may enhance or detract from test scores on tests involving timed items (Gopaul-McNicol, 1993). In a more general sense, Hoffman (1962) questioned the value of timed tests of ability, particularly those tests that employed multiple-choice items. He believed such tests relied too heavily on testtakers' quickness of response and as such discriminated against the individual who is characteristically a "deep, brooding thinker."

Culture exerts effects over many aspects of nonverbal behavior. For example, a child may present as noncommunicative and having only minimal language skills when verbally examined. This finding may be due to the fact that the child is from a culture where elders are revered and where children speak to adults only when they are spoken to—and then only in as short a phrase as possible. Clearly, it is incumbent upon test users to be knowledgeable about aspects of an assessee's culture that are relevant to the assessment. Dr. Nathaniel V. Mohatt touched on such issues in his discussion of the culturally sensitive issues that were considered in the development of a new test designed primarily for use with Alaskan Natives (see this chapter's *Meet an Assessment Professional*).

> **JUST THINK . . .**
>
> Play the role of a therapist in the Freudian tradition and cite one example of a student's or an instructor's public behavior that you believe may be telling about that individual's private motivation. No naming names!

> **JUST THINK . . .**
>
> What type of test is best suited for administration to people who are "deep, brooding thinkers"? How practical for group administration would such tests be?

**Standards of evaluation** Suppose that master chefs representing nations around the globe entered a contest designed to crown "the best chicken soup in the world." Who do you think would win? The answer to that question hinges on the evaluative standard to be employed. If the sole judge of the contest was the owner of a kosher delicatessen on the Lower East Side of Manhattan, it is conceivable that the entry that came closest to the "Jewish mother homemade" variety might well be declared the winner. However, other judges might have other standards and preferences. For example, soup connoisseurs from Arabic cultures might prefer chicken soup with fresh lemon juice in the recipe. Judges from India might be inclined to give their vote to a chicken soup flavored with curry and other Asian spices. For Japanese and Chinese judges, soy sauce might be viewed as an indispensable ingredient. Ultimately, the judgment of which soup is best will probably be very much a matter of personal preference and the standard of evaluation employed.

Somewhat akin to judgments concerning the best chicken soup recipe, judgments related to certain psychological traits can also be culturally relative. For example, whether specific patterns of behavior are considered to be male- or female-appropriate will depend on the prevailing societal standards regarding masculinity and femininity. In some societies, for example, it is role-appropriate for women to fight wars and put food on the table while the men are occupied in more domestic activities. Whether specific patterns of behavior are considered to be psychopathological also depends on the prevailing societal standards. In Sudan, for example, there are tribes that live among cattle because they regard the animals as sacred. Judgments as to who might be the best

## Meet Dr. Nathaniel V. Mohatt

A good example of my approach to psychological testing and assessment is the development of the Awareness of Connectedness Scale (N. V. Mohatt et al., 2011). In developing the Awareness of Connectedness Scale (ACS) we began with the premise that scientific measurement tools for assessing risk, resiliency, and change can and should be based on cultural notions of disorder, wellness, and healing. Without looking into local culture and incorporating cultural understandings into our research, we run the risk of psychological science becoming a tool of intellectual and cultural colonialism, whereby we overlay our own culture's notions on another's without regard for the insights and explanatory power of their viewpoint. This problem is particularly important to attend to when working with Native American and other colonized people, as any furthering of colonial-like practices can cause more harm, regardless of how good our intentions may be.

**Nathaniel V. Mohatt, Ph.D., Yale University School of Medicine, Department of Psychiatry, Division of Prevention and Community Research**

The ACS arose out of a long-term research relationship between Alaska Native communities and researchers at the University of Alaska Fairbanks. The seed research that informed the development of the ACS was the People Awakening project, a community-based participatory research study examining pathways to sobriety among Alaska Native people (G. V. Mohatt et al., 2004). Out of this qualitative research emerged a model of protective factors that promote resilience and sobriety, one of which was the notion of the reciprocal interconnectedness of a person to their family, community, and natural environment. This variable is similarly discussed throughout the literature describing American Indian and Alaska Native world views, but had no equivalent in the field of psychological measurement. Furthermore, the Center for Alaska Native Health Research and communities across Alaska have been actively developing prevention programs for a number of years based on the findings from the original People Awakening project. Measuring awareness of connectedness was necessary to test the People Awakening theory of protective factors and evaluate the effectiveness of substance abuse and suicide prevention programs that seek to foster this awareness as a culture-based protective factor.

*Read more of what Dr. Mohatt had to say—his complete essay—at www.mhhe.com/cohentesting8.*

employee, manager, or leader may differ as a function of culture, as might judgments regarding intelligence, wisdom, courage, and other psychological variables.

Cultures differ from one another in the extent to which they are *individualist* or *collectivist* (Markus & Kitayama, 1991). Generally speaking, an **individualist culture** (typically associated with the dominant culture in countries such as the United States and Great Britain) is characterized by value being placed on traits such as self-reliance, autonomy, independence, uniqueness, and competitiveness. In a **collectivist culture** (typically associated with the dominant culture in many countries throughout Asia, Latin America and Africa), value is placed on traits such as conformity, cooperation, interdependence, and striving toward group goals. As a consequence of being raised in one or another of these types of cultures, people may develop certain characteristic aspects of their sense of self. Markus and Kitayama (1991) believe that people raised in Western culture tend to see themselves as having a unique constellation of traits that are stable over time and through situations. The person raised in an individualist culture exhibits behavior that is "organized and made meaningful primarily by reference to one's own internal repertoire of thoughts, feelings, and action, rather than by reference to the thoughts, feelings, and actions of others" (Markus & Kitayama, 1991, p. 226). By contrast, people raised in a collectivist culture see themselves as part of a larger whole, with much greater connectedness to others. And rather than seeing their own traits as stable over time and through situations, the person raised in a collectivist culture believes that "one's behavior is determined, contingent on, and, to a large extent organized by what the actor perceives to be the thoughts, feelings, and actions of *others* in the relationship" (Markus & Kitayama, 1991, p. 227, emphasis in the original).

**JUST THINK . . .**

When considering tools of evaluation that purport to measure the trait of assertiveness, what are some culture-related considerations that should be kept in mind?

Consider in a clinical context, for example, a psychiatric diagnosis of dependent personality disorder. To some extent the description of this disorder reflects the values of an individualist culture in deeming overdependence on others to be pathological. Yet the clinician making such a diagnosis would, ideally, be aware that such a belief foundation is contradictory to a guiding philosophy for many people from a collectivist culture wherein dependence and submission may be integral to fulfilling role obligations (Chen et al., 2009). In the workplace, individuals from collectivist cultures may be penalized in some performance ratings because they are less likely to attribute success in their jobs to themselves. Rather, they are more likely to be self-effacing and self-critical (Newman et al., 2004). The point is clear: cultural differences carry with them important implications for assessment.

A challenge inherent in the assessment enterprise concerns tempering test- and assessment-related outcomes with good judgment regarding the cultural relativity of those outcomes. In practice, this means raising questions about the applicability of assessment-related findings to specific individuals. It therefore seems prudent to supplement questions such as "How intelligent is this person?" or "How assertive is this individual?" with other questions, such as: "How appropriate are the norms or other standards that will be used to make this evaluation?" "To what extent has the assessee been assimilated by the culture from which the test is drawn, and what influence might such assimilation (or lack of it) have on the test results?" "What research has been done on the test to support the applicability of findings with it for use in evaluating this particular asssessee?" These are the types of questions that are being raised not only by responsible test users but also by courts of law.

## Tests and Group Membership

Tests and other evaluative measures administered in vocational, educational, counseling, and other settings leave little doubt that people differ from one another on an individual basis and also from group to group on a collective basis. What happens when groups systematically differ in terms of scores on a particular test? The answer, in a word, is *conflict.*

On the face of it, questions such as "What student is best qualified to be admitted to this school?" or "Which job candidate should get the job?" are rather straightforward. On the other hand, societal concerns about fairness both to individuals and to groups of individuals have made the answers to such questions matters of heated debate, if not lawsuits and civil disobedience. Consider the case of a person who happens to be a member of a particular group—cultural or otherwise—who fails to obtain a desired outcome (such as attainment of employment or admission to a university). Suppose it is further observed that most other people from that same group have also failed to obtain that same prized outcome. What may well happen is that the criteria being used to judge attainment of the prized outcome becomes the subject of intense scrutiny, sometimes by a court or a legislature.

In vocational assessment, test users are sensitive to legal and ethical mandates concerning the use of tests with regard to hiring, firing, and related decision making. If a test is used to evaluate a candidate's ability to do a job, one point of view is that the test should do just that—regardless of the group membership of the testtaker. According to this view, scores on a test of job ability should be influenced only by job-related variables. That is, scores should not be affected by variables such as group membership, hair length, eye color, or any other variable extraneous to the ability to perform the job. Although this rather straightforward view of the role of tests in personnel selection may seem consistent with principles of equal opportunity, it has attracted charges of unfairness and claims of discrimination. Why?

Claims of test-related discrimination made against major test publishers may be best understood as evidence of the great complexity of the assessment enterprise rather than as a conspiracy to use tests to discriminate against individuals from certain groups. In vocational assessment, for example, conflicts may arise from disagreements about the criteria for performing a particular job. The potential for controversy looms over almost all selection criteria that an employer sets, regardless of whether the criteria are physical, educational, psychological, or experiential.

The critical question with regard to hiring, promotion, and other selection decisions in almost any work setting is: "What criteria must be met to do this job?" A state police department may require all applicants for the position of police officer to meet certain physical requirements, including a minimum height of 5 feet 4 inches. A person who is 5 feet 2 inches tall is therefore barred from applying. Because such police force evaluation policies have the effect of systematically excluding members of cultural groups where the average height of adults is less than 5 feet 4 inches, the result may be a class-action lawsuit charging discrimination. Whether the police department's height requirement is reasonable and job related, and whether discrimination actually occurred, are complex questions that are usually left for the courts to resolve. Compelling arguments may be presented on both sides, as benevolent, fair-minded, knowledgeable, and well-intentioned people may have honest differences about the necessity of the prevailing height requirement for the job of police officer.

**JUST THINK . . .**

What might be a fair and equitable way to determine the minimum required height, if any, for police officers in your community?

Beyond the variable of height, it would seem that variables such as appearance and religion should have little to do with what job one is qualified to perform. However, it is precisely such factors that keep some group members from entry into many jobs and careers. Consider in this context observant Jews. Their appearance and dress is not mainstream. The food they eat must be kosher. They are unable to work or travel on weekends. Given the established selection criteria for many positions in corporate America, candidates who are members of the group known as observant Jews are effectively excluded, regardless of their ability to perform the work (Korman, 1988; Mael, 1991; Zweigenhaft, 1984).

General differences among groups of people also extend to psychological attributes such as measured intelligence. Unfortunately, the mere suggestion that such differences in psychological variables exist arouses skepticism if not charges of discrimination, bias, or worse. This is especially true when the observed group differences are deemed responsible for blocking one or another group from employment or educational opportunities.

If systematic differences related to group membership were found to exist on job ability test scores, then what, if anything, should be done? One view is that nothing needs to be done. According to this view, the test was designed to measure job ability, and it does what it was designed to do. In support of this view is evidence suggesting that group differences in scores on professionally developed tests do reflect differences in real-world performance (Gottfredson, 2000; Halpern, 2000; Hartigan & Wigdor, 1989; Kubiszyn et al., 2000; Neisser et al., 1996; Schmidt, 1988; Schmidt & Hunter, 1992).

**JUST THINK . . .**

What should be done if a test adequately assesses a skill required for a job but is discriminatory?

A contrasting view is that efforts should be made to "level the playing field" between groups of people. The term **affirmative action** refers to voluntary and mandatory efforts undertaken by federal, state, and local governments, private employers, and schools to combat discrimination and to promote equal opportunity for all in education and employment (American Psychological Association, 1996a, p. 2). Affirmative action seeks to create equal opportunity actively, not passively. One impetus to affirmative action is the view that "policies that appear to be neutral with regard to ethnicity or gender can operate in ways that advantage individuals from one group over individuals from another group" (Crosby et al., 2003, p. 95).

In assessment, one way of implementing affirmative action is by altering test-scoring procedures according to set guidelines. For example, an individual's score on a test could be revised according to the individual's group membership (McNemar, 1975). While proponents of this approach view such remedies as necessary to address past inequities, others condemn manipulation of test scores as introducing "inequity in equity" (Benbow & Stanley, 1996).

**JUST THINK . . .**

What are your thoughts on the manipulation of test scores as a function of group membership to advance certain social goals? Should membership in a particular cultural group trigger an automatic increase (or decrease) in test scores?

As sincerely committed as they may be to principles of egalitarianism and fair play, test developers and test users must ultimately look to society at large—and, more specifically, to laws, administrative regulations, and other rules and professional codes of conduct—for guidance in the use of tests and test scores.

**Psychology, tests, and public policy** Few people would object to using psychological tests in academic and applied contexts that obviously benefit human welfare. Then again, few people are aware of the everyday use of psychological tests in such ways. More typically, members of the general public become acquainted with the use of psychological tests in high-profile contexts, such as when an individual or a group has a great deal to gain or to lose as a result of a test score. In such situations, tests and other tools of assessment are portrayed as instruments that can have a momentous and immediate impact on one's life. In such situations, tests may be perceived by the everyday person as tools used to deny people things they very much want or need. Denial of educational advancement, dismissal from a job, denial of parole, and denial of custody are some of the more threatening consequences that the public may associate with psychological tests and assessment procedures.

Members of the public call upon government policy-makers to protect them from perceived threats. Legislators pass laws, administrative agencies make regulations, judges hand down rulings, and citizens call for referenda regarding prevailing public policies. In the section that follows, we broaden our view of the assessment enterprise beyond the concerns of the profession. Legal and ethical considerations with regard to assessment are a matter of concern to the public at large.

## Legal and Ethical Considerations

**Laws** are rules that individuals must obey for the good of the society as a whole—or rules thought to be for the good of society as a whole. Some laws are and have been relatively uncontroversial. For example, the law that mandates driving on the right side of the road has not been a subject of debate, a source of emotional soul-searching, or a stimulus to civil disobedience. For safety and the common good, most people are willing to relinquish their freedom to drive all over the road. Even visitors from countries where it is common to drive on the other side of the road will readily comply with this law when driving in the United States.

Although rules of the road may be relatively uncontroversial, there are some laws that are very controversial. Consider in this context laws pertaining to abortion, capital punishment, euthanasia, affirmative action, busing . . . the list goes on. Exactly how laws regulating matters like these should be written and interpreted are issues of heated controversy. So too is the role of testing and assessment in such matters.

Whereas a body of laws is a body of rules, a body of **ethics** is a body of principles of right, proper, or good conduct. Thus, for example, an ethic of the Old West was "Never shoot 'em in the back." Two well-known principles subscribed to by seafarers are "Women and children leave first in an emergency" and "A captain goes down with his ship."[3] The ethics of journalism dictate that reporters present all sides of a controversial issue. A principle of ethical research is that the researcher should never fudge data; all data must be reported accurately.

To the extent that a **code of professional ethics** is recognized and accepted by members of a profession, it defines the *standard of care* expected of members of that profession. In this context, we may define **standard of care** as the level at which the average, reasonable, and prudent professional would provide diagnostic or therapeutic services under the same or similar conditions.

Members of the public and members of the profession have not always been on "the same side of the fence" with respect to issues of ethics and law. Let's review how and why this has been the case.

**JUST THINK . . .**

List five ethical guidelines that you think should govern the professional behavior of psychologists involved in psychological testing and assessment.

### The Concerns of the Public

The assessment enterprise has never been very well understood by the public, and even today we might hear criticisms based on a misunderstanding of testing (e.g., "The only thing tests measure is the ability to take tests"). Possible consequences of public misunderstanding include fear, anger, legislation, litigation, and administrative regulations.

---

3. We leave the question of what to do when the captain of the ship is a woman to a volume dedicated to an in-depth exploration of seafaring ethics.

Concern about the use of psychological tests first became widespread in the aftermath of World War I, when various professionals (as well as nonprofessionals) sought to adapt group tests developed by the military for civilian use in schools and industry. Reflecting growing public discomfort with the burgeoning assessment industry were popular magazine articles featuring stories with titles such as "The Abuse of Tests" (see Haney, 1981). Less well known were voices of reason that offered constructive ways to correct what was wrong with assessment practices.

The widespread military testing during World War II in the 1940s did not attract as much popular attention as the testing undertaken during World War I. Rather, an event that took place on the other side of the globe had a far more momentous effect on testing in the United States: the launching of a satellite into space (see Figure 2–4). About a year after the Soviet Union's launch of *Sputnik*, Congress passed the National Defense Education Act, which provided federal money to local schools for the purpose of testing ability and aptitude to identify gifted and academically talented students. This event triggered a proliferation of large-scale testing programs in the schools. At the same time, the use of ability tests and personality tests for personnel selection increased in government, the military, and business. The wide and growing use of

**Figure 2–4**
**The Launch of a Satellite . . . and Renewed Interest in Testing**

*On October 4, 1957, scientists in the country then known as the Union of Soviet Socialist Republics launched a satellite (they called it* Sputnik*) into space. The event was greeted with surprise, if not shock, by most Americans. The prospect of a cold-war enemy having a satellite orbiting Earth 24 hours a day was most unsettling. The launch caused widespread concern about the ability of the United States to compete in the new frontier of space. More emphasis would have to be placed on education, particularly in subjects such as math, science, engineering, and physics. And greater efforts would have to be made to identify the gifted children who would one day apply such knowledge in the race to space.*

tests led to renewed public concern, reflected in magazine articles such as "Testing: Can Everyone Be Pigeonholed?" (*Newsweek,* July 20, 1959) and "What the Tests Do Not Test" (*New York Times Magazine,* October 2, 1960). The upshot of such concern was congressional hearings on the subject of testing (Amrine, 1965).

The fires of public concern about testing were again fanned in 1969 when widespread media attention was given to the publication of an article, in the prestigious *Harvard Educational Review,* entitled "How Much Can We Boost IQ and Scholastic Achievement?" Its author, Arthur Jensen, argued that "genetic factors are strongly implicated in the average Negro–white intelligence difference" (1969, p. 82). What followed was an outpouring of public and professional attention to nature-versus-nurture issues in addition to widespread skepticism about what intelligence tests were really measuring. By 1972 the U.S. Select Committee on Equal Education Opportunity was preparing for hearings on the matter. However, according to Haney (1981), the hearings "were canceled because they promised to be too controversial" (p. 1026).

The extent of public concern about psychological assessment is reflected in the extensive involvement of the government in many aspects of the assessment process in recent decades. Assessment has been affected in numerous and important ways by activities of the legislative, executive, and judicial branches of federal and state governments. A sampling of some landmark legislation and litigation is presented in Table 2–1.

**Table 2–1**
**Some Significant Legislation and Litigation**

| Legislation | Significance |
| --- | --- |
| Americans with Disabilities Act of 1990 | Employment testing materials and procedures must be essential to the job and not discriminate against persons with handicaps. |
| Civil Rights Act of 1964 (amended in 1991), also known as the Equal Opportunity Employment Act | It is an unlawful employment practice to adjust the scores of, use different cutoff scores for, or otherwise alter the results of employment-related tests on the basis of race, religion, sex, or national origin. |
| Family Education Rights and Privacy Act (1974) | Parents and eligible students must be given access to school records, and have a right to challenge findings in records by a hearing. |
| Health Insurance Portability and Accountability Act of 1996 (HIPAA) | New federal privacy standards limit the ways in which health care providers and others can use patients' personal information. |
| Education for All Handicapped Children (PL 94-142) (1975 and then amended several times thereafter, including IDEA of 1997 and 2004) | Screening is mandated for children suspected to have mental or physical handicaps. Once identified, an individual child must be evaluated by a professional team qualified to determine that child's special educational needs. The child must be reevaluated periodically. Amended in 1986 to extend disability-related protections downward to infants and toddlers. |
| Individuals with Disabilities Education Act (IDEA) Amendments of 1997 (PL 105-17) | Children should not be inappropriately placed in special education programs due to cultural differences. Schools should accommodate existing test instruments and other alternate means of assessment for the purpose of gauging the progress of special education students as measured by state- and district-wide assessments. |
| The No Child Left Behind (NCLB) Act of 2001 | This reauthorization of the Elementary and Secondary Education Act of 2001 was designed to "close the achievement gaps between minority and nonminority students and between disadvantaged children and their more advantaged peers" by, among other things, setting strict standards for school accountability and establishing periodic assessments to gauge the progress of school districts in improving academic achievement. The "battle cry" driving this legislation was "Demographics are not destiny!" However, by 2012, it was clear that many, perhaps the majority of states, sought or will seek waivers to opt out of NCLB and what has been viewed as its demanding bureaucratic structure, and overly ambitious goals. |

| Litigation | Significance |
|---|---|
| *Hobson v. Hansen* (1967) | U.S. Supreme Court ruled that ability tests developed on Whites could not lawfully be used to track Black students in the school system. To do so could result in resegregation of desegregated schools. |
| *Tarasoff v. Regents of the University of California* (1974) | Therapists (and presumably psychological assessors) must reveal privileged information if a third party is endangered. In the words of the Court, "Protective privilege ends where the public peril begins." |
| *Larry P. v. Riles* (1979 and reaffirmed by the same judge in 1986) | California judge ruled that the use of intelligence tests to place Black children in special classes had a discriminatory impact because the tests were "racially and culturally biased." |
| *Debra P. v. Turlington* (1981) | Federal court ruled that minimum competency testing in Florida was unconstitutional because it perpetuated the effects of past discrimination. |
| *Griggs v. Duke Power Company* (1971) | Black employees brought suit against a private company for discriminatory hiring practices. The U.S. Supreme Court found problems with "broad and general testing devices" and ruled that tests must "fairly measure the knowledge or skills required by a particular job." |
| *Albemarle Paper Company v. Moody* (1976) | An industrial psychologist at a paper mill found that scores on a general ability test predicted measures of job performance. However, as a group, Whites scored better than Blacks on the test. The U.S. District Court found the use of the test to be sufficiently job related. An appeals court did not. It ruled that discrimination had occurred, however unintended. |
| *Regents of the University of California v. Bakke* (1978) | When Alan Bakke, who had been denied admission, learned that his test scores were higher than those of some minority students who had gained admission to the University of California at Davis medical school, he sued. A highly divided U.S. Supreme Court agreed that Bakke should be admitted, but it did not preclude the use of diversity considerations in admission decisions. |
| *Allen v. District of Columbia* (1993) | Blacks scored lower than Whites on a city fire department promotion test based on specific aspects of firefighting. The court found in favor of the fire department, ruling that "the promotional examination . . . was a valid measure of the abilities and probable future success of those individuals taking the test." |
| *Adarand Constructors, Inc. v. Pena et al.* (1995) | A construction firm competing for a federal contract brought suit against the federal government after it lost a bid to a minority-controlled competitor, which the government had retained instead in the interest of affirmative action. The U.S. Supreme Court, in a close (5–4) decision, found in favor of the plaintiff, ruling that the government's affirmative action policy violated the equal protection clause of the 14th Amendment. The Court ruled, "Government may treat people differently because of their race only for the most compelling reasons." |
| *Jaffee v. Redmond* (1996) | Communication between a psychotherapist and a patient (and presumably a psychological assessor and a client) is privileged in federal courts. |
| *Grutter v. Bollinger* (2003) | In a highly divided decision, the U.S. Supreme Court approved the use of race in admissions decisions on a time-limited basis to further the educational benefits that flow from a diverse student body. |
| *Mitchell v. State*, 192 P.3d 721 (Nev. 2008) | Does a court order for a compulsory psychiatric examination of the defendant in a criminal trial violate that defendant's Fifth Amendment right to avoid self-incrimination? Given the particular circumstances of the case (see Leahy et al., 2010), the Nevada Supreme Court ruled that the defendant's right to avoid self-incrimination was not violated by the trial court's order to have him undergo a psychiatric evaluation. |

**Legislation**  Although the legislation summarized in Table 2–1 was enacted at the federal level, states also have passed legislation that affects the assessment enterprise. In the 1970s numerous states enacted **minimum competency testing programs:** formal testing programs designed to be used in decisions regarding various aspects of students' education. The data from such programs was used in decision making about grade promotions, awarding of diplomas, and identification of areas for remedial instruction. These laws grew out of grassroots support for the idea that high-school graduates should have, at the very least, "minimal competencies" in areas such as reading, writing, and arithmetic.

**Truth-in-testing legislation** was also passed at the state level beginning in the 1980s. The primary objective of these laws was to give testtakers a way to learn the criteria by which they are being judged. To meet that objective, some laws mandate the disclosure of answers to postsecondary and professional school admissions tests within 30 days of the publication of test scores. Some laws require that information relevant to a test's development and technical soundness be kept on file. Some truth-in-testing laws require providing descriptions of (1) the test's purpose and its subject matter, (2) the knowledge and skills the test purports to measure, (3) procedures for ensuring accuracy in scoring, (4) procedures for notifying testtakers of errors in scoring, and (5) procedures for ensuring the testtaker's confidentiality. Truth-in-testing laws create special difficulties for test developers and publishers, who argue that it is essential for them to keep the test items secret. They note that there may be a limited item pool for some tests and that the cost of developing an entirely new set of items for each succeeding administration of a test is prohibitive.

JUST THINK . . .

How might truth-in-testing laws be modified to better protect both the interest of testtakers and that of test developers?

Some laws mandate the involvement of the executive branch of government in their application. For example, Title VII of the Civil Rights Act of 1964 created the Equal Employment Opportunity Commission (EEOC) to enforce the act. The EEOC has published sets of guidelines concerning standards to be met in constructing and using employment tests. In 1978 the EEOC, the Civil Service Commission, the Department of Labor, and the Justice Department jointly published the *Uniform Guidelines on Employee Selection Procedures.* Here is a sample guideline:

> The use of any test which adversely affects hiring, promotion, transfer or any other employment or membership opportunity of classes protected by Title VII constitutes discrimination unless (a) the test has been validated and evidences a high degree of utility as hereinafter described, and (b) the person giving or acting upon the results of the particular test can demonstrate that alternative suitable hiring, transfer or promotion procedures are unavailable for . . . use.

Note that here the definition of discrimination as exclusionary coexists with the proviso that a valid test evidencing "a high degree of utility" (among other criteria) will not be considered discriminatory. Generally, however, the public has been quick to label a test as unfair and discriminatory regardless of its utility. As a consequence, a great public demand for proportionality by group membership in hiring and college admissions now coexists with a great lack of proportionality in skills across groups. Gottfredson (2000) noted that although selection standards can often be improved, the manipulation of such standards "will produce only lasting frustration, not enduring solutions." She recommended that enduring solutions be sought by addressing the problems related to gaps in skills between groups. She argued against addressing the problem by lowering hiring and admission standards or by legislation designed to make hiring and admissions decisions a matter of group quotas.

JUST THINK . . .

How can government and the private sector address problems related to gaps in skills between groups?

In Texas, state law was enacted mandating that the top 10% of graduating seniors at each Texas high school be admitted to a state university regardless of SAT scores. This means that, regardless of the quality of education in any particular Texas high school, a senior in the top 10% of the graduating class is guaranteed college admission regardless of how he or she might score on a nationally administered measure. In California, the use of skills tests in the public sector decreased following the passage of Proposition 209, which banned racial preferences (Rosen, 1998). One consequence has been the deemphasis on the Law School Admissions Test (LSAT) as a criterion for being accepted by the University of California at Berkeley law school. Additionally, the law school stopped weighing grade point averages from undergraduate schools in their admission criteria, so that a 4.0 from any California state school "is now worth as much as a 4.0 from Harvard" (Rosen, 1998, p. 62).

Gottfredson (2000) makes the point that those who advocate reversal of achievement standards obtain "nothing of lasting value by eliminating valid tests." For her, lowering standards amounts to hindering progress "while providing only the illusion of progress." Rather than reversing achievement standards, society is best served by action to reverse other trends with deleterious effects (such as trends in family structure). In the face of consistent gaps between members of various groups, Gottfredson emphasized the need for skills training, not a lowering of achievement standards or an unfounded attack on tests.

State and federal legislatures, executive bodies, and courts have been involved in many aspects of testing and assessment. There has been little consensus about whether validated tests on which there are racial differences can be used to assist with employment-related decisions. Courts have also been grappling with the role of diversity in criteria for admission to colleges, universities, and professional schools. For example, in 2003 the question before the U.S. Supreme Court in the case of *Grutter v. Bollinger* was "whether diversity is a compelling interest that can justify the narrowly tailored use of race in selecting applicants for admission to public universities." One of the questions to be decided in that case was whether or not the University of Michigan Law School was using a **quota system,** a selection procedure whereby a fixed number or percentage of applicants from certain backgrounds were selected.[4]

**Litigation**   Rules governing citizens' behavior stem not only from legislatures but also from interpretations of existing law in the form of decisions handed down by courts. This is why law resulting from **litigation** (the court-mediated resolution of legal matters of a civil, criminal or administrative nature) can impact our daily lives. Examples of some court cases that have affected the assessment enterprise were presented in Table 2–1 under the "Litigation" heading. It is also true that litigation can result in bringing an important and timely matter to the attention of legislators, thus serving as a stimulus to the creation of new legislation. This is exactly what happened in the cases of *PARC v. Commonwealth of Pennsylvania* (1971) and *Mills v. Board of Education of District of Columbia* (1972). In the PARC case, the Pennsylvania Association for Retarded Children brought suit because children with mental retardation in that state had been denied access to public education. In *Mills,* a similar lawsuit was filed on behalf of children with behavioral, emotional, and learning impairments. Taken together, these two cases had the effect of jump-starting similar litigation in several other jurisdictions and alerting Congress to the need for federal law to ensure appropriate educational opportunities for children with disabilities.

Litigation has sometimes been referred to as "judge-made law" because it typically comes in the form of a ruling by a court. And although judges do, in essence, create law by their rulings, these rulings are seldom made in a vacuum. Rather, judges typically rely on prior rulings and on other people—most notably, expert witnesses—to assist in their judgments. A psychologist acting as an expert witness in criminal litigation may testify on matters such as the competence of a defendant to stand trial, the competence of a witness to give testimony, or the sanity of a defendant entering a plea of "not guilty by reason of insanity." A psychologist acting as an expert witness in a civil matter could

---

4. A detailed account of *Grutter v. Bollinger* is presented on the companion website to this text at *www.mhhe .com/cohentesting8.*

conceivably offer opinions on many different types of issues ranging from the parenting skills of a parent in a divorce case to the capabilities of a factory worker prior to sustaining a head injury on the job. In a malpractice case, an expert witness might testify about how reasonable and professional the actions taken by a fellow psychologist were and whether any reasonable and prudent practitioner would have engaged in the same or similar actions (Cohen, 1979).

The issues on which expert witnesses can be called upon to give testimony are as varied as the issues that reach courtrooms for resolution. And so, some important questions arise with respect to expert witnesses. For example: Who is qualified to be an expert witness? How much weight should be given to the testimony of an expert witness? Questions such as these have themselves been the subject of litigation.

A landmark case heard by the U.S. Supreme Court in June 1993 has implications for the admissibility of expert testimony in court. The case was *Daubert v. Merrell Dow Pharmaceuticals*. The origins of this case can be traced to Mrs. Daubert's use of the prescription drug Bendectin to relieve nausea during pregnancy. The plaintiffs sued the manufacturer of this drug, Merrell Dow Pharmaceuticals, when their children were born with birth defects. They claimed that Mrs. Daubert's use of Bendectin had caused their children's birth defects.

Attorneys for the Dauberts were armed with research that they claimed would prove that Bendectin causes birth defects. However, the trial judge ruled that the research failed to meet the criteria for admissibility. In part because the evidence the Dauberts wished to present was not deemed admissible, the trial judge ruled against the Dauberts.

The Dauberts appealed to the next higher court. That court, too, ruled against them and in favor of Merrell Dow. Once again, the plaintiffs appealed, this time to the U.S. Supreme Court. A question before the Court was whether the judge in the original trial had acted properly by not allowing the plaintiffs' research to be admitted into evidence. To understand whether the trial judge acted properly, it is important to understand (1) a ruling that was made in the 1923 case of *Frye v. the United States* and (2) a law subsequently passed by Congress, Rule 702 in the *Federal Rules of Evidence* (1975).

In *Frye*, the Court held that scientific research is admissible as evidence when the research study or method enjoys general acceptance. General acceptance could typically be established by the testimony of experts and by reference to publications in peer-reviewed journals. In short, if an expert witness claimed something that most other experts in the same field would agree with then, under *Frye*, the testimony could be admitted into evidence. Rule 702 changed that by allowing more experts to testify regarding the admissibility of the original expert testimony. Beyond expert testimony indicating that some research method or technique enjoyed general acceptance in the field, other experts were now allowed to testify and present their opinions with regard to the admissibility of the evidence. So, an expert might offer an opinion to a jury concerning the acceptability of a research study or method regardless of whether that opinion represented the opinions of other experts. Rule 702 was enacted to assist juries in their fact-finding by helping them to understand the issues involved.

Presenting their case before the Supreme Court, the attorneys for the Dauberts argued that Rule 702 had wrongly been ignored by the trial judge. The attorneys for the defendant, Merrell Dow Pharmaceuticals, countered that the trial judge had ruled appropriately. The defendant argued that high standards of evidence admissibility were necessary to protect juries from "scientific shamans who, in the guise of their purported expertise, are willing to testify to virtually any conclusion to suit the needs of the litigant with resources sufficient to pay their retainer."

*...the Ancients measured facial beauty by the* millihelen, *a unit equal to that necessary to launch one ship....*

The Supreme Court ruled that the *Daubert* case be retried and that the trial judge should be given wide discretion in deciding what does and does not qualify as scientific evidence. In effect, federal judges were charged with a *gatekeeping* function with respect to what expert testimony would or would not be admitted into evidence. The *Daubert* ruling superseded the long-standing policy, set forth in *Frye*, of admitting into evidence only scientific testimony that had won general acceptance in the scientific community. Opposing expert testimony, whether or not such testimony had won general acceptance in the scientific community, would be admissible.

In *Daubert*, the Supreme Court viewed factors such as general acceptance in the scientific community or publication in a peer-reviewed journal as only some of many possible factors for judges to consider. Other factors judges might consider included the extent to which a theory or technique had been tested and the extent to which the theory or technique might be subject to error. In essence, the Supreme Court's ruling in *Daubert* gave trial judges a great deal of leeway in deciding what juries would be allowed to hear.

Subsequent to *Daubert*, the Supreme Court has ruled on several other cases that in one way or another clarify or slightly modify its position in *Daubert*. For example, in the case of *General Electric Co. v. Joiner* (1997), the Court emphasized that the trial court had a duty to exclude unreliable expert testimony as evidence. In the case of *Kumho Tire Company Ltd. v. Carmichael* (1999), the Supreme Court expanded the principles expounded in *Daubert* to include the testimony of *all* experts, whether or not the experts claimed scientific research as a basis for their testimony. Thus, for example, a psychologist's testimony based on personal experience in independent practice (rather than findings from a formal research study) could be admitted into evidence at the discretion of the trial judge (Mark, 1999).

Whether or not *Frye* or *Daubert* will be relied on by the court depends on the individual jurisdiction in which a legal proceeding occurs. Some jurisdictions still rely on the *Frye* standard when it comes to admitting expert testimony, and some subscribe to *Daubert*. As an example, consider the Missouri case of *Zink vs. State* (2009). After David Zink rear-ended a woman's car in traffic, Zink kidnapped the woman, and then raped, mutilated, and murdered her. Zink was subsequently caught, tried, convicted, and sentenced to death. In an appeal proceeding, Zink argued that the death penalty should be set aside because of his mental disease. Zink's position was that he was not adequately represented by his attorney, because during the trial, his defense attorney had failed to present "hard" evidence of a mental disorder as indicated by a PET scan (a type of neuroimaging tool that will be discussed in Chapter 16). The appeals court denied Zink's claim, noting that the PET scan failed to meet the *Frye* standard for proving mental disorder (Haque & Guyer, 2010).

The implications of *Daubert* for psychologists and others who might have occasion to provide expert testimony in a trial are wide-ranging (Ewing & McCann, 2006). More specifically, discussions of the implications of *Daubert* for psychological experts can be found in cases involving mental capacity (Frolik, 1999; Poythress, 2004; Bumann, 2010), claims of emotional distress (McLearen et al., 2004), personnel decisions (Landy, 2007), child custody and termination of parental rights (Bogacki & Weiss, 2007; Gould, 2006; Krauss & Sales, 1999), and numerous other matters (Grove & Barden, 1999; Lipton, 1999; Mossman, 2003; Posthuma et al., 2002; Saldanha, 2005; Saxe & Ben-Shakhar, 1999; Slobogin, 1999; Stern, 2001; Tenopyr, 1999). One concern is that *Daubert* has not been applied consistently across jurisdictions and within jurisdictions (Sanders, 2010).

## The Concerns of the Profession

As early as 1895 the American Psychological Association (APA), in its infancy, formed its first committee on mental measurement. The committee was charged with investigating various aspects of the relatively new practice of testing. Another APA committee on measurement was formed in 1906 to further study various testing-related issues and problems. In 1916 and again in 1921, symposia dealing with various issues surrounding the expanding uses of tests were sponsored (*Mentality Tests*, 1916; *Intelligence and Its Measurement*, 1921). In 1954, APA published its *Technical Recommendations for Psychological Tests and Diagnostic Tests*, a document that set forth testing standards and technical recommendations. The following year, another professional organization, the National Educational Association (working in collaboration with the National Council on Measurements Used in Education—now known as the National Council on Measurement) published its *Technical Recommendations for Achievement Tests*. Collaboration between these professional organizations led to the development of rather detailed testing standards and guidelines that would be periodically updated in future years.

Expressions of concern about the quality of tests being administered could also be found in the work of several professionals, acting independently. Anticipating the present-day *Standards*, Ruch (1925), a measurement specialist, proposed a number of standards for tests and guidelines for test development. He also wrote of "the urgent need for a fact-finding organization which will undertake impartial, experimental, and statistical evaluations of tests" (Ruch, 1933). History records that one team of measurement experts even took on the (overly) ambitious task of attempting to rank all published tests designed for use in educational settings. The result was a pioneering book (Kelley, 1927) that provided test users with information needed to compare the merits of published tests. However, given the pace at which test instruments were being published, this resource required regular updating. And so, Oscar Buros was not the first measurement professional to undertake a comprehensive testing of the tests. He was, however, the most tenacious in updating and revising the information.

The APA and related professional organizations in the United States have made available numerous reference works and publications designed to delineate ethical, sound practice in the field of psychological testing and assessment.[5] Along the way, these professional organizations have tackled a variety of thorny questions, such as the questions cited in the next *Just Think*.

**JUST THINK . . .**

Who should be privy to test data? Who should be able to purchase psychological test materials? Who is qualified to administer, score, and interpret psychological tests? What level of expertise in psychometrics qualifies someone to administer which types of test?

**Test-user qualifications** Should just anyone be allowed to purchase and use psychological test materials? If not, then who should be permitted to use psychological tests? As early as 1950 an APA Committee on Ethical Standards for Psychology published a report called *Ethical Standards for the Distribution of Psychological Tests and Diagnostic Aids.* This report defined three levels of tests in terms of the degree to which the test's use required knowledge of testing and psychology.

*Level A:* Tests or aids that can adequately be administered, scored, and interpreted with the aid of the manual and a general orientation to the kind of institution or organization in which one is working (for instance, achievement or proficiency tests).

*Level B:* Tests or aids that require some technical knowledge of test construction and use and of supporting psychological and educational fields such as statistics, individual differences, psychology of adjustment, personnel psychology, and guidance (e.g., aptitude tests and adjustment inventories applicable to normal populations).

*Level C:* Tests and aids that require substantial understanding of testing and supporting psychological fields together with supervised experience in the use of these devices (for instance, projective tests, individual mental tests).

The report included descriptions of the general levels of training corresponding to each of the three levels of tests. Although many test publishers continue to use this three-level classification, some do not. In general, professional standards promulgated by professional organizations state that psychological tests should be used only by qualified persons. Furthermore, there is an ethical mandate to take reasonable steps to prevent the misuse of the tests and the information they provide. The obligations of professionals to testtakers are set forth in a document called the *Code of Fair Testing Practices in Education.* Jointly authored and/or sponsored by the Joint Committee of Testing Practices (a coalition of APA, AERA, NCME, the American Association for Measurement and Evaluation in Counseling and Development, and the American Speech-Language Hearing Association), this document presents standards for educational test developers in four areas: (1) developing/selecting tests, (2) interpreting scores, (3) striving for fairness, and (4) informing testtakers.

Beyond promoting high standards in testing and assessment among professionals, APA has initiated or assisted in litigation to limit the use of psychological tests to qualified personnel. Skeptics label such measurement-related legal action as a kind of jockeying for turf, done solely for financial gain. A more charitable and perhaps more realistic view is that such actions benefit society at large. It is essential to the survival of the assessment enterprise that certain assessments be conducted by people qualified to conduct them by virtue of their education, training, and experience.

---

5. Unfortunately, although organizations in many other countries have verbalized concern about ethics and standards in testing and assessment, relatively few organizations have taken meaningful and effective action in this regard (Leach & Oakland, 2007).

A psychologist licensing law designed to serve as a model for state legislatures has been available from APA since 1987. The law contains no definition of psychological testing. In the interest of the public, the profession of psychology, and other professions that employ psychological tests, it may now be time for that model legislation to be rewritten—with terms such as *psychological testing* and *psychological assessment* clearly defined and differentiated. Terms such as *test-user qualifications* and *psychological assessor qualifications* must also be clearly defined and differentiated. It seems that legal conflicts regarding psychological test usage partly

**JUST THINK . . .**

Is it essential for the terms *psychological testing* and *psychological assessment* to be defined and differentiated in state licensing laws?

stem from confusion of the terms *psychological testing* and *psychological assessment.* People who are not considered professionals by society may be qualified to use psychological tests (psychological testers). However, these same people may not be qualified to engage in psychological assessment. As we argued in Chapter 1, psychological assessment requires certain skills, talents, expertise, and training in psychology and measurement over and above that required to engage in psychological testing. In the past, psychologists have been lax in differentiating psychological testing from psychological assessment. However, continued laxity may prove to be a costly indulgence, given current legislative and judicial trends.

**Testing people with disabilities** Challenges analogous to those concerning testtakers from linguistic and cultural minorities are present when testing people with disabling conditions. Specifically, these challenges may include (1) transforming the test into a form that can be taken by the testtaker, (2) transforming the responses of the testtaker so that they are scorable, and (3) meaningfully interpreting the test data.

The nature of the transformation of the test into a form ready for administration to the individual with disabling conditions will, of course, depend on the nature of the disability. Then, too, some test stimuli do not translate easily. For example, if a critical aspect of a test item contains artwork to be analyzed, there may be no meaningful way to translate this item for use with testtakers who are blind. With respect to any

**JUST THINK . . .**

If the form of a test is changed or adapted for a specific type of administration to a particular individual or group, can the scores obtained by that individual or group be interpreted in a "business as usual" manner?

test converted for use with a population for which the test was not originally intended, choices must inevitably be made regarding exactly how the test materials will be modified, what standards of evaluation will be applied, and how the results will be interpreted. Professional assessors do not always agree on the answers to such questions.

Another complex issue—this one, ethically charged— has to do with a request by a terminally ill individual for assistance in quickening the process of dying. In Oregon, the first state to enact "Death with Dignity" legislation, a request for assistance in dying may be granted only contingent on the findings of a psychological evaluation; life or death literally hangs in the balance of such assessments. Some ethical and related issues surrounding this phenomenon are discussed in greater detail in this chapter's *Everyday Psychometrics.*

**Computerized test administration, scoring, and interpretation** Computer-assisted psychological assessment (CAPA) has become more the norm than the exception. An ever-growing number of psychological tests can be purchased on disc or administered and scored online. In many respects, the relative simplicity, convenience, and range of

## Life-or-Death Psychological Assessment

The state of Oregon has the distinction—dubious to some people, depending on one's values—of having enacted the nation's first aid-in-dying law. Oregon's Death with Dignity Act (ODDA) provides that a patient with a medical condition thought to give that patient 6 months or less to live may end his or her own life by voluntarily requesting a lethal dose of medication. The law requires that two physicians corroborate the terminal diagnosis and stipulates that either may request a psychological evaluation of the patient by a state-licensed psychologist or psychiatrist in order to ensure that the patient is competent to make the life-ending decision and to rule out impaired judgment due to psychiatric disorder. Assistance in dying will be denied to persons "suffering from a psychiatric or psychological disorder, or depression causing impaired judgement" (ODDA, 1997).

The ODDA was hotly debated prior to its passage by referendum, and it remains controversial today. Critics of the law question whether suicide is ever a rational choice under any circumstances, and they fear that state-condoned aid in dying will serve to destigmatize suicide in general (Callahan, 1994; see also Richman, 1988). It is argued that the first duty of health and mental health professionals is to do no harm (Jennings, 1991). Some fear that professionals willing to testify to almost anything (so-called **hired guns**) will corrupt the process by providing whatever professional opinion is desired by those who will pay their fees. Critics also point with concern to the experience of the Dutch death-with-dignity legislation. In the Netherlands, relatively few individuals requesting physician-assisted suicide are referred for psychological assessment. Further, the highest court of that land ruled that "in rare cases, physician-assisted suicide is possible even for individuals suffering only from mental problems rather than from physical illnesses" (Abeles & Barlev, 1999, p. 233). On moral and religious grounds, it has been argued that death should be viewed as the province solely of Divine, not human, intervention.

Supporters of death-with-dignity legislation argue that life-sustaining equipment and methods can extend life beyond a time when it is meaningful and that the first obligation of health and mental health professionals is to relieve suffering (Latimer, 1991; Quill et al., 1992; Weir, 1992). Additionally, they may point to the dogged determination of people intent on dying and to stories of how many terminally ill people have struggled to end their lives using all kinds of less-than-sure methods, enduring even greater suffering in the process. In marked contrast to

**Sigmund Freud (1856–1939)**

*It has been said that Sigmund Freud made a "rational decision" to end his life. Suffering from terminal throat cancer, having great difficulty in speaking, and experiencing increasing difficulty in breathing, the founder of psychoanalysis asked his physician for a lethal dose of morphine. For years it has been debated whether a decision to die, even made by a terminally ill patient, can ever truly be "rational." Today, in accordance with death-with-dignity legislation, the responsibility for evaluating just how rational such a choice is falls on mental health professionals.*

such horror stories, the first patient to die under the ODDA is said to have described how the family "could relax and say what a wonderful life we had. We could look back at all the lovely things because we knew we finally had an answer" (cited in Farrenkopf & Bryan, 1999, p. 246).

Professional associations such as the American Psychological Association and the American Psychiatric

*(continued)*

## Life-or-Death Psychological
## Assessment *(continued)*

Association have long promulgated codes of ethics requiring the prevention of suicide. The enactment of the law in Oregon has placed clinicians in that state in a uniquely awkward position. Clinicians who for years have devoted their efforts to suicide prevention have been thrust into the position of being a potential party to, if not a facilitator of, physician-assisted suicide—regardless of how the aid-in-dying process is referred to in the legislation. Note that the Oregon law scrupulously denies that its objective is the legalization of physician-assisted suicide. In fact, the language of the act mandates that action taken under it "shall not, for any purpose, constitute suicide, assisted suicide, mercy killing or homicide, under the law." The framers of the legislation perceived it as a means by which a terminally ill individual could exercise some control over the dying process. Couched in these terms, the sober duty of the clinician drawn into the process may be made more palatable or even ennobled.

The ODDA provides for various records to be kept regarding patients who die under its provisions. Each year since the Act first took effect, the collected data is published in

an annual report. So, for example, in the 2010 report we learn that the reasons most frequently cited for seeking to end one's life were loss of autonomy, decreasing ability to participate in activities that made life enjoyable, loss of dignity, and loss of control of bodily functions. In 2010, 96 prescriptions for lethal medications were prescribed and 59 people had opted to end their life by ingesting the medications.

Psychologists and psychiatrists called upon to make death-with-dignity competency evaluations may accept or decline the responsibility (Haley & Lee, 1998). Judging from one survey of 423 psychologists in clinical practice in Oregon (Fenn & Ganzini, 1999), many of the psychologists who could be asked to make such a life-or-death assessment might decline to do so. About one-third of the sample responded that an ODDA assessment would be outside the scope of their practice. Another 53% of the sample said they would either refuse to perform the assessment and take no further action or refuse to perform the assessment themselves and refer the patient to a colleague.

Guidelines for the ODDA assessment process were offered by Farrenkopf and Bryan (1999), and they are as follows.

### The ODDA Assessment Process

*1. Review of Records and Case History*
With the patient's consent, the assessor will gather records from all relevant sources, including medical and mental health records. A goal is to understand the patient's current functioning in the context of many factors, ranging from the current medical condition and prognosis to the effects of medication and substance use.

*2. Consultation with Treating Professionals*
With the patient's consent, the assessor may consult with the patient's physician and other professionals involved in the case to better understand the patient's current functioning and current situation.

*3. Patient Interviews*
Sensitive but thorough interviews with the patient will explore the reasons for the aid-in-dying request, including the pressures and values motivating the request. Other areas to explore include: (a) the patient's understanding of his or her medical condition, the prognosis, and the treatment alternatives; (b) the patient's experience of physical pain, limitations of functioning, and changes over

time in cognitive, emotional, and perceptual functioning; (c) the patient's characterization of his or her quality of life, including exploration of related factors including personal identity, role functioning, and self-esteem; and (d) external pressures on the patient, such as personal or familial financial inability to pay for continued treatment.

*4. Interviews with Family Members and Significant Others*
With the permission of the patient, separate interviews should be conducted with the patient's family and significant others. One objective is to explore from their perspective how the patient has adjusted in the past to adversity and how the patient has changed and adjusted to his or her current situation.

*5. Assessment of Competence*
Like the other elements of this overview, this aspect of the assessment is complicated, and only the barest of guidelines can be presented here. In general, the assessor seeks to understand the patient's reasoning and decision-making process, including all information relevant to the decision and its consequences. Some formal tests of competency are available (Appelbaum & Grisso, 1995a, 1995b; Lavin, 1992),

but the clinical and legal applicability of such tests to an ODDA assessment has yet to be established.

### 6. Assessment of Psychopathology

To what extent is the decision to end one's life a function of pathological depression, anxiety, dementia, delirium, psychosis, or some other pathological condition? This is a question the assessor addresses using not only interviews but formal tests. Examples of the many possible instruments the assessor might employ include intelligence tests, personality tests, neuropsychological tests, symptom checklists, and depression and anxiety scales; refer to the appendix in Farrenkopf and Bryan (1999) for a complete list of these tests.

### 7. Reporting Findings and Recommendations

Findings, including those related to the patient's mental status and competence, family support and pressures, and anything else relevant to the patient's aid-in-dying request, should be reported. If treatable conditions were found, treatment recommendations relevant to those conditions may be made. Nontreatment types of recommendations may include recommendations for legal advice, estate planning, or other resources. In Oregon, a Psychiatric/Psychological Consultant's Compliance Form with the consultant's recommendations should be completed and sent to the Oregon Health Division.

potential testing activities that computer technology brings to the testing industry have been a great boon. Of course, every rose has its thorns.

For assessment professionals, some major issues with regard to CAPA are as follows.

- *Access to test administration, scoring, and interpretation software.* Despite purchase restrictions on software and technological safeguards to guard against unauthorized copying, software may still be copied. Unlike test kits, which may contain manipulatable objects, manuals, and other tangible items, a computer-administered test may be easily copied and duplicated.

- *Comparability of pencil-and-paper and computerized versions of tests.* Many tests once available only in a paper-and-pencil format are now available in computerized form as well. In many instances the comparability of the traditional and the computerized forms of the test has not been researched or has only insufficiently been researched.

- *The value of computerized test interpretations.* Many tests available for computerized administration also come with computerized scoring and interpretation procedures. Thousands of words are spewed out every day in the form of test interpretation results, but the value of these words in many cases is questionable.

- *Unprofessional, unregulated "psychological testing" online.* A growing number of Internet sites purport to provide, usually for a fee, online psychological tests. Yet the vast majority of the tests offered would not meet a psychologist's standards. Assessment professionals wonder about the long-term effect of these largely unprofessional and unregulated "psychological testing" sites. Might they, for example, contribute to more public skepticism about psychological tests?

Imagine being administered what has been represented to you as a "psychological test," only to find that the test is not bona fide. The online availability of myriad tests of uncertain quality that purport to measure psychological variables increases the possibility of this happening. To help remedy such potential problems, a Florida-based organization called the International Test Commission developed the "International Guidelines on Computer-Based and

> **JUST THINK . . .**
>
> What differences in the test results may exist as a result of the same test being administered orally, online, or by means of a paper-and-pencil examination? What differences in the testtaker's experience may exist as a function of test administration method?

Internet-Delivered Testing" (Coyne & Bartram, 2006). These guidelines address technical, quality, security, and related issues. Although not without limitations (Sale, 2006), these guidelines clearly are a step forward in nongovernmental regulation.

Let's now consider some other rights of testtakers.

## The Rights of Testtakers

As prescribed by the *Standards* and in some cases by law, some of the rights that test users accord to testtakers are the right of informed consent, the right to be informed of test findings, the right to privacy and confidentiality, and the right to the least stigmatizing label.

**The right of informed consent**   Testtakers have a right to know why they are being evaluated, how the test data will be used, and what (if any) information will be released to whom. With full knowledge of such information, testtakers give their **informed consent** to be tested. The disclosure of the information needed for consent must, of course, be in language the testtaker can understand. Thus, for a testtaker as young as 2 or 3 years of age or an individual who is mentally retarded with limited language ability, a disclosure before testing might be worded as follows: "I'm going to ask you to try to do some things so that I can see what you know how to do and what things you could use some more help with" (APA, 1985, p. 85).

Competency in providing informed consent has been broken down into several components: (1) Being able to evidence a choice as to whether one wants to participate; (2) demonstrating a factual understanding of the issues; (3) being able to reason about the facts of a study, treatment, or whatever it is to which consent is sought, and (4) appreciating the nature of the situation (Appelbaum & Roth, 1982; Roth et al., 1977).

Competency to provide consent may be assessed informally, and in fact many physicians engage in such informal assessment. Marson et al. (1997) cautioned that informal assessment of competency may be idiosyncratic and unreliable. As an alternative, many standardized instruments are available (Sturman, 2005). One such instrument is the MacArthur Competence Assessment Tool-Treatment (Grisso & Appelbaum, 1998). Also known as the MacCAT-T, it consists of structured interviews based on the four components of competency listed above (Grisso et al., 1997). Other instruments have been developed that are performance based and yield information on decision-making competence (Finucane & Gullion, 2010).

Another consideration related to competency is the extent to which persons diagnosed with psychopathology may be incompetent to provide informed consent (Sturman, 2005). So, for example, individuals diagnosed with dementia, bipolar disorder, and schizophrenia are likely to have competency impairments that may affect their ability to provide informed consent. By contrast, individuals with major depression may retain the competency to give truly informed consent (Grisso & Appelbaum, 1995; Palmer et al., 2007; Vollmann et al., 2003). Competence to provide informed consent may be improved by training (Carpenter et al., 2000; Dunn et al., 2002; Palmer et al., 2007). Therefore, clinicians should not necessarily assume that patients are not capable of consent based solely on their diagnosis.

If a testtaker is incapable of providing an informed consent to testing, such consent may be obtained from a parent or a legal representative. Consent must be in written rather than oral form. The written form should specify (1) the general purpose of the testing, (2) the specific reason it is being undertaken in the present case, and (3) the general type of instruments to be administered. Many school districts now routinely send home such forms before testing children. Such forms typically include the option to have the child assessed privately if a parent so desires. In instances where testing is legally mandated (as in a court-ordered situation), obtaining informed consent to test may be considered more of a courtesy (undertaken in part for reasons of establishing good rapport) than a necessity.

One gray area with respect to the testtaker's right of fully informed consent before testing involves research and experimental situations wherein the examiner's complete disclosure of all facts pertinent to the testing (including the experimenter's hypothesis and so forth) might irrevocably contaminate the test data. In some instances, deception is used to create situations that occur relatively rarely. For example, a deception might be created to evaluate how an emergency worker might react under emergency conditions. Sometimes deception involves the use of confederates to simulate social conditions that can occur during an event of some sort.

For situations in which it is deemed advisable not to obtain fully informed consent to evaluation, professional discretion is in order. Testtakers might be given a minimum amount of information before the testing. For example, "This testing is being undertaken as part of an experiment on obedience to authority." A full disclosure and debriefing would be made after the testing. Various professional organizations have created policies and guidelines regarding deception in research. For example, the APA *Ethical Principles of Psychologists and Code of Conduct* (2002) provides that psychologists (a) do not use deception unless it is absolutely necessary, (b) do not use deception at all if it will cause participants emotional distress, and (c) fully debrief participants.[6]

**The right to be informed of test findings**  In a bygone era, the inclination of many psychological assessors, particularly many clinicians, was to tell testtakers as little as possible about the nature of their performance on a particular test or test battery. In no case would they disclose diagnostic conclusions that could arouse anxiety or precipitate a crisis. This orientation was reflected in at least one authoritative text that advised testers to keep information about test results superficial and focus only on "positive" findings. This was done so that the examinee would leave the test session feeling "pleased and satisfied" (Klopfer et al., 1954, p. 15). But all that has changed, and giving realistic information about test performance to examinees is not only ethically and legally mandated but may be useful from a therapeutic perspective as well. Testtakers have a right to be informed, in language they can understand, of the nature of the findings with respect to a test they have taken. They are also entitled to know what recommendations are being made as a consequence of the test data. If the test results, findings, or recommendations made on the basis of test data are voided for any reason (such as irregularities in the test administration), testtakers have a right to know that as well.

Because of the possibility of untoward consequences of providing individuals with information about themselves—ability, lack of ability, personality, values— the communication of results of a psychological test is a most important part of the evaluation process. With sensitivity to the situation, the test user will inform the testtaker (and the parent or the legal representative or both) of the purpose of the test, the meaning of the score relative to those of other testtakers, and the possible limitations and margins of error of the test. And regardless of whether such reporting is done in

> **JUST THINK . . .**
>
> Describe a scenario where knowledge of the experimenter's hypotheses would probably invalidate the data gathered.

---

6. A detailed presentation of exactly how APA's *Ethical Principles of Psychologists* impacts the professional conduct of users of tests and measurements can be found on this text's companion website, *www.mhhe .com/cohentesting8*.

person or in writing, a qualified professional should be available to answer any further questions that testtakers (or their parents or legal representatives) have about the test scores. Ideally, counseling resources will be available for those who react adversely to the information presented.

**The right to privacy and confidentiality**　　The concept of the **privacy right** "recognizes the freedom of the individual to pick and choose for himself the time, circumstances, and particularly the extent to which he wishes to share or withhold from others his attitudes, beliefs, behavior, and opinions" (Shah, 1969, p. 57). When people in court proceedings "take the Fifth" and refuse to answer a question put to them on the grounds that the answer might be self-incriminating, they are asserting a right to privacy provided by the Fifth Amendment to the Constitution. The information withheld in such a manner is termed *privileged;* it is information that is protected by law from disclosure in a legal proceeding. State statutes have extended the concept of **privileged information** to parties who communicate with each other in the context of certain relationships, including the lawyer–client relationship, the doctor–patient relationship, the priest– penitent relationship, and the husband–wife relationship. In most states, privilege is also accorded to the psychologist–client relationship.

Privilege is extended to parties in various relationships because it has been deemed that the parties' right to privacy serves a greater public interest than would be served if their communications were vulnerable to revelation during legal proceedings. Stated another way, it is for the social good if people feel confident that they can talk freely to their attorneys, clergy, physicians, psychologists, and spouses. Professionals such as psychologists who are parties to such special relationships have a legal and ethical duty to keep their clients' communications confidential.

**Confidentiality** may be distinguished from *privilege* in that, whereas "confidentiality concerns matters of communication outside the courtroom, privilege protects clients from disclosure in judicial proceedings" (Jagim et al., 1978, p. 459). Privilege is not absolute. There are occasions when a court can deem the disclosure of certain information necessary and can order the disclosure of that information. Should the psychologist or other professional so ordered refuse, he or she does so under the threat of going to jail, being fined, and other legal consequences.

Privilege in the psychologist–client relationship belongs to the client, not the psychologist. The competent client can direct the psychologist to disclose information to some third party (such as an attorney or an insurance carrier), and the psychologist is obligated to make the disclosure. In some rare instances the psychologist may be ethically (if not legally) compelled to disclose information if that information will prevent harm either to the client or to some endangered third party. An illustrative case would be the situation where a client details a plan to commit suicide or homicide. In such an instance the psychologist would be legally and ethically compelled to take reasonable action to prevent the client's intended outcome from occurring. Here, the preservation of life would be deemed an objective more important than the nonrevelation of privileged information.

A wrong judgment on the part of the clinician regarding the revelation of confidential communication may lead to a lawsuit or worse. A landmark U.S. Supreme Court case in this area was the 1974 case of *Tarasoff v. Regents of the University of California.* In that case, a therapy patient had made known to his psychologist his intention to kill an unnamed but readily identifiable girl two months before the murder. The Court held that "protective privilege ends where the public peril begins," and so the therapist had a duty to warn the endangered girl of her peril. Clinicians may have a duty to warn endangered third parties not only of potential violence but of potential AIDS infection from an HIV-positive client (Buckner & Firestone, 2000; Melchert & Patterson, 1999) as well as other threats to physical well-being.

Another ethical mandate with regard to confidentiality involves the safekeeping of test data. Test users must take reasonable precautions to safeguard test records. If these data are stored in a filing cabinet, then the cabinet should be locked and preferably made of steel. If these data are stored in a computer, electronic safeguards must be taken to ensure only authorized access. The individual or institution should have a reasonable policy covering the length of time that records are stored and when, if ever, the records will be deemed to be outdated, invalid, or useful only from an academic perspective. In general, it is not a good policy to maintain all records in perpetuity. Policies in conformance with privacy laws should also be in place governing the conditions under which requests for release of records to a third party will be honored. Some states have enacted law that describes, in detail, procedures for storing and disposing of patient records.

Relevant to the release of assessment-related information is the Health Insurance Portability and Accountability Act of 1996 (HIPAA), which took effect in April 2003. These federal privacy standards limit the ways that health care providers, health plans, pharmacies, and hospitals can use patients' personal medical information. For example, personal health information may not be used for purposes unrelated to health care.

**JUST THINK . . .**

Describe key features of a model law designed to guide psychologists in the storage and disposal of patient records.

In part due to the decision of the U.S. Supreme Court in the case of *Jaffee v. Redmond* (1996), HIPAA singled out "psychotherapy notes" as requiring even more stringent protection than other records. The ruling in *Jaffee* affirmed that communications between a psychotherapist and a patient were privileged in federal courts. The HIPAA privacy rule cited *Jaffee* and defined privacy notes as "notes recorded (in any medium) by a health care provider who is a mental health professional documenting or analyzing the contents of conversation during a private counseling session or a group, joint, or family counseling session and that are separated from the rest of the individual's medical record." Although "results of clinical tests" were specifically *excluded* in this definition, we would caution assessment professionals to obtain specific consent from assessees before releasing assessment-related information. This is particularly essential with respect to data gathered using assessment tools such as the interview, behavioral observation, and role play.

**The right to the least stigmatizing label** The *Standards* advise that the least stigmatizing labels should always be assigned when reporting test results. To better appreciate the need for this standard, consider the case of Jo Ann Iverson.[7] Jo Ann was 9 years old and suffering from claustrophobia when her mother brought her to a state hospital in Blackfoot, Idaho, for a psychological evaluation. Arden Frandsen, a psychologist employed part-time at the hospital, conducted an evaluation of Jo Ann, during the course of which he administered a Stanford-Binet Intelligence Test. In his report, Frandsen classified Jo Ann as "feeble-minded, at the high-grade moron level of general mental ability." Following a request from Jo Ann's school guidance counselor, a copy of the psychological report was forwarded to the school—and embarrassing rumors concerning Jo Ann's mental condition began to circulate.

---

7. See *Iverson v. Frandsen*, 237 F. 2d 898 (Idaho, 1956) or Cohen (1979), pp. 149–150.

Jo Ann's mother, Carmel Iverson, brought a libel (defamation) suit against Frandsen on behalf of her daughter.[8] Mrs. Iverson lost the lawsuit. The court ruled in part that the psychological evaluation "was a professional report made by a public servant in good faith, representing his best judgment." But although Mrs. Iverson did not prevail in her lawsuit, we can certainly sympathize with her anguish at the thought of her daughter going through life with a label such as "high-grade moron"—this despite the fact that the psychologist had probably merely copied that designation from the test manual. We would also add that the Iversons may have prevailed in their lawsuit had the cause of action been breach of confidentiality and had the defendant been the guidance counselor; there was uncontested testimony that it was from the guidance counselor's office, and not that of the psychologist, that the rumors concerning Jo Ann first emanated.

While on the subject of the rights of testtakers, let's not forget about the rights—of sorts—of students of testing and assessment. Having been introduced to various aspects of the assessment enterprise, you have the right to learn more about technical aspects of measurement. Exercise that right in the succeeding chapters.

---

## Self-Assessment

Test your understanding of elements of this chapter by seeing if you can explain each of the following terms, expressions, abbreviations, events, or names in terms of their significance in the context of psychological testing and assessment:

affirmative action
*Albemarle Paper Company v. Moody*
Alfred Binet
James McKeen Cattell
Charles Darwin
*Code of Fair Testing Practices in Education*
code of professional ethics
collectivist culture
confidentiality
culture
culture-specific test
*Debra P. v. Turlington*
ethics
eugenics
Francis Galton
Henry H. Goddard

*Griggs v. Duke Power Company*
HIPAA
hired gun
*Hobson v. Hansen*
individualist culture
informed consent
*Jaffee v. Redmond*
*Larry P. v. Riles*
laws
litigation
minimum competency testing programs
Christiana D. Morgan
Henry A. Murray
ODDA
Karl Pearson
privacy right

privileged information
projective test
psychoanalysis
Public Law 105-17
quota system
Hermann Rorschach
self-report
*Sputnik*
standard of care
*Tarasoff v. Regents of the University of California*
truth-in-testing legislation
David Wechsler
Lightner Witmer
Robert S. Woodworth
Wilhelm Max Wundt

---

8. An interesting though tangential aspect of this case was that Iverson had brought her child in with a presenting problem of claustrophobia. The plaintiff questioned whether the administration of an intelligence test under these circumstances was unauthorized and beyond the scope of the consultation. However, the defendant psychologist proved to the satisfaction of the Court that the administration of the Stanford-Binet was necessary to determine whether Jo Ann had the mental capacity to respond to psychotherapy.

# 3

# *A Statistics Refresher*

From the red-pencil number circled at the top of your first spelling test to the computer printout of your college entrance examination scores, tests and test scores touch your life. They seem to reach out from the paper and shake your hand when you do well and punch you in the face when you do poorly. They can point you toward or away from a particular school or curriculum. They can help you to identify strengths and weaknesses in your physical and mental abilities. They can accompany you on job interviews and influence a job or career choice.

In your role as a student, you have probably found that your relationship to tests has been primarily that of a testtaker. But as a psychologist, teacher, researcher, or employer, you may find that your relationship with tests is primarily that of a test user—the person who breathes life and meaning into test scores by applying the knowledge and skill to interpret them appropriately. You may one day create a test, whether in an academic or a business setting, and then have the responsibility for scoring and interpreting it. In that situation, or even from the perspective of one who would take that test, it's essential to understand the theory underlying test use and the principles of test-score interpretation.

> **JUST THINK . . .**
>
> For most people, test scores are an important fact of life. But what makes those numbers so meaningful? In general terms, what information, ideally, should be conveyed by a test score?

Test scores are frequently expressed as numbers, and statistical tools are used to describe, make inferences from, and draw conclusions about numbers.[1] In this statistics refresher, we cover scales of measurement, tabular and graphic presentations of data, measures of central tendency, measures of variability, aspects of the normal curve, and standard scores. If these statistics-related terms look painfully familiar to you, we ask your indulgence and ask you to remember that overlearning is the key to retention. Of course, if any of these terms appear unfamiliar, we urge you to learn more about them. Feel free to supplement the discussion here with a review of these and related terms in any good elementary statistics text. The brief review of statistical concepts that follows can in no way replace a sound grounding in basic statistics gained through an introductory course in that subject.

---

1. Of course, a test score may be expressed in other forms, such as a letter grade or a pass–fail designation. Unless stated otherwise, terms such as *test score, test data, test results,* and *test scores* are used throughout this book to refer to numeric descriptions of test performance.

# Scales of Measurement

We may formally define **measurement** as the act of assigning numbers or symbols to characteristics of things (people, events, whatever) according to rules. The rules used in assigning numbers are guidelines for representing the magnitude (or some other characteristic) of the object being measured. Here is an example of a measurement rule: *Assign the number 12 to all lengths that are exactly the same length as a 12-inch ruler.* A **scale** is a set of numbers (or other symbols) whose properties model empirical properties of the objects to which the numbers are assigned.[2]

There are various ways in which a scale can be categorized. One way of categorizing a scale is according to the type of variable being measured. Thus, a scale used to measure a continuous variable might be referred to as a *continuous scale*, whereas a scale used to measure a discrete variable might be referred to as a *discrete scale*. If, for example, research subjects were to be categorized as either female or male, the categorization scale would be said to be discrete because it would not be meaningful to categorize a subject as anything other than female or male.[3] In contrast, a continuous scale exists when it is theoretically possible to divide any of the values of the scale. A distinction must be made, however, between what is theoretically possible and what is practically desirable. The units into which a continuous scale will actually be divided may depend on such factors as the purpose of the measurement and practicality. In measurement to install venetian blinds, for example, it is theoretically possible to measure by the millimeter or even by the micrometer. But is such precision necessary? Most installers do just fine with measurement by the inch.

**JUST THINK . . .**

What is another example of a measurement rule?

Measurement always involves *error*. In the language of assessment, **error** refers to the collective influence of all of the factors on a test score or measurement beyond those specifically measured by the test or measurement. As we will see, there are many different sources of error in measurement. Consider, for example, the score someone received on a test in American history. We might conceive of part of the score as reflecting the testtaker's knowledge of American history and part of the score as reflecting error. The error part of the test score may be due to many different factors. One source of error might have been a distracting thunderstorm going on outside at the time the test was administered. Another source of error was the particular selection of test items the instructor chose to use for the test. Had a different item or two been used in the test, the testtaker's score on the test might have been

**JUST THINK . . .**

The *scale* with which we are all perhaps most familiar is the common bathroom scale. How are a psychological test and a bathroom scale alike? How are they different? Your answer may change as you read on.

---

2. David L. Streiner reflected, "Many terms have been used to describe a collection of items or questions—*scale, test, questionnaire, index, inventory,* and a host of others—with no consistency from one author to another" (2003a, p. 217, emphasis in the original). Streiner proposed to refer to questionnaires of theoretically like or related items as scales and those of theoretically unrelated items as *indexes*. He acknowledged that, as it stands now, counterexamples of each term could readily be found.

3. Perhaps a disclaimer is in order here. The authors recognize that if all females were labeled "1" and all males were labeled "2," then some people—for example, individuals born with a gender-related genetic abnormality, and persons in the midst of a transgender transformation—might intuitively seem to qualify as "1.5." But such exceptions aside, all cases on a discrete scale must lie on a point on the scale, and it is theoretically impossible for a case to lie *between* two points on the scale.

higher or lower. Error is very much an element of all measurement, and it is an element for which any theory of measurement must surely account.

Measurement using continuous scales always involves error. To illustrate why, let's go back to the scenario involving venetian blinds. The length of the window measured to be 35.5 inches could, in reality, be 35.7 inches. The measuring scale is conveniently marked off in grosser gradations of measurement. Most scales used in psychological and educational assessment are continuous and therefore can be expected to contain this sort of error. The number or score used to characterize the trait being measured on a continuous scale should be thought of as an approximation of the "real" number. Thus, for example, a score of 25 on some test of anxiety should not be thought of as a precise measure of anxiety. Rather, it should be thought of as an approximation of the real anxiety score had the measuring instrument been calibrated to yield such a score. In such a case, perhaps the score of 25 is an approximation of a real score of, say, 24.7 or 25.44.

It is generally agreed that there are four different levels or scales of measurement. Within these levels or scales of measurement, assigned numbers convey different kinds of information. Accordingly, certain statistical manipulations may or may not be appropriate, depending upon the level or scale of measurement.[4]

The French word for black is *noir* (pronounced "'nwăre"). We bring this up here only to call attention to the fact that this word is a useful acronym for remembering the four levels or scales of measurement. Each letter in *noir* is the first letter of the succeedingly more rigorous levels: N stands for *nominal, o* for *ordinal, i* for *interval,* and *r* for *ratio* scales.

### Nominal Scales

**Nominal scales** are the simplest form of measurement. These scales involve classification or categorization based on one or more distinguishing characteristics, where all things measured must be placed into mutually exclusive and exhaustive categories. For example, in the specialty area of clinical psychology, a nominal scale in use for many years was the *Diagnostic and Statistical Manual of Mental Disorders IV-TR* (American Psychiatric Association, 2000). Each disorder listed in that manual was assigned its own number. Thus, for example, the number 303.00 identified alcohol intoxication, and the number 307.00 identified stuttering. But these numbers were used exclusively for classification purposes and could not be meaningfully added, subtracted, ranked, or averaged. Hence, the middle number between these two diagnostic codes, 305.00, did *not* identify an intoxicated stutterer.

---

4. For the purposes of our statistics refresher, we present what Nunnally (1978) called the "fundamentalist" view of measurement scales, which "holds that 1. there are distinct types of measurement scales into which all possible measures of attributes can be classified, 2. each measure has some 'real' characteristics that permit its proper classification, and 3. once a measure is classified, the classification specifies the types of mathematical analyses that can be employed with the measure" (p. 24). Nunnally and others have acknowledged that alternatives to the "fundamentalist" view may also be viable.

Individual test items may also employ nominal scaling, including *yes/no* responses. For example, consider the following test items:

*Instructions:* Answer either *yes* or *no*.

Are you actively contemplating suicide? _____

Are you currently under professional care for a psychiatric disorder? _____

Have you ever been convicted of a felony? _____

**JUST THINK . . .**

What are some other examples of nominal scales?

In each case, a *yes* or *no* response results in the placement into one of a set of mutually exclusive groups: suicidal or not, under care for psychiatric disorder or not, and felon or not. Arithmetic operations that can legitimately be performed with nominal data include counting for the purpose of determining how many cases fall into each category and a resulting determination of proportion or percentages.[5]

## Ordinal Scales

Like nominal scales, **ordinal scales** permit classification. However, in addition to classification, rank ordering on some characteristic is also permissible with ordinal scales. In business and organizational settings, job applicants may be rank-ordered according to their desirability for a position. In clinical settings, people on a waiting list for psychotherapy may be rank-ordered according to their need for treatment. In these examples, individuals are compared with others and assigned a rank (perhaps 1 to the best applicant or the most needy wait-listed client, 2 to the next, and so forth).

Although he may have never used the term *ordinal scale,* Alfred Binet, a developer of the intelligence test that today bears his name, believed strongly that the data derived from an intelligence test are ordinal in nature. He emphasized that what he tried to do with his test was not to *measure* people (as one might measure a person's height), but merely to *classify* (and rank) people on the basis of their performance on the tasks. He wrote:

> I have not sought . . . to sketch a method of measuring, in the physical sense of the word, but only a method of classification of individuals. The procedures which I have indicated will, if perfected, come to classify a person before or after such another person, or such another series of persons; but I do not believe that one may measure one of the intellectual aptitudes in the sense that one measures a length or a capacity. Thus, when a person studied can retain seven figures after a single audition, one can class him, from the point of his memory for figures, after the individual who retains eight figures under the same conditions, and before those who retain six. It is a classification, not a measurement . . . we do not measure, we classify. (Binet, cited in Varon, 1936, p. 41)

Assessment instruments applied to the individual subject may also use an ordinal form of measurement. The Rokeach Value Survey uses such an approach. In that test, a list of personal values—such as freedom, happiness, and wisdom—are put in order according to their perceived importance to the testtaker (Rokeach, 1973). If a set of 10 values is rank ordered, then the testtaker would assign a value of "1" to the most important and "10" to the least important.

Ordinal scales imply nothing about how much greater one ranking is than another. Even though ordinal scales may employ numbers or "scores" to represent the rank ordering, the numbers do not indicate units of measurement. So, for example, the

---

5. We hasten to add that there are other ways to analyze nominal data (Gokhale & Kullback, 1978; Kranzler & Moursund, 1999). However, these advanced methods of analysis are beyond the scope of this book.

performance difference between the first-ranked job applicant and the second-ranked applicant may be small while the difference between the second- and third-ranked applicants may be large. On the Rokeach Value Survey, the value ranked "1" may be handily the most important in the mind of the testtaker. However, ordering the values that follow may be difficult to the point of being almost arbitrary.

Ordinal scales have no absolute zero point. In the case of a test of job performance ability, every testtaker, regardless of standing on the test, is presumed to have *some* ability. No testtaker is presumed to have zero ability. Zero is without meaning in such a test because the number of units that separate one testtaker's score from another's is simply not known. The scores are ranked, but the actual number of units separating one score from the next may be many, just a few, or practically none. Because there is no zero point on an ordinal scale, the ways in which data from such scales can be analyzed statistically are limited. One cannot average the qualifications of the first- and third-ranked job applicants, for example, and expect to come out with the qualifications of the second-ranked applicant.

**JUST THINK . . .**

What are some other examples of ordinal scales?

## Interval Scales

In addition to the features of nominal and ordinal scales, **interval scales** contain equal intervals between numbers. Each unit on the scale is exactly equal to any other unit on the scale. But like ordinal scales, interval scales contain no absolute zero point. With interval scales, we have reached a level of measurement at which it *is* possible to average a set of measurements and obtain a meaningful result.

Scores on many tests, such as tests of intelligence, are analyzed statistically in ways appropriate for data at the interval level of measurement. The difference in intellectual ability represented by IQs of 80 and 100, for example, is thought to be similar to that existing between IQs of 100 and 120. However, if an individual were to achieve an IQ of 0 (something that is not even possible, given the way most intelligence tests are structured), that would not be an indication of zero (the total absence of) intelligence. Because interval scales contain no absolute zero point, a presumption inherent in their use is that no testtaker possesses none of the ability or trait (or whatever) being measured.

**JUST THINK . . .**

What are some other examples of interval scales?

## Ratio Scales

In addition to all the properties of nominal, ordinal, and interval measurement, a **ratio scale** has a true zero point. All mathematical operations can meaningfully be performed because there exist equal intervals between the numbers on the scale as well as a true or absolute zero point.

In psychology, ratio-level measurement is employed in some types of tests and test items, perhaps most notably those involving assessment of neurological functioning. One example is a test of hand grip, where the variable measured is the amount of pressure a person can exert with one hand (see Figure 3–1). Another example is a timed test of perceptual-motor ability that requires the testtaker to assemble a jigsaw-like puzzle. In such an instance, the time taken to successfully complete the puzzle is the measure that is recorded. Because there is a true zero point on this scale (that is, 0 seconds), it is meaningful to say that a testtaker who completes the assembly in 30 seconds has taken half the time of a testtaker who completed it in 60 seconds. In this example, it is meaningful to speak of a true zero point on the scale—but in theory only. Why? *Just think . . .*

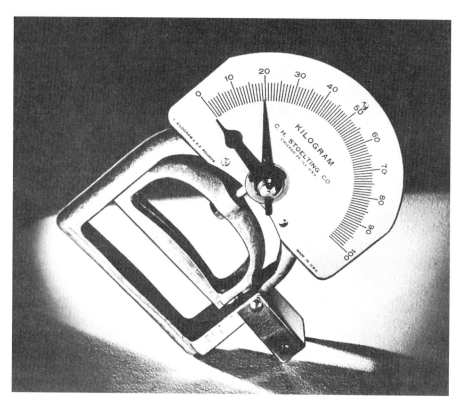

**Figure 3–1**
**Ratio-Level Measurement in the Palm of One's Hand**

*Pictured above is a **dynamometer,** an instrument used to measure strength of hand grip. The examinee is instructed to squeeze the grips as hard as possible. The squeezing of the grips causes the gauge needle to move and reflect the number of pounds of pressure exerted. The highest point reached by the needle is the score. This is an example of ratio-level measurement. Someone who can exert 10 pounds of pressure (and earns a score of 10) exerts twice as much pressure as a person who exerts 5 pounds of pressure (and earns a score of 5). On this test it is possible to achieve a score of 0, indicating a complete lack of exerted pressure. Although it is meaningful to speak of a score of 0 on this test, we have to wonder about its significance. How might a score of 0 result? One way would be if the testtaker genuinely had paralysis of the hand. Another way would be if the testtaker was uncooperative and unwilling to comply with the demands of the task. Yet another way would be if the testtaker was attempting to malinger or "fake bad" on the test. Ratio scales may provide us "solid" numbers to work with, but some interpretation of the test data yielded may still be required before drawing any "solid" conclusions.*

♦
**JUST THINK . . .**
What are some other examples of ratio scales?

No testtaker could ever obtain a score of zero on this assembly task. Stated another way, no testtaker, not even The Flash (a comic-book superhero whose power is the ability to move at superhuman speed), could assemble the puzzle in zero seconds.

## Measurement Scales in Psychology

The ordinal level of measurement is most frequently used in psychology. As Kerlinger (1973, p. 439) put it: "Intelligence, aptitude, and personality test scores are, *basically and strictly speaking,* ordinal. These tests indicate with more or less accuracy not the amount of intelligence, aptitude, and personality traits of individuals, but rather the rank-order positions of the individuals." Kerlinger allowed that "most psychological and educational scales approximate interval equality fairly well," though he cautioned that if ordinal measurements are treated as if they were interval measurements, then the test user must "be constantly alert to the possibility of *gross* inequality of intervals" (pp. 440–441).

Why would psychologists want to treat their assessment data as interval when those data would be better described as ordinal? Why not just say that they are ordinal? The attraction of interval measurement for users of psychological tests is the flexibility with which such data can be manipulated statistically. What kinds of statistical manipulation? you may ask.

In this chapter we discuss the various ways in which test data can be described or converted to make those data more manageable and understandable. Some of the techniques we'll describe, such as the computation of an average, can be used if data are assumed to be interval- or ratio-level in nature but not if they are ordinal- or nominal-level. Other techniques, such as those involving the creation of graphs or tables, may be used with ordinal- or even nominal-level data.

## Describing Data

Suppose you have magically changed places with the professor teaching this course and that you have just administered an examination that consists of 100 multiple-choice items (where 1 point is awarded for each correct answer). The distribution of scores for the 25 students enrolled in your class could theoretically range from 0 (none correct) to 100 (all correct). A **distribution** may be defined as a set of test scores arrayed for recording or study. The 25 scores in this distribution are referred to as *raw scores.* As its name implies, a **raw score** is a straightforward, unmodified accounting of performance that is usually numerical. A raw score may reflect a simple tally, as in *number of items responded to correctly on an achievement test.* As we will see later in this chapter, raw scores can be converted into other types of scores. For now, let's assume it's the day after the examination and that you are sitting in your office looking at the raw scores listed in Table 3–1. What do you do next?

One task at hand is to communicate the test results to your class. You want to do that in a way that will help students understand how their performance on the test compared to the performance of other students. Perhaps the first step is to organize the data by transforming it from a random listing of raw scores into something that immediately conveys a bit more information. Later, as we will see, you may wish to transform the data in other ways.

> **JUST THINK . . .**
>
> In what way do most of your instructors convey test-related feedback to students? Is there a better way they could do this?

### Frequency Distributions

The data from the test could be organized into a distribution of the raw scores. One way the scores could be distributed is by the frequency with which they occur. In a **frequency distribution,** all scores are listed alongside the number of times each score occurred. The scores might be listed in tabular or graphic form. Table 3–2 lists the frequency of occurrence of each score in one column and the score itself in the other column.

**Table 3–1**
**Data from Your Measurement Course Test**

| Student | Score (number correct) |
|---|---|
| Judy | 78 |
| Joe | 67 |
| Lee-Wu | 69 |
| Miriam | 63 |
| Valerie | 85 |
| Diane | 72 |
| Henry | 92 |
| Esperanza | 67 |
| Paula | 94 |
| Martha | 62 |
| Bill | 61 |
| Homer | 44 |
| Robert | 66 |
| Michael | 87 |
| Jorge | 76 |
| Mary | 83 |
| "Mousey" | 42 |
| Barbara | 82 |
| John | 84 |
| Donna | 51 |
| Uriah | 69 |
| Leroy | 61 |
| Ronald | 96 |
| Vinnie | 73 |
| Bianca | 79 |

**Table 3–2**
**Frequency Distribution of Scores from Your Test**

| Score | $f$ (frequency) |
|---|---|
| 96 | 1 |
| 94 | 1 |
| 92 | 1 |
| 87 | 1 |
| 85 | 1 |
| 84 | 1 |
| 83 | 1 |
| 82 | 1 |
| 79 | 1 |
| 78 | 1 |
| 76 | 1 |
| 73 | 1 |
| 72 | 1 |
| 69 | 2 |
| 67 | 2 |
| 66 | 1 |
| 63 | 1 |
| 62 | 1 |
| 61 | 2 |
| 51 | 1 |
| 44 | 1 |
| 42 | 1 |

Often, a frequency distribution is referred to as a *simple frequency distribution* to indicate that individual scores have been used and the data have not been grouped. Another kind of frequency distribution used to summarize data is a *grouped frequency distribution*. In a **grouped frequency distribution,** test-score intervals, also called *class intervals,* replace the actual test scores. The number of class intervals used and the size or *width* of each class interval (i.e., the range of test scores contained in each class interval) are for the test user to decide. But how?

In most instances, a decision about the size of a class interval in a grouped frequency distribution is made on the basis of convenience. Of course, virtually any decision will represent a trade-off of sorts. A convenient, easy-to-read summary of the

| Table 3–3 | Class Interval | $f$ (frequency) |
|-----------|---------------|-----------------|
| **A Grouped Frequency Distribution** | 95–99 | 1 |
| | 90–94 | 2 |
| | 85–89 | 2 |
| | 80–84 | 3 |
| | 75–79 | 3 |
| | 70–74 | 2 |
| | 65–69 | 5 |
| | 60–64 | 4 |
| | 55–59 | 0 |
| | 50–54 | 1 |
| | 45–49 | 0 |
| | 40–44 | 2 |

data is the trade-off for the loss of detail. To what extent must the data be summarized? How important is detail? These types of questions must be considered. In the grouped frequency distribution in Table 3–3, the test scores have been grouped into 12 class intervals, where each class interval is equal to 5 points.[6] The highest class interval (95 to 99) and the lowest class interval (40 to 44) are referred to, respectively, as the upper and lower limits of the distribution. Here, the need for convenience in reading the data outweighs the need for great detail, so such groupings of data seem logical.

Frequency distributions of test scores can also be illustrated graphically. A **graph** is a diagram or chart composed of lines, points, bars, or other symbols that describe and illustrate data. With a good graph, the place of a single score in relation to a distribution of test scores can be understood easily. Three kinds of graphs used to illustrate frequency distributions are the histogram, the bar graph, and the frequency polygon (Figure 3–2). A **histogram** is a graph with vertical lines drawn at the true limits of each test score (or class interval), forming a series of contiguous rectangles. It is customary for the test scores (either the single scores or the midpoints of the class intervals) to be placed along the graph's horizontal axis (also referred to as the *abscissa* or X-axis) and for numbers indicative of the frequency of occurrence to be placed along the graph's vertical axis (also referred to as the *ordinate* or Y-axis). In a **bar graph,** numbers indicative of frequency also appear on the Y-axis, and reference to some categorization (e.g., yes/no/maybe, male/female) appears on the X-axis. Here the rectangular bars typically are not contiguous. Data illustrated in a **frequency polygon** are expressed by a continuous line connecting the points where test scores or class intervals (as indicated on the X-axis) meet frequencies (as indicated on the Y-axis).

Graphic representations of frequency distributions may assume any of a number of different shapes (Figure 3–3). Regardless of the shape of graphed data, it is a good idea for the consumer of the information contained in the graph to examine it carefully—and, if need be, critically. Consider, in this context, this chapter's *Everyday Psychometrics.*

As we discuss in detail later in this chapter, one graphic representation of data of particular interest to measurement professionals is the *normal* or *bell-shaped curve.* Before getting to that, however, let's return to the subject of distributions and how we can describe and characterize them. One way to describe a distribution of test scores is by a measure of central tendency.

6. Technically, each number on such a scale would be viewed as ranging from as much as 0.5 below it to as much as 0.5 above it. For example, the "real" but hypothetical width of the class interval ranging from 95 to 99 would be the difference between 99.5 and 94.5, or 5. The true upper and lower limits of the class intervals presented in the table would be 99.5 and 39.5, respectively.

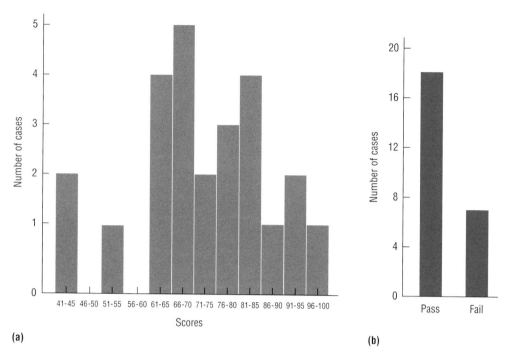

(a)

(b)

## Figure 3–2
### Graphic Illustrations of Data from Table 3–3

*A histogram (a), a bar graph (b), and a frequency polygon (c) all may be used to graphically convey information about test performance. Of course, the labeling of the bar graph and the specific nature of the data conveyed by it depend on the variables of interest. In (b), the variable of interest is the number of students who passed the test (assuming, for the purpose of this illustration, that a raw score of 65 or higher had been arbitrarily designated in advance as a passing grade).*

*Returning to the question posed earlier—the one in which you play the role of instructor and must communicate the test results to your students—which type of graph would best serve your purpose? Why?*

*As we continue our review of descriptive statistics, you may wish to return to your role of professor and formulate your response to challenging related questions, such as "Which measure(s) of central tendency shall I use to convey this information?" and "Which measure(s) of variability would convey the information best?"*

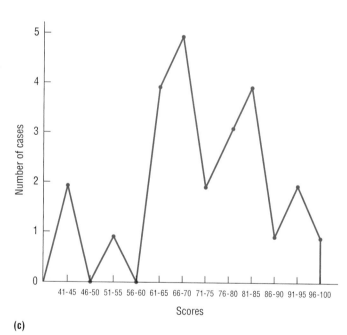

(c)

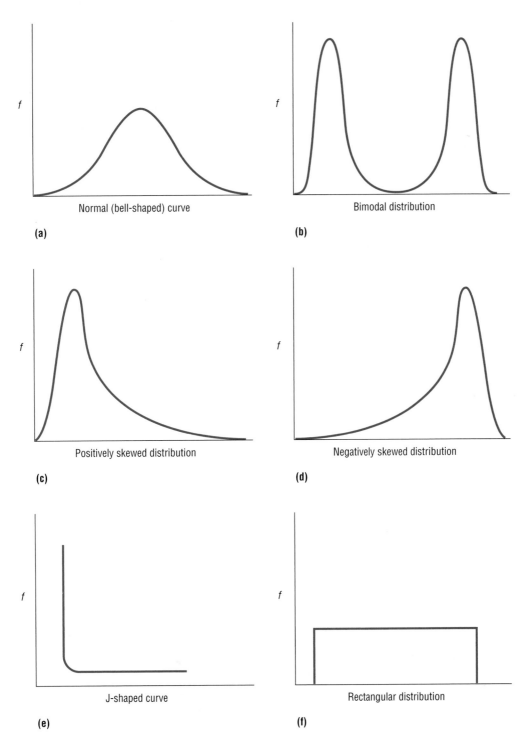

**Figure 3–3**
**Shapes That Frequency Distributions Can Take**

## Consumer (of Graphed Data), Beware!

One picture is worth a thousand words, and one purpose of representing data in graphic form is to convey information at a glance. However, although two graphs may be accurate with respect to the data they represent, their pictures—and the impression drawn from a glance at them—may be vastly different. As an example, consider the following hypothetical scenario involving a hamburger restaurant chain we'll call "The Charred House."

The Charred House chain serves very charbroiled, microscopically thin hamburgers formed in the shape of little triangular houses. In the 10-year period since its founding in 1993, the company has sold, on average, 100 million burgers per year. On the chain's tenth anniversary, The Charred House distributes a press release proudly announcing "Over a Billion Served."

Reporters from two business publications set out to research and write a feature article on this hamburger restaurant chain. Working solely from sales figures as compiled from annual reports to the shareholders, Reporter 1 focuses her story on the differences in yearly sales. Her article is entitled "A Billion Served—But Charred House Sales Fluctuate from Year to Year," and its graphic illustration is reprinted here.

Quite a different picture of the company emerges from Reporter 2's story, entitled "A Billion Served—And Charred House Sales Are as Steady as Ever," and its accompanying graph. The latter story is based on a diligent analysis of comparable data for the same number of hamburger chains in the same areas of the country over the same time period. While researching the story, Reporter 2 learned that yearly fluctuations in sales are common to the entire industry and that the annual fluctuations observed in the Charred House figures were—relative to other chains—insignificant.

Compare the graphs that accompanied each story. Although both are accurate insofar as they are based on the correct numbers, the impressions they are likely to leave are quite different.

Incidentally, custom dictates that the intersection of the two axes of a graph be at 0 and that all the points on the Y-axis be in equal and proportional intervals from 0. This custom is followed in Reporter 2's story, where the first point on the ordinate is 10 units more than 0, and

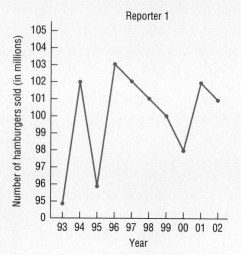

**(a)**   The Charred House Sales over a 10-Year Period

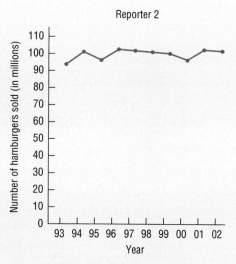

**(b)**   The Charred House Sales over a 10-Year Period

each succeeding point is also 10 more units away from 0. However, the custom is violated in Reporter 1's story, where the first point on the ordinate is 95 units more than 0, and each succeeding point increases only by 1. The fact that the custom is violated in Reporter 1's story should serve as a warning to evaluate pictorial representations of data all the more critically.

## Measures of Central Tendency

A **measure of central tendency** is a statistic that indicates the average or midmost score between the extreme scores in a distribution. The center of a distribution can be defined in different ways. Perhaps the most commonly used measure of central tendency is the *arithmetic mean* (or, more simply, **mean**), which is referred to in everyday language as the "average." The mean takes into account the actual numerical value of every score. In special instances, such as when there are only a few scores and one or two of the scores are extreme in relation to the remaining ones, a measure of central tendency other than the mean may be desirable. Other measures of central tendency we review include the *median* and the *mode.* Note that, in the formulas to follow, the standard statistical shorthand called "summation notation" (*summation* meaning "the sum of") is used. The Greek uppercase letter sigma, $\Sigma$, is the symbol used to signify "sum"; if $X$ represents a test score, then the expression $\Sigma X$ means "add all the test scores."

**The arithmetic mean**    The **arithmetic mean,** denoted by the symbol $\overline{X}$ (and pronounced "X bar"), is equal to the sum of the observations (or test scores, in this case) divided by the number of observations. Symbolically written, the formula for the arithmetic mean is $\overline{X} = \sum(X/n)$, where $n$ equals the number of observations or test scores. The arithmetic mean is typically the most appropriate measure of central tendency for interval or ratio data when the distributions are believed to be approximately normal. An arithmetic mean can also be computed from a frequency distribution. The formula for doing this is

$$\overline{X} = \frac{\sum(fX)}{n}$$

where $\Sigma(fX)$ means "multiply the frequency of each score by its corresponding score and then sum." An estimate of the arithmetic mean may also be obtained from a grouped frequency distribution using the same formula, where $X$ is equal to the midpoint of the class interval. Table 3–4 illustrates a calculation of the mean from a grouped frequency distribution. After doing the math you will find that, using the grouped data, a mean of 71.8 (which may be rounded to 72) is calculated. Using the raw scores, a mean of 72.12 (which also may be rounded to 72) is calculated. Frequently, the choice of statistic will depend on the required degree of precision in measurement.

> **JUST THINK . . .**
>
> Imagine that a thousand or so engineers took an extremely difficult pre-employment test. A handful of the engineers earned very high scores but the vast majority did poorly, earning extremely low scores. Given this scenario, what are the pros and cons of using the mean as a measure of central tendency for this test?

**The median**    The **median,** defined as the middle score in a distribution, is another commonly used measure of central tendency. We determine the median of a distribution of scores by ordering the scores in a list by magnitude, in either ascending or descending order. If the total number of scores ordered is an odd number, then the median will be the score that is exactly in the middle, with one-half of the remaining scores lying above it and the other half of the remaining scores lying below it. When the total number of scores ordered is an even number, then the median can be calculated by determining the arithmetic mean of the two middle scores. For example, suppose that 10 people

**Table 3–4**
**Calculating the Arithmetic Mean from a Grouped Frequency Distribution**

| Class Interval | f | X (midpoint of class interval) | fX |
|---|---|---|---|
| 95–99 | 1 | 97 | 97 |
| 90–94 | 2 | 92 | 184 |
| 85–89 | 2 | 87 | 174 |
| 80–84 | 3 | 82 | 246 |
| 75–79 | 3 | 77 | 231 |
| 70–74 | 2 | 72 | 144 |
| 65–69 | 5 | 67 | 335 |
| 60–64 | 4 | 62 | 248 |
| 55–59 | 0 | 57 | 000 |
| 50–54 | 1 | 52 | 52 |
| 45–49 | 0 | 47 | 000 |
| 40–44 | 2 | 42 | 84 |
| | $\Sigma f = 25$ | | $\Sigma (fX) = 1{,}795$ |

To estimate the arithmetic mean of this grouped frequency distribution,

$$\overline{X} = \frac{\Sigma(fX)}{n} = \frac{1795}{25} = 71.80$$

To calculate the mean of this distribution using raw scores,

$$\overline{X} = \frac{\Sigma X}{n} = \frac{1803}{25} = 72.12$$

took a preemployment word-processing test at The Rochester Wrenchworks (TRW) Corporation. They obtained the following scores, presented here in descending order:

66
65
61
59
53
52
41
36
35
32

The median of these data would be calculated by obtaining the average (that is, the arithmetic mean) of the two middle scores, 53 and 52 (which would be equal to 52.5). The median is an appropriate measure of central tendency for ordinal, interval, and ratio data. The median may be a particularly useful measure of central tendency in cases where relatively few scores fall at the high end of the distribution or relatively few scores fall at the low end of the distribution.

Suppose not 10 but rather tens of thousands of people had applied for jobs at The Rochester Wrenchworks. It would be impractical to find the median by simply ordering the data and finding the midmost scores, so how would the median score be identified? For our purposes, the answer is simply that there are advanced methods for doing so. There are also techniques for identifying the median in other sorts of distributions, such as a grouped frequency distribution and a distribution wherein various scores are identical. However, instead of delving into such new and complex territory, let's resume our discussion of central tendency and consider another such measure.

**The mode**   The most frequently occurring score in a distribution of scores is the **mode**.[7] As an example, determine the mode for the following scores obtained by another TRW job applicant, Bruce. The scores reflect the number of words Bruce word-processed in seven 1-minute trials:

43   34   45   51   42   31   51

It is TRW policy that new hires must be able to word-process at least 50 words per minute. Now, place yourself in the role of the corporate personnel officer. Would you hire Bruce? The most frequently occurring score in this distribution of scores is 51. If hiring guidelines gave you the freedom to use any measure of central tendency in your personnel decision making, then it would be your choice as to whether or not Bruce is hired. You could hire him and justify this decision on the basis of his modal score (51). You also could *not* hire him and justify this decision on the basis of his mean score (below the required 50 words per minute). Ultimately, whether Rochester Wrenchworks will be Bruce's new home away from home will depend on other job-related factors, such as the nature of the job market in Rochester and the qualifications of competing applicants. Of course, if company guidelines dictate that only the mean score be used in hiring decisions, then a career at TRW is not in Bruce's immediate future.

Distributions that contain a tie for the designation "most frequently occurring score" can have more than one mode. Consider the following scores—arranged in no particular order—obtained by 20 students on the final exam of a new trade school called the Home Study School of Elvis Presley Impersonators:

51   49   51   50   66   52   53   38   17   66

33   44   73   13   21   91   87   92   47   3

These scores are said to have a **bimodal distribution** because there are two scores (51 and 66) that occur with the highest frequency (of two). Except with nominal data, the mode tends not to be a very commonly used measure of central tendency. Unlike the arithmetic mean, which has to be calculated, the value of the modal score is not calculated; one simply counts and determines which score occurs most frequently. Because the mode is arrived at in this manner, the modal score may be totally atypical—for instance, one at an extreme end of the distribution—which nonetheless occurs with the greatest frequency. In fact, it is theoretically possible for a bimodal distribution to have two modes, each of which falls at the high or the low end of the distribution—thus violating the expectation that a measure of central tendency should be . . . well, central (or indicative of a point at the middle of the distribution).

Even though the mode is not calculated in the sense that the mean is calculated, and even though the mode is not necessarily a unique point in a distribution (a distribution can have two, three, or even more modes), the mode can still be useful in conveying certain types of information. The mode is useful in analyses of a qualitative or verbal nature.

---

7. If adjacent scores occur equally often and more often than other scores, custom dictates that the mode be referred to as the average.

For example, when assessing consumers' recall of a commercial by means of interviews, a researcher might be interested in which word or words were mentioned most by interviewees.

The mode can convey a wealth of information *in addition to* the mean. As an example, suppose you wanted an estimate of the number of journal articles published by clinical psychologists in the United States in the past year. To arrive at this figure, you might total the number of journal articles accepted for publication written by each clinical psychologist in the United States, divide by the number of psychologists, and arrive at the arithmetic mean. This calculation would yield an indication of the average number of journal articles published. Whatever that number would be, we can say with certainty that it would be more than the mode. It is well known that most clinical psychologists do not write journal articles. The mode for publications by clinical psychologists in any given year is zero. In this example, the arithmetic mean would provide us with a precise measure of the average number of articles published by clinicians. However, what might be lost in that measure of central tendency is that, proportionately, very few of all clinicians do most of the publishing. The mode (in this case, a mode of zero) would provide us with a great deal of information at a glance. It would tell us that, regardless of the mean, most clinicians do not publish.

**JUST THINK . . .**

Devise your own example to illustrate how the mode, and not the mean, can be the most useful measure of central tendency.

Because the mode is not calculated in a true sense, it is a nominal statistic and cannot legitimately be used in further calculations. The median is a statistic that takes into account the order of scores and is itself ordinal in nature. The mean, an interval-level statistic, is generally the most stable and useful measure of central tendency.

## Measures of Variability

**Variability** is an indication of how scores in a distribution are scattered or dispersed. As Figure 3–4 illustrates, two or more distributions of test scores can have the same mean even though differences in the dispersion of scores around the mean can be wide. In both distributions A and B, test scores could range from 0 to 100. In distribution A, we see that the mean score was 50 and the remaining scores were widely distributed around the mean. In distribution B, the mean was also 50 but few people scored higher than 60 or lower than 40.

Statistics that describe the amount of variation in a distribution are referred to as **measures of variability.** Some measures of variability include the range, the interquartile range, the semi-interquartile range, the average deviation, the standard deviation, and the variance.

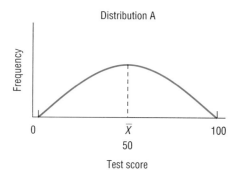
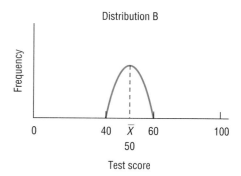

**Figure 3–4**
**Two Distributions with Differences in Variability**

**The range**   The **range** of a distribution is equal to the difference between the highest and the lowest scores. We could describe distribution B of Figure 3–3, for example, as having a range of 20 if we knew that the highest score in this distribution was 60 and the lowest score was 40 (60 − 40 = 20). With respect to distribution A, if we knew that the lowest score was 0 and the highest score was 100, the range would be equal to 100 − 0, or 100. The range

**JUST THINK . . .**

Devise two distributions of test scores to illustrate how the range can overstate or understate the degree of variability in the scores.

is the simplest measure of variability to calculate, but its potential use is limited. Because the range is based entirely on the values of the lowest and highest scores, one extreme score (if it happens to be the lowest or the highest) can radically alter the value of the range. For example, suppose distribution B included a score of 90. The range of this distribution would now be equal to 90 − 40, or 50. Yet, in looking at the data in the graph for distribution B, it is clear that the vast majority of scores tend to be between 40 and 60.

As a descriptive statistic of variation, the range provides a quick but gross description of the spread of scores. When its value is based on extreme scores in a distribution, the resulting description of variation may be understated or overstated. Better measures of variation include the interquartile range and the semi-interquartile range.

**The interquartile and semi-interquartile ranges**   A distribution of test scores (or any other data, for that matter) can be divided into four parts such that 25% of the test scores occur in each quarter. As illustrated in Figure 3–5, the dividing points between the four quarters in the distribution are the **quartiles.** There are three of them, respectively labeled $Q_1$, $Q_2$, and $Q_3$. Note that *quartile* refers to a specific point whereas *quarter* refers to an interval. An individual score may, for example, fall *at* the third quartile or *in* the third quarter (but *not* "in" the third quartile or "at" the third quarter). It should come as

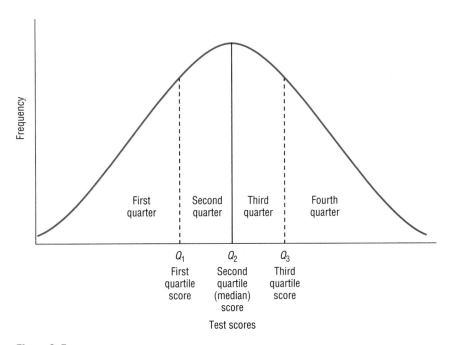

**Figure 3–5**
**A Quartered Distribution**

no surprise to you that $Q_2$ and the median are exactly the same. And just as the median is the midpoint in a distribution of scores, so are quartiles $Q_1$ and $Q_3$ the *quarter-points* in a distribution of scores. Formulas may be employed to determine the exact value of these points.

The **interquartile range** is a measure of variability equal to the difference between $Q_3$ and $Q_1$. Like the median, it is an ordinal statistic. A related measure of variability is the **semi-interquartile range,** which is equal to the interquartile range divided by 2. Knowledge of the relative distances of $Q_1$ and $Q_3$ from $Q_2$ (the median) provides the seasoned test interpreter with immediate information as to the shape of the distribution of scores. In a perfectly symmetrical distribution, $Q_1$ and $Q_3$ will be exactly the same distance from the median. If these distances are unequal then there is a lack of symmetry. This lack of symmetry is referred to as *skewness,* and we will have more to say about that shortly.

**The average deviation**  Another tool that could be used to describe the amount of variability in a distribution is the **average deviation,** or AD for short. Its formula is

$$\mathrm{AD} = \frac{\sum |x|}{n}$$

The lowercase italic $x$ in the formula signifies a score's deviation from the mean. The value of $x$ is obtained by subtracting the mean from the score ($X -$ mean $= x$). The bars on each side of $x$ indicate that it is the *absolute value* of the deviation score (ignoring the positive or negative sign and treating all deviation scores as positive). All the deviation scores are then summed and divided by the total number of scores ($n$) to arrive at the average deviation. As an exercise, calculate the average deviation for the following distribution of test scores:

85   100   90   95   80

Begin by calculating the arithmetic mean. Next, obtain the absolute value of each of the five deviation scores and sum them. As you sum them, note what would happen if you did not ignore the plus or minus signs: All the deviation scores would then sum to 0. Divide the sum of the deviation scores by the number of measurements (5). Did you obtain an AD of 6? The AD tells us that the five scores in this distribution varied, on average, 6 points from the mean.

**JUST THINK . . .**

After reading about the standard deviation, explain in your own words how an understanding of the *average deviation* can provide a "stepping-stone" to better understanding the concept of a *standard deviation.*

The average deviation is rarely used. Perhaps this is so because the deletion of algebraic signs renders it a useless measure for purposes of any further operations. Why, then, discuss it here? The reason is that a clear understanding of what an average deviation measures provides a solid foundation for understanding the conceptual basis of another, more widely used measure: the *standard deviation.* Keeping in mind what an average deviation is, what it tells us, and how it is derived, let's consider its more frequently used "cousin," the standard deviation.

**The standard deviation**  Recall that, when we calculated the average deviation, the problem of the sum of all deviation scores around the mean equaling zero was solved by employing only the absolute value of the deviation scores. In calculating the standard deviation, the same problem must be dealt with, but we do so in a different way. Instead of using the absolute value of each deviation score, we use the square of each score.

With each score squared, the sign of any negative deviation becomes positive. Because all the deviation scores are squared, we know that our calculations won't be complete until we go back and obtain the square root of whatever value we reach.

We may define the **standard deviation** as a measure of variability equal to the square root of the average squared deviations about the mean. More succinctly, it is equal to the square root of the *variance.* The **variance** is equal to the arithmetic mean of the squares of the differences between the scores in a distribution and their mean. The formula used to calculate the variance ($s^2$) using deviation scores is

$$s^2 = \frac{\sum x^2}{n}$$

Simply stated, the variance is calculated by squaring and summing all the deviation scores and then dividing by the total number of scores. The variance can also be calculated in other ways. For example: From raw scores, first calculate the summation of the raw scores squared, divide by the number of scores, and then subtract the mean squared. The result is

$$s^2 = \frac{\sum X^2}{n} - \overline{X}^2$$

The variance is a widely used measure in psychological research. To make meaningful interpretations, the test-score distribution should be approximately normal. We'll have more to say about "normal" distributions later in the chapter. At this point, think of a normal distribution as a distribution with the greatest frequency of scores occurring near the arithmetic mean. Correspondingly fewer and fewer scores relative to the mean occur on both sides of it.

For some hands-on experience with—and to develop a sense of mastery of—the concepts of variance and standard deviation, why not allot the next 10 or 15 minutes to calculating the standard deviation for the test scores shown in Table 3–1? Use both formulas to verify that they produce the same results. Using deviation scores, your calculations should look similar to these:

$$s^2 = \frac{\sum x^2}{n}$$

$$s^2 = \frac{\sum (X - \text{mean})^2}{n}$$

$$s^2 = \frac{[(78 - 72.12)^2 + (67 - 72.12)^2 + \cdots + (79 - 72.12)^2]}{25}$$

$$s^2 = \frac{4972.64}{25}$$

$$s^2 = 198.91$$

Using the raw-scores formula, your calculations should look similar to these:

$$s^2 = \frac{\sum X^2}{n} - \overline{X}^2$$

$$s^2 = \frac{[(78)^2 + (67)^2 + \cdots + (79)^2]}{25} - 5201.29$$

$$s^2 = \frac{135005}{25} - 5201.29$$

$$s^2 = 5400.20 - 5201.29$$

$$s^2 = 198.91$$

In both cases, the standard deviation is the square root of the variance ($s^2$). According to our calculations, the standard deviation of the test scores is 14.10. If $s = 14.10$, then 1 standard deviation unit is approximately equal to 14 units of measurement or (with reference to our example and rounded to a whole number) to 14 test-score points. The test data did not provide a good normal curve approximation. Test professionals would describe these data as "positively skewed." *Skewness*, as well as related terms such as *negatively skewed* and *positively skewed*, are covered in the next section. Once you are "positively familiar" with terms like *positively skewed*, you'll appreciate all the more the section later in this chapter entitled "The Area Under the Normal Curve." There you will find a wealth of information about test-score interpretation in the case when the scores are *not* skewed—that is, when the test scores are approximately normal in distribution.

The symbol for standard deviation has variously been represented as $s$, $S$, SD, and the lowercase Greek letter sigma ($\sigma$). One custom (the one we adhere to) has it that $s$ refers to the sample standard deviation and $\sigma$ refers to the population standard deviation. The number of observations in the sample is $n$, and the denominator $n - 1$ is sometimes used to calculate what is referred to as an "unbiased estimate" of the population value (though it's actually only *less* biased; see Hopkins & Glass, 1978). Unless $n$ is 10 or less, the use of $n$ or $n - 1$ tends not to make a meaningful difference.

Whether the denominator is more properly $n$ or $n - 1$ has been a matter of debate. Lindgren (1983) has argued for the use of $n - 1$, in part because this denominator tends to make correlation formulas simpler. By contrast, most texts recommend the use of $n - 1$ only when the data constitute a sample; when the data constitute a population, $n$ is preferable. For Lindgren (1983), it doesn't matter whether the data are from a sample or a population. Perhaps the most reasonable convention is to use $n$ either when the entire population has been assessed or when no inferences to the population are intended. So, when considering the examination scores of one class of students—including all the people about whom we're going to make inferences—it seems appropriate to use $n$.

Having stated our position on the $n$ versus $n - 1$ controversy, our formula for the population standard deviation follows. In this formula, $\overline{X}$ represents a sample mean and $M$ a population mean:

$$\sqrt{\frac{\sum(X - M)^2}{n}}$$

The standard deviation is a very useful measure of variation because each individual score's distance from the mean of the distribution is factored into its computation. You will come across this measure of variation frequently in the study and practice of measurement in psychology.

## Skewness

Distributions can be characterized by their **skewness,** or the nature and extent to which symmetry is absent. Skewness is an indication of how the measurements in a distribution are distributed. A distribution has a **positive skew** when relatively few of the scores fall at the high end of the distribution. Positively skewed examination results may indicate that the test was too difficult. More items that were easier would have been desirable in order to better discriminate at the lower end of the distribution of test scores. A distribution has a **negative skew** when relatively few of the scores fall at the low end of the distribution. Negatively skewed examination results may indicate that the test was too easy. In this case, more items of a higher level of difficulty would make it possible to better discriminate between scores at the upper end of the distribution. (Refer to Figure 3–3 for graphic examples of skewed distributions.)

The term *skewed* carries with it negative implications for many students. We suspect that *skewed* is associated with *abnormal*, perhaps because the skewed distribution deviates from the symmetrical or so-called normal distribution. However, the presence or absence of symmetry in a distribution (skewness) is simply one characteristic by which a distribution can be described. Consider in this context a hypothetical Marine Corps Ability and Endurance Screening Test administered to all civilians seeking to enlist in the U.S. Marines. Now look again at the graphs in Figure 3–3. Which graph do you think would best describe the resulting distribution of test scores? (No peeking at the next paragraph before you respond.)

No one can say with certainty, but if we had to guess, then we would say that the Marine Corps Ability and Endurance Screening Test data would look like graph C, the positively skewed distribution in Figure 3–3. We say this assuming that a level of difficulty would have been built into the test to ensure that relatively few assessees would score at the high end of the distribution. Most of the applicants would probably score at the low end of the distribution. All of this is quite consistent with the advertised objective of the Marines, who are only looking for a *few* good men. You know: *the few, the proud*. Now, a question regarding this positively skewed distribution: Is the skewness a good thing? A bad thing? An abnormal thing? In truth, it is probably none of these things—it just *is*. By the way, although they may not advertise it as much, the Marines are also looking for (an unknown quantity of) good women. But here we are straying a bit too far from skewness.

Various formulas exist for measuring skewness. One way of gauging the skewness of a distribution is through examination of the relative distances of quartiles from the median. In a positively skewed distribution, $Q_3 - Q_2$ will be greater than the distance of $Q_2 - Q_1$. In a negatively skewed distribution, $Q_3 - Q_2$ will be less than the distance of $Q_2 - Q_1$. In a distribution that is symmetrical, the distances from $Q_1$ and $Q_3$ to the median are the same.

## Kurtosis

The term testing professionals use to refer to the steepness of a distribution in its center is **kurtosis.** To the root *kurtic* is added to one of the prefixes *platy-*, *lepto-*, or *meso-* to describe the peakedness/flatness of three general types of curves (Figure 3–6). Distributions are generally described as **platykurtic** (relatively flat), **leptokurtic** (relatively peaked), or— somewhere in the middle—**mesokurtic.** Distributions that have high kurtosis are characterized by a high peak and "fatter" tails compared to a normal distribution. In contrast, lower kurtosis values indicate a distribution with a rounded peak and thinner tails. Many methods exist for measuring kurtosis. According to the original definition, the normal bell-shaped curve (see graph A from Figure 3–3) would

**JUST THINK . . .**

Like skewness, reference to the kurtosis of a distribution can provide a kind of "shorthand" description of a distribution of test scores. Imagine and describe the kind of test that might yield a distribution of scores that form a platykurtic curve.

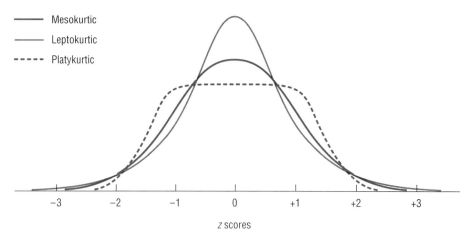

**Figure 3–6**
**The Kurtosis of Curves**

have a kurtosis value of 3. In other methods of computing kurtosis, a normal distribution would have kurtosis of 0, with positive values indicating higher kurtosis and negative values indicating lower kurtosis. It is important to keep the different methods of calculating kurtosis in mind when examining the values reported by researchers or computer programs. So, given that this can quickly become an advanced-level topic and that this book is of a more introductory nature, let's move on. It's time to focus on a type of distribution that happens to be the standard against which all other distributions (including all of the kurtic ones) are compared: the normal distribution.

## The Normal Curve

Before delving into the statistical, a little bit of the historical is in order. Development of the concept of a normal curve began in the middle of the eighteenth century with the work of Abraham DeMoivre and, later, the Marquis de Laplace. At the beginning of the nineteenth century, Karl Friedrich Gauss made some substantial contributions. Through the early nineteenth century, scientists referred to it as the "Laplace-Gaussian curve." Karl Pearson is credited with being the first to refer to the curve as the *normal curve*, perhaps in an effort to be diplomatic to all of the people who helped develop it. Somehow the term *normal curve* stuck—but don't be surprised if you're sitting at some scientific meeting one day and you hear this distribution or curve referred to as *Gaussian*.

Theoretically, the **normal curve** is a bell-shaped, smooth, mathematically defined curve that is highest at its center. From the center it tapers on both sides approaching the *X*-axis *asymptotically* (meaning that it approaches, but never touches, the axis). In theory, the distribution of the normal curve ranges from negative infinity to positive infinity. The curve is perfectly symmetrical, with no skewness. If you folded it in half at the mean, one side would lie exactly on top of the other. Because it is symmetrical, the mean, the median, and the mode all have the same exact value.

Why is the normal curve important in understanding the characteristics of psychological tests? Our *Close-Up* provides some answers.

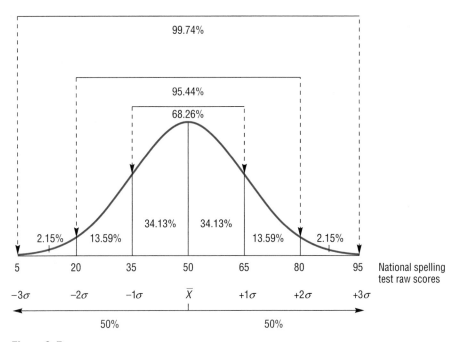

**Figure 3–7**
**The Area Under the Normal Curve**

## *The Area Under the Normal Curve*

The normal curve can be conveniently divided into areas defined in units of standard deviation. A hypothetical distribution of National Spelling Test scores with a mean of 50 and a standard deviation of 15 is illustrated in Figure 3–7. In this example, a score equal to 1 standard deviation above the mean would be equal to 65 ($\overline{X} + 1s = 50 + 15 = 65$).

Before reading on, take a minute or two to calculate what a score exactly at 3 standard deviations below the mean would be equal to. How about a score exactly at 3 standard deviations above the mean? Were your answers 5 and 95, respectively? The graph tells us that 99.74% of all scores in these normally distributed spelling-test data lie between ±3 standard deviations. Stated another way, 99.74% of all spelling test scores lie between 5 and 95. This graph also illustrates the following characteristics of all normal distributions.

- 50% of the scores occur above the mean and 50% of the scores occur below the mean.

- Approximately 34% of all scores occur between the mean and 1 standard deviation above the mean.

- Approximately 34% of all scores occur between the mean and 1 standard deviation below the mean.

- Approximately 68% of all scores occur between the mean and ±1 standard deviation.

- Approximately 95% of all scores occur between the mean and ±2 standard deviations.

# The Normal Curve
# and Psychological Tests

**S**cores on many psychological tests are often approximately normally distributed, particularly when the tests are administered to large numbers of subjects. Few, if any, psychological tests yield precisely normal distributions of test scores (Micceri, 1989). As a general rule (with ample exceptions), the larger the sample size and the wider the range of abilities measured by a particular test, the more the graph of the test scores will approximate the normal curve. A classic illustration of this was provided by E. L. Thorndike and his colleagues (1927). They compiled intelligence test scores from several large samples of students. As you can see in Figure 1, the distribution of scores closely approximated the normal curve.

Following is a sample of more varied examples of the wide range of characteristics that psychologists have found to be approximately normal in distribution.

- The strength of handedness in right-handed individuals, as measured by the Waterloo Handedness Questionnaire (Tan, 1993).

- Scores on the Women's Health Questionnaire, a scale measuring a variety of health problems in women across a wide age range (Hunter, 1992).

- Responses of both college students and working adults to a measure of intrinsic and extrinsic work motivation (Amabile et al., 1994).

- The intelligence-scale scores of girls and women with eating disorders, as measured by the Wechsler Adult Intelligence Scale–Revised and the Wechsler Intelligence Scale for Children–Revised (Ranseen & Humphries, 1992).

- The intellectual functioning of children and adolescents with cystic fibrosis (Thompson et al., 1992).

- Decline in cognitive abilities over a one-year period in people with Alzheimer's disease (Burns et al., 1991).

- The rate of motor-skill development in developmentally delayed preschoolers, as measured by the Vineland Adaptive Behavior Scale (Davies & Gavin, 1994).

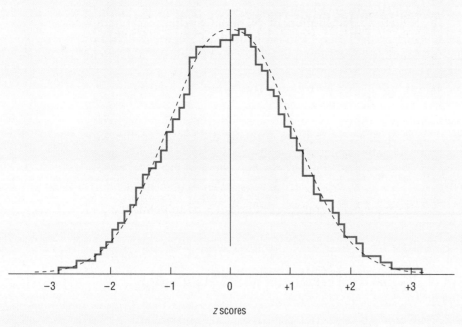

*z* scores

**Figure 1**
**Graphic Representation of Thorndike et al. Data**

*The solid line outlines the distribution of intelligence test scores of sixth-grade students (N = 15,138). The dotted line is the theoretical normal curve (Thorndike et al., 1927).*

- Scores on the Swedish translation of the Positive and Negative Syndrome Scale, which assesses the presence of positive and negative symptoms in people with schizophrenia (von Knorring & Lindstrom, 1992).
- Scores of psychiatrists on the Scale for Treatment Integration of the Dually Diagnosed (people with both a drug problem and another mental disorder); the scale examines opinions about drug treatment for this group of patients (Adelman et al., 1991).
- Responses to the Tridimensional Personality Questionnaire, a measure of three distinct personality features (Cloninger et al., 1991).
- Scores on a self-esteem measure among undergraduates (Addeo et al., 1994).

In each case, the researchers made a special point of stating that the scale under investigation yielded something close to a normal distribution of scores. Why? One benefit of a normal distribution of scores is that it simplifies the interpretation of individual scores on the test. In a normal distribution, the mean, the median, and the mode take on the same value. For example, if we know that the average score for intellectual ability of children with cystic fibrosis is a particular value and that the scores are normally distributed, then we know quite a bit more. We know that the average is the most common score and the score below and above which half of all the scores fall. Knowing the mean and the standard deviation of a scale and that it is approximately normally distributed tells us that (1) approximately two-thirds of all testtakers' scores are within a standard deviation of the mean and (2) approximately 95% of the scores fall within 2 standard deviations of the mean.

The characteristics of the normal curve provide a ready model for score interpretation that can be applied to a wide range of test results.

A normal curve has two *tails*. The area on the normal curve between 2 and 3 standard deviations above the mean is referred to as a **tail.** The area between −2 and −3 standard deviations below the mean is also referred to as a tail. Let's digress here momentarily for a "real-life" tale of the tails to consider along with our rather abstract discussion of statistical concepts.

As observed in a thought-provoking article entitled "Two Tails of the Normal Curve," an intelligence test score that falls within the limits of either tail can have momentous consequences in terms of the tale of one's life:

> Individuals who are mentally retarded or gifted share the burden of deviance from the norm, in both a developmental and a statistical sense. In terms of mental ability as operationalized by tests of intelligence, performance that is approximately two standard deviations from the mean (i.e., IQ of 70–75 or lower or IQ of 125–130 or higher) is one key element in identification. Success at life's tasks, or its absence, also plays a defining role, but the primary classifying feature of both gifted and retarded groups is intellectual deviance. These individuals are out of sync with more average people, simply by their difference from what is expected for their age and circumstance. This asynchrony results in highly significant consequences for them and for those who share their lives. None of the familiar norms apply, and substantial adjustments are needed in parental expectations, educational settings, and social and leisure activities. (Robinson et al., 2000, p. 1413)

Robinson et al. (2000) convincingly demonstrated that knowledge of the areas under the normal curve can be quite useful to the interpreter of test data. This knowledge can tell us not only something about where the score falls among a distribution of scores but also something about a *person* and perhaps even something about the people who share that person's life. This knowledge might also convey something about how impressive, average, or lackluster the individual is with respect to a particular discipline or ability. For example, consider a high-school student whose score on a national, well-reputed spelling test is close to 3 standard deviations above the mean. It's a good bet that this student would know how to spell words like *asymptotic* and *leptokurtic*.

Just as knowledge of the areas under the normal curve can instantly convey useful information about a test score in relation to other test scores, so can knowledge of standard scores.

## Standard Scores

Simply stated, a **standard score** is a raw score that has been converted from one scale to another scale, where the latter scale has some arbitrarily set mean and standard deviation. Why convert raw scores to standard scores?

Raw scores may be converted to standard scores because standard scores are more easily interpretable than raw scores. With a standard score, the position of a testtaker's performance relative to other testtakers is readily apparent.

Different systems for standard scores exist, each unique in terms of its respective mean and standard deviations. We will briefly describe *z* scores, *T* scores, stanines, and some other standard scores. First for consideration is the type of standard score scale that may be thought of as the *zero plus or minus one scale*. This is so because it has a mean set at 0 and a standard deviation set at 1. Raw scores converted into standard scores on this scale are more popularly referred to as *z* scores.

### z Scores

A ***z* score** results from the conversion of a raw score into a number indicating how many standard deviation units the raw score is below or above the mean of the distribution. Let's use an example from the normally distributed "National Spelling Test" data in Figure 3–7 to demonstrate how a raw score is converted to a *z* score. We'll convert a raw score of 65 to a *z* score by using the formula

$$z = \frac{X - \overline{X}}{s} = \frac{65 - 50}{15} = \frac{15}{15} = 1$$

In essence, a *z* score is equal to the difference between a particular raw score and the mean divided by the standard deviation. In the preceding example, a raw score of 65 was found to be equal to a *z* score of +1. Knowing that someone obtained a *z* score of 1 on a spelling test provides context and meaning for the score. Drawing on our knowledge of areas under the normal curve, for example, we would know that only about 16% of the other testtakers obtained higher scores. By contrast, knowing simply that someone obtained a raw score of 65 on a spelling test conveys virtually no usable information because information about the context of this score is lacking.

In addition to providing a convenient context for comparing scores on the same test, standard scores provide a convenient context for comparing scores on different tests. As an example, consider that Crystal's raw score on the hypothetical Main Street Reading Test was 24 and that her raw score on the (equally hypothetical) Main Street Arithmetic Test was 42. Without knowing anything other than these raw scores, one might conclude that Crystal did better on the arithmetic test than on the reading test. Yet more informative than the two raw scores would be the two *z* scores.

Converting Crystal's raw scores to $z$ scores based on the performance of other students in her class, suppose we find that her $z$ score on the reading test was 1.32 and that her $z$ score on the arithmetic test was $-0.75$. Thus, although her raw score in arithmetic was higher than in reading, the $z$ scores paint a different picture. The $z$ scores tell us that, relative to the other students in her class (and assuming that the distribution of scores is relatively normal), Crystal performed above average on the reading test and below average on the arithmetic test. An interpretation of exactly how much better she performed could be obtained by reference to tables detailing distances under the normal curve as well as the resulting percentage of cases that could be expected to fall above or below a particular standard deviation point (or $z$ score).

## T Scores

If the scale used in the computation of $z$ scores is called a *zero plus or minus one scale,* then the scale used in the computation of T **scores** can be called a *fifty plus or minus ten scale;* that is, a scale with a mean set at 50 and a standard deviation set at 10. Devised by W. A. McCall (1922, 1939) and named a $T$ score in honor of his professor E. L. Thorndike, this standard score system is composed of a scale that ranges from 5 standard deviations below the mean to 5 standard deviations above the mean. Thus, for example, a raw score that fell exactly at 5 standard deviations below the mean would be equal to a $T$ score of 0, a raw score that fell at the mean would be equal to a $T$ of 50, and a raw score 5 standard deviations above the mean would be equal to a $T$ of 100. One advantage in using $T$ scores is that none of the scores is negative. By contrast, in a $z$ score distribution, scores can be positive and negative; this can make further computation cumbersome in some instances.

## Other Standard Scores

Numerous other standard scoring systems exist. Researchers during World War II developed a standard score with a mean of 5 and a standard deviation of approximately 2. Divided into nine units, the scale was christened a **stanine,** a term that was a contraction of the words *standard* and *nine.*

Stanine scoring may be familiar to many students from achievement tests administered in elementary and secondary school, where test scores are often represented as stanines. Stanines are different from other standard scores in that they take on whole values from 1 to 9, which represent a range of performance that is half of a standard deviation in width (Figure 3–8). The 5th stanine indicates performance in the average range, from 1/4 standard deviation below the mean to 1/4 standard deviation above the mean, and captures the middle 20% of the scores in a normal distribution. The 4th and 6th stanines are also 1/2 standard deviation wide and capture the 17% of cases below and above (respectively) the 5th stanine.

Another type of standard score is employed on tests such as the Scholastic Aptitude Test (SAT) and the Graduate Record Examination (GRE). Raw scores on those tests are converted to standard scores such that the resulting distribution has a mean of 500 and a standard deviation of 100. If the letter $A$ is used to represent a standard score from a college or graduate school admissions test whose distribution has a mean of 500 and a standard deviation of 100, then the following is true:

$$(A = 600) = (z = 1) = (T = 60)$$

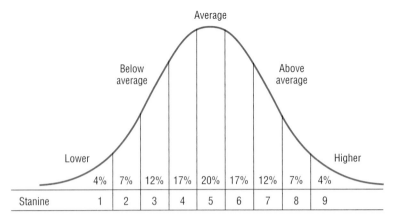

Average

Below
average

Above
average

Lower

Higher

| | 4% | 7% | 12% | 17% | 20% | 17% | 12% | 7% | 4% |
| Stanine | 1 | 2 | 3 | 4 | 5 | 6 | 7 | 8 | 9 |

**Figure 3–8**
**Stanines and the Normal Curve**

Have you ever heard the term *IQ* used as a synonym for one's score on an intelligence test? Of course you have. What you may not know is that what is referred to variously as IQ, deviation IQ, or deviation intelligence quotient is yet another kind of standard score. For most IQ tests, the distribution of raw scores is converted to IQ scores, whose distribution typically has a mean set at 100 and a standard deviation set at 15. Let's emphasize *typically* because there is some variation in standard scoring systems, depending on the test used. The typical mean and standard deviation for IQ tests results in approximately 95% of deviation IQs ranging from 70 to 130, which is 2 standard deviations below and above the mean. In the context of a normal distribution, the relationship of deviation IQ scores to the other standard scores we have discussed so far (*z*, *T*, and *A* scores) is illustrated in Figure 3–9.

Standard scores converted from raw scores may involve either linear or nonlinear transformations. A standard score obtained by a **linear transformation** is one that retains a direct numerical relationship to the original raw score. The magnitude of differences between such standard scores exactly parallels the differences between corresponding raw scores. Sometimes scores may undergo more than one transformation. For example, the creators of the SAT did a second linear transformation on their data to convert *z* scores into a new scale that has a mean of 500 and a standard deviation of 100.

A **nonlinear transformation** may be required when the data under consideration are not normally distributed yet comparisons with normal distributions need to be made. In a nonlinear transformation, the resulting standard score does not necessarily have a direct numerical relationship to the original, raw score. As the result of a nonlinear transformation, the original distribution is said to have been *normalized*.

**Normalized standard scores**    Many test developers hope that the test they are working on will yield a normal distribution of scores. Yet even after very large samples have been tested with the instrument under development, skewed distributions result. What should be done?

One alternative available to the test developer is to normalize the distribution. Conceptually, **normalizing a distribution** involves "stretching" the skewed curve into the shape of a normal curve and creating a corresponding scale of standard scores, a scale that is technically referred to as a **normalized standard score scale.**

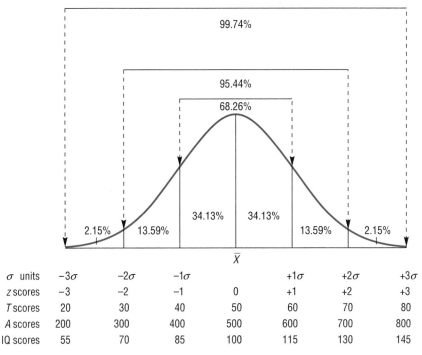

| | | | | | | | |
|---|---|---|---|---|---|---|---|
| $\sigma$ units | $-3\sigma$ | $-2\sigma$ | $-1\sigma$ | | $+1\sigma$ | $+2\sigma$ | $+3\sigma$ |
| $z$ scores | $-3$ | $-2$ | $-1$ | 0 | $+1$ | $+2$ | $+3$ |
| $T$ scores | 20 | 30 | 40 | 50 | 60 | 70 | 80 |
| $A$ scores | 200 | 300 | 400 | 500 | 600 | 700 | 800 |
| IQ scores | 55 | 70 | 85 | 100 | 115 | 130 | 145 |

**Figure 3–9**
**Some Standard Score Equivalents**

*Note that the values presented here for the IQ scores assume that the intelligence test scores have a mean of 100 and a standard deviation of 15. This is true for many, but not all, intelligence tests. If a particular test of intelligence yielded scores with a mean other than 100 and/or a standard deviation other than 15, then the values shown for IQ scores would have to be adjusted accordingly.*

Normalization of a skewed distribution of scores may also be desirable for purposes of comparability. One of the primary advantages of a standard score on one test is that it can readily be compared with a standard score on another test. However, such comparisons are appropriate only when the distributions from which they derived are the same. In most instances, they are the same because the two distributions are approximately normal. But if, for example, distribution A were normal and distribution B were highly skewed, then $z$ scores in these respective distributions would represent different amounts of area subsumed under the curve. A $z$ score of $-1$ with respect to normally distributed data tells us, among other things, that about 84% of the scores in this distribution were higher than this score. A $z$ score of $-1$ with respect to data that were very positively skewed might mean, for example, that only 62% of the scores were higher.

For test developers intent on creating tests that yield normally distributed measurements, it is generally preferable to fine-tune the test according to difficulty or other relevant variables so that the resulting distribution will approximate the normal curve. That usually is a better bet than attempting to normalize skewed distributions.

**JUST THINK . . .**

Apply what you have learned about frequency distributions, graphing frequency distributions, measures of central tendency, measures of variability, and the normal curve and standard scores to the question of the data listed in Table 3–1. How would you communicate the data from Table 3–1 to the class? Which type of frequency distribution might you use? Which type of graph? Which measure of central tendency? Which measure of variability? Might reference to a normal curve or to standard scores be helpful? Why or why not?

This is so because there are technical cautions to be observed before attempting normalization. For example, transformations should be made only when there is good reason to believe that the test sample was large enough and representative enough and that the failure to obtain normally distributed scores was due to the measuring instrument.

## Correlation and Inference

Central to psychological testing and assessment are inferences (deduced conclusions) about how some things (such as traits, abilities, or interests) are related to other things (such as behavior). A **coefficient of correlation** (or **correlation coefficient**) is a number that provides us with an index of the strength of the relationship between two things. An understanding of the concept of correlation and an ability to compute a coefficient of correlation is therefore central to the study of tests and measurement.

### The Concept of Correlation

Simply stated, **correlation** is an expression of the degree and direction of correspondence between two things. A coefficient of correlation ($r$) expresses a linear relationship between two (and only two) variables, usually continuous in nature. It reflects the degree of concomitant variation between variable $X$ and variable $Y$. The *coefficient of correlation* is the numerical index that expresses this relationship: It tells us the extent to which $X$ and $Y$ are "co-related."

The meaning of a correlation coefficient is interpreted by its sign and magnitude. If a correlation coefficient were a person asked "What's your sign?," it wouldn't answer anything like "Leo" or "Pisces." It would answer "plus" (for a positive correlation), "minus" (for a negative correlation), or "none" (in the rare instance that the correlation coefficient was exactly equal to zero). If asked to supply information about its magnitude, it would respond with a number anywhere at all between $-1$ and $+1$. And here is a rather intriguing fact about the magnitude of a correlation coefficient: It is judged by its absolute value. This means that to the extent that we are impressed by correlation coefficients, a correlation of $-.99$ is every bit as impressive as a correlation of $+.99$. To understand why, you need to know a bit more about correlation.

"Ahh . . . a perfect correlation! Let me count the ways." Well, actually there are only *two* ways. The two ways to describe a perfect correlation between two variables are as either $+1$ or $-1$. If a correlation coefficient has a value of $+1$ or $-1$, then the relationship between the two variables being correlated is perfect—without error in the statistical sense. And just as perfection in almost anything is difficult to find, so too are perfect correlations. It's challenging to try to think of any two variables in psychological work that are perfectly correlated. Perhaps that is why, if you look in the margin, you are asked to "just think" about it.

JUST THINK . . .

Can you name two variables that are perfectly correlated? How about two *psychological* variables that are perfectly correlated?

If two variables simultaneously increase or simultaneously decrease, then those two variables are said to be *positively* (or directly) correlated. The height and weight of normal, healthy children ranging in age from birth to 10 years tend to be positively or directly correlated. As children get older, their height and their weight generally increase simultaneously.

A positive correlation also exists when two variables simultaneously decrease. For example, the less a student prepares for an examination, the lower that student's score on the examination. A *negative* (or inverse) correlation occurs when one variable increases while the other variable decreases. For example, there tends to be an inverse relationship between the number of miles on your car's odometer (mileage indicator) and the number of dollars a car dealer is willing to give you on a trade-in allowance; all other things being equal, as the mileage increases, the number of dollars offered on trade-in decreases.

If a correlation is zero, then absolutely no relationship exists between the two variables. And some might consider "perfectly no correlation" to be a third variety of perfect correlation; that is, a perfect noncorrelation. After all, just as it is nearly impossible in psychological work to identify two variables that have a perfect correlation, so it is nearly impossible to identify two variables that have a zero correlation. Most of the time, two variables will be fractionally correlated. The fractional correlation may be extremely small but seldom "perfectly" zero.

As we stated in our introduction to this topic, correlation is often confused with causation. It must be emphasized that a correlation coefficient is merely an index of the relationship between two variables, *not* an index of the causal relationship between two variables. If you were told, for example, that from birth to age 9 there is a high positive correlation between hat size and spelling ability, would it be appropriate to conclude that hat size causes spelling ability? Of course not. The period from birth to age 9 is a time of maturation in *all* areas, including physical size and cognitive abilities such as spelling. Intellectual development parallels physical development during these years, and a relationship clearly exists between physical and mental growth. Still, this doesn't mean that the relationship between hat size and spelling ability is causal.

**JUST THINK . . .**

Could a correlation of zero between two variables also be considered a "perfect" correlation? Can you name two variables that have a correlation that is exactly zero?

Although correlation does not imply causation, there *is* an implication of prediction. Stated another way, if we know that there is a high correlation between $X$ and $Y$, then we should be able to predict—with various degrees of accuracy, depending on other factors—the value of one of these variables if we know the value of the other.

## The Pearson r

Many techniques have been devised to measure correlation. The most widely used of all is the **Pearson r,** also known as the *Pearson correlation coefficient* and the *Pearson product-moment coefficient of correlation.* Devised by Karl Pearson (Figure 3–10), $r$ can be the statistical tool of choice when the relationship between the variables is linear and when the two variables being correlated are continuous (that is, they can theoretically take any value). Other correlational techniques can be employed with data that are discontinuous and where the relationship is nonlinear. The formula for the Pearson $r$ takes into account the relative position of each test score or measurement with respect to the mean of the distribution.

A number of formulas can be used to calculate a Pearson $r$. One formula requires that we convert each raw score to a standard score and then multiply each pair of standard scores. A mean for the sum of the products is calculated, and that mean is the value of the Pearson $r$. Even from this simple verbal conceptualization of the Pearson $r$, it can be seen that the sign of the resulting $r$ would be a function of the sign and the magnitude of the standard scores used. If, for example, negative standard score values

**Figure 3–10**
**Karl Pearson (1857–1936)**

*Pictured here with his daughter is Karl Pearson, whose name has become synonymous with correlation. History records, however, that it was actually Sir Francis Galton who should be credited with developing the concept of correlation (Magnello & Spies, 1984). Galton experimented with many formulas to measure correlation, including one he labeled* r. *Pearson, a contemporary of Galton's, modified Galton's* r, *and the rest, as they say, is history. The Pearson* r *eventually became the most widely used measure of correlation.*

for measurements of $X$ always corresponded with negative standard score values for $Y$ scores, the resulting $r$ would be positive (because the product of two negative values is positive). Similarly, if positive standard score values on $X$ always corresponded with positive standard score values on $Y$, the resulting correlation would also be positive. However, if positive standard score values for $X$ corresponded with negative standard score values for $Y$ and vice versa, then an inverse relationship would exist and so a negative correlation would result. A zero or near-zero correlation could result when some products are positive and some are negative.

The formula used to calculate a Pearson $r$ from raw scores is

$$r = \frac{\Sigma(X - \overline{X})(Y - \overline{Y})}{\sqrt{[\Sigma(X - \overline{X})^2][\Sigma(Y - \overline{Y})^2]}}$$

This formula has been simplified for shortcut purposes. One such shortcut is a deviation formula employing "little $x$," or $x$ in place of $X - \overline{X}$, and "little $y$," or $y$ in place of $Y - \overline{Y}$:

$$r = \frac{\Sigma xy}{\sqrt{(\Sigma x^2)(\Sigma y^2)}}$$

Another formula for calculating a Pearson $r$ is

$$r = \frac{N\Sigma XY - (\Sigma X)(\Sigma Y)}{\sqrt{N\Sigma X^2 - (\Sigma X)^2}\ \sqrt{N\Sigma Y^2 - (\Sigma Y)^2}}$$

Although this formula looks more complicated than the previous deviation formula, it is easier to use. Here $N$ represents the number of paired scores; $\Sigma XY$ is the sum of the product of the paired $X$ and $Y$ scores; $\Sigma X$ is the sum of the $X$ scores;

$\Sigma\ Y$ is the sum of the $Y$ scores; $\Sigma\ X^2$ is the sum of the squared $X$ scores; and $\Sigma\ Y^2$ is the sum of the squared $Y$ scores. Similar results are obtained with the use of each formula.

The next logical question concerns what to do with the number obtained for the value of $r$. The answer is that you ask even more questions, such as "Is this number statistically significant, given the size and nature of the sample?" or "Could this result have occurred by chance?" At this point, you will need to consult tables of significance for Pearson $r$—tables that are probably in the back of your old statistics textbook. In those tables you will find, for example, that a Pearson $r$ of .899 with an $N = 10$ is significant at the .01 level (using a two-tailed test). You will recall from your statistics course that significance at the .01 level tells you, with reference to these data, that a correlation such as this could have been expected to occur merely by chance only one time or less in a hundred if $X$ and $Y$ are not correlated in the population. You will also recall that significance at either the .01 level or the (somewhat less rigorous) .05 level provides a basis for concluding that a correlation does indeed exist. Significance at the .05 level means that the result could have been expected to occur by chance alone five times or less in a hundred.

The value obtained for the coefficient of correlation can be further interpreted by deriving from it what is called a **coefficient of determination,** or $r^2$. The coefficient of determination is an indication of how much variance is shared by the $X$- and the $Y$-variables. The calculation of $r^2$ is quite straightforward. Simply square the correlation coefficient and multiply by 100; the result is equal to the percentage of the variance accounted for. If, for example, you calculated $r$ to be .9, then $r^2$ would be equal to .81. The number .81 tells us that 81% of the variance is accounted for by the $X$- and $Y$-variables. The remaining variance, equal to $100(1 - r^2)$, or 19%, could presumably be accounted for by chance, error, or otherwise unmeasured or unexplainable factors.[8]

Before moving on to consider another index of correlation, let's address a logical question sometimes raised by students when they hear the Pearson $r$ referred to as the *product-moment coefficient of correlation.* Why is it called that? The answer is a little complicated, but here goes.

In the language of psychometrics, a *moment* describes a deviation about a mean of a distribution. Individual deviations about the mean of a distribution are referred to as *deviates.* Deviates are referred to as the *first moments* of the distribution. The *second moments* of the distribution are the moments squared. The *third moments* of the distribution are the moments cubed, and so forth. The computation of the Pearson $r$ in one of its many formulas entails multiplying corresponding standard scores on two measures. One way of conceptualizing standard scores is as the first moments of a distribution. This is because standard scores are deviates about a mean of zero. A formula that entails the multiplication of two corresponding standard scores can therefore be conceptualized as one that entails the computation of the *product* of corresponding *moments.* And there you have the reason $r$ is called *product-moment correlation.* It's probably all more a matter of psychometric trivia than anything else, but we think it's cool to know. Further, you can now understand the rather "high-end" humor contained in the cartoon.

---

8. On a technical note, Ozer (1985) cautioned that the actual estimation of a coefficient of determination must be made with scrupulous regard to the assumptions operative in the particular case. Evaluating a coefficient of determination solely in terms of the variance accounted for may lead to interpretations that underestimate the magnitude of a relation.

YOU STANDARD SCORES ARE A BUNCH OF DEVIATES ABOUT A MEAN OF ZERO!

## The Spearman Rho

The Pearson *r* enjoys such widespread use and acceptance as an index of correlation that if for some reason it is not used to compute a correlation coefficient, mention is made of the statistic that was used. There are many alternative ways to derive a coefficient of correlation. One commonly used alternative statistic is variously called a **rank-order correlation coefficient,** a **rank-difference correlation coefficient,** or simply **Spearman's rho.** Developed by Charles Spearman, a British psychologist (Figure 3–11), this coefficient of correlation is frequently used when the sample size is small (fewer

**Figure 3–11**
**Charles Spearman (1863–1945)**

*Charles Spearman is best known as the developer of the Spearman rho statistic and the Spearman-Brown prophecy formula, which is used to "prophesize" the accuracy of tests of different sizes. Spearman is also credited with being the father of a statistical method called factor analysis, discussed later in this text.*

than 30 pairs of measurements) and especially when both sets of measurements are in ordinal (or rank-order) form. Special tables are used to determine whether an obtained rho coefficient is or is not significant.

## Graphic Representations of Correlation

One type of graphic representation of correlation is referred to by many names, including a **bivariate distribution**, a **scatter diagram**, a **scattergram**, or—our favorite—a **scatterplot**. A *scatterplot* is a simple graphing of the coordinate points for values of the X-variable (placed along the graph's horizontal axis) and the Y-variable (placed along the graph's vertical axis). Scatterplots are useful because they provide a quick indication of the direction and magnitude of the relationship, if any, between the two variables. Figure 3–12 and Figure 3–13 offer a quick course in eyeballing the nature and degree of correlation by means of scatterplots. To distinguish positive from negative correlations, note the direction of the curve. And to estimate the strength of magnitude of the correlation, note the degree to which the points form a straight line.

Scatterplots are useful in revealing the presence of *curvilinearity* in a relationship. As you may have guessed, **curvilinearity** in this context refers to an "eyeball gauge" of how curved a graph is. Remember that a Pearson r should be used only if the relationship between the variables is linear. If the graph does not appear to take the form of a straight line, the chances are good that the relationship is not linear (Figure 3–14). When the relationship is nonlinear, other statistical tools and techniques may be employed.[9]

A graph also makes the spotting of outliers relatively easy. An **outlier** is an extremely atypical point located at a relatively long distance—an outlying distance—from the rest of the coordinate points in a scatterplot (Figure 3–15). Outliers stimulate interpreters of test data to speculate about the reason for the atypical score. For example, consider an outlier on a scatterplot that reflects a correlation between hours each member of a fifth-grade class spent studying and their grades on a 20-item spelling test. And let's say that one student studied for 10 hours and received a failing grade. This outlier on the scatterplot might raise a red flag and compel the test user to raise some important questions, such as "How effective are this student's study skills and habits?" or "What was this student's state of mind during the test?"

In some cases, outliers are simply the result of administering a test to a very small sample of testtakers. In the example just cited, if the test were given statewide to fifth-graders and the sample size were much larger, perhaps many more low scorers who put in large amounts of study time would be identified.

As is the case with very low raw scores or raw scores of zero, outliers can sometimes help identify a testtaker who did not understand the instructions, was not able to follow the instructions, or was simply oppositional and did not follow the instructions. In other cases, an outlier can provide a hint of some deficiency in the testing or scoring procedures.

People who have occasion to use or make interpretations from graphed data need to know if the range of scores has been restricted in any way. To understand why this is so necessary to know, consider Figure 3–16. Let's say that graph A describes the relationship between Public University entrance test scores for 600 applicants

---

9. The specific statistic to be employed will depend at least in part on the suspected reason for the nonlinearity. For example, if it is believed that the nonlinearity is due to one distribution being highly skewed because of a poor measuring instrument, then the skewed distribution may be statistically normalized and the result may be a correction of the curvilinearity. If—even after graphing the data—a question remains concerning the linearity of the correlation, a statistic called "eta squared" ($\eta^2$) can be used to calculate the exact degree of curvilinearity.

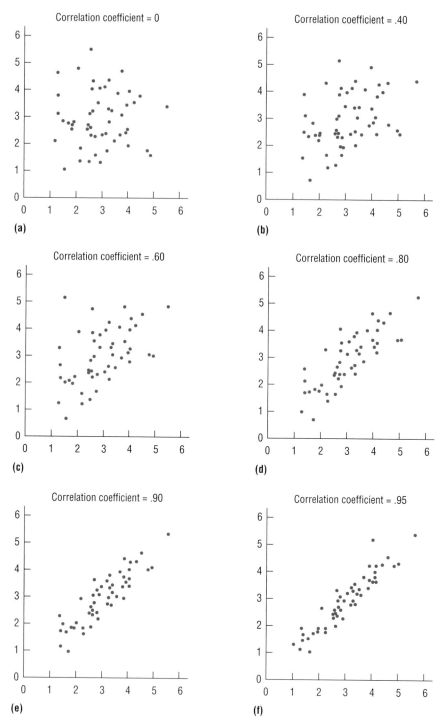

**Figure 3–12**
**Scatterplots and Correlations for Positive Values of *r***

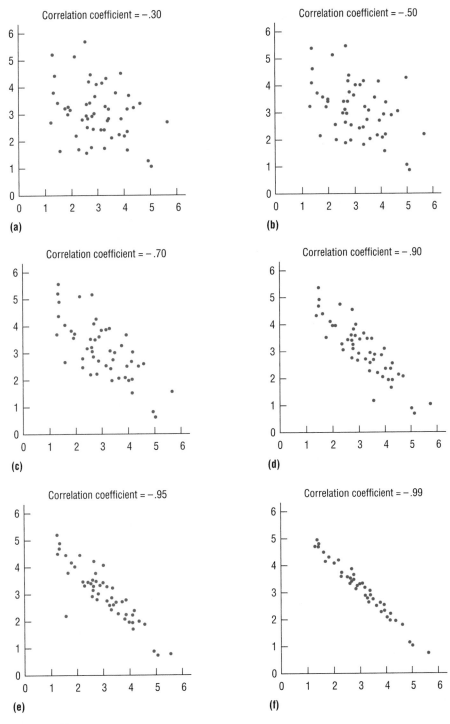

**Figure 3–13**
**Scatterplots and Correlations for Negative Values of *r***

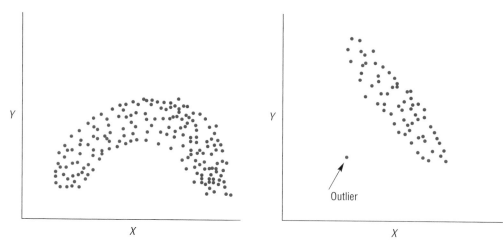

**Figure 3–14**
**Scatterplot Showing a Nonlinear Correlation**

**Figure 3–15**
**Scatterplot Showing an Outlier**

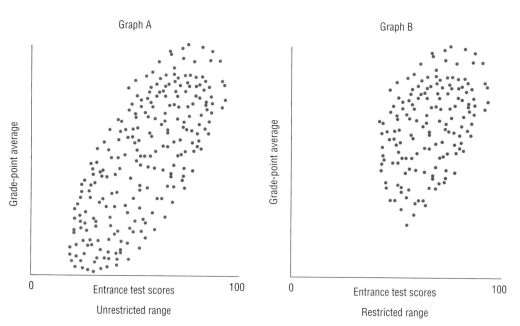

**Figure 3–16**
**Two Scatterplots Illustrating Unrestricted and Restricted Ranges**

(all of whom were later admitted) and their grade point averages at the end of the first semester. The scatterplot indicates that the relationship between entrance test scores and grade point average is both linear and positive. But what if the admissions officer had accepted only the applications of the students who scored within the top half or so on the entrance exam? To a trained eye, this scatterplot (graph B) appears to indicate a weaker correlation than that indicated in graph A—an effect attributable exclusively to the restriction of range. Graph B is less a straight line than graph A, and its direction is not as obvious.

## Meta-Analysis

Generally, the best estimate of the correlation between two variables is most likely to come not from a single study alone but from analysis of the data from several studies. One option to facilitate understanding of the research across a number of studies is to present the range of statistical values calculated from a number of different studies of the same phenomenon. Viewing all of the data from a number of studies that attempted to determine the correlation between variable X and variable Y, for example, might lead the researcher to conclude that "The correlation between variable *X* and variable *Y* ranges from .73 to .91." Another option might be to combine statistically the information across the various studies; that is what is done using a statistical technique called *meta-analysis.* Using this technique, researchers raise (and strive to answer) the question: "Combined, what do all of these studies tell us about the matter under study?" **Meta-analysis** may be defined as a family of techniques used to statistically combine information across studies to produce single estimates of the data under study. The estimates derived, referred to as **effect size,** may take several different forms. In most meta-analytic studies, effect size is typically expressed as a correlation coefficient.[10] Meta-analysis facilitates the drawing of conclusions and the making of statements like, "the typical therapy client is better off than 75% of untreated individuals" (Smith & Glass, 1977, p. 752), there is "about 10% increased risk for antisocial behavior among children with incarcerated parents, compared to peers" (Murray et al., 2012), and "GRE and UGPA [undergraduate grade point average] are generalizably valid predictors of graduate grade point average, 1st-year graduate grade point average, comprehensive examination scores, publication citation counts, and faculty ratings" (Kuncel et al., 2001, p. 162).

A key advantage of meta-analysis over simply reporting a range of findings is that, in meta-analysis, more weight can be given to studies that have larger numbers of subjects. This weighting process results in more accurate estimates (Hunter & Schmidt, 1990). Some advantages to meta-analyses are: (1) meta-analyses can be replicated; (2) the conclusions of meta-analyses tend to be more reliable and precise than the conclusions from single studies; (3) there is more focus on effect size rather than statistical significance alone; and (4) meta-analysis promotes **evidence-based practice,** which may be defined as professional practice that is based on clinical and research findings (Sánchez-Meca & Marin-Martinez, 2010). Despite these and other advantages, meta-analysis is, at least to some degree, art as well as science (Hall & Rosenthal, 1995). The value of any meta-analytic investigation is very much a matter of the skill and ability of the meta-analyst (Kavale, 1995), and use of an inappropriate meta-analytic method can lead to misleading conclusions (Kisamore & Brannick, 2008).

It may be helpful at this time to review this statistics refresher to make certain that you indeed feel "refreshed" and ready to continue. We will build on your knowledge of basic statistical principles in the chapters to come, and it is important to build on a rock-solid foundation. Of course, as our guest assessment professional, psychologist and psychoanalyst Benoît Verdon reminds us, it is sometimes important, especially in

---

10. More generally, *effect size* refers to an estimate of the strength of the relationship (or the size of the differences) between groups. In a typical study using two groups (an experimental group and a control group) effect size, ideally reported with confidence intervals, is helpful in determining the effectiveness of some sort of intervention (such as a new form of therapy, a drug, a new management approach, and so forth). In practice, many different procedures may be used to determine effect size, and the procedure selected will be based on the particular research situation.

## Meet Dr. Benoît Verdon

What we learn about an individual through tests, must always be interpreted within that individual's own life story. Our understanding of an assessee's psychological strengths and weaknesses as reflected by tests provides only an imperfect snapshot; it is incumbent upon the clinician to consider potential sources of change. . . .

Assessors must have a mastery of not only administrative techniques, but scoring and interpretative skills vis-à-vis their tools. Especially in a clinical context, it is also desirable for clinicians to be able to distance themselves from what might be termed "statistical objectification" of data, the better to be able to make sense of such data as it specifically relates to assessees. Data from different tests may, at times, appear contradictory. In such instances, a dynamic and coherent analysis of all of the data, along with an understanding of the limits of the data, is essential. . . .

**Benoît Verdon, Ph.D., Independent Practitioner, and Professor, Paris Descartes University, France.**

*Read more of what Dr. Verdon had to say— his complete essay—at www.mhhe.com/ cohentesting8.*

a clinical context, to "look beyond the numbers." Especially in the clinical arena, where the data may sometimes appear contradictory, the judgment of a clinician skilled in assessment can help shed new light on the meaning of the test scores, and bring new understanding and clarity to the clinical picture.

## Self-Assessment

Test your understanding of elements of this chapter by seeing if you can explain each of the following terms, expressions, and abbreviations:

| | | |
|---|---|---|
| arithmetic mean | coefficient of correlation | dynamometer |
| average deviation | coefficient of determination | effect size |
| bar graph | correlation | error |
| bimodal distribution | curvilinearity | evidence-based practice |
| bivariate distribution | distribution | frequency distribution |

frequency polygon
graph
grouped frequency distribution
histogram
interquartile range
interval scale
kurtosis
leptokurtic
linear transformation
mean
measurement
measure of central tendency
measure of variability
median
mesokurtic
meta-analysis
mode

negative skew
nominal scale
nonlinear transformation
normal curve
normalized standard
    score scale
normalizing a distribution
ordinal scale
outlier
Pearson $r$
platykurtic
positive skew
quartile
range
rank-order/rank-difference
    correlation coefficient
ratio scale

raw score
scale
scatter diagram
scattergram
scatterplot
semi-interquartile
    range
skewness
Spearman's rho
standard deviation
standard score
stanine
$T$ score
tail
variability
variance
$z$ score

# 4

# *Of Tests and Testing*

*Is this person competent to stand trial?*

*Who should be hired, transferred, promoted, or fired?*

*Who should gain entry to this special program or be awarded a scholarship?*

*Which parent shall have custody of the children?*

Every day, throughout the world, critically important questions like these are addressed through the use of tests. The answers to these kinds of questions are likely to have a significant impact on many lives.

If they are to sleep comfortably at night, assessment professionals must have confidence in the tests and other tools of assessment they employ. They need to know, for example, what does and does not constitute a "good test."

Our objective in this chapter is to overview the elements of a good test. As background, we begin by listing some basic assumptions about assessment. Aspects of these fundamental assumptions will be elaborated later in this chapter as well as in subsequent chapters.

> **JUST THINK . . .**
>
> What's a "good test"? Outline some elements or features that you believe are essential to a good test before reading on.

## Some Assumptions About Psychological Testing and Assessment

### *Assumption 1: Psychological Traits and States Exist*

A **trait** has been defined as "any distinguishable, relatively enduring way in which one individual varies from another" (Guilford, 1959, p. 6). **States** also distinguish one person from another but are relatively less enduring (Chaplin et al., 1988). The trait term that an observer applies, as well as the strength or magnitude of the trait presumed to be present, is based on observing a sample of behavior. Samples of behavior may be obtained in a number of ways, ranging from direct observation to the analysis of self-report statements or pencil-and-paper test answers.

The term *psychological trait,* much like the term *trait* alone, covers a wide range of possible characteristics. Thousands of psychological trait terms can be found in the

English language (Allport & Odbert, 1936). Among them are psychological traits that relate to intelligence, specific intellectual abilities, cognitive style, adjustment, interests, attitudes, sexual orientation and preferences, psychopathology, personality in general, and specific personality traits. New concepts or discoveries in research may bring new trait terms to the fore. For example, a trait term seen in the professional literature on human sexuality is *androgynous* (referring to an absence of primacy of male or female characteristics). Cultural evolution may bring new trait terms into common usage, as it did in the 1960s when people began speaking of the degree to which women were *liberated* (or freed from the constraints of gender-dependent social expectations). A more recent example is the trait term *New Age*, used in the popular culture to refer to a particular nonmainstream orientation to spirituality and health.

Few people deny that psychological traits exist. Yet there has been a fair amount of controversy regarding just *how* they exist. For example, do traits have a physical existence, perhaps as a circuit in the brain? Although some have argued in favor of such a conception of psychological traits (Allport, 1937; Holt, 1971), compelling evidence to support such a view has been difficult to obtain. For our purposes, a psychological trait exists only as a **construct**—an informed, scientific concept developed or *constructed* to describe or explain behavior. We can't see, hear, or touch constructs, but we can infer their existence from *overt behavior*. In this context, **overt behavior** refers to an observable action or the product of an observable action, including test- or assessment-related responses. A challenge facing test developers is to construct tests that are at least as telling as observable behavior such as that illustrated in Figure 4–1.

The phrase *relatively enduring* in our definition of *trait* is a reminder that a trait is not expected to be manifested in behavior 100% of the time So, for example, we may become more agreeable and conscientious as we age, and perhaps become less prone

**Figure 4–1**
**Measuring Sensation Seeking**

*The psychological trait of sensation seeking has been defined as "the need for varied, novel, and complex sensations and experiences and the willingness to take physical and social risks for the sake of such experiences" (Zuckerman, 1979, p. 10). A 22-item Sensation-Seeking Scale (SSS) seeks to identify people who are high or low on this trait. Assuming the SSS actually measures what it purports to measure, how would you expect a random sample of people lining up to bungee jump to score on the test as compared with another age-matched sample of people shopping at the local mall? What are the comparative advantages of using paper-and-pencil measures, such as the SSS, and using more performance-based measures, such as the one pictured here?*

to "sweat the small stuff" (Lüdtke et al., 2009; Roberts et al., 2003; Roberts et al., 2006) Yet there also seems to be rank-order stability in personality traits. This is evidenced by relatively high correlations between trait scores at different time points (Lüdtke et al., 2009; Roberts & Del Vecchio, 2000).

Whether a trait manifests itself in observable behavior, and to what degree it manifests, is presumed to depend not only on the strength of the trait in the individual but also on the nature of the situation. Stated another way, exactly how a particular trait manifests itself is, at least to some extent, situation-dependent. For example, a violent parolee may be prone to behave in a rather subdued way with her parole officer and much more violently in the presence of her family and friends. John may be viewed as dull and cheap by his wife but as charming and extravagant by his business associates, whom he keenly wants to impress.

The context within which behavior occurs also plays a role in helping us select appropriate trait terms for observed behavior. Consider how we might label the behavior of someone who is kneeling and praying aloud. Such behavior might be viewed as either religious or deviant, depending on the context in which it occurs. A person who is doing this inside a church or upon a prayer rug may be described as *religious,* whereas another person engaged in the exact same behavior at a venue such as a sporting event or a movie theater might be viewed as deviant or *paranoid.*

**JUST THINK . . .**

Give another example of how the same behavior in two different contexts may be viewed in terms of two different traits.

The definitions of *trait* and *state* we are using also refer to *a way in which one individual varies from another.* Attributions of a trait or state term are relative. For example, in describing one person as *shy,* or even in using terms such as *very shy* or *not shy,* most people are making an unstated comparison with the degree of shyness they could reasonably expect the average person to exhibit under the same or similar circumstances. In psychological assessment, assessors may also make such comparisons with respect to the hypothetical average person. Alternatively, assessors may make comparisons among people who, because of their membership in some group or for any number of other reasons, are decidedly not average.

**JUST THINK . . .**

Is the strength of a particular psychological trait the same across all situations or environments? What are the implications of one's answer to this question for assessment?

As you might expect, the reference group with which comparisons are made can greatly influence one's conclusions or judgments. For example, suppose a psychologist administers a test of shyness to a 22-year-old male who earns his living as an exotic dancer. The interpretation of the test data will almost surely differ as a function of the reference group with which the testtaker is compared—that is, other males in his age group or other male exotic dancers in his age group.

## Assumption 2: Psychological Traits and States Can Be Quantified and Measured

Once it's acknowledged that psychological traits and states do exist, the specific traits and states to be measured and quantified need to be carefully defined. Test developers and researchers, much like people in general, have many different ways of looking at and defining the same phenomenon. Just think, for example, of the different ways a term such as *aggressive* is used. We speak of an aggressive salesperson, an aggressive killer, and an aggressive waiter, to name but a few contexts. In each of these different contexts, *aggressive* carries with it a different meaning. If a personality test yields a score purporting to provide information about how aggressive a testtaker is, a first step in understanding the meaning of that score is understanding how *aggressive* was defined by the test developer. More specifically, what types of behaviors are presumed to be indicative of someone who is aggressive as defined by the test? One test developer may define aggressive behavior as "the number of self-reported acts of physically harming others." Another test developer might define it as the number of observed acts of aggression, such as pushing, hitting, or kicking, that occur in a playground stetting. Other test developers may define "aggressive behavior" in vastly different ways. Ideally, the test developer has provided test users with a clear operational definition of the construct under study.

Once having defined the trait, state, or other construct to be measured, a test developer considers the types of item content that would provide insight into it. From a universe of behaviors presumed to be indicative of the targeted trait, a test developer has a world of possible items that can be written to gauge the strength of that trait in testtakers.[1] For example, if the test developer deems knowledge of American history to be one component of intelligence in U.S. adults, then the item *Who was the second president of the United States?* may appear on the test. Similarly, if social judgment is deemed to be indicative of adult intelligence, then it might be reasonable to include the item *Why should guns in the home always be inaccessible to children?*

Suppose we agree that an item tapping knowledge of American history and an item tapping social judgment are both appropriate for an adult intelligence test. One question that arises is: Should both items be given equal weight? That is, should we place more importance on—and award more points for—an answer keyed "correct" to one or the other of these two items? Perhaps a correct response to the social judgment question should earn more credit than a correct response to the American history question. Weighting the comparative value of a test's items comes about as the result of a complex interplay among many factors, including technical considerations, the way a construct has been defined for the purposes of the test, and the value society (and the test developer) attaches to the behaviors evaluated.

**JUST THINK . . .**

On an adult intelligence test, what type of item should be given the most weight? What type of item should be given the least weight?

Measuring traits and states by means of a test entails developing not only appropriate test items but also appropriate ways to score the test and interpret the results. For many varieties of psychological tests, some number representing the score on the test is derived from the examinee's responses. The test score is presumed to represent the strength of the targeted ability or trait or state and is frequently based on **cumulative scoring.**[2] Inherent in cumulative scoring is the assumption that the more the testtaker responds in a particular direction as keyed by the test manual as correct or consistent with a particular trait, the higher that testtaker is presumed to be on the targeted ability or trait. You were probably first introduced to cumulative scoring early in elementary school when you observed that your score on a weekly spelling test had everything to do with how many words you spelled correctly or incorrectly. The score reflected the extent to which you had successfully mastered the spelling assignment for the week. On the basis of that score, we might predict that you would spell those words correctly if called upon to do so. And in the context of such prediction, consider the next assumption.

---

1. In the language of psychological testing and assessment, the word *domain* is substituted for *world* in this context. Assessment professionals speak, for example, of **domain sampling,** which may refer to either (1) a sample of behaviors from all possible behaviors that could conceivably be indicative of a particular construct or (2) a sample of test items from all possible items that could conceivably be used to measure a particular construct.

2. Other models of scoring are discussed in Chapter 8.

## Assumption 3: Test-Related Behavior Predicts Non-Test-Related Behavior

Many tests involve tasks such as blackening little grids with a number. 2 pencil or simply pressing keys on a computer keyboard. The objective of such tests typically has little to do with predicting future grid-blackening or key-pressing behavior. Rather, the objective of the test is to provide some indication of other aspects of the examinee's behavior. For example, patterns of answers to true–false questions on one widely used test of personality are used in decision making regarding mental disorders.

The tasks in some tests mimic the actual behaviors that the test user is attempting to understand. By their nature, however, such tests yield only a sample of the behavior that can be expected to be emitted under nontest conditions. The obtained sample of behavior is typically used to make predictions about future behavior, such as work performance of a job applicant. In some forensic (legal) matters, psychological tests may be used not to predict behavior but to *postdict* it—that is, to aid in the understanding of behavior that has already taken place. For example, there may be a need to understand a criminal defendant's state of mind at the time of the commission of a crime. It is beyond the capability of any known testing or assessment procedure to reconstruct someone's state of mind. Still, behavior samples may shed light, under certain circumstances, on someone's state of mind in the past. Additionally, other tools of assessment—such as case history data or the defendant's personal diary during the period in question—might be of great value in such an evaluation.

**JUST THINK . . .**

In practice, tests have proven to be good predictors of some types of behaviors and not-so-good predictors of other types of behaviors. For example, tests have *not* proven to be as good at predicting violence as had been hoped. Why do you think it is so difficult to predict violence by means of a test?

## Assumption 4: Tests and Other Measurement Techniques Have Strengths and Weaknesses

Competent test users understand a great deal about the tests they use. They understand, among other things, how a test was developed, the circumstances under which it is appropriate to administer the test, how the test should be administered and to whom, and how the test results should be interpreted. Competent test users understand and appreciate the limitations of the tests they use as well as how those limitations might be compensated for by data from other sources. All of this may sound quite commonsensical, and it probably is. Yet this deceptively simple assumption—that test users know the tests they use and are aware of the tests' limitations—is emphasized repeatedly in the codes of ethics of associations of assessment professionals.

## Assumption 5: Various Sources of Error Are Part of the Assessment Process

In everyday conversation, we use the word *error* to refer to mistakes, miscalculations, and the like. In the context of assessment, error need not refer to a deviation, an oversight, or something that otherwise violates expectations. To the contrary, *error* traditionally refers to something that is more than expected; it is actually a component of the measurement process. More specifically, *error* refers to a long-standing assumption that factors other than what a test attempts to measure will influence performance on the test. Test scores are always subject to questions about the degree to which the measurement process includes error. For example, an intelligence test score could be subject to debate concerning the degree to which the obtained score truly reflects the examinee's intelligence and the degree to which it was due to factors other than intelligence. Because error is a variable that must be taken account of in any assessment, we often speak of **error variance,** that is, the component of a test score attributable to sources other than the trait or ability measured.

There are many potential sources of error variance. Whether or not an assessee has the flu when taking a test is a source of error variance. In a more general sense, then, assessees themselves are sources of error variance. Assessors, too, are sources of error variance. For example, some assessors are more professional than others in the extent to which they follow the instructions governing how and under what conditions a test should be administered. In addition to assessors and assessees, measuring instruments themselves are another source of error variance. Some tests are simply better than others in measuring what they purport to measure.

Instructors who teach the undergraduate measurement course will occasionally hear a student refer to error as "creeping into" or "contaminating" the measurement process. Yet measurement professionals tend to view error as simply an element in the process of measurement, one for which any theory of measurement must surely account. In what is referred to as **classical test theory (CTT;** also variously referred to as **true score theory**) the assumption is made that each testtaker has a *true* score on a test that would be obtained but for the action of measurement error. Alternatives to CTT exist, such as a model of measurement based on item response theory (IRT, to be discussed later). However, whether CTT, IRT, or some other model of measurement is used, the model must have a way of accounting for measurement error. There is more on CTT and its alternatives in Chapter 5.

## Assumption 6: Testing and Assessment Can Be Conducted in a Fair and Unbiased Manner

If we had to pick the one of these seven assumptions that is more controversial than the remaining six, this one is it. Decades of court challenges to various tests and testing programs have sensitized test developers and users to the societal demand for fair tests used in a fair manner. Today all major test publishers strive to develop instruments that are fair when used in strict accordance with guidelines in the test manual. However, despite the best efforts of many professionals, fairness-related questions and problems do occasionally arise. One source of fairness-related problems is the test user who attempts to use a particular test with people whose background and experience are different from the background and experience of people for whom the test was intended. Some potential problems related to test fairness are more political than psychometric. For example, heated debate on selection, hiring, and access or denial of access to various opportunities often surrounds affirmative action programs. In many cases the real question for debate is not "Is this test or assessment procedure fair?" but rather "What do we as a society wish to accomplish by the use of this test or assessment procedure?" In all questions about tests with regard to fairness, it is important to keep in mind that tests are tools. And just like other, more familiar tools (hammers, ice picks, wrenches, and so on), they can be used properly or improperly.

> **JUST THINK . . .**
>
> Do you believe that testing can be conducted in a fair and unbiased manner?

## Assumption 7: Testing and Assessment Benefit Society

At first glance, the prospect of a world devoid of testing and assessment might seem appealing, especially from the perspective of a harried student preparing for a week of midterm examinations. Yet a world without tests would most likely be more a nightmare than a dream. In such a world, people could present themselves as surgeons, bridge builders, or airline pilots regardless of their background, ability, or professional credentials. In a world without tests or other assessment procedures, personnel might be hired on the basis of nepotism rather than documented merit. In a world without tests, teachers and school administrators could arbitrarily place children in different types of special classes simply because that is where they believed the children belonged. In a world without tests, there would be a great need for instruments to diagnose educational difficulties in reading and math and point the way to remediation. In a world without tests, there would be no instruments to diagnose neuropsychological impairments. In a world without tests, there would be no practical way for the military to screen thousands of recruits with regard to many key variables.

**JUST THINK . . .**

How else might a world without tests or other assessment procedures be different from the world today?

Considering the many critical decisions that are based on testing and assessment procedures, we can readily appreciate the need for tests, especially good tests. And that, of course, raises one critically important question . . .

## What's a "Good Test"?

Logically, the criteria for a good test would include clear instructions for administration, scoring, and interpretation. It would also seem to be a plus if a test offered economy in the time and money it took to administer, score, and interpret it. Most of all, a good test would seem to be one that measures what it purports to measure.

Beyond simple logic, there are technical criteria that assessment professionals use to evaluate the quality of tests and other measurement procedures. Test users often speak of the *psychometric soundness* of tests, two key aspects of which are *reliability* and *validity*.

### Reliability

A good test or, more generally, a good measuring tool or procedure is *reliable*. As we will explain in Chapter 5, the criterion of reliability involves the *consistency* of the measuring tool: the precision with which the test measures and the extent to which error is present in measurements. In theory, the perfectly reliable measuring tool consistently measures in the same way.

To exemplify reliability, visualize three digital scales labeled A, B, and C. To determine if they are reliable measuring tools, we will use a standard 1-pound gold bar that has been certified by experts to indeed weigh 1 pound and not a fraction of an ounce more or less. Now, let the testing begin.

Repeated weighings of the 1-pound bar on Scale A register a reading of 1 pound every time. No doubt about it, Scale A is a reliable tool of measurement. On to Scale B. Repeated weighings of the bar on Scale B yield a reading of 1.3 pounds. Is this scale reliable? It sure is! It may be consistently inaccurate by three-tenths of a pound, but there's no taking away the fact that it is reliable. Finally, Scale C. Repeated weighings of the bar on Scale C register a different weight every time. On one weighing, the gold bar weighs in at 1.7 pounds. On the next weighing, the weight registered is 0.9 pound. In short, the weights registered are all over the map. Is this scale reliable? Hardly. This scale is neither reliable nor accurate. Contrast it to Scale B, which also did not record the weight of the gold standard correctly. Although inaccurate, Scale B was consistent in terms of how much the registered weight deviated from the true weight. By contrast, the weight registered by Scale C deviated from the true weight of the bar in seemingly random fashion.

Whether we are measuring gold bars, behavior, or anything else, unreliable measurement is to be avoided. We want to be reasonably certain that the measuring tool or test that we are using is consistent. That is, we want to know that it yields the same numerical measurement every time it measures the same thing under the same conditions. Psychological tests, like other tests and instruments, are reliable to varying degrees. As you might expect, however, reliability is a necessary but not sufficient element of a good test. In addition to being reliable, tests must be reasonably accurate. In the language of psychometrics, tests must be *valid*.

## Validity

A test is considered valid for a particular purpose if it does, in fact, measure what it purports to measure. In the gold bar example cited earlier, the scale that consistently indicated that the 1-pound gold bar weighed 1 pound is a valid scale. Likewise, a test of reaction time is a valid test if it accurately measures reaction time. A test of intelligence is a valid test if it truly measures intelligence. Well, yes, but . . .

Although there is relatively little controversy about the definition of a term such as *reaction time*, a great deal of controversy exists about the definition of intelligence. Because there is controversy surrounding the definition of intelligence, the validity of any test purporting to measure this variable is sure to be closely scrutinized by critics. If the definition of intelligence on which the test is based is sufficiently different from the definition of intelligence on other accepted tests, then the test may be condemned as not measuring what it purports to measure.

Questions regarding a test's validity may focus on the items that collectively make up the test. Do the items adequately sample the range of areas that must be sampled to adequately measure the construct? Individual items will also come under scrutiny in an investigation of a test's validity. How do individual items contribute to or detract from the test's validity? The validity of a test may also be questioned on grounds related to the interpretation of resulting test scores. What do these scores really tell us about the targeted construct? How are high scores on the test related to testtakers' behavior? How are low scores on the test related to testtakers' behavior? How do scores on this test relate to scores on other tests purporting to measure the same construct? How do scores on this test relate to scores on other tests purporting to measure opposite types of constructs?

We might expect one person's score on a valid test of introversion to be inversely related to that same person's score on a valid test of extraversion; that is, the higher the introversion test score, the lower the extraversion test score, and vice versa. As we will see when we discuss validity in

**JUST THINK . . .**

Why might a test shown to be valid for use for a particular purpose with members of one population not be valid for use for that same purpose with members of another population?

greater detail in Chapter 6, questions concerning the validity of a particular test may be raised at every stage in the life of a test. From its initial development through the life of its use with members of different populations, assessment professionals may raise questions regarding the extent to which a test is measuring what it purports to measure.

## Other Considerations

A good test is one that trained examiners can administer, score, and interpret with a minimum of difficulty. A good test is a useful test, one that yields actionable results that will ultimately benefit individual testtakers or society at large. In "putting a test to the test," there are a number of ways to evaluate just how good a test really is (see this chapter's *Everyday Psychometrics*).

## Putting Tests to the Test

For experts in the field of testing and assessment, certain questions occur almost reflexively in evaluating a test or measurement technique. As a student of assessment, you may not be expert yet, but consider the questions that follow when you come across mention of any psychological test or other measurement technique.

### Why Use This Particular Instrument or Method?

Typically there will be a choice of measuring instruments when it comes to measuring a particular psychological or educational variable, and the test user must therefore choose from many available tools. Why use one over another? Answering this question typically entails raising other questions, such as: What is the objective of using a test and how well does the test under consideration meet that objective? Who is this test designed for use with (age of testtakers? reading level? etc.) and how appropriate is it for the targeted testtakers? How is what the test measures defined? For example, if a test user seeks a test of "leadership," how is "leadership" defined by the test developer (and how close does this definition match the test user's definition of leadership for the purposes of the assessment)? What type of data will be generated from using this test, and what other types of data will it be necessary to generate if this test is used? Do alternate forms of this test exist? Answers to questions about specific instruments may be found in published sources of information (such as test catalogues, test manuals, and published test reviews) as well as unpublished sources (correspondence with test developers and publishers and with colleagues who have used the same or similar tests). Answers to related questions about the use of a particular instrument may be found elsewhere—for example, in published guidelines. This brings us to another question to "put to the test."

### Are There Any Published Guidelines for the Use of This Test?

Measurement professionals make it their business to be aware of published guidelines from professional associations and related organizations for the use of tests and measurement techniques. Sometimes a published guideline for the use of a particular test will list other measurement tools that should also be used along with it. For example, consider the case of psychologists called upon to provide input to a court in the matter of a child custody decision.

More specifically, the court has asked the psychologist for expert opinion regarding an individual's parenting capacity. Many psychologists who perform such evaluations use a psychological test as part of the evaluation process. However, the psychologist performing such an evaluation is—or should be—aware of the guidelines promulgated by the American Psychological Association's Committee on Professional Practice and Standards. These guidelines describe three types of assessments relevant to a child custody decision: (1) the assessment of parenting capacity, (2) the assessment of psychological and developmental needs of the child, and (3) the assessment of the goodness of fit between the parent's capacity and the child's needs. According to these guidelines, an evaluation of a parent—or even of two parents—is not sufficient to arrive at an opinion regarding custody. Rather, an educated opinion about who should be awarded custody can be arrived at only after evaluating (1) the parents (or others seeking custody), (2) the child, and (3) the goodness of fit between the needs and capacity of each of the parties.

In this example, published guidelines inform us that any instrument the assessor selects to obtain information about parenting capacity must be supplemented with other instruments or procedures designed to support any expressed opinion, conclusion, or recommendation. In everyday practice, these other sources of data will be derived using other tools of psychological assessment such as interviews, behavioral observation, and case history or document analysis. Published guidelines and research may also provide useful information regarding how likely the use of a particular test or measurement technique is to meet the *Daubert* or other standards set by courts (see, for example, Yañez & Fremouw, 2004).

### Is This Instrument Reliable?

Earlier we introduced you to the psychometric concept of reliability and noted that it concerned the consistency of measurement. Research to determine whether a particular instrument is reliable starts with a careful reading of the test's manual and of published research on the test, test reviews, and related sources. However, it does not necessarily end with such research.

Measuring reliability is not always a straightforward matter. As an example, consider one of the tests that might be used in the evaluation of parenting capacity, the Bricklin Perceptual Scales (BPS; Bricklin, 1984).

The BPS was designed to explore a child's perception of father and mother. A measure of one type of reliability, referred to as *test-retest reliability,* would indicate how consistent a child's perception of father and mother is over time. However, the BPS test manual contains no reliability data because, as Bricklin (1984, p. 42) opined, "There are no reasons to expect the measurements reported here to exhibit any particular degree of stability, since they should vary in accordance with changes in the child's perceptions." This assertion has not stopped others (Gilch-Pesantez, 2001; Speth, 1992) and even Bricklin himself many years later (Bricklin & Halbert, 2004) from exploring the test-retest reliability of the BPS. Whether or not one accepts Bricklin's opinion as found in the original test manual, such opinions illustrate the great complexity of reliability questions. They also underscore the need for multiple sources of data to strengthen arguments regarding the confirmation or rejection of a hypothesis.

### Is This Instrument Valid?

Validity, as you have learned, refers to the extent to which a test measures what it purports to measure. And as was the case with questions concerning a particular instrument's reliability, research to determine whether a particular instrument is valid starts with a careful reading of the test's manual as well as published research on the test, test reviews, and related sources. Once again, as you might have anticipated, there will not necessarily be any simple answers at the end of this preliminary research.

As with reliability, questions related to the validity of a test can be complex and colored more in shades of gray than black or white. For example, even if data from a test such as the BPS were valid for the purpose of gauging children's perceptions of their parents, the data would be invalid as the sole source on which to base an opinion regarding child custody (Brodzinsky, 1993; Heinze & Grisso, 1996). The need for multiple sources of data on which to base an opinion stems not only from the ethical mandates published in the form of guidelines from professional associations but also from the practical demands of meeting a burden of proof in court. In sum, what starts as research to determine the validity of an individual instrument for a particular objective may end with research as to which *combination* of instruments will best achieve that objective.

### Is This Instrument Cost-Effective?

During World Wars I and II, the military needed to quickly screen hundreds of thousands of recruits for intelligence. It may have been desirable to individually administer a Binet intelligence test to each recruit, but it would have taken a great deal of time—too much time, given the demands of war—and it would not have been very cost-effective. Instead, the armed services developed group measures of intelligence that could be administered quickly and that addressed its needs more efficiently than an individually administered test. In this instance, it could be said that group tests had greater *utility* than individual tests. The concept of *test utility* is discussed in greater depth in Chapter 7.

### What Inferences May Reasonably Be Made from This Test Score, and How Generalizable Are the Findings?

In evaluating a test, it is critical to consider the inferences that may reasonably be made as a result of administering that test. Will we learn something about a child's readiness to begin first grade? about whether one is harmful to oneself or others? about whether an employee has executive potential? These represent but a small sampling of critical questions for which answers must be inferred on the basis of test scores and other data derived from various tools of assessment.

Intimately related to considerations regarding the inferences that can be made are those regarding the generalizability of the findings. As you learn more and more about test norms, for example, you will discover that the population of people used to help develop a test has a great effect on the generalizability of findings from an administration of the test. Many other factors may affect the generalizability of test findings. For example, if the items on a test are worded in such a way as to be less comprehensible by members of a specific group, then the use of that test with members of that group could be questionable. Another issue regarding the generalizability of findings concerns how a test was administered. Most published tests include explicit directions for testing conditions and test administration procedures that must be followed to the letter. If a test administration deviates in any way from these directions, the generalizability of the findings may be compromised. Culture is a variable that must be taken account of in the development of new tests as well as the administration, scoring, and interpretation of any test. The role of culture, too often overlooked in testing and assessment, will be emphasized and elaborated on at various points throughout this book.

Although you may not yet be an expert in measurement, you are now aware of the types of questions experts ask when evaluating tests. It is hoped that you can now appreciate that simple questions such as "What's a good test?" don't necessarily have simple answers.

If the purpose of a test is to compare the performance of the testtaker with the performance of other testtakers, a good test is one that contains adequate *norms*. Also referred to as *normative data*, norms provide a standard with which the results of measurement can be compared. Let's explore the important subject of norms in a bit more detail.

## Norms

We may define **norm-referenced testing and assessment** as a method of evaluation and a way of deriving meaning from test scores by evaluating an individual testtaker's score and comparing it to scores of a group of testtakers. In this approach, the meaning of an individual test score is understood relative to other scores on the same test. A common goal of norm-referenced tests is to yield information on a testtaker's standing or ranking relative to some comparison group of testtakers.

*Norm* in the singular is used in the scholarly literature to refer to behavior that is usual, average, normal, standard, expected, or typical. Reference to a particular variety of norm may be specified by means of modifiers such as *age*, as in the term *age norm. Norms* is the plural form of norm, as in the term *gender norms*. In a psychometric context, **norms** are the test performance data of a particular group of testtakers that are designed for use as a reference when evaluating or interpreting individual test scores. As used in this definition, the "particular group of testtakers" may be defined broadly (for example, "a sample representative of the adult population of the United States") or narrowly (for example, "female inpatients at the Bronx Community Hospital with a primary diagnosis of depression"). A **normative sample** is that group of people whose performance on a particular test is analyzed for reference in evaluating the performance of individual testtakers.

Whether broad or narrow in scope, members of the normative sample will all be typical with respect to some characteristic(s) of the people for whom the particular test was designed. A test administration to this representative sample of testtakers yields a distribution (or distributions) of scores. These data constitute the *norms* for the test and typically are used as a reference source for evaluating and placing into context test scores obtained by individual testtakers. The data may be in the form of raw scores or converted scores.

The verb *to norm*, as well as related terms such as **norming**, refer to the process of deriving norms. *Norming* may be modified to describe a particular type of norm derivation. For example, **race norming** is the controversial practice of norming on the basis of race or ethnic background. Race norming was once engaged in by some government agencies and private organizations, and the practice resulted in the establishment of different cutoff scores for hiring by cultural group. Members of one cultural group would have to attain one score to be hired, whereas members of another cultural group would have to attain a different score. Although initially instituted in the service of affirmative action objectives (Greenlaw & Jensen, 1996), the practice was outlawed by the Civil Rights Act of 1991. The Act left unclear a number of issues, however, including "whether, or under what circumstances, in the development of an assessment procedure, it is lawful to adjust item content to minimize group differences" (Kehoe & Tenopyr, 1994, p. 291).

Norming a test, especially with the participation of a nationally representative normative sample, can be a very expensive proposition. For this reason, some test manuals provide what are variously known as **user norms** or **program norms,** which "consist of descriptive statistics based on a group of testtakers in a given period of time rather than norms obtained by formal sampling methods" (Nelson, 1994, p. 283). Understanding how norms are derived through "formal sampling methods" requires some discussion of the process of sampling.

## Sampling to Develop Norms

The process of administering a test to a representative sample of testtakers for the purpose of establishing norms is referred to as **standardization** or **test standardization.** As will be clear from this chapter's *Close-Up,* a test is said to be *standardized* when it has clearly specified procedures for administration and scoring, typically including normative data. To understand how norms are derived, an understanding of sampling is necessary.

**Sampling**    In the process of developing a test, a test developer has targeted some defined group as the population for which the test is designed. This population is the complete universe or set of individuals with at least one common, observable characteristic. The common observable characteristic(s) could be just about anything. For example, it might be *high-school seniors who aspire to go to college,* or *the 16 boys and girls in Mrs. Perez's day-care center,* or *all housewives with primary responsibility for household shopping who have purchased over-the-counter headache remedies within the last two months.*

To obtain a distribution of scores, the test developer could have the test administered to every person in the targeted population. If the total targeted population consists of something like the 16 boys and girls in Mrs. Perez's day-care center, it may well be feasible to administer the test to each member of the targeted population. However, for tests developed to be used with large or wide-ranging populations, it is usually impossible, impractical, or simply too expensive to administer the test to everyone, nor is it necessary.

The test developer can obtain a distribution of test responses by administering the test to a **sample** of the population—a portion of the universe of people deemed to be representative of the whole population. The size of the sample could be as small as one person, though samples that approach the size of the population reduce the possible sources of error due to insufficient sample size. The process of selecting the portion of the universe deemed to be representative of the whole population is referred to as **sampling.**

Subgroups within a defined population may differ with respect to some characteristics, and it is sometimes essential to have these differences proportionately represented in the sample. Thus, for example, if you devised a public opinion test and wanted to sample the opinions of Manhattan residents with this instrument, it would be desirable to include in your sample people representing different subgroups (or strata) of the population, such as Blacks, Whites, Asians, other non-Whites, males, females, the poor, the middle class, the rich, professional people, business people, office workers, skilled and unskilled laborers, the unemployed, homemakers, Catholics, Jews, members of other religions, and so forth—all in proportion to the current occurrence of these strata in the population of people who reside on the island of Manhattan. Such sampling, termed **stratified sampling,** would help prevent sampling bias and ultimately aid in the interpretation of the findings. If such sampling were *random* (that is, if every member of the population had the same chance of being included in the sample), then the procedure would be termed **stratified-random sampling.**

> **JUST THINK . . .**
>
> Truly random sampling is relatively rare. Why do you think this is so?

# How "Standard" Is *Standard* in Measurement?

The foot, a unit of distance measurement in the United States, probably had its origins in the length of a British king's foot used as a standard—one that measured about 12 inches, give or take. It wasn't so very long ago that different localities throughout the world all had different "feet" to measure by. We have come a long way since then, especially with regard to standards and standardization in measurement . . . haven't we?

Perhaps. However, in the field of psychological testing and assessment, there's still more than a little confusion when it comes to the meaning of terms like *standard* and *standardization*. Questions also exist concerning what is and is not *standardized*. To address these and related questions, a close-up look at the word *standard* and its derivatives seems very much in order.

The word *standard* can be a noun or an adjective, and in either case it may have multiple (and quite different) definitions. As a noun, *standard* may be defined as *that which others are compared to or evaluated against*. One may speak, for example, of a test with exceptional psychometric properties as being "the standard against which all similar tests are judged." An exceptional textbook on the subject of psychological testing and assessment—take the one you are reading, for example—may be judged "the standard against which all similar textbooks are judged." Perhaps the most common use of *standard* as a noun in the context of testing and assessment is in the title of that well-known manual that sets forth ideals of professional behavior against which any practitioner's behavior can be judged: *The Standards for Educational and Psychological Testing*, usually referred to simply as *the Standards*.

As an adjective, *standard* often refers to *what is usual, generally accepted, or commonly employed*. One may speak, for example, of the *standard* way of conducting a particular measurement procedure, especially as a means of contrasting it to some newer or experimental measurement procedure. For example, a researcher experimenting with a new, multimedia approach to conducting a mental status examination might conduct a study to compare the value of this approach to the *standard* mental status examination interview.

In some areas of psychology, there has been a need to create a new *standard unit of measurement* in the interest of better understanding or quantifying particular phenomena. For example, in studying alcoholism and associated

**Figure 1**
**Ben's Cold Cut Preference Test (CCPT)**

*Ben owns a small "deli boutique" that sells 10 varieties of private-label cold cuts. Ben had read somewhere that if a test has clearly specified methods for test administration and scoring, then it must be considered "standardized." He then went on to create his own "standardized test"— the Cold Cut Preference Test (CCPT). The CCPT consists of only two questions: "What would you like today?" and a follow-up question, "How much of that would you like?" Ben scrupulously trains his only employee (his wife—it's literally a "mom and pop" business) on "test administration" and "test scoring" of the CCPT. So, just think: Does the CCPT really qualify as a "standardized test"?*

problems, many researchers have adopted the concept of a *standard drink*. The notion of a "standard drink" is designed to facilitate communication and to enhance understanding regarding alcohol consumption patterns (Aros et al., 2006;

Gill et al., 2007), intervention strategies (Hwang, 2006; Podymow et al., 2006), and costs associated with alcohol consumption (Farrell, 1998). Regardless of whether it is beer, wine, liquor, or any other alcoholic beverage, reference to a "standard drink" immediately conveys information to the knowledgeable researcher about the amount of alcohol in the beverage.

The verb "to standardize" refers to *making or transforming something into something that can serve as a basis of comparison or judgment.* One may speak, for example, of the efforts of researchers to *standardize* an alcoholic beverage that contains 15 milliliters of alcohol as a "standard drink." For many of the variables commonly used in assessment studies, there is an attempt to *standardize* a definition. As an example, Anderson (2007) sought to standardize exactly what is meant by "creative thinking." Well known to any student who has ever taken a nationally administered achievement test or college admission examination is the standardizing of tests. But what does it mean to say that a test is "standardized"? Some "food for thought" regarding an answer to this deceptively simple question can be found in Figure 1.

Test developers *standardize* tests by developing replicable procedures for administering the test and for scoring and interpreting the test. Also part of *standardizing* a test is developing norms for the test. Well, not necessarily . . . whether or not norms for the test must be developed in order for the test to be deemed "standardized" is debatable. It is true that almost any "test" that has clearly specified procedures for administration, scoring, and interpretation can be considered "standardized." So even Ben the deli guy's CCPT (described in Figure 1) might be deemed a "standardized test" according to some. This is so because the test is "standardized" to the extent that the "test items" are clearly specified (presumably along with "rules" for "administering" them and rules for "scoring and interpretation"). Still, many assessment professionals would hesitate to refer to Ben's CCPT as a "standardized test." Why?

Traditionally, assessment professionals have reserved the term **standardized test** for those tests that have clearly specified procedures for administration, scoring, and interpretation in addition to norms. Such tests also come with manuals that are as much a part of the test package as the test's items. Ideally, the test manual, which may be published in one or more booklets, will provide potential test users with all of the information they need to use the test in a responsible fashion. The test manual enables the test user to administer the test in the "standardized" manner in which it was designed to be administered; all test users should be able to replicate the test administration as prescribed by the test developer. Ideally, there will be little deviation from examiner to examiner in the way that a standardized test is administered, owing to the rigorous preparation and training that all potential users of the test have undergone prior to administering the test to testtakers.

If a standardized test is designed for scoring by the test user (in contrast to computer scoring), the test manual will ideally contain detailed scoring guidelines. If the test is one of ability that has correct and incorrect answers, the manual will ideally contain an ample number of examples of correct, incorrect, or partially correct responses, complete with scoring guidelines. In like fashion, if it is a test that measures personality, interest, or any other variable that is *not* scored as correct or incorrect, then ample examples of potential responses will be provided along with complete scoring guidelines. We would also expect the test manual to contain detailed guidelines for interpreting the test results, including samples of both appropriate and inappropriate generalizations from the findings.

Also from a traditional perspective, we think of standardized tests as having undergone a *standardization* process. Conceivably, the term *standardization* could be applied to "standardizing" all the elements of a standardized test that need to be standardized. Thus, for a standardized test of leadership, we might speak of standardizing the definition of leadership, standardizing test administration instructions, standardizing test scoring, standardizing test interpretation, and so forth. Indeed, one definition of standardization as applied to tests is "the process employed to introduce objectivity and uniformity into test administration, scoring and interpretation" (Robertson, 1990, p. 75). Another and perhaps more typical use of *standardization,* however, is reserved for that part of the test development process during which norms are developed. It is for this very reason that the terms *test standardization* and *test norming* have been used interchangeably by many test professionals.

Assessment professionals develop and use standardized tests to benefit testtakers, test users, and/or society at large. Although there is conceivably some benefit to Ben in gathering data on the frequency of orders for a pound or two of bratwurst, this type of data gathering does not require a "standardized test." So, getting back to Ben's CCPT . . . although some writers would staunchly defend the CCPT as a "standardized test" (simply because any two questions with clearly specified guidelines for administration and scoring would make the "cut"), practically speaking this is simply not the case from the perspective of most assessment professionals.

There are a number of other ambiguities in psychological testing and assessment when it comes to the use of the

*(continued)*

## How "Standard" Is *Standard* in Measurement? *(continued)*

word *standard* and its derivatives. Consider, for example, the term *standard score*. Some test manuals and books reserve the term *standard score* for use with reference to *z* scores. Raw scores (as well as *z* scores) linearly transformed to any other type of standard scoring systems—that is, transformed to a scale with an arbitrarily set mean and standard deviation—are differentiated from *z* scores by the term *standardized.* For these authors, a *z* score would still be referred to as a "standard score" whereas a *T* score, for example, would be referred to as a "standardized score."

For the purpose of tackling another "nonstandard" use of the word *standard,* let's digress for just a moment to images of the great American pastime of baseball. Imagine, for a moment, all of the different ways that players can be charged with an error. There really isn't one type of error that could be characterized as *standard* in the game of baseball. Now, back to psychological testing and assessment—where there also isn't just one variety of error that could be characterized as "standard." No, there isn't one . . . there are lots of them! One speaks, for example, of the *standard error of measurement* (also known as the *standard error of a score*) the *standard error of estimate* (also known as the *standard error of prediction*), the *standard error of the mean,* and the *standard error of the difference.* A table briefly summarizing the main differences between these terms is presented here, although they are discussed in greater detail elsewhere in this book.

| Type of "Standard Error" | What Is It? |
| --- | --- |
| Standard error of measurement | A statistic used to estimate the extent to which an observed score deviates from a true score |
| Standard error of estimate | In regression, an estimate of the degree of error involved in predicting the value of one variable from another |
| Standard error of the mean | A measure of sampling error |
| Standard error of the difference | A statistic used to estimate how large a difference between two scores should be before the difference is considered statistically significant |

We conclude by encouraging the exercise of critical thinking upon encountering the word *standard*. The next time you encounter the word *standard* in any context, give some thought to how standard that "standard" really is. Certainly with regard to this word's use in the context of psychological testing and assessment, what is presented as "standard" usually turns out to be not as standard as we might expect.

Two other types of sampling procedures are *purposive sampling* and *incidental sampling.* If we arbitrarily select some sample because we believe it to be representative of the population, then we have selected what is referred to as a **purposive sample.** Manufacturers of products frequently use purposive sampling when they test the appeal of a new product in one city or market and then make assumptions about how that product would sell nationally. For example, the manufacturer might test a product in a market such as Cleveland because, on the basis of experience with this particular product, "how goes Cleveland, so goes the nation." The danger in using such a purposive sample is that the sample, in this case Cleveland residents, may no longer be representative of the nation. Alternatively, this sample may simply not be representative of national preferences with regard to the particular product being test-marketed.

Often a test user's decisions regarding sampling wind up pitting what is ideal against what is practical. It may be ideal, for example, to use 50 chief executive officers from any of the *Fortune 500* companies (that is, the top 500 companies in terms of income) as a sample in an experiment. However, conditions may dictate that it is practical for the experimenter only to use 50 volunteers recruited from the local Chamber of Commerce. This important distinction between what is *ideal* and what is *practical* in sampling brings us to a discussion of what has been referred to variously as an *incidental sample* or a *convenience sample.*

Ever hear the old joke about a drunk searching for money he lost under the lamppost? He may not have lost his money there, but that is where the light is. Like the drunk searching for money under the lamppost, a researcher may sometimes employ a sample that is not necessarily the most appropriate but is simply the most convenient. Unlike the drunk, the researcher employing this type of sample is doing so not as a result of poor judgment but because of budgetary limitations or other constraints. An **incidental sample** or **convenience sample** is one that is convenient or available for use. You may have been a party to incidental sampling if you have ever been placed in a subject pool for experimentation with introductory psychology students. It's not that the students in such subject pools are necessarily the most appropriate subjects for the experiments, it's just that they are the most available. Generalization of findings from incidental samples must be made with caution.

If incidental or convenience samples were clubs, they would not be considered very exclusive clubs. By contrast, there are many samples that are exclusive, in a sense, because they contain many exclusionary criteria. Consider, for example, the group of children and adolescents who served as the normative sample for one well-known children's intelligence test. The sample was selected to reflect key demographic variables representative of the U.S. population according to the latest available census data. Still, some groups were deliberately excluded from participation. Who?

- Persons tested on any intelligence measure in the six months prior to the testing
- Persons not fluent in English or who are primarily nonverbal
- Persons with uncorrected visual impairment or hearing loss
- Persons with upper-extremity disability that affects motor performance
- Persons currently admitted to a hospital or mental or psychiatric facility
- Persons currently taking medication that might depress test performance
- Persons previously diagnosed with any physical condition or illness that might depress test performance (such as stroke, epilepsy, or meningitis)

Our general description of the norming process for a standardized test continues in what follows and, to varying degrees, in subsequent chapters. A highly recommended way to supplement this study and gain a great deal of firsthand knowledge about norms for intelligence tests, personality tests, and other tests is to peruse the technical manuals of major standardized instruments. By going to the library and consulting a few of these manuals, you will discover not only the "real life" way that normative samples are described but also the many varied ways that normative data can be presented.

> **JUST THINK . . .**
>
> Why do you think each of these groups of people were excluded from the standardization sample of a nationally standardized intelligence test?

**Developing norms for a standardized test**  Having obtained a sample, the test developer administers the test according to the standard set of instructions that will be used with the test. The test developer also describes the recommended setting for giving the test. This may be as simple as making sure that the room is quiet and well lit or as complex as providing a specific set of toys to test an infant's cognitive skills. Establishing a standard set of instructions and conditions under which the test is given makes the test scores of the normative sample more comparable with the scores of future testtakers. For example, if a test of concentration ability is given to a normative sample in the summer with the windows open near people mowing the grass and arguing about whether the hedges need trimming, then the normative sample probably won't concentrate well. If a testtaker then completes the concentration test under quiet, comfortable conditions, that person may well do much better than the normative group, resulting in a high standard score. That high score would not be very helpful in understanding the testtaker's concentration abilities because it would reflect the differing conditions under which the tests were taken. This example illustrates how important it is that the normative sample take the test under a standard set of conditions, which are then replicated (to the extent possible) on each occasion the test is administered.

After all the test data have been collected and analyzed, the test developer will summarize the data using descriptive statistics, including measures of central tendency and variability. In addition, it is incumbent on the test developer to provide a precise description of the standardization sample itself. Good practice dictates that the norms be developed with data derived from a group of people who are presumed to be representative of the people who will take the test in the future. After all, if the normative group is very different from future testtakers, the basis for comparison becomes questionable at best. In order to best assist future users of the test, test developers are encouraged to "provide information to support recommended interpretations of the results, including the nature of the content, norms or comparison groups, and other technical evidence" (*Code of Fair Testing Practices in Education*, 2004, p. 4).

In practice, descriptions of normative samples vary widely in detail. Test authors wish to present their tests in the most favorable light possible. Shortcomings in the standardization procedure or elsewhere in the process of the test's development therefore may be given short shrift or totally overlooked in a test's manual. Sometimes, although the sample is scrupulously defined, the generalizability of the norms to a particular group or individual is questionable. For example, a test carefully normed on school-age children who reside within the Los Angeles school district may be relevant only to a lesser degree to school-age children who reside within the Dubuque, Iowa, school district. How many children in the standardization sample were English speaking? How many were of Hispanic origin? How does the elementary school curriculum in Los Angeles differ from the curriculum in Dubuque? These are the types of questions that must be raised before the Los Angeles norms are judged to be generalizable to the children of Dubuque. Test manuals sometimes supply prospective test users with guidelines for establishing *local norms* (discussed shortly), one of many different ways norms can be categorized.

One note on terminology is in order before moving on. When the people in the normative sample are the same people on whom the test was standardized, the phrases *normative sample* and *standardization sample* are often used interchangeably. Increasingly, however, new norms for standardized tests for specific groups of testtakers are developed some time after the original standardization. That is, the test remains standardized based on data from the original standardization sample; it's just that new normative data are developed based on an administration of the test to a new normative sample. Included in this new normative sample may be groups of people who were underrepresented in the original standardization sample data. For example, with the changing demographics of a state such as California, and the increasing numbers of people identified as "Hispanic" in that state, an updated normative sample for a California-statewide test might well include a higher proportion of individuals of Hispanic origin. In such a scenario, the normative sample for the new norms clearly would not be identical to the standardization sample, so it would be inaccurate to use the terms *standardization sample* and *normative sample* interchangeably.

## Types of Norms

Some of the many different ways we can classify norms are as follows: *age norms, grade norms, national norms, national anchor norms, local norms, norms from a fixed reference group, subgroup norms,* and *percentile norms. Percentile norms* are the raw data from a test's standardization sample converted to percentile form. To better understand them, let's backtrack for a moment and review what is meant by *percentiles*.

**Percentiles** In our discussion of the median, we saw that a distribution could be divided into quartiles where the median was the second quartile $(Q_2)$, the point at or below which 50% of the scores fell and above which the remaining 50% fell. Instead of dividing a distribution of scores into quartiles, we might wish to divide the distribution into *deciles,* or 10 equal parts. Alternatively, we could divide a distribution into 100 equal parts—100 *percentiles.* In such a distribution, the $x$th percentile is equal to the score at or below which $x$% of scores fall. Thus, the 15th percentile is the score at or below which 15% of the scores in the distribution fall. The 99th percentile is the score at or below which 99% of the scores in the distribution fall. If 99% of a particular standardization sample answered fewer than 47 questions on a test correctly, then we could say that a raw score of 47 corresponds to the 99th percentile on this test. It can be seen that a percentile is a ranking that conveys information about the relative position of a score within a distribution of scores. More formally defined, a **percentile** is an expression of the percentage of people whose score on a test or measure falls below a particular raw score.

Intimately related to the concept of a percentile as a description of performance on a test is the concept of *percentage correct.* Note that *percentile* and *percentage correct* are *not* synonymous. A percentile is a converted score that refers to a percentage of testtakers. **Percentage correct** refers to the distribution of raw scores—more specifically, to the number of items that were answered correctly multiplied by 100 and divided by the total number of items.

Because percentiles are easily calculated, they are a popular way of organizing all test-related data, including standardization sample data. Additionally, they lend themselves to use with a wide range of tests. Of course, every rose has its thorns. A problem with using percentiles with normally distributed scores is that real differences between raw scores may be minimized near the ends of the distribution and exaggerated in the middle of the distribution. This distortion may even be worse with highly skewed data. In the normal distribution, the highest frequency of raw scores occurs in the middle. That being the case, the differences between all those scores that cluster in the middle might be quite small, yet even the smallest differences will appear as differences in percentiles. The reverse is true at the extremes of the distributions, where differences between raw scores may be great, though we would have no way of knowing that from the relatively small differences in percentiles.

**Age norms** Also known as **age-equivalent scores, age norms** indicate the average performance of different samples of testtakers who were at various ages at the time the test was administered. If the measurement under consideration is height in inches, for example, then we know that scores (heights) for children will gradually increase at various rates as a function of age up to the middle to late teens. With the graying of America, there has been increased interest in performance on various types of psychological tests, particularly neuropsychological tests, as a function of advancing age.

Carefully constructed age norm tables for physical characteristics such as height enjoy widespread acceptance and are virtually noncontroversial. This is not the case, however, with respect to age norm tables for psychological characteristics such as intelligence. Ever since the introduction of the Stanford-Binet to this country in the early twentieth century, the idea of identifying the "mental age" of a testtaker has had great intuitive appeal. The child of any chronological age whose performance on a valid test of intellectual ability indicated that he or she had intellectual ability similar to that of the average child of some other age was said to have the mental age of the norm group in which his or her test score fell. The reasoning here was that, irrespective of chronological age, children with the same mental age could be expected to read the same level of material, solve the same kinds of math problems, reason with a similar level of judgment, and so forth.

Increasing sophistication about the limitations of the mental age concept has prompted assessment professionals to be hesitant about describing results in terms of mental age. The problem is that "mental age" as a way to report test results is too broad and too inappropriately generalized. To understand why, consider the case of a 6-year-old who, according to the tasks sampled on an intelligence test, performs intellectually like a 12-year-old. Regardless, the 6-year-old is likely not to be very similar at all to the average 12-year-old socially, psychologically, and in many other key respects. Beyond such obvious faults in mental age analogies, the mental age concept has also been criticized on technical grounds.[3]

**Grade norms** Designed to indicate the average test performance of testtakers in a given school grade, **grade norms** are developed by administering the test to representative samples of children over a range of consecutive grade levels (such as first through sixth grades). Next, the mean or median score for children at each grade level is calculated. Because the school year typically runs from September to June—10 months—fractions in the mean or median are easily expressed as decimals. Thus, for example, a sixth-grader performing exactly at the average on a grade-normed test administered during the fourth month of the school year (December) would achieve a grade-equivalent score of 6.4. Like age norms, grade norms have great intuitive appeal. Children learn and develop at varying rates but in ways that are in some aspects predictable. Perhaps because of this fact, grade norms have widespread application, especially to children of elementary school age.

---

3. For many years, IQ (intelligence quotient) scores on tests such as the Stanford-Binet were calculated by dividing mental age (as indicated by the test) by chronological age. The quotient would then be multiplied by 100 to eliminate the fraction. The distribution of IQ scores had a mean set at 100 and a standard deviation of approximately 16. A child of 12 with a mental age of 12 had an IQ of 100 ($12/12 \times 100 = 100$). The technical problem here is that IQ standard deviations were not constant with age. At one age, an IQ of 116 might be indicative of performance at 1 standard deviation above the mean, whereas at another age an IQ of 121 might be indicative of performance at 1 standard deviation above the mean.

Now consider the case of a student in 12th grade who scores "6" on a grade-normed spelling test. Does this mean that the student has the same spelling abilities as the average sixth-grader? The answer is no. What this finding means is that the student and a hypothetical, average sixth-grader answered the same fraction of items correctly on that test. Grade norms do not provide information as to the content or type of items that a student could or could not answer correctly. Perhaps the primary use of grade norms is as a convenient, readily understandable gauge of how one student's performance compares with that of fellow students in the same grade.

One drawback of grade norms is that they are useful only with respect to years and months of schooling completed. They have little or no applicability to children who are not yet in school or to children who are out of school. Further, they are not typically designed for use with adults who have returned to school. Both grade norms and age norms are referred to more generally as **developmental norms,** a term applied broadly to norms developed on the basis of any trait, ability, skill, or other characteristic that is presumed to develop, deteriorate, or otherwise be affected by chronological age, school grade, or stage of life.

**JUST THINK . . .**

Some experts in testing have called for a moratorium on the use of grade-equivalent as well as age-equivalent scores because such scores may so easily be misinterpreted. What is your opinion on this issue?

**National norms**   As the name implies, **national norms** are derived from a normative sample that was nationally representative of the population at the time the norming study was conducted. In the fields of psychology and education, for example, national norms may be obtained by testing large numbers of people representative of different variables of interest such as age, gender, racial/ethnic background, socioeconomic strata, geographical location (such as North, East, South, West, Midwest), and different types of communities within the various parts of the country (such as rural, urban, suburban).

If the test were designed for use in the schools, norms might be obtained for students in every grade to which the test aimed to be applicable. Factors related to the representativeness of the school from which members of the norming sample were drawn might also be criteria for inclusion in or exclusion from the sample. For example, is the school the student attends publicly funded, privately funded, religiously oriented, military, or something else? How representative are the pupil/teacher ratios in the school under consideration? Does the school have a library, and if so, how many books are in it? These are only a sample of the types of questions that could be raised in assembling a normative sample to be used in the establishment of national norms. The precise nature of the questions raised when developing national norms will depend on whom the test is designed for and what the test is designed to do.

Norms from many different tests may all claim to have nationally representative samples. Still, close scrutiny of the description of the sample employed may reveal that the sample differs in many important respects from similar tests also claiming to be based on a nationally representative sample. For this reason, it is always a good idea to check the manual of the tests under consideration to see exactly how comparable the tests are. Two important questions that test users must raise as consumers of test-related information are "What are the differences between the tests I am considering for use in terms of their normative samples?" and "How comparable are these normative samples to the sample of testtakers with whom I will be using the test?"

**National anchor norms** Even the most casual survey of catalogues from various test publishers will reveal that, with respect to almost any human characteristic or ability, there exist many different tests purporting to measure the characteristic or ability. Dozens of tests, for example, purport to measure reading. Suppose we select a reading test designed for use in grades 3 to 6, which, for the purposes of this hypothetical example, we call the Best Reading Test (BRT). Suppose further that we want to compare findings obtained on another national reading test designed for use with grades 3 to 6, the hypothetical XYZ Reading Test, with the BRT. An equivalency table for scores on the two tests, or **national anchor norms,** could provide the tool for such a comparison. Just as an anchor provides some stability to a vessel, so national anchor norms provide some stability to test scores by anchoring them to other test scores.

The method by which such equivalency tables or national anchor norms are established typically begins with the computation of percentile norms for each of the tests to be compared. Using the **equipercentile method,** the equivalency of scores on different tests is calculated with reference to corresponding percentile scores. Thus, if the 96th percentile corresponds to a score of 69 on the BRT and if the 96th percentile corresponds to a score of 14 on the XYZ, then we can say that a BRT score of 69 is equivalent to an XYZ score of 14. We should note that the national anchor norms for our hypothetical BRT and XYZ tests must have been obtained on the same sample—each member of the sample took both tests, and the equivalency tables were then calculated on the basis of these data.[4] Although national anchor norms provide an indication of the equivalency of scores on various tests, technical considerations entail that it would be a mistake to treat these equivalencies as precise equalities (Angoff, 1964, 1966, 1971).

**Subgroup norms** A normative sample can be segmented by any of the criteria initially used in selecting subjects for the sample. What results from such segmentation are more narrowly defined **subgroup norms.** Thus, for example, suppose criteria used in selecting children for inclusion in the XYZ Reading Test normative sample were age, educational level, socioeconomic level, geographic region, community type, and handedness (whether the child was right-handed or left-handed). The test manual or a supplement to it might report normative information by each of these subgroups. A community school board member might find the regional norms to be most useful, whereas a psychologist doing exploratory research in the area of brain lateralization and reading scores might find the handedness norms most useful.

**Local norms** Typically developed by test users themselves, **local norms** provide normative information with respect to the local population's performance on some test. A local company personnel director might find some nationally standardized test useful in making selection decisions but might deem the norms published in the test manual to be far afield of local job applicants' score distributions. Individual high schools may wish to develop their own school norms (local norms) for student scores on an examination that is administered statewide. A school guidance center may find that locally derived norms for a particular test—say, a survey of personal values—are more useful in counseling students than the national norms printed in the manual. Some test users use abbreviated forms of existing tests, which requires new norms. Some test users substitute one subtest for another within a larger test, thus creating the need for new norms. There are many different scenarios that would lead the prudent test user to develop local norms.

---

4. When two tests are normed from the same sample, the norming process is referred to as *co-norming.*

## Fixed Reference Group Scoring Systems

Norms provide a context for interpreting the meaning of a test score. Another type of of aid in providing a context for interpretation is termed a **fixed reference group scoring system.** Here, the distribution of scores obtained on the test from one group of testtakers—referred to as the *fixed reference group*—is used as the basis for the calculation of test scores for future administrations of the test. Perhaps the test most familiar to college students that exemplifies the use of a fixed reference group scoring system is the SAT. This test was first administered in 1926. Its norms were then based on the mean and standard deviation of the people who took the test at the time. With passing years, more colleges became members of the College Board, the sponsoring organization for the test. It soon became evident that SAT scores tended to vary somewhat as a function of the time of year the test was administered. In an effort to ensure perpetual comparability and continuity of scores, a fixed reference group scoring system was put into place in 1941. The distribution of scores from the 11,000 people who took the SAT in 1941 was immortalized as a standard to be used in the conversion of raw scores on future administrations of the test.[5] A new fixed reference group, which consisted of the more than 2 million testtakers who completed the SAT in 1990, began to be used in 1995. A score of 500 on the SAT corresponds to the mean obtained by the 1990 sample, a score of 400 corresponds to a score that is 1 standard deviation below the 1990 mean, and so forth. As an example, suppose John took the SAT in 1995 and answered 50 items correctly on a particular scale. And let's say Mary took the test in 2008 and, just like John, answered 50 items correctly. Although John and Mary may have achieved the same raw score, they would not necessarily achieve the same scaled score. If, for example, the 2008 version of the test was judged to be somewhat easier than the 1995 version, then scaled scores for the 2008 testtakers would be calibrated downward. This would be done so as to make scores earned in 2008 comparable to scores earned in 1995.

Test items common to each new version of the SAT and each previous version of it are employed in a procedure (termed *anchoring*) that permits the conversion of raw scores on the new version of the test into *fixed reference group scores*. Like other fixed reference group scores, including Graduate Record Examination scores, SAT scores are most typically interpreted by local decision-making bodies with respect to local norms. Thus, for example, college admissions officers usually rely on their own independently collected norms to make selection decisions. They will typically compare applicants' SAT scores to the SAT scores of students in their school who completed or failed to complete their program. Of course, admissions decisions are seldom made on the basis of the SAT (or any other single test) alone. Various criteria are typically evaluated in admissions decisions.

## Norm-Referenced Versus Criterion-Referenced Evaluation

One way to derive meaning from a test score is to evaluate the test score in relation to other scores on the same test. As we have pointed out, this approach to evaluation is referred to as *norm-referenced.* Another way to derive meaning from a test score is to evaluate it on the basis of whether or not some criterion has been met. We may define a **criterion** as a standard on which a judgment or decision may be based.

---

5. Conceptually, the idea of a *fixed reference group* is analogous to the idea of a *fixed reference foot*, the foot of the English king that also became immortalized as a measurement standard (Angoff, 1962).

**Criterion-referenced testing and assessment** may be defined as a method of evaluation and a way of deriving meaning from test scores by evaluating an individual's score with reference to a set standard. Some examples:

- To be eligible for a high-school diploma, students must demonstrate at least a sixth-grade reading level.

- To earn the privilege of driving an automobile, would-be drivers must take a road test and demonstrate their driving skill to the satisfaction of a state-appointed examiner.

- To be licensed as a psychologist, the applicant must achieve a score that meets or exceeds the score mandated by the state on the licensing test.

- To conduct research using human subjects, many universities and other organizations require researchers to successfully complete an online course that presents testtakers with ethics-oriented information in a series of modules, followed by a set of forced-choice questions.

The criterion in criterion-referenced assessments typically derives from the values or standards of an individual or organization. For example, in order to earn a black belt in karate, students must demonstrate a black-belt level of proficiency in karate and meet related criteria such as those related to self-discipline and focus. Each student is evaluated individually to see if all of these criteria are met. Regardless of the level of performance of all the testtakers, only students who meet all the criteria will leave the *dojo* (training room) with a brand-new black belt.

**JUST THINK . . .**

List other examples of a criterion that must be met in order to gain privileges or access of some sort.

Criterion-referenced testing and assessment goes by other names. Because the focus in the criterion-referenced approach is on how scores relate to a particular content area or domain, the approach has also been referred to as **domain-** or **content-referenced testing and assessment.**[6] One way of conceptualizing the difference between norm-referenced and criterion-referenced approaches to assessment has to do with the area of focus regarding test results. In norm-referenced interpretations of test data, a usual area of focus is how an individual performed relative to other people who took the test. In criterion-referenced interpretations of test data, a usual area of focus is the testtaker's performance: what the testtaker can or cannot do; what the testtaker has or has not learned; whether the testtaker does or does not meet specified criteria for inclusion in some group, access to certain privileges, and so forth. Because criterion-referenced tests are frequently used to gauge achievement or mastery, they are sometimes referred to as *mastery tests*. The criterion-referenced approach has enjoyed widespread acceptance in the field of computer-assisted education programs. In such programs, mastery of segments of materials is assessed before the program user can proceed to the next level.

---

6. Although acknowledging that content-referenced interpretations can be referred to as criterion-referenced interpretations, the 1974 edition of the *Standards for Educational and Psychological Testing* also noted a technical distinction between interpretations so designated: "*Content-referenced* interpretations are those where the score is directly interpreted in terms of performance at each point on the achievement continuum being measured. *Criterion-referenced* interpretations are those where the score is directly interpreted in terms of performance at any given point on the continuum of an *external* variable. An external criterion variable might be grade averages or levels of job performance" (p. 19; footnote in original omitted).

"Has this flight trainee mastered the material she needs to be an airline pilot?" This is the type of question that an airline personnel office might seek to address with a mastery test on a flight simulator. If a standard, or criterion, for passing a hypothetical "Airline Pilot Test" (APT) has been set at 85% correct, then trainees who score 84% correct or less will not pass. It matters not whether they scored 84% or 42%. Conversely, trainees who score 85% or better on the test will pass whether they scored 85% or 100%. All who score 85% or better are said to have mastered the skills and knowledge necessary to be an airline pilot. Taking this example one step further, another airline might find it useful to set up three categories of findings based on criterion-referenced interpretation of test scores:

85% or better correct = pass

75% to 84% correct = retest after a two-month refresher course

74% or less = fail

How should cut scores in mastery testing be determined? How many and what kinds of test items are needed to demonstrate mastery in a given field? The answers to these and related questions have been tackled in diverse ways (Cizek & Bunch, 2007; Ferguson & Novick, 1973; Geisenger & McCormick, 2010; Glaser & Nitko, 1971; Panell & Laabs, 1979).

Critics of the criterion-referenced approach argue that if it is strictly followed, potentially important information about an individual's performance relative to other testtakers is lost. Another criticism is that although this approach may have value with respect to the assessment of mastery of basic knowledge, skills, or both, it has little or no meaningful application at the upper end of the knowledge/skill continuum. Thus, the approach is clearly meaningful in evaluating whether pupils have mastered basic reading, writing, and arithmetic. But how useful is it in evaluating doctoral-level writing or math? Identifying stand-alone originality or brilliant analytic ability is *not* the stuff of which criterion-oriented tests are made. By contrast, brilliance and superior abilities are recognizable in tests that employ norm-referenced interpretations. They are the scores that trail off all the way to the right on the normal curve, past the third standard deviation.

Norm-referenced and criterion-referenced are two of many ways that test data may be viewed and interpreted. However, these terms are *not* mutually exclusive, and the use of one approach with a set of test data does not necessarily preclude the use of the other approach for another application. In a sense, all testing is ultimately normative, even if the scores are as seemingly criterion-referenced as pass–fail. This is so because even in a pass–fail score there is an inherent acknowledgment of a continuum of abilities. At some point in that continuum, a dichotomizing cutoff point has been applied. We should also make the point that some so-called norm-referenced assessments are made with subject samples wherein "the norm is hardly the norm." In a similar vein, when dealing with special or extraordinary populations, the criterion level that is set by a test may also be "far from the norm" in the sense of being average with regard to the general population. To get a sense what we mean by such statements, just think of the norm for everyday skills related to playing basketball, and then imagine how those norms might be with a subject sample limited exclusively to players on NBA teams. Now, meet two sports psychologists who have worked in a professional assessment capacity with the Chicago Bulls in this chapter's *Meet an Assessment Professional.*

> **JUST THINK . . .**
>
> For licensing of physicians, psychologists, engineers, and other professionals, would you advocate that your state use criterion- or norm-referenced assessment? Why?

## Meet Dr. Steve Julius
## and Dr. Howard W. Atlas

The Chicago Bulls of the 1990s is considered one of the great dynasties in sports, as witnessed by their six world championships in that decade. . . .

The team benefited from great individual contributors, but like all successful organizations, the Bulls were always on the lookout for ways to maintain a competitive edge. The Bulls . . . were one of the first NBA franchises to apply personality testing and behavioral interviewing to aid in the selection of college players during the annual draft, as well as in the evaluation of goodness-of-fit when considering the addition of free agents. The purpose of this effort was not to rule out psychopathology, but rather to evaluate a range of competencies (e.g., resilience, relationship to authority, team orientation) that were deemed necessary for success in the league, in general, and the Chicago Bulls, in particular.

[The team utilized] commonly used and well-validated personality assessment tools and techniques from the world of business (e.g., 16PF–fifth edition). . . . Eventually, sufficient data was collected to allow for the validation of a regression formula, useful as a prediction tool in its own right. In addition to selection, the information collected on the athletes often is used to assist the coaching staff in their efforts to motivate and instruct players, as well as to create an atmosphere of collaboration.

*Read more of what Dr. Atlas and Dr. Julius had to say—their complete essay—at www.mhhe .com/cohentesting8.*

Steve Julius, Ph.D., Sports Psychologist, Chicago Bulls

Howard W. Atlas, Ed.D., Sports Psychologist, Chicago Bulls

## Culture and Inference

Along with statistical tools designed to help ensure that prediction and inferences from measurement are reasonable, there are other considerations. It is incumbent upon responsible test users not to lose sight of culture as a factor in test administration, scoring, and interpretation. So, in selecting a test for use, the responsible test user does some advance research on the test's available norms to check on how appropriate they are for use with the targeted testtaker population. In interpreting data from

**Table 4–1**
**Culturally Informed Assessment: Some "Do's" and "Don'ts"**

| Do | Do *Not* |
|---|---|
| Be aware of the cultural assumptions on which a test is based | Take for granted that a test is based on assumptions that impact all groups in much the same way |
| Consider consulting with members of particular cultural communities regarding the appropriateness of particular assessment techniques, tests, or test items | Take for granted that members of all cultural communities will automatically deem particular techniques, tests, or test items appropriate for use |
| Strive to incorporate assessment methods that complement the worldview and lifestyle of assessees who come from a specific cultural and linguistic population | Take a "one-size-fits-all" view of assessment when it comes to evaluation of persons from various cultural and linguistic populations |
| Be knowledgeable about the many alternative tests or measurement procedures that may be used to fulfill the assessment objectives | Select tests or other tools of assessment with little or no regard for the extent to which such tools are appropriate for use with a particular assessee. |
| Be aware of equivalence issues across cultures, including equivalence of language used and the constructs measured | Simply assume that a test that has been translated into another language is automatically equivalent in every way to the original |
| Score, interpret, and analyze assessment data in its cultural context with due consideration of cultural hypotheses as possible explanations for findings | Score, interpret, and analyze assessment in a cultural vacuum |

psychological tests, it is frequently helpful to know about the culture of the testtaker, including something about the era or "times" that the testtaker experienced. In this regard, think of the words of the famous anthropologist Margaret Mead (1978, p. 71), who, in recalling her youth, wrote: "We grew up under skies which no satellite had flashed." In interpreting assessment data from assessees of different generations, it would seem useful to keep in mind whether "satellites had or had not flashed in the sky." In other words, historical context should not be lost sight of in evaluation (Rogler, 2002).

> **JUST THINK . . .**
>
> What event in recent history may have relevance when interpreting data from a psychological assessment?

It seems appropriate to conclude a chapter entitled "Of Tests and Testing" with the introduction of the term *culturally informed assessment* and with some guidelines for accomplishing it (Table 4–1). Think of these guidelines as a list of themes that may be repeated in different ways as you continue to learn about the assessment enterprise. To supplement this list, see the guidelines published by the American Psychological Association (2003). For now, let's continue to build a sound foundation in testing and assessment with a discussion of the psychometric concept of *reliability* in Chapter 5.

## Self-Assessment

Test your understanding of elements of this chapter by seeing if you can explain each of the following terms, expressions, and abbreviations:

age-equivalent scores
age norms
classical test theory (CTT)
construct

content-referenced testing and
    assessment
convenience sample
criterion

criterion-referenced testing and
    assessment
cumulative scoring
developmental norms

domain-referenced testing and
    assessment
domain sampling
equipercentile method
error variance
fixed reference group scoring
    system
grade norms
incidental sample
local norms
national anchor norms
national norms

norm
normative sample
norming
norm-referenced testing and
    assessment
overt behavior
percentage correct
percentile
program norms
purposive sampling
race norming
sample

sampling
standardization
standardized test
state
stratified-random
    sampling
stratified sampling
subgroup norms
test standardization
trait
true score theory
user norms

# 5

# *Reliability*

In everyday conversation, *reliability* is a synonym for *dependability* or *consistency*. We speak of the train that is so reliable you can set your watch by it. If we're lucky, we have a reliable friend who is always there for us in a time of need.

Broadly speaking, in the language of psychometrics *reliability* refers to consistency in measurement. And whereas in everyday conversation reliability always connotes something positive, in the psychometric sense it really only refers to something that is consistent—not necessarily consistently good or bad, but simply consistent.

It is important for us, as users of tests and consumers of information about tests, to know how reliable tests and other measurement procedures are. But reliability is not an all-or-none matter. A test may be reliable in one context and unreliable in another. There are different types and degrees of reliability. A **reliability coefficient** is an index of reliability, a proportion that indicates the ratio between the true score variance on a test and the total variance. In this chapter, we explore different kinds of reliability coefficients, including those for measuring test-retest reliability, alternate-forms reliability, split-half reliability, and inter-scorer reliability.

## The Concept of Reliability

Recall from our discussion of classical test theory that a score on an ability test is presumed to reflect not only the testtaker's true score on the ability being measured but also error.[1] In its broadest sense, error refers to the component of the observed test score that does not have to do with the testtaker's ability. If we use $X$ to represent an observed score, $T$ to represent a true score, and $E$ to represent error, then the fact that an observed score equals the true score plus error may be expressed as follows:

$$X = T + E$$

---

1. Ability is frequently used for illustrative purposes as a trait being measured. However, unless stated otherwise, the principles to which we refer with respect to ability tests also hold true with respect to other types of tests, such as tests for personality. Thus, according to the true score model, it is also true that the magnitude of the presence of a certain psychological trait (such as extraversion) as measured by a test of extraversion will be due to (1) the "true" amount of extraversion and (2) other factors.

A statistic useful in describing sources of test score variability is the **variance** $(\sigma^2)$—the standard deviation squared. This statistic is useful because it can be broken into components. Variance from true differences is **true variance,** and variance from irrelevant, random sources is **error variance.** If $\sigma^2$ represents the total variance, the true variance, and the error variance, then the relationship of the variances can be expressed as

$$\sigma^2 = \sigma^2_{th} + \sigma^2_{e}$$

In this equation, the total variance in an observed distribution of test scores $(\sigma^2)$ equals the sum of the true variance $(\sigma^2_{th})$ plus the error variance $(\sigma^2_{e})$. The term **reliability** refers to the proportion of the total variance attributed to true variance. The greater the proportion of the total variance attributed to true variance, the more reliable the test. Because true differences are assumed to be stable, they are presumed to yield consistent scores on repeated administrations of the same test as well as on equivalent forms of tests. Because error variance may increase or decrease a test score by varying amounts, consistency of the test score—and thus the reliability—can be affected.

In general, the term **measurement error** refers to, collectively, all of the factors associated with the process of measuring some variable, other than the variable being measured. To illustrate, consider an English-language test on the subject of 12th-grade algebra being administered, in English, to a sample of 12th-grade students, newly arrived to the United States from China. The students in the sample are all known to be "whiz kids" in algebra. Yet for some reason, all of the students receive failing grades on the test. Do these failures indicate that these students really are not "whiz kids" at all? Possibly. But a researcher looking for answers regarding this outcome would do well to evaluate the English-language skills of the students. Perhaps this group of students did not do well on the algebra test because they could neither read nor understand what was required of them. In such an instance, the fact that the test was written and administered in English could have contributed in large part to the measurement error in this evaluation. Stated another way, although the test was designed to evaluate one variable (knowledge of algebra), scores on it may have been more reflective of another variable (knowledge of and proficiency in English language). This source of measurement error (the fact that the test was written and administered in English) could have been eliminated by translating the test and administering it in the language of the testtakers.

Measurement error, much like error in general, can be categorized as being either *systematic* or *random.* **Random error** is a source of error in measuring a targeted variable caused by unpredictable fluctuations and inconsistencies of other variables in the measurement process. Sometimes referred to as "noise," this source of error fluctuates from one testing situation to another with no discernible pattern that would systematically raise or lower scores. Examples of random error that could conceivably affect test scores range from unanticipated events happening in the immediate vicinity of the test environment (such as a lightning strike or a spontaneous "occupy the university" rally), to unanticipated physical events happening within the testtaker (such as a sudden and unexpected surge in the testtaker's blood sugar or blood pressure).

**JUST THINK . . .**

What might be a source of random error inherent in all the tests an assessor administers in his or her private office?

In contrast to random error, **systematic error** refers to a source of error in measuring a variable that is typically constant or proportionate to what is presumed to be the true value of the variable being measured. For example, a 12-inch ruler may be found to be, in actuality, a tenth of one inch longer than 12 inches. All of the 12-inch measurements previously taken with that ruler were systematically off by one-tenth of an inch; that is, anything measured to be exactly 12 inches with that ruler was, in reality, 12 and one-tenth inches. In this example, it is the measuring instrument itself that has been found to be a source of systematic error. Once a systematic error becomes known, it becomes predictable—as well as fixable. Note also that a systematic source of error does not affect score consistency. So, for example, suppose a measuring instrument such as the official weight scale used on *The Biggest Loser* television program consistently underweighed by 5 pounds everyone who stepped on it. Regardless of this (systematic) error, the relative standings of all of the contestants weighed on that scale would remain unchanged. A scale underweighing all contestants by 5 pounds simply amounts to a constant being subtracted from every "score." Although weighing contestants on such a scale would not yield a true (or valid) weight, such a systematic error source would not change the variability of the distribution or affect the measured reliability of the instrument. In the end, the individual crowned "the biggest loser" would indeed be the contestant who lost the most weight—it's just that he or she would actually weigh 5 pounds more than the weight measured by the show's official scale. Now moving from the realm of reality television back to the realm of psychological testing and assessment, let's take a closer look at the source of some error variance commonly encountered during testing and assessment.

**JUST THINK . . .**

What might be a source of systematic error inherent in all the tests an assessor administers in his or her private office?

## Sources of Error Variance

Sources of error variance include test construction, administration, scoring, and/or interpretation.

**Test construction**   One source of variance during test construction is **item sampling** or **content sampling,** terms that refer to variation among items within a test as well as to variation among items between tests. Consider two or more tests designed to measure a specific skill, personality attribute, or body of knowledge. Differences are sure to be found in the way the items are worded and in the exact content sampled. Each of us has probably walked into an achievement test setting thinking "I hope they ask this question" or "I hope they don't ask that question." If the only questions on the examination were the ones we hoped would be asked, we might achieve a higher score on that test than on another test purporting to measure the same thing. The higher score would be due to the specific content sampled, the way the items were worded, and so on. The extent to which a testtaker's score is affected by the content sampled on a test and by the way the content is sampled (that is, the way in which the item is constructed) is a source of error variance. From the perspective of a test creator, a challenge in test development is to maximize the proportion of the total variance that is true variance and to minimize the proportion of the total variance that is error variance.

**Test administration**   Sources of error variance that occur during test administration may influence the testtaker's attention or motivation. The testtaker's reactions to those influences are the source of one kind of error variance. Examples of untoward influences during administration of a test include factors related to the *test environment:* room temperature, level of lighting, and amount of ventilation and noise, for instance. A relentless fly may develop a tenacious attraction to an examinee's face. A wad of gum on the seat of the chair may make itself known only after the testtaker sits down on it. Other environment-related variables include the instrument used to enter responses and even the writing surface on which responses are entered. A pencil with a dull or broken point can make it difficult to blacken the little grids. The writing surface on a school desk may be riddled with heart carvings, the legacy of past years' students who felt compelled to express their eternal devotion to someone now long forgotten.

Other potential sources of error variance during test administration are *testtaker variables*. Pressing emotional problems, physical discomfort, lack of sleep, and the effects of drugs or medication can all be sources of error variance. A testtaker may, for whatever reason, make a mistake in entering a test response. For example, the examinee might blacken a "b" grid when he or she meant to blacken the "d" grid. An examinee may simply misread a test item. For example, an examinee might read the question "Which is not a source of error variance?" as "Which is a source of error variance?" Other simple mistakes can have score-depleting consequences. Responding to the fifth item on a multiple-choice test, for example, the testtaker might blacken the grid for the sixth item. Just one skipped question will result in every subsequent test response being out of sync. Formal learning experiences, casual life experiences, therapy, illness, and changes in mood or mental state are other potential sources of testtaker-related error variance.

*Examiner-related variables* are potential sources of error variance. The examiner's physical appearance and demeanor—even the presence or absence of an examiner—are some factors for consideration here. Some examiners in some testing situations might knowingly or unwittingly depart from the procedure prescribed for a particular test. On an oral examination, some examiners may unwittingly provide clues by emphasizing key words as they pose questions. They might convey information about the correctness of a response through head nodding, eye movements, or other nonverbal gestures. Clearly, the level of professionalism exhibited by examiners is a source of error variance.

**Test scoring and interpretation**   In many tests, the advent of computer scoring and a growing reliance on objective, computer-scorable items have virtually eliminated error variance caused by scorer differences. However, not all tests can be scored from grids blackened by no. 2 pencils. Individually administered intelligence tests, some tests of personality, tests of creativity, various behavioral measures, essay tests, portfolio assessment, situational behavior tests, and countless other tools of assessment still require scoring by trained personnel.

Manuals for individual intelligence tests tend to be very explicit about scoring criteria, lest examinees' measured intelligence vary as a function of who is doing the testing and scoring. In some tests of personality, examinees are asked to supply open-ended responses to stimuli such as pictures, words, sentences, and inkblots, and it is the examiner who must then quantify or qualitatively evaluate responses. In one test of creativity, examinees might be given the task of creating as many things as they can out of a set of blocks. Here, it is the examiner's task to determine which block constructions will be awarded credit and which will not. For a behavioral measure of social skills in an inpatient psychiatric service, the scorers or raters might be asked to rate patients with respect to the variable "social relatedness." Such a behavioral measure might require the rater to check *yes* or *no* to items like *Patient says "Good morning" to at least two staff members.*

Scorers and scoring systems are potential sources of error variance. A test may employ objective-type items amenable to computer scoring of well-documented reliability. Yet even then, a technical glitch might contaminate the data. If subjectivity is involved in scoring, then the scorer (or rater) can be a source of error variance. Indeed, despite rigorous scoring criteria set forth in many of the better-known tests of intelligence, examiner/scorers occasionally still are confronted by situations where an examinee's response lies in a gray area. The element of subjectivity in scoring may be much greater in the administration of certain nonobjective-type personality tests, tests of creativity (such as the block test just described), and certain academic tests (such as

**JUST THINK . . .**

Can you conceive of a test item on a rating scale requiring human judgment that all raters will score the same 100% of the time?

essay examinations). Subjectivity in scoring can even enter into behavioral assessment. Consider the case of two behavior observers given the task of rating one psychiatric inpatient on the variable of "social relatedness." On an item that asks simply whether two staff members were greeted in the morning, one rater might judge the patient's eye contact and mumbling of something to two staff members to qualify as a *yes* response. The other observer might feel strongly that a *no* response to the item is appropriate. Such problems in scoring agreement can be addressed through rigorous training designed to make the consistency—or reliability—of various scorers as nearly perfect as can be.

**JUST THINK . . .**

Recall your score on the most recent test you took. What percentage of that score do you think represented your "true" ability, and what percentage of that score was represented by error? Now, hazard a guess as to what type(s) of error were involved.

**Other sources of error**   Surveys and polls are two tools of assessment commonly used by researchers who study public opinion. In the political arena, for example, researchers trying to predict who will win an election may sample opinions from representative voters and then draw conclusions based on their data. However, in the "fine print" of those conclusions is usually a disclaimer that the conclusions may be off by plus or minus a certain percent. This fine print is a reference to the margin of error the researchers estimate to exist in their study. The error in such research may be a result of sampling error—the extent to which the population of voters in the study actually was representative of voters in the election. The researchers may not have gotten it right with respect to demographics, political party affiliation, or other factors related to the population of voters. Alternatively, the researchers may have gotten such factors right but simply did not include enough people in their sample to draw the conclusions that they did. This bring us to another type of error, called methodological error. So, for example, the interviewers may not have been trained properly, the wording in the questionnaire may have been ambiguous, or the items may have somehow been biased to favor one or another of the candidates. Can such sources of error be serious enough to affect the outcome of a poll? For the answer to that question, consider the research that led to the publication of the image presented in Figure 5–1. Popular pollsters seldom provide methodological details sufficient to determine what type of measurement error may have affected their poll.

**Figure 5–1**
**A Classic Case of Measurement Error (and Journalistic Poor Judgment)**

*The 1948 presidential election in the United States featured Democrat Harry Truman (the vice president under Franklin Roosevelt who became president when Roosevelt died in office) against the Republican, crime-fighting governor of New York, Thomas Dewey. A famous opinion research company (Gallup), not to mention publications such as the* New York Times *and* Life *magazine all viewed Truman as the underdog in the election. One newspaper, the* Chicago Daily Tribune, *even went so far as to publish the news of Truman's electoral demise. This now-classic photo depicts a jubilant President Truman holding a copy of the paper with an erroneous headline.*

Certain types of assessment situations lend themselves to particular varieties ~stematic and nonsystematic error. For example, consider assessing the extent ~ement between partners regarding the quality and quantity of physical and ~gical abuse in their relationship. As Moffitt et al. (1997) observed, "Because ~use usually occurs in private, there are only two persons who 'really' know ~ on behind closed doors: the two members of the couple" (p. 47). Potential ~s of nonsystematic error in such an assessment situation include forgetting, ~ling to notice abusive behavior, and misunderstanding instructions regarding reporting. A number of studies (O'Leary & Arias, 1988; Riggs et al., 1989; Straus, 1979) have suggested that underreporting or overreporting of perpetration of abuse also may contribute to systematic error. Females, for example, may underreport abuse because of fear, shame, or social desirability factors and overreport abuse if they are seeking help. Males may underreport abuse because of embarrassment and social desirability factors and overreport abuse if they are attempting to justify the report.

Just as the amount of abuse one partner suffers at the hands of the other may never be known, so the amount of test variance that is true relative to error may never be known. A so-called true score, as Stanley (1971, p. 361) put it, is "not the ultimate fact in the book of the recording angel." Further, the utility of the methods used for estimating true versus error variance is a hotly debated matter (see Collins, 1996; Humphreys, 1996; Williams & Zimmerman, 1996a, 1996b). Let's take a closer look at such estimates and how they are derived.

# Reliability Estimates

## *Test-Retest Reliability Estimates*

A ruler made from the highest-quality steel can be a very reliable instrument of measurement. Every time you measure something that is exactly 12 inches long, for example, your ruler will tell you that what you are measuring is exactly 12 inches long. The reliability of this instrument of measurement may also be said to be stable over time. Whether you measure the 12 inches today, tomorrow, or next year, the ruler is still going to measure 12 inches as 12 inches. By contrast, a ruler constructed of putty might be a very unreliable instrument of measurement. One minute it could measure some known 12-inch standard as 12 inches, the next minute it could measure it as 14 inches, and a week later it could measure it as 18 inches. One way of estimating the reliability of a measuring instrument is by using the same instrument to measure the same thing at two points in time. In psychometric parlance, this approach to reliability evaluation is called the *test-retest method*, and the result of such an evaluation is an estimate of *test-retest reliability*.

**Test-retest reliability** is an estimate of reliability obtained by correlating pairs of scores from the same people on two different administrations of the same test. The test-retest measure is appropriate when evaluating the reliability of a test that purports to measure something that is relatively stable over time, such as a personality trait. If the characteristic being measured is assumed to fluctuate over time, then there would be little sense in assessing the reliability of the test using the test-retest method.

As time passes, people change. For example, people may learn new things, forget some things, and acquire new skills. It is generally the case (although there are exceptions) that, as the time interval between administrations of the same test increases, the correlation between the scores obtained on each testing decreases. The passage of time can be a source of error variance. The longer the time that passes, the greater the likelihood that the reliability coefficient will be lower. When the interval between testing is greater than six months, the estimate of test-retest reliability is often referred to as the **coefficient of stability.**

An estimate of test-retest reliability from a math test might be low if the testtakers took a math tutorial before the second test was administered. An estimate of test-retest reliability from a personality profile might be low if the testtaker suffered some emotional trauma or received counseling during the intervening period. A low estimate of test-retest reliability might be found even when the interval between testings is relatively brief. This may well be the case when the testings occur during a time of great developmental change with respect to the variables they are designed to assess. An evaluation of a test-retest reliability coefficient must therefore extend beyond the magnitude of the obtained coefficient. If we are to come to proper conclusions about the reliability of the measuring instrument, evaluation of a test-retest reliability estimate must extend to a consideration of possible intervening factors between test administrations.

An estimate of test-retest reliability may be most appropriate in gauging the reliability of tests that employ outcome measures such as reaction time or perceptual judgments (including discriminations of brightness, loudness, or taste). However, even in measuring variables such as these, and even when the time period between the two administrations of the test is relatively small, various factors (such as experience, practice, memory, fatigue, and motivation) may intervene and confound an obtained measure of reliability.[2]

## Parallel-Forms and Alternate-Forms Reliability Estimates

If you have ever taken a makeup exam in which the questions were not all the same as on the test initially given, you have had experience with different forms of a test. And if you have ever wondered whether the two forms of the test were really equivalent, you have wondered about the *alternate-forms* or *parallel-forms* reliability of the test. The degree of the relationship between various forms of a test can be evaluated by means of an alternate-forms or parallel-forms coefficient of reliability, which is often termed the **coefficient of equivalence.**

Although frequently used interchangeably, there is a difference between the terms *alternate forms* and *parallel forms.* **Parallel forms** of a test exist when, for each form of the test, the means and the variances of observed test scores are equal. In theory, the means of scores obtained on parallel forms correlate equally with the true score. More practically, scores obtained on parallel tests correlate equally with other measures. The term **parallel forms reliability** refers to an estimate of the extent to which item sampling and other errors have affected test scores on versions of the same test when, for each form of the test, the means and variances of observed test scores are equal.

**Alternate forms** are simply different versions of a test that have been constructed so as to be parallel. Although they do not meet the requirements for the legitimate designation "parallel," alternate forms of a test are typically designed to be equivalent with respect to variables such as content and level of difficulty. The term **alternate forms reliability** refers to an estimate of the extent to which these different forms of the same test have been affected item sampling error, or other error.

> **JUST THINK . . .**
>
> You missed the midterm examination and have to take a makeup exam. Your classmates tell you that they found the midterm impossibly difficult. Your instructor tells you that you will be taking an alternate form, not a parallel form, of the original test. How do you feel about that?

---

2. Although we may refer to a number as the summary statement of the reliability of individual tools of measurement, any such index of reliability can be meaningfully interpreted only in the context of the process of measurement—the unique circumstances surrounding the use of the ruler, the test, or some other measuring instrument in a particular application or situation.

Obtaining estimates of alternate-forms reliability and parallel-forms reliability is similar in two ways to obtaining an estimate of test-retest reliability: (1) Two test administrations with the same group are required, and (2) test scores may be affected by factors such as motivation, fatigue, or intervening events such as practice, learning, or therapy (although not as much as when the same test is administered twice). An additional source of error variance, item sampling, is inherent in the computation of an alternate- or parallel-forms reliability coefficient. Testtakers may do better or worse on a specific form of the test not as a function of their true ability but simply because of the particular items that were selected for inclusion in the test.[3]

Developing alternate forms of tests can be time-consuming and expensive. Imagine what might be involved in trying to create sets of equivalent items and then getting the same people to sit for repeated administrations of an experimental test! On the other hand, once an alternate or parallel form of a test has been developed, it is advantageous to the test user in several ways. For example, it minimizes the effect of memory for the content of a previously administered form of the test.

◆
JUST THINK . . .

From the perspective of the test user, what are other possible advantages of having alternate or parallel forms of the same test?

Certain traits are presumed to be relatively stable in people over time, and we would expect tests measuring those traits—alternate forms, parallel forms, or otherwise—to reflect that stability. As an example, we expect that there will be, and in fact there is, a reasonable degree of stability in scores on intelligence tests. Conversely, we might expect relatively little stability in scores obtained on a measure of state anxiety (anxiety felt at the moment).

An estimate of the reliability of a test can be obtained without developing an alternate form of the test and without having to administer the test twice to the same people. Deriving this type of estimate entails an evaluation of the internal consistency of the test items. Logically enough, it is referred to as an **internal consistency estimate of reliability** or as an **estimate of inter-item consistency.** There are different methods of obtaining internal consistency estimates of reliability. One such method is the *split-half estimate.*

## Split-Half Reliability Estimates

An estimate of **split-half reliability** is obtained by correlating two pairs of scores obtained from equivalent halves of a single test administered once. It is a useful measure of reliability when it is impractical or undesirable to assess reliability with two tests or to administer a test twice (because of factors such as time or expense). The computation of a coefficient of split-half reliability generally entails three steps:

*Step 1.* Divide the test into equivalent halves.

*Step 2.* Calculate a Pearson *r* between scores on the two halves of the test.

*Step 3.* Adjust the half-test reliability using the Spearman-Brown formula (discussed shortly).

When it comes to calculating split-half reliability coefficients, there's more than one way to split a test—but there are some ways you should never split a test. Simply dividing the test in the middle is not recommended because it's likely that this procedure

---

3. According to classical test theory, the effect of such factors on test scores is indeed presumed to be measurement error. There are alternative models in which the effect of such factors on fluctuating test scores would not be considered error. Atkinson (1981), for example, discussed such alternatives in the context of personality assessment.

would spuriously raise or lower the reliability coefficient. Different amounts of fatigue for the first as opposed to the second part of the test, different amounts of test anxiety, and differences in item difficulty as a function of placement in the test are all factors to consider.

One acceptable way to split a test is to randomly assign items to one or the other half of the test. Another acceptable way to split a test is to assign odd-numbered items to one half of the test and even-numbered items to the other half. This method yields an estimate of split-half reliability that is also referred to as **odd-even reliability**.[4] Yet another way to split a test is to divide the test by content so that each half contains items equivalent with respect to content and difficulty. In general, a primary objective in splitting a test in half for the purpose of obtaining a split-half reliability estimate is to create what might be called "mini-parallel-forms," with each half equal to the other—or as nearly equal as humanly possible—in format, stylistic, statistical, and related aspects.

Step 2 in the procedure entails the computation of a Pearson $r$, which requires little explanation at this point. However, the third step requires the use of the Spearman-Brown formula.

**The Spearman-Brown formula**    The **Spearman-Brown formula** allows a test developer or user to estimate internal consistency reliability from a correlation of two halves of a test. It is a specific application of a more general formula to estimate the reliability of a test that is lengthened or shortened by any number of items. Because the reliability of a test is affected by its length, a formula is necessary for estimating the reliability of a test that has been shortened or lengthened. The general Spearman-Brown ($r_{SB}$) formula is

$$r_{SB} = \frac{nr_{xy}}{1 + (n-1)r_{xy}}$$

where $r_{SB}$ is equal to the reliability adjusted by the Spearman-Brown formula, $r_{xy}$ is equal to the Pearson $r$ in the original-length test, and $n$ is equal to the number of items in the revised version divided by the number of items in the original version.

By determining the reliability of one half of a test, a test developer can use the Spearman-Brown formula to estimate the reliability of a whole test. Because a whole test is two times longer than half a test, $n$ becomes 2 in the Spearman-Brown formula for the adjustment of split-half reliability. The symbol $r_{hh}$ stands for the Pearson $r$ of scores in the two half tests:

$$r_{SB} = \frac{2r_{hh}}{1 + r_{hh}}$$

Usually, but not always, reliability increases as test length increases. Ideally, the additional test items are equivalent with respect to the content and the range of difficulty of the original items. Estimates of reliability based on consideration of the entire test therefore tend to be higher than those based on half of a test. Table 5–1 shows half-test correlations presented alongside adjusted reliability estimates for the whole test. You can see that all the adjusted correlations are higher than the unadjusted correlations. This is so because Spearman-Brown estimates are based on a test that is twice as long as

---

4. One precaution here: With respect to a group of items on an achievement test that deals with a single problem, it is usually desirable to assign the whole group of items to one half of the test. Otherwise—if part of the group were in one half and another part in the other half—the similarity of the half scores would be spuriously inflated. In this instance, a single error in understanding, for example, might affect items in both halves of the test.

| Table 5–1 Odd-Even Reliability Coefficients before and after the Spearman-Brown Adjustment* | Grade | Half-Test Correlation (unadjusted $r$) | Whole-Test Estimate ($r_{SB}$) |
|---|---|---|---|
| | K | .718 | .836 |
| | 1 | .807 | .893 |
| | 2 | .777 | .875 |

*For scores on a test of mental ability

the original half test. For the data from the kindergarten pupils, for example, a half-test reliability of .718 is estimated to be equivalent to a whole-test reliability of .836.

If test developers or users wish to shorten a test, the Spearman-Brown formula may be used to estimate the effect of the shortening on the test's reliability. Reduction in test size for the purpose of reducing test administration time is a common practice in certain situations. For example, the test administrator may have only limited time with a particular testtaker or group of testtakers. Reduction in test size may be indicated in situations where boredom or fatigue could produce responses of questionable meaningfulness.

**JUST THINK . . .**

What are other situations in which a reduction in test size or the time it takes to administer a test might be desirable? What are the arguments against reducing test size?

A Spearman-Brown formula could also be used to determine the number of items needed to attain a desired level of reliability. In adding items to increase test reliability to a desired level, the rule is that the new items must be equivalent in content and difficulty so that the longer test still measures what the original test measured. If the reliability of the original test is relatively low, then it may be impractical to increase the number of items to reach an acceptable level of reliability. Another alternative would be to abandon this relatively unreliable instrument and locate—or develop—a suitable alternative. The reliability of the instrument could also be raised in some way. For example, the reliability of the instrument might be raised by creating new items, clarifying the test's instructions, or simplifying the scoring rules.

Internal consistency estimates of reliability, such as that obtained by use of the Spearman-Brown formula, are inappropriate for measuring the reliability of heterogeneous tests and speed tests. The impact of test characteristics on reliability is discussed in detail later in this chapter.

## Other Methods of Estimating Internal Consistency

In addition to the Spearman-Brown formula, other methods used to obtain estimates of internal consistency reliability include formulas developed by Kuder and Richardson (1937) and Cronbach (1951). **Inter-item consistency** refers to the degree of correlation among all the items on a scale. A measure of inter-item consistency is calculated from a single administration of a single form of a test. An index of inter-item consistency, in turn, is useful in assessing the **homogeneity** of the test. Tests are said to be homogeneous if they contain items that measure a single trait. As an adjective used to describe test items, *homogeneity* (derived from the Greek words *homos*, meaning "same," and *genos*, meaning "kind") is the degree to which a test measures a single factor. In other words, homogeneity is the extent to which items in a scale are unifactorial.

In contrast to test homogeneity, **heterogeneity** describes the degree to which a test measures different factors. A *heterogeneous* (or nonhomogeneous) test is composed of items that measure more than one trait. A test that assesses knowledge only of

3-D television repair skills could be expected to be more homogeneous in content than a general electronics repair test. The former test assesses only one area whereas the latter assesses several, such as knowledge not only of 3-D televisions but also of digital video recorders, Blu-Ray players, MP3 players, satellite radio receivers, and so forth.

The more homogeneous a test is, the more inter-item consistency it can be expected to have. Because a homogeneous test samples a relatively narrow content area, it is to be expected to contain more inter-item consistency than a heterogeneous test. Test homogeneity is desirable because it allows relatively straightforward test-score interpretation. Testtakers with the same score on a homogeneous test probably have similar abilities in the area tested. Testtakers with the same score on a more heterogeneous test may have quite different abilities.

Although a homogeneous test is desirable because it so readily lends itself to clear interpretation, it is often an insufficient tool for measuring multifaceted psychological variables such as intelligence or personality. One way to circumvent this potential source of difficulty has been to administer a series of homogeneous tests, each designed to measure some component of a heterogeneous variable.[5]

**The Kuder-Richardson formulas** Dissatisfaction with existing split-half methods of estimating reliability compelled G. Frederic Kuder and M. W. Richardson (1937; Richardson & Kuder, 1939) to develop their own measures for estimating reliability. The most widely known of the many formulas they collaborated on is their **Kuder-Richardson formula 20,** or KR-20, so named because it was the 20th formula developed in a series. Where test items are highly homogeneous, KR-20 and split-half reliability estimates will be similar. However, KR-20 is the statistic of choice for determining the inter-item consistency of dichotomous items, primarily those items that can be scored right or wrong (such as multiple-choice items). If test items are more heterogeneous, KR-20 will yield lower reliability estimates than the split-half method. Table 5–2 summarizes items on a sample heterogeneous test (the HERT), and Table 5–3 summarizes HERT performance for 20 testtakers. Assuming the difficulty level of all the items on the test to be about the same, would you expect a split-half (odd-even) estimate of reliability to be fairly high or low? How would the KR-20 reliability estimate compare with the odd-even estimate of reliability—would it be higher or lower?

We might guess that, because the content areas sampled for the 18 items from this "Hypothetical Electronics Repair Test" are ordered in a manner whereby odd and even items tap the same content area, the odd-even reliability estimate will probably be quite high. Because of the great heterogeneity of content areas when taken as a whole, it could reasonably be predicted that the KR-20 estimate of reliability will be lower than the odd-even one. How is KR-20 computed? The following formula may be used:

$$r_{KR20} = \left(\frac{k}{k-1}\right)\left(1 - \frac{\sum pq}{\sigma^2}\right)$$

where $r_{KR20}$ stands for the Kuder-Richardson formula 20 reliability coefficient, $k$ is the number of test items, $\sigma^2$ is the variance of total test scores, $p$ is the proportion of

---

5. As we will see elsewhere throughout this textbook, important decisions are seldom made on the basis of one test only. Psychologists frequently rely on a **test battery**—a selected assortment of tests and assessment procedures—in the process of evaluation. A test battery is typically composed of tests designed to measure different variables.

**Table 5–2**

**Content Areas Sampled for 18 Items of the Hypothetical Electronics Repair Test (HERT)**

| Item Number | Content Area |
|---|---|
| 1 | 3-D television |
| 2 | 3-D television |
| 3 | Digital video recorder (DVR) |
| 4 | Digital video recorder (DVR) |
| 5 | Blu-Ray player |
| 6 | Blu-Ray player |
| 7 | Smart phone |
| 8 | Smart phone |
| 9 | Computer |
| 10 | Computer |
| 11 | Compact disc player |
| 12 | Compact disc player |
| 13 | Satellite radio receiver |
| 14 | Satellite radio receiver |
| 15 | Video camera |
| 16 | Video camera |
| 17 | MP3 player |
| 18 | MP3 player |

**Table 5–3**

**Performance on the 18-Item HERT by Item for 20 Testtakers**

| Item Number | Number of Testtakers Correct |
|---|---|
| 1 | 14 |
| 2 | 12 |
| 3 | 9 |
| 4 | 18 |
| 5 | 8 |
| 6 | 5 |
| 7 | 6 |
| 8 | 9 |
| 9 | 10 |
| 10 | 10 |
| 11 | 8 |
| 12 | 6 |
| 13 | 15 |
| 14 | 9 |
| 15 | 12 |
| 16 | 12 |
| 17 | 14 |
| 18 | 7 |

testtakers who pass the item, $q$ is the proportion of people who fail the item, and $\Sigma\, pq$ is the sum of the $pq$ products over all items. For this particular example, $k$ equals 18. Based on the data in Table 5–3, $\Sigma\, pq$ can be computed to be 3.975. The variance of total test scores is 5.26. Thus, $r_{KR20} = .259$.

An approximation of KR-20 can be obtained by the use of the 21st formula in the series developed by Kuder and Richardson, a formula known as—you guessed it—KR-21. The KR-21 formula may be used if there is reason to assume that all the test items have approximately the same degree of difficulty. Let's add that this assumption is seldom justified. Formula KR-21 has become outdated in an era of calculators and computers. Way back when, KR-21 was sometimes used to estimate KR-20 only because it required many fewer calculations.

Numerous modifications of Kuder-Richardson formulas have been proposed through the years. The one variant of the KR-20 formula that has received the most acceptance and is in widest use today is a statistic called coefficient alpha. You may even hear it referred to as *coefficient α−20*. This expression incorporates both the Greek letter alpha (α) and the number 20, the latter a reference to KR-20.

**Coefficient alpha** Developed by Cronbach (1951) and subsequently elaborated on by others (such as Kaiser & Michael, 1975; Novick & Lewis, 1967), **coefficient alpha** may be thought of as the mean of all possible split-half correlations, corrected by the Spearman-Brown formula. In contrast to KR-20, which is appropriately used only on tests with dichotomous items, coefficient alpha is appropriate for use on tests containing nondichotomous items. The formula for coefficient alpha is

$$r_\alpha = \left( \frac{k}{k-1} \right) \left( 1 - \frac{\sum \sigma_i^2}{\sigma^2} \right)$$

where $r_a$ is coefficient alpha, $k$ is the number of items, is the variance of one item, $\Sigma$ is the sum of variances of each item, and $\sigma^2$ is the variance of the total test scores.

Coefficient alpha is the preferred statistic for obtaining an estimate of internal consistency reliability. A variation of the formula has been developed for use in obtaining an estimate of test-retest reliability (Green, 2003). Essentially, this formula yields an estimate of the mean of all possible test-retest, split-half coefficients. Coefficient alpha is widely used as a measure of reliability, in part because it requires only one administration of the test.

Unlike a Pearson $r$, which may range in value from $-1$ to $+1$, coefficient alpha typically ranges in value from 0 to 1. The reason for this is that, conceptually, coefficient alpha (much like other coefficients of reliability) is calculated to help answer questions about how *similar* sets of data are. Here, similarity is gauged, in essence, on a scale from 0 (absolutely no similarity) to 1 (perfectly identical). It is possible, however, to conceive of data sets that would yield a negative value of alpha (Streiner, 2003b). Still, because negative values of alpha are theoretically impossible, it is recommended under such rare circumstances that the alpha coefficient be reported as zero (Henson, 2001). Also, a myth about alpha is that "bigger is always better." As Streiner (2003b) pointed out, a value of alpha above .90 may be "too high" and indicate redundancy in the items.

In contrast to coefficient alpha, a Pearson $r$ may be thought of as dealing conceptually with both dissimilarity and similarity. Accordingly, an $r$ value of $-1$ may be thought of as indicating "perfect dissimilarity." In practice, most reliability coefficients—regardless of the specific type of reliability they are measuring—range in value from 0 to 1. This is generally true, although it is possible to conceive of exceptional cases in which data sets yield an $r$ with a negative value.

**Average proportional distance (APD)** A relatively new measure for evaluating the internal consistency of a test is the *average proportional distance* (APD) method (Sturman et al., 2009). Rather than focusing on similarity between scores on items of a test (as do split-half methods and Cronbach's alpha), the APD is a measure that focuses on the degree of *difference* that exists between item scores. Accordingly, we define the **average proportional distance method** as a measure used to evaluate the internal consistency of a test that focuses on the degree of difference that exists between item scores.

To illustrate how the APD is calculated, consider the (hypothetical) "3-Item Test of Extraversion" (3-ITE). As conveyed by the title of the 3-ITE, it is a test that has only three items. Each of the items is a sentence that somehow relates to extraversion. Testtakers are instructed to respond to each of the three items with reference to the following 7-point scale: 1 = Very strongly disagree, 2 = Strongly disagree, 3 = Disagree, 4 = Neither Agree nor Disagree, 5 = Agree, 6 = Strongly agree, and 7 = Very strongly agree.

Typically, in order to evaluate the inter-item consistency of a scale, the calculation of the APD would be calculated for a group of testtakers. However, for the purpose of illustrating the calculations of this measure, let's look at how the APD would be calculated for one testtaker. Yolanda scores 4 on Item 1, 5 on Item 2, and 6 on Item 3. Based on Yolanda's scores, the APD would be calculated as follows:

*Step 1*: Calculate the absolute difference between scores for all of the items.

*Step 2*: Average the difference between scores.

*Step 3*: Obtain the APD by dividing the average difference between scores by the number of response options on the test, minus one.

So, for the 3-ITE, here is how the calculations would look using Yolanda's test scores:

*Step 1*: Absolute difference between Items 1 and 2 = 1

Absolute difference between Items 1 and 3 = 2

Absolute difference between Items 2 and 3 = 1

*Step 2*: In order to obtain the average difference (AD), add up the absolute differences in Step 1 and divide by the number of items as follows:

$$AD = \frac{1 + 2 + 1}{3} = \frac{4}{3} = 1.33$$

*Step 3*: To obtain the average proportional distance (APD), divide the average difference by 6 (the 7 response options in our ITE scale minus 1). Using Yolanda's data, we would divide 1.33 by 6 to get .22. Thus, the APD for the ITE is .22. But what does this mean?

The general "rule of thumb" for interpreting an APD is that an obtained value of .2 or lower is indicative of excellent internal consistency, and that a value of .25 to .2 is in the acceptable range. A calculated APD of .25 is suggestive of problems with the internal consistency of the test. These guidelines are based on the assumption that items measuring a single construct such as extraversion should ideally be correlated with one another in the .6 to .7 range. Let's add that the expected inter-item correlation may vary depending on the variables being measured, so the ideal correlation values are not set in stone. In the case of the 3-ITE, the data for our one subject suggests that the scale has acceptable internal consistency. Of course, in order to make any meaningful conclusions about the internal consistency of the 3-ITE, the instrument would have to be tested with a large sample of testtakers.

One potential advantage of the APD method over using Cronbach's alpha is that the APD index is not connected to the number of items on a measure. Cronbach's alpha will be higher when a measure has more than 25 items (Cortina, 1993). Perhaps the best course of action when evaluating the internal consistency of a given measure is to analyze and integrate the information using several indices, including Cronbach's alpha, mean inter-item correlations, and the APD.

Before proceeding, let's emphasize that all indices of reliability provide an index that is a characteristic of a particular group of test scores, not of the test itself (Caruso, 2000; Yin & Fan, 2000). Measures of reliability are estimates, and estimates are subject to error. The precise amount of error inherent in a reliability estimate will vary with various factors, such as the sample of testtakers from which the data were drawn. A reliability index published in a test manual might be very impressive. However, keep in mind that the reported reliability was achieved with a particular group of testtakers. If a new group of testtakers is sufficiently different from the group of testtakers on whom the reliability studies were done, the reliability coefficient may not be as impressive—and may even be unacceptable.

## Measures of Inter-Scorer Reliability

When being evaluated, we usually would like to believe that the results would be the same no matter who is doing the evaluating.[6] For example, if you take a road test for a driver's license, you would like to believe that whether you pass or fail is solely a matter of your performance behind the wheel and not a function of who is sitting in the passenger's seat. Unfortunately, in some types of tests under some conditions, the score may be more a function of the scorer than of anything else. This was demonstrated back in 1912, when researchers presented one pupil's English composition to a convention of teachers and volunteers graded the papers. The grades ranged from a low of 50% to a high of 98% (Starch & Elliott, 1912). With this as background, it can be appreciated that certain tests lend themselves to scoring in a way that is more consistent than with other tests. It is meaningful, therefore, to raise questions about the degree of consistency, or reliability, that exists between scorers of a particular test.

Variously referred to as *scorer reliability, judge reliability, observer reliability,* and *inter-rater reliability,* **inter-scorer reliability** is the degree of agreement or consistency between two or more scorers (or judges or raters) with regard to a particular measure. Reference to levels of inter-scorer reliability for a particular test may be published in the test's manual or elsewhere. If the reliability coefficient is high, the prospective test user knows that test scores can be derived in a systematic, consistent way by various scorers with sufficient training. A responsible test developer who is unable to create a test that can be scored with a reasonable degree of consistency by trained scorers will go back to the drawing board to discover the reason for this problem. If, for example, the problem is a lack of clarity in scoring criteria, then the remedy might be to rewrite the scoring criteria section of the manual to include clearly written scoring rules. Inter-rater consistency may be promoted by providing raters with the opportunity for group discussion along with practice exercises and information on rater accuracy (Smith, 1986).

Inter-scorer reliability is often used when coding nonverbal behavior. For example, a researcher who wishes to quantify some aspect of nonverbal behavior, such as depressed mood, would start by composing a checklist of behaviors that constitute depressed mood (such as looking downward and moving slowly). Accordingly, each subject would be given a depressed mood score by a rater. Researchers try to guard against such ratings being products of the rater's individual biases or idiosyncrasies in judgment. This can be accomplished by having at least one other individual observe and rate the same behaviors. If consensus can be demonstrated in the ratings, the researchers can be more confident regarding the accuracy of the ratings and their conformity with the established rating system.

**JUST THINK . . .**

Can you think of a measure in which it might be desirable for different judges, scorers, or raters to have different views on what is being judged, scored, or rated?

Perhaps the simplest way of determining the degree of consistency among scorers in the scoring of a test is to calculate a coefficient of correlation. This correlation coefficient is referred to as a **coefficient of inter-scorer reliability.**

---

6. We say "usually" because exceptions do exist. Thus, for example, if you go on a job interview and the employer/interviewer is a parent or other loving relative, you might reasonably expect that the evaluation you receive would not be the same were the evaluator someone else. On the other hand, if the employer/interviewer is someone with whom you have had an awkward run-in, it may be time to revisit Monster.com, the newspaper "want ads," or any other possible source of an employment lead.

# Using and Interpreting a Coefficient of Reliability

We have seen that, with respect to the test itself, there are basically three approaches to the estimation of reliability: (1) test-retest, (2) alternate or parallel forms, and (3) internal or inter-item consistency. The method or methods employed will depend on a number of factors, such as the purpose of obtaining a measure of reliability.

Another question that is linked in no trivial way to the purpose of the test is, "How high should the coefficient of reliability be?" Perhaps the best "short answer" to this question is: "On a continuum relative to the purpose and importance of the decisions to be made on the basis of scores on the test." Reliability is a mandatory attribute in all tests we use. However, we need more of it in some tests, and we will admittedly allow for less of it in others. If a test score carries with it life-or-death implications, then we need to hold that test to some high standards—including relatively high standards with regard to coefficients of reliability. If a test score is routinely used in combination with many other test scores and typically accounts for only a small part of the decision process, that test will not be held to the highest standards of reliability. As a rule of thumb, it may be useful to think of reliability coefficients in a way that parallels many grading systems: In the .90s rates a grade of A (with a value of .95 higher for the most important types of decisions), in the .80s rates a B (with below .85 being a clear B−), and anywhere from .65 through the .70s rates a weak, "barely passing" grade that borders on failing (and unacceptable). Now, let's get a bit more technical with regard to the purpose of the reliability coefficient.

## *The Purpose of the Reliability Coefficient*

If a specific test of employee performance is designed for use at various times over the course of the employment period, it would be reasonable to expect the test to demonstrate reliability across time. It would thus be desirable to have an estimate of the instrument's test-retest reliability. For a test designed for a single administration only, an estimate of internal consistency would be the reliability measure of choice. If the purpose of determining reliability is to break down the error variance into its parts, as shown in Figure 5–2, then a number of reliability coefficients would have to be calculated.

**Figure 5–2**
**Sources of Variance in a Hypothetical Test**

*In this hypothetical situation, 5% of the variance has not been identified by the test user. It is possible, for example, that this portion of the variance could be accounted for by* **transient error,** *a source of error attributable to variations in the testtaker's feelings, moods, or mental state over time. Then again, this 5% of the error may be due to other factors that are yet to be identified.*

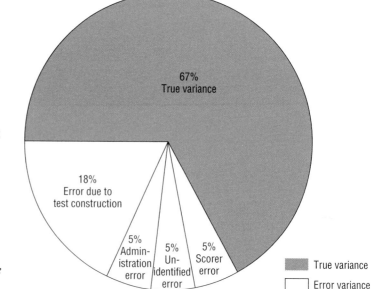

Note that the various reliability coefficients do not all reflect the same sources of error variance. Thus, an individual reliability coefficient may provide an index of error from test construction, test administration, or test scoring and interpretation. A coefficient of inter-rater reliability, for example, provides information about error as a result of test scoring. Specifically, it can be used to answer questions about how consistently two scorers score the same test items. Table 5–4 summarizes the different kinds of error variance that are reflected in different reliability coefficients.

## The Nature of the Test

Closely related to considerations concerning the purpose and use of a reliability coefficient are those concerning the nature of the test itself. Included here are considerations such as whether (1) the test items are homogeneous or heterogeneous in nature; (2) the characteristic, ability, or trait being measured is presumed to be dynamic or static; (3) the range of test scores is or is not restricted; (4) the test is a speed or a power test; and (5) the test is or is not criterion-referenced.

Some tests present special problems regarding the measurement of their reliability. For example, a number of psychological tests have been developed for use with infants to help identify children who are developing slowly or who may profit from early intervention of some sort. Measuring the internal consistency reliability or the inter-scorer reliability of such tests is accomplished in much the same way as it is with other tests. However, measuring test-retest reliability presents a unique problem. The abilities of the very young children being tested are fast-changing. It is common knowledge that

**Table 5–4**
**Summary of Reliability Types**

| Type of Reliability | Purpose | Typical uses | Number of Testing Sessions | Sources of Error Variance | Statistical Procedures |
|---|---|---|---|---|---|
| Test-retest | To evaluate the stability of a measure | When assessing the stability of various personality traits | 2 | Administration | Pearson *r* or Spearman rho |
| Alternate-forms | To evaluate the relation-ship between different forms of a measure | When there is a need for different forms of a test (e.g., makeup tests) | 1 or 2 | Test construction or administration | Pearson *r* or Spearman rho |
| Internal consistency | To evaluate the extent to which items on a scale relate to one another | When evaluating the homogeneity of a measure (i.e., all items are tapping a single construct) | 1 | Test construction | Pearson *r between equivalent test halves with Spearman Brown correction or Kuder-Richardson for dichotomous items, or coefficient alpha for multipoint items or APD* |
| Inter-scorer | To evaluate the level of agreement between rat-ers on a measure | Interviews or coding of behavior. Used when researchers need to show that there is con-sensus in the way that different raters view a particular behavior pattern (and hence no observer bias). | 1 | Scoring and interpretation | Cohen's kappa, Pearson *r* or Spearman rho |

cognitive development during the first months and years of life is both rapid and uneven. Children often grow in spurts, sometimes changing dramatically in as little as days (Hetherington & Parke, 1993). The child tested just before and again just after a developmental advance may perform very differently on the two testings. In such cases, a marked change in test score might be attributed to error when in reality it reflects a genuine change in the testtaker's skills. The challenge in gauging the test-retest reliability of such tests is to do so in such a way that it is not spuriously lowered by the testtaker's actual developmental changes between testings. In attempting to accomplish this, developers of such tests may design test-retest reliability studies with very short intervals between testings, sometimes as little as four days.

**Homogeneity versus heterogeneity of test items** Recall that a test is said to be *homogeneous* in items if it is functionally uniform throughout. Tests designed to measure one factor, such as one ability or one trait, are expected to be homogeneous in items. For such tests, it is reasonable to expect a high degree of internal consistency. By contrast, if the test is *heterogeneous* in items, an estimate of internal consistency might be low relative to a more appropriate estimate of test-retest reliability.

**Dynamic versus static characteristics** Whether what is being measured by the test is *dynamic* or *static* is also a consideration in obtaining an estimate of reliability. A **dynamic characteristic** is a trait, state, or ability presumed to be ever-changing as a function of situational and cognitive experiences. If, for example, one were to take hourly measurements of the dynamic characteristic of anxiety as manifested by a stockbroker throughout a business day, one might find the measured level of this characteristic to change from hour to hour. Such changes might even be related to the magnitude of the Dow Jones average. Because the true amount of anxiety presumed to exist would vary with each assessment, a test-retest measure would be of little help in gauging the reliability of the measuring instrument. Therefore, the best estimate of reliability would be obtained from a measure of internal consistency. Contrast this situation to one in which hourly assessments of this same stockbroker are made on a trait, state, or ability presumed to be relatively unchanging (a **static characteristic**), such as intelligence. In this instance, obtained measurement would not be expected to vary significantly as a function of time, and either the test-retest or the alternate-forms method would be appropriate.

**JUST THINK . . .**

Provide another example of both a dynamic characteristic and a static characteristic that a psychological test could measure.

**Restriction or inflation of range** In using and interpreting a coefficient of reliability, the issue variously referred to as **restriction of range** or **restriction of variance** (or, conversely, **inflation of range** or **inflation of variance**) is important. If the variance of either variable in a correlational analysis is restricted by the sampling procedure used, then the resulting correlation coefficient tends to be lower. If the variance of either variable in a correlational analysis is inflated by the sampling procedure, then the resulting correlation coefficient tends to be higher. Refer back to Figure 3–16 on page 114 (Two Scatterplots Illustrating Unrestricted and Restricted Ranges) for a graphic illustration.

Also of critical importance is whether the range of variances employed is appropriate to the objective of the correlational analysis. Consider, for example, a published educational test designed for use with children in grades 1 through 6. Ideally, the manual for this test should contain not one reliability value covering all the testtakers in grades 1 through 6 but instead reliability values for testtakers at each grade level. Here's another example: A corporate personnel officer employs a certain screening test in the hiring process.

For future testing and hiring purposes, this personnel officer maintains reliability data with respect to scores achieved by job applicants—as opposed to hired employees—in order to avoid restriction of range effects in the data. This is so because the people who were hired typically scored higher on the test than any comparable group of applicants.

**Speed tests versus power tests**   When a time limit is long enough to allow testtakers to attempt all items, and if some items are so difficult that no testtaker is able to obtain a perfect score, then the test is a **power test.** By contrast, a **speed test** generally contains items of uniform level of difficulty (typically uniformly low) so that, when given generous time limits, all testtakers should be able to complete all the test items correctly. In practice, however, the time limit on a speed test is established so that few if any of the testtakers will be able to complete the entire test. Score differences on a speed test are therefore based on performance speed because items attempted tend to be correct.

A reliability estimate of a speed test should be based on performance from two independent testing periods using one of the following: (1) test-retest reliability, (2) alternate-forms reliability, or (3) split-half reliability from *two separately timed* half tests. If a split-half procedure is used, then the obtained reliability coefficient is for a half test and should be adjusted using the Spearman-Brown formula.

Because a measure of the reliability of a speed test should reflect the consistency of response speed, the reliability of a speed test should not be calculated from a single administration of the test with a single time limit. If a speed test is administered once and some measure of internal consistency, such as the Kuder-Richardson or a split-half correlation, is calculated, the result will be a spuriously high reliability coefficient. To understand why the KR-20 or split-half reliability coefficient will be spuriously high, consider the following example.

When a group of testtakers completes a speed test, almost all the items completed will be correct. If reliability is examined using an odd-even split, and if the testtakers completed the items in order, then testtakers will get close to the same number of odd as even items correct. A testtaker completing 82 items can be expected to get approximately 41 odd and 41 even items correct. A testtaker completing 61 items may get 31 odd and 30 even items correct. When the numbers of odd and even items correct are correlated across a group of testtakers, the correlation will be close to 1.00. Yet this impressive correlation coefficient actually tells us nothing about response consistency.

Under the same scenario, a Kuder-Richardson reliability coefficient would yield a similar coefficient that would also be, well, equally useless. Recall that KR-20 reliability is based on the proportion of testtakers correct ($p$) and the proportion of testtakers incorrect ($q$) on each item. In the case of a speed test, it is conceivable that $p$ would equal 1.0 and $q$ would equal 0 for many of the items. Toward the end of the test—when many items would not even be attempted because of the time limit—$p$ might equal 0 and $q$ might equal 1.0. For many, if not a majority, of the items, then, the product $pq$ would equal or approximate 0. When 0 is substituted in the KR-20 formula for $\Sigma\,pq$, the reliability coefficient is 1.0 (a meaningless coefficient in this instance).

**Criterion-referenced tests**   A **criterion-referenced test** is designed to provide an indication of where a testtaker stands with respect to some variable or criterion, such as an educational or a vocational objective. Unlike norm-referenced tests, criterion-referenced tests tend to contain material that has been mastered in hierarchical fashion. For example, the would-be pilot masters on-ground skills before attempting to master in-flight skills. Scores on criterion-referenced tests tend to be interpreted in pass–fail (or, perhaps more accurately, "master-failed-to-master") terms, and any scrutiny of performance on individual items tends to be for diagnostic and remedial purposes.

Traditional techniques of estimating reliability employ measures that take into account scores on the entire test. Recall that a test-retest reliability estimate is based on the correlation between the total scores on two administrations of the same test. In alternate-forms reliability, a reliability estimate is based on the correlation between the two total scores on the two forms. In split-half reliability, a reliability estimate is based on the correlation between scores on two halves of the test and is then adjusted using the Spearman-Brown formula to obtain a reliability estimate of the whole test. Although there are exceptions, such traditional procedures of estimating reliability are usually not appropriate for use with criterion-referenced tests. To understand why, recall that reliability is defined as the proportion of total variance ($\sigma^2$) attributable to true variance ($\sigma^2_{th}$). Total variance in a test score distribution equals the sum of the true variance plus the error variance ($\sigma_e^2$)

$$\sigma^2 = \sigma^2_{th} + \sigma^2_e$$

A measure of reliability, therefore, depends on the variability of the test scores: how different the scores are from one another. In criterion-referenced testing, and particularly in mastery testing, how different the scores are from one another is seldom a focus of interest. In fact, individual differences between examinees on total test scores may be minimal. The critical issue for the user of a mastery test is whether or not a certain criterion score has been achieved.

As individual differences (and the variability) decrease, a traditional measure of reliability would also decrease, regardless of the stability of individual performance. Therefore, traditional ways of estimating reliability are not always appropriate for criterion-referenced tests, though there may be instances in which traditional estimates can be adopted. An example might be a situation in which the same test is being used at different stages in some program—training, therapy, or the like—and so variability in scores could reasonably be expected. Statistical techniques useful in determining the reliability of criterion-referenced tests are discussed in great detail in many sources devoted to that subject (for example, Hambleton & Jurgensen, 1990).

Are there models of measurement other than the true score model? As we will see in what follows, the answer to that question is yes. Before proceeding, however, take a moment to review a "real-life" application of reliability in measurement in this chapter's *Everyday Psychometrics*.

## *The True Score Model of Measurement and Alternatives to It*

Thus far—and throughout this book, unless specifically stated otherwise—the model we have assumed to be operative is **classical test theory** (**CTT**), also referred to as the true score (or classical) model of measurement. CTT is the most widely used and accepted model in the psychometric literature today—rumors of its demise have been greatly exaggerated (Zickar & Broadfoot, 2009). One of the reasons it has remained the most widely used model has to do with its simplicity, especially when one considers the complexity of other proposed models of measurement. Comparing CTT to IRT, for example, Streiner (2010) mused, "CTT is much simpler to understand than IRT; there aren't formidable-looking equations with exponentiations, Greek letters, and other arcane symbols" (p. 185). Additionally, the CTT notion that everyone has a "true score" on a test has had, and continues to have, great intuitive appeal. Of course, exactly how to define this elusive *true score* has been a matter of sometimes contentious debate. For our purposes, we will define **true score** as a value that according to classical test theory genuinely reflects an individual's ability (or trait) level as measured by a particular test. Let's emphasize here that this value is indeed very test dependent. A person's "true score" on one intelligence test, for example, can vary greatly from that same person's

## The Reliability Defense and the Breathalyzer Test

Breathalyzer is the generic name for a number of different instruments used by law enforcement agencies to determine if a suspect, most typically the operator of a motor vehicle, is legally drunk. The driver is required to blow into a tube attached to the breathalyzer. The breath sample then mixes with a chemical that is added to the machine for each new test. The resulting mixture is automatically analyzed for alcohol content in the breath. The value for the alcohol content in the breath is then converted to a value for blood alcohol level. Whether the testtaker is deemed to be legally drunk will vary from state to state as a function of the state law regarding the blood alcohol level necessary for a person to be declared intoxicated.

In New Jersey, the blood alcohol level required for a person to be declared legally drunk is one-tenth of 1 percent (.10%). Drivers in New Jersey found guilty of a first drunk-driving offense face fines and surcharges amounting to about $3,500, mandatory detainment in an Intoxicated Driver Resource Center, suspension of driving privileges for a minimum of six months, and a maximum of 30 days' imprisonment. Two models of a breathalyzer (Models 900 and 900A made by National Draeger, Inc.) have been used in New Jersey since the 1950s. Well-documented test-retest reliability regarding the 900 and 900A breathalyzers indicate that the instruments have a margin of error of about one-hundredth of a percentage point. This means that an administration of the test to a testtaker who in reality has a blood alcohol level of .10% (a "true score," if you will) might yield a test score anywhere from a low of .09% to a high of .11%.

A driver in New Jersey who was convicted of driving drunk appealed the decision on grounds relating to the test-retest reliability of the breathalyzer. The breathalyzer had indicated that the driver's blood alcohol level was .10%. The driver argued that the law did not take into account the margin of error inherent in the measuring instrument. However, the state supreme court ruled against the driver, finding that the legislature must have taken into consideration such error when it wrote the law.

Another issue related to the use of breathalyzers concerns where and when they are administered. In some states the test is most typically administered at police headquarters, not at the scene of the arrest. Expert witnesses were once retained on behalf of defendants to calculate what the defendant's blood alcohol was at the actual time of the arrest. Working backward from the time the test was administered, and figuring in values for

*A suspect being administered a breathalyzer test*

variables such as what the defendant had to drink and when as well as the defendant's weight, they could calculate a blood alcohol level at the time of arrest. If that level was lower than the level required for a person to be declared legally drunk, the case might be dismissed. However, in some states, such as New Jersey, this defense would not be entertained. In these states, higher courts have ruled that because the legislature was aware that breathalyzer tests would not be administered at the arrest scene, it had intended the measured blood alcohol level to apply at the time of the test's administration at police headquarters.

One final reliability-related issue regarding breathalyzers involves inter-scorer reliability. When using the 900 and 900A models, the police officer who makes the arrest also records the measured blood alcohol level. Although the vast majority of police officers are honest when it comes to such recording, there is potential for abuse. A police officer who wished to save face on a drunk-driving arrest, or even a police officer who simply wanted to add to a record of drunk-driving arrests, could record an incorrect breathalyzer value to ensure a conviction. In 1993 a police officer in Camden County, New Jersey, was convicted of and sent to prison for recording incorrect breathalyzer readings (Romano, 1994). Such an incident is representative of extremely atypical "error" entering into the assessment process.

"true score" on another intelligence test. Similarly, if "Form D" of an ability test contains items that the testtaker finds to be much more difficult than those on "Form E" of that test, then there is a good chance that the testtaker's true score on Form D will be lower than that on Form E. The same holds for true scores obtained on different tests of personality. One's true score on one test of extraversion, for example, may not bear much resemblance to one's true score on another test of extraversion. Comparing a testtaker's scores on two different tests purporting to measure the same thing requires a sophisticated knowledge of the properties of each of the two tests, as well as some rather complicated statistical procedures designed to equate the scores.

Another aspect of the appeal of CTT is that its assumptions allow for its application in most situations (Hambleton & Swaminathan, 1985). The fact that CTT assumptions are rather easily met and therefore applicable to so many measurement situations can be advantageous, especially for the test developer in search of an appropriate model of measurement for a particular application. Still, in psychometric parlance, CTT assumptions are characterized as "weak"—this precisely because its assumptions are so readily met. By contrast, the assumptions in another model of measurement, item response theory (IRT), are more difficult to meet. As a consequence, you may read of IRT assumptions being characterized in terms such as "strong," "hard," "rigorous," and "robust." A final advantage of CTT over any other model of measurement has to do with its compatibility and ease of use with widely used statistical techniques (as well as most currently available data analysis software). Factor analytic techniques, whether exploratory or confirmatory, are all "based on the CTT measurement foundation" (Zickar & Broadfoot, 2009, p. 52).

For all of its appeal, measurement experts have also listed many problems with CTT. For starters, one problem with CTT has to do with its assumption concerning the equivalence of all items on a test; that is, all items are presumed to be contributing equally to the score total. This assumption is questionable in many cases, and particularly questionable when doubt exists as to whether the scaling of the instrument in question is genuinely interval level in nature. Another problem has to do with the length of tests that are developed using a CTT model. Whereas test developers favor shorter rather than longer tests (as do most testtakers), the assumptions inherent in CTT favor the development of longer rather than shorter tests. For these reasons, as well as others, alternative measurement models have been developed. Below we briefly describe domain sampling theory and generalizability theory. We will then describe in greater detail, item response theory (IRT), a measurement model that some believe is a worthy successor to CTT (Borsbroom, 2005; Harvey & Hammer, 1999).

**Domain sampling theory and generalizability theory**    The 1950s saw the development of a viable alternative to CTT. It was originally referred to as *domain sampling theory* and is better known today in one of its many modified forms as *generalizability theory.* As set forth by Tryon (1957), the theory of domain sampling rebels against the concept of a true score existing with respect to the measurement of psychological constructs. Whereas those who subscribe to CTT seek to estimate the portion of a test score that is attributable to error, proponents of **domain sampling theory** seek to estimate the extent to which specific sources of variation under defined conditions are contributing to the test score. In domain sampling theory, a test's reliability is conceived of as an objective measure of how precisely the test score assesses the domain from which the test draws a sample (Thorndike, 1985). A *domain* of behavior, or the universe of items that could conceivably measure that behavior, can be thought of as a hypothetical construct: one that shares certain characteristics with (and is measured by) the sample of items that make up the test. In theory, the items in the domain are thought to have the same means and variances of those in the test that samples from the domain. Of the three types of estimates of reliability, measures of internal consistency are perhaps the most compatible with domain sampling theory.

In one modification of domain sampling theory called *generalizability theory*, a "universe score" replaces that of a "true score" (Shavelson et al., 1989). Developed by Lee J. Cronbach (1970) and his colleagues (Cronbach et al., 1972), **generalizability theory** is based on the idea that a person's test scores vary from testing to testing because of variables in the testing situation. Instead of conceiving of all variability in a person's scores as error, Cronbach encouraged test developers and researchers to describe the details of the particular test situation or **universe** leading to a specific test score. This universe is described in terms of its **facets,** which include things like the number of items in the test, the amount of training the test scorers have had, and the purpose of the test administration. According to generalizability theory, given the exact same conditions of all the facets in the universe, the exact same test score should be obtained. This test score is the **universe score,** and it is, as Cronbach noted, analogous to a true score in the true score model. Cronbach (1970) explained as follows:

> "What is Mary's typing ability?" This must be interpreted as "What would Mary's word processing score on this be if a large number of measurements on the test were collected and averaged?" The particular test score Mary earned is just one out of a universe of possible observations. If one of these scores is as acceptable as the next, then the mean, called the universe score and symbolized here by $M_p$ (mean for person $p$), would be the most appropriate statement of Mary's performance in the type of situation the test represents.
>
> The universe is a collection of possible measures "of the same kind," but the limits of the collection are determined by the investigator's purpose. If he needs to know Mary's typing ability on May 5 (for example, so that he can plot a learning curve that includes one point for that day), the universe would include observations on that day and on that day only. He probably does want to generalize over passages, testers, and scorers—that is to say, he would like to know Mary's ability on May 5 without reference to any particular passage, tester, or scorer. . . .
>
> The person will ordinarily have a different universe score for each universe. Mary's universe score covering tests on May 5 will not agree perfectly with her universe score for the whole month of May. . . . Some testers call the average over a large number of comparable observations a "true score"; e.g., "Mary's true typing rate on 3-minute tests." Instead, we speak of a "universe score" to emphasize that what score is desired depends on the universe being considered. For any measure there are many "true scores," each corresponding to a different universe.
>
> When we use a single observation as if it represented the universe, we are generalizing. We generalize over scorers, over selections typed, perhaps over days. If the observed scores from a procedure agree closely with the universe score, we can say that the observation is "accurate," or "reliable," or "generalizable." And since the observations then also agree with each other, we say that they are "consistent" and "have little error variance." To have so many terms is confusing, but not seriously so. The term most often used in the literature is "reliability." The author prefers "generalizability" because that term immediately implies "generalization to what?" . . . There is a different degree of generalizability for each universe. The older methods of analysis do not separate the sources of variation. They deal with a single source of variance, or leave two or more sources entangled. (Cronbach, 1970, pp. 153–154)

How can these ideas be applied? Cronbach and his colleagues suggested that tests be developed with the aid of a generalizability study followed by a decision study. A **generalizability study** examines how generalizable scores from a particular test are if the test is administered in different situations. Stated in the language of generalizability theory, a generalizability study examines how much of an impact different facets of the universe have on the test score. Is the test score affected by group as opposed to individual administration? Is the test score affected by the time of day in which the test is administered? The influence of particular facets on the test score is represented by **coefficients of generalizability.** These coefficients are similar to reliability coefficients in the true score model.

After the generalizability study is done, Cronbach et al. (1972) recommended that test developers do a decision study, which involves the application of information from the generalizability study. In the **decision study,** developers examine the usefulness of test scores in helping the test user make decisions. In practice, test scores are used to guide a variety of decisions, from placing a child in special education to hiring new employees to discharging mental patients from the hospital. The decision study is designed to tell the test user how test scores should be used and how dependable those scores are as a basis for decisions, depending on the context of their use. Why is this so important? Cronbach (1970) noted:

> The decision that a student has completed a course or that a patient is ready for termination of therapy must not be seriously influenced by chance errors, temporary variations in performance, or the tester's choice of questions. An erroneous favorable decision may be irreversible and may harm the person or the community. Even when reversible, an erroneous unfavorable decision is unjust, disrupts the person's morale, and perhaps retards his development. Research, too, requires dependable measurement. An experiment is not very informative if an observed difference could be accounted for by chance variation. Large error variance is likely to mask a scientifically important outcome. Taking a better measure improves the sensitivity of an experiment in the same way that increasing the number of subjects does. (p. 152)

Generalizability has not replaced CTT. Perhaps one of its chief contributions has been its emphasis on the fact that a test's reliability does not reside within the test itself. From the perspective of generalizability theory, a test's reliability is very much a function of the circumstances under which the test is developed, administered, and interpreted.

**Item response theory (IRT)**   Another alternative to the true score model is **item response theory** (**IRT;** Lord & Novick, 1968; Lord, 1980). The procedures of item response theory provide a way to model the probability that a person with *X* ability will be able to perform at a level of *Y.* Stated in terms of personality assessment, it models the probability that a person with *X* amount of a particular personality trait will exhibit *Y* amount of that trait on a personality test designed to measure it. Because so often the psychological or educational construct being measured is physically unobservable (stated another way, is *latent*) and because the construct being measured may be a *trait* (it could also be something else, such as an ability), a synonym for IRT in the academic literature is **latent-trait theory.** Let's note at the outset, however, that IRT is not a term used to refer to a single theory or method. Rather, it refers to a family of theories and methods—and quite a large family at that—with many other names used to distinguish specific approaches. There are well over a hundred varieties of IRT models. Each model is designed to handle data with certain assumptions and data characteristics.

Examples of two characteristics of items within an IRT framework are the *difficulty* level of an item and the item's level of *discrimination;* items may be viewed as varying in terms of these, as well as other, characteristics. "Difficulty" in this sense refers to the attribute of not being easily accomplished, solved, or comprehended. In a mathematics test, for example, a test item tapping basic addition ability will have a lower difficulty level than a test item tapping basic algebra skills. The characteristic of *difficulty* as applied to a test item may also refer to *physical* difficulty—that is, how hard or easy it is for a person to engage in a particular activity. Consider in this context three items on a hypothetical "Activities of Daily Living Questionnaire" (ADLQ), a true–false questionnaire designed to tap the extent to which respondents are physically able to participate in activities of daily living. Item 1 of this test is *I am able to walk from room to room in my home.* Item 2 is *I require assistance to sit, stand, and walk.* Item 3 is *I am able to jog one mile a day, seven days a week.* With regard to difficulty related to mobility, the respondent who answers *true* to item 1 and *false* to item 2 may be presumed to have more mobility than the respondent who answers *false* to item 1 and *true* to item 2. In classical test theory, each of these items might be scored with 1 point awarded to responses indicative of mobility and 0 points for responses indicative of a lack of mobility. Within IRT, however, responses indicative of mobility (as opposed to a lack of mobility or impaired mobility) may be assigned different weights. A *true* response to item 1 may therefore earn more points than a *false* response to item 2, and a *true* response to item 3 may earn more points than a *true* response to item 1.

In the context of IRT, **discrimination** signifies the degree to which an item differentiates among people with higher or lower levels of the trait, ability, or whatever it is that is being measured. Consider two more ADLQ items: item 4, *My mood is generally good*; and item 5, *I am able to walk one block on flat ground.* Which of these two items do you think would be more discriminating in terms of the respondent's physical abilities? If you answered "item 5" then you are correct. And if you were developing this questionnaire within an IRT framework, you would probably assign differential weight to the value of these two items. Item 5 would be given more weight for the purpose of estimating a person's level of physical activity than item 4. Again, within the context of classical test theory, all items of the test might be given equal weight and scored, for example, 1 if indicative of the ability being measured and 0 if not indicative of that ability.

A number of different IRT models exist to handle data resulting from the administration of tests with various characteristics and in various formats. For example, there are IRT models designed to handle data resulting from the administration of tests with **dichotomous test items** (test items or questions that can be answered with only one of two alternative responses, such as *true–false, yes–no,* or *correct–incorrect* questions). There are IRT models designed to handle data resulting from the administration of tests with **polytomous test items** (test items or questions with three or more alternative responses, where only one is scored correct or scored as being consistent with a targeted trait or other construct). Other IRT models exist to handle other types of data.

In general, latent-trait models differ in some important ways from CTT. For example, in CTT, no assumptions are made about the frequency distribution of test scores. By contrast, such assumptions are inherent in latent-trait models. As Allen and Yen (1979, p. 240) have pointed out, "Latent-trait theories propose models that describe how the latent trait influences performance on each test item. Unlike test scores or true scores, latent traits theoretically can take on values from $-\infty$ to $+\infty$ [negative infinity to positive infinity]." Some IRT models have very specific and stringent assumptions about the underlying distribution. In one group of IRT models developed by the Danish mathematician Georg Rasch, each item on the test is assumed to have an equivalent relationship with the construct being measured by the test. A shorthand reference to these types of models is "Rasch," so reference to the **Rasch model** is a reference to an IRT model with very specific assumptions about the underlying distribution.

The psychometric advantages of IRT have made this model appealing, especially to commercial and academic test developers and to large-scale test publishers. It is

# Item Response Theory (IRT)

Psychological and educational constructs such as intelligence, leadership, depression, self-esteem, math ability, and reading comprehension cannot be observed or touched or measured in the same physical sense that (say) fabric can be observed, touched, and measured. How then are psychological and educational constructs to be measured by tests? Different models and methods have been proposed in response to this important question. One approach focuses on the relationship between a testtaker's response to an individual test item and that testtaker's standing, in probabilistic terms, on the construct being measured. This approach is *item response theory*. The effective use of this approach requires that certain assumptions be met.

## Assumptions in Using IRT

For most applications in educational and psychological testing, there are three assumptions made regarding data to be analyzed within an IRT framework. These are the assumptions of (1) *unidimensionality,* (2) *local independence,* and (3) *monotonicity.*

### Unidimensionality
The **unidimensionality assumption** posits that the set of items measures a single continuous latent construct. This construct is referred to by the Greek letter *theta* ($\theta$). Stated another way, it is a person's *theta level* that gives rise to a response to the items in the scale. Here, **theta level** (sometimes referred to simply as "theta") is a reference to the degree of the underlying ability or trait that the testtaker is presumed to bring to the test. For example, a person's response to the question, "To what extent are you feeling fatigued right now?" should depend solely on that person's fatigue level (or theta level of fatigue) and not any other factor. The assumption of unidimensionality does not preclude that the set of items may have a number of minor dimensions (which, in turn, might be measured by subscales). However, it does assume that one dominant dimension explains the underlying structure.

### Local Independence
Before explaining what local *independence* means, it might be helpful to explain what is meant by local *dependence.* When we say that items on a test are "locally dependent," we mean that these items are all dependent on some factor that is different from what the test as a whole is measuring. For example, a test of reading comprehension might contain several reading passages on different topics. A testtaker might find all of the items dealing with a particular reading passage much easier (or much more difficult) than all of the other reading passages on the test. We would describe the items associated with that passage as *locally dependent* because they are more related to each other than to the other items on the test.

From a measurement perspective, locally dependent items on such a test may be measuring some factor other than the construct of "reading comprehension" as that construct is measured by the other items on the test. Such a situation might arise in the case where the testtaker is particularly proficient (or deficient) in whatever the subject of that particular passage is. For example, if the reading passage is about fishing and the testtaker happens to be a professional fisherman, then the passage might actually be measuring something other than reading comprehension. Locally dependent items have high inter-item correlations. In an effort to control for such local dependence, test developers may sometimes combine the responses to a set of locally dependent items into a separate subscale within the test.

With this background regarding what it means when test items are locally *dependent,* you may be able to anticipate that local *independence* is quite the opposite. The assumption of **local independence** means that (a) there is a systematic relationship between all of the test items and (b) that relationship has to do with the theta level of the testtaker. When the assumption of local independence is met, it means that differences in responses to items are reflective of differences in the underlying trait or ability.

### Monotonicity
The **assumption of monotonicity** means that the probability of endorsing or selecting an item response indicative of higher levels of theta should increase as the underlying level of theta increases. So, for example, we would expect that an extraverted respondent, in contrast to an introverted respondent, would be more likely to answer *true* to an item like *I love to party with friends on weekends*.

IRT models tend to be robust; that is, they tend to be resistant to minor violations of these three assumptions. In the "real world" it is actually difficult, if not impossible, to find data that rigorously conforms to these assumptions. Still, the better the data meets these three assumptions, the better the IRT model will fit the data and shed light on the construct being measured. With an understanding of the applicable assumptions firmly in mind, let's proceed to illustrate how IRT can work in practice.

## IRT in Practice

The probabilistic relationship between a testtaker's response to a test item and that testtaker's level on the latent construct being measured by the test is expressed in graphic form by what has been variously referred to as an **item characteristic curve (ICC)**, an *item response curve*, a *category response curve*, or an *item trace line*. An example of such a graph—we'll refer to it here as an ICC—is presented in Figure 1, the ICC for one true–false item ("I am unhappy some of the time") on a clinical measure of depressive symptoms. The "latent trait" being measured is depressive symptomatology, so theta ($\theta$) is used to label the horizontal axis. For the purposes of this illustration, let's say that the mean depression level of the study population is set at 0 and the standard deviation is set at 1. The numbers along the $\theta$-axis are expressed in standard deviation units ranging from 3 standard deviations below the mean to 3 standard deviations above the mean. This scale is akin to *z* scores, and in theory, theta scores could range from negative infinity to positive infinity. A score of 2 on the item depicted in Figure 1 would indicate that a testtaker's level of depressive symptoms falls 2 standard deviations above the population mean, a score indicating that the testtaker is experiencing severe depressive symptoms.

The vertical axis in Figure 1 indicates the probability, bounded between 0 and 1, that a person will select

one of the item's response categories. Thus, the two response curves in Figure 1 indicate that the probability of responding *false* or *true* to the item "I am unhappy some of the time" depends on the respondent's level of depressive symptomatology. As would be expected, testtakers who are indeed depressed would have a high probability of selecting *true* for this item, whereas those with lower depressive symptomatology would be more likely to select *false*.

Another useful feature of IRT is that it enables test users to better understand the range over theta for which an item is most useful in discriminating among groups of testtakers. The IRT tool used to make such determinations is the **information function** (or *information curve*), which is illustrated in Figure 2. Graphs of the information function provide insight into what items work best with testtakers at a particular theta level as compared to other items on the test. Traditionally in such graphs, theta is set on the horizontal axis and information magnitude (that is, precision) on the vertical axis.

Figure 2 provides a glimpse at what is referred to in the language of IRT as *information* (the precision of measurement) of three test items for evaluating testtakers at different levels of theta. Presumably, the more information, the better the predictions made. As can be seen from the graph, the item "I don't seem to care what happens to me" is informative for measuring *high levels* of depressive symptomatology. The item "I am unhappy some of the time" is informative for measuring *moderate* depressive

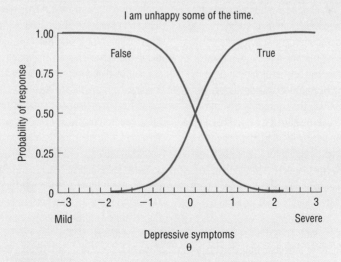

**Figure 1**
**ICC for One True–False Item on a Measure of Depressive Symptomatology**

*(continued)*

# Item Response Theory (IRT) *(continued)*

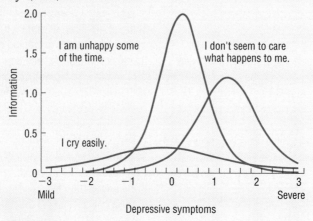

**Figure 2**
**Information Function for Three Test Items on a Measure of Depressive Symptomatology**

symptomatology. The item "I cry easily" is not informative for measuring any level relative to the other items.

An item information curve can be a very useful tool for test developers. It is used, for example, to reduce the total number of test items in a "long form" of a test and so create a new and effective "short form." Shorter versions of tests are created through selection of the most informative set of items (questions) that are relevant for the population under study. For example, a researcher working with a clinically depressed population might select only items with information curves that are peaked in the high levels of depressive symptoms.

An information curve can also be useful in terms of raising "red flags" regarding test items that are particularly low in information; that is, test items that evidence relatively little ability to discriminate between testtakers from various groups. Items with low information (that is, little discriminative ability) prompt the test developer to consider the possibility that (1) the content of the item does not match the construct measured by the other items in the scale, (2) the item is poorly worded and needs to be rewritten, (3) the item is too complex for the educational level of the population, (4) the placement of the item in the test is out of context, or (5) cultural factors may be operating to weaken the item's ability to discriminate between groups.

To elaborate on the latter point, consider the item "I cry easily." Such an item might have little discriminative value if administered to Ethiopian testtakers—despite the fact that members of this sample might otherwise evidence signs of extreme depression on other tools of assessment

such as a clinical interview. The reason for this discrepancy involves cultural teachings regarding the outward expression of emotion. Researchers exploring emotional suffering in postwar Ethiopia have noted that authoritative religious sources in the area caution against any outward expression of distress (Nordanger, 2007). In fact, the Ethiopians studied had been taught that crying can engender negative spiritual and physical consequences.

Figure 3 provides an illustration of how individual item information functions can be summed across all of the items in a scale to produce what would then be referred to as a scale (or test) information function. The test information function presented in Figure 3 is for a 57-item measure of depression. Along with the information magnitude indicated along the vertical axis in the graph, the associated reliability ($r$) is provided. Overall, the scale is highly reliable for measuring moderate to severe levels of depression (i.e., when the curve is above reliability $r = .90$). However, the information function shows that scale precision worsens for measuring persons with low levels of depressive symptomatology.

Let's step back at this juncture and contrast IRT to classical test theory with regard to the evaluation of a test's reliability. From the classical perspective, we might check the reliability of this 57-item scale by using, for example, an index of internal consistency such as coefficient alpha. If we did, we would find that the estimated coefficient alpha in a psychiatric sample was .92—quite high. But does this indicate that the depression scale is reliable in the assessment of any level of depressive symptomatology?

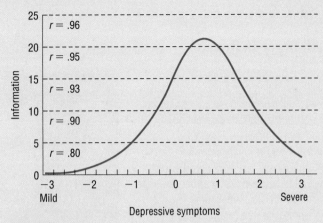

**Figure 3**
**Scale Information Function for a 57-Item Measure of Depressive Symptomatology**

The test information curve tells us that the depression scale is highly reliable for assessing moderate to severe levels of depressive symptomatology but has poor precision for assessing mild levels of depressive symptoms. Thus, under the IRT framework, the precision of a scale varies depending on what levels of the construct are being measured. We can illustrate this using another kind of test—say, one that measures educational achievement in mathematics. A test of advanced calculus may be very precise for differentiating among excellent math students but have low precision (or high measurement error) in differentiating students with more limited mathematical knowledge and abilities; testtakers in the latter group would quite likely answer every item on the test incorrectly. So, although an evaluation of this test's internal consistency might suggest it was highly reliable, an IRT-savvy test user might respond by asking: "Yes, but reliable for use with whom?" In many situations, then, an IRT measure of precision will be more useful than a single indicator of internal consistency.

a model that in recent years has found increasing application in standardized tests, professional licensing examinations, and questionnaires used in behavioral and social sciences (De Champlain, 2010). However, the mathematical sophistication of the approach has made it out of reach for many everyday users of tests such as classroom teachers or "mom and pop" employers (Reise & Henson, 2003). To learn more about the approach that has fostered "new rules of measurement" for ability testing (Roid, 2006), read this chapter's *Close-Up*. Also, in our *Meet an Assessment Professional* feature, you will meet a "real life" user of IRT, Dr. Bryce B. Reeve.

## Reliability and Individual Scores

The reliability coefficient helps the test developer build an adequate measuring instrument, and it helps the test user select a suitable test. However, the usefulness of the reliability coefficient does not end with test construction and selection. By employing the reliability coefficient in the formula for the standard error of measurement, the test user now has another descriptive statistic relevant to test interpretation, this one useful in estimating the precision of a particular test score.

## Meet Dr. Bryce B. Reeve

I use my skills and training as a psychometrician to design questionnaires and studies to capture the burden of cancer and its treatment on patients and their families. . . . The types of questionnaires I help to create measure a person's health-related quality of life (HRQOL). HRQOL is a multidimensional construct capturing such domains as physical functioning, mental well-being, and social well-being. Different cancer types and treatments for those cancers may have different impact on the magnitude and which HRQOL domain is affected. All cancers can impact a person's mental health with documented increases in depressive symptoms and anxiety. . . . There may also be positive impacts of cancer as some cancer survivors experience greater social well-being and appreciation of life. Thus, our challenge is to develop valid and precise measurement tools that capture these changes in patients' lives. Psychometrically strong measures also allow us to evaluate the impact of new behavioral or pharmacological interventions developed to improve quality of life. Because many patients in our research studies are ill, it is important to have very brief questionnaires to minimize their burden responding to a battery of questionnaires.

. . . we . . . use both qualitative and quantitative methodologies to design . . . HRQOL instruments. We use qualitative methods like focus groups and cognitive interviewing to make sure we have captured the experiences and perspectives of cancer patients and to write questions that are comprehendible to people with low literacy skills or people of different cultures. We use quantitative methods to examine how well individual questions and scales perform for measuring the HRQOL domains. Specifically, we use classical test theory, factor analysis, and item response theory (IRT) to: (1) develop and refine questionnaires; (2) identify the performance of instruments across different age groups, males and females, and cultural/racial groups; and (3) to develop

**Bryce B. Reeve, Ph.D., U.S. National Cancer Institute**

item banks which allow for creating standardized questionnaires or administering computerized adaptive testing (CAT).

I use IRT models to get an in-depth look as to how questions and scales perform in our cancer research studies. [Using IRT], we were able to reduce a burdensome 21-item scale down to a brief 10-item scale. . . .

Differential item function (DIF) is a key methodology to identify . . . biased items in questionnaires. I have used IRT modeling to examine DIF in item responses on many HRQOL questionnaires. It is especially important to evaluate DIF in questionnaires that have been translated to multiple languages for the purpose of conducting international research studies. An instrument may be translated to have the same words in multiple languages, but the words themselves may have entirely different meaning to people of different cultures. For example, researchers at the University of Massachusetts found Chinese respondents gave lower satisfaction ratings of their medical doctors than non-Chinese. In a review of the translation, the "Excellent" response category translated into Chinese as "God-like." IRT modeling gives me the ability to not only detect DIF items, but the flexibility to correct for bias as well. I can use IRT to look at unadjusted and adjusted IRT scores to see the effect of the DIF item without removing the item from the scale if the item is deemed relevant. . . .

The greatest challenges I found to greater application or acceptance of IRT methods in health care research are the complexities of the models themselves and lack of easy-to-understand resources and tools to train researchers. Many researchers have been trained in classical test theory statistics, are comfortable interpreting these statistics, and can use readily available software to generate easily familiar summary statistics, such as Cronbach's coefficient $\alpha$ or item-total correlations.

In contrast, IRT modeling requires an advanced knowledge of measurement theory to understand the mathematical complexities of the models, to determine whether the assumptions of the IRT models are met, and to choose the model from within the large family of IRT models that best fits the data and the measurement task at hand. In addition, the supporting software and literature are not well adapted for researchers outside the field of educational testing.

*Read more of what Dr. Reeve had to say—his complete essay—at www.mhhe.com/cohentesting8.*

## The Standard Error of Measurement

The *standard error of measurement,* often abbreviated as *SEM* or $SE_M$, provides a measure of the precision of an observed test score. Stated another way, it provides an estimate of the amount of error inherent in an observed score or measurement. In general, the relationship between the SEM and the reliability of a test is inverse; the higher the reliability of a test (or individual subtest within a test), the lower the SEM.

To illustrate the utility of the SEM, let's revisit The Rochester Wrenchworks (TRW) and reintroduce Mary (from Cronbach's excerpt earlier in this chapter), who is now applying for a job as a word processor. To be hired at TRW as a word processor, a candidate must be able to word-process accurately at the rate of 50 words per minute. The personnel office administers a total of seven brief word-processing tests to Mary over the course of seven business days. In words per minute, Mary's scores on each of the seven tests are as follows:

$$52 \quad 55 \quad 39 \quad 56 \quad 35 \quad 50 \quad 54$$

If you were in charge of hiring at TRW and you looked at these seven scores, you might logically ask, "Which of these scores is the best measure of Mary's 'true' word-processing ability?" And more to the point, "Which is her 'true' score?"

The "true" answer to this question is that we cannot conclude with absolute certainty from the data we have exactly what Mary's true word-processing ability is. We can, however, make an educated guess. Our educated guess would be that her true word-processing ability is equal to the mean of the distribution of her word-processing scores plus or minus a number of points accounted for by error in the measurement process. We do not know how many points are accounted for by error in the measurement process. The best we can do is estimate how much error entered into a particular test score.

The **standard error of measurement** is the tool used to estimate or infer the extent to which an observed score deviates from a true score. We may define the standard error of measurement as the standard deviation of a theoretically normal distribution of test scores obtained by one person on equivalent tests. Also known as the **standard error of a score** and denoted by the symbol $\sigma_{meas}$, the standard error of measurement is an index of the extent to which one individual's scores vary over tests presumed to be parallel. In accordance with the true score model, an obtained test score represents one point in the theoretical distribution of scores the testtaker could have obtained. But where on the continuum of possible scores is this obtained score? If the standard deviation for the distribution of test scores is known (or can be calculated) and if an estimate of the reliability of the test is known (or can be calculated), then an estimate of the standard error of a particular score (that is, the standard error of measurement) can be determined by the following formula:

$$\sigma_{meas} = \sigma\sqrt{1 - r_{xx}}$$

where $\sigma_{meas}$ is equal to the standard error of measurement, $\sigma$ is equal to the standard deviation of test scores by the group of testtakers, and $r_{xx}$ is equal to the reliability coefficient of the test. The standard error of measurement allows us to estimate, with a specific level of confidence, the range in which the true score is likely to exist.

If, for example, a spelling test has a reliability coefficient of .84 and a standard deviation of 10, then

$$\sigma_{meas} = 10\sqrt{1 - .84} = 4$$

In order to use the standard error of measurement to estimate the range of the true score, we make an assumption: If the individual were to take a large number of equivalent tests, scores on those tests would tend to be normally distributed, with the individual's true score as the mean. Because the standard error of measurement functions like a standard deviation in this context, we can use it to predict what would happen if an individual took additional equivalent tests:

- approximately 68% (actually, 68.26%) of the scores would be expected to occur within $\pm 1\sigma_{meas}$ of the true score;
- approximately 95% (actually, 95.44%) of the scores would be expected to occur within $\pm 2\sigma_{meas}$ of the true score;
- approximately 99% (actually, 99.74%) of the scores would be expected to occur within $\pm 3\sigma_{meas}$ of the true score.

Of course, we don't know the true score for any individual testtaker, so we must estimate it. The best estimate available of the individual's true score on the test is the test score already obtained. Thus, if a student achieved a score of 50 on one spelling test and if the test had a standard error of measurement of 4, then—using 50 as the point estimate—we can be:

- 68% (actually, 68.26%) confident that the true score falls within $50 \pm 1\sigma_{meas}$ (or between 46 and 54, including 46 and 54);
- 95% (actually, 95.44%) confident that the true score falls within $50 \pm 2\sigma_{meas}$ (or between 42 and 58, including 42 and 58);
- 99% (actually, 99.74%) confident that the true score falls within $50 \pm 3\sigma_{meas}$ (or between 38 and 62, including 38 and 62).

The standard error of measurement, like the reliability coefficient, is one way of expressing test reliability. If the standard deviation of a test is held constant, then the smaller the $\sigma_{meas}$, the more reliable the test will be; as $r_{xx}$ increases, the $\sigma_{meas}$ decreases. For example, when a reliability coefficient equals .64 and $\sigma$ equals 15, the standard error of measurement equals 9:

$$\sigma_{meas} = 15\sqrt{1 - .64} = 9$$

With a reliability coefficient equal to .96 and $\sigma$ still equal to 15, the standard error of measurement decreases to 3:

$$\sigma_{meas} = 15\sqrt{1 - .96} = 3$$

In practice, the standard error of measurement is most frequently used in the interpretation of individual test scores. For example, intelligence tests are given as part of the assessment of individuals for mental retardation. One of the criteria for mental retardation is an IQ score of 70 or below (when the mean is 100 and the standard deviation is 15) on an individually administered intelligence test (American Psychiatric Association, 1994). One question that could be asked about these tests is how scores that are close to the cutoff value of 70 should be treated. Specifically, how high above 70 must a score be for us to conclude confidently that the individual is unlikely to be retarded? Is 72 clearly above the retarded range, so that if the person were to take a parallel form of the test, we could be confident that the second score would be above 70? What about a score of 75? A score of 79?

Useful in answering such questions is an estimate of the amount of error in an observed test score. The standard error of measurement provides such an estimate. Further, the standard error of measurement is useful in establishing what is called a **confidence interval:** a range or band of test scores that is likely to contain the true score.

Consider an application of a confidence interval with one hypothetical measure of adult intelligence. The manual for the test provides a great deal of information relevant to the reliability of the test as a whole as well as more specific reliability-related information for each of its subtests. As reported in the manual, the standard deviation is 3 for the subtest scaled scores and 15 for IQ scores. Across all of the age groups in the normative sample, the average reliability coefficient for the Full Scale IQ (FSIQ) is .98, and the average standard error of measurement for the FSIQ is 2.3.

Knowing an individual testtaker's FSIQ score and his or her age, we can calculate a confidence interval. For example, suppose a 22-year-old testtaker obtained a FSIQ of 75. The test user can be 95% confident that this testtaker's true FSIQ falls in the range of 70 to 80. This is so because the 95% confidence interval is set by taking the observed score of 75, plus or minus 1.96, multiplied by the standard error of measurement. In the test manual we find that the standard error of measurement of the FSIQ for a 22-year-old testtaker is 2.37. With this information in hand, the 95% confidence interval is calculated as follows:

$$75 \pm 1.96\sigma_{meas} = 75 \pm 1.96(2.37) = 75 \pm 4.645$$

The calculated interval of 4.645 is rounded to the nearest whole number, 5. We can therefore be 95% confident that this testtaker's true FSIQ on this particular test of intelligence lies somewhere in the range of the observed score of 75 plus or minus 5, or somewhere in the range of 70 to 80.

In the interest of increasing your SEM "comfort level," consider the data presented in Table 5–5. These are SEMs for selected age ranges and selected types of IQ measurements as reported in the *Technical Manual for the Stanford-Binet Intelligence Scales*, fifth edition (SB5). When presenting these and related data, Roid (2003c, p. 65) noted: "Scores that are more precise and consistent have smaller differences between true and observed scores, resulting in lower SEMs." Given this, *just think:* What hypotheses come to mind regarding SB5 IQ scores at ages 5, 10, 15, and 80+?

The standard error of measurement can be used to set the confidence interval for a particular score or to determine whether a score is significantly different from a

**Table 5-5**
**Standard Errors of Measurement of SB5 IQ Scores at Ages 5, 10, 15, and 80+**

| IQ Type | Age (in years) | | | |
|---|---|---|---|---|
| | 5 | 10 | 15 | 80+ |
| Full Scale IQ | 2.12 | 2.60 | 2.12 | 2.12 |
| Nonverbal IQ | 3.35 | 2.67 | 3.00 | 3.00 |
| Verbal IQ | 3.00 | 3.35 | 3.00 | 2.60 |
| Abbreviated Battery IQ | 4.24 | 5.20 | 4.50 | 3.00 |

criterion (such as the cutoff score of 70 described previously). But the standard error of measurement cannot be used to compare scores. So, how do test users compare scores?

## The Standard Error of the Difference Between Two Scores

Error related to any of the number of possible variables operative in a testing situation can contribute to a change in a score achieved on the same test, or a parallel test, from one administration of the test to the next. The amount of error in a specific test score is embodied in the standard error of measurement. But scores can change from one testing to the next for reasons other than error.

True differences in the characteristic being measured can also affect test scores. These differences may be of great interest, as in the case of a personnel officer who must decide which of many applicants to hire. Indeed, such differences may be hoped for, as in the case of a psychotherapy researcher who hopes to prove the effectiveness of a particular approach to therapy. Comparisons between scores are made using the **standard error of the difference,** a statistical measure that can aid a test user in determining how large a difference should be before it is considered statistically significant. As you are probably aware from your course in statistics, custom in the field of psychology dictates that if the probability is more than 5% that the difference occurred by chance, then, for all intents and purposes, it is presumed that there was no difference. A more rigorous standard is the 1% standard. Applying the 1% standard, no statistically significant difference would be deemed to exist unless the observed difference could have occurred by chance alone less than one time in a hundred.

The standard error of the difference between two scores can be the appropriate statistical tool to address three types of questions:

1. How did this individual's performance on test 1 compare with his or her performance on test 2?

2. How did this individual's performance on test 1 compare with someone else's performance on test 1?

3. How did this individual's performance on test 1 compare with someone else's performance on test 2?

As you might have expected, when comparing scores achieved on the different tests, it is essential that the scores be converted to the same scale. The formula for the standard error of the difference between two scores is

$$\sigma_{\text{diff}} = \sqrt{\sigma^2_{\text{meas 1}} + \sigma^2_{\text{meas 2}}}$$

where $\sigma_{\text{diff}}$ is the standard error of the difference between two scores, is the squared standard error of measurement for test 1, and is the squared standard error of measurement for test 2. If we substitute reliability coefficients for the standard errors of measurement of the separate scores, the formula becomes

$$\sigma_{\text{diff}} = \sigma\sqrt{2 - r_1 - r_2}$$

where $r_1$ is the reliability coefficient of test 1, $r_2$ is the reliability coefficient of test 2, and $\sigma$ is the standard deviation. Note that both tests would have the same standard deviation because they must be on the same scale (or be converted to the same scale) before a comparison can be made.

The standard error of the difference between two scores will be larger than the standard error of measurement for either score alone because the former is affected by measurement error in both scores. This also makes good sense: If two scores each contain error such that in each case the true score could be higher or lower, then we would want the two scores to be further apart before we conclude that there is a significant difference between them.

The value obtained by calculating the standard error of the difference is used in much the same way as the standard error of the mean. If we wish to be 95% confident that the two scores are different, we would want them to be separated by 2 standard errors of the difference. A separation of only 1 standard error of the difference would give us 68% confidence that the two true scores are different.

As an illustration of the use of the standard error of the difference between two scores, consider the situation of a corporate personnel manager who is seeking a highly responsible person for the position of vice president of safety. The personnel officer in this hypothetical situation decides to use a new published test we will call the Safety-Mindedness Test (SMT) to screen applicants for the position. After placing an ad in the employment section of the local newspaper, the personnel officer tests 100 applicants for the position using the SMT. The personnel officer narrows the search for the vice president to the two highest scorers on the SMT: Moe, who scored 125, and Larry, who scored 134. Assuming the measured reliability of this test to be .92 and its standard deviation to be 14, should the personnel officer conclude that Larry performed significantly better than Moe? To answer this question, first calculate the standard error of the difference:

$$\sigma_{\text{diff}} = 14\sqrt{2 - .92 - .92} = 14\sqrt{.16} = 5.6$$

Note that in this application of the formula, the two test reliability coefficients are the same because the two scores being compared are derived from the same test.

What does this standard error of the difference mean? For any standard error of the difference, we can be:

- 68% confident that two scores differing by $1\sigma_{\text{diff}}$ represent true score differences;
- 95% confident that two scores differing by $2\sigma_{\text{diff}}$ represent true score differences;
- 99.7% confident that two scores differing by $3\sigma_{\text{diff}}$ represent true score differences.

Applying this information to the standard error of the difference just computed for the SMT, we see that the personnel officer can be:

- 68% confident that two scores differing by 5.6 represent true score differences;
- 95% confident that two scores differing by 11.2 represent true score differences;
- 99.7% confident that two scores differing by 16.8 represent true score differences.

**JUST THINK . . .**

With all of this talk about Moe, Larry, and Curly, please tell us that you have not forgotten about Mary. You know, Mary from the Cronbach quote on page 167—yes, that Mary. Should she get the job at TRW? If your instructor thinks it would be useful to do so, do the math before responding.

The difference between Larry's and Moe's scores is only 9 points, not a large enough difference for the personnel officer to conclude with 95% confidence that the two individuals have true scores that differ on this test. Stated another way: If Larry and Moe were to take a parallel form of the SMT, then the personnel officer could not be 95% confident that, at the next testing, Larry would again outperform Moe. The personnel officer in this example would have to resort to other means to decide whether Moe, Larry, or someone else would be the best candidate for the position (Curly has been patiently waiting in the wings).

As a postscript to the preceding example, suppose Larry got the job primarily on the basis of data from our hypothetical SMT. And let's further suppose that it soon became all too clear that Larry was the hands-down absolute worst vice president of safety that the company had ever seen. Larry spent much of his time playing practical jokes on fellow corporate officers, and he spent many of his off-hours engaged in his favorite pastime, flagpole sitting. The personnel officer might then have very good reason to question how well the instrument called the Safety-Mindedness Test truly measured safety-mindedness. Or, to put it another way, the personnel officer might question the *validity* of the test. Not coincidentally, the subject of test validity is taken up in the next chapter.

## Self-Assessment

Test your understanding of elements of this chapter by seeing if you can explain each of the following terms, expressions, and abbreviations:

alternate forms
alternate-forms reliability
assumption of local
    independence (in IRT)
assumption of monotonicity (in
    IRT)
assumption of unidimensionality
    (in IRT)
average proportional distance
    (APD)
classical test theory (CTT)
coefficient alpha
coefficient of equivalence
coefficient of generalizability
coefficient of inter-scorer
    reliability
coefficient of stability
confidence interval
content sampling
criterion-referenced test
decision study
dichotomous test item
discrimination
domain sampling theory

dynamic characteristic
error variance
estimate of inter-item consistency
facet
generalizability study
generalizability theory
heterogeneity
homogeneity
inflation of range/variance
information function
inter-item consistency
internal consistency estimate of
    reliability
inter-scorer reliability
item characteristic curve (ICC)
item response theory (IRT)
item sampling
Kuder-Richardson formula 20
latent-trait theory
measurement error
odd-even reliability
parallel forms
parallel-forms reliability
polytomous test item

power test
random error
Rasch model
reliability
reliability coefficient
restriction of range/variance
Spearman-Brown formula
speed test
split-half reliability
standard error of a score
standard error of measurement
standard error of the
    difference
static characteristic
systematic error
test battery
test-retest reliability
theta level (in IRT)
transient error
true score
true variance
universe
universe score
variance

# 6

# *Validity*

In everyday language we say that something is valid if it is sound, meaningful, or well grounded on principles or evidence. For example, we speak of a valid theory, a valid argument, or a valid reason. In legal terminology, lawyers say that something is valid if it is "executed with the proper formalities" (Black, 1979), such as a valid contract and a valid will. In each of these instances, people make judgments based on evidence of the meaningfulness or the veracity of something. Similarly, in the language of psychological assessment, *validity* is a term used in conjunction with the meaningfulness of a test score—what the test score truly means.

## The Concept of Validity

**Validity,** as applied to a test, is a judgment or estimate of how well a test measures what it purports to measure in a particular context. More specifically, it is a judgment based on evidence about the appropriateness of inferences drawn from test scores.[1] An **inference** is a logical result or deduction. Characterizations of the validity of tests and test scores are frequently phrased in terms such as "acceptable" or "weak." These terms reflect a judgment about how adequately the test measures what it purports to measure.

Inherent in a judgment of an instrument's validity is a judgment of how useful the instrument is for a particular purpose with a particular population of people. As a shorthand, assessors may refer to a particular test as a "valid test." However, what is really meant is that the test has been shown to be valid for a particular use with a particular population of testtakers at a particular time. No test or measurement technique is "universally valid" for all time, for all uses, with all types of testtaker populations. Rather, tests may be shown to be valid within what we would characterize as *reasonable boundaries* of a contemplated usage. If those boundaries are exceeded, the validity of the test may be called into question.

> **JUST THINK . . .**
>
> Why is the phrase *valid test* sometimes misleading?

---

1. Recall from Chapter 1 that the word *test* is used throughout this book in the broadest possible sense. It may therefore also apply to measurement procedures and processes that, strictly speaking, would not be referred to colloquially as "tests."

Further, to the extent that the validity of a test may diminish as the culture or the times change, the validity of a test must be proven again from time to time.

**Validation** is the process of gathering and evaluating evidence about validity. Both the test developer and the test user may play a role in the validation of a test for a specific purpose. It is the test developer's responsibility to supply validity evidence in the test manual. It may sometimes be appropriate for test users to conduct their own **validation studies** with their own groups of testtakers. Such *local validation studies* may yield insights regarding a particular population of testtakers as compared to the norming sample described in a test manual. **Local validation studies** are absolutely necessary when the test user plans to alter in some way the format, instructions, language, or content of the test. For example, a local validation study would be necessary if the test user sought to transform a nationally standardized test into Braille for administration to blind and visually impaired testtakers. Local validation studies would also be necessary if a test user sought to use a test with a population of testtakers that differed in some significant way from the population on which the test was standardized.

**JUST THINK . . .**

Local validation studies require professional time and know-how, and they may be costly. For these reasons, they might not be done even if they are desirable or necessary. What would you recommend to a test user who is in no position to conduct such a local validation study but who nonetheless is contemplating the use of a test that requires one?

One way measurement specialists have traditionally conceptualized validity is according to three categories:

1. *Content validity.* This is a measure of validity based on an evaluation of the subjects, topics, or content covered by the items in the test.

2. *Criterion-related validity.* This is a measure of validity obtained by evaluating the relationship of scores obtained on the test to scores on other tests or measures

3. *Construct validity.* This is a measure of validity that is arrived at by executing a comprehensive analysis of

   a. how scores on the test relate to other test scores and measures, and

   b. how scores on the test can be understood within some theoretical framework for understanding the construct that the test was designed to measure.

In this classic conception of validity, referred to as the *trinitarian* view (Guion, 1980), it might be useful to visualize construct validity as being "umbrella validity" because every other variety of validity falls under it. Why construct validity is the overriding variety of validity will become clear as we discuss what makes a test valid and the methods and procedures used in validation. Indeed, there are many ways of approaching the process of test validation, and these different plans of attack are often referred to as *strategies*. We speak, for example, of *content validation strategies, criterion-related validation strategies,* and *construct validation strategies.*

Trinitarian approaches to validity assessment are not mutually exclusive. That is, each of the three conceptions of validity provides evidence that, with other evidence, contributes to a judgment concerning the validity of a test. Stated another way, all three types of validity evidence contribute to a unified picture of a test's validity. A test user may not need to know about all three. Depending on the use to which a test is being put, one type of validity evidence may be more relevant than another.

The trinitarian model of validity is not without its critics (Landy, 1986). Messick (1995), for example, condemned this approach as fragmented and incomplete. He called for a unitary view of validity, one that takes into account everything from the implications of test scores in terms of societal values to the consequences of test use. However, even in the so-called unitary view, different elements of validity may come to the fore for scrutiny, and so an understanding of those elements in isolation is necessary.

In this chapter we discuss content validity, criterion-related validity, and construct validity; three now-classic approaches to judging whether a test measures what it purports to measure. Let's note at the outset that, although the trinitarian model focuses on three types of validity, you are likely to come across other varieties of validity in your readings. For example, you are likely to come across terms such as *predictive validity* and *concurrent validity*. We discuss these terms later in this chapter in the context of *criterion-related validity*. Another term you may come across in the literature is *face validity* (see Figure 6–1). In fact, you will come across that term right now . . .

## Face Validity

**Face validity** relates more to what a test *appears* to measure to the person being tested than to what the test actually measures. Face validity is a judgment concerning how relevant the test items appear to be. Stated another way, if a test definitely appears to measure what it purports to measure "on the face of it," then it could be said to be high in face validity. A paper-and-pencil personality test labeled The Introversion/Extraversion Test, with items that ask respondents whether they have acted in an introverted or an extraverted way in particular situations, may be perceived by respondents as a highly face-valid test. On the other hand, a personality test in which respondents are asked to report what they see in inkblots may be perceived as a test with low face validity. Many respondents would be left wondering how what they said they saw in the inkblots really had anything at all to do with personality.

**Figure 6–1**
**Face Validity and Comedian Rodney Dangerfield**

*Rodney Dangerfield (1921–2004) was famous for complaining, "I don't get no respect." Somewhat analogously, the concept of face validity has been described as the "Rodney Dangerfield of psychometric variables" because it has "received little attention—and even less respect—from researchers examining the construct validity of psychological tests and measures" (Bornstein et al., 1994, p. 363). By the way, the tombstone of this beloved stand-up comic and film actor reads: "Rodney Dangerfield . . . There goes the neighborhood."*

In contrast to judgments about the reliability of a test and judgments about the content, construct, or criterion-related validity of a test, judgments about face validity are frequently thought of from the perspective of the testtaker, not the test user. A test's *lack* of face validity could contribute to a lack of confidence in the perceived effectiveness of the test—with a consequential decrease in the testtaker's cooperation or motivation to do his or her best. In a corporate environment, lack of face validity may lead to unwillingness of administrators or managers to "buy in" to the use of a particular test (see this chapter's *Meet an Assessment Professional*). In a similar vein, parents may object to having their children tested with instruments that lack ostensible validity. Such concern might stem from a belief that the use of such tests will result in invalid conclusions.

**JUST THINK . . .**

What is the value of face validity from the perspective of the test user?

In reality, a test that lacks face validity may still be relevant and useful. However, if the test is not perceived as relevant and useful by testtakers, parents, legislators, and others, then negative consequences may result. These consequences may range from poor testtaker attitude to lawsuits filed by disgruntled parties against a test user and test publisher. Ultimately, face validity may be more a matter of public relations than psychometric soundness. Still, it is important nonetheless, and (much like Rodney Dangerfield) deserving of respect.

## Content Validity

**Content validity** describes a judgment of how adequately a test samples behavior representative of the universe of behavior that the test was designed to sample. For example, the universe of behavior referred to as *assertive* is very wide-ranging. A content-valid, paper-and-pencil test of assertiveness would be one that is adequately representative of this wide range. We might expect that such a test would contain items sampling from hypothetical situations at home (such as whether the respondent has difficulty in making her or his views known to fellow family members), on the job (such as whether the respondent has difficulty in asking subordinates to do what is required of them), and in social situations (such as whether the respondent would send back a steak not done to order in a fancy restaurant). Ideally, test developers have a clear (as opposed to "fuzzy") vision of the construct being measured, and the clarity of this vision can be reflected in the content validity of the test (Haynes et al., 1995). In the interest of ensuring content validity, test developers strive to include key components of the construct targeted for measurement, and exclude content irrelevant to the construct targeted for measurement.

With respect to educational achievement tests, it is customary to consider a test a content-valid measure when the proportion of material covered by the test approximates the proportion of material covered in the course. A cumulative final exam in introductory statistics would be considered content-valid if the proportion and type of introductory statistics problems on the test approximates the proportion and type of introductory statistics problems presented in the course.

The early stages of a test being developed for use in the classroom—be it one classroom or those throughout the state or the nation—typically entail research exploring the universe of possible instructional objectives for the course. Included among the many possible sources of information on such objectives are course syllabi, course textbooks, teachers of the course, specialists who develop curricula, and professors and supervisors who train teachers in the particular subject area. From the pooled information (along with the judgment of the test developer), there emerges a **test blueprint** for the "structure" of the evaluation—that is, a plan regarding the types of information to be covered

## Meet Dr. Adam Shoemaker

In the "real world," tests require buy-in from test administrators and candidates. While the reliability and validity of the test are always of primary importance, the test process can be short-circuited by administrators who don't know how to use the test or who don't have a good understanding of test theory. So at least half the battle of implementing a new testing tool is to make sure administrators know how to use it, accept the way that it works, and feel comfortable that it is tapping the skills and abilities necessary for the candidate to do the job.

Here's an example: Early in my company's history of using online assessments, we piloted a test that had acceptable reliability and criterion validity. We saw some strongly significant correlations between scores on the test and objective performance numbers, suggesting that this test did a good job of distinguishing between high and low performers on the job. The test proved to be unbiased and showed no demonstrable adverse impact against minority groups. However, very few test administrators felt comfortable using the assessment because most people felt that the skills that it tapped were not closely related to the skills needed for the job. Legally, ethically, and statistically, we were on firm ground, but we could never fully achieve "buy-in" from the people who had to administer the test.

On the other hand, we also piloted a test that showed very little criterion validity at all. There were no significant correlations between scores on the test and performance outcomes; the test was unable to distinguish between a high and a low performer. Still . . . the test administrators loved this test because it "looked" so much like the job. That is, it had high face validity and tapped skills that seemed to be precisely the kinds of skills that were needed on the job. From a legal, ethical, and statistical perspective, we knew we could not use this test to select employees, but we continued to use it to provide a "realistic job preview" to candidates. That

**Adam Shoemaker, Ph.D., Human Resources Consultant for Talent Acquisition, Tampa, Florida**

way, the test continued to work for us in really showing candidates that this was the kind of thing they would be doing all day at work. More than a few times, candidates voluntarily withdrew from the process because they had a better understanding of what the job involved long before they even sat down at a desk.

The moral of this story is that as scientists, we have to remember that reliability and validity are super important in the development and implementation of a test . . . but as human beings, we have to remember that the test we end up using must also be easy to use and appear face valid for both the candidate and the administrator.

*Read more of what Dr. Shoemaker had to say—his complete essay—at www.mhhe.com/cohentesting8.*

by the items, the number of items tapping each area of coverage, the organization of the items in the test, and so forth (see Figure 6–2). In many instances the test blueprint represents the culmination of efforts to adequately sample the universe of content areas that conceivably could be sampled in such a test.[2]

For an employment test to be content-valid, its content must be a representative sample of the job-related skills required for employment. Behavioral observation is one technique frequently used in blueprinting the content areas to be covered in certain types of employment tests. The test developer will observe successful veterans on that job, note the behaviors necessary for success on the job, and design the test to include a representative sample of those behaviors. Those same workers (as well as their supervisors and others) may subsequently be

**Figure 6–2**
**Building a Test from a Test Blueprint**

*An architect's blueprint usually takes the form of a technical drawing or diagram of a structure, sometimes written in white lines on a blue background. The blueprint may be thought of as a plan of a structure, typically detailed enough so that the structure could actually be constructed from it. Somewhat comparable to the architect's blueprint is the test blueprint of a test developer. Seldom, if ever, on a blue background and written in white, it is nonetheless a detailed plan of the content, organization, and quantity of the items that a test will contain—sometimes complete with "weightings" of the content to be covered (He, 2011; Spray & Huang, 2000; Sykes & Hou, 2003). A test administered on a regular basis may require "item-pool management" to manage the creation of new items and the output of old items in a manner that is consistent with the test's blueprint (Ariel et al., 2006; van der Linden et al., 2000).*

---

2. The application of the concept of *blueprint* and of *blueprinting* is, of course, not limited to achievement tests. Blueprinting may be used in the design of a personality test, an attitude measure, an employment test, or any other test. The judgments of experts in the field are often employed in order to construct the best possible test blueprint.

called on to act as experts or judges in rating the degree to which the content of the test is a representative sample of the required job-related skills. At that point, the test developer will want to know about the extent to which the experts or judges agree. A description one such method for quantifying the degree of agreement between such raters follows.

**The quantification of content validity**  The measurement of content validity is important in employment settings, where tests used to hire and promote people are carefully scrutinized for their relevance to the job, among other factors (Russell & Peterson, 1997). Courts often require evidence that employment tests are work related. Several methods for quantifying content validity have been created (for example, James et al., 1984; Lindell et al., 1999; Tinsley & Weiss, 1975). One method of measuring content validity, developed by C. H. Lawshe, is essentially a method for gauging agreement among raters or judges regarding how essential a particular item is. Lawshe (1975) proposed that, for each item, each rater respond to the following question: "Is the skill or knowledge measured by this item

- essential
- useful but not essential
- not necessary

to the performance of the job?" (p. 567). For each item, the number of panelists stating that the item is essential is noted. According to Lawshe, if more than half the panelists indicate that an item is essential, that item has at least some content validity. Greater levels of content validity exist as larger numbers of panelists agree that a particular item is essential. Using these assumptions, Lawshe developed a formula termed the **content validity ratio (CVR)**:

$$CVR = \frac{n_e - (N/2)}{N/2}$$

where CVR = content validity ratio, $n_e$ = number of panelists indicating "essential," and $N$ = total number of panelists. Assuming a panel of 10 experts, the following three examples illustrate the meaning of the CVR when it is negative, zero, and positive.

1. *Negative CVR:* When fewer than half the panelists indicate "essential," the CVR is negative. Assume 4 of 10 panelists indicated "essential"; then

$$CVR = \frac{4 - (10/2)}{10/2} = -0.2$$

2. *Zero CVR:* When exactly half the panelists indicate "essential," the CVR is zero:

$$CVR = \frac{5 - (10/2)}{10/2} = 0.0$$

3. *Positive CVR:* When more than half but not all the panelists indicate "essential," the CVR ranges between .00 and .99. Suppose that 9 of 10 indicated "essential"; then

$$CVR = \frac{9 - (10/2)}{10/2} = 0.80$$

In validating a test, the content validity ratio is calculated for each item. Lawshe recommended that if the amount of agreement observed is more than 5% likely to occur

| Number of Panelists | Minimum Value |
|---|---|
| 5 | .99 |
| 6 | .99 |
| 7 | .99 |
| 8 | .75 |
| 9 | .78 |
| 10 | .62 |
| 11 | .59 |
| 12 | .56 |
| 13 | .54 |
| 14 | .51 |
| 15 | .49 |
| 20 | .42 |
| 25 | .37 |
| 30 | .33 |
| 35 | .31 |
| 40 | .29 |

**Table 6–1**
**Minimum Values of the Content Validity Ratio to Ensure That Agreement Is Unlikely to Be Due to Chance**

Source: Lawshe (1975).

by chance, then the item should be eliminated. The minimal CVR values corresponding to this 5% level are presented in Table 6–1. In the case of 10 panelists, an item would need a minimum CVR of .62. In our third example (in which 9 of 10 panelists agreed), the CVR of .80 is significant and so the item could be retained. Subsequently, in our discussion of criterion-related validity, our attention shifts from an index of validity based not on test content but on test scores. First, some perspective on culture as it relates to a test's validity.

**Culture and the relativity of content validity**  Tests are often thought of as either valid or not valid. A history test, for example, either does or does not accurately measure one's knowledge of historical fact. However, it is also true that what constitutes historical fact depends to some extent on who is writing the history. Consider, for example, a momentous event in the history of the world, one that served as a catalyst for World War I. Archduke Franz Ferdinand was assassinated on June 28, 1914, by a Serb named Gavrilo Princip (Figure 6–3). Now think about how you would answer the following multiple-choice item on a history test:

Gavrilo Princip was

    a.  a poet

    b.  a hero

    c.  a terrorist

    d.  a nationalist

    e.  all of the above

For various textbooks in the Bosnian region of the world, choice "e"—that's right, "all of the above"—is the "correct" answer. Hedges (1997) observed that textbooks in areas of Bosnia and Herzegovina that were controlled by different ethnic groups imparted widely varying characterizations of the assassin. In the Serb-controlled region of the country, history textbooks—and presumably the tests constructed to measure students' learning—regarded Princip as a "hero and poet." By contrast, Croatian students might read that Princip was an assassin trained to commit a terrorist act. Muslims in the region were taught that Princip was a nationalist whose deed sparked anti-Serbian rioting.

**JUST THINK . . .**

The passage of time sometimes serves to place historical figures in a different light. How might the textbook descriptions of Gavrilo Princip have changed in these regions?

**Figure 6–3**
**Cultural Relativity, History, and Test Validity**

*Austro-Hungarian Archduke Franz Ferdinand and his wife, Sophia, are pictured (left) as they left Sarajevo's City Hall on June 28, 1914. Moments later, Ferdinand would be assassinated by Gavrilo Princip, shown in custody at right. The killing served as a catalyst for World War I and is discussed and analyzed in history textbooks in every language around the world. Yet descriptions of the assassin Princip in those textbooks—and ability test items based on those descriptions—vary as a function of culture.*

A history test considered valid in one classroom, at one time, and in one place will not necessarily be considered so in another classroom, at another time, and in another place. Consider a test containing the true-false item, "Colonel Claus von Stauffenberg is a hero." Such an item is useful in illustrating the cultural relativity affecting item scoring. In 1944, von Stauffenberg, a German officer, was an active participant in a bomb plot to assassinate Germany's leader, Adolf Hitler. When the plot (popularized in the film, *Operation Valkyrie*) failed, von Stauffenberg was executed and promptly villified in Germany as a despicable traitor. Today, the light of history shines favorably on von Stauffenberg, and he is perceived as a hero in Germany. A German postage stamp with his face on it was issued to honor von Stauffenberg's 100th birthday.

Politics is another factor that may well play a part in perceptions and judgments concerning the validity of tests and test items. In many countries throughout the world, a response that is keyed incorrect to a particular test item can lead to consequences far more dire than a deduction in points towards the total test score. Sometimes, even constructing a test with a reference to a taboo topic can have dire consequences for the test developer. For example, one Palestinian professor who included items pertaining to governmental corruption on an examination was tortured by authorities as a result ("Brother Against Brother," 1997). Such scenarios bring new meaning to the term *politically correct* as it applies to tests, test items, and testtaker responses.

**JUST THINK . . .**

Commercial test developers who publish widely used history tests must maintain the content validity of their tests. What challenges do they face in doing so?

# Criterion-Related Validity

**Criterion-related validity** is a judgment of how adequately a test score can be used to infer an individual's most probable standing on some measure of interest—the measure of interest being the criterion. Two types of validity evidence are subsumed under the heading *criterion-related validity*. **Concurrent validity** is an index of the degree to which a test score is related to some criterion measure obtained at the same time (concurrently). **Predictive validity** is an index of the degree to which a test score predicts some criterion measure. Before we discuss each of these types of validity evidence in detail, it seems appropriate to raise (and answer) an important question.

## What Is a Criterion?

We were first introduced to the concept of a criterion in Chapter 4, where, in the context of defining criterion-referenced assessment, we defined a criterion broadly as a standard on which a judgment or decision may be based. Here, in the context of our discussion of criterion-related validity, we will define a **criterion** just a bit more narrowly as the standard against which a test or a test score is evaluated. So, for example, if a test purports to measure the trait of athleticism, we might expect to employ "membership in a health club" or any generally accepted measure of physical fitness as a criterion in evaluating whether the athleticism test truly measures athleticism. Operationally, a criterion can be most anything: *pilot performance in flying a Boeing 767, grade on examination in Advanced Hairweaving, number of days spent in psychiatric hospitalization*; the list is endless. There are no hard-and-fast rules for what constitutes a criterion. It can be a test score, a specific behavior or group of behaviors, an amount of time, a rating, a psychiatric diagnosis, a training cost, an index of absenteeism, an index of alcohol intoxication, and so on. Whatever the criterion, ideally it is relevant, valid, and uncontaminated. Let's explain.

**Characteristics of a criterion**    An adequate criterion is *relevant*. By this we mean that it is pertinent or applicable to the matter at hand. We would expect, for example, that a test purporting to advise testtakers whether they share the same interests of successful actors to have been validated using the interests of successful actors as a criterion.

An adequate criterion measure must also be *valid* for the purpose for which it is being used. If one test ($X$) is being used as the criterion to validate a second test ($Y$), then evidence should exist that test $X$ is valid. If the criterion used is a rating made by a judge or a panel, then evidence should exist that the rating is valid. Suppose, for example, that a test purporting to measure depression is said to have been validated using as a criterion the diagnoses made by a blue-ribbon panel of psychodiagnosticians. A test user might wish to probe further regarding variables such as the credentials of the "blue-ribbon panel" (that is, their educational background, training, and experience) and the actual procedures used to validate a diagnosis of depression. Answers to such questions would help address the issue of whether the criterion (in this case, the diagnoses made by panel members) was indeed valid.

Ideally, a criterion is also *uncontaminated*. **Criterion contamination** is the term applied to a criterion measure that has been based, at least in part, on predictor measures. As an example, consider a hypothetical "Inmate Violence Potential Test" (IVPT) designed to predict a prisoner's potential for violence in the cell block. In part, this evaluation entails ratings from fellow inmates, guards, and other staff in order to come up with a number that represents each inmate's violence potential. After all of the inmates in the study have been given scores on this test, the study authors then attempt to validate the test by asking guards to rate each inmate on their violence potential. Because the guards' opinions were used to formulate the inmate's test score in the first place (the predictor variable), the guards' opinions cannot be used as a criterion against which to judge the soundness of the test. If the guards' opinions were used both as a predictor and as a criterion, then we would say that criterion contamination had occurred.

Here is another example of criterion contamination. Suppose that a team of researchers from a company called Ventura International Psychiatric Research (VIPR) just completed a study of how accurately a test called the MMPI-2-RF predicted psychiatric diagnosis in the psychiatric population of the Minnesota state hospital system. As we will see in Chapter 13, the MMPI-2-RF is, in fact, a widely used test. In this study, the predictor is the MMPI-2-RF, and the criterion is the psychiatric diagnosis that exists in the patient's record. Further, let's suppose that while all the data are being analyzed at VIPR headquarters, someone informs these researchers that the diagnosis for every patient in the Minnesota state hospital system was determined, at least in part, by an MMPI-2-RF test score. Should they still proceed with their analysis? The answer is no. Because the predictor measure has contaminated the criterion measure, it would be of little value to find, in essence, that the predictor can indeed predict itself.

When criterion contamination does occur, the results of the validation study cannot be taken seriously. There are no methods or statistics to gauge the extent to which criterion contamination has taken place, and there are no methods or statistics to correct for such contamination.

Now, let's take a closer look at concurrent validity and predictive validity.

## Concurrent Validity

If test scores are obtained at about the same time as the criterion measures are obtained, measures of the relationship between the test scores and the criterion provide evidence of concurrent validity. Statements of concurrent validity indicate the extent to which test scores may be used to estimate an individual's present standing on a criterion. If, for example, scores (or classifications) made on the basis of a psychodiagnostic test were to be validated against a criterion of already diagnosed psychiatric patients, then the process would be one of concurrent validation. In general, once the validity of the inference from the test scores is established, the test may provide a faster, less expensive way to offer a diagnosis or a classification decision. A test with satisfactorily demonstrated concurrent validity may therefore be appealing to prospective users because it holds out the potential of savings of money and professional time.

Sometimes the concurrent validity of a particular test (let's call it Test A) is explored with respect to another test (we'll call Test B). In such studies, prior research has satisfactorily demonstrated the validity of Test B, so the question becomes: "How well does Test A compare with Test B?" Here, Test B is used as the *validating criterion*. In some studies, Test A is either a brand-new test or a test being used for some new purpose, perhaps with a new population.

Here is a real-life example of a concurrent validity study in which a group of researchers explored whether a test validated for use with adults could be used with adolescents. The Beck Depression Inventory (BDI; Beck et al., 1961, 1979; Beck & Steer, 1993) and its revision, the Beck Depression Inventory-II (BDI-II; Beck et al., 1996) are self-report measures used to identify symptoms of depression and quantify their severity. Although the BDI had been widely used with adults, questions were raised regarding its appropriateness for use with adolescents. Ambrosini et al. (1991) conducted a concurrent validity study to explore the utility of the BDI with adolescents.

> **JUST THINK . . .**
>
> What else might these researchers have done to explore the utility of the BDI with adolescents?

They also sought to determine if the test could successfully differentiate patients with depression from those without depression in a population of adolescent outpatients. Diagnoses generated from the concurrent administration of an instrument previously validated for use with adolescents were used as the criterion validators. The findings suggested that the BDI is valid for use with adolescents.

We now turn our attention to another form of criterion validity, one in which the criterion measure is obtained not concurrently but at some future time.

## Predictive Validity

Test scores may be obtained at one time and the criterion measures obtained at a future time, usually after some intervening event has taken place. The intervening event may take varied forms, such as training, experience, therapy, medication, or simply the passage of time. Measures of the relationship between the test scores and a criterion measure obtained at a future time provide an indication of the *predictive validity* of the test; that is, how accurately scores on the test predict some criterion measure. Measures of the relationship between college admissions tests and freshman grade point averages, for example, provide evidence of the predictive validity of the admissions tests.

In settings where tests might be employed—such as a personnel agency, a college admissions office, or a warden's office—a test's high predictive validity can be a useful aid to decision makers who must select successful students, productive workers, or good parole risks. Whether a test result is valuable in decision making depends on how well the test results improve selection decisions over decisions made without knowledge of test results. In an industrial setting where volume turnout is important, if the use of a personnel selection test can enhance productivity to even a small degree, then that enhancement will pay off year after year and may translate into millions of dollars of increased revenue. And in a clinical context, no price could be placed on a test that could save more lives from suicide or by providing predictive accuracy over and above existing tests with respect to such acts. Unfortunately, the difficulties inherent in developing such tests are numerous and multifaceted (Mulvey & Lidz, 1984; Murphy, 1984; Petrie & Chamberlain, 1985). This chapter's *Close-Up* was written with the objective of imparting a sense of what is involved in predictive validity studies.

Judgments of criterion-related validity, whether concurrent or predictive, are based on two types of statistical evidence: *the validity coefficient* and *expectancy data*.

**The validity coefficient**    The **validity coefficient** is a correlation coefficient that provides a measure of the relationship between test scores and scores on the criterion measure. The correlation coefficient computed from a score (or classification) on a psychodiagnostic test and the criterion score (or classification) assigned by psychodiagnosticians is one example of a validity coefficient. Typically, the Pearson correlation coefficient is used to determine the validity between the two measures. However, depending on variables such as the type of data, the sample size, and the shape of the distribution, other correlation coefficients could be used. For example, in correlating self-rankings of performance on some job with rankings made by job supervisors, the formula for the Spearman rho rank-order correlation would be employed.

Like the reliability coefficient and other correlational measures, the validity coefficient is affected by restriction or inflation of range. And as in other correlational studies, a key issue is whether the range of scores employed is appropriate to the objective of the correlational analysis. In situations where, for example, attrition in the number of subjects has occurred over the course of the study, the validity coefficient may be adversely affected.

# Base Rates and Predictive Validity

**W**hen evaluating the predictive validity of a test, researchers must take into consideration the base rate of the occurrence of the variable in question, both as that variable exists in the general population and as it exists the sample being studied. Some definitions of terminology commonly used when discussing predictive validity will be helpful here. Generally, a **base rate** is the extent to which a particular trait, behavior, characteristic, or attribute exists in the population (expressed as a proportion). In psychometric parlance, a **hit rate** may be defined as the proportion of people a test accurately identifies as possessing or exhibiting a particular trait, behavior, characteristic, or attribute. For example, *hit rate* could refer to the proportion of people accurately predicted to be able to perform work at the graduate school level or to the proportion of neurological patients accurately identified as having a brain tumor. In like fashion, a **miss rate** may be defined as the proportion of people the test fails to identify as having, or not having, a particular characteristic or attribute. Here, a *miss* amounts to an inaccurate prediction. The category of *misses* may be further subdivided. A **false positive** is a miss wherein the test predicted that the testtaker did possess the particular characteristic or attribute being measured when in fact the testtaker did not. A **false negative** is a miss wherein the test predicted that the testtaker did not possess the particular characteristic or attribute being measured when the testtaker actually did.

To evaluate the predictive validity of a test, a test targeting a particular attribute may be administered to a sample of research subjects in which approximately half of the subjects possess or exhibit the targeted attribute and the other half do not. Questions may subsequently arise about the appropriateness of using such a test in which the base rate of the occurrence of the targeted attribute in the population being tested is substantially less than 50%. Such questions arose, for example, with regard to the use of a test called the Child Abuse Potential Inventory (CAP; Milner, 1986).

The CAP was designed to be a screening aid in the identification of adults at high risk for physically abusing children. A high score on the CAP, especially in combination with confirmatory evidence from other sources, might prompt the test user to probe further with regard to the testtaker's history of, or present intentions regarding, child abuse. Another use of the CAP is as an outcome measure in programs designed to prevent physical abuse of children (Milner, 1989b). Participants would be administered the CAP upon entry to the program and again upon exit.

Predictive validity research conducted with the CAP has "demonstrated an uncanny hit rate (about 90%) in discriminating abusers from nonabusers" (Melton & Limber, 1989, p. 1231). Yet as the author of the CAP has pointed out, "The reported 90% hit rate was determined in studies using groups that consisted of equal numbers of abusers and nonabusers that by design contain base rates of 50% which are optimal for classification purposes" (Milner, 1991, p. 80). Thus, as the base rate for child abuse decreases, the number of false positives in the group indicated as abusive will increase while the number of false negatives in the group indicated as nonabusive will decrease. If these facts related to base rates and predictive validity are not known and appreciated by the test user, a potential exists for misuse of tests such as the CAP.

The base rate for child abuse in the general population is about 2–3% annually (Finkelhor & Dziuba-Leatherman, 1994). This base rate is low relative to the 50% base rate that prevailed in the predictive validity studies with the CAP. This fact must therefore be considered in any use of the CAP with members of the general population.

With this background, consider a study conducted by Milner et al. (1986) with 220 adults, including 110 known abusers and 110 nonabusers. All subjects completed the CAP, and the test was scored. Fully 82.7% of the abusers and 88.2% of the nonabusers were correctly classified using the CAP (Table 1). Working down the columns of Table 1, note that of the 110 known abusers, 19 were incorrectly classified as nonabusers. Of the 110 known nonabusers, 13 were incorrectly identified as abusers. Of course, in most applications of the CAP, one would not know whether the person being tested was an actual child abuser; that would probably be the reason for administering the test.

**Table 1**
**Application of the CAP in a Population with a High Base Rate of Child Abuse**

|  | Actual Status | | |
| --- | --- | --- | --- |
|  | Abuser | Nonabuser | Row Totals |
| *CAP results indicate:* | | | |
| Abuser | 91 | 13 | 104 |
| Nonabuser | 19 | 97 | 116 |
| **Column Totals** | **110** | **110** | **220** |

*(continued)*

# Base Rates and Predictive Validity
## (continued)

To gain an understanding of the errors that would be made, look at Table 1 again, but this time work across the rows. When the CAP indicates that a person is an abuser, the finding is correct 87.5% of the time (91 of 104 instances). When the CAP indicates that a person is not an abuser, it is correct 83.6% of the time (97 of 116 instances).

The picture changes dramatically, however, in a low base-rate environment. For the purposes of this example, let's say that physical child abuse occurs in 5% of the population. In a hypothetical study, we test 1,000 people using the CAP. Because physical child abuse occurs in 5% of the population, we would expect 50 or so of our testtakers to be abusers. And let's say further that, just as in the Milner et al. (1986) study, 82.7% of the abusers and 88.2% of the nonabusers are correctly identified in our study (Table 2). Working down the columns in Table 2, if 82.7% of the abusers are correctly identified, then 41 will be identified as abusers and the remaining 9 will be identified as nonabusers. If the test has an 88.2% accuracy rate for nonabusers, 838 of the nonabusers will be correctly identified, and the remaining 112 will be identified as abusers.

Now look at Table 2 again, this time working across the rows. If the CAP score indicates that the individual is an abuser, it is probably *incorrect*. Most of the people (73.2% of them, in this example) with CAP scores indicating that they

are abusers are, in reality, not abusers. This inaccuracy is entirely the product of working with a low base-rate sample. Even if the CAP were more accurate, using test results to identify abusers will still result in many identified abusers being wrongly classified because abuse is a low base-rate phenomenon. Stated another way, when the nonabusing population is much larger than the abusing population, the chances are that most of the mistakes will be made in classifying the nonabusing population.

Place yourself in the seat of the judge or the jury hearing a physical child abuse case. A psychologist testifies that the CAP, which has an accuracy rate of 85–90%, indicates that the defendant is a physical abuser. The psychologist attempts an explanation about population base rates and the possibility of error. Still, what might stick in your mind about the psychologist's testimony? Many people would reason that, if the CAP is right more than 85% of the time, and if the defendant is *identified* as a child abuser, there must be at least an 85% chance that the defendant *is* a child abuser. This conclusion, as you know now, would be incorrect and could result in justice not being served (Melton & Limber, 1989).

This example illustrates that the test developer's intended use of the test must be respected. Lacking any compelling psychometric evidence to deviate from the test developer's intended use of the test, such deviations may result in harm to the testtaker. The example further serves as a reminder that, when data about the accuracy and consistency of a test are collected, the data are collected using a sampling of people from a particular population. Conclusions drawn from those psychometric data are applicable only to groups of people from a similar population.

Joel Milner, the author of the CAP, urged users of his test to keep in mind that it is inappropriate to use any single psychological test as a diagnostic criterion. Milner (1991) reminded readers that "data from multiple sources, such as several tests, client interviews, collateral interviews, direct observations, and case histories should be used in making decisions regarding child abuse and treatment" (p. 81).

**Table 2**
**Application of the CAP in a Population with a Low Base Rate of Child Abuse**

|  | Actual Status | | |
|---|---|---|---|
|  | Abuser | Nonabuser | Row Totals |
| CAP results indicate: |  |  |  |
| Abuser | 41 | 112 | 153 |
| Nonabuser | 9 | 838 | 847 |
| **Column totals** | **50** | **950** | **1,000** |

The problem of restricted range can also occur through a self-selection process in the sample employed for the validation study. Thus, for example, if the test purports to measure something as technical or as dangerous as oil-barge firefighting skills, it may well be that the only people who reply to an ad for the position of oil-barge firefighter are those who are actually highly qualified for the position. Accordingly, the range of the distribution of scores on this test of oil-barge firefighting skills would be restricted. For less technical or dangerous positions, a self-selection factor might be operative if the test developer selects a group of newly hired employees to test (with the expectation that criterion measures will be available for this group at some subsequent date). However, because the newly hired employees have probably already passed some formal or informal evaluation in the process of being hired, there is a good chance that ability to do the job will be higher among this group than among a random sample of ordinary job applicants. Consequently, scores on the criterion measure that is later administered will tend to be higher than scores on the criterion measure obtained from a random sample of ordinary job applicants. Stated another way, the scores will be restricted in range.

Whereas it is the responsibility of the test developer to report validation data in the test manual, it is the responsibility of test users to read carefully the description of the validation study and then to evaluate the suitability of the test for their specific purposes. What were the characteristics of the sample used in the validation study? How matched are those characteristics to the people for whom an administration of the test is contemplated? For a specific test purpose, are some subtests of a test more appropriate than the entire test?

How high should a validity coefficient be for a user or a test developer to infer that the test is valid? There are no rules for determining the minimum acceptable size of a validity coefficient. In fact, Cronbach and Gleser (1965) cautioned against the establishment of such rules. They argued that validity coefficients need to be large enough to enable the test user to make accurate decisions within the unique context in which a test is being used. Essentially, the validity coefficient should be high enough to result in the identification and differentiation of testtakers with respect to target attribute(s), such as employees who are likely to be more productive, police officers who are less likely to misuse their weapons, and students who are more likely to be successful in a particular course of study.

**Incremental validity**    Test users involved in predicting some criterion from test scores are often interested in the utility of multiple predictors. The value of including more than one predictor depends on a couple of factors. First, of course, each measure used as a predictor should have criterion-related predictive validity. Second, additional predictors should possess **incremental validity,** defined here as the degree to which an additional predictor explains something about the criterion measure that is not explained by predictors already in use.

Incremental validity may be used when predicting something like academic success in college. Grade point average (GPA) at the end of the first year may be used as a measure of academic success. A study of potential predictors of GPA may reveal that time spent in the library and time spent studying are highly correlated with GPA. How much sleep a student's roommate allows the student to have during exam periods correlates with GPA to a smaller extent. What is the most accurate but most efficient way to predict GPA? One approach, employing the principles of incremental validity, is to start with the best predictor: the predictor that is most highly correlated with GPA. This may be time spent studying. Then, using multiple regression techniques, one would examine the usefulness of the other predictors.

Even though time in the library is highly correlated with GPA, it may not possess incremental validity if it overlaps too much with the first predictor, time spent studying. Said another way, if time spent studying and time in the library are so highly

JUST THINK . . .

From your own personal experience, what is a nonobvious predictor of GPA that is probably not correlated with time spent studying?

correlated with each other that they reflect essentially the same thing, then only one of them needs to be included as a predictor. Including both predictors will provide little new information. By contrast, the variable of how much sleep a student's roommate allows the student to have during exams may have good incremental validity. This is so because it reflects a different aspect of preparing for exams (resting) from the first predictor (studying). Incremental validity has been used to improve the prediction of job performance for Marine Corps mechanics (Carey, 1994) and the prediction of child abuse (Murphy-Berman, 1994). In both instances, predictor measures were included only if they demonstrated that they could explain something about the criterion measure that was not already known from the other predictors.

**Expectancy data**   Expectancy data provide information that can be used in evaluating the criterion-related validity of a test. Using a score obtained on some test(s) or measure(s), expectancy tables illustrate the likelihood that the testtaker will score within some interval of scores on a criterion measure—an interval that may be seen as "passing," "acceptable," and so on. An **expectancy table** shows the percentage of people within specified test-score intervals who subsequently were placed in various categories of the criterion (for example, placed in "passed" category or "failed" category). An expectancy table may be created from a scatterplot according to the steps listed in Figure 6–4. An expectancy table showing the relationship between scores on a subtest of the Differential Aptitude Test (DAT) and course grades in American history for 11th-grade boys is presented in Table 6–2. You can see that, of the students who scored between 40 and 60, 83% scored 80 or above in their American history course.

To illustrate how an expectancy table might be used by a corporate personnel office, suppose that on the basis of various test scores and personal interviews, personnel experts rated all applicants for a manual labor position entailing piecework as *excellent, very good, average, below average,* or *poor.* In this example, then, the test score is actually a rating made by personnel experts on the basis of a number of test scores and a personal interview. Let's further suppose that, because of a severe labor scarcity at the time, all the applicants were hired—which, by the way, is a dream come true for a researcher interested in conducting a validation study of the assessment procedure. Floor supervisors were not informed of the composite score obtained by the newly hired workers. The floor supervisors provided the criterion measure by rating each employee's performance as either *satisfactory* or *unsatisfactory.* Figure 6–5 is the resulting **expectancy chart,** or graphic representation of an expectancy table.

As illustrated in the expectancy chart, of all applicants originally rated *excellent,* 94% were rated *satisfactory* on the job. By contrast, among applicants originally rated *poor,* only 17% were rated *satisfactory* on the job. In general, this expectancy chart tells us that the higher the initial rating, the greater the probability of job success. Stated another way, it tells us that the lower the initial rating, the greater the probability of job failure. The company experimenting with such a rating system could reasonably expect to improve its productivity by using this rating system. Specifically, job applicants who obtained ratings of *average* or higher would be the only applicants hired.

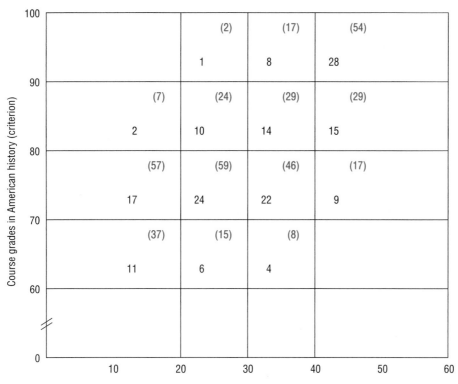

Language usage raw scores from the Differential Aptitude Tests
( ) percentage of points per cell

**Figure 6–4**
**Seven Steps to an Expectancy Table**

1. Draw a scatterplot such that each point in the plot represents a particular test score–criterion score combination. The criterion should be on the Y-axis.

2. Draw grid lines in such a way as to summarize the number of people who scored within a particular interval.

3. Count the number of points in each cell ($n_i$), as shown in the figure.

4. Count the total number of points within each vertical interval ($N_v$). This number represents the number of people scoring within a particular test score interval.

5. Convert each cell frequency to a percentage ($n_i/N_v$). This represents the percentage of people obtaining a particular test score–criterion score combination. Write the percentages in the cells. Enclose the percentages in parentheses to distinguish them from the frequencies.

6. On a separate sheet, create table headings and subheadings and copy the percentages into the appropriate cell tables as shown in Table 6–2. Be careful to put the percentages in the correct cell tables. (Note that it's easy to make a mistake at this stage because the percentages of people within particular score intervals are written vertically in the scatterplot but horizontally in the table.)

7. If desired, write the number and percentage of cases per test-score interval. If the number of cases in any one cell is very small, it is more likely to fluctuate in subsequent charts. If cell sizes are small, the user could create fewer cells or accumulate data over several years.

**Table 6–2**
**DAT Language Usage Subtest Scores and American History Grade for 171 Eleventh-Grade Boys**
**(Showing Percentage of Students Obtaining Course Grades in the Interval Shown)**

| | Course Grade Interval | | | | Cases per Test-Score Interval | |
|---|---|---|---|---|---|---|
| Test Score | 0–69 | 70–79 | 80–89 | 90–100 | $N_v$ | % |
| 40 and above | 0 | 17 | 29 | 54 | 52 | 100 |
| 30–39 | 8 | 46 | 29 | 17 | 48 | 100 |
| 0–29 | 15 | 59 | 24 | 2 | 41 | 100 |
| Below 20 | 37 | 57 | 7 | 0 | 30 | 101* |

*Total sums to more than 100% because of rounding.

Source: From the *Manual of Differential Aptitude Tests,* Fifth Edition, Form C (DAT 5). Copyright © 1990 NCS Pearson, Inc. Reproduced with permission. All rights reserved. "Differential Aptitude Tests" and "DAT" are trademarks, in the U.S. and/or other countries, of Pearson Education, Inc., or its affiliate(s).

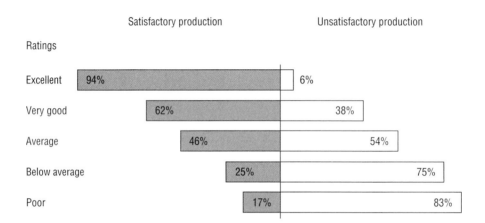

**Figure 6–5**
**Expectancy Chart for Test Ratings and Job Performance**

## Construct Validity

**Construct validity** is a judgment about the appropriateness of inferences drawn from test scores regarding individual standings on a variable called a *construct*. A **construct** is an informed, scientific idea developed or hypothesized to describe or explain behavior. *Intelligence* is a construct that may be invoked to describe why a student performs well in school. *Anxiety* is a construct that may be invoked to describe why a psychiatric patient paces the floor. Other examples of constructs are *job satisfaction, personality, bigotry, clerical aptitude, depression, motivation, self-esteem, emotional adjustment, potential dangerousness, executive potential, creativity,* and *mechanical comprehension,* to name but a few.

Constructs are unobservable, presupposed (underlying) traits that a test developer may invoke to describe test behavior or criterion performance. The researcher investigating a test's construct validity must formulate hypotheses about the expected behavior of high scorers and low scorers on the test. These hypotheses give rise to a tentative theory about the nature of the construct the test was designed to measure. If the test is a valid measure of the construct, then high scorers and low scorers will behave as predicted by the theory. If high scorers and low scorers on the test do not behave as predicted, the investigator will need to reexamine the nature of the construct itself or hypotheses made about it. One possible reason for obtaining results contrary to those predicted by the theory is that the test simply does not measure the construct. An alternative explanation could lie in the theory that generated hypotheses about the construct. The theory may need to be reexamined.

In some instances, the reason for obtaining contrary findings can be traced to the statistical procedures used or to the way the procedures were executed. One procedure may have been more appropriate than another, given the particular assumptions. Thus, although confirming evidence contributes to a judgment that a test is a valid measure of a construct, evidence to the contrary can also be useful. Contrary evidence can provide a stimulus for the discovery of new facets of the construct as well as alternative methods of measurement.

Increasingly, construct validity has been viewed as the unifying concept for all validity evidence (American Educational Research Association et al., 1999). As we noted at the outset, all types of validity evidence, including evidence from the content- and criterion-related varieties of validity, come under the umbrella of construct validity. Let's look at the types of evidence that might be gathered.

## Evidence of Construct Validity

A number of procedures may be used to provide different kinds of evidence that a test has construct validity. The various techniques of construct validation may provide evidence, for example, that

- the test is homogeneous, measuring a single construct;
- test scores increase or decrease as a function of age, the passage of time, or an experimental manipulation as theoretically predicted;
- test scores obtained after some event or the mere passage of time (that is, posttest scores) differ from pretest scores as theoretically predicted;
- test scores obtained by people from distinct groups vary as predicted by the theory;
- test scores correlate with scores on other tests in accordance with what would be predicted from a theory that covers the manifestation of the construct in question.

A brief discussion of each type of construct validity evidence and the procedures used to obtain it follows.

**Evidence of homogeneity**   When describing a test and its items, **homogeneity** refers to how uniform a test is in measuring a single concept. A test developer can increase test homogeneity in several ways. Consider, for example, a test of academic achievement that contains subtests in areas such as mathematics, spelling, and reading comprehension. The Pearson $r$ could be used to correlate average subtest scores with the average total test score. Subtests that in the test developer's judgment do not correlate very well with the test as a whole might have to be reconstructed (or eliminated) lest the test not measure the construct *academic achievement*. Correlations between subtest scores and total test score are generally reported in the test manual as evidence of homogeneity.

One way a test developer can improve the homogeneity of a test containing items that are scored dichotomously (for example, true–false) is by eliminating items that do not show significant correlation coefficients with total test scores. If all test items show significant, positive correlations with total test scores and if high scorers on the test tend to pass each item more than low scorers do, then each item is probably measuring the same construct as the total test. Each item is contributing to test homogeneity.

The homogeneity of a test in which items are scored on a multipoint scale can also be improved. For example, some attitude and opinion questionnaires require respondents to indicate level of agreement with specific statements by responding, for example, *strongly agree, agree, disagree,* or *strongly disagree.* Each response is assigned a numerical score, and items that do not show significant Spearman rank-order correlation coefficients are eliminated. If all test items show significant, positive correlations with total test scores, then each item is most likely measuring the same construct that the test as a whole is measuring (and is thereby contributing to the test's homogeneity). Coefficient alpha may also be used in estimating the homogeneity of a test composed of multiple-choice items (Novick & Lewis, 1967).

As a case study illustrating how a test's homogeneity can be improved, consider the Marital Satisfaction Scale (MSS; Roach et al., 1981). Designed to assess various aspects of married people's attitudes toward their marital relationship, the MSS contains an approximately equal number of items expressing positive and negative sentiments with respect to marriage. For example, *My life would seem empty without my marriage* and *My marriage has "smothered" my personality.* In one stage of the development of this test, subjects indicated how much they agreed or disagreed with the various sentiments in each of 73 items by marking a 5-point scale that ranged from *strongly agree* to *strongly disagree.* Based on the correlations between item scores and total score, the test developers elected to retain 48 items with correlation coefficients greater than .50, thus creating a more homogeneous instrument.

Item-analysis procedures have also been employed in the quest for test homogeneity. One item-analysis procedure focuses on the relationship between testtakers' scores on individual items and their score on the entire test. Each item is analyzed with respect to how high scorers versus low scorers responded to it. If it is an academic test and if high scorers on the entire test for some reason tended to get that particular item wrong while low scorers on the test as a whole tended to get the item right, the item is obviously not a good one. The item should be eliminated in the interest of test homogeneity, among other considerations. If the test is one of marital satisfaction, and if individuals who score high on the test as a whole respond to a particular item in a way that would indicate that they are not satisfied whereas people who tend not to be satisfied respond to the item in a way that would indicate that they are satisfied, then again the item should probably be eliminated or at least reexamined for clarity.

**JUST THINK . . .**

Is it possible for a test to be *too* homogeneous in item content?

Although test homogeneity is desirable because it assures us that all the items on the test tend to be measuring the same thing, it is not the be-all and end-all of construct validity. Knowing that a test is homogeneous contributes no information about how the construct being measured relates to other constructs. It is therefore important to report evidence of a test's homogeneity along with other evidence of construct validity.

**Evidence of changes with age**  Some constructs are expected to change over time. *Reading rate,* for example, tends to increase dramatically year by year from age 6 to the early teens. If a test score purports to be a measure of a construct that could be expected to change over time, then the test score, too, should show the same progressive changes with age to be considered a valid measure of the construct. For example, if children in grades 6, 7, 8, and 9 took a test of eighth-grade vocabulary, then we would expect that the total number of items scored as correct from all the test protocols would increase as a function of the higher grade level of the testtakers.

Some constructs lend themselves more readily than others to predictions of change over time. Thus, although we may be able to predict that a gifted child's scores on a test of reading skills will increase over the course of the testtaker's years of elementary and secondary education, we may not be able to predict with such confidence how a newlywed couple will score through the years on a test of marital satisfaction. This fact does not relegate a construct such as *marital satisfaction* to a lower stature than *reading ability*. Rather, it simply means that measures of marital satisfaction may be less stable over time or more vulnerable to situational events (such as in-laws coming to visit and refusing to leave for three months) than is reading ability. Evidence of change over time, like evidence of test homogeneity, does not in itself provide information about how the construct relates to other constructs.

**Evidence of pretest–posttest changes**    Evidence that test scores change as a result of some experience between a pretest and a posttest can be evidence of construct validity. Some of the more typical intervening experiences responsible for changes in test scores are formal education, a course of therapy or medication, and on-the-job experience. Of course, depending on the construct being measured, almost any intervening life experience could be predicted to yield changes in score from pretest to posttest. Reading an inspirational book, watching a TV talk show, undergoing surgery, serving a prison sentence, or the mere passage of time may each prove to be a potent intervening variable.

Returning to our example of the Marital Satisfaction Scale, one investigator cited in Roach et al. (1981) compared scores on that instrument before and after a sex therapy treatment program. Scores showed a significant change between pretest and posttest. A second posttest given eight weeks later showed that scores remained stable (suggesting the instrument was reliable), whereas the pretest–posttest measures were still significantly different. Such changes in scores in the predicted direction after the treatment program contribute to evidence of the construct validity for this test.

We would expect a decline in marital satisfaction scores if a pretest were administered to a sample of couples shortly after they took their nuptial vows and a posttest were administered shortly after members of the couples consulted their respective divorce attorneys sometime within the first five years of marriage. The experimental group in this study would consist of couples who consulted a divorce attorney within the first five years of marriage. The design of such pretest–posttest research ideally should include a control group to rule out alternative explanations of the findings.

> **JUST THINK . . .**
>
> Might it have been advisable to have simultaneous testing of a matched group of couples who did not participate in sex therapy and simultaneous testing of a matched group of couples who did not consult divorce attorneys? In both instances, would there have been any reason to expect any significant changes in the test scores of these two control groups?

**Evidence from distinct groups**    Also referred to as the **method of contrasted groups,** one way of providing evidence for the validity of a test is to demonstrate that scores on the test vary in a predictable way as a function of membership in some group. The rationale here is that if a test is a valid measure of a particular construct, then test scores from groups of people who would be presumed to differ with respect to that construct should have correspondingly different test scores. Consider in this context a test of depression wherein the higher the test score, the more depressed the testtaker is presumed to be. We would expect individuals psychiatrically hospitalized for depression to score higher on this measure than a random sample of Walmart shoppers.

Now, suppose it was your intention to provide construct validity evidence for the Marital Satisfaction Scale by showing differences in scores between distinct groups. How might you go about doing that?

Roach and colleagues (1981) proceeded by identifying two groups of married couples, one relatively satisfied in their marriage, the other not so satisfied. The groups were identified by ratings by peers and professional marriage counselors. A $t$ test on the difference between mean score on the test was significant ($p < .01$)—evidence to support the notion that the Marital Satisfaction Scale is indeed a valid measure of the construct *marital satisfaction.*

In a bygone era, the method many test developers used to create distinct groups was deception. For example, if it had been predicted that more of the construct would be exhibited on the test in question if the subject felt highly anxious, an experimental situation might be designed to make the subject feel highly anxious. Virtually any feeling state the theory called for could be induced by an experimental scenario that typically involved giving the research subject some misinformation. However, given the ethical constraints of contemporary psychologists and the reluctance of academic institutions and other sponsors of research to condone deception in human research, the method of obtaining distinct groups by creating them through the dissemination of deceptive information is seldom allowed today.

**Convergent evidence**    Evidence for the construct validity of a particular test may converge from a number of sources, such as other tests or measures designed to assess the same (or a similar) construct. Thus, if scores on the test undergoing construct validation tend to correlate highly in the predicted direction with scores on older, more established, and already validated tests designed to measure the same (or a similar) construct, this would be an example of **convergent evidence.**[3]

Convergent evidence for validity may come not only from correlations with tests purporting to measure an identical construct but also from correlations with measures purporting to measure related constructs. Consider, for example, a new test designed to measure the construct *test anxiety.* Generally speaking, we might expect high positive correlations between this new test and older, more established measures of test anxiety. However, we might also expect more moderate correlations between this new test and measures of general anxiety.

Roach et al. (1981) provided convergent evidence of the construct validity of the Marital Satisfaction Scale by computing a validity coefficient between scores on it and scores on the Marital Adjustment Test (Locke & Wallace, 1959). The validity coefficient of .79 provided additional evidence of their instrument's construct validity.

**Discriminant evidence**    A validity coefficient showing little (that is, a statistically insignificant) relationship between test scores and/or other variables with which scores on the test being construct-validated should *not* theoretically be correlated provides **discriminant evidence** of construct validity (also known as *discriminant validity*). In the course of developing the Marital Satisfaction Scale (MSS), its authors correlated scores on that instrument with scores on the Marlowe-Crowne Social Desirability Scale

---

3. Data indicating that a test measures the same construct as other tests purporting to measure the same construct are also referred to as evidence of **convergent validity.** One question that may be raised here concerns the necessity for the new test if it simply duplicates existing tests that measure the same construct. The answer, generally speaking, is a claim that the new test has some advantage over the more established test. For example, the new test may be shorter and capable of being administered in less time without significant loss in reliability or validity. On a practical level, the new test may be less costly.

(Crowne & Marlowe, 1964). Roach et al. (1981) hypothesized that high correlations between these two instruments would suggest that respondents were probably not answering items on the MSS entirely honestly but instead were responding in socially desirable ways. But the correlation between the MSS and the social desirability measure did not prove to be significant, so the test developers concluded that social desirability could be ruled out as a primary factor in explaining the meaning of MSS test scores.

In 1959 an experimental technique useful for examining both convergent and discriminant validity evidence was presented in *Psychological Bulletin.* This rather technical procedure, called the **multitrait-multimethod matrix,** is presented in our companion online workbook to this textbook. Here, let's simply point out that *multitrait* means "two or more traits" and *multimethod* means "two or more methods." The multitrait-multimethod matrix (Campbell & Fiske, 1959) is the matrix or table that results from correlating variables (traits) within and between methods. Values for any number of traits (such as aggressiveness or extraversion) as obtained by various methods (such as behavioral observation or a personality test) are inserted into the table, and the resulting matrix of correlations provides insight with respect to both the convergent and the discriminant validity of the methods used.[4]

**Factor analysis**   Both convergent and discriminant evidence of construct validity can be obtained by the use of factor analysis. **Factor analysis** is a shorthand term for a class of mathematical procedures designed to identify *factors* or specific variables that are typically attributes, characteristics, or dimensions on which people may differ. In psychometric research, factor analysis is frequently employed as a data reduction method in which several sets of scores and the correlations between them are analyzed. In such studies, the purpose of the factor analysis may be to identify the factor or factors in common between test scores on subscales within a particular test, or the factors in common between scores on a series of tests. In general, factor analysis is conducted on either an exploratory or a confirmatory basis. **Exploratory factor analysis** typically entails "estimating, or extracting factors; deciding how many factors to retain; and rotating factors to an interpretable orientation" (Floyd & Widaman, 1995, p. 287). By contrast, in **confirmatory factor analysis,** researchers test the degree to which a hypothetical model (which includes factors) fits the actual data.

A term commonly employed in factor analysis is **factor loading,** which is "a sort of metaphor. Each test is thought of as a vehicle carrying a certain amount of one or more abilities" (Tyler, 1965, p. 44). Factor loading in a test conveys information about the extent to which the factor determines the test score or scores. A new test purporting to measure bulimia, for example, can be factor-analyzed with other known measures of bulimia, as well as with other kinds of measures (such as measures of intelligence, self-esteem, general anxiety, anorexia, or perfectionism). High factor loadings by the new test on a "bulimia factor" would provide convergent evidence of construct validity. Moderate to low factor loadings by the new test with respect to measures of other eating disorders such as anorexia would provide discriminant evidence of construct validity.

Factor analysis frequently involves technical procedures so complex that few contemporary researchers would attempt to conduct one without the aid of a prepackaged computer program. But although the actual data analysis has become work for computers, humans still tend to be very much involved in the *naming* of factors

---

4. For an interesting real-life application of the multitrait-multimethod technique as used to better understand tests, see Storholm et al. (2011). The researchers used this technique to explore construct validity-related questions regarding a test called the Compulsive Sexual Behavior Inventory.

once the computer has identified them. Thus, for example, suppose a factor analysis identified a common factor being measured by two hypothetical instruments, a "Bulimia Test" and an "Anorexia Test." This common factor would have to be named. One factor analyst looking at the data and the items of each test might christen the common factor an *eating disorder factor*. Another factor analyst examining exactly the same materials might label the common factor a *body weight preoccupation factor*. A third analyst might name the factor a *self-perception disorder factor*. Which of these is correct?

From a statistical perspective, it is simply impossible to say what the common factor should be named. Naming factors that emerge from a factor analysis has more to do with knowledge, judgment, and verbal abstraction ability than with mathematical expertise. There are no hard-and-fast rules. Factor analysts exercise their own judgment about what factor name best communicates the meaning of the factor. Further, even the criteria used to identify a common factor, as well as related technical matters, can be a matter of debate, if not heated controversy (see, for example, Bartholomew, 1996a, 1996b; Maraun, 1996a, 1996b, 1996c; McDonald, 1996a, 1996b; Mulaik, 1996a, 1996b; Rozeboom, 1996a, 1996b; Schönemann, 1996a, 1996b; Steiger, 1996a, 1996b).

Factor analysis is a subject rich in technical complexity. Its uses and applications can vary as a function of the research objectives as well as the nature of the tests and the constructs under study. Factor analysis is the subject of our *Close-Up* in Chapter 10.

## Validity, Bias, and Fairness

In the eyes of many laypeople, questions concerning the validity of a test are intimately tied to questions concerning the fair use of tests and the issues of bias and fairness. Let us hasten to point out that validity, fairness in test use, and test bias are three separate issues. It is possible, for example, for a valid test to be used fairly or unfairly.

JUST THINK . . .

What might be an example of a valid test used in an unfair manner?

### Test Bias

For the general public, the term *bias* as applied to psychological and educational tests may conjure up many meanings having to do with prejudice and preferential treatment (Brown et al., 1999). For federal judges, the term *bias* as it relates to items on children's intelligence tests is synonymous with "too difficult for one group as compared to another" (Sattler, 1991). For psychometricians, **bias** is a factor inherent in a test that systematically prevents accurate, impartial measurement.

Psychometricians have developed the technical means to identify and remedy bias, at least in the mathematical sense. As a simple illustration, consider a test we will call the "flip-coin test" (FCT). The "equipment" needed to conduct this test is a two-sided coin. One side ("heads") has the image of a profile and the other side ("tails") does not. The FCT would be considered biased if the instrument (the coin) were weighted so that either heads or tails appears more frequently than by chance alone. If the test in question were an intelligence test, the test would be considered biased if it were constructed so that people who had brown eyes consistently and systematically obtained higher scores than people with green eyes—assuming, of course, that in reality people with brown eyes are not generally more intelligent than people with green eyes.

*Systematic* is a key word in our definition of test bias. We have previously looked at sources of *random* or chance variation in test scores. *Bias* implies *systematic* variation.

Another illustration: Let's suppose we need to hire 50 secretaries and so we place an ad in the newspaper. In response to the ad, 200 people reply, including 100 people who happen to have brown eyes and 100 people who happen to have green eyes. Each of the 200 applicants is individually administered a hypothetical test we will call the "Test of Secretarial Skills" (TSS). Logic tells us that eye color is probably not a relevant variable with respect to performing the duties of a secretary. We would therefore have no reason to believe that green-eyed people are better secretaries than brown-eyed people or vice versa. We might reasonably expect that, after the tests have been scored and the selection process has been completed, an approximately equivalent number of brown-eyed and green-eyed people would have been hired (that is, approximately 25 brown-eyed people and 25 green-eyed people). But what if it turned out that 48 green-eyed people were hired and only 2 brown-eyed people were hired? Is this evidence that the TSS is a biased test?

Although the answer to this question seems simple on the face of it—"Yes, the test is biased because they should have hired 25 and 25!"—a truly responsible answer to this question would entail statistically troubleshooting the test and the entire selection procedure (see Berk, 1982). One reason some tests have been found to be biased has more to do with the design of the research study than the design of the test. For example, if there are too few testtakers in one of the groups (such as the minority group—literally), this methodological problem will make it appear as if the test is biased when in fact it may not be. A test may justifiably be deemed biased if some portion of its variance stems from some factor(s) that are irrelevant to performance on the criterion measure; as a consequence, one group of testtakers will systematically perform differently from another. Prevention during test development is the best cure for test bias, though a procedure called *estimated true score transformations* represents one of many available *post hoc* remedies (Mueller, 1949; see also Reynolds & Brown, 1984).[5]

**Rating error**  A **rating** is a numerical or verbal judgment (or both) that places a person or an attribute along a continuum identified by a scale of numerical or word descriptors known as a **rating scale.** Simply stated, a **rating error** is a judgment resulting from the intentional or unintentional misuse of a rating scale. Thus, for example, a **leniency error** (also known as a **generosity error**) is, as its name implies, an error in rating that arises from the tendency on the part of the rater to be lenient in scoring, marking, and/or grading. From your own experience during course registration, you might be aware that a section of a particular course will quickly be filled if it is being taught by a professor with a reputation for leniency errors in end-of-term grading.

At the other extreme is a **severity error.** Movie critics who pan just about everything they review may be guilty of severity errors. Of course, that is only true if they review a wide range of movies that might consensually be viewed as good and bad.

Another type of error might be termed a **central tendency error.** Here the rater, for whatever reason, exhibits a general and systematic reluctance to giving ratings at either

> **JUST THINK . . .**
>
> What factor do you think might account for the phenomenon of raters whose ratings always seem to fall victim to the central tendency error?

---

5. Lest you think that there is something not quite right about transforming data under such circumstances, we add that even though *transformation* is synonymous with *change,* the change referred to here is merely a change in form, not meaning. Data may be transformed to place them in a more useful form, not to change their meaning.

the positive or the negative extreme. Consequently, all of this rater's ratings would tend to cluster in the middle of the rating continuum.

One way to overcome what might be termed *restriction-of-range rating errors* (central tendency, leniency, severity errors) is to use **rankings,** a procedure that requires the rater to measure individuals against one another instead of against an absolute scale. By using rankings instead of ratings, the rater (now the "ranker") is forced to select first, second, third choices, and so forth.

**Halo effect** describes the fact that, for some raters, some ratees can do no wrong. More specifically, a halo effect may also be defined as a tendency to give a particular ratee a higher rating than he or she objectively deserves because of the rater's failure to discriminate among conceptually distinct and potentially independent aspects of a ratee's behavior. Just for the sake of example—and not for a moment because we believe it is even in the realm of possibility—let's suppose Lady Gaga consented to write and deliver a speech on multivariate analysis. Her speech probably would earn much higher all-around ratings if given before the founding chapter of the Lady Gaga Fan Club than if delivered before and rated by the membership of, say, the Royal Statistical Society. This would be true even in the highly improbable case that the members of each group were equally savvy with respect to multivariate analysis. We would expect the halo effect to be operative at full power as Lady Gaga spoke before her diehard fans.

Criterion data may also be influenced by the rater's knowledge of the ratee's race or sex (Landy & Farr, 1980). Males have been shown to receive more favorable evaluations than females in traditionally masculine occupations. Except in highly integrated situations, ratees tend to receive higher ratings from raters of the same race (Landy & Farr, 1980). Returning to our hypothetical Test of Secretarial Skills (TSS) example, a particular rater may have had particularly great—or particularly distressing—prior experiences with green-eyed (or brown-eyed) people and so may be making extraordinarily high (or low) ratings on that irrational basis.

Training programs to familiarize raters with common rating errors and sources of rater bias have shown promise in reducing rating errors and increasing measures of reliability and validity. Lecture, role playing, discussion, watching oneself on videotape, and computer simulation of different situations are some of the many techniques that could be brought to bear in such training programs. We revisit the subject of rating and rating error in our discussion of personality assessment later. For now, let's take up the issue of test fairness.

## Test Fairness

In contrast to questions of test bias, which may be thought of as technically complex statistical problems, issues of test fairness tend to be rooted more in thorny issues involving values (Halpern, 2000). Thus, although questions of test bias can sometimes be answered with mathematical precision and finality, questions of fairness can be grappled with endlessly by well-meaning people who hold opposing points of view. With that caveat in mind, and with exceptions most certainly in the offing, we will define **fairness** in a psychometric context as the extent to which a test is used in an impartial, just, and equitable way.[6]

---

6. On a somewhat more technical note, Ghiselli et al. (1981, p. 320) observed that "fairness refers to whether a difference in mean predictor scores between two groups represents a useful distinction for society, relative to a decision that must be made, or whether the difference represents a bias that is irrelevant to the objectives at hand." For those interested, some more practical guidelines regarding fairness, at least as construed by legislative bodies and the courts were offered by Russell (1984).

Some uses of tests are patently unfair in the judgment of any reasonable person. During the cold war, the government of what was then called the Soviet Union used psychiatric tests to suppress political dissidents. People were imprisoned or institutionalized for verbalizing opposition to the government. Apart from such blatantly unfair uses of tests, what constitutes a fair and an unfair use of tests is a matter left to various parties in the assessment enterprise. Ideally, the test developer strives for fairness in the test development process and in the test's manual and usage guidelines. The test user strives for fairness in the way the test is actually used. Society strives for fairness in test use by means of legislation, judicial decisions, and administrative regulations.

Fairness as applied to tests is a difficult and complicated subject. However, it is possible to discuss some rather common misunderstandings regarding what are sometimes perceived as unfair or even biased tests. Some tests, for example, have been labeled "unfair" because they discriminate among groups of people.[7] The reasoning here goes something like this: "Although individual differences exist, it is a truism that all people are created equal. Accordingly, any differences found among groups of people on any psychological trait must be an artifact of an unfair or biased test." Because this belief is rooted in faith as opposed to scientific evidence—in fact, it flies in the face of scientific evidence—it is virtually impossible to refute. One either accepts it on faith or does not.

We would all like to believe that people are equal in every way and that all people are capable of rising to the same heights given equal opportunity. A more realistic view would appear to be that each person is capable of fulfilling a personal potential. Because people differ so obviously with respect to physical traits, one would be hard put to believe that psychological differences found to exist between individuals—and groups of individuals—are purely a function of inadequate tests. Again, although a test is not inherently unfair or biased simply because it is a tool by which group differences are found, the *use* of the test data, like the use of any data, can be unfair.

Another misunderstanding of what constitutes an unfair or biased test is that it is unfair to administer to a particular population a standardized test that did not include members of that population in the standardization sample. In fact, the test may well be biased, but that must be determined by statistical or other means. The sheer fact that no members of a particular group were included in the standardization sample does not *in itself* invalidate the test for use with that group.

A final source of misunderstanding is the complex problem of remedying situations where bias or unfair test usage has been found to occur. In the area of selection for jobs, positions in universities and professional schools, and the like, a number of different preventive measures and remedies have been attempted. As you read about the tools used in these attempts in this chapter's *Everyday Psychometrics,* form your own opinions regarding what constitutes a fair use of employment and other tests in a selection process.

If performance differences are found between identified groups of people on a valid and reliable test used for selection purposes, some hard questions may have to be dealt with if the test is to continue to be used. Is the problem due to some technical deficiency in the test, or is the test in reality too good at identifying people of different levels of ability? Regardless, is the test being used fairly? If so, what might society do to remedy the skill disparity between different groups as reflected on the test?

---

7. The verb *to discriminate* here is used in the psychometric sense, meaning *to show a statistically significant difference between individuals or groups with respect to measurement.* The great difference between this statistical, scientific definition and other colloquial definitions (such as *to treat differently and/or unfairly because of group membership*) must be kept firmly in mind in discussions of bias and fairness.

# Adjustment of Test Scores
# by Group Membership:
# Fairness in Testing or Foul Play?

Any test, regardless of its psychometric soundness, may be knowingly or unwittingly used in a way that has an adverse impact on one or another group. If such adverse impact is found to exist and if social policy demands some remedy or an affirmative action program, then psychometricians have a number of techniques at their disposal to create change. Table 1 lists some of these techniques.

Although psychometricians have the tools to institute special policies through manipulations in test development, scoring, and interpretation, there are few clear guidelines in this controversial area (Brown, 1994; Gottfredson, 1994, 2000; Sackett & Wilk, 1994). The waters are further muddied by the fact that some of the guidelines seem to have contradictory implications. For example, although racial preferment in employee selection (disparate impact) is unlawful, the use of valid and unbiased selection procedures virtually guarantees disparate impact. This state of affairs will change only when racial disparities in job-related skills and abilities are minimized (Gottfredson, 1994).

In 1991, Congress enacted legislation effectively barring employers from adjusting testtakers' scores for the purpose of making hiring or promotion decisions. Section 106 of the Civil Rights Act of 1991 made it illegal for employers "in connection with the selection or referral of applicants or candidates for employment or promotion to adjust the scores of, use different cutoffs for, or otherwise alter the results of employment-related tests on the basis of race, color, religion, sex, or national origin."

The law prompted concern on the part of many psychologists who believed it would adversely affect various societal groups and might reverse social gains. Brown (1994, p. 927) forecast that "the ramifications of the Act are more far-reaching than Congress envisioned when it considered the amendment and could mean that many personality tests and physical ability tests that rely on separate scoring for men and women are outlawed in employment selection." Arguments in favor of group-related test-score adjustment have been made on philosophical as well as technical grounds. From a philosophical perspective, increased minority representation is socially valued to the point that minority preference in test scoring is warranted. In the same vein, minority preference is viewed both as a remedy for past societal wrongs and as a contemporary guarantee of proportional workplace representation. From a more technical perspective, it is argued that some tests require adjustment in scores because (1) the tests are biased, and a given score on them does not necessarily carry the same meaning for all testtakers; and/or (2) "a particular way of using a test is at odds with an espoused position as to what constitutes fair use" (Sackett & Wilk, 1994, p. 931).

In contrast to advocates of test-score adjustment are those who view such adjustments as part of a social agenda for preferential treatment of certain groups. These opponents of test-score adjustment reject the subordination of individual effort and ability to group membership as criteria in the assignment of test scores (Gottfredson, 1988, 2000). Hunter and Schmidt (1976, p. 1069) described the unfortunate consequences for all parties involved in a college selection situation wherein poor-risk applicants were accepted on the basis of score adjustments or quotas. With reference to the employment setting, Hunter and Schmidt (1976) described one case in which entrance standards were lowered so more members of a particular group could be hired. However, many of these new hires did not pass promotion tests—with the result that the company was sued for discriminatory promotion practice. Yet another consideration concerns the feelings of "minority applicants who are selected under a quota system but who also would have been selected under unqualified individualism and must therefore pay the price, in lowered prestige and self-esteem" (Jensen, 1980, p. 398).

A number of psychometric models of fairness in testing have been presented and debated in the scholarly literature (Hunter & Schmidt, 1976; Petersen & Novick, 1976; Schmidt & Hunter, 1974; Thorndike, 1971). Despite a wealth of research and debate, a long-standing question in the field of personnel psychology remains: "How can group differences on cognitive ability tests be reduced while retaining existing high levels of reliability and criterion-related validity?"

According to Gottfredson (1994), the answer probably will not come from measurement-related research because differences in scores on many of the tests in question arise principally from differences in job-related abilities. For Gottfredson (1994, p. 963), "the biggest contribution personnel psychologists can make in the long run may be to insist collectively and candidly that their measurement tools are neither the cause of nor the cure for racial differences in job skills and consequent inequalities in employment."

**Table 1**
**Psychometric Techniques for Preventing or Remedying Adverse Impact and/or Instituting an Affirmative Action Program**

*Some of these techniques may be preventive if employed in the test development process, and others may be employed with already established tests. Some of these techniques entail direct score manipulation; others, such as banding, do not. Preparation of this table benefited from Sackett and Wilk (1994), and their work should be consulted for more detailed consideration of the complex issues involved.*

| Technique | Description |
| --- | --- |
| Addition of Points | A constant number of points is added to the test score of members of a particular group. The purpose of the point addition is to reduce or eliminate observed differences between groups. |
| Differential Scoring of Items | This technique incorporates group membership information, not in adjusting a raw score on a test but in deriving the score in the first place. The application of the technique may involve the scoring of some test items for members of one group but not scoring the same test items for members of another group. This technique is also known as *empirical keying by group.* |
| Elimination of Items Based on Differential Item Functioning | This procedure entails removing from a test any items found to inappropriately favor one group's test performance over another's. Ideally, the intent of the elimination of certain test items is not to make the test easier for any group but simply to make the test fairer. Sackett and Wilk (1994) put it this way: "Conceptually, rather than asking 'Is this item harder for members of Group X than it is for Group Y?' these approaches ask 'Is this item harder for members of Group X with true score Z than it is for members of Group Y with true score Z?'" |
| Differential Cutoffs | Different cutoffs are set for members of different groups. For example, a passing score for members of one group is 65, whereas a passing score for members of another group is 70. As with the addition of points, the purpose of differential cutoffs is to reduce or eliminate observed differences between groups. |
| Separate Lists | Different lists of testtaker scores are established by group membership. For each list, test performance of testtakers is ranked in top-down fashion. Users of the test scores for selection purposes may alternate selections from the different lists. Depending on factors such as the allocation rules in effect and the equivalency of the standard deviation within the groups, the separate-lists technique may yield effects similar to those of other techniques, such as the addition of points and differential cutoffs. In practice, the separate list is popular in affirmative action programs where the intent is to overselect from previously excluded groups. |
| Within-Group Norming | Used as a remedy for adverse impact if members of different groups tend to perform differentially on a particular test, within-group norming entails the conversion of all raw scores into percentile scores or standard scores based on the test performance of one's own group. In essence, an individual testtaker is being compared only with other members of his or her own group. When race is the primary criterion of group membership and separate norms are established by race, this technique is known as *race-norming.* |
| Banding | The effect of banding of test scores is to make equivalent all scores that fall within a particular range or band. For example, thousands of raw scores on a test may be transformed to a stanine having a value of 1 to 9. All scores that fall within each of the stanine boundaries will be treated by the test user as either equivalent or subject to some additional selection criteria. A *sliding band* (Cascio et al., 1991) is a modified banding procedure wherein a band is adjusted ("slid") to permit the selection of more members of some group than would otherwise be selected. |
| Preference Policies | In the interest of affirmative action, reverse discrimination, or some other policy deemed to be in the interest of society at large, a test user might establish a policy of preference based on group membership. For example, if a municipal fire department sought to increase the representation of female personnel in its ranks, it might institute a test-related policy designed to do just that. A key provision in this policy might be that when a male and a female earn equal scores on the test used for hiring, the female will be hired. |

Beyond the workplace and personnel psychology, what role, if any, should measurement play in promoting diversity? As Haidt et al. (2003) reflected, there are several varieties of diversity, some perceived as more valuable than others. Do we need to develop more specific measures designed, for example, to discourage "moral diversity" while encouraging "demographic diversity"? These types of questions have implications in a number of areas from academic admission policies to immigration.

---

**JUST THINK . . .**

How do *you* feel about the use of various procedures to adjust test scores on the basis of group membership? Are these types of issues best left to measurement experts?

Our discussion of issues of test fairness and test bias may seem to have brought us far afield of the seemingly cut-and-dried, relatively nonemotional subject of test validity. However, the complex issues accompanying discussions of test validity, including issues of fairness and bias, must be wrestled with by us all. For further consideration of the philosophical issues involved, we refer you to the solitude of your own thoughts and the reading of your own conscience.

## Self-Assessment

Test your understanding of elements of this chapter by seeing if you can explain each of the following terms, expressions, and abbreviations:

base rate
bias
central tendency error
concurrent validity
confirmatory factor analysis
construct
construct validity
content validity
content validity ratio (CVR)
convergent evidence
convergent validity
criterion
criterion contamination
criterion-related validity
discriminant evidence
expectancy chart
expectancy data

expectancy table
exploratory factor analysis
face validity
factor analysis
factor loading
fairness
false negative
false positive
generosity error
halo effect
hit rate
homogeneity
incremental validity
inference
intercept bias
leniency error
local validation study

method of contrasted groups
miss rate
multitrait-multimethod matrix
predictive validity
ranking
rating
rating error
rating scale
severity error
slope bias
test blueprint
validation
validation study
validity
validity coefficient

# 7

# *Utility*

In everyday language, we use the term *utility* to refer to the usefulness of some thing or some process. In the language of psychometrics, *utility* (also referred to as *test utility*) means much the same thing; it refers to how useful a test is. More specifically, it refers to the practical value of using a test to aid in decision making. An overview of some frequently raised utility-related questions would include the following:

- How useful is this test in terms of cost efficiency?
- How useful is this test in terms of savings in time?
- What is the *comparative utility* of this test? That is, how useful is this test as compared to another test?
- What is the *clinical utility* of this test? That is, how useful is it for purposes of diagnostic assessment or treatment?
- What is the *diagnostic utility* of this neurological test? That is, how useful is it for classification purposes?
- How useful is this medical school admissions test used in assigning a limited number of openings to an overwhelming number of applicants?
- How useful is the addition of another test to the test battery already in use for screening purposes?
- How useful is this personnel test as a tool for the selection of new employees?
- Is this particular personnel test used for promoting middle-management employees more useful than using no test at all?
- Is the time and money it takes to administer, score, and interpret this personnel promotion test battery worth it as compared to simply asking the employee's supervisor for a recommendation as to whether the employee should be promoted?
- How useful is the training program in place for new recruits?
- How effective is this particular clinical technique?
- Should this new intervention be used in place of an existing intervention?

# What Is Utility?

We may define **utility** in the context of testing and assessment as the usefulness or practical value of testing to improve efficiency. Note that in this definition, "testing" refers to anything from a single test to a large-scale testing program that employs a battery of tests. For simplicity and convenience, in this chapter we often refer to the utility of one individual test. Keep in mind, however, that such discussion is applicable and generalizable to the utility of large-scale testing programs that may employ many tests or test batteries. *Utility* is also used to refer to the usefulness or practical value of a training program or intervention. We may speak, for example, of the utility of adding a particular component to an existing corporate training program or clinical intervention. Throughout this chapter, however, our discussion and illustrations will focus primarily on utility as it relates to testing.

**JUST THINK . . .**

Based on everything that you have read about tests and testing so far in this book, how do you think you would go about making a judgment regarding the utility of a test?

If your response to our *Just Think* question about judging a test's utility made reference to the reliability of a test or the validity of a test, then you are correct—well, partly. Judgments concerning the utility of a test are made on the basis of test reliability and validity data as well as on other data.

## Factors That Affect a Test's Utility

A number of considerations are involved in making a judgment about the utility of a test. Here we will review how a test's psychometric soundness, costs, and benefits can all affect a judgment concerning a test's utility.

**Psychometric soundness** By psychometric soundness, we refer—as you probably know by now—to the reliability and validity of a test. A test is said to be psychometrically sound for a particular purpose if reliability and validity coefficients are acceptably high. How can an index of utility be distinguished from an index of reliability or validity? The short answer to that question is as follows: An index of reliability can tell us something about how consistently a test measures what it measures; and an index of validity can tell us something about whether a test measures what it purports to measure. But an index of utility can tell us something about the practical value of the information derived from scores on the test. Test scores are said to have utility if their use in a particular situation helps us to make better decisions—better, that is, in the sense of being more cost-effective.

In previous chapters on reliability and validity, it was noted that reliability sets a ceiling on validity. It is tempting to draw the conclusion that a comparable relationship exists between validity and utility and conclude that "validity sets a ceiling on utility." In many instances, such a conclusion would certainly be defensible. After all, a test must be valid to be useful. Of what practical value or usefulness is a test for a specific purpose if the test is not valid for that purpose?

Unfortunately, few things about utility theory and its application are simple and uncomplicated. Generally speaking, the higher the criterion-related validity of test scores for making a particular decision, the higher the utility of the test is likely to be. However, there are exceptions to this general rule. This is so because many factors may enter into an estimate of a test's utility, and there are great variations in the ways in which the utility of a test is determined. In a study of the utility of a test used for personnel selection, for example, the selection ratio may be very high. We'll review the concept of a selection ratio (introduced in the previous chapter) in greater detail later in this chapter. For now, let's simply note that if the selection ratio is very high, most people who apply for the job are being hired. Under such circumstances, the validity of the test may have little to do with the test's utility.

What about the other side of the coin? Would it be accurate to conclude that "a valid test is a useful test"? At first blush this statement may also seem perfectly logical and true. But once again—we're talking about utility theory here, and this can be very complicated stuff—the answer is no; it is *not* the case that "a valid test is a useful test." People often refer to a particular test as "valid" if scores on the test have been shown to be good indicators of how the person will score on the criterion.

An example from the published literature may help to further illustrate how a valid tool of assessment may have questionable utility. One way of monitoring the drug use of cocaine users being treated on an outpatient basis is through regular urine tests. As an alternative to that monitoring method, researchers developed a patch which, if worn day and night, could detect cocaine use through sweat. In a study designed to explore the utility of the sweat patch with 63 opiate-dependent volunteers who were seeking treatment, investigators found a 92% level of agreement between a positive urine test for cocaine and a positive test on the sweat patch for cocaine. On the face of it, these results would seem to be encouraging for the developers of the patch. However, this high rate of agreement occurred only when the patch had been untampered with and properly applied by research participants—which, as it turned out, wasn't all that often. Overall, the researchers felt compelled to conclude that the sweat patch had limited utility as a means of monitoring drug use in outpatient treatment facilities (Chawarski et al., 2007). This study illustrates that even though a test may be psychometrically sound, it may have little utility—particularly if the targeted testtakers demonstrate a tendency to "bend, fold, spindle, mutilate, destroy, tamper with," or otherwise fail to scrupulously follow the test's directions.

Another utility-related factor does not necessarily have anything to do with the behavior of targeted testtakers. In fact, it typically has more to do with the behavior of the test's targeted *users*.

**Costs** Mention the word *costs* and what comes to mind? Usually words like *money* or *dollars*. In considerations of test utility, factors variously referred to as *economic, financial,* or *budget-related* in nature must certainly be taken into account. In fact, one of the most basic elements in any utility analysis is the financial cost of the selection device (or training program or clinical intervention) under study. However, the meaning of "cost" as applied to test utility can extend far beyond dollars and cents (see this chapter's *Everyday Psychometrics*). Briefly, **cost** in the context of test utility refers to disadvantages, losses, or expenses in both economic and noneconomic terms.

As used with respect to test utility decisions, the term *costs* can be interpreted in the traditional, economic sense; that is, relating to expenditures associated with testing or not testing. If testing is to be conducted, then it may be necessary to allocate funds to purchase (1) a particular test, (2) a supply of blank test protocols, and (3) computerized test processing, scoring, and interpretation from the test publisher or some independent service. Associated costs of testing may come in the form of (1) payment to professional personnel and staff associated with test administration, scoring, and interpretation, (2) facility rental, mortgage, and/or other charges related to the usage of the test facility, and (3) insurance, legal, accounting, licensing, and other routine costs of doing business. In some settings, such as private clinics, these costs may be offset by revenue, such as fees paid by testtakers. In other settings, such as research organizations, these costs will be paid from the test user's funds, which may in turn derive from sources such as private donations or government grants.

## Rethinking the "Costs" of Testing— and of Not Testing

Consider the following scenario: In the course of a basketball game with friends, a man trips, complains of pain in his leg, and sits out the rest of the game. Minute by minute the pain in his leg seems to worsen. Instead of going home, the man decides to go to a local hospital emergency room. By now he's in so much pain that he can't even drive. One of the man's basketball buddies drives his injured friend to the hospital.

After taking the patient's history and performing a physical examination, the emergency room physician suspects that the man has a broken leg. The physician orders a diagnostic test—in this case, an X-ray—to confirm the diagnosis. The patient must pay about $100 for the test. The physician could have ordered a number of other diagnostic imaging tests, such as an MRI, which also would have confirmed the diagnosis. However, an MRI would have cost the patient about $800 and, in most such cases, would have yielded exactly the same diagnostic information. The physician informs the man that, in the rather extraordinary event that the X-ray indicates the bone was not broken but shattered, a more elaborate (and expensive) test such as an MRI will be ordered.

About an hour later, the results are in. The man has, indeed, broken his leg. The good news is that it is a clean break—the bone is not shattered—and the leg can be set. The man leaves the hospital with a cast and crutches. It takes time, but the story has a happy ending. Months later, he is back on his feet and yes, back on the basketball court.

Now consider an alternative scenario involving the same man who broke his leg during a basketball game. Instead of arranging an emergency medical visit, the man makes his way home, believing the cost of the exam will outweigh its benefits. He decides to treat his injury with bed rest and ice packs placed on his leg. After days and weeks go by, things gradually get better, but not really all that much better. Without the benefit of testing to yield an accurate diagnosis

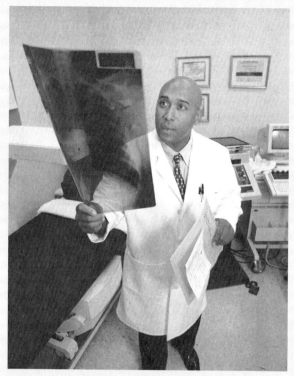

*The cost of this X-ray might be $100 or so . . . but what is the cost of not having this diagnostic procedure done?*

leading to the appropriate intervention, the man has done permanent damage to his body. The pain is much less, but it will never go away completely. The man walks with a limp, cannot really run, and has difficulty negotiating stairs. His basketball-playing days are over. He probably saved a couple of hundred dollars in medical expenses . . . but at what cost? Was it worth it?

The moral of the story is that there are sometimes costs associated with *not* testing. Further, the costs of not testing can be staggering—and not merely in financial terms.

The economic costs listed here are the easy ones to calculate. Not so easy to calculate are other economic costs, particularly those associated with not testing or testing with an instrument that turns out to be ineffective. As an admittedly far-fetched example, what if skyrocketing fuel costs prompted a commercial airline to institute cost-cutting methods?[1] What if one of the cost-cutting methods the airline instituted was the cessation of its personnel assessment program? Now, all personnel—including pilots and equipment repair personnel—would be hired and trained with little or no evaluation. Alternatively, what if the airline simply converted its current hiring and training program to a much less expensive program with much less rigorous (and perhaps ineffective) testing for all personnel? What economic (and noneconomic) consequences do you envision might result from such action? Would cost-cutting actions such as those described previously be prudent from a business perspective?

One need not hold an M.B.A. or an advanced degree in consumer psychology to understand that such actions on the part of the airline would probably not be effective. The resulting cost savings from elimination of such assessment programs would pale in comparison to the probable losses in customer revenue once word got out about the airline's strategy for cost cutting; loss of public confidence in the safety of the airline would almost certainly translate into a loss of ticket sales. Additionally, such revenue losses would be irrevocably compounded by any safety-related incidents (with their attendant lawsuits) that occurred as a consequence of such imprudent cost cutting.

In this example, mention of the variable of "loss of confidence" brings us to another meaning of "costs" in terms of utility analyses; that is, costs in terms of loss. Noneconomic costs of drastic cost cutting by the airline might come in the form of harm or injury to airline passengers and crew as a result of incompetent pilots flying the plane and incompetent ground crews servicing the planes. Although people (and most notably insurance companies) do place dollar amounts on the loss of life and limb, for our purposes we can still categorize such tragic losses as noneconomic in nature.

Other noneconomic costs of testing can be far more subtle. Consider, for example, a published study that examined the utility of taking four X-ray pictures as compared to two X-ray pictures in routine screening for fractured ribs among potential child abuse victims. Hansen et al. (2008) found that a four-view series of X-rays differed significantly from the more traditional, two-view series in terms of the number of fractures identified. These researchers recommended the addition of two more views in the routine X-ray protocols for possible physical abuse. Stated another way, these authors found diagnostic utility in adding two X-ray views to the more traditional protocol. The financial cost of using the two additional X-rays was seen as worth it, given the consequences and potential costs of failing to diagnose the injuries. Here, the (noneconomic) cost concerns the risk of letting a potential child abuser continue to abuse a child without detection.

Our featured test user in this chapter, Dr. Erik Viirre, has had a wealth of experience in determining whether certain tests and technologies have value. In the excerpt from his *Meet an Assessment Professional* essay reprinted here, Dr. Viirre describes how the addition of a cell phone–like task to a driving simulation had the effect of impairing driving performance, thus attesting to the value of eye-movement detection technologies in automobiles.

**JUST THINK . . .**

How would you describe the noneconomic cost of a nation's armed forces using ineffective screening mechanisms to screen military recruits?

**Benefits**   Judgments regarding the utility of a test may take into account whether the benefits of testing justify the costs of administering, scoring, and interpreting the test. So, when evaluating the utility of a particular test, an evaluation is made of the costs

---

1. This example may not be all that far-fetched. See *www.usatoday.com/travel/flights/2008-03-06-fine_N.htm*.

## Meet Dr. Erik Viirre

. . . we carried out a study (Tsai et al., 2007) where we combined the Paced Auditory Serial Addition Task (PASAT) with a driving simulator. The idea was to examine the combination of driving (a visual and psychomotor task), with a pure auditory task. We examined eye movement activity during the driving task with driving alone and with driving and the PASAT. The Paced Auditory Serial Addition Task requires the subject to listen to spoken numbers and respond verbally with the sum of the two most recently heard numbers. Thus the combination was like driving while talking on the phone.

We found a number of effects, including that trying to do the PASAT interfered with subjects' ability to maintain driving performance, especially when the auditory task was very rapid. Importantly, we were also able to detect changes in eye movement activity. During driving alone, subjects visually scanned the scene they observed, checking other lanes, checking their rearview mirror and reading their instruments. By contrast, during the task of doing the driving simulation and the PASAT simultaneously, there were dramatic changes in eye movement activity, *despite the fact that the visual task was exactly the same.* Here, subjects ignored their rearview mirror and instruments and had a very restricted range of eye movements.

Through our research we hope to develop recommendations on the importance of the relative workload of a variety of tasks. In addition, with our physiologic measurements, we hope to

**Erik Viirre, M.D., Ph.D., Associate Adjunct Professor, School of Medicine, University of California, San Diego UCSD**

develop technologies that will assess people in real-time during performance of their tasks. For example, eye movement detection technologies have now been implemented in new cars to assess the driver's state of focus and alertness. Work such as ours supports the argument that these technologies have value.

*Read more of what Dr. Viirre had to say—his entire essay, complete with illustrations—at www.mhhe.com/cohentesting8.*

incurred by testing as compared to the benefits accrued from testing. Here, **benefit** refers to profits, gains, or advantages. As we did in discussing costs associated with testing (and not testing), we can view *benefits* in both economic and noneconomic terms.

From an economic perspective, the cost of administering tests can be minuscule when compared to the economic benefits—or financial returns in dollars and cents—that a successful testing program can yield. For example, if a new personnel testing program results in the selection of employees who produce significantly more than other employees, then the program will have been responsible for greater productivity on the part of the new employees. This greater productivity may lead to greater overall company profits. If a new method of quality control in a food-processing plant results in higher quality products and less product being trashed as waste, the net result will be greater profits for the company.

There are also many potential noneconomic benefits to be derived from thoughtfully designed and well-run testing programs. In industrial settings, a partial list of such noneconomic benefits—many carrying with them economic benefits as well—would include:

- an increase in the quality of workers' performance;
- an increase in the quantity of workers' performance;
- a decrease in the time needed to train workers;
- a reduction in the number of accidents;
- a reduction in worker turnover.

The cost of administering tests can be well worth it if the result is certain noneconomic benefits, such as a good work environment. As an example, consider the admissions program in place at most universities. Educational institutions that pride themselves on their graduates are often on the lookout for ways to improve the way that they select applicants for their programs. Why? Because it is to the credit of a university that their graduates succeed at their chosen careers. A large portion of happy, successful graduates enhances the university's reputation and sends the message that the university is doing something right. Related benefits to a university that has students who are successfully going through its programs may include high morale and a good learning environment for students, high morale of and a good work environment for the faculty, and reduced load on counselors and on disciplinary personnel and boards. With fewer students leaving the school before graduation for academic reasons, there might actually be less of a load on admissions personnel as well; the admissions office will not be constantly working to select students to replace those who have left before completing their degree programs. A good work environment and a good learning environment are not necessarily things that money can buy. Such outcomes can, however, result from a well-administered admissions program that consistently selects qualified students who will keep up with the work and "fit in" to the environment of a particular university.

One of the economic benefits of a diagnostic test used to make decisions about involuntary hospitalization of psychiatric patients is a benefit to society at large. Persons are frequently confined involuntarily for psychiatric reasons if they are harmful to themselves or others. Tools of psychological assessment such as tests, case history data, and interviews may be used to make a decision regarding involuntary psychiatric hospitalization. The more useful such tools of assessment are, the safer society will be from individuals intent on inflicting harm or injury.

> **JUST THINK . . .**
>
> Provide an example of another situation in which the stakes involving the utility of a tool of psychological assessment are high.

Clearly, the potential noneconomic benefit derived from the use of such diagnostic tools is great. It is also true, however, that the potential economic *costs* are great when errors are made. Errors in clinical determination made in cases of involuntary hospitalization may cause people who are not threats to themselves or others to be denied their freedom. The stakes involving the utility of tests can indeed be quite high.

How do professionals in the field of testing and assessment balance variables such as psychometric soundness, benefits, and costs? How do they come to a judgment regarding the utility of a specific test? How do they decide that the benefits (however defined) outweigh the costs (however defined) and that a test or intervention indeed has utility? There are formulas that can be used with values that can be filled in, and there are tables that can be used with values to be looked up. We will introduce you to such methods in this chapter. But let's preface our discussion of utility analysis by emphasizing that other, less definable elements—such as prudence, vision, and, for lack of a better (or more technical) term, *common sense*—must be ever-present in the process. A psychometrically sound test of practical value is worth paying for, even when the dollar cost is high, if the potential benefits of its use are also high or if the potential costs of *not* using it are high. We have discussed "costs" and "benefits" at length in order to underscore that such matters cannot be considered solely in monetary terms.

## Utility Analysis

### *What Is a Utility Analysis?*

A **utility analysis** may be broadly defined as a family of techniques that entail a cost–benefit analysis designed to yield information relevant to a decision about the usefulness and/or practical value of a tool of assessment. Note that in this definition, we used the phrase "family of techniques." This is so because a utility analysis is not one specific technique used for one specific objective. Rather, *utility analysis* is an umbrella term covering various possible methods, each requiring various kinds of data to be inputted and yielding various kinds of output. Some utility analyses are quite sophisticated, employing high-level mathematical models and detailed strategies for weighting the different variables under consideration (Roth et al., 2001). Other utility analyses are far more straightforward and can be readily understood in terms of answers to relatively uncomplicated questions, such as: "Which test gives us more bang for the buck?"

In a most general sense, a utility analysis may be undertaken for the purpose of evaluating whether the benefits of using a test (or training program or intervention) outweigh the costs. If undertaken to evaluate a test, the utility analysis will help make decisions regarding whether:

- one test is preferable to another test for use for a specific purpose;
- one tool of assessment (such as a test) is preferable to another tool of assessment (such as behavioral observation) for a specific purpose;
- the addition of one or more tests (or other tools of assessment) to one or more tests (or other tools of assessment) that are already in use is preferable for a specific purpose;
- no testing or assessment is preferable to any testing or assessment.

If undertaken for the purpose of evaluating a training program or intervention, the utility analysis will help make decisions regarding whether:

- one training program is preferable to another training program;
- one method of intervention is preferable to another method of intervention;
- the addition or subtraction of elements to an existing training program improves the overall training program by making it more effective and efficient;
- the addition or subtraction of elements to an existing method of intervention improves the overall intervention by making it more effective and efficient;
- no training program is preferable to a given training program;
- no intervention is preferable to a given intervention.

The endpoint of a utility analysis is typically an educated decision about which of many possible courses of action is optimal. For example, in a now-classic utility analysis, Cascio and Ramos (1986) found that the use of a particular approach to assessment in selecting managers could save a telephone company more than $13 million over four years (see also Cascio, 1994, 2000).

Whether reading about utility analysis in this chapter or in other sources, a solid foundation in the language of this endeavor—both written and graphic—is essential. Toward that end, we hope you find the detailed case illustration presented in our *Close-Up* helpful.

## How Is a Utility Analysis Conducted?

The specific objective of a utility analysis will dictate what sort of information will be required as well as the specific methods to be used. Here we will briefly discuss two general approaches to utility analysis. The first is an approach that employs data that should actually be quite familiar.

**Expectancy data** Some utility analyses will require little more than converting a scatterplot of test data to an expectancy table (much like the process described in the previous chapter). An expectancy table can provide an indication of the likelihood that a testtaker will score within some interval of scores on a criterion measure—an interval that may be categorized as "passing," "acceptable," or "failing." For example, with regard to the utility of a new and experimental personnel test in a corporate setting, an expectancy table can provide vital information to decision makers. An expectancy table might indicate, for example, that the higher a worker's score is on this new test, the greater the probability that the worker will be judged successful. In other words, the test is working as it should and, by instituting this new test on a permanent basis, the company could reasonably expect to improve its productivity.

Tables that could be used as an aid for personnel directors in their decision-making chores were published by H. C. Taylor and J. T. Russell in the *Journal of Applied Psychology* in 1939. Referred to by the names of their authors, the **Taylor-Russell tables** provide an estimate of the extent to which inclusion of a particular test in the selection system will improve selection. More specifically, the tables provide an estimate of the percentage of employees hired by the use of a particular test who will be successful at their jobs, given different combinations of three variables: the test's validity, the selection ratio used, and the base rate.

The value assigned for the test's validity is the computed validity coefficient. The *selection ratio* is a numerical value that reflects the relationship between the number of people to be hired and the number of people available to be hired. For instance, if there are 50 positions and 100 applicants, then the selection ratio is 50/100, or .50. As used here, *base rate* refers to the percentage of people hired under the existing system for a particular position. If, for example, a firm employs 25 computer programmers and 20 are considered successful, the base rate would be .80. With knowledge of the validity coefficient of a particular test along with the selection ratio, reference to the Taylor-Russell tables provides the personnel officer with an estimate of how much using the test would improve selection over existing methods.

A sample Taylor-Russell table is presented in Table 7–1. This table is for the base rate of .60, meaning that 60% of those hired under the existing system are successful in their work. Down the left-hand side are validity coefficients for a test that could be used to help select employees. Across the top are the various selection ratios. They reflect the proportion of the people applying for the jobs who will be hired. If a new test is

# Utility Analysis: An Illustration

Like factor analysis, discriminant analysis, psychoanalysis, and other specific approaches to analysis and evaluation, utility analysis has its own vocabulary. It even has its own images in terms of graphic representations of various phenomena. As a point of departure for learning about the words and images associated with utility analysis, we present a hypothetical scenario involving utility-related issues that arise in a corporate personnel office. The company is a South American package delivery company called Federale (pronounced *fed-a-rally*) Express (FE). The question at hand concerns the cost-effectiveness of adding a new test to the process of hiring delivery drivers. Consider the following details.

Dr. Wanda Carlos, the personnel director of Federale Express, has been charged with the task of evaluating the utility of adding a new test to the procedures currently in place for hiring delivery drivers. Current FE policy states that drivers must possess a valid driver's license and have no criminal record. Once hired, the delivery driver is placed on probation for three months, during which time on-the-job supervisory ratings (OTJSRs) are collected on random work days. If scores on the OTJSRs are satisfactory at the end of the probationary period, then the new delivery driver is deemed "qualified." Only qualified drivers attain permanent employee status and benefits at Federale Express.

The new evaluation procedure to be considered from a cost–benefit perspective is the Federale Express Road Test (FERT). The FERT is a procedure that takes less than one hour and entails the applicant driving an FE truck in actual traffic to a given destination, parallel parking, and then driving back to the start point. Does the FERT evidence criterion-related validity? If so, what cut score instituted to designate passing and failing scores would provide the greatest utility? These are preliminary questions that Dr. Carlos seeks to answer "on the road" to tackling issues of utility. They will be addressed in a study exploring the predictive validity of the FERT.

Dr. Carlos conducts a study in which a new group of drivers is hired based on FE's existing requirements: possession of a valid driver's license and no criminal record. However, to shed light on the question of the value of adding a new test to the process, these new hires must also take the FERT. So, subsequent to their hiring and after taking the FERT, these new employees are all placed on probation for the usual period of three months. During this probationary period, the usual on-the-job supervisory ratings (OTJSRs) are collected on randomly selected work days. The total scores the new employees achieve on the OTJSRs will be used to address not only the question of whether the new hire is qualified

but also questions concerning the added value of the FERT in the hiring process.

The three-month probationary period for the new hires is now over, and Dr. Carlos has accumulated quite a bit of data including scores on the predictor measure (the FERT) and scores on the criterion measure (the OTJSR). Looking at these data, Dr. Carlos wonders aloud about setting a cut score for the FERT . . . but does she even need to set a cut score? What if FE hired as many new permanent drivers as they need by a process of *top-down selection* with regard to OTJSRs? **Top-down selection** is a process of awarding available positions to applicants whereby the highest scorer is awarded the first position, the next highest scorer the next position, and so forth until all positions are filled. Dr. Carlos decides against a top-down hiring policy based on her awareness of its possible adverse impact. Top-down selection practices may carry with them unintended discriminatory effects (Cascio et al., 1995; De Corte & Lievens, 2005; McKinney & Collins, 1991; Zedeck et al., 1996).

For assistance in setting a cut score for hiring and in answering questions related to the utility of the FERT, Dr. Carlos purchases a (hypothetical) computer program entitled *Utility Analysis Made Easy.* This program contains definitions for a wealth of utility-related terms and also provides the tools for automatically creating computer-generated, utility-related tables and graphs. In what follows we learn, along with Dr. Carlos, how utility analysis can be "made easy" (or, at the very least, somewhat less complicated). After entering all of the data from this study, she enters the command *set cut score,* and what pops up is a table (Table 1) and this prompt:

*There is no single, all-around best way to determine the cut score to use on the FERT. The cut score chosen will reflect the goal of the selection process. In this case, consider which of the following four options best reflects the company's hiring policy and objectives. For some companies, the best cut score may be no cut score (Option 1).*

### (1) Limit the cost of selection by not using the FERT.

*This goal could be appropriate (a) if Federale Express just needs "bodies" to fill positions in order to continue operations, (b) if the consequences of hiring unqualified personnel are not a major consideration; and/or (c) if the size of the applicant pool is equal to or smaller than the number of openings.*

**Table 1**
**Hits and Misses**

| Term | General Definition | What It Means in This Study | Implication |
|---|---|---|---|
| Hit | A correct classification | A passing score on the FERT is associated with satisfactory performance on the OTJSR, and a failing score on the FERT is associated with unsatisfactory performance on the OTJSR. | The predictor test has successfully predicted performance on the criterion; it has successfully predicted on-the-job outcome. A qualified driver is hired; an unqualified driver is not hired. |
| Miss | An incorrect classification; a mistake | A passing score on the FERT is associated with unsatisfactory performance on the OTJSR, and a failing score on the FERT is associated with satisfactory performance on the OTJSR. | The predictor test has not predicted performance on the criterion; it has failed to predict the on-the-job outcome. A qualified driver is not hired; an unqualified driver is hired. |
| Hit rate | The proportion of people that an assessment tool accurately identifies as possessing or exhibiting a particular trait, ability, behavior, or attribute | The proportion of FE drivers with a passing FERT score who perform satisfactorily after three months based on OTJSRs. Also, the proportion of FE drivers with a failing FERT score who do not perform satisfactorily after three months based on OTJSRs. | The proportion of qualified drivers with a passing FERT score who actually gain permanent employee status after three months on the job. Also, the proportion of unqualified drivers with a failing FERT score who are let go after three months. |
| Miss rate | The proportion of people that an assessment tool inaccurately identifies as possessing or exhibiting a particular trait, ability, behavior, or attribute | The proportion of FE drivers with a passing FERT score who perform unsatisfactorily after three months based on OTJSRs. Also, the proportion of FE drivers with a failing FERT score who perform satisfactorily after three months based on OTJSRs. | The proportion of drivers whom the FERT inaccurately predicted to be qualified. Also, the proportion of drivers whom the FERT inaccurately predicted to be unqualified |
| False positive | A specific type of *miss* whereby an assessment tool falsely indicates that the testtaker possesses or exhibits a particular trait, ability, behavior, or attribute | The FERT indicates that the new hire will perform successfully on the job but, in fact, the new driver does not. | A driver who is hired is not qualified |
| False negative | A specific type of *miss* whereby an assessment tool falsely indicates that the testtaker does not possess or exhibit a particular trait, ability, behavior, or attribute | The FERT indicates that the new hire will not perform successfully on the job but, in fact, the new driver would have performed successfully. | FERT says to not hire but driver would have been rated as qualified. |

*(2) Ensure that qualified candidates are not rejected.*

*To accomplish this goal, set a FERT cut score that ensures that no one who is rejected by the cut would have been deemed qualified at the end of the probationary period. Stated another way, set a cut score that yields the lowest false negative rate. The emphasis in such a scenario is on weeding out the "worst" applicants; that is, those applicants who will definitely be deemed unqualified at the end of the probationary period.*

*(3) Ensure that all candidates selected will prove to be qualified.*

*To accomplish this goal, set a FERT cut score that ensures that everyone who "makes the cut" on the FERT is rated as qualified at*

*the end of the probationary period; no one who "makes the cut" is rated as unqualified at the end of the probationary period. Stated another way, set a cut score that yields the lowest false positive rate. The emphasis in such a scenario is on selecting only the best applicants; that is, those applicants who will definitely be deemed qualified at the end of the probationary period.*

*(4) Ensure, to the extent possible, that qualified candidates will be selected and unqualified candidates will be rejected.*

*This objective can be met by setting a cut score on the FERT that is helpful in (a) selecting for permanent positions those drivers who performed satisfactorily on the OTJSR, (b) eliminating from*

*(continued)*

# Utility Analysis:
## An Illustration *(continued)*

consideration those drivers who performed unsatisfactorily on the OTJSR, and (c) reducing the miss rate as much as possible. This approach to setting a cut score will yield the highest hit rate while allowing for FERT-related "misses" that may be either of the false-positive or false-negative variety. Here, false positives are seen as no better or worse than false negatives and vice versa.

It is seldom possible to "have it all ways." In other words, it is seldom possible to have the lowest false positive rate, the lowest false negative rate, the highest hit rate, and not incur any costs of testing. Which of the four listed objectives represents the best "fit" with your policies and the company's hiring objectives? Before responding, it may be helpful to review Table 1.

After reviewing Table 1 and all of the material on terms including *hit, miss, false positive,* and *false negative,* Dr. Carlos elects to *continue* and is presented with the following four options from which to choose.

1. Select applicants without using the FERT.
2. Use the FERT to select with the lowest false negative rate.
3. Use the FERT to select with the lowest false positive rate.
4. Use the FERT to yield the highest hit rate and lowest miss rate.

Curious about the outcome associated with each of these four options, Dr. Carlos wishes to explore all of them. She begins by selecting Option 1: *Select applicants without using the FERT.* Immediately, a graph (*Close-Up* Figure 1) and this prompt pop up:

Generally speaking, base rate *is defined as the proportion of people in the population that possess a particular trait, behavior, characteristic, or attribute. In this study,* base rate *refers to the proportion of new hire drivers who would go on to perform satisfactorily on the criterion measure (the OTJSRs) and be deemed "qualified" regardless of whether or not a test such as the FERT existed (and regardless of their score on the FERT if it were administered). The base rate is represented in Figure 1 (and in all subsequent graphs) by the number of drivers whose OTJSRs fall above the dashed horizontal line (a line that refers to minimally acceptable performance on the OTJSR) as compared to the total number of scores. In other words, the base rate is equal to the ratio of qualified applicants to the total number of applicants.*

Without the use of the FERT, it is estimated that about one-half of all new hires would exhibit satisfactory performance; that is, the base rate would be .50. Without use of the FERT, the miss rate

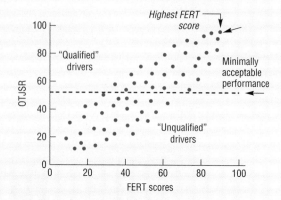

**Figure 1**
**Base Rate Data for Federale Express**

*Before the use of the FERT, any applicant with a valid driver's license and no criminal record was hired for a permanent position as an FE driver. Drivers could be classified into two groups based on their on-the-job supervisory ratings (OTJSRs): those whose driving was considered to be satisfactory (located above the dashed horizontal line) and those whose driving was considered to be unsatisfactory (below the dashed line). Without use of the FERT, then, all applicants were hired and the selection ratio was 1.0; 60 drivers were hired out of the 60 applicants. However, the base rate of successful performance shown in Figure 1 was only .50. This means that only half of the drivers hired (30 of 60) were considered "qualified" drivers by their supervisor. This also shows a miss rate of .50, because half of the drivers turned out to perform below the minimally accepted level.*

*Yet because scores on the FERT and the OTJSRs are positively correlated, the FERT can be used to help select the individuals who are likely to be rated as qualified drivers. Thus, using the FERT is a good idea, but how should it be used? One method would entail top-down selection. That is, a permanent position could be offered first to the individual with the highest score on the FERT (top, rightmost case in Figure 1), followed by the individual with the next highest FERT score, and so on until all available positions are filled. As you can see in the figure, if permanent positions are offered only to individuals with the top 20 FERT scores, then OTJSR ratings of the permanent hires will mostly be in the satisfactory performer range. However, as previously noted, such a top-down selection policy can be discriminatory.*

*would also be .50—this because half of all drivers hired would be deemed unqualified based on the OTJSRs at the end of the probationary period.*

Dr. Carlos considers the consequences of a 50% miss rate. She thinks about the possibility of an increase in customer complaints regarding the level of service. She envisions an increase in at-fault accidents and costly lawsuits. Dr. Carlos is pleasantly distracted from these potential nightmares when she inadvertently leans on her keyboard and it furiously begins to beep. Having rejected Option 1, she "presses on" and next explores what outcomes would be associated with Option 2: *Use the FERT to select with the lowest false negative rate.* Now, another graph (*Close-Up* Figure 2) appears along with this text:

*This graph, as well as all others incorporating FERT cut-score data, have FERT (predictor) scores on the horizontal axis (which increase from left to right), and OTJSR (criterion) scores on the vertical axis (with scores increasing from the bottom toward the top). The selection ratio provides an indication of the competitiveness of the position; it is directly affected by the cut score used in selection. As the cut score is set farther to the right, the selection ratio goes down. The practical implication of the decreasing selection ratio is that hiring becomes more selective; this means that there is more competition for a position and that the proportion of people actually hired (from all of those who applied) will be less.[2] As the cut score is set farther to the left, the selection ratio goes up; hiring becomes less selective, and chances are that more people will be hired.[3]*

*Using a cut score of 18 on the FERT, as compared to not using the FERT at all, reduces the miss rate from 50% to 45% (see Figure 2). The major advantage of setting the cut score this low is that the false negative rate falls to zero; no potentially qualified drivers will be rejected based on the FERT. Use of this FERT cut score also increases the base rate of successful performance from .50 to .526. This means that the percentage of hires who will be rated as "qualified" has increased from 50% without use of the FERT to 52.6% with the FERT. The selection ratio associated with using 18 as the cut score is .95, which means that 95% of drivers who apply are selected.*

Dr. Carlos appreciates that the false negative rate is zero and thus no potentially qualified drivers are turned away based on FERT score. She also believes that a 5% reduction

2. It may help you to remember this if you think: "Selection ratio down, fewer employees around." Of course it works the opposite way when it comes to cut scores: "Cut score low, more employees to know."

3. It may help you to remember this if you think: "Selection ratio high, more employees say 'Hi!'" Of course, it works the opposite way when it comes to cut scores: "Cut score high, bid applicants good-bye."

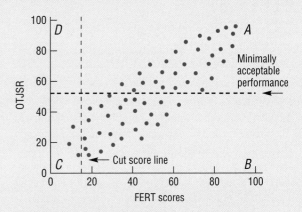

**Figure 2
Selection with Low Cut Score and High Selection Ratio**

*As we saw in Figure 1, without the use of the FERT, only half of all the probationary hires would be rated as satisfactory drivers by their supervisors. Now we will consider how to improve selection by using the FERT. For ease of reference, each of the quadrants in Figure 2 (as well as the remaining Close-Up graphs) have been labeled, A, B, C, or D. The selection ratio in this and the following graphs may be defined as being equal to the ratio of the number of people who are hired on a permanent basis (qualified applicants as determined by FERT score) compared to the total number of people who apply.*

*The total number of applicants for permanent positions was 60, as evidenced by all of the dots in all of the quadrants. In quadrants A and B, just to the right of the vertical Cut score line (set at 18), are the 57 FE drivers who were offered permanent employment. We can also see that the false positive rate is zero because no scores fall in quadrant D; thus, no potentially qualified drivers will be rejected based on use of the FERT with a cut score of 18. The selection ratio in this scenario is 57/60, or .95. We can therefore conclude that 57 applicants (95% of the 60 who originally applied) would have been hired on the basis of their FERT scores with a cut score set at 18 (resulting in a "high" selection ratio of 95%); only three applicants would not be hired based on their FERT scores. These three applicants would also be rated as unqualified by their supervisors at the end of the probationary period. We can also see that, by removing the lowest-scoring applicants, the base rate of successful performance improves slightly as compared to not using the FERT at all. Instead of having a successful performance base rate of only .50 (as was the case when all applicants were hired), now the base rate of successful performance is .526. This is so because 30 drivers are still rated as qualified based on OTJSRs while the number of drivers hired has been reduced from 60 to 57.*

*(continued)*

## Utility Analysis:
## An Illustration *(continued)*

in the miss rate is better than no reduction at all. She wonders, however, whether this reduction in the miss rate is statistically significant. She would have to formally analyze these data to be certain but, after simply "eyeballing" these findings, a decrease in the miss rate from 50% to 45% does not seem significant. Similarly, an increase in the number of qualified drivers of only 2.6% through the use of a test for selection purposes does not, on its face, seem significant. It simply does not seem prudent to institute a new personnel selection test at real cost and expense to the company if the only benefit of the test is to reject the lowest-scoring 3 of 60 applicants—when, in reality, 30 of the 60 applicants will be rated as "unqualified."

Dr. Carlos pauses to envision a situation in which reducing the false negative rate to zero might be prudent; it might be ideal if she were testing drivers for drug use, because she would definitely not want a test to indicate a driver is drug-free if that driver had been using drugs. Of course, a test with a false negative rate of zero would likely also have a high false positive rate. But then she could retest any candidate who received a positive result with a second, more expensive, more accurate test—this to ensure that the initial positive result was correct and not a testing error. As Dr. Carlos mulls over these issues, a colleague startles her with a friendly query: "How's that FERT researching coming?"

Dr. Carlos says, "Fine," and smoothly reaches for her keyboard to select Option 3: *Use the FERT to select with the lowest false positive rate.* Now, another graph (*Close-Up* Figure 3) and another message pop up:

> Using a cut score of 80 on the FERT, as compared to not using the FERT at all, results in a reduction of the miss rate from 50% to 40% (see Figure 3) but also reduces the false positive rate to zero. Use of this FERT cut score also increases the base rate of successful performance from .50 to 1.00. This means that the percentage of drivers selected who are rated as "qualified" increases from 50% without use of the FERT to 100% when the FERT is used with a cut score of 80. The selection ratio associated with using 80 as the cut score is .10, which means that 10% of applicants are selected.

Dr. Carlos likes the idea of the "100% solution" entailed by a false positive rate of zero. It means that 100% of the applicants selected by their FERT scores will turn out to be qualified drivers. At first blush, this solution seems optimal. However, there is, as they say, a fly in the ointment. Although

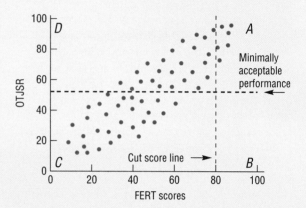

**Figure 3**
**Selection with High Cut Score and Low Selection Ratio**

*As before, the total number of applicants for permanent positions was 60, as evidenced by all of the dots in all of the quadrants. In quadrants A and B, just to the right of the vertical Cut score line (set at a FERT score of 80), are the 6 FE drivers who were offered permanent employment. The selection ratio in this scenario is 6/60, or .10. We can therefore conclude that 6 applicants (10% of the 60 who originally applied) would have been hired on the basis of their FERT scores with the cut score set at 80 (and with a "low" selection ratio of 10%). Note also that the base rate improves dramatically, from .50 without use of the FERT to 1.00 with a FERT cut score set at 80. This means that all drivers selected when this cut score is in place will be qualified. Although only 10% of the drivers will be offered permanent positions, all who are offered permanent positions will be rated qualified drivers on the OTJSR. Note, however, that even though the false positive rate drops to zero, the overall miss rate only drops to .40. This is so because a substantial number (24) of qualified applicants would be denied permanent positions because their FERT scores were below 80.*

the high cut score (80) results in the selection of only qualified candidates, the selection ratio is so stringent that only 10% of those candidates would actually be hired. Dr. Carlos envisions the consequences of this low selection ratio. She sees herself as having to recruit and test at least 100 applicants for every 10 drivers she actually hires. To meet her company goal of hiring 60 drivers, for example, she would have to recruit about 600 applicants for testing. Attracting that many applicants to the company is a venture that has some obvious (as well as some less obvious) costs. Dr. Carlos sees her recruiting budget dwindle as she repeatedly writes checks for classified advertising in newspapers. She sees herself purchasing airline tickets and making hotel reservations in order to attend various job fairs, far and wide. Fantasizing about the applicants she will attract at one of those job fairs, she is abruptly brought back to the here-and-now by the friendly voice of a fellow staff member asking her if she wants to go to lunch. Still half-steeped in thought about a potential budget crisis, Dr. Carlos responds, "Yes, just give me ten dollars . . . I mean, ten minutes."

As Dr. Carlos takes the menu of a local hamburger haunt from her desk to review, she still can't get the "100% solution" out of her mind. Although clearly attractive, she has reservations (about the solution, not for the restaurant). Offering permanent positions to only the top-performing applicants could easily backfire. Competing companies could be expected to also offer these applicants positions, perhaps with more attractive benefit packages. How many of the top drivers hired would actually stay at Federale Express? Hard to say. What is not hard to say, however, is that the use of the "100% solution" has essentially brought Dr. Carlos full circle back to the top-down hiring policy that she sought to avoid in the first place. Also, scrutinizing Figure 3, Dr. Carlos sees that—even though the base rate with this cut score is 100%—the percentage of misclassifications (as compared to not using any selection test) is reduced only by a measly 10%. Further, there would be many qualified drivers who would also be cut by this cut score. In this instance, then, a cut score that scrupulously seeks to avoid the hiring of unqualified drivers also leads to rejecting a number of qualified applicants. Perhaps in the hiring of "super responsible" positions—say, nuclear power plant supervisors—such a rigorous selection policy could be justified. But is such rigor really required in the selection of Federale Express drivers?

Hoping for a more reasonable solution to her cut-score dilemma and beginning to feel hungry, Dr. Carlos leafs through the burger menu while choosing Option 4 on her computer screen: *Use the FERT to yield the highest hit rate and lowest miss rate.* In response to this selection, another graph (*Close-Up* Figure 4) along with the following message is presented:

*Using a cut score of 48 on the FERT results in a reduction of the miss rate from 50% to 15% as compared to not using the FERT (see Figure 4). False positive and false negative rates are both fairly low at .167 and .133, respectively. Use of this cut score also*

*increases the base rate from .50 (without use of the FERT) to .839. This means that the percentage of hired drivers who are rated as "qualified" at the end of the probationary period has increased from 50% (without use of the FERT) to 83.9%. The selection ratio associated with using 48 as the cut score is .517, which means that 51.7% of applicants will be hired.*

Although a formal analysis would have to be run, Dr. Carlos again "eyeballs" the findings and, based on her extensive experience, strongly suspects that these results are statistically significant. Moreover, these findings would seem to be of practical significance. As compared to not using the FERT, use of the FERT with a cut score of 48 could reduce misclassifications from 50% to 15%.

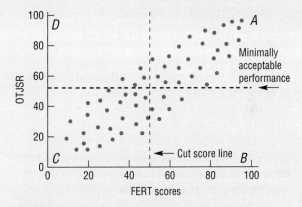

**Figure 4**
**Selection with Moderate Cut Score and Moderate Selection Ratio**

*Again, the total number of applicants was 60. In quadrants A and B, just to the right of the vertical Cut Score line (set at 48), are the 31 FE drivers who were offered permanent employment at the end of the probationary period. The selection ratio in this scenario is therefore equal to 31/60, or about .517. This means that slightly more than half of all applicants will be hired based on the use of 48 as the FERT cut score. The selection ratio of .517 is a moderate one. It is not as stringent as is the .10 selection ratio that results from a cut score of 80, nor is it as lenient as the .95 selection ratio that results from a cut score of 18. Note also that the cut score set at 48 effectively weeds out many of the applicants who won't receive acceptable performance ratings. Further, it does this while retaining many of the applicants who will receive acceptable performance ratings. With a FERT cut score of 48, the base rate increases quite a bit: from .50 (as was the case without using the FERT) to .839. This means that about 84% (83.9%, to be exact) of the hired drivers will be rated as qualified when the FERT cut score is set to 48 for driver selection.*

*(continued)*

## Utility Analysis:
## An Illustration *(continued)*

Such a reduction in misclassifications would almost certainly have positive cost–benefit implications for FE. Also, the percentage of drivers who are deemed qualified at the end of the probationary period would rise from 50% (without use of the FERT) to 83.9% (using the FERT with a cut score of 48). The implications of such improved selection are many and include better service to customers (leading to an increase in business volume), less costly accidents, and fewer costs involved in hiring and training new personnel.

Yet another benefit of using the FERT with a cut score of 48 concerns recruiting costs. Using a cut score of 48, FE would need to recruit only 39 or so qualified applicants for every 20 permanent positions it needed to fill. Now, anticipating real savings in her annual budget, Dr. Carlos returns the hamburger menu to her desk drawer and removes instead the menu from her favorite (pricey) steakhouse.

Dr. Carlos decides that the moderate cut-score solution is optimal for FE. She acknowledges that this solution doesn't reduce any of the error rates to zero. However, it produces relatively low error rates overall. It also yields a relatively high hit rate; about 84% of the drivers hired will be qualified at the end of the probationary period. Dr. Carlos believes that the costs associated with recruitment and testing using this FERT cut score will be more than compensated by the evolution of a work force that evidences satisfactory performance and has fewer accidents. As she peruses the steakhouse menu and mentally debates the pros and cons of sautéed onions, she also wonders about the dollars-and-cents utility of using the FERT. Are all of the costs associated with instituting the FERT as part of FE hiring procedures worth the benefits?

Dr. Carlos puts down the menu and begins to calculate the company's **return on investment** (the ratio of benefits to costs). She estimates the cost of each FERT to be about $200, including the costs associated with truck usage, gas, and supervisory personnel time. She further estimates that FE will test 120 applicants per year in order to select approximately 60 new hires based on a moderate FERT cut score. Given the cost of each test ($200) administered individually to 120 applicants, the total to be spent on testing annually will be about $24,000. So, is it worth it? Considering all of the possible benefits previously listed that could result from a significant reduction of the misclassification rate, Dr. Carlos's guess is, "Yes, it would be worth it." Of course, decisions like that aren't made with guesses. So continue reading—later in this chapter, a formula will be applied that will prove Dr. Carlos right. In fact, the moderate cut score shown in Figure 4 would produce a return on investment of 12.5 to 1. And once Dr. Carlos gets wind of these projections, you can bet it will be surf-and-turf-tortilla time at Federale Express.

introduced to help select employees in a situation with a selection ratio of .20 and if the new test has a predictive validity coefficient of .55, then the table shows that the base rate will increase to .88. This means that, rather than 60% of the hired employees being expected to perform successfully, a full 88% can be expected to do so. When selection ratios are low, as when only 5% of the applicants will be hired, even tests with low validity coefficients, such as .15, can result in improved base rates.

One limitation of the Taylor-Russell tables is that the relationship between the predictor (the test) and the criterion (rating of performance on the job) must be linear. If, for example, there is some point at which job performance levels off, no matter how high the score on the test, use of the Taylor-Russell tables would be inappropriate. Another limitation of the Taylor-Russell tables is the potential difficulty of identifying a criterion score that separates "successful" from "unsuccessful" employees.

The potential problems of the Taylor-Russell tables were avoided by an alternative set of tables (Naylor & Shine, 1965) that provided an indication of the difference in average criterion scores for the selected group as compared with the original group.

**Table 7-1**
**Taylor-Russell Table for a Base Rate of .60**

| Validity $(\rho_{xy})$ | Selection Ratio | | | | | | | | | | |
|---|---|---|---|---|---|---|---|---|---|---|---|
| | .05 | .10 | .20 | .30 | .40 | .50 | .60 | .70 | .80 | .90 | .95 |
| .00 | .60 | .60 | .60 | .60 | .60 | .60 | .60 | .60 | .60 | .60 | .60 |
| .05 | .64 | .63 | .63 | .62 | .62 | .62 | .61 | .61 | .61 | .60 | .60 |
| .10 | .68 | .67 | .65 | .64 | .64 | .63 | .63 | .62 | .61 | .61 | .60 |
| .15 | .71 | .70 | .68 | .67 | .66 | .65 | .64 | .63 | .62 | .61 | .61 |
| .20 | .75 | .73 | .71 | .69 | .67 | .66 | .65 | .64 | .63 | .62 | .61 |
| .25 | .78 | .76 | .73 | .71 | .69 | .68 | .66 | .65 | .63 | .62 | .61 |
| .30 | .82 | .79 | .76 | .73 | .71 | .69 | .68 | .66 | .64 | .62 | .61 |
| .35 | .85 | .82 | .78 | .75 | .73 | .71 | .69 | .67 | .65 | .63 | .62 |
| .40 | .88 | .85 | .81 | .78 | .75 | .73 | .70 | .68 | .66 | .63 | .62 |
| .45 | .90 | .87 | .83 | .80 | .77 | .74 | .72 | .69 | .66 | .64 | .62 |
| .50 | .93 | .90 | .86 | .82 | .79 | .76 | .73 | .70 | .67 | .64 | .62 |
| .55 | .95 | .92 | .88 | .84 | .81 | .78 | .75 | .71 | .68 | .64 | .62 |
| .60 | .96 | .94 | .90 | .87 | .83 | .80 | .76 | .73 | .69 | .65 | .63 |
| .65 | .98 | .96 | .92 | .89 | .85 | .82 | .78 | .74 | .70 | .65 | .63 |
| .70 | .99 | .97 | .94 | .91 | .87 | .84 | .80 | .75 | .71 | .66 | .63 |
| .75 | .99 | .99 | .96 | .93 | .90 | .86 | .81 | .77 | .71 | .66 | .63 |
| .80 | 1.00 | .99 | .98 | .95 | .92 | .88 | .83 | .78 | .72 | .66 | .63 |
| .85 | 1.00 | 1.00 | .99 | .97 | .95 | .91 | .86 | .80 | .73 | .66 | .63 |
| .90 | 1.00 | 1.00 | 1.00 | .99 | .97 | .94 | .88 | .82 | .74 | .67 | .63 |
| .95 | 1.00 | 1.00 | 1.00 | 1.00 | .99 | .97 | .92 | .84 | .75 | .67 | .63 |
| 1.00 | 1.00 | 1.00 | 1.00 | 1.00 | 1.00 | 1.00 | 1.00 | .86 | .75 | .67 | .63 |

Source: Taylor and Russell (1939).

Use of the **Naylor-Shine tables** entails obtaining the difference between the means of the selected and unselected groups to derive an index of what the test (or some other tool of assessment) is adding to already established procedures.

Both the Taylor-Russell and the Naylor-Shine tables can assist in judging the utility of a particular test, the former by determining the increase over current procedures and the latter by determining the increase in average score on some criterion measure. With both tables, the validity coefficient used must be one obtained by concurrent validation procedures—a fact that should not be surprising because it is obtained with respect to current employees hired by the selection process in effect at the time of the study.

If hiring decisions were made solely on the basis of variables such as the validity of an employment test and the prevailing selection ratio, then tables such as those offered by Taylor and Russell and Naylor and Shine would be in wide use today. The fact is that many other kinds of variables might enter into hiring and other sorts of personnel selection decisions (including decisions relating to promotion, transfer, layoff, and firing). Some additional variables might include, for example, applicants' minority status, general physical or mental health, or drug use. Given that many variables may affect a personnel selection decision, of what use is a given test in the decision process?

> **JUST THINK . . .**
>
> In addition to testing, what types of assessment procedures might employers use to help them make judicious personnel selection decisions?

Expectancy data, such as that provided by the Taylor-Russell tables or the Naylor-Shine tables could be used to shed light on many utility-related decisions, particularly those confined to questions concerning the validity of an employment test and the selection ratio employed. Table 7–2 presents a brief summary of some of the uses, advantages, and disadvantages of these approaches. In many instances, however, the purpose of a utility analysis is to answer a question related to costs and benefits in terms of dollars and cents. When such questions are raised, the answer may be found by using the Brogden-Cronbach-Gleser formula.

**Table 7–2**
**Most Everything You Ever Wanted to Know about Utility Tables**

| Instrument | What It Tells Us | Example | Advantages | Disadvantages |
|---|---|---|---|---|
| Expectancy table or chart | Likelihood that individuals who score within a given range on the predictor will perform successfully on the criterion | A school psychologist uses an expectancy table to determine the likelihood that students who score within a particular range on an aptitude test will succeed in regular classes as opposed to special education classes. | Easy-to-use graphical display; can aid in decision making regarding a specific individual or a group of individuals scoring in a given range on the predictor | Dichotomizes performance into successful and unsuccessful categories, which is not realistic in most situations; does not address monetary issues such as cost of testing or return on investment of testing |
| Taylor-Russell tables | Increase in base rate of successful performance that is associated with a particular level of criterion-related validity | A human resources manager of a large computer store uses the Taylor-Russell tables to help decide whether applicants for sales positions should be administered an extraversion inventory prior to hire. The manager wants to increase the portion of the sales force that is considered successful (i.e., consistently meets sales quota). By using an estimate of the test's validity (e.g., by using a value of .20 based on research by Conte & Gintoft, 2005), the current base rate, and selection ratio, the manager can estimate whether the increase in proportion of the sales force that do successfully meet their quotas will justify the cost of testing all sales applicants. | Easy-to-use shows the relationships between selection ratio, criterion-related validity, and existing base rate; facilitates decision making with regard to test use and/or recruitment to lower the selection ratio | Relationship between predictor and criterion must be linear; does not indicate the likely average increase in performance with use of the test; difficulty identifying a criterion value to separate successful and unsuccessful performance; dichotomizes performance into successful versus unsuccessful, which is not realistic in most situations; does not consider the cost of testing in comparison to benefits |
| Naylor-Shine tables | Likely average increase in criterion performance as a result of using a particular test or intervention; also provides selection ratio needed to achieve a particular increase in criterion performance | The provost at a private college estimates the increase in applicant pool (and corresponding decrease in selection ratio) that is needed in order to improve the mean performance of students it selects by 0.50 standardized units while still maintaining its enrollment figures. | Provides information (i.e., average performance gain) needed to use the Brogden-Cronbach-Gleser utility formula; does not dichotomize criterion performance; useful either for showing average performance gain or to show selection ratio needed for a particular performance gain; facilitates decision making with regard to likely increase in performance with test use and/or recruitment needed to lower the selection ratio | Overestimates utility unless top-down selection is used;[a] utility expressed in terms of performance gain based on standardized units, which can be difficult to interpret in practical terms; does not address monetary issues such as cost of testing or return on investment |

a. Boudreau (1988).

**The Brogden-Cronbach-Gleser formula** The independent work of Hubert E. Brogden (1949) and a team of decision theorists (Cronbach & Gleser, 1965) has been immortalized in the **Brogden-Cronbach-Gleser formula,** used to calculate the dollar amount of a *utility gain* resulting from the use of a particular selection instrument under specified conditions. In general, **utility gain** refers to an estimate of the benefit (monetary or otherwise) of using a particular test or selection method. The Brogden-Cronbach-Gleser (BCG) formula is:

$$\text{utility gain} = (N)(T)(r_{xy})(\text{SD}_y)(\bar{Z}_m) - (N)(C)$$

In the first part of the formula, $N$ represents the number of applicants selected per year, $T$ represents the average length of time in the position (i.e., tenure), $r_{xy}$ represents the (criterion-related) validity coefficient for the given predictor and criterion, $\text{SD}_y$ represents the standard deviation of performance (in dollars) of employees, and $\bar{Z}_m$ represents the mean (standardized) score on the test for selected applicants. The second part of the formula represents the cost of testing, which takes into consideration the number of applicants ($N$) multiplied by the cost of the test for each applicant ($C$). A difficulty in using this formula is estimating the value of $\text{SD}_y$, a value that is, quite literally, estimated (Hunter et al., 1990). One recommended way to estimate $\text{SD}_y$ is by setting it equal to 40% of the mean salary for the job (Schmidt & Hunter, 1998).

The BCG formula can be applied to the question raised in this chapter's *Close-Up* about the utility of the FERT. Suppose 60 Federale Express (FE) drivers are selected per year and that each driver stays with FE for one and a half years. Let's further suppose that the standard deviation of performance of the drivers is about $9,000 (calculated as 40% of annual salary), that the criterion-related validity of FERT scores is .40, and that the mean standardized FERT score for applicants is +1.0. Applying the *benefits* part of the BCG formula, the benefits are $324,000 (60 × 1.5 × .40 × $9,000 × 1.0). When the costs of testing ($24,000) are subtracted from the financial benefits of testing ($324,000), it can be seen that the utility gain amounts to $300,000.

So, would it be wise for a company to make an investment of $24,000 to receive a return of about $300,000? Most people (and corporations) would be more than willing to invest in something if they knew that the return on their investment would be more than $12.50 for each dollar invested. Clearly, with such a return on investment, using the FERT with the cut score illustrated in Figure 4 of the *Close-Up* does provide a cost-effective method of selecting delivery drivers.

By the way, a modification of the BCG formula exists for researchers who prefer their findings in terms of *productivity gains* rather than financial ones. Here, **productivity gain** refers to an estimated increase in work output. In this modification of the formula, the value of the standard deviation of productivity, $\text{SD}_p$, is substituted for the value of the standard deviation of performance in

> **JUST THINK . . .**
>
> When might it be better to present utility gains in productivity terms rather than financial terms?

dollars, $\text{SD}_y$ (Schmidt et al., 1986). The result is a formula that helps estimate the percent increase in output expected through the use of a particular test. The revised formula is:

$$\text{productivity gain} = (N)(T)(r_{xy})(\text{SD}_p)(\bar{Z}_m) - (N)(C)$$

**Decision theory and test utility** Perhaps the most oft-cited application of statistical decision theory to the field of psychological testing is Cronbach and Gleser's *Psychological Tests and Personnel Decisions* (1957, 1965). The idea of applying statistical decision theory to questions of test utility was conceptually appealing and promising, and an authoritative textbook of the day reflects the great enthusiasm with which this marriage of enterprises was greeted:

> The basic decision-theory approach to selection and placement . . . has a number of advantages over the more classical approach based upon the correlation model. . . . There is no question but that it is a more general and better model for handling this kind of decision task, and we predict that in the future problems of selection and placement will be treated in this context more frequently—perhaps to [the] eventual exclusion of the more stereotyped correlational model. (Blum & Naylor, 1968, p. 58)

Stated generally, Cronbach and Gleser (1965) presented (1) a classification of decision problems; (2) various selection strategies ranging from single-stage processes to sequential analyses; (3) a quantitative analysis of the relationship between test utility, the selection ratio, cost of the testing program, and expected value of the outcome; and (4) a recommendation that in some instances job requirements be tailored to the applicant's ability instead of the other way around (a concept they refer to as *adaptive treatment*).

Let's illustrate decision theory in action. To do so, recall the definition of five terms that you learned in the previous chapter: *base rate, hit rate, miss rate, false positive,* and *false negative.* Now, imagine that you developed a procedure called the Vapor Test (VT), which was designed to determine if alive-and-well subjects are indeed breathing. The procedure for the VT entails having the examiner hold a mirror under the subject's nose and mouth for a minute or so and observing whether the subject's breath fogs the mirror. Let's say that 100 introductory psychology students are administered the VT, and it is concluded that 89 were, in fact, breathing (whereas 11 are deemed, on the basis of the VT, not to be breathing). Is the VT a good test? Obviously not. Because the base rate is 100% of the (alive-and-well) population, we really don't even need a test to measure the characteristic *breathing.* If for some reason we did need such a measurement procedure, we probably wouldn't use one that was inaccurate in approximately 11% of the cases. A test is obviously of no value if the hit rate is higher *without* using it. One measure of the value of a test lies in the extent to which its use improves on the hit rate that exists without its use.

As a simple illustration of decision theory applied to testing, suppose a test is administered to a group of 100 job applicants and that some cutoff score is applied to distinguish applicants who will be hired (applicants judged to have passed the test) from applicants whose employment application will be rejected (applicants judged to have failed the test). Let's further suppose that some criterion measure will be applied some time later to ascertain whether the newly hired person was considered a success or a failure at the job. In such a situation, if the test is a perfect predictor (if its validity coefficient is equal to 1), then two distinct types of outcomes can be identified: (1) Some applicants will score at or above the cutoff score on the test and be successful at the job, and (2) some applicants will score below the cutoff score and would not have been successful at the job.

In reality, few, if any, employment tests are perfect predictors with validity coefficients equal to 1. Consequently, two additional types of outcomes are possible: (3) Some applicants will score at or above the cutoff score, be hired, and fail at the job (the criterion), and (4) some applicants who scored below the cutoff score and were not hired could have been successful at the job. People who fall into the third category could be categorized as *false positives,* and those who fall into the fourth category could be categorized as *false negatives.*

In this illustration, logic alone tells us that if the selection ratio is, say, 90% (9 out of 10 applicants will be hired), then the cutoff score will probably be set lower than if the selection ratio is 5% (only 5 of the 100 applicants will be hired). Further, if the selection ratio is 90%, then it is a good bet that the number of false positives (people hired who will fail on the criterion measure) will be greater than if the selection ratio is 5%. Conversely, if the selection ratio is only 5%, it is a good bet that the number of false negatives (people not hired who could have succeeded on the criterion measure) will be greater than if the selection ratio is 90%.

Decision theory provides guidelines for setting optimal cutoff scores. In setting such scores, the relative seriousness of making false-positive or false-negative selection decisions is frequently taken into account. Thus, for example, it is a prudent policy for an airline personnel office to set cutoff scores on tests for pilots that might result in a false negative (a pilot who is truly qualified being rejected) as opposed to a cutoff score that would allow a false positive (a pilot who is truly unqualified being hired).

In the hands of highly skilled researchers, principles of decision theory applied to problems of test utility have led to some enlightening and impressive findings. For example, Schmidt et al. (1979) demonstrated in dollars and cents how the utility of a company's selection program (and the validity coefficient of the tests used in that program) can play a critical role in the profitability of the company. Focusing on one employer's population of computer programmers, these researchers asked supervisors to rate (in terms of dollars) the value of good, average, and poor programmers. This information was used in conjunction with other information, including these facts: (1) Each year the employer hired 600 new programmers, (2) the average programmer remained on the job for about 10 years, (3) the Programmer Aptitude Test currently in use as part of the hiring process had a validity coefficient of .76, (4) it cost about $10 per applicant to administer the test, and (5) the company currently employed more than 4,000 programmers.

Schmidt et al. (1979) made a number of calculations using different values for some of the variables. For example, knowing that some of the tests previously used in the hiring process had validity coefficients ranging from .00 to .50, they varied the value of the test's validity coefficient (along with other factors such as different selection ratios that had been in effect) and examined the relative efficiency of the various conditions. Among their findings was that the existing selection ratio and selection process provided a great gain in efficiency over a previous situation (when the selection ratio was 5% and the validity coefficient of the test used in hiring was equal to .50). This gain was equal to almost $6 million per year. Multiplied over, say, 10 years, that's $60 million. The existing selection ratio and selection process provided an even greater gain in efficiency over a previously existing situation in which the test had no validity at all and the selection ratio was .80. Here, in one year, the gain in efficiency was estimated to be equal to over $97 million.

By the way, the employer in the previous study was the U.S. government. Hunter and Schmidt (1981) applied the same type of analysis to the national workforce and made a compelling argument with respect to the critical relationship between valid tests and measurement procedures and our national productivity. In a subsequent study, Schmidt, Hunter, and their colleagues found that substantial increases in work output or reductions in payroll costs would result from using valid measures of cognitive ability as opposed to non-test procedures (Schmidt et al., 1986).

**JUST THINK . . .**

What must happen in society at large if the promise of decision theory in personnel selection is to be fulfilled?

Employers are reluctant to use decision theory–based strategies in their hiring practices because of the complexity of their application and the threat of legal challenges. Thus, although decision theory approaches to assessment hold great promise, this promise has yet to be fulfilled.

## Some Practical Considerations

A number of practical matters must be considered when conducting utility analyses. For example, as we have noted elsewhere, issues related to existing base rates can affect the accuracy of decisions made on the basis of tests. Particular attention must be paid to this factor when the base rates are extremely low or high because such a situation may render the test useless as a tool of selection. Focusing for the purpose of this discussion on the area of personnel selection, some other practical matters to keep in mind involve assumptions about the pool of job applicants, the complexity of the job, and the cut score in use.

**The pool of job applicants**   If you were to read a number of articles in the utility analysis literature on personnel selection, you might come to the conclusion that there exists, "out there," what seems to be a limitless supply of potential employees just waiting to be evaluated and possibly selected for employment. For example, utility estimates such as those derived by Schmidt et al. (1979) are based on the assumption that there will be a ready supply of viable applicants from which to choose and fill positions. Perhaps for some types of jobs and in some economic climates that is, indeed, the case. There are certain jobs, however, that require such unique skills or demand such great sacrifice that there are relatively few people who would even apply, let alone be selected. Also, the pool of possible job applicants for a particular type of position may vary with the economic climate. It may be that in periods of high unemployment there are significantly more people in the pool of possible job applicants than in periods of high employment.

Closely related to issues concerning the available pool of job applicants is the issue of how many people would actually *accept* the employment position offered to them even if they were found to be a qualified candidate. Many utility models, somewhat naively, are constructed on the assumption that all of the people selected by a personnel test accept the position that they are offered. In fact, many of the top performers on the test are people who, because of their superior and desirable abilities, are also being offered positions by one or more other potential employers. Consequently, the top performers on the test are probably the least likely of all of the job applicants to actually be hired. Utility estimates based on the assumption that all people selected will actually accept offers of employment thus tend to overestimate the utility of the measurement tool. These estimates may have to be adjusted downward as much as 80% in order to provide a more realistic estimate of the utility of a tool of assessment used for selection purposes (Murphy, 1986).

◆
**JUST THINK . . .**

What is an example of a type of job that requires such unique skills that there are probably relatively few people in the pool of qualified employees?

**The complexity of the job**   In general, the same sorts of approaches to utility analysis are put to work for positions that vary greatly in terms of complexity. The same sorts of data are gathered, the same sorts of analytic methods may be applied, and the same sorts of utility models may be invoked for corporate positions ranging from assembly line worker to computer programmer. Yet as Hunter et al. (1990) observed, the more complex the job, the more people differ on how well or poorly they do that job. Whether or not the same utility models apply to jobs of varied complexity, and whether or not the same utility analysis methods are equally applicable, remain matters of debate.

**The cut score in use**   Also called a *cutoff score,* we have previously defined a **cut score** as a (usually numerical) reference point derived as a result of a judgment and used to divide a set of data into two or more classifications, with some action to be taken or some inference to be made on the basis of these classifications. In discussions of utility theory and utility analysis, reference is frequently made to different types of cut scores. For example, a distinction can be made between a *relative cut score* and a *fixed cut score.* A **relative cut score** may be defined as a reference point—in a distribution of test scores used to divide a set of data into two or more classifications—that is set based on norm-related considerations rather than on the relationship of test scores to a criterion. Because this type of cut score is set with reference to the performance of a group (or some target segment of a group), it is also referred to as a **norm-referenced cut score.**

As an example of a relative cut score, envision your instructor announcing on the first day of class that, for each of the four examinations to come, the top 10% of all scores on each test would receive the grade of A. In other words, the cut score in use would depend on the performance of the class as a whole. Stated another way, the cut score in use would be *relative* to the scores achieved by a targeted group (in this case, the entire class and in particular the top 10% of the class). The actual test score used to define who would and would not achieve the grade of A on each test could be quite different for each of the four tests, depending upon where the boundary line for the 10% cutoff fell on each test.

In contrast to a relative cut score is the **fixed cut score,** which we may define as a reference point—in a distribution of test scores used to divide a set of data into two or more classifications—that is typically set with reference to a judgment concerning a minimum level of proficiency required to be included in a particular classification. Fixed cut scores may also be referred to as *absolute cut scores.* An example of a fixed cut score might be the score achieved on the road test for a driver's license. Here the performance of other would-be drivers has no bearing upon whether an individual testtaker is classified as "licensed" or "not licensed." All that really matters here is the examiner's answer to this question: "Is this driver able to meet (or exceed) the fixed and absolute score on the road test necessary to be licensed?"

A distinction can also be made between the terms *multiple cut scores* and *multiple hurdles* as used in decision-making processes. **Multiple cut scores** refers to the use of two or more cut scores with reference to one predictor for the purpose of categorizing testtakers. So, for example, your instructor may have multiple cut scores in place every time an examination is administered, and each class member will be assigned to one category (e.g., A, B, C, D, or F) on the basis of scores on that examination. That is, meeting or exceeding one cut score will result in an A for the examination, meeting or exceeding another cut score will result in a B for the examination, and so forth. This is an example of multiple cut scores being used with a single predictor. Of course, we may also speak of multiple cut scores being used in an evaluation that entails several predictors wherein applicants must meet the requisite cut score on every predictor to be considered for the position. A more sophisticated but cost-effective multiple cut-score method can involve several "hurdles" to overcome.

> **JUST THINK . . .**
>
> Can both relative and absolute cut scores be used within the same evaluation? If so, provide an example.

At every stage in a multistage (or **multiple hurdle**) selection process, a cut score is in place for each predictor used. The cut score used for each predictor will be designed to ensure that each applicant possess some minimum level of a specific attribute or skill. In this context, *multiple hurdles* may be thought of as one collective element of a multistage decision-making process in which the achievement of a particular cut score on one test is necessary in order to advance to the next stage of evaluation in the selection process. In applying to colleges or professional schools, for example, applicants may have to successfully meet some standard in order to move to the next stage in a series of stages. The process might begin, for example, with the *written application* stage in which individuals who turn in incomplete applications are eliminated from further consideration. This is followed by what might be termed an *additional materials* stage in which individuals with low test scores, GPAs, or poor letters of recommendation are eliminated. The final stage in the process might be a *personal interview* stage. Each of these stages entails unique demands (and cut scores) to be successfully met, or hurdles to be overcome, if an applicant is to proceed to the next stage. Switching gears considerably, another example of a selection process that entails multiple hurdles is presented in Figure 7–1.

Multiple-hurdle selection methods assume that an individual must possess a certain minimum amount of knowledge, skill, or ability for each attribute measured by a predictor to be successful in the desired position. But is that really the case? Could it be that a very high score in one stage of a multistage evaluation compensates for or "balances out" a relatively low score in another stage of the evaluation? In what is referred to as a **compensatory model of selection,** an assumption is made that high scores on one attribute can, in fact, "balance out" or compensate for low scores on another attribute. According to this model, a person strong in some areas and weak in others can perform as successfully in a position as a person with moderate abilities in all areas relevant to the position in question.

Intuitively, the compensatory model is appealing, especially when post-hire training or other opportunities are available to develop proficiencies and help an applicant

**Figure 7–1**
**"There She Goes . . ." Over Yet Another Hurdle**

*Contestants in this pageant must exhibit more than beauty if they are to be crowned "Miss America." Beyond the swimsuit competition, contestants are judged on talent, responses to interview questions, and other variables. Only by "making the cut" and "clearing each hurdle" in each category of the judging will one of the 50 contestants emerge as the pageant winner.*

compensate for any areas of deficiency. For instance, with reference to the delivery driver example in this chapter's *Close-Up*, consider an applicant with strong driving skills but weak customer service skills. All it might take for this applicant to blossom into an outstanding employee is some additional education (including readings and exposure to videotaped models) and training (role-play and on-the-job supervision) in customer service.

When a compensatory selection model is in place, the individual or entity making the selection will, in general, differentially weight the predictors being used in order to arrive at a total score. Such differential weightings may reflect value judgments made on the part of the test developers regarding the relative importance of different criteria used in hiring. For example, a safe driving history may be weighted higher in the selection formula than is customer service. This weighting might be based on a company-wide "safety first" ethic. It may also be based on a company belief that skill in driving safely is less amenable to education and training than skill in customer service. The total score on all of the predictors will be used to make the decision to select or reject. The statistical tool that is ideally suited for making such selection decisions within the framework of a compensatory model is multiple regression. Other tools, as we will see in what follows, are used to set cut scores.

**JUST THINK . . .**

It is possible for a corporate employer to have in place personnel selection procedures that use both cutoff scores at one stage of the decision process and a compensatory approach at another? Can you think of an example?

## Methods for Setting Cut Scores

If you have ever had the experience of earning a grade of B when you came oh-so-close to the cut score needed for a grade A, then you have no doubt spent some time pondering the way that cut scores are determined. In this exercise, you are not alone. Educators, researchers, corporate statisticians, and others with diverse backgrounds have spent countless hours questioning, debating, and—judging from the nature of the heated debates in the literature—agonizing about various aspects of cut scores. No wonder; cut scores applied to a wide array of tests may be used (usually in combination with other tools of measurement) to make various "high-stakes" (read "life-changing") decisions, a partial listing of which would include:

- who gets into what college, graduate school, or professional school;
- who is certified or licensed to practice a particular occupation or profession;
- who is accepted for employment, promoted, or moved to some desirable position in a business or other organization;
- who will advance to the next stage in evaluation of knowledge or skills;
- who is legally able to drive an automobile;
- who is legally competent to stand trial;
- who is legally competent to make a last will;
- who is considered to be legally intoxicated;
- who is not guilty by reason of insanity;
- which foreign national will earn American citizenship.

Page upon page in journal articles, books, and other scholarly publications contain writings that wrestle with issues regarding the optimal method of "making the cut" with

JUST THINK . . .

What if there were a "true cut-score theory" for setting cut scores that was analogous to the "true score theory" for tests? What might it look like?

cut scores. One thoughtful researcher raised the question that served as the inspiration for our next *Just Think* exercise (see Reckase, 2004). So, after you have given due thought to that exercise, read on and become acquainted with various methods in use today for setting fixed and relative cut scores. Although no one method has won universal acceptance, some methods are more popular than others.

## The Angoff Method

Devised by William Angoff (1971), the **Angoff method** for setting fixed cut scores can be applied to personnel selection tasks as well as to questions regarding the presence or absence of a particular trait, attribute, or ability. When used for purposes of personnel selection, experts in the area provide estimates regarding how testtakers who have at least minimal competence for the position should answer test items correctly. As applied for purposes relating to the determination of whether or not testtakers possess a particular trait, attribute, or ability, an expert panel makes judgments concerning the way a person with that trait, attribute, or ability would respond to test items. In both cases, the judgments of the experts are averaged to yield cut scores for the test. Persons who score at or above the cut score are considered high enough in the ability to be hired or to be sufficiently high in the trait, attribute, or ability of interest. This relatively simple technique has wide appeal (Cascio et al., 1988; Maurer & Alexander, 1992) and works well—that is, as long as the experts agree. The Achilles heel of the Angoff method is when there is low inter-rater reliability and major disagreement regarding how certain populations of testtakers should respond to items. In such scenarios, it may be time for "Plan B," a strategy for setting cut scores that is driven more by data and less by subjective judgments.

## The Known Groups Method

Also referred to as the *method of contrasting groups,* the **known groups method** entails collection of data on the predictor of interest from groups known to possess, and *not* to possess, a trait, attribute, or ability of interest. Based on an analysis of this data, a cut score is set on the test that best discriminates the two groups' test performance. How does this work in practice? Consider the following example.

A hypothetical online college called Internet Oxford University (IOU) offers a remedial math course for students who have not been adequately prepared in high school for college-level math. But who needs to take remedial math before taking regular math? To answer that question, senior personnel in the IOU Math Department prepare a placement test called the "Who Needs to Take Remedial Math? Test" (WNTRMT). The next question is, "What shall the cut score on the WNTRMT be?" That question will be answered by administering the test to a selected population and then setting a cut score based on the performance of two contrasting groups: (1) students who successfully completed college-level math, and (2) students who failed college-level math.

Accordingly, the WNTRMT is administered to all incoming freshmen. IOU collects all test data and holds it for a semester (or two). It then analyzes the scores of two approximately equal-sized groups of students who took college-level math courses: a group who passed the course and earned credit, and a group who did not earn credit

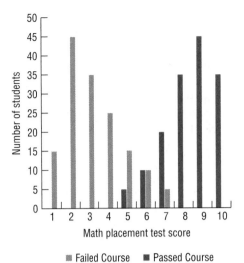

Figure 7–2
**Scores on IOU's WMTRMT**

■ Failed Course  ■ Passed Course

for the course because their final grade was a D or an F. IOU statisticians will now use these data to choose the score that best discriminates the two groups from each other, which is the score at the point of *least* difference between the two groups. As shown in Figure 7–2, the two groups are indistinguishable at a score of 6. Consequently, now and forever more (or at least until IOU conducts another study), the cutoff score on the IOU shall be 6.

The main problem with using known groups is that determination of where to set the cutoff score is inherently affected by the composition of the contrasting groups. No standard set of guidelines exist for choosing contrasting groups. In the IOU example, the university officials could have chosen to contrast just the A students with the F students when deriving a cut score; this would definitely have resulted in a different cutoff score. Other types of problems in choosing scores from contrasting groups occur in other studies. For example, in setting cut scores for a clinical measure of depression, just how depressed do respondents from the depressed group have to be? How "normal" should the respondents in the nondepressed group be?

### IRT-Based Methods

The methods described thus far for setting cut scores are based on classical test score theory. In this theory, cut scores are typically set based on testtakers' performance across all the items on the test; some portion of the total number of items on the test must be scored "correct" (or in a way that indicates the testtaker possesses the target trait or attribute) in order for the testtaker to "pass" the test (or be deemed to possess the targeted trait or attribute). Within an item response theory (IRT) framework, however, things can be done a little differently. In the IRT framework, each item is associated with a particular level of difficulty. In order to "pass" the test, the testtaker must answer items that are deemed to be above some minimum level of difficulty, which is determined by experts and serves as the cut score.

There are several IRT-based methods for determining the difficulty level reflected by a cut score (Karantonis & Sireci, 2006; Wang, 2003). For example, a technique that has found application in setting cut scores for licensing examinations is the

**item-mapping method.** It entails the arrangement of items in a histogram, with each column in the histogram containing items deemed to be of equivalent value. Judges who have been trained regarding minimal competence required for licensure are presented with sample items from each column and are asked whether or not a minimally competent licensed individual would answer those items correctly about half the time. If so, that difficulty level is set as the cut score; if not, the process continues until the appropriate difficulty level has been selected. Typically, the process involves several rounds of judgments in which experts may receive feedback regarding how their ratings compare to ratings made by other experts.

An IRT-based method of setting cut scores that is more typically used in academic applications is the **bookmark method** (Lewis et al., 1996; see also Mitzel et al., 2000). Use of this method begins with the training of experts with regard to the minimal knowledge, skills, and/or abilities that testtakers should possess in order to "pass." Subsequent to this training, the experts are given a book of items, with one item printed per page, such that items are arranged in an ascending order of difficulty. The expert then places a "bookmark" between the two pages (that is, the two items) that are deemed to separate testtakers who have acquired the minimal knowledge, skills, and/or abilities from those who have not. The bookmark serves as the cut score. Additional rounds of bookmarking with the same or other judges may take place as necessary. Feedback regarding placement may be provided, and discussion among experts about the bookmarkings may be allowed. In the end, the level of difficulty to use as the cut score is decided upon by the test developers. Of course, none of these procedures are free of possible drawbacks. Some concerns raised about the bookmarking method include issues regarding the training of experts, possible floor and ceiling effects, and the optimal length of item booklets (Skaggs et al., 2007).

## Other Methods

Our overview of cut-score setting has touched on only a few of the many methods that have been proposed, implemented, or experimented with; many other methods exist. For example, Hambleton and Novick (1973) presented a decision-theoretic approach to setting cut scores. In his book *Personnel Psychology,* R. L. Thorndike (1949) proposed a norm-referenced method for setting cut scores called the *method of predictive yield.* The **method of predictive yield** was a technique for setting cut scores which took into account the number of positions to be filled, projections regarding the likelihood of offer acceptance, and the distribution of applicant scores. Another approach to setting cut scores employs a family of statistical techniques called **discriminant analysis** (also referred to as *discriminant function analysis*). These techniques are typically used to shed light on the relationship between identified variables (such as scores on a battery of tests) and two (and in some cases more) naturally occurring groups (such as persons judged to be successful at a job and persons judged unsuccessful at a job).

Given the importance of setting cut scores and how much can be at stake for individuals "cut" by them, research and debate on the issues involved are likely to continue—at least until that hypothetical "true score theory for cut scores" alluded to earlier in this chapter is identified and welcomed by members of the research community.

In this chapter we have focused on the possible benefits of testing and how to assess those benefits. In so doing, we have touched on several aspects of test development and construction. In the next chapter, we delve more deeply into the details of these important elements of testing and assessment.

# Self-Assessment

Test your understanding of elements of this chapter by seeing if you can explain each of the following terms, expressions, and abbreviations:

absolute cut score
Angoff method
benefit (as related to test utility)
bookmark method
Brogden-Cronbach-Gleser formula
compensatory model of selection
cost (as related to test utility)
cut score

discriminant analysis
fixed cut score
item-mapping method
known groups method
method of contrasting groups
method of predictive yield
multiple cut scores
multiple hurdle (selection process)

norm-referenced cut score
productivity gain
relative cut score
return on investment
top-down selection
utility (test utility)
utility analysis
utility gain

# 8

# *Test Development*

Allll tests are not created equal. The creation of a good test is not a matter of chance. It is the product of the thoughtful and sound application of established principles of *test development*. In this context, **test development** is an umbrella term for all that goes into the process of creating a test.

In this chapter, we introduce the basics of test development and examine in detail the processes by which tests are assembled. We explore, for example, ways that test items are written, and ultimately selected for use. Although we focus on tests of the published, standardized variety, much of what we have to say also applies to custom-made tests such as those created by teachers, researchers, and employers.

The process of developing a test occurs in five stages:

1.   test conceptualization;
2.   test construction;
3.   test tryout;
4.   item analysis;
5.   test revision.

Once the idea for a test is conceived (**test conceptualization**), *test construction* begins. As we are using this term, **test construction** is a stage in the process of test development that entails writing test items (or re-writing or revising existing items), as well as formatting items, setting scoring rules, and otherwise designing and building a test. Once a preliminary form of the test has been developed, it is administered to a representative sample of testtakers under conditions that simulate the conditions that the final version of the test will be administered under (**test tryout**). The data from the tryout will be collected and testtakers' performance on the test as a whole and on each item will be analyzed. Statistical procedures, referred to as *item analysis,* are employed to assist in making judgments about which items are good as they are, which items need to be revised, and which items should be discarded. The analysis of the test's items may include analyses of item reliability, item validity, and item discrimination. Depending on the type of test, item-difficulty level may be analyzed as well.

Next in the sequence of events in test development is *test revision*. Here, **test revision** refers to action taken to modify a test's content or format for the purpose of improving the test's effectiveness as a tool of measurement. This action is usually based on item

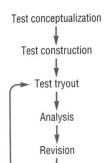

**Figure 8–1**
**The Test Development Process**

analyses, as well as related information derived from the test tryout. The revised version of the test will then be tried out on a new sample of testtakers. After the results are analyzed the test will be further revised if necessary—and so it goes (see Figure 8–1). Although the test development process described is fairly typical today, let's note that there are many exceptions to it, both with regard to tests developed in the past, and some contemporary tests. Some tests are conceived of and constructed but neither tried-out, nor item-analyzed, nor revised.

**JUST THINK . . .**

Can you think of a classic psychological test from the past that has never undergone test tryout, item analysis, or revision? What about so-called psychological tests found on the Internet?

## Test Conceptualization

The beginnings of any published test can probably be traced to thoughts—self-talk, in behavioral terms. The test developer says to himself or herself something like: "There ought to be a test designed to measure [fill in the blank] in [such and such] way." The stimulus for such a thought could be almost anything. A review of the available literature on existing tests designed to measure a particular construct might indicate that such tests leave much to be desired in psychometric soundness. An emerging social phenomenon or pattern of behavior might serve as the stimulus for the development of a new test. If, for example, celibacy were to become a widely practiced lifestyle, then we might witness the development of a variety of tests related to celibacy. These tests might measure variables such as reasons for adopting a celibate lifestyle, commitment to a celibate lifestyle, and degree of celibacy by specific behaviors. The analogy with medicine is straightforward: Once a new disease comes to the attention of medical researchers, they attempt to develop diagnostic tests to assess its presence or absence as well as the severity of its manifestations in the body.

The development of a new test may be in response to a need to assess mastery in an emerging occupation or profession. For example, new tests may be developed to assess mastery in fields such as high-definition electronics, environmental engineering, and wireless communications.

**JUST THINK . . .**

What is a "hot topic" today that developers of psychological tests should be working on? What aspects of this topic might be explored by means of a psychological test?

### Some Preliminary Questions

Regardless of the stimulus for developing the new test, a number of questions immediately confront the prospective test developer.

- *What is the test designed to measure?* This is a deceptively simple question. Its answer is closely linked to how the test developer defines the construct being measured and how that definition is the same as or different from other tests purporting to measure the same construct.

- *What is the objective of the test?* In the service of what goal will the test be employed? In what way or ways is the objective of this test the same as or different from other tests with similar goals? What real-world behaviors would be anticipated to correlate with testtaker responses?

- *Is there a need for this test?* Are there any other tests purporting to measure the same thing? In what ways will the new test be better than or different from existing ones? Will there be more compelling evidence for its reliability or validity? Will it be more comprehensive? Will it take less time to administer? In what ways would this test *not* be better than existing tests?

- *Who will use this test?* Clinicians? Educators? Others? For what purpose or purposes would this test be used?

- *Who will take this test?* Who is this test for? Who needs to take it? Who would find it desirable to take it? For what age range of testtakers is the test designed? What reading level is required of a testtaker? What cultural factors might affect testtaker response?

- *What content will the test cover?* Why should it cover this content? Is this coverage different from the content coverage of existing tests with the same or similar objectives? How and why is the content area different? To what extent is this content culture-specific?

- *How will the test be administered?* Individually or in groups? Is it amenable to both group and individual administration? What differences will exist between individual and group administrations of this test? Will the test be designed for or amenable to computer administration? How might differences between versions of the test be reflected in test scores?

- *What is the ideal format of the test?* Should it be true–false, essay, multiple-choice, or in some other format? Why is the format selected for this test the best format?

- *Should more than one form of the test be developed?* On the basis of a cost–benefit analysis, should alternate or parallel forms of this test be created?

- *What special training will be required of test users for administering or interpreting the test?* What background and qualifications will a prospective user of data derived from an administration of this test need to have? What restrictions, if any, should be placed on distributors of the test and on the test's usage?

- *What types of responses will be required of testtakers?* What kind of disability might preclude someone from being able to take this test? What adaptations or accommodations are recommended for persons with disabilities?

- *Who benefits from an administration of this test?* What would the testtaker learn, or how might the testtaker benefit, from an administration of this test? What would the test user learn, or how might the test user benefit? What social benefit, if any, derives from an administration of this test?

- *Is there any potential for harm as the result of an administration of this test?* What safeguards are built into the recommended testing procedure to prevent any sort of harm to any of the parties involved in the use of this test?

- *How will meaning be attributed to scores on this test?* Will a testtaker's score be compared to those of others taking the test at the same time? To those of others in a criterion group? Will the test evaluate mastery of a particular content area?

This last question provides a point of departure for elaborating on issues related to test development with regard to norm- versus criterion-referenced tests.

**Norm-referenced versus criterion-referenced tests: Item development issues** Different approaches to test development and individual item analyses are necessary, depending upon whether the finished test is designed to be norm-referenced or criterion-referenced. Generally speaking, for example, a good item on a norm-referenced achievement test is an item for which high scorers on the test respond correctly. Low scorers on the test tend to respond to that same item incorrectly. On a criterion-oriented test, this same pattern of results may occur: High scorers on the test get a particular item right whereas low scorers on the test get that same item wrong. However, that is not what makes an item good or acceptable from a criterion-oriented perspective. Ideally, each item on a criterion-oriented test addresses the issue of whether the testtaker—a would-be physician, engineer, piano student, or whoever—has met certain criteria. In short, when it comes to criterion-oriented assessment, being "first in the class" does not count and is often irrelevant. Although we can envision exceptions to this general rule, norm-referenced comparisons typically are insufficient and inappropriate when knowledge of mastery is what the test user requires.

Criterion-referenced testing and assessment are commonly employed in licensing contexts, be it a license to practice medicine or to drive a car. Criterion-referenced approaches are also employed in educational contexts in which mastery of particular material must be demonstrated before the student moves on to advanced material that conceptually builds on the existing base of knowledge, skills, or both.

In contrast to techniques and principles applicable to the development of norm-referenced tests (many of which are discussed in this chapter), the development of criterion-referenced instruments derives from a conceptualization of the knowledge or skills to be mastered. For purposes of assessment, the required cognitive or motor skills may be broken down into component parts. The test developer may attempt to sample criterion-related knowledge with regard to general principles relevant to the criterion being assessed. Experimentation with different items, tests, formats, or measurement procedures will help the test developer discover the best measure of mastery for the targeted skills or knowledge.

In general, the development of a criterion-referenced test or assessment procedure may entail exploratory work with at least two groups of testtakers: one group known to have mastered the knowledge or skill being measured and another group known *not* to have mastered such knowledge or skill. For example, during the development of a criterion-referenced written test for a driver's license, a preliminary version of the test may be administered to one group of people who have been driving about 15,000 miles per year for 10 years and who have perfect safety records (no accidents and no moving violations). The second group of testtakers might be a group of adults matched in demographic and related respects to the first group but who have never had any instruction in driving or driving experience. The items that best discriminate between these two groups would be considered "good" items. The preliminary exploratory experimentation done in test development need not have anything at all to do with flying, but you wouldn't know that from its name . . .

> **JUST THINK . . .**
>
> Suppose you were charged with developing a criterion-referenced test to measure mastery of Chapter 8 of this book. Explain, in as much detail as you think sufficient, how you would go about doing that. It's OK to read on before answering (in fact, you are encouraged to do so).

## Pilot Work

In the context of test development, terms such as **pilot work**, *pilot study,* and *pilot research* refer, in general, to the preliminary research surrounding the creation of a prototype of the test. Test items may be pilot studied (or piloted) to evaluate whether they should be included in the final form of the instrument. In developing a structured interview to measure introversion/extraversion, for example, pilot research may involve open-ended interviews with research subjects believed for some reason (perhaps on the basis of an existing test) to be introverted or extraverted. Additionally, interviews with parents, teachers, friends, and others who know the subject might also be arranged. Another type of pilot study might involve physiological monitoring of the subjects (such as monitoring of heart rate) as a function of exposure to different types of stimuli.

In pilot work, the test developer typically attempts to determine how best to measure a targeted construct. The process may entail literature reviews and experimentation as well as the creation, revision, and deletion of preliminary test items. After pilot work comes the process of test construction. Keep in mind, however, that depending on the nature of the test, as well as the nature of the changing responses to it by testtakers, test users, and the community at large, the need for further pilot research and test revision is always a possibility.

## Test Construction

Pilot work is a necessity when constructing tests or other measuring instruments for publication and wide distribution. Of course, pilot work need not be part of the process of developing teacher-made tests for classroom use (see this chapter's *Everyday Psychometrics*). As you read about more formal aspects of professional test construction, think about which (if any) technical procedures might lend themselves to modification for everyday use by classroom teachers.

### Scaling

We have previously defined *measurement* as the assignment of numbers according to rules. **Scaling** may be defined as the process of setting rules for assigning numbers in measurement. Stated another way, scaling is the process by which a measuring device is designed and calibrated and by which numbers (or other indices)—scale values—are assigned to different amounts of the trait, attribute, or characteristic being measured.

Historically, the prolific L. L. Thurstone (Figure 8–2) is credited for being at the forefront of efforts to develop methodologically sound scaling methods. He adapted psychophysical scaling methods to the study of psychological variables such as attitudes and values (Thurstone, 1959; Thurstone & Chave, 1929). Thurstone's (1925) article entitled "A Method of Scaling Psychological and Educational Tests" introduced, among other things, the notion of absolute scaling—a procedure for obtaining a measure of item difficulty across samples of testtakers who vary in ability.

**Types of scales** In common parlance, scales are instruments used to measure something, such as weight. In psychometrics, scales may also be conceived of as instruments used to measure. Here, however, that *something* being measured is likely to be a trait, a state, or an ability. When we think of types of scales, we think of the different ways that scales can be categorized. In Chapter 3, for example, we saw that scales can be meaningfully categorized along a continuum of level of measurement and be referred to as nominal, ordinal, interval, or ratio. But we might also characterize scales in other ways.

If the testtaker's test performance as a function of age is of critical interest, then the test might be referred to as an *age-based scale*. If the testtaker's test performance as a

## Psychometrics in the Classroom

Many concerns of professors and students about testing are psychometric. Professors want to give—and students want to take—tests that are reliable and valid measures of student knowledge. Even students who have not taken a course in psychological testing and assessment seem to understand psychometric issues regarding the tests administered in the classroom. As an illustration, consider each of the following pairs of statements. The first statement in each pair is a criticism of a classroom test you may have heard (or said yourself); the second is that criticism translated into the language of psychometrics.

> "I spent all last night studying Chapter 3, and there wasn't one item on that test from that chapter!"
>
> *Translation:* "I question the examination's content validity!"
>
> "The instructions on that essay test weren't clear, and I think it affected my grade."
>
> *Translation:* "There was excessive error variance related to the test administration procedures."
>
> "I wrote the same thing my friend did for this short-answer question—how come she got full credit and the professor took three points off my answer?"
>
> *Translation:* "I have grave concerns about rater error affecting reliability."
>
> "I didn't have enough time to finish; this test didn't measure what I know—only how fast I could write!"
>
> *Translation:* "I wish the person who wrote this test had paid more attention to issues related to criterion-related validity and the comparative efficacy of speed as opposed to power tests!"

Like their students, professors have concerns about the tests they administer. They want their examination questions to be clear, relevant, and representative of the material covered. They sometimes wonder about the length of their examinations. Their concern is to cover voluminous amounts of material while still providing enough time for students to give thoughtful consideration to their answers.

For most published psychological tests, these types of psychometric concerns would be addressed in a formal way during the test development process. In the classroom, however, rigorous psychometric evaluation of the dozen or so tests that any one instructor may administer during the course of a semester is impractical. Classroom tests are typically created for the purpose of testing just one group of students during one semester. Tests change to reflect changes in lectures and readings as courses evolve. Also, if tests are reused, they are in danger of becoming measures of who has seen or heard about the examination before taking it rather than measures of how well the students know the course material. Of course, although formal psychometric evaluation of classroom tests may be impractical, informal methods are frequently used.

Concerns about content validity are routinely addressed, usually informally, by professors in the test development process. For example, suppose an examination containing 50 multiple-choice questions and five short essays is to cover the reading and lecture material on four broad topics. The professor might systematically include 12 or 13 multiple-choice questions and at least one short essay from each topic area. The professor might also draw a certain percentage of the questions from the readings and a certain percentage from the lectures. Such a deliberate approach to content coverage may well boost the test's content validity, although no formal evaluation of the test's content validity will be made. The professor may also make an effort to inform the students that all textbook boxes and appendices and all instructional media presented in class (such as videotapes) are fair game for evaluation.

Criterion-related validity is difficult to establish on many classroom tests because no obvious criterion reflects the level of the students' knowledge of the material. Exceptions may exist for students in a technical or applied program who take an examination for licensure or certification. Informal assessment of something akin to criterion validity may occur on an individual basis in a student–professor chat wherein a student who obtained the lowest score in a class may demonstrate to the professor an unambiguous lack of understanding of the material. It is also true that the criterion validity of the test may be called into question by the same method. A chat with the student who scored the highest might reveal that this student doesn't have a clue about the material the test was designed to tap. Such a finding would give the professor pause.

The construct validity of classroom tests is often assessed informally, as when an anomaly in test performance may call attention to issues related to construct validity. For example, consider a group of students who have a history of performing at an above-average level on exams. Now suppose that all the students in this group perform poorly on a particular exam. If all these students report not

*(continued)*

## Psychometrics in the Classroom
*(continued)*

having studied for the test or just not having understood the text material, then there is an adequate explanation for their low scores. However, if the students report that they studied and understood the material as usual, then one might explain the outcome by questioning the exam's construct validity.

Aspects of a classroom test's reliability can also be informally assessed. For example, a discussion with students can shed light on the test's internal consistency. Then again, if the test was designed to be heterogeneous, then low internal consistency ratings might be desirable. On essay tests, inter-rater reliability can be explored by providing a group of volunteers with the criteria used in grading the essays and letting them grade some. Such an exercise might clarify the scoring criteria. In the rare instance when the same classroom test is given twice or in an alternate form, a discussion of the test-retest or alternate-forms reliability can be conducted.

Have you ever taken an exam in which one student quietly asks for clarification of a specific question and the professor then announces to the entire class the response to the student's question? This professor is attempting to reduce administration error (and increase reliability) by providing the same experience for all testtakers. When grading short-answer or essay questions, professors may try to reduce rater error by several techniques. For example, they may ask a colleague to help decipher a student's poor handwriting or re-grade a set of essays (without seeing the original grades). Professors also try to reduce administration error and increase reliability by eliminating items that many students misunderstand.

Tests developed for classroom use may not be perfect. Few, if any, tests for any purpose are. Still, most professors are always on the lookout for ways—formal and informal—to make the tests they administer as psychometrically sound as possible.

function of grade is of critical interest, then the test might be referred to as a *grade-based scale*. If all raw scores on the test are to be transformed into scores that can range from 1 to 9, then the test might be referred to as a *stanine* scale. A scale might be described in still other ways. For example, it may be categorized as *unidimensional* as opposed to *multidimensional*. It may be categorized as *comparative* as opposed to *categorical*. This is just a sampling of the various ways in which scales can be categorized.

Given that scales can be categorized in many different ways, it would be reasonable to assume that there are many different methods of scaling. Indeed, there are; there is no one method of scaling. There is no best type of scale. Test developers scale a test in the manner they believe is optimally suited to their conception of the measurement of the trait (or whatever) that is being measured.

**Scaling methods** Generally speaking, a testtaker is presumed to have more or less of the characteristic measured by a (valid) test as a function of the test score. The higher or lower the score, the more or less of the characteristic the testtaker presumably possesses. But how are numbers assigned to responses so that a test score can be calculated? This is done through scaling the test items, using any one of several available methods.

For example, consider a moral-issues opinion measure called the Morally Debatable Behaviors Scale–Revised (MDBS-R; Katz et al., 1994). Developed to be "a practical means of assessing what people believe, the strength of their convictions, as well as individual differences in moral tolerance" (p. 15), the MDBS-R contains 30 items. Each item contains a brief description of a moral issue or behavior on which testtakers express their opinion by means of a 10-point scale that ranges from "never justified" to "always justified." Here is a sample.

**Figure 8–2**
**L. L. Thurstone (1887–1955)**

*Among his many achievements in the area of scaling was Thurstone's (1927) influential article "A Law of Comparative Judgment." One of the few "laws" in psychology. This was Thurstone's proudest achievement (Nunnally, 1978, pp. 60–61). Of course, he had many achievements from which to choose. Thurstone's adaptations of scaling methods for use in psychophysiological research and the study of attitudes and values have served as models for generations of researchers (Bock & Jones, 1968). He is also widely considered to be one of the primary architects of modern factor analysis.*

**Cheating on taxes if you have a chance is:**

| 1 | 2 | 3 | 4 | 5 | 6 | 7 | 8 | 9 | 10 |
|---|---|---|---|---|---|---|---|---|---|
| never justified | | | | | | | | | always justified |

The MDBS-R is an example of a **rating scale,** which can be defined as a grouping of words, statements, or symbols on which judgments of the strength of a particular trait, attitude, or emotion are indicated by the testtaker. Rating scales can be used to record judgments of oneself, others, experiences, or objects, and they can take several forms (Figure 8–3).

On the MDBS-R, the ratings that the testtaker makes for each of the 30 test items are added together to obtain a final score. Scores range from a low of 30 (if the testtaker indicates that all 30 behaviors are never justified) to a high of 300 (if the testtaker indicates that all 30 situations are always justified). Because the final test score is obtained by summing the ratings across all the items, it is termed a **summative scale.**

One type of summative rating scale, the **Likert scale** (Likert, 1932), is used extensively in psychology, usually to scale attitudes. Likert scales are relatively easy to construct. Each item presents the testtaker with five alternative responses (sometimes seven), usually on an agree–disagree or approve–disapprove continuum. If Katz et al. had used a Likert scale, an item on their test might have looked like this:

**Cheating on taxes if you have a chance.**

This is (check one):

| _____ | _____ | _____ | _____ | _____ |
|---|---|---|---|---|
| never justified | rarely justified | sometimes justified | usually justified | always justified |

*Rating Scale Item A*
How did you feel about what you saw on television?

*Rating Scale Item B*
I believe I would like the work of a lighthouse keeper.
True    False    (circle one)

*Rating Scale Item C*
Please rate the employee on ability to cooperate and get along with fellow employees:
Excellent _____ / _____ / _____ / _____ / _____ / _____ / _____ / Unsatisfactory

**Figure 8–3**
**The Many Faces of Rating Scales**

*Rating scales can take many forms. "Smiley" faces, such as those illustrated here as Item A, have been used in social-psychological research with young children and adults with limited language skills. The faces are used in lieu of words such as positive, neutral, and negative.*

Likert scales are usually reliable, which may account for their widespread popularity. Likert (1932) experimented with different weightings of the five categories but concluded that assigning weights of 1 (for endorsement of items at one extreme) through 5 (for endorsement of items at the other extreme) generally worked best.

The use of rating scales of any type results in ordinal-level data. With reference to the Likert scale item, for example, if the response *never justified* is assigned the value 1, *rarely justified* the value 2, and so on, then a higher score indicates greater permissiveness with regard to cheating on taxes. Respondents could even be ranked with regard to such permissiveness. However, the difference in permissiveness between the opinions of a pair of people who scored 2 and 3 on this scale is not necessarily the same as the difference between the opinions of a pair of people who scored 3 and 4.

**JUST THINK . . .**

It's debatable, but which form of the Morally Debatable Behaviors Scale worked best for you? Why?

Rating scales differ in the number of dimensions underlying the ratings being made. Some rating scales are *unidimensional,* meaning that only one dimension is presumed to underlie the ratings. Other rating scales are *multidimensional,* meaning that more than one dimension is thought to guide the testtaker's responses. Consider in this context an item from the MDBS-R regarding marijuana use. Responses to this item, particularly responses in the low to middle range, may be interpreted in many different ways. Such responses may reflect the view (a) that people should not engage in illegal activities, (b) that people should not take risks with their health, or (c) that people should avoid activities that could lead to contact with a bad crowd. Responses to this item may also reflect other attitudes and beliefs, such as those related to the beneficial use of marijuana as an adjunct to chemotherapy for cancer patients. When more than one dimension is tapped by an item, multidimensional scaling techniques are used to identify the dimensions.

Another scaling method that produces ordinal data is the **method of paired comparisons.** Testtakers are presented with pairs of stimuli (two photographs, two objects, two statements), which they are asked to compare. They must select one of the stimuli according to some rule; for example, the rule that they agree more with one statement than the other, or the rule that they find one stimulus more appealing than the other. Had Katz et al. used the method of paired comparisons, an item on their scale might have looked like the one that follows.

**Select the behavior that you think would be more justified:**

a. cheating on taxes if one has a chance
b. accepting a bribe in the course of one's duties

For each pair of options, testtakers receive a higher score for selecting the option deemed more justifiable by the majority of a group of judges. The judges would have been asked to rate the pairs of options before the distribution of the test, and a list of the options selected by the judges would be provided along with the scoring instructions as an answer key. The test score would reflect the number of times the choices of a testtaker agreed with those of the judges. If we use Katz et al.'s (1994) standardization sample as the judges, then the more justifiable option is cheating on taxes. A testtaker might receive a point toward the total score for selecting option "a" but no points for selecting option "b." An advantage of the method of paired comparisons is that it forces testtakers to choose between items.

Sorting tasks are another way that ordinal information may be developed and scaled. Here, stimuli such as printed cards, drawings, photographs, or other objects are typically presented to testtakers for evaluation. One method of sorting, **comparative scaling,** entails judgments of a stimulus in comparison with every other stimulus on the scale. A version of the MDBS-R that employs comparative scaling might feature 30 items, each printed on a separate index card. Testtakers would be asked to sort the cards from most justifiable to least justifiable. Comparative scaling could also be accomplished by providing testtakers with a list of 30 items on a sheet of paper and asking them to rank the justifiability of the items from 1 to 30.

> **JUST THINK . . .**
>
> Under what circumstance might it be advantageous for tests to contain items presented as a sorting task?

Another scaling system that relies on sorting is **categorical scaling.** Stimuli are placed into one of two or more alternative categories that differ quantitatively with respect to some continuum. In our running MDBS-R example, testtakers might be given 30 index cards, on each of which is printed one of the 30 items. Testtakers would be asked to sort the cards into three piles: those behaviors that are never justified, those that are sometimes justified, and those that are always justified.

A **Guttman scale** (Guttman, 1944a,b, 1947) is yet another scaling method that yields ordinal-level measures. Items on it range sequentially from weaker to stronger expressions of the attitude, belief, or feeling being measured. A feature of Guttman scales is that all respondents who agree with the stronger statements of the attitude will also agree with milder statements. Using the MDBS-R scale as an example, consider the following statements that reflect attitudes toward suicide.

**Do you agree or disagree with each of the following:**

a. All people should have the right to decide whether they wish to end their lives.
b. People who are terminally ill and in pain should have the option to have a doctor assist them in ending their lives.
c. People should have the option to sign away the use of artificial life-support equipment before they become seriously ill.
d. People have the right to a comfortable life.

If this were a perfect Guttman scale, then all respondents who agree with "a" (the most extreme position) should also agree with "b," "c," and "d." All respondents who disagree with "a" but agree with "b" should also agree with "c" and "d," and so forth. Guttman scales are developed through the administration of a number of items to a target group. The resulting data are then analyzed by means of **scalogram analysis**, an item-analysis procedure and approach to test development that involves a graphic mapping of a testtaker's responses. The objective for the developer of a measure of attitudes is to obtain an arrangement of items wherein endorsement of one item automatically connotes endorsement of less extreme positions. It is not always possible to do this. Beyond the measurement of attitudes, Guttman scaling or scalogram analysis (the two terms are used synonymously) appeals to test developers in consumer psychology, where an objective may be to learn if a consumer who will purchase one product will purchase another product.

All the foregoing methods yield ordinal data. The method of equal-appearing intervals, first described by Thurstone (1929), is one scaling method used to obtain data that are presumed to be interval in nature. Again using the example of attitudes about the justifiability of suicide, let's outline the steps that would be involved in creating a scale using Thurstone's equal-appearing intervals method.

1. A reasonably large number of statements reflecting positive and negative attitudes toward suicide are collected, such as *Life is sacred, so people should never take their own lives* and *A person in a great deal of physical or emotional pain may rationally decide that suicide is the best available option.*

2. Judges (or experts in some cases) evaluate each statement in terms of how strongly it indicates that suicide is justified. Each judge is instructed to rate each statement on a scale as if the scale were interval in nature. For example, the scale might range from 1 (the statement indicates that suicide is never justified) to 9 (the statement indicates that suicide is always justified). Judges are instructed that the 1-to-9 scale is being used as if there were an equal distance between each of the values—that is, as if it were an interval scale. Judges are cautioned to focus their ratings on the statements, not on their own views on the matter.

3. A mean and a standard deviation of the judges' ratings are calculated for each statement. For example, if fifteen judges rated 100 statements on a scale from 1 to 9 then, for each of these 100 statements, the fifteen judges' ratings would be averaged. Suppose five of the judges rated a particular item as a 1, five other judges rated it as a 2, and the remaining five judges rated it as a 3. The average rating would be 2 (with a standard deviation of 0.816).

4. Items are selected for inclusion in the final scale based on several criteria, including (a) the degree to which the item contributes to a comprehensive measurement of the variable in question and (b) the test developer's degree of confidence that the items have indeed been sorted into equal intervals. Item means and standard deviations are also considered. Items should represent a wide range of attitudes reflected in a variety of ways. A low standard deviation is indicative of a good item; the judges agreed about the meaning of the item with respect to its reflection of attitudes toward suicide.

5. The scale is now ready for administration. The way the scale is used depends on the objectives of the test situation. Typically, respondents are asked to select those statements that most accurately reflect their own attitudes. The values of the items that the respondent selects (based on the judges' ratings) are averaged, producing a score on the test.

The method of equal-appearing intervals is an example of a scaling method of the *direct estimation* variety. In contrast to other methods that involve *indirect estimation*, there is no need to transform the testtaker's responses into some other scale.

The particular scaling method employed in the development of a new test depends on many factors, including the variables being measured, the group for whom the test is intended (children may require a less complicated scaling method than adults, for example), and the preferences of the test developer.

## Writing Items

In the grand scheme of test construction, considerations related to the actual writing of the test's items go hand in hand with scaling considerations. The prospective test developer or item writer immediately faces three questions related to the test blueprint:

- What range of content should the items cover?
- Which of the many different types of item formats should be employed?
- How many items should be written in total and for each content area covered?

When devising a standardized test using a multiple-choice format, it is usually advisable that the first draft contain approximately twice the number of items that the final version of the test will contain.[1] If, for example, a test called "American History: 1940 to 1990" is to have 30 questions in its final version, it would be useful to have as many as 60 items in the item pool. Ideally, these items will adequately sample the domain of the test. An **item pool** is the reservoir or well from which items will or will not be drawn for the final version of the test.

A comprehensive sampling provides a basis for content validity of the final version of the test. Because approximately half of these items will be eliminated from the test's final version, the test developer needs to ensure that the final version also contains items that adequately sample the domain. Thus, if all the questions about the Persian Gulf War from the original 60 items were determined to be poorly written, then the test developer should either rewrite items sampling this period or create new items. The new or rewritten items would then also be subjected to tryout so as not to jeopardize the test's content validity. As in earlier versions of the test, an effort is made to ensure adequate sampling of the domain in the final version of the test. Another consideration here is whether or not alternate forms of the test will be created and, if so, how many. Multiply the number of items required in the pool for one form of the test by the number of forms planned, and you have the total number of items needed for the initial item pool.

How does one develop items for the item pool? The test developer may write a large number of items from personal experience or academic acquaintance with the subject matter. Help may also be sought from others, including experts. For psychological tests designed to be used in clinical settings, clinicians, patients, patients' family members, clinical staff, and others may be interviewed for insights that could assist in item writing. For psychological tests designed to be used by personnel psychologists, interviews with members of a targeted industry or organization will likely be of great value.

---

1. Common sense and the practical demands of the situation may dictate that fewer items be written for the first draft of a test. If, for example, the final draft were to contain 1,000 items, then creating an item pool of 2,000 items might be an undue burden. If the test developer is a knowledgeable and capable item writer, it might be necessary to create only about 1,200 items for the item pool.

**JUST THINK . . .**

If you were going to develop a pool of items to cover the subject of "academic knowledge of what it takes to develop an item pool," how would you go about doing it?

For psychological tests designed to be used by school psychologists, interviews with teachers, administrative staff, educational psychologists, and others may be invaluable. Searches through the academic research literature may prove fruitful, as may searches through other databases.

Considerations related to variables such as the purpose of the test and the number of examinees to be tested at one time enter into decisions regarding the format of the test under construction.

**Item format**    Variables such as the form, plan, structure, arrangement, and layout of individual test items are collectively referred to as **item format.** Two types of item format we will discuss in detail are the *selected-response format* and the *constructed-response format.* Items presented in a **selected-response format** require testtakers to select a response from a set of alternative responses. Items presented in a **constructed-response format** require testtakers to supply or to create the correct answer, not merely to select it.

If a test is designed to measure achievement and if the items are written in a selected-response format, then examinees must select the response that is keyed as correct. If the test is designed to measure the strength of a particular trait and if the items are written in a selected-response format, then examinees must select the alternative that best answers the question with respect to themselves. As we further discuss item formats, for the sake of simplicity we will confine our examples to achievement tests. The reader may wish to mentally substitute other appropriate terms for words such as *correct* for personality or other types of tests that are not achievement tests.

Three types of selected-response item formats are *multiple-choice, matching,* and *true–false.* An item written in a **multiple-choice format** has three elements: (1) a stem, (2) a correct alternative or option, and (3) several incorrect alternatives or options variously referred to as *distractors* or *foils.* Two illustrations follow (despite the fact that you are probably all too familiar with multiple-choice items).

### Item A

| | | |
|---|---|---|
| Stem | ⟶ | A psychological test, an interview, and a case study are: |
| Correct alt. | ⟶ | a. psychological assessment tools |
| | | ⌐ b. standardized behavioral samples |
| Distractors | ⟶ | ⎢ c. reliable assessment instruments |
| | | ⌐ d. theory-linked measures |

Now consider Item B:

### Item B

A good multiple-choice item in an achievement test:

a.  has one correct alternative

b.  has grammatically parallel alternatives

c.  has alternatives of similar length

d.  has alternatives that fit grammatically with the stem

e.  includes as much of the item as possible in the stem to avoid unnecessary repetition

f.  avoids ridiculous distractors

g. is not excessively long

h. all of the above

i. none of the above

If you answered "h" to Item B, you are correct. As you read the list of alternatives, it may have occurred to you that Item B violated some of the rules it set forth!

In a **matching item,** the testtaker is presented with two columns: *premises* on the left and *responses* on the right. The testtaker's task is to determine which response is best associated with which premise. For very young testtakers, the instructions will direct them to draw a line from one premise to one response. Testtakers other than young children are typically asked to write a letter or number as a response. Here's an example of a matching item one might see on a test in a class on modern film history:

*Directions:* Match an actor's name in Column X with a film role the actor played in Column Y. Write the letter of the film role next to the number of the corresponding actor. Each of the roles listed in Column Y may be used once, more than once, or not at all.

| Column X | Column Y |
|---|---|
| _____ 1. Anthony Hopkins | a. Anton Chigurh |
| _____ 2. Javier Bardem | b. The Jackal |
| _____ 3. Mark Wahlberg | c. Storm |
| _____ 4. Mike Myers | d. Hannibal Lecter |
| _____ 5. Charlize Theron | e. Austin Powers |
| _____ 6. Natalie Portman | f. Micky Ward |
| _____ 7. George Lazenby | g. Danny Archer |
| _____ 8. Jesse Eisenberg | h. Nina Sayers |
| _____ 9. Sigourney Weaver | i. Mark Zuckerberg |
| _____ 10. Leonardo DiCaprio | j. Aileen Wuornos |
| _____ 11. Halle Berry | k. James Bond |
| | l. Ellen Ripley |
| | m. John Book |

You may have noticed that the two columns contain different numbers of items. If the number of items in the two columns were the same, then a person unsure about one of the actor's roles could merely deduce it by matching all the other options first. A perfect score would then result even though the testtaker did not actually know all the answers. Providing more options than needed minimizes such a possibility. Another way to lessen the probability of chance or guessing as a factor in the test score is to state in the directions that each response may be a correct answer once, more than once, or not at all.

Some guidelines should be observed in writing matching items for classroom use. The wording of the premises and the responses should be fairly short and to the point. No more than a dozen or so premises should be included; otherwise, some students will forget what they were looking for as they go through the lists. The lists of premises and responses should both be homogeneous—that is, lists of the same sort of thing. Our film school example provides a homogeneous list of premises (all names of actors) and a homogeneous list of responses (all names of film characters). Care must be taken to ensure that one and only one premise is matched to one and only one response. For example, adding the name of actors Sean Connery, Roger Moore, David Niven, Timothy Dalton, Pierce Brosnan, or Daniel Craig to the premise column as it now exists would be inadvisable, regardless of what character's name was added to the response column. Do you know why?

At one time or another, Connery, Moore, Niven, Dalton, Brosnan, and Craig all played the role of James Bond (response "k"). As the list of premises and responses currently stands, the match to response "k" is premise "7" (this Australian actor played Agent 007 in the film *On Her Majesty's Secret Service*). If in the future the test developer wanted to substitute the name of another actor—say, Daniel Craig for George Lazenby—then it would be prudent to review the columns to confirm that Craig did not play any of the other characters in the response list and that James Bond still was not played by any actor in the premise list besides Craig.[2]

A multiple-choice item that contains only two possible responses is called a **binary-choice item.** Perhaps the most familiar binary-choice item is the **true–false item.** As you know, this type of selected-response item usually takes the form of a sentence that requires the testtaker to indicate whether the statement is or is not a fact. Other varieties of binary-choice items include sentences to which the testtaker responds with one of two responses, such as *agree or disagree, yes or no, right or wrong,* or *fact or opinion.*

A good binary choice contains a single idea, is not excessively long, and is not subject to debate; the correct response must undoubtedly be one of the two choices. Like multiple-choice items, binary-choice items are readily applicable to a wide range of subjects. Unlike multiple-choice items, binary-choice items cannot contain distractor alternatives. For this reason, binary-choice items are typically easier to write than multiple-choice items and can be written relatively quickly. A disadvantage of the binary-choice item is that the probability of obtaining a correct response purely on the basis of chance (guessing) on any one item is .5, or 50%.[3] In contrast, the probability of obtaining a correct response by guessing on a four-alternative multiple-choice question is .25, or 25%.

Moving from a discussion of the selected-response format to the constructed variety, three types of constructed-response items are the *completion item,* the *short answer,* and the *essay.*

A **completion item** requires the examinee to provide a word or phrase that completes a sentence, as in the following example:

The standard deviation is generally considered the most useful measure of _____.

A good completion item should be worded so that the correct answer is specific. Completion items that can be correctly answered in many ways lead to scoring problems. (The correct completion here is *variability.*) An alternative way of constructing this question would be as a short-answer item:

What descriptive statistic is generally considered the most useful measure of variability?

A completion item may also be referred to as a **short-answer item.** It is desirable for completion or short-answer items to be written clearly enough that the testtaker can respond succinctly—that is, with a short answer. There are no hard-and-fast rules

---

2. Here's the entire answer key: 1-d, 2-a, 3-f, 4-e, 5-j, 6-h, 7-k, 8-i, 9-l, 10-g, 11-c.

3. We note in passing, however, that although the probability of guessing correctly on an individual binary-choice item on the basis of chance alone is .5, the probability of guessing correctly on a *sequence* of such items decreases as the number of items increases. The probability of guessing correctly on two such items is equal to $.5^2$, or 25%. The probability of guessing correctly on ten such items is equal to $.5^{10}$, or .001. This means there is a one-in-a-thousand chance that a testtaker would guess correctly on ten true–false (or other binary-choice) items on the basis of chance alone.

for how short an answer must be to be considered a short answer; a word, a term, a sentence, or a paragraph may qualify. Beyond a paragraph or two, the item is more properly referred to as an essay item. We may define an **essay item** as a test item that requires the testtaker to respond to a question by writing a composition, typically one that demonstrates recall of facts, understanding, analysis, and/or interpretation.

Here is an example of an essay item:

> Compare and contrast definitions and techniques of classical and operant conditioning. Include examples of how principles of each have been applied in clinical as well as educational settings.

An essay item is useful when the test developer wants the examinee to demonstrate a depth of knowledge about a single topic. In contrast to selected-response and constructed-response items such as the short-answer item, the essay question not only permits the restating of learned material but also allows for the creative integration and expression of the material in the testtaker's own words. The skills tapped by essay items are different from those tapped by true–false and matching items. Whereas these latter types of items require only recognition, an essay requires recall, organization, planning, and writing ability. A drawback of the essay item is that it tends to focus on a more limited area than can be covered in the same amount of time when using a series of selected-response items or completion items. Another potential problem with essays can be subjectivity in scoring and inter-scorer differences. A review of some advantages and disadvantages of these different item formats, especially as used in academic classroom settings, is presented in Table 8–1.

**Writing items for computer administration** A number of widely available computer programs are designed to facilitate the construction of tests as well as their administration, scoring, and interpretation. These programs typically make use of two advantages of digital media: the ability to store items in an *item bank* and the ability to individualize testing through a technique called *item branching.*

An **item bank** is a relatively large and easily accessible collection of test questions. Instructors who regularly teach a particular course sometimes create their own item bank of questions that they have found to be useful on examinations. One of the many potential advantages of an item bank is accessibility to a large number of test items conveniently classified by subject area, item statistics, or other variables. And just as funds may be added to or withdrawn from a more traditional bank, so items may be added to, withdrawn from, and even modified in an item bank (see this chapter's *Close-Up*).

The term **computerized adaptive testing (CAT)** refers to an interactive, computer-administered test-taking process wherein items presented to the testtaker are based in part on the testtaker's performance on previous items. As in traditional test administration, the test might begin with some sample, practice items. However, the computer may not permit the testtaker to continue with the test until the practice items have been responded to in a satisfactory

> **JUST THINK . . .**
>
> If an item bank is sufficiently large, does it makes sense to publish the entire bank of items in advance to the testtakers before the test?

manner and the testtaker has demonstrated an understanding of the test procedure. Using CAT, the test administered may be different for each testtaker, depending on the test performance on the items presented. Each item on an achievement test, for example, may have a known difficulty level. This fact as well as other data (such as a statistical allowance for blind guessing) may be factored in when it comes time to tally a final score on the items administered. Note that we do not say "final score on the test" because what constitutes "the test" may well be different for different testtakers.

**Table 8–1**

**Some Advantages and Disadvantages of Various Item Formats**

| Format of Item | Advantages | Disadvantages |
|---|---|---|
| Multiple-choice | • Can sample a great deal of content in a relatively short time.<br>• Allows for precise interpretation and little "bluffing" other than guessing. This, in turn, may allow for more content-valid test score interpretation than some other formats.<br>• May be machine- or computer-scored. | • Does not allow for expression of original or creative thought.<br>• Not all subject matter lends itself to reduction to one and only one answer keyed correct.<br>• May be time-consuming to construct series of good items.<br>• Advantages of this format may be nullified if item is poorly written or if a pattern of correct alternatives is discerned by the testtaker. |
| Binary-choice items (such as true/false) | • Can sample a great deal of content in a relatively short time.<br>• Test consisting of such items is relatively easy to construct and score.<br>• May be machine- or computer-scored. | • Susceptibility to guessing is high, especially for "test-wise" students who may detect cues to reject one choice or the other.<br>• Some wordings, including use of adverbs such as *typically* or *usually*, can be interpreted differently by different students.<br>• Can be used only when a choice of dichotomous responses can be made without qualification. |
| Matching | • Can effectively and efficiently be used to evaluate testtakers' recall of related facts.<br>• Particularly useful when there are a large number of facts on a single topic.<br>• Can be fun or game-like for testtaker (especially the well-prepared testtaker).<br>• May be machine- or computer-scored. | • As with other items in the selected-response format, testtakers need only *recognize* a correct answer and not recall it or devise it.<br>• One of the choices may help eliminate one of the other choices as the correct response.<br>• Requires pools of related information and is of less utility with distinctive ideas. |
| Completion or short-answer (fill-in-the-blank) | • Wide content area, particularly of questions that require factual recall, can be sampled in relatively brief amount of time.<br>• This type of test is relatively easy to construct.<br>• Useful in obtaining picture of what testtaker is able to generate as opposed to merely recognize since testtaker must generate response. | • Useful only with responses of one word or a few words.<br>• May demonstrate only recall of circumscribed facts or bits of knowledge.<br>• Potential for inter-scorer reliability problems when test is scored by more than one person.<br>• Typically hand-scored. |
| Essay | • Useful in measuring responses that require complex, imaginative, or original solutions, applications, or demonstrations.<br>• Useful in measuring how well testtaker is able to communicate ideas in writing.<br>• Requires testtaker to generate entire response, not merely recognize it or supply a word or two. | • May not sample wide content area as well as other tests do.<br>• Testtaker with limited knowledge can attempt to bluff with confusing, sometimes long and elaborate writing designed to be as broad and ambiguous as possible.<br>• Scoring can be time-consuming and fraught with pitfalls.<br>• When more than one person is scoring, inter-scorer reliability issues may be raised.<br>• May rely too heavily on writing skills, even to the point of confounding writing ability with what is purportedly being measured.<br>• Typically hand-scored. |

The advantages of CAT have been well documented (Weiss & Vale, 1987). Only a sample of the total number of items in the item pool is administered to any one testtaker. On the basis of previous response patterns, items that have a high probability of being answered in a particular fashion ("correctly" if an ability test) are not presented, thus providing economy in terms of testing time and total number of items presented. Computerized adaptive testing has been found to reduce the number of test items that need to be administered by as much as 50% while simultaneously reducing measurement error by 50%.

CAT tends to reduce *floor effects* and *ceiling effects*. A **floor effect** refers to the diminished utility of an assessment tool for distinguishing testtakers at the low end of the ability, trait, or other attribute being measured. A test of ninth-grade mathematics, for

## Designing an Item Bank

**D**eveloping an item bank is more work than simply writing items for a test. Many questions and issues need to be resolved relating to the development of such a bank and to the maintenance of a satisfactory pool of items. These questions and issues relate to the items, the test, the system, the use to which the item bank will be put, and the cost.

I. Items
   A. Acquisition and development
      1. Develop/use your own item collection or use collections of others?
         a. If develop your own item collection, what development procedures will be followed?
         b. If use collections of others, will the items be leased or purchased? Is the classification scheme sufficiently documented, and can the item format specifications be easily transferred and used?
      2. What types of items will be permitted?
         a. Will open-ended (constructed-response) items, opinion questions, instructional objectives, or descriptions of performance tasks be included in the bank?
         b. Will all the items be made to fit a common format (for example, all multiple-choice with options "a," "b," "c," and "d")?
         c. Must the items be calibrated, validated or otherwise carry additional information?
      3. What will be the size of the item collection?
         a. How many items per objective or subtopic (collection depth)?
         b. How many different topics (collection breadth)?
      4. What review, tryout, and editing procedures will be used?
         a. Who will perform the review and editing?
         b. Will there be a field tryout, and if so, what statistics will be gathered, and what criteria will be used for inclusion in the bank?
   B. Classification
      1. How will the subject matter classifications be performed?
         a. Will the classification by subject matter use fixed categories, keywords, or some combination of the two?
         b. Who will be responsible for preparing, expanding, and refining the taxonomy?
         c. How detailed will the taxonomy be? Will it be hierarchically or nonhierarchically arranged?
         d. Who will assign classification indices to each item, and how will this assignment be verified?

      2. What other assigned information about the items will be stored in the item bank?
      3. What measured information about the items will be stored in the bank? How will the item measures be calculated?*
   C. Management
      1. Will provision be made for updating the classification scheme and items? If so:
         a. Who will be permitted to make additions, deletions, and revisions?
         b. What review procedures will be followed?
         c. How will the changes be disseminated?
         d. How will duplicate (or near-duplicate) items be detected and eliminated?
         e. When will a revision of an item be trivial enough that item statistics from a previous version can be aggregated with revisions from the current version?
         f. Will item statistics be stored from each use, or from last use, or will they be aggregated across uses?
      2. How will items be handled that require pictures, graphs, special characters, or other types of enhanced printing?
      3. How will items that must accompany other items be handled, such as a series of questions about the same reading passage?

II. Tests
   A. Assembly
      1. Must the test constructor specify the specific items to appear on the test, or will the items be selected by computer?
      2. If the items are selected by computer:
         a. How will one item be selected out of several that match the search specification (randomly, time since last usage, frequency of previous use)?
         b. What happens if no item meets the search specifications?
         c. Will a test constructor have the option to reject a selected item, and if so, what will be the mechanism for doing so?
         d. What precautions will be taken to ensure that examinees who are tested more than once do not receive the same items?

*This question is the subject of considerable controversy and discussion in the technical measurement literature.

*(continued)*

## Designing an Item Bank *(continued)*

3. What item or test parameters can be specified for test assembly (item format restrictions, limits on difficulty levels, expected score distribution, expected test reliability, and so on)?
4. What assembly procedures will be available (options to multiple-choice items placed in random order, the test items placed in random order, different items on each test)?
5. Will the system print tests, or only specify which items to use? If the former, how will the tests be printed or duplicated, and where will the answers be displayed?

B. Administration, scoring, and reporting
1. Will the system be capable of online test administration? If so:
   a. How will access be managed?
   b. Will test administration be adaptive, and if so, using what procedures?
2. Will the system provide for test scoring? If so:
   a. What scoring formula will be used (rights only, correction for guessing, partial credit for some answers, weighting by discrimination values)?
   b. How will constructed responses be evaluated (offline by the instructor, online or offline by examiners comparing their answers to a key, online by computer with or without employing a spelling algorithm)?
3. Will the system provide for test reporting? If so:
   a. What records will be kept (the tests themselves, individual student item responses, individual student test scores, school or other group scores) and for how long? Will new scores for individuals and groups supplement or replace old scores?
   b. What reporting options (content and format) will be available?
   c. To whom will the reports be sent?

C. Evaluation
1. Will reliability and validity data be collected? If so, what data will be collected by whom, and how will they be used?
2. Will norms be made available, and if so, based on what norm-referenced measures?

III. System
A. Acquisition and development
1. Who will be responsible for acquisition and development, given what resources, and operating under what constraints?
2. Will the system be transportable to others? What levels and degree of documentation will be available?

B. Software and hardware
1. What aspects of the system will be computer-assisted?
   a. Where will the items be stored (computer, paper, card file)?
   b. Will requests be filled using a batch, online, or manual mode?
2. Will a microcomputer be used, and if so, what special limits does such a choice place on item text, item bank size, and test development options?
3. Will items be stored as one large collection, or will separate files be maintained for each user?
4. How will the item banking system be constructed (from scratch; by piecing together word processing, database management, and other general-purpose programs; by adopting existing item banking systems)?
5. What specific equipment will be needed (for storage, retrieval, interactions with the system, and so on)?
6. How user- and maintenance-friendly will the equipment and support programs be?
7. Who will be responsible for equipment maintenance?

C. Monitoring and training
1. What system features will be monitored (number of items per classification category, usage by user group, number of revisions until a user is satisfied, distribution of test lengths or other test characteristics, and so on)?
2. Who will monitor the system, train users, and give support (initially and ongoing)?
3. How will information be disseminated about changes in system procedures?

D. Access and security
1. Who will have access to the items and other information in the bank (authors/owners, teachers, students)? Who can request tests?
2. Will users have direct access to the system, or must they go through an intermediary?
3. What procedures will be followed to secure the contents of the item bank (if they are to be secure)?
4. Where will the contents of the item bank be housed (centrally, or will each user also have a copy)?
5. Who will have access to score reports?

IV. Use and Acceptance
A. General
1. Who decides to what uses the item bank will be put? And will these uses be those the test users need and want?

2. Who will develop the tests, and who will be allowed to use the system? Will those people be acceptable to the examinees and recipients of the test information?
3. Will the system be able to handle the expected demand for use?
4. Is the output of the system likely to be used and used as intended?
5. How will user acceptance and item bank credibility be enhanced?

B. Instructional improvement. If this is an intended use:
1. Will the item bank be part of a larger instructional or decision-making system?
2. Which textbooks, curriculum guidelines, and other materials, if any, will be keyed to the bank's items? Who will make that decision, and how will the assignments be validated?
3. Will items be available for drill and practice as well as for testing?
4. Will information be available to users that will assist in the diagnosis of educational needs?

C. Adaptive testing. If this is an option:
1. How will test administrations be scheduled?
2. How will the items be selected to ensure testing efficiency yet maintain content representation and avoid duplication between successive test administrations?
3. What criteria will be used to terminate testing?
4. What scoring procedures will be followed?

D. Certification of competence. If this is an intended use:
1. Will the item bank contain measures that cover all the important component skills of the competence being assessed?

2. How many attempts at passing the test will be allowed? When? How will these attempts be monitored?

E. Program and curriculum evaluation. If this is an intended use:
1. Will it be possible to implement the system to provide reliable measures of student achievement in a large number of specific performance areas?
2. Will the item bank contain measures that cover all the important stated objectives of the curriculum? That go beyond the stated objectives of the curriculum?
3. Will the item bank yield commensurable data that permit valid comparisons over time?

F. Testing and reporting requirements imposed by external agencies. If meeting these requirements is an intended use:
1. Will the system be able to handle requirements for program evaluation, student selection for specially funded programs, assessing educational needs, and reporting?
2. Will the system be able to accommodate minor modifications in the testing and reporting requirements?

V. Costs
A. Cost feasibility
1. What are the (fixed, variable) costs (financial, time, space, equipment, and supplies) to create and support the system?
2. Are those costs affordable?

B. Cost comparisons
1. How do the item banking system costs compare with the present or other testing systems that achieve the same goals?
2. Do any expanded capabilities justify the extra cost? Are any restricted capabilities balanced by cost savings?

Source: Millman and Arter (1984).

example, may contain items that range from easy to hard for testtakers having the mathematical ability of the average ninth-grader. However, testtakers who have not yet achieved such ability might fail all of the items; because of the floor effect, the test would not provide any guidance as to the relative mathematical ability of testtakers in this group. If the item bank contained some less difficult items, these could be pressed into service to minimize the floor effect and provide discrimination among the low-ability testtakers.

As you might expect, a **ceiling effect** refers to the diminished utility of an assessment tool for distinguishing testtakers at the high end of the ability, trait, or other attribute being measured. Returning to our example of the ninth-grade mathematics test, what would happen if all of the testtakers answered all of the items correctly? It is likely that the test user would conclude that the test was too easy for this group of testtakers and so discrimination was impaired by a ceiling effect. If the item bank contained some items that were more difficult, these could

**JUST THINK . . .**

Provide an example of how a floor effect in a test of integrity might occur when the sample of testtakers consisted of prison inmates convicted of fraud.

be used to minimize the ceiling effect and enable the test user to better discriminate among these high-ability testtakers.

◆
**JUST THINK . . .**

Provide an example of a ceiling effect in a test that measures a personality trait.

The ability of the computer to tailor the content and order of presentation of test items on the basis of responses to previous items is referred to as **item branching.** A computer that has stored a bank of achievement test items of different difficulty levels can be programmed to present items according to an algorithm or rule. For example, one rule might be "don't present an item of the next difficulty level until two consecutive items of the current difficulty level are answered correctly." Another rule might be "terminate the test when five consecutive items of a given level of difficulty have been answered incorrectly." Alternatively, the pattern of items to which the testtaker is exposed might be based not on the testtaker's response to preceding items but on a random drawing from the total pool of test items. Random presentation of items reduces the ease with which testtakers can memorize items on behalf of future testtakers.

Item-branching technology may be applied when constructing tests not only of achievement but also of personality. For example, if a respondent answers an item in a way that suggests he or she is depressed, the computer might automatically probe for depression-related symptoms and behavior. The next item presented might be designed to probe the respondents' sleep patterns or the existence of suicidal ideation.

◆
**JUST THINK . . .**

Try your hand at writing a couple of true–false items that could be used to detect nonpurposive or random responding on a personality test.

Item-branching technology may be used in personality tests to recognize nonpurposive or inconsistent responding. For example, on a computer-based true–false test, if the examinee responds *true* to an item such as "I summered in Baghdad last year," then there would be reason to suspect that the examinee is responding nonpurposively, randomly, or in some way other than genuinely. And if the same respondent responds *false* to the identical item later on in the test, the respondent is being inconsistent as well. Should the computer recognize a nonpurposive response pattern, it may be programmed to respond in a prescribed way— for example, by admonishing the respondent to be more careful or even by refusing to proceed until a purposive response is given.

## Scoring Items

Many different test scoring models have been devised. Perhaps the model used most commonly—owing, in part, to its simplicity and logic—is the cumulative model. Typically, the rule in a cumulatively scored test is that the higher the score on the test, the higher the testtaker is on the ability, trait, or other characteristic that the test purports to measure. For each testtaker response to targeted items made in a particular way, the testtaker earns cumulative credit with regard to a particular construct.

In tests that employ **class scoring** or (also referred to as **category scoring),** testtaker responses earn credit toward placement in a particular class or category with other testtakers whose pattern of responses is presumably similar in some way. This approach is used by some diagnostic systems wherein individuals must exhibit a certain number of symptoms to qualify for a specific diagnosis. A third scoring model, *ipsative scoring,* departs radically in rationale from either cumulative or class models. A typical objective in **ipsative scoring** is comparing a testtaker's score on one scale within a test to another scale within that same test.

Consider, for example, a personality test called the Edwards Personal Preference Schedule (EPPS), which is designed to measure the relative strength of different psychological needs. The EPPS ipsative scoring system yields information on the strength of various needs in relation to the strength of other needs of the testtaker. The test does not yield information on the strength of a testtaker's need relative to the presumed strength of that need in the general population. Edwards constructed his test of 210 pairs of statements in a way such that respondents were "forced" to answer *true* or *false* or *yes* or *no* to only one of two statements. Prior research by Edwards had indicated that the two statements were equivalent in terms of how socially desirable the responses were. Here is a sample of an EPPS-like forced-choice item, to which the respondents would indicate which is "more true" of themselves:

I feel depressed when I fail at something.

I feel nervous when giving a talk before a group.

On the basis of such an ipsatively scored personality test, it would be possible to draw only intra-individual conclusions about the testtaker. Here's an example: "John's need for achievement is higher than his need for affiliation." It would not be appropriate to draw inter-individual comparisons on the basis of an ipsatively scored test. It would be inappropriate, for example, to compare two testtakers with a statement like "John's need for achievement is higher than Jane's need for achievement."

Once the test developer has decided on a scoring model and has done everything else necessary to prepare the first draft of the test for administration, the next step is test tryout.

## Test Tryout

Having created a pool of items from which the final version of the test will be developed, the test developer will try out the test. The test should be tried out on people who are similar in critical respects to the people for whom the test was designed. Thus, for example, if a test is designed to aid in decisions regarding the selection of corporate employees with management potential at a certain level, it would be appropriate to try out the test on corporate employees at the targeted level.

Equally important are questions about the number of people on whom the test should be tried out. An informal rule of thumb is that there should be no fewer than 5 subjects and preferably as many as 10 for each item on the test. In general, the more subjects in the tryout the better. The thinking here is that the more subjects employed, the weaker the role of chance in subsequent data analysis. A definite risk in using too few subjects during test tryout comes during factor analysis of the findings, when what we might call phantom factors—factors that actually are just artifacts of the small sample size—may emerge.

The test tryout should be executed under conditions as identical as possible to the conditions under which the standardized test will be administered; all instructions, and everything from the time limits allotted for completing the test to the atmosphere at the test site, should be as similar as possible. As Nunnally (1978, p. 279) so aptly phrased it, "If items for a personality inventory are being administered in an atmosphere that encourages frankness and the eventual test is to be administered in an atmosphere where subjects will be reluctant to say bad things about themselves, the item analysis will tell a faulty story." In general, the test developer endeavors to ensure that differences in response to the test's items are due in fact to the items, not to extraneous factors.

> **JUST THINK . . .**
>
> How appropriate would it be to try out a "management potential" test on a convenience sample of introductory psychology students?

In Chapter 4, we dealt in detail with the important question "What is a good test?" Now is a good time to raise a related question.

## What Is a Good Item?

In the same sense that a good test is reliable and valid, a good test item is reliable and valid. Further, a good test item helps to discriminate testtakers. That is, a good test item is one that is answered correctly by high scorers on the test as a whole. An item that is answered incorrectly by high scorers on the test as a whole is probably not a good item. Conversely, a good test item is one that is answered incorrectly by low scorers on the test as a whole, and an item that is answered correctly by low scorers on the test as a whole may not be a good item.

How does a test developer identify good items? After the first draft of the test has been administered to a representative group of examinees, the test developer analyzes test scores and responses to individual items. The different types of statistical scrutiny that the test data can potentially undergo at this point are referred to collectively as **item analysis.** Although item analysis tends to be regarded as a quantitative endeavor, it may also be qualitative, as we shall see.

**JUST THINK . . .**

Well, do a bit more than think: Write one good item in any format, along with a brief explanation of why you think it is a good item. The item should be for a new test you are developing called the American History Test, which will be administered to ninth-graders.

# Item Analysis

Statistical procedures used to analyze items may become quite complex, and our treatment of this subject should be viewed as only introductory. We briefly survey some procedures typically used by test developers in their efforts to select the best items from a pool of tryout items. The criteria for the best items may differ as a function of the test developer's objectives. Thus, for example, one test developer might deem the best items to be those that optimally contribute to the internal reliability of the test. Another test developer might wish to design a test with the highest possible criterion-related validity and then select items accordingly. Among the tools test developers might employ to analyze and select items are

- an index of the item's difficulty
- an index of the item's reliability
- an index of the item's validity
- an index of item discrimination

**JUST THINK . . .**

Apply these item-analysis statistics to a test of personality. Make translations in phraseology as you think about how statistics such as an item-difficulty index or an item-validity index could be used to help identify good items for a personality test (not for an achievement test).

Assume for the moment that you got carried away on the previous *Just Think* exercise and are now the proud author of 100 items for a ninth-grade-level American History Test (AHT). Let's further assume that this 100-item (draft) test has been administered to 100 ninth-graders. Hoping in the long run to standardize the test and have it distributed by a commercial test publisher, you have a more immediate, short-term goal: to select the 50 best of the 100 items you originally created. How might that short-term goal be achieved? As we will see, the answer lies in item-analysis procedures.

## The Item-Difficulty Index

Suppose every examinee answered item 1 of the AHT correctly. Can we say that item 1 is a good item? What if no one answered item 1 correctly? In either case, item 1 is not a good item. If everyone gets the item right then the item is too easy; if everyone gets the item wrong, the item is too difficult. Just as the test as a whole is designed to provide an index of degree of knowledge about American history, so each individual item on the test should be passed (scored as correct) or failed (scored as incorrect) on the basis of testtakers' differential knowledge of American history.[4]

An index of an item's difficulty is obtained by calculating the proportion of the total number of testtakers who answered the item correctly. A lowercase italic "p" ($p$) is used to denote item difficulty, and a subscript refers to the item number (so $p_1$ is read "item-difficulty index for item 1"). The value of an item-difficulty index can theoretically range from 0 (if no one got the item right) to 1 (if everyone got the item right). If 50 of the 100 examinees answered item 2 correctly, then the item-difficulty index for this item would be equal to 50 divided by 100, or .5 ($p_2 = .5$). If 75 of the examinees got item 3 right, then $p_3$ would be equal to .75 and we could say that item 3 was easier than item 2. Note that the larger the item-difficulty index, the easier the item. Because $p$ refers to the percent of people passing an item, the higher the $p$ for an item, the easier the item. The statistic referred to as an **item-difficulty index** in the context of achievement testing may be an **item-endorsement index** in other contexts, such as personality testing. Here, the statistic provides not a measure of the percent of people passing the item but a measure of the percent of people who said yes to, agreed with, or otherwise endorsed the item.

An index of the difficulty of the average test item for a particular test can be calculated by averaging the item-difficulty indices for all the test's items. This is accomplished by summing the item-difficulty indices for all test items and dividing by the total number of items on the test. For maximum discrimination among the abilities of the testtakers, the optimal average item difficulty is approximately .5, with individual items on the test ranging in difficulty from about .3 to .8. Note, however,

**JUST THINK . . .**

Create an achievement test item having to do with any aspect of psychological testing and assessment that you believe would yield a $p$ of 0 if administered to every member of your class.

that the possible effect of guessing must be taken into account when considering items of the selected-response variety. With this type of item, the optimal average item difficulty is usually the midpoint between 1.00 and the chance success proportion, defined as the probability of answering correctly by random guessing. In a true–false item, the probability of guessing correctly on the basis of chance alone is 1/2, or .50. Therefore, the optimal item difficulty is halfway between .50 and 1.00, or .75. In general, the midpoint representing the optimal item difficulty is obtained by summing the chance success proportion and 1.00 and then dividing the sum by 2, or

$$.5 + 1.00 = 1.5$$

$$\frac{1.5}{2} = .60$$

---

4. An exception here may be a **giveaway item.** Such an item might be inserted near the beginning of an achievement test to spur motivation and a positive test-taking attitude and to lessen testtakers' test-related anxiety. In general, however, if an item analysis suggests that a particular item is too easy or too difficult, the item must be either rewritten or discarded.

For a five-option multiple-choice item, the probability of guessing correctly on any one item on the basis of chance alone is equal to 1/5, or .20. The optimal item difficulty is therefore .60:

$$.20 + 1.00 = 1.20$$

$$\frac{1.20}{2} = .60$$

### The Item-Reliability Index

The **item-reliability index** provides an indication of the internal consistency of a test (Figure 8–4); the higher this index, the greater the test's internal consistency. This index is equal to the product of the item-score standard deviation (*s*) and the correlation (*r*) between the item score and the total test score.

**Factor analysis and inter-item consistency** A statistical tool useful in determining whether items on a test appear to be measuring the same thing(s) is factor analysis. Through the judicious use of factor analysis, items that do not "load on" the factor that they were written to tap (that is, items that do not appear to be measuring what they were designed to measure) can be revised or eliminated. If too many items appear to be tapping a particular area, the weakest of such items can be eliminated. Additionally, factor analysis can be useful in the test interpretation process, especially when comparing the constellation of responses to the items from two or more groups. Thus, for example, if a particular personality test is administered to two groups of hospitalized psychiatric patients, each group with a different diagnosis, then the same items may be found to load on different factors in the two groups. Such information will compel the responsible test developer to revise or eliminate certain items from the test or to describe the differential findings in the test manual.

**JUST THINK . . .**

An achievement test on the subject of test development is designed to have two items that load on a factor called "item analysis." Write these two test items.

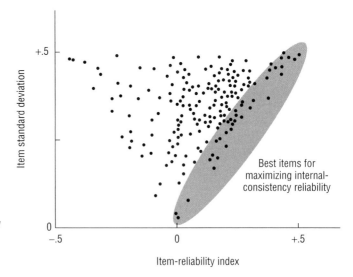

**Figure 8–4**
**Maximizing Internal-Consistency Reliability**

Source: Allen and Yen (1979).

## The Item-Validity Index

The **item-validity index** is a statistic designed to provide an indication of the degree to which a test is measuring what it purports to measure. The higher the item-validity index, the greater the test's criterion-related validity. The item-validity index can be calculated once the following two statistics are known:

- the item-score standard deviation
- the correlation between the item score and the criterion score

The item-score standard deviation of item 1 (denoted by the symbol $s_1$) can be calculated using the index of the item's difficulty ($p_1$) in the following formula:

$$s_1 = \sqrt{p_1(1 - p_1)}$$

The correlation between the score on item 1 and a score on the criterion measure (denoted by the symbol $r_{1C}$) is multiplied by item 1's item-score standard deviation ($s_1$), and the product is equal to an index of an item's validity ($s_1 r_{1C}$). Calculating the item-validity index will be important when the test developer's goal is to maximize the criterion-related validity of the test. A visual representation of the best items on a test (if the objective is to maximize criterion-related validity) can be achieved by plotting each item's item-validity index and item-reliability index (Figure 8–5).

## The Item-Discrimination Index

Measures of item discrimination indicate how adequately an item separates or discriminates between high scorers and low scorers on an entire test. In this context, a multiple-choice item on an achievement test is a good item if most of the high scorers answer correctly and most of the low scorers answer incorrectly. If most of the high scorers fail a particular item, these testtakers may be making an alternative interpretation of a response intended to serve as a distractor. In such a case, the test developer should interview the examinees to understand better the basis for the choice and then

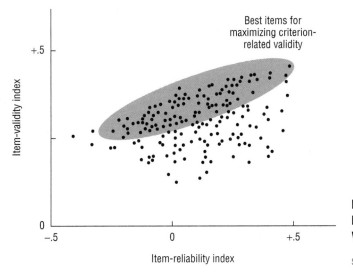

**Figure 8–5**
**Maximizing Criterion-Related Validity**

Source: Allen and Yen (1979).

appropriately revise (or eliminate) the item. Common sense dictates that an item on an achievement test is not doing its job if it is answered correctly by respondents who least understand the subject matter. Similarly, an item on a test purporting to measure a particular personality trait is not doing its job if responses indicate that people who score very low on the test as a whole (indicating absence or low levels of the trait in question) tend to score very high on the item (indicating that they are very high on the trait in question—contrary to what the test as a whole indicates).

The **item-discrimination index** is a measure of item discrimination, symbolized by a lowercase italic "d" ($d$). This estimate of item discrimination, in essence, compares performance on a particular item with performance in the upper and lower regions of a distribution of continuous test scores. The optimal boundary lines for what we refer to as the "upper" and "lower" areas of a distribution of scores will demarcate the upper and lower 27% of the distribution of scores—provided the distribution is normal (Kelley, 1939). As the distribution of test scores becomes more platykurtic (flatter), the optimal boundary line for defining upper and lower increases to near 33% (Cureton, 1957). Allen and Yen (1979, p. 122) assure us that "for most applications, any percentage between 25 and 33 will yield similar estimates."

The item-discrimination index is a measure of the difference between the proportion of high scorers answering an item correctly and the proportion of low scorers answering the item correctly; the higher the value of $d$, the greater the number of high scorers answering the item correctly. A negative $d$-value on a particular item is a red flag because it indicates that low-scoring examinees are more likely to answer the item correctly than high-scoring examinees. This situation calls for some action such as revising or eliminating the item.

◆───────────────
**JUST THINK . . .**

Write two items on the subject of test development. The first item to be one that you will predict will have a very high $d$, and the second to be one that you predict will have a high negative $d$.

Suppose a history teacher gave the AHT to a total of 119 students who were just weeks away from completing ninth grade. The teacher isolated the upper ($U$) and lower ($L$) 27% of the test papers, with a total of 32 papers in each group. Data and item-discrimination indices for Items 1 through 5 are presented in Table 8–2. Observe that 20 testtakers in the $U$ group answered Item 1 correctly and that 16 testtakers in the $L$ group answered Item 1 correctly. With an item-discrimination index equal to .13, Item 1 is probably a reasonable item because more $U$-group members than $L$-group members answered it correctly. The higher the value of $d$, the more adequately the item discriminates the higher-scoring from the lower-scoring testtakers. For this reason, Item 2 is a better item than Item 1 because Item 2's item-discrimination index is .63. The highest possible value of $d$ is $+1.00$. This value indicates that all members of the $U$ group answered the item correctly whereas all members of the $L$ group answered the item incorrectly.

If the same proportion of members of the $U$ and $L$ groups pass the item, then the item is not discriminating between testtakers at all and $d$, appropriately enough, will

**Table 8–2**
**Item-Discrimination Indices for Five Hypothetical Items**

| Item | $U$ | $L$ | $U - L$ | $n$ | $d[(U - L)/n]$ |
|------|-----|-----|---------|-----|----------------|
| 1 | 20 | 16 | 4 | 32 | .13 |
| 2 | 30 | 10 | 20 | 32 | .63 |
| 3 | 32 | 0 | 32 | 32 | 1.00 |
| 4 | 20 | 20 | 0 | 32 | 0.00 |
| 5 | 0 | 32 | −32 | 32 | −1.00 |

be equal to 0. The lowest value that an index of item discrimination can take is −1. A $d$ equal to –1 is a test developer's nightmare: It indicates that all members of the $U$ group failed the item and all members of the $L$ group passed it. On the face of it, such an item is the worst possible type of item and is in dire need of revision or elimination. However, through further investigation of this unanticipated finding, the test developer might learn or discover something new about the construct being measured.

**Analysis of item alternatives** The quality of each alternative within a multiple-choice item can be readily assessed with reference to the comparative performance of upper and lower scorers. No formulas or statistics are necessary here. By charting the number of testtakers in the $U$ and $L$ groups who chose each alternative, the test developer can get an idea of the effectiveness of a distractor by means of a simple eyeball test. To illustrate, let's analyze responses to five items on a hypothetical test, assuming that there were 32 scores in the upper level ($U$) of the distribution and 32 scores in the lower level ($L$) of the distribution. Let's begin by looking at the pattern of responses to item 1. In each case, ♦ denotes the correct alternative.

### Alternatives

| Item 1 | | ♦a | b | c | d | e |
|---|---|---|---|---|---|---|
| | $U$ | 24 | 3 | 2 | 0 | 3 |
| | $L$ | 10 | 5 | 6 | 6 | 5 |

The response pattern to Item 1 indicates that the item is a good one. More $U$ group members than $L$ group members answered the item correctly, and each of the distractors attracted some testtakers.

### Alternatives

| Item 2 | | a | b | c | d | ♦e |
|---|---|---|---|---|---|---|
| | $U$ | 2 | 13 | 3 | 2 | 12 |
| | $L$ | 6 | 7 | 5 | 7 | 7 |

Item 2 signals a situation in which a relatively large number of members of the $U$ group chose a particular distractor choice (in this case, "b"). This item could probably be improved upon revision, preferably one made after an interview with some or all of the $U$ students who chose "b."

### Alternatives

| Item 3 | | a | b | ♦c | d | e |
|---|---|---|---|---|---|---|
| | $U$ | 0 | 0 | 32 | 0 | 0 |
| | $L$ | 3 | 2 | 22 | 2 | 3 |

Item 3 indicates a most desirable pattern of testtaker response. All members of the $U$ group answered the item correctly, and each distractor attracted one or more members of the $L$ group.

### Alternatives

| Item 4 | | a | ♦b | c | d | e |
|---|---|---|---|---|---|---|
| | $U$ | 5 | 15 | 0 | 5 | 7 |
| | $L$ | 4 | 5 | 4 | 4 | 14 |

Item 4 is more difficult than Item 3; fewer examinees answered it correctly. Still, this item provides useful information because it effectively discriminates higher-scoring from lower-scoring examinees. For some reason, one of the alternatives ("e") was particularly effective—perhaps too effective—as a distractor to students in the low-scoring group. The test developer may wish to further explore why this was the case.

**Alternatives**

| Item 5 | a | b | c | ♦d | e |
|--------|---|---|---|----|---|
| *U* | 14 | 0 | 0 | 5 | 13 |
| *L* | 7 | 0 | 0 | 16 | 9 |

Item 5 is a poor item because more *L* group members than *U* group members answered the item correctly. Furthermore, none of the examinees chose the "b" or "c" distractors.

Before moving on to a consideration of the use of item-characteristic curves in item analysis, let's pause to "bring home" the real-life application of some of what we have discussed so far. In his capacity as a consulting industrial/organizational psychologist, our featured test user in this chapter, Dr. Scott Birkeland, has had occasion to create tests and improve them with item-analytic methods. He shares some of his thoughts in his *Meet an Assessment Professional* essay, an excerpt of which is presented here.

## Item-Characteristic Curves

As you may have surmised from the introduction to item response theory (IRT) that was presented in Chapter 5, IRT can be a powerful tool not only for understanding how test items perform but also for creating or modifying individual test items, building new tests, and revising existing tests. We will have more to say about that later in the chapter. For now, let's review how *item-characteristic curves (ICCs)* can play a role in decisions about which items are working well and which items are not. Recall that an **item-characteristic curve** is a graphic representation of item difficulty and discrimination.

Figure 8–6 presents several ICCs with ability plotted on the horizontal axis and probability of correct response plotted on the vertical axis. Note that the extent to which an item discriminates high- from low-scoring examinees is apparent from the slope of the curve. The steeper the slope, the greater the item discrimination. An item may also vary in terms of its difficulty level. An easy item will shift the ICC to the left along the ability axis, indicating that many people will likely get the item correct. A difficult item will shift the ICC to the right along the horizontal axis, indicating that fewer people will answer the item correctly. In other words, it takes high ability levels for a person to have a high probability of their response being scored as correct.

Now focus on the item-characteristic curve for Item A. Do you think this is a good item? The answer is that it is not. The probability of a testtaker's responding correctly is high for testtakers of low ability and low for testtakers of high ability. What about Item B; is it a good test item? Again, the answer is no. The curve tells us that testtakers of moderate ability have the highest probability of answering this item correctly. Testtakers with the greatest amount of ability—as well as their counterparts at the other end of the ability spectrum—are unlikely to respond correctly to this item. Item B may be one of those items to which people who know too much (or think too much) are likely to respond incorrectly.

Item C is a good test item because the probability of responding correctly to it increases with ability. What about Item D? Its ICC profiles an item that discriminates at only one point on the continuum of ability. The probability is great that all testtakers at or above this point will respond correctly to the item, and the probability of an incorrect response is great for testtakers who fall below that particular point in ability. An item such as D therefore has excellent discriminative ability and would be useful in a test designed, for example, to select applicants on the basis of some cutoff score. However, such an item might not be desirable in a test designed to provide detailed information on testtaker ability across all ability levels. This might be the case, for example, in a diagnostic reading or arithmetic test.

## Meet Dr. Scott Birkeland

I also get involved in developing new test items. Given that these tests are used with real-life candidates, I place a high level of importance on a test's face validity. I want applicants who take the tests to walk away feeling as though the questions that they answered were truly relevant for the job for which they applied. Because of this, each new project leads to the development of new questions so that the tests "look and feel right" for the candidates. For example, if we have a reading and comprehension test, we make sure that the materials that the candidates read are materials that are similar to what they would actually read on the job. This can be a challenge in that by having to develop new questions, the test development process takes more time and effort. In the long run, however, we know that this enhances the candidates' reactions to the testing process. Additionally, our research suggests that it enhances the test's predictability.

Once tests have been developed and administered to candidates, we continue to look for ways to improve them. This is where statistics comes into play. We conduct item level analyses of each question to determine if certain questions are performing better than others. I am often amazed at the power of a simple item analysis (i.e., calculating item difficulty and item discrimination). Oftentimes, an item analysis will flag a question, causing me to go back and

Scott Birkeland, Ph.D., Stang Decision Systems, Inc.

re-examine the item only to find something about it to be confusing. An item analysis allows us to fix those types of issues and continually enhance the quality of a test.

*Read more of what Dr. Birkeland had to say—his complete essay—at www.mhhe.com/cohentesting8.*

## *Other Considerations in Item Analysis*

**Guessing**   In achievement testing, the problem of how to handle testtaker **guessing** is one that has eluded any universally acceptable solution. Methods designed to detect guessing (S.-R. Chang et al., 2011), minimize the effects of guessing (Kubinger et al., 2010), and statistically correct for guessing (Espinosa & Gardeazabal, 2010) have been proposed, but no such method has achieved universal acceptance. Perhaps it is because the issues surrounding guessing are more complex than they appear at first glance. To better appreciate the complexity of the issues, consider the following three criteria that any correction for guessing must meet as well as the other interacting issues that must be addressed:

1.  A correction for guessing must recognize that, when a respondent guesses at an answer on an achievement test, the guess is not typically made on a totally random basis. It is more reasonable to assume that the testtaker's guess is based on

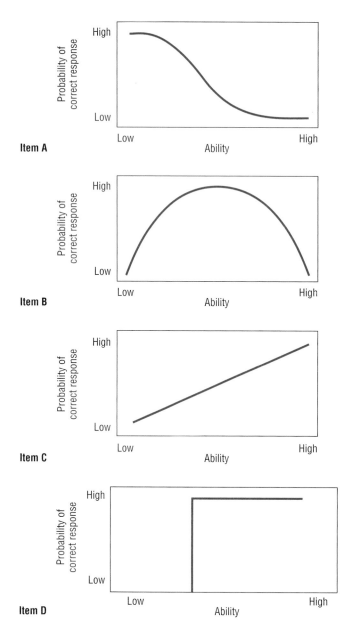

**Figure 8–6**
**Some Sample Item-Characteristic Curves**

*For simplicity, we have omitted scale values for the axes. The vertical axis in such a graph lists probability of correct response in values ranging from 0 to 1. Values for the horizontal axis, which we have simply labeled "ability," are total scores on the test. In other sources, you may find the vertical axis of an item-characteristic curve labeled something like "proportion of examinees who respond correctly to the item" and the horizontal axis labeled "total test score."*

Source: Ghiselli et al. (1981).

some knowledge of the subject matter and the ability to rule out one or more of the distractor alternatives. However, the individual testtaker's amount of knowledge of the subject matter will vary from one item to the next.

2. A correction for guessing must also deal with the problem of omitted items. Sometimes, instead of guessing, the testtaker will simply omit a response to an item. Should the omitted item be scored "wrong"? Should the omitted item be excluded from the item analysis? Should the omitted item be scored as if the testtaker had made a random guess? Exactly how should the omitted item be handled?

3. Just as some people may be luckier than others in front of a Las Vegas slot machine, so some testtakers may be luckier than others in guessing the choices that are keyed correct. Any correction for guessing may seriously underestimate or overestimate the effects of guessing for lucky and unlucky testtakers.

In addition to proposed interventions at the level of test scoring through the use of corrections for guessing (referred to as formula scores), intervention has also been proposed at the level of test instructions. Testtakers may be instructed to provide an answer only when they are certain (no guessing) or to complete all items and guess when in doubt. Individual differences in testtakers' willingness to take risks result in problems for this approach to guessing (Slakter et al., 1975). Some people who don't mind taking risks may guess even when instructed not to do so. Others who tend to be reluctant to take risks refuse to guess under any circumstances. This creates a situation in which predisposition to take risks can affect one's test score.

To date, no solution to the problem of guessing has been deemed entirely satisfactory. The responsible test developer addresses the problem of guessing by including in the test manual (1) explicit instructions regarding this point for the examiner to convey to the examinees and (2) specific instructions for scoring and interpreting omitted items.

**JUST THINK . . .**

The prevailing logic among measurement professionals is that when testtakers guess at an answer on a personality test in a selected-response format, the testtaker is making the best choice. Why should professionals continue to believe this? Alternatively, why might they modify their view?

Guessing on responses to personality and related psychological tests is not thought of as a great problem. Although it may sometimes be difficult to choose the most appropriate alternative on a selected-response format personality test (particularly one with forced-choice items), the presumption is that the testtaker does indeed make the best choice.

**Item fairness**    Just as we may speak of biased tests, we may speak of biased test items. The term **item fairness** refers to the degree, if any, a test item is biased. A **biased test item** is an item that favors one particular group of examinees in relation to another when differences in group ability are controlled (Camilli & Shepard, 1985). Many different methods may be used to identify biased test items. In fact, evidence suggests that the choice of item-analysis method may affect determinations of item bias (Ironson & Subkoviak, 1979).

Item-characteristic curves can be used to identify biased items. Specific items are identified as biased in a statistical sense if they exhibit differential item functioning. Differential item functioning is exemplified by different shapes of item-characteristic curves for different groups (say, men and women) when the two groups do not differ in total test score (Mellenbergh, 1994). If an item is to be considered fair to different groups of testtakers, the item-characteristic curves for the different groups should not be significantly different:

> The essential rationale of this ICC criterion of item bias is that any persons showing the same ability as measured by the whole test should have the same probability of passing any given item that measures that ability, regardless of the person's race, social class, sex, or any other background characteristics. In other words, the same proportion of persons from each group should pass any given item of the test, provided that the persons all earned the same total score on the test. (Jensen, 1980, p. 444)

Establishing the presence of differential item functioning requires a statistical test of the null hypothesis of no difference between the item-characteristic curves of the two groups. The pros and cons of different statistical tests for detecting differential item functioning have long been a matter of debate (Raju et al., 1993). What is not a matter of debate is that items exhibiting significant difference in item-characteristic curves must be revised or eliminated from the test. If a relatively large number of items biased in favor of one group coexist with approximately the same number of items biased in favor of another group, it cannot be claimed that the test measures the same abilities in the two groups. This is true even though overall test scores of the individuals in the two groups may not be significantly different (Jensen, 1980).

**JUST THINK . . .**

Write an item that is purposely designed to be biased in favor of one group over another. Members of what group would do well on this item? Members of what group would do poorly on this item?

**Speed tests**   Item analyses of tests taken under speed conditions yield misleading or uninterpretable results. The closer an item is to the end of the test, the more difficult it may appear to be. This is because testtakers simply may not get to items near the end of the test before time runs out.

In a similar vein, measures of item discrimination may be artificially high for late-appearing items. This is so because testtakers who know the material better may work faster and are thus more likely to answer the later items. Items appearing late in a speed test are consequently more likely to show positive item-total correlations because of the select group of examinees reaching those items.

Given these problems, how can items on a speed test be analyzed? Perhaps the most obvious solution is to restrict the item analysis of items on a speed test only to the items completed by the testtaker. However, this solution is not recommended, for at least three reasons: (1) Item analyses of the later items would be based on a progressively smaller number of testtakers, yielding progressively less reliable results; (2) if the more knowledgeable examinees reach the later items, then part of the analysis is based on all testtakers and part is based on a selected sample; and (3) because the more knowledgeable testtakers are more likely to score correctly, their performance will make items occurring toward the end of the test appear to be easier than they are.

If speed is not an important element of the ability being measured by the test, and because speed as a variable may produce misleading information about item performance, the test developer ideally should administer the test to be item-analyzed with generous time limits to complete the test. Once the item analysis is completed, norms should be established using the speed conditions intended for use with the test in actual practice.

**JUST THINK . . .**

Provide an example of what, in your opinion is the best, as well as the worst, use of a speed test.

## Qualitative Item Analysis

Test users have had a long-standing interest in understanding test performance from the perspective of testtakers (Fiske, 1967; Mosier, 1947). The calculation of item-validity, item-reliability, and other such *quantitative* indices represents one approach to understanding testtakers. Another general class of research methods is referred to as *qualitative*. In contrast to quantitative methods, **qualitative methods** are techniques of data generation and analysis that rely primarily on verbal rather than mathematical or statistical procedures. Encouraging testtakers—on a group or individual basis—to discuss aspects of their test-taking experience is, in essence, eliciting or generating "data" (words).

These data may then be used by test developers, users, and publishers to improve various aspects of the test.

**Qualitative item analysis** is a general term for various nonstatistical procedures designed to explore how individual test items work. The analysis compares individual test items to each other and to the test as a whole. In contrast to statistically based procedures, qualitative methods involve exploration of the issues through verbal means such as interviews and group discussions conducted with testtakers and other relevant parties. Some of the topics researchers may wish to explore qualitatively are summarized in Table 8–3.

**Table 8–3**
**Potential Areas of Exploration by Means of Qualitative Item Analysis**

*This table lists sample topics and questions of possible interest to test users. The questions could be raised either orally or in writing shortly after a test's administration. Additionally, depending upon the objectives of the test user, the questions could be placed into other formats, such as true–false or multiple choice. Depending upon the specific questions to be asked and the number of testtakers being sampled, the test user may wish to guarantee the anonymity of the respondents.*

| Topic | Sample Question |
|---|---|
| *Cultural Sensitivity* | Did you feel that any item or aspect of this test was discriminatory with respect to any group of people? If so, why? |
| *Face Validity* | Did the test appear to measure what you expected it would measure? If not, what was contrary to your expectations? |
| *Test Administrator* | Did the behavior of the test administrator affect your performance on this test in any way? If so, how? |
| *Test Environment* | Did any conditions in the room affect your performance on this test in any way? If so, how? |
| *Test Fairness* | Do you think the test was a fair test of what it sought to measure? Why or why not? |
| *Test Language* | Were there any instructions or other written aspects of the test that you had difficulty understanding? |
| *Test Length* | How did you feel about the length of the test with respect to (a) the time it took to complete and (b) the number of items? |
| *Testtaker's Guessing* | Did you guess on any of the test items? What percentage of the items would you estimate you guessed on? Did you employ any particular strategy for guessing, or was it basically random? |
| *Testtaker's Integrity* | Do you think that there was any cheating during this test? If so, please describe the methods you think may have been used. |
| *Testtaker's Mental/Physical State Upon Entry* | How would you describe your mental state going into this test? Do you think that your mental state in any way affected the test outcome? If so, how? How would you describe your physical state going into this test? Do you think that your physical state in any way affected the test outcome? If so, how? |
| *Testtaker's Mental/Physical State During the Test* | How would you describe your mental state as you took this test? Do you think that your mental state in any way affected the test outcome? If so, how? How would you describe your physical state as you took this test? Do you think that your physical state in any way affected the test outcome? If so, how? |
| *Testtaker's Overall Impressions* | What is your overall impression of this test? What suggestions would you offer the test developer for improvement? |
| *Testtaker's Preferences* | Did you find any part of the test educational, entertaining, or otherwise rewarding? What, specifically, did you like or dislike about the test? Did you find any part of the test anxiety-provoking, condescending, or otherwise upsetting? Why? |
| *Testtaker's Preparation* | How did you prepare for this test? If you were going to advise others how to prepare for it, what would you tell them? |

One cautionary note: Providing testtakers with the opportunity to describe a test can be like providing students with the opportunity to describe their instructors. In both cases, there may be abuse of the process, especially by respondents who have extra-test (or extra-instructor) axes to grind. Respondents may be disgruntled for any number of reasons, from failure to prepare adequately for the test to disappointment in their test performance. In such cases, the opportunity to evaluate the test is an opportunity to lash out. The test, the administrator of the test, and the institution, agency, or corporation responsible for the test administration may all become objects of criticism. Testtaker questionnaires, much like other qualitative research tools, must be interpreted with an eye toward the full context of the experience for the respondent(s).

**"Think aloud" test administration** An innovative approach to cognitive assessment entails having respondents verbalize thoughts as they occur. Although different researchers use different procedures (Davison et al., 1997; Hurlburt, 1997; Klinger, 1978), this general approach has been employed in a variety of research contexts, including studies of adjustment (Kendall et al., 1979; Sutton-Simon & Goldfried, 1979), problem solving (Duncker, 1945; Kozhevnikov et al., 2007; Montague, 1993), educational research and remediation (Muñoz et al., 2006; Randall et al., 1986; Schellings et al., 2006), clinical intervention (Gann & Davison, 1997; Haaga et al., 1993; Schmitter-Edgecombe & Bales, 2005; White et al., 1992), and jury modeling (Wright & Hall, 2007).

Cohen et al. (1988) proposed the use of **"think aloud" test administration** as a qualitative research tool designed to shed light on the testtaker's thought processes during the administration of a test. On a one-to-one basis with an examiner, examinees are asked to take a test, thinking aloud as they respond to each item. If the test is designed to measure achievement, such verbalizations may be useful in assessing not only if certain students (such as low or high scorers on previous examinations) are misinterpreting a particular item but also *why* and *how* they are misinterpreting the item. If the test is designed to measure personality or some aspect of it, the "think aloud" technique may also yield valuable insights regarding the way individuals perceive, interpret, and respond to the items.

**JUST THINK (ALOUD) . . .**

How might thinking aloud to evaluate test items be more effective than thinking silently?

**Expert panels** In addition to interviewing testtakers individually or in groups, **expert panels** may also provide qualitative analyses of test items. A **sensitivity review** is a study of test items, typically conducted during the test development process, in which items are examined for fairness to all prospective testtakers and for the presence of offensive language, stereotypes, or situations. Since the 1990s or so, sensitivity reviews have become a standard part of test development (Reckase, 1996). For example, in an effort to root out any possible bias in the Stanford Achievement Test series, the test publisher formed an advisory panel of twelve minority group members, each a prominent member of the educational community. Panel members met with the publisher to obtain an understanding of the history and philosophy of the test battery and to discuss and define the problem of bias. Some of the possible forms of content bias that may find their way into any achievement test were identified as follows (Stanford Special Report, 1992, pp. 3–4).

*Status:* Are the members of a particular group shown in situations that do not involve authority or leadership?

*Stereotype:* Are the members of a particular group portrayed as uniformly having certain (1) aptitudes, (2) interests, (3) occupations, or (4) personality characteristics?

*Familiarity:* Is there greater opportunity on the part of one group to (1) be acquainted with the vocabulary or (2) experience the situation presented by an item?

*Offensive Choice of Words:* (1) Has a demeaning label been applied, or (2) has a male term been used where a neutral term could be substituted?

*Other:* Panel members were asked to be specific regarding any other indication of bias they detected.

On the basis of qualitative information from an expert panel or testtakers themselves, a test user or developer may elect to modify or revise the test. In this sense, revision typically involves rewording items, deleting items, or creating new items. Note that there is another meaning of test revision beyond that associated with a stage in the development of a new test. After a period of time, many existing tests are scheduled for republication in new versions or editions. The development process that the test undergoes as it is modified and revised is called, not surprisingly, *test revision.* The time, effort, and expense entailed by this latter variety of test revision may be quite extensive. For example, the revision may involve an age extension of the population for which the test is designed for use—upward for older testtakers and/or downward for younger testtakers—and corresponding new validation studies.

**JUST THINK . . .**

Is there any way that expert panels might introduce more error into the test development process?

# Test Revision

We first consider aspects of test revision as a stage in the development of a new test. Later we will consider aspects of test revision in the context of modifying an existing test to create a new edition. Much of our discussion of test revision in the development of a brand-new test may also apply to the development of subsequent editions of existing tests, depending on just how "revised" the revision really is.

## Test Revision as a Stage in New Test Development

Having conceptualized the new test, constructed it, tried it out, and item-analyzed it both quantitatively and qualitatively, what remains is to act judiciously on all the information and mold the test into its final form. A tremendous amount of information is generated at the item-analysis stage, particularly given that a developing test may have hundreds of items. On the basis of that information, some items from the original item pool will be eliminated and others will be rewritten. How is information about the difficulty, validity, reliability, discrimination, and bias of test items—along with information from the item-characteristic curves—integrated and used to revise the test?

There are probably as many ways of approaching test revision as there are test developers. One approach is to characterize each item according to its strengths and weaknesses. Some items may be highly reliable but lack criterion validity, whereas other items may be purely unbiased but too easy. Some items will be found to have many weaknesses, making them prime candidates for deletion or revision. For example, very difficult items have a restricted range; all or almost all testtakers get them wrong. Such items will tend to lack reliability and validity because of their restricted range, and the same can be said of very easy items.

Test developers may find that they must balance various strengths and weaknesses across items. For example, if many otherwise good items tend to be somewhat easy, the test developer may purposefully include some more difficult items even if they have other problems. Those more difficult items may be specifically targeted for rewriting. The purpose of the test also influences the blueprint or plan for the revision. For example, if the test will be used to influence major decisions about educational placement or employment, the test developer should be scrupulously concerned with item bias. If there is a need to identify the most highly skilled individuals among those being tested, items demonstrating excellent item discrimination, leading to the best possible test discrimination, will be made a priority.

As revision proceeds, the advantage of writing a large item pool becomes more and more apparent. Poor items can be eliminated in favor of those that were shown on the test tryout to be good items. Even when working with a large item pool, the revising test developer must be aware of the domain the test should sample. For some aspects of the domain, it may be particularly difficult to write good items, and indiscriminate deletion of all poorly functioning items could cause those aspects of the domain to remain untested.

Having balanced all these concerns, the test developer comes out of the revision stage with a better test. The next step is to administer the revised test under standardized conditions to a second appropriate sample of examinees. On the basis of an item analysis of data derived from this administration of the second draft of the test, the test developer may deem the test to be in its finished form. Once the test is in finished form, the test's norms may be developed from the data, and the test will be said to have been "standardized" on this (second) sample. Recall from Chapter 4 that a standardization sample represents the group(s) of individuals with whom examinees' performance will be compared. All of the guidelines presented in that chapter for selecting an appropriate standardization sample should be followed.

## JUST THINK . . .

Surprise! An international publisher is interested in publishing your American History Test. You've just been asked which population demographic characteristics you think are most important to be represented in your international standardization sample. Your response?

When the item analysis of data derived from a test administration indicates that the test is not yet in finished form, the steps of revision, tryout, and item analysis are repeated until the test is satisfactory and standardization can occur. Once the test items have been finalized, professional test development procedures dictate that conclusions about the test's validity await a cross-validation of findings. We'll discuss *cross-validation* shortly; for now, let's briefly consider some of the issues surrounding the development of a new edition of an existing test.

## Test Revision in the Life Cycle of an Existing Test

Time waits for no person. We all get old, and tests get old, too. Just like people, some tests seem to age more gracefully than others. For example, as we will see when we study projective techniques in Chapter 13, the Rorschach Inkblot Test seems to have held up quite well over the years. By contrast, the stimulus materials for another projective technique, the Thematic Apperception Test (TAT), are showing their age. There comes a time in the life of most tests when the test will be revised in some way or its publication will be discontinued. When is that time?

No hard-and-fast rules exist for when to revise a test. The American Psychological Association (APA, 1996b, Standard 3.18) offered the general suggestions that an existing test be kept in its present form as long as it remains "useful" but that it should be revised "when significant changes in the domain represented, or new conditions of test use and interpretation, make the test inappropriate for its intended use."

Practically speaking, many tests are deemed to be due for revision when any of the following conditions exist.

1. The stimulus materials look dated and current testtakers cannot relate to them.

2. The verbal content of the test, including the administration instructions and the test items, contains dated vocabulary that is not readily understood by current testtakers.

3. As popular culture changes and words take on new meanings, certain words or expressions in the test items or directions may be perceived as inappropriate or even offensive to a particular group and must therefore be changed.

4. The test norms are no longer adequate as a result of group membership changes in the population of potential testtakers.

5. The test norms are no longer adequate as a result of age-related shifts in the abilities measured over time, and so an age extension of the norms (upward, downward, or in both directions) is necessary.

6. The reliability or the validity of the test, as well as the effectiveness of individual test items, can be significantly improved by a revision.

7. The theory on which the test was originally based has been improved significantly, and these changes should be reflected in the design and content of the test.

The steps to revise an existing test parallel those to create a brand-new one. In the test conceptualization phase, the test developer must think through the objectives of the revision and how they can best be met. In the test construction phase, the proposed changes are made. Test tryout, item analysis, and test revision (in the sense of making final refinements) follow. All this sounds relatively easy and straightforward, but creating a revised edition of an existing test can be a most ambitious undertaking. For example, recalling the revision of a test called the Strong Vocational Interest Blank, Campbell (1972) reflected that the process of conceiving the revision started about ten years prior to actual revision work, and the revision work itself ran for another ten years. Butcher (2000) echoed these thoughts in an article that provided a detailed "inside view" of the process of revising a widely used personality test called the MMPI. Others have also noted the sundry considerations that must be kept in mind when conducting or contemplating the revision of an existing instrument (Adams, 2000; Cash et al., 2004; Okazaki & Sue, 2000; Prinzie et al., 2007; Reise et al., 2000; Silverstein & Nelson, 2000; Vickers-Douglas et al., 2005).

Once the successor to an established test is published, there are inevitably questions about the equivalence of the two editions. For example, does a measured full-scale IQ of 110 on the first edition of an intelligence test mean exactly the same thing as a full-scale IQ of 110 on the second edition? A number of researchers have advised caution in comparing results from an original and a revised edition of a test, despite similarities in appearance (Reitan & Wolfson, 1990; Strauss et al., 2000). Even if the content of individual items does not change, the context in which the items appear may change, thus opening up the possibility of significant differences in testtakers' interpretation of the meaning of the items. Simply developing a computerized version of a test may make a difference, at least in terms of test scores achieved by members of different populations (Ozonoff, 1995).

Formal item-analysis methods must be employed to evaluate the stability of items between revisions of the same test (Knowles & Condon, 2000). Ultimately, scores on a test and on its updated version may not be directly comparable. As Tulsky and

**JUST THINK . . .**

Why can the process of creating a revision to an established test take years to complete?

Ledbetter (2000) summed it up in the context of original and revised versions of tests of cognitive ability: "Any improvement or decrement in performance between the two cannot automatically be viewed as a change in examinee performance" (p. 260).

A key step in the development of all tests—brand-new or revised editions—is cross-validation. Next we discuss that important process as well as a more recent trend in test publishing, *co-validation.*

**Cross-validation and co-validation**   The term **cross-validation** refers to the revalidation of a test on a sample of testtakers other than those on whom test performance was originally found to be a valid predictor of some criterion. We expect that items selected for the final version of the test (in part because of their high correlations with a criterion measure) will have smaller item validities when administered to a second sample of testtakers. This is so because of the operation of chance. The decrease in item validities that inevitably occurs after cross-validation of findings is referred to as **validity shrinkage.** Such shrinkage is expected and is viewed as integral to the test development process. Further, such shrinkage is infinitely preferable to a scenario wherein (spuriously) high item validities are published in a test manual as a result of inappropriately using the identical sample of testtakers for test standardization and cross-validation of findings. When such scenarios occur, test users will typically be let down by lower-than-expected test validity. The test manual accompanying commercially prepared tests should outline the test development procedures used. Reliability information, including test-retest reliability and internal consistency estimates, should be reported along with evidence of the test's validity. Articles discussing cross-validation of tests are often published in scholarly journals. For example, Bank et al. (2000) provided a detailed account of the cross-validation of an instrument used to screen for cognitive impairment in older adults.

Not to be confused with "cross-validation," **co-validation** may be defined as a test validation process conducted on two or more tests using the same sample of testtakers. When used in conjunction with the creation of norms or the revision of existing norms, this process may also be referred to as **co-norming.** A current trend among test publishers who publish more than one test designed for use with the same population is to co-validate and/or co-norm tests. Co-validation of new tests and revisions of existing tests can be beneficial in various ways to all parties in the assessment enterprise. Co-validation is beneficial to test publishers because it is economical. During the process of validating a test, many prospective testtakers must first be identified. In many instances, after being identified as a possible participant in the validation study, a person will be prescreened for suitability by means of a face-to-face or telephone interview. This costs money, which is charged to the budget for developing the test. Both money and time are saved if the same person is deemed suitable in the validation studies for multiple tests and can be scheduled to participate with a minimum of administrative preliminaries. Qualified examiners to administer the test and other personnel to assist in scoring, interpretation, and statistical analysis must also be identified, retained, and scheduled to participate in the project. The cost of retaining such professional personnel on a per-test basis is minimized when the work is done for multiple tests simultaneously.

Beyond benefits to the publisher, co-validation can hold potentially important benefits for test users and testtakers. Many tests that tend to be used together are published by the same publisher. For example, the fourth edition of the Wechsler Adult Intelligence Scale (WAIS-IV) and the fourth edition of the Wechsler Memory Scale (WMS-IV) might be used together in the clinical evaluation of an adult. And let's suppose that, after an evaluation using these two tests, differences in measured memory ability emerged as a function of the test used. Had these two tests been normed on different samples, then sampling error would be one possible reason for the observed differences in measured memory. However, because the two tests were normed on the same population, sampling error as a causative factor has been virtually eliminated. A clinician might thus look to factors such as differences in the way that the two tests measure memory. One test, for example, might measure short-term memory using the recall of number sequences. The other test might measure the same variable using recalled comprehension of short reading passages. How each test measures the variable under study may yield important diagnostic insights.

On the other hand, consider two co-normed tests that are almost identical in how they measure the variable under study. With sampling error minimized by the co-norming process, a test user can be that much more confident that the scores on the two tests are comparable.

**Quality assurance during test revision**   Once upon a time, a long time ago in Manhattan, one of this text's authors (Cohen) held the title of senior psychologist at Bellevue Hospital. Among other duties, senior psychologists supervised clinical psychology interns in all phases of their professional development, including the administration of psychological tests:

> One day, in the course of reviewing a test protocol handed in by an intern, something very peculiar caught my eye. On a subtest that had several tasks scored on the basis of number of seconds to completion, all of the recorded times on the protocol were in multiples of 5 (as in 10 seconds, 15 seconds, etc.). I had never seen a protocol like that. All of the completed protocols I had seen previously had recorded completion times with no identifiable pattern or multiple (like 12 seconds, 17 seconds, 9 seconds, etc.). Curious about the way that the protocol had been scored, I called in the intern to discuss it.
>
> As it turned out, the intern had not equipped herself with either a stopwatch or a watch with a second-hand before administering this test. She had ignored this mandatory bit of preparation prior to test administration. Lacking any way to record the exact number of seconds it took to complete each task, the intern said she had "estimated" the number of seconds. Estimating under such circumstances is not permitted because it violates the standardized procedure set forth in the manual. Beyond that, estimating could easily result in the testtaker either earning or failing to earn bonus points for (inaccurately) timed scores. The intern was advised of the error of her ways, and the patient was retested.

Well, that's one "up close and personal" example of quality control in psychological testing at a large municipal hospital. But what mechanisms of quality assurance are put into place by test publishers in the course of standardizing a new test or restandardizing an existing test? Let's take a brief look at some quality control mechanisms for examiners, protocol scoring, and data entry. For the purpose of illustration, we draw some examples from procedures followed by the developers of the Wechsler Intelligence Scale for Children, Fourth Edition (WISC-IV; Wechsler, 2003).

The examiner is the front-line person in test development, and it is critically important that examiners adhere to standardized procedures. In developing a new test or in restandardizing or renorming an existing test, test developers seek to employ examiners who have experience testing members of the population targeted for the test. For example, the developers of the WISC-IV sought to

> recruit examiners with extensive experience testing children and adolescents. Potential examiners completed a questionnaire by supplying information about their educational and professional experience, administration experience with various intellectual measures, certification, and licensing status. Those selected as potential standardization examiners were very familiar with childhood assessment practices. (Wechsler, 2003, p. 22)

Although it might be desirable for every examiner to hold a doctoral degree, this is simply not feasible given that many thousands of tests may have to be individually administered. The professional time of doctoral-level examiners tends to be at a premium—not to mention their fees. Regardless of education or experience, all examiners will be trained to administer the instrument. Training will typically take the form of written guidelines for test administration and may involve everything from classroom instruction to practice test administrations on site to videotaped demonstrations to be reviewed at home. Publishers may evaluate potential examiners by a quiz or other means to determine how well they have learned what they need to know. During the standardization of the WISC-IV, examiners were required to submit a review case prior to testing additional children. And during the course of the test's standardization, all persons selected as examiners received a periodic newsletter advising them of potential problems in test administration. The newsletter was designed to provide an ongoing way to maintain quality assurance in test administration.

In the course of test development, examiners may be involved to greater or lesser degrees in the final scoring of protocols. Regardless of whether it is the examiner or a "dedicated scorer," all persons who have responsibility for scoring protocols will typically undergo training. As with examiner training, the training for scorers may take many forms, from classroom instruction to videotaped demonstrations.

Quality assurance in the restandardization of the WISC-IV was in part maintained by having two qualified scorers rescore each protocol collected during the national tryout and standardization stages of test development. If there were discrepancies in scoring, the discrepancies were resolved by yet another scorer, referred to as a *resolver*. According to the manual, "The resolvers were selected based on their demonstration of exceptional scoring accuracy and previous scoring experience" (Wechsler, 2003, p. 22).

Another mechanism for ensuring consistency in scoring is the *anchor protocol*. An **anchor protocol** is a test protocol scored by a highly authoritative scorer that is designed as a model for scoring and a mechanism for resolving scoring discrepancies. A discrepancy between scoring in an anchor protocol and the scoring of another protocol is referred to as **scoring drift.** Anchor protocols were used for quality assurance in the development of the WISC-IV:

> If two independent scorers made the same scoring error on a protocol, comparison to the anchor score revealed the scoring drift. Scorers received feedback immediately to prevent repetition of the error and to correct for scoring drift. (Wechsler, 2003, p. 23)

Once protocols are scored, the data from them must be entered into a database. For quality assurance during the data entry phase of test development, test developers may employ computer programs to seek out and identify any irregularities in score reporting. For example, if a score on a particular subtest can range from a low of 1 to a high of 10, any score reported out of that range would be flagged by the computer. Additionally, a proportion of protocols can be randomly selected to make certain that the data entered from them faithfully match the data they originally contained.

## The Use of IRT in Building and Revising Tests

In the previous chapter, we noted that item response theory (IRT) could be applied in the evaluation of the utility of tests and testing programs. Here, let's briefly elaborate on the possible roles of IRT in test construction, as well as some of its pros and cons vis-à-vis classical test theory (CTT). As can be seen from Table 8–4, one of the *disadvantages* of applying CTT in test development is the extent to which item statistics are dependent upon characteristics (strength of traits or ability level) of the group of people tested. Stated another way, "all CTT-based statistics are sample dependent"

**Table 8–4**
**Some Advantages and Disadvantages of Classical Test Theory (CTT) and Item Response Theory (IRT)***

| Theory | Advantages | Disadvantages |
|---|---|---|
| Classical Test Theory | 1. Smaller sample sizes are required for testing, so CTT is especially useful if only a small sample of testtakers is available. | 1. Item statistics and overall psychometric properties of a test are dependent on the samples which have been administered the test. |
| | 2. CTT utilizes relatively simple mathematical models. | 2. Tests developed using CTT may be longer (that is, require more items) than tests developed using IRT. |
| | 3. Assumptions underlying CTT are "weak" allowing CTT wide applicability | 3. One often violated assumption is that each item of a test contributes equally to the total test score. |
| | 4. Most researchers are familiar with this basic approach to test development. | |
| | 5. Many data analysis and statistics-related software packages are built from a CTT perspective or are readily compatible with it. | |
| Item Response Theory | 1. Item statistics are independent of the samples which have been administered the test. | 1. The techniques used to test item response models are relatively complicated and unfamiliar to most researchers. |
| | 2. Test items can be matched to ability levels (as in computerized adaptive testing) thus resulting in relatively short tests that are still reliable and valid. | 2. Sample sizes need to be relatively large to properly test IRT models (200 or more is a good rule-of-thumb). |
| | 3. IRT models facilitate advanced psychometric tools and methods, holding out the promise of greater precision in measurement under certain circumstances. | 3. Assumptions for use of IRT are characterized as "hard" or "strong" making IRT inappropriate for use in many applications. |
| | | 4. As compared to CTT-based statistics-related software, there are much fewer IRT-based packages currently available. |

*For a more detailed comparison of CTT to IRT, consult the sources used to synthesize this table (De Champlain, 2010; Hambleton & Jones, 1993; Streiner, 2010; and Zickar & Broadfoot, 2009).

(De Champlain, 2010, p. 112). To elaborate, consider a hypothetical "Perceptual-Motor Ability Test" (PMAT), and the characteristics of items on that test with reference to different groups of testtakers. From a CTT perspective, a PMAT item might be judged to be very *high* in difficulty when it is administered to a sample of people known to be very low in perceptual-motor ability. From that same perspective, that same PMAT item might be judged to be very *low* in difficulty when administered to a group of people known to be very high in perceptual-motor ability. Because the way that an item is viewed is so dependent on the group of testtakers taking the test, the ideal situation, at least from the CTT perspective, is one in which all testtakers represent a truly random sample of how well the trait or ability being studied is represented in the population. Using IRT, test developers evaluate individual item performance with reference to item-characteristic curves (ICCs). ICCs provide information about the relationship between the performance of individual items and the presumed underlying ability (or trait) level in the testtaker.

Three of the many possible applications of IRT in building and revising tests include (1) evaluating existing tests for the purpose of mapping test revisions, (2) determining measurement equivalence across testtaker populations, and (3) developing item banks.

**Evaluating the properties of existing tests and guiding test revision** IRT information curves can help test developers evaluate how well an individual item (or entire test) is working to measure different levels of the underlying construct. Developers can use these information curves to weed out uninformative questions or to eliminate redundant items that provide duplicate levels of information. Information curves allow test developers to tailor an instrument to provide high information (that is, precision). As an illustration, refer back to the information curve for a measure of depression in Figure 3 of the *Close-Up* in Chapter 5 (page 173). Now suppose the test developer wanted to increase precision so that level of depression could better be measured across all levels of theta. The graph suggests that this could be accomplished by adding more items to the test (or by adding more response options to existing items) that differentiate among people with mild depressive symptoms. Adding appropriate items (or response options) will both broaden the range and increase the height of the curve across the underlying construct—thus reflecting increased precision in measurement.

**Determining measurement equivalence across testtaker populations** Test developers often aspire to have their tests become so popular that they will be translated into other languages and used in many places throughout the world. But how do they assure that their tests are tapping into the same construct regardless of who in the world is responding to the test items? One tool to help ensure that the same construct is being measured, no matter what language the test has been translated into, is IRT.

Despite carefully translated test items, it sometimes happens that even though the words may be linguistically equivalent, members of different populations—typically members of populations other than the population for which the test was initially developed—may interpret the items differently. As we saw in Chapter 5, for example, response rates to a measure of depression from people of different cultures may not necessarily depend on how depressed the testtaker is. Rather, response rates may vary more as a function of how much the prevailing culture sanctions outward expression of emotion. This phenomenon, wherein an item functions differently in one group of testtakers as compared to another group of testtakers known to have the same (or similar) level of the underlying trait, is referred to as **differential item functioning (DIF).** Instruments containing such items may have reduced validity for between-group comparisons because their scores may indicate a variety of attributes other than those the scale is intended to measure.

In a process known as **DIF analysis,** test developers scrutinize group-by-group item response curves, looking for what are termed *DIF items.* **DIF items** are those items that respondents from different groups at the same level of the underlying trait have different probabilities of endorsing as a function of their group membership. DIF analysis has been used to evaluate measurement equivalence in item content across groups that vary by culture, gender, and age. It has even been used to explore differential item functioning as a function of different patterns of guessing on the part of members of different groups (DeMars & Wise, 2010). Yet another application of DIF analysis has to do with the evaluation of item-ordering effects, and the effects of different test administration procedures (such as paper-and-pencil test administration versus computer-administered testing).

**Developing item banks** Developing an item bank is not simply a matter of collecting a large number of items. Typically, each of the items assembled as part of an item bank, whether taken from an existing test (with appropriate permissions, if necessary) or written especially for the item bank, have undergone rigorous qualitative and quantitative evaluation (Reeve et al., 2007). As can be seen from Figure 8–7, many item banking efforts begin with the collection of appropriate items from existing instruments (Instruments A, B, and C). New items may also be written when existing measures are either not available or do not tap targeted aspects of the construct being measured.

All items available for use as well as new items created especially for the item bank constitute the item pool. The item pool is then evaluated by content experts, potential respondents, and survey experts using a variety of qualitative and quantitative methods. Individual items in an item pool may be evaluated by cognitive testing procedures whereby an interviewer conducts one-on-one interviews with respondents in an effort to identify any ambiguities associated with the items. Item pools may also be evaluated by groups of respondents, which allows for discussion of the clarity and relevance of each item, among other item characteristics. The items that "make the cut" after such scrutiny constitute the preliminary item bank.

The next step in creating the item bank is the administration of all of the questionnaire items to a large and representative sample of the target population. For ease in data analysis, group administration by computer is preferable. However, depending upon the content and method of administration required by the items, the questionnaire (or portions of it) may be administered individually using paper-and-pencil methods.

After administration of the preliminary item bank to the entire sample of respondents, responses to the items are evaluated with regard to several variables such as validity, reliability, domain coverage, and differential item functioning. The final item bank will consist of a large set of items all measuring a single domain (that is, a single trait or ability). A test developer may then use the banked items to create one or more tests with a fixed number of items. For example, a teacher may create two different versions of a math test in order to minimize efforts by testtakers to cheat. The item bank can also be used for purposes of computerized-adaptive testing.

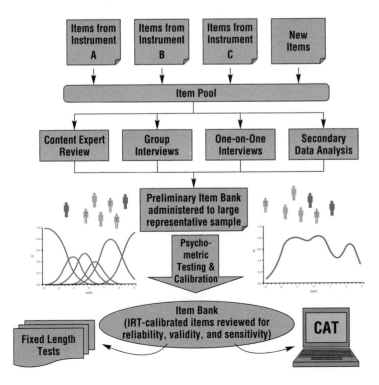

**Figure 8–7**
**The Use of IRT to Create Item Banks**

When used within a CAT environment, a testtaker's response to an item may automatically trigger which item is presented to the testtaker next. The software has been programmed to present the item next that will be most informative with regard to the testtaker's standing on the construct being measured. This programming is actually based on near-instantaneous construction and analysis of IRT information curves. The process continues until the testing is terminated.

Because of CAT's widespread appeal, the technology is being increasingly applied to a wide array of tests. It is also becoming available on many different platforms ranging from the Internet to handheld devices to computer-assisted telephone interviewing.

Our survey of how tests are built has taken us from a test developer's first thoughts regarding what new test needs to be created, all the way through to the development of a large item bank. In the following chapters, we will be exploring various aspects of many different types of tests, beginning with tests of *intelligence*. Prior to that, however, some background regarding this somewhat elusive construct is presented in Chapter 9.

## Self-Assessment

Test your understanding of elements of this chapter by seeing if you can explain each of the following terms, expressions, and abbreviations:

anchor protocol
biased test item
binary-choice item
categorical scaling
category scoring
ceiling effect
class scoring
comparative scaling
completion item
computerized adaptive testing (CAT)
co-norming
constructed-response format
co-validation
cross-validation
DIF analysis
differential item functioning (DIF)
DIF items
essay item
expert panel

floor effect
giveaway item
guessing
Guttman scale
ipsative scoring
item analysis
item bank
item branching
item-characteristic curve (ICC)
item-difficulty index
item-discrimination index
item-endorsement index
item fairness
item format
item pool
item-reliability index
item-validity index
Likert scale
matching item
method of paired comparisons

multiple-choice format
pilot work
qualitative item analysis
qualitative methods
rating scale
scaling
scalogram analysis
scoring drift
selected-response format
sensitivity review
short-answer item
summative scale
test conceptualization
test construction
test development
test revision
test tryout
"think aloud" test administration
true–false item
validity shrinkage

# 9

# *Intelligence and Its Measurement*

**F**or as long as there has been a discipline of psychology, psychologists have had differing definitions of intelligence and how best to measure it.

In this chapter we look at the varied ways intelligence has been defined and survey the ways it has been measured. We conclude with a discussion of a few major issues surrounding the practice of measuring intelligence, including the relationship between culture and intelligence. In Chapter 10, we will look more closely at the "nuts and bolts" of intelligence tests and focus on some representative tests. The measurement of intelligence and other ability- and achievement-related constructs in preschool and educational settings is the subject of Chapter 11. We begin, however, by raising a question that logically precedes consideration of intelligence measurement issues.

## What Is Intelligence?

We may define **intelligence** as a multifaceted capacity that manifests itself in different ways across the life span. In general, intelligence includes the abilities to:

- acquire and apply knowledge
- reason logically
- plan effectively
- infer perceptively
- make sound judgments and solve problems
- grasp and visualize concepts
- pay attention
- be intuitive
- find the right words and thoughts with facility
- cope with, adjust to, and make the most of new situations

All of that having been said, please do not interpret these descriptions of intelligence as the "last word" on

> **JUST THINK . . .**
> How do *you* define intelligence?

the matter. Rather, think of these descriptions as a point of departure for reflection on the meaning of a most intriguing term—one that, as we will see, is paradoxically both simple and complex.

Most people believe they can recognize intelligence when it is expressed in observable behavior. Nonetheless, a widely accepted definition of this "readily observable" entity has remained elusive—this despite the fact that we design tests to measure it and effect life-changing consequences on the basis of those test results. But maybe intelligence isn't observable at all; maybe it is, as Henry Goddard (1947) conceived it, "the degree of availability of one's experiences for the solution of his present problems and the anticipation of future ones."

When words fail, the search for an adequate and widely acceptable definition of intelligence has led to avenues that could be characterized as less semantic and more physical. In search of answers, behavioral scientists have conducted cerebral glucose metabolism studies (Haier, 1993) and other such research on brain physiology (Vernon, 1993). More recently, brain-mapping studies using sophisticated neuropsychological imaging techniques have been used to explore various aspects of human abilities (see, for example, Hu et al., 2011; Kreifelts et al., 2010). Despite such efforts, devising a widely acceptable definition of intelligence has historically been (Neisser, 1979; Neisser et al., 1996), and today remains, a challenge.

## Intelligence Defined: Views of the Lay Public

Research conducted by Sternberg and his associates (Sternberg, 1981, 1982; Sternberg & Detterman, 1986; Sternberg et al., 1981) sought to shed light on how intelligence is defined by laypeople and psychologists. In one study, a total of 476 people (students, commuters, supermarket shoppers, people who answered newspaper ads, and people randomly selected from phone books) were asked to list behaviors they associated with "intelligence," "academic intelligence," "everyday intelligence," and "unintelligence." After a list of various behaviors characterizing intelligence was generated, 28 nonpsychologists in the New Haven area were asked to rate on a scale of 1 (low) to 9 (high) how characteristic each of the behaviors was for the ideal "intelligent" person, the ideal "academically intelligent" person, and the ideal "everyday intelligent" person. The views of 140 doctoral-level research psychologists who were experts in the area of intelligence were also solicited. These experts were themselves involved in research on intelligence in major universities and research centers around the United States.

All people polled in Sternberg's study had definite ideas about intelligence and the lack of it. For the nonpsychologists, the behaviors most commonly associated with intelligence were "reasons logically and well," "reads widely," "displays common sense," "keeps an open mind," and "reads with high comprehension." Leading the list of most frequently mentioned behaviors associated with unintelligence were "does not tolerate diversity of views," "does not display curiosity," and "behaves with insufficient consideration of others."

Sternberg and his colleagues grouped the list of 250 behaviors characterizing intelligence and unintelligence into subsets that were most strongly related to each other. The analysis indicated that the nonpsychologists and the experts conceived of intelligence in general as practical problem-solving ability (such as "listens to all sides of an argument"), verbal ability ("displays a good vocabulary"), and social competence ("is on time for appointments"). Each specific type of intelligence was characterized by various descriptors. "Academic intelligence" included verbal ability, problem-solving ability, and social competence as well as specific behaviors associated with acquiring academic skills (such as "studying hard"). "Everyday intelligence" included practical problem-solving ability, social competence, character, and interest in learning and culture.

In general, the researchers found a surprising degree of similarity between the experts' and laypeople's conceptions of intelligence. With respect to academic intelligence, however, the experts tended to stress motivation ("is persistent," "highly dedicated and motivated in chosen pursuits") whereas laypeople stressed the interpersonal and social aspects of intelligence ("sensitivity to other people's needs and desires," "is frank and honest with self and others").

In another study (Siegler & Richards, 1980), students enrolled in college developmental psychology classes were asked to list behaviors associated with intelligence in infancy, childhood, and adulthood. Perhaps not surprisingly, different conceptions of intelligence as a function of developmental stage were noted. In infancy, intelligence was associated with physical coordination, awareness of people, verbal output, and attachment. In childhood, verbal facility, understanding, and characteristics of learning were most often listed. Verbal facility, use of logic, and problem solving were most frequently associated with adult intelligence.

A study conducted with first-, third-, and sixth-graders (Yussen & Kane, 1980) suggested that children also have notions about intelligence as early as first grade. Younger children's conceptions tended to emphasize interpersonal skills (acting nice, being helpful, being polite), whereas older children emphasized academic skills (reading well).

## Intelligence Defined: Views of Scholars and Test Professionals

In a symposium published in the *Journal of Educational Psychology* in 1921, seventeen of the country's leading psychologists addressed the following questions: (1) *What is intelligence?* (2) *How can it best be measured in group tests?* and (3) *What should be the next steps in the research?* No two psychologists agreed (Thorndike et al., 1921). Six years later, Spearman (1927, p. 14) would reflect: "In truth, intelligence has become . . . a word with so many meanings that finally it has none." And decades after the symposium was first held, Wesman (1968, p. 267) concluded that there appeared to be "no more general agreement as to the nature of intelligence or the most valid means of measuring intelligence today than was the case 50 years ago."

**JUST THINK . . .**

Must professionals agree on a definition of intelligence?

As Neisser (1979) observed, although the *Journal* felt that the symposium would generate vigorous discussion, it generated more heat than light and led to a general increase in exasperation with discussion on the subject. Symptomatic of that exasperation was an unfortunate statement by an experimental psychologist and historian of psychology, Edwin G. Boring. Boring (1923, p. 5), who was not a psychometrician, attempted to quell the argument by pronouncing that "intelligence is what the tests test." Although such a view is not entirely devoid of merit (see Neisser, 1979, p. 225), it is an unsatisfactory, incomplete, and circular definition. In what follows we record the thoughts of some other behavioral scientists through history and up to contemporary times.

**Francis Galton**   Among other accomplishments, Sir Francis Galton is remembered as the first person to publish on the heritability of intelligence, thus framing the contemporary nature–nurture debate (McGue, 1997). Galton (1883) believed that the most intelligent persons were those equipped with the best sensory abilities. This position was intuitively appealing because, as Galton observed, "The only information that reaches us concerning outward events appears to pass through the avenues of our senses; and the more perceptive the senses are of difference, the larger is the field upon which our judgment and intelligence can act" (p. 27). Following this logic, tests of visual acuity or hearing ability are, in a sense, tests of intelligence. Galton attempted to measure this sort of intelligence in many of the sensorimotor and other perception-related tests he devised. In this respect he anticipated later physiological research exploring, for example, the relationship between intelligence and speed of neural conductivity (Reed & Jensen, 1992, 1993) and speed of information processing (Sheppard, 2008).

◆
**JUST THINK . . .**

What was wrong with the logic behind Galton's definition of the most intelligent people?

**Alfred Binet**   Although his test at the turn of the century had the effect of launching the testing movement—for intelligence and other characteristics—Alfred Binet did not leave us an explicit definition of intelligence. He did, however, write about the components of intelligence. For Binet, these components included reasoning, judgment, memory, and abstraction (Varon, 1936). As we will see, in later years there would be no shortage of opinion among scholars regarding exactly what the components—or factors—in intelligence are, how these factors should be grouped or organized, and how they could best be assessed.

In papers critical of Galton's approach to intellectual assessment, Binet and a colleague called for more complex measurements of intellectual ability (Binet & Henri, 1895a, 1895b, 1895c). Galton had viewed intelligence as a number of distinct processes or abilities that could be assessed only by separate tests. In contrast, Binet argued that when one solves a particular problem, the abilities used cannot be separated because they interact to produce the solution. For example, memory and concentration interact when a subject is asked to repeat digits presented orally. When analyzing a testtaker's response to such a task, it is difficult to determine the relative contribution of memory and concentration to the successful solution. This difficulty in determining the relative contribution of distinct abilities is the reason Binet called for more complex measurements of intelligence.

**David Wechsler**   David Wechsler's conceptualization of intelligence can perhaps best be summed up in his own words:

> Intelligence, operationally defined, is the aggregate or global capacity of the individual to act purposefully, to think rationally and to deal effectively with his environment. It is aggregate or global because it is composed of elements or abilities which, though not entirely independent, are qualitatively differentiable. By measurement of these abilities, we ultimately evaluate intelligence. But intelligence is not identical with the mere sum of these abilities, however inclusive. . . . The only way we can evaluate it quantitatively is by the measurement of the various aspects of these abilities. (1958, p. 7)

In this definition we see an acknowledgment of the complexity of intelligence and its conceptualization as an "aggregate" or "global" capacity. Elsewhere Wechsler added that there are nonintellective factors that must be taken into account when assessing intelligence (Kaufman, 1990). Included among those factors are "capabilities more of the nature of conative, affective, or personality traits [that] include such traits as drive, persistence, and goal awareness [as well as] an individual's potential to perceive and respond to social, moral and aesthetic values" (Wechsler, 1975, p. 136). Ultimately, however, Wechsler was of the opinion that the best way to measure this global ability was by measuring aspects of several "qualitatively differentiable" abilities. Wechsler (1974) wrote of two such "differentiable" abilities, which he conceived as being primarily *verbal-* or *performance-*based in nature. Historically, users of Wechsler tests have interpreted test data with reference to individual subtest scores as well as the Verbal, Performance, and Full Scale scores, with the IQ calculated on the basis of these indices. Clinicians were trained to look for diagnostically significant discrepancies within and between these many indices—yet all within the Verbal–Performance framework. However, as early as the 1950s, alternative, multifactor models of what the Wechsler-Bellevue (Cohen, 1952a, 1952b) and the WAIS (Cohen, 1957a, 1957b) seemed to be measuring were in evidence.

**JUST THINK . . .**

What is the role of personality in measured intelligence?

In the years that followed, test users and theorists would wonder whether data derived from Wechsler tests might fit better conceptually with alternative models of cognitive ability (Hishinuma & Yamakawa, 1993; Kaufman, 1990, 1994a, 1994b; Sattler, 1992; Shaw et al., 1993; Smith et al., 1993). The question "How many factors are there *really* on the Wechsler tests?" seemed to have been transformed from a passing academic interest to a pressing user obsession. The issue was addressed in the development of a later edition of the Wechsler Adult Intelligence Scale (the WAIS-III), as evidenced by extensive exploratory and confirmatory factor-analytic investigations described in the test's technical manual. A result of these investigations was that, in addition to the traditional Verbal–Performance dichotomy, WAIS-III users would be able to group test data by four factors: verbal comprehension, working memory, perceptual organization, and processing speed. Based on these four factors, four *index scores* could be derived from the test data. As we will see in Chapter 10 (when we discuss the current incarnation of the Wechsler adult scale, the WAIS-IV), the conceptualization of intelligence in terms of a Verbal–Performance dichotomy is more a matter of historical interest than present-day reality.

**Jean Piaget** Since the early 1960s, the theoretical research of the Swiss developmental psychologist Jean Piaget (1954, 1971) has commanded attention from developmental psychologists around the world. Piaget's research focused on the development of cognition in children: how children think, how they understand themselves and the world around them, and how they reason and solve problems.

For Piaget, intelligence may be conceived of as a kind of evolving biological adaptation to the outside world. As cognitive skills are gained, adaptation (at a symbolic level) increases, and mental trial and error replaces physical trial and error. Yet, according to Piaget, the process of cognitive development occurs neither solely through maturation nor solely through learning. He believed that, as a consequence of interaction with the environment, psychological structures become reorganized. Piaget described four stages of cognitive development through which, he theorized, all of us pass during our lifetimes. Although individuals can move through these stages at different rates and ages, he believed that their order was unchangeable. Piaget viewed the unfolding of these stages of cognitive development as the result of the interaction of biological factors and learning.

According to this theory, biological aspects of mental development are governed by inherent maturational mechanisms. As individual stages are reached and passed through, the child also has experiences within the environment. Each new experience, according to Piaget, requires some form of cognitive organization or reorganization in a mental structure called a *schema*. More specifically, Piaget used the term **schema** to refer to an organized action or mental structure that, when applied to the world, leads to knowing or understanding. Infants are born with several simple **schemata** (the plural of schema), including sucking and grasping. Learning initially by grasping and by putting almost anything in their mouths, infants use these schemata to understand and appreciate their world. As the infant grows older, schemata become more complicated and are tied less to overt action than to mental transformations. For example, adding a series of numbers requires mental transformation of numbers to arrive at the correct sum. Infants, children, and adults continue to apply schemata to objects and events to achieve understanding, and these schemata are constantly adjusted.

Piaget hypothesized that learning occurs through two basic mental operations: **assimilation** (actively organizing new information so that it fits in with what already is perceived and thought) and **accommodation** (changing what is already perceived or thought so that it fits with new information). For example, a child who sees a butterfly and calls it a "bird" has assimilated the idea of butterfly into an already existing mental structure, "bird." However, when the new concept of "butterfly"—separate from "bird"—has also been formed, the mental operation of *accommodation* has been employed. Piaget also stressed the importance of physical activities and social peer interaction in promoting a disequilibrium by which mental structures change, and new information, perceptions, and communication skills are acquired.

**JUST THINK . . .**

Provide a recent, personal example of assimilation and accommodation at work in your own mind.

The four periods of cognitive development, each representing a more complex form of cognitive organization, are outlined in Table 9–1. The stages range from the sensorimotor period, wherein infants' thoughts are dominated by their perceptions, to the formal operations period, wherein an individual has the ability to construct theories and make logical deductions without direct experience.

**Table 9–1**
**Piaget's Stages of Cognitive Development**

| Stage | Age Span | Characteristics of Thought |
|---|---|---|
| Sensorimotor Period | Birth–2 years of age | Child develops ability to exhibit goal-directed, intentional behavior; develops the capacity to coordinate and integrate input from the five senses; acquires the capacity to recognize the world and its objects as permanent entities (that is, the infant develops "object permanence"). |
| Preoperational Period | 2–6 years of age | Child's understanding of concepts is based largely on what is seen; the child's comprehension of a situation, an event, or an object is typically based on a single, usually the most obvious, perceptual aspect of the stimulus; thought is irreversible (child focuses on static states of reality and cannot understand relations between states; for example, child believes the quantities of a set of beads change if the beads are pushed together or spread apart); animistic thinking (attributing human qualities to nonhuman objects and events). |
| Concrete Operations Period | 7–12 years of age | Reversibility of thought now appears; conservation of thought (certain attributes of the world remain stable despite some modification in appearance); part–whole problems and serial ordering tasks can now be solved (able to put ideas in rank order); can deal only with relationships and things with which he or she has direct experience; able to look at more than one aspect of a problem and able to clearly differentiate between present and historical time. |
| Formal Operations Period | 12 years of age and older | Increased ability to abstract and to deal with ideas independent of his or her own experience; greater capacity to generate hypotheses and test them in a systematic fashion ("if-then" statements, more alternatives); able to think about several variables acting together and their combined effects; can evaluate own thought; applies learning to new problems in a deductive way. |

A major thread running through the theories of Binet, Wechsler, and Piaget is a focus on interactionism. **Interactionism** refers to the complex concept by which heredity and environment are presumed to interact and influence the development of one's intelligence. As we will see, other theorists have focused on other aspects of intelligence. In **factor-analytic theories,** the focus is squarely on identifying the ability or groups of abilities deemed to constitute intelligence. In **information-processing theories,** the focus is on identifying the specific mental processes that constitute intelligence.

## Factor-Analytic Theories of Intelligence

Factor analysis is a group of statistical techniques designed to determine the existence of underlying relationships between sets of variables, including test scores. In search of a definition of intelligence, theorists have used factor analysis to study correlations between tests measuring varied abilities presumed to reflect the underlying attribute of intelligence.

As early as 1904, the British psychologist Charles Spearman pioneered new techniques to measure intercorrelations between tests. He found that measures of intelligence tended to correlate to various degrees with each other. Spearman (1927) formalized these observations into an influential theory of general intelligence that postulated the existence of a general intellectual ability factor (denoted by an italic lowercase $g$) that is partially tapped by all other mental abilities. This theory is sometimes referred to as a **two-factor theory of intelligence,** with $g$ representing the portion of the variance that all intelligence tests have in common and the remaining portions of the variance being accounted for either by specific components ($s$), or by error components ($e$) of this general factor (Figure 9–1). Tests that exhibited high positive correlations with other intelligence tests were thought to be highly saturated with $g$, whereas tests with low or moderate correlations with other intelligence tests were viewed as possible

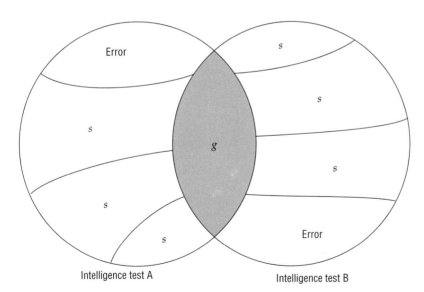

**Figure 9–1**
**Spearman's Two-Factor Theory of Intelligence**

*Here, g stands for a general intelligence factor and s stands for a specific factor of intelligence (specific to a single intellectual activity only).*

measures of specific factors (such as visual or motor ability). The greater the magnitude of $g$ in a test of intelligence, the better the test was thought to predict overall intelligence.

Spearman (1927) conceived of the basis of the $g$ factor as some type of general electrochemical mental energy available to the brain for problem solving. In addition, it was associated with facility in thinking of one's own experience and in making observations and extracting principles. It was $g$ rather than $s$ that was assumed to afford the best prediction of overall intelligence. Abstract-reasoning problems were thought to be the best measures of $g$ in formal tests. As Spearman and his students continued their research, they acknowledged the existence of an intermediate class of factors common to a group of activities but not to all. This class of factors, called **group factors,** is neither as general as $g$ nor as specific as $s$. Examples of these broad group factors include linguistic, mechanical, and arithmetical abilities.

Other theorists attempted to "dig deeper," to be even more specific about identifying and describing factors other than $g$ in intelligence. The number of factors listed to define intelligence in a factor-analytic theory of intelligence may depend, in part, on just how specific the theory is in terms of defining discrete cognitive abilities. These abilities may be conceived of in many ways, from very broad to highly specific. As an example, consider that one researcher has identified an ability "to repeat a chain of verbally presented numbers" that he labels "Factor R." Another researcher analyzes Factor R into three "facilitating abilities" or subfactors, which she labels "ability to process sound" (R1), "ability to retain verbally presented stimuli" (R2), and "speed of processing verbally presented stimuli" (R3). Both researchers present factor-analytic evidence to support their respective positions.[1] Which of these two models will prevail? All other things being equal, it will probably be the model that is perceived as having the greater real-world application, the greater intuitive appeal in terms of how intelligence should be defined, and the greater amount of empirical support.

Many multiple-factor models of intelligence have been proposed. Some of these models, such as that developed by Guilford (1967), have sought to explain mental activities by deemphasizing, if not eliminating, any reference to $g$. Thurstone (1938) initially conceived of intelligence as being composed of seven "primary abilities." However, after designing tests to measure these abilities and noting a moderate correlation between the tests, Thurstone became convinced it was difficult, if not impossible, to develop an intelligence test that did not tap $g$. Gardner (1983, 1994) developed a theory of multiple (seven, actually) intelligences: logical-mathematical, bodily-kinesthetic, linguistic, musical, spatial, interpersonal, and intrapersonal. Gardner (1983) described the last two as follows:

> Interpersonal intelligence is the ability to understand other people: what motivates them, how they work, how to work cooperatively with them. Successful sales people, politicians, teachers, clinicians, and religious leaders are all likely to be individuals with high degrees of interpersonal intelligence. Intrapersonal intelligence, a seventh kind of intelligence, is a correlative ability, turned inward. It is a capacity to form an accurate, veridical model of oneself and to be able to use that model to operate effectively in life. (p. 9)

Aspects of Gardner's writings, particularly his descriptions of **interpersonal intelligence** and **intrapersonal intelligence,** have found expression in popular books

---

1. Recall that factor analysis can take many forms. In exploratory factor analysis, the researcher essentially explores what relationships exist. In confirmatory factor analysis, the researcher is typically testing the viability of a proposed model or theory. Some factor-analytic studies are conducted on the subtests of a single test (such as a Wechsler test), whereas other studies are conducted on subtests from two (or more) tests (such as the current versions of a Wechsler test and the Binet test). The type of factor analysis employed by a theorist may well be the tool that presents that theorist's conclusions in the best possible light.

written by others on the subject of so-called **emotional intelligence.** But whether or not constructs related to empathy and self-understanding qualify more for the study of emotion and personality than the study of intelligence has been a subject of debate (Davies et al., 1998).

**JUST THINK . . .**

Is it possible to develop an intelligence test that does not tap *g*?

In recent years, a theory of intelligence first proposed by Raymond B. Cattell (1941, 1971) and subsequently modified by Horn (Cattell & Horn, 1978; Horn & Cattell, 1966, 1967) has received increasing attention from test developers as well as test users (see this chapter's *Meet an Assessment Professional*). As originally conceived by Cattell, the theory postulated the existence of two major types of cognitive abilities: crystallized intelligence and fluid intelligence. The abilities that make up **crystallized intelligence** (symbolized *Gc*) include acquired skills and knowledge that are dependent on exposure to a particular culture as well as on formal and informal education (vocabulary, for example). Retrieval of information and application of general knowledge are conceived of as elements of crystallized intelligence. The abilities that make up **fluid intelligence** (symbolized *Gf*) are nonverbal, relatively culture-free, and independent of specific instruction (such as memory for digits). Through the years, Horn (1968, 1985, 1988, 1991, 1994) proposed the addition of several factors: visual processing (*Gv*), auditory processing (*Ga*), quantitative processing (*Gq*), speed of processing (*Gs*), facility with reading and writing (*Grw*), short-term memory (*Gsm*), and long-term storage and retrieval (*Glr*). According to Horn (1989; Horn & Hofer, 1992), some of the abilities (such as *Gv*) are **vulnerable abilities** in that they decline with age and tend not to return to preinjury levels following brain damage. Others of these abilities (such as *Gq*) are **maintained abilities;** they tend not to decline with age and may return to preinjury levels following brain damage.

Another influential multiple-intelligences model based on factor-analytic studies is the **three-stratum theory of cognitive abilities** (Carroll, 1997). In geology, a stratum is a layer of rock formation having the same composition throughout. Strata (the plural of *stratum*) are illustrated in Figure 9–2, along with a representation of each of the three strata in Carroll's theory. The top stratum or level in Carroll's model is *g*, or

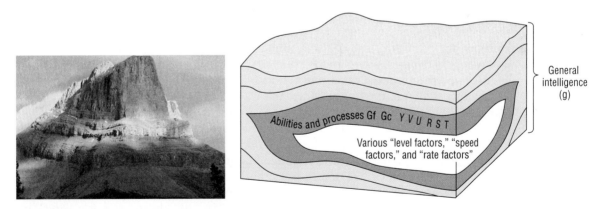

**Figure 9–2**
**Strata in Geology and Carroll's Three-Stratum Theory**

*Erosion can bare multiple levels of strata on a cliff. In psychology, theory can bare the strata of hypothesized mental structure and function. In Carroll's three-stratum theory of cognitive ability, the first level is* g, *followed by a stratum made up of eight abilities and processes, followed by a stratum containing what Carroll refers to as varying "level factors" and "speed factors."*

general intelligence. The second stratum is composed of eight abilities and processes: fluid intelligence (*Gf*), crystallized intelligence (*Gc*), general memory and learning (*Y*), broad visual perception (*V*), broad auditory perception (*U*), broad retrieval capacity (*R*), broad cognitive speediness (*S*), and processing/decision speed (*T*). Below each of the abilities in the second stratum are many "level factors" and/or "speed factors"—each

**JUST THINK . . .**

Moving from an analogy based on geology to one based on chemistry, think of the periodic table, which lists all known elements. Will it ever be possible to develop a comparable, generally agreed-upon "periodic table" of human abilities?

different, depending on the second-level stratum to which they are linked. For example, three factors linked to *Gf* are general reasoning, quantitative reasoning, and Piagetian reasoning. A speed factor linked to *Gf* is speed of reasoning. Four factors linked to *Gc* are language development, comprehension, spelling ability, and communication ability. Two speed factors linked to *Gc* are oral fluency and writing ability. The three-stratum theory is a **hierarchical model,** meaning that all of the abilities listed in a stratum are subsumed by or incorporated in the strata above.

Desire for a comprehensive, agreed-upon conceptualization of human cognitive abilities has led some researchers to try to extract elements of existing models to create a new, more complete model. Using factor analysis as well as other statistical tools, these researchers have attempted to modify and reconfigure existing models to better fit empirical evidence. One such modification that has gained increasing attention blends the Cattell-Horn theory with Carroll's three-stratum theory. Although this blending was not initiated by Cattell or Horn or Carroll, it is nonetheless referred to as the Cattell-Horn-Carroll **(CHC) model** of cognitive abilities.

**The CHC model**  The Cattell-Horn and Carroll models are similar in several respects, among them the designation of broad abilities (second-stratum level in Carroll's theory) that subsume several narrow abilities (first-stratum level in Carroll's theory). Still, any prospective integration of the Cattell-Horn and Carroll models must somehow account for the differences between these two models. One difference involves the existence of a general intellectual (*g*) factor. For Carroll, *g* is the third-stratum factor, subsuming *Gf*, *Gc*, and the remaining six other broad, second-stratum abilities. By contrast, *g* has no place in the Cattell-Horn model. Another difference between the two models concerns whether or not abilities labeled "quantitative knowledge" and "reading/writing ability" should each be considered a distinct, broad ability as they are in the Cattell-Horn model. For Carroll, all of these abilities are first-stratum, narrow abilities. Other differences between the two models include the notation, the specific definitions of abilities, and the grouping of narrow factors related to memory.

An integration of the Cattell-Horn and Carroll models was proposed by Kevin S. McGrew (1997). On the basis of additional factor-analytic work, McGrew and Flanagan (1998) subsequently modified McGrew's initial CHC model. In its current form, the McGrew-Flanagan CHC model features ten "broad-stratum" abilities and over seventy "narrow-stratum" abilities, with each broad-stratum ability subsuming two or more narrow-stratum abilities. The ten broad-stratum abilities, with their "code names" in parentheses, are labeled as follows: fluid intelligence (*Gf*), crystallized intelligence (*Gc*), quantitative knowledge (*Gq*), reading/writing ability (*Grw*), short-term memory (*Gsm*), visual processing (*Gv*), auditory processing (*Ga*), long-term storage and retrieval (*Glr*), processing speed (*Gs*), and decision/reaction time or speed (*Gt*).

The McGrew-Flanagan CHC model makes no provision for the general intellectual ability factor (*g*). To understand the reason for this omission, it is important to understand why the authors undertook to create the model in the first place. The model was the product of efforts designed to improve the practice of psychological assessment in education (sometimes referred to as **psychoeducational assessment**) by identifying tests from different batteries that could be used to provide a comprehensive assessment of a student's abilities. Having identified key abilities, the authors made recommendations for **cross-battery assessment** of students, or assessment that employs tests from different test batteries and entails interpretation of data from specified subtests to provide a comprehensive assessment. According to these authors, $g$ was not employed in their CHC model because it lacked utility in psychoeducational evaluations. They explained:

> The exclusion of $g$ does not mean that the integrated model does not subscribe to a separate general human ability or that $g$ does not exist. Rather, it was omitted by McGrew (1997) (and is similarly omitted in the current integrated model) since it has little practical relevance to cross-battery assessment and interpretation. (McGrew & Flanagan, 1998, p. 14)

Other differences between the Cattell-Horn and Carroll models were resolved more on the basis of factor-analytic studies than judgments regarding practical relevance to cross-battery assessment. The abilities labeled "quantitative knowledge" and "reading/writing" were conceived of as distinct broad abilities, much as they were by Horn and Cattell. McGrew and Flanagan drew heavily on Carroll's (1993) writings for definitions of many of the broad and narrow abilities listed and also for the codes for these abilities.

McGrew (2009) called on intelligence researchers to adopt CHC as a consensus model, thus allowing for a common nomenclature and theoretical framework. Toward that end, he established an online archive of over 460 correlation matrices that formed the basis of Carroll's factor-analytic work.[2] This resource was designed to allow researchers to test the CHC model using confirmatory factor analysis, a more powerful statistical technique than the exploratory factor analysis employed by Carroll.

> **JUST THINK . . .**
>
> Do you agree that $g$ has little practical relevance in educational settings?

At the very least, CHC theory as formulated by McGrew and Flanagan has great value from a heuristic standpoint. It compels practitioners and researchers alike to think about exactly how many human abilities really need to be measured and about how narrow or how broad an approach is optimal in terms of being clinically useful. Further, it stimulates researchers to revisit other existing theories that may be ripe for reexamination by means of statistical methods like factor analysis. The best features of such theories might then be combined with the goal of developing a clinically useful and actionable model of human abilities.

## The Information-Processing View

Another approach to conceptualizing intelligence derives from the work of the Russian neuropsychologist Aleksandr Luria (1966a, 1966b, 1970, 1973, 1980). This approach focuses on the mechanisms by which information is processed—*how* information is processed, rather than *what* is processed. Two basic types of information-processing styles, simultaneous and successive, have been distinguished (Das et al., 1975; Luria, 1966a, 1966b). In **simultaneous** (or **parallel**) **processing,** information is integrated all at one time. In **successive** (or **sequential**) **processing,** each bit of information is individually processed in sequence. As its name implies, sequential processing is logical and analytic

---

2. The archived data is available through the Woodcock-Muñoz Foundation's Human Cognitive Abilities (WMF HCA) project at *http://www.iapsych.com/wmfhcaarchive/map.htm*

in nature; piece by piece and one piece after the other, information is arranged and rearranged so that it makes sense. In trying to anticipate who the murderer is while watching *Law & Order,* for example, one's thinking could be characterized as sequential. The viewer constantly integrates bits of information that will lead to a solution of the "whodunnit?" problem. Memorizing a telephone number or learning the spelling of a new word is typical of the types of tasks that involve acquisition of information through successive processing.

By contrast, *simultaneous* processing may be described as "synthesized." Information is integrated and synthesized at once and as a whole. As you stand before and appreciate a painting in an art museum, the information conveyed by the painting is processed in a manner that, at least for most of us, could reasonably be described as simultaneous. Of course, art critics and connoisseurs may be exceptions to this general rule. In general, tasks that involve the simultaneous mental representations of images or information involve simultaneous processing. Map reading is another task that is typical of such processing.

Some tests—such as the Kaufman Assessment Battery for Children, second edition (KABC-II; discussed in Chapter 11)—rely heavily on this concept of a distinction between successive and simultaneous information processing. The strong influence of an information-processing perspective is also evident in the work of others (Das, 1972; Das et al., 1975; Naglieri, 1989, 1990; Naglieri & Das, 1988) who have developed the **PASS model** of intellectual functioning, where PASS is an acronym for planning, attention, simultaneous, and successive. In this model, *planning* refers to strategy development for problem solving; *attention* (also referred to as *arousal*) refers to receptivity to information; and *simultaneous* and *successive* refer to the type of information processing employed. Proponents of the PASS model have argued that existing tests of intelligence do not adequately assess planning. Naglieri and Das (1997) developed the Cognitive Assessment System (CAS), a cognitive ability test expressly designed to tap PASS factors. Although these test authors presented evidence to support the construct validity of the CAS, and some other studies have been similarly supportive (Huang et al., 2010; Feiz et al., 2010), questions remain as to whether the test actually measures what it purports to measure (Keith & Kranzler, 1999; Keith et al., 2001; Kranzler & Keith, 1999; Kranzler et al., 2000).

Robert Sternberg proposed another information-processing approach to intelligence, arguing that "the essence of intelligence is that it provides a means to govern ourselves so that our thoughts and actions are organized, coherent, and responsive to both our internally driven needs and to the needs of the environment" (Sternberg, 1986, p. 141). He proposed a triarchic theory of intelligence with three principal elements: metacomponents, performance components, and knowledge-acquisition components. Metacomponents are involved in planning what one is going to do, monitoring what one is doing, and evaluating what one has done upon completion. Performance components administer the instructions of metacomponents. Knowledge-acquisition components are involved in "learning how to do something in the first place" (Sternberg, 1994, p. 221). Elaborating on cross-cultural research suggesting that not all intelligence is of the variety that can be measured by IQ tests, Sternberg (1997b) introduced the notion of *successful intelligence.* **Successful intelligence** is gauged by the extent to which one effectively adapts, shares, shapes, and selects environments in a way that conforms to both personal and societal standards of success. Achieving success in most any culture is thought to depend on one's analytic, creative, and practical abilities, as well as an overall ability to capitalize on strengths and to compensate for shortcomings.

**JUST THINK. . .**

What kinds of tasks might be on a test purporting to measure "successful intelligence"? How might such tasks be useful in cross-cultural measurements of "successful intelligence"?

Now that you have some background on the various ways in which intelligence has been conceptualized, let's briefly look at some of the ways developers have endeavored to measure it. In the chapters that follow, we will look more closely at specific tests created to measure intelligence.

## Measuring Intelligence

The measurement of intelligence entails sampling an examinee's performance on different types of tests and tasks as a function of developmental level. At all developmental levels, the intellectual assessment process also provides a standardized situation from which the examinee's approach to the various tasks can be closely observed. It therefore provides an opportunity for an assessment that in itself can have great utility in settings as diverse as schools, the military, and business organizations. Of course, as our guest assessment professional, Dr. Barbara Pavlo, will tell you, obtaining an estimate of a client's measured intelligence is part of a typical clinical evaluation (see *Meet an Assessment Professional*).

### Types of Tasks Used in Intelligence Tests

In infancy (the period from birth through 18 months), intellectual assessment consists primarily of measuring sensorimotor development. This includes, for example, the measurement of nonverbal motor responses such as turning over, lifting the head, sitting up, following a moving object with the eyes, imitating gestures, and reaching for a group of objects (Figure 9–3). The examiner who attempts to assess the intellectual

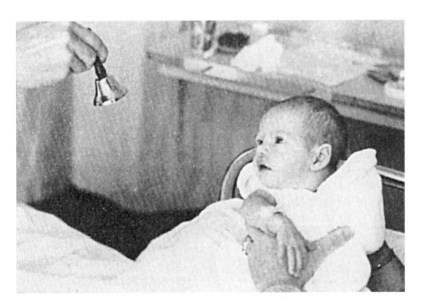

**Figure 9–3**
**Testing the Alerting Response**

*One assessment technique common to infant development tests is a test of the alerting response. The* **alerting** **response** *indicates an infant's capacity for responsiveness. It is deemed to be present when the infant's eyes brighten and widen—in contrast to the orienting response, which defines the response of turning in the direction of a stimulus. Here, the child is exhibiting an alerting response to the sound of the bell.*

## Meet Dr. Barbara C. Pavlo

"What tools of assessment do I use?" Perhaps a better question would be, "What tools of assessment *don't* I use?" I probably use interviews the most (sometimes structured, more often semi-structured) with written tests such as Beck's test (for assessment of depression and anxiety) a close second. But depending on the assessment objective, I can also use various other tools such as case history document analysis, behavioral observation, figure drawing analysis, and evaluations that employ role play. Each tool of assessment, including tests of intelligence, tests of personality, and tests used for neuropsychological screening can play an important role in providing key pieces to a psychological puzzle. Great artisans, craft people, and others who have earned respect and admiration for doing what they do have mastered the art of using the tools available to them to best advantage. Why should it be different for psychologists?

How do I use assessment data? I use it in the development, implementation, and fine-tuning of interventions. It helps greatly in terms of decisions concerning where to focus therapeutic efforts. It can be extremely useful in enlightening patients with little insight into their own condition. With some patients, a test can serve as a kind of "icebreaker" that opens floodgates of memories that had previously been stored and shelved neatly away. Most people who seek psychotherapy are eager to learn more about themselves, and valid tests, skillfully administered and interpreted, can put them on the fast track to doing just that. Moreover, when used in a so-called dynamic (test-intervention-retest) manner, tests can provide feedback to clients regarding their progress. And by the way, it's very

**Barbara C. Pavlo, Psy.D., Independent Practice, West Hills, California**

nice (and very useful) for therapists to get that feedback too. . . .

Many students aspiring to become psychologists go through school with visions of seeing themselves conducting psychotherapy. Relatively few students go through school with visions of seeing themselves administering psychological tests. This is unfortunate given the potentially great role psychological tests can play not only in clinical diagnosis and intervention, but in research. Take it from one who also gave little thought to assessment when she was an aspiring psychologist: This stuff is important, you need to know it, and the better you know it, the better your chances for success in whatever area of psychology you choose to work in.

*Read more of what Dr. Pavlo had to say— her complete essay—at www.mhhe.com/ cohentesting8.*

and related abilities of infants must be skillful in establishing and maintaining rapport with examinees who do not yet know the meaning of words like *cooperation* and *patience*. Typically, measures of infant intelligence rely to a great degree on information obtained from a structured interview with the examinee's parents, guardians, or other caretakers.

The focus in evaluation of the older child shifts to verbal and performance abilities. More specifically, the child may be called on to perform tasks designed to yield a measure of general fund of information, vocabulary, social judgment, language, reasoning, numerical concepts, auditory and visual memory, attention, concentration, and spatial visualization. The administration of many of the items may be preceded, as prescribed by the test manual, with teaching items designed to provide the examinee with practice in what is required by a particular test item.

In a bygone era, many intelligence tests were scored and interpreted with reference to the concept of mental age. **Mental age** is an index that refers to the chronological age equivalent of one's performance on a test or a subtest. This index was typically derived by reference to norms that indicate the age at which most testtakers are able to pass or otherwise meet some criterion performance.

Especially when individually administered by a trained professional, tests administered to children, much like tests individually administered to adults, afford the examiner a unique opportunity to observe an examinee's reactions to success, failure, and frustration. The examiner can see, up close, the examinee's general approach to problem solving and the test situation with its varied demands. Keen observation of such verbal and nonverbal behavior can yield a wealth of insights that in many cases will help bring to light hitherto unidentified assets and deficits and also help clarify ambiguities that arise in the test data. For schoolchildren, such observation may be useful in the service of a variety of objectives ranging from the individual tailoring of teaching agendas to class placement decisions.

According to Wechsler (1958), adult intelligence scales should tap abilities such as retention of general information, quantitative reasoning, expressive language and memory, and social judgment. The types of tasks used to reach these measurement objectives on the Wechsler scale for adults are the same as many of the tasks used on the Wechsler scales for children, although the content of specific items may vary. The fact that similar stimulus materials are used with children and adults has caused some to question whether children tend to be more motivated when presented with such materials (Marquette, 1976; Schaie, 1978) and whether the tasks fail to capture an adequate sampling of skills acquired by adults (Wesman, 1968). Publishers of intelligence tests have made available series of tests that can be used through a period that not quite, but almost, spans cradle to grave.

Note that tests of intelligence are seldom administered to adults for purposes of educational placement. Rather, they may be given to obtain clinically relevant information or some measure of learning potential and skill acquisition. Data from the administration of an adult intelligence test may be used to evaluate the faculties of an impaired individual (or one suspected of being senile, traumatized, or otherwise impaired) for the purpose of judging that person's competency to make important decisions (such as those regarding a will, a contract, or other legal matter). Insurance companies rely on such data to make determinations regarding disability. Data from adult intelligence tests may also be used to help make decisions about vocational and career decisions and transitions.

**JUST THINK . . .**

How else might data from adult intelligence tests be used?

More basic than age as a factor to consider when developing a test of intelligence is the foundation or theory of the test. Let's consider the role of theory in the development and the interpretation of data from intelligence tests.

## Theory in Intelligence Test Development and Interpretation

How one measures intelligence depends in large part on what one conceives intelligence to be. A chapter in Galton's (1869) *Hereditary Genius* entitled "Classification of Men

According to Their Natural Gifts" discussed sensory and other differences between people, which he believed were inherited. Perhaps not surprisingly, many Galtonian measures of cognitive ability were perceptual or sensorimotor in nature. Although Alfred Binet did write about the nature of intelligence, the formal theory with which the original Binet test is best associated is Carl Spearman's (1904) "universal unity of the intellective function," with $g$ as its centerpiece.

David Wechsler wrote extensively on what intelligence is, and he usually emphasized that it is multifaceted and consists not only of cognitive abilities but also of factors related to personality. Still, because his original test (the Wechsler-Bellevue, or W-B, Scale) as well as many of the Wechsler tests that followed provided for the calculation of a Verbal IQ and a Performance IQ, some have misinterpreted his position as representing a two-factor theory of intelligence: verbal abilities and performance abilities. Commenting on the development of the W-B and on the Verbal subtests (numbered 1 through 6) and the Performance subtests (numbered 7 through 11), Matarazzo (1972) explained:

> The grouping of the subtests into Verbal (1 to 6) and Performance (7 to 11), while intending to emphasize a dichotomy as regards possible types of ability called for by the individual tests, does *not* imply that these are the only abilities involved in the tests. Nor does it presume that there are different kinds of intelligence, e.g., verbal, manipulative, etc. It merely implies that these are different ways in which intelligence may manifest itself. The subtests are different measures of intelligence, not measures of different kinds of intelligence, and the dichotomy into Verbal and Performance areas is only one of several ways in which the tests could be grouped. (p. 196, emphasis in the original)

**JUST THINK . . .**

Name one factor that you believe is common to all intelligence tests. Explain why it is a common factor.

In an accompanying footnote, Matarazzo pointed out that the verbal and performance areas presumably coincided with the so-called primary factors of mental ability first postulated by Thurstone (1938). Regardless, decades of factor-analytic research on the Wechsler tests have pointed to the existence of more than two factors being tapped. Exactly how many factors are tapped by the various Wechsler tests and what they should be called have been matters of heated debate. And that brings us to an important point about theory and intelligence tests: Different theorists with different ideas about what factors are key in a theory of intelligence can look for (and probably find) their preferred factors in most widely used tests of intelligence.

**JUST THINK . . .**

Outline notes for your very own version of a "Thorndike Test of Intelligence." How will test items be grouped? What types of items would be found in each grouping? What types of summary scores might be reported for each testtaker? What types of interpretations would be made from the test data?

Beyond putting new interpretation-related templates over existing tests, new tests may be developed to measure the abilities and related factors described in a theory. Imagine what it might be like to develop a test of intelligence from a theory of intelligence. In fact, don't imagine it; try your hand at it! As an exercise in converting a theory of intelligence into a test of intelligence, consider the multifactor theory of intelligence developed by a pioneer in psychometrics, E. L. Thorndike. According to Thorndike (Thorndike et al., 1909; Thorndike et al., 1921), intelligence can be conceived in terms of three clusters of ability: social intelligence (dealing with people), concrete intelligence (dealing with objects), and abstract intelligence (dealing with verbal and mathematical symbols). Thorndike also incorporated a general mental ability factor ($g$) into the theory, defining it as the total number of modifiable neural connections or "bonds" available in the brain. For Thorndike, one's ability to learn is determined by the number and speed of the bonds that can be marshaled. No major test of intelligence was ever developed based on Thorndike's multifactor theory. *This is your moment!* Complete the *Just Think* exercise just above before reading on.

Even in the course of completing this *Just Think* exercise, you may have encountered some questions or issues about how a theory about intelligence can actually be applied in the development of an intelligence test. Well, welcome to the "real world," where test developers have long grappled with many questions and issues regarding intelligence in theory and intelligence in practice.

# Intelligence: Some Issues

## *Nature versus Nurture*

Although most behavioral scientists today believe that measured intellectual ability represents an interaction between (1) innate ability and (2) environmental influences, such a belief was not always popular. As early as the seventeenth century, *preformationism* began to gain a foothold, as scientists of the day made discoveries that seemed to support this doctrine. **Preformationism** holds that all living organisms are preformed at birth: All of an organism's structures, including intelligence, are preformed at birth and therefore cannot be improved upon. In 1672 one scientist reported that butterflies were preformed inside their cocoons and that their maturation was a result of an unfolding. In that same year, another scientist, this one studying chick embryos, generalized from his studies to draw a similar conclusion about humans (Malphigi, *De Formatione Pulli in Ovo*, 1672; cited in Needham, 1959, p. 167).

The invention of the compound microscope in the late seventeenth century provided a new tool with which preformationists could attempt to gather supportive evidence. Scientists confirmed their expectations by observing semen under the microscope. Various investigators "claimed to have seen a microscopic horse in the semen of a horse, an animalcule with very large ears in the semen of a donkey, and minute roosters in the semen of a rooster" (Hunt, 1961, p. 38; see Figure 9–4).

The influence of preformationist theory waned slowly as evidence inconsistent with it was brought forth. For example, the theory could not explain the regeneration

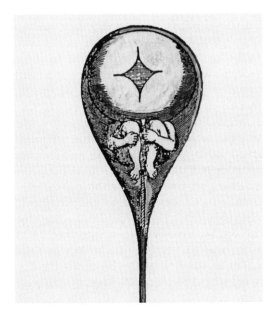

**Figure 9–4**
**A Human Sperm Cell According to a Preformationist**

*This is how Nicolaas Hartsoeker, a Dutch physicist and inventor of a type of microscope hypothesized the existence of homunculi (little men) to exist in human sperm in a 1694 essay entitled, "Essay on Dioptrics." Although it has been claimed that the drawing was a reproduction of what Hartsoeker saw through his microscope, Hill (1984) argued that Hartsoeker's drawings were designed to only suggest the possible appearance of homunculi.*

of limbs by crayfish and other organisms. With the progression of work in the area of genetics, preformationism as the dominant theory of development was slowly replaced by *predeterminism.* **Predeterminism** is the doctrine that holds that one's abilities are predetermined by genetic inheritance and that no amount of learning or other intervention can enhance what has been genetically encoded to unfold in time.

Experimental work with animals was often cited in support of the predeterminist position. For example, a study by Carmichael (1927) showed that newborn salamanders and frogs that had been anesthetized and deprived of an opportunity to swim swam at about the same time as unanesthetized controls. Carmichael's work did not take into consideration the influence of the environment in the swimming behavior of salamanders and frogs. In parallel studies with humans, Dennis and Dennis (1940) observed the development of walking behavior in Hopi Indian children. Comparisons were made between children who spent much of their first year of life bound to a cradle board and children who had spent no such time constricted. Their conclusion was that there was no significant difference between the two groups of children at time of onset of walking and that walking was not a skill that could be enhanced by practice. Walking was thus "proven" to be a human activity that unfolded with maturation.

Another proponent of the predeterminist view was Arnold Gesell. Generalizing from early twin studies that showed that practice had little effect on tasks such as climbing stairs, cutting with scissors, building with cubes, and buttoning buttons, Gesell (with Helen Thompson, 1929) concluded that "training does not transcend maturation." For Gesell, it was primarily the maturation of neural mechanisms, not learning or experience, that was most important in the development of what might be referred to as intelligence. Gesell described mental development as a "progressive morphogenesis of patterns of behavior" (Gesell et al., 1940, p. 7) and argued that behavior patterns are determined by "innate processes of growth" that he viewed as synonymous with maturation (Gesell, 1945). Gesell (1954, p. 335) described infancy as "the period in which the individual realizes his racial inheritance" and argued that this inheritance was "the end product of evolutionary processes that trace back to an extremely remote antiquity."

Is intelligence genetically encoded, unfolding with maturation? Or does the learning environment account for our intelligence? Nature–nurture questions like these have been raised for as long as there have been concepts of intelligence and tests to measure those concepts—sometimes amid great publicity and controversy. Galton firmly believed that genius was hereditary, a belief that was expressed in works such as *Hereditary Genius* (1869) and *English Men of Science* (1874). Galton came to these conclusions not on the basis of intelligence tests (which had not yet been devised) but rather on the basis of family histories of eminent people. In doing so, he greatly minimized the role of environmental enrichment.

Richard Dugdale, another predeterminist, argued that degeneracy, like genius, was also inherited. Dugdale (1877) traced the immoral, lecherous lineage of the infamous Jukes family and hypothesized that the observed trail of poverty, harlotry, and laziness was a matter of heredity. Complementing the work of Dugdale was Henry Goddard's book, *The Kallikak Family* (1912), another work based on faulty research that purported to document the role of heredity in feeblemindedness (discussed in our Chapter 2 *Close-Up*). Geneticists of the day refuted the idea that feeblemindedness was the product of a single gene. Experimentation with simple organisms such as fruit flies had suggested that inheritance of even simple traits was a very complex matter. A basic flaw in Goddard's argument lay in the fact that he conceptualized feeblemindedness as the product of a recessive gene. Even if this were true, a feebleminded son or daughter would have had to inherit the gene from *both* parents—the "normal" one as well as the "feebleminded" one.

By the mid-1920s, Goddard had begun to distance himself from theories of mental defect based on heredity. Still, he seemed forever haunted by his work, which ardent eugenicists continued to cite in support of their causes.

Based on his testing of a sample of Mexican and Native American children, Lewis M. Terman—the father of the American version of Binet's test—concluded that people from these cultures were genetically inferior. The noted English statistician Karl Pearson wrote that, as compared with the native British, immigrating Jews were "somewhat inferior physiologically and mentally" (Pearson & Moul, 1925, p. 126). Such observations seem flawed, even prejudiced—if not racist—by current standards, yet they reflected the prevailing beliefs of the day.

**JUST THINK . . .**

Eugenics remains very much alive in the twenty-first century. What accounts for its appeal? How can assessment professionals shed light on the issues?

Although a scholarly consideration of the role of environmental and cultural factors (not to mention language barriers) is lacking in the writings of many behavioral scientists of the early twentieth century, a research literature that shed light on the environment side of the hereditary–environment issue subsequently began to mount. It was found, for example, that when identical twins are reared apart they still show remarkably similar intelligence test scores, though not as similar as if they had been reared together (Johnson, 1963; Newman et al., 1937). Children born to poverty-stricken parents but then adopted at an early age by better-educated, middle-class families tend to have higher intelligence test scores than their counterparts who are not adopted by families of higher socioeconomic status—although the natural mothers with the higher IQs tend to have the children with the higher IQs, irrespective of the family in which the adopted child is raised (Leahy, 1932, 1935). A more recent study focusing on related nature–nurture issues concluded that level of parental education, rather than parental income, was of primary importance in predicting the IQ of Portuguese adolescents (Lemos et al., 2011).

To be sure, nature–nurture questions regarding intelligence have a long history of debate and controversy (see, for example, Deary et al., 2009; Frumkin, 1997; Herrnstein & Murray, 1994; Lynn, 1997; Neisser et al., 1996; Reed, 1997; Velden, 1997). One contemporary group of researchers who believe that intelligence and related abilities have a very strong basis in genetics is the architect of a **Verbal, Perceptual, and Image Rotation (VPR) model** of the structure of mental abilities. The VPR model, conceived by Wendy Johnson and her associates (Johnson et al., 2007; Johnson & Bouchard, 2005a; 2005b), is a hierarchical one with a $g$ factor that contributes to verbal, perceptual, and image rotation abilities as well as to eight abilities of a more specialized nature. In one study employing twin data, Johnson et al. (2007) estimated that genetic influences accounted for much of the variance in measured mental abilities.

In general, proponents of the "nurture" side of the nature–nurture controversy emphasize the crucial importance of factors such as prenatal and postnatal environment, socioeconomic status, educational opportunities, and parental modeling with respect to intellectual development. Proponents of this view characteristically suspect that opposing arguments that champion the role of nature in the controversy are based more on political leanings and the like than on sound, impartial scientific inquiry and analysis. Somewhere between the rhetoric arguing that heredity plays *no* part in intelligence (Kamin, 1974) and assertions such as "Nature has color-coded groups of individuals so that statistically reliable predictions of their adaptability to intellectually rewarding and effective lives can easily be made and profitably be used by the pragmatic man-in-the-street" (Shockley, 1971, p. 375) lies the middle ground of the interactionist position: that

**Figure 9–5**
**What Does It Take to Win?**

*During the 1998 Winter Olympics in Nagano, Japan, the world looked on as Tara Lipinski became the youngest figure skater in Olympic history to win the gold. What does it take to do that? To what extent is such an accomplishment a matter of genes, training, motivation, and other factors?*

intelligence, as measured by intelligence tests, is the result of the interaction between heredity and environment.

**Inheritance and interactionism**   People differ in intelligence levels just as they differ in blood pressure levels, cerebrospinal fluid levels, sensitivity to pain (Sheffield et al., 2000), and many other characteristics. Once that is understood, it is natural to wonder *why* people differ in intellectual abilities. According to the interactionist view, people inherit a certain intellectual potential. Exactly how much of that genetic potential is realized depends partially on the type of environment in which it is nurtured. No one to date has inherited X-ray vision or the ability to fly. You might spend your entire life in libraries or on mountaintops visiting gurus, but all your studies cannot result in acquiring the ability to fly or to see through things because those abilities are not encoded in your genetic makeup.

The interactionist perspective on intellectual development can be conceived as an extremely optimistic one. According to this view, we are free to become all that we can be. The notion that we can use the environment to push our genetic potential to the limit can be illustrated most graphically by reference to dedicated athletes (Figure 9–5).

One interactionist perspective focuses on the differential impact of hereditary and environment as a result of one's developmental stage. There is research to suggest that the hereditary influence on intelligence increased from 41% in childhood, to 55% in adolescence, and to 66% in late adolescence and early adulthood (Haworth et al., 2010). A possible explanation for this counterintuitive finding was that, as they age, people increasingly modify their environment to complement genetic tendencies. At the risk of oversimplification, "we create experiences that suit our genes." Further support for this variety of interactionism comes from a study that examined the genetic underpinnings of many lifetime experiences of twins (Vinkhuyzen et al., 2010). These researchers found that genetics had a relatively strong effect on many childhood experiences (e.g., being bullied in primary school), social environment and behavior (e.g., having children), leisure time activities (e.g., current musical activity), and various life events.

## The Stability of Intelligence

Although research on the stability of measured intelligence in young children has yielded mixed findings (Dougherty & Haith, 1997; Lamp & Krohn, 1990; Smith et al., 1988; Wesman, 1968), intelligence does seem to be stable for much of one's adult life (Birren & Schaie, 1985; Shock et al., 1984; Youngjohn & Crook, 1993). Using archival intelligence test data from World War II, Gold et al. (1995) administered the same intelligence test to a sample of 326 veterans some 40 years later. In general, the data pointed to stability in measured intelligence over time. Increases in vocabulary were noted, as were decreases in arithmetic, verbal analogies, and other nonverbal skills. The researchers concluded that young adult intelligence was the most important determinant of cognitive performance as an older adult. Longitudinal research on adult intelligence, especially with older subjects, can be complicated by many factors: the extent to which one remains mentally active (Kaufman, 1990), physical health (Birren, 1968; Palmore, 1970), and myriad other potentially confounding factors (ranging from medication to personality). It is also important to distinguish between *group* similarities and differences in cognitive abilities over time and *intra-individual* similarities and differences. Full Scale IQs may seem to remain the same over time, although the individual abilities assessed may change significantly (Smith, Smith, et al., 2000).

Ivnik and colleagues (Ivnik et al., 1995; Malec et al., 1993) noted that, in many studies conducted over time, group means and standard deviations would seem to point to the conclusion that cognitive abilities are remarkably stable over the course of adult life. However, in a sample of normal adults, a focus on aging-related, within-individual variability in cognitive abilities may lead to a different conclusion. Ivnik et al. (1995) found verbal intellectual skills to be highly stable over time, with delayed free recall of newly learned information being the least stable of the cognitive abilities they surveyed. The researchers concluded: "These data challenge the assumption that normal persons' cognitive abilities are stable over long periods of time. In actuality, none of the general cognitive abilities measured in this study is absolutely stable, although some are more stable than others" (p. 160).

In later adulthood, especially after age 75, a decline in cognitive abilities has been noted (Nettelbeck & Rabbit, 1992; Ryan et al., 1990; Storandt, 1994). One study compared the performance of medical doctors over the age of 75 to the performance of younger colleagues on measures of cognitive ability. The performance of the elder physicians was about 26% lower than that of the younger group (Powell, 1994). The fact that cognitive abilities decline in older adulthood may come as no surprise. What might well come as a surprise is that some aspects of that decline may begin as early as one's 20s or 30s (Salthouse, 2009).

A popular stereotype that once existed about very bright children was "early ripe, early rot." A longitudinal study initiated by Terman at Stanford University in 1921 would subsequently expose this belief as myth. Terman and his colleagues identified 1,528 children (with an average age of 11) whose measured intelligence placed them within the top 1% in the country in intellectual functioning.[3] Terman followed these children for the remainder of his own life, taking measures of achievement, physical and social development, books read, character traits, and recreational interests. He conducted interviews with parents, teachers, and the subjects themselves. Some of the findings were published four years after the study had begun (Terman et al., 1925), although other researchers continued to collect and analyze data (Oden, 1968; Sears, 1977; Holahan & Sears, 1995). In general, the Terman studies suggested that gifted children tended to maintain their superior intellectual ability.

**JUST THINK . . .**

How might your life differ if you believed that your measured IQ was significantly higher than it actually is? By the way, to better understand the stimulus for this exercise, read footnote 3.

---

3. The children followed in the Terman study were humorously referred to as **"Termites."** One Termite, Lee Cronbach, would himself later earn his place as a luminary in the field of psychometrics. However, as Hirsch (1997) reported, Cronbach believed that serious errors were made in the scoring of the Termites' intelligence test protocols. Cronbach (cited in Hirsch, 1997, p. 214) reflected that "Terman was looking for high IQs and his assistants provided them. . . . Sears [a Stanford colleague of Terman] has found and recalculated my own IQ and it turns out that I have lived my life with an IQ that was 10 points too high."

In contrast to Terman's conclusion is more recent work that suggests there may be a point at which gifted children cease to pursue or exploit their gift. Winner (2000) writes that child prodigies may become "frozen into expertise." By this she meant that the public acclaim garnered by these prodigies may make it increasingly difficult for them to break away from their acknowledged expertise. Also, after having been pushed so hard by family or others to achieve at an early age, gifted children may lose motivation as adults (Winner, 1996).

From the Terman studies, we also know that the gifted tend to have lower mortality rates and to be in better physical and mental health than their nongifted counterparts. They tend to hold moderate political and social views and tend to be successful in educational and vocational pursuits. They commit less crime than the nongifted. This all sounds fine. But just as there is usually another side to other gifts, such as fame or fortune, there is another side to being gifted—see this chapter's *Everyday Psychometrics.*

## The Construct Validity of Tests of Intelligence

The evaluation of a test's construct validity proceeds on the assumption that one knows in advance exactly what the test is supposed to measure. For intelligence tests, it is essential to understand how the test developer defined intelligence. If, for example, *intelligence* were defined in a particular intelligence test as Spearman's $g$, then we would expect factor analysis of this test to yield a single large common factor. Such a factor would indicate that the different questions or tasks on the test largely reflected the same underlying characteristic (intelligence, or $g$). By contrast, if intelligence were defined by a test developer in accordance with Guilford's theory, then no one factor would be expected to dominate. Instead, one would anticipate many different factors reflecting a diverse set of abilities. Recall that, from Guilford's perspective, there is no single underlying intelligence for the different test items to reflect. This means that there would be no basis for a large common factor.

In a sense, a compromise between Spearman and Guilford is Thorndike. Thorndike's theory of intelligence leads us to look for one central factor reflecting $g$ along with three additional factors representing social, concrete, and abstract intelligences. In this case, an analysis of the test's construct validity would ideally suggest that testtakers' responses to specific items reflected in part a general intelligence but also different types of intelligence: social, concrete, and abstract.

## Other Issues

Measured intelligence may vary as a result of factors related to the measurement process. Just a few of the many factors that can affect measured intelligence are a test author's definition of intelligence, the diligence of the examiner, the amount of feedback the examiner gives the examinee (Vygotsky, 1978), the amount of previous practice or coaching the examinee has had, and the competence of the person interpreting the test data. There are many other factors that can cause measured intelligence to vary. One of those factors is what has become known as the "Flynn effect."

**The Flynn effect**   James R. Flynn, while at the Department of Political Studies at the University of Otago in Dunedin, New Zealand, published findings that caused those who study and use intelligence tests in the United States to take notice. In his article entitled "The Mean IQ of Americans: Massive Gains 1932 to 1978," Flynn (1984) presented compelling evidence of what might be termed *intelligence inflation.* He found that measured intelligence seems to rise on average, year by year, starting with

## Being Gifted

### Who Is Gifted?

An informal answer to the question "Who is gifted?" might be "one whose performance is consistently remarkable in any positively valued area" (Witty, 1940, p. 516). Criteria for **giftedness** cited in legislation such as PL 95-561 include intellectual ability ("consistently superior"), creative thinking, leadership ability, ability in performing arts, and mechanical or other psychomotor aptitudes. To that list, others have added many other variables ranging from diversity of interests to love of metaphors, abstract ideas, and novelty. The origin of giftedness is a matter of debate, but factors such as heredity, atypical brain organization (Hassler & Gupta, 1993; O'Boyle et al., 1994), and environmental influences, including family environment (Gottfried et al., 1994), are frequently cited.

### Identifying the Gifted

Tests of intelligence may aid in the identification of members of special populations at all points in the possible range of human abilities—including that group of exceptional people collectively referred to as "the gifted." As you may suspect, exactly who is identified as gifted may sometimes vary as a function of the measuring instrument. Wechsler tests of intelligence are commonly used. They contain subtests that are labeled "Verbal" and subtests that are labeled "Performance." A composite or Full Scale score thought to reflect overall intelligence has in some cases been used (sometimes along with other measures) to identify the gifted.

The Wechsler Full Scale score has been questioned because it obscures superior performance on individual subtests if the record as a whole is not superior. The Full Scale score further obscures a significant discrepancy, if one exists, between the Verbal and Performance scores. Additionally, each of the subtests does not contribute equally to overall intelligence. In one study that employed gifted students as subjects, Malone et al. (1991) cautioned that their findings might be affected by a **ceiling effect.** That is, some of the test items were not sufficiently challenging—had too low a "ceiling"—to accurately gauge the gifted students' ability. A greater range of items at the high end of the difficulty continuum would have been preferable. Malone et al. (1991, p. 26) further cautioned that "the use of the overall IQ score to classify students as gifted, or as a criterion for acceptance into special advanced programs, may contribute to the lack of recognition of the ability of some students."

*Anyone who has ever watched the* E! True Hollywood Story *knows that fame isn't always all that it seems to be. In each episode of that series, viewers are taken on a journey through what may be referred to as the "flip side of Hollywood's walk of fame." The inevitable moral of each story is that fame, fortune, and other gifts can come with a price. Giftedness is no exception. After some background about what giftedness is and how it is identified, we present some considerations about its possible costs.*

Identification of the gifted should ideally be made not simply on the basis of an intelligence test but also on the basis of the goals of the program for which the test is being conducted. Thus, for example, if an assessment program is undertaken to identify gifted writers, common sense indicates that a component of the assessment program should be a writing sample taken from the examinee and evaluated by an authority. It is true, however, that the most effective and most frequently used instrument for identifying gifted children is an intelligence test.

*(continued)*

## Being Gifted *(continued)*

School systems screening for candidates for gifted programs might employ a group test for the sake of economy. A group test frequently employed for this purpose is the Otis-Lennon School Ability Test. To screen for social abilities or aptitudes, tests such as the Differential Aptitude Test or Guilford et al.'s (1974) Structure-of-Intellect (SOI) test may be administered. Creativity might be assessed through the use of the SOI, through personality and biographical inventories (Davis, 1989), or through other measures of creative thinking.

Other tools of assessment used to identify the gifted include case studies, behavior rating scales, and nominating techniques. A **nominating technique** is a method of peer appraisal in which members of a class, team, work unit, or other type of group are asked to select (or nominate) people in response to a question or statement. Class members, parents, or teachers might be asked questions such as "Who has the most leadership ability?" "Who has the most original ideas?" and "Who would you most like to help you with this project?" Although teacher nomination is a widely used method of identifying gifted children, it is not necessarily the most reliable one (French, 1964; Gallagher, 1966; Jacobs, 1970; Tuttle & Becker, 1980). The gifted child may be a misbehaving child whose misbehavior is due to boredom with the low level of the material presented. The gifted child may ask questions of or make comments to the teacher that the teacher doesn't understand or misconstrues as smart-alecky. Clark (1988) outlined specific behaviors that gifted children may display in the classroom.

### The Pros and Cons of Giftedness

Most people can readily appreciate and list many benefits of being gifted. Depending on the nature of their gifts, gifted children may, for example, read at an age when their nongifted peers are learning the alphabet, do algebra at an age when their nongifted peers are learning addition, or

play a musical instrument with expert proficiency at an age when their nongifted peers are struggling with introductory lessons. The gifted child can earn admiration and respect, and the gifted adult may add to that a certain level of financial freedom.

The downside of being gifted is not as readily apparent. As Plucker and Levy (2001) remind us,

> many talented people are not happy, regardless of whether they become experts in their fields. The literature contains a growing number of studies of underachievers who fail to develop their talents and achieve personal fulfillment. Furthermore, even the happiest, most talented individuals must face considerable personal and professional roadblocks emanating from their talent. The process of achieving professional success and personal happiness and adjustment involves overcoming many common, interrelated challenges. (p. 75)

Plucker and Levy (2001) cited the widely held assumption that "the gifted will do just fine" as a challenge to be overcome. Other challenges that must frequently be overcome by gifted individuals include depression and feelings of isolation (Jacobsen, 1999), sometimes to the point of suicidal ideation, gestures, or action (Weisse, 1990). Such negative feeling states may arise, at least in part, as a result of cultural pressure to be average or "normal" and even from stigma associated with talent and giftedness (Cross et al., 1991, 1993). Plucker and Levy add that there are self-imposed pressures, which often lead to long hours of study or practice—not without consequence:

> Being talented, or exceptional in almost any other way, entails a number of personal sacrifices. These sacrifices are not easy, especially when the issue is maintaining relationships, having a family, or maintaining a desirable quality of life. We would all like to believe that a person can work hard and develop his or her talent with few ramifications, but this is simply not realistic. (Plucker & Levy, 2001, p. 75)

the year for which the test is normed. The rise in measured IQ is not accompanied by any academic dividend and so is not thought to be due to any actual rise in "true intelligence." The phenomenon has since been well documented not only in the United States but in other countries as well (Flynn, 1988, 2007). The **Flynn effect** is thus a shorthand reference to the progressive rise in intelligence test scores that is expected to occur on a normed test intelligence from the date when the test was first normed. According to Flynn (2000), the exact amount of the rise in IQ will vary as a function of several factors, such as how culture-specific the items are and whether the measure used is one of fluid or crystallized intelligence.

Beyond being a phenomenon of academic interest, the Flynn effect has wide-ranging, real-world implications and consequences. Flynn (2000) sarcastically advised examiners who want the children they test to be eligible for special services to use the most recently normed version of an intelligence test. On the other hand, examiners who want the children they test to escape the stigma of any labeling were advised to use "the oldest test they can get away with," which should, according to Flynn, allow for at least 10 points' leeway in measured intelligence. At the very least, examiners who use intelligence tests to make important decisions need to be aware of a possible Flynn effect, especially at the beginning or near the end of the test's norming cycle (Kanaya et al., 2003).

> **JUST THINK . . .**
>
> What is your opinion regarding the ethics of Flynn's advice to psychologists and educators who examine children for placement in special classes?

There are numerous other, everyday potential consequences of the Flynn effect ranging from eligibility for special services at school to eligibility for social security benefits. One potential consequence of the Flynn effect has to do with an issue of no less importance than whether one will live or die. Soon after the U.S. Supreme Court ruled it illegal to execute a person who suffers from mental retardation (*Atkins v. Virginia*, 2002), many criminal defense attorneys started familiarizing themselves with the Flynn effect, and investigating whether or not clients accused of capital crimes had been evaluated with an older test—one that spuriously inflated measured intelligence, thereby making such defendants eligible for execution (Fletcher et al., 2010). As might be expected, the ethics of such defense tactics have been questioned, especially because there seems to be sufficient variability in the Flynn effect leading researchers to conclude that not everyone's scores are affected in the same way (Hagan et al., 2010; Zhou et al., 2010).

From a less applied, and more academic perspective, consideration of the Flynn effect can be used to shed light on theories, and to help support or disprove them. For example, Cattell (1971) wrote that fluid intelligence (a product of heredity) formed the basis for crystallized intelligence (a product of learning and the environment). If Cattell was correct, we might expect generational gains in IQ to be due to increased crystallized intelligence—this as a result of factors such as improvements in education, greater educational opportunities for people, and greater cognitive demands in the workplace (Colom et al., 2007). However, according to Flynn (2009), most of the observed increases in IQ have been in the realm of fluid intelligence. Some research has been designed to address this issue (Rindermann et al., 2010) but the results have been equivocal, with partial support for both Cattell and Flynn.

> **JUST THINK . . .**
>
> In your opinion, are generational gains in measured intelligence due more to factors related more to heredity, environment, or some combination of both?

Now let's briefly consider some other factors that—to a greater or lesser degree—may play a role in measured intelligence: personality, gender, family environment, and culture.

**Personality** Sensitive to the manifestations of intelligence in *all* human behavior, Alfred Binet had conceived of the study of intelligence as being synonymous with the study of personality. David Wechsler (1958) also believed that all tests of intelligence measure traits of personality, such as drive, energy level, impulsiveness, persistence, and goal awareness. More contemporary researchers have also taken note of the great overlap between intelligence and personality (Ackerman & Heggestad, 1997;

**JUST THINK . . .**

To what extent are measured intelligence and measured personality reciprocal in nature? That is, can one's personality affect measured intelligence? Can one's intelligence affect measured personality?

Chamorro-Premuzic & Furnham, 2006; Furnham et al., 2007; Reeve et al., 2005; Sternberg et al., 2003). The concept of "street efficacy" is one that would certainly seem to lie at the crossroads of intelligence and personality—if not firmly within the bounds of each (see Figure 9–6).

Longitudinal and cross-sectional studies of children have explored the relationship between various personality characteristics and measured intelligence. Aggressiveness with peers, initiative, high need for achievement, competitive striving, curiosity, self-confidence, and emotional stability are some personality factors associated with gains in measured intelligence over time. Passivity, dependence, and maladjustment are some of the factors present in children whose measured intellectual ability has not increased over time.

In discussions of the role of personality in the measured intelligence of infants, the term *temperament* (rather than *personality*) is typically employed. In this context, **temperament** may be defined as the distinguishing manner of the child's observable actions and reactions. Evidence suggests that infants differ quite markedly in temperament on a number of dimensions, including vigor of responding, general activity rate, restlessness during sleep, irritability, and "cuddliness" (Chess & Thomas, 1973). Temperament can affect an infant's measured intellectual ability in that irritable, restless children who do not enjoy being held have a negative reciprocal influence on their parents—and perhaps on test administrators as well. Parents are less likely to want to pick such children up and spend more time with them. They may therefore be less likely to engage in activities with them that are known to stimulate intellectual

**Figure 9–6**
**"Knowing" the Streets**

*A person who "knows his (or her) way around the streets" is referred to as "streetwise" or as possessing "street smarts." This characteristic—which has absolutely nothing to do with map-reading ability—may also be thought of as street efficacy, which has been formally defined as "the perceived ability to avoid violent confrontations and to be safe in one's neighborhood" (Sharkey, 2006). Question: Is this characteristic a personality trait, an aspect of intelligence, or something of a "hybrid"?*

development, such as talking to them (White, 1971). One longitudinal study that began with assessment of temperament at age 3 and followed subjects through a personality assessment at age 21 concluded that differences in temperament were associated with differences in health risk–related behaviors such as dangerous driving, alcohol dependence, unsafe sex, and violent crime (Caspi et al., 1997).

**Gender**  A great deal of research has been conducted on differences between males and females with regard to cognitive, motor, and other abilities related to intelligence. Although some differences have been found consistently, their exact significance has been a matter of controversy (Halpern, 1997). For examples, males may have the edge when it comes to the *g* factor in intelligence (Jackson & Rushton, 2006; Lynn & Irwing, 2004), especially when only the highest-scoring group on an ability test is considered (Deary et al., 2007). Males also tend to outperform females on tasks requiring visual spatialization. However, there is suggestive evidence indicating that more experience in spatialization might be all that is required to bridge this gender gap (Chan, 2007). Girls may generally outperform on language skill–related tasks, although these differences may be minimized when the assessment is conducted by computer (Horne, 2007). On the basis of their research on motor performance with a population of "typically developing children," Larson et al. (2007) concluded that motor development follows a gender-specific developmental course. They advocated the use of separate gender and age norms when clinically assessing motor function in children. Reasons advanced to account for observed gender differences have been psychosocial (Eccles, 1987) as well as physiological (Hines et al., 1992; Larson et al., 2007; Shaywitz et al., 1995).

**Family environment**  To what extent does family environment contribute to measured intelligence? The answer to this relatively straightforward question is complicated in part by the intrusion of nature–nurture issues, or issues of family environment versus genetic inheritance (Baumrind, 1993; Jackson, 1993; Scarr, 1992, 1993). At a minimum, we can begin by stating what we hope is the obvious: Children thrive in a loving home where their safety and welfare are of the utmost concern and where they are given ample opportunity for learning and growth. Beyond that, other environmental factors may affect measured intelligence, such as the presence of resources (Gottfried, 1984), parental use of language (Hart & Risley, 1992), parental expression of concern about achievement (Honzik, 1967), and parental explanation of discipline policies in a warm, democratic home environment (Baldwin et al., 1945; Kent & Davis, 1957; Sontag et al., 1958). Divorce may bring with it many negative consequences ranging from the loss of residential stability to the loss of parental and extended family supports. As such, divorce may have significant consequences in the life of a child ranging from impaired school achievement to impaired social problem-solving ability (Guidubaldi & Duckworth, 2001).

> **JUST THINK . . .**
>
> What role would you attribute to your own family environment with regard to your intellectual abilities?

Let's also note that some have contended that "family environment" begins in the womb and that a "maternal effects" model may more satisfactorily integrate data than a "family effects" model (Devlin et al., 1997). In this regard, it has been reported that "twins, and especially monozygotic twins, can experience radically different intrauterine environments even though they share the womb at the same time" (B. Price, cited in McGue, 1997, p. 417).

**Culture**  Much of our discussion about the relationship between culture and psychological assessment in general applies to any consideration of the role of culture in measured intelligence. A culture provides specific models for thinking, acting, and feeling. Culture enables people to survive both physically and socially and to master and control the world around them (Chinoy, 1967). Because values may differ radically between cultural and subcultural groups, people from different cultural groups can have radically different views about what constitutes intelligence (Super, 1983; Wober, 1974). Because different cultural groups value and promote different types of abilities and pursuits, testtakers from different cultural groups can be expected to bring to a test situation differential levels of ability, achievement, and motivation. These differential levels may even find expression in measured perception and perceptual-motor skills.

Consider, for example, an experiment conducted with children who were members of a rural community in eastern Zambia. Serpell (1979) tested Zambian and English research subjects on a task involving the reconstruction of models using pencil and paper, clay, or wire. The English children did best on the paper-and-pencil reconstructions because those were the materials with which they were most familiar. By contrast, the Zambian children did best using wire because that was the medium with which they were most familiar. Both groups of children did about equally well using clay. Any conclusions about the subjects' ability to reconstruct models would have to be qualified with regard to the particular instrument used. This point could be generalized with regard to the use of most any instrument of evaluation or assessment; is it really tapping the ability it purports to tap, or is it tapping something else—especially when used with culturally different subjects or testtakers?

Items on a test of intelligence tend to reflect the culture of the society where the test is employed. To the extent that a score on such a test reflects the degree to which testtakers have been integrated into the society and the culture, it would be expected that members of subcultures (as well as others who, for whatever reason, choose not to identify themselves with the mainstream society) would score lower. In fact, Blacks (Baughman & Dahlstrom, 1968; Dreger & Miller, 1960; Lesser et al., 1965; Shuey, 1966), Hispanics (Gerry, 1973; Holland, 1960; Lesser et al., 1965; Mercer, 1976; Murray, 2007; Simpson, 1970), and Native Americans (Cundick, 1976) tend to score lower on intelligence tests than Whites or Asians (Flynn, 1991). These findings are controversial on many counts—ranging from the great diversity of the people who are grouped under each of these categories, to sampling differences (Zuckerman, 1990), as well as related definitional issues (Daley & Onwuegbuzie, 2011; Sternberg et al., 2005). The meaningfulness of such findings can be questioned further when claims of genetic difference are made owing to the difficulty of separating the effects of genes from effects of the environment. For an authoritative and readable account of the complex issues involved in making such separations, see Neisser et al. (1996).

Alfred Binet shared with many others the desire to develop a measure of intelligence as untainted as possible by factors such as prior education and economic advantages. The Binet-Simon test was designed to separate "natural intelligence from instruction" by "disregarding, insofar as possible, the degree of instruction which the subject possesses" (Binet & Simon, 1908/1961, p. 93). This desire to create what might be termed a **culture-free intelligence test** has resurfaced with various degrees of fervor throughout history. One assumption inherent in the development of such tests is that if cultural factors can be controlled then differences between cultural groups will be lessened. A related assumption is that the effect of culture can be controlled through the elimination of verbal items and the exclusive reliance on nonverbal, performance items. Nonverbal items were thought to represent the best available means for determining the cognitive ability of

**JUST THINK . . .**

Is it possible to create a culture-free test of intelligence? Is it desirable to create one?

minority group children and adults. However logical this assumption may seem on its face, it has not been borne out in practice (see, e.g., Cole & Hunter, 1971; McGurk, 1975).

Exclusively nonverbal tests of intelligence have not lived up to the high expectations of their developers. They have not been found to have the same high level of predictive validity as more verbally loaded tests. This may be due to the fact that nonverbal items do not sample the same psychological processes as do the more verbally loaded, conventional tests of intelligence. Whatever the reason, nonverbal tests tend not to be very good at predicting success in various academic and business settings. Perhaps this is so because such settings require at least some verbal facility.

The idea of developing a truly culture-free test has had great intuitive appeal but has proven to be a practical impossibility. All tests of intelligence reflect, to a greater or lesser degree, the culture in which they were devised and will be used. Stated another way, intelligence tests differ in the extent to which they are *culture-loaded.*

**Culture loading** may be defined as the extent to which a test incorporates the vocabulary, concepts, traditions, knowledge, and feelings associated with a particular culture. A test item such as "Name three words for snow" is a highly culture-loaded item—one that draws heavily from the Eskimo culture, where many words exist for snow. Testtakers from Brooklyn would be hard put to come up with more than one word for snow (well, maybe two, if you count *slush*).

Soon after it became evident that no test could legitimately be called "culture free," a number of tests referred to as *culture fair* began to be published. We may define a **culture-fair intelligence test** as a test or assessment process designed to minimize the influence of culture with regard to various aspects of the evaluation procedures, such as administration instructions, item content, responses required of testtakers, and interpretations made from the resulting data. Table 9–2 lists techniques used to reduce the culture loading of tests. Note that—in contrast to the factor-analytic concept of *factor loading,* which can be quantified—the *culture loading* of a test tends to involve more of a subjective, qualitative, nonnumerical judgment.

The rationale for culture-fair test items was to include only those tasks that seemed to reflect experiences, knowledge, and skills common to all different cultures. In addition, all the tasks were designed to be motivating to all groups (Samuda, 1982). An attempt

**Table 9–2**
**Ways of Reducing the Culture Loading of Tests**

| Culture Loaded | Culture Loading Reduced |
| --- | --- |
| Paper-and-pencil tasks | Performance tests |
| Printed instructions | Oral instructions |
| Oral instructions | Pantomime instructions |
| No preliminary practice | Preliminary practice items |
| Reading required | Purely pictorial |
| Pictorial (objects) | Abstract figural |
| Written response | Oral response |
| Separate answer sheet | Answers written on test itself |
| Language | Nonlanguage |
| Speed tests | Power tests |
| Verbal content | Nonverbal content |
| Specific factual knowledge | Abstract reasoning |
| Scholastic skills | Nonscholastic skills |
| Recall of past-learned information | Solving novel problems |
| Content graded from familiar to rote | All item content highly familiar |
| Difficulty based on rarity of content | Difficulty based on complexity of relation education |

Source: Jensen (1980).

was made to minimize the importance of factors such as verbal skills thought to be responsible for the lower mean scores of various minority groups. Therefore, the culture-fair tests tended to be nonverbal and to have simple, clear directions administered orally by the examiner. The nonverbal tasks typically consisted of assembling, classifying, selecting, or manipulating objects and drawing or identifying geometric designs. Some sample items from the Cattell Culture Fair Test are illustrated in this chapter's *Close-up.*

Reducing culture loading of intelligence tests seems to lead to a parallel decrease in the value of the test. Culture-fair tests have been found to lack the hallmark of traditional tests of intelligence: predictive validity. Not only that, minority group members still tended to score lower on these tests than did majority group members. Various subcultural characteristics have been presumed to penalize unfairly some minority group members who take intelligence tests that are culturally loaded with American White, middle-class values. Some have argued, for example, that Americans living in urban ghettos share common beliefs and values that are quite different from those of mainstream America. Included among these common beliefs and values, for example, are a "live for today" orientation and a reliance on slang in verbal communication. Native Americans also share a common subculture with core values that may negatively influence their measured intelligence. Central to these values is the belief that individuals should be judged in terms of their relative contribution to the group, not in terms of their individual accomplishments. Native Americans also value their relatively unhurried, present time–oriented lifestyle (Foerster & Little Soldier, 1974).

Frustrated by their seeming inability to develop culture-fair equivalents of traditional intelligence tests, some test developers attempted to develop equivalents of traditional intelligence tests that were culture-specific. Expressly developed for members of a particular cultural group or subculture, such tests were thought to be able to yield a more valid measure of mental development. One culture-specific intelligence test developed expressly for use with Blacks was the Black Intelligence Test of Cultural Homogeneity (Williams, 1975), a 100-item multiple-choice test. Keeping in mind that many of the items on this test are now dated, here are three samples:[4]

1.  *Mother's Day* means
    a.  Black independence day.
    b.  a day when mothers are honored.
    c.  a day the welfare checks come in.
    d.  every first Sunday in church.

2.  *Blood* means
    a.  a vampire.
    b.  a dependent individual.
    c.  an injured person.
    d.  a brother of color.

3.  The following are popular brand names. Which one does not belong?
    a.  Murray's
    b.  Dixie Peach
    c.  Royal Crown
    d.  Preparation H

---

4. The answers keyed correct are as follows: 1(c), 2(d), and 3(d).

## Culture-Fair, Culture-Loaded

**W**hat types of test items are thought to be "culture-fair"—or at least more culture-fair than other, more culture-loaded items? The items reprinted below from the Culture Fair Test of Intelligence (Cattell, 1940) are a sample. As you look at them, think about how culture-fair they really are.

**Mazes**

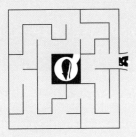

**Classification**
Pick out the two odd items in each row of figures.

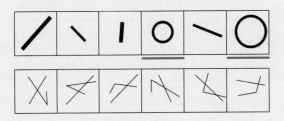

**Figure Matrices**
Choose from among the six alternatives the one that most logically completes the matrix pattern above it.

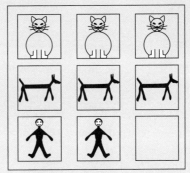

**Series**
Choose one figure from the six on the right that logically continues the series of three figures at the left.

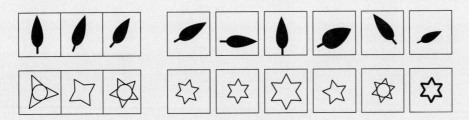

*Items from the Culture Fair Test of Intelligence (Cattell, 1940)*

In contrast to items designed to be culture-fair, consider the items on the Cultural/Regional Uppercrust Savvy Test (CRUST; Herlihy, 1977). This tongue-in-cheek test of intelligence was intentionally designed for illustrative purposes to be culture loaded. Members of society's upper crust should have no problem at all achieving a perfect score.

*(continued)*

## Culture-Fair,
## Culture-Loaded *(continued)*

1. When you are "posted" at the country club, (a) you ride horses with skill, (b) you are elected to the governance board, (c) you are publicly announced as not having paid your dues, (d) a table is reserved for you in the dining room whether you use it or not.

2. An arabesque in ballet is (a) an intricate leap, (b) a posture in which the dancer stands on one leg, the other extended backward, (c) a series of steps performed by a male and a female dancer, (d) a bow similar to a curtsy.

3. The *Blue Book* is (a) the income tax guidelines, (b) a guide to pricing used cars, (c) a booklet used for writing essay exams, (d) a social register listing 400 prominent families.

4. Brookline is located (a) in suburban Boston, (b) on Cape Cod, (c) between Miami Beach and Fort Lauderdale, (d) on the north shore of Chicago.

5. Beef Wellington is (a) the king's cut of roast beef, (b) tenderloin in a pastry crust lined with pâté, (c) an hors d'oeuvre flavored with sherry, (d) roast beef with béarnaise sauce.

6. Choate is (a) a gelded colt used in fox hunts, (b) a prep school, (c) an imported brandy, (d) the curator of the Metropolitan Museum of Art.

7. The most formal dress for men is (a) white tie, (b) black tie, (c) tuxedo, (d) décolletage.

8. *The Stranger* is (a) the [ethnically different] family who moved into the neighborhood, (b) Howard Hughes, (c) a book by Camus, (d) an elegant restaurant in San Francisco.

9. Waterford is (a) a health spa for the hep set, (b) a "fat farm," (c) hand-cut crystal from Ireland, (d) the Rockefeller family estate in upper New York.

10. Dining *alfresco* means (a) by candlelight, (b) a buffet supper, (c) at a sidewalk cafe, (d) outdoors.

According to Herlihy (1977), the answers keyed correct are 1(c), 2(b), 3(d), 4(a), 5(b), 6(b), 7(a), 8(c), 9(c), 10(d).

As you read the previous items, you may be asking yourself, "Is this really an intelligence test? Should I be taking this seriously?" If you were thinking such questions, you are in good company. At the time, many psychologists probably asked themselves the same questions. In fact, a parody of the BITCH (the test's acronym) was published in the May 1974 issue of *Psychology Today* (p. 101) and was called the "S.O.B. (Son of the Original BITCH) Test." However, the Williams (1975) test was purported to be a genuine culture-specific test of intelligence standardized on 100 Black high-school students in the St. Louis area. Williams was awarded $153,000 by the National Institute of Mental Health to develop the BITCH.

In what was probably one of the few published studies designed to explore the test's validity, the Wechsler Adult Intelligence Scale (WAIS) and the BITCH were both administered to Black ($n = 17$) and White ($n = 116$) applicants for a job with the Portland, Oregon, police department. The Black subjects performed much better on the test than did the White subjects, with a mean score that exceeded the White mean score by 2.83 standard deviations. The White mean IQ as measured by the WAIS exceeded the Black mean IQ by about 1.5 standard deviations. None of the correlations between the BITCH score and any of the following variables for either the Black or the White testtakers differed significantly from zero: WAIS Verbal IQ, WAIS Performance IQ, WAIS Full Scale IQ, and years of education. Even though the Black sample in this study had an average of more than 2.5 years of college education, and even though their overall mean on the WAIS was about 20 points higher than for Blacks in general, their scores on the BITCH fell below the average of the standardization sample (high-school pupils ranging in age from 16 to 18). What, then, is the BITCH measuring? The study authors, Matarazzo and Wiens (1977), concluded that the test was measuring that variable we characterized earlier in this chapter as being "at the cross-roads of intelligence and personality": *streetwiseness.*

Many of the tests designed to be culture-specific did yield higher mean scores for the minority group for which they were specifically designed. Still, they lacked predictive validity and provided little useful, practical information.[5] The knowledge required to score high on all of the culture-specific and culture-reduced tests has not been seen as relevant for educational purposes within our pluralistic society. Such tests have low predictive validity for the criterion of success in academic as well as vocational settings.

At various phases in the life history of the development of an intelligence test, a number of approaches to reduce cultural bias may be employed. Panels of experts may evaluate the potential bias inherent in a newly developed test, and those items judged to be biased may be eliminated. The test may be devised so that relatively few verbal instructions are needed to administer it or to demonstrate how to respond. Related efforts can be made to minimize any possible language bias. A tryout or pilot testing with ethnically mixed samples of testtakers may be undertaken. If differences in scores emerge solely as a function of ethnic group membership, individual items may be studied further for possible bias.

Major tests of intelligence have undergone a great deal of scrutiny for bias in many investigations. Procedures range from analysis of individual items to analysis of the test's predictive validity. Only when it can be reasonably concluded that a test is as free as it can be of systematic bias is it made available for use. Of course, even if a test is free of bias, other potential sources of bias still exist. These sources include the criterion for referral for assessment, the conduct of the assessment, the scoring of items (particularly those items that are somewhat subjective), and, finally, the interpretation of the findings.

---

5. Perhaps the most psychometrically sound of the instruments designed especially for use with Black subjects was the Listening Comprehension Test (Carver, 1968/1969, 1969; Orr & Graham, 1968). On this test, however, Blacks tended to score lower than Whites even when the groups were matched with respect to socioeconomic status.

# A Perspective

So many decades after the publication of the 1921 symposium, professionals still debate the nature of intelligence and how it should be measured. In the wake of the controversial book *The Bell Curve* (Herrnstein & Murray, 1994), the American Psychological Association commissioned a panel to write a report on intelligence that would carry psychology's official imprimatur. The panel's report reflected wide disagreement with regard to the definition of intelligence but noted that "such disagreements are not cause for dismay. Scientific research rarely begins with fully agreed definitions, though it may eventually lead to them" (Neisser et al., 1996, p. 77).

There has been no shortage of controversy when it comes to the subject of intelligence, beginning with how that word is defined. A trend in recent years has been to be much more liberal when defining and allowing for behavior presumed to be indicative of intelligence in the real world. So, for example, we read discussions of "managerial intelligence" by no less an authority than Robert Sternberg (1997a). Such work also reflects a trend toward context orientation in terms of defining intelligence. There seems to be more interest in specific types of intelligence, as opposed to $g$. Still, disagreement over "the issue of the one versus the many" (Sternberg & Berg, 1986, p. 157) shows no sign of abating.

Another issue that is not going to go away concerns group differences in measured intelligence. Human beings certainly do differ in size, shape, and color, and it is thus reasonable to consider that there is also a physical basis for differences in intellectual ability, so discerning where and how nature can be differentiated from nurture is a laudable academic pursuit. Still, such differentiation remains not only a complex business but one potentially fraught with social, political, and even legal consequences. Claims about group differences can and have been used as political and social tools to oppress religious, ethnic, or other minority group members. This is most unfortunate because, as Jensen (1980) observed, variance attributable to group differences is far less than variance attributable to individual differences. Echoing this sentiment is the view that "what matters for the next person you meet (to the extent that test scores matter at all) is that person's own particular score, not the mean of some reference group to which he or she happens to belong" (Neisser et al., 1996, p. 90).

The relationship between intelligence and a wide range of social outcomes has been well documented. Scores on intelligence tests, especially when used with other indicators, have value in predicting outcomes such as school performance, years of education, and even social status and income. Measured intelligence is negatively correlated with socially undesirable outcomes such as juvenile crime. For these and related reasons, we would do well to concentrate research attention on the environmental end of the heredity–environment spectrum. We need to find ways of effectively boosting measured intelligence through environmental interventions, the better to engender hope and optimism.

Unfairly maligned by some and unduly worshipped by others, intelligence has endured—and will continue to endure—as a key construct in psychology and psychological assessment. For this reason, professionals who administer intelligence tests have a great responsibility, one for which thorough preparation is a necessity. That being said, we press on to the following chapter, which examines some widely used tests of intelligence.

**JUST THINK . . .**

In a "real-life" competitive job market, what part—if any—does the "mean of the reference group" play in employment decisions?

# Self-Assessment

Test your understanding of elements of this chapter by seeing if you can explain each of the following terms, expressions, and abbreviations:

accommodation
alerting response
assimilation
ceiling effect
CHC model
cross-battery assessment
crystallized intelligence
culture-fair intelligence test
culture-free intelligence test
culture loading
emotional intelligence
factor-analytic theories (of intelligence)
fluid intelligence
Flynn effect
*g* (factor of intelligence)
*Gf* and *Gc*

giftedness
group factors
hierarchical model
information-processing theories (of intelligence)
intelligence
interactionism
interpersonal intelligence
intrapersonal intelligence
maintained abilities
mental age
nominating technique
parallel processing
PASS model
predeterminism
preformationism
psychoeducational assessment

schema
schemata
sequential processing
*s* factor (of intelligence)
simultaneous processing
successful intelligence
successive processing
temperament
"Termites"
three-stratum theory of cognitive abilities
two-factor theory of intelligence
Verbal, Perceptual, and Image Rotation (VPR) model
vulnerable abilities

# 10

# *Tests of Intelligence*

A test developer's conception of intelligence is, in a sense, both the starting point and the ending point in the development of a test of intelligence. To the extent that a test developer conceives of intelligence in terms of mental structures, the test will be designed to shed light on those structures. To the extent that a test developer conceives of intelligence in terms of processes, the test will be designed to shed light on those processes.

Beginning with initial considerations of item content and item format, continuing with considerations of scoring and interpretation, and following with plans for revising the test, the conception of intelligence at the test's foundation remains a guiding force—one that is reflected in decisions about almost every aspect of the test. It is evident in the final form of the test and in the uses to which the test will be put.

In this chapter, we look at a sampling of individual and group tests of intelligence.[1] As evidenced by reference volumes such as *Tests in Print,* many different intelligence tests exist. From the test user's standpoint, several considerations figure into a test's appeal:

- The theory (if any) on which the test is based
- The ease with which the test can be administered
- The ease with which the test can be scored
- The ease with which results can be interpreted for a particular purpose
- The adequacy and appropriateness of the norms
- The acceptability of the published reliability and validity indices
- The test's utility in terms of costs versus benefits

Some tests of intelligence were constructed on the basis of a theory. For example, Louis L. Thurstone conceived of intelligence as composed of what he termed *primary mental abilities* (PMAs). Thurstone (1938) developed and published the Primary Mental Abilities test, which consisted of separate tests, each designed to measure one PMA: verbal meaning,

---

1. Our objective in this and succeeding chapters is to provide a brief description of a small but representative sample of tests in various categories. We selected for discussion only a few tests for illustrative purposes. Readers are asked not to draw any conclusions about the value of any particular test on the basis of its inclusion in or omission from our discussion.

perceptual speed, reasoning, number facility, rote memory, word fluency, and spatial relations. Although the test was not widely used, this early model of multiple abilities inspired other theorists and test developers to explore various components of intelligence and ways to measure them.

An intelligence test may be developed on the basis of one theory but reconceptualized in terms of another theory. For example, in Chapter 9 you were introduced to a theory of intelligence that contains features of the Cattell-Horn model and the Carroll three-stratum model, a theory now referred to as the Cattell-Horn-Carroll (CHC) theory. As receptivity to CHC has grown, books and manuals have been published illustrating how this model can be used to supplement findings from other well-known ability tests.

**JUST THINK . . .**

In everyday living, mental abilities tend to operate in unison rather than in isolation. How useful is it, therefore, to attempt to isolate and measure "primary mental abilities"?

Historically, some tests seem to have been developed more as a matter of necessity than anything else. In the early 1900s, for example, Alfred Binet was charged with the responsibility of developing a test to screen for children with developmental disabilities in the Paris schools. Binet collaborated with Theodore Simon to create the world's first formal test of intelligence in 1905. Adaptations and translations of Binet's work soon appeared in many countries throughout the world. The original Binet-Simon Scale was in use in the United States as early as 1908 (Goddard, 1908, 1910). By 1912 a modified version had been published that extended the age range of the test downward to 3 months (Kuhlmann, 1912). However, it was the work of Lewis Madison Terman at Stanford University that culminated in the ancestor of what we know now as the Stanford-Binet Intelligence Scale.

In 1916 Terman published a translation and "extension" of the Binet-Simon Intelligence Scale. The publication included new items he had devised on the basis of years of research in addition to a methodological approach that included normative studies. Terman's efforts helped garner worldwide recognition and success for Binet's test (Minton, 1988). Let's take a closer look at how the Binet test has evolved over time (see Table 10–1).

**Table 10–1**
**The Stanford-Binet over Time**

| Year | Advantages | Limitations |
|---|---|---|
| 1916 | Contains alternate items at most age levels<br>Shares items to maintain continuity with earlier versions<br>Emphasizes abstraction and novel problem solving<br>Extends range of items relative to Binet-Simon<br>Based on extensive research literature<br>Extensive standardization performed | Inadequately measures adult mental capacity<br>Has inadequate scoring and administrative procedures at some points<br>Measures only single factor ($g$)<br>Has nonuniform IQ standard deviation<br>Has single test form<br>Is verbally loaded |
| 1937 | Contains alternate items at most levels<br>Shares items to maintain continuity with earlier versions<br>Extends range of items<br>Based on extensive research literature<br>Contains more performance tests at earlier age levels<br>Contains more representative norms<br>Includes parallel form<br>Uses toys to make test more engaging for young children<br>Verbal items allow subjects to display fluency, imagination, unusual or advanced concepts, and complex linguistic usage | Some items have ambiguous scoring rules<br>Form M lacks vocabulary<br>Has longer administration time than 1916 version<br>Measures only single factor ($g$)<br>Has nonuniform IQ standard deviation<br>IQs not comparable across ages<br>Sample had higher SES and higher percentage of urban children than general population<br>Has unequal coverage of different abilities at different levels<br>Is verbally loaded |

*(continued)*

**Table 10–1**
(*continued*)

| Year | Advantages | Limitations |
|---|---|---|
| 1960/1973 | Administers several varied tests to each examinee to keep children interested<br>Retains best items from Forms L and M<br>Has better layout than previous versions<br>Manual presents clear scoring rules<br>Contains alternate items at each age level<br>Shares items to maintain continuity with earlier versions<br>Eliminates items that are no longer appropriate<br>Based on extensive research literature<br>Presents stimulus material in spiral-bound book<br>Has uniform IQ standard deviation<br>Uses toys to make test more engaging for young children | Has inadequate ceiling for adolescents and highly gifted examinees<br>Measures only single factor ($g$)<br>Separates scoring standards from items<br>Is verbally loaded |
| 1986 | Contains both a general composite score and several factor scores<br>Shares items to maintain continuity with earlier versions<br>Easel format with directions, scoring criteria, and stimuli makes administration easier<br>Emphasizes abstraction and novel problem solving; emphasizes verbal reasoning less compared with prior versions<br>Technical Manual reports extensive validity studies<br>Has flexible administration procedures<br>Contains higher ceilings for advanced adolescents than Form L-M<br>Number of basic concepts in preschool-level tests compares favorably with other tests for that age range<br>Contains understandable age-level instructions for young children<br>Uses adaptive testing (routing) to economize on administration time and reduce examinee frustration<br>Uses explicit theoretical framework as guide for item development and alignment of subtests within modeled hierarchy<br>Has wider age range than prior versions (2-0 through 23)<br>Creatively extends many classic item types | Less gamelike than earlier versions; yields less information from styles and strategies due to decreased examiner/examinee interaction<br>Contains no toys<br>Norming sample overrepresents managerial/professional and college-educated adults and their children<br>Has possible lack of comparability in the content of area scores at different ages due to variability of subtests used in their computation<br>Has psychometric rather than developmental emphasis<br>Has standard deviation of 16 rather than 15 for composite scores; $M = 50$, $SD = 8$ for subtests<br>Contains subjectivity (examiner preference) when determining subtests used to compute composite score<br>Unable to diagnose mild retardation before age 4 and moderate retardation before age 5 |
| 2003 | More gamelike than earlier versions with colorful artwork, toys, and manipulatives<br>Matches norms to 2000 U.S. Census<br>Contains nonverbal as well as verbal routing test<br>Contains both a general composite score and several factor scores<br>Shares items to maintain continuity with earlier versions<br>Covers age range of 2-0 through 85+<br>Change-sensitive scores allow for evaluation of extreme performance<br>Has easel format with directions, scoring criteria, and stimuli, for easy administration<br>Has equal balance of verbal and nonverbal content in all factors<br>Contains Nonverbal IQ<br>Has standard deviation of 15 for composite scores, allowing easy comparison with other tests; $M = 10$, $SD = 3$ for subtests<br>Uses adaptive testing (routing) to economize on administration time and reduce examinee frustration<br>Uses explicit theoretical framework as guide for item development and alignment of subtests within modeled hierarchy<br>Extends low-end items, allowing earlier identification of individuals with delays or cognitive difficulties<br>Extends high-end items to measure gifted adolescents and adults | Not cited |

Source: From the *Stanford-Binet Intelligence Scales*, Fifth Edition, "Assessment Service Bulletin 1: History of the Stanford-Binet Intelligence Scales: Content and Psychometrics," by Kirk A. Becker, © 2003, Austin: PRO-ED. Used with permission.

# The Stanford-Binet Intelligence Scales

Although the first edition of the **Stanford-Binet** was certainly not without major flaws (such as lack of representativeness of the standardization sample), it also contained some important innovations. It was the first published intelligence test to provide organized and detailed administration and scoring instructions. It was also the first American test to employ the concept of IQ. And it was the first test to introduce the concept of an **alternate item,** an item to be substituted for a regular item under specified conditions (such as the situation in which the examiner failed to properly administer the regular item).

In 1926, Lewis Terman began a collaboration with a Stanford colleague, Maude Merrill, in a project to revise the test. The project would take 11 years to complete. Innovations in the 1937 scale included the development of two equivalent forms, labeled *L* (for Lewis) and *M* (for Maude, according to Becker, 2003), as well as new types of tasks for use with preschool-level and adult-level testtakers.[2] The manual contained many examples to aid the examiner in scoring. The test authors went to then-unprecedented lengths to achieve an adequate standardization sample (Flanagan, 1938), and the test was praised for its technical achievement in the areas of validity and especially reliability. A serious criticism of the test remained: lack of representation of minority groups during the test's development.

Another revision of the Stanford-Binet was well under way at the time of Terman's death at age 79 in 1956. This edition of the Stanford-Binet, the 1960 revision, consisted of only a single form (labeled *L-M*) and included the items considered to be the best from the two forms of the 1937 test, with no new items added to the test. A major innovation, however, was the use of the *deviation IQ* tables in place of the ratio IQ tables. Earlier versions of the Stanford-Binet had employed the *ratio IQ,* which was based on the concept of mental age (the age level at which an individual appears to be functioning intellectually). The **ratio IQ** is the ratio of the testtaker's mental age divided by his or her chronological age, multiplied by 100 to eliminate decimals. As illustrated by the formula for its computation, those were the days, now long gone, when an **IQ** (for **intelligence quotient**) really was a quotient:

$$\text{ratio IQ} = \frac{\text{mental age}}{\text{chronological age}} \times 100$$

A child whose mental age and chronological age were equal would thus have an IQ of 100. Beginning with the third edition of the Stanford-Binet, the deviation IQ was used in place of the ratio IQ. The **deviation IQ** reflects a comparison of the performance of the individual with the performance of others of the same age in the standardization sample. Essentially, test performance is converted into a standard score with a mean of 100 and a standard deviation of 16. If an individual performs at the same level as the average person of the same age, the deviation IQ is 100. If performance is a standard deviation above the mean for the examinee's age group, the deviation IQ is 116.

Another revision of the Stanford-Binet was published in 1972. As with previous revisions, the quality of the standardization sample was criticized. Specifically, the manual was vague about the number of minority individuals in the standardization sample, stating only that a "substantial portion" of Black and Spanish-surnamed

---

2. L. M. Terman left no clue to what initials would have been used for Forms L and M if his co-author's name had not begun with the letter *M.*

individuals was included. The 1972 norms may also have overrepresented the West, as well as large urban communities (Waddell, 1980).

The fourth edition of the Stanford-Binet Intelligence Scale (SB:FE; Thorndike et al., 1986) represented a significant departure from previous versions of the Stanford-Binet in theoretical organization, test organization, test administration, test scoring, and test interpretation. Previously, different items were grouped by age and the test was referred to as an **age scale.** The Stanford-Binet: Fourth Edition (SB:FE) was a *point scale.* In contrast to an age scale, a **point scale** is a test organized into subtests by category of item, not by age at which most testtakers are presumed capable of responding in the way that is keyed as correct. The SB:FE manual contained an explicit exposition of the theoretical model of intelligence that guided the revision. The model was one based on the Cattell-Horn (Horn & Cattell, 1966) model of intelligence. A *test composite*—formerly described as a deviation IQ score—could also be obtained. In general, a **test composite** may be defined as a test score or index derived from the combination of, and/or a mathematical transformation of, one or more subtest scores. This brief review brings us to the point at which the fifth edition was published. Let's take a closer look at it.

## The Stanford-Binet Intelligence Scales: Fifth Edition

The fifth edition of the Stanford-Binet (SB5; Roid, 2003a) was designed for administration to assessees as young as 2 and as old as 85 (or older). The test yields a number of composite scores, including a Full Scale IQ derived from the administration of ten subtests. Subtest scores all have a mean of 10 and a standard deviation of 3. Other composite scores are an Abbreviated Battery IQ score, a Verbal IQ score, and a Nonverbal IQ score. All composite scores have a mean set at 100 and a standard deviation of 15. In addition, the test yields five Factor Index scores corresponding to each of the five factors that the test is presumed to measure (see Table 10–2).

**Table 10–2**
**CHC and Corresponding SB5 Factors**

| CHC Factor Name | SB5 Factor Name | Brief Definition | Sample SB5 Subtest |
|---|---|---|---|
| Fluid Intelligence (*Gf*) | Fluid Reasoning (FR) | Novel problem solving; understanding of relationships that are not culturally bound | Object Series/Matrices (nonverbal) Verbal Analogies (verbal) |
| Crystallized Knowledge (*Gc*) | Knowledge (KN) | Skills and knowledge acquired by formal and informal education | Picture Absurdities (nonverbal) Vocabulary (verbal) |
| Quantitative Knowledge (*Gq*) | Quantitative Reasoning (QR) | Knowledge of mathematical thinking including number concepts, estimation, problem solving, and measurement | Verbal Quantitative Reasoning (verbal) Nonverbal Quantitative Reasoning (nonverbal) |
| Visual Processing (*Gv*) | Visual-Spatial Processing (VS) | Ability to see patterns and relationships and spatial orientation as well as the gestalt among diverse visual stimuli | Position and Direction (verbal) Form Board (nonverbal) |
| Short-Term Memory (*Gsm*) | Working Memory (WM) | Cognitive process of temporarily storing and then transforming or sorting information in memory | Memory for Sentences (verbal) Delayed Response (nonverbal) |

The SB5 was based on the Cattell-Horn-Carroll (CHC) theory of intellectual abilities. In fact, according to Roid (2003c), a factor analysis of the early Forms L and M showed that "the CHC factors were clearly recognizable in the early editions of the Binet scales" (Roid et al., 1997, p. 8). The SB5 measures five CHC factors by different types of tasks and subtests at different levels. The five CHC factor names (with abbreviations) alongside their SB5 equivalents are summarized in Table 10–2. Also provided in that table is a brief definition of the cognitive ability being measured by the SB5 as well as illustrative SB5 verbal and nonverbal subtests designed to measure that ability.

In designing the SB5, an attempt was made to strike an equal balance between tasks requiring facility with language (both expressive and receptive) and tasks that minimize demands on facility with language. In the latter category are subtests that use pictorial items with brief vocal directions administered by the examiner. The examinee response to such items may be made in the form of nonvocal pointing, gesturing, or manipulating.

> **JUST THINK . . .**
>
> We live in a society where ability to express oneself in language is highly prized. Should verbal self-expression skills be given more weight on any measure of general ability or intelligence?

**Standardization**   After about five years in development and extensive item analysis to address possible objections on the grounds of gender, racial/ethnic, cultural, or religious bias, the final standardization edition of the test was developed. Some 500 examiners from all 50 states were trained to administer the test. Examinees in the norming sample were 4,800 subjects from age 2 to over 85. The sample was nationally representative according to year-2000 U.S. Census data stratified with regard to age, race/ethnicity, geographic region, and socioeconomic level. No accommodations were made for persons with special needs in the standardization sample, although such accommodations were made in separate studies. Persons were excluded from the standardization sample (although included in separate validity studies) if they had limited English proficiency, severe medical conditions, severe sensory or communication deficits, or severe emotional/behavior disturbance (Roid, 2003c).

**Psychometric soundness**   To determine the reliability of the SB5 Full Scale IQ with the norming sample, an internal-consistency reliability formula designed for the sum of multiple tests (Nunnally, 1967, p. 229) was employed. The calculated coefficients for the SB5 Full Scale IQ were consistently high (.97 to .98) across age groups, as was the reliability for the Abbreviated Battery IQ (average of .91). Test-retest reliability coefficients reported in the manual were also high. The test-retest interval was only 5 to 8 days—shorter by some 20 to 25 days than the interval employed on other, comparable tests. Inter-scorer reliability coefficients reported in the SB5 Technical Manual ranged from .74 to .97 with an overall median of .90. Items showing especially poor inter-scorer agreement had been deleted during the test development process.

Content-related evidence of validity for SB5 items was established in various ways, ranging from expert input to empirical item analysis. Criterion-related evidence was presented in the form of both concurrent and predictive data. For the concurrent studies, Roid (2003c) studied correlations between the SB5 and the SB:FE as well as between the SB5 and all three of the then-current major Wechsler batteries (WPPSI-R, WISC-III, and WAIS-III). The correlations were high when comparing the SB5 to the SB:FE and, perhaps as expected, generally less so when comparing to the Wechsler tests. Roid (2003c) attributed the difference in part to the varying extents to which the SB5 and the Wechsler tests were presumed to tap $g$. To establish evidence for predictive validity, correlations with measures of achievement (the Woodcock Johnson III Test of Achievement and the Wechsler Individual Achievement Test, among other tests) were employed and the detailed findings reported in the manual. Roid (2003c) presented a number of factor-analytic studies in support of the construct validity of the SB5. However, exactly how many factors best account for what the test is measuring has been a matter of some debate. Some believe as little as one factor, *g,* best describes what the test measures (Canivez, 2008; DiStefano & Dombrowski, 2006). One study of high-achieving third-graders supported a model with 4 factors (Williams et al., 2010). Using a clinical population in her study, another researcher concluded that "the five factor model on which the SB5 was constructed does not reliably hold true across clinical samples." With regard to her clinical sample, she concluded, "Roid's findings were not generalizable" (Chase, 2005, p. 64). At the very least, it can be said that questions have been raised regarding the utility of the SB-5's five factor model, especially with regard to its applicability to clinical populations.

**Test administration**   Developers of intelligence tests, particularly tests designed for use with children, have traditionally been sensitive to the need for **adaptive testing,** or testing individually tailored to the testtaker. Other terms used to refer to adaptive testing include *tailored testing, sequential testing, branched testing,* and *response-contingent testing.* As employed in intelligence tests, adaptive testing might entail beginning a subtest with a question in the middle range of difficulty. If the testtaker responds correctly to the item, an item of greater difficulty is posed next. If the testtaker responds incorrectly to the item, an item of lesser difficulty is posed. Computerized adaptive testing is in essence designed "to mimic automatically what a wise examiner would do" (Wainer, 1990, p. 10).

Adaptive testing helps ensure that the early test or subtest items are not so difficult as to frustrate the testtaker and not so easy as to lull the testtaker into a false sense of security or a state of mind in which the task will not be taken seriously enough. Three other advantages of beginning an intelligence test or subtest at an optimal level of difficulty are that (1) it allows the test user to collect the maximum amount of information in the minimum amount of time, (2) it facilitates rapport, and (3) it minimizes the potential for examinee fatigue from being administered too many items.

After the examiner has established a rapport with the testtaker, the examination formally begins with an item from what is called a *routing test.* A **routing test** may be defined as a task used to direct or route the examinee to a particular level of questions. A purpose of the routing test, then, is to direct an examinee to test items that have a high probability of being at an optimal level of difficulty. There are two routing tests on the SB5, each of which may be referred to by either their activity names (Object Series/ Matrices and Vocabulary) or their factor-related names (Nonverbal Fluid Reasoning and Verbal Knowledge). By the way, these same two subtests—and only these—are administered for the purpose of obtaining the Abbreviated Battery IQ score.

The routing tests, as well as many of the other subtests, contain **teaching items,** which are designed to illustrate the task required and assure the examiner that the examinee understands. Qualitative aspects of an examinee's performance on teaching items may be recorded as examiner observations on the test protocol. However, performance on teaching items is not formally scored, and performance on such items in no way enters into calculations of any other scores.

Now for a sampling of "nuts-and-bolts" information on administering the SB5. All of the test items for the SB5 are contained in three item books. Item Book 1 contains the first two (routing) subtests. After the second subtest has been administered, the examiner has recorded estimated ability scores designed to identify an appropriate start point in Item Books 2 and 3. The examiner administers the next four nonverbal subtests of an appropriate level from Item Book 2. These subtests are labeled Knowledge,

Quantitative Reasoning, Visual-Spatial Processing, and Working Memory. The examiner then administers the final four verbal subtests from Item Book 3, again starting at an appropriate level. The four verbal subtests are labeled Fluid Reasoning, Quantitative Reasoning, Visual-Spatial Processing, and Working Memory.

Although many of the subtests for the verbal and nonverbal tests share the same name, they involve different tasks. For example, a *verbal measure* of Working Memory is a test called Memory for Sentences, in which the examinee's task is to repeat brief phrases and sentences. A *nonverbal measure* of Working Memory, known as Delayed Response, involves a totally different task, one reminiscent of the shell game or three-card monte (when played with cards) wagered on by passersby on many city streets (see Figure 10–1). Such street games, as well as the more standardized SB5 task, draw on visual memory and possibly verbal mediation. The latter process is presumed to occur because, during the "delay," the examinee (or onlooker of the game) *subvocalizes* (verbalizes in thought, not aloud) the name of the hidden object and the path it takes while being manipulated. The convergent validity of both the verbal and nonverbal working memory subtests of the SB5 has been supported by correlations with other tests presumed to be measuring the same respective variables (Pomplun & Custer, 2005).

Some of the ways that the items of a subtest in intelligence and other ability tests are described by assessment professionals have parallels in your home. For example, there is the *floor*. In intelligence testing parlance, the term **floor** refers to the lowest level of the items on a subtest. So, for example, if the items on a particular subtest run the gamut of ability from *developmentally delayed* at one end of the spectrum to *intellectually gifted* at the other, then the lowest-level item at the former end would be considered the *floor* of the subtest. The highest-level item of the subtest is the **ceiling.** On the Binet, another useful term is *basal level*, which is used to describe a subtest with reference to a specific testtaker's performance. Many Binet subtests have rules for establishing

**Figure 10–1**
**Watch Closely and Win a Prize**

*Players of shell games know they must follow the hidden object as its position is changed under one of three shells or cups. In the new SB5 subtest called Delayed Response, the examiner places objects under cups and then manipulates the position of the cups. The examinee's task is to locate the hidden object after a brief delay. On the SB5, the "prize" for successful performance comes in the form of raw score points that figure into the calculation of one's measured intelligence, not—as above—a monetary return on a wager.*

a **basal level,** or a base-level criterion that must be met for testing on the subtest to continue. For example, a rule for establishing a basal level might be "Examinee answers two consecutive items correctly." If and when examinees fail a certain number of items in a row, a **ceiling level** is said to have been reached and testing is discontinued.[3]

**JUST THINK . . .**

In what way(s) might an examiner misuse or abuse the obligation to prompt examinees? How could such misuse or abuse be prevented?

For each subtest on the SB5, there are explicit rules for where to *start,* where to *reverse,* and where to *stop* (or *discontinue*). For example, an examiner might start at the examinee's estimated present ability level. The examiner might reverse if the examinee scores 0 on the first two items from the start point. The examiner would discontinue testing (stop) after a certain number of item failures after reversing. The manual also provides explicit rules for prompting examinees. If a vague or ambiguous response is given on some verbal items in subtests such as Vocabulary, Verbal Absurdities, or Verbal Analogies, the examiner is encouraged to give the examinee a prompt such as "Tell me more."

Although a few of the subtests are timed, most of the SB5 items are not. The test was constructed this way to accommodate testtakers with special needs and to fit the item response theory model used to calibrate the difficulty of items.

**Scoring and interpretation**   The test manual contains explicit directions for administering, scoring, and interpreting the test in addition to numerous examples of correct and incorrect responses useful in the scoring of individual items. Scores on the individual items of the various subtests are tallied to yield raw scores on each of the various subtests. The scorer then employs tables found in the manual to convert each of the raw subtest scores into a standard score. From these standard scores, composite scores are derived.

When scored by a knowledge test user, an administration of the SB5 may yield much more than a number for a Full Scale IQ and related composite scores: The test may yield a wealth of valuable information regarding the testtaker's strengths and weaknesses with respect to cognitive functioning. This information may be used by clinical and academic professionals in interventions designed to make a meaningful difference in the quality of examinees' lives.

Various methods of profile analysis have been described for use with all major tests of cognitive ability (see, for example, Kaufman & Lichtenberger, 1999). These methods tend to have in common the identification of significant differences between subtest, composite, or other types of index scores as well as a detailed analysis of the factors analyzing those differences. In identifying these significant differences, the test user relies not only on statistical calculations (or tables, if available) but also on the normative data described in the test manual. Large differences between the scores under analysis should be uncommon or infrequent. The SB5 Technical Manual contains various tables designed to assist the test user in analysis. For example, one such table is "Differences Between SB5 IQ Scores and Between SB5 Factor Index Scores Required for Statistical Significance at .05 Level by Age."

---

3. Experienced clinicians who have had occasion to test the limits of an examinee will tell you that this assumption is not always correct. **Testing the limits** is a procedure that involves administering test items beyond the level at which the test manual dictates discontinuance. The procedure may be employed when an examiner has reason to believe that an examinee can respond correctly to items at the higher level. On a standardized ability test such as the SB:FE, the discontinue guidelines must be respected, at least in terms of scoring. Testtakers do not earn formal credit for passing the more difficult items. Rather, the examiner would simply note on the protocol that testing the limits was conducted with regard to a particular subtest and then record the findings.

In addition to formal scoring and analysis of significant difference scores, the occasion of an individually administered test affords the examiner an opportunity for behavioral observation. More specifically, the assessor is alert to the assessee's **extra-test behavior.** The way the examinee copes with frustration; how the examinee reacts to items considered very easy; the amount of support the examinee seems to require; the general approach to the task; how anxious, fatigued, cooperative, distractible, or compulsive the examinee appears to be—these are the types of behavioral observations that will supplement formal scores. The SB5 record form includes a checklist form of notable examinee behaviors. Included is a brief, yes–no questionnaire with items such as *Examinee's English usage was adequate for testing* and *Examinee was adequately cooperative.* There is also space to record notes and observations regarding the examinee's physical appearance, mood, and activity level, current medications, and related variables. Examiners may also note specific observations during the assessment. For example, when administering Memory for Sentences, there is usually no need to record an examinee's verbatim response. However, if the examinee produced unusual elaborations on the stimulus sentences, good judgment on the part of the examiner dictates that verbatim responses be recorded. Unusual responses on this subtest may also cue the examiner to possible hearing or speech problems.

A long-standing custom with regard to Stanford-Binet Full Scale scores is to convert them into nominal categories designated by certain cutoff boundaries for quick reference. Through the years, these categories have had different names. For the SB5, here are the cutoff boundaries with their corresponding nominal categories:

| Measured IQ Range | Category |
|---|---|
| 145–160 | Very gifted or highly advanced |
| 130–144 | Gifted or very advanced |
| 120–129 | Superior |
| 110–119 | High average |
| 90–109 | Average |
| 80–89 | Low average |
| 70–79 | Borderline impaired or delayed |
| 55–69 | Mildly impaired or delayed |
| 40–54 | Moderately impaired or delayed |

With reference to this list, Roid (2003b) cautioned that "the important concern is to describe the examinee's skills and abilities in detail, going beyond the label itself" (p. 150). The primary value of such labels is as a shorthand reference in some psychological reports. For example, in a summary statement at the end of a detailed SB5 report, a school psychologist might write, "In summary, Theodore presents as a well-groomed, engaging, and witty fifth-grader who is functioning in the high average range of intellectual ability."

**JUST THINK . . .**

Not that very long ago, *moron*, a word with pejorative connotations, was one of the categories in use. What, if anything, can test developers do to guard against the use of classification categories with pejorative connotations?

## The Wechsler Tests

David Wechsler designed a series of individually administered intelligence tests to assess the intellectual abilities of people from preschool through adulthood. A general description of the various types of tasks measured in current as well as past revisions of these tests is presented in Table 10–3.

Traditionally, whether it was the Wechsler adult scale, the child scale, or the preschool scale, an examiner familiar with one Wechsler test would not have a great deal of difficulty navigating any other Wechsler test. Although this is probably still true, the Wechsler tests have shown a clear trend away from such uniformity. For example, until recently all Wechsler scales yielded, among other possible composite scores, a Full Scale IQ (a measure of general intelligence), a Verbal IQ (calculated on the basis of scores on subtests categorized as verbal), and a Performance IQ (calculated on the basis of scores on subtests categorized as nonverbal). All of that changed in 2003 with the publication of the fourth edition of the children's scale (discussed in greater detail later in the chapter), a test that dispensed with the long-standing Wechsler dichotomy of Verbal and Performance subtests.

Regardless of the changes instituted to date, there remains a great deal of commonality between the scales. The Wechsler tests are all point scales that yield deviation IQs with a mean of 100 (interpreted as average) and a standard deviation of 15. On each of the Wechsler tests, a testtaker's performance is compared with scores earned by others in that age group. The tests have in common clearly written manuals that provide descriptions of each of the subtests, including the rationale for their inclusion. The manuals also contain clear, explicit directions for administering subtests as well as a number of standard prompts for dealing with a variety of questions, comments, or other contingencies. There are similar starting, stopping, and discontinue guidelines and explicit scoring instructions with clear examples. For test interpretation, all the Wechsler manuals come with myriad statistical charts that can prove very useful when it comes time for the assessor to make recommendations on the basis of the assessment. In addition, a number of aftermarket publications authored by various assessment professionals are available to supplement guidelines presented in the test manuals.

In general, the Wechsler tests have been evaluated favorably from a psychometric standpoint. Although the coefficients of reliability will vary as a function of the specific type of reliability assessed, reported reliability estimates for the Wechsler tests in various categories (internal consistency, test-retest reliability, inter-scorer reliability) tend to be satisfactory and, in many cases, more than satisfactory. Wechsler manuals also typically contain a great deal of information on validity studies, usually in the form of correlational studies or factor-analytic studies.

Three Wechsler intelligence tests in use at this writing are the Wechsler Adult Intelligence Scale-Fourth Edition (WAIS-IV) for ages 16 through 90 years 11 months; the Wechsler Intelligence Scale for Children-Fourth Edition (WISC-IV) for ages 6 through 16 years 11 months; and the Wechsler Preschool and Primary Scale of Intelligence–Third Edition (WPPSI-III) for ages 3 years to 7 years 3 months. Because these (as well as other) tests are revised periodically, readers are advised to check and see if a newer version of any of these tests has been published since this edition of our text was published.

### The Wechsler Adult Intelligence Scale–Fourth Edition (WAIS-IV)

The predecessors of the WAIS-IV, from the most recent on back, were the WAIS-III, the WAIS-R, the WAIS, the W-B II (Wechsler-Bellevue II), and the W-B I (Wechsler-Bellevue I). As you will see in our brief historical review, long before "the W-B" had become a television network, this abbreviation was used to refer to the first in a long line of Wechsler tests.

**Table 10–3**
**General Types of Items Used in Wechsler Tests**

*A listing of the subtests specific to individual Wechsler scales is presented in Table 10–6.*

| Subtest | Description |
|---|---|
| **Information** | *In what continent is Brazil?* Questions such as these, which are wide-ranging and tap general knowledge, learning, and memory, are asked. Interests, education, cultural background, and reading skills are some influencing factors in the score achieved. |
| **Comprehension** | In general, these questions tap social comprehension, the ability to organize and apply knowledge, and what is colloquially referred to as "common sense." An illustrative question is *Why should children be cautious in speaking to strangers?* |
| **Similarities** | *How are a pen and a pencil alike?* This is the general type of question that appears in this subtest. Pairs of words are presented to the examinee, and the task is to determine how they are alike. The ability to analyze relationships and engage in logical, abstract thinking are two cognitive abilities tapped by this type of test. |
| **Arithmetic** | Arithmetic problems are presented and solved verbally. At lower levels, the task may involve simple counting. Learning of arithmetic, alertness and concentration, and short-term auditory memory are some of the intellectual abilities tapped by this test. |
| **Vocabulary** | The task is to define words. This test is thought to be a good measure of general intelligence, although education and cultural opportunity clearly contribute to success on it. |
| **Receptive Vocabulary** | The task is to select from four pictures what the examiner has said aloud. This tests taps auditory discrimination and processing, auditory memory, and the integration of visual perception and auditory input. |
| **Picture Naming** | The task is to name a picture displayed in a book of stimulus pictures. This test taps expressive language and word retrieval ability. |
| **Digit Span** | The examiner verbally presents a series of numbers, and the examinee's task is to repeat the numbers in the same sequence or backward. This subtest taps auditory short-term memory, encoding, and attention. |
| **Letter-Number Sequencing** | Letters and numbers are orally presented in a mixed-up order. The task is to repeat the list with numbers in ascending order and letters in alphabetical order. Success on this subtest requires attention, sequencing ability, mental manipulation, and processing speed. |
| **Picture Completion** | The subject's task here is to identify what important part is missing from a picture. For example, the testtaker might be shown a picture of a chair with one leg missing. This subtest draws on visual perception abilities, alertness, memory, concentration, attention to detail, and ability to differentiate essential from nonessential detail. Because respondents may point to the missing part, this test provides a good nonverbal estimate of intelligence. However, successful performance on a test such as this still tends to be highly influenced by cultural factors. |
| **Picture Arrangement** | In the genre of a comic-strip panel, this subtest requires the testtaker to re-sort a scrambled set of cards with pictures on them into a story that makes sense. Because the testtaker must understand the whole story before a successful re-sorting will occur, this subtest is thought to tap the ability to comprehend or "size up" a situation. Additionally, attention, concentration, and ability to see temporal and cause-and-effect relationships are tapped. |
| **Block Design** | A design with colored blocks is illustrated either with blocks themselves or with a picture of the finished design, and the examinee's task is to reproduce the design. This test draws on perceptual-motor skills, psychomotor speed, and the ability to analyze and synthesize. Factors that may influence performance on this test include the examinee's color vision, frustration tolerance, and flexibility or rigidity in problem solving. |
| **Object Assembly** | The task here is to assemble, as quickly as possible, a cut-up picture of a familiar object. Some of the abilities called on here include pattern recognition, assembly skills, and psychomotor speed. Useful qualitative information pertinent to the examinee's work habits may also be obtained here by careful observation of the approach to the task. For example, does the examinee give up easily or persist in the face of difficulty? |
| **Coding** | If you were given the dot-and-dash equivalents of several letters in Morse code and then had to write out letters in Morse code as quickly as you could, you would be completing a coding task. The Wechsler coding task involves using a code from a printed key. The test is thought to draw on factors such as attention, learning ability, psychomotor speed, and concentration ability. |
| **Symbol Search** | The task is to visually scan two groups of symbols, one search group and one target group, and determine whether the target symbol appears in the search group. The test is presumed to tap cognitive processing speed. |
| **Matrix Reasoning** | A nonverbal analogy-like task involving an incomplete matrix designed to tap perceptual organizing abilities and reasoning. |
| **Word Reasoning** | The task is to identify the common concept being described with a series of clues. This test taps verbal abstraction ability and the ability to generate alternative concepts. |
| **Picture Concepts** | The task is to select one picture from two or three rows of pictures to form a group with a common characteristic. It is designed to tap the ability to abstract as well as categorical reasoning ability. |
| **Cancellation** | The task is to scan either a structured or an unstructured arrangement of visual stimuli and mark targeted images within a specified time limit. This subtest taps visual selective attention and related abilities. |

**The test's heritage**   In the early 1930s, Wechsler's employer, Bellevue Hospital in Manhattan, needed an instrument for evaluating the intellectual capacity of its multilingual, multinational, and multicultural clients. Dissatisfied with existing intelligence tests, Wechsler began to experiment. The eventual result was a test of his own, the W-B I, published in 1939. This new test borrowed from existing tests in format though not in content.

Unlike the most popular individually administered intelligence test of the time, the Stanford-Binet, the W-B I was a point scale, not an age scale. The items were classified by subtests rather than by age. The test was organized into six verbal subtests and five performance subtests, and all the items in each test were arranged in order of increasing difficulty. An equivalent alternate form of the test, the W-B II, was created in 1942 but was never thoroughly standardized (Rapaport et al., 1968). Unless a specific reference is made to the W-B II, references here (and in the literature in general) to the Wechsler-Bellevue (or the W-B) refer only to the Wechsler-Bellevue I (W-B I).

Research comparing the W-B to other intelligence tests of the day suggested that the W-B measured something comparable to what other intelligence tests measured. Still, the test suffered from some problems: (1) The standardization sample was rather restricted; (2) some subtests lacked sufficient inter-item reliability; (3) some of the subtests were made up of items that were too easy; and (4) the scoring criteria for certain items were too ambiguous. Sixteen years after the publication of the W-B, a new Wechsler scale for adults was published: the Wechsler Adult Intelligence Scale (WAIS; Wechsler, 1955).

Like the W-B, the WAIS was organized into Verbal and Performance scales. Scoring yielded a Verbal IQ, a Performance IQ, and a Full Scale IQ. As a result of many improvements over its W-B predecessor, the WAIS would quickly become the standard against which other adult tests were compared. A revision of the WAIS, the WAIS-R, was published in 1981 shortly after Wechsler's death in May of that same year. In addition to new norms and updated materials, the WAIS-R test administration manual mandated the alternate administration of verbal and performance tests. In 1997 the third edition of the test (the WAIS-III) was published, with authorship credited to David Wechsler.

The WAIS-III contained updated and more user-friendly materials. In some cases, test materials were made physically larger to facilitate viewing by older adults. Some items were added to each of the subtests that extended the test's floor in order to make the test more useful for evaluating people with extreme intellectual deficits. Extensive research was designed to detect and eliminate items that may have contained cultural bias. Norms were expanded to include testtakers in the age range of 74 to 89. The test was co-normed with the Wechsler Memory Scale-Third Edition (WMS-III), thus facilitating comparisons of memory with other indices of intellectual functioning when both the WAIS-III and the WMS-III were administered. The WAIS-III yielded a Full Scale (composite) IQ as well as four Index Scores—Verbal Comprehension, Perceptual Organization, Working Memory, and Processing Speed—used for more in-depth interpretation of findings.

**JUST THINK . . .**

Why is it important to demonstrate that a new version of an intelligence test is measuring much the same thing as a previous version of the test? Why might it be desirable for the test to measure something that was *not* measured by the previous version of the test?

**The test today**   The WAIS-IV is the most recent edition to the family of Wechsler adult scales. It is made up of subtests that are designated either as *core* or *supplemental*. A **core subtest** is one that is administered to obtain a composite score. Under usual circumstances, a **supplemental subtest** (also sometimes referred to as an **optional subtest**) is used for purposes such as providing additional clinical information or extending the number of abilities or processes sampled. There are, however, situations in which a supplemental subtest can be used *in place of* a core subtest. The latter types of situation arise when, for some reason, the use of a score on a particular core subtest would be questionable. So, for example, a supplemental subtest might be substituted for a core subtest if:

- the examiner incorrectly administered a core subtest
- the assessee had been inappropriately exposed to the subtest items prior to their administration
- the assessee evidenced a physical limitation that affected the assessee's ability to effectively respond to the items of a particular subtest

The WAIS-IV contains ten core subtests (Block Design, Similarities, Digit Span, Matrix Reasoning, Vocabulary, Arithmetic, Symbol Search, Visual Puzzles, Information, and Coding) and five supplemental subtests (Letter-Number Sequencing, Figure Weights, Comprehension, Cancellation, and Picture Completion). Longtime users of previous versions of the Wechsler series of adult tests will note the absence of four subtests (Picture Arrangement, Object Assembly, Coding Recall, and Coding Copy-Digit Symbol) and the addition of three new subtests (Visual Puzzles, Figure Weights, and Cancellation). Visual Puzzles and Figure Weights are both timed subtests scored on the WAIS-IV Perceptual Reasoning Scale. In Visual Puzzles, the assessee's task is to identify the parts that went into making a stimulus design. In Figure Weights, the assessee's task is to determine what needs to be added to balance a two-sided scale—one that is reminiscent of the "blind justice" type of scale. In Cancellation, a timed subtest used in calculating the Processing Speed Index, the assessee's task is to draw lines through targeted pairs of colored shapes (while not drawing lines through nontargeted shapes presented as distractors).[4]

Improvements in the WAIS-IV over earlier versions of the test include more explicit administration instructions as well as the expanded use of demonstration and sample items—this in an effort to provide assessees with practice in doing what is required, in addition to feedback on their performance. Practice items (or teaching items, as they are also called) are presumed to pay dividends in terms of ensuring that low scores are actually due to a deficit of some sort and not simply to a misunderstanding of directions. As is now customary in the development of most tests of cognitive ability, all of the test items were thoroughly reviewed to root out any possible cultural bias. The WAIS-IV also represents an improvement over its predecessor in terms of its "floor" and "ceiling." The floor of an intelligence test is the lowest level of intelligence the test purports to measure. The WAIS-III had a Full Scale IQ floor of 45; the WAIS-IV has a Full Scale IQ floor of 40. The ceiling of an intelligence test is the highest level of intelligence the test purports to measure. The WAIS-III had a Full Scale IQ ceiling of 155; the WAIS-IV has a Full Scale IQ ceiling of 160. If interest in measuring such extremes in intelligence grows, we can expect to see comparable "home improvements" (in the floors and ceilings) in future versions of this and comparable tests.

Because of longer life expectancies, normative data was extended to include information for testtakers up to age 90 years, 11 months. Other changes in the WAIS-IV

---

4. Sample items from all three of these subtests have been posted on the publisher's website. Visit http://pearsonassess.com and navigate to the material on the WAIS-IV to find the folder labeled "New Subtests."

as compared to the previous edition of this test reflect greater sensitivity to the needs of older adults. These improvements include:

- enlargement of the images in the Picture Completion, Symbol Search, and Coding subtests
- the recommended nonadministration of certain supplemental tests that tap short-term memory, hand-eye coordination, and/or motor speed for testtakers above the age of 69 (this to reduce testing time and to minimize testtaker frustration)
- an average reduction in overall test administration time from 80 to 67 minutes (accomplished primarily by shortening the number of items the testtaker must fail before a subtest is discontinued)

In a bygone era, testtakers' subtest scores on Wechsler tests were used to calculate a Verbal IQ, a Performance IQ, and a Full Scale IQ; that is not the case with the WAIS-IV. As with its predecessor, the WAIS-III, factor-analytic methods were used to help identify the factors that the test seemed to be loading on. The developers of the WAIS-IV deemed the subtests to be loading on four factors: Verbal Comprehension, Working Memory, Perceptual Reasoning, and Processing Speed.[5] Subtests that loaded heavily on any one of these factors were grouped together, and scores on these subtests were used to calculate corresponding index scores. Subtests that loaded less on a particular factor were designated as supplemental with regard to the measurement of that factor (see Table 10–4). As a result, scoring of subtests yields four index scores: a Verbal Comprehension Index, a Working Memory Index, a Perceptual Reasoning Index, and a Processing Speed Index. There is also a fifth index score, the General Ability Index (GAI), which is a kind of "composite of two composites." It is calculated using the Verbal Comprehension and Perceptual Reasoning indexes. The GAI is useful to clinicians as an overall index of intellectual ability.

Another composite score that has clinical application is the Cognitive Proficiency Index (CPI). Comprised of the Working Memory Index and the Processing Speed Index, the CPI is used to identify problems related to working memory or processing speed (Dumont & Willis, 2001). Some researchers have suggested that it can be used in conjunction with the GAI as an aid to better understanding and identifying various learning disabilities (Weiss et al., 2010). Like the GAI and the Full Scale IQ (FSIQ), the CPI was calibrated to have a mean of 100 and a standard deviation of 15.

**Table 10–4**
**WAIS-IV Subtests Grouped According to Indexes**

| Verbal Comprehension Scale | Perceptual Reasoning Scale | Working Memory Scale | Processing Speed Scale |
|---|---|---|---|
| Similarities[a] | Block Design[a] | Digit Span[a] | Symbol Search[a] |
| Vocabulary[a] | Matrix Reasoning[a] | Arithmetic[a] | Coding[a] |
| Information[a] | Visual Puzzles[a] | Letter-Number Sequencing (ages 16–69)[b] | Cancellation (ages 16–69)[b] |
| Comprehension[b] | Picture Completion[b] | | |
| | Figure Weights (ages 16–69)[b] | | |

[a] Core subtest.
[b] Supplemental subtest.

5. The WAIS-IV factor called "Perceptual Reasoning" is the same factor that was called "Perceptual Organization" on the WAIS-III.

**Standardization and norms**   The WAIS-IV standardization sample consisted of 2,200 adults from the age of 16 to 90 years, 11 months. The sample was stratified on the basis of 2005 U.S. Census data with regard to variables such as age, sex, race/ethnicity, educational level, and geographic region. Consistent with census data, there were more females than males in the older age bands. As compared to the WAIS-III standardization sample, the WAIS-IV sample is older, more diverse, and has an improved standard of living.

Following a Wechsler tradition, most subtest raw scores for each age group were converted to percentiles and then to a scale with a mean of 10 and a standard deviation of 3. Another Wechsler tradition, beginning with the WAIS-R, called for scaled scores for each subtest to be based on the performance of a "normal" (or, at least, nondiagnosed and nonimpaired) reference group of testtakers 20–34 years old. According to Tulsky et al. (1997), this was done as a consequence of David Wechsler's conviction that "optimal performance tended to occur at these ages" (p. 40). However, the practice was found to contribute to a number of problems in WAIS-R test interpretation, especially with older testtakers (Ivnik et al., 1992; Ryan et al., 1990; Tulsky et al., 1997). Beginning with the WAIS-III and continuing with the WAIS-IV, the practice of deriving norms on a hypothesized "optimal performance" reference group was abandoned. Scores obtained by the testtaker's same-age normative group would serve as the basis for the testtaker's scaled score.[6]

**Psychometric soundness**   The manual for the WAIS-IV (Coalson & Raiford, 2008) presents data from a number of studies attesting to the reliability, validity, and overall psychometric soundness of the test. For example, high internal consistency reliability estimates were found for all subtests and composite scores for which an estimate of internal consistency is appropriate.[7]

The validity of the WAIS-IV was established by a number of means such as concurrent validity studies and convergent and discriminative validity studies. Additionally, qualitative studies were conducted on the problem-solving strategies testtakers used in responding to questions in order to confirm that they were the same processes targeted for assessment. Independent researchers have noted that although there is comparability between WAIS-IV and SB5 scores in the middle range of intelligence, some discrepancies exist between scores achieved on these tests at the extreme ends of the distribution. For example, in one study, individuals known to be intellectually disabled were found to earn WAIS full scale scores that were roughly 16 points higher than those earned on the SB5 (Silverman et al., 2010).

The enthusiasm with which the professional community received the Wechsler adult scale prompted a "brand extension" of sorts downward. The result would be a series of Wechsler intelligence tests for children.

> **JUST THINK . . .**
>
> Give some thought to your own problem-solving processes. Answer the question "What is the square root of 81?" Now, answer the question "What did you have for dinner last evening?" How are the processes of thought you used to respond to these two questions different? For example, did one of the questions evoke more mental imagery than the other question?

---

6. However, such reference group scores (derived from the performance of adults from age 20 through age 34 years, 11 months) are still published in the WAIS-IV manual. Presumably, these norms are there for research purposes—or for examiners who seek to determine how an individual testtaker's performance compares with adults in this age group.

7. An estimate of internal consistency would not be appropriate for speeded subtests, such as those subtests used to calculate the Processing Speed Index.

## The Wechsler Intelligence Scale for Children–Fourth Edition (WISC-IV)

**Background**   The Wechsler Intelligence Scale for Children (WISC) was first published in 1949. It represented a downward extension of the W-B and incorporated many items contemplated for use in the (never-published) W-B II. Although it was generally received as a reliable instrument that correlated well with other tests of intelligence, the WISC was not without its flaws. The standardization sample contained only White children, and some of the test items were viewed as perpetuating gender and cultural stereotypes. Furthermore, parts of the test manual were so unclear that it led to ambiguities in the administration and scoring of the test. A revision of the WISC, called the Wechsler Intelligence Scale for Children–Revised (WISC-R), was published in 1974. The WISC-R included non-Whites in the standardization sample, and test material pictures were more balanced culturally. The test's language was modernized and "child-ized"; for example, the word *cigars* in an arithmetic item was replaced with *candy bars.* There were also innovations in the administration and scoring of the test. For example, Verbal and Performance tests were administered in alternating fashion, a practice that would also be extended to the WAIS-III and the WPPSI-R.

The revision of the WISC-R yielded the Wechsler Intelligence Scale for Children-III, published in 1991. This revision was undertaken to update and improve test items as well as the norms. For example, easier items were added to the Arithmetic scale to assess counting ability. At the other end of the Arithmetic scale, relatively difficult, multistep word problems were added. A Symbol Search subtest was introduced in the WISC-III. The test was added as the result of research on controlled attention, and it was thought to tap *freedom from distractibility.*

**The test today**   Published in 2003, the WISC-IV represents the culmination of a five-year research program involving several research stages from conceptual development through final assembly and evaluation. Perhaps most noteworthy in the introduction to the fourth edition is a noticeable "warming" to the CHC model of intelligence—qualified by a reminder that Carroll (1997), much like Wechsler and others, believed *g* to be very much alive and well in the major instruments designed to measure intelligence:

> Based on the most comprehensive factor-analytic investigation of cognitive ability measures to date, Carroll (1993, 1997) concluded that evidence for a general factor of intelligence was overwhelming. Thus, the trend toward an emphasis on multiple, more narrowly defined cognitive abilities has not resulted in rejection of an underlying, global aspect of general intelligence. Despite continuing debate over the existence of a single, underlying construct of intelligence, the results of factor-analytic research converge in the identification of 8 to 10 broad domains of intelligence. . . . (Wechsler, 2003, p. 2)

Also emphasized in the manual is that cognitive functions are interrelated, making it difficult if not impossible to obtain a "pure" measure of a function. A test purporting to measure *processing speed*, for example, may involve multiple abilities, such as visual discrimination ability and motor ability. Further, questions were raised regarding the desirability of even trying to isolate specific abilities for measurement, because in "real life," cognitive tasks are rarely performed in isolation. This point was made by Wechsler himself:

> the attributes and factors of intelligence, like the elementary particles in physics, have at once collective and individual properties; that is, they appear to behave differently when alone from what they do when operating in concert. (1975, p. 138)

**JUST THINK . . .**

The last *C* in the CHC model belongs to Carroll, and Carroll is a firm believer in *g*. Cattell and Horn, the first *C* and the *H* in CHC, are no fans of *g*. It goes to show the strange bedfellows that can come together when a theory named for three people was not actually developed by those three people. Your thoughts?

Consistent with the foregoing, the developers of the WISC-IV revised the test so that it now yields a measure of general intellectual functioning (a Full Scale IQ, or FSIQ) as well as four index scores: a Verbal Comprehension Index, a Perceptual Reasoning Index, a Working Memory Index, and a Processing Speed Index. Each of these indexes is based on scores on three to five subtests. It is the scores from each index, based on the core subtests only, that combine to yield the Full Scale IQ.

From an administration of the WISC-IV it is also possible to derive up to seven *process scores* by using tables supplied in the Administration and Scoring Manual. A **process score** may be generally defined as an index designed to help understand the way the testtaker processes various kinds of information. In what many would view as a momentous departure from previous versions of the test, the WISC-IV does *not* yield separate Verbal and Performance IQ scores.

Examiners familiar with previous versions of the WISC may be surprised by some of the other changes instituted in this edition. The subtests known as Picture Arrangement, Object Assembly, and Mazes have all been eliminated. Separate norms are now presented for Block Design, with and without time bonuses. In part, these separate norms represent an acknowledgment that certain cultures value speeded tasks more than others. The subtests Information, Arithmetic, and Picture Completion— formerly core subtests—are now supplemental subtests. On the WISC-IV, there are 10 core subtests and five supplemental subtests.

After pilot work and national tryouts using preliminary versions of the new scale, a standardization edition of the WISC-IV was created and administered to a stratified sample of 2,200 subjects ranging in age from 6 years to 16 years 11 months. The sample was stratified to be representative of U.S. Census data for the year 2000 with regard to key variables such as age, gender, race/ethnicity, parent education level, and geographic region. Persons who were not fluent in English or who suffered from any of a variety of physical or mental conditions that might depress test performance were excluded from participation in the standardization sample (see Wechsler, 2003, p. 24, for a complete list of exclusionary criteria). Quality assurance procedures were put in place for qualifying examiners, scoring procedures, and data entry. All items were reviewed qualitatively for possible bias by reviewers as well as quantitatively by means of IRT bias analysis methodologies.

The manual for the WISC-IV presents a number of studies as evidence of the psychometric soundness of the test. In terms of reliability, evidence is presented to support the test's internal consistency and its test-retest stability. Additionally, evidence of excellent inter-scorer agreement (low to high .90s) is presented. Evidence for the validity of the test comes in the form of a series of factor-analytic studies and of several correlational studies that focused on WISC-IV scores as compared to scores achieved on other tests. Detailed data are presented in the test manual.

**The WISC-IV compared to the SB5**   Although the SB5 can be used with testtakers who are both much younger and much older than the testtakers who can be tested with the WISC-IV, comparisons between the Binet and the WISC have become something akin to a tradition among assessors who test children.

Both tests were published in 2003. Both tests are individually administered instruments that take about an hour or so of test administration time to yield a Full Scale IQ composite score based on the administration of 10 subtests. The WISC-IV also contains five supplemental tests (add about 30 minutes for the administration of the "extended battery"); the SB5 contains none. With the SB5, an Abbreviated Battery IQ can be obtained from the administration of two subtests. The WISC-IV contains no such short forms, although this fact has not stopped many assessors from devising their own "short form" or finding a way to construct one from some aftermarket publication. Both tests contain child-friendly materials, and both tests have optional available software for scoring and report writing.

The norming sample for testtakers ages 6 through 16 was 2,200 for both tests. The WISC-IV included parent education as one stratifying variable that the SB5 did not. The SB5 included socioeconomic status and testtaker education as stratifying variables that the WISC-IV did not. The test developers for both tests included exclusionary criteria in the norming sample, and separate validity studies with some of these exceptional samples were conducted for both tests. Consult the respective manuals for differences between the two tests in terms of these separate validity studies because they did, in fact, employ different kinds of samples.

JUST THINK . . .

The SB5 and the WISC-IV are similar in many respects except with regard to exclusionary criteria and the populations on which separate validity studies were conducted. Why do you think that is? What are the implications of these differences for test users who test members of exceptional populations?

The developers of both the WISC-IV and the SB5 were obvious fans of the CHC model of intelligence. Still, both seemed to accept the model only to the extent that they could still find a place for $g$ at the top of the hierarchy. The two tests employ some similar and some dissimilar kinds of subtests. As a whole, both tests may be interpreted with respect to several cognitive and nonverbal indices that are drawn, to greater or lesser degrees, from the CHC model (see Table 10–5).

In our discussion comparing the WAIS-IV to the SB5, we noted that there seemed to be comparability between the scores, except at the extreme range of the scores; testtakers known to have intellectual deficits tended to earn scores that were higher on the WAIS-IV as compared to the SB5. A parallel result was found in a WISC-III/SB5 comparison study that employed children known to be gifted as subjects. The scores of the subjects on the SB5 were found to be significantly lower (Minton & Pratt, 2006).

## The Wechsler Preschool and Primary Scale of Intelligence– Third Edition (WPPSI-III)

Project Head Start—as well as other 1960s programs for preschool children who were culturally different or exceptional (defined in this context as atypical in ability; i.e., gifted or developmentally delayed)—fostered interest in the development of new tests for preschoolers (Zimmerman & Woo-Sam, 1978). The Stanford-Binet traditionally had been the test of choice for use with preschoolers. A question before the developers

**Table 10–5**

**Cognitive and Nonverbal Factors on the WISC-IV Compared to the Stanford-Binet 5**

| | WISC-IV | SB5 |
|---|---|---|
| **Cognitive Factors** | Working Memory<br>Processing Speed<br>Verbal Comprehension<br>Perceptual Reasoning | Working Memory<br>Visual-Spatial Processing<br>Knowledge<br>Fluid Reasoning<br>Quantitative Reasoning |
| **Nonverbal Factors** | Working Memory<br>Processing Speed<br>Perceptual Reasoning | Working Memory<br>Visual-Spatial Processing<br>Fluid Reasoning<br>Quantitative Reasoning<br>Knowledge |

of the WISC was whether or not that test should be restandardized for children under 6. Alternatively, should an entirely new test be developed? Wechsler (1967) decided that a new scale should be developed and standardized especially for children under age 6. The new test was the WPPSI (the Wechsler Preschool and Primary Scale of Intelligence), usually pronounced "whipsy." Its publication in 1967 extended the age range of the Wechsler series of intelligence tests downward to age 4.

The WPPSI was the first major intelligence test that "adequately sampled the total population of the United States, including racial minorities" (Zimmerman & Woo-Sam, 1978, p. 10). This advantage contributed greatly to the success of the WPPSI, especially in an era when standardized tests were under attack for inadequate minority representation in standardization samples. A revision of the WPPSI, the WPPSI-R, was published in 1989. It was designed to assess the intelligence of children from ages 3 years through 7 years 3 months. New items were developed to extend the range of the test both upward and downward.

Published in 2002, the WPPSI-III extended the age range of children who could be tested with this instrument downward to 2 years 6 months. The technical manual for this instrument contained the same sort of historical introduction to intelligence testing as the WISC-IV. However, instead of arriving at the conclusion that it was time to drop Wechsler's traditional Verbal/Performance dichotomy, as was done with the WISC-IV, the utility of the dichotomy was reaffirmed in the WPPSI-III manual. Accordingly, three composite scores may be obtained: Verbal IQ, Performance IQ, and Full Scale IQ.

The WPPSI-III was changed in many ways from its previous edition. Five subtests (Arithmetic, Animal Pegs, Geometric Design, Mazes, and Sentences) were dropped. Seven new subtests were added: Matrix Reasoning, Picture Concepts, Word Reasoning, Coding, Symbol Search, Receptive Vocabulary, and Picture Naming. On the WPPSI-III, subtests are labeled *core, supplemental,* or *optional,* and some tests have different labels at different age levels (for example, *supplemental* at one age level and *optional* at another age level). Core subtests are required for the calculation of composite scores. Supplemental subtests are used to provide a broader sampling of intellectual functioning; they may also substitute for a core subtest if a core subtest for some reason was not administered or was administered but is not usable. Supplemental subtests are also used to derive additional scores, such as a *Processing Speed Quotient.* Optional subtests may not be used to substitute for core subtests but may be used in the derivation of optional scores such as a *General Language Composite.* A complete list of all the subtests on all of the Wechsler scales, including the WPPSI-III, the WISC-IV, and the WAIS-IV, is presented in Table 10–6.

**JUST THINK . . .**

David Wechsler believed that the factors of intelligence, much like elementary particles in physics, have both collective and individual properties. Most of the time, Wechsler tests seem to have as their goal the measurement of the collective properties "acting in concert." However, with the incorporation of Symbol Search and Coding on the WPPSI-III, the test developers seem to be striving for a "purer" measure of processing speed. What are your thoughts on the apparent mixing of the measurement of the collective and individual properties of factors in intellectual ability?

The structure of the WPPSI-III reflects the interest of the test developers in enhancing measures of fluid reasoning and processing speed. Three of the new tests (Matrix Reasoning, Picture Concepts, and Word Reasoning) were designed to tap fluid reasoning, and two of the new tests (Coding and Symbol Search) were designed to tap processing speed. In an effort to reduce the confounding effects of speed on cognitive ability, the test developers discontinued the practice of awarding bonus points to Block Design and Object Assembly scores for quick, successful performance. The test developers hoped that their incorporation of the Symbol Search and Coding subtests would provide a less confounded measure of processing speed.

**Table 10–6**
**The Wechsler Tests at a Glance**

| Subtest | WPPSI-III | WISC-IV | WAIS-IV |
|---|---|---|---|
| Information | X | X | X |
| Comprehension | X | X | X |
| Similarities | X | X | X |
| Arithmetic | — | X | X |
| Vocabulary | X | X | X |
| Receptive Vocabulary[a] | X | — | — |
| Picture Naming | X | — | — |
| Digit Span | X | X | X |
| Letter-Number Sequencing | — | X | X |
| Picture Completion | X | X | X |
| Picture Arrangement | — | X | — |
| Block Design | X | X | X |
| Object Assembly | X | — | — |
| Coding | X | X | X |
| Symbol Search | X | X | X |
| Matrix Reasoning | X | X | X |
| Word Reasoning | X | X | — |
| Picture Concepts | X | X | — |
| Cancellation | — | X | X |
| Visual Puzzles | — | — | X |
| Figure Weights | — | — | X |

[a] Consult the individual test manual to see whether a particular subtest is a core subtest or a supplemental (or optional) subtest. For example, on the WPPSI-III, some subtests function as one type of test at one age level and as another type of test at another age level: Receptive Vocabulary is a *core* verbal subtest for testtakers up to 3 years 11 months but an *optional* verbal subtest for ages 4 years and over; Picture Naming is a *supplemental* verbal subtest for testtakers up to 3 years 11 months but an *optional* verbal subtest for ages 4 years and over.

If you have ever watched *Trading Spaces, This Old House,* or *Extreme Makeover: Home Edition,* you know that any reality television show that deals with home renovation will give proper attention to the floors and ceilings. Well, it's that way when renovating intelligence tests, too. The designers of the WPPSI-III added easier items as well as more difficult ones to each of the retained subtests. They concluded that the improved subtest floors and ceilings made the WPPSI-III "a more accurate measure of cognitive functioning for children with significant developmental delays, as well as for children suspected of being intellectually gifted" (Wechsler, 2002, p. 17).

◆
**JUST THINK . . .**

Why is it important for independent researchers to attempt to verify some of the findings regarding the psychometric soundness of major tests?

After pilot work and a national tryout of the WPPSI-III in development, a standardization edition of the test was created. The test was administered to a stratified sample of 1,700 children between the ages of 2 years 6 months and 7 years 3 months and also to samples of children from special groups. The sample was selected in proportion to year-2000 U.S. Census data stratified on the variables of age, sex, race/ethnicity, parent education level, and geographic region. As has become the custom when revising major intelligence scales, a number of steps were taken to guard against item bias. Included were statistical methods as well as reviews by bias experts. A number of quality assurance procedures were put in place, including anchor protocols, to ensure that tests were scored and that data were entered properly. As has also become customary, a number of studies attesting to the psychometric soundness of the scale are presented in the technical manual.

So how does the WPPSI-III compare to its chief competitor, the SB5? Quite favorably—at least according to research conducted in Australia with "36 typically developing 4-year-old children" (Garred & Gilmore, 2009). These researchers found significant correlations among all WPPSI-III and SB5 composite scores, although a number of the subjects had notably different performance on subtests. Interestingly, in terms of preference, the preschoolers in this sample tended to prefer taking the SB5 over the WPPSI-III.

## Short Forms

An issue related to Wechsler tests but certainly not exclusive to them is the development and use of short forms. The term **short form** refers to a test that has been abbreviated in length, typically to reduce the time needed for test administration, scoring, and interpretation. Sometimes, particularly when the testtaker is believed to have an atypically short attention span or other problems that would make administration of the complete test impossible, a sampling of representative subtests is administered. Arguments for such use of Wechsler scales have been made with reference to testtakers from the general population (Kaufman et al., 1991), the elderly (Paolo & Ryan, 1991), and others (Benedict et al., 1992; Boone, 1991; Grossman et al., 1993; Hayes, 1999; Randolph et al., 1993; Sweet et al., 1990). A seven-subtest short form of the WAIS-III is sometimes used by clinicians, and it seems to demonstrate acceptable psychometric characteristics (Ryan & Ward, 1999; Schoop et al., 2001).

Short forms of intelligence tests are nothing new. In fact, they have been around almost as long as the long forms. Soon after the Binet-Simon reached the United States, a short form of it was proposed (Doll, 1917). Today, school psychologists with long waiting lists for assessment appointments, forensic psychologists working in an overburdened criminal justice system, and health insurers seeking to pay less for assessment services are some of the groups to whom the short form appeals.

In 1958 David Wechsler endorsed the use of short forms but only for screening purposes. Years later, perhaps in response to the potential for abuse of short forms, he took a much dimmer view of reducing the number of subtests just to save time. He advised those claiming that they did not have the time to administer the entire test to "find the time" (Wechsler, 1967, p. 37).

Some literature reviews on the validity of short forms have tended to support Wechsler's admonition to "find the time." Watkins (1986) concluded that short forms may be used for screening purposes only, not to make placement or educational decisions. From a historical perspective, Smith, McCarthy, and Anderson (2000) characterized views on the transfer of validity from the parent form to the short form as "overly optimistic." In contrast to some critics who have called for the abolishment of short forms altogether, Smith et al. (2000) argued that the standards for the validity of a short form must be high. They suggested a series of procedures to be used in the development of valid short forms. Silverstein (1990) provided an incisive review of the history of short forms, focusing on four issues: (1) how to abbreviate the original test; (2) how to select subjects; (3) how to estimate scores on the original test; and (4) the criteria to apply when comparing the short form with the original. Ryan and Ward (1999) advised that anytime a short form is used, the score should be reported on the official record with the abbreviation "Est" next to it, indicating that the reported value is only an estimate.

From a psychometric standpoint, the validity of a test is affected by and is somewhat dependent on the test's reliability. Changes in a test that lessen its reliability may also lessen its validity. Reducing the number of items in a test typically reduces the test's reliability and hence its validity. For that reason, decisions made on the basis of data derived from administrations of a test's short form must, in general, be made with caution (Nagle & Bell, 1993). In fact, when data from the administration of a short form clearly suggest the need for intervention or placement, the best practice may be to "find the time" to administer the full form of the test.

**The Wechsler Abbreviated Scale of Intelligence (WASI)**    Against a backdrop in which many practitioners view short forms as desirable and many psychometricians urge caution in their use, the Wechsler Abbreviated Scale of Intelligence (WASI) was published in 1999. Because many test users find the appeal of a short form irresistible, many different short forms have been devised informally from longer forms of tests—short forms with varying degrees of psychometric soundness and seldom with any normative data. The WASI was designed to answer the need for a short instrument to screen intellectual ability in testtakers from 6 to 89 years of age. The test comes in a two-subtest form (consisting of Vocabulary and Block Design) that takes about 15 minutes to administer and a four-subtest form that takes about 30 minutes to administer. The four subtests (Vocabulary, Block Design, Similarities, and Matrix Reasoning) are WISC- and WAIS-type subtests that had high correlations with Full Scale IQ on those tests and are thought to tap a wide range of cognitive abilities. The WASI yields measures of Verbal IQ, Performance IQ, and Full Scale IQ. Consistent with many other intelligence tests, the Full Scale IQ was set at 100 with a standard deviation of 15.

The WASI was standardized with 2,245 cases including 1,100 children and 1,145 adults. The manual presents evidence for satisfactory psychometric soundness, although some reviewers of this test were not completely satisfied with the way the validity research was conducted and reported (Keith et al., 2001). However, other reviewers have found that the psychometric qualities of the WASI, as well as its overall usefulness, far exceed those of comparable, brief measures of intelligence (Lindskog & Smith, 2001).

**Other Short Forms**    In addition to the WASI, a number of other abbreviated tests of intelligence have been developed. Some of the more widely used tests include the Kaufman Brief Intelligence Scale–Second Edition (KBIT-2) and the Wide Range Intelligence Test (WRIT). High correlations between the WASI, the KBIT, and the WRIT speak to the convergent validity of these tests (Canivez et al., 2009). Given such findings, abbreviated intelligence tests may well provide a viable alternative to full-length tests under circumstances where there are time constraints or other extenuating circumstances.

## The Wechsler Tests in Perspective

Read the manual for a recently developed Wechsler intelligence test, and the chances are good that you will find illustrations of exemplary practices in test development. Qualified examiners can learn to administer the tests relatively quickly, and examinees tend to find the test materials engaging. A number of computer-assisted scoring and interpretive aids are available for each of the tests, as are a number of manuals and guides. Moreover, the test developers are evidently making efforts to keep the scoring and interpretation of the tests fresh. Witness the efforts of the developers of the WISC-IV, who reexamined the traditional Wechsler verbal–performance dichotomy and transformed it into a model that is more conducive to analysis by means of the more contemporary, multiple-factor conceptualization of intelligence.

In becoming acquainted with the Wechsler tests and also the SB5, you have probably noticed that the statistical technique of factor analysis plays a key role in the test development process. For an "up close and personal" look at this technique, take a moment to read this chapter's *Close-Up*.

# Factor Analysis*

To measure characteristics of physical objects, there may be some disagreement about the best methods to use, but there is little disagreement about which dimensions are being measured. We know, for example, that we are measuring length when we use a ruler, and we know that we are measuring temperature when we use a thermometer. Such certainty is not always present in measuring psychological dimensions such as personality traits, attitudes, and cognitive abilities.

Psychologists may disagree about what to name the dimensions being measured and about the number of dimensions being measured. Consider a personality trait that one researcher refers to as *niceness.* Another researcher views *niceness* as a vague term that lumps together two related but independent traits called *friendliness* and *kindness.* Yet another researcher claims that *kindness* is too general and must be dichotomized into *kindness to friends* and *kindness to strangers.* Who is right? Is everybody right? If researchers are ever going to build on each others' findings, there needs to be some way of reaching consensus about what is being measured. Toward that end, factor analysis can be helpful.

An assumption of factor analysis is that things that co-occur tend to have a common cause. Note here that "tend to" does *not* mean "always." Fevers, sore throats, stuffy noses, coughs, and sneezes may *tend to* occur at the same time in the same person, but they do not always co-occur. When these symptoms do co-occur, they may be caused by one thing: the virus that causes the common cold. Although the virus is one thing, its manifestations are quite diverse.

In psychological assessment research, we measure a diverse set of abilities, behaviors, and symptoms and then attempt to deduce which underlying dimensions cause or account for the variations in behavior and symptoms observed in large groups of people. We measure the relations among various behaviors, symptoms, and test scores with correlation coefficients. We then use factor analysis to discover patterns of correlation coefficients that suggest the existence of underlying psychological dimensions.

All else being equal, a simple theory is better than a complicated theory. Factor analysis helps us discover the smallest number of psychological dimensions (or factors) that can account for the various behaviors, symptoms,

and test scores we observe. For example, imagine that we create four different tests to measure people's knowledge of vocabulary, grammar, multiplication, and geometry. If the correlations between all of these tests were zero (i.e., high scorers on one test are no more likely than low scorers to score high on the other tests), then the factor analysis would suggest to us that we have measured four distinct abilities.

Of course, you probably recognize that it is most unlikely that the correlations between these tests would be zero. Therefore, imagine that the correlation between the vocabulary and grammar tests were quite high (i.e., high scorers on vocabulary were likely also to score high on grammar, and low scorers on vocabulary were likely to score low on grammar), and suppose also a high correlation between multiplication and geometry. Furthermore, the correlations between the verbal tests and the mathematics tests were zero. Factor analysis would suggest that we have measured not four distinct abilities but two. The researcher interpreting the results of this factor analysis would have to use his or her best judgment in deciding what to call these two abilities. In this case, it would seem reasonable to call them *language ability* and *mathematical ability.*

Now imagine that the correlations between all four tests were equally high—for example, that vocabulary was as strongly correlated with geometry as it was with grammar. In this case, factor analysis suggests that the simplest explanation for this pattern of correlations is that there is just one factor that causes all these tests to be equally correlated. We might call this factor *general academic ability.*

In reality, if you were to actually measure these four abilities, the results would not be so clear-cut. It is likely that all of the correlations would be positive and substantially above zero. It is likely that the verbal subtests would correlate more strongly with each other than with the mathematical subtests. It is likely that factor analysis would suggest that language and mathematical abilities are distinct from but not entirely independent of each other—in other words, that language abilities and mathematics abilities are substantially correlated, suggesting that a general academic (or intellectual) ability influences performance in all academic areas.

Factor analysis can help researchers decide how best to summarize large amounts of information about people by using just a few scores. For example, when we ask parents to complete questionnaires about their children's behavior problems, the questionnaires can have hundreds of items.

*Prepared by W. Joel Schneider.

*(continued)*

# Factor Analysis *(continued)*

It would take too long and would be too confusing to review every item. Factor analysis can simplify the information while minimizing the loss of detail. Here is an example of a short questionnaire that factor analysis can be used to summarize.

On a scale of 1 to 5, compared to other children his or her age, my child:

1. gets in fights frequently at school
2. is defiant to adults
3. is very impulsive
4. has stomachaches frequently
5. is anxious about many things
6. appears sad much of the time

If we give this questionnaire to a large, representative sample of parents, we can calculate the correlations between the items. Table 1 illustrates what we might find.

Note that all of the perfect 1.00 correlations in this table are used to emphasize the fact that each item correlates perfectly with itself. In the analysis of the data, the software would ignore these correlations and analyze only all of the correlations below this diagonal "line of demarcation" of 1.00 correlations.

Using the set of correlation coefficients presented in Table 1, factor analysis suggests that there are two factors measured by this behavior rating scale. The logic of factor analysis suggests that the reason Items 1 through 3 have high correlations with each other is that each has a high correlation with the first factor. Similarly, Items 4 through 6 have high correlations with each other because they have high correlations with the second factor. The correlations of the items with the hypothesized factors are called *factor loadings.* The factor loadings for this hypothetical example are presented in Table 2.

Factor analysis tells us which items *load* on which factors, but it cannot interpret the meaning of the factors. Researchers usually look at all the items that load on a factor and use their intuition or knowledge of theory to identify what the items have in common. In this case, Factor 1 could receive any number of names, such as *Conduct Problems, Acting Out,* or *Externalizing Behaviors.* Factor 2 might also go by various names, such as *Mood Problems, Negative Affectivity,* or *Internalizing Behaviors.* Thus, the problems on this behavior rating scale can be summarized fairly efficiently with just two scores. In this

**Table 1**
**A Sample Table of Correlations**

| | 1 | 2 | 3 | 4 | 5 | 6 |
|---|---|---|---|---|---|---|
| 1. gets in fights frequently at school | 1.00 | | | | | |
| 2. is defiant to adults | .81 | 1.00 | | | | |
| 3. is very impulsive | .79 | .75 | 1.00 | | | |
| 4. has stomachaches frequently | .42 | .38 | .36 | 1.00 | | |
| 5. is anxious about many things | .39 | .34 | .34 | .77 | 1.00 | |
| 6. appears sad much of the time | .37 | .34 | .32 | .77 | .74 | 1.00 |

**Table 2**
**Factor Loadings for Our Hypothetical Example**

| | Factor 1 | Factor 2 |
|---|---|---|
| 1. gets in fights frequently at school | .91 | .03 |
| 2. is defiant to adults | .88 | −.01 |
| 3. is very impulsive | .86 | −.01 |
| 4. has stomachaches frequently | .02 | .89 |
| 5. is anxious about many things | .01 | .86 |
| 6. appears sad much of the time | −.02 | .87 |

example, a reduction of six scores to two scores may not seem terribly useful. In actual behavior rating scales, factor analysis can reduce the overwhelming complexity of hundreds of different behavior problems to a more manageable number of scores that help professionals more easily conceptualize individual cases.

Factor analysis also calculates the correlation among factors. If a large number of factors are identified and if there are substantial correlations among factors, then this new correlation matrix can also be factor-analyzed to obtain *second-order factors.* These factors, in turn, can be analyzed to obtain *third-order factors.* Theoretically, it is possible to have even higher-order factors, but most researchers rarely find it necessary to go beyond third-order factors. The *g* factor from intelligence test data is an example of a third-order factor that emerges because all tests of cognitive abilities are positively correlated. In our previous example, the two factors have a correlation of .46, suggesting that children who have externalizing problems are also at risk of having internalizing problems. It is therefore reasonable to calculate a second-order factor score that measures the overall level of behavior problems.

This example illustrates the most commonly used type of factor analysis: *exploratory factor analysis.* Exploratory factor analysis is helpful when we wish to summarize data efficiently, when we are not sure how many factors are present in our data, or when we are not sure which items load on which factors. In short, when we are exploring or looking for factors, we may use exploratory factor analysis. When we think we have found factors and seek to *confirm* this, we may use another variety of factor analysis.

Researchers can use *confirmatory factor analysis* to test highly specific hypotheses. For example, a researcher might want to know if the two different types of items on the WISC-IV Digit Span subtest measure the same ability or two different abilities. On the Digits Forward type of item, the child must repeat a string of digits in the same order in which they were heard. On the Digits Backward type of item, the child must repeat the string of digits in reverse order. Some researchers believe that repeating numbers verbatim

measures auditory short-term memory and that repeating numbers in reverse order measures executive control, the ability to allocate attentional resources efficiently to solve multistep problems. Typically, clinicians add the raw scores of both types of items to produce a single score. If the two item types measure different abilities, then adding the raw scores together is kind of like adding apples and oranges, peaches and pears . . . you get the idea. If, however, the two items measure the same ability, then adding the scores together may yield a more reliable score than the separate scores.

Confirmatory factor analysis may be used to determine whether the two item types measure different abilities. We would need to identify or invent several additional tests that are likely to measure the two separate abilities we believe are measured by the two types of Digit Span items. Usually, three tests per factor is sufficient. Let's call the short-term memory tests STM1, STM2, and STM3. Similarly, we can call the executive control tests EC1, EC2, and EC3.

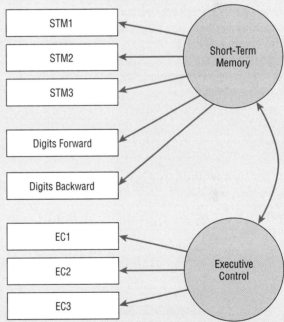

**Figure 2**

*This path diagram is a graphical representation of the hypothesis that* Both Digits Forward and Digits Backward measure short-term memory and are distinct from executive control. *Note that the curved arrow indicates the possibility that the two factors might be correlated.*

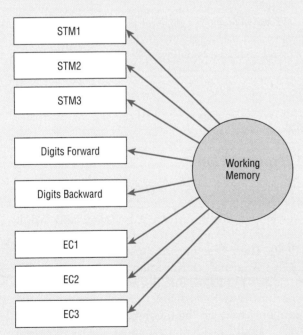

**Figure 1**

*This path diagram is a graphical representation of the hypothesis that* All of the tests measure the same ability.

*(continued)*

## Factor Analysis *(continued)*

Next, we specify the hypotheses, or models, we wish to test. There are three of them:

1. *All of the tests measure the same ability.* A graphical representation of a hypothesis in confirmatory factor analysis is called a *path diagram.* Tests are drawn with rectangles, and hypothetical factors are drawn with ovals. The correlations between tests and factors are drawn with arrows. The path diagram for this hypothesis is presented in Figure 1.

2. *Both Digits Forward and Digits Backward measure short-term memory and are distinct from executive control.* The path diagram for this hypothesis is presented in Figure 2.

3. *Digits Forward and Digits Backward measure different abilities.* The path diagram for this hypothesis is presented in Figure 3.

Confirmatory factor analysis produces a number of statistics, called *fit statistics,* that tell us which of the models or hypotheses we tested are most in agreement with the data. Studying the results, we can select the model that provides the best fit with the data or perhaps even generate a new model. Actually, factor analysis can quickly become a lot more complicated than described here, but for now, let's hope this is helpful.

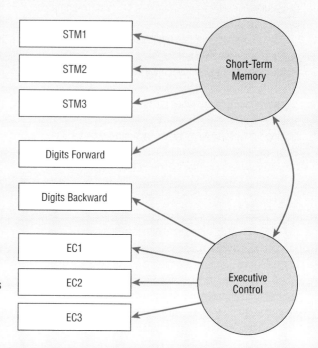

**Figure 3**
*This path diagram is a graphical representation of the hypothesis that* Digits Forward and Digits Backward *measure different abilities.*

## Other Measures of Intelligence

### Tests Designed for Individual Administration

In recent years, a growing number of tests purporting to measure intelligence have become available to test users. Some of these tests were developed by Alan and Nadeen Kaufman. This husband-wife team developed the Kaufman Adolescent and Adult Intelligence Test (KAIT; Kaufman & Kaufman, 1993) and the Kaufman Brief Intelligence Test (K-BIT; Kaufman & Kaufman, 1990). Their first flagship test was the Kaufman Assessment Battery for Children (K-ABC; Kaufman & Kaufman, 1983a, 1983b). The K-ABC departed conceptually from previously published intelligence tests with its focus on information processing and, more specifically, with its distinction between sequential and simultaneous processing. The Kaufmans drew on the theoretical writings of A. R. Luria (1966b) in the design of the K-ABC, as did Jack Naglieri and J. P. Das (Naglieri & Das, 1997) in the development of their test called the Cognitive Assessment System. Another test battery that deviated in many ways from prior measures of cognitive ability is the Differential Ability Scales (DAS). Widely used in educational settings, the DAS is discussed in more detail in Chapter 11.

An estimate of intelligence can be derived from an assessee's paper-and-pencil rendering of a human figure and other drawings, according to some researchers and clinicians (Bardos, 1993; Buck, 1948; Holtzman, 1993; Naglieri, 1993). Many methods have been proposed for obtaining such estimates, the best-known of which is the Goodenough-Harris scoring system (Harris, 1963). A long-standing controversy, however, is whether the Goodenough system is indeed "good enough." Although there is evidence that the system is reliable (Kamphaus & Pleiss, 1993; Scott, 1981), questions remain about its validity (Aikman et al., 1992; Motta et al., 1993a, 1993b; Sattler, 1992). Figure drawings hold out the promise of less time needed for evaluation, especially when the same drawings may be used for personality assessment. However, their use to assess intelligence—even as a screening device—remains controversial.

**JUST THINK . . .**

Using a drawing of a human figure to gauge intelligence has been controversial on many counts. Comment on the practice with regard to the face validity of such a measure (all puns aside).

## Tests Designed for Group Administration

The Stanford revision of the Binet-Simon test was published in 1916, and only one year later, many psychologists were compelled to start thinking about how such a test could be adapted for group administration. To understand why, we need to take a brief historical look at testing in the military.

**Group tests in the military**   On April 6, 1917, the United States entered World War I. On April 7, the president of the American Psychological Association, Robert M. Yerkes, began efforts to mobilize psychologists to help in the war effort. By late May, the APA committee that would develop group tests for the military had their first meeting. There was little debate among the participants about the nature of intelligence, only a clear sense of urgency about developing instruments for the military to identify both the "unfit" and those of "exceptionally superior ability."

Whereas the development of a major intelligence or ability test today might take three to five years, the committee had two tests ready in a matter of weeks and a final form of those tests ready for the printer on July 7. One test became known as the **Army Alpha test.** This test would be administered to Army recruits who could read. It contained tasks such as general information questions, analogies, and scrambled sentences to reassemble. The other test was the **Army Beta test,** designed for administration to foreign-born recruits with poor knowledge of English or to illiterate recruits (defined as "someone who could not read a newspaper or write a letter home"). It contained tasks such as mazes, coding, and picture completion (wherein the examinee's task was to draw in the missing element of the picture). Both tests were soon administered in army camps by teams of officers and enlisted men. By 1919 nearly 2 million recruits had been tested, 8,000 of whom had been recommended for immediate discharge on the basis of the test results. Other recruits had been assigned to various units in the Army based on their Alpha or Beta test results. For example, recruits who scored in the low but acceptable range were likely to draw duty that involved digging ditches or similar kinds of assignments.

If one dream drove the development of the Army Alpha and Beta tests, it was for the Army, other organizations, and society as a whole to run smoothly and efficiently as a result of the proper allocation of human resources—all thanks to tests. Some psychometric scrutiny of the Alpha and Beta tests supported their use. The tests were reliable enough, and they seemed to correlate acceptably with external criteria such as

Stanford-Binet Full Scale IQ scores and officers' ratings of men on "practical soldier value." Yerkes (1921) provided this explanation of what he thought the test actually measured:

> The tests give a reliable index of a man's ability to learn, to think quickly and accurately, and to comprehend instructions. They do not measure loyalty, bravery, dependability, or the emotional traits that make a man "carry on." A man's value to the service is measured by his intelligence plus other necessary qualifications. (p. 424)

An original objective of the Alpha and Beta tests was to measure the ability to be a good soldier. However, after the war, that objective seemed to get lost in the shuffle as the tests were used in various aspects of civilian life to measure general intelligence. An Army Alpha or Beta test was much easier to obtain, administer, and interpret than a Stanford-Binet test, and it was also much cheaper. Thousands of unused Alpha and Beta booklets became government surplus that almost anyone could buy. The tests were administered, scored, and interpreted by many who lacked the background and training to use them properly. The utopian vision of a society in which individuals contributed according to their abilities as determined by tests would never materialize. To the contrary, the misuse of tests soured many members of the public and the profession on the use of tests, particularly group tests.

The military's interest in psychological testing during the 1920s and 1930s was minimal. It was only when the threat of a second world war loomed that interest in group intelligence testing reemerged; this led to development of the Army General Classification Test (AGCT). During the course of World War II, the AGCT would be administered to more than 12 million recruits. Other, more specialized tests were also developed by military psychologists. An assessment unit discretely named the Office of Strategic Services (OSS) developed innovative measures for selecting spies and secret agents to work abroad. By the way, the OSS was a predecessor to today's Central Intelligence Agency (CIA).

JUST THINK . . .

James Bond aside, what qualities do you think a real secret agent needs to have? How might you measure these qualities in an applicant?

Today, group tests are still administered to prospective recruits, primarily for screening purposes. In general, we may define a **screening tool** as an instrument or procedure used to identify a particular trait or constellation of traits at a gross or imprecise level. Data derived from the process of screening may be explored in more depth by more individualized methods of assessment. Various types of screening instruments are used in many different settings. For example, in the following chapter we see how screening tools such as behavior checklists are used in preschool settings to identify young children to be evaluated with more individualized, in-depth procedures.

In the military, the long tradition of using data from screening tools as an aid to duty and training assignments continues to this day. Such data also serve to mold the nature of training experiences. For example, data from group testing have indicated a downward trend in the mean intelligence level of recruits since the inception of an all-volunteer army. In response to such findings, the military has developed new weapons training programs that incorporate, for example, simpler vocabulary in programmed instruction.

Included among many group tests used today by the armed forces are the Officer Qualifying Test (a 115-item multiple-choice test used by the U.S. Navy as an admissions test to Officer Candidate School), the Airman Qualifying Exam (a 200-item multiple-choice test given to all U.S. Air Force volunteers), and the Armed Services Vocational Aptitude Battery (ASVAB). The ASVAB is administered to prospective new recruits in all the armed services. It is also made available to high-school students and other young adults who seek guidance and counseling about their future education and career plans.

Annually, hundreds of thousands of people take the ASVAB, making it perhaps the most widely used multiple aptitude test in the United States. It is administered by school counselors and at various walk-in centers at no cost to the testtaker. In the context of a career exploration program, the ASVAB is designed to help testtakers learn about their interests, abilities, and personal preferences in relation to career opportunities in military and civilian settings. Illustrative items from each of the ten subtests are presented in this chapter's *Everyday Psychometrics*.

Through the years, various forms of the ASVAB have been produced, some for exclusive use in schools and some for exclusive use in the military. A set of 100 selected items included in the subtests of Arithmetic Reasoning, Numerical Operations, Word Knowledge, and Paragraph Comprehension make up a measure within the ASVAB called the Armed Forces Qualification Test (AFQT). The AFQT is a measure of general ability used in the selection of recruits. The different armed services employ different cutoff scores in making accept/reject determinations for service, which are based also on such considerations as their preset quotas for particular demographic groups. In addition to the AFQT score, ten aptitude areas are also tapped on the ASVAB, including general technical, general mechanics, electrical, motor-mechanics, science, combat operations, and skill-technical. These are combined to assess aptitude in five separate career areas, including clerical, electronics, mechanics, skill-technical (medical, computers), and combat operations.

The test battery is continually reviewed and improved on the basis of data regarding how predictive scores are of actual performance in various occupations and military training programs. The ASVAB has been found to predict success in computer programming and computer operating roles (Besetsny et al., 1993), multi-tasking in Navy sailors (Hambrick et al., 2011), and grades in military technical schools across a variety of fields (Earles & Ree, 1992; Ree & Earles, 1990). A review of validity studies supports the construct, content, and criterion-related validity of the ASVAB as a device to guide training and selection decisions (Welsh et al., 1990). In general, the test has been deemed quite useful for selection and placement decisions regarding personnel in the armed forces (Chan et al., 1999).

**Group tests in the schools**    Perhaps no more than a decade or two ago, approximately two-thirds of all school districts in the United States used group intelligence tests on a routine basis to screen 90% of their students. The other 10% were administered individual intelligence tests. Litigation and legislation surrounding the routine use of group intelligence tests have altered this picture somewhat. Still, the group intelligence test, now also referred to as a *school ability test,* is by no means extinct. In many states, legal mandates prohibit the use of group intelligence data alone for class assignment purposes. However, group intelligence test data can, when combined with other data, be extremely useful in developing a profile of a child's intellectual assets.

Group intelligence test results provide school personnel with valuable information for instruction-related activities and increased understanding of the individual pupil. One primary function of data from a group intelligence test is to alert educators to students who might profit from more extensive assessment with individually administered ability tests. The individually administered intelligence test, along with other tests, may point the way to placement in a special class, a program for the gifted, or some other program. Group intelligence test data can also help a school district plan educational goals for all children.

## The Armed Services Vocational Aptitude Battery (ASVAB): A Test You Can Take

If you would like firsthand experience in taking an ability test that can be useful in vocational guidance, do what about 900,000 other people do each year and take the Armed Services Vocational Aptitude Battery (ASVAB). Uncle Sam makes this test available to you free of charge—along with other elements of a career guidance package, including a workbook and other printed materials and test scoring and interpretation. Although one objective is to get testtakers "into boots" (that is, into the military), taking the test entails no obligation of military service. For more information about how you can take the ASVAB, contact your school's counseling office or a military recruiter. Meanwhile, you may wish to warm up with the following ten sample items representing each of the ten ASVAB subtests.

I.  General Science
    *Included here are general science questions, including questions from the areas of biology and physics.*
    1.  An eclipse of the sun throws the shadow of the
        a.  moon on the sun.
        b.  moon on the earth.
        c.  earth on the sun.
        d.  earth on the moon.

II. Arithmetic Reasoning
    *The task here is to solve arithmetic problems. Testtakers are permitted to use (government-supplied) scratch paper.*
    2.  It costs $0.50 per square yard to waterproof canvas. What will it cost to waterproof a canvas truck that is 15' × 24'?
        a.  $6.67
        b.  $18.00
        c.  $20.00
        d.  $180.00

III. Word Knowledge
    *Which of four possible definitions best defines the underlined word?*
    3.  Rudiments most nearly means
        a.  politics.
        b.  minute details.
        c.  promotion opportunities.
        d.  basic methods and procedures.

IV. Paragraph Comprehension
    *A test of reading comprehension and reasoning.*
    4.  Twenty-five percent of all household burglaries can be attributed to unlocked windows or doors. Crime is the result of opportunity plus desire. To prevent crime, it is each individual's responsibility to
        a.  provide the desire.
        b.  provide the opportunity.
        c.  prevent the desire.
        d.  prevent the opportunity.

V.  Numerical Operations
    *This speeded test contains simple arithmetic problems that the testtaker must solve quickly; it is one of two speeded tests on the ASVAB.*
    5.  $6 - 5 =$
        a.  1
        b.  4
        c.  2
        d.  3

VI. Coding Speed
    *This subtest contains coding items that measure perceptual/ motor speed, among other factors.*
    KEY

| green . . . 2715 | man . . . 3451 | salt . . . 4586 |
| hat . . . 1413 | room . . . 2864 | tree . . . 5927 |

|   |      | a.   | b.   | c.   | d.   | e.   |
|---|------|------|------|------|------|------|
| 6. | room | 1413 | 2715 | 2864 | 3451 | 4586 |

VII. Auto and Shop Information
*This test assesses knowledge of automobile shop practice and the use of tools.*

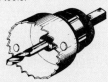

7. What tool is shown above?
   a. hole saw
   b. keyhole saw
   c. counter saw
   d. grinding saw

VIII. Mathematics Knowledge
*This is a test of ability to solve problems using high-school-level mathematics. Use of scratch paper is permitted.*
8. If $3X = -5$, then $X =$
   a. $-2$
   b. $-5/3$
   c. $-3/5$
   d. $3/5$

IX. Mechanical Comprehension
*Knowledge and understanding of general mechanical and physical principles are probed by this test.*

9. Liquid is being transferred from the barrel to the bucket by
   a. capillary action.
   b. gravitational forces.
   c. fluid pressure in the hose.
   d. water pressure in the barrel.

X. Electronics Information
*Here, knowledge of electrical, radio, and electronics information is assessed.*

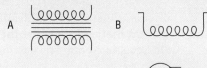

10. Which of the above is the symbol for a transformer?
   a. A
   b. B
   c. C
   d. D

---

Answer Key
1. b
2. c
3. d
4. d
5. Why are you looking this one up?
6. c
7. a
8. b
9. b
10. a

Group intelligence tests in the schools are used in special forms as early as the kindergarten level. The tests are administered to groups of 10 to 15 children, each of whom receives a test booklet that includes printed pictures and diagrams. For the most part, simple motor responses are required to answer items. Oversized alternatives in the form of pictures in a multiple-choice test might appear on the pages, and it is the child's job to circle or place an $X$ on the picture that represents the correct answer to the item presented orally by the examiner. During such testing in small groups, the testtakers will be carefully monitored to make certain they are following the directions.

The California Test of Mental Maturity, the Kuhlmann-Anderson Intelligence Tests, the Henmon-Nelson Tests of Mental Ability, and the Cognitive Abilities Test are some of the many group intelligence tests available for use in school settings. The first group intelligence test to be used in U.S. schools was the Otis-Lennon School Ability Test, formerly the Otis Mental Ability Test. In its current edition, the test is designed to measure abstract thinking and reasoning ability and to assist in school evaluation and placement decision-making. This nationally standardized test yields Verbal and Nonverbal score indexes as well as an overall School Ability Index (SAI).

In general, group tests are useful screening tools when large numbers of examinees must be evaluated either simultaneously or within a limited time frame. More specific advantages—and disadvantages—of traditional group testing are listed in Table 10–7. We qualify group testing with *traditional* because more contemporary forms of group testing, especially testing with all testtakers seated at a computer station, might more aptly be termed *individual assessment simultaneously administered in a group* rather than *group testing.*

**JUST THINK. . .**

How has the dynamics of what has traditionally been referred to as "group testing" changed as a result of the administration of tests to groups of testtakers using personal computers?

Regardless of the number of students to whom a psychological test is administered to in the schools, all reports of psychological testing and assessment must be meaningful and actionable. Toward that end, consider the recommendations of our guest assessment professional, Dr. Rebecca Anderson (see this chapter's *Meet an Assessment Professional*).

**Table 10–7**
**The Pros and Cons of Traditional Group Testing**

| Advantages of Group Tests | Disadvantages of Group Tests |
|---|---|
| Large numbers of testtakers can be tested at one time, offering efficient use of time and resources. | All testtakers, regardless of ability, typically must start on the same item, end on the same item, and be exposed to every item on the test. Opportunity for adaptive testing is minimized. |
| Testtakers work independently at their own pace. | Testtakers must be able to work independently and understand what is expected of them, with little or no opportunity for questions or clarification once testing has begun. |
| Test items are typically in a format easily scored by computer or machine. | Test items may not be in more innovative formats or any format involving examiner manipulation of materials or examiner–examinee interaction. |
| The test administrator need not be highly trained, as task may require little beyond reading instructions, keeping time, and supervising testtakers. | Opportunity for assessor observation of testtaker's extra-test behavior is lost. |
| Test administrator may have less effect on the examinee's score than a test administrator in a one-on-one situation. | Opportunity for learning about assessee through assessor–assessee interaction is lost. |
| Group testing is less expensive than individual testing on a per-testtaker basis. | The information from a group test may not be as detailed and actionable as information from an individual test administration. |
| Group testing has proven value for screening purposes. | Instruments designed expressly for screening are occasionally used for making momentous decisions. |
| Group tests may be normed on large numbers of people more easily than an individual test. | In any test-taking situation, testtakers are assumed to be motivated to perform and follow directions. The opportunity to verify these assumptions may be minimized in large-scale testing programs. The testtaker who "marches to the beat of a different drummer" is at a greater risk of obtaining a score that does not accurately approximate his or her hypothetical true score. |
| Group tests work well with people who can read, follow directions, grip a pencil, and do not require a great deal of assistance. | Group tests may not work very well with people who cannot read, who cannot grip a pencil (such as very young children), who "march to the beat of a different drummer," or who have exceptional needs or requirements. |

## Meet Dr. Rebecca Anderson

In my opinion, one of the most important components of an evaluation is generating a report that is reader friendly and provides useful information for parents and teachers who are directly working with the child. A key component of the evaluation is the summary, which should provide a concise picture of the child's strengths and areas of difficulty. Moreover, the recommendations section is a critical element of the report and should provide useful information on ways to support the child's social/emotional and educational success. I try to give recommendations that are accessible to staff and provide tangible tools and suggestions that can be implemented both at home and at school. I often list additional resources (such as books, internet sites, handouts) specific to the child's area of deficiency.

Realistically, when working within the schools, there are strict timelines, which prohibit extensive evaluations. I think one of the biggest challenges relates to the time and effort that goes into a student's evaluation. Schools are often under budget restrictions and want things done quickly. As a rule of thumb, I conduct more thorough evaluations on students who are receiving an initial evaluation in order to determine the nature of the presenting problem. Less time is required for re-evaluation of students who are already receiving specialized support services.

**Rebecca Anderson, Ph.D., Independent Practice, Consulting School Psychologist**

An additional obstacle in the assessment process is accessing parents and staff. I make several efforts to contact parents. If unsuccessful, I note that parental information was unavailable at the time of the evaluation. Ideally, school psychologists would be given ample time and resources and have access to parents and all relevant school personnel, but the reality is that we do the best we can with the time allotted and available resources.

*Read more of what Dr. Anderson had to say—her complete essay—at www.mhhe.com/cohentesting8.*

## Measures of Cognitive Style and Specific Intellectual Abilities

Widely used measures of general intelligence sample only a small realm of the many human abilities that may be conceived of as contributing to an individual's intelligence. There are many known intellectual abilities and talents that are not—or are only indirectly—assessed by popular intelligence tests. There are, for example, tests available to measure very specific abilities such as critical thinking, music, or art appreciation. There is also an evolving knowledge base regarding what are called *cognitive styles.* A **cognitive style** is a psychological dimension that characterizes the consistency with which one acquires and processes information (Ausburn & Ausburn, 1978; Messick, 1976). Examples of cognitive styles include Witkin et al.'s (1977) field dependence

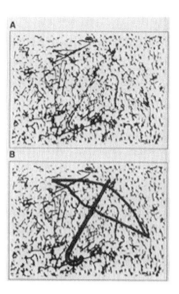

**FIGURE 10–2**
**An Item from the Degraded Pictures Test**

*Seated in front of a computer screen, the testtaker's task is to distinguish degraded line drawings of common objects set against background visual "noise." After a picture such as that shown in "A" is presented, testtakers are instructed to press a key as soon as they recognize an image within the picture. The image then disappears from the screen and the testtaker must type in the name of the image that they think they saw. For this item, as illustrated in the less degraded version (Item B), the correct answer would be "umbrella."*

versus field independence dimension, the reflection versus impulsivity dimension (Messer, 1976), and the visualizer versus verbalizer dimension (Kirby et al., 1988; Paivio, 1971). Researching the latter dimension, and using measurement tools such as the Degraded Pictures Test (see Figure 10–2), Maria Kozhevnikov and her colleagues (2005) demonstrated that visual processers can usefully be further subdivided into those that do well on *object* imagery tasks, and those that do well on *spatial* imagery tasks. Building on these and related findings, she proposed the existence of new component of intelligence called *visual-object ability* (Blazhenkova & Kozhevnikov, 2010). According to Kozhevnikov and her colleagues, **visual-object ability** reflects the ability to process information about the visual appearance of objects as well as the pictorial properties of the object (such as shape, color, and texture).

Interestingly, although most intelligence tests do not measure creativity, tests designed to measure creativity may well measure variables related to intelligence. For example, some component abilities of creativity are thought to be originality in problem solving, originality in perception, and originality in abstraction. To the extent that tests of intelligence tap these components, measures of creativity may also be thought of as tools for assessing intelligence. We conclude this chapter with a relatively brief survey of some measures of creativity.

**Measures of creativity.** A number of tests and test batteries are available to measure creativity in children and adults. In fact, some universities, such as the University of Georgia and the State University College of New York at Buffalo, maintain libraries containing several hundred of these tests. What types of tasks are featured on these tests? And what do these tests really measure?

Four terms common to many measures of creativity are *originality, fluency, flexibility,* and *elaboration. Originality* refers to the ability to produce something that is innovative or nonobvious. It may be something abstract like an idea or something tangible and visible like artwork or a poem. *Fluency* refers to the ease with which responses are reproduced and is usually measured by the total number of responses produced. For example, an item in a test of word fluency might be *In the next thirty seconds, name as many words as you can that begin with the letter w. Flexibility* refers to the variety of ideas presented and the ability to shift from one approach to another. *Elaboration* refers to the richness of detail in a verbal explanation or pictorial display.

A criticism frequently leveled at group standardized intelligence tests (as well as at other ability and achievement tests) is that evaluation of test performance is too heavily focused on whether the answer is correct. The heavy emphasis on correct response leaves little room for the evaluation of processes such as originality, fluency, flexibility, and elaboration. Stated another way, on most achievement tests the thought process typically required is *convergent thinking*. **Convergent thinking** is a deductive reasoning process that entails recall and consideration of facts as well as a series of logical judgments to narrow down solutions and eventually arrive at one solution. In his structure-of-intellect model, Guilford (1967) drew a distinction between the intellectual processes of *convergent* and *divergent* thinking. **Divergent thinking** is a reasoning process in which thought is free to move in many different directions, making several solutions possible. Divergent thinking requires flexibility of thought, originality, and imagination. There is much less emphasis on recall of facts than in convergent thinking. Guilford's model has served to focus research attention not only on the products but also on the process of creative thought.

Guilford (1954) described several tasks designed to measure creativity, such as Consequences ("Imagine what would happen if . . .") and Unusual Uses (for example, "Name as many uses as you can think of for a rubber band"). Included in Guilford et al.'s (1974) test battery, the Structure-of-Intellect Abilities, are verbally oriented tasks (such as Word Fluency) and nonverbally oriented tasks (such as Sketches).

A number of other tests are available to tap various aspects of creativity. For example, based on the work of Mednick (1962), the Remote Associates Test (RAT) presents the testtaker with three words; the task is to find a fourth word associated with the other three. The Torrance (1966, 1987a, 1987b) Tests of Creative Thinking consist of word-based, picture-based, and sound-based test materials. In a subtest of different sounds, for example, the examinee's task is to respond with the thoughts that each sound conjures up. Each subtest is designed to measure various characteristics deemed important in the process of creative thought.

> **JUST THINK . . .**
> Based on this brief description of the RAT and the Torrance Tests, demonstrate your own creativity by creating a new RAT or Torrance Test item that is unmistakably one from the twenty-first century.

It is interesting that many tests of creativity do not fare well when evaluated by traditional psychometric procedures. For example, the test-retest reliability estimates for some of these tests tend to border on the unacceptable range. Some have wondered aloud whether tests of creativity should be judged by different standards from other tests. After all, creativity may differ from other abilities in that it may be highly susceptible to emotional or physical health, motivation, and related factors—even more so than other abilities. This fact would explain tenuous reliability and validity estimates.

> **JUST THINK . . .**
> Should tests of creativity be held to different psychometric standards from other ability tests?

As you read about various human abilities and how they all might be related to that intangible construct *intelligence,* you may have said to yourself, "Why doesn't anyone create a test that measures all these diverse aspects of intelligence?"

Although no one has undertaken that ambitious project, in recent years test packages have been developed to test not only intelligence but also related abilities in educational settings. These test packages, called *psychoeducational batteries,* are discussed in the chapter that follows, along with other tests used to measure academic skills and abilities.

## Self-Assessment

Test your understanding of elements of this chapter by seeing if you can explain each of the following terms, expressions, and abbreviations:

adaptive testing
AFQT
age scale
alternate item
Army Alpha test
Army Beta test
ASVAB
basal level
Binet, Alfred
ceiling
ceiling level
cognitive style
convergent thinking

core subtest
deviation IQ
divergent thinking
extra-test behavior
floor
IQ (intelligence quotient)
optional subtest
point scale
process score
RAT
ratio IQ
routing test
screening tool

short form
Stanford-Binet
supplemental subtest
Terman, Lewis
teaching item
test composite
testing the limits
visual-object ability
WAIS-IV
WASI
Wechsler, David
WISC-IV
WPPSI-III

# 11

# *Assessment for Education*

W hat word comes to mind first when you think of the word *school?*

If the word *test* came to mind, it would certainly be understandable. Dozens—maybe even hundreds—of tests are administered to students over the course of their academic career. Included are teacher-made tests, state-mandated tests, psychologist-recommended tests, and assorted other tests. Why so many tests?

> **JUST THINK . . .**
>
> How many tests would you estimate you have taken since you first entered preschool or elementary school?

## The Role of Testing and Assessment in Education

Educators are interested in answers to diverse questions as students progress through school. If they had a "wish list" of questions they would like you, the student, to answer, a small sampling of the questions on that list might be as follows:

*How much of this course material have you actually learned?*

*Have you mastered the material in this course?*

*How does the knowledge you acquired in this course compare to the knowledge acquired by your classmates?*

*Are you having difficulties learning any material, and if so, why?*

*How good is the fit between you and the educational program that you seek enrollment in?*

From the perspective of students, perhaps the most obvious reason testing occurs is to ensure that knowledge being shared by the teacher (in the classroom, on the Internet, or however and wherever teaching is taking place) has indeed been received and learned by the student. But educators are also interested in helping students better their learning skills. Toward that end, educators may administer tests designed to pinpoint possible areas of learning difficulty. There are other circumstances wherein educators have a compelling interest in knowing the extent to which their students—or prospective students—are prepared to learn more advanced material. In such cases, tests variously referred to as "readiness" or "aptitude" tests may be administered. Yet another reason testing occurs in classrooms is very simple: the testing is required by law. And speaking of testing in the schools and the law, let's consider the (legislation-driven) exploding popularity of RtI. That upper case *R*, lower case *t*, and upper case *I* stands for . . .

## Response to Intervention (RtI)

**Background** In the mid-1970s, the federal mandate to identify and assist children with learning problems defined a learning disability as a "severe discrepancy between achievement and intellectual ability" (*Procedures for Evaluating Specific Learning Disabilities*, 1977, p. 65083). For decades thereafter, a specific learning disability (SLD) was diagnosed if a significant discrepancy existed between the child's measured intellectual ability (usually on an intelligence test) and the level of achievement that could reasonably be expected from the child in one or more areas (including oral expression, listening comprehension, written expression, basic reading skills, reading comprehension, mathematics calculation, and mathematics reasoning). However, all of that changed with a new definition of SLD and new diagnostic guidelines.

As defined in 2007 by Public Law 108-147, a **specific learning disability** is "a disorder in one or more of the basic psychological processes involved in understanding or in using language, spoken or written, which disorder may manifest itself in the imperfect ability to listen, think, speak, read, write, spell, or do mathematical calculations." Also, as reauthorized in 2004 and enacted into law in 2006, the Individuals with Disabilities Education Act (IDEA) no longer mandated that state-adopted criteria for defining SLD be made on the basis of a severe discrepancy between intellectual ability and achievement. Rather, it required states to allow "the use of a process based on the child's *response to* scientific, research-based *intervention*" (emphasis added). Although academics had been writing about "response to intervention" in the interim period (see, for example, Dwairy, 2004), all of a sudden the rush to understand and apply this model was on. By 2008 most states had in place legislative or regulatory policies that changed their existing special educations to require RtI (Zirkel & Krohn, 2008).

**JUST THINK . . .**

Why do you think there has been so much disagreement and controversy over the definition of the term *learning disability*? Why is it so important to "get it right"?

**The RtI model** Based on the definition presented on the federally funded website of the National Center on Response to Intervention (2011, p. 2), we may define the **response to intervention model** as a multilevel prevention framework applied in educational settings that is designed to maximize student achievement through the use of data that identifies students at risk for poor learning outcomes combined with evidence-based intervention and teaching that is adjusted on the basis of student responsiveness. A simpler description of this model of teaching and assessment is: (a) Teachers provide evidence-based instruction, (b) student learning of that instruction is regularly evaluated, (c) intervention, if required, occurs in some form of appropriate adjustment in the instruction, (d) reevaluation of learning takes place, and (e) intervention and reassessment occur as necessary.

The model is *multilevel* because there are at least three levels of intervention (or teaching). The first level is the classroom environment wherein all students are being taught whatever it is that the teacher is teaching. The second level of intervention is one in which a small group of learners who have failed to make adequate progress in the classroom have been segregated for special teaching. The third level of intervention is individually tailored and administered instruction for students who have failed to respond to the second level of intervention.

By providing intervention (teaching or remedial instruction, as the case may be) appropriate to the level of the student's needs, the objective of RtI is to accelerate the learning process for all students. In addition, RtI doubles as a process in place that will identify students with learning disabilities. In this sense, RtI is seen by many as superior to the more traditional, referral-based process—which has been characterized as a "wait to fail" process (Fletcher et al., 2002). However, questions regarding the exact nature of a learning disability and the relationship between measured intelligence and academic learning have hardly gone away (Büttner & Hasselhorn, 2011; Collier, 2011; Davis & Broitman, 2011; Goldstein, 2011; Kane et al., 2011; Maehler & Schuchardt, 2009; Swanson, 2011).

**Implementing RtI**  Owing at least in part to the federal mandate, the RtI-related literature has been burgeoning (see, for example, Fuchs & Fuchs, 2006; Gustafson et al., 2011; Jackson et al., 2009; Johnston, 2011; Mesmer & Duhon, 2011; Petscher et al., 2011; Speece et al., 2011; Tran et al., 2011; Wixon, 2011). Still, because the law left implementation of RtI to the states and school districts, many important questions remain regarding exactly how RtI is to be implemented. Some states and school districts employ what has been referred to as a *problem-solving model*. In this context, **problem-solving model** refers to the use of interventions tailored to students' individual needs that are selected by a multidisciplinary team of school professionals. By contrast, other states and school districts rely more on a more general intervention policy, one selected by the school's administration and designed to address the needs of multiple students. Some schools have put in place a hybrid of these two approaches. That is, some standard school policy is applied to all students, but there are provisions to allow for the problem-solving approach with certain students under certain conditions.

Many critical questions remain regarding exactly how RtI is to be implemented. Some of these questions include: What criteria should be used in moving students from one level to the other in the multilevel model? What tests should be used to assess learning and response to intervention? What are the respective roles of school personnel such as classroom teachers, school psychologists, reading teachers, and guidance counselors in implementing RtI?

Tests and measurement procedures designed to answer RtI-related questions are being developed, and tests already published are being suggested as useful within an RtI model (see, for example, Coleman & Johnsen, 2011; Penner-Williams et al., 2009; Watson et al., 2011; Willcutt et al., 2011). With reference to the question regarding the respective roles of school personnel, it is useful to keep in mind that the same legislation (IDEA) that mandated RtI also encouraged the use of multiple sources of input with regard to the diagnosis of disability. More specifically, IDEA mandated that no single measure be used "as the sole criterion for determining whether a child is a child with a disability." In a comment designed to clarify the intent of the law, the Department of Education wrote that "an evaluation must include a variety of assessment tools and strategies and cannot rely on any single procedure as the sole criterion for determining eligibility for special education and related services." In diagnosing (and treating) disabilities, particularly learning disabilities, it is useful to employ not only various tools of assessment, but input from various school personnel, as well as parents, and other relevant sources of information. The term **integrative assessment** has been used to describe a multidisciplinary approach to evaluation that assimilates input from relevant sources. Judging from the essay written by our guest professional in this chapter, school psychologist Eliane Hack (see *Meet an Assessment Professional*), integrative assessment is very much a part of the assessment program at her school.

## Meet Eliane Hack, M.A.

Imagine reading an intriguing mystery novel. The author has laid out the core clues of the case. You, the reader, have your own theories mapped out in your mind. You turn the page to read further, only to discover that the next page is missing. Several pages have been ripped out! You only have one perspective of the story. The solution is therefore incomplete. The same is true for psychoeducational testing that does not incorporate an interdisciplinary approach. In school-based assessments, there will be many team members who contribute vital information in piecing together a child's learning profile. An assessment that does not include multiple measures from various data sources and disciplines is not a full assessment.

With the reauthorization of the *Response to Intervention (RtI)* guidelines in New York State, interdisciplinary testing takes on a whole new meaning. Now, more than ever, the information from classroom and reading teachers holds a great deal of weight in the identification of a specific learning disability. A balance must exist between standardized testing and data supporting response (or nonresponse) to intervention. Whereas school psychologists previously relied more heavily on a discrepancy formula for eligibility into special education, the RtI process urges evaluators to consider external factors that may impede learning. In essence, RtI looks to "even the playing field" by systematically providing intensive levels of intervention before ultimately determining that a disability is "within" a child. Going with the earlier "detective" theme, imagine Sherlock Holmes, or his more modern counterpart, Dr. House. Both used methods of measurement and reasoning to form a hypothesis. They then test the hypothesis to see if it holds weight. To relate this back to the identification of learning disabilities, the interdisciplinary team will focus on a specific target area of intervention. Let's say they are focusing on sight-word recognition. The teacher and interventionists will be responsible for

**Eliane Hack, M.A., School Psychologist, Queensbury Elementary School, Queensbury, NY**

measuring improvement in sight-word vocabulary with additional intervention (either a specific reading program or targeted strategy). After several weeks of intervention and monitoring, results are reviewed. With this information, the team will determine if the same intervention should continue, a new intervention should be introduced, or a higher level of intervention is necessary. After plotting out several data points, it may be evident that the child has not responded to the intervention. At this point, a team can more appropriately discuss the need for a comprehensive psychoeducational evaluation. RtI is an important step in the process of ruling out that a learning difficulty is not due to lack of instruction, or environmental, cultural, or economic disadvantage. Students with these types of disadvantages are oftentimes misidentified as needing special education support, when truly they were in need of specific academic interventions for a more short-term period. RtI seeks to close this gap.

As an undergraduate school psychology intern, my advisor impressed upon me that the most important skill of a school psychologist is the ability to see the obvious. In a field where children are often represented by test scores and data, it is important to consider the real-world impact for what these scores suggest, and not to lose sight of the fact that a child is more than a set of numbers. Sometimes test scores help explain a deficit, and sometimes they make it more mysterious. One should never underestimate the power of confounding variables! Equally, one should never assume the overall power of a single test score. Interdisciplinary evaluations are a good way to get a more complete picture of a child, but the most indispensable skill for professionals across all education-related fields is to see through to the obvious.

*Read more of what school psychologist Eliane Hack had to say—her complete essay—at www .mhhe.com/cohentesting8.*

RtI is what has been termed a "dynamic" model. To understand what is meant by that, it is necessary to understand what is meant by "dynamic assessment."

## Dynamic Assessment

Although originally developed for use with children, a dynamic approach to assessment may be used with testtakers of any age. It is an approach to assessment that departs from reliance on, and can be contrasted to, fixed (so-called "static") tests. Dynamic assessment encompasses an approach to exploring learning potential that is based on a test-intervention-retest model. The theoretical underpinnings of this approach can be traced to the work of Budoff (1967, 1987), Feuerstein (1977, 1981), and Vygotsky (1978).

Budoff explored differences between deficits identified by standardized tests that seemed to be due to differences in education versus mental deficiency. He did this by determining whether training could improve test performance. Feuerstein's efforts focused on the extent to which teaching of principles and strategies (or mediated learning) modified cognition. Based on this research, he and his colleagues developed a dynamic system of assessment tasks called The Learning Potential Assessment Device (LPAD; Feuerstein et al., 1979). The LPAD was designed to yield information about the nature and amount of intervention required to enhance a child's performance. Vygotsky (see Figure 11–1) introduced the concept of a **zone of proximal development** or "the distance between the actual developmental level as determined by individual problem-solving, and the level of potential development as determined through problem-solving under adult guidance or in collaboration with more capable peers" (1978, p. 86). The "zone" referred to is, in essence, the area between a testtaker's ability as measured by a formal test and what might be possible as the result of instruction, "guidance," or related intervention. It may be thought of as an index of learning potential that will vary depending upon factors such as the extent of the testtaker's abilities and the nature of the task.

Dynamic assessment procedures differ from more traditional assessment procedures in several key ways. Whereas examiners administering tests in the traditional ways are taught to scrupulously maintain neutrality, dynamic

**Figure 11–1**
**Lev Semyonovitch Vygotsky (1896–1934)**

*Now viewed as a celebrated researcher in the history of Soviet psychology and a present-day influence in American education and psychology, Vygotsky was hardly celebrated in his homeland during his lifetime. He labored under strict government regulation and censorship and widespread anti-Semitism (Etkind, 1994). He worked for very little pay, lived in the basement of the institute in which he worked, and suffered ill health—succumbing at the age of 38 from years of living with tuberculosis. Although his political views were Marxist, he was hardly embraced by the authorities. In the end his works were banned by the government and, as Zinchenko (2007) put it, "he was lucky to have managed to die in his own bed."*

*Vygotsky's impact on the behavioral science community will be long felt years after the relatively brief decade or so that his psychology laboratory was active. His published writings stimulated thought in diverse fields, including educational psychology, developmental psychology, and physiological psychology. A. R. Luria was a contemporary of Vygotsky, and Vygotsky was believed to have had a great influence on Luria's thinking (Radzikhovskii & Khomskaya, 1981). In his own autobiography, Luria referred to Vygotsky as a genius.*

assessors—especially when intervening with teaching, coaching, or other "guidance"—are hardly neutral. To the contrary, their goal may be to do everything in their power to help the testtaker master material in preparation for retesting. Depending upon the assessor's particular approach to dynamic assessment, variations may be introduced into the assessment that are designed to better understand or remediate the obstacles to learning. These variations may take any number of different forms, such as clues or prompts delivered in verbal or nonverbal ways. Of course, the great diversity of approaches to dynamic assessment in terms of the goals pursued and the specific techniques and methods used make it difficult to judge the validity of this approach (Beckmann, 2006).

Dynamic assessment is, as you might expect, consistent with the response to intervention model (Wagner & Compton, 2011; Fuchs et al., 2011). For her doctoral dissertation, Emily Duvall (2011) conducted a pilot study with third-graders wherein a state-mandated standardized test was redesigned for purposes of dynamic assessment. She reported that employing dynamic assessment not only facilitated the goal of illuminating the progress that learning disabled children make as a result of intervention, but offered valuable and actionable data to multiple stakeholders (the children being assessed, their parents, teachers, and the school administration).

Of course, before rushing off to convert any standardized tests into a form amenable to dynamic assessment, it is important to acquire a sound understanding of and appreciation for the benefits of such tests as they were developed. Toward that end, we now proceed to describe and survey a small sampling of some standardized (as well as nonstandardized) achievement tests, aptitude tests, and related tools of assessment.

## Achievement Tests

**Achievement tests** are designed to measure accomplishment. An achievement test for a first-grader might have as its subject matter the English language alphabet, whereas an achievement test for a college student might contain questions relating to principles of psychological assessment. In short, achievement tests are designed to measure the degree of learning that has taken place as a result of exposure to a relatively defined learning experience. "Relatively defined learning experience" may mean something as broad as *what was learned from four years of college,* or something much narrower, such as *how to prepare dough for use in making pizza.* In most educational settings, achievement tests are used to gauge student progress toward instructional objectives, compare an individual's accomplishment to peers, and help determine what instructional activities and strategies might best propel the students toward educational objectives.

A test of achievement may be standardized nationally, regionally, or locally, or it may not be standardized at all. The pop quiz on the anatomy of a frog given by your high-school biology teacher qualifies as an achievement test every bit as much as a statewide examination in biology.

Like other tests, achievement tests vary widely with respect to their psychometric soundness. A sound achievement test is one that adequately samples the targeted subject matter and reliably gauges the extent to which the examinees have learned it.

Scores on achievement tests may be put to varied uses. They may help school personnel make decisions about a student's placement in a particular class, acceptance into a program, or advancement to a higher grade level. Achievement test data can be helpful in gauging the quality of instruction in a particular class, school, school district, or state. Achievement tests are sometimes used to screen for difficulties, and in such instances they may precede the administration of more specific tests designed to identify areas that may require remediation. One general way of categorizing achievement tests is in terms of how general their content is in nature.

### *Measures of General Achievement*

Measures of general achievement may survey learning in one or more academic areas. Tests that cover a number of academic areas are typically divided into several subtests and are referred to as *achievement batteries.* Such batteries may be individually administered or group administered. They may consist of a few subtests, as does the Wide Range Achievement Test–4 (Wilkinson & Robertson, 2006) with its measures of reading, spelling, arithmetic, and (new to the fourth edition) reading comprehension. A general measure of achievement may be quite comprehensive, as is the Sequential Tests of Educational Progress (STEP) battery. Used in kindergarten through grade 12, the STEP battery includes achievement subtests in reading, vocabulary, mathematics, writing skills, study skills, science, and social studies, as well as a behavior inventory, an educational environment questionnaire, and an activities inventory. Because it is frequently used to identify gifted children, any of the "five steps" may be administered at or above the testtaker's grade level.

Some batteries, such as the SRA California Achievement Tests, span kindergarten through grade 12, whereas others are grade- or course-specific. Some batteries are constructed to provide both norm-referenced and criterion-referenced analyses. Others are concurrently normed with scholastic aptitude tests to enable a comparison between achievement and aptitude. Some batteries are constructed with practice tests that may be administered several days before actual testing to help students familiarize themselves with test-taking procedures. Other batteries contain **locator tests,** or routing tests, pretests administered to determine the level of the actual test most appropriate for administration.

One popular instrument appropriate for use with persons age 4 through adult (age 50 is the age limit) is the Wechsler Individual Achievement Test–Third Edition, otherwise known as the WIAT-III (Psychological Corporation, 2009). Designed for use in the schools as well as clinical and research settings, this battery contains a total of 16 subtests, although not every subtest will be administered to every testtaker. The test was nationally standardized on 3,000 student and adult testtakers, and the manual provides comprehensive normative information. The test has been favorably reviewed regarding its potential to yield actionable data relating to student achievement in academic areas such as reading, writing, and mathematics, as well as skill in listening and speaking (Vaughan-Jensen et al., 2011).

Of the many available achievement batteries, the test most appropriate for use is the one most consistent with the educational objectives of the individual teacher or school system. For a particular purpose, a battery that focuses on achievement in a few select areas may be preferable to one that attempts to sample achievement in several areas. On the other hand, a test that samples many areas may be advantageous when an individual comparison of performance across subject areas is desirable. If a school or a local school district undertakes to follow the progress of a group of students as measured by a particular achievement battery, then the battery of choice will be one that spans the targeted subject areas in all the grades to be tested. If ability to distinguish individual areas of difficulty is of primary concern, then achievement tests with strong diagnostic features will be chosen.

Although achievement batteries sampling a wide range of areas, across grades, and standardized on large, national samples of students have much to recommend them, they also have certain drawbacks. For example, such tests usually take years to develop. In the interim, many of the items, especially in fields such as social studies and science, may become outdated. When selecting such a test, there are certain "musts," as well as certain "desirables," to keep in mind. Psychometric soundness— that is, well-documented reliability and validity data for members of the population to whom the test will be administered—is a must when evaluating the suitability of any nationally standardized test for a local administration. Another "must" is that possible sources of bias in the test have been minimized. In the "desirables" category, it is a plus if the test is relatively easy to administer and score. Further, it is desirable for the content to be up-to-date, as well as engaging and relevant for its targeted audience of testtakers.

## Measures of Achievement in Specific Subject Areas

Whereas achievement batteries tend to be standardized instruments, most measures of achievement in specific subject areas are teacher-made tests. Every time a teacher gives a quiz, a test, or a final examination in a course, a test in a specific subject area has been created. Still, there are a number of standardized instruments designed to gauge achievement in specific areas.

At the elementary-school level, the acquisition of basic skills such as reading, writing, and arithmetic is emphasized. Tests to measure achievement in reading come in many different forms. For example, there are tests for individual or group administration and for silent or oral reading. The tests may vary in the theory of cognitive ability on which they are based and in the type of subtest data they yield. In general, the tests present the examinee with words, sentences, or paragraphs to be read silently or aloud, and reading ability is assessed by variables such as comprehension and vocabulary. When the material is read aloud, accuracy and speed are measured. Tests of reading comprehension also vary with respect to the intellectual demands placed on the examinee beyond mere comprehension of the words read. Thus, some tests might require the examinee to simply recall facts from a passage whereas others might require interpretation and the making of inferences.

At the secondary school level, one popular battery is the Cooperative Achievement Test. It consists of a series of separate achievement tests in areas as diverse as English, mathematics, literature, social studies, science, and foreign languages. Each test was standardized on different populations appropriate to the grade level, with samples randomly selected and stratified according to public, parochial, and private schools. In general, the tests tend to be technically sound instruments. Assessment of achievement in high-school students may involve evaluation of minimum competencies, often as a requirement for a high-school diploma (see this chapter's *Close-Up*).

At the college level, state legislatures are becoming more interested in mandating end-of-major outcomes assessment in state colleges and universities. Apparently taxpayers want confirmation that their education tax dollars are being well spent. Thus, for example, undergraduate psychology students attending a state-run institution could be required in their senior year to sit for a final—in the literal sense—examination encompassing a range of subject matter that could be described as "everything that an undergraduate psychology major should know." And if that sounds formidable to you, be advised that the task of developing such examinations is all the more formidable.

Another use for achievement tests at the college level, as well as for adults, is placement. The advanced placement program developed by the College Entrance Examination Board offers high-school students the opportunity to achieve college credit for work completed in high school. Successful completion of the advanced placement test may result in advanced standing, advanced course credit, or both, depending on the college policy. Since its inception, the advanced placement program has resulted in advanced credit or standing for more than 100,000 high-school students in approximately 2,000 colleges.

Tests of English proficiency or English as a second language are yet another example of a specific variety of achievement test. Data from such tests are currently used in the placement of college applicants in appropriate levels of English as a Second Language (ESL) programs.

Achievement tests at the college or adult level may also assess whether college credit should be awarded for learning acquired outside a college classroom. Numerous programs are designed to systematically assess whether

**JUST THINK . . .**

There have been growing calls for "English only" in some American communities and states. If such demands find their way into legislation, how might that affect the ways English proficiency test results are used?

# Tests of Minimum Competency

Soon after the United States became an independent nation, one citizen commented in a book entitled *Letters from an American Farmer* that a "pleasing uniformity of decent competence appears throughout our habitations" (Crèvecoeur, 1762/1951, cited in Lerner, 1981). Over 200 years later, widespread dissatisfaction with the *lack* of competence in this country has become evident. At about the time of the nation's bicentennial celebration, a grassroots movement aimed at eradicating illiteracy and anumeracy began taking shape. By 1980, legislation had been passed in 38 states requiring the schools to administer a test to determine whether secondary-school graduates had developed "minimum competence." Exactly what constituted minimum competence varied from one jurisdiction to the next, but it generally referred to some basic knowledge of reading, writing, and arithmetic. The movement has gained momentum with the realization that the illiterate and anumerate often wind up not just unemployed but unemployable. The unfortunate consequence is that too many of these individuals require public assistance or, alternatively, turn to crime—some finding their way to jail.

A minimum competency testing program is designed to ensure that a student who is awarded a high-school diploma has at least acquired the minimal skills to become a productive member of society. Such minimal skills include filling out an employment application, writing checks, balancing a checkbook, and interpreting a bank statement.

As an example of one test of minimum competency, we focus attention on the Alabama High School Graduation Exam (AHSGE). A publication of the Alabama State Department of Education (Teague, 1983) sets forth detailed specifications for items to be used in the AHSGE. The skills that are tested are based on ninth-grade minimum competencies in the areas of Reading, Language, and Mathematics. Some of the skills listed in the area of Language are as follows.

- *Observe pronoun-antecedent agreement.* The student chooses the pronoun that agrees with its antecedent.

- *Use correct forms of nouns and verbs.* The student chooses the correct form of nouns (singular and/or plural) and verbs (regular and/or irregular) and selects verbs that agree with the subjects.

- *Include in a message or request all necessary information (who, what, when, where, how, or why).* The student demonstrates knowledge about the information necessary in a message or request.

- *Determine what information is missing from a message, an announcement, or a process explanation; or what information is irrelevant.*

- *Identify question marks, periods, and exclamation points to punctuate sentences.*

- *Identify words frequently used in daily activities.* The student recognizes frequently used words that are spelled incorrectly.

- *Complete a common form, such as a driver's license application or change of address form.*

- *Identify the proper format of a friendly letter.*

- *Identify the proper format of a business letter.* The student demonstrates knowledge of the proper format of a business letter, which includes punctuation and capitalization. (Test questions refer to business letters reproduced in the test booklet; an example appears at the end of this *Close-Up*.)

Although minimum competency may seem like a good idea, it has not gone unchallenged in the courts. Who should determine the skills involved in minimum competence and the lack of it? What consequence should result from being found not minimally competent? Will a minimum competence requirement for a high-school diploma motivate the academically unmotivated? In 1979 a federal judge in Florida found the scheduled application of that state's minimum competency law unconstitutional. Condemning the judge's decision, Lerner (1981) wrote that "disputes over empirical questions cannot be resolved by judicial fiat," and she went on to document that (1) substantial numbers of Americans are failing to master basic skills, such as reading; (2) the consequences of such deficits warrant action; and (3) the actions recommended by minimum competence advocates offer reasonable hope of bringing about the desired change (see also Lerner, 1980). Critics (such as Airasian et al., 1979; Haney & Madaus, 1978; Tyler, 1978) object primarily on the grounds of the potential for abuse inherent in such programs, though some criticisms have also been voiced regarding the psychometric soundness of the instruments.

120 Drewry Road
Monroeville, Alabama 36460

Miss Ann Andrews, Director
Parks and Recreation
Monroeville, Alabama 36460

Dear Miss Andrews:

Our class would like to use the Community House for our senior prom. The tentative date for the prom is April 30, 2009. Please let me know if the ballroom is available on this date and the charges for the use of this facility.

yours truly,

Jan Austin

1. What part of the letter is the salutation?

   a. Jan Austin
   *b. Dear Miss Andrews:
   c. yours truly,
   d. Miss Ann Andrews

2. Which part of the letter has an error in punctuation?

   a. The salutation
   b. The closing
   c. The signature
   *d. The heading

3. Which part of the letter has an error in capitalization?

   *a. The closing
   b. The body
   c. The inside address
   d. The heading

4. Which part of this business letter has been omitted?

   *a. The date of the letter
   b. The salutation
   c. The closing
   d. The inside address

**Sample Items Designed to Evaluate the Testtaker's Knowledge of the Format for a Business Letter**

sufficient knowledge has been acquired to qualify for course credit. The College Level Examination Program (CLEP) is based on the premise that knowledge may be obtained through independent study and sources other than formal schooling. The program includes exams in subjects ranging from African American history to tests and measurement. The Proficiency Examination Program (PEP) offered by the American College Testing Program is another service designed to assess achievement and skills learned outside the classroom.

The special needs of adults with a wide variety of educational backgrounds are addressed in tests such as the Adult Basic Learning Examination (ABLE), a test intended for use with examinees age 17 and older who have not completed eight years of formalized schooling. Developed in consultation with experts in the field of adult education, the test is designed to assess achievement in the areas of vocabulary, reading, spelling, and arithmetic.

**JUST THINK . . .**

Is there an extracurricular life experience for which you should be given college credit? What would a test that measures what you learned from that experience look like?

Achievement tests in nationwide use may test for information or concepts that are not taught within a specific school's curriculum. Some children will do well on such items anyway, having been exposed to the concepts or information independently. Performance on a school achievement test therefore does not depend entirely on school achievement. Concern about such issues has led to an interest in **curriculum-based assessment (CBA),** a term used to refer to assessment of information acquired from teachings at school. **Curriculum-based measurement (CBM),** a type of CBA, is characterized by the use of standardized measurement procedures to derive local norms to be used in the evaluation of student performance on curriculum-based tasks.

Before leaving the topic of achievement tests, let's make the point that achievement test items may be characterized by the type of mental processes required by the testtaker to successfully retrieve the information needed to respond to the item. More specifically, there are at least two distinctly different types of achievement test items: *fact-based items* and *conceptual items.* Here is an example of a fact-based test item; that is, one that draws primarily on rote memory:

1. One type of item that could be used in an achievement test is an item that requires

    a. remote memory
    b. rote memory
    c. memory loss
    d. mnemonic loss

Alternatively, achievement test items can require that the respondent not only know and understand relevant facts but also be able to apply them. Because respondents must draw on and apply knowledge related to a particular concept, these types of achievement test items are referred to as *conceptual* in nature. Here's one example of a conceptual type of item on an achievement test designed to measure mastery of the material in this chapter:

2. Which of the following testtakers would be a likely candidate for the CLEP?

    a. an illiterate migrant farmworker
    b. a child factory worker
    c. a learning-disabled third-grader
    d. a carpenter with little formal education

The correct response to item 1 is "b"—an alternative that could be arrived at by rote memory alone. Item 2 requires a bit more than rote memory; it requires *applying* knowledge related to what the CLEP is. Choice "a" can be eliminated because a written test would not be appropriate for administration to an illiterate testtaker. Choices "b" and "c" can be eliminated because the CLEP is administered to adults. A knowledgeable respondent could arrive at the correct alternative, "d," either by the process of elimination or by application of the knowledge of what the CLEP is and with whom it is designed to be used.

Let's move—but not very far—from the subject of achievement tests to the subject of aptitude tests. Before doing so, try your hand (and mind) on this *Just Think* exercise.

**JUST THINK . . .**

"Achievement tests measure learned knowledge, whereas aptitude tests measure innate potential." Why is this belief a myth?

# Aptitude Tests

We are all constantly acquiring information through everyday life experiences and formal learning experiences (such as coursework in school). The primary difference between achievement tests and aptitude tests is that **aptitude tests** tend to focus more on informal learning or life experiences whereas achievement tests tend to focus on the learning that has occurred as a result of relatively structured input. Keeping this distinction in mind, consider the following two items; the first is from a hypothetical achievement test, and the second is from a hypothetical aptitude test.

1. A correlation of .7 between variables $X$ and $Y$ in a predictive validity study accounts for what percentage of the variance?

   a. 7%

   b. 70%

   c. .7%

   d. 49%

   e. 25%

2. o is to O as x is to

   a. /

   b. %

   c. X

   d. Y

At least on the face of it, Item 1 appears to be more dependent on formal learning experiences than does Item 2. The successful completion of Item 1 hinges on familiarity with the concept of correlation and the knowledge that the variance accounted for by a correlation coefficient is equal to the square of the coefficient (in this case, $.7^2$, or .49—choice "d"). The successful completion of Item 2 requires experience with the concept of size as well as the ability to grasp the concept of analogies. The latter abilities tend to be gleaned from life experiences (witness how quickly you determined that the correct answer was choice "c").

Interestingly, the label *achievement* or *aptitude* for a test may depend not simply on the types of items contained in the test but also on the intended *use* of the test. It is possible for two tests containing the same or similar items to be called by different names: one could be labeled an aptitude test while the other is labeled an achievement test. In the preceding examples, a nonverbal analogy item represented an aptitude test item. However, this same item could very well have been used to represent an achievement test item—one administered to test knowledge acquired, for example, at a seminar on conceptual thinking. Similarly, the first item, presented as an illustrative achievement test item, might well be used to assess aptitude (in statistics or psychology, for example) were it included in a test not expressly designed to measure achievement in this area. Whether a test is seen as measuring aptitude or achievement is a context-based judgment—that is, the judgment will be based, at least in part, on whether or not the testtaker is presumed to have prior exposure or formal learning related to the test's content.

> **JUST THINK . . .**
>
> Create an item for an aptitude test that will compel testtakers to draw on life experience rather than classroom learning for a response.

Aptitude tests, also referred to as **prognostic tests,** are typically used to make predictions. Some aptitude tests have been used to measure readiness to:

- enter a particular preschool program
- enter elementary school
- successfully complete a challenging course of study in secondary school
- successfully complete college-level work
- successfully complete graduate-level work, including a course of study at a professional or trade school

Achievement tests may also be used for predictive purposes. For example, an individual who performs well on a first-semester foreign-language achievement test might be considered a good candidate for the second term's work. The operative assumption here is that an individual who was able to master certain basic skills should be able to master more advanced skills. Understanding what students have already mastered can help school authorities better anticipate what content and skills they are ready to learn. When such assumptions are operative, it can be readily understood that achievement tests—as well as test items that tap achievement—are used in ways akin to aptitude tests.

**JUST THINK . . .**

Well beyond measuring readiness to participate in higher education, tests such as the SAT and the GRE have been praised as "levelers" that "level the playing field." Scores on these tests are blind to what school the testtakers are from as well as the grades received.

Typically, when measures of achievement tests are used to make predictions, the measures tend to draw on narrower and more formal learning experiences than do aptitude tests. For example, a measure of achievement in a course entitled Basic Conversational French might be used as a predictor of achievement for a course entitled Advanced Conversational French. Aptitude tests tend to draw on a broader fund of information and abilities and may be used to predict a wider variety of variables.

In the following sections, we survey some aptitude tests used from the preschool level through the graduate school level and beyond. Let's note here an "unwritten rule" of terminology regarding reference to aptitude tests. At the preschool and elementary school level, you may hear references to **readiness tests.** Here, "readiness" presumably refers to the physical factors, personality factors, and other factors that are judged necessary for a child to be ready to learn. As the level of education climbs, however, the term *readiness* is dropped in favor of the term *aptitude*—this despite the fact that readiness is very much implied at all levels. So, for example, the Graduate Record Examination (GRE), given in college and used as a predictor of ability to do graduate-level work, might have been called the "GSRE" or "Graduate School Readiness Examination." So—are you ready to learn about readiness for learning at the preschool level?

## The Preschool Level

The first five years of life—the span of time referred to as the *preschool period*—is a time of profound change. Basic reflexes develop, and the child passes a number of sensorimotor milestones, such as crawling, sitting, standing, walking, running, and grasping. Usually between 18 and 24 months, the child becomes capable of symbolic thought and develops language skills. By age 2, the average child has a vocabulary of more than 200 words. Of course, all such observations about the development of children are of more than mere academic interest to professionals charged with the responsibility of psychological assessment. At the preschool level, such assessment is largely a matter of determining whether a child's cognitive, emotional, and social development is in line with age-related expectations, and whether any problems likely to hamper learning ability are evident.

In the mid-1970s, Congress enacted Public Law (PL) 94-142, which mandated the professional evaluation of children age 3 and older suspected of having physical or mental disabilities in order to determine their special educational needs. The law also provided federal funds to help states meet those needs. In 1986, a set of amendments to PL 94-142 known as PL 99-457 extended downward to birth the obligation of states toward children with disabilities. It further mandated that, beginning with the school year 1990–1991, all disabled children from ages 3 to 5 were to be provided with a free, appropriate education. The law was expanded in scope in 1997 with the passage of PL 105-17. Among other things, PL 105-17 was intended to give greater attention to diversity issues, especially as a factor in evaluation and assignment of special services. PL 105-17 also mandated that infants and toddlers with disabilities must receive services in the home or in other natural settings, and that such services were to be continued in preschool programs.

In 1999, attention deficit hyperactivity disorder (ADHD) was officially added to the list of disabling conditions that can qualify a child for special services. This, combined with other federal legislation and a growing movement toward "full-service schools" that dispense health and psychological services in addition to education (Reeder et al., 1997), signaled a growing societal reliance on infant and preschool assessment techniques.

The tools of preschool assessment are, with age-appropriate variations built into them, the same types of tools used to assess school-age children and adults. These tools include, among others, checklists and rating scales, tests, and interviews.

**Checklists and rating scales** Checklists and rating scales are tools of assessment commonly used with preschoolers, although their use is certainly not exclusive to this population. In general, a **checklist** is a questionnaire on which marks are made to indicate the presence or absence of a specified behavior, thought, event, or circumstance. The individual doing the "checking" of the boxes on a checklist may be a professional (such as a psychologist or a teacher), an observer (such as a parent or other caretaker), or even the subject of the checklist himself or herself. Checklists can cover a wide array of item content and still be relatively economical and quick to administer.

A *rating scale* is quite similar in definition and sometimes even identical in form to a checklist. The definitional differences between the two terms is technically rather subtle, and for all practical purposes, blurred. The difference involves the degree to which actual rating is involved. For our purposes, we will define a **rating scale** as a form completed by an evaluator (a rater, judge, or examiner) to make a judgment of relative standing with regard to a specified variable or list of variables. As with a checklist, the targeted judgment may have to do with the presence or absence of a particular event or even its frequency.

Have you ever been evaluated by a checklist or rating scale? If you answered no, you are probably incorrect. This is because one of the very first things that most of us are greeted with upon entry to the world is a checklist related to our appearance, behavior, and overall health (see this chapter's *Everyday Psychometrics*).

Three commonly used checklists and rating scales are the Achenbach Child Behavior Checklist (CBCL), the Connors Rating Scales–Revised (CRS-R), and the Behavior Assessment System for Children–2 (BASC-2). The CBCL comes in versions appropriate for use with children from ages 1½ to 5 years (CBCL/1½-5) and for use

## First Impressions

It's been said that every person in contemporary society is a number. We are represented by a Social Security number, a driver's license number, and myriad others. Before these, however, we are represented by what is called an **Apgar number.** The Apgar number is a score on a rating scale developed by physician Virginia Apgar (1909–1974), an obstetrical anesthesiologist who saw a need for a simple, rapid method of evaluating newborn infants and determining what immediate action, if any, is necessary.

As first presented in the early 1950s, the Apgar evaluation is conducted at 1 minute after birth to assess how well the infant tolerated the birthing process. The evaluation is conducted again at 5 minutes after birth to assess how well the infant is adapting to the environment. Each evaluation is made with respect to the same five variables; each variable can be scored on a range from 0 to 2; and each score (at 1 minute and 5 minutes) can range from 0 to 10. The five variables are heart rate, respiration, color, muscle tone, and reflex irritability, the last measure being obtained by response to a stimulus such as a mild pinch. For example, with respect to the variable of reflex irritability, the infant will earn a score of 2 for a vigorous cry in response to the stimulus, a score of 1 for a grimace, and a score of 0 if it shows no reflex irritability. Few babies are "perfect 10s" on their 1-minute Apgar; many are 7s, 8s, and 9s. An Apgar score below 7 or 8 may indicate the need for assistance in being stabilized. A very low Apgar score, in the 0-to-3 range, may signal a more enduring problem such as neurological deficit. By the way, a useful acronym for remembering the five variables is the name "APGAR" itself: A stands for activity (or muscle tone), P for pulse (or heart rate), G for grimace (or reflex irritability), A for appearance (or color), and R for respiration.

Moving from the realm of the medical to the realm of the psychological, another evaluation, one far less formal, takes place shortly after birth, by the child's mother. Judith Langlois and colleagues (1995) studied the relationship between infant attractiveness and maternal behavior and attitudes using a sample of 173 mothers and their firstborn infants (86 girls and 87 boys). Approximately one-third of the sample was identified as White, one-third was African American, and one-third was Mexican American. For the record, the mean first Apgar score for the infants in the study was 8.36 and the mean second Apgar score was 9.04.

To gauge attractiveness, the investigators used judges' ratings of photographs taken a standard distance from each

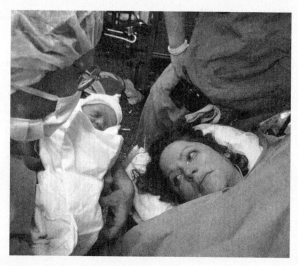

**Welcome to the World of Evaluation**

*Only seconds after birth, a newborn infant is given its first formal evaluation by the hospital staff. The infant's next evaluation, conducted by the mother, may be no less momentous in its consequences*

infant's face while the child was either sleeping or had an otherwise neutral expression. Maternal behavior during feeding and play was directly observed by trained raters in the hospital. A second set of observations was recorded around the time of the infant's three-month birthday. A measure developed by Parke and Sawin (1975) called the Parent Attitude Questionnaire was used to assess maternal attitudes both in the hospital and approximately three months later out of the hospital. The researchers found that although all of the infants studied received adequate care, the attractive infants received more positive treatment and attitudes from their mothers than did the unattractive infants. The mothers of the attractive infants were more affectionate and playful. The mothers of less attractive infants were more likely to be attentive to other people rather than to their infant. These mothers were also more likely to engage in routine caregiving than in affectionate behavior. The attitudes of the mothers of less attractive infants, particularly during the first assessment, were also more negative than those of mothers of more attractive infants. At the time of the first assessment, the mothers of the less attractive infants were more likely than the mothers of more attractive infants to endorse the belief that their infant was interfering with their lives. Approximately three months later, the mothers of the less attractive infants, as compared with the mothers of more attractive infants, were more likely to endorse the belief that their infants needed more stimulation, although they no longer differed in beliefs regarding interference with their lives.

These findings are consistent with prior research suggesting that attractive children are treated less harshly by adults than unattractive children are (Berkowitz & Frodi, 1979; Dion, 1979; Elder et al., 1985) and that mothers of children with physical anomalies may behave less desirably toward their children than mothers whose children had no such anomalies (Allen et al., 1990; Barden et al., 1989; Field & Vega-Lahr, 1984). Fathers, too, may behave differently as a function of the attractiveness of their offspring. Parke et al. (1977) found quality of paternal caregiving to 3-month-old infants to be significantly and positively correlated with infant attractiveness.

Langlois et al. (1995) cautioned that their correlational findings should not be interpreted as being indicative of cause and effect; the results cannot be used to support statements indicating that attractiveness causes or affects maternal behavior and attitudes. However, it does seem that—whatever the reason—infant attractiveness tends to predict maternal behavior and attitudes. The researchers also wondered whether the results of their study would generalize to families of other income levels and what effect the birth of additional children might have on the main findings. It may be that the mothers' relative inexperience with the range of infant behaviors led them to be more influenced by appearance than mothers who have had other children.

From moments after birth and onward, evaluation—both formal and informal—is very much a fact of life. We may define **informal evaluation** as a typically nonsystematic, relatively brief, and "off-the-record" assessment leading to the formation of an opinion or attitude conducted by any person, in any way, for any reason, in an unofficial context that is not subject to the ethics or other standards of an evaluation by a professional. The process of informal evaluation has not received a great deal of attention in the psychological assessment literature. Accordingly, the nature and extent of the influence of informal evaluations by people (such as parents, teachers, supervisors, personnel in the criminal justice system, and others) is largely unknown. On the one hand, considering the need for privacy, perhaps it is best that such private evaluations remain that way. On the other hand, research such as that conducted by Langlois and her colleagues brings to light the everyday implications of such informal evaluations, implications that may ultimately help to improve the quality of life for many people.

with children through young adults, ages 4 to 18 (CBCL/4–18). Parents and others with a close relationship to the subject provide information for competence items covering the subject's activities, social relations, and school performance. The checklist also contains items that describe specific behavioral and emotional problems in addition to open-ended items for reporting additional problems. The protocols are hand-scored, machine-scored, or computer-scored on both competence and clinical scales. A **syndrome** may be defined as a set of co-occurring emotional and behavioral problems. The CBCL has an eight-syndrome structure, with syndromes designated as (1) Anxious/Depressed, (2) Withdrawn/Depressed, (3) Somatic Complaints, (4) Social Problems, (5) Thought Problems, (6) Attention Problems, (7) Rule-Breaking Behavior, and (8) Aggressive Behavior. A large-scale study employing CBCL parent ratings of over 58,000 16- to 18-year-olds was interpreted as supporting the CBCL's eight-syndrome structure in 30 societies around the world (Ivanova et al., 2007a; see also Ivanova et al., 2007b). Other research attests to the psychometric soundness of the scales (Nakamura et al., 2009).

The Connors (CRS-R) may be used to screen for ADHD and other behavior problems. It comes in different versions for use throughout the life span, and each version has a long form (15 to 20 minutes' administration time) and a short form (5 to 10 minutes' administration time). There is a parent version and a teacher version for use with children ages 3 to 17. An adolescent self-report version is for use by respondents ages 12 to 17. The CRS-R is particularly well suited for monitoring ADHD treatment (Kollins et al., 2004).

Designed for use from preschool through adolescence, the BASC-2 utilizes teacher and parent ratings to identify adaptive difficulties on 16 scales ranging from activities of daily living to study skills. An additional Self-Report of Personality (SRP) may also be administered if the respondents are believed to have sufficient insight into their own behavior with regard to variables such as interpersonal relations, self-esteem, and sensation seeking.

Most checklists and rating scales serve the purpose of screening tools. In preschool assessment, screening tools may be used as a first step in identifying children who are said to be *at risk*. This term came into vogue as an alternative to diagnostic labels that might have a detrimental effect (Smith & Knudtson, 1990). Today, what a child is actually at risk *for* may vary in terms of the context of the discussion and the state in which the child resides. *At risk* has been used to refer to preschool children who may not be ready for first grade. The term has also been applied to children who are believed to be not functioning within normal limits. In a most general sense, **at risk** refers to children who have documented difficulties in one or more psychological, social, or academic areas and for whom intervention is or may be required. The need for intervention may be decided on the basis of a more complete evaluation, often involving psychological tests.

**Psychological tests**  At the earliest levels, cognitive, emotional, and social attributes are gauged by scales that assess the presence or absence of various developmental achievements through such means as observation and parental (or caretaker) interviews. By age 2, the child enters a challenging period for psychological assessors. Language and conceptual skills are beginning to emerge, yet the kinds of verbal and performance tests traditionally used with older children and adults are inappropriate. The attention span of the preschooler is short. Ideally, test materials are colorful, engaging, and attention-sustaining. Approximately one hour is a good rule-of-thumb limit for an entire test session with a preschooler; less time is preferable. As testing time increases, so does the possibility of fatigue and distraction. Of course, with assessee fatigue and distraction comes a higher potential for an underestimation of the assessee's ability.

Motivation of the young child may vary from one test session to the next, and this is something of which the examiner must be aware. Particularly desirable are tests that are relatively easy to administer and have simple start/discontinue rules. Also very desirable are tests that allow ample opportunity to make behavioral observations. Dual-easel test administration format (Figure 11–2), sample and teaching items for each subtest, and dichotomous scoring (for example, right/wrong) all may facilitate test administration with very young children.

Data from infant intelligence tests, especially when combined with other information (such as birth history, emotional and social history, health history, data on the quality of the physical and emotional environment, and measures of adaptive behavior) have proved useful to health professionals when questions about developmental disability and related deficits have been raised. Infant intelligence tests have also proved useful in helping to define the abilities—as well as the extent of disability—in older, psychotic children. Furthermore, the tests have been in use for a number of years by many adoption agencies that will disclose and interpret such information to prospective adoptive parents. Infant tests also have wide application in research. They can play a

**Figure 11–2**
**A Dual-Easel Format in Test Administration**

*Easel format in the context of test administration refers to test materials, usually some sort of book that contains test-stimulus materials and that can be folded and placed on a desk; the examiner turns the pages to reveal to the examinee, for example, objects to identify or designs to copy. When corresponding test administration instructions or notes are printed on the reverse side of the test-stimulus pages for the examiner's convenience during test administration, the format is sometimes referred to as dual easel.*

key role, for example, in selecting infants for specialized early educational experiences or in measuring the outcome of educational, therapeutic, or prenatal care interventions.

Tests such as the WPPSI-III and the SB5, as well as others, may be used to gauge developmental strengths and weaknesses by sampling children's performance in cognitive, motor, and social/behavioral content areas. However, the question arises, "What is the meaning of a score on an infant intelligence test?" Whereas some of the developers of infant tests (such as Cattell, 1940; Gesell et al., 1940) claimed that such tests can predict future intellectual ability because they measure the developmental precursors to such ability, others have insisted that performance on such tests at best reflects the infant's physical and neuropsychological intactness. The research literature supports a middle ground between these extreme positions. In general, the tests have not been found to predict performance on child or adult intelligence tests— tests that tap vastly different types of abilities and thought processes. However, the predictive ability of infant intelligence tests does tend to increase with the extremes of the infant's performance. The test interpreter can say with authority more about the future performance of an infant whose performance was either profoundly below age expectancy or significantly precocious. Still, infancy is a developmental period of many spurts and lags, and infants who are slow or precocious at this age might catch up or fall back in later years. Perhaps the great value of preschool tests lies in their ability to help identify children who are in a very low range of functioning and in need of intervention.

**Other measures** Many other instruments and assessment techniques are available for use with preschoolers, including interviews, case history methods, portfolio evaluation, and role-play methods. There are instruments, for example, to measure temperament (Fullard et al., 1984; Gagne et al., 2011; McDevitt & Carey, 1978), language skills (Smith, Myers-Jennings, & Coleman, 2000), the family environment in general (Moos & Moos, 1994; Pritchett et al., 2011), and specific aspects of parenting and caregiving (Arnold et al., 1993; Lovejoy et al., 1999). Drawings may be analyzed for insights they can provide with respect to the child's personality. Some techniques are very specialized and would be used only under rather extraordinary conditions or in the context of research with a very specific focus. An example of the latter is the Child Sexual Behavior Inventory (Friedrich et al., 2001), a 38-item behavior checklist that may be helpful in identifying sexually abused children as young as 2 years old. In sum, many different types of instruments are available for use with preschoolers to help evaluate a wide variety of areas related to personal, social, and academic development.

## The Elementary-School Level

The age at which a child is mandated by law to enter school varies from state to state. Yet individual children of the same chronological age may vary widely in how ready they are to separate from their parents and begin academic learning. Children entering the educational system come from a wide range of backgrounds and experiences, and their rates of physiological, psychological, and social development also vary widely. School readiness tests provide educators with a yardstick by which to assess pupils' abilities in areas as diverse as general information and sensorimotor skills. One of many instruments designed to assess children's readiness and aptitude for formal education is the Metropolitan Readiness Tests (MRTs).

**The Metropolitan Readiness Tests (sixth edition; MRT6)** The MRT6 (Nurss, 1994) is a test battery that assesses the development of the reading and mathematics skills important in the early stages of formal school learning. The test is divided into two levels: Level I (individually administered), for use with beginning and middle kindergarteners, and Level II (group administered), which spans the end of kindergarten through first grade (Table 11–1). There are two forms of the test at each level. The tests are orally administered in several sessions and are untimed, though administration time typically runs about 90 minutes. A practice test (especially useful with young children who have had minimal or no prior test-taking experience) may be administered several days before the actual examination to help familiarize students with the procedures and format.

Normative data for the current edition of the MRTs are based on a national sample of approximately 30,000 children. The standardization sample was stratified according to geographic region, socioeconomic factors, prior school experience, and ethnic background. Data were obtained from both public and parochial schools and from both large and small schools. Split-half reliability coefficients for both forms of both levels of the MRT as well as Kuder-Richardson measures of internal consistency were in the acceptably high range. Content validity was developed through an extensive review of the literature, an analysis of the skills involved in the reading process, and the development of test items that reflected those skills. Items were reviewed by minority

**Table 11-1**
**The Metropolitan Readiness Tests**

*Level I*

*Auditory Memory:* Four pictures containing familiar objects are presented. The examiner reads aloud several words. The child must select the picture that corresponds to the same sequence of words that were presented orally.

*Rhyming:* The examiner supplies the names of each of the pictures presented and then gives a fifth word that rhymes with one of them. The child must select the picture that rhymes with the examiner's word.

*Letter Recognition:* The examiner names different letters, and the child must identify each from the series presented in the test booklet.

*Visual Matching:* A sample is presented, and the child must select the choice that matches the sample.

*School Language and Listening:* The examiner reads a sentence, and the child selects the picture that describes what was read. The task involves some inference making and awareness of relevancy of detail.

*Quantitative Language:* The test assesses comprehension of quantitative terms and knowledge of ordinal numbers and simple mathematical operations.

*Level II*

*Beginning Consonants:* Four pictures representing familiar objects are presented in the test booklet and are named by the examiner. The examiner then supplies a fifth word (not presented), and the child must select the picture that begins with the same sound.

*Sound-Letter Correspondence:* A picture is presented, followed by a series of letters. The examiner names the picture, and the child selects the choice that corresponds to the beginning sound of the pictured item.

*Visual Matching:* As in the corresponding subtest at Level I, a model is presented, and the child must select the choice that matches the model.

*Finding Patterns:* A stimulus consisting of several symbols is presented, followed by a series of representative options. The child must select the option that contains the same sequence of symbols, even though they are presented in a larger grouping with more distractions.

*School Language:* As in the School Language and Listening Test at Level I, the child must select the picture that corresponds to an orally presented sentence.

*Listening:* Material is orally presented, and the child must select the picture that reflects comprehension of and drawing conclusions about the stimulus material.

*Quantitative Concepts and Quantitative Operations:* Two optional tests designed to gauge knowledge of basic mathematical concepts and operations.

---

consultants in an attempt to reduce, if not eliminate, any potential ethnic bias. The predictive validity of MRT scores has been examined with reference to later school achievement indices, and the obtained validity coefficients have been relatively high.

## The Secondary-School Level

Perhaps the most obvious example of an aptitude test widely used in the schools at the secondary level is the SAT, which until 1993 went by the name Scholastic Aptitude Test. The test has been of value not only in the college selection process but also as an aid to high-school guidance and job placement counselors; it has value in helping students decide whether further academics, vocational training, or some other course of action would be most advisable. SAT data is also used by organizations and government agencies in determining who will receive scholarship grants and other such awards.

What is collectively referred to as "the SAT" is actually a number of tests that consist of (1) a multipart test referred to as the SAT (which contains measures of reading, writing, and mathematics) and (2) SAT subject tests. Reading is measured through reading comprehension tasks as measured by short passages followed by sentence completion items. The mathematics section probes knowledge of subjects such as algebra, geometry, basic statistics, and probability. The writing portion of the exam tests knowledge of grammar, usage, and word choice, and is tested through both multiple-choice items and an essay question. The SAT Subject tests are one-hour-long tests designed to measure achievement in specific subject areas such as English, History and Social Studies, Mathematics, Science, and Languages. Colleges may require or recommend taking a specific subject test for purposes of admission or placement or simply to advise students about course selection.

The SAT always seems to be a "work in progress" with regard to its constantly evolving form and nature. Still, a longstanding controversy exists regarding its developer's claim that SAT scores, combined with a consideration of high-school grade-point average, yields the best available predictor of academic success in college. Critics of the SAT have cited everything from differential functioning of items as a function of race (Santelices & Wilson, 2010) to the effects of daylight savings time (Gaski & Sagarin, 2011) as possible sources of adverse effects on SAT scores. It has also been claimed that SAT scores *over*predict the first-year college grade-point averages of African American and Latino students (Zwick & Himelfarb, 2011).

On the bright side, students who take the test more than once can now decide which institution will receive which results. Prior to 2009, students had no such choice and all test results were forwarded to all of the institutions they listed. For the most current information about the SAT, including sample questions and videos, visit the College Board's informative website at *www.collegeboard.com*.

The ACT Assessment, commonly referred to by its three letters ("A-C-T") and *not* by rhyming it with "fact," serves a purpose that is similar to the SAT's. Formerly known as the American College Testing Program, the ACT was developed at the University of Iowa. This college entrance examination was an outgrowth of the Iowa Tests of Educational Development. The test is curriculum-based, with questions directly based on typical high-school subject areas. One study comparing the ACT with the SAT found that the tests were highly correlated with each other in many respects and that both were highly correlated with general intelligence (Koenig et al., 2008). Scores on the ACT may be predictive of creativity as well as academic success (Dollinger, 2011). Such findings are noteworthy in light of assertions that the lack of creativity-related items on college aptitude tests is a critical omission. In this vein, Kaufman (2010) proposed that the inclusion of creativity items on college aptitude tests may be a way to further reduce possible bias.

Although most colleges and universities in the United States require SAT or ACT scores before an applicant is considered for admission, how much do they really rely on them for making college entrance decisions? Probably less than most people believe. Institutions of higher learning in this country differ widely with respect to their admission criteria. Even among schools that require SAT or ACT test scores, varying weights are accorded to the scores with respect to admission decisions. Scores on the SAT or ACT, along with other criteria (such as grade-point average), are designed to help admissions committees determine which of many candidates will do well at their institution. And given the competition for a finite number of seats at institutions of higher learning, these tests also serve a "gatekeeping" function—serving both to award seats to students with documented academic potential and to preserve an institution's reputation for selectivity. However, SAT and ACT test scores can be balanced by other admissions criteria designed to achieve other goals of admissions committees, such as the encouragement of diversity on campus. Motivation and interest, which are clearly necessary to sustain a student through an undergraduate or graduate course of study, may be judged by less standardized means such as letters written by the candidates themselves, letters of recommendation, and personal interviews.

## The College Level and Beyond

If you are a college student planning to pursue further education after graduation, you are probably familiar with the letters G-R-E (which together form an acronym that is very much on the minds of many graduate-school-bound students).

**The Graduate Record Examinations (GRE)**    This long-standing rite of passage for students seeking admission to graduate school has a General Test form as well as specific subject tests. The General Test contains verbal and quantitative sections as well as analytical writing sections. The verbal subtest taps, among other things, the ability to analyze and evaluate written materials as well as the ability to recognize relationships between concepts. The quantitative subtest taps, among other things, knowledge of basic mathematical concepts and the ability to reason quantitatively. The analytical writing subtest taps, among other things, critical thinking and the ability to articulate and argue ideas effectively in standard written English. The General Test may be taken by paper and pencil or by computer at a test center. If it is taken by computer, testtakers use an "elementary word processor" devised by the test developer so that persons familiar with one or another commercially available word-processing programs will not have an advantage. Essays written by respondents may be sent in their entirety to graduate institutions receiving GRE test reports.

Perhaps because of the potentially momentous importance of GRE test results, a number of independent researchers have critically examined the test with regard to various psychometric variables. One comprehensive meta-analysis of the relevant literature focused on the use of the GRE along with undergraduate grade-point average as predictors of graduate success. The researchers concluded that the GRE was a valid predictor of several important criterion measures (ranging from graduate grade-point average to faculty ratings) across disciplines (Kuncel et al., 2001). Other researchers have argued that the GRE has limited utility in predicting other variables related to success in graduate school. These outcomes include the quality of a dissertation, creativity, practical abilities, research skills, and teaching ability (Sternberg & Williams, 1997).

Experience tells us that many readers of this book have more than a casual interest in one specific GRE subject test: *Psychology.* "How do I prepare for it?" is a common question. Here is a four-step preparation program you may wish to consider:

- *Step 1:* Visit the official GRE website maintained by Educational Testing Service (ETS) at *www.ets.org/gre.* Navigate to the *Subject Tests,* and then click on *Psychology.* Use this resource to the fullest to get all the information you can about the current form of the test, even a practice sample of the test.

- *Step 2:* Dust off your introductory psychology textbook and then reread it, review it, do whatever you need to in order to relearn it. If for some reason you no longer have that textbook, or if you took introductory psychology ages ago, ask your instructor to recommend a current text that provides a comprehensive review of the field. Then, read that textbook diligently from cover to cover.

- *Step 3:* Many students have praise for some commercially available review books. There are many available. Spend an evening at your favorite bookstore browsing through the ones available; identify the one that you think will work best for you, and buy it. Typically, these exam preparation books contain a number of sample tests that may be helpful in pinpointing areas that will require extra study.

- *Step 4:* Use all of the resources available to you (textbooks in your personal library, books in your school library, the Internet, etc.) to "fill in the gaps" of knowledge you have identified. Additionally, you may find it helpful to read about effective test preparation and test-taking strategies (see, for example, Loken et al., 2004).

After you have made your best effort to prepare for the test, know that you have the authors' best wishes for luck with it. Or, in psychological and psychometric terms, *may the content sampled on the test match the content you have learned in preparing to take it, and may that information be readily accessed!*

**The Miller Analogies Test (MAT)** Another widely used examination is the Miller Analogies Test. This is a 100-item, multiple-choice analogy test that draws not only on the examinee's ability to perceive relationships but also on general intelligence, vocabulary, and academic learning. As an example, complete the following analogy:

*Classical conditioning* is to *Pavlov* as *operant conditioning* is to

    a. Freud

    b. Rogers

    c. Skinner

    d. Jung

    e. Dr. Phil

Successful completion of this item demands not only the ability to understand the relationship between classical conditioning and Pavlov but also the knowledge that it was B. F. Skinner (choice "c") whose name—of those listed—is best associated with operant conditioning.

The MAT has been cited as one of the most cost-effective of all existing aptitude tests when it comes to forecasting success in graduate school (Kuncel & Hezlett, 2007a). However, as most readers are probably aware, the use of most any aptitude test, even in combination with other predictors, tends to engender controversy (see, for example, Brown, 2007; Kuncel & Hezlett, 2007b; Lerdau & Avery, 2007; Sherley, 2007).

**Other aptitude tests** Applicants for training in certain professions and occupations may be required to take specialized entrance examinations. For example, undergraduate students interested in pursuing a career in medicine, including podiatry or osteopathy, will probably be required to sit for the Medical College Admission Test (MCAT). A high rate of attrition among students studying to become physicians in the 1920s was the stimulus for the development of this test in 1928. Since that time, the test has gone through a number of revisions. The various versions of the test "demonstrate that the definition of aptitude for medical education reflects the professional and social mores and values of the time" (McGaghie, 2002, p. 1085). In its present form, the MCAT consists of four sections: Verbal Reasoning, Physical Sciences, Writing Sample, and Biological Sciences. One group of investigators examined the ability of the MCAT to predict performance in medical school and medical licensing examinations in a sample of 7,859 medical school matriculants. The authors concluded that the "obtained predictive validity coefficients are impressive" (Callahan et al., 2011).

Numerous other aptitude tests have been developed to assess specific kinds of academic, professional, and/or occupational aptitudes. Some of the more widely used tests are described briefly in Table 11–2. There are also a number of lesser known (and less widely used) aptitude tests. For example, the Seashore Measures of Musical Talents (Seashore, 1938) is a now-classic measure of musical aptitude administered with the aid

**Table 11–2**
**Some Entrance Examinations for Professional or Occupational Training**

| Entrance Examination and Website for More Information | Brief Description |
|---|---|
| Medical College Admission Test (MCAT) *www.aamc.org* | Designed to assess problem solving, critical thinking, and writing skills, as well as knowledge of science concepts prerequisite to the study of medicine. |
| Law School Admission Test (LSAT) *www.lsac.org* | A standardized measure of acquired reading and verbal reasoning skills. Includes measures of reading comprehension, analytical reasoning, and logical reasoning, as well as a writing sample. |
| Veterinary College Admission Test (VCAT) *www.tpcweb.com* (follow links) | Assesses five content areas: biology, chemistry, verbal ability, quantitative ability, and reading comprehension. |
| Dental Admission Test (DAT) *www.ada.org* | Conducted by the American Dental Association, this test may be computer administered almost any day of the year. Includes four sections: Natural Sciences (biology, general chemistry, organic chemistry), Perceptual Ability (including angle discrimination tasks), Reading Comprehension, and Quantitative Reasoning (including algebra, various conversions, probability and statistics, geometry, trigonometry, and applied mathematics). |
| Pharmacy College Admission Test (PCAT) *marketplace.psychcorp.com* (follow links) | Contains five subtests: Verbal (including vocabulary with analogies and antonyms), Quantitative (arithmetic, fractions, decimals, percentages, algebra, and reasoning), Biology, Chemistry (basic organic and inorganic), Reading Comprehension (analyze and interpret passages). |
| Optometry Admission Test (OAT) *www.opted.org* | Contains four subtests: Natural Sciences (tapping knowledge of biology, general chemistry, and organic chemistry), Reading Comprehension, Physics, and Quantitative Reasoning. |
| Allied Health Professions Admission Test (AHPAT) *www.tpcweb.com* (follow links) | Assesses ability in five content areas: biology, chemistry, verbal ability, quantitative ability, and reading comprehension. Designed for use with aspiring physical and occupational therapists, physician's assistants, and other members of allied health professions. |
| Entrance Examination for Schools of Nursing (RNEE) *www.tpcweb.com* (follow links) | Voted by the authors of this textbook as "Test with Trickiest Acronym," the RNEE assesses ability in five content areas: physical sciences, numerical ability, life sciences, verbal ability, and reading comprehension. |
| Accounting Program Admission Test (APAT) *www.tpcweb.com* (follow links) | Measures student achievement in elementary accounting by means of 75 multiple-choice questions, 60% of which deal with financial accounting and the remaining 40% of which deal with managerial accounting. |
| Graduate Management Admission Test *www.mba.com* | Measures basic verbal and mathematical and analytical writing skills through three subtests: Analytical Writing Assessment, the Quantitative section, and the Verbal section. |

of a record (if you can find a record player) or prerecorded tape. The six subtests measure specific aspects of musical talent (for example, comparing different notes and rhythms on variables such as loudness, pitch, time, and timbre). The Horn Art Aptitude Inventory is a measure designed to gauge various aspects of the respondent's artistic aptitude.

> **JUST THINK . . .**
>
> "Art is in the eye of the beholder."
> Considering this bit of wisdom, how is it possible to determine if someone truly has an aptitude for art?

## Diagnostic Tests

By the early twentieth century, it was recognized that tests of intelligence could be used to do more than simply measure cognitive ability. Binet and Simon (1908/1961) wrote of their concept of "mental orthopedics," whereby intelligence test data could be used to improve learning. Today a distinction is made between tests and test data used primarily for *evaluative* purposes and tests and test data used primarily for *diagnostic* purposes. The term **evaluative,** as used in phrases such as *evaluative purposes* or **evaluative information,** is typically applied to tests or test data that are used to make judgments (such as pass–fail and admit–reject decisions). By contrast, **diagnostic information,** as used in educational contexts (and related phrases such as *diagnostic purposes*) is typically applied to tests or test data used to pinpoint a student's difficulty, usually for remedial purposes. In an educational context, a **diagnostic test** is a tool used to identify areas of deficit to be targeted for intervention.[1]

A diagnostic reading test may, for example, contain a number of subtests. Each subtest is designed to analyze a specific knowledge or skill required for reading. The objective of each of these subtests might be to bring into focus the specific problems that need to be addressed if the testtaker is to read at an appropriate grade level. By the way, the line between "diagnostic" and "evaluative" testing is not carved in stone; diagnostic information can be used for evaluative purposes, and information from evaluative tests can provide diagnostic information. For example, on the basis of a child's performance on a diagnostic reading test, a teacher or an administrator might make a class placement decision.

Diagnostic tests do not necessarily provide information that will answer questions concerning *why* a learning difficulty exists. Other educational, psychological, and perhaps medical examinations are needed to answer that question. In general, diagnostic tests are administered to students who have already demonstrated their problem with a particular subject area through their poor performance either in the classroom or on some achievement test. For this reason, diagnostic tests may contain simpler items than achievement tests designed for use with members of the same grade.

## Reading Tests

The ability to read is integral to virtually all classroom learning, so it is not surprising that a number of diagnostic tests are available to help pinpoint difficulties in acquiring this skill. Some of the many tests available to help pinpoint reading difficulties include the Stanford Diagnostic Reading Test, the Metropolitan Reading Instructional Tests, the Diagnostic Reading Scales, and the Durrell Analysis of Reading Test. For illustrative purposes we briefly describe one such diagnostic battery, the Woodcock Reading Mastery Tests.

**The Woodcock Reading Mastery Tests-Revised (WRMT-III; Woodcock, 2011)**  This paper-and-pencil measure of reading readiness, reading achievement, and reading difficulties takes between 15 and 45 minutes to administer the entire battery. It can be used with children as young as 4½, adults as old as 80, and most everyone in between. This edition of the test was standardized on a nationally representative sample totaling over 3,300 testtakers. Users of prior editions of this popular test will recognize many of the subtests on the WRMT-III (with revised artwork to be more engaging ), including:

*Letter Identification:* Items that measure the ability to name letters presented in different forms. Both cursive and printed as well as uppercase and lowercase letters are presented.

*Word Identification:* Words in isolation arranged in order of increasing difficulty. The student is asked to read each word aloud.

---

1. In a clinical context, the same term may be used to refer to a tool of assessment designed to yield a psychiatric diagnosis.

*Word Attack:* Nonsense syllables that incorporate phonetic as well as structural analysis skills. The student is asked to pronounce each nonsense syllable.

*Word Comprehension:* Items that assess word meaning by using a four-part analogy format.

*Passage Comprehension:* Phrases, sentences, or short paragraphs, read silently, in which a word is missing. The student must supply the missing word.

Three subtests new to the third edition are *Phonological Awareness, Listening Comprehension,* and *Oral Reading Fluency.* All of the subtests taken together are used to derive a picture of the testtaker's reading-related strengths and weaknesses, as well as an actionable plan for reading remediation when necessary. The test comes in parallel forms, useful for establishing a baseline and then monitoring postintervention progress.

### Math Tests

The Stanford Diagnostic Mathematics Test, Fourth Edition (SDMT4) and the KeyMath 3 Diagnostic System (KeyMath3-DA) are two of many tests that have been developed to help diagnose difficulties with arithmetic and mathematical concepts. Items on such tests typically test everything from knowledge of basic concepts and operations through applications entailing increasingly advanced problem-solving skills. The KeyMath3-DA (Connolly, 2007) is a standardized test that may be administered to children as young as 4½ and adults as old as 21. According to the website of the test's publisher (Pearson Assessments), the test's development included "a review of state math standards and National Council of Teachers of Mathematics publications," which led to the creation of "a comprehensive blueprint reflecting essential mathematics content, existing curriculum priorities, and national math standards" ("KeyMath," 2011). The test comes in two forms, each containing 10 subtests. Test protocols can either be hand-scored or computer-scored. Because the KeyMath3-DA is individually administered, it is ideally administered by a qualified examiner who is skillful in establishing and maintaining rapport with testtakers and knowledgeable in following the test's standardized procedures.

The SDMT-4 is a standardized test that can provide useful diagnostic insights with regard to the mathematical abilities of children just entering school to just entering college. The test, available in different forms, is amenable for individual or group administration. It contains both multiple-choice and (optional) free-response items. The latter items are designed to provide the examiner with a firsthand understanding of the reasoning, strategies, and methods applied by testtakers to solve different kinds of problems. Test protocols may be hand-scored or centrally scored by the test's publisher. Since 2003 an online version of the SDMT-4 has been available.

## Psychoeducational Test Batteries

**Psychoeducational test batteries** are test kits that generally contain two types of tests: those that measure abilities related to academic success and those that measure educational achievement in areas such as reading and arithmetic. Data derived from these batteries allow for normative comparisons (how the student compares with other students within the same age group), as well as an evaluation of the testtaker's own strengths and weaknesses—all the better to plan educational interventions. Let's begin with a brief look at one psychoeducational battery, the Kaufman Assessment Battery for Children (K-ABC), as well as the extensively revised second edition of the test, the KABC-II.

### The Kaufman Assessment Battery for Children (K-ABC) and the Kaufman Assessment Battery for Children, Second Edition (KABC-II)

Developed by a husband-and-wife team of psychologists, the K-ABC was designed for use with testtakers from age 2½ through age 12½. Subtests measuring both intelligence and achievement are included. The K-ABC intelligence subtests are divided into two groups, reflecting the two kinds of information-processing skills identified by Luria and his students (Das et al., 1975; Luria, 1966a, 1966b): *simultaneous skills* and *sequential skills* (see Chapter 9). Table 11–3 presents the particular learning and teaching styles that reflect the two types of intelligence measured by the K-ABC. Scores on the simultaneous and sequential subtests are combined into a Mental Processing Composite, which is analogous to the IQ measure calculated on other tests.

Factor-analytic studies of the K-ABC have confirmed the presence of a factor researchers label *simultaneous processing* and a factor labeled *sequential processing.* Perhaps surprisingly, it is an achievement factor that researchers have had difficulty finding. Kaufman (1993) found evidence for the presence of an achievement factor, but independent researchers have different ideas about what that third factor is. Good and Lane (1988) identified the third factor of the K-ABC as *verbal comprehension and reading achievement.* Kaufman and McLean (1986) identified it as *achievement and reading ability.* Keith and Novak (1987) identified it as *reading achievement and verbal reasoning.* Whatever the factor is, the K-ABC Achievement Scale has been shown to predict achievement (Lamp & Krohn, 2001). In addition to questions about what the elusive third factor actually measures, questions have also been raised about whether or not sequential and simultaneous learning are entirely independent (Bracken, 1985; Keith, 1985).

Recommendations for teaching based on Kaufman and Kaufman's (1983a, 1983b) concept of *processing strength* can be derived from the K-ABC test findings. It may be recommended, for example, that a student whose strength is processing sequentially should be taught using the teaching guidelines for sequential learners. Students who do not have any particular processing strength may be taught using a combination of methods. This model of test interpretation and consequential intervention may engender great enthusiasm on the basis of its intuitive appeal. However, research findings related to this approach have been mixed (Ayres & Cooley, 1986; Good et al., 1989; McCloskey, 1989; Salvia & Hritcko, 1984). Good et al. (1993) concluded that educational decisions based on a child's processing style as defined by the K-ABC did not improve the quality of those decisions.

**JUST THINK . . .**

How realistic is it to expect that children can be taught a variety of subjects by classroom teachers in a way that is individually tailored to each child's unique processing strength as measured by a test?

The next generation of the K-ABC was published in 2004. In the abbreviation for the title of this test, the authors dropped the hyphen between the *K* and the *ABC* and instead inserted a hyphen between the *C* and the roman numeral *II* (KABC-II). But that was only the beginning; there are changes in the age range covered, the structure of the test, and even the conceptual underpinnings of the test.

The age range for the second edition of the test was extended upward (ages 3 to 18) in order to expand the possibility of making ability/achievement comparisons with the same test through high school. Structurally, 10 new subtests were created, 8 of the existing subtests were removed, and only 8 of the original subtests remained. Such

**Table 11–3**
**Characteristics and Teaching Guidelines for Sequential and Simultaneous Learners**

### Learner Characteristics

| The Sequential Learner | The Simultaneous Learner |
|---|---|
| The sequential learner solves problems best by mentally arranging small amounts of information in consecutive, linear, step-by-step order. He/she is most at home with verbal instructions and cues because the ability to interpret spoken language depends to a great extent on the sequence of words. | The simultaneous learner solves problems best by mentally integrating and synthesizing many parallel pieces of information at the same time. He/she is most at home with visual instructions and cues because the ability to interpret the environment visually depends on perceiving and integrating many details at once. |

Sequential processing is especially important in

- learning and retaining basic arithmetic facts
- memorizing lists of spelling words
- making associations between letters and their sounds
- learning the rules of grammar, the chronology of historical events
- remembering details
- following a set of rules, directions, steps
- solving problems by breaking them down into their components or steps

Simultaneous processing is especially important in

- recognizing the shape and physical appearance of letters and numbers
- interpreting the overall effect or meaning of pictures and other visual stimuli, such as maps and charts
- understanding the overall meaning of a story or poem
- summarizing, comparing, evaluating
- comprehending mathematical or scientific principles
- solving problems by visualizing them in their entirety

Sequential learners who are weak in simultaneous processing may have difficulty with

- sight word recognition
- reading comprehension
- understanding mathematical or scientific principles
- using concrete, hands-on materials
- using diagrams, charts, maps
- summarizing, comparing, evaluating

Simultaneous learners who are weak in sequential processing may have difficulty with

- word attack, decoding, phonics
- breaking down science or arithmetic problems into parts
- interpreting the parts and features of a design or drawing
- understanding the rules of games
- understanding and following oral instructions
- remembering specific details and sequence of a story

### Teaching Guidelines

**For the Sequential Learner**

1. Present material step by step, gradually approaching the overall concept or skill. Lead up to the big question with a series of smaller ones. Break the task into parts.
2. Get the child to verbalize what is to be learned. When you teach a new word, have the child say it, aloud or silently. Emphasize verbal cues, directions, and memory strategies.
3. Teach and rehearse the steps required to do a problem or complete a task. Continue to refer back to the details or steps already mentioned or mastered. Offer a logical structure or procedure by appealing to the child's verbal/temporal orientation.

For example, the sequential learner may look at one or two details of a picture but miss the visual image as a whole. To help such a student toward an overall appreciation of the picture, start with the parts and work up to the whole. Rather than beginning with "What does the picture show?" or "How does the picture make you feel?" first ask about details:

"What is the little boy in the corner doing?"
"Where is the dog?"
"What expression do you see on the woman's face?"
"What colors are used in the sky?"

Lead up to questions about the overall interpretation or appreciation:

"How do all these details give you clues about what is happening in this picture?"
"How does this picture make you feel?"

The sequential learner prefers a step-by-step teaching approach, one that may emphasize the gradual accumulation of details.

**For the Simultaneous Learner**

1. Present the overall concept or question before asking the child to solve the problem. Continue to refer back to the task, question, or desired outcome.
2. Get the child to visualize what is to be learned. When you teach a new word, have the child write it and picture it mentally, see it on the page in the mind's eye. Emphasize visual cues, directions, and memory strategies.
3. Make tasks concrete wherever possible by providing manipulative materials, pictures, models, diagrams, graphs. Offer a sense of the whole by appealing to the child's visual/spatial orientation.

The simultaneous learner may react to a picture as a whole but may miss details. To help such a student notice that parts contribute to the total visual image, begin by establishing an overall interpretation or reaction:

"What does the picture show?"
"How does the picture make you feel?"

Then consider the details:

"What is the expression on the woman's face?"
"What is the little boy in the corner doing?"
"What colors are used in the sky?"

Relate the details to the student's initial interpretation:

"How do these details explain why the picture made you feel the way it did?"

The simultaneous learner responds best to a holistic teaching approach that focuses on groups of details or images and stresses the overall meaning or configuration of the task.

Source: From Kaufman Sequential or Simultaneous (K-SOS). Copyright © 1984 NCS Pearson, Inc. Reproduced with permission. All rights reserved.

significant structural changes in the test must be kept in mind by test users making comparisons between testtaker K-ABC scores and KABC-II scores.

Conceptually, the grounding of the K-ABC in Luria's theory of sequential versus simultaneous processing theory was expanded. In addition, a grounding in the Cattell-Horn-Carroll (CHC) theory was added. This dual theoretical foundation provides the examiner with a choice as to which model of test interpretation is optimal for the particular situation. As stated in the publisher's promotional materials, you can choose the Cattell-Horn-Carroll model for children from a mainstream cultural and language background; if Crystallized Ability would not be a fair indicator of the child's cognitive ability, then you can choose the Luria model, which excludes verbal ability. Administer the same subtests on four or five ability scales. Then, interpret the results based on your chosen model. Either approach gives you a global score that is highly valid and that shows small differences between ethnic groups in comparison with other comprehensive ability batteries.

In general, reviewers of the KABC-II found it to be a psychometrically sound instrument for measuring cognitive abilities. However, few evidenced ease with its new, dual theoretical basis. For example, Thorndike (2007) wondered aloud about assessing two distinct sets of processes and abilities without adequately explaining "how a single test can measure two distinct constructs" (p. 520). Braden and Ouzts (2007) expressed their concern that combining the two interpretive models "smacks of trying to have (and market) it both ways" (p. 519). Bain and Gray (2008) were disappointed that the test manual did not contain sample reports based on each of the models.

**JUST THINK . . .**

What are your thoughts regarding a psychoeducational test battery that has a dual theoretical basis?

Some reviewers raised questions about the variable (or variables) that were actually being measured by the KABC-II. For example, Reynolds et al. (2007) questioned the extent to which certain supplemental tests could best be conceived as measures of specific abilities or measures of multiple abilities. In general, however, they were satisfied that for "school-age children, the KABC-II is closely aligned with the five CHC broad abilities it is intended to measure" (p. 537). Other researchers have confirmed that the KABC-II is indeed tapping the broad CHC abilities (Morgan et al., 2009).

Another widely known and widely used psychoeducational test battery is the Woodcock-Johnson III.

## The Woodcock-Johnson III (WJ III)

The WJ III (Woodcock et al., 2000) is a psychoeducational test package consisting of two co-normed batteries: Tests of Achievement and Tests of Cognitive Abilities, both of which are based on the Cattell-Horn-Carroll (CHC) theory of cognitive abilities. The WJ III was designed for use with persons as young as 2 years and as old as "90+," according to the test manual. The WJ III yields a measure of general intellectual ability ($g$) as well as measures of specific cognitive abilities, achievement, scholastic aptitude, and oral language. Along with other assessment techniques (including, for example, parent or guardian interviews, analysis of response to prior teaching or interventions, portfolio evaluation, and analysis of data from other standardized tests), the WJ III may be used to diagnose SLDs and to plan educational programs and interventions. The Tests of Achievement are packaged in parallel forms designated A and B, each of which is divided into a standard battery (12 subtests) and an extended battery (10 additional subtests). As illustrated in Table 11–4, interpretation of an achievement test is based on the testtaker's performance on clusters of tests in specific curricular areas.

**Table 11–4**
**WJ III Tests of Achievement**

| Curricular Area | Cluster | Standard Battery—Forms A & B | Extended Battery—Forms A & B |
|---|---|---|---|
| Reading | Basic Skills | Test 1 Letter-Word Identification | Test 13 Word Attack |
| | Fluency | Test 2 Reading Fluency | |
| | Comprehension | Test 9 Passage Comprehension | Test 17 Reading Vocabulary |
| | Broad | Tests 1, 2, 9 | |
| Oral Language | Oral Expression | Test 3 Story Recall | Test 14 Picture Vocabulary |
| | Listening Comprehension | Test 4 Understanding Directions | Test 15 Oral Comprehension |
| Mathematics | Calculation Skills | Test 5 Calculation | |
| | Fluency | Test 6 Math Fluency | |
| | Reasoning | Test 10 Applied Problems | Test 18 Quantitative Concepts |
| | Broad | Tests 5, 6, 10 | |
| Written Language | Basic Skills | Test 7 Spelling | Test 16 Editing |
| | Fluency | Test 8 Writing Fluency | |
| | Expression | Test 11 Writing Samples | |
| | Broad | Tests 7, 8, 11 | |
| Knowledge | | | Test 19 Academic Knowledge |
| Supplemental | | Test 12 Story Recall-Delayed | Test 20 Spelling of Sounds |
| | | Handwriting Legibility Scale | Test 21 Sound Awareness |
| | | | Test 22 Punctuation & Capitalization |

The Tests of Cognitive Abilities may also be divided into a standard battery (10 subtests) and an extended battery (10 additional subtests). As illustrated in Table 11–5, the subtests tapping cognitive abilities are conceptualized in terms of broad cognitive factors, primary narrow abilities, and cognitive performance clusters.

When using either the achievement or the cognitive abilities tests, the standard battery might be appropriate for screenings or brief reevaluations. The extended battery would likely be used to provide a more comprehensive and detailed assessment, complete with diagnostic information. In any case, cluster scores are used to help evaluate performance level, gauge educational progress, and identify individual strengths and weaknesses.

According to the test manual, the WJ III was normed on a sample of 8,818 subjects from ages 24 months to "90+" years who were representative of the population of the United States. Age-based norms are provided by month from ages 24 months to 19 years and by year after that. Grade-based norms are provided for kindergarten through grade 12, two-year college, and four-year college, including graduate school. Procedures for analysis of reliabilities for each subtest were appropriate, depending upon the nature of the tests. For example, the reliability of tests that were not speeded and that did not have multiple-point scoring systems was analyzed by means of the split-half method, corrected for length using the Spearman-Brown correction formula. The test manual also presents concurrent validity data. Support for the validity of various aspects of the test has also come from independent researchers. For example, Floyd et al. (2003) found that certain cognitive clusters were significantly related to mathematics achievement in a large, nationally representative sample of children and adolescents.

Scoring of the WJ III is accomplished with the aid of software provided in the test kit. Data from the raw scores are entered, and the program produces a summary report (in English or Spanish) and a table of scores, including all derived scores for tests administered as well as clusters of tests. The program also provides age/grade profiles and standard score/percentile rank profiles. Optional interpretive software is

**Table 11–5**
**WJ III Tests of Cognitive Abilities***

| Broad Cognitive Factor | Test (Standard & Extended) | Primary Narrow Ability | Cognitive Performance |
|---|---|---|---|
| Comprehension-Knowledge *(Gc)* | Test 1 Verbal Comprehension<br>Test 11 General Information | Lexical knowledge, language development<br>General (verbal) information | Verbal ability |
| Long-Term Retrieval *(Glr)* | Test 2 Visual-Auditory Learning<br>Test 12 Retrieval Fluency<br>*Test 10 Visual-Auditory<br>Learning—Delayed* | Associate memory<br>Ideational fluency<br>Associative memory | Thinking ability |
| Visual-Spatial Thinking *(Gv)* | Test 3 Spatial Relations<br>Test 13 Picture Recognition<br>*Test 19 Planning (Gv/Gf)* | Visualization, spatial relations<br>Visual memory<br>*Spatial scanning, general sequential reasoning* | Thinking ability |
| Auditory Processing *(Ga)* | Test 4 Sound Blending<br>Test 14 Auditory Attention<br>*Test 8 Incomplete Words* | Phonetic coding, synthesis<br>Speech-sound discrimination, resistance to<br>    auditory stimulus distortion<br>*Phonetic coding, analysis* | Thinking ability |
| Fluid Reasoning *(Gf)* | Test 5 Concept Formation<br>Test 15 Analysis-Synthesis<br>*Test 19 Planning (Gv/Gf)* | Induction<br>General sequential reasoning<br>*Spatial scanning, general sequential reasoning* | Thinking ability |
| Processing Speed *(Gs)* | Test 6 Visual Matching<br>Test 16 Decision Speed<br>*Test 18 Rapid Picture Naming*<br>*Test 20 Pair Cancellation* | Perceptual speed<br>Semantic processing speed<br>*Naming facility*<br>*Attention and concentration* | Cognitive efficiency |
| Short-Term Memory *(Gsm)* | Test 7 Numbers Reversed<br>Test 17 Memory for Words<br>*Test 9 Auditory Working Memory* | Working memory<br>Memory span<br>*Working memory* | Cognitive efficiency |

*Tests shown in italics are not part of the factor or cognitive performance cluster.

also available (Riverside Publishing, 2001). This software features checklist protocols (a teacher checklist, a parent checklist, a self-report checklist, and a classroom observation form) in a form that integrates the checklist data into the report. The test publisher has also made available optional training materials, including CD-ROMs and videos, for assistance in administering and using the battery.

Independent reviews of the WJ III have been very favorable in many respects. Two detailed reviews were published in the *Fifteenth Mental Measurements Yearbook* (see Cizek, 2003; Sandoval, 2003).

## Other Tools of Assessment in Educational Settings

Beyond traditional achievement, aptitude, and diagnostic instruments lies a wide universe of other instruments and techniques of assessment that may be used in the service of students and society at large. Let's take a look at a sampling of these approaches, beginning with performance, portfolio, and authentic assessment.

### *Performance, Portfolio, and Authentic Assessment*

For many years the very broad label *performance assessment* has vaguely referred to any type of assessment that requires the examinee to do more than choose the correct response from a small group of alternatives. Thus, for example, essay questions and the development of an art project are examples of performance tasks. By contrast, true–false questions and multiple-choice test items would not be considered performance tasks.

Among testing and assessment professionals, contemporary usage of performance-related terms focuses less on the type of item or task involved and more on the knowledge, skills, and values that the examinee must marshal and exhibit. Additionally, there is a growing tendency to speak of performance tasks and performance assessment in the context of a particular domain of study, where experts in that domain are typically required to set the evaluation standards. For example, a performance task for an architecture student might be to create a blueprint of a contemporary home. The overall quality of the student's work—together with the knowledge, skill, and values inherent in it—will be judged according to standards set by architects acknowledged by the community of architects to have expertise in the construction of contemporary homes. In keeping with these trends, particularly in educational and work settings, we will define a **performance task** as a work sample designed to elicit representative knowledge, skills, and values from a particular domain of study. **Performance assessment** will be defined as an evaluation of performance tasks according to criteria developed by experts from the domain of study tapped by those tasks.

One of many possible types of performance assessment is portfolio assessment. *Portfolio* has many meanings in different contexts. It may refer to a portable carrying case, most typically used to carry artwork, drawings, maps, and the like. Bankers and investors use it as a shorthand reference to one's financial holdings. In the language of psychological and educational assessment, **portfolio** is synonymous with *work sample*. **Portfolio assessment** refers to the evaluation of one's work samples. In many educational settings, dissatisfaction with some more-traditional methods of assessment has led to calls for more performance-based evaluations. *Authentic assessment* (discussed subsequently) is one name given to this trend toward more performance-based assessment. When used in the context of like-minded educational programs, portfolio assessment and authentic assessment are techniques designed to target academic teachings to real-world settings external to the classroom.

> **JUST THINK . . .**
>
> What might your personal portfolio, detailing all that you have learned about psychological testing and assessment to date, look like?

Consider, for example, how students could use portfolios to gauge their progress in a high-school algebra course. They could be instructed to devise their own personal portfolios to illustrate all they have learned about algebra. An important aspect of portfolio assessment is the freedom of the person being evaluated to select the content of the portfolio. Some students might include narrative accounts of their understanding of various algebraic principles. Other students might reflect in writing on the ways algebra can be used in daily life. Still other students might attempt to make a convincing case that they can do some types of algebra problems that they could not do before taking the course. Throughout, the portfolio may be illustrated with items such as gas receipts (complete with algebraic formulas for calculating mileage), paychecks (complete with formulas used to calculate an hourly wage and taxes), and other items limited only by the student's imagination. The illustrations might go from simple to increasingly complex—providing compelling evidence for the student's grasp of the material.

Innovative use of the portfolio method to assess giftedness (Hadaway & Marek-Schroer, 1992) and reading (Henk, 1993), among many other characteristics, can be found in the scholarly literature. Portfolios have also been applied at the college and graduate level as devices to assist students with career decisions (Bernhardt et al., 1993). Benefits of the portfolio approach include engaging students in the assessment process, giving them the opportunity to think generatively, and encouraging them to think about learning as an ongoing and integrated process. A key drawback, however, is the penalty such a technique may levy on the noncreative student. Typically, exceptional portfolios are creative efforts. A person whose strengths do not lie in creativity may have learned the course material but be unable to adequately demonstrate that learning in such a medium. Another drawback, this one from the other side of the instructor's desk, concerns the evaluation of portfolios. Typically, a great deal of time and thought must be devoted to their evaluation. In a lecture class of 300 people, for example, portfolio assessment would be impractical. Also, it is difficult to develop reliable criteria for portfolio assessment, given the great diversity of work products. Hence, inter-rater reliability in portfolio assessment can become a problem.

A related form of assessment is *authentic assessment,* also known as *performance-based assessment* (Baker et al., 1993) as well as other names. We may define **authentic assessment** in educational contexts as evaluation of relevant, meaningful tasks that may be conducted to evaluate learning of academic subject matter but that demonstrate the student's transfer of that study to real-world activities. Authentic assessment of students' writing skills, for example, would therefore be based on writing samples rather than on responses to multiple-choice tests. Authentic assessment of students' reading would be based on tasks that involve reading—preferably "authentic" reading, such as an article in a local newspaper as opposed to a piece contrived especially for the purposes of assessment. Students in a college-level psychopathology course might be asked to identify patients' psychiatric diagnoses on the basis of videotaped interviews with the patients.

Authentic assessment is thought to increase student interest and the transfer of knowledge to settings outside the classroom. A drawback is that the assessment might assess prior knowledge and experience, not simply what was learned in the classroom. For example, students from homes where there has been a long-standing interest in legislative activities may well do better on an authentic assessment of reading skills that employs an article on legislative activity. Additionally, authentic skill may inadvertently entail the assessment of some skills that have little to do with classroom learning. For example, authentic assessment of learning a cooking school lesson on filleting fish may be confounded with an assessment of the would-be chef's perceptual-motor skills.

## Peer Appraisal Techniques

One method of obtaining information about an individual is by asking that individual's peer group to make the evaluation. Techniques employed to obtain such information are termed **peer appraisal** methods. A teacher, a supervisor, or some other group leader may be interested in peer appraisals for a variety of reasons. Peer appraisals can help call needed attention to an individual who is experiencing academic, personal, social, or work-related difficulties—difficulties that, for whatever reason, have not come to the attention of the person in charge. Peer appraisals allow the individual in charge to view members of a group from a different perspective: the perspective of those who work, play, socialize, eat lunch, and walk home with the person being evaluated. In addition to providing information about behavior that is rarely observable, peer appraisals supply information about the group's dynamics: who takes which roles under what conditions. Knowledge of an individual's place within the group is an important aid in guiding the group to optimal efficiency.

Peer appraisal techniques may be used in university settings as well as in grade-school, industrial, and military settings. Such techniques tend to be most useful in settings where the individuals doing the rating have functioned as a group long enough to be able to evaluate each other on specific variables. The nature of peer appraisals may change as a function of changes in the assessment situation and the membership of the group. Thus, for example, an individual who is rated as the shyest in the classroom can theoretically be quite gregarious—and perhaps even be rated the rowdiest—in a peer appraisal undertaken at an after-school center.

One method of peer appraisal that can be employed in elementary school (as well as other) settings is called the Guess Who? technique. Brief descriptive sentences (such as "This person is the most friendly") are read or handed out in the form of questionnaires to the class, and the children are instructed to guess who. Whether negative attributes should be included in the peer appraisal (for example, "This person is the least friendly") must be decided on an individual basis, considering the potential negative consequences such an appraisal could have on a member of the group.

The *nominating* technique is a method of peer appraisal in which individuals are asked to select or nominate other individuals for various types of activities. A child being interviewed in a psychiatric clinic may be asked, "Who would you most like to go to the moon with?" as a means of determining which parent or other individual is most important to the child. Members of a police department might be asked, "Who would you most like as your partner for your next tour of duty and why?" as a means of finding out which police officers are seen by their peers as especially competent or incompetent.

The results of a peer appraisal can be graphically illustrated. One graphic method of organizing such data is the **sociogram.** Figures such as circles or squares are drawn to represent different individuals, and lines and arrows are drawn to indicate various types of interaction. At a glance, the sociogram can provide information such as who is popular in the group, who tends to be rejected by the group, and who is relatively neutral in the opinion of the group. Nominating techniques have been the most widely researched of the peer appraisal techniques, and they have generally been found to be highly reliable and valid. Still, the careful user of such techniques must be aware that an individual's perceptions within a group are constantly changing. Anyone who has ever watched reality television shows such as *Survivor* or *The Apprentice* is certainly aware of such group dynamics. As some members leave the group and others join it, the positions and roles the members hold within the group change. New alliances form, and as a result, all group members may be looked at in a new light. It is therefore important to periodically update and verify information.

## Measuring Study Habits, Interests, and Attitudes

Academic performance is the result of a complex interplay of a number of factors. Ability and motivation are inseparable partners in the pursuit of academic success. A number of instruments designed to look beyond ability and toward factors such as study habits, interests, and attitudes have been published. For example, the Study Habits Checklist, designed for use with students in grades 9 through 14, consists of 37 items that assess study habits with respect to note taking, reading material, and general study practices. In the development of the test, potential items were presented for screening to 136 Phi Beta Kappa members at three colleges. This procedure was based on the premise that good students are the best judges of important and effective study techniques (Preston, 1961). The judges were asked to evaluate the items according to their usefulness to students having difficulty with college course material. Although the judges conceded that they did not always engage in these practices themselves, they identified the techniques they deemed the most useful in study activities. Standardization for the Checklist took place in 1966, and percentile norms were based on a sample of several thousand high-school and college students residing in Pennsylvania. In one validity study, 302 college freshmen who had demonstrated learning difficulties and had been referred to a learning skills center were evaluated with the Checklist. As predicted, it was found that these students demonstrated poor study practices, particularly in the areas of note taking and proper use of study time (Bucofsky, 1971).

If a teacher knows a child's areas of interest, instructional activities engaging those interests can be employed. The What I Like to Do Interest Inventory consists of 150 forced-choice items that assess four areas of interests: academic interests, artistic interests, occupational interests, and interests in leisure time (play) activities. Included in the test materials are suggestions for designing instructional activities that are consonant with the designated areas of interest.

Attitude inventories used in educational settings assess student attitudes toward a variety of school-related factors. Interest in student attitudes is based on the premise that "positive reactions to school may increase the likelihood that students will stay in school, develop a lasting commitment to learning, and use the school setting to advantage" (Epstein & McPartland, 1978, p. 2). Some instruments assess attitudes in specific subject areas, whereas others, such as the Survey of School Attitudes and the Quality of School Life Scales, are more general in scope.

**JUST THINK . . .**

While we're on the subject of study habits, skills, and attitudes, this seems an appropriate time to raise a question about how these variables are related to another, more global variable: *personality*. Are one's study habits, skills, and attitudes a part of one's personality? Why might it be useful to think about them as such?

The Survey of Study Habits and Attitudes (SSHA) and the Study Attitudes and Methods Survey combine the assessment of attitudes with the assessment of study methods. The SSHA, intended for use in grades 7 through college, consists of 100 items tapping poor study skills and attitudes that could affect academic performance. Two forms are available, Form H for grades 7 to 12 and Form C for college, each requiring 20 to 25 minutes to complete. Students respond to items on the following 5-point scale: *rarely, sometimes, frequently, generally,* or *almost always.* Test items are divided into six areas: Delay Avoidance, Work Methods, Study Habits, Teacher Approval, Education Acceptance, and Study Attitudes. The test yields a study skills score, an attitude score, and a total orientation score.

As you *just think* about the questions raised regarding study and personality, *just know* that you will learn about personality and its assessment in the next two chapters.

## Self-Assessment

Test your understanding of elements of this chapter by seeing if you can explain each of the following terms, expressions, names, and abbreviations:

| | | |
|---|---|---|
| achievement test | evaluative information | problem-solving model |
| Apgar number | informal evaluation | prognostic test |
| aptitude test | integrative assessment | psychoeducational test battery |
| at risk | K-ABC | rating scale |
| authentic assessment | KABC-II | readiness test |
| checklist | LPAD | response to intervention model |
| curriculum-based assessment (CBA) | locator test | sociogram |
| curriculum-based measurement (CBM) | peer appraisal | specific learning disability (SLD) |
| | performance assessment | syndrome |
| | performance task | Vygotsky, Lev |
| diagnostic information | portfolio | WJ III |
| diagnostic test | portfolio assessment | zone of proximal development |

# 12

# *Personality Assessment: An Overview*

In a 1950s rock 'n' roll classic song entitled "Personality," singer Lloyd Price described the subject of that song with the words *walk, talk, smile,* and *charm.* In so doing, Price used the term *personality* the way most people tend to use it. For laypeople, *personality* refers to components of an individual's makeup that can elicit positive or negative reactions from others. Someone who consistently tends to elicit positive reactions from others is thought to have a "good personality." Someone who consistently tends to elicit not-so-good reactions from others is thought to have a "bad personality" or, perhaps worse yet, "no personality." We also hear of people described in other ways, with adjectives such as *aggressive, warm,* or *cold.* For professionals in the field of behavioral science, the terms tend to be better-defined, if not more descriptive.

## Personality and Personality Assessment

### *Personality*

Dozens of different definitions of personality exist in the psychology literature. Some definitions appear to be all-inclusive. For example, McClelland (1951, p. 69) defined personality as "the most adequate conceptualization of a person's behavior in all its detail." Menninger (1953, p. 23) defined it as "the individual as a whole, his height and weight and love and hates and blood pressure and reflexes; his smiles and hopes and bowed legs and enlarged tonsils. It means all that anyone is and that he is trying to become." Some definitions focus narrowly on a particular aspect of the individual (Goldstein, 1963), whereas others view the individual in the context of society (Sullivan, 1953). Some theorists avoid any definition at all. For example, Byrne (1974, p. 26) characterized the entire area of personality psychology as "psychology's garbage bin in that any research which doesn't fit other existing categories can be labeled 'personality.'"

In their widely read and authoritative textbook *Theories of Personality,* Hall and Lindzey (1970, p. 9) wrote: "It is our conviction that *no substantive definition of personality can be applied with any generality*" and "*Personality is defined by the particular empirical concepts which are a part of the theory of personality employed by the observer*" [emphasis in the original]. Noting that there were important theoretical differences in many

JUST THINK . . .

Despite great effort, a definition of personality itself—much like a definition of intelligence—has been somewhat elusive. Why do you think this is so?

theories of personality, Hall and Lindzey encouraged their readers to select a definition of personality from the many presented and adopt it as their own.

For our purposes, we will define **personality** as an individual's unique constellation of psychological traits that is relatively stable over time. We view this definition as one that has the advantage of parsimony yet still is flexible enough to incorporate a wide variety of variables. Included in this definition, then, are variables on which individuals may differ, such as values, interests, attitudes, worldview, acculturation, sense of humor, cognitive and behavioral styles, and personality states.

## Personality Assessment

**Personality assessment** may be defined as the measurement and evaluation of psychological traits, states, values, interests, attitudes, worldview, acculturation, sense of humor, cognitive and behavioral styles, and/or related individual characteristics. In this chapter we overview the process of personality assessment, including different approaches to the construction of personality tests. In Chapter 13, we will focus on various methods of personality assessment, including objective, projective, and behavioral methods. Before all that, however, some background is needed regarding the use of the terms *trait, type,* and *state.*

## Traits, Types, and States

**Personality traits**   Just as no consensus exists regarding the definition of personality, there is none regarding the definition of *trait.* Theorists such as Gordon Allport (1937) have tended to view personality traits as real physical entities that are "bona fide mental structures in each personality" (p. 289). For Allport, a trait is a "generalized and focalized neuropsychic system (peculiar to the individual) with the capacity to render many stimuli functionally equivalent, and to initiate and guide consistent (equivalent) forms of adaptive and expressive behavior" (p. 295). Robert Holt (1971) wrote that there "*are* real structures inside people that determine their behavior in lawful ways" (p. 6), and he went on to conceptualize these structures as changes in brain chemistry that might occur as a result of learning: "Learning causes submicroscopic structural changes in the brain, probably in the organization of its biochemical substance" (p. 7). Raymond Cattell (1950) also conceptualized traits as mental structures, but for him *structure* did not necessarily imply actual physical status.

Our own preference is to shy away from definitions that elevate *trait* to the status of physical existence. We view psychological traits as attributions made in an effort to identify threads of consistency in behavioral patterns. In this context, a definition of **personality trait** offered by Guilford (1959, p. 6) has great appeal: "Any distinguishable, relatively enduring way in which one individual varies from another."

This relatively simple definition has some aspects in common with the writings of other personality theorists such as Allport (1937), Cattell (1950, 1965), and Eysenck (1961). The word *distinguishable* indicates that behaviors labeled with different trait terms are actually different from one another. For example, a behavior labeled "friendly" should be distinguishable from a behavior labeled "rude." The *context,* or the situation in which the behavior is displayed, is important in applying trait terms to behaviors. A behavior present in one context may be labeled with one trait term, but the same behavior exhibited in another context may be better described using another trait term.

For example, if we observe someone involved in a lengthy, apparently interesting conversation, we would observe the context before drawing any conclusions about the person's traits. A person talking with a friend over lunch may be demonstrating friendliness, whereas that same person talking to that same friend during a wedding ceremony may be considered rude. Thus, the trait term selected by an observer is dependent both on the behavior itself and on the context in which it appears.

**JUST THINK . . .**

What is another example of how the trait term selected by an observer is dependent both on the behavior emitted as well as the context of that behavior?

A measure of behavior in a particular context may be obtained using varied tools of psychological assessment. For example, using naturalistic observation, an observer could watch the assessee interact with co-workers during break time. Alternatively, the assessee could be administered a self-report questionnaire that probes various aspects of the assessee's interaction with co-workers during break time.

In his definition of trait, Guilford did not assert that traits represent enduring ways in which individuals vary from one another. Rather, he said *relatively enduring. Relatively* emphasizes that exactly how a particular trait manifests itself is, at least to some extent, dependent on the situation. For example, a "violent" parolee generally may be prone to behave in a rather subdued way with his parole officer and much more violently in the presence of his family and friends. Allport (1937) addressed the issue of cross-situational consistency of traits—or lack of it—as follows:

> Perfect consistency will never be found and must not be expected. . . . People may be ascendant and submissive, perhaps submissive only towards those individuals bearing traditional symbols of authority and prestige; and towards everyone else aggressive and domineering. . . . The ever-changing environment raises now one trait and now another to a state of active tension. (p. 330)

For years personality theorists and assessors have assumed that personality traits are relatively enduring over the course of one's life. Roberts and DelVecchio (2000) explored the endurance of traits by means of a meta-analysis of 152 longitudinal studies. These researchers concluded that trait consistency increases in a steplike pattern until one is 50 to 59 years old, at which time such consistency peaks. Their findings may be interpreted as compelling testimony to the relatively enduring nature of personality traits over the course of one's life. Do you think the physically aggressive hockey player pictured in Figure 12-1 will still be as physically aggressive during his retirement years?

Returning to our elaboration of Guilford's definition, note that *trait* is described as a way in which one individual varies from another. Let's emphasize here that the attribution of a trait term is always a *relative* phenomenon. For instance, some behavior described as "patriotic" may differ greatly from other behavior also described as "patriotic." There are no absolute standards. In describing an individual as patriotic, we are, in essence, making an unstated comparison with the degree of patriotic behavior that could reasonably be expected to be exhibited under the same or similar circumstances.

Classic research on the subject of cross-situational consistency in traits has pointed to a *lack* of consistency with regard to traits such as honesty (Hartshorne & May, 1928), punctuality (Dudycha, 1936), conformity (Hollander & Willis, 1967), attitude toward authority (Burwen & Campbell, 1957), and introversion/extraversion (Newcomb, 1929). These are the types of studies cited by Mischel (1968, 1973, 1977, 1979) and others who have been critical of the predominance of the concept of traits in personality theory. Such critics may also allude to the fact that some undetermined

**Figure 12–1**
**Trait Aggressiveness and Flare-ups on the Ice**

*Bushman and Wells (1998) administered a self-report measure of trait aggressiveness (the Physical Aggression subscale of the Aggression Questionnaire) to 91 high-school team hockey players before the start of the season. The players responded to items such as "Once in a while I cannot control my urge to strike another person" presented in Likert scale format ranging from 1 to 5 (where 1 corresponded to "extremely uncharacteristic of me" and 5 corresponded to "extremely characteristic of me"). At the end of the season, trait aggressiveness scores were examined with respect to minutes served in the penalty box for aggressive penalties such as fighting, slashing, and tripping. The preseason measure of trait aggressiveness predicted aggressive penalty minutes served. The study is particularly noteworthy because the test data were used to predict real-life aggression, not a laboratory analogue of aggression such as the administration of electric shock. The authors recommended that possible applications of the Aggression Questionnaire be explored in other settings where aggression is a problematic behavior.*

portion of behavior exhibited in public may be governed more by societal expectations and cultural role restrictions than by an individual's personality traits (Barker, 1963; Goffman, 1963). Research designed to shed light on the primacy of individual differences, as opposed to situational factors in behavior, is methodologically complex (Golding, 1975), and a definitive verdict as to the primacy of the trait or the situation is simply not in.

**Personality types**   Having defined personality as a unique constellation of traits, we might define a **personality type** as a constellation of traits that is similar in pattern to one identified category of personality within a taxonomy of personalities. Whereas traits are frequently discussed as if they were *characteristics* possessed by an individual, types are more clearly *descriptions* of people. So, for example, describing an individual as "depressed" is different from describing that individual as a "depressed type." The latter term has more far-reaching implications regarding characteristic aspects of the individual, such as the person's worldview, activity level, capacity to enjoy life, and level of social interest.

At least since Hippocrates' classification of people into four types (melancholic, phlegmatic, choleric, and sanguine), there has been no shortage of personality typologies through the ages. A typology devised by Carl Jung (1923) became the basis for the Myers-Briggs Type Indicator (MBTI; Myers & Briggs, 1943/1962). An assumption guiding the development of this test was that people exhibit definite preferences in the way that they perceive or become aware of—and judge or arrive at conclusions about—people, events, situations, and ideas. According to Myers (1962, p. 1), these differences in perception and judging result in "corresponding differences in their reactions, in their interests, values, needs, and motivations, in what they do best, and in what they like to do." For example, in one study designed to better understand the personality of chess players, the Myers-Briggs Type Indicator was administered to 2,165 chess players, including players at the masters and senior masters level.

The chess players were found to be significantly more introverted, intuitive, and thinking (as opposed to feeling) than members of the general population. The investigator also found masters to be more judgmental than the general population (Kelly, 1985).

**JUST THINK . . .**

What are the possible benefits of classifying people into types? What possible problems may arise from doing so?

John Holland (Figure 12–2) argued that most people can be categorized as one of the following six personality types: Artistic, Enterprising, Investigative, Social, Realistic, or Conventional (Holland, 1973, 1985, 1997, 1999). His Self-Directed Search test (SDS; Holland et al., 1994) is a self-administered, self-scored, and self-interpreted aid used to type people according to this system and to offer vocational guidance. Another personality typology, this one having only two categories, was devised by cardiologists Meyer Friedman and Ray Rosenman (1974; Rosenman et al., 1975). They conceived of a **Type A personality,** characterized by competitiveness, haste, restlessness, impatience, feelings of being time-pressured, and strong needs for achievement and dominance. A **Type B personality** has the opposite of the Type A's traits: mellow or laid-back. A 52-item self-report inventory called the Jenkins Activity Survey (JAS; Jenkins et al., 1979) has been used to type respondents as Type A or Type B personalities.

The personality typology that has attracted the most attention from researchers and practitioners alike is associated with scores on a test called the MMPI (as well as

**Figure 12–2**
**John L. Holland (1919–2008)**

*John Holland was well known for the employment-related personality typology he developed, as well as the Self-Directed Search (SDS), a measure of one's interests and perceived abilities. The test is based on Holland's theory of vocational personality. At the heart of this theory is the view that occupational choice has a great deal to do with one's personality and self-perception of abilities. Holland's work was the subject of controversy in the 1970s. Critics asserted that measured differences between the interests of men and women were an artifact of sex bias. Holland argued that such differences reflected valid variance. As the author of Holland's obituary in* American Psychologist *recalled, "He did not bend willy-nilly in the winds of political correctness" (Gottfredson, 2009, p. 561).*

all of its successors—discussed later in this chapter). Data from the administration of these tests, as with others, are frequently discussed in terms of the patterns of scores that emerge on the subtests. This pattern is referred to as a *profile*. In general, a **profile** is a narrative description, graph, table, or other representation of the extent to which a person has demonstrated certain targeted characteristics as a result of the administration or application of tools of assessment.[1] In the term **personality profile,** the targeted characteristics are typically traits, states, or types. With specific reference to the MMPI, different profiles of scores are associated with different patterns of behavior. So, for example, a particular MMPI profile designated as "2–4–7" is associated with a type of individual who has a history of alcohol abuse alternating with sobriety and self-recrimination (Dahlstrom, 1995).

**Personality states**   The word **state** has been used in at least two distinctly different ways in the personality assessment literature. In one usage, a personality state is an inferred psychodynamic disposition designed to convey the dynamic quality of id, ego, and superego in perpetual conflict. Assessment of these psychodynamic dispositions may be made through the use of various psychoanalytic techniques such as free association, word association, symbolic analysis of interview material, dream analysis, and analysis of slips of the tongue, accidents, jokes, and forgetting.

Presently, a more popular usage of the term *state*—and the one we use in the discussion that follows—refers to the transitory exhibition of some personality trait. Put another way, the use of the word *trait* presupposes a relatively enduring behavioral predisposition, whereas the term *state* is indicative of a relatively temporary predisposition (Chaplin et al., 1988). Thus, for example, your friend may be accurately described as being "in an anxious state" before her midterms, though no one who knows her well would describe her as "an anxious person."

**JUST THINK . . .**

You experience "butterflies" in your stomach just before asking someone to whom you are attracted to accompany you to the movies. Would this feeling better be characterized as a state or a trait?

Measuring personality states amounts, in essence, to a search for and an assessment of the strength of traits that are relatively transitory or fairly situation specific. Relatively few personality tests seek to distinguish traits from states. Pathbreaking work in this area was done by Charles D. Spielberger and his associates (Spielberger et al., 1980). These researchers developed a number of personality inventories designed to distinguish various states from traits. In the manual for the State-Trait Anxiety Inventory (STAI), for example, we find that state anxiety refers to a transitory experience of tension because of a particular situation. By contrast, trait anxiety or anxiety proneness refers to a relatively stable or enduring personality characteristic. The STAI test items consist of short descriptive statements, and subjects are instructed to indicate either (1) how they feel right now or at this moment (and to indicate the intensity of the feeling), or (2) how they generally feel (and to record the frequency of the feeling). The test-retest reliability coefficients reported in the manual are consistent with the theoretical premise that trait anxiety is the more enduring characteristic, whereas state anxiety is transitory.

---

1. The verb *to profile* refers to the creation of such a description. The term **profile analysis** refers to the interpretation of patterns of scores on a test or test battery. Profile analysis is frequently used to generate diagnostic hypotheses from intelligence test data. The noun **profiler** refers to an occupation: one who creates personality profiles of crime suspects to assist law enforcement personnel in capturing the profiled suspects. More on the work of profilers in Chapter 14.

# Personality Assessment: Some Basic Questions

For what type of employment is a person with this type of personality best suited?

Is this individual sufficiently well adjusted for military service?

What emotional and other adjustment-related factors may be responsible for this student's level of academic achievement?

What pattern of traits and states does this psychotherapy client evince, and to what extent may this pattern be deemed pathological?

How has this patient's personality been affected by neurological trauma?

These questions are a sampling of the kind that might lead to a referral for personality assessment. Collectively, these types of referral questions provide insight into a more general question in a clinical context: Why assess personality?

We might raise the same question in the context of basic research and find another wide world of potential applications for personality assessment. For example, aspects of personality could be explored in identifying determinants of knowledge about health (Beier & Ackerman, 2003), in categorizing different types of commitment in intimate relationships (Frank & Brandstaetter, 2002), in determining peer response to a team's weakest link (Jackson & LePine, 2003), or even in the service of national defense to identify those prone to terrorism. Personality assessment is a staple in developmental research, be it tracking trait development over time (McCrae et al., 2002) or studying some uniquely human characteristic such as moral judgment (Eisenberg et al., 2002). From a health psychology perspective, there are a number of personality variables (such as perfectionism, self-criticism, dependency, and neuroticism) that have been linked to physical and psychological disorders (Flett & Hewitt, 2002; Klein et al., 2011; Kotov et al., 2010; Zuroff et al., 2004; Sturman, 2011). In the corporate world, personality assessment is a key tool of the human resources department, relied on to aid in hiring, firing, promoting, transferring, and related decisions. Perhaps as long as there have been tests to measure people's interests, there have been questions regarding how those interests relate to personality (Larson et al., 2002). In military organizations around the world, leadership is a sought-after trait, and personality tests help identify who has it (see, for example, Bradley et al., 2002; Handler, 2001). In the most general sense, basic research involving personality assessment helps to validate or invalidate theories of behavior and to generate new hypotheses.

Tangentially, let's note that a whole other perspective on the *why* of personality assessment emerges with a consideration of cross-species research (see Figure 12–3). Gosling, Kwan, & John, (2003) viewed their research on the personality of dogs as paving the way for future research in previously uncharted areas such as the exploration of environmental effects on personality.

Beyond the *why* of personality assessment are several other questions that must be addressed in any overview of the enterprise. Approaches to personality assessment differ in terms of *who* is being assessed, *what* is being assessed, *where* the assessment is conducted, and *how* the assessment is conducted. Let's take a closer look at each of these related issues.

> **JUST THINK . . .**
>
> What differences in terms of accuracy and reliability of report would you expect when one is reporting on one's own personality as opposed to when another person is reporting about someone's personality?

## Who?

*Who is being assessed, and who is doing the assessing?* Some methods of personality assessment rely on the assessee's own self-report. Assessees may respond to interview

**Figure 12–3**
**Simply Lovable!**

*Gosling, Kwan, & John (2003) examined a comprehensive array of dog-relevant personality traits in a carefully designed study that even controlled for the potentially biasing effects of factors such as preconceived personality stereotypes based on breed and appearance. The researchers concluded that differences in personality among dogs exist and can be reliably measured. These findings dovetail with those of other researchers who have advanced the idea that differences in the personalities of animals not only exist but are heritable (Weiss et al., 2002).[2]*

questions, answer questionnaires in writing, blacken squares on computer answer forms, or sort cards with various terms on them—all with the ultimate objective of providing the assessor with a personality-related self-description. By contrast, other methods of personality assessment rely on informants other than the person being assessed to provide personality-related information. So, for example, parents or teachers may be asked to participate in the personality assessment of a child by providing ratings, judgments, opinions, and impressions relevant to the child's personality.

**The self as the primary referent**  People typically undergo personality assessment so that they, as well as the assessor, can learn something about who they are. In many instances, the assessment or some aspect of it requires **self-report,** or a process wherein

_____

2. Thanks to Sheena, the beloved, loving, and indescribably wonderful companion to one of the authors (RJC), for graciously posing for this photo.

information about assessees is supplied by the assessees themselves. Self-reported information may be obtained in the form of diaries kept by assessees or in the form of responses to oral or written questions or test items. In some cases, the information sought by the assessor is so private that only the individual assessees themselves are capable of providing it. For example, when researchers investigated the psychometric soundness of the Sexual Sensation Seeking Scale with a sample of college students, only the students themselves could provide the highly personal information needed. The researchers viewed their reliance on self-report as a possible limitation of the study, but noted that this methodology "has been the standard practice in this area of research because no gold standard exists for verifying participants' reports of sexual behaviors" (Gaither & Sellbom, 2003, p. 165).

Self-report methods are very commonly used to explore an assessee's *self-concept*. **Self-concept** may be defined as one's attitudes, beliefs, opinions, and related thoughts about oneself. Inferences about an assessee's self-concept may be derived from many tools of assessment. However, the tool of choice is typically a dedicated **self-concept measure;** that is, an instrument designed to yield information relevant to how an individual sees him- or herself with regard to selected psychological variables. Data from such an instrument are usually interpreted in the context of how others may see themselves on the same or similar variables. In the Beck Self-Concept Test (BST; Beck & Stein, 1961), named after senior author, psychiatrist Aaron T. Beck, respondents are asked to compare themselves to other people on variables such as looks, knowledge, and the ability to tell jokes.

A number of self-concept measures for children have been developed. Some representative tests include the Tennessee Self-Concept Scale and the Piers-Harris Self-Concept Scale. The latter test contains 80 self-statements (such as "I don't have any friends") to which respondents from grades 3 to 12 respond either *yes* or *no* as the statement applies to them. Factor analysis has suggested that the items cover six general areas of self-concept: behavior, intellectual and school status, physical appearance and attributes, anxiety, popularity, and happiness and satisfaction. The Beck Self-Concept Test was extended down as one component of a series called the Beck Youth Inventories–Second Edition (BYI-II) developed by senior author, psychologist Judith Beck (Aaron T. Beck's daughter). In addition to a self-concept measure, the BYI-II includes inventories to measures depression, anxiety, anger, and disruptive behavior in children and adolescents aged 7 to 18 years.

Some measures of self-concept are based on the notion that states and traits related to self-concept are to a large degree context-dependent—that is, ever-changing as a result of the particular situation (Callero, 1992). The term **self-concept differentiation** refers to the degree to which a person has different self-concepts in different roles (Donahue et al., 1993). People characterized as *highly differentiated* are likely to perceive themselves quite differently in various roles. For example, a highly differentiated businessman in his 40s may perceive himself as motivated and hard-driving in his role at work, conforming and people-pleasing in his role as son, and emotional and passionate in his role as husband. By contrast, people whose concept of self is not very differentiated tend to perceive themselves similarly across their social roles. According to Donahue et al. (1993), people with low levels of self-concept differentiation tend to be healthier psychologically, perhaps because of their more unified and coherent sense of self.

**JUST THINK . . .**

Highly differentiated or not very differentiated in self-concept—which do *you* think is preferable? Why?

Assuming that assessees have reasonably accurate insight into their own thinking and behavior, and assuming that they are motivated to respond to test items honestly, self-report measures can be extremely valuable. An assessee's candid and accurate self-report can illustrate what that individual is thinking, feeling, and doing. Unfortunately, some assessees may intentionally or unintentionally paint distorted pictures of themselves in self-report measures.

Consider what would happen if employers were to rely on job applicants' representations concerning their personality and their suitability for a particular job. Employers might be led to believe they have found a slew of perfect applicants. Many job applicants—as well as people in contexts as diverse as high-school reunions, singles bars, and child custody hearings—attempt to "fake good" in their presentation of themselves to other people.

**JUST THINK . . .**

Has anyone you know engaged in "faking good" or "faking bad" behavior (in or out of the context of assessment)? Why?

The other side of the "faking good" coin is "faking bad." Litigants in civil actions who claim injury may seek high awards as compensation for their alleged pain, suffering, and emotional distress—all of which may be exaggerated and dramatized for the benefit of a judge and jury. The accused in a criminal action may view time in a mental institution as preferable to time in prison (or capital punishment) and strategically choose an insanity defense—with accompanying behavior and claims to make such a defense as believable as possible. A homeless person who prefers the environs of a mental hospital to that of the street may attempt to fake bad on tests and in interviews if failure to do so will result in discharge. In the days of the military draft, it was not uncommon for draft resisters to fake bad on psychiatric examinations in their efforts to be deferred.

Some testtakers truly may be impaired with regard to their ability to respond accurately to self-report questions. They may lack insight, for example, because of certain medical or psychological conditions at the time of assessment. By contrast, other testtakers seem blessed with an abundance of self-insight that they can convey with ease and expertise on self-report measures. It is for this latter group of individuals that self-report measures, according to Burisch (1984), will not reveal anything the testtaker does not already know. Of course, Burisch may have overstated the case. Even people with an abundance of self-insight can profit from taking the time to reflect about their own thoughts and behaviors, especially if they are unaccustomed to doing so.

**Another person as the referent** In some situations, the best available method for the assessment of personality, behavior, or both involves reporting by a third party such as a parent, teacher, peer, supervisor, spouse, or trained observer. Consider, for example, the assessment of a child for emotional difficulties. The child may be unable or unwilling to complete any measure (self-report, performance, or otherwise) that will be of value in making a valid determination concerning that child's emotional status. Even case history data may be of minimal value because the problems may be so subtle as to become evident only after careful and sustained observation. In such cases, the use of a test in which the testtaker or respondent is an informant—but not the subject of study—may be valuable. In basic personality research, this third-party approach to assessment has been found useful, especially when the third-party reporter knows the subject of the evaluation very well. Proceeding under the assumption that spouses should be familiar enough with each other to serve as good informants, one study examined self- versus spouse ratings on personality-related variables (South et al., 2011). Self and spousal ratings were found to be significantly correlated, and this relationship was stronger than that typically found between self- and peer ratings in personality research.

**JUST THINK . . .**

Do you believe meaningful insights are better derived through self-assessment or through assessment by someone else? Why?

The Personality Inventory for Children (PIC) and its revision, the PIC-2 (pronounced "pick two"), are examples of a kind of standardized interview of a child's parent. Although the child is the subject of the test, the respondent is the parent (usually the mother), guardian, or other adult qualified to respond with reference to the child's characteristic behavior. The test consists of a series of true–false items designed to be free of racial and gender bias. The items may be administered by computer or paper and pencil. Test results yield scores that provide clinical information and shed light on the validity of the testtaker's response patterns. A number of studies attest to the validity of the PIC for its intended purpose (Kline et al., 1992; Kline et al., 1993; Lachar & Wirt, 1981; Lachar et al., 1985; Wirt et al., 1984). However, as with any test that relies on the observations and judgment of a rater, some concerns about this instrument have also been expressed (Achenbach, 1981; Cornell, 1985).

In general, there are many cautions to consider when one person undertakes to evaluate another. These cautions are by no means limited to the area of personality assessment. Rather, in any situation when one individual undertakes to rate another individual, it is important to understand the dynamics of the situation. Although a rater's report can provide a wealth of information about an assessee, it may also be instructive to look at the source of that information.

Raters may vary in the extent to which they are, or strive to be, scrupulously neutral, favorably generous, or harshly severe in their ratings. Generalized biases to rate in a particular direction are referred to in terms such as **leniency error** or **generosity error** and **severity error.** A general tendency to rate everyone near the midpoint of a rating scale is termed an **error of central tendency.** In some situations, a particular set of circumstances may create a certain bias. For example, a teacher might be disposed to judging one pupil very favorably because that pupil's older sister was teacher's pet in a prior class. This variety of favorable response bias is sometimes referred to as a **halo effect.**

Raters may make biased judgments, consciously or unconsciously, simply because it is in their own self-interest to do so (see Figure 12–4). Therapists who passionately believe in the efficacy of a particular therapeutic approach may be more disposed than others to see the benefits of that approach. Proponents of alternative approaches may be more disposed to see the negative aspects of that same treatment.

Numerous other factors may contribute to bias in a rater's ratings. The rater may feel competitive with, physically attracted to, or physically repelled by the subject of the ratings. The rater may not have the proper background, experience, and trained eye needed for the particular task. Judgments may be limited by the rater's general level of conscientiousness and willingness to devote the time and effort required to do the job properly. The rater may harbor biases concerning various stereotypes. Subjectivity based on the rater's own personal preferences and taste may also enter into judgments. Features that rate a "perfect 10" in one person's opinion may represent more like a "mediocre 5" in the eyes of another person. If such marked diversity of opinion occurs frequently with regard to a particular instrument, we would expect it to be reflected in low inter-rater reliability coefficients. It would probably be desirable to take another look at the criteria used to make ratings and how specific they are.

When another person is the referent, an important factor to consider with regard to ratings is the *context* of the evaluation. Different raters may have different perspectives on the individual they are rating because of the context in which they typically view that person. A parent may indicate on a rating scale that a child is hyperactive, whereas the same child's teacher may indicate on the same rating scale that the child's activity level is within normal limits. Can they both be right?

The answer is yes, according to one meta-analysis of 119 articles in the scholarly literature (Achenbach et al., 1987). Different informants may have different perspectives

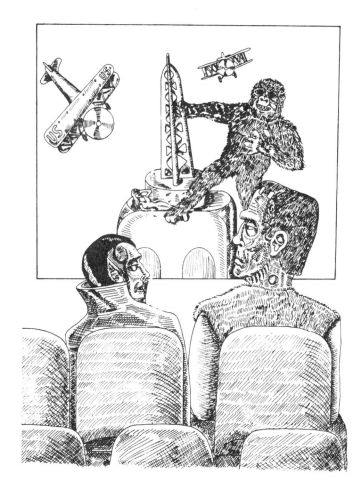

**Figure 12–4
Ratings in One's Own
Self-Interest**

*"Monsters and screamers have
always worked for me; I give it
'thumbs up,' Roger."*

on the subjects being evaluated. These different perspectives derive from observing and interacting with the subjects in different contexts. The study also noted that raters tended to agree more about the difficulties of young children (ages 6 to 11) than about those of older children and adolescents. Raters also tended to show more agreement about children exhibiting self-control problems (such as hyperactivity and mistreating other children) in contrast to "overcontrol" problems (such as anxiety or depression). The researchers urged professionals to view the differences in evaluation that arise from different perspectives as something more than error in the evaluation process. They urged professionals to employ context-specific differences in treatment plans. Many of their ideas regarding context-dependent evaluation and treatment were incorporated into Achenbach's (1993) Multiaxial Empirically Based Assessment system. The system is an approach to the assessment of children and adolescents that incorporates cognitive and physical assessments of the subject, self-report of the subject, and ratings by parents and teachers. Additionally, performance measures of the child alone, with the family, or in the classroom may be included.

**JUST THINK . . .**

Imagining that it was *you* who was being rated, how might you be rated differently on the same variable in different contexts?

Regardless whether the self or another person is the subject of study, one element of any evaluation that must be kept in mind by the assessor is the cultural context.

**The cultural background of assessees** Test developers and users have shown increased sensitivity to issues of cultural diversity. A number of concerns have been raised regarding the use of personality tests and other tools of assessment with members of culturally and linguistically diverse populations (Anderson, 1995; Campos, 1989; Greene, 1987; Hill et al., 2010; Irvine & Berry, 1983; López & Hernandez, 1987; Nye et al., 2008; Sundberg & Gonzales, 1981; Widiger & Samuel, 2009). How fair or generalizable is a particular instrument or measurement technique with a member of a particular cultural group? How a test was developed, how it is administered, and how scores on it are interpreted are all questions to be raised when considering the appropriateness of administering a particular personality test to members of culturally and linguistically diverse populations. We continue to explore these and related questions later in this chapter and throughout this book. In Chapter 14, for example, we consider in detail the meaning of the term *culturally informed psychological assessment.*

## What?

*What is assessed when a personality assessment is conducted?* For many personality tests, it is meaningful to answer this question with reference to the primary content area sampled by the test and to that portion of the test devoted to measuring aspects of the testtaker's general response style.

**Primary content area sampled**   Personality measures are tools used to gain insight into a wide array of thoughts, feelings, and behaviors associated with all aspects of the human experience. Some tests are designed to measure particular traits (such as introversion) or states (such as test anxiety), whereas others focus on descriptions of behavior, usually in particular contexts. For example, an observational checklist may concentrate on classroom behaviors associated with movement in order to assess a child's hyperactivity. Extended discussion of behavioral measures is presented in Chapter 13.

Many contemporary personality tests, especially tests that can be scored and interpreted by computer, are designed to measure not only some targeted trait or other personality variable but also some aspect of the testtaker's response style. For example, in addition to scales labeled *Introversion* and *Extraversion,* a test of introversion/extraversion might contain other scales. Such additional scales could be designed to shed light on how honestly testtakers responded to the test, how consistently they answered the questions, and other matters related to the validity of the test findings. These measures of response pattern are also known as *measures of response set* or *response style.* Let's take a look at some different testtaker response styles as well as the scales used to identify them.

**Testtaker response styles**   Response style refers to a tendency to respond to a test item or interview question in some characteristic manner regardless of the content of the item or question. For example, an individual may be more apt to respond *yes* or *true* than *no* or *false* on a short-answer test. This particular pattern of responding is characterized as **acquiescent.** Table 12–1 shows a listing of other identified response styles.

**Impression management** is a term used to describe the attempt to manipulate others' impressions through "the selective exposure of some information (it may be false information) . . . coupled with suppression of [other] information" (Braginsky et al., 1969, p. 51). In the process of personality assessment, assessees might employ any number of impression management strategies for any number of reasons. Delroy Paulhus (1984, 1986, 1990) and his colleagues (Kurt & Paulhus, 2008; Paulhus & Holden, 2010; Paulhus & Levitt, 1987) have explored impression management in test-taking as well as the related phenomena of enhancement (the claiming of positive attributes), denial (the repudiation of negative attributes), and self-deception—"the tendency to give favorably biased but honestly held self-descriptions" (Paulhus & Reid, 1991, p. 307).

**Table 12–1**
**A Sampling of Test Response Styles**

| Response Style Name | Explanation: A Tendency to . . . |
|---|---|
| Socially desirable responding | present oneself in a favorable (socially acceptable or desirable) light |
| Acquiescence | agree with whatever is presented |
| Nonacquiescence | disagree with whatever is presented |
| Deviance | make unusual or uncommon responses |
| Extreme | make extreme, as opposed to middle, ratings on a rating scale |
| Gambling/cautiousness | guess—or not guess—when in doubt |
| Overly positive | claim extreme virtue through self-presentation in a superlative manner (Butcher & Han, 1995) |

Testtakers who engage in impression management are exhibiting, in the broadest sense, a response style (Jackson & Messick, 1962).

**JUST THINK . . .**

On what occasion did you attempt to manage a particular impression for a friend, a family member, or an acquaintance? Why did you feel the need to do so? Would you consider your effort successful?

Some personality tests contain items designed to detect different types of response styles. So, for example, a *true* response to an item like "I summer in Baghdad" would raise a number of questions, such as: Did the testtaker understand the instructions? Take the test seriously? Respond *true* to all items? Respond randomly? Endorse other infrequently endorsed items? Analysis of the entire protocol will help answer such questions.

Responding to a personality test in an inconsistent, contrary, or random way, or attempting to fake good or bad, may affect the validity of the interpretations of the test data. Because a response style can affect the validity of the outcome, one particular type of response style measure is referred to as a *validity scale*. We may define a **validity scale** as a subscale of a test designed to assist in judgments regarding how honestly the testtaker responded and whether observed responses were products of response style, carelessness, deliberate efforts to deceive, or unintentional misunderstanding. Validity scales can provide a kind of shorthand indication of how honestly, diligently, and carefully a testtaker responded to test items. Some tests, such as the MMPI and its revision (to be discussed shortly), contain multiple validity scales. Although there are those who question the utility of formally assessing response styles (Costa & McCrae, 1997; Rorer, 1965), perhaps the more common view is that response styles are themselves important for what they reveal about testtakers. As Nunnally (1978, p. 660) observed: "To the extent that such stylistic variables can be measured independently of content relating to nonstylistic variables or to the extent that they can somehow be separated from the variance of other traits, they might prove useful as measures of personality traits."

## *Where?*

*Where are personality assessments conducted?* Traditional sites for personality assessment, as well as other varieties of assessment, are schools, clinics, hospitals, academic research laboratories, employment counseling and vocational selection centers, and the offices of psychologists and counselors. In addition to such traditional venues, contemporary assessors may be found observing behavior and making assessments in natural settings, ranging from the assessee's own home (Marx, 1998; McElwain, 1998; Polizzi, 1998) to the incarcerated assessee's prison cell (Glassbrenner, 1998) and other settings where the

## Meet Dr. Eric A. Zillmer

Given that terrorism on a grand scale has become increasingly possible, it is important for psychologists to understand the terrorist's frame of mind. Military personnel, behavioral scientists, and psychologists may find themselves progressively more involved as consultants to the military, security firms, federal and state governments, intelligence agencies, and the police in their fight against the potential threat of terrorism. Thus, it has become increasingly more relevant to the behavioral and social sciences to study the terrorists decision-making process, the social context under which terror acts occur, and the specific personalities that may be involved in terrorist atrocities.

Related to my expertise in this area, I was invited by the Pentagon in November of 2006 to visit the Naval base at Guantanamo Bay, Cuba [see Figure 12–5], to take a firsthand look at the facilities, meet medical staff and behavioral science consultants to interrogators, and review policies and practices pertinent to detainee care and management.

**Eric A. Zillmer, Psy.D., Carl R. Pacifico Professor of Neuropsychology, Drexel University**

*Read more of what Dr. Zillmer had to say— his complete essay—at www.mhhe.com/ cohentesting8.*

assessee is held captive (see *Meet an Assessment Professional* and Figure 12–5). As we will see in the discussion of behavioral assessment in Chapter 13, behavioral observation may be undertaken just about anywhere.

### How?

*How are personality assessments structured and conducted?* Let's look at various facets of this multidimensional question, beginning with issues of scope and theory. We then discuss procedures and item formats that may be employed, the frame of reference of the assessment, and scoring and interpretation.

**Scope and theory** One dimension of the *how* of personality assessment concerns its scope. The scope of an evaluation may be very wide, seeking to take a kind of general inventory of an individual's personality. The California Psychological Inventory (CPI 434) is an example of an instrument with a relatively wide scope. This test contains 434 true–false items—but then you knew that from its title—and is designed to yield information on many personality-related variables such as responsibility, self-acceptance, and dominance. It was originally conceived to measure enduring

**Figure 12–5**
**Psychological Assessment at Camp Delta, Guantanamo Bay, Cuba**

*Dr. Eric Zillmer discusses issues facing psychologists who are stationed at Guantanamo Bay, Cuba, with other civilian and military personnel as he leaves Camp Delta.*

personality traits across cultural groups, and predict the behavior of generally well-functioning people (Boer et al., 2008).

In contrast to instruments and procedures designed to inventory personality as a whole are instruments that are much narrower in terms of what they purport to measure. An instrument may be designed to focus on as little as one particular aspect of personality. For example, consider tests designed to measure a personality variable called *locus of control* (Rotter, 1966; Wallston et al., 1978). **Locus** (meaning "place" or "site") **of control** is a person's perception about the source of things that happen to him or her. In general, people who see themselves as largely responsible for what happens to them are said to have an *internal* locus of control. People who are prone to attribute what happens to them to external factors (such as fate or the actions of others) are said to have an *external* locus of control. A person who believes in the value of seatbelts, for example, would be expected to score closer to the internal than to the external end of the continuum of locus of control as opposed to a nonbuckling counterpart.

**JUST THINK . . .**

Suppose you would like to learn as much as you can about the personality of an assessee from one personality test that is narrow in scope. On what single aspect of personality do you believe it would be most important to focus?

To what extent is a personality test theory-based or relatively atheoretical? Instruments used in personality testing and assessment vary in the extent to which they are based on a theory of personality. Some are based entirely on a theory, and some are relatively atheoretical. An example of a theory-based instrument is the Blacky Pictures Test (Blum, 1950). This test consists of cartoonlike pictures of a dog named Blacky in various situations, and each image is designed to elicit fantasies associated with various psychoanalytic themes. For example, one card depicts Blacky with a knife hovering over his tail, a scene (according to the test's author) designed to elicit material related to the psychoanalytic concept of castration anxiety. The respondent's task is to make up stories in response to such cards, and the stories are then analyzed according to the guidelines set forth by Blum (1950). The test is seldom used today; we cite it here as a particularly dramatic and graphic illustration of how a personality theory (in this case, psychoanalytic theory) can saturate a test.

The other side of the theory saturation coin is the personality test that is relatively atheoretical. The single most popular personality test in use today is atheoretical: the Minnesota Multiphasic Personality Inventory (MMPI), in both its original and revised forms. Streiner (2003a) referred to this test as "the epitome of an atheoretical, 'dust bowl empiricism' approach to the development of a tool to measure personality traits" (p. 218). You will better appreciate this comment when we discuss the MMPI and its subsequent revisions later in this chapter. For now, let's simply point out one advantage of an atheoretical tool of personality assessment: It allows test users, should they so desire, to impose their own theoretical preferences on the interpretation of the findings.

Pursuing another aspect of the *how* of personality assessment, let's turn to a nuts-and-bolts look at the methods used.

**Procedures and item formats**  Personality may be assessed by many different methods, such as face-to-face interviews, computer-administered tests, behavioral observation, paper-and-pencil tests, evaluation of case history data, evaluation of portfolio data, and recording of physiological responses. The equipment required for assessment varies greatly, depending upon the method employed. In one technique, for example, all that may be required is a blank sheet of paper and a pencil. The assessee is asked to draw a person, and the assessor makes inferences about the assessee's personality from the drawing. Other approaches to assessment, whether in the interest of basic research or for more applied purposes, may be far more elaborate in terms of the equipment they require (Figure 12–6).

**Figure 12–6**
**Learning About Personality in the Field—Literally**

*During World War II, the assessment staff of the Office of Strategic Services (OSS) selected American secret agents using a variety of measures. One measure used to assess leadership ability and emotional stability in the field was a simulation that involved rebuilding a blown bridge. Candidates were deliberately supplied with insufficient materials for rebuilding the bridge. In some instances, "assistants" who were actually confederates of the experimenter further frustrated the candidates' efforts.*

Measures of personality vary in terms of the degree of *structure* built into them. For example, personality may be assessed by means of an interview, but it may also be assessed by a **structured interview.** In the latter method, the interviewer must typically follow an interview guide and has little leeway in terms of posing questions not in that guide. The variable of structure is also applicable to the tasks assessees are instructed to perform. In some approaches to personality assessment, the tasks are straightforward, highly structured, and unambiguous. Here is one example of the instructions used for such a task: *Copy this sentence in your own handwriting.* Such instructions might be used if the assessor was attempting to learn something about the assessee by handwriting analysis, also referred to as **graphology** (see Figure 12–7). Intuitively appealing as a method of deriving insights into personality, graphology seems not to have lived up to its promise (Dazzi & Pedrabissi, 2009; Fox, 2011; Gawda, 2008; Thiry, 2009).

In other approaches to personality, what is required of the assessee is not so straightforward, not very structured, and intentionally ambiguous. One example of a highly unstructured task is as follows: Hand the assessee one of a series of inkblots and ask, *What might this be?*

**JUST THINK . . .**

Straightforward or ambiguous? Which approach to personality assessment has more appeal to you in your (future) role as an assessor? Why?

The same personality trait or construct may be measured with different instruments in different ways. Consider the many possible ways of determining how *aggressive* a person is. Measurement of this trait could be made in different ways: a paper-and-pencil test; a computerized test; an interview with the assessee; an interview with family, friends, and associates of the assessee; analysis of official records and other case history data; behavioral observation; and laboratory experimentation.

**Figure 12–7**
**Three Faces (and Three Handwritings) of Eve**

Three Faces of Eve *was a fact-based, 1957 film classic about three of the personalities—there were more over the course of the woman's lifetime—manifested by a patient known as "Eve White," "Eve Black," and "Jane." Prior to making that film, the 20th Century–Fox legal department insisted that the patient on whom the screenplay was based sign three separate contracts, one for each of her personalities. Accordingly, the patient was asked to elicit "Eve White," "Eve Black," and "Jane," and then sign an agreement while manifesting each of these respective personalities. According to Aubrey Solomon, co-author of The Films of 20th Century–Fox (Thomas & Solomon, 1989) and commentator on the DVD release of the film, the three signatures on the three separate contracts were all distinctly different— presumably because they were a product of three distinctly different personalities.*

Of course, criteria for what constitutes the trait measured—in this case, aggression—would have to be rigorously defined in advance. After all, psychological traits and constructs can and have been defined in many different ways, and virtually all such definitions tend to be context-dependent. For example, *aggressive* may be defined in ways ranging from hostile and assaultive (as in the "aggressive inmate") to bold and enterprising (as in the "aggressive salesperson"). This personality trait, like many others, may or may not be socially desirable; it depends entirely on the context.

In personality assessment, as well as in assessment of other areas, information may be gathered and questions answered in a variety of ways. For example, a researcher or practitioner interested in learning about the degree to which respondents are field-dependent may construct an elaborate tilting chair/tilting room device—the same one you may recall from Chapter 1 (Figure 1–6). In the interests of time and expense, an equivalent process administered by paper and pencil or computer may be more practical for everyday use. In this chapter's *Everyday Psychometrics*, we illustrate some of the more common item formats employed in the study of personality and related psychological variables. Keep in mind that, although we are using these formats to illustrate different ways that personality has been studied, some are employed in other areas of assessment as well.

**Frame of reference**   Another variable relevant to the *how* of personality measurement concerns the *frame of reference* of the assessment. In the context of item format and assessment in general, **frame of reference** may be defined as aspects of the focus of exploration such as the time frame (the past, the present, or the future) as well as other contextual issues that involve people, places, and events. Perhaps for most measures of personality, the frame of reference for the assessee may be described in phrases such as *what is* or *how I am right now*. However, some techniques of measurement are easily adapted to tap alternative frames of reference, such as *what I could be ideally, how I am in the office, how others see me, how I see others,* and so forth. Obtaining self-reported information from different frames of reference is, in itself, a way of developing information related to states and traits. For example, in comparing self-perception in the present versus what is anticipated for the future, assessees who report that they will become better people may be presumed to be more optimistic than assessees who report a reverse trend.

Representative of methodologies that can be readily applied in the exploration of varied frames of reference is the **Q-sort technique.** Originally developed by Stephenson (1953), the Q-sort is an assessment technique in which the task is to sort a group of statements, usually in perceived rank order ranging from *most descriptive* to *least descriptive*. The statements, traditionally presented on index cards, may be sorted in ways designed to reflect various perceptions. They may, for example, reflect how respondents see themselves or how they would like to see themselves. Illustrative statements are *I am confident, I try hard to please others,* and *I am uncomfortable in social situations.*

One of the best-known applications of Q-sort methodology in clinical and counseling settings was advocated by the personality theorist and psychotherapist Carl Rogers. Rogers (1959) used the Q-sort to evaluate the discrepancy between the perceived actual self and the ideal self. At the beginning of psychotherapy, clients might be asked to sort cards twice, once according to how they perceived themselves to be and then according to how they would ultimately like to be. The larger the discrepancy between the sortings, the more goals would have to be set in therapy. Presumably, retesting the client who successfully completed a course of therapy would reveal much less discrepancy between the present and idealized selves.

## Some Common Item Formats

How may personality be assessed? Here are some of the more typical types of item formats.

### ITEM 1

I enjoy being out and among other people.     TRUE     FALSE

This item illustrates the true–false format. Was your reaction something like "been there, done that" when you saw this item?

### ITEM 2

Working with fellow community members on organizing and staging a blood drive.     LIKE     DISLIKE

This two-choice item is designed to elicit information about the respondent's likes and dislikes. It is a common format in interest inventories, particularly those used in vocational counseling.

### ITEM 3

How I feel when I am out and among other people

| | |
|---|---|
| Warm     __:__:__:__:__:__ | Cold |
| Tense     __:__:__:__:__:__ | Relaxed |
| Weak     __:__:__:__:__:__ | Strong |
| Brooks Brothers suit     __:__:__:__:__:__ | Hawaiian shirt |

This item format, called a **semantic differential** (Osgood et al., 1957), is characterized by bipolar adjectives separated by a seven-point rating scale on which respondents select one point to indicate their response. This type of item is useful for gauging the strength, degree, or magnitude of the direction of a particular response and has applications ranging from self-concept descriptions to opinion surveys.

### ITEM 4

I enjoy being out and among other people.

or

I have an interest in learning about art.

### ITEM 5

I am depressed too much of the time.

or

I am anxious too much of the time.

These are two examples of items written in a **forced-choice format,** where ideally each of the two choices (there may be more than two choices) is equal in social desirability. The Edwards Personal Preference Schedule (Edwards, 1953) is a classic forced-choice test. Edwards (1957a, 1957b, 1966) described in detail how he determined the items in this test to be equivalent in social desirability.

### ITEM 6

naughty

needy

negativistic

New Age

nerdy

nimble

nonproductive

numb

This illustrates an item written in an adjective checklist format. Respondents check the traits that apply to them.

### ITEM 7

Complete this sentence.

I feel as if I _____.

Respondents are typically instructed to finish the sentence with their "real feelings" in what is called a sentence completion item. The Rotter Incomplete Sentence Blank (Rotter & Rafferty, 1950) is a standardized test that employs such items, and the manual features normative data (Rotter et al., 1992).

### ITEM 8

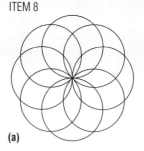     

(a)                                          (b)

Can you distinguish the figure labeled (b) in the figure labeled (a)? This type of item is found in embedded-figures tests. Identifying hidden figures is a skill thought to tap the same field dependence/independence variable tapped by more elaborate apparatuses such as the tilting chair/tilting room illustrated in Figure 1–6.

ITEM 9

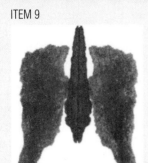

This is an item reminiscent of one of the Rorschach inkblots. We will have much more to say about the Rorschach in the following chapter.

ITEM 10

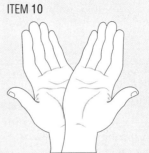

Much like the Rorschach test, which uses inkblots as ambiguous stimuli, many other tests ask the respondent to "project" onto an ambiguous stimulus. This item is reminiscent of one such projective technique called the Hand Test. Respondents are asked to tell the examiner what they think the hands might be doing.

Beyond its application in initial assessment and reevaluation of a therapy client, the Q-sort technique has also been used extensively in basic research in the area of personality and other areas. Some highly specialized Q-sorts include the Leadership Q-Test (Cassel, 1958) and the Tyler Vocational Classification System (Tyler, 1961). The former test was designed for use in military settings and contains cards with statements that the assessee is instructed to sort in terms of their perceived importance to effective leadership. The Tyler Q-sort contains cards on which occupations are listed; the cards are sorted in terms of the perceived desirability of each occupation. One feature of Q-sort methodology is the ease with which it can be adapted for use with a wide population range for varied clinical and research purposes. Q-sort methodology has been used to measure a wide range of variables (for example, Bradley & Miller, 2010; Fowler & Westen, 2011; Huang & Shih, 2011). It has been used to measure attachment security with children as young as preschoolers (DeMulder et al., 2000). An adaptation of Q-sort methodology has even been used to measure attachment security in rhesus monkeys (Warfield et al., 2011).

Two other item presentation formats that are readily adaptable to different frames of reference are the *adjective checklist* format and the *sentence completion* format. With the adjective checklist method, respondents simply check off on a list of adjectives those that apply to themselves (or to people they are rating). Using the same list of adjectives, the frame of reference can easily be changed by changing the instructions. For example, to gauge various states, respondents can be asked to check off adjectives indicating how they feel *right now*. Alternatively, to gauge various traits, they may be asked to check off adjectives indicative of how they have felt for the last year or so. A test called, simply enough, the Adjective Check List (Gough, 1960; Gough & Heilbrun, 1980) has been used in a wide range of research studies to study assessees' perceptions of themselves or others. For example, the instrument has been used to study managers' self-perceptions (Hills, 1985), parents' perceptions of their children (Brown, 1972), and clients' perceptions of their therapists (Reinehr, 1969). The sheer simplicity of the measure makes it adaptable for use in a wide range of applications (e.g., Ledesma et al., 2011; Redshaw & Martin, 2009; Tsaousis & Georgiades, 2009).

As implied by the label ascribed to these types of tests, the testtaker's task in responding to an item written in a *sentence completion* format is to complete an incomplete sentence. Items may tap how assessees feel about themselves, as in this sentence completion item: *I would describe my feeling about myself as* _____. Items may tap how assessees feel about others, as in *My classmates are* _____. More on sentence completion methods in the following chapter; right now, let's briefly overview *how* personality tests are scored and interpreted.

◆

**JUST THINK . . .**

Envision and describe an assessment scenario in which it would be important to obtain the assessee's perception of others.

**Scoring and interpretation** Personality measures differ with respect to the way conclusions are drawn from the data they provide. For some paper-and-pencil measures, a simple tally of responses to targeted items is presumed to provide a measure of the strength of a particular trait. For other measures, a computer programmed to apply highly technical manipulations of the data is required for purposes of scoring and interpretation. Yet other measures may require a highly trained clinician reviewing a verbatim transcript of what the assessee said in response to certain stimuli such as inkblots or pictures.

It is also meaningful to dichotomize measures with respect to the *nomothetic* versus *idiographic* approach. The **nomothetic approach** to assessment is characterized by efforts to learn how a limited number of personality traits can be applied to all people. According to a nomothetic view, certain personality traits exist in all people to varying degrees. The assessor's task is to determine what the strength of each of these traits are in the assessee. An assessor who uses a test such as the 16 PF, Fifth Edition (Cattell et al., 1993), probably subscribes to the nomothetic view. This is so because the 16PF was designed to measure the strength of 16 *personality factors* (which is what "PF" stands for) in the testtaker. Similarly, tests purporting to measure the "Big 5" personality traits are very much in the nomothetic tradition.

In contrast to a nomothetic view is the idiographic one. An **idiographic approach** to assessment is characterized by efforts to learn about each individual's unique constellation of personality traits, with no attempt to characterize each person according to any particular set of traits. The idea here is not to see where one falls on the continuum of a few traits deemed to be universal, but rather to understand the specific traits unique to the makeup of the individual. The idiographic orientation is evident in assessment procedures that are more flexible not only in terms not only of listing the observed traits but also of naming new trait terms.[3] The idiographic approach to personality assessment was described in detail by Allport (1937; Allport & Odbert, 1936). Methods of assessment used by proponents of this view tend to be more like tools such as the case study and personal records rather than tests. Of these two different approaches, most contemporary psychologists seem to favor the nomothetic approach.

Another dimension related to how meaning is attached to test scores has to do with whether inter-individual or intra-individual comparisons are made with respect to test scores. Most common in personality assessment is the *normative* approach, whereby a testtaker's responses and the presumed strength of a measured trait are interpreted relative to the strength of that trait in a sample of a larger population. However, you

---

3. Consider in this context the adjective *New Age* used as a personality trait (referring to a belief in spirituality). A personality assessment conducted with an idiographic orientation would be flexible enough to characterize the assessee as New Age should this trait be judged applicable. Nomothetic instruments developed prior to the emergence of such a new trait term would subsume cognitive and behavioral characteristics of the term under whatever existing trait (or traits) in the nomothetic system were judged appropriate. So, for example, a nomothetic system that included *spiritual* as one of its core traits might subsume "New Age" under "spiritual." At some point, if trends and usage warrant it, an existing nomothetic instrument could be revised to include a new trait term.

may recall that an alternative to the normative approach in test interpretation is the *ipsative* approach. In the ipsative approach, a testtaker's responses, as well as the presumed strength of measured traits, are interpreted relative to the strength of measured traits for that same individual. On a test that employs ipsative scoring procedures, two people with the same score for a particular trait or personality characteristic may differ markedly with regard to the magnitude of that trait or characteristic relative to members of a larger population.

**JUST THINK . . .**

Place yourself in the role of a human resources executive for a large airline. As part of the evaluation process, all new pilots will be given a personality test. You are asked whether the test should be ipsative or normative in nature. Your response?

Concluding our overview of the *how* of personality assessment, and to prepare for discussing the ways in which personality tests are developed, let's review some issues in personality test development and use.

**Issues in personality test development and use**  Many of the issues inherent in the test development process mirror the basic questions just discussed about personality assessment in general. What testtakers will this test be designed to be used with? Will the test entail self-report? Or will it require the use of raters or judges? If raters or judges are needed, what special training or other qualifications must they have? How will a reasonable level of inter-rater reliability be ensured? What content area will be sampled by the test? How will issues of testtaker response style be dealt with? What item format should be employed, and what is the optimal frame of reference? How will the test be scored and interpreted?

As previously noted, personality assessment that relies exclusively on self-report is a two-edged sword. On the one hand, the information is from "the source." Respondents are in most instances presumed to know themselves better than anyone else does and therefore should be able to supply accurate responses about themselves. On the other hand, the consumer of such information has no way of knowing with certainty which self-reported information is entirely true, partly true, not really true, or an outright lie. Consider a response to a single item on a personality inventory written in a true–false format. The item reads: *I tend to enjoy meeting new people.* A respondent indicates *true.* In reality, we do not know whether the respondent (1) enjoys meeting new people; (2) honestly believes that he or she enjoys meeting new people but really does not (in which case, the response is more the product of a lack of insight than a report of reality); (3) does not enjoy meeting new people but would like people to think that he or she does; or (4) did not even bother to read the item, is not taking the test seriously, and is responding *true* or *false* randomly to each item.

Building validity scales into self-report tests is one way that test developers have attempted to deal with the potential problems. In recent years, there has been some debate about whether validity scales should be included in personality tests. In arguing the case for the inclusion of validity scales, it has been asserted that "detection of an attempt to provide misleading information is a vital and absolutely necessary component of the clinical interpretation of test results" and that using any instrument without validity scales "runs counter to the basic tenets of clinical assessment" (Ben-Porath & Waller, 1992, p. 24). By contrast, the authors of the widely used Revised NEO Personality Inventory (NEO PI-R), Paul T. Costa Jr. and Robert R. McCrae, perceived no need to include any validity scales in their instrument and have been unenthusiastic about the use of such scales in other tests (McCrae & Costa, 1983; McCrae et al., 1989; Piedmont & McCrae, 1996; Piedmont et al., 2000). Referring to validity scales as SD (social desirability) scales, Costa and McCrae (1997) opined:

> SD scales typically consist of items that have a clearly desirable response. We know that people who are trying falsely to appear to have good qualities will endorse many such

items, and the creators of SD scales wish to infer from this that people who endorse many SD items are trying to create a good impression. That argument is formally identical to asserting that presidential candidates shake hands, and therefore people who shake hands are probably running for president. In fact, there are many more common reasons for shaking hands, and there is also a more common reason than impression management for endorsing SD items—namely, because the items are reasonably accurate self-descriptions. (p. 89)

◆

**JUST THINK . . .**

Having read about some of the pros and cons of using validity scales in personality assessment, where do you stand on the issue? Feel free to revise your opinion as you learn more.

According to Costa and McCrae, assessors can affirm that self-reported information is reasonably accurate by consulting external sources such as peer raters. Of course, the use of raters necessitates certain other precautions to guard against rater error and bias. Education regarding the nature of various types of rater error and bias has been a key weapon in the fight against intentional or unintentional inaccuracies in ratings. Training sessions may be designed to accomplish several objectives, such as clarifying terminology to increase the reliability of ratings. A term like *satisfactory,* for example, may have different meanings to different raters. During training, new raters can observe and work with more experienced raters to become acquainted with aspects of the task that may not be described in the rater's manual, to compare ratings with more experienced raters, and to discuss the thinking that went into the ratings.

To include or not include a validity scale in a personality test is definitely an issue that must be dealt with. What about the language in which the assessment is conducted? At first blush, this would appear to be a non-issue. Well, yes and no. If an assessee is from a culture different from the culture in which the test was developed, or if the assessee is fluent in one or more languages, then language may well become an issue. Words tend to lose—or gain—something in translation, and some words and expressions are not readily translatable into other languages. Consider the following true–false item from a popular personality test: *I am known for my prudence and common sense.* If you are a bilingual student, translate that statement from English as an exercise in test-item translation before reading on.

A French translation of this item is quite close, adding only an extra first-person possessive pronoun ("par ma prudence et *mon* bon sens"); however, the Filipino translation of this item would read *I can be relied on to decide carefully and well on matters* (McCrae et al., 1998, p. 176).

In addition to sometimes significant differences in the meaning of individual items, the traits measured by personality tests sometimes have different meanings as well. Acknowledging this fact, McCrae et al. (1998, p. 183) cautioned that "personality-trait relations reported in Western studies should be considered promising hypotheses to be tested in new cultures."

The broader issue relevant to the development and use of personality tests with members of a culture different from the culture in which the test was normed concerns the applicability of the norms. For example, a number of MMPI studies conducted with members of groups from diverse backgrounds yield findings in which minority group members tend to present with more psychopathology than majority group members (see, for example, Montgomery & Orozco, 1985; Whitworth & Unterbrink, 1994). Such differences have elicited questions regarding the appropriateness of the use of the test with members of different populations (Dana, 1995; Dana & Whatley, 1991; Malgady et al., 1987).

A test may well be appropriate for use with members of culturally different populations. As López (1988, p. 1096) observed, "To argue that the MMPI is culturally biased, one needs to go beyond reporting that ethnic groups differ in their group profiles." López noted that many of the studies showing differences between the groups did not control for psychopathology. Accordingly, there may well have been actual differences across the groups in psychopathology. The size of the sample used in the research and the appropriateness of the statistical analysis are other extracultural factors to consider when evaluating cross-cultural research. Of course, if culture and "learned meanings" (Rohner, 1984, pp. 119–120), as opposed to psychopathology, are found to account for differences in measured psychopathology with members of a particular cultural group, then the continued use of the measures with members of that cultural group must be questioned.

Armed with some background information regarding the nature of personality and its assessment, let's take a closer look at the process of developing instruments designed to assess personality.

## Developing Instruments to Assess Personality

Tools such as *logic, theory,* and *data reduction methods* (such as factor analysis) are frequently used in the process of developing personality tests. Another tool in the test development process may be a *criterion group.* As we will see, most personality tests employ two or more of these of these tools in the course of their development.

### Logic and Reason

Notwithstanding the grumblings of skeptics, there is a place for logic and reason in psychology, at least when it comes to writing items for a personality test. Logic and reason may dictate what content is covered by the items. Indeed, the use of logic and reason in the development of test items is sometimes referred to as the *content* or *content-oriented* approach to test development. So, for example, if you were developing a true–false test of extraversion, logic and reason might dictate that one of the items might be something like *I consider myself an outgoing person.*

Efforts to develop such content-oriented, face-valid items can be traced at least as far back as an instrument used to screen World War I recruits for personality and adjustment problems. The Personal Data Sheet (Woodworth, 1917), later known as the Woodworth Psychoneurotic Inventory, contained items designed to elicit self-report of fears, sleep disorders, and other problems deemed symptomatic of a pathological condition referred to then as psychoneuroticism. The greater the number of problems reported, the more psychoneurotic the respondent was presumed to be.

A great deal of clinically actionable information can be collected in relatively little time using such self-report instruments—provided, of course, that the testtaker has the requisite insight and responds with candor. A highly trained professional is not required for administration of the test. A plus in the digital age is that a computerized report of the findings can be available in minutes. Moreover, such instruments are particularly well suited to clinical settings in managed care environments, where drastic cost cutting has led to reductions in orders for assessment, and insurers are reluctant to authorize assessments. In such environments, the preferred use of psychological tests has traditionally been to identify conditions of "medical necessity" (Glazer et al., 1991). Quick, relatively inexpensive tests, wherein assessees report specific problems have won favor with insurers.

A typical companion to logic, reason, and intuition in item development is research. A review of the literature on the aspect of personality that test items are designed to tap will frequently be very helpful to test developers. In a similar vein, clinical experience can be helpful in item creation. So, for example, clinicians with ample experience in treating people diagnosed with antisocial personality disorder could be expected to have their own ideas about which items will work best on a test designed to identify people with the disorder. A related aid in the test development process is correspondence with experts on the subject matter of the test. Included here are experts who have researched and published on the subject matter, as well as experts who have known to have amassed great clinical experience on the subject matter. Yet another possible tool in test development—sometimes even the guiding force—is psychological theory.

## Theory

As we noted earlier, personality measures differ in the extent to which they rely on a particular theory of personality in their development as well as their interpretation. If psychoanalytic theory was the guiding force behind the development of a new test designed to measure antisocial personality disorder, for example, the items might look quite different than the items developed solely on the basis of logic and reason. One might find, for example, items designed to tap ego and superego defects that might result in a lack of mutuality in interpersonal relationships. Given that dreams are thought to reveal unconscious motivation, there might even be items probing the respondent's dreams; interpretations of such responses would be made from a psychoanalytic perspective. As with the development of tests using logic and reason, research, clinical experience, and the opinions of experts might be used in the development of a personality test that is theory-based.

## Data Reduction Methods

Data reduction methods represent another class of widely used tool in contemporary test development. Data reduction methods include several types of statistical techniques collectively known as factor analysis or cluster analysis. One use of data reduction methods in the design of personality measures is to aid in the identification of the minimum number of variables or factors that account for the intercorrelations in observed phenomena.

Let's illustrate the process of data reduction with a simple example related to painting your apartment. You may not have a strong sense of the exact color that best complements your "student-of-psychology" decor. Your investment in a subscription to *Architectural Digest* proved to be no help at all. You go to the local paint store and obtain free card samples of every shade of paint known to humanity—thousands of color samples. Next, you undertake an informal factor analysis of these thousands of color samples. You attempt to identify the minimum number of variables or factors that account for the intercorrelations among all of these colors. You discover that there are three factors (which might be labeled "primary" factors) and four more factors (which might be labeled "secondary" or "second-order" factors), the latter set of factors being combinations of the first set of factors. Because all colors can be reduced to three primary colors and their combinations, the three primary factors would correspond to the three primary colors, red, yellow, and blue (which you might christen factor *R*, factor *Y*, and factor *B*), and the four secondary or second-order factors would correspond to all the possible combinations that could be made from the primary factors (factors *RY, RB, YB,* and *RYB*).

The paint sample illustration might be helpful to keep in mind as we review how factor analysis is used in test construction and personality assessment. In a way analogous to the factoring of all those shades of paint into three primary colors, think of all personality traits being factored into what one psychologist referred to as "the most important individual differences in human transactions" (Goldberg, 1993, p. 26). After all the factoring is over and the dust has settled, how many personality-related terms do you think would remain? Stated another way, just how many *primary* factors of personality are there?

As the result of a pioneering research program in the 1940s, Raymond Bernard Cattell's answer to the question posed above was "16." Cattell (1946, 1947, 1948a, 1948b) reviewed previous research by Allport and Odbert (1936), which suggested that there were more than 18,000 personality trait names and terms in the English language. Of these, however, only about a quarter were "real traits of personality" or words and terms that designated "generalized and personalized determining tendencies— consistent and stable modes of an individual's adjustment to his environment . . . not . . . merely temporary and specific behavior" (Allport, 1937, p. 306).

Cattell added to the list some trait names and terms employed in the professional psychology and psychiatric literature and then had judges rate "just distinguishable" differences between all the words (Cattell, 1957). The result was a reduction in the size of the list to 171 trait names and terms. College students were asked to rate their friends with respect to these trait names and terms, and the factor-analyzed results of that rating further reduced the number of names and terms to 36, which Cattell referred to as *surface traits*. Still more research indicated that 16 basic dimensions or *source traits* could be distilled. In 1949, Cattell's research culminated in the publication of a test called the Sixteen Personality Factor (16 PF) Questionnaire. Revisions of the test were published in 1956, 1962, 1968, and 1993. In 2002, supplemental updated norms were published (Maraist & Russell, 2002).

Over the years, many questions have been raised regarding (1) whether the 16 factors identified by Cattell do indeed merit the description as the "source traits" of personality, and (2) whether, in fact, the 16 PF measures 16 distinct factors. Although some research supports Cattell's claims, give or take a factor or two depending on the sample (Cattell & Krug, 1986; Lichtenstein et al., 1986), serious reservations regarding these assertions have also been expressed (Eysenck, 1985, 1991; Goldberg, 1993). Some have argued that the 16 PF may be measuring fewer than 16 factors, because several of the factors are substantially intercorrelated.

With colors in the paint store, we can be certain that there are three that are primary. But with regard to personality factors, certainty doesn't seem to be in the cards. Some theorists have argued that the primary factors of personality can be narrowed down to three (Eysenck, 1991), or maybe four, five, or six (Church & Burke, 1994). At least four different five-factor models exist (Johnson & Ostendorf, 1993; Costa & McCrae, 1992a), and Waller and Zavala (1993) made a case for a seven-factor model. Costa and McCrae's five-factor model (with factors that have come to be known as "the Big Five," sometimes also expressed as "the Big 5"). has gained the greatest following. Interestingly, using factor analysis in the 1960s, Raymond Cattell had also derived five factors from his "primary 16" (H. Cattell, 1996). A side-by-side comparison of "Cattell's five" with the Big Five shows strong similarity between the two sets of derived factors (Table 12–2). Still, Cattell believed in the primacy of the 16 factors he originally identified.

**The Big Five**    The Revised NEO Personality Inventory (NEO PI-R; Costa & McCrae, 1992a) is widely used in both clinical applications and a wide range of research that involves personality assessment. Based on a five-dimension (or factor) model of personality, the NEO PI-R is a measure of five major dimensions (or "domains") of personality and a total of 30 elements or *facets* that define each domain.

**Table 12–2**
**The Big Five Compared to Cattell's Five**

| The Big Five | Cattell's Five (circa 1960) |
| --- | --- |
| Extraversion | Introversion/Extraversion |
| Neuroticism | Low Anxiety/High Anxiety |
| Openness | Tough-Mindedness/Receptivity |
| Agreeableness | Independence/Accommodation |
| Conscientiousness | Low Self-Control/High Self-Control |

Cattell expressed what he viewed as the source traits of personality in terms of bipolar dimensions. The 16 personality factors measured by the test today are: Warmth (Reserved vs. Warm), Reasoning (Concrete vs. Abstract), Emotional Stability (Reactive vs. Emotionally Stable), Dominance (Deferential vs. Dominant), Liveliness (Serious vs. Lively), Rule-Consciousness (Expedient vs. Rule-Conscious), Social Boldness (Shy vs. Socially Bold), Sensitivity (Utilitarian vs. Sensitive), Vigilance (Trusting vs. Vigilant), Abstractedness (Grounded vs. Abstracted), Privateness (Forthright vs. Private), Apprehension (Self-Assured vs. Apprehensive), Openness to Change (Traditional vs. Open to Change), Self-Reliance (Group-Oriented vs. Self-Reliant), Perfectionism (Tolerates Disorder vs. Perfectionistic), and Tension (Relaxed vs. Tense).

The original version of the test was called the NEO Personality Inventory (NEO-PI; Costa & McCrae, 1985), where NEO was an acronym for the first three domains measured: Neuroticism, Extraversion, and Openness. The NEO PI-R provides for the measurement of two additional domains: Agreeableness and Conscientiousness. Stated briefly, the *Neuroticism* domain (now referred to as the *Emotional Stability* factor) taps aspects of adjustment and emotional stability, including how people cope in times of emotional turmoil. The *Extraversion* domain taps aspects of sociability, how proactive people are in seeking out others, as well as assertiveness. *Openness* (also referred to as the Intellect factor) refers to openness to experience as well as active imagination, aesthetic sensitivity, attentiveness to inner feelings, preference for variety, intellectual curiosity, and independence of judgment. *Agreeableness* is primarily a dimension of interpersonal tendencies that include altruism, sympathy toward others, friendliness, and the belief that others are similarly inclined. *Conscientiousness* is a dimension of personality that has to do with the active processes of planning, organizing, and following through. Each of these major dimensions or domains of personality may be subdivided into individual traits or facets measured by the NEO PI-R. Psychologists have found value in using these dimensions to describe a wide range of behavior attributable to personality (Chang et al., 2011).

The NEO PI-R is designed for use with persons 17 years of age and older and is essentially self-administered. Computerized scoring and interpretation are available. Validity and reliability data are presented in the manual. A more detailed description of this test prepared by the test authors (Costa and McCrae) is presented in the companion website to this text, *www.mhhe.com/cohentesting8*.

Perhaps due to the enthusiasm with which psychologists have embraced "the Big 5," a number of tests other than the NEO PI-R have been developed to measure it. One such instrument is The Big Five Inventory (BFI; John et al., 1991). This test is made publicly available for noncommercial purposes to researchers and students. It consists of only 44 items, which makes it relatively quick to administer. Another instrument, the Ten Item Personality Inventory (TIPI; Gosling, Rentfrow, & Swann, 2003), contains only two items for each of the Big 5 dimensions. Educated on matters of test construction and test validity, you may now be asking yourself how a test with so few items could possibly be valid. And if that is the case, you may want to read an article by Jonason et al. (2011), which actually has some favorable things to say about the construct validity of the TIPI. A nonverbal measure of the Big-5 has also been developed.

And once again, educated on matters of test construction as you are, you may be asking yourself something like, "How in blazes did they do that?!" The Five-Factor Nonverbal Personality Questionnaire (FF-NPQ) is administered by showing respondents illustrations of behaviors indicative of the Big-5 dimensions. Respondents are then asked to gauge the likelihood of personally engaging in those behaviors (Paunonen et al., 2004). One study compared the performance of monozygotic (identical) twins on verbal and nonverbal measures of the Big-5. The researchers concluded that the performance of the twins was similar on the measures and that the similarities were attributable to shared genes rather than shared environments (Moore et al., 2010). Such studies fueled speculation regarding the heritability of psychological traits.

We began our discussion of personality test development methods with a note that many personality tests have used two or more of these strategies in their process of development. At this point you may begin to appreciate how, as well as why, two or more tools might be used. A pool of items for an objective personality measure could be created, for example, on the basis of logic or theory, or both logic and theory. The items might then be arranged into scales on the basis of factor analysis. The draft version of the test could be administered to a criterion group and to a control group to see if responses to the items differ as a function of group membership. But here we are getting just a bit ahead of ourselves. We need to define, discuss, and illustrate what is meant by *criterion group* in the context of developing personality tests.

## Criterion Groups

A **criterion** may be defined as a standard on which a judgment or decision can be made. With regard to scale development, a **criterion group** is a reference group of testtakers who share specific characteristics and whose responses to test items serve as a standard according to which items will be included in or discarded from the final version of a scale. The process of using criterion groups to develop test items is referred to as **empirical criterion keying** because the scoring or keying of items has been demonstrated empirically to differentiate among groups of testtakers. The shared characteristic of the criterion group to be researched—a psychiatric diagnosis, a unique skill or ability, a genetic aberration, or whatever—will vary as a function of the nature and scope of the test. Development of a test by means of empirical criterion keying may be summed up as follows:

1.  Create a large, preliminary pool of test items from which the test items for the final form of the test will be selected.

2.  Administer the preliminary pool of items to at least two groups of people:

    Group 1: A criterion group composed of people known to possess the trait being measured.

    Group 2: A randomly selected group of people (who may or may not possess the trait being measured)

3.  Conduct an item analysis to select items indicative of membership in the criterion group. Items in the preliminary pool that discriminate between membership in the two groups in a statistically significant fashion will be retained and incorporated in the final form of the test.

4.  Obtain data on test performance from a standardization sample of testtakers who are representative of the population from which future testtakers will come. The test performance data for Group 2 members on items incorporated into the

final form of the test may be used for this purpose if deemed appropriate. The performance of Group 2 members on the test would then become the standard against which future testtakers will be evaluated. After the mean performance of Group 2 members on the individual items (or scales) of the test has been identified, future testtakers will be evaluated in terms of the extent to which their scores deviate in either direction from the Group 2 mean.

At this point you may ask, "But what about that initial pool of items? How is it created?" The answer is that the test developer may have found inspiration for each of the items from reviews of journals and books, interviews with patients, or consultations with colleagues or known experts. The test developer may have relied on logic or reason alone to write the items, or on other tests. Alternatively, the test developer may have relied on none of these and simply let imagination loose and committed to paper whatever emerged. An interesting aspect of test development by means of empirical criterion keying is that the content of the test items does not have to relate in a logical, rational, direct, or face-valid way to the measurement objective. Burisch (1984, p. 218) captured the essence of empirical criterion keying when he stated flatly, "If shoe size as a predictor improves your ability to predict performance as an airplane pilot, use it."[4] Burisch went on to offer this tongue-in-cheek description of how criterion groups could be used to develop an "M-F" test to differentiate males from females:

> Allegedly not knowing where the differences were, he or she would never dream of using an item such as "I can grow a beard if I want to" or "In a restaurant I tend to prefer the ladies' room to the men's room." Rather, a heterogeneous pool of items would be assembled and administered to a sample of men and women. Next, samples would be compared item by item. Any item discriminating sufficiently well would qualify for inclusion in the M-F test. (p. 214)

Now imagine that it is the 1930s. A team of researchers is keenly interested in devising a paper-and-pencil test that will improve reliability in psychiatric diagnosis. Their idea is to use empirical criterion keying to create the instrument. A preliminary version of the test will be administered (1) to several criterion groups of adult inpatients, each group homogeneous with respect to psychiatric diagnosis, and (2) to a group of randomly selected normal adults. Using item analysis, items useful in differentiating members of the various clinical groups from members of the normal group will be retained to make up the final form of the test. The researchers envision that future users of the published test will be able to derive diagnostic insights by comparing a testtaker's response pattern to that of testtakers in the normal group.

And there you have the beginnings of a relatively simple idea that would, in time, win widespread approval from clinicians around the world. It is an idea for a test that stimulated the publication of thousands of research studies, and an idea that led to the development of a test that would serve as a model for countless other instruments devised through the use of criterion group research. The test, originally called the Medical and Psychiatric Inventory (Dahlstrom & Dahlstrom, 1980), is the MMPI. Years after its tentative beginnings, the test's senior author recalled that "it was difficult to persuade a publisher to accept the MMPI" (Hathaway, cited in Dahlstrom & Welsh, 1960, p. vii). However, the University of Minnesota Press was obviously persuaded,

---

4. It should come as no surprise, however, that any scale that is the product of such wildly empirical procedures would be expected to be extremely high in heterogeneity of item content and profoundly low in internal consistency measures.

because in 1943 it published the test under a new name, the Minnesota Multiphasic Personality Inventory (MMPI). The rest, as they say, is history.

In the next few pages, we describe the development of the original MMPI as well as its more contemporary progeny, the MMPI-2, the MMPI-2 Restructured Form (the MMPI-2-RF), and the MMPI-A.

**The MMPI**  The MMPI was the product of a collaboration between psychologist Starke R. Hathaway and psychiatrist/neurologist John Charnley McKinley (Hathaway & McKinley, 1940, 1942, 1943, 1951; McKinley & Hathaway, 1940, 1944). It contained 566 true–false items and was designed as an aid to psychiatric diagnosis with adolescents and adults 14 years of age and older. Research preceding the selection of test items included review of textbooks, psychiatric reports, and previously published personality test items. In this sense, the beginnings of the MMPI can be traced to an approach to test development that was based on logic and reason.

A listing of the 10 clinical scales of the MMPI is presented in Table 12–3 along with a description of the corresponding criterion group. Each of the diagnostic categories listed for the 10 clinical scales were popular diagnostic categories in the 1930s. Members of the clinical criterion group for each scale were presumed to have met the criteria for inclusion in the category named in the scale. MMPI clinical scale items were derived empirically by administration to clinical criterion groups and normal control groups. The items that successfully differentiated between the two groups were retained in the final version of the test (Welsh & Dahlstrom, 1956). Well, it's actually a bit more complicated than that, and you really should know some of the details . . .

To understand the meaning of *normal control group* in this context, think of an experiment. In experimental research, an experimenter manipulates the situation so that the experimental group is exposed to something (the independent variable) and the control group is not. In the development of the MMPI, members of the criterion groups were drawn from a population of people presumed to be members of a group with a shared diagnostic label. Analogizing an experiment to this test development situation, it is as if the experimental treatment for the criterion group members was

**Table 12–3**
**The Clinical Criterion Groups for MMPI Scales**

| Scale | Clinical Criterion Group |
|---|---|
| 1. Hypochondriasis (Hs) | Patients who showed exaggerated concerns about their physical health |
| 2. Depression (D) | Clinically depressed patients; unhappy and pessimistic about their future |
| 3. Hysteria (Hy) | Patients with conversion reactions |
| 4. Psychopathic deviate (Pd) | Patients who had histories of delinquency and other antisocial behavior |
| 5. Masculinity-femininity (Mf) | Minnesota draftees, airline stewardesses, and male homosexual college students from the University of Minnesota campus community |
| 6. Paranoia (Pa) | Patients who exhibited paranoid symptomatology such as ideas of reference, suspiciousness, delusions of persecution, and delusions of grandeur |
| 7. Psychasthenia (Pt) | Anxious, obsessive-compulsive, guilt-ridden, and self-doubting patients |
| 8. Schizophrenia (Sc) | Patients who were diagnosed as schizophrenic (various subtypes) |
| 9. Hypomania (Ma) | Patients, most diagnosed as manic-depressive, who exhibited manic symptomatology such as elevated mood, excessive activity, and easy distractibility |
| 10. Social introversion (Si) | College students who had scored at the extremes on a test of introversion/extraversion |

Note that these same 10 clinical scales formed the core not only of the original MMPI, but of its 1989 revision, the MMPI-2. The clinical scales did undergo some modification for the MMPI-2, such as editing and reordering, and nine items were eliminated. Still, the MMPI-2 retained the 10 original clinical scale names, despite the fact that some of them (such as "Psychopathic Deviate") are relics of a bygone era. Perhaps that accounts for why convention has it that these scales be referred to by scale numbers only, not their names.

membership in the category named. By contrast, members of the **control group** were normal (that is, nondiagnosed) people who ostensibly received no such experimental treatment.

The normal control group, also referred to as the standardization sample, consisted of approximately 1,500 subjects. Included were 724 people who happened to be visiting friends or relatives at University of Minnesota hospitals, 265 high-school graduates seeking precollege guidance at the University of Minnesota Testing Bureau, 265 skilled workers participating in a local Works Progress Administration program, and 243 medical (nonpsychiatric) patients. The clinical criterion group for the MMPI was, for the most part, made up of psychiatric inpatients at the University of Minnesota Hospital. We say "for the most part" because Scale 5 (Masculinity-Femininity) and Scale 0 (Social Introversion) were not derived in this way.

The number of people included in each diagnostic category was relatively low by contemporary standards. For example, the criterion group for Scale 7 (Psychasthenia) contained only 20 people, all diagnosed as psychasthenic.[5] Two of the "clinical" scales (Scale 0 and Scale 5) did not even use members of a clinical population in the criterion group. The members of the Scale 0 (Social Introversion) clinical criterion group were college students who had earned extreme scores on a measure of introversion-extraversion. Scale 5 (Masculinity-Femininity) was designed to measure neither masculinity nor femininity; rather, it was originally developed to differentiate heterosexual from homosexual males. Due to a dearth of items that effectively differentiated people on this variable, the test developers broadened the definition of Scale 5 and added items that discriminated between normal males (soldiers) and females (airline personnel). Some of the items added to this scale were obtained from the Attitude Interest Scale (Terman & Miles, 1936). Hathaway and McKinley had also attempted to develop a scale to differentiate lesbians from female heterosexuals but were unable to do so.

By the 1930s, research on the Personal Data Sheet (Woodworth, 1917) as well as other face-valid, logic-derived instruments had brought to light problems inherent in self-report methods. Hathaway and McKinley (1943) evinced a keen awareness of such problems. They built into the MMPI three validity scales: the L scale (the Lie scale), the F scale (the Frequency scale—or, perhaps more accurately, the "Infrequency" scale), and the K (Correction) scale. Note that these scales were not designed to measure validity in the technical, psychometric sense. There is, after all, something inherently self-serving, if not suspect, about a test that purports to gauge its own validity! Rather, *validity* here was a reference to a built-in indicator of the operation of testtaker response styles (such as carelessness, deliberate efforts to deceive, or unintentional misunderstanding) that could affect the test results.

The L scale contains 15 items that, if endorsed, could reflect somewhat negatively on the testtaker. Two examples: "I do not always tell the truth" and "I gossip a little at times"

5. *Psychasthenia* (literally, *loss of strength* or *weakness* of the *psyche* or *mind*) is a now-antiquated term and psychiatric diagnosis. As used in the 1930s, it referred to an individual unable to think properly or focus concentration owing to conditions such as obsessive thoughts, excessive doubts, and phobias. A person with this diagnosis was said to be *psychasthenic.*

(Dahlstrom et al., 1972, p. 109). The willingness of the examinee to reveal *anything* negative of a personal nature will be called into question if the score on the L scale does not fall within certain limits.

The 64 items on the F scale (1) are infrequently endorsed by members of nonpsychiatric populations (that is, normal people) and (2) do not fit into any known pattern of deviance. A response of *true* to an item such as the following would be scored on the F scale: "It would be better if almost all laws were thrown away" (Dahlstrom et al., 1972, p. 115). An elevated F score may mean that the respondent did not take the test seriously and was just responding to items randomly. Alternatively, the individual with a high F score may be a very eccentric individual or someone who was attempting to fake bad. Malingerers in the armed services, people intent on committing fraud with respect to health insurance, and criminals attempting to cop a psychiatric plea are some of the groups of people who might be expected to have elevated F scores on their profiles.

> **JUST THINK . . .**
> Try your hand at writing a good L-scale item.

Like the L score and the F score, the K score is a reflection of the frankness of the testtaker's self-report. An elevated K score is associated with defensiveness and the desire to present a favorable impression. A low K score is associated with excessive self-criticism, desire to detail deviance, or desire to fake bad. A *true* response to the item "I certainly feel useless at times" and a *false* response to "At times I am all full of energy" (Dahlstrom et al., 1972, p. 125) would be scored on the K scale. The K scale is sometimes used to correct scores on five of the clinical scales. The scores are statistically corrected for an individual's overwillingness or unwillingness to admit deviance.

Another scale that bears on the validity of a test administration is the *Cannot Say* scale, also referred to simply as the ? (question mark) scale. This scale is a simple frequency count of the number of items to which the examinee responded *cannot say* or failed to mark any response. Items may be omitted or marked *cannot say* for many reasons, including respondent indecisiveness, defensiveness, carelessness, and lack of experience relevant to the item. Traditionally, the validity of an answer sheet with a *cannot say* count of 30 or higher is called into question and deemed uninterpretable (Dahlstrom et al., 1972). Even for test protocols with a *cannot say* count of 10, caution has been urged in test interpretation. High *cannot say* scores may be avoided by a proctor's emphasis in the initial instructions to answer *all* items.

The MMPI contains 550 true–false items, 16 of which are repeated on some forms of the test (for a total of 566 items administered). Scores on each MMPI scale are reported in the form of *T* scores which, you may recall, have a mean set at 50 and a standard deviation set at 10. A score of 70 on any MMPI clinical scale is 2 standard deviations above the average score of members of the standardization sample, and a score of 30 is 2 standard deviations below their average score.

In addition to the clinical scales and the validity scales, there are MMPI content scales, supplementary scales, and Harris-Lingoes subscales. As the name implies, the *content scales,* such as the Wiggins Content Scales (after Wiggins, 1966), are composed of groups of test items of similar content. Examples of content scales on the MMPI include the scales labeled Depression and Family Problems. In a sense, content scales "bring order" and face validity to groups of items, derived from empirical criterion keying, that ostensibly have no relation to one another.

*Supplementary scales* is a catch-all phrase for the hundreds of different MMPI scales that have been developed since the test's publication. These scales have been devised by different researchers using a variety of methods and statistical procedures, most notably factor analysis. There are supplementary scales that are fairly consistent with the original objectives of the MMPI, such as scales designed to shed light on alcoholism and ego strength. And then there are dozens of other supplementary scales, ranging from "Success in Baseball" to—well, you name it![6]

The publisher of the MMPI makes available for computerized scoring only a limited selection of the many hundreds of supplementary scales that have been developed and discussed in the professional literature. One of them, the Harris-Lingoes subscales (often referred to simply as the Harris scales), are groupings of items into subscales (with labels such as Brooding and Social Alienation) that were designed to be more internally consistent than the umbrella scale from which the subscale was derived.

Historically administered by paper and pencil, the MMPI is today administered by many methods: online, offline on disk, or by index cards. An audio version for semiliterate testtakers is also available, with instructions recorded on audiocassette. Testtakers respond to items by answering *true* or *false.* Items left unanswered are construed as *cannot say.* In the version of the test administered using individual items printed on cards, testtakers are instructed to sort the cards into three piles labeled *true, false,* and *cannot say.* At least a sixth-grade reading level is required to understand all the items. There are no time limits, and the time required to administer 566 items is typically between 60 and 90 minutes.

It is possible to score MMPI answer sheets by hand, but the process is labor intensive and rarely done. Computer scoring of protocols is accomplished by software on personal computers, by computer transmission to a scoring service via modem, or by physically mailing the completed form to a computer scoring service. Computer output may range from a simple numerical and graphic presentation of scores to a highly detailed narrative report complete with analysis of scores on selected supplementary scales.

Soon after the MMPI was published, it became evident that the test could not be used to neatly categorize testtakers into diagnostic categories. When testtakers had elevations in the pathological range of two or more scales, diagnostic dilemmas arose. Hathaway and McKinley (1943) had urged users of their test to opt for *configural interpretation* of scores—that is, interpretation based not on scores of single scales but on the pattern, profile, or configuration of the scores. However, their proposed method for profile interpretation was extremely complicated, as were many of the proposed adjunctive and alternative procedures.

Paul Meehl (1951) proposed a 2-point code derived from the numbers of the clinical scales on which the testtaker achieved the highest (most pathological) scores. If a testtaker achieved the highest score on Scale 1 and the second-highest score on Scale 2, then that testtaker's 2-point code type would be 12. The 2-point code type for a highest score on Scale 2 and a second-highest score on Scale 1 would be 21. Because each digit in the code is interchangeable, a code of 12 would be interpreted in exactly the same way as a code of 21. By the way, a code of 12 (or 21) is indicative of an individual in physical pain. An assumption here is that each score in the 2-point code type exceeds an elevation of $T = 70$. If the scale score does not exceed 70, this is indicated by the use of a prime (') after the scale number. Meehl's system had great appeal for many MMPI users.

---

6. Here, the astute reader will begin to appreciate just how far from its original intended purpose the MMPI has strayed. In fact, the MMPI in all of its forms has been used for an extraordinarily wide range of adventures that are only tangentially related to the objective of psychiatric diagnosis.

Before long, a wealth of research mounted on the interpretive meanings of the 40 code types that could be derived using 10 scales and two interchangeable digits.[7]

Another popular approach to scoring and interpretation came in the form of **Welsh codes**—referred to as such because they were created by Welsh (1948, 1956), not because they were written in Welsh (although to the uninitiated, they may be equally incomprehensible). Here is an example of a Welsh code:

$$6* \underline{78}''' \ 1\text{-}53/4\text{:}2\# \ \underline{90} \ F'L\text{-}/K$$

To the seasoned Welsh code user, this expression provides information about a testtaker's scores on the MMPI clinical and validity scales.

Students interested in learning more about the MMPI need not expend a great deal of effort in tracking down sources. Chances are your university library is teeming with books and journal articles written on or about this multiphasic (many-faceted) instrument. Of course, you may also want to go well beyond this historical introduction by becoming better acquainted with this test's more contemporary revisions, the MMPI-2, the MMPI-2 Restructured Form, and the MMPI-A. A barebones overview of those instruments follows.

**The MMPI-2**   Much of what has already been said about the MMPI in terms of its general structure, administration, scoring, and interpretation is applicable to the MMPI-2. The most significant difference between the two tests is the more representative standardization sample (normal control group) used in the norming of the MMPI-2. Approximately 14% of the MMPI items were rewritten to correct grammatical errors and to make the language more contemporary, nonsexist, and readable. Items thought to be objectionable to some testtakers were eliminated. Added were items addressing topics such as drug abuse, suicide potential, marital adjustment, attitudes toward work, and Type A behavior patterns.[8] In all, the MMPI-2 contains a total of 567 true–false items, including 394 items that are identical to the original MMPI items, 66 items that were modified or rewritten, and 107 new items. The suggested age range of testtakers for the MMPI-2 is 18 years and older, as compared to 14 years and older for the MMPI. The reading level required (sixth-grade) is the same as for the MMPI. The MMPI-2, like its predecessor, may be administered online, offline by paper and pencil, or by audiocassette, and it takes about the same length of time to administer.

The 10 clinical scales of the MMPI are identical to those on the MMPI-2, as is the policy of referring to them primarily by number. Content component scales were added to the MMPI-2 to provide more focused indices of content. For example, Family Problems content was subdivided into Family Discord and Familial Alienation content.

The three original validity scales of the MMPI were retained in the MMPI-2, and three new validity scales were added: Back-Page Infrequency (Fb), True Response Inconsistency (TRIN), and Variable Response Inconsistency (VRIN). The Back-Page Infrequency scale contains items seldom endorsed by testtakers who are candid, deliberate, and diligent in their approach to the test. Of course, some testtakers' diligence wanes as the test wears on and so, by the "back pages" of the test, a random or inconsistent pattern of responses may become evident. The Fb scale is designed to detect such a pattern.

---

7. In addition to 2-point coding systems, at least one 3-point coding system was proposed. As you might expect, in that system the first number was the highest score, the second number was the second-highest score, and the third number was the third-highest score.

8. Recall from our discussion of psychological types earlier in this chapter (p.397) what constitutes Type A and Type B behavior.

**Figure 12–8**
**James Butcher (1933– ) and Friend**

*That's Jim, today better known as the senior author of the MMPI-2, to your right as an Army infantryman at Outpost Yoke in South Korea in 1953. Returning to civilian life, Jim tried various occupations, including salesman and private investigator. He later earned a Ph.D. at the University of North Carolina, where he had occasion to work with W. Grant Dahlstrom and George Welsh (as in MMPI "Welsh code"). Butcher's first teaching job was at the University of Minnesota, where he looked forward to working with Starke Hathaway and Paul Meehl. But he was disappointed to learn that "Hathaway had moved on to the pursuit of psychotherapy research and typically disclaimed any expertise in the test. . . . Hathaway always refused to become involved in teaching people about the test. Meehl had likewise moved on to other venues"* (Butcher, 2003, p. 233).

**◆ JUST THINK . . .**

To maintain continuity with the original test, the MMPI-2 used the same names for the clinical scales. Some of these scale names, such as *Psychasthenia*, are no longer used. If you were in charge of the MMPI's revision, what would your recommendation have been for dealing with this issue related to MMPI-2 scale names?

The TRIN scale is designed to identify acquiescent and nonacquiescent response patterns. It contains 23 pairs of items worded in opposite forms. Consistency in responding dictates that, for example, a *true* response to the first item in the pair is followed by a *false* response to the second item in the pair. The VRIN scale is designed to identify indiscriminate response patterns. It, too, is made up of item pairs, where each item in the pair is worded in either opposite or similar form.

The senior author of the MMPI-2, James Butcher (Figure 12–8),[9] developed yet another validity scale after the publication of that test. The S scale is a validity scale designed to detect self-presentation in a superlative manner (Butcher & Han, 1995; Lanyon, 1993a, 1993b; Lim & Butcher, 1996).

Another proposed validity scale, this one designed to detect malingerers in personal injury claims, was proposed by Paul R. Lees-Haley and his colleagues (1991). Referred to as the FBS or Faking Bad Scale, this scale was originally developed as a means to detect malingerers who submitted bogus personal injury claims. In the years since its development, the FBS Scale has found support from some, most notably

---

9. Pictured to the right of James Butcher is his buddy, Dale Moss, who was killed in the war. The authors pause at this juncture to remember and express gratitude to all the people in all branches of the military and government who have sacrificed for this country.

Ben-Porath et al. (2009). However, it also has its critics—among them, James Butcher and his colleagues. Butcher et al. (2008) argued that factors other than malingering (such as genuine physical or psychological problems) could contribute to endorsement of items that were keyed as indicative of malingering. They cautioned that the "lack of empirical verification of the 43 items selected by Lees-Haley, including examination of the items' performance across broad categories of people, argues against its widespread dissemination" (pp. 194–195).

**JUST THINK . . .**

Of all of the proposed validity scales for the MMPI-2, which do you think is the best indicator of whether the test scores are truly indicative of the testtaker's personality?

A nagging criticism of the original MMPI was the lack of representation of the standardization sample of the U.S. population. This criticism was addressed in the standardization of the MMPI-2. The 2,600 individuals (1,462 females, 1,138 males) from seven states who made up the MMPI-2 standardization sample had been matched to 1980 U.S. Census data on the variables of age, gender, minority status, social class, and education (Butcher, 1990). Whereas the original MMPI did not contain any non-Whites in the standardization sample, the MMPI-2 sample was 81% White and 19% non-White. Age of subjects in the sample ranged from 18 years to 85 years. Formal education ranged from 3 years to 20+ years, with more highly educated people and people working in the professions overrepresented in the sample. Median annual family income for females in the sample was $25,000 to $30,000. Median annual family income for males in the sample was $30,000 to $35,000.

As with the original MMPI, the standardization sample data provided the basis for transforming the raw scores obtained by respondents into $T$ scores for the MMPI-2. However, a technical adjustment was deemed to be in order. The $T$ scores used for standardizing the MMPI clinical scales and content scales were linear $T$ scores. For the MMPI-2, linear $T$ scores were also used for standardization of the validity scales, the supplementary scales, and Scales 5 and 0 of the clinical scales. However, a different $T$ score was used to standardize the remaining eight clinical scales as well as all of the content scales; these scales were standardized with uniform $T$ scores ($UT$ scores). The $UT$ scores were used in an effort to make the $T$ scores corresponding to percentile scores more comparable across the MMPI-2 scales (Graham, 1990; Tellegen & Ben-Porath, 1992).

Efforts to address concerns about the MMPI did not end with the publication of the MMPI-2. Before long, research was under way to revise the MMPI-2. These efforts were evident in the publication of restructured clinical scales (Tellegen et al., 2003) and culminated more recently in the publication of the MMPI-2 Restructured Form (MMPI-2-RF).

**The MMPI-2-RF**   The need to rework the clinical scales of the MMPI-2 was perceived by Tellegen et al. (2003) as arising, at least in part, from two basic problems with the structure of the scales. One basic problem was overlapping items. The method of test development initially used to create the MMPI, empirical criterion keying, practically ensured there would be some item overlap. But just how much item overlap was there? Per pair of clinical scales, it has been observed that there is an average of more than six overlapping items in the MMPI-2 (Greene, 2000; Helmes & Reddon, 1993). Item overlap between the scales can decrease the distinctiveness and discriminant validity of individual scales and can also contribute to difficulties in determining the meaning of elevated scales.

A second problem with the basic structure of the test could also be characterized in terms of overlap—one that is more conceptual in nature. Here, reference is made to the pervasive influence of a factor that seemed to permeate all of the clinical scales.

The factor has been described in different ways with different terms such as anxiety, malaise, despair, and maladjustment. It is a factor that is thought to be common to most forms of psychopathology yet unique to none. Exploring the issue of why entirely different approaches to psychotherapy had comparable results, Jerome Frank (1974) focused on what he viewed as this common factor in psychopathology, which he termed *demoralization:*

> Only a small proportion of persons with psychopathology come to therapy; apparently something else must be added that interacts with their symptoms. This state of mind, which may be termed "demoralization," results from persistent failure to cope with internally or externally induced stresses. . . . Its characteristic features, not all of which need to be present in any one person, are feelings of impotence, isolation, and despair. (p. 271)

Dohrenwend et al. (1980) perpetuated the use of Frank's concept of demoralization in their discussion of a nonspecific distress factor in psychopathology. Tellegen (1985) also made reference to demoralization when he wrote of a factor that seemed to inflate correlations between measures within clinical inventories. Many of the items on all of the MMPI and MMPI-2 clinical scales, despite their heterogeneous content, seemed to be saturated with the demoralization factor. Concern about the consequences of this overlapping has a relatively long history (Welsh, 1952; Rosen, 1962; Adams & Horn, 1965). In fact, the history of efforts to remedy the problem of insufficient discriminant validity and discriminative efficiency of the MMPI clinical scales is almost as long as the long history of the test itself.

One goal of the restructuring was to make the clinical scales of the MMPI-2 more distinctive and meaningful. As described in detail in a monograph supplement to the MMPI-2 administration and scoring manual, Tellegen et al. (2003) attempted to (1) identify the "core components" of each clinical scale, (2) create revised scales to measure these core components (referred to as "seed scales"), and (3) derive a final set of Revised Clinical (RC) scales using the MMPI-2 item pool. Another objective of the restructuring was, in essence, to extract the demoralization factor from the existing MMPI-2 clinical scales and create a new Demoralization scale. This new scale was described as one that "measures a broad, emotionally colored variable that underlies much of the variance common to the MMPI-2 Clinical Scales" (Tellegen et al., 2003, p. 11).

Employing the MMPI-2 normative sample as well as three additional clinical samples in their research, Tellegen et al. (2003) made the case that their restructuring procedures were psychometrically sound and had succeeded in improving both convergent and discriminant validity. According to their data, the restructured clinical (RC) scales were less intercorrelated than the original clinical scales, and their convergent and discriminant validity were greater than those original scales. Subsequent to the development of the RC scales, additional scales were developed. For example, the test authors developed scales to measure clinically significant factors that were not directly assessed by the RC scales, such as suicidal ideation. They also saw a need to develop scales tapping higher-order dimensions to provide a framework for organizing and interpreting findings. These higher-order scales were labeled Emotional/Internalizing Dysfunction, Thought Dysfunction, and Behavioral/Externalizing Dysfunction. The finished product was published in 2008 and called the MMPI-2 Restructured Form (MMPI-2-RF; Ben-Porath & Tellegen, 2008). It contains a total of 338 items and 50 scales, some of which are summarized in Table 12–4.

Since the publication of Tellegen et al.'s (2003) monograph, Tellegen, Ben-Porath, and their colleagues have published a number of other articles that provide support for various aspects of the psychometric adequacy of the RC scales and the MMPI-2-RF.

**Table 12–4**
**Description of a Sampling of MMPI-2-RF Scales**

*Clinical Scales Group*

*There are a total of nine clinical scales. The RCd, RC1, RC2, and RC3 scales were introduced by Tellegen et al. (2003). Gone from the original MMPI (and MMPI-2) clinical scales is the Masculinity-Femininity Scale.*

| Scale Name | Scale Description |
|---|---|
| Demoralization (RCd) | General malaise, unhappiness, and dissatisfaction |
| Somatic Complaints (RC1) | Diffuse complaints related to physical health |
| Low Positive Emotions (RC2) | A "core" feeling of vulnerability in depression |
| Cynicism (RC3) | Beliefs nonrelated to self that others are generally ill-intentioned and not to be trusted |
| Antisocial Behavior (RC4) | Acting in violation of societal or social rules |
| Ideas of Persecution (RC6) | Self-referential beliefs that one is in danger or threatened by others |
| Dysfunctional Negative Emotions (RC7) | Disruptive anxiety, anger, and irritability |
| Aberrant Experiences (RC8) | Psychotic or psychotic-like thoughts, perceptions, or experiences |
| Hypomanic Activation (RC9) | Over-activation, grandiosity, impulsivity, or aggression |

*Validity Scales Group*

*There are a total of eight validity scales, which is one more validity scale than in the previous edition of the test. The added validity scale is Infrequent Somatic Response (Fs).*

| Scale Name | Scale Description |
|---|---|
| Variable Response Inconsistency-Revised (VRIN-r) | Random responding |
| True Response Inconsistency-Revised (TRIN-r) | Fixed responding |
| Infrequent Responses-Revised (F-r) | Infrequent responses compared to the general population |
| Infrequent Psychopathology Responses-Revised (Fp-r) | Infrequent responses characteristic of psychiatric populations |
| Infrequent Somatic Responses (Fs) | Infrequent somatic complaints from patients with medical problems |
| Symptom Validity (aka Fake Bad Scale-Revised; FBS-r) | Somatic or mental complaints with little or no credibility |
| Uncommon Virtues (aka Lie Scale-Revised; L-r) | Willingness to reveal anything negative about oneself |
| Adjustment Validity (aka Defensiveness Scale-Revised; K-r) | Degree to which the respondent is self-critical |

*Specific Problem (SP) Scales Group*

*There are a total of 20 scales that measure problems. These SP scales are grouped as relating to Internalizing, Externalizing, or Interpersonal issues and are subgrouped according to the clinical scale on which they shed light.*

| Scale Name | Scale Description |
|---|---|
| Suicidal/Death Ideation (SUI)[a] | Respondent reports self-related suicidal thoughts or actions |
| Helplessness/Hopelessness (HLP)[a] | Pervasive belief that problems are unsolvable and/or goals unattainable |
| Self-Doubt (SFD)[a] | Lack of self-confidence, feelings of uselessness |
| Inefficacy (NFC)[a] | Belief that one is indecisive or incapable of accomplishment |
| Cognitive Complaints (COG)[a] | Concentration and memory difficulties |
| Juvenile Conduct Problems (JCP)[b] | Difficulties at home or school, stealing |
| Substance Abuse (SUB)[b] | Current and past misuse of alcohol and drugs |
| Sensitivity/Vulnerability (SNV)[c] | Taking things too hard, being easily hurt by others |

*(continued)*

**Table 12–4**

*(continued)*

| | |
|---|---|
| Stress/Worry (STW)[c] | Preoccupation with disappointments, difficulty with time pressure |
| Anxiety (AXY)[c] | Pervasive anxiety, frights, frequent nightmares |
| Anger Proneness (ANP)[c] | Being easily angered, impatient with others |
| Behavior-Restricting Fears (BRF)[c] | Fears that significantly inhibit normal behavior |
| Multiple Specific Fears (MSF)[c] | Various specific fears, such as a fear of blood or a fear of thunder |
| Juvenile Conduct Problems (JCP)[c] | Difficulties at home or school, stealing |
| Aggression (AGG)[d] | Physically aggressive, violent behavior |
| Activation (ACT)[d] | Heightened excitation and energy level |

*Interest Scales Group*

*There are two scales that measure interests: the AES scale and the MEC scale.*

| Scale Name | Scale Description |
|---|---|
| Aesthetic-Literary Interests (AES) | Interest in literature, music, and/or the theater |
| Mechanical-Physical Interests (MEC) | Fixing things, building things, outdoor pursuits, sports |

*PSY-5 Scales Group*

*These five scales are revised versions of MMPI-2 measures.*

| Scale Name | Scale Description |
|---|---|
| Aggressiveness-Revised (AGGR-r) | Goal-directed aggression |
| Psychoticism-Revised (PSYC-r) | Disconnection from reality |
| Disconstraint-Revised (DISC-r) | Undercontrolled behavior |
| Negative Emotionality/Neuroticism-Revised (NEGE-r) | Anxiety, insecurity, worry, and fear |
| Introversion/Low Positive Emotionality-Revised (INTR-r) | Social disengagement and absence of joy or happiness |

Note: Overview based on Ben-Porath et al. (2007) and related materials; consult the MMPI-2-RF test manual (and updates) for a complete list and description of all the test's scales.
[a] Internalizing scale that measures facets of Demoralization (RCd).
[b] Internalizing scale that measures facets of Antisocial Behavior (RC4).
[c] Internalizing scale that measures facets of Dysfunctional Negative Emotions (RC7).
[d] Internalizing scale that measures facets of Hypomanic Activation (RC9).

Studies from independent researchers have also provided support for some of the claims made regarding the RC scales' reduced item intercorrelations and increased convergent and discriminant validity (Simms et al., 2005; Wallace & Liljequist, 2005). Other authors have obtained support for the Somatic Complaints RC scale, the Cynicism RC scale, and the VRIN-r and TRIN-r validity scales (Handel et al., 2010; Ingram et al., 2011; Thomas & Locke, 2010). Osberg et al. (2008) compared the MMPI-2 clinical scales with the RC scales in terms of psychometric properties and diagnostic efficiency and reported mixed results.

The restructuring of a test as iconic at the MMPI has not made everyone happy. For example, Rogers et al. (2006) and Nichols (2006) took issue with aspects of the logic of the restructuring, the restructuring procedures employed, and the result of the restructuring. One of the concerns expressed by Nichols was that Tellegen and colleagues had gone too far in terms of extracting the demoralization factor (Dem) from the clinical scales. Addressing

**JUST THINK . . .**

What is a scale that you think should have been added to the restructured MMPI-2?

what he viewed as the overextraction of depressive variance from each of the clinical scales, Nichols (2006, p. 137) asserted that "the depression-biased Dem was used to extract unwanted variance from the Depression scale (Scale 2), thereby assuring that significant core depressive variance would be lost rather than preserved in a restructured scale (RC2)."

The arguments of Nichols and other critics were rebutted by Tellegen et al. (2006), among others. To appreciate the tenor of some of the rebuttals, consider Weed's (2006) response to Nichols' comments about the restructuring of the depression scale:

> The MMPI-2 Clinical Scales are not models of psychopathology by any conventional sense of the term. No effort was made, for example, to guarantee that the most important features of depression were reflected within Clinical Scale D, let alone in careful balance. Furthermore, no effort was made to prevent the inclusion of items with content that lacked theoretical relevance to Major Depression.... Scale D is not a neatly ordered multivariate model of depression; it is a dimensional cacophony, probably overrepresenting facets here and underrepresenting there, and certainly comprising both good items and poorly performing items.
>
> Nichols's characterization thus inaccurately recasts a grave flaw of the MMPI-2 Clinical Scales in a benign or even favorable light. Rather than highlighting their internal chaos, Nichols describes the scales as reflecting "syndromal complexity," a phrase that might sound euphemistic if it were not clear that he is serious. One might as well speak of the Clinical Scales as being "charmingly free of typical psychometric restraints," characterized by "sassy heterogeneity," or filled to the brim with "intrascale insouciance." (p. 218)

Well . . . lest the present authors be accused of being insouciant (or otherwise indifferent) about providing some "nuts-and-bolts" information about the MMPI-2-RF, we hasten to note that the test manual reports evidence of the instrument's psychometric soundness. The MMPI-2-RF technical manual provides empirical correlates of test scores based on various criteria in various settings including clinical and nonclinical samples. The MMPI-2-RF can still be hand-scored and hand-profiled, although computerized score reporting (with or without a computerized narrative report) is available.

**The MMPI-A**   Although its developers had recommended the original MMPI for use with adolescents, test users had evinced skepticism of this recommendation through the years. Early on it was noticed that adolescents as a group tended to score somewhat higher on the clinical scales than adults, a finding that left adolescents as a group in the unenviable position of appearing to suffer from more psychopathology than adults. In part for this reason, separate MMPI norms for adolescents were developed. In the 1980s, while the MMPI was being revised to become the MMPI-2, the test developers had a choice of simply renorming the MMPI-2 for adolescents or creating a new instrument. They opted to develop a new test that was in many key respects a downward extension of the MMPI-2.

The Minnesota Multiphasic Personality Inventory–Adolescent (MMPI-A; Butcher et al., 1992) is a 478-item, true–false test designed for use in clinical, counseling, and school settings for the purpose of assessing psychopathology and identifying personal, social, and behavioral problems. The individual items of the MMPI-A largely parallel the MMPI-2, although there are 88 fewer items. Some of the MMPI-2 items were discarded, others were rewritten, and some completely new ones were added. In its written (as opposed to audiocassette) form, the test is designed for administration to testtakers in the 14- to 18-year-old age range who have at least a sixth-grade reading ability. As with the MMPI-2, versions of the test are available for administration by computer, by paper and pencil, and by audiocassette. The time required for an administration of all the items typically is between 45 and 60 minutes.

The MMPI-A contains 16 basic scales, including 10 clinical scales (identical in name and number to those of the MMPI-2) and six validity scales (actually, a total of eight validity scales given that the F scale is subdivided into F, $F_1$, and $F_2$ scales). The validity scales are Variable Response Inconsistency (VRIN), True Response Inconsistency (TRIN), Infrequency (F), Infrequency 1 ($F_1$, specifically applicable to the clinical scales), Infrequency 2 ($F_2$, specifically applicable to the content and supplementary scales), Lie (L), Defensiveness (K), and Cannot Say (?).

In addition to basic clinical and validity scales, the MMPI-A contains six supplementary scales (dealing with areas such as alcohol and drug use, immaturity, anxiety, and repression), 15 content scales (including areas such as conduct problems and school problems), 28 Harris-Lingoes scales, and three scales labeled Social Introversion. As with the MMPI-2, uniform $T$ ($UT$) scales were employed for use with all the content scales and eight of the clinical scales (Scales 5 and 0 excluded) in order to make percentile scores comparable across scales.

The normative sample for the MMPI-A consisted of 805 adolescent males and 815 adolescent females drawn from schools in California, Minnesota, New York, North Carolina, Ohio, Pennsylvania, Virginia, and Washington. The objective was to obtain a sample that was nationally representative in terms of demographic variables such as ethnic background, geographic region of the United States, and urban/rural residence. Concurrent with the norming of the MMPI-A, a clinical sample of 713 adolescents was tested for the purpose of obtaining validity data. However, no effort was made to ensure representativeness of the clinical sample. Subjects were all drawn from the Minneapolis area, most from drug and alcohol treatment centers.

**JUST THINK . . .**

Your comments on the norming of the MMPI-A?

In general, the MMPI-A has earned high marks from test reviewers and may well have quickly become the most widely used measure of psychopathology in adolescents. More information about this test can be obtained from an authoritative book entitled *A Beginner's Guide to the MMPI—A* (Williams & Butcher, 2011). Chapters variously introduce readers to the history of the MMPI-A and set the test in the contemporary context of the digital age. The test's scales are described and guidelines for test administration are presented. The book also covers culture-related issues, as well as guidelines for interpreting scores and sharing information with testtakers, parents and others. When supplemented with the insights of others with more "arms length" distance from the test (e.g., Martin & Finn, 2010; Stokes et al., 2009; Zubeidat et al., 2011), the Williams and Butcher *Guide* can be an invaluable reference work for students of the MMPI-A.

**The MMPI and its revisions and progeny in perspective** The MMPI burst onto the psychology scene in the 1940s and was greeted as an innovative, well-researched, and highly appealing instrument by both clinical practitioners and academic researchers. Today, we can look back at its development and be even more impressed, as it was developed without the benefit of high-speed computers. The number of research studies that have conducted on this test number in the thousands, and few psychological tests are better known throughout the world. Through the years, various weaknesses in the test have been discovered, and remedies have been proposed as a consequence. The latest "restructuring" of the MMPI represents an effort not only to improve the test and bring it into the twenty-first century but also to maintain continuity with the voluminous research addressing its previous forms. There can be little doubt

**JUST THINK . . .**

What should the next version of the MMPI look like? In what ways should it be different than the MMPI-2-RF?

that the MMPI is very much a "work in progress" that will be continually patched, restructured, and otherwise re-innovated to maintain that continuity.

## Personality Assessment and Culture

Every day, assessment professionals across the United States are routinely called on to evaluate personality and related variables of people from culturally and linguistically diverse populations. Yet personality assessment is anything but routine with children, adolescents, and adults from Native American, Hispanic, Asian, African American, and other cultures that may have been underrepresented in the development, standardization, and interpretation protocols of the measures used. Especially with members of culturally and linguistically diverse populations, a routine and business-as-usual approach to psychological testing and assessment is inappropriate, if not irresponsible. What is required is a professionally trained assessor capable of conducting a meaningful assessment, with sensitivity to how culture relates to the behaviors and cognitions being measured (López, 2000).

Before any tool of personality assessment—an interview, a test, a protocol for behavioral observation, a portfolio, or something else—can be employed, and before data derived from an attempt at measurement can be imbued with meaning, the assessor will ideally consider some important issues with regard to assessment of a particular assessee. Many of these issues relate to the level of acculturation, values, identity, worldview, and language of the assessee. Professional exploration of these areas is capable of yielding not only information necessary as a prerequisite for formal personality assessment but a wealth of personality-related information in its own right.

### *Acculturation and Related Considerations*

**Acculturation** is an ongoing process by which an individual's thoughts, behaviors, values, worldview, and identity develop in relation to the general thinking, behavior, customs, and values of a particular cultural group. The process of acculturation begins at birth, a time at which the newborn infant's family or caretakers serve as agents of the culture.[10] In the years to come, other family members, teachers, peers, books, films, theater, newspapers, television and radio programs, and other media serve as agents of acculturation. Through the process of acculturation, one develops culturally accepted ways of thinking, feeling, and behaving.

A number of tests and questionnaires have been developed to yield insights regarding assessees' level of acculturation to their native culture or the dominant culture. A sampling of these measures is presented in Table 12–5. As you survey this list, keep in mind that the amount of psychometric research done on these instruments varies. Some of these instruments may be little more than content valid, if that. In such cases, let the buyer beware. Should you wish to use any of these measures, you may wish to look up more information about it in a resource such as the *Mental Measurements Yearbook*. Perhaps the most appropriate use of many of these tests would be to derive hypotheses for future testing by means of other tools of assessment. Unless compelling

---

10. The process of acculturation may begin before birth. It seems reasonable to assume that nutritional and other aspects of the mother's prenatal care may have implications for the newborn infant's tastes and other preferences.

**Table 12–5**
**Some Published Measures of Acculturation**

| Target Population | Reference Sources |
| --- | --- |
| African-American | Baldwin (1984) |
| | Baldwin & Bell (1985) |
| | Klonoff & Landrine (2000) |
| | Obasi & Leong (2010) |
| | Snowden & Hines (1999) |
| Asian | Kim et al. (1999) |
| | Suinn et al. (1987) |
| Asian-American | Gim Chung et al. (2004) |
| | Wolfe et al. (2001) |
| Asian (East & South) | Barry (2001) |
| | Inman et al. (2001) |
| Asian Indian | Sodowsky & Carey (1988) |
| Central American | Wallen et al. (2002) |
| Chinese | Yao (1979) |
| Cuban | Garcia & Lega (1979) |
| Deaf culture | Maxwell-McCaw & Zea (2011) |
| Eskimo | Chance (1965) |
| Hawaiian | Bautista (2004) |
| | Hishinuma et al. (2000) |
| Iranian | Shahim (2007) |
| Japanese-American | Masuda et al. (1970) |
| | Padilla et al. (1985) |
| Khmer | Lim et al. (2002) |
| Latino/Latina | Murguia et al. (2000) |
| | Zea et al. (2003) |
| Mexican-American | Cuéllar et al. (1995) |
| | Franco (1983) |
| | Mendoza (1989) |
| | Ramirez (1984) |
| Muslim American | Bagasra (2010) |
| Native American | Garrett & Pichette (2000) |
| | Howe Chief (1940) |
| | Roy (1962) |
| Puerto Rican | Tropp et al. (1999) |
| | Cortes et al. (2003) |
| Vietnamese | Nguyen & von Eye (2002) |
| Population nonspecific measures | Sevig et al. (2000) |
| | Smither & Rodriguez-Giegling (1982) |
| | Stephenson (2000) |
| | Unger et al. (2002) |
| | Wong-Rieger & Quintana (1987) |

evidence exists to attest to the use of a particular instrument with members of a specific population, data derived from any of these tests and questionnaires should not be used alone to make selection, treatment, placement, or other momentous decisions. Some of our own thoughts on assessing acculturation and related variables are presented in this chapter's *Close-Up*.

Intimately entwined with acculturation is the learning of *values*. **Values** are that which an individual prizes or the ideals an individual believes in. An early systematic treatment of the subject of values came in a book entitled *Types of Men* (Spranger, 1928), which listed different types of people based on whether they valued things like truth, practicality, and power. The book served as an inspiration for a yet more systematic

## Assessing Acculturation and Related Variables

A number of important questions regarding acculturation and related variables can be raised with regard to assessees from culturally diverse populations. Many general types of interview questions may yield rich insights regarding the overlapping areas of acculturation, values, worldview, and identity. A sampling of such questions follows. Before actually posing these or other questions with assessees, some caveats are in order. Keep in mind the critical importance of rapport when conducting an interview. Be sensitive to cultural differences in readiness to engage in self-disclosure about family or other matters that may be perceived as too personal to discuss with a stranger. Be ready and able to change the wording of these questions should you need to facilitate the assessee's understanding of them or to change the order of these questions should an assessee answer more than one question in the same response. Listen carefully and do not hesitate to probe for more information if you perceive value in doing so. Finally, note that the relevance of each of these questions will vary with the background and unique socialization experiences of each assessee.

- Describe yourself.
- Describe your family. Who lives at home?
- Describe roles in your family, such as the role of mother, the role of father, the role of grandmother, the role of child, and so forth.
- What traditions, rituals, or customs were passed down to you by family members?
- What traditions, rituals, or customs do you think it is important to pass to the next generation?
- With regard to your family situation, what obligations do you see yourself as having?
- What obligations does your family have to you?
- What role does your family play in everyday life?
- How does the role of males and females differ from your own cultural perspective?
- What kind of music do you like?
- What kinds of foods do you eat most routinely?
- What do you consider fun things to do? When do you do these things?
- Describe yourself in the way that you think most other people would describe you. How would you say your own self-description would differ from that description?

- How might you respond to the question "Who are you?" with reference to your own sense of personal identity?
- With which cultural group or groups do you identify most? Why?
- What aspect of the history of the group with which you most identify is most significant to you? Why?
- Who are some of the people who have influenced you most?
- What are some things that have happened to you in the past that have influenced you most?
- What sources of satisfaction are associated with being you?
- What sources of dissatisfaction or conflict are associated with being you?
- What do you call yourself when asked about your ethnicity?
- What are your feelings regarding your racial and ethnic identity?
- Describe your most pleasant memory as a child.
- Describe your least pleasant memory as a child.
- Describe the ways in which you typically learn new things. In what ways might cultural factors have influenced this learning style?
- Describe the ways you typically resolve conflicts with other people. What influence might cultural factors have on this way of resolving conflicts?
- How would you describe your general view of the world?
- How would you characterize human nature in general?
- How much control do you believe you have over the things that happen to you? Why?
- How much control do you believe you have over your health? Your mental health?
- What are your thoughts regarding the role of work in daily life? Has your cultural identity influenced your views about work in any way? If so, how?
- How would you characterize the role of doctors in the world around you?
- How would you characterize the role of lawyers in the world around you?
- How would you characterize the role of politicians in the world around you?
- How would you characterize the role of spirituality in your daily life?
- What are your feelings about the use of illegal drugs?

*(continued)*

## Assessing Acculturation and Related Variables *(continued)*

- What is the role of play in daily life?
- How would you characterize the ideal relationship between human beings and nature?
- What defines a person who has power?
- What happens when one dies?
- Do you tend to live your life more in the past, the present, or the future? What influences on you do you think helped shape this way of living?

- How would you characterize your attitudes and feelings about the older people in your family? About older people in society in general?
- Describe your thinking about the local police and the criminal justice system.
- How do you see yourself 10 years from now?

treatment of the subject (Allport et al., 1951). Before long, a number of different systems for listing and categorizing values had been published.

Rokeach (1973) differentiated what he called *instrumental* from *terminal* values. **Instrumental values** are guiding principles to help one attain some objective. Honesty, imagination, ambition, and cheerfulness are examples of instrumental values. **Terminal values** are guiding principles and a mode of behavior that is an endpoint objective. A comfortable life, an exciting life, a sense of accomplishment, and self-respect are some examples of terminal values. Other value-categorization systems focus on values in specific contexts, such as employment settings. Values such as financial reward, job security, or prestige may figure prominently in decisions regarding occupational choice and employment or feelings of job satisfaction.

Writing from an anthropological/cultural perspective, Kluckhohn (1954, 1960; Kluckhohn & Strodtbeck, 1961) conceived of values as answers to key questions with which civilizations must grapple. So, for example, from questions about how the individual should relate to the group, values emerge about individual versus group priorities. In one culture, the answers to such questions might take the form of norms and sanctions that encourage strict conformity and little competition among group members. In another culture, norms and sanctions may encourage individuality and competition among group members. In this context, one can begin to appreciate how members of different cultural groups can grow up with vastly different values, ranging from views on various "isms" (such as individualism versus collectivism) to views on what is trivial and what is worth dying for. The different values people from various cultures bring to the assessment situation may translate into widely varying motivational and incentive systems. Understanding an individual's values is an integral part of understanding personality.

Also intimately tied to the concept of acculturation is the concept of personal *identity.* **Identity** in this context may be defined as a set of cognitive and behavioral characteristics by which individuals define themselves as members of a particular group. Stated simply, identity refers to one's sense of self. Levine and Padilla (1980) defined **identification** as a process by which an individual assumes a pattern of behavior characteristic of other people, and referred to it as one of the "central issues that ethnic minority groups must deal with" (p. 13). Echoing this sentiment, Zuniga (1988) suggested that a question such as "What do you call yourself when asked about your ethnicity?" might be used as an icebreaker when assessing identification. She went on:

> How a minority client handles their response offers evidence of their comfortableness with their identity. A Mexican-American client who responds by saying, "I am an American, and I am just like everyone else," displays a defensiveness that demands gentle probing. One client sheepishly declared that she always called herself Spanish. She used this self-designation since she felt the term "Mexican" was dirty. (p. 291)

Another key culture-related personality variable concerns how an assessee tends to view the world. As its name implies, **worldview** is the unique way people interpret and make sense of their perceptions as a consequence of their learning experiences, cultural background, and related variables.

Our overview of personality began with a consideration of some superficial, lay perspectives on this multifaceted subject. We made reference to the now-classic rock oldie *Personality* and its "definition" of personality in terms of observable variables such as *walk, talk, smile,* and *charm.* Here, at the end of the chapter, we have come a long way in considering more personal, nonobservable elements of personality in the form of constructs such as *worldview, identification, values,* and *acculturation.* In the chapter that follows, we continue to broaden our perspective regarding tools that may be used to assess personality.

---

## Self-Assessment

Test your understanding of elements of this chapter by seeing if you can explain each of the following terms, expressions, and abbreviations:

| | | |
|---|---|---|
| acculturation | instrumental values | Q-sort technique |
| acquiescent response style | leniency error | response style |
| Big Five | locus of control | self-concept |
| control group | MMPI | self-concept differentiation |
| criterion | MMPI-2 | self-concept measure |
| criterion group | MMPI-2-RF | self-report |
| empirical criterion keying | MMPI-A | semantic differential |
| error of central tendency | NEO PI-R | severity error |
| forced-choice format | nomothetic approach | state |
| frame of reference | personality | structured interview |
| generosity error | personality assessment | terminal values |
| graphology | personality profile | Type A personality |
| halo effect | personality trait | Type B personality |
| identification | personality type | validity scale |
| identity | profile | values |
| idiographic approach | profile analysis | Welsh code |
| impression management | profiler | worldview |

# 13

# *Personality Assessment Methods*

**S**ome people see the world as filled with love and goodness, where others see hate and evil. Some people equate *living* with behavioral excess, whereas others strive for moderation in all things. Some people have relatively realistic perceptions of themselves. Other people labor under grossly distorted self-images and inaccurate perceptions of family, friends, and acquaintances. For psychologists and others interested in exploring differences among people with regard to these and other dimensions, many different tools are available. In this chapter, we survey some of the tools of personality assessment, including projective methods of assessment and behavioral approaches to assessment. We begin with a consideration of methods that are typically characterized as "objective" in nature.

## Objective Methods

Usually administered by paper-and-pencil means or by computer, **objective methods of personality assessment** characteristically contain short-answer items for which the assessee's task is to select one response from the two or more provided. The scoring is done according to set procedures involving little, if any, judgment on the part of the scorer. As with tests of ability, objective methods of personality assessment may include items written in a multiple-choice, true–false, or matching format.

Whereas a particular response on an objective ability test may be scored *correct* or *incorrect*, a response on an objective personality test is scored with reference to either the personality characteristic(s) being measured or the validity of the respondent's pattern of responses. For example, on a personality test where a *true* response is deemed indicative of the presence of a particular trait, a number of *true* responses to *true–false* items will be interpreted with reference to the presumed strength of that trait in the testtaker. Well, maybe.

If the respondent has also responded *true* to items indicative of the *absence* of the trait as well as to items rarely endorsed as such by testtakers, then the validity of the protocol will be called into question. Scrutiny of the protocol may suggest an irregularity of some sort. For example, the items may have been responded to inconsistently, in random fashion, or with a *true* response to all questions. As we have seen, some objective personality tests are constructed with validity scales or other devices (such as a forced-choice format) designed to detect or deter response patterns that would call into question the meaningfulness of the scores.

Objective personality tests share many advantages with objective tests of ability. The items can be answered quickly, allowing the administration of many items covering varied aspects of the trait or traits the test is designed to assess. If the items on an objective test are well written, then they require little explanation; this makes

JUST THINK . . .

What possible explanations exist for someone exhibiting inconsistency on an objective personality test?

them well suited for both group and computerized administration. Objective items can usually be scored quickly and reliably by varied means, from hand scoring (usually with the aid of a template held over the test form) to computer scoring. Analysis and interpretation of such tests may be almost as fast as scoring, especially if conducted by computer and custom software.

## How Objective Are Objective Methods of Personality Assessment?

Although objective personality test items share many characteristics with objective measures of ability, we hasten to add that the adjective *objective* is something of a misnomer when applied to personality testing and assessment. With reference to short-answer items on *ability* tests, the term *objective* gained favor because all items contained only one correct response. Well, that was not always true, either, but that's the way they were designed.

In contrast to the scoring of, say, essay tests, the scoring of objective, multiple-choice tests of ability left little room for emotion, bias, or favoritism on the part of the test scorer. Scoring was dispassionate and—for lack of a better term—objective. But unlike objective ability tests, objective personality tests typically contain no one correct answer. Rather, the selection of a particular choice from multiple-choice items provides information relevant to something about the testtaker—such as the presence, absence, or strength of a personality-related variable. Yes, the scoring of such tests can still be dispassionate and objective. However, the "objectivity" of the score derived from a so-called objective test of personality can be a matter of debate. Consider, for example, a personality test written in an objective test format designed to detect the existence of an unresolved oedipal conflict. The extent to which these test results will be viewed as "objective" is inextricably linked to one's views about the validity of psychoanalytic theory and, more specifically, the construct *oedipal conflict.*

Another issue related to the use of the adjective *objective* with *personality test* concerns self-report and the distinct *lack* of objectivity that can be associated with self-report. Testtakers' self-reports of what they like or dislike, what they agree or disagree with, what they do or do not do, and so forth can be anything but "objective," for many reasons. Some respondents may lack the insight to respond in what could reasonably be described as an objective manner. Some respondents respond in a manner that they believe will place them in the best or worst possible light—depending on the impression they wish to manage and their objectives in submitting to the evaluation. In other words, they can attempt to manage a desired impression by faking good or faking bad.

Ultimately, the term *objective* as applied to most personality tests may be best thought of as a shorthand description for a test format. Objective personality tests are objective in the sense that they employ a short-answer (typically multiple-choice) format, one that provides little, if any, room for discretion in terms of scoring. To describe a personality test as objective serves to distinguish it from projective and other measurement methods rather than to impart information about the reality, tangibility, or objectivity of scores derived from it.

# Projective Methods

Suppose the lights in your classroom were dimmed and everyone was told to stare at the clean chalkboard for a minute or so. And suppose everyone was then asked to take out some paper and write down what they thought could be seen on the chalkboard (other than the chalkboard itself). If you examined what each of your fellow students wrote, you might find as many different things as there were students responding. You could assume that the students saw on the chalkboard—or, more accurately, *projected* onto the chalkboard—something that was not really there but rather was in (or on) their own minds. You might further assume that each student's response to the blank chalkboard reflected something very telling and unique about that student's personality structure.

The **projective hypothesis** holds that an individual supplies structure to unstructured stimuli in a manner consistent with the individual's own unique pattern of conscious and unconscious needs, fears, desires, impulses, conflicts, and ways of perceiving and responding. In like manner, we may define the **projective method** as a technique of personality assessment in which some judgment of the assessee's personality is made on the basis of performance on a task that involves supplying some sort of structure to unstructured or incomplete stimuli. Almost any relatively unstructured stimulus will do for this purpose. In a scene in Shakespeare's play *Hamlet*, Polonius and Hamlet discuss what can be seen in clouds. Indeed, clouds could be used as a projective stimulus.[1] But psychologists, slaves to practicality (and scientific methods) as they are, have developed projective measures of personality that are more reliable than clouds and more portable than chalkboards. Inkblots, pictures, words, drawings, and other things have been used as projective stimuli.

**JUST THINK . . .**

Be creative and name some non-obvious thing that could be used as a projective stimulus for personality assessment purposes. How might a projective test using what you named be administered, scored, and interpreted?

Unlike self-report methods, projective tests are *indirect* methods of personality assessment; assessees aren't being directly asked to disclose information about themselves. Rather, their task is to talk about something else (like inkblots or pictures). Through such indirect responses the assessor draws inferences about the personality of assessees. On such a task, the ability—and presumably the inclination—of examinees to fake is greatly minimized. Also minimized on some projective tasks is the testtaker's need for great proficiency in the English language. For example, minimal language skills are required to respond to or create a drawing. For that reason, and because some projective methods may be less linked to culture than are other measures of personality, proponents of projective testing believe that there is a promise of cross-cultural utility with these tests that has yet to be fulfilled. Proponents of projective measures also argue that a major advantage of such measures is that they tap unconscious as well as conscious material. In the words of the man who coined the term *projective methods*, "the most important things about an individual are what he cannot or will not say" (Frank, 1939, p. 395).[2]

---

1. In fact, clouds *have* been used as projective stimuli. Wilhelm Stern's Cloud Picture Test, in which subjects were asked to tell what they saw in pictures of clouds, was one of the earliest projective measures.

2. The first published use of the term *projective methods* that we are aware of was in an article entitled "Projective Methods in the Psychological Study of Children" by Ruth Horowitz and Lois Barclay Murphy (1938). However, these authors had read Lawrence K. Frank's (1939) as-yet-unpublished manuscript and credited him for having "applied the term 'projective methods.'"

Projective tests were born in the spirit of rebellion against normative data and through attempts by personality researchers to break down the study of personality into the study of specific traits of varying strengths. This orientation is exemplified by Frank (1939), who reflected: "It is interesting to see how the students of personality have attempted to meet the problem of individuality with methods and procedures designed for study of uniformities and norms that ignore or subordinate individuality, treating it as a troublesome deviation which derogates from the real, the superior, and only important central tendency, mode, average, etc." (pp. 392–393).

In contrast to methods of personality assessment that focused on the individual from a statistics-based, normative perspective, projective techniques were once the technique of choice for focusing on the individual from a purely clinical perspective—a perspective that examined the unique way an individual projects onto an ambiguous stimulus "his way of seeing life, his meanings, significances, patterns, and especially his feelings" (Frank, 1939, p. 403). Somewhat paradoxically, years of clinical experience with these tests and a mounting volume of research data have led the interpretation of responses to projective stimuli to become increasingly norm-referenced.

## Inkblots as Projective Stimuli

*Spill some ink in the center of a blank, white sheet of paper and fold it over. Allow to dry.* There you have the recipe for an inkblot. Inkblots are not only used by assessment professionals as projective stimuli, they are very much associated with psychology itself in the public eye. The most famous inkblot test is, of course . . .

**The Rorschach**  Hermann Rorschach (Figure 13–1) developed what he called a "form interpretation test" using inkblots as the forms to be interpreted. In 1921 he published his monograph on the technique, *Psychodiagnostics.* In the last section of that monograph, Rorschach proposed applications of his test to personality assessment. He provided 28 case studies employing normal (well, undiagnosed) subjects and people with various psychiatric diagnoses (including neurosis, psychosis, and manic-depressive illness) to illustrate his test. Rorschach died suddenly and unexpectedly at the age of 38, just

**Figure 13–1**
**Hermann Rorschach (1884–1922)**

*Rorschach was a Swiss psychiatrist whose father had been an art teacher and whose interests included art as well as psychoanalysis—particularly the work of Carl Jung, who had written extensively on methods of bringing unconscious material to light. In 1913, Rorschach published papers on how analysis of a patient's artwork could provide insights into personality. Rorschach's inkblot test was published in 1921, and it was not an immediate success. Rorschach died of peritonitis the following year at the age of 38, unaware of the great legacy he would leave. For more on Hermann Rorschach, read his Test Developer Profile on this book's companion website at www.mhhe.com /cohentesting8.*

a year after his book was published. A paper co-authored by Rorschach and Emil Oberholzer entitled "The Application of the Form Interpretation Test" was published posthumously in 1923.

Like Rorschach, we will refer to his test as just that—a *test*. However, there has been a bit of a controversy about whether the instrument Rorschach created is best referred to as a test, a method, a technique, or something else. For example, Goldfried et al. (1971) view the Rorschach as a structured interview, and Korchin and Schuldberg (1981) regard it as "less of a test" and more "an open and flexible arena for studying interpersonal transactions" (p. 1151). There has also been debate about whether or not the Rorschach is properly considered a projective instrument (Acklin, 1995; Aronow et al., 1995; Moreland et al., 1995b; Ritzler, 1995). For example, Rorschach authority John Exner once argued that the inkblots are "not completely ambiguous," that the task does not necessarily "force projection," and that "unfortunately, the Rorschach has been erroneously mislabeled a projective test for far too long" (1989, pp. 526–527; see also Exner, 1997). Regardless, *Rorschach* remains virtually synonymous with *projective test* among assessment professionals and, no matter how else referred to, it certainly qualifies as a "test."

The Rorschach consists of 10 bilaterally symmetrical (that is, mirror-imaged if folded in half) inkblots printed on separate cards. Five inkblots are achromatic (meaning without color, or black-and-white). Two inkblots are black, white, and red. The remaining three inkblots are multicolored. The test comes with the cards only; there is no test manual or any administration, scoring, or interpretation instructions. There is no rationale for why some of the inkblots are achromatic and others are chromatic (with color). Unlike most psychological test kits, which today are published complete with test manual and optional carrying case, this test contains 10 cards packaged in a cardboard box; that's it. For any old-school clinician who uses the Rorschach, a computer-administered version of this test would somehow seem gauche and inappropriate. Of course, that's not to say that it hasn't been tried (Padawer, 2001). But even computerized scoring and interpretation of Rorschach protocols, let alone a computerized administration of the test, may be frowned upon by Rorschach purists (Andronikof, 2005).

**JUST THINK . . .**

Why might a Rorschach purist object to the administration of the test by computer?

To fill the need for a test manual and instructions for administration, scoring, and interpretation, a number of manuals and handbooks set forth a variety of methods (such as Aronow & Reznikoff, 1976, 1983; Beck, 1944, 1945, 1952, 1960; Exner, 1974, 1978, 1986, 2003; Exner & Weiner, 1982; Klopfer & Davidson, 1962; Lerner, 1991, 1996a, 1996b; Piotrowski, 1957). The system most widely used is the "comprehensive system" devised by Exner. Before describing Exner's scoring system, however, here is a general overview of the process of administering, scoring, and interpreting the Rorschach.

Inkblot cards (similar in some respects to the one shown in Figure 13–2) are initially presented to the testtaker one at a time in numbered order from 1 to 10. The testtaker is instructed to tell what is on each of the cards with a question such as "What might this be?" Testtakers have a great deal of freedom with the Rorschach. They may, for example, rotate the cards and vary the number and length of their responses to each card. The examiner records all relevant information, including the testtaker's verbatim responses, nonverbal gestures, the length of time before the first response to each card, the position of the card, and so forth. The examiner does not engage in any discussion concerning the testtaker's responses during the initial administration of the cards. Every effort is made to provide the testtaker with the opportunity to *project*, free from any outside distractions.

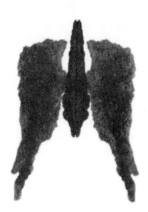

**Figure 13–2
A Rorschach-like Inkblot**

After the entire set of cards has been administered once, a second administration, referred to as the **inquiry,** is conducted. During the inquiry, the examiner attempts to determine what features of the inkblot played a role in formulating the testtaker's **percept** (perception of an image). Questions such as "What made it look like [whatever]?" and "How do you see [whatever it is that the testtaker reported seeing]?" are asked in an attempt to clarify what was seen and which aspects of the inkblot were most influential in forming the perception. The inquiry provides information that is useful in scoring and interpreting the responses. The examiner also learns whether the testtaker remembers earlier responses, whether the original percept is still seen, and whether any new responses are now perceived.

A third component of the administration, referred to as **testing the limits,** may also be included. This procedure enables the examiner to restructure the situation by asking specific questions that provide additional information concerning personality functioning. If, for example, the testtaker has utilized the entire inkblot when forming percepts throughout the test, the examiner might want to determine if details within the inkblot could be elaborated on. Under those conditions, the examiner might say, "Sometimes people use a part of the blot to see something." Alternatively, the examiner might point to a specific area of the card and ask, "What does this look like?"

Other objectives of limit-testing procedures are (1) to identify any confusion or misunderstanding concerning the task, (2) to aid the examiner in determining if the testtaker is able to refocus percepts given a new frame of reference, and (3) to see if a testtaker made anxious by the ambiguous nature of the task is better able to perform given this added structure. At least one Rorschach researcher has advocated the technique of trying to elicit one last response from testtakers who think they have already given as many responses as they are going to give (Cerney, 1984). The rationale was that endings have many meanings, and the one last response may provide a source of questions and inferences applicable to treatment considerations.

> **JUST THINK . . .**
>
> Under what conditions would you think it advisable to engage in a testing the limits procedure? Under what conditions would it be inadvisable?

Hypotheses concerning personality functioning will be formed by the assessor on the basis of all the variables outlined (such as the content of the response, the location of the response, the length of time to respond) as well as many additional ones. In general, Rorschach protocols are scored according to several categories, including location, determinants, content, popularity, and form. *Location* is the part of the inkblot that was utilized in forming the percept. Individuals may use the entire inkblot, a large section, a small section, a minute detail, or white spaces. *Determinants* are the qualities of the inkblot that determine what the individual perceives. Form, color, shading, or movement that the individual attributes to the inkblot are all considered determinants. *Content* is the content category of the response. Different scoring systems vary in some of the categories scored. Some typical content areas include human figures, animal figures, anatomical parts, blood, clouds, X-rays, and sexual responses. *Popularity* refers to the frequency with which a certain response has been found to correspond with a particular inkblot or section of an inkblot. A popular response is one that has frequently been obtained from the general population. A rare response is one that has been perceived infrequently by the general population. The *form* of a response is how accurately the individual's perception matches or fits the corresponding part of the inkblot. Form level may be evaluated as being adequate or inadequate or as good or poor.

The scoring categories are considered to correspond to various aspects of personality functioning. Hypotheses concerning aspects of personality are based both on the number of responses that fall within each category and on the interrelationships among the categories. For example, the number of whole responses (using the entire inkblot) in a Rorschach record is typically associated with conceptual thought process. Form level is associated with reality testing. Accordingly, psychotic patients would be expected to achieve low scores for form level. Human movement has been associated with creative imagination. Color responses have been associated with emotional reactivity.

◆
**JUST THINK . . .**

How would you expect the responses of a group of people such as abstract artists to differ from a group of matched controls on the Form category?

Patterns of response, recurrent themes, and the interrelationships among the different scoring categories are all considered in arriving at a final description of the individual from a Rorschach protocol. Data concerning the responses of various clinical and nonclinical groups of adults, adolescents, and children have been compiled in various books and research publications.

Rorschach's form interpretation test was in its infancy at the time of its developer's death. The orphaned work-in-progress found a receptive home in the United States, where it was nurtured by various groups of supporters, each with its own vision of how the test should be administered, scored, and interpreted. In this sense, the Rorschach is, as McDowell and Acklin (1996, p. 308) characterized it, "an anomaly in the field of psychological measurement when compared to objective and other projective techniques."

◆
**JUST THINK . . .**

"If the Rorschach has anything at all going for it, it has great intuitive appeal." Argue this view—pro or con.

Widely referred to simply as "the Rorschach," as if this instrument were a standardized test, Rorschach practitioners and researchers have for many years employed a variety of Rorschach scoring and interpretation systems—on some occasions picking and choosing interpretive criteria from one or more of each. Consider in this context a study by Saunders (1991) that focused on Rorschach indicators of child abuse. Reporting on how he scored the protocols, Saunders wrote: "Rorschach protocols were scored using Rapaport et al.'s (1945–1946) system as the basic framework, but special scores of four different types were added. I borrowed two of these additional measures from other researchers . . . and developed the other two specifically for this study" (p. 55). Given the variation that existed in terminology and in administration and scoring practices, one readily appreciates how difficult it might be to muster consistent and credible evidence for the test's psychometric soundness.[3]

---

3. Partly in response to such criticisms of the Rorschach, another inkblot test, the Holtzman Inkblot Technique (HIT; Holtzman et al., 1961), was designed to be more psychometrically sound. A description of Wayne Holtzman's HIT, as well as speculation as to why it never achieved the popularity and acceptance of the Rorschach, can be found in the supplementary material for this chapter presented on this book's companion website, *www.mhhe.com/cohentesting8*.

In a book that reviewed several Rorschach systems, John E. Exner Jr. (Figure 13–3) wrote of the advisability of approaching "the Rorschach problem through a research integration of the systems" (1969, p. 251). Exner would subsequently develop such an integration—a **comprehensive system,** as he called it (Exner 1974, 1978, 1986, 1990, 1991, 1993a, 1993b, 2003; Exner & Weiner, 1982, 1995; see also Handler, 1996)—for the test's administration, scoring, and interpretation. Exner's system has been well received by clinicians and is the single system most used and most taught today. However, to inextricably link the fate of the Rorschach to Exner's system would be unfair, at least according to Bornstein and Masling (2005); Exner's system has much to recommend it, but so do several other systems.

Prior to the development of Exner's system and its widespread adoption by clinicians and researchers, evaluations of the Rorschach's psychometric soundness tended to be mixed at best. Exner's system brought a degree of uniformity to Rorschach use and thus facilitated "apples-to-apples" (or "bats-to-bats") comparison of research studies. Yet, regardless of the scoring system employed, there were a number of reasons why the evaluation of the psychometric soundness of the Rorschach was a tricky business. For example, because each inkblot is considered to have a unique stimulus quality, evaluation of reliability by a split-half method would be inappropriate. Of historical interest in this regard is the work of Hans Behn-Eschenburg, who attempted to develop, under Hermann Rorschach's direction (Eichler, 1951), a similar but not alternate form of the test. The need for such an "analogous" set of cards was recognized by Rorschach himself:

> Frequently occasion arises when the test must be repeated with the same subject. Such situations appear when one wishes to test normals in various moods, manic-depressives in different stages, schizophrenics in various conditions, or in testing patients before and after psychoanalysis, etc. Or a control test on a normal may be desired. If the test is repeated with the same plates, conscious or unconscious memory enters to warp

**Figure 13–3**
**John Ernest Exner, Jr. (1928–2006)**

*In their obituary of John E. Exner Jr., Erdberg and Weiner (2007, p. 54) wrote: "Many psychologists bounce around a bit before they lock in on the specialty that becomes the focus of their professional life. That was not the case with John Exner. He first laid hands on a set of blots from the Rorschach Inkblot Test in 1953, and his fascination with the instrument anchored his career from then on. Through five decades, 14 books, more than 60 journal articles, and countless workshop and conference presentations, John Exner and the Rorschach became synonymous." Among other accomplishments, Exner was the founding curator of the Hermann Rorschach Museum and Archives in Bern, Switzerland. One of his last publications before his death at the age of 77 from leukemia was an article entitled "A New U.S. Adult Nonpatient Sample." In that article Exner discussed implications for modifying Comprehensive System interpretive guidelines based on new data (Exner, 2007).*

the result. Analogous series of plates, different from the usual ones but satisfying the prerequisites for the individual plates of the basic series, are necessary for these situations. (Rorschach, 1921/1942, p. 53)

The "analogous series of plates" was referred to as "the Behn-Rorschach" or simply "the Behn." Some early research studies sought to compare findings on the "classic" Rorschach with findings on the Behn.

As Exner observed, traditional test-retest reliability procedures may be inappropriate for use with the Rorschach. This is so because of the effect of familiarity in response to the cards and because responses may reflect transient states as opposed to enduring traits. Exner (1983) reflected that "some Comprehensive System scores defy the axiom that something cannot be valid unless it is also reliable" (p. 411).

**JUST THINK . . .**

Do scores on a test such as the Rorschach defy the axiom that the score cannot be valid unless it is reliable?

The widespread acceptance of Exner's system has advanced the cause of Rorschach reliability—well, inter-scorer reliability, anyway. Exner, as well as others, have provided ample evidence that acceptable levels of inter-scorer reliability can be attained with the Rorschach. Using Exner's system, McDowell and Acklin (1996) reported an overall mean percentage agreement of 87% among Rorschach scorers. Still, as these researchers cautioned, "The complex types of data developed by the Rorschach introduce formidable obstacles to the application of standard procedures and canons of test development" (pp. 308–309). Far more pessimistic about such "formidable obstacles" and far less subtle in their conclusions were Hunsley and Bailey (1999). After reviewing the literature on the clinical utility of the Rorschach, they wrote of "meager support from thousands of publications" and expressed doubt that evidence would ever be developed that the Rorschach or Exner's comprehensive system could "contribute, in routine clinical practice, to scientifically informed psychological assessment" (p. 274).

Countering such pessimism were other reviews of the literature that were far more favorable (Bornstein, 1998, 1999; Ganellen, 1996, 2007; Hughes et al., 2007; Meyer & Handler, 1997; Viglione, 1999). One review of several meta-analyses indicated that the Rorschach validity coefficients were similar to those of the MMPI and the WAIS (Meyer & Archer, 2001). In their meta-analysis designed to compare the validity of the Rorschach with that of the MMPI, Hiller et al. (1999) concluded that "on average, both tests work about equally well when used for purposes deemed appropriate by experts" (p. 293). In a similar vein, Stricker and Gold (1999, p. 240) reflected that, "A test is not valid or invalid; rather, there are as many validity coefficients as there are purposes for which the test is used. The Rorschach can demonstrate its utility for several purposes and can be found wanting for several others." Stricker and Gold (1999) went on to argue for an approach to assessment that incorporated many different types of methods:

> Arguably, Walt Whitman's greatest poem was entitled "Song of Myself." We believe that everything that is done by the person being assessed is a song of the self. The Rorschach is one instrument available to the clinician, who has the task of hearing all of the music. (p. 249)

Decades ago, Jensen (1965, p. 509) opined that "the rate of scientific progress in clinical psychology might well be measured by the speed and thoroughness with which it gets over the Rorschach." If this statement were true, then the rate of scientific progress in clinical psychology could be characterized as a crawl. Publications supporting its use dot the contemporary literature (e.g., Bram, 2010; Keddy & Erdberg, 2010; Mishra et al., 2010; Weizmann-Henelius et al., 2009), although controversies still rage (e.g., Del Giudice, 2010a, 2010b; Kottke et al., 2010). The Rorschach remains one of the most frequently used and frequently taught psychological tests. It is widely used in forensic work and generally accepted by the courts. One reviewer concluded his evaluation of the status of the Rorschach at age 75 with words that seem applicable many years later: "Widely used and highly valued by clinicians and researchers in many countries of the world, it appears despite its fame not yet to have received the academic respect it deserves and, it can be hoped, will someday enjoy" (Weiner, 1997, p. 17).

**JUST THINK . . .**

Do you count yourself among those assessment professionals who hope that the Rorschach will some day enjoy academic respect? Why or why not?

## Pictures as Projective Stimuli

Look at Figure 13–4. Now make up a story about it. Your story should have a beginning, a middle, and an end. Write it down, using as much paper as you need. Bring the story to class with you and compare it with other students' stories. What does your story reveal about your needs, fears, desires, impulse control, ways of viewing the world—your personality? What do the stories written by your classmates reveal about them? This exercise introduces you to the use of pictures as projective stimuli. Pictures used as projective stimuli may be photos of real people, animals, objects, or anything. They may be paintings, drawings, etchings, or any other variety of picture.

One of the earliest uses of pictures as projective stimuli came at the beginning of the twentieth century. Differences as a function of gender were found in the stories that children gave in response to nine pictures (Brittain, 1907). The author reported that the girls in the study were more interested in religious and moral themes than the boys. Another early experiment using pictures and a storytelling technique investigated children's imagination. Differences in themes as a function of age were observed (Libby, 1908). In 1932, a psychiatrist working at the Clinic for Juvenile Research in Detroit developed the Social Situation Picture Test (Schwartz, 1932), a projective instrument

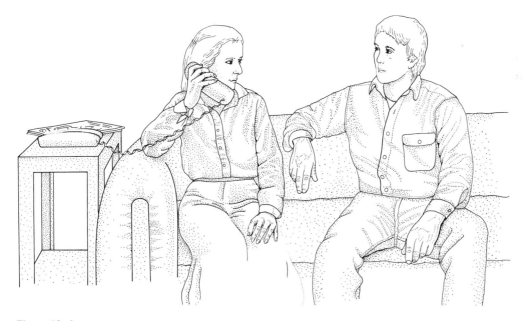

**Figure 13–4**
**Ambiguous Picture for Use in Projective Storytelling Task**

**Figure 13–5**
**Christiana D. Morgan (1897–1967)**

*On the box cover of the widely used TAT and in numerous other measurement-related books and articles, the authorship of the TAT is listed as "Henry A. Murray, Ph.D., and the Staff of the Harvard Psychological Clinic." However, the first articles describing the TAT were written by Christiana D. Morgan (Morgan, 1938) or by Morgan and Murray with Morgan listed as senior author (Morgan & Murray, 1935, 1938). In a mimeographed manuscript in the Harvard University archives, an early version of the test was titled the "Morgan-Murray Thematic Apperception Test" (White et al., 1941). Wesley G. Morgan (1995) noted that, because Christiana Morgan "had been senior author of the earlier publications, a question is raised about why her name was omitted as an author of the 1943 version" (p. 238). Morgan (1995) took up that and related questions in a brief but fascinating account of the origin and history of the TAT images. More on the life of Christiana Morgan can be found in* Translate This Darkness: The Life of Christiana Morgan *(Douglas, 1993). Her Test Developer Profile can be found on this book's companion website at www.mhhe.com/cohentesting8.*

designed for use with juvenile delinquents. Working at the Harvard Psychological Clinic in 1935, Christiana D. Morgan (Figure 13–5) and Henry A. Murray (Figure 13–6) published the Thematic Apperception Test (TAT)—pronounced by saying the letters, not by rhyming with *cat*—the instrument that has come to be the most widely used of all the picture storytelling projective tests.

**The Thematic Apperception Test (TAT)** The TAT was originally designed as an aid to eliciting fantasy material from patients in psychoanalysis (Morgan & Murray, 1935). The stimulus materials consisted, as they do today, of 31 cards, one of which is blank. The 30 picture cards, all black-and-white, contain a variety of scenes designed to present the testtaker with "certain classical human situations" (Murray, 1943). Some of the pictures contain a lone individual, some contain a group of people, and some contain no people. Some of the pictures appear to be almost as real as a photograph; others are surrealistic drawings. Testtakers are introduced to the examination with the cover story that it is a test of imagination in which it is their task to tell what events led up to the scene in the picture, what is happening at that moment, and what the outcome will be. Testtakers are also asked to describe what the people depicted in the cards are thinking

**Figure 13–6**
**Henry A. Murray (1893–1988)**

*Henry Murray is perhaps best known for the influential theory of personality he developed, as well as for his role as author of the Thematic Apperception Test. Biographies of Murray have been written by Anderson (1990) and Robinson (1992). Murray's Test Developer Profile can be found on this book's companion website at www.mhhe.com/cohentesting8.*

and feeling. If the blank card is administered, examinees are instructed to imagine that there is a picture on the card and then proceed to tell a story about it.

In the TAT manual, Murray (1943) also advised examiners to attempt to find out the source of the examinee's story. It is noteworthy that the noun *apperception* is derived from the verb **apperceive,** which may be defined as *to perceive in terms of past perceptions.* The source of a story could be a personal experience, a dream, an imagined event, a book, an episode of *The Daily Show*—really almost anything.

In everyday clinical practice, examiners tend to take liberties with various elements pertaining to the administration, scoring, and interpretation of the TAT. For example, although 20 cards is the recommended number for presentation, in practice an examiner might administer as few as one or two cards or as many as all 31. If a clinician is assessing a patient who has a penchant for telling stories that fill reams of the clinician's notepad, it's probably a good bet that fewer cards will be administered. If, on the other hand, a patient tells brief, one-or two-sentence stories, more cards may be administered in an attempt to collect more raw data with which to work. Some of the cards are suggested for use with adult males, adult females, or both, and some are suggested for use with children. This is so because certain pictorial representations lend themselves more than others to identification and projection by members of these groups. In one study involving 75 males (25 each of 11-, 14-, and 17-year-olds), Cooper (1981) identified the 10 most productive cards for use with adolescent males. In practice, however, any card—be it one recommended for use with males, with females, or with children—may be administered to any subject. The administering clinician selects the cards that are believed likely to elicit responses pertinent to the objective of the testing.

The raw material used in deriving conclusions about the individual examined with the TAT are (1) the stories as they were told by the examinee, (2) the clinician's notes about the way or the manner in which the examinee responded to the cards, and (3) the clinician's notes about extra-test

> **JUST THINK . . .**
>
> Describe a picture on a card that would really get *you* talking. After describing the card, imagine what story you might tell in response to it.

behavior and verbalizations. The last two categories of raw data (test and extra-test behavior) are sources of clinical interpretations for almost any individually administered test. Analysis of the story content requires special training. One illustration of how a testtaker's behavior during testing may influence the examiner's interpretations of the findings was provided by Sugarman (1991, p. 140), who told of a "highly narcissistic patient [who] demonstrated contempt and devaluation of the examiner (and presumably others) by dictating TAT stories complete with spelling and punctuation as though the examiner was a stenographer."

A number of systems for interpreting TAT data exist (for example, Thompson, 1986; Jenkins, 2008; Westen et al., 1988). Many interpretive systems incorporate, or are to some degree based on, Henry Murray's concepts of **need** (determinants of behavior arising from within the individual), **press** (determinants of behavior arising from within the environment), and **thema** (a unit of interaction between needs and press). In general, the guiding principle in interpreting TAT stories is that the testtaker is identifying with someone (the protagonist) in the story and that the needs, environmental demands, and conflicts of the protagonist in the story are in some way related to the concerns, hopes, fears, or desires of the examinee.

**JUST THINK . . .**

Would testtaker identification with the depicted characters or scenes increase if the TAT were redone today in a different media, such as scenes shot on film or video?

In his discussion of the TAT from the perspective of a clinician, William Henry (1956) examined each of the cards in the test with regard to such variables as *manifest stimulus demand, form demand, latent stimulus demand, frequent plots,* and *significant variations.* To get an idea of how some of these terms are used, look again at Figure 13–5—a picture that is *not* a TAT card—and then review Tables 13–1 and 13–2, which are descriptions of the card and some responses to the card from college-age respondents. Although a clinician may obtain bits of information from the stories told about every individual card, the clinician's final impressions will usually derive from a consideration of the overall patterns of themes that emerge.

As with the Rorschach and many other projective techniques, a debate between academics and practitioners regarding the psychometric soundness of the TAT has been unceasing through the years. Because of the general lack of standardization and uniformity with which administration, scoring, and interpretation procedures tend to be applied in everyday clinical practice, concern on psychometric grounds is clearly justified. However, in experimental tests where trained examiners use the same procedures and scoring systems, inter-rater reliability coefficients can range from adequate to impressive (Stricker & Healy, 1990).

**JUST THINK . . .**

Why are split-half, test-retest, and alternate-form reliability measures inappropriate for use with the TAT?

Research suggests that situational factors—including who the examiner is, how the test is administered, and the testtaker's experiences prior to and during the test's administration—may affect test responses. Additionally, transient internal need states such as hunger, thirst, fatigue, and higher-than-ordinary levels of sexual tension can affect a testtaker's responses. Different TAT cards have different stimulus "pulls" (Murstein & Mathes, 1996). Some pictures are more likely than others to elicit stories with themes of despair, for example. Given that the pictures have different stimulus "pulls" or, more technically stated, different latent stimulus demands, it becomes difficult, if not impossible, to determine the inter-item (read "inter-card") reliability of the test. Card 1 might reliably elicit themes of need for achievement, whereas card 16, for example, might not typically elicit any such themes. The possibility of widely variable story lengths in response to the cards presents yet another challenge to the documentation of inter-item reliability.

## Table 13–1
## A Description of the Sample TAT-like Picture

**Author's Description**

A male and a female are seated in close proximity on a sofa. The female is talking on the phone. There is an end table with a magazine on it next to the sofa.

**Manifest Stimulus Demand**

Some explanation of the nature of the relationship between these two persons and some reason the woman is on the phone are required. Less frequently noted is the magazine on the table and its role in this scene.

**Form Demand**

Two large details, the woman and the man, must be integrated. Small details include the magazine and the telephone.

**Latent Stimulus Demand**

This picture is may elicit attitudes toward heterosexuality as well as material relevant to the examinee with regard to optimism–pessimism, security–insecurity, dependence–independence, passivity–assertiveness, and related continuums. Alternatively, attitudes toward family and friends may be elicited, with the two primary figures being viewed as brother and sister, the female talking on the phone to a family member, and so on.

**Frequent Plots**

We haven't administered this card to enough people to make judgments about what constitutes "frequent plots." We have, however, provided a sampling of plots (Table 13–2).

**Significant Variations**

Just as we cannot provide information on frequent plots, we cannot report data on significant variations. We would guess, however, that most college students viewing this picture would perceive the two individuals in it as being involved in a heterosexual relationship. Were that to be the case, a significant variation would be a story in which the characters are not involved in a heterosexual relationship (for example, they are employer/employee). Close clinical attention will also be paid to the nature of the relationship of the characters to any "introduced figures" (persons not pictured in the card but introduced into the story by the examinee). The "pull" of this card is to introduce the figure to whom the woman is speaking. What is the phone call about? How will the story be resolved?

## Table 13–2
## Some Responses to the Sample Picture

| Respondent | Story |
|---|---|
| 1. (Male) | This guy has been involved with this girl for a few months. Things haven't been going all that well. He's suspected that she's been seeing a lot of guys. This is just one scene in a whole evening where the phone hasn't stopped ringing. Pretty soon he is just going to get up and leave. |
| 2. (Female) | This couple is dating. They haven't made any plans for the evening, and they are wondering what they should do. She is calling up another couple to ask if they want to get together. They will go out with the other couple and have a good time. |
| 3. (Male) | This girl thinks she is pregnant and is calling the doctor for the results of her test. This guy is pretty worried because he has plans to finish college and go to graduate school. He is afraid she will want to get married, and he doesn't want to get trapped into anything. The doctor will tell her she isn't pregnant, and he'll be really relieved. |
| 4. (Female) | This couple has been dating for about two years, and they're very much in love. She's on the phone firming up plans for a down payment on a hall that's going to cater the wedding. That's a bridal magazine on the table over there. They look like they're really in love. I think things will work out for them even though the odds are against it—the divorce rates and all. |
| 5. (Male) | These are two very close friends. The guy has a real problem and needs to talk to someone. He is feeling really depressed and that he is all alone in the world. Every time he starts to tell her how he feels, the phone rings. Pretty soon he will leave feeling like no one has time for him and even more alone. I don't know what will happen to him, but it doesn't look good. |

Conflicting opinions are presented in the scholarly literature concerning the validity of the TAT, including the validity of its assumptions and the validity of various applications (Barends et al., 1990; Cramer, 1996; Gluck, 1955; Hibbard et al., 1994; Kagan, 1956; Keiser & Prather, 1990; Mussen & Naylor, 1954; Ronan et al., 1995; Worchel & Dupree, 1990). Some have argued that as much motivational information could be obtained through much simpler, self-report methods. However, one meta-analysis of this literature concluded that there was little relation between TAT-derived data and that derived from self-report (Spangler, 1992). McClelland et al. (1989) distinguished the products of self-report and TAT-derived motivational information, arguing that self-report measures yielded "self-attributed motives" whereas the TAT was capable of yielding "implicit motives." Drawing partially on McClelland et al. (1989), we may define an **implicit motive** as a nonconscious influence on behavior typically acquired on the basis of experience.

◆
**JUST THINK . . .**

If someone asked you about your "need to achieve," what would you say? How might what you say differ from the "implicit" measure of need for achievement that would emerge from your TAT protocol?

A study by Peterson et al. (2008) provided partial support not only for the projective hypothesis but also for the value of the TAT in clinical assessment. The research subjects were 126 introductory psychology students (70 female, 56 male) whose average age was about 19½. All subjects completed a demographic questionnaire and were pre-evaluated by self-report measures of personality and mood. Subjects were then exposed to rock music with suicide-related lyrics. The specific songs used were *Dirt, Desperate Now,* and *Fade to Black.* Subjects next completed a memory test for the music they had heard. They also completed self-report measures of personality and mood (again), and a picture storytelling task using three TAT cards. Of particular interest among the many findings was the fact that measured personality traits predicted the level of suicide-related responding in the TAT stories told. Participants who wrote stories with higher levels of suicide-related responding (a) tended to believe that suicidal thinking was valid, and that suicide-related lyrics in songs were potentially harmful, (b) felt more sad, angry, and isolated while listening to the music, and, (c) were more likely to report negative affect states after listening to the music. One unexpected finding from this study was that

> after listening to music with suicide lyrics, many participants wrote projective stories with altruistic themes. . . . There is a vast literature relating exposure to violence in music, video games, and movies to increased aggression but Meier [et al.] 2006 reported that this relationship does not occur for individuals who score high on measures of agreeableness. Indeed, such individuals respond to aggression-related cues by accessing pro-social thoughts. (Peterson et al., 2008, p. 167)

Although the relationship between expression of fantasy stories and real-life behavior is tentative at best, and although the TAT is highly susceptible to faking, the test is widely used by practitioners. The rationale of the TAT, and of many similar published picture story tests (see Table 13–3), has great intuitive appeal. It does make sense that people would project their own motivation when asked to construct a story from an ambiguous stimulus. Another appeal for users of this test is that it is the clinician who tailors the test administration by selecting the cards and the nature of the inquiry—a feature most welcome by many practitioners in an era of computer-adaptive testing and computer-generated narrative summaries. And so it is with the TAT, as it is many other projective tools of assessment, the test must ultimately be judged by a different standard that is more clinically than psychometrically oriented, if its contribution to personality assessment is to be fully appreciated.

**Table 13–3**
**Some Picture Story Tests**

| Picture-Story Test | Description |
| --- | --- |
| Thompson (1949) modification of the original TAT | Designed specifically for use with African American testtakers, with pictures containing both Black and White protagonists. |
| TEMAS (Malgady et al., 1984) | Designed for use with urban Hispanic children, with drawings of scenes relevant to their experience. |
| Children's Apperception Test (CAT; Bellak, 1971) (first published in 1949) | Designed for use with ages 3 to 10 and based on the idea that animals engaged in various activities were useful in stimulating projective storytelling by children. |
| Children's Apperception Test-Human (CAT-H; Bellak & Bellak, 1965) | A version of the CAT based on the idea that depending on the maturity of the child, a more clinically valuable response might be obtained with humans instead of animals in the pictures. |
| Senior Apperception Technique (SAT; Bellak & Bellak, 1973) | Picture-story test depicting images relevant to older adults. |
| The Picture Story Test (Symonds, 1949) | For use with adolescents, with pictures designed to elicit adolescent-related themes such as coming home late and leaving home. |
| Education Apperception Test (Thompson & Sones, 1973) and the School Apperception Method (Solomon & Starr, 1968) | Two independent tests, listed here together because both were designed to tap school-related themes. |
| The Michigan Picture Test (Andrew et al., 1953) | For ages 8 to 14, contains pictures designed to elicit various themes ranging from conflict with authority to feelings of personal inadequacy. |
| Roberts Apperception Test for Children (RATC; McArthur & Roberts, 1982) | Designed to elicit a variety of developmental themes such as family confrontation, parental conflict, parental affection, attitudes toward school, and peer action. |
| Children's Apperceptive Story-Telling Test (CAST; Schneider, 1989) | Theory-based test based on the work of Alfred Adler. |
| Blacky Pictures Test (Blum, 1950) | Psychoanalytically based, cartoon-like items featuring Blacky the Dog. |
| Make a Picture Story Method (Shneidman, 1952) | For ages 6 and up, respondents construct their own pictures from cutout materials included in the test kit and then tell a story. |

**Other tests using pictures as projective stimuli**   Following the publication of the TAT and its subsequent embrace by many clinicians, there has been no shortage of other, TAT-like tests published. The rationale for creating some of these tests has to do with their proposed contribution in terms of greater testtaker identification with the images depicted in the cards. So, for example, one group of TAT-like tests designed for use with the elderly features seniors in the pictures (Bellak & Bellak, 1973; Starr & Weiner, 1979; Wolk & Wolk, 1971). The assumption made by these test authors is that pictures featuring seniors will be more relevant to the elderly and thus elicit verbal responses that more accurately reflect inner conflicts. Verdon (2011) raised some important questions regarding the assumptions inherent in the use of such instruments. One question he raised had to do with the appropriateness of treating the elderly as a group when it comes to measures such as the TAT. He wrote, "We must never forget that these persons too were once children, adolescents, and young adults, and that their past experiences of pleasure and pain, hope and disenchantment are still present in their mental lives. For this reason, we must be careful not to consider the elderly population as a homogeneous clinical entity whose mental characteristics and concerns would have nothing more to do with those of their past" (p. 62). Verdon questioned whether cards shown to elderly testtakers must necessarily depict elderly figures if they are to elicit themes linked to loss or helplessness; the original TAT cards could do that, and may even be more effective at doing so. Verdon cautioned:

if the material does match real life situations too closely, little room is left for fantasy, and the persons' discourse can be taken literally, as supposedly reflecting actual problems of their daily lives. On the other hand . . . if both actor and narrator of the scene are one, we run the risk of attributing a positive value to a story that is in fact conventional, where conflicts are avoided or minimized. (Verdon, 2011, p. 25)

There are other types of projective instruments, not quite like the TAT, that also use pictures as projective stimuli. One such projective technique, the Hand Test (Wagner, 1983), consists of nine cards with pictures of hands on them and a tenth blank card. The testtaker is asked what the hands on each card might be doing. When presented with the blank card, the testtaker is instructed to imagine a pair of hands on the card and then describe what they might be doing. Testtakers may make several responses to each card, and all responses are recorded. Responses are interpreted according to 24 categories such as affection, dependence, and aggression.

Another projective technique, the Rosenzweig Picture-Frustration Study (Rosenzweig, 1945, 1978), employs cartoons depicting frustrating situations (Figure 13–7). The testtaker's task is to fill in the response of the cartoon figure being frustrated. The test, which is based on the assumption that the testtaker will identify with the person being frustrated, is available in forms for children, adolescents, and adults. Young children respond orally to the pictures, whereas older testtakers may respond either orally or in writing. An inquiry period is suggested after administration of all of the pictures in order to clarify the responses.

Test responses are scored in terms of the type of reaction elicited and the direction of the aggression expressed. The direction of the aggression may be *intropunitive* (aggression turned inward), *extrapunitive* (outwardly expressed), or *inpunitive* (aggression is evaded so as to avoid or gloss over the situation). Reactions are grouped into categories such as *obstacle dominance* (in which the response concentrates on the frustrating barrier), *ego defense* (in which attention is focused on protecting the frustrated person), and *need persistence* (in which attention is focused on solving the frustrating problem). For each scoring category, the percentage of responses is calculated and compared with normative data. A group conformity rating (GCR) is derived representing the degree to which one's responses conform to or are typical of those of the standardization group.

**Figure 13–7**
**Sample Item from the Rosenzweig**
**Picture-Frustration Study**

This test has captured the imagination of researchers for decades, although questions remain concerning how reactions to cartoons depicting frustrating situations are related to real-life situations.

One variation of the picture story method may appeal to old school clinicians as well as to clinicians who thrive on normative data with all of the companion statistics. The Apperceptive Personality Test (APT; Karp et al., 1990) represents an attempt to address some long-standing criticisms of the TAT as a projective instrument while introducing objectivity into the scoring system. The test consists of eight stimulus cards "depicting recognizable people in everyday settings" (Holmstrom et al., 1990, p. 252), including males and females of different ages as well as minority group members. This, by the way, is in contrast to the TAT stimulus cards, some of which depict fantastic or unreal types of scenes.[4] Another difference between the APT and the TAT is the emotional tone and draw of the stimulus cards. A long-standing criticism of the TAT cards has been their negative or gloomy tone, which may restrict the range of affect projected by a testtaker (Garfield & Eron, 1948; Ritzler et al., 1980). After telling a story about each of the APT pictures orally or in writing, testtakers respond to a series of multiple-choice questions. In addition to supplying quantitative information, the questionnaire segment of the test was designed to fill in information gaps from stories that are too brief or cryptic to otherwise score. Responses are thus subjected to both clinical and actuarial interpretation and may, in fact, be scored and interpreted with computer software.

> **JUST THINK . . .**
>
> For the purposes of a test such as the TAT, why might the depiction of contemporary "regular" people on the cards work better or worse than the images currently on them?

Every picture tells a story—well, hopefully for the sake of the clinician or researcher trying to collect data by means of a picture-story projective test. Otherwise, it may be time to introduce another type of test, one where words themselves are used as projective stimuli.

## Words as Projective Stimuli

Projective techniques that employ words or open-ended phrases and sentences are referred to as *semistructured* techniques because, although they allow for a variety of responses, they still provide a framework within which the subject must operate. Perhaps the two best-known examples of verbal projective techniques are *word association tests* and *sentence completion tests*.

**Word association tests**   **Word association** is a task that may be used in personality assessment in which an assessee verbalizes the first word that comes to mind in response to a stimulus word. A **word association test** may be defined as a semistructured, individually administered, projective technique of personality assessment that involves the presentation of a list of stimulus words, to each of which an assessee responds verbally or in writing with whatever comes immediately to mind first upon first exposure to the stimulus word. Responses are then analyzed on the basis of content and other variables. The first attempt to investigate word association was made by Galton (1879). Galton's method consisted of presenting a series of unrelated stimulus words and instructing the subject to respond with the first word that came to mind. Continued interest in the phenomenon of word association resulted in additional studies.

---

4. Murray et al. (1938) believed that fantastic or unreal types of stimuli might be particularly effective in tapping unconscious processes.

Precise methods were developed for recording the responses given and the length of time elapsed before obtaining a response (Cattell, 1887; Trautscholdt, 1883). Cattell and Bryant (1889) were the first to use cards with stimulus words printed on them. Kraepelin (1895) studied the effect of physical states (such as hunger and fatigue) and of practice on word association. Mounting experimental evidence led psychologists to believe that the associations individuals made to words were not chance happenings but rather the result of the interplay between one's life experiences, attitudes, and unique personality characteristics.

Jung (1910) maintained that, by selecting certain key words that represented possible areas of conflict, word association techniques could be employed for psychodiagnostic purposes. Jung's experiments served as an inspiration to the creators of the Word Association Test developed by Rapaport et al. (1945–1946) at the Menninger Clinic. This test consisted of three parts. In the first part, each stimulus word was administered to the examinee, who had been instructed to respond quickly with the first word that came to mind. The examiner recorded the length of time it took the subject to respond to each item. In the second part of the test, each stimulus word was again presented to the examinee. The examinee was instructed to reproduce the original responses. Any deviation between the original and this second response was recorded, as was the length of time before reacting. The third part of the test was the inquiry. Here the examiner asked questions to clarify the relationship that existed between the stimulus word and the response (for example, "What were you thinking about?" or "What was going through your mind?"). In some cases, the relationship may have been obvious; in others, however, the relationship between the two words may have been extremely idiosyncratic or even bizarre.

Rapaport et al.'s test consisted of 60 words, some considered neutral by the test authors (for example, *chair, book, water, dance, taxi*) and some characterized as "traumatic." In the latter category were "words that are likely to touch upon sensitive personal material according to clinical experience, and also words that attract associative disturbances" (Rapaport et al., 1968, p. 257). Examples of words so designated were *love, girlfriend, boyfriend, mother, father, suicide, fire, breast*, and *masturbation.*

Responses on the Word Association Test were evaluated with respect to variables such as popularity, reaction time, content, and test-retest responses. Normative data were provided regarding the percentage of occurrence of certain responses for college students and schizophrenic groups. For example, to the word *stomach*, 21% of the college group responded with "ache" and 13% with "ulcer." Ten percent of the schizophrenic group responded with "ulcer." To the word *mouth*, 20% of the college sample responded with "kiss," 13% with "nose," 11% with "tongue," 11% with "lips," and 11% with "eat." In the schizophrenic group, 19% responded with "teeth," and 10% responded with "eat." The test does not enjoy widespread clinical use today but is more apt to be found in the occasional research application.

The Kent-Rosanoff Free Association Test (Kent & Rosanoff, 1910) represented one of the earliest attempts to develop a standardized test using words as projective stimuli.[5] The test consisted of 100 stimulus words, all

**JUST THINK . . .**

As compared to the 1940s, how emotion-arousing do you think the "traumatic" stimuli on the Word Association Test are by contemporary standards? Why?

---

5. The term **free association** refers to the technique of having subjects relate all their thoughts as they are occurring and is most frequently used in psychoanalysis; the only structure imposed is provided by the subjects themselves. The technique employed in the Kent-Rosanoff is that of **word association** (not free association), in which the examinee relates the first word that comes to mind in response to a stimulus word. The term *free association* in the test's title is, therefore, a misnomer.

commonly used and believed to be neutral with respect to emotional impact. The standardization sample consisted of 1,000 normal adults who varied in geographic location, educational level, occupation, age, and intellectual capacity. Frequency tables based on the responses of these 1,000 cases were developed. These tables were used to evaluate examinees' responses according to the clinical judgment of psychopathology. Psychiatric patients were found to have a lower frequency of popular responses than the normal subjects in the standardization group. However, as it became apparent that the individuality of responses may be influenced by many variables other than psychopathology (such as creativity, age, education, and socioeconomic factors), the popularity of the Kent-Rosanoff as a differential diagnostic instrument diminished. Damaging, too, was research indicating that scores on the Kent-Rosanoff were unrelated to other measures of psychotic thought (Ward et al., 1991). Still, the test endures as a standardized instrument of word association responses and, more than 90 years after its publication, continues to be used in experimental research and clinical practice.

**JUST THINK . . .**

Quick! The first thought that comes into your mind when you hear the term . . . *word association.*

**Sentence completion tests**   Other projective techniques that use verbal material as projective stimuli are *sentence completion tests.* In general, **sentence completion** refers to a task in which the assessee is asked to finish an incomplete sentence or phrase. A **sentence completion test** is a semistructured projective technique of personality assessment that involves the presentation of a list of words that begin a sentence and the assessee's task is to respond by finishing each sentence with whatever word or words come to mind. To obtain some firsthand experience with sentence completion items, how might you complete the following sentences?

I like to _____.

Someday, I will _____.

I will always remember the time _____.

I worry about _____.

I am most frightened when _____.

My feelings are hurt _____.

My mother _____.

I wish my parents _____.

Sentence completion tests may contain items that, like the sample items just presented, are quite general and appropriate for administration in a wide variety of settings. Alternatively, **sentence completion stems** (the part of the sentence completion item that is not blank, but must be created by the testtaker) may be developed for use in specific types of settings (such as school or business) or for specific purposes. Sentence completion tests may be relatively atheoretical or linked very closely to some theory. As an example of the latter, the Washington University Sentence Completion Test (Loevinger et al., 1970) was based on the writings of Loevinger and her colleagues in the area of self-concept development.

A number of standardized sentence completion tests are available to the clinician. One such test, the Rotter[6] Incomplete Sentences Blank (Rotter & Rafferty, 1950) may be

_____

6. The *o* sound in *Rotter* is long, as in *rote.*

the most popular of all. The Rotter was developed for use with populations from grade 9 through adulthood and is available in three levels: high school (grades 9 through 12), college (grades 13 through 16), and adult. Testtakers are instructed to respond to each of the 40 incomplete sentence items in a way that expresses their "real feelings." The manual suggests that responses on the test be interpreted according to several categories: family attitudes, social and sexual attitudes, general attitudes, and character traits. Each response is evaluated on a seven-point scale that ranges from *need for therapy* to *extremely good adjustment.* According to the psychometric studies quoted in the test manual, the Rotter is a reliable and valid instrument.

In general, a sentence completion test may be a useful and straightforward way to obtain information from an honest and verbally expressive testtaker about diverse topics. The tests may tap interests, educational aspirations, future goals, fears, conflicts, needs—just about anything the testtaker cares to be candid about. The tests have a high degree of face validity. However, with this high degree of face validity comes a certain degree of transparency about the objective of the test. For this reason, sentence completion tests are perhaps the most vulnerable of all the projective methods to faking on the part of an examinee intent on making a good—or a bad—impression.

**JUST THINK . . .**

Is there a way that sentence completion tests could be made "less transparent" and thus less vulnerable to faking?

## Sounds as Projective Stimuli

Let's state at the outset that this section is included more as a fascinating footnote in the history of projectives than as a description of widely used tests. The history of the use of sound as a projective stimulus is fascinating because of its origins in the laboratory of a then-junior fellow of Harvard University. You may be surprised to learn that it was a behaviorist whose name has seldom been uttered in the same sentence as the term *projective test* by any contemporary psychologist: B. F. Skinner (Figure 13–8). The device was something "like auditory inkblots" (Skinner, 1979, p. 175).

**Figure 13–8**
**Projective Test Pioneer B. F. Skinner . . . *What?!***

*Working at the Harvard Psychological Clinic with the blessing of (and even some financial support from) Henry Murray, B. F. Skinner (who today is an icon of behaviorism) evinced great enthusiasm for an auditory projective test he had developed. He believed the technique had potential as "a device for snaring out complexes" (Skinner, 1979, p. 176). A number of well-known psychologists of the day apparently agreed. For example, Joseph Zubin, in correspondence with Skinner, wrote that Skinner's technique had promise "as a means for throwing light on the less objective aspects of the Rorschach experiment" (Zubin, 1939). Of course, if the test really had that much promise, Skinner would probably be getting equal billing in this chapter with Murray and Rorschach.*

The time was the mid-1930's. Skinner's colleagues Henry Murray and Christiana Morgan were working on the TAT in the Harvard Psychological Clinic. Psychoanalytic theory was very much in vogue. Even behaviorists were curious about Freud's approach, and some were even undergoing psychoanalysis themselves. Switching on the equipment in his laboratory in the biology building, the rhythmic noise served as a stimulus for Skinner to create words that went along with it. This inspired Skinner to think of an application for sound, not only in behavioral terms but in the elicitation of "latent" verbal behavior that was significant "in the Freudian sense" (Skinner, 1979, p. 175). Skinner created a series of recorded sounds much like muffled, spoken vowels, to which people would be instructed to associate. The sounds, packaged as a device he called a *verbal summator,* presumably would act as a stimulus for the person to verbalize certain unconscious material. Henry Murray, by the way, liked the idea and supplied Skinner with a room at the clinic in which to test subjects. Saul Rosenzweig also liked the idea; he and David Shakow renamed the instrument the *tautophone* (from the Greek *tauto,* meaning "repeating the same") and did research with it (Rutherford, 2003). Their instructions to subjects were as follows:

> Here is a phonograph. On it is a record of a man's voice saying different things. He speaks rather unclearly, so I'll play over what he says a number of times. You'll have to listen carefully. As soon as you have some idea of what he's saying, tell me at once. (Shakow & Rosenzweig, 1940, p. 217)

As recounted in detail by Rutherford (2003), there was little compelling evidence to show that the instrument could differentiate between members of clinical and nonclinical groups. Still, a number of other auditory projective techniques were developed. There was the Auditory Apperception Test (Stone, 1950), in which the subject's task was to respond by creating a story based on three sounds played on a phonograph record. Other researchers produced similar tests, one called an auditory sound association test (Wilmer & Husni, 1951) and the other referred to as an auditory apperception test (Ball & Bernardoni, 1953). Henry Murray also got into the act with his Azzageddi test (Davids & Murray, 1955), named for a Herman Melville character. Unlike other auditory projectives, the Azzageddi presented subjects with spoken paragraphs.

So why aren't test publishers today punching out CDs with projective sounds at a pace to match the publication of inkblots and pictures? Rutherford (2003) speculated that a combination of factors conspired to cause the demise of auditory projective methods. The tests proved not to differentiate between different groups of subjects who took it. Responses to the auditory stimuli lacked the complexity and richness of responses to inkblots, pictures, and other projective stimuli. None of the available scoring systems was very satisfactory. Except for use with the blind, auditory projective tests were seen as redundant and not as good as the TAT.

**JUST THINK . . .**

Are you surprised that early in his career B. F. Skinner experimented with a projective instrument that was psychoanalytically grounded? Why or why not?

## *The Production of Figure Drawings*

A relatively quick, easily administered projective technique is the analysis of drawings. Drawings can provide the psychodiagnostician with a wealth of clinical hypotheses to be confirmed or discarded as the result of other findings (Figure 13–9). The use of drawings in clinical and research settings has extended beyond the area of personality assessment. Attempts have been made to use artistic productions as a source of information about intelligence, neurological intactness, visual-motor coordination,

*Drawing by a 25-year-old schoolteacher after becoming engaged. Previously, she had entered psychotherapy because of problems relating to men and a block against getting married. The position of the hands was interpreted as indicating a fear of sexual intercourse.*

*Drawing by a male with a "Don Juan" complex—a man who pursued one affair after another. The collar pulled up to guard the neck and the excessive shading of the buttocks suggests a fear of being attacked from the rear. It is possible that this man's Don Juanism is an outward defense against a lack of masculinity—even feelings of effeminacy—with which he may be struggling inside.*

*Drawing by an authoritarian and sadistic male who had been head disciplinarian of a reformatory for boys before he was suspended for child abuse. His description of this picture was that it "looked like a Prussian or a Nazi general."*

*The manacled hands, tied feet, exposed buttocks, and large foot drawn to the side of the drawing taken together are reflective, according to Hammer, of masochistic, homosexual, and exhibitionistic needs.*

*This drawing by an acutely paranoid, psychotic man was described by Hammer (1981, p. 170) as follows: "The savage mouth expresses the rage-filled projections loose within him. The emphasized eyes and ears with the eyes almost emanating magical rays reflect the visual and auditory hallucinations the patient actually experiences. The snake in the stomach points up his delusion of a reptile within, eating away and generating venom and evil."*

**Figure 13–9**
**Some Sample Interpretations Made from Figure Drawings**

Source: Hammer (1981).

cognitive development, and even learning disabilities (Neale & Rosal, 1993). Figure drawings are an appealing source of diagnostic data because the instructions for them can be administered individually or in a group by nonclinicians such as teachers, and no materials other than a pencil and paper are required.

**Figure-drawing tests**  In general, a **figure drawing test** may be defined as a projective method of personality assessment whereby the assessee produces a drawing that is analyzed on the basis of its content and related variables. The classic work on the use of figure drawings as a projective stimulus is a book entitled *Personality Projection in the Drawing of the Human Figure* by Karen Machover (1949). Machover wrote that

> the human figure drawn by an individual who is directed to "draw a person" [is] related intimately to the impulses, anxieties, conflicts, and compensations characteristic of that individual. In some sense, the figure drawn is the person, and the paper corresponds to the environment. (p. 35)

The instructions for administering the Draw A Person (DAP) test are quite straightforward. The examinee is given a pencil and a blank sheet of 8½-by-11-inch white paper and told to draw a person. Inquiries on the part of the examinee concerning how the picture is to be drawn are met with statements such as "Make it the way you think it should be" or "Do the best you can." Immediately after the first drawing is completed, the examinee is handed a second sheet of paper and instructed to draw a picture of a person of the sex opposite that of the person just drawn.[7] Subsequently, many clinicians will ask questions about the drawings, such as "Tell me a story about that figure," "Tell me about that boy/girl, man/lady," "What is the person doing?" "How is the person feeling?" "What is nice or not nice about the person?" Responses to these questions are used in forming various hypotheses and interpretations about personality functioning.

Traditionally, DAP productions have been formally evaluated through analysis of various characteristics of the drawing. Attention has been given to such factors as the length of time required to complete the picture, placement of the figures, the size of the figure, pencil pressure used, symmetry, line quality, shading, the presence of erasures, facial expressions, posture, clothing, and overall appearance. Various hypotheses have been generated based on these factors (Knoff, 1990a). For example, the *placement* of the figure on the paper is seen as representing how the individual functions within the environment. The person who draws a tiny figure at the bottom of the paper might have a poor self-concept or might be insecure or depressed. The individual who draws a picture that cannot be contained on one sheet of paper and goes off the page is considered to be impulsive. Unusually light pressure suggests character disturbance (Exner, 1962). According to Buck (1948, 1950), placement of drawing on the right of the page suggests orientation to the future; placement to the left suggests an orientation to the past. Placement at the upper right suggests a desire to suppress an unpleasant past as well as excessive optimism about the future. Placement to the lower left suggests depression with a desire to flee into the past.

Another variable of interest to those who analyze figure drawings is the *characteristics* of the individual drawn. For example, unusually large eyes or large ears suggest suspiciousness, ideas of reference, or other paranoid characteristics (Machover, 1949; Shneidman, 1958). Unusually large breasts drawn by a male may be interpreted as unresolved oedipal problems with maternal dependence (Jolles, 1952). Long and conspicuous ties suggest sexual aggressiveness, perhaps overcompensating for fear of impotence (Machover, 1949). Button emphasis suggests dependent, infantile, inadequate personality (Halpern, 1958).

---

7. When instructed simply to "draw a person," most people will draw a person of the same sex, so it is deemed clinically significant if the assessee draws a person of the opposite sex when given this instruction. Rierdan and Koff (1981) found that, in some cases, children are uncertain of the sex of the figure drawn. They hypothesized that in such cases "the child has an indefinite or ill-defined notion of sexual identity" (p. 257).

JUST THINK . . .

Draw a person. Contemplate what that drawing tells about you on the basis of what you have read.

The House-Tree-Person test (HTP; Buck, 1948) is another projective figure-drawing test. As the name of the test implies, the testtaker's task is to draw a picture of a house, a tree, and a person. In much the same way that different aspects of the human figure are presumed to be reflective of psychological functioning, the ways in which an individual represents a house and a tree are considered symbolically significant. Another test, this one thought to be of particular value in learning about the examinee in relation to her or his family, is the Kinetic Family Drawing (KFD). Derived from Hulse's (1951, 1952) Family Drawing Test, an administration of the KFD (Burns & Kaufman, 1970, 1972) begins with the presentation of an 8½-by-11-inch sheet of paper and a pencil with an eraser. The examinee, usually though not necessarily a child, is instructed as follows:

> Draw a picture of everyone in your family, including you, DOING something. Try to draw whole people, not cartoons or stick people. Remember, make everyone DOING something—some kind of actions. (Burns & Kaufman, 1972, p. 5)

In addition to yielding graphic representations of each family member for analysis, this procedure may yield important information in the form of examinee verbalizations while the drawing is being executed. After the examinee has completed the drawing, a rather detailed inquiry follows. The examinee is asked to identify each of the figures, talk about their relationship, and detail what they are doing in the picture and why. A number of formal scoring systems for the KFD are available. Related techniques include a school adaptation called the Kinetic School Drawing (KSD; Prout & Phillips, 1974); a test that combines aspects of the KFD and the KSD called the Kinetic Drawing System (KDS; Knoff & Prout, 1985); and the Collaborative Drawing Technique (D. K. Smith, 1985), a test that provides an occasion for family members to collaborate on the creation of a drawing—presumably all the better to "draw together."

JUST THINK . . .

How might another creative medium (such as clay modeling) be structured to supply projective information?

Like other projective techniques thought to be clinically useful, figure-drawing tests have had a rather embattled history with regard to their perceived psychometric soundness (Joiner & Schmidt, 1997). In general, the techniques are vulnerable with regard to the assumptions that drawings are essentially self-representations (Tharinger & Stark, 1990) and represent something far more than drawing ability (Swensen, 1968). Although a number of systems have been devised to score figure drawings, solid support for the validity of such approaches has been elusive (Watson et al., 1967). Experience and expertise do not necessarily correlate with greater clinical accuracy in drawing interpretation. Karen Machover (cited in Watson, 1967) herself reportedly had "grave misgivings" (p. 145) about the misuse of her test for diagnostic purposes.

To be sure, the clinical use of figure drawings has its academic defenders (Riethmiller & Handler, 1997a, 1997b). Waehler (1997), for example, cautioned that tests are not foolproof and that a person who comes across as rife with pathology in an interview might well seem benign on a psychological test. He went on to advise that figure drawings "can be considered more than 'tests'; they involve tasks that can also serve as stepping-off points for clients and examiners to discuss and clarify the picture" (p. 486).

## Projective Methods in Perspective

Used enthusiastically by many clinicians and criticized harshly by many academics, projective methods continue to occupy a rather unique habitat in the psychological landscape. Lilienfeld et al. (2000) raised serious questions regarding whether that habitat is worth maintaining. These authors focused their criticism on scoring systems for the Rorschach, the TAT, and figure drawings. They concluded that there was empirical support for only a relatively small number of Rorschach and TAT indices. They found even fewer compelling reasons to justify the continued use of figure drawings. Some of their assertions with regard to the Rorschach and the TAT—as well as the response of a projective test user and advocate, Stephen Hibbard (2003)—are presented in Table 13–4. Hibbard commented only on the Rorschach and the TAT because of his greater experience with these tests as opposed to figure drawings.

In general, critics have attacked projective methods on grounds related to the *assumptions* inherent in their use, the *situational variables* that attend their use, and several *psychometric considerations*—most notably, a paucity of data to support their reliability and validity.

**Assumptions** Bernard Murstein's (1961) criticisms regarding the basic assumptions of projectives are as relevant today as they were when they were first published decades ago. Murstein dismissed the assumption that the more ambiguous the stimuli, the more subjects reveal about their personality. For Murstein the projective stimulus is only one aspect of the "total stimulus situation." Environmental variables, response sets, reactions to the examiner, and related

> **JUST THINK . . .**
>
> Suppose a Rorschach card or a TAT card elicited much the same response from *most* people. Would that be an argument for or against the use of the card?

**Table 13–4**
**The Cons and Pros (or Cons Rebutted) of Projective Methods**

| Lilienfeld et al. (2000) on the Cons | Hibbard (2003) in Rebuttal |
|---|---|
| Projective techniques tend not to provide incremental validity above more structured measures, as is the argument of proponents of the projective hypothesis as stated by Dosajh (1996). | Lilienfeld et al. presented an outmoded caricature of projection and then proceeded to attack it. Dosajh has not published on any of the coding systems targeted for criticism. None of the authors who developed coding systems that were attacked espouse a view of projection similar to Dosajh's. Some of the criticized authors have even positioned their systems as nonprojective. |
| The norms for Exner's Comprehensive System (CS) are in error. They may overpathologize normal individuals and may even harm clients. | Evidence is inconclusive as to error in the norms. Observed discrepancies may have many explanations. Overpathologization may be a result of "drift" similar to that observed in the measurement of intelligence (Flynn effect). |
| There is limited support for the generalizability of the CS across different cultures. | More cross-cultural studies do need to be done, but the same could be said for most major tests. |
| Four studies are cited to support the deficiency of the test-retest reliability of the CS. | Only three of the four studies cited are in *refereed journals* (for which submitted manuscripts undergo critical review and may be selected or rejected for publication), and none of these three studies are bona fide test-retest reliability studies. |
| With regard to the TAT, there is no point in aggregating scores into a scale in the absence of applying internal consistency reliability criteria. | This assertion is incorrect because "each subunit of an aggregated group of predictors of a construct could be unrelated to the other, but when found in combination, they might well predict important variance in the construct" (p. 264). |
| TAT test-retest reliability estimates have been "notoriously problematic" (p. 41). | ". . . higher retest reliability would accrue to motive measures if the retest instructions permitted participants to tell stories with the same content as previously" (p. 265). |
| Various validity studies with different TAT scoring systems can be faulted on methodological grounds. | Lilienfeld et al. (2000) misinterpreted some studies they cited and did not cite other studies. For example, a number of relevant validity studies in support of Cramer's (1991) Defense Mechanism Manual coding system for the TAT were not cited. |

*Note: Interested readers are encouraged to read the full text of Lilienfeld et al. (2000) and Hibbard (2003), as the arguments made by each are far more detailed than the brief samples presented here.*

factors all contribute to response patterns. In addition, Murstein asserted that projection on the part of the assessee does not increase along with increases in the ambiguity of projective stimuli.

Another assumption inherent in projective testing concerns the supposedly idiosyncratic nature of the responses evoked by projective stimuli. In fact, similarities in the response themes of different subjects to the same stimuli suggest that the stimulus material may not be as ambiguous and amenable to projection as previously assumed. Some consideration of the stimulus properties and the ways they affect the subject's responses is therefore indicated. Also, the assumption that projection is greater onto stimulus material that is similar to the subject (in physical appearance, gender, occupation, and so on) has also been found questionable. This latter point was more recently made by one supporter of projectives and the projective hypothesis, French psychologist Benoît Verdon (whom you may recall "meeting" in Chapter 3). Verdon (2011) argued that the latent stimulus demand of projective stimuli such as inkblots and pictures superseded their manifest stimulus demand.

Now consider these assumptions inherent in projective testing:

- Every response provides meaning for personality analysis.
- A relationship exists between the strength of a need and its manifestation on projective instruments.
- Testtakers are unaware of what they are disclosing about themselves.
- A projective protocol reflects sufficient data concerning personality functioning for formulation of judgments.
- There is a parallel between behavior obtained on a projective instrument and behavior displayed in social situations.

Murstein dismissed these assumptions as "cherished beliefs" accepted "without the support of sufficient research validation" (p. 343). Still, proponents of projectives argue that the ambiguous nature of a task such as inkblot interpretation make for test results that are less subject to faking, especially "faking good." This latter assumption is evident in the writings of advocates for the use of the Rorschach in forensic applications (Gacono et al., 2008). The test's presumed utility in bypassing "volitional controls" prompted Weiss et al. (2008) to recommend it for preemployment screening of police personnel. Support for the assumption that the Rorschach test frustrates testtakers' efforts to fake good comes from a study conducted in China with college student subjects (Cai & Shen, 2007). The researchers concluded that the Rorschach was superior to the Tennessee Self-Concept Scale as a measure of self-concept because subjects were unable to manage favorable impressions.

Although studies such as these could be cited to support the use of the Rorschach as a means to lessen or negate the role of impression management in personality assessment, even that assumption remains controversial (Conti, 2007; Fahs, 2004; Ganellen, 2008; Gregg, 1998; Whittington, 1998; Yell, 2008). At the very least, it can be observed that as a measurement method, the Rorschach provides a stimulus that is less susceptible than others to socially conventional responding. It may also be useful in obtaining insights into the respondent's unique way of perceiving and organizing novel stimuli.

Another assumption underlying the use of projective tests is that something called "the unconscious" exists. Though the term *unconscious* is widely used as if its existence were a given, some academicians have questioned whether in fact the unconscious exists in the same way that, say, the liver exists. The scientific studies typically cited to support the existence of the unconscious (or, perhaps more accurately, the efficacy of the construct *unconscious*) have used a wide array of methodologies; see, for example, Diven (1937), Erdelyi (1974), Greenspoon (1955), and Razran (1961). The conclusions of each of these types of studies are subject to alternative explanations. Also subject to alternative explanation are conclusions about the existence of the unconscious based on experimental testing of predictions derived from hypnotic phenomena, from signal detection theory, and from specific personality theories (Brody, 1972). More generally, many interpretive systems for the Rorschach and other projective instruments are based on psychodynamic theory, which itself has no shortage of critics.

**Situational variables** Proponents of projective techniques have claimed that such tests are capable of illuminating the mind's recesses much like X-rays illuminate the body. Frank (1939) conceptualized projective tests as tapping personality patterns without disturbing the pattern being tapped. If that were true, then variables related to the test situation should have no effect on the data obtained. However, situational variables such as the examiner's presence or absence have significantly affected the responses of experimental subjects. For example, TAT stories written in private are likely to be less guarded, less optimistic, and more affectively involved than those written in the presence of the examiner (Bernstein, 1956). The age of the examiner is likely to affect projective protocols (Mussen & Scodel, 1955), as are the specific instructions (Henry & Rotter, 1956) and the subtle reinforcement cues provided by the examiner (Wickes, 1956).

Masling (1960) reviewed the literature on the influence of situational and interpersonal variables in projective testing and concluded that there was strong evidence for a role of situational and interpersonal influences in projection. Masling concluded that subjects utilized every available cue in the testing situation, including cues related to the actions or the appearance of the examiner. Moreover, Masling argued that examiners also relied on situational cues, in some instances over and above what they were taught. Examiners appeared to interpret projective data with regard to their own needs and expectations, their own subjective feelings about the person being tested, and their own constructions regarding the total test situation. Masling (1965) experimentally demonstrated that Rorschach examiners—through postural, gestural, and facial cues—are capable of unwittingly eliciting the responses they expect.

In any given clinical situation, many variables may be placed in the mix. The interaction of these variables may influence clinical judgments. So it is that research has suggested that even in situations involving objective (not projective) tests or simple history taking, the effect of the clinician's training (Chapman & Chapman, 1967; Fitzgibbons & Shearn, 1972) and role perspective (Snyder et al., 1976) as well as the patient's social class (Hollingshead & Redlich, 1958; Lee, 1968; Routh & King, 1972) and motivation to manage a desired impression (Edwards & Walsh, 1964; Wilcox & Krasnoff, 1967) are capable of influencing ratings of pathology (Langer & Abelson, 1974) and related conclusions (Batson, 1975). These and other variables are given wider latitude in the projective test situation, where the examiner may be at liberty to choose not only the test and extra-test data on which interpretation will be focused but also the scoring system that will be used to arrive at that interpretation.

**Psychometric considerations** The psychometric soundness of many widely used projective instruments has yet to be demonstrated. Critics of projective techniques have called attention to variables such as uncontrolled variations in protocol length, inappropriate subject samples, inadequate control groups, and poor external criteria as factors contributing to spuriously increased ratings of validity.

**JUST THINK . . .**

Projective tests have been around for a long time because of their appeal to many clinicians. Citing their advantages, argue the case that these tests should be around for a long time to come.

There are methodological obstacles in researching projectives because many test-retest or split-half methods are inappropriate. It is, to say the least, a challenge to design and execute validity studies that effectively rule out, limit, or statistically take into account all of the unique situational variables that attend the administration of such tests.

The debate between academicians who argue that projective tests are not technically sound instruments and clinicians who find such tests useful has been raging ever since projectives came into widespread use. Frank (1939) responded to those who would reject projective methods because of their lack of technical rigor:

> These leads to the study of personality have been rejected by many psychologists because they do not meet psychometric requirements for validity and reliability, but they are being employed in association with clinical and other studies of personality where they are finding increasing validation in the consistency of results for the same subject when independently assayed by each of these procedures. . . .
>
> If we face the problem of personality, in its full complexity, as an active dynamic process to be studied as a *process* rather than as entity or aggregate of traits, factors, or as static organization, then these projective methods offer many advantages for obtaining data on the process of organizing experience which is peculiar to each personality and has a life career. (Frank, 1939, p. 408; emphasis in the original)

**Objective Tests and Projective Tests: How Meaningful Is the Dichotomy?**   So-called objective tests are affected by response styles, malingering and other sources of test bias (Meyer & Kurtz, 2006). Further, testtakers may lack sufficient insight or perspective to respond "objectively" to objective test items. And as Meehl (1945) mused, so-called objective test items may, in a sense, serve as projective stimuli for some testtakers. Too, projective tests, given the vulnerability of some of their assumptions, may not be as projective as they were once thought to be. In fact, many projective tests feature scoring systems that entail rather "objective" coding (Weiner, 2005). And so the question arises: How meaningful is the objective versus projective dichotomy?

Weiner (2005) characterized the objective versus projective dichotomy as misleading. Truth in labeling is not served by characterizing one class of tests as "objective" (in the face of many questions regarding their objectivity), and another class of tests as something "other than objective." Observers might conclude that one group of tests is indeed objective, while the other group of tests must be "subjective."

As an alternative to the objective/projective dichotomy, Weiner (2005) suggested substituting the terms *structured*, in place of objective, and *unstructured*, in place of projective. The more structured a test is, the more likely it is to tap relatively conscious aspects of personality. By contrast, unstructured or ambiguous tests are more likely to access material beyond immediate, conscious awareness (Stone & Dellis, 1960; Weiner & Kuehnle, 1998). As intuitively appealing as Weiner's recommendations are, old habits die hard.

If a special section in the September–October (2011) issue of the *Journal of Personality Assessment* is any indicator, the objective versus projective dichotomy is still very much intact. The special section was devoted to articles on a new test called the Adult Attachment Projective Picture System (George & West, 2011; Webster & Joubert, 2011; Finn, 2011b; Lis et al., 2011).

Regardless what they are called, clinicians and others interested in understanding the personality of assessees use tests and other tools of assessment toward that end. This chapter's featured test user, Anthony Bram (see *Meet an Assessment Professional*)

## Meet Dr. Anthony Bram

Typically, patients are referred to me when they have not responded well to first- or second-line treatment interventions, be it medication or a certain kind of therapy. Thus, those referred for assessment tend to be more complex; something has not yet been understood about the patient through standard psychiatric interviewing or in the course of therapy. Or perhaps something has gone awry in the relationship between the patient and therapist. My role is to be a consultant to the referring clinician and/or the patient. I try to elicit their specific questions and then answer them using the test data. I rely on my knowledge of the tests, inference-making, personality theories, and empirical research to synthesize the test data in a way that will answer the questions. . . .

**Anthony Bram, Ph.D., Private Practice, Lexington, Massachusetts, and Clinical Instructor, Harvard Medical School/Cambridge Health Alliance**

The core test battery that I use is a traditional one involving a Wechsler intelligence test (WAIS-IV or WISC-IV), Rorschach, Thematic Apperception Test (TAT), and a self-report personality inventory such as the MMPI-2, MCMI-III, or PAI. I may add other tests or scales depending on the referral questions. In addition to the scores and themes derived from the tests themselves, I consider the *patient–examiner relationship* to be a crucial data source. This notion transcends the commonly stated truism that the purpose of the testing relationship is to establish 'rapport' so that the patient will give her best effort to complete the evaluation as data. I have learned that it is useful to attune to my interaction with the patient, noticing what I say or do that encourages versus impedes her collaboration, openness, and reflectiveness. Shectman and Harty (1986) have aptly described the patient-examiner relationship as a "screen test" for psychotherapy: What facilitates collaboration with the examiner will have implications for what it will take to create an alliance in psychotherapy. Given the magnitude of research evidence that the alliance is the most robust predictor of psychotherapy outcome, data from the patient-examiner

relationship can contribute to vital treatment implications (Horvath et al., 2011). In the evaluation of the adolescent referenced above, the patient-examiner relationship was essential data. I learned that encouraging curiosity and self-reflection actually shut her down and led to her dismissiveness of me and the tests. On the other hand, not taking the bait of her provocative behaviors (such as her sitting in my chair or responding sarcastically to questions), and giving her breaks and space led to her increased cooperation and openness to share with me her painful internal experience. This was extrapolated effectively to what would help overcome her difficulties establishing a therapeutic alliance (Bram, 2010).

For me, the challenge and fun of psychological assessment involves putting all of these pieces together like a puzzle. When the data from different tests converge strongly, it is a bit easier. We can be highly confident in our inferences if a person's MMPI-2 profile is elevated on scales indicating severe depression, there are many morbid percepts on the Rorschach, and TAT stories are consistently bleak. The greater challenge comes in synthesizing data that appear incongruous. Consider the example of a

*(continued)*

## Meet Dr. Anthony Bram
*(continued)*

successful businessman who was hospitalized because of severe depression including suicidal thoughts (Bram & Peebles, in preparation). After a short time on the inpatient unit, he reported that his symptoms were gone and he was ready to be discharged. At the same time, his inpatient team was perplexed because his report of symptoms disappearing seemed sudden and not in response to treatment efforts. Despite their efforts to connect with him, they were having difficulty getting to know him and, given his previous level of suicidality, were uneasy about letting him leave without a better understanding of his condition and needs. The team referred him for testing to clarify what was making it so difficult to engage him in a meaningful way. On the performance-based Rorschach and TAT, what stood out most were his powerful dependency longings. This thematic content involves passive reliance on another for caretaking. On the self-report MCMI-III, his profile was not elevated on the Dependency scale; he had not endorsed statements describing excessive needs to rely on others. How do we make sense of this discrepancy? A common mistake would be to

consider that one test was right, and the other wrong. The challenge is to synthesize the findings to capture a complex, nuanced understanding that will illuminate the referral question.

A closer look at his TAT and Rorschach content revealed that his attitude toward dependency was laden with disgust, shame, and guilt. Thus, my synthesis was that the patient had intense longings to be taken care of but that he had difficulty accepting them and thus he disavowed them on self-report. This contributed to an appreciation of how difficult it must have been for him to be in the vulnerable, dependent position of a hospital patient. He needed to convince himself and his team that was really okay and did not need anything so he could get out of there as soon as he could. With this formulation, his team was less apt to view him negatively as evasive and resistant and, instead, be more empathic with his dilemma around needing and accepting help.

*Read more of what Dr. Bram had to say— his complete essay—at www.mhhe.com/ cohentesting8.*

views using tests and other tools of assessment as a "disciplined approach to making inferences . . . about how a person is 'put together' psychologically." For him, tests are used to learn about critical psychological capacities such as logical reasoning, reality perception, social relatedness, and emotional regulation.

## Behavioral Assessment Methods

Traits, states, motives, needs, drives, defenses, and related psychological constructs have no tangible existence. They are constructs whose existence must be inferred from behavior. In the traditional approach to clinical assessment, tests as well as other tools are employed to gather data. From these data, diagnoses and inferences are made concerning the existence and strength of psychological constructs. The traditional approach to assessment might therefore be labeled a *sign* approach because test responses are deemed to be signs or clues to underlying personality or ability. In contrast to this traditional approach is an alternative philosophy of assessment that may be termed the *sample* approach. The sample approach focuses on the behavior itself. Emitted behavior is viewed not as a sign of something but rather as a sample to be interpreted in its own right.

The emphasis in **behavioral assessment** is on "what a person *does* in situations rather than on inferences about what attributes he *has* more globally" (Mischel, 1968, p. 10). Predicting what a person will do is thought to entail an understanding of the assessee with respect to both antecedent conditions and consequences of a particular situation (Smith & Iwata, 1997). Upon close scrutiny, however, the trait concept is still present in many behavioral measures, though more narrowly defined and more closely linked to specific situations (Zuckerman, 1979).

To illustrate behavioral observation as an assessment strategy, consider the plight of the single female client who presents herself at the university counseling center. She complains that even though all her friends tell her how attractive she is, she has great difficulty meeting men—so much so that she doesn't even want to try anymore. A counselor confronted with such a client might, among other things, (1) interview the client about this problem, (2) administer an appropriate test to the client, (3) ask the client to keep a detailed diary of her thoughts and behaviors related to various aspects of her efforts to meet men, including her expectations, and (4) accompany the client on a typical night out to a singles bar or similar venue and observe her behavior. The latter two strategies come under the heading of behavioral observation. With regard to the diary, the client is engaging in self-observation. In the scenario of the night out, the counselor is doing the actual observation.

The more traditional administration of a psychological test or test battery to a client such as this single woman might yield signs that then could be inferred to relate to the problem. For example, if a number of the client's TAT stories involved themes of demeaning, hostile, or otherwise unsatisfactory heterosexual encounters as a result of venturing out into the street, a counselor might make an interpretation at a deeper or second level of inference. For example, a counselor, especially one with a psychoanalytic orientation, might reach a conclusion something like this:

> The client's expressed fear of going outdoors, and ultimately her fear of meeting men, might in some way be related to an unconscious fear of promiscuity—a fear of becoming a streetwalker.

Such a conclusion in turn would have implications for treatment. Many hours of treatment might be devoted to uncovering the "real" fear so that it is apparent to the client herself and ultimately dealt with effectively.

In contrast to the sign approach, the clinician employing the sample or behavioral approach to assessment might examine the behavioral diary that the client kept and design an appropriate therapy program on the basis of those records. Thus, for example, the antecedent conditions under which the client would feel most distraught and unmotivated to do anything about the problem might be delineated and worked on in counseling sessions.

An advantage of the sign approach over the sample approach is that—in the hands of a skillful, perceptive clinician—the client might be put in touch with feelings that even she was not really aware of before the assessment. The client may have been consciously (or unconsciously) avoiding certain thoughts and images (those attendant on the expression of her sexuality, for example), and this inability to deal with those thoughts and images may indeed have been a factor contributing to her ambivalence about meeting men.

Behavioral assessors seldom make such deeper-level inferences. For example, if sexuality is not raised as an area of difficulty by the client (in an interview, a diary, a checklist, or by some other behavioral assessment technique), this problem area may well be ignored or given short shrift. Behavioral assessors do, however, tend to be more empirical in their approach, as they systematically assess the client's presenting problem both from the perspective of the client and from the perspective of one observing the client in social situations and the environment in general. The behavioral assessor does not search the Rorschach or other protocols for clues to treatment. Rather, the behaviorally oriented counselor or clinician relies much more on what the client *does* and *has done* for guideposts to treatment. In a sense, the behavioral approach does not require as much clinical creativity as the sign approach. Perhaps for that reason, the behavioral approach may be considered less an art than a science (at least as compared to some other clinical approaches). It is certainly science-based in that it relies on relatively precise methods of proven validity (Haynes & Kaholokula, 2008).

Early on, the shift away from traditional psychological tests by behaviorally oriented clinicians compelled some to call for a way to integrate such tests in behavioral evaluations. This view is typified by the wish that "psychological tests should be able to provide the behavior therapist with information that should be of value in doing behavior therapy. This contention is based on the assumption that the behavior on any psychological test should be lawful" (Greenspoon & Gersten, 1967, p. 849). Accordingly, psychological tests could be useful, for example, in helping the behavior therapist identify the kinds of contingent stimuli that would be most effective with a given patient. For example, patients with high percentages of color or color/form responses on the Rorschach and with IQs over 90 might be most responsive to positive verbal contingencies (such as *good, excellent,* and so forth). By contrast, patients with high percentages of movement or vista (three-dimensional) responses on the Rorschach and IQs over 90 might be most responsive to negative verbal contingencies (such as *no* or *wrong*). Such innovative efforts to narrow a widening schism in the field of clinical assessment have failed to ignite experimental enthusiasm, perhaps because more direct ways exist to assess responsiveness to various contingencies.

JUST THINK . . .

Is there a way to integrate traditional psychological testing and assessment and behavioral assessment?

Differences between traditional and behavioral approaches to assessment have to do with varying assumptions about the nature of personality and the causes of behavior. The data from traditional assessment are used primarily to describe, classify, or diagnose, whereas the data from a behavioral assessment are typically more directly related to the formulation of a specific treatment program. Some of the other differences between the two approaches are summarized in Table 13–5.

## The Who, What, When, Where, Why, and How of It

The name says it all: *Behavior* is the focus of assessment in behavioral assessment—not traits, states, or other constructs presumed to be present in various strengths—just behavior. This will become clear as we survey the *who, what, when, where, why,* and *how* of behavioral assessment.

**Who?**   *Who* is the assessee? The person being assessed may be, for example, a patient on a closed psychiatric ward, a client seeking help at a counseling center, or a subject in an academic experiment. Regardless of whether the assessment is for research, clinical, or other purposes, the hallmark of behavioral assessment is the intensive study of individuals.

**Table 13-5**
**Differences Between Behavioral and Traditional Approaches to Psychological Assessment**

| | Behavioral | Traditional |
|---|---|---|
| *Assumptions* | | |
| Conception of personality | Personality constructs mainly employed to summarize specific behavior patterns, if at all | Personality as a reflection of enduring, underlying states or traits |
| Causes of behavior | Maintaining conditions sought in current environment | Intrapsychic, or within the individual |
| *Implications* | | |
| Role of behavior | Important as a sample of person's repertoire in a specific situation | Behavior assumes importance only insofar as it indexes underlying causes |
| Role of history | Relatively unimportant except, for example, to provide a retrospective baseline | Crucial in that present conditions seen as products of the past |
| Consistency of behavior | Behavior thought to be specific to the situation | Behavior expected to be consistent across time and settings |
| *Uses of data* | To describe target behaviors and maintain conditions<br>To select the appropriate treatment<br>To evaluate and revise treatment | To describe personality functioning and etiology<br>To diagnose or classify<br>To make prognosis; to predict |
| *Other characteristics* | | |
| Level of inferences | Low | Medium to high |
| Comparisons | More emphasis on intraindividual or idiographic | More emphasis on interindividual or nomothetic |
| Methods of assessment | More emphasis on direct methods (e.g., observations of behavior in natural environment) | More emphasis on indirect methods (e.g., interviews and self-report) |
| Timing of assessment | More ongoing; prior, during, and after treatment | Pre- and perhaps posttreatment, or strictly to diagnose |
| Scope of assessment | Specific measures and of more variables (e.g., of target behaviors in various situations, of side effects, context, strengths as well as deficiencies) | More global measures (e.g., of cure, or improvement) but only of the individual |

Source: Hartmann et al. (1979).

This is in contrast to mass testing of groups of people to obtain normative data with respect to some hypothesized trait or state.

*Who* is the assessor? Depending on the circumstances, the assessor may be a highly qualified professional or a technician/assistant trained to conduct a particular assessment. Technicians are frequently employed to record the number of times a targeted behavior is exhibited. In this context, the assessor may also be a classroom teacher recording, for example, the number of times a child leaves her or his seat. An assessor in behavioral assessment may also be the assessee. Assessees are frequently directed to maintain behavioral diaries, complete behavioral checklists, or engage in other activities designed to monitor their own behavior.

**What?** *What* is measured in behavioral assessment? Perhaps not surprisingly, the behavior or behaviors targeted for assessment will vary as a function of the objectives of the assessment. What constitutes a targeted behavior will typically be described in sufficient detail prior to any assessment. For the purposes of assessment, the targeted behavior must be measurable—that is, quantifiable in some way. Examples of such measurable behaviors can range from the number of seconds elapsed before a child calls out in class to the number of degrees body temperature is altered. Note that descriptions of targeted behaviors in behavioral assessment typically begin with the phrase *the number of*. In studies that focus on physiological variables such as muscle tension or autonomic responding, special equipment is required to obtain the behavioral measurements.

**When?** *When* is an assessment of behavior made? One response to this question is that assessment of behavior is typically made at times when the problem behavior is most likely to be elicited. So, for example, if a pupil is most likely to get into verbal and physical altercations during lunch, a behavioral assessor would focus on lunch hour as a time to assess behavior.

Another way to address the *when* question has to do with the various schedules with which behavioral assessments may be made. For example, one schedule of assessment is referred to as *frequency* or *event recording*. Each time the targeted behavior occurs, it is recorded. Another schedule of assessment is referred to as *interval recording*. Assessment according to this schedule occurs only during predefined intervals of time (for example, every other minute, every 48 hours, every third week). Beyond merely tallying the number of times a particular behavior occurs, the assessor may also maintain a record of the *intensity* of the behavior. Intensity of a behavior may be gauged by observable and quantifiable events such as the *duration* of the behavior, stated in number of seconds, minutes, hours, days, weeks, months, or years. Alternatively, it may be stated in terms of some ratio or percentage of time that the behavior occurs during a specified interval of time. One method of recording the frequency and intensity of target behavior is **timeline followback (TLFB) methodology** (Sobell & Sobell, 1992, 2000). TLFB was originally designed for use in the context of a clinical interview for the purpose of assessing alcohol abuse. Respondents were presented with a specific calendar time period and asked to recall aspects of their drinking. A feature of TLFB is that respondents are prompted with memory aids (such as memorable dates including birthdays, holidays, events in the news, and events of personal importance) to assist in recall of the targeted behavior during the defined timeline. From the recalled information, patterns regarding the targeted behavior (such as substance abuse versus abstinence) emerge. The technique may be particularly useful in identifying antecedent stimuli that cue the undesired behavior. The method has been used to evaluate problem behaviors as diverse as gambling (Weinstock et al., 2004; Weinstock, Ledgerwood, & Petry, 2007; Weinstock, Whelan, et al., 2007), maternal smoking (Stroud et al., 2009), HIV risk behaviors (Copersino et al., 2010), and alcohol/medication (Garnier et al., 2009), though its utility will vary by situation (Shiffman, 2009). Another assessment methodology entails recording problem behavior-related events (such as drinking, smoking, and so forth) not retrospectively, but as they occur. This is accomplished by means of a handheld computer used to maintain an electronic diary of behavior. Referred to as **ecological momentary assessment,** this methodology was used to analyze the immediate antecedents of cigarette smoking (Shiffman et al., 2002).

**JUST THINK . . .**

You are a behavior therapist who has a client who is a compulsive gambler. You advise the client to keep a record of his behavior. Do you advise that this self-monitoring be kept on a frequency basis or an interval schedule? Why?

**Where?** *Where* does the assessment take place? In contrast to the administration of psychological tests, behavioral assessment may take place just about anywhere—preferably in the environment where the targeted behavior is most likely to occur naturally. For example, a behavioral assessor studying the obsessive-compulsive habits of a patient might wish to visit the patient at home to see firsthand the variety and intensity of the behaviors exhibited. Does the patient check the oven for gas left on, for example? If so, how many times per hour? Does the patient engage in excessive hand-washing? If so, to what extent? These and related questions may be raised and answered effectively through firsthand observation in the patient's home. In some instances, when virtual reality is deemed preferable to reality, the assessment may involve stimuli created in a laboratory setting, rather than a "real life" setting (see, for example, Bordnick et al., 2008).

**Why?**   *Why* conduct behavioral assessment? In general, data derived from behavioral assessment may have several advantages over data derived by other means. Data derived from behavioral assessment can be used:

- to provide behavioral baseline data with which other behavioral data (accumulated after the passage of time, after intervention, or after some other event) may be compared
- to provide a record of the assessee's behavioral strengths and weaknesses across a variety of situations
- to pinpoint environmental conditions that are acting to trigger, maintain, or extinguish certain behaviors
- to target specific behavioral patterns for modification through interventions
- to create graphic displays useful in stimulating innovative or more effective treatment approaches

In the era of managed care and frugal third-party payers, let's also note that insurance companies tend to favor behavioral assessments over more traditional assessments. This is because behavioral assessment is typically not linked to any particular theory of personality, and patient progress tends to be gauged on the basis of documented behavioral events.

**How?**   *How* is behavioral assessment conducted? The answer to this question will vary, of course, according to the purpose of the assessment. In some situations, the only special equipment required will be a trained observer with pad and pencil. In other types of situations, highly sophisticated recording equipment may be necessary.

Another key *how* question relates to the analysis of data from behavioral assessment. The extent to which traditional psychometric standards are deemed applicable to behavioral assessment is a controversial issue, with two opposing camps. One camp may be characterized as accepting traditional psychometric assumptions about behavioral assessment, including assumptions about the measurement of reliability (Russo et al., 1980) and validity (Haynes, Follingstad, & Sullivan, 1979; Haynes et al., 1981). Representative of this position are statements such as that made by Bellack and Hersen (1988) that "the reliability, validity, and utility of any procedure should be paramount, regardless of its behavioral or nonbehavioral development" (p. 614).

> **JUST THINK . . .**
>
> Imagine that you are a NASA psychologist studying the psychological and behavioral effects of space travel on astronauts. What types of behavioral measures might you employ, and what special equipment would you need—or design—to obtain those measures?

Cone (1977) championed the traditionalist approach to behavioral assessment in an article entitled "The Relevance of Reliability and Validity for Behavioral Assessment." However, as the years passed, Cone (1986, 1987) would become a leading proponent of an alternative position, one in which traditional psychometric standards are rejected as inappropriate yardsticks for behavioral assessment. Cone (1981) wrote, for example, that "a truly behavioral view of assessment is based on an approach to the study of behavior so radically different from the customary individual differences model that a correspondingly different approach must be taken in evaluating the adequacy of behavioral assessment procedures" (p. 51).

> **JUST THINK . . .**
>
> Do traditional psychometric standards apply to behavioral assessment?

Others, too, have questioned the utility of traditional approaches to test reliability in behavioral assessment, noting that "the assessment tool may be precise, but the behavior being measured may have changed" (Nelson et al., 1977, p. 428). Based on the conceptualization of each behavioral assessment as an experiment unto itself, Dickson (1975) wrote: "If one assumes that each target for assessment represents a single experiment, then what is needed is the scientific method of experimentation and research, rather than a formalized schedule for assessment. . . . Within this framework, each situation is seen as unique, and the reliability of the approach is not a function of standardization techniques . . . but rather is a function of following the experimental method in evaluation" (pp. 376–377).

## Varieties of Behavioral Assessment

Behavioral assessment may be accomplished through various means, including behavioral observation and behavior rating scales, analogue studies, self-monitoring, and situational performance methods. Let's briefly take a closer look at each of these as well as related methods.

**Behavioral observation and rating scales**    *A child psychologist observes a client in a playroom through a one-way mirror. A family therapist views a videotape of a troubled family attempting to resolve a conflict. A school psychologist observes a child interacting with peers in the school cafeteria.* These are all examples of the use of an assessment technique termed **behavioral observation.** As its name implies, this technique involves watching the activities of targeted clients or research subjects and, typically, maintaining some kind of record of those activities. Researchers, clinicians, or counselors may themselves serve as observers, or they may designate trained assistants or other people (such as parents, siblings, teachers, and supervisors) as the observers. Even the observed person can be the behavior observer, although in such cases the term *self-observation* is more appropriate than *behavioral observation.*

In some instances, behavioral observation employs mechanical means, such as a video recording of an event. Recording behavioral events relieves the clinician, the researcher, or any other observer of the need to be physically present when the behavior occurs and allows for detailed analysis of it at a more convenient time. Factors noted in behavioral observation will typically include the presence or absence of specific, targeted behaviors, behavioral excesses, behavioral deficits, behavioral assets, and the situational antecedents and consequences of the observed behaviors. Of course, because the people doing the observing and rating are human themselves, behavioral observation isn't always as cut and dried as it may appear (see this chapter's *Everyday Psychometrics*).

Behavioral observation may take many forms. The observer may, in the tradition of the naturalist, record a running narrative of events using tools such as pencil and paper, a video, film, or still camera, or a cassette recorder. Mehl and Pennebaker (2003), for example, used such a naturalistic approach in their study of student social life. They tracked the conversations of 52 undergraduates across two two-day periods by means of a computerized recorder.

Another form of behavioral observation employs what is called a *behavior rating scale*—a preprinted sheet on which the observer notes the presence or intensity of targeted behaviors, usually by checking boxes or filling in coded terms. Sometimes the user of a behavior rating form writes in coded descriptions of various behaviors. The code is preferable to a running narrative because it takes far less time to enter the data and thus frees the observer to enter data relating to any of hundreds of possible

## Confessions of a Behavior Rater

In discussions of behavioral assessment, the focus is often placed squarely on the individual being evaluated. Only infrequently, if ever, is reference made to the thoughts and feelings of the person responsible for evaluating the behavior of another. What follows are the hypothetical thoughts of one behavior rater. We say hypothetical because these ideas are not really one person's thoughts but instead a compilation of thoughts of many people responsible for conducting behavioral evaluations.

The behavior raters interviewed for this feature were all on the staff at a community-based inpatient/outpatient facility in Brewster, New York. One objective of this facility is to prepare its adolescent and adult members for a constructive, independent life. Members live in residences with varying degrees of supervision, and their behavior is monitored on a 24-hour basis. Each day, members are issued an eight-page behavior rating sheet referred to as a CDR (clinical data recorder), which is circulated to supervising staff for rating through the course of the day. The staff records behavioral information on variables such as activities, social skills, support needed, and dysfunctional behavior.

On the basis of behavioral data, certain medical or other interventions may be recommended. Because behavioral monitoring is daily and consistent, changes in patient behavior as a function of medication, activities, or other variables are quickly noted and intervention strategies adjusted. In short, the behavioral data may significantly affect the course of a patient's institutional stay—everything from amount of daily supervision to privileges to date of discharge is influenced by the behavioral data. Both patients and staff are aware of this fact of institutional life; therefore, both patients and staff take the completion of the CDR very seriously. With that as background, here are some private thoughts of a behavior rater.

I record behavioral data in the presence of patients, and the patients are usually keenly aware of what I am doing. After I am through coding patients' CDRs for the time they are with me, other staff members will code them with respect to the time they spend with the patient. And so it goes. It is as if each patient is keeping a detailed diary of his or her life; only, it is we, the staff, who are keeping that diary for them.

Sometimes, especially for new staff, it feels odd to be rating the behavior of fellow human beings. One morning, perhaps out of empathy for a patient, I tossed a blank CDR to a patient and

*A member receives training in kitchen skills for independent living as a staff member monitors behavior.*

jokingly offered to let him rate my behavior. By dinner, long after I had forgotten that incident in the morning, I realized the patient was coding me for poor table manners. Outwardly, I laughed. Inwardly, I was really a bit offended. Subsequently, I told a joke to the assembled company that in retrospect probably was not in the best of taste. The patient coded me for being socially offensive. Now, I was genuinely becoming self-conscious. Later that evening, we drove to a local video store to return a tape we had rented, and the patient coded me for reckless driving. My discomfort level rose to the point where I thought it was time to end the joke. In retrospect, I had experienced firsthand the self-consciousness and discomfort some of our patients had experienced as their every move was monitored on a daily basis by staff members.

Even though patients are not always comfortable having their behavior rated—and indeed many patients have outbursts with

*(continued)*

## Confessions of a Behavior Rater
*(continued)*

staff members that are in one way or another related to the rating system—it is also true that the system seems to work. Sometimes, self-consciousness is what is needed for people to get better. Here, I think of Sandy, a bright young man who gradually became fascinated by the CDR and soon spent much of the day asking staff members various questions about it. Before long, Sandy asked if he could be allowed to code his own CDR. No one had ever asked to do that before, and a staff meeting was held to mull over the consequences of such an action. As an experiment, it was decided that this patient would be allowed to code his own CDR. The experiment paid off. Sandy's self-coding kept him relatively "on track" with regard

to his behavioral goals, and he found himself trying even harder to get better as he showed signs of improvement. Upon discharge, Sandy said he would miss tracking his progress with the CDR.

Instruments such as the CDR can and probably have been used as weapons or rewards by staff. Staff may threaten patients with a poor behavioral evaluation. Overly negative evaluations in response to dysfunctional behavior that is particularly upsetting to the staff is also an ever-present possibility. Yet all the time you are keenly aware that the system works best when staff code patients' behavior consistently and fairly.

behaviors, not just the ones printed on the sheets. For example, a number of coding systems for observing the behavior of couples and families are available. Two such systems are the Marital Interaction Coding System (Weiss & Summers, 1983) and the Couples Interaction Scoring System (Notarius & Markman, 1981). Handheld data-entry devices are frequently used today to facilitate the work of the observer.

Behavior rating scales and systems may be categorized in different ways. A continuum of *direct* to *indirect* applies to the setting in which the observed behavior occurs and how closely that setting approximates the setting in which the behavior naturally occurs. The more natural the setting, the more direct the measure; the more removed from the natural setting, the less direct the measure (Shapiro & Skinner, 1990). According to this categorization, for example, assessing a firefighter's actions and reactions while fighting a real fire would provide a *direct* measure of firefighting ability. Assessing a firefighter's actions and reactions while fighting a simulated fire would provide a less direct (or more *indirect*) measure of firefighting ability. Still further down the direct-to-indirect continuum would be verbally asking the firefighter about how he or she might react to hypothetical situations that could occur during a fire. Shapiro and Skinner (1990) also distinguished between *broad-band instruments*, designed to measure a wide variety of behaviors, and *narrow-band instruments*, which may focus on behaviors related to single, specific constructs. A broad-band instrument might measure, for example, general firefighter ability, while a narrow-band instrument might measure proficiency in one particular aspect of those abilities, such as proficiency in administering cardiopulmonary resuscitation (CPR).

**Self-monitoring** Self-monitoring may be defined as the act of systematically observing and recording aspects of one's own behavior and/or events related to that behavior. Self-monitoring is different from self-report. As noted by Cone (1999, p. 411), self-monitoring

> relies on observations of *the* behavior of clinical interest . . . at the *time* . . . and *place* . . . of its actual occurrence. In contrast, self-report uses stand-ins or surrogates (verbal descriptions, reports) of the behavior of interest that are obtained at a time and place different from the time and place of the behavior's actual occurrence. (emphasis in the original)

Self-monitoring may be used to record specific thoughts, feelings, or behaviors. The utility of self-monitoring depends in large part on the competence, diligence, and motivation of the assessee, although a number of ingenious methods have been devised to assist in the process or to ensure compliance (Barton et al., 1999; Bornstein et al., 1986; Wilson & Vitousek, 1999). For example, just as you may hear a signal in a car if you fail to buckle your seatbelt, handheld computers have been programmed to beep as a cue to observe and record behavior (Shiffman et al., 1997).

Self-monitoring is both a tool of assessment and a tool of intervention. In some instances, the very act of self-monitoring (of smoking, eating, anxiety, and panic, for example) may be therapeutic. Practical issues that must be considered include the methodology employed, the targeting of specific thoughts, feelings, or behaviors, the sampling procedures put in place, the actual self-monitoring devices and procedures, and the training and preparation (Foster et al., 1999).

Any discussion of behavioral assessment, and particularly self-monitoring, would be incomplete without mention of the psychometric issue of *reactivity* (Jackson, 1999). **Reactivity** refers to the possible changes in an assessee's behavior, thinking, or performance that may arise in response to being observed, assessed, or evaluated. For example, if you are on a weight-loss program and are self-monitoring your food intake, you may be more inclined to forgo the cheesecake than to consume it. In this case, reactivity has a positive effect on the assessee's behavior. There are many instances in which reactivity may have a negative effect on an assessee's behavior or performance. For example, we have previously noted how the presence of third parties during an evaluation may adversely effect an assessee's performance on tasks that require memory or attention (Gavett et al., 2005). Education, training, and adequate preparation are some of the tools used to counter the effects of reactivity in self-monitoring. In addition, post-self-monitoring interviews on the effects of reactivity can provide additional insights about the occurrence of the targeted thoughts or behaviors as well as any reactivity effects.

> **JUST THINK . . .**
>
> Create an original example to illustrate how self-monitoring can be a tool of assessment as well as an intervention.

**Analogue studies** The behavioral approach to clinical assessment and treatment has been likened to a researcher's approach to experimentation. The behavioral assessor proceeds in many ways like a researcher; the client's problem is the dependent variable, and the factor (or factors) responsible for causing or maintaining the problem behavior is the independent variable. Behavioral assessors may use the phrase *functional analysis of behavior* to convey the process of identifying the dependent and independent variables with respect to the presenting problem. However, just as experimenters must frequently employ independent and dependent variables that imitate those variables in the real world, so must behavioral assessors.

An **analogue study** is a research investigation in which one or more variables are similar or analogous to the real variable that the investigator wishes to examine. This definition is admittedly very broad, and the term *analogue study* has been used in various ways. It has been used, for example, to describe research conducted with white rats when the experimenter really wishes to learn about humans. It has been used to describe research conducted with full-time students when the experimenter really wishes to learn about people employed full-time in business settings. It has been used to describe research on aggression defined as the laboratory administration of electric shock when the experimenter really wishes to learn about real-world aggression outside the laboratory.

More specific than the term *analogue study* is **analogue behavioral observation,** which, after Haynes (2001b), may be defined as the observation of a person or persons in an environment designed to increase the chance that the assessor can observe targeted behaviors and interactions. The person or persons in this definition may be clients (including individual children and adults, families, or couples) or research subjects (including students, co-workers, or any other research sample). The targeted behavior, of course, depends on the objective of the research. For a client who avoids hiking because of a fear of snakes, the behavior targeted for assessment (and change) is the fear reaction to snakes, most typically elicited while hiking. This behavior may be assessed (and treated) in analogue fashion within the confines of a clinician's office, using a backdrop of a scene that might be encountered while hiking, photos of snakes, videos of snakes, live snakes that are caged, and live snakes that are not caged.

**JUST THINK . . .**

As a result of a car accident, a client of a behavior therapist claims not to be able to get into a car and drive again. The therapist wishes to assess this complaint by means of analogue behavioral observation. How should the therapist proceed?

A variety of environments have been designed to increase the assessor's chances of observing the targeted behavior (see, for example, Heyman, 2001; Mori & Armendariz, 2001; Norton & Hope, 2001; and Roberts, 2001). Questions about how analogous some analogue studies really are have been raised, along with questions regarding their ultimate utility (Haynes, 2001a).

Situational performance measures and role-play measures both may be thought of as analogue approaches to assessment. Let's take a closer look at each.

**Situational performance measures**  If you have ever applied for a part-time clerical job and been required to take a word processing test, you have had firsthand experience with *situational performance measures.* Broadly stated, a **situational performance measure** is a procedure that allows for observation and evaluation of an individual under a standard set of circumstances. A situational performance measure typically involves performance of some specific task under actual or simulated conditions. The road test you took to obtain your driver's license was a situational performance measure that involved an evaluation of your driving skills in a real car on a real road in real traffic. On the other hand, situational performance measures used to assess the skills of prospective space-traveling astronauts are done in rocket simulators in laboratories firmly planted on Mother Earth. Common to all situational performance measures is that the construct they measure is thought to be more accurately assessed by examining behavior directly than by asking subjects to describe their behavior. If simply asked about how they would perform, some respondents may be motivated to misrepresent themselves to manage a more favorable impression. Also, it is very possible that the respondents really do not know how they will perform under particular circumstances. Verbal speculation about how one would perform under particular circumstances, particularly high stress circumstances, is often quite different than what actually occurs.

The **leaderless group technique** is a situational assessment procedure wherein several people are organized into a group for the purpose of carrying out a task as an observer records information related to individual group members' initiative, cooperation, leadership, and related variables. Usually, all group members know they are being evaluated and that their behavior is being observed and recorded. Purposely vague instructions are typically provided to the group, and no one is placed in the position of leadership or authority. The group determines how it will accomplish the task and who will be responsible for what duties. The leaderless group situation provides an opportunity to observe the degree of cooperation exhibited by each individual group member and the extent to which each is able to function as part of a team.

The leaderless group technique has been employed in military and industrial settings. Its use in the military developed out of attempts by the U.S. Office of Strategic Services (OSS Assessment Staff, 1948) to assess leadership as well as other personality traits. The procedure was designed to aid in the establishment of cohesive military units—cockpit crews, tank crews, and so forth—in which members would work together well and could each make a significant contribution. Similarly, the procedure is used in industrial and organizational settings to identify people who work well together and those with superior managerial skills and "executive potential."

The self-managed work-group approach challenges traditional conceptions of manager and worker. How does one manage a group that is supposed to manage itself? One approach is to try to identify *unleaders,* who act primarily as facilitators in the workplace and are able to balance a hands-off management style with a style that is more directive when necessary (Manz & Sims, 1984).

**JUST THINK . . .**

You are a management consultant to a major corporation with an assignment: Create a situational performance measure designed to identify an *unleader.* Briefly outline your plan.

**Role play**    The technique of **role play,** or acting an improvised or partially improvised part in a simulated situation, can be used in teaching, therapy, and assessment. Police departments, for example, routinely prepare rookies for emergencies by having them play roles, such as an officer confronted by a criminal holding a hostage at gunpoint. Part of the prospective police officer's final exam may be successful performance on a role-playing task. A therapist might use role play to help a feuding couple avoid harmful shouting matches and learn more effective methods of conflict resolution. That same couple's successful resolution of role-played issues may be one of a therapist's criteria for terminating therapy.

A large and growing literature exists on role play as a method of assessment. In general, role play can provide a relatively inexpensive and highly adaptable means of assessing various behavior "potentials." We cautiously say "potentials" because of the uncertainty that role-played behavior will then be elicited in a naturalistic situation (Kern et al., 1983; Kolotkin & Wielkiewicz, 1984). Bellack et al. (1990) employed role play for both evaluative and instructional purposes with psychiatric inpatients who were being prepared for independent living. While acknowledging the benefits of role play in assessing patients' readiness to return to the community, these authors cautioned that "the ultimate validity criterion for any laboratory- or clinic-based assessment is unobtrusive observation of the target behavior in the community" (p. 253).

**JUST THINK . . .**

Describe a referral for evaluation that would ideally lend itself to the use of role play as a tool of assessment.

**Psychophysiological methods**    The search for clues to understanding and predicting human behavior has led researchers to the study of physiological indices such as heart rate and blood pressure. These and other indices are known to be influenced by psychological factors—hence the term **psychophysiological** to describe these variables as well as the methods used to study them. Whether these methods are properly regarded as *behavioral* in nature is debatable. Still, these techniques do tend to be associated with behaviorally oriented clinicians and researchers.

Perhaps the best known of all psychophysiological methods used by psychologists is *biofeedback.* **Biofeedback** is a generic term that may be defined broadly as a class of psychophysiological assessment techniques designed to gauge, display, and record a continuous monitoring of selected biological processes such as pulse and blood pressure.

Depending on how biofeedback instrumentation is designed, many different biological processes—such as heart rate, respiration rate, muscle tone, electrical resistance of the skin, and brain waves—may be monitored and "fed back" to the assessee via visual displays, such as lights and scales, or auditory stimuli, such as bells and buzzers. Perhaps the variety of biofeedback most familiar to students is the electrocardiogram. You may have heard this measure of heart rate referred to in physicians' offices as an "EKG." Less familiar may be varieties of biofeedback that measure brainwaves (the electroencephalogram or EEG), and muscle tone (the electromyogram or EMG).

The use of biofeedback with humans was inspired by reports that animals given rewards (and hence feedback) for exhibiting certain involuntary responses (such as heart rate) could successfully modify those responses (Miller, 1969). Early experimentation with humans demonstrated a capacity to produce certain types of brain waves on command (Kamiya, 1962, 1968). Since that time, different varieties of biofeedback have been experimented with in a wide range of therapeutic and assessment-related applications (Forbes et al., 2011; French et al., 1997; Hazlett et al., 1997; Henriques et al., 2011; Hermann et al., 1997; Lofthouse et al., 2011; Zhang et al., 1997; see Figure 13–10).

The **plethysmograph** is a biofeedback instrument that records changes in the volume of a part of the body arising from variations in blood supply. Investigators have used this device to explore changes in blood flow as a dependent variable. For example, Kelly (1966) found significant differences in the blood supplies of normal, anxiety-ridden, and psychoneurotic groups (the anxiety group having the highest mean) by using a plethysmograph to measure blood supply in the forearm.

A **penile plethysmograph** is also an instrument designed to measure changes in blood flow, but more specifically blood flow to the penis. Because the volume of blood in the penis increases with male sexual arousal, the penile plethysmograph has found application in the assessment of adolescent and adult male sexual offenders (Clift et al., 2009; Lanyon & Thomas, 2008). In one study, subjects who were convicted rapists demonstrated more sexual arousal to descriptions of rape and less arousal to consenting-sex stories than did control subjects (Quinsey et al., 1984). Offenders who continue to deny deviant sexual object choices may be confronted with **phallometric data** (the record from a study conducted with a penile plethysmograph) as a means of compelling them to speak more openly about their thoughts and behavior (Abel et al., 1986). Phallometric data also has treatment and program evaluation applications. In one such type of application, the offender—a rapist, a child molester, an exhibitionist, or some other sexual offender—is exposed to visual and/or auditory stimuli depicting scenes of normal and deviant behavior while penile tumescence is simultaneously gauged. Analysis of phallometric data is then used to evaluate improvement as a result of intervention.

In the public eye, the best-known of all psychophysiological measurement tools is what is commonly referred to as a *lie detector* or **polygraph** (literally, "more than one graph"). Although not commonly associated with psychological assessment, the lie detection industry has been characterized as "one of the most important branches of applied psychology" (Lykken, 1981, p. 4). This is especially true today, given the frequency with which such tests are administered, as well as the potential consequences as a result of such tests.

Based on the assumption that detectable physical changes occur when an individual lies, the polygraph provides a continuous written record (variously referred to as a *tracing,* a *graph,* a *chart,* or a *polygram*) of several physiological indices (typically respiration, galvanic skin response, and blood volume/pulse rate) as an interviewer and instrument operator (known as a *polygrapher* or *polygraphist*) asks the

**Figure 13–10**
**What Emotion Would You Like to Experience Today?**

*A document dated June 7, 2011, filed in the United States Patent and Trademark Office, claimed that a newly invented biofeedback device can "accurately induce an emotion desired by a user." Lee, Goudarzi, et al.'s (2011) apparatus outputs biofeedback to the user consistent with the emotional state that the user would like to be in. At this writing, there has been no independent validation of these claims. However, if this device really works as claimed, how might it be used in clinical assessment and practice?*

assessee a series of yes–no questions. Judgments of the truthfulness of the responses are made either informally by surveying the charts or more formally by means of a scoring system.

**JUST THINK . . .**

Polygraph evidence is not admissible in most courts, yet law enforcement agencies and the military continue to use it as a tool of evaluation. Your thoughts?

The reliability of judgments made by polygraphers has long been, and today remains, a matter of great controversy (Alpher & Blanton, 1985; Iacono & Lykken, 1997). Different methods of conducting polygraphic examinations exist (Lykken, 1981), and polygraphic equipment is not standardized (Abrams, 1977; Skolnick, 1961). A problem with the method is a high false-positive rate for lying. The procedure "may label more than 50% of the innocent subjects as guilty" (Kleinmuntz & Szucko, 1984, p. 774). In light of the judgments that polygraphers are called upon to make, their education, training, and background requirements seem minimal. One may qualify as a polygrapher after as few as six weeks of training. From the available psychometric and related data, it seems reasonable to conclude that the promise of a machine purporting to detect dishonesty remains unfulfilled.

**Unobtrusive measures**   A type of measure quite different from any we have discussed so far is the *nonreactive* or *unobtrusive* variety (Webb et al., 1966). In many instances, an **unobtrusive measure** is a telling physical trace or record. In one study, it was garbage—literally (Cote et al., 1985). Because of their nature, unobtrusive measures do not necessarily require the presence or cooperation of respondents when measurements are being conducted.

In a now-classic book that was almost entitled *The Bullfighter's Beard*,[8] Webb et al. (1966) listed numerous examples of unobtrusive measures, including the following:

- The popularity of a museum exhibit can be measured by examination of the erosion of the floor around it relative to the erosion around other exhibits.
- The amount of whiskey consumption in a town can be measured by counting the number of empty bottles in trashcans.
- The degree of fear induced by session of telling ghost stories can be measured by noting the shrinking diameter of a circle of seated children.

**JUST THINK . . .**

Webb et al. (1966) argued that unobtrusive measures can usefully complement other research techniques such as interviews and questionnaires. What unobtrusive measure could conceivably be used to complement a questionnaire on student study habits?

One team of researchers used wrappers left on trays at fast-food restaurants to estimate the caloric intake of restaurant patrons (Stice et al., 2004). These researchers had hoped to expand their study by developing a comparably unobtrusive way to gather information on caloric intake in the home. However, they were unable to devise any ethically acceptable way to so. In another innovative use of a "telling record," researchers used college yearbook photos to study the relationship between positive emotional expression and other variables, such as personality and life outcome (see this chapter's *Close-Up*).

## Issues in Behavioral Assessment

The psychometric soundness of tools of behavioral assessment can be evaluated, but how best to do that is debatable. More specifically, questions arise about the appropriateness of various models of measurement. You may recall that classical test theory and generalizability theory conceptualize test-score variation in somewhat different ways. In generalizability theory, rather than trying to estimate a single true score, consideration is given to how test scores would be expected to shift across situations as a result of changes in the characteristic being measured. It is for this and related reasons that generalizability theory seems more applicable to behavioral assessment than to the measurement of personality traits. Behavior changes across situations, necessitating an approach to reliability that can account for those changes. In contrast, personality traits are assumed by many to be relatively stable across

---

8. Webb et al. (1966) explained that the provocative, if uncommunicative, title *The Bullfighter's Beard* was a "title drawn from the observation that toreadors' beards are longer on the day of the fight than on any other day. No one seems to know if the toreador's beard really grows faster that day because of anxiety or if he simply stands further away from the blade, shaking razor in hand. Either way, there were not enough American aficionados to get the point" (p. v). The title they finally settled on was *Unobtrusive Measures: Nonreactive Research in the Social Sciences*.

## Personality, Life Outcomes, and College Yearbook Photos

Few people would be shocked to learn that individual differences in emotion are associated with differences in personality. Yet it will probably surprise many to learn that interpersonal differences in emotion may well have a pervasive effect on the course of one's life. In one study, it was observed that a tendency to express uncontrolled anger in early childhood was associated with ill temper across the lifespan and with several negative life outcomes, such as lower educational attainment, lower-status jobs, erratic work patterns, lower military rank, and divorce (Caspi et al., 1987). Suggestive findings such as these have prompted other investigators to wonder about the possible effects of positive emotions on personality and life outcomes.

Positive emotions have many beneficial effects, ranging from the broadening of thoughts and action repertoires (Cunningham, 1988; Frederickson, 1998; Isen, 1987) to the facilitation of the approach of other people (Berry & Hansen, 1996; Frijda & Mesquita, 1994; Ruch, 1993). A smile may send the message that one is friendly and nonthreatening (Henley & LaFrance, 1984; Keating et al., 1981) and may lead to positive attributions about one's sociability, friendliness, likability, and stability (Borkenau & Liebler, 1992; Frank et al., 1993; Matsumoto & Kudoh, 1993). On the basis of such findings and related research, Harker and Keltner (2001) hypothesized that positive emotional expression would predict higher levels of well-being across adulthood. They tested the hypothesis by examining the relationship of individual differences in positive emotional expression to personality and other variables.

A measure of positive emotional expression was obtained by coding judges' ratings of college yearbook photographs of women who participated in a longitudinal research project (Helson, 1967; Helson et al., 1984). These coded judgments were analyzed with respect to personality data on file (such as the subjects' responses to the Adjective Check List at ages 21, 27, 43, and 52) and life outcome data (including well-being as measured by the California Psychological Inventory, marital status, and the Marital Tensions Checklist).

Consistent with the researchers' hypothesis, positive emotional expression as evidenced in the college yearbook photos was found to correlate positively with life outcomes such as marital satisfaction and sense of personal well-being. This was the case even when the possible confounding influences of physical attractiveness or social desirability in responding were controlled for in the analysis of the data. The researchers cautioned, however,

*Is there a relationship between emotion expressed in college yearbook photos and personality and life outcomes? According to one study, the answer is yes. Researchers found that positive emotional expression in women's college photos predicted favorable outcomes in marriage and personal well-being up to 30 years later.*

that the measure of emotional expression used in the study (the yearbook photo) consisted of a single instance of very limited behavior. They urged future researchers to consider the use of different measures of emotional expression obtained in different contexts. The researchers also cautioned that their findings are limited to research with women. Smiling may have different implications for the lives of men (Stoppard & Gruchy, 1993). In fact, smiling was negatively correlated with positive outcomes for a sample of male cadets at West Point (Mueller & Mazur, 1996).

This thought-provoking study was, according to Harker and Keltner (2001), "one of the first to document that individual differences in expression relate to personality and may be stable aspects of personality" (p. 121).

situations. Personality traits are therefore presumed to be more appropriately measured by instruments with assumptions that are consistent with the true score model.

Regardless of whether behavioral measures are evaluated in accordance with classical test theory, generalizability theory, or something else (such as a Skinnerian experimental analysis), it would seem there are some things on which everyone can agree. One is that there must be an acceptable level of inter-rater reliability among behavior observers or raters. A potential source of error in behavioral ratings may arise when a dissimilarity in two or more of the observed behaviors (or other things being rated) leads to a more favorable or unfavorable rating than would have been made had the dissimilarity not existed (Maurer & Alexander, 1991). A behavioral rating may be excessively positive (or negative) because a prior rating was excessively negative (or positive). This source of error is referred to as a **contrast effect.**

Contrast effects have been observed in interviews (Schuh, 1978), in behavioral diaries and checklists (Maurer et al., 1993), in laboratory-based performance evaluations (Smither et al., 1988), and in field performance evaluations (Ivancevich, 1983). The contrast effect may even be at work in some judgments at the Olympics (see Figure 13–11). In one study of employment interviews, as much as 80% of the total variance was thought to be due to contrast effects (Wexley et al., 1972).

**JUST THINK . . .**

How might a contrast effect be operative in a university classroom?

To combat potential contrast effects and other types of rating error, rigorous training of raters is necessary. However, such training may be costly in terms of time and labor. For example, teaching professionals how to use the behavior observation and coding system of the Marital Interaction Coding System took "two to three months of weekly instruction and practice to learn how to use its 32 codes" (Fredman & Sherman, 1987, p. 28). Another approach to minimizing error and improving inter-rater reliability among behavioral raters is to employ a **composite judgment,** which is, in essence, an averaging of multiple judgments.

Some types of observer bias cannot practically or readily be remedied. For example, in behavioral observation involving the use of video equipment, it would on many occasions be advantageous if multiple cameras and recorders could be used to cover various angles of the ongoing action, to get close-ups, and so forth. The economic practicality of the situation (let alone other factors, such as the number of hours required

**Figure 13–11**
**The Contrast Effect at the Rink**

*Figure skating judges, like other behavior raters, are only human. Skaters who give performances worthy of extremely high marks may not always get what they deserve, simply because the skater who performed just before they did excelled by contrast. Ratings may be more favorable when the performance just prior to theirs was very poor. Because of this contrast effect, the points earned by a skater may depend to some degree on the quality of the preceding skater's performance.*

to watch footage from multiple views) is that it is seldom feasible to have more than one camera in a fixed position recording the action. The camera is in a sense biased in that one fixed position because in many instances it is recording information that may be quite different from the information that would have been obtained had it been placed in another position—or if multiple recordings were being made.

As we have already noted in the context of self-monitoring, *reactivity* is another possible issue with regard to behavioral assessment; people react differently in experimental than in natural situations. Microphones, cameras, and one-way mirrors may in themselves alter the behavior of persons being observed. For example, some patients under videotaped observation may attempt to minimize the amount of psychopathology they are willing to record for posterity; others under the same conditions may attempt to exaggerate it. One possible solution to the problem of reactivity is the use of hidden observers or clandestine recording techniques, although such methods raise serious ethical issues. Many times, all that is required to solve the problem of reactivity is an adaptation period. People being observed may adjust to the idea and begin to behave in their typical ways. Most clinicians are aware from personal experience that a recording device in the therapy room might put off some patients at first, but in only a matter of minutes the chances are good that it will be ignored.

Some of the other possible limitations of behavioral approaches include the equipment costs (some of the electronics can be expensive) and the cost of training behavioral assessors (Kenny et al., 2008). If training is not sufficient, another "cost"—one that few behavioral assessors are willing to pay—may be unwanted variables in their reports such as observer error or bias.

## A Perspective

More than a half-century ago, Theodor Reik's influential book *Listening with the Third Ear* intrigued clinicians with the possibilities of evaluation and intervention by means of skilled interviewing, active listening, and artful, depth-oriented interpretation. In one vignette, a female therapy patient recounted a visit to the dentist that involved an injection and a tooth extraction. While speaking, she remarked on a book in Reik's bookcase that was "standing on its head"—to which Reik responded, "But why did you not tell me that you had had an abortion?" (Reik, 1948, p. 263). Reflecting on this dazzling exhibition of clinical intuition, Masling (1997) wrote, "We would all have liked to have had Reik's magic touch, the ability to discern what is hidden and secret, to serve as oracle" (p. 259).

Historically, society has called upon mental health professionals to make diagnostic judgments and intervention recommendations, and often on the basis of relatively little information. Early on, psychological tests, particularly in the area of personality assessment, promised to empower clinicians—mere mortals—to play the oracular role society imposed and expected. Soon, two very different philosophies of test design and use emerged. The clinical approach relied heavily on the clinician's judgment and intuition. This approach was criticized for its lack of preset and uniformly applied rules for drawing clinical conclusions and making predictions. By contrast, the statistical or actuarial approach relied heavily on standardization, norms, and preset, uniformly applied rules and procedures. Duels between various members of these two camps were common for many years and have been reviewed in detail elsewhere (Marchese, 1992).

It seems fair to say that in those situations where data are insufficient to formulate rules for decision making and prediction, the clinical approach wins out over the actuarial. For the most part, however, it is the actuarial approach that has been most enthusiastically embraced by contemporary practitioners. This is so for a number of reasons, chief among them a passionate desire to make assessment more a science than an art. And that desire may simply reflect the fact that much as we would like it to be different, most of us are not oracles. Without reliable and valid tools, it is difficult if not impossible to spontaneously and consistently see through to what Reik (1952) characterized as the "secret self." Even with good tools, it's a challenge.

The actuarial approach encourages the retention only of hypotheses and predictions that have proven themselves. Conversely, it enables practitioners to quickly discover and discard untenable hypotheses and predictions (Masling, 1997). Of course, in many instances, skill in clinical assessment can be conceptualized as an internalized, less formal, and more creative version of the actuarial approach.

The actuarial approach to personality assessment is increasingly common. Even projective instruments, once the bastion of the "old school" clinical approach, are increasingly published with norms, and scrupulously researched. There have even been efforts—very respectable efforts—to apply sophisticated IRT models to, of all things, TAT data (Tuerlinckx et al., 2002). But swaying long-held opinions about the invalidity of projective assessment will not come easy. There is in academic psychology a climate of opinion that "continues as though nothing has changed and clinicians were still reading tea leaves" (Masling, 1997, p. 263).

If the oracle-like, clinical orientation is characterized as the *third ear approach,* we might characterize the contemporary orientation as a *van Gogh approach;* in a sense, an ear has been dispatched. The day of the all-knowing oracle has passed. Today, it is incumbent upon the responsible clinician to rely on norms, inferential statistics, and related essentials of the actuarial approach. Sound clinical judgment is still desirable, if not mandatory. However, it is required less for the purpose of making off-the-cuff interpretations and predictions and more for the purpose of organizing and interpreting information from different tools of assessment. We'll have more to say on this point as we move to the next chapter.

---

## Self-Assessment

Test your understanding of elements of this chapter by seeing if you can explain each of the following terms, expressions, and abbreviations:

analogue behavioral observation
analogue study
apperceive
behavioral assessment
behavioral observation
biofeedback
composite judgment
comprehensive system (Exner)
contrast effect
ecological momentary assessment
figure drawing test
free association
functional analysis of behavior
implicit motive
inquiry (on the Rorschach)

leaderless group technique
need (Murray)
objective methods of personality assessment
penile plethysmograph
percept (on the Rorschach)
phallometric data
plethysmograph
polygraph
press (Murray)
projective hypothesis
projective method
psychophysiological (assessment methods)
reactivity
role play

Rorschach test
self-monitoring
sentence completion
sentence completion stem
sentence completion test
situational performance measure
TAT
testing the limits (on the Rorschach)
thema (Murray)
timeline followback (TLFB) methodology
unobtrusive measure
word association
word association test

# 14

# *Clinical and Counseling Assessment*

**C**linical psychology is the branch of psychology that has as its primary focus the prevention, diagnosis, and treatment of abnormal behavior. Clinical psychologists receive training in psychological assessment and psychotherapy and are employed in hospitals, public and private mental health centers, independent practice, and academia. Like clinical psychology, **counseling psychology** is a branch of psychology that is concerned with the prevention, diagnosis, and treatment of abnormal behavior. Clinical psychologists tend to focus their research and treatment efforts on the more severe forms of behavior pathology, whereas counseling psychologists focus more on "everyday" types of concerns and problems, such as those related to marriage, family, academics, and career. Members of both professions strive to foster personal growth in their clients. The tools employed in the process of assessment overlap considerably.

All the tests and measures we have covered so far—intelligence, personality, self-concept, cognitive style—would be appropriate for discussion in this chapter, for all have potential application in clinical and counseling contexts. In an introductory text such as this, however, choices must be made as to coverage and organization. We have organized the material in this chapter to best convey to the reader how tools of assessment such as the interview, the case history, and psychological tests are used in clinical contexts. Our discussion will sample some of the many special applications of clinical assessment. We will see, for example, how clinical assessment is useful in forensic work, in custody evaluations, and in evaluations of child abuse and neglect. Interwoven throughout, as has been our custom throughout this book, is attention to cultural aspects of the subjects we discuss. We begin with an overview of psychological assessment, including discussion of some general issues related to the diagnosis of mental disorders.

## An Overview

Clinical assessment may be undertaken for various reasons and to answer a variety of important questions. For the clinical psychologist working in a hospital, clinic, or other clinical setting, tools of assessment are frequently used to clarify the psychological problem, make a diagnosis, and/or design a treatment plan.

*Does this patient have a mental disorder?* and *If so, what is the diagnosis?* are typical questions that require answers. In many cases, tools of assessment, including an interview, a test, and case history data, can provide those answers. Let's briefly explore how tests and other tools of assessment can be used in clinical settings.

Before or after interviewing a patient, a clinician may administer tests such as a Wechsler intelligence test and the MMPI-2-RF to obtain estimates of the patient's intellectual functioning and level of psychopathology. The data derived may provide the clinician with initial hypotheses about the nature of the individual's difficulties, which will then guide the interview. Alternatively, test data can confirm or refute hypotheses made on the basis of the clinical interview. Interview and test data will be supplemented with case history data, especially if the patient will not or cannot cooperate. The clinician may interview people who know the patient—such as family members, co-workers, and friends—and obtain records relevant to the case.

**JUST THINK . . .**

Clinicians approach assessment in different ways. Some prefer little more than a referral to begin with (so that their findings will not be shaped in any way by others' impressions or case history data), whereas other clinicians prefer to obtain as much information as they can prior to interviewing and administering any tests. Your preference?

The tools may be used to address questions such as *What is this person's current level of functioning? How does this level of functioning compare with that of other people of the same age?* Consider the example of an individual who is suspected of suffering from dementia caused by Alzheimer's disease. The patient has experienced a steady and progressive loss of cognitive skills over a period of months. A diagnosis of dementia may involve tracking the individual's performance with repeated administrations of tests of cognitive ability, including memory. If dementia is present, a progressive decline in test performance will be noted. Periodic testing with various instruments may also provide information about the kinds of activities the patient should be advised to pursue as well as the kinds of activities the patient should be encouraged to curtail or give up entirely. Ideally, case history data will provide some way to estimate the patient's level of **premorbid functioning** (or level of psychological and physical performance prior to the development of a disorder, an illness, or a disability).

*What type of treatment shall this patient be offered?* Tools of assessment can help guide decisions relating to treatment. Patients found to be high in intelligence, for example, tend to make good candidates for insight-oriented methods that require high levels of abstract ability. A person who complains of being depressed may be asked periodically to complete a measure of depression. If such a person is an inpatient, trends in the depth of depression as measured by the instrument may contribute to critical decisions regarding level of supervision within the institution, strength of medication administered, and date of discharge.

*How can this person's personality best be described?* Gaining an understanding of the individual need not focus on psychopathology. People who do not have any mental disorder sometimes seek psychotherapy for personal growth or support in coping with a difficult set of life circumstances. In such instances, interviews and personality tests geared more to the normal testtaker might be employed.

Researchers may raise a wide variety of other assessment-related questions, including *Which treatment approach is most effective?* or *What kind of client tends to benefit most from a particular kind of treatment?* A researcher may believe, for example, that people with a field-dependent cognitive style would be most likely to benefit from a cognitive-behavioral approach to treatment and that people with a field-independent cognitive style would be most likely to benefit from a humanistic approach to treatment. The researcher would use a variety of assessment tools to combine subjects into treatment groups and then to measure outcome in psychotherapy.

Counseling psychologists who do employment counseling may use a wide variety of assessment tools to help determine not only what occupations a person might enjoy but also which occupations would be sufficiently challenging yet not overwhelming. School psychologists and counseling psychologists working in a school setting may assist students with a wide variety of problems, including those related to studying. Here, behavioral measures, including self-monitoring, might be employed to better understand exactly how, when, and where the student engages in study behavior. The answer to related questions such as *Why am I not doing well in school?* may in part be found in diagnostic educational tests, such as those designed to identify problem areas in reading and reading comprehension. Another part of the answer may be obtained through other tools of assessment, including the interview, which may focus on aspects of the student's motivation and other life circumstances.

**JUST THINK . . .**

Cite another example or two to illustrate how a tool of assessment could be used in a clinical or counseling setting.

## The Diagnosis of Mental Disorders

Frequently an objective of clinical assessment is to diagnose mental disorders. The reference source used for making such diagnoses is the American Psychiatric Association's *Diagnostic and Statistical Manual (DSM)*. *DSM-IV* was published in 1994, and a text revision (*DSM-IV-TR*) was published in 2000. At this writing, the *DSM-V* is in preparation and scheduled to be published in the near future. The *DSM* names and describes all known mental disorders. *DSM-IV-TR* includes a category called *Conditions not attributable to a mental disorder that are a focus of attention or treatment*. A *DSM* diagnosis immediately conveys a great deal of descriptive information about the nature of the behavioral deviance, deficits, or excesses in the diagnosed person.

Some clinical psychologists, most vocally the behaviorally oriented clinicians, have expressed dissatisfaction with *DSM-IV-TR* on many grounds. Perhaps their chief concern is that the manual is firmly rooted in the medical model. Patterns of thinking and behavior are not described in *DSM-IV-TR* as just that—patterns of thinking and behavior—but rather in ways akin to describing diseases. This diagnostic system has also been criticized for being relatively unreliable. Different clinicians interviewing the same patient may well come up with different diagnoses. Further, even when all clinicians concur on a diagnosis, the *DSM-IV-TR* provides no guidance as to what method of treatment will be optimally effective. From a cultural perspective, the *DSM-IV-TR* may have been built on a foundation with insufficient sensitivity to certain cultures, especially with regard to the discussion of dissociative disorders (Lewis-Fernandez, 1998).

Proponents of the DSM believe that this diagnostic system is useful because of the wealth of information conveyed by a psychiatric diagnosis. They argue that perfect inter-diagnostician reliability cannot be achieved, owing to the nature of the subject matter. In response to the medical model criticism, *DSM* supporters maintain that the diagnostic system is useful whether or not any

**JUST THINK . . .**

Should a diagnostic manual provide clinicians with guidance as to what method of treatment will be optimally effective?

particular diagnostic category is actually a disease. Each of the disorders listed is associated with pain, suffering, or disability. The classification system, it is argued, provides useful subject headings under which practitioners can search for (or add to) the research literature with respect to the different diagnostic categories.

In *DSM-IV-TR,* diagnoses are coded according to five *axes* (dimensions). The types of disorders subsumed under each axis are as follows:

*Axis I:* Disorders of infancy, childhood, and adolescence; dementias such as those caused by Alzheimer's disease; disorders arising out of drug use; mood and anxiety disorders; and schizophrenia. Also included here are conditions that may be the focus of treatment (such as academic or social problems) but are not attributable to mental disorder.

*Axis II:* Mental retardation and personality disorders.

*Axis III:* Physical conditions that may affect mental functioning—from migraine headaches to allergies—are included here.

*Axis IV:* Different problems or sources of stress may occur in an individual's life at any given time. Financial, legal, marital, occupational, or other problems may precipitate behavior ranging from starting to smoke after having quit to attempting suicide. The presence of such problems is noted on this axis.

*Axis V:* This axis calls for a global rating of overall functioning. At the high end of this scale are ratings indicative of no symptoms and everyday concerns. At the low end of this scale are ratings indicative of people who are a clear and present danger to themselves or others and must therefore be confined in a secure facility.

*DSM-IV-TR* diagnoses are descriptive and atheoretical. This is appropriate for an authoritative reference work designed to provide common language for clinicians and researchers with varied theoretical orientations toward the etiology and treatment of mental disorders (Widiger & Clark, 2000). The first two axes contain all the diagnostic categories of mental disorders, and the remaining three axes provide additional information regarding an individual's level of functioning and current life situation. Multiple diagnoses are possible. An individual may be diagnosed, for example, as exhibiting behavior indicative of disorders listed on both Axis I and Axis II.

In the course of the debate regarding *DSM-IV-TR,* a variety of intriguing issues related to categorizing mental disorders have been raised (Kupfer et al., 2002). Perhaps one of the most basic questions is, "What is a disorder?" This deceptively simple question has generated heated rhetoric (Clark, 1999; Spitzer, 1999). The third edition of the *DSM* was the first edition of that manual to contain a definition of mental disorder, and the definition it offered of *disorder* was criticized by many. As an alternative, Jerome C. Wakefield (1992b) conceptualized mental disorder as a "harmful dysfunction." For Wakefield, a disorder is a harmful failure of internal mechanisms to perform their naturally selected functions. Wakefield's position is an **evolutionary view of mental disorder** because the internal mechanisms that break down or fail are viewed as having been acquired through the Darwinian process of natural selection. For Wakefield, the attribution of disorder entails two things: (1) a scientific judgment that such an evolutionary failure exists; and (2) a value judgment that this failure is harmful to the individual (Wakefield, 1992a).

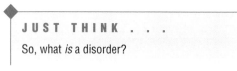

JUST THINK . . .

So, what *is* a disorder?

To better understand an evolutionary view of a disorder, consider the work of Schjelderup-Ebbe (1921), who coined the term "pecking order." This comparative psychologist noticed that when hens were defeated in dominance contests, they became severely withdrawn, "depressed" if you will. There are some cross-species behavioral similarities under such conditions of loss. For example, visualize the manner in which many athletes or teams carry themselves off the field of play when they lose, as compared to when they win. Bowed heads, slumped postures, and dejected looks communicate a mental withdrawal from competition. According to the social rank theory of depression (Price, 1969, 1972), a yielding mechanism has been triggered that prompts the individual to disengage; he or she is no longer a competitor for resources and status. From an evolutionary perspective, such withdrawal mechanisms occurred to prevent the individual from sustaining further injury. It is a course of action that has been termed an "involuntary defeat strategy" (Sloman & Gilbert, 2000). Adaptive in the short term, this strategy is counterproductive in the long term (Sloman & Price, 1987). The social rank theory can also account for the high degree of overlap, or comorbidity, between depression and anxiety. Individuals who are in an involuntarily subordinate position are not only depressed but vigilant and preoccupied with others who are perceived as more powerful. Many studies have now demonstrated that defeat and involuntary subordination are linked to depression, anxiety, and suicidal ideation (Gilbert & Allan, 1998; Sturman, 2011; Sturman & Mongrain, 2008; Taylor, 2011a, 2011b).

In contrast to the evolutionary view of disorder are myriad other views. Klein (1999) argued that "proper evolutionary function" is not known and that behavior labeled "disordered" may be the product of various involuntary causes (such as disease) or even voluntary causes (such as role-playing or malingering). Others have weighed in on this controversial issue by illuminating the role of culture (Kirmayer & Young, 1999) and by championing alternative vantage points, such as focusing on the issue at the level of the neuron (Richters & Hinshaw, 1999). Some have suggested that the concept of disorder is so broad that it need not have any defining properties (Lilienfeld & Marino, 1995, 1999).

**The Making of *DSM-V***   The first step in the development of the *DSM-V* was to convene a *DSM-V* Research Planning Conference in 1999. Planning work groups were created at this time that would cover, among other things, developmental issues, gaps in the current diagnostic system, disability, cultural issues, and neuroscience. Between 2004 and 2008, a series of 13 conferences was held to address various diagnostic questions and set the research agenda for *DSM-V*. The conferences were attended by participants from around the world, setting a decidedly international tone. A task force for the *DSM-V* was established in 2006 and included diagnostic work groups composed of leading experts. From 2007 onward, the work groups met regularly to discuss strengths and weaknesses of the *DSM-IV*, review the literature, and analyze existing data. Based on their research and clinical experience, the work groups put forward draft diagnostic criteria for the *DSM-V*. Some of the proposed changes for the new manual are presented in Table 14–1. From April 2010 to December 2011, field trials were conducted in large, academic medical centers as well as smaller clinical practices to test the reliability, validity, and

**Table 14–1**
**Changes Proposed for *DSM-V***

| Diagnostic Category | Proposed Disorders | Disorders to Be Eliminated |
| --- | --- | --- |
| Disorders usually first diagnosed in infancy, childhood or adolescence | Language Impairment<br>Late Language Emergence<br>Specific Language Impairment<br>Social Communication Disorder<br>Voice Disorder | Expressive Language Disorder<br>Mixed Receptive-Expressive Language Disorder<br>Communication Disorder—Not Otherwise Specified |
| Mood Disorders | Premenstrual Dysphoric Disorder<br>Mixed Features Specifier<br>Mixed Anxiety Depression | Mixed Episode<br>Bipolar I Disorder—Single Manic Episode<br>Mood Disorder—Not Otherwise Specified |
| Somatoform Disorders | Simple Somatic Symptom Disorder<br>Illness Anxiety Disorder | Hypochondriasis (being replaced by Illness Anxiety Disorder) |

clinical utility of the diagnostic criteria for the proposed mental disorders. The data from the field trials was analyzed by the work groups and informed their decisions on which diagnostic criteria to include in the *DSM-V*.

The *DSM-V* field trials were unique because *continuous* measures (as opposed to *categorical* measures) were used with each disorder listed. *DSM-IV* had been developed with categorical measures; either a person had a particular disorder or not. *DSM-V* added a continuous (also referred to as a *dimensional* measure) of severity of the disorder. This addition was based on the idea that mental disorders could be better understood as existing on a continuum of severity (as opposed to an all-or-none state). Such continuous measures could be used to establish a baseline of severity for any of the disorders listed. This baseline could be useful in tracking changes over time. For instance, a clinician would be able to obtain a measure of the severity level of depression before and after intervention (such as individual therapy, group therapy, or medication). One meta-analysis of 58 studies concluded that the adoption of a continuous approach (in contrast to a categorical approach) could result in a 15% increase in reliability and a 37% increase in validity (Markon et al., 2011).

Changes for the new *DSM* were also proposed in the area of personality disorders. Potential problems with a categorical approach to personality disorder have long been recognized. The psychiatrist and philosopher Karl Jaspers (1923) wrote that "there is no sharp line to be drawn between different types, nor between what is healthy and what is not." The empirical evidence has tended to support Jaspers' claim. Individuals who meet criteria for one personality disorder may well meet criteria for another (Marinangeli et al., 2000). Also, there is no clear dividing point in the distribution of symptoms between individuals meeting criteria for a personality disorder and "normal" individuals (Widiger, 1993). Indeed, many individuals show some symptoms of personality disorder but not enough to be diagnosed. All of these considerations led the *DSM-V* work group for personality disorders to adopt a hybrid categorical-dimensional approach. The work group proposed that six personality disorders (antisocial, avoidant, borderline, narcissistic, obsessive-compulsive, and schizotypal disorder) be diagnosed in categorical fashion. However, the *DSM-V* would also contain a Personality Disorder Trait Specified (PDTS) diagnosis, which would take into account the degree of disturbance that existed with regard to a particular personality trait.

Many of the proposed changes in the *DSM-V* addressed the criticism that its predecessor was not sufficiently *biopsychosocial* in orientation (Denton, 2007). To understand that criticism, a more general knowledge of *biopsychosocial assessment* is necessary.

**Biopsychosocial assessment** Beginning in 2009, federal mandates required that television broadcasting would not only change from analog to digital in nature but also be broadcast in a "wide screen" format. Likewise, if advocates of the biopsychosocial approach had their way, conceptualizations of mental disorder would be in "wide screen"—providing consumers of such data with the "big picture" view of disorders.

As its name implies, **biopsychosocial assessment** is a multidisciplinary approach to assessment that includes exploration of relevant biological, psychological, social, cultural, and environmental variables for the purpose of evaluating how such variables may have contributed to the development and maintenance of a presenting problem. Rather than being exclusively medical or even psychological in orientation, this approach encourages input from virtually any discipline that can provide relevant insights when such input can be put to use in better understanding the problem and effectively intervening to remedy it (Campbell & Rohrbaugh, 2006; Ingham et al., 2008). Studies focusing on various aspects of physical health, for example, have noted that psychological factors such as **fatalism** (the belief that what happens in life is largely beyond a person's control; Caplan & Schooler, 2003), **self-efficacy** (confidence in one's own ability to accomplish a task) and **social support** (expressions of understanding, acceptance, empathy, love, advice, guidance, care, concern, or trust from friends, family, community caregivers, or others in one's social environment; Keefe et al., 2002) may play key roles. One key tool of biopsychosocial assessment, as with clinical assessment in general, is the interview.

**JUST THINK . . .**

From your own experience, how has social support been helpful to you in times when you were feeling physically ill? Do you think psychological factors such as social support actually help in feeling better?

## The Interview in Clinical Assessment

Except in rare circumstances, such as when an assessee is totally noncommunicative, an interview is likely to be part of every clinician's or counselor's individual assessment. In a clinical situation, for example, an interview may be conducted to arrive at a diagnosis, to pinpoint areas that must be addressed in psychotherapy, or to determine whether an individual will harm himself or others. In a typical counseling application, an interview is conducted to help the interviewee learn more about him- or herself, the better to make potentially momentous life choices. Usually conducted face-to-face, interviewers learn about interviewees not only from *what* they say but also from *how* they say it and from how they present themselves during the interview.

Often, an interview will guide decisions about what else needs to be done to assess an individual. If symptoms or complaints are described by the interviewee in a vague or inconsistent manner, a test designed to screen in a general way for psychopathology may be indicated. If an interviewee complains of memory problems, a standardized memory test may be administered. If the interviewee is unable to describe the frequency with which a particular problem occurs, a period of self-monitoring may be in order. Interviews are frequently used early on in independent practice settings to solidify a **therapeutic contract,** an agreement between client and therapist setting forth goals, expectations, and mutual obligations with regard to a course of therapy.

Seasoned interviewers endeavor to create a positive, accepting climate in which to conduct the interview. They may use open-ended questions initially and then closed questions to obtain specific information. The effective interviewer conveys understanding to the interviewee verbally or nonverbally. Ways of conveying that understanding include attentive posture and facial expression as well as frequent statements acknowledging or summarizing what the interviewee is trying to say. Sometimes interviewers attempt to convey attentiveness by head nodding and vocalizations such as "um-hmm." However, here the interviewer must exercise caution. Such vocalizations and head nodding have been observed to act as reinforcers that increase the emission of certain interviewee verbalizations (Greenspoon, 1955). For example, if a therapist said "um-hmm" every time an interviewee brought up material related to the subject of mother, then—other things being equal—the interviewee might spend more time talking about mother than if not reinforced for bringing up that topic.

**Types of interviews** Interviews may be typed with respect to a number of different variables. One such variable is *content*. The content of some interviews, such as a general, "getting-to-know-you" interview, can be wide ranging. By contrast, other interviews focus narrowly on particular content. Another variable on which interviews differ is *structure*. A highly structured interview is one in which all

**JUST THINK . . .**

What is another subtle way that an interviewer might inadvertently (or deliberately) encourage an interviewee to spend more time on a particular topic?

the questions asked are prepared in advance. In an interview with little structure, few or no questions are prepared in advance, leaving interviewers the freedom to delve into subject areas as their judgment dictates. An advantage of a structured interview is that it provides a uniform method of exploration and evaluation. A structured interview, much like a test, may therefore be employed as a standardized pre/post measure of outcome. In fact, many research studies that explore the efficacy of a new medication, an approach to therapy, or some other intervention employ structured interviews as outcome measures.

Many structured interviews are available for use by assessment professionals. For example, the Structured Clinical Interview for *DSM-IV* (SCID) is a semistructured interview designed to assist clinicians and researchers in diagnostic decision-making. It is used to assess disorders on Axis I of the *DSM-IV* (major mental disorders) and requires 1 to 2 hours to administer. The SCID-II is used to assess Axis II personality disorders and requires 30 minutes to 1 hour to administer. The Schedule for Affective Disorders and Schizophrenia (SADS) is a standardized interview designed to detect schizophrenia and disorders of affect (such as major depression, bipolar disorder, and anxiety disorders). The Structured Interview of Reported Symptoms-2 (SIRS-2; Rogers et al., 2010) is used primarily in efforts to detect malingering.

In addition to content and structure, interviews may differ in *tone*. In one type of interview—not very common—the interviewer intentionally tries to make the interviewee feel stressed. **Stress interview** is the general name applied to any interview where one objective is to place the interviewee in a pressured state for some particular reason. The stress may be induced to test for some aspect of personality (such as aggressiveness or hostility) that might be elicited only under such conditions. Screening for work in the security or intelligence fields might entail stress interviews if a criterion of the job is the ability to remain cool under pressure. The source of the stress varies as a function of the purpose of the evaluation; possible sources may emanate from the interviewer as disapproving facial expressions, critical remarks, condescending reassurances, relentless probing, or seeming incompetence. Other sources of stress may emanate from the "rules of the game," such as unrealistic time limits for complying with demands.

**JUST THINK . . .**

Why might it be desirable to subject an interviewee to a stress interview? What ethical constraints are there to stress interviews?

Interviewee *state of consciousness* is another variable related to interview type. Most interviews are conducted with the interviewee in an ordinary, everyday, waking state of consciousness. On occasion, however, a particular situation may call for a very specialized interview in which the state of consciousness of the interviewee is deliberately altered. A **hypnotic interview** is one conducted while the interviewee is under hypnosis. Hypnotic interviews may be conducted as part of a therapeutic assessment or intervention when the interviewee has been an eyewitness to a crime or related situations. In all such cases, the prevailing belief is that the hypnotic state will focus the interviewee's concentration and enhance recall (McConkey & Sheehan, 1996; Reiser, 1980, 1990; Vingoe, 1995).

Critics of hypnotic interviewing suggest that any gains in recall may be offset by losses in accuracy and other possible negative outcomes (Kebbell & Wagstaff, 1998). Hypnotic interview procedures may inadvertently make interviewees more confident of their memories, regardless of their correctness (Dywan & Bowers, 1983; Sheehan et al., 1984). As compared to nonhypnotized interviewees, hypnotized interviewees may be more suggestible to leading questions and thus more vulnerable to distortion of memories (Putnam, 1979; Zelig & Beidleman, 1981). Some researchers believe that hypnosis of witnesses may inadvertently produce memory distortion that is irreversible

(Diamond, 1980; Orne, 1979). As a result, witnesses who have been hypnotized to enhance memory may be banned from testifying (Laurence & Perry, 1988; Perry & Laurence, 1990). A new technique, similar to hypnotic interviewing involves focused meditation with eyes closed (Wagstaff et al., 2011). The researchers reported that their focused meditation technique increased memory yet was resistant to report of misleading information.

An interview procedure designed to retain the best features of a hypnotic interview but without the hypnotic induction has been developed by Fisher and colleagues (Fisher & Geiselman, 1992; Fisher et al., 1987; Fisher et al., 1989; Mello & Fisher, 1996). In the **cognitive interview,** rapport is established and the interviewee is encouraged to use imagery and focused retrieval to recall information. If the interviewee is an eyewitness to a crime, he or she may be asked to shift perspective and describe events from the viewpoint of the perpetrator. Much like what typically occurs in hypnosis, a great deal of control of the interview shifts to the interviewee. And unlike many police interviews, there is an emphasis on open-ended rather than closed questions, and interviewees are allowed to speak without interruption (Kebbell & Wagstaff, 1998). The same term, by the way, has been applied to a questionnaire design procedure whereby draft survey questions are posed to research subjects using a "think aloud" paradigm and the resulting data is analyzed to improve the survey questions (Beatty & Willis, 2007). A meta-analysis of 65 experiments showed that the use of a cognitive interview led to large and significant increases in recalling correct details, although there was also a small increase in erroneous details (Memon et al., 2010). Since 2009, cognitive interviewing has been incorporated into police interview training programs in the United Kingdom.

The **collaborative interview** allows the interviewee wide latitude to interact with the interviewer. It is almost as if the boundary between professional assessor and lay assessee has been diminished and both are participants working closely together—collaborating—on a common mission of discovery, clarification, and enlightenment. In an initial contact prior to a formal assessment by tests and other means, an interviewee might be invited to help frame objectives. What should be accomplished by the assessment? The interviewee is very much an active participant in collaborative assessment. Descriptions of an essentially collaborative assessment process may be found in the writings of Dana (1982), Finn (1996), Fischer (1994), and others. What they have in common is "empowerment of the person through a participatory, collaborative role in the assessment process" (Allen, 2002, p. 221).

Regardless of the specific type of interview conducted, certain "standard" questions are typically raised, during the initial intake interview, with regard to several areas. These questions are followed by additional queries as clinical judgment dictates.

> **JUST THINK . . .**
>
> In what innovative way would you like to participate or collaborate in your own clinical or counseling interview, where you are the interviewee?

*Demographic data:* Name, age, sex, religion, number of persons in family, race, occupation, marital status, socioeconomic status, address, telephone numbers.

*Reason for referral:* Why is this individual requesting or being sent for psychological assessment? Who is the referral source?

*Past medical history:* What events are significant in this individual's medical history?

*Present medical condition:* What current medical complaints does this individual have? What medications are currently being used?

*Familial medical history:* What chronic or familial types of disease are present in the family history?

*Past psychological history:* What traumatic events has this individual suffered? What psychological problems (such as disorders of mood or disorders of thought content) have troubled this individual?

*Past history with medical or psychological professionals:* What similar contacts for assessment or intervention has this individual had? Were these contacts satisfactory in the eyes of the assessee? If not, why not?

*Current psychological conditions:* What psychological problems are currently troubling this person? How long have these problems persisted? What is causing these problems? What are the psychological strengths of this individual?

Throughout the interview, the interviewer may jot down subjective impressions about the interviewee's general appearance (appropriate?), personality (sociable? suspicious? shy?), mood (elated? depressed?), emotional reactivity (appropriate? blunted?), thought content (hallucinations? delusions? obsessions?), speech (normal conversational? slow and rambling? rhyming? singing? shouting?), and judgment (regarding such matters as prior behavior and plans for the future). During the interview, any chance actions by the patient that may be relevant to the purpose of the assessment are noted.[1]

A parallel to the general physical examination conducted by a physician is a special clinical interview conducted by a clinician called a **mental status examination.** This examination, used to screen for intellectual, emotional, and neurological deficits, typically includes questioning or observation with respect to each area discussed in the following list.

*Appearance:* Are the patient's dress and general appearance appropriate?

*Behavior:* Is anything remarkably strange about the patient's speech or general behavior during the interview? Does the patient exhibit facial tics, involuntary movements, difficulties in coordination or gait?

*Orientation:* Is the patient oriented to person? That is, does he know who he is? Is the patient oriented to place? That is, does she know where she is? Is the patient oriented to time? That is, does he or she know the year, the month, and the day?

*Memory:* How is the patient's memory of recent and long-past events?

*Sensorium:* Are there any problems related to the five senses?

*Psychomotor activity:* Does there appear to be any abnormal retardation or quickening of motor activity?

*State of consciousness:* Does consciousness appear to be clear, or is the patient bewildered, confused, or stuporous?

*Affect:* Is the patient's emotional expression appropriate? For example, does the patient (inappropriately) laugh while discussing the death of an immediate family member?

*Mood:* Throughout the interview, has the patient generally been angry? Depressed? Anxious? Apprehensive?

*Personality:* In what terms can the patient best be described? Sensitive? Stubborn? Apprehensive?

---

1. Tangentially we note the experience of the senior author (RJC) while conducting a clinical interview in the Bellevue Hospital Emergency Psychiatric Service. Throughout the intake interview, the patient sporadically blinked his left eye. At one point in the interview, the interviewer said, "I notice that you keep blinking your left eye"—in response to which the interviewee said, "Oh, this . . ." as he proceeded to remove his (glass) eye. Once he regained his breath, the interviewer noted this vignette on the intake sheet.

*Thought content:* Is the patient hallucinating—seeing, hearing, or otherwise experiencing things that aren't really there? Is the patient delusional—expressing untrue, unfounded beliefs (such as the delusion that someone follows him everywhere)? Does the patient appear to be obsessive—does the patient appear to think the same thoughts over and over again?

*Thought processes:* Is there under- or overproductivity of ideas? Do ideas seem to come to the patient abnormally slowly or quickly? Is there evidence of loosening of associations? Are the patient's verbal productions rambling or disconnected?

*Intellectual resources:* What is the estimated intelligence of the interviewee?

*Insight:* Does the patient realistically appreciate her situation and the necessity for professional assistance if such assistance is necessary?

*Judgment:* How appropriate has the patient's decision-making been with regard to past events and future plans?

A mental status examination begins the moment the interviewee enters the room. The examiner takes note of the examinee's appearance, gait, and so forth. **Orientation** is assessed by straightforward questions such as "What is your name?" "Where are you now?" and "What is today's date?" If the patient is indeed oriented to person, place, and time, the assessor may note in the record of the assessment "Oriented $\times$ 3" (read "**oriented times 3**").

Different kinds of questions based on the individual examiner's own preferences will be asked in order to assess different areas in the examination. For example, to assess intellectual resources, questions may range from those of general information (such as "What is the capital of New York?") to arithmetic calculations ("What is 81 divided by 9?") to proverb interpretations ("What does this saying mean: People who live in glass houses shouldn't throw stones?"). Insight may be assessed, for example, simply by asking the interviewee why he or she is being interviewed. The interviewee who has little or no appreciation of the reason for the interview indicates little insight. An alternative explanation, however, might be that the interviewee is malingering.

As a result of a mental status examination, a clinician might be better able to diagnose the interviewee if, in fact, the purpose of the interview is diagnostic. The outcome of such an examination might be, for example, a decision to hospitalize or not to hospitalize or perhaps a request for a deeper-level psychological or neurological examination.

> **JUST THINK . . .**
>
> A clinical interviewer conducts a mental status examination and determines that the interviewee is extremely depressed, possibly to the point of being a danger to himself. How might this clinical impression be validated?

**Psychometric aspects of the interview**   After an interview, an interviewer usually reaches some conclusions about the interviewee. Those conclusions, like test scores, can be evaluated for their reliability and validity.

If more than one interviewer conducts an interview with the same individual, inter-rater reliability for interview data could be represented by the degree of agreement between the different interviewers' conclusions. One study explored the diagnosis of schizophrenia through two different types of interviews, one structured and one unstructured. Perhaps not surprisingly, Lindstrom et al. (1994) found that structured interviews yielded higher inter-rater reliability even though the content of the two types of interviews was similar.

Consistent with these findings, the inter-rater reliability of interview data may be increased when different interviewers consider specific issues systematically. Systematic and specific consideration of different interview issues can be fostered in various ways—for instance, by having interviewers complete a scale that rates the interviewee on targeted variables at the conclusion of the interview. In one study, family members were interviewed by several psychologists for the purpose of diagnosing depression. The actual content of the interviews was left to the discretion of the interviewers, although all interviewers completed the same rating scale at the conclusion of the interview. Completion of the post-interview rating scale improved inter-rater reliability (Miller et al., 1994).

In general, when an interview is undertaken for diagnostic purposes, the reliability and validity of the diagnostic conclusions made on the basis of the interview data are likely to increase when the diagnostic criteria are clear and specific. Efforts to increase inter-rater reliability for diagnostic purposes are evident in the third revision of the *Diagnostic and Statistical Manual* (*DSM-III*), published in 1980. Although its predecessor, *DSM-II* (1968), provided descriptive information about the disorders listed, the descriptions were inconsistent in specific detail and in some cases were rather vague. For example, this is the *DSM-II* description of paranoid personality:

> This behavioral pattern is characterized by hypersensitivity, rigidity, unwarranted suspicion, jealousy, envy, excessive self-importance, and a tendency to blame others and ascribe evil motives to them. These characteristics often interfere with the patient's ability to maintain satisfactory interpersonal relations. Of course, the presence of suspicion itself does not justify the diagnosis, because suspicion may be warranted in some cases. (American Psychiatric Association, 1968, p. 42)

A description such as this may be helpful in communicating the nature of the disorder, but because of its nonspecificity and openness to interpretation, it is of only minimal value for diagnostic purposes. In an effort to bolster the reliability and validity of psychiatric diagnoses, the *DSM-III* (American Psychiatric Association, 1980) provided specific diagnostic guidelines, including reference to a number of symptoms that had to be present for the diagnosis to be made. The diagnostic criteria for paranoid personality disorder, for example, listed eight ways in which suspicion might be displayed, at least three of which must be present for the diagnosis to be made. It listed four ways in which hypersensitivity might be displayed, two of which had to be present for the diagnosis to be made. It listed four ways in which restricted affect might be displayed, two of which had to be present for the diagnosis to be made (American Psychiatric Association, 1980). This trend toward increased specificity in diagnostic descriptions continued in an interim revision of *DSM-III* (published in 1987 and referred to as *DSM-III-R*) as well as in the more recent revisions, *DSM-IV* (American Psychiatric Association, 1994) and *DSM-IV-TR*. Presumably, the trend will also be evident in *DSM-V*.

Evaluating the consistency of conclusions drawn from two interviews separated by some period of time produces a coefficient of reliability that conceptually parallels a coefficient of test-retest reliability. As an example, consider a study of the reliability of a semi-structured interview for the diagnosis of alcoholism and commonly co-occurring disorders such as substance dependence, substance abuse, depression, and antisocial personality disorder. Bucholz et al. (1994) found that some disorders (substance dependence and depression) were diagnosed with greater test-retest reliability than were other disorders (substance abuse and antisocial personality disorder).

Criterion validity of conclusions made on the basis of interviews concerns psychometricians as much as the criterion validity of conclusions made on the basis of test data. The degree to which an interviewer's findings or conclusions concur with other test results or other behavioral evidence reflects on the criterion-related validity of the conclusions. Consider in this context a study that compared the accuracy of two different tools of assessment in predicting the behavior of probationers: an objective test and a structured interview. Harris (1994) concluded that the structured interview was much more accurate in predicting the criterion (later behavior of probationers) than was the test. In another study, this one having as a criterion the accurate reporting of the subject's drug use, a paper-and-pencil test was also pitted against an interview. The written test was found to be more criterion-valid than the interview, perhaps because people may be more disposed to admit to illegal drug use in writing than in a face-to-face interview (McElrath, 1994).

**JUST THINK . . .**

Do you think it is true that people are more apt to admit socially disapproved behavior in a written test as opposed to a face-to-face interview? What factors are operative in each situation?

An interview is a dynamic interaction between two or more people. On occasion, interviews may seem to develop lives of their own. Ultimately, the nature and form of any interview is determined by many factors, such as:

- the interview referral question
- the context and setting of the interview (clinic, prison, practitioner's office, etc.)
- the nature and quality of background information available to the interviewer
- time constraints and any other limiting factors
- the interviewee's previous experience, if any, with similar types of interviews
- the motivation, willingness, and abilities of the interviewee
- the motivation, willingness, and abilities of the interviewer
- cultural aspects of the interview

What do we mean by this last point? It will be taken up again shortly in our discussion of *culturally informed assessment*.

## Case History Data

Biographical and related data about an assessee may be obtained by interviewing the assessee and/or significant others in that person's life. Additional sources of case history data include hospital records, school records, military records, employment records, and related documents. All such data are combined in an effort to obtain an understanding of the assessee, including insights into observed behavior patterns.[2] Case history data may be invaluable in helping a therapist develop a meaningful context in which to interpret data from other sources, such as interview transcripts and reports of psychological testing.

**JUST THINK . . .**

How might the contents of an assessee's home video library be a useful source of information in assembling a case history?

## Psychological Tests

Clinicians and counselors may have occasion to use many different tests in the course of their practices, and nearly all of the tests we have described could be employed in clinical or counseling assessment. Some tests are designed primarily to be of diagnostic

---

2. For an example of a case study from the psychology literature, the interested reader is referred to "Socially Reinforced Obsessing: Etiology of a Disorder in a Christian Scientist" (Cohen & Smith, 1976), wherein the authors suggest that a woman's exposure to Christian Science predisposed her to an obsessive disorder. The article stirred some controversy and elicited a number of comments (for example, Coyne, 1976; Halleck, 1976; London, 1976; McLemore & Court, 1977), including one from a representative of the Christian Science Church (Stokes, 1977)—all rebutted by Cohen (1977, 1979, pp. 76–83).

assistance to clinicians. One such test is the Millon Clinical Multiaxial Inventory–III (MCMI-III; Millon et al., 1994), a 175-item true–false test that yields scores related to enduring personality features as well as acute symptoms. As implied in the name of this *multiaxial* test, it can yield information that can assist clinicians in making diagnoses based on the multiaxial *DSM*.

In addition to tests that are used for general diagnostic purposes, thousands of tests focus on specific traits, states, interests, attitudes, and related variables. Depression is perhaps the most common mental health problem and reason for psychiatric hospitalization. A diagnosis of depression is a most serious matter, as this condition is a key risk factor in suicide. Given the critical importance of depression, many instruments have been developed to measure it and provide insights with respect to it.

Perhaps the most widely used test to measure the severity of depression is the Beck Depression Inventory–II (BDI-II; Beck et al., 1996). This is a self-report measure consisting of 21 items, each tapping a specific symptom or attitude associated with depression. For each item, testtakers circle one of four statements that best describes their feelings over the past two weeks. The statements reflect different intensities of feeling and are weighted in their scoring accordingly. Beck et al. (1996) presented data to document their assertion that, on average, patients with mood disorders obtain higher scores on the BDI-II than patients with anxiety, adjustment, or other disorders. Additionally, they presented data to support their claim that, on average, patients with more serious depressive disorders score higher on the BDI-II than patients with less serious forms of depression. However, because the items are so transparent and the test outcome is so easily manipulated by the testtaker, it is usually recommended that the BDI-II be used only with patients who have no known motivation to fake good or fake bad. Further, because the BDI-II contains no validity scales, it is probably advisable to administer it along with other tests that do have validity scales, such as the MMPI-2-RF.

The Center for Epidemiological Studies Depression scale (CES-D) is another widely used self-report measure of depressive symptoms. The CES-D consists of 20 items, although shorter versions of the scale have been developed as screening tools for depression (Andresen et al., 1994; Melchior et al., 1993; Shrout & Yager, 1989; Turvey et al., 1999). Santor et al. (1995) compared the test characteristic curves of the BDI and CES-D and found the CES-D to be more discriminating in determining symptom severity in both a college and a depressed outpatient sample. A revised version of the CESD, the CESD-R, has shown promise as a reliable and valid instrument in a large community sample consisting of 7,389 people (Van Dam & Earleywine, 2011).

Of course, it does not necessarily take a test specifically developed to measure depression in order to learn that someone is depressed or emotionally labile. Our guest professional in this chapter, Dr. Joel Goldberg, learned this (clinical) fact of life early in his career while reviewing psychological test results with a colleague (see this chapter's *Meet an Assessment Professional*).

Whether assessment is undertaken for general or more specific diagnostic purposes, it is usually good practice to use more than one tool of assessment to meet the assessment objective. Often, more than one test is administered to an assessee. The phrase used to describe the group of tests administered is *test battery.*

**The psychological test battery**  If you are a culinary aficionado, or if you are a fan of *Iron Chef* on the Food Network, then you will know that the word *batter* refers to a beaten liquid mixture that typically contains a number of ingredients. Somewhat similar in meaning to this definition of batter is one definition of the word *battery:* an

## Meet Dr. Joel Goldberg

Early in my weeks of internship training, one of the psychiatric residents, with whom I had begun to develop a growing friendship, referred a patient to me for psychological assessment. Tragically, soon after, a member of that resident's family died. The resident was subsequently absent from work for a period of seven days, which is the traditional period of mourning (*shivah*) in the Jewish faith. Over that time, I had completed the assessment of his patient. Upon the resident's return, I arranged to review the results with him as a way of consulting about the case findings. The review would also serve to help him in learning more about the test instruments employed, and their effectiveness. As I reviewed the case materials, I showed him the Thematic Apperception Test (TAT) cards that I had administered, reading aloud his patient's accompanying stories, and then making interpretations about the apparent underlying issues. When I came to Card 14, my colleague began to sob; his typically kind and gentle facial expression grew clouded, and tears began to flood. The darkness of the TAT card, with its image of a solitary figure, had elicited a poignant outpouring of sadness. The resident then shared his feelings of grief over the recent loss of his dear family member. He remarked on how he appreciated the power of the TAT instrument in revealing the depth of his mourning, which he had been attempting to mask in his first days back to work. For my own part, up until that time, I had learned about the administration and psychometrics of test instruments and I

**Joel Goldberg, Ph.D., Director of Clinical Training, Department of Psychology, York University, and Independent Practice**

had interpreted a number of cases as part of my clinical practicum training. Still, it was not until that very unanticipated moment that I truly became aware of, and fully appreciated the potential of psychological assessment for uncovering human experience.

*Read more of what Dr. Goldberg had to say—his complete essay—at mhhe.com/cohentesting8.*

array or grouping of like things to be used together. When psychological assessors speak of a **test battery,** they are referring to a group of tests administered together to gather information about an individual from a variety of instruments.

    *Personality test battery* refers to a group of personality tests. The term *projective test battery* also refers to a group of personality tests, though this term is more specific because it additionally tells us that the battery is confined to projective techniques (such as the Rorschach, the TAT, and figure drawings). In shoptalk among clinicians, if the type of battery referred to is left unspecified, or if the clinician refers to a battery of tests as a **standard battery,** what is usually being referred to is a group of tests including one intelligence test, at least one personality test, and a test designed to screen for neurological deficit (discussed in the following chapter).

Each test in the standard battery provides the clinician with information that goes beyond the specific area the test is designed to tap. Thus, for example, a test of intelligence may yield information not only about intelligence but also about personality and neurological functioning. Conversely, information about intelligence and neurological functioning can be gleaned from personality test data (and here we refer specifically to projective tests rather than personality inventories). The insistence on using a battery of tests and not a single test was one of the many contributions of psychologist David Rapaport in his now-classic work, *Diagnostic Psychological Testing* (Rapaport et al., 1945–1946). At a time when using a battery of tests might mean using more than one projective test, Rapaport argued that assessment would be incomplete if there weren't "right or wrong answers" to at least one of the tests administered. Here, Rapaport was referring to the need for inclusion of at least one test of intellectual ability.

Today, the utility of using multiple measures is a given. However, judging by the lack of attention given to cultural variables that has traditionally been evident in textbooks on assessment other than this one, what is not yet "a given" is attention to the notion of being *culturally informed* when conducting clinical (or other) assessments.

## Culturally Informed Psychological Assessment

We may define **culturally informed psychological assessment** as an approach to evaluation that is keenly perceptive of and responsive to issues of acculturation, values, identity, worldview, language, and other culture-related variables as they may impact the evaluation process or the interpretation of resulting data. We offer this definition not as the last word on the subject but rather as a first step designed to promote constructive and scholarly dialogue about what culturally sensitive psychological assessment really is and all that it can be.

When planning an assessment in which there is some question regarding the projected impact of culture, language, or some related variable on the validity of the assessment, the culturally sensitive assessor can do a number of things. One is to carefully read any existing case history data. Such data may provide answers to key questions regarding the assessee's level of acculturation and other factors useful to know about in advance of any formal assessment. Family, friends, clergy, professionals, and others who know the assessee may be able to provide valuable information about culture-related variables prior to the assessment. In some cases, it may be useful to enlist the aid of a local cultural advisor as preparation for the assessment. (One administrative note here: If any such informants are to be used, it will be necessary to have signed permission forms authorizing the exchange of information related to the assessee.)

We should also note that assessment experts themselves may disagree on key assessment-related issues regarding individuals who are members of particular groups. Consider, for example, the opinion of two experts regarding one widely used personality test, the MMPI-2. In an article entitled "Culturally Competent MMPI Assessment of Hispanic Populations," Dana (1995, p. 309) advised that "the MMPI-2 is neither better nor worse than [its predecessor] the

**JUST THINK . . .**

Is cultural competence a realistic and achievable goal? If so, what are the criteria for achieving it? Is a culturally competent assessor capable of assessing people from any culture or only those from the culture in which they are "competent"? Would you consider yourself culturally competent to assess someone from the same culture as yourself?

MMPI for Hispanics." By contrast, Velasquez et al. (1997, p. 111) wrote, *"Counselors should always apply the MMPI-2, and not the MMPI, to Chicano clients"* (emphasis in the original). On the basis of clinical experience, Velasquez et al. (1997) concluded that, as compared to the MMPI, the MMPI-2 "lessens the chances of overpathologization of Chicanos" (p. 111).

We might well consider such factual disagreements as only the tip of the iceberg when it comes to the potential for disagreement about what constitutes culturally competent assessment. It is better (and more realistic), we think, to aspire to culturally informed or culturally sensitive psychological assessment. With specific reference to the disagreement just cited, it would be useful to be informed about, or have a sensitivity to, the possibility of overpathologization of test results. Prior to the formal assessment, the assessor may consider a screening interview with the assessee in which rapport is established and various culture-related issues are discussed.

The *Close-Up* in Chapter 12 listed some of the questions that could be raised during such an interview. During the formal assessment, the assessor keeps in mind all the cultural information acquired, including any customs regarding personal space, eye contact, and so forth. After the assessment, the culturally sensitive assessor might reevaluate the data and conclusions for any possible adverse impact of culture-related factors. So, for example, with the cautions of Velasquez et al. (1997) firmly in mind, an assessor who happened to have administered the MMPI and not the MMPI-2 to a Chicano client might revisit the protocol and its interpretation with an eye toward identifying any possible overpathologization.

Translators are frequently used in clinic emergency rooms, crisis intervention cases, and other such situations. Whenever a translator is used, the interviewer must be wary not only of the interviewee's translated words but of their intensity as well (Draguns, 1984). Members of the assessee's family are frequently enlisted to serve as translators, although this practice may not be desirable under some circumstances. For example, in some cultures a younger person translating the words of an older person, particularly with regard to certain topics (such as sexual matters), may be perceived as very awkward if not disrespectful (Ho, 1987). Case study and behavioral observation data must be interpreted with sensitivity to the meaning of the historical or behavioral data in a cultural context (Longabaugh, 1980; Williams, 1986). Ultimately, a key aspect of culturally informed psychological assessment is to raise important questions regarding the generalizability and appropriateness of the evaluative measures employed.

If you just happen to be thinking about the *Just Think* question just raised, you are probably not alone. Students frequently are curious about how a culturally informed approach to assessment is acquired. Although there are no hard-and-fast rules, our own view is that formal instruction should occur in the context of a curriculum with three major components: a foundation in basic assessment, a foundation in culture issues in assessment, and supervised training and experience. A more detailed model curriculum, one informed by descriptions of existing programs (Allen, 2002; Hansen, 2002; López, 2002; Dana et al., 2002), as well as other sources (such as Sue & Sue, 2003), is presented on this text's companion website at *www.mhhe.com/cohentesting8*.

As you will see in the website presentation of the model curriculum, a subcomponent of both the "foundation in cultural issues in assessment" and the "supervised training and experience" components of the curriculum is **shifting cultural lenses** (Kleinman & Kleinman, 1991). The meaning of this term has been explained and illustrated memorably by Steven Regeser López, who teaches a core course in culturally informed assessment at UCLA. In his course, López (2002) draws on lessons he learned from driving public highways in Mexico, most of which have only two lanes, one in each

> **JUST THINK . . .**
>
> How can culturally informed assessment best be taught?

direction. Frequently, traffic will back up on one lane due to a slow-moving vehicle. Drivers who wish to pass slow-moving vehicles may be assisted by other drivers in front of them, who use their turn signals to indicate when it is safe to pass. A blinking right turn signal indicates that it is *not* safe to pass because of oncoming traffic or visibility issues in the opposing lane. A blinking left turn signal indicates that it *is* safe to pass. Large trucks may have printed on their rear mudflaps the word *siga* ("continue") by the left turn signal light or *alto* ("stop") by the right one. Besides signaling other drivers when it is safe to pass, turn signals have the same meaning as they do in the United States: an indication of an intention to turn.

In a class exercise that uses slides of highway scenes as well as close-ups of turn signals, López asks students to interpret the meaning of a blinking turn signal in different traffic scenarios: Does it mean pass, don't pass, or turning? Students quickly appreciate that the meaning of the blinking signal can be interpreted correctly only from cues in a specific context. López (2002) next builds on this lesson:

> I then translate this concrete example into more conceptual terms. In discerning the appropriate meaning, one must first entertain both sets of meanings or apply both sets of cultural lenses. Then one collects data to test both ideas. Ultimately, one weights the available evidence and then applies the meaning that appears to be most appropriate. It is important to note that whatever decision is made, there usually exists some degree of uncertainty. By collecting evidence to test the two possible meanings, the psychologist attempts to reduce uncertainty. With multiple assessments over time, greater certainty can be achieved. (pp. 232–233)

The notion of shifting cultural lenses is intimately tied to critical thinking and hypothesis testing. Interview data may suggest, for example, that a client is suffering from some form of psychopathology that involves delusional thinking. A shift in cultural lenses, however, permits the clinician to test an alternative hypothesis: that the observed behavior is culture-specific and arises from long-held family beliefs. The process of culturally informed psychological assessment demands such lens shifting with all forms of gathering information, including the interview.

## Cultural Aspects of the Interview

When an interview is conducted in preparation for counseling or psychotherapy, it may be useful to explore a number of culture-related issues. To what extent does the client feel different from other people, and how much of a problem is this? What conflicts, if any, are evident with regard to motivation to assimilate versus commitment to a particular culture? To what extent does the client feel different as an individual vis-à-vis the cultural group with which she or he identifies most? What role, if any, does racism or prejudice play as an obstacle to this client's adjustment? What role, if any, do the dominant culture's standards (such as physical attractiveness) play in this client's adjustment? In what ways have culture-related factors affected this client's feelings of self-worth? What potential exists for cultural loss or feelings of rootlessness and loss of native heritage as a function of efforts to assimilate? Questions regarding physical health may also be appropriate, especially if the client is from a cultural group that has a documented tendency to express emotional distress through physical symptoms (Cheung & Lau, 1982; Kleinman & Lin, 1980).

The misspelled **ADRESSING** is an easy-to-remember acronym that may help the assessor recall various sources of cultural influence when assessing clients. As proposed by Pamela Hays (Hays, 1996; Hays & Iwamasa, 2006; Hays & LeVine, 2001), the letters in ADRESSING stand

**JUST THINK . . .**

What other culture-related issues may need to be explored in a clinical or counseling interview?

for *a*ge, *d*isability, *r*eligion, *e*thnicity, *s*ocial status (including variables such as income, occupation, and education), *s*exual orientation, *i*ndigenous heritage, *n*ational origin, and *g*ender. How, for example, might a particular disability affect one's worldview in a particular context? Why might a deeply religious person feel strongly about a particular issue? These are the types of questions that could be raised by considering the ADRESSING acronym in the assessment of clients.

Whether using an interview, a test, or some other tool of assessment with a culturally different assessee, the assessor needs to be aware of ostensibly psychopathological responses that may be fairly commonplace in a particular culture. For example, claims of spirit involvement are not uncommon among some groups of depressed Native Americans (Johnson & Johnson, 1965) as well as others (Matchett, 1972). Diagnostic conclusions and judgments should attempt to distinguish veritable psychological and behavioral problems from behavior that may be deviant by the standards of the dominant culture but customary by the standards of the assessee's culture.

## Cultural Considerations and Managed Care

Here, *culture* refers both to (1) a kind of clash in cultures between that of the care-driven one of mental health professionals and the more bureaucratic, cost-savings one of managed care agencies, and (2) the need for culturally informed approaches to clinical services to be built into managed care guidelines. Before elaborating, let's backtrack for a moment and explain what *managed care* is.

In general, **managed care** may be defined as a health care system wherein the products and services provided to patients by a network of participating health care providers are mediated by an administrative agency of the insurer that works to keep costs down by fixing schedules of reimbursement to service providers. The majority of all health care in the United States is delivered through a managed-care system (Sanchez & Turner, 2003). For this reason, any overview of contemporary clinical assessment would be incomplete without reference to managed care and the profound effect it has exerted on the way that clinical assessment is conducted.

**JUST THINK . . .**

From your own knowledge and experience, how would you characterize "the culture of managed care"?

Steadily rising health care costs have led to budget crises and attendant cutbacks by administrators of managed care. One area of service for which managed care has been particularly reluctant to reimburse is psychological testing and assessment. Despite long-standing and compelling evidence for the utility of these services in health care settings (Kubiszyn et al., 2000), the result of nonpayment or underpayment of claims for psychological assessment and other mental health services has been a cutback in services rendered (Hartston, 2008; Riaz, 2006). Further, it has been shown that compared to public health care such as Medicare or Medicaid, psychological services offered through managed care have both greater preauthorization requirements and lower rates of reimbursement (Gasquoine, 2010). Providers of mental health services are frustrated in that what they offer is so inextricably linked to the dictates of economic reality and third-party decisions (Donald, 2001; Gittell, 2008; Rosenberg & DeMaso, 2008). Questions have been raised as to whether recipients of services are being adequately served. This is particularly true of service recipients (and would-be recipients) in rural and impoverished areas (Turchik et al., 2007).

The current situation has deteriorated to what might be termed a clash of cultures (Cohen et al., 2006). Providers of mental health services may perceive managed care organizations as compelling them to vary in unacceptable ways from established standards of care and professional ethics. Perhaps worse yet, providers themselves may not recognize the ways that managed care practices negatively affect their own behavior and possibly even that of their clients. Cohen et al. (2006) wrote of "the common practice of colluding with clients in embellishing or misrepresenting their [clients'] difficulties to gain additional benefits, thus modeling dishonest behavior . . . diagnoses seemed to serve as little more than bargaining chips for gaining reimbursement" (p. 257). The study authors feared that such trends would have increasingly negative consequences:

> We worry that the diagnostic language games practitioners feel compelled to play will empty diagnostic categories of any content or clinical utility. Furthermore, when practitioners draw their clients into these language games, the credibility of the profession erodes and public confidence in its knowledge base diminishes. (Cohen et al., 2006, p. 257)

Another potential negative consequence of this culture clash is that many experienced clinicians work under a managed care system just long enough to leave it. While working in a managed care environment, many clinicians aspire to build a private, fee-for-service practice base. The endgame is to leave managed care for the more lucrative and bureaucracy-free world of independent practice as soon as the practitioner's income base is sustainable. If this trend continues, a two-tier system of service delivery will emerge: one where less experienced service providers accept insurance reimbursement and more experienced service providers do not. Turchik et al. (2007) presented some possible strategies and practical suggestions for coping with the obstacles to quality service presented by managed care. For example, they noted that many managed care agencies have an appeal process in place for requesting a reevaluation of any service denials, and they urged clinicians to take full advantage of such processes. These authors also recommended ways of *not* coping with the demands of managed care or low budgets—such as by circumventing copyright laws and copying tests to avoid the cost of purchasing new ones, using psychological tests that are not current or psychometrically sound, or arranging to have psychological assessments conducted by unqualified clinicians.

JUST THINK . . .

List as many changes that you can think of that need to be made in the managed care approach to psychological assessment if this approach is to be optimally effective for service recipients.

The emergence of such a two-tier system would probably compound existing problems with the current managed care system regarding the need for culturally responsive approaches. Managed care has not been known for acknowledging or being sensitive to the need for different approaches to assessment and intervention on the basis of cultural background. If anything, it has been quite the opposite. That is, a "one size fits all" policy seems to be in place for mental health services; policies, once put in place, apply to everyone regardless of cultural background. Commentators on this state of affairs have made recommendations for change (Chin, 2003; Dana, 1998; Moffic & Kinzie, 1996) and, indeed, some change has occurred (see, e.g., Arthur et al., 2005). However, the need is still great for culturally responsive assessments and interventions within managed care environments.

## Special Applications of Clinical Measures

Clinical measures have application in a wide variety of research-related and applied settings. In this chapter, our modest objective is to provide only a small sample of the varied ways that clinical measures are used. Toward that end, let's begin with a brief look at some of the ways that clinicians evaluate various aspects of addiction and substance abuse.

## The Assessment of Addiction and Substance Abuse

Assessment for drug addiction and for alcohol and substance abuse has become routine in a number of settings. Whether an individual is seeking outpatient psychotherapy services, being admitted for inpatient services, or even seeking employment, being screened for drug use may be a prerequisite. Such screening can take varied forms, from straightforward physical tests involving the analysis of urine or blood samples to much more imaginative laboratory procedures that involve the analysis of psychophysiological responses (Carter & Tiffany, 1999; Lang et al., 1993; Sayette et al., 2000).

Exploration of personal history with drugs and alcohol may be accomplished by means of questionnaires or face-to-face interviews. However, such direct procedures are highly subject to impression management and all the other potential drawbacks of a self-report instrument. A number of tests and scales have been developed to assist in the assessment of abuse and addiction (see Table 14–2). The MMPI-2-RF, for example, contains three scales that provide information about substance abuse potential. The oldest of these three scales is the MacAndrew Alcoholism Scale (MacAndrew, 1965), since revised and usually referred to simply as the MAC-R. This scale was originally constructed to aid in differentiating alcoholic from nonalcoholic psychiatric patients.

Behavior associated with substance abuse or its potential has also been explored by analogue means, such as role play. The Situational Competency Test (Chaney et al., 1978), the Alcohol Specific Role Play Test

> **JUST THINK . . .**
>
> In your opinion, what are some personality traits that "often serve as pathways to substance abuse"?

**Table 14–2**
**Common Measures of Substance Abuse**

| Name of Measure | No. Items | Description of Items | Comment |
|---|---|---|---|
| MacAndrew Alcoholism Scale (MAC) and MacAndrew Alcoholism Scale-Revised (MAC-R) | 49 | Personality and attitude variables thought to underlie alcoholism | The MAC was derived from the MMPI. The MAC-R was derived from the MMPI-2. Neither scale assesses alcoholism directly. Both were designed to differentiate alcoholics from non-alcoholics empirically. |
| Addiction Potential Scale (APS) | 39 | Personality traits thought to underlie drug or alcohol abuse | Items were derived from the MMPI-2. Like the MAC-R, it does not assess alcoholism directly. |
| Addiction Acknowledgment Scale (AAS) | 13 | Direct acknowledgment of substance abuse | A face-valid, self-report of substance abuse derived from the MMPI-2. Endorsement of items is an admission of drug use. |
| Addiction Severity Index (ASI) | 200 | Raters assess severity of addiction in 7 problem areas: medical condition, employment functioning, drug use, alcohol use, illegal activity, family/social relations, and psychiatric functioning | The ASI was first developed by McLellan et al. (1980) and is currently in its 6th edition (ASI-6). It is a semi-structured interview that is useful at intake and follow-up. |
| Michigan Alcohol Screening Test (MAST) | 24 | Lifetime alcohol-related problems | Widely used to screen for problem drinking. Shorter versions have been created as well as a 22-item revised version (MAST-R) |

(Abrams et al., 1991), and the Cocaine Risk Response Test (Carroll, 1998; Carroll et al., 1999) are all measures that contain audiotaped role-play measures. In the latter test, assessees are asked to orally respond with a description of what they would do under certain conditions—conditions known to prompt cocaine use in regular cocaine users. One scenario involves having had a difficult week followed by cravings for cocaine to reward oneself. Another scenario takes place at a party where people are using cocaine in the next room. Assessees are asked to candidly detail their thinking and behavior in response to these and other situations. Of course, the value of the information elicited will vary as a function of many factors, among them the purpose of the assessment and the candor with which assessees respond. One might expect assessees to be straightforward in their responses if they were self-referred for addiction treatment. On the other hand, assessees might be less than straightforward if, for example, they were court-referred on suspicion of probation violation.

Efforts to reduce widespread substance abuse have led researchers to consider how culture may contribute to the problem and how culturally informed intervention may be part of the solution. Using a wide variety of measures, researchers have explored substance abuse in the context of variables such as cultural identity and generational status (Ames & Stacy, 1998; Chappin & Brook, 2001; Duclos, 1999; Kail & DeLaRosa, 1998; Karlsen et al., 1998; Lessinger, 1998; O'Hare & Van Tran, 1998; Pilgrim et al., 1999), religious beliefs (Corwyn & Benda, 2000; Klonoff & Landrine, 1999), and sexual orientation (Kippax et al., 1998). Recovery from drug addiction has itself been conceptualized as a socially mediated process of **reacculturation** that can result in a new sense of identity (Hurst, 1997).

**JUST THINK . . .**

Why is it useful to conceptualize recovery from drug addiction as reacculturation?

An important ethical consideration when assessing substance abusers, especially in research contexts, concerns obtaining fully informed consent to assessment. McCrady and Bux (1999) noted that substance abusers may be high or intoxicated at the time of consent and so their ability to attend to and comprehend the requirements of the research might be compromised. Further, because their habit may have thrust them into desperate financial straits, any payment offered to substance abusers for participation in a research study may appear coercive. Procedures to maximize comprehension of consent and minimize the appearance of coercion are necessary elements of the consent process.

## Forensic Psychological Assessment

The word *forensic* means "pertaining to or employed in legal proceedings," and the term **forensic psychological assessment** can be defined broadly as the theory and application of psychological evaluation and measurement in a legal context. Psychologists, psychiatrists, and other health professionals may be called on by courts, corrections and parole personnel, attorneys, and others involved in the criminal justice system to offer expert opinion. With respect to criminal proceedings, the opinion may, for example, concern an individual's competency to stand trial or his or her criminal responsibility (that is, sanity) at the time a crime was committed. With respect to a civil

**JUST THINK . . .**

When you envision a psychologist testifying in court, what topic do you see the psychologist speaking on?

proceeding, the opinion may involve issues as diverse as the extent of emotional distress suffered in a personal injury suit, the suitability of one or the other parent in a custody proceeding, or the testamentary capacity (capacity to make a last will and testament) of a person before death.

Before discussing assessment-related aspects in some of the many areas of forensic psychology, it is important to note that there are major differences between forensic and general clinical practice. Perhaps the biggest difference is that, in the forensic situation, the clinician may be the client of a third party (such as a court) and not of the assessee. This fact, as well as its implications with respect to issues such as confidentiality, must be made clear to the assessee. Another difference between forensic and general clinical practice is that the patient may have been compelled to undergo assessment. Unlike the typical client seeking therapy, for example, the assessee is not highly motivated to be truthful. Consequently, it is imperative that the assessor rely not only on the assessee's representations but also on all available documentation, such as police reports and interviews with persons who may have pertinent knowledge. The mental health professional who performs forensic work would do well to be educated in the language of the law:

> To go into court and render the opinion that a person is not responsible for a crime because he is psychotic is to say nothing of value to the judge or jury. However, to go into the same court and state that a man is not responsible because as a result of a mental disorder, namely, paranoid schizophrenia, "he lacked substantial capacity to conform his behavior to the requirements of the law"—because he was hearing voices that told him he must commit the crime to protect his family from future harm—would be of great value to the judge or jury. It is not because the man had a psychosis that he is not responsible; it is how his illness affected his behavior and his ability to form the necessary criminal intent or to have the *mens rea*, or guilty mind, that is important. (Rappeport, 1982, p. 333)

Forensic assessors are sometimes placed in the role of psychohistorians, especially in cases involving questions of capacity to testify. In such cases, assessors may be called on to offer opinions about people they have never personally interviewed or observed—a situation that seldom if ever arises in nonforensic assessments. Forensic assessment frequently entails rendering opinions about momentous matters such as whether a person is competent to stand trial, is criminally responsible, or is ready for parole. Some have challenged the role of mental health professionals in these and related matters, citing the unreliability of psychiatric diagnosis and the invalidity of various assessment tools for use with such objectives (Faust & Ziskin, 1988a, 1988b; see also Matarazzo, 1990, for a response). Nonetheless, judges, juries, district attorneys, the police, and other members of the criminal justice system rely on mental health professionals to provide them with their best judgments concerning such critical questions. One such question that is raised frequently concerns the prediction of dangerousness (Lally, 2003).

**Dangerousness to oneself or others**   An official determination that a person is dangerous to self or others is legal cause to deprive that individual of liberty. The individual so judged will, on a voluntary or involuntary basis, undergo psychotherapeutic intervention, typically in a secure treatment facility, until such time that he or she is no longer judged to be dangerous. This is so because the state has a compelling duty to protect its citizens from danger. The duty extends to protecting suicidal people, who are presumed to be suffering from mental disorder, from acting on self-destructive impulses. Mental health professionals play a key role in decisions about who is and is not considered dangerous.

The determination of dangerousness is ideally made on the basis of multiple data sources, including interview data, case history data, and formal testing. When dealing with potentially homicidal or suicidal assessees, the professional assessor must have knowledge of the risk factors associated

**JUST THINK . . .**

During the course of a counseling assessment, a counselor learns that an HIV-infected patient is planning to have unprotected sexual contact with an identified party. Is it the counselor's duty to warn that party?

with such violent acts. Risk factors may include a history of previous attempts to commit the act, drug/alcohol abuse, and unemployment. If given an opportunity to interview the potentially dangerous individual, the assessor will typically explore the assessee's ideation, motivation, and imagery associated with the contemplated violence. Additionally, questions will be raised that relate to the availability and lethality of the method and means by which the violent act would be perpetrated. The assessor will assess how specific and detailed the plan, if any, is. The assessor may also explore the extent to which helping resources such as family, friends, or roommates can prevent violence from occurring. If the assessor determines that a homicide is imminent, the assessor has a legal **duty to warn** the endangered third party—a duty that overrides the privileged communication between psychologist and client. As stated in the landmark 1974 case *Tarasoff v. the Regents of the University of California,* "Protective privilege ends where the public peril begins" (see Cohen, 1979, for elaboration of this and related principles).

Dangerousness manifests itself in sundry ways in varied settings, from the school playground to the post office lobby. Working together, members of the legal and mental health communities strive to keep people reasonably safe from themselves and others while not unduly depriving any citizens of their right to liberty. Toward that end, a rather large literature dealing with the assessment of dangerousness, including suicide, has emerged (see, for example, Baumeister, 1990; Blumenthal & Kupfer, 1990; Catalano et al., 1997; Copas & Tarling, 1986; Gardner et al., 1996; Jobes et al., 1997; Kapusta, 2011; Lewinsohn et al., 1996; Lidz et al., 1993; Monahan, 1981; Olweus, 1979; Pisani et al., 2011; Rice & Harris, 1995; Steadman, 1983; van Praag et al., 1990; Wagner, 1997; Webster et al., 1994) along with a number of tests (Beck et al., 1989; Eyman & Eyman, 1990; Linehan et al., 1983; Patterson et al., 1983; Reynolds, 1987; Rothberg & Geer-Williams, 1992; Williams et al., 1996) and clinical interview guidelines (Sommers-Flanagan & Sommers-Flanagan, 1995; Truant et al., 1991; Wollersheim, 1974).

Despite the best efforts of many scholars, the prediction of dangerousness must be considered more an art than a science at present. Historically, clinicians have not been very accurate in their predictions of dangerousness. On a brighter note, many people and organizations are working to better the odds of successfully predicting dangerousness. As pointed out in this chapter's *Close-Up,* among the organizations committed to the application of behavioral science to issues of dangerousness is the U.S. Secret Service.

**Competency to stand trial**   *Competency* in the legal sense has many different meanings. One may speak, for example, of competence to make a will, enter into a contract, commit a crime, waive constitutional rights, consent to medical treatment . . . the list goes on. Before convicted murderer Gary Gilmore was executed in Utah, he underwent an examination designed to determine whether or not he was competent to be executed. That is so because the law mandates that a certain propriety exists with respect to state-ordered executions: It would not be morally proper to execute insane persons.

**Competence to stand trial** has to do largely with a defendant's ability to understand the charges against him and assist in his own defense. As stated in the Supreme Court's ruling in *Dusky v. United States,* a defendant must have "sufficient present ability to consult with his lawyer with a reasonable degree of rational . . . [and] factual understanding of the proceedings against him." This "understand and assist" requirement, as it has come to be called, is in effect an extension of the constitutional prohibition against trials *in absentia;* a defendant must be not only physically present during the trial but mentally present as well.

## Assessment of Dangerousness and the Secret Service

The Secret Service is charged by federal law with a number of responsibilities, including investigation of crimes of counterfeiting, forgery, and fraud involving computers and financial institutions. It is perhaps best known for its protective functions and its duty to protect the following people and their families: the president of the United States, the vice president, former presidents and vice presidents, major candidates for or successors to these offices, and visiting foreign heads of state.

Law enforcement agencies have evinced a great deal of interest in terms of how behavioral science, and more specifically knowledge of dangerousness, can be applied to crime prevention. In Los Angeles, where the stalking of celebrities is a well-publicized problem, the police department established a threat management unit (Lane, 1992). When members of Congress or their staffs receive threats, the matter may be referred to a similar police unit established by the U.S. Capitol Police. Additionally, "the United States Marshals Service has initiated systematic efforts to formulate a protective investigative function to analyze inappropriate communications to, and to evaluate and manage potential threats against, federal judicial officials" (Coggins et al., 1998, p. 53).

The Secret Service has been exemplary in its efforts to integrate behavioral research and clinical expertise into its policies and practices, including its risk assessment and protective activities. In the course of attempting to prevent a highly specific crime from taking place, some of the things the Service must do are (1) identify and investigate people who may pose a risk to a protectee; (2) make a determination of the level of risk the identified people pose; and (3) implement a case management program for those identified as possibly posing a genuine risk. To meet these and related objectives with maximum effectiveness, the service established a behavioral research program. The head of that program is Margaret Coggins, Ph.D., and much of what we say here about that program is derived from a publication by Coggins and her colleagues (1998).

Charged with duties that require very specialized assessments of dangerousness on a regular basis, the Secret Service has a history of receiving input from clinical and forensic professionals. In 1980, the agency contracted with the Institute of Medicine to sponsor a conference of clinicians and behavioral scientists that addressed

*The Secret Service relies on research on the assessment of dangerousness in fulfilling its protective mission.*

such issues as the prediction of dangerousness, case management of dangerous persons, and agent training needs (Takeuchi et al., 1981). Another conference in 1982 extended the agenda to issues such as the development of an internal research program on the assessment of people who threatened protectees and training for agents in the assessment and management of mentally ill threateners (Institute of Medicine, 1984). The Secret Service's behavioral research program evolved out of these conferences. The research program now studies diverse matters such as risk assessment issues, factors in agent decision making, and attitudes of mental health professionals toward the Secret Service in terms of their effect on reporting threats to the Service's protectees. A collaboration between researchers

*(continued)*

## Assessment of Dangerousness
## and the Secret Service *(continued)*

and practitioners was forged in order to achieve the program objectives:

> Special agents and researchers, both internal Secret Service staff and external consultants, work together to identify practical study questions, prioritize areas of inquiry, design study methodologies, collect and analyze data, and disseminate research findings. Agents play a key role in ensuring that relevant investigative, risk assessment, and case management concerns are brought forward for study, and their participation in research design and data collection lends internal credibility to the importance of incorporating study findings into practice. Similarly, research staff and scholars from the academic and scientific communities ensure that principles of scientific integrity guide the research process and are instrumental in protecting the external validity of the data and findings according to rigorous standards of peer review. (Coggins et al., 1998, p. 61)

The case study is a potentially useful tool of assessment and research, particularly in efforts to identify factors related to an individual's potential for violence against a Secret Service protectee. The Secret Service's Exceptional Case Study Project (ECSP) was designed to study persons who have either attacked or approached with lethal means an individual targeted on the basis of public status. Variables selected for study include behavior, thinking, planning, mental status, motivation, and communication patterns. One noteworthy finding from such research could be paraphrased in terms of the aphorism "actions speak louder than words." Indeed, prior behavior has been found to take precedence over threatening statements as a factor related to potential for violence (Vossekuil & Fein, 1997). This finding is consistent with the findings of psychiatrist Park Dietz in his research on individuals who stalk Hollywood celebrities. Dietz et al. (1991) concluded that there was little relation between writing a threatening letter to the celebrity and attempting to physically approach the celebrity. People who wrote such letters were no more or less likely to attempt to approach the celebrity than people who did not make threats.

Behavioral science, and in particular assessment-related research, has much to offer the Secret Service and other organizations involved in law enforcement and crime prevention. This is true even though the Secret Service's "operational mission always takes precedence over academic or scientific interest" (Coggins et al., 1998, p. 68).

The competency requirement protects an individual's right to choose and assist counsel, the right to act as a witness on one's own behalf, and the right to confront opposing witnesses. The requirement also increases the probability that the truth of the case will be developed because the competent defendant is able to monitor continuously the testimony of witnesses and help bring discrepancies in testimony to the attention of the court. In general, persons who are mentally retarded, psychotic, or suffering from a debilitating neurological disorder are persons held to be incompetent to stand trial. However, it cannot be overemphasized that any one of these three diagnoses is not in itself sufficient for a person to be found incompetent. Stated another way: It is possible for a person to be mentally retarded, psychotic, or suffering from a debilitating neurological disorder—or all three—and still be found competent to stand trial. The person will be found to be incompetent if and only if she is unable to understand the charges against her and is unable to assist in her own defense.

A number of instruments have been developed as aids in evaluating whether a defendant meets the understand-and-assist requirement. For example, researchers at Georgetown University Law School enumerated 13 criteria of competency to stand trial. Six of the criteria were characterized as "factual," and seven were characterized as "inferential." In general, the factual criteria had to do with clinical judgments regarding the defendant's ability to understand the charges and relevant legal procedures. The inferential criteria focused more on clinical judgments concerning the defendant's ability to communicate with counsel and make informed decisions. Interested readers will find a listing of all 13 criteria as well as a more detailed description of the criteria in Bukatman et al.'s (1971) *American Journal of Psychiatry* article. An earlier volume of that same journal contained a presentation of another instrument used to assess competency to stand trial. The Competency Screening Test (Lipsitt et al., 1971) is a 22-item instrument written in a sentence completion format. The defendant's competency is clinically evaluated by the quality of responses to sentence stems such as "If the jury finds me guilty, I _____." The test is scored on a three-point scale ranging from 0 to 2, with appropriate responses scored 2, marginally appropriate responses scored 1, and clearly inappropriate responses scored 0. For example, consider this item: *When I go to court, the lawyer will . . ."* A 2-point response would be "defend me." Such a response indicates that the assessee has a clear understanding of the lawyer's role. By contrast, a 0-point response might be "have me guillotined," which would be indicative of an inappropriate perception of the lawyer's role. Lipsitt et al. reported the inter-rater reliability among trained scorers of this test to be $r = .93$. They also reported that their test was successful in discriminating seriously disturbed, state-hospitalized men from control groups consisting of students, community adults, club members, and civilly committed hospitalized patients.

Other tests of competency to stand trial include the Fitness Interview Test (FIT; Roesch et al., 1984), the MacArthur Competence Assessment Tool–Criminal Adjudication (MacCAT-CA; Hoge et al., 1999; Poythress et al., 1999) and the Evaluation of Competency to Stand Trial–Revised (ECST-R; Rogers et al., 2004). Although the FIT was developed in accordance with Canadian legal standards it has been widely used in the United States. The FIT is an idiographic measure, thus limiting comparisons between testtakers. By contrast, the MacCAT-CA and ECST-R both employ a nomothetic approach; scores from defendants on competency to stand trial can be compared to other defendants (Zapf & Roesch, 2011).

**Criminal responsibility**    "Not guilty by reason of insanity" is a plea to a criminal charge that we have all heard. But stop and think about the meaning of the legal term **insanity** to mental health professionals and the evaluation procedures by which psychological assessors could identify the insane. The insanity defense has its roots in the idea that

JUST THINK . . .

Should measures of competency ideally be idiographic or nomothetic?

only blameworthy persons (that is, those with a criminal mind) should be punished. Possibly exempt from blame, therefore, are children, mental incompetents, and others who may be irresponsible, lack control of their actions, or have no conception that what they are doing is criminal. As early as the sixteenth century, it was argued in an English court that an offending act should not be considered a felony if the offender had no conception of good and evil. By the eighteenth century, the focus had shifted from good and evil as a criterion for evaluating criminal responsibility to the issue of whether the defendant "doth not know what he is doing no more than . . . a wild beast."

Judicial history was made in nineteenth-century England when in 1843 Daniel M'Naghten was found not guilty by reason of insanity after attempting to assassinate the British prime minister. (He mistakenly shot and killed the prime minister's secretary.) M'Naghten was acquitted. According to the court, he could not be held accountable for the crime if, "at the time of the committing of the act, the party accused was laboring under such a defect of reason from disease of the mind as not to know the nature and quality of the act he was doing, or if he did know it, that he did not know he was doing what was wrong."

The decision in the *M'Naghten* case has come to be referred to as the *right or wrong test,* or the **M'Naghten standard.** To the present day, this test of sanity is used in England as well as in a number of jurisdictions in the United States. However, a problem with the right or wrong test is that it does not provide for the acquitting of persons who know right from wrong yet still are unable to control impulses to commit criminal acts. In 1954, an opinion written by the U.S. Court of Appeal for the District of Columbia in the case of *Durham v. United States* held that a defendant was not culpable for criminal action "if his unlawful act was the product of a mental disease or defect" (the **Durham standard**). Still another standard of legal insanity, set forth by the American Law Institute (ALI) in 1956, has become one of the most widely used throughout the United States (Weiner, 1980). With slight alterations from one jurisdiction to another, the **ALI standard** provides as follows:

> A person is not responsible for criminal conduct, i.e., [is] insane if, at the time of such conduct, as a result of a mental disease or defect, he lacks substantial capacity either to appreciate the criminality (wrongfulness) of his conduct, or to conform his conduct to the requirements of the law.
>
> As used in this article, the terms "mental disease or defect" do not include an abnormality manifested only by repeated criminal or otherwise antisocial conduct.

In clinical practice, defendants who are mentally retarded, psychotic, or neurologically impaired are likely to be the ones found not guilty by reason of insanity. However, as was the case with considerations of competency to stand trial, the mere fact that a person is judged to be mentally retarded, psychotic, or neurologically impaired is in itself no guarantee that the individual will be found not guilty. Other criteria, such as the ALI standards cited, must be met.

**JUST THINK . . .**

Should mental health professionals be involved in determining who is not guilty by reason of insanity? Should the insanity plea be eliminated as a legal defense in criminal proceedings?

To help determine if the ALI standards are met, a number of instruments such as the Rogers Criminal Responsibility Assessment Scale (RCRAS) have been developed. Psychologist Richard Rogers and his colleagues (Rogers & Cavanaugh, 1980, 1981; Rogers et al., 1981) designed the RCRAS as a systematic and empirical approach to insanity evaluations. This instrument consists of 25 items tapping both psychological and situational variables. The items are scored with respect to five scales: reliability (including malingering), organic factors, psychopathology, cognitive control, and behavioral control. After scoring, the examiner employs a hierarchical decision model to arrive at a decision concerning the assessee's sanity. Validity studies done with this scale (for example, Rogers et al., 1983; Rogers et al., 1984) have shown it to be useful in discriminating between sane and insane patients/defendants.

**Readiness for parole or probation**   Some people convicted of a crime will pay their dues to society and go on to lead fulfilling, productive lives after their incarceration. At the other extreme are career criminals who will violate laws at the first opportunity upon their release—or escape—from prison. Predicting who is ready for parole or probation and the possible outcome of such a release has proved to be no easy task. Still, attempts have been made to develop measures that are useful in parole and probation decisions.

A person with a diagnosis of psychopathy (a **psychopath**) is four times more likely than a nonpsychopath to fail on release from prison (Hart et al., 1988). A classic work by Cleckley (1976) provided a detailed profile of psychopaths. They are people with few inhibitions who may pursue pleasure or money with callous disregard for the welfare of others. Based on a factor-analytic study of Cleckley's description of persons with psychopathy, Robert D. Hare (1980) developed a 22-item Psychopathy Checklist (PCL) that reflects personality characteristics as rated by the assessor (such as callousness, impulsiveness, and empathy) in addition to prior history as gleaned from the assessee's records (such as "criminal versatility"). In the revised version of the test, the Revised

Psychopathy Checklist (PCL-R; Hare, 1985), two items from the original PCL were omitted because of their relatively low correlation with the rest of the scale, and the scoring criteria for some of the remaining items were modified. Hare et al. (1990) report that the two forms are equivalent.

In one study that employed a maximum-security psychiatric sample, the PCL correctly identified 80% of the violent recidivists (Harris et al., 1989). A version of the PCL specially modified for use with young male offenders produced scores that correlated significantly with variables such as number of conduct disorder symptoms, previous violent offenses, violent recidivism, and violent behavior within the maximum-security institution in which the study was conducted (Forth et al., 1990). In another study, psychopathy ratings were found to predict outcome for both temporary absence and parole release. Psychopaths were recommitted four times more frequently than nonpsychopaths (Serin et al., 1990).

## Diagnosis and evaluation of emotional injury

**Emotional injury,** or psychological harm or damage, is a term sometimes used synonymously with mental suffering, pain and suffering, and emotional harm. In cases involving charges such as discrimination, harassment, malpractice, stalking, and unlawful termination of employment, psychological assessors may be responsible for evaluating alleged emotional injury. Such an evaluation will be designed to shed light on an individual's functioning prior and subsequent to the alleged injury (Melton et al., 1997). The court will evaluate the findings in light of all of the evidence and make a determination regarding whether the alleged injury exists and, if so, the magnitude of the damage.

Many tools of assessment—including the interview, the case study, and psychological tests—may be used in the process of evaluating and diagnosing claims of emotional injury. Interviews may be conducted with the person claiming the injury as well as with others who have knowledge relevant to the claim. Case study materials include documents such as physician or therapist records, school records, military records, employment records, and police records. The specific psychological tests used in an emotional injury evaluation will vary with the preferences of the assessor. In one study in which 140 forensic psychologists returned a survey dealing with assessment practices, it was found that no two practitioners routinely used exactly the same combination of tests to assess emotional injury (Boccaccini & Brodsky, 1999). The reasons given for the use of specific tests and test batteries most frequently involved established norms, personal clinical experience, the widespread acceptance of the instrument, research support, and content. Greater consistency in test selection would be desirable. Such consistency could be achieved by studying the incremental validity that each test adds to the task of assessing different types of emotional injury in specific contexts.

> **JUST THINK . . .**
>
> Why would greater consistency be desirable in instruments used to evaluate emotional injury?

## Profiling

Contemporary films and television shows in the detective genre, not to mention occasional, high profile news stories, have provided many of us with some familiarity with the term *profiling.* Now referred to by the FBI as "criminal investigative analysis," and by some in the mental health field simply as "investigative psychology," **profiling** may be defined as a crime-solving process that draws upon psychological and criminological expertise applied to the study of crime scene evidence.

At the core of profiling is the assumption that perpetrators of serial crimes (usually involving murder, some sort of ritual, and/or sexual violation) leave more than physical evidence at a crime scene; they leave psychological clues about who they are, personality traits they possess, and how they think. The hope is that these behavior-related clues will help investigators effect an arrest. Hypotheses typically made by profilers from crime-scene evidence usually relate to perpetrators' organization and planning skills and to the degrees of control, emotion, and risk that appear evident (O'Toole, 2004). The primary tools of assessment employed in profiling are interviews (both from witnesses and about witnesses) and case study material (such as autopsy reports and crime-scene photos and reports). The Behavioral Science Unit of the FBI (now part of the National Center for the Analysis of Violent Crime) maintains a database of such material.

To date, most of the highly publicized cases for which profilers have been employed have not involved persons with advanced degrees in psychology as the profiler. Rather, the profilers in such cases have tended to be psychologically savvy individuals with a background in law enforcement and/or criminology. Whether or not criminal profiling is more the province of psychologists or criminologists is debatable (Alison & Barrett, 2004; Coupe, 2006; see also Hicks & Sales, 2006). Indeed, some have called for the "professionalization" of what is currently "an ill-formed forensic discipline" (Alison et al., 2004, p. 71). It has further been noted that, to be effective in their work, profilers must have attained a degree of competence in the knowledge of diverse cultures (Palermo, 2002).

Profiling can be viewed with skepticism by behavioral scientists who find aspects of it theoretically and methodologically questionable (Cox, 2006; Snook et al., 2007; Woodworth & Porter, 2000). The process may also be looked at with skepticism by law enforcement officials who question its utility in crime solving (Gregory, 2005). For students who are interested in learning more about psychological evaluation as it has been applied to profiling, a table posted on our companion website presents brief descriptions of a sampling of published work on the subject.

**JUST THINK . . .**

Should profiling be a specialty area of psychology that is taught in graduate schools with forensic psychology graduate programs? Why or why not?

## Custody Evaluations

As the number of divorces in this country continues to climb, so does the number of custody proceedings. Before the 1920s, it was fairly commonplace for the father to be granted custody of the children (Lamb, 1981). The pendulum swung, however, with the widespread adoption of what was referred to as the "tender years" doctrine and the belief that the child's interest would be best served if the mother were granted custody. But with the coming of age of the dual-career household, the courts have begun to be more egalitarian in their custody decisions (McClure-Butterfield, 1990). Courts have recognized that the best interest of the child may be served by father custody, mother custody, or joint custody. Psychological assessors can assist the court in making such decisions through the use of a **custody evaluation**—a psychological assessment of parents or guardians and their parental capacity and/or of children and their parental needs and preferences—usually undertaken for the purpose of assisting a court in making a decision about awarding custody. Ideally, one impartial expert in the mental health field should be responsible for assessing *all* family members and submitting a report to the court (Gardner, 1982). More often than not, however, the husband has his expert, the wife has her expert, and a battle, often bitter in tone, is on (Benjamin & Gollan, 2003).

**Evaluation of the parent** The evaluation of parental capacity typically involves a detailed interview that focuses primarily on various aspects of child rearing, though tests of intelligence, personality, and adjustment may be employed if questions remain after the interview. The assessor might begin with open-ended questions, designed to let the parent ventilate some of his or her feelings, and then proceed to more specific questions tapping a wide variety of areas, including

- the parent's own childhood: happy? abused?
- the parent's own relationship with parents, siblings, peers
- the circumstances that led up to the marriage and the degree of forethought that went into the decision to have (or adopt) children
- the adequacy of prenatal care and attitudes toward the pregnancy
- the parent's description of the child
- the parent's self-evaluation as a parent, including strengths and weaknesses
- the parent's evaluation of his or her spouse in terms of strengths and weaknesses as a parent
- the quantity and quality of time spent caring for and playing with children
- the parent's approach to discipline
- the parent's receptivity to the child's peer relationships

During the course of the interview, the assessor may find evidence that the interviewee really does not want custody of the children but is undertaking the custody battle for some other reason. For example, custody may be nothing more than another issue to bargain over with respect to the divorce settlement. Alternatively, for example, parents might be embarrassed to admit—to themselves or others—that custody of the children is not desired. Sometimes a parent, emotionally scathed by all that has gone on before the divorce, may be employing the custody battle as a technique of vengeance—to threaten to take away that which is most prized and adored by the spouse. The clinician performing the evaluation must appreciate that such ill-motivated intentions do underlie some custody battles. In the best interest of the children, it is the obligation of the clinician to report such findings.

In certain cases an assessor may deem it desirable to assess any of many variables related to marriage and family life. A wide variety of such instruments is available, including those designed to measure adjustment (Beier & Sternberg, 1977; Epstein et al., 1983; Locke & Wallace, 1959; McCubbin et al., 1985a; McCubbin et al., 1985b; Spanier, 1976; Spanier & Filsinger, 1983; Udry, 1981), assets (Olson et al., 1985), preferences (Price et al., 1982), intimacy (Waring & Reddon, 1983), jealousy (Bringle et al., 1979), communication (Bienvenu, 1978), feelings (Lowman, 1980), satisfaction (Roach et al., 1981; Snyder, 1981), stability (Booth & Edwards, 1983), trust (Larzelere & Huston, 1980), expectancies (Notarius & Vanzetti, 1983; Sabatelli, 1984), parenting ability (Bavolek, 1984), coping strategies (McCubbin et al., 1985a; McCubbin et al., 1985b; Straus, 1979), strength of family ties (Bardis, 1975), family interpersonal environment (Kinston et al., 1985; Moos & Moos, 1981; Robin et al., 1990), children's attitudes toward parents (Hudson, 1982), and overall quality of family life (Beavers, 1985; Olson & Barnes, 1985).

**Evaluation of the child**   The court will be interested in knowing whether the child in a custody proceeding has a preference with respect to future living and visitation arrangements. Toward that end, the psychological assessor can be of assistance with a wide variety of tests and techniques. Most authorities agree that the preferences of children under the age of 5 are too unreliable and too influenced by recent experiences to be accorded much weight. However, if intelligence test data indicate that the child who is chronologically 5 years old is functioning at a higher level, then those preferences may be accorded greater weight. This is particularly true if evidence attesting to the child's keen social comprehension is presented to the court. Some methods that can

**Figure 14–1**
**Projective Techniques Used in Custody Evaluation**

*The picture on the left is from the Children's Apperception Test-H (Bellak & Bellak, 1965), and the one on the right is from* The Boys and Girls Book about Divorce *(Gardner, 1971). These, as well as TAT and other pictures used as projective stimuli, may be useful in evaluating children's parental preferences.*

be useful in assessing a child's parental preference include structured play exercises with dolls that represent the child and other family members, figure drawings of family members followed by storytelling about the drawings, and the use of projective techniques such as the TAT and related tests (Figure 14–1).

Specially constructed sentence completion items can also be of value in the assessment of parental preferences. For example, the following items might be useful in examining children's differing perceptions of each parent:

Mothers _____.

If I do something wrong, my father _____.

It is best for children to live with _____.

Fathers _____.

Mommies are bad when _____.

I like to hug _____.

I don't like to hug _____.

Daddies are bad when _____.

The last time I cried _____.

My friends think that my mother _____.

My friends think that my father _____.

Sometimes impromptu innovation on the part of the examiner is required. In performing a custody evaluation on a 5-year-old child, one of this text's authors (RJC) noted that the child seemed to identify strongly with the main character in *E.T., The Extraterrestrial.* The child had seen the film three times, came into the test session carrying two *E.T.* bubble-gum cards, and identified as "E.T." the picture he drew when instructed to draw a person. To obtain a measure of parental preference, the examiner took four figures and represented them as "E.T.," "E.T.'s mother," "E.T.'s father," and "E.T.'s sister." An empty cardboard box was then labeled a "spaceship," and the child was told that E.T. (stranded on earth and longing to return to his home planet) had the opportunity to go home but that the spaceship had room for only two other passengers.

The child boarded his mother and his sister in addition to "E.T." The child told the examiner that E.T.'s father would "wave goodbye."

The data-gathering process for the evaluation begins the moment the child and the parent(s) come into the office. The assessor takes careful note of the quality of the interaction between the parent(s) and the child. The child will then be interviewed alone and asked about the nature and quality of the relationship. If the child expresses a strong preference for one parent or the other, the assessor must evaluate how meaningful that preference is. For example, a child who sees his rancher father only every other weekend might have a good ol' time on the brief occasions they are together and express a preference for living there—unaware that life in the country would soon become just as routine as life in the city with Mom. If children do not express a preference, insight into their feelings can be obtained by using the tests described earlier combined with skillful interviewing. Included among the topics for discussion will be the child's physical description of the parents and living quarters. Questions will be asked about the routine aspects of life (such as "Who makes breakfast for you?") and about recreation, parental visitation, parental involvement with the children's education, their general well-being, and their siblings and friends.

Before leaving the subject of custody, let's note that children are not the only subject of custody battles. Recent years have witnessed an increasing number of custody disputes over dogs, cats, and other family pets. In most states, pets are considered by law not as living creatures, but simply as property—much like furniture or golf clubs.

> **JUST THINK . . .**
>
> How might hand puppets be used as a tool of assessment with very young children involved in a custody dispute?

Many pet lovers would like the legislature and courts to recognize that pets are living entities and that as such, consideration in custody disputes should also be given to what is in the best interest of the pet. Psychologists may find themselves embroiled in this new type of custody battle in the years to come.

## Child Abuse and Neglect

A legal mandate exists in most states for many licensed professionals to report *child abuse* and *child neglect* when they have knowledge of it. The legal definitions of child abuse and child neglect vary from state to state. Typically, definitions of **abuse** refer to the creation of conditions that may give rise to abuse of a child (a person under the state-defined age of majority) by an adult responsible for the care of that person. The abuse may be in the form of (1) the infliction or allowing of infliction of physical injury or emotional impairment that is nonaccidental, (2) the creation or allowing the creation of substantial risk of physical injury or emotional impairment that is nonaccidental, or (3) the committing or allowing of a sexual offense to be committed against a child. Typical definitions of **neglect** refer to a failure on the part of an adult responsible for the care of a child to exercise a minimum degree of care in providing the child with food, clothing, shelter, education, medical care, and supervision.

A number of excellent general sources for the study of child abuse and child neglect are currently available (see, for example, Board of Professional Affairs, 1999; Cicchetti & Carlson, 1989; Ellerstein, 1981; Fischer, 1999; Fontana et al., 1963; Helfer & Kempe, 1988; Kelley, 1988; Reece & Groden, 1985). Resources are also available to assist professionals in recognizing specific forms of child abuse such as head injury (Billmire & Myers, 1985), eye injury (Gammon, 1981), mouth injury (Becker et al., 1978), emotional trauma (Brassard et al., 1986), burns (Alexander et al., 1987;

Lung et al., 1977), bites (American Board of Forensic Odontology, 1986), fractures (Worlock et al., 1986), poisoning (Kresel & Lovejoy, 1981), sexual abuse (Adams-Tucker, 1982; Faller, 1988; Friedrich et al., 1986; Sanfilippo et al., 1986; Sebold, 1987), and shaken infant syndrome (Dykes, 1986). What follows are some brief, very general guidelines for the assessment of physical and emotional signs of child abuse.

**Physical signs of abuse and neglect**   Although psychologists and other mental health professionals without medical credentials typically do not have occasion to physically examine children, a knowledge of physical signs of abuse and neglect is important.

Many signs of abuse take the form of physical injuries. During an evaluation, these injuries may be described by abused children or abusing adults as the result of an accident. The knowledgeable professional needs a working familiarity with the various kinds of injuries that may signal more ominous causes. Consider, for example, the case of injury to the face. In most veritable accidents, only one side of the face is injured. It may therefore be significant if a child evidences injury on both sides of the face—both eyes and both cheeks. Marks on the skin may be telling. Grab marks made by an adult-size hand and marks that form a recognizable pattern (such as the tines of a fork, a cord or rope, or human teeth) may be especially revealing. Burns from a cigarette or lighter may be in evidence as marks on the soles of the feet, the palms of the hands, the back, or the buttocks. Burns from scalding water may be in evidence as a glove-like redness on the hands or feet. Any bone fracture or dislocation should be investigated, as should head injuries, particularly when a patch of hair appears to be missing. In some instances, the head injury may have resulted from being held by the hair.

Physical signs that may or may not indicate neglect include dress that is inappropriate for the season, poor hygiene, and lagging physical development. Physical signs indicative of sexual abuse are not present in the majority of cases. In many instances, there is no penetration or only partial penetration by the abusing adult, and no physical scars. In young children, physical signs that may or may not indicate sexual abuse include difficulty in sitting or walking; itching or reported pain or discomfort of genital areas; stained, bloody, or torn underclothing; and foreign objects in orifices. In older children, the presence of sexually transmitted diseases or a pregnancy may or may not signal child sexual abuse.

**Emotional and behavioral signs of abuse and neglect**   Emotional and behavioral indicators may reflect something other than child abuse and neglect. Child abuse or neglect is only one of several possible explanations underlying the appearance of such signs. Fear of going home or fear of adults in general and reluctance to remove outer garments may be signs of abuse. Other possible emotional and behavioral signs of abuse include:

- unusual reactions or apprehension in response to other children crying
- low self-esteem
- extreme or inappropriate moods
- aggressiveness
- social withdrawal
- nail biting, thumb sucking, or other habit disorders

Possible emotional and behavioral signs of neglect include frequent lateness to or absence from school, chronic fatigue, and chronic hunger. Age-inappropriate behavior may also be a sign of neglect. Most typically, this is seen as the result of a child taking on many adult roles with younger children owing to the absence of a caregiver at home.

Possible emotional and behavioral signs of sexual abuse in children under 8 years of age may include fear of sleeping alone, eating disorders, enuresis, encopresis, sexual acting out, change in school behavior, tantrums, crying spells, sadness, and suicidal thoughts. These signs may also be present in older children, along with other possible signs such as memory problems, emotional numbness, violent fantasies, hyperalertness, self-mutilation, and sexual concerns or preoccupations, which may be accompanied by guilt or shame.

Interviews, behavioral observation, and psychological tests are all used in identifying child abuse. However, professionals disagree about the appropriate tools for such an assessment, particularly when it involves identifying sexual abuse. One technique involves observing children while they play with **anatomically detailed dolls** (ADDs), which are dolls with accurately represented genitalia. Sexually abused children may, on average, engage ADDs in more sexually oriented activities than other children, but differences between groups of abused and nonabused children tend not to be significant. Many nonabused children play in a sexually explicit way with ADDs, so such play is not necessarily diagnostic of sexual abuse (Elliott et al., 1993; Wolfner et al., 1993).

Human-figure drawings are also used to assess sexual and physical abuse, though their accuracy in distinguishing abused from nonabused children is a subject of debate (Burgess et al., 1981; Chantler et al., 1993; Kelley, 1985). Questionnaires designed for administration to a child who may have been abused (Mannarino et al., 1994) or to adults such as teachers or parents who know that child well (Chantler et al., 1993) have been explored, although no thoroughly validated instruments have been developed to date. In short, no widely accepted, reliable, and valid set of techniques for the assessment of sexual abuse is available. Professionals who have occasion to conduct assessments for sexual abuse have been advised to integrate information from many assessment tools and to select those tools on a case-by-case basis.

**Issues in reporting child abuse and neglect** Child abuse, when it occurs, is a tragedy. A claim of child abuse when in fact there has been no such abuse is also a tragedy—one that can scar irrevocably an accused but innocent individual for life. It is incumbent on professionals who undertake the weighty obligation of assessing a child for potential abuse not to approach their task with any preconceived notions because such notions can be conveyed to the child

> **JUST THINK . . .**
>
> What obstacles do test developers face as they attempt to develop psychometrically sound instruments to assess sexual abuse in children?

and perceived as the right answer to questions (King & Yuille, 1987; White et al., 1988). Children from the ages of about 2 to 7 are highly suggestible, and their memory is not as well developed as that of older children. It is possible that events that occurred after the alleged incident—including events referred to only in conversations—may be confused with the actual incident (Ceci et al., 1987; Goodman & Reed, 1986; Loftus & Davies, 1984). Related considerations regarding the psychological examination of a child for abuse have been discussed in detail by Weissman (1991). Sensitivity to the rights of all parties in a child abuse proceeding, including the rights of the accused, is critical to making certain that justice is served.

**Risk assessment** In an effort to prevent child abuse, test developers have sought to create instruments useful in identifying parents and others who may be at risk for abusing children. The Child Abuse Potential Inventory (CAP; Milner et al., 1986; Milner, 1991) has demonstrated impressive validity in identifying abusers. Another test, the Parenting Stress Index (PSI; Loyd & Abidin, 1985), measures stress associated with the parental role. Parents are asked to reflect on their relationship with one child at a time. Some of the items focus on child characteristics that could engender stress, such as activity level and mood. Other PSI items reflect potentially stressful aspects of the parent's life, such as lack of social support and marital problems (Gresham, 1989).

The test's authors report internal consistency reliability coefficients ranging from .89 to .95 for factors and total scores. Test-retest reliability coefficients range from .71 to .82 over three weeks and from .55 to .70 over a one-year interval (Loyd & Abidin, 1985). With respect to the test's validity, parents who physically abuse their children tend to score higher on the PSI than parents who do not (Wantz, 1989).

What are the appropriate uses of measures like the CAP and the PSI? Although positive relationships exist between child abuse and scores on the tests, the tests cannot be used to identify or prosecute child abusers in a legal context (Gresham, 1989). Because child abuse is a low base-rate phenomenon, even the use of highly reliable instruments will produce many false positives. In this instance, a false positive is an erroneous identification of the assessee as an abuser. For some parents, high levels of stress as measured by the PSI may indeed lead to physical abuse; however, for most parents they will not. Some parent–child relationships, such as those involving children with disabilities, are inherently stressful (Innocenti et al., 1992; Orr et al., 1993). Still, most parents manage to weather the relationship without inflicting any harm. Some parents who experience high levels of stress as a result of their relationship with a child may themselves be harmed—and stressed even more—to hear from a mental health official that they are at risk for child abuse. For that reason, great caution is called for in interpreting and acting on the results of a test designed to assess risk for child abuse.

On the other hand, high CAP or PSI scores may well point the way to an abusive situation, and they should alert concerned professionals to be watchful for signs of abuse. A second appropriate use of such scores concerns the allocation of resources designed to reduce parenting stress. Parents who score high on the CAP and the PSI could be given priority for placement in a parenting skills class, individualized parent training, child care assistance, and other such programs. If reducing the stress of the parent will reduce the risk of child abuse, everything that can possibly be done to reduce the parental stress should be attempted.

**JUST THINK . . .**

Other than by administering a psychological test, how else might professionals identify parents who are extremely stressed?

As we have seen throughout this book, there are many different tools of assessment and many different ways the tools can be used. If these tools have anything at all in common, it is that their use by a professional will at some time or another culminate in a written report. In clinical and counseling settings, that report is referred to simply as the **psychological report.**

## The Psychological Report

A critical component of any testing or assessment procedure is the reporting of the findings. The high reliability or validity of a test or assessment procedure may be cast to the wind if the assessment report is not written in an organized and readable fashion. Of course, what constitutes an organized and readable report will vary as a function of the goal of the assessment and the audience for whom the report is intended. A psychoanalyst's report exploring a patient's unresolved oedipal conflict designed for presentation to the New York Psychoanalytic Society will look and sound quite different from a school psychologist's report to a teacher concerning a child's hyperactive behavior in the classroom.

Psychological reports may be as different as the reasons for undertaking the assessment. Reports may differ on a number of variables, such as the extent to which conclusions rely on one or another assessment procedure and the specificity of recommendations made, if any. Still, some basic elements are common to most clinical reports. We focus our attention on those elements in this chapter's *Everyday Psychometrics*. It should be clear, however, that report writing is a necessary skill in educational, organizational, and other settings—any setting where psychological assessment takes place.

## The Barnum Effect

The showman P. T. Barnum is credited with having said, "There's a sucker born every minute." Psychologists, among others, have taken P. T. Barnum's words about the widespread gullibility of people quite seriously. In fact, *Barnum effect* is a term that should be familiar to any psychologist called on to write a psychological report. Before reading on to find out exactly what the Barnum effect is, imagine that you have just completed a computerized personality test and that the printout describing the results reads as follows:

> You have a strong need for other people to like you and for them to admire you. You have a tendency to be critical of yourself. You have a great deal of unused capacity that you have not turned to your advantage. Although you have some personality weaknesses, you are generally able to compensate for them. Your sexual adjustment has presented some problems for you. Disciplined and controlled on the outside, you tend to be worrisome and insecure inside. At times you have serious doubts as to whether you have made the right decision or done the right thing. You prefer a certain amount of change and variety and become dissatisfied when hemmed in by restrictions and limitations. You pride yourself on being an independent thinker and do not accept others' opinions without satisfactory proof. You have found it unwise to be too frank in revealing yourself to others. At times you are extraverted, affable, and sociable, whereas at other times you are introverted, wary, and reserved. Some of your aspirations tend to be pretty unrealistic.

Still imagining that the preceding test results had been formulated specifically for you, please rate the accuracy of the description in terms of how well it applies to you personally.

*I feel that the interpretation was:*

excellent

good

average

poor

very poor

Now that you have completed the exercise, we can say: "Welcome to the ranks of those who have been subject to the Barnum effect." This psychological profile is, as you have no doubt noticed, vague and general. The same paragraph (sometimes with slight modifications) has been used in a number of psychological studies (Forer, 1949; Jackson et al., 1982; Merrens & Richards, 1970; Sundberg, 1955; Ulrich et al., 1963) with similar findings: People tend to accept vague and general personality descriptions as uniquely applicable to themselves without realizing that the same description could be applied to just about anyone.

The finding that people tend to accept vague personality descriptions as accurate descriptions of themselves came to be known as the **Barnum effect** after psychologist Paul Meehl's (1956) condemnation of

**JUST THINK . . .**

Write one paragraph—a vague and general personality description—that could be used to study the Barnum effect. Here's a hint: You may use the daily horoscope column in your local newspaper for assistance in finding the words.

# Elements of a Typical Report of Psychological Assessment

There is no single, universally accepted style or form for a psychological report. Most assessors develop a style and form that they believe best suits the specific objectives of the assessment. Generally, however, most clinical reports contain the elements listed and briefly discussed below.

## Demographic Data

Included here are all or some of the following: the patient's name, address, telephone number, education, occupation, religion, marital status, date of birth, place of birth, ethnic membership, citizenship, and date of testing. The examiner's name may also be listed with such identifying material.

## Reason for Referral

Why was this patient referred for psychological assessment? This section of the report may sometimes be as short as one sentence (for example, "Johnny was referred for evaluation to shed light on the question of whether his inattention in class is due to personality, neurological, or other difficulties"). Alternatively, this section of the report may be extended with all relevant background information (for example, "Johnny complained of hearing difficulties in his fourth-grade class, according to a note in his records"). If all relevant background information is not covered in the *Reason for Referral* section of the report, it may be covered in a separate section labeled *Background* (not illustrated here) or in a later section labeled *Findings*.

## Tests Administered

Here the examiner simply lists the names of the tests that were administered. Thus, for example, this section of the report may be as brief as the following:

- Wechsler Intelligence Scale for Children-IV (1/8/09, 1/12/09)
- Bender Visual-Motor Gestalt Test-2 (1/8/09)
- Rorschach Test (1/12/09)
- Thematic Apperception Test (1/12/09)
- Sentence Completion Test (1/8/09)
- Figure drawings (1/8/09)
- In-class behavioral observation (1/7/09)

Note that the date of the test administration has been inserted next to the name of each test administered. This is a good idea under any circumstances and is particularly

important if testing was executed over the course of a number of days, weeks, or longer. In this example, the WISC-IV was administered over the course of two testing sessions on two days. The Bender-2, Sentence Completion Test, and figure drawings were administered on 1/8/09; and the Rorschach and TAT were administered on 1/12/09. Evaluation and assessment procedures other than those commonly referred to as "tests" may also be listed here. So, for example, the in-class behavioral observation that took place on 1/7/09 is listed under *Tests Administered*.

Also in this section, the examiner might place the names and the dates of tests known to have been previously administered to the examinee. If the examiner has a record of the findings (or, better yet, the original test protocols) from prior testing, this information may be integrated into the next section of the report, *Findings*.

## Findings

Here the examiner reports not only findings (for example, "On the WISC-IV Johnny achieved a Verbal IQ of 100 and a Performance IQ of 110, yielding a Full Scale IQ of 106") but also all extra-test considerations, such as observations concerning the examinee's motivation ("the examinee did/ did not appear to be motivated to do well on the tests"), the examinee's level of fatigue, the nature of the relationship and rapport with the examiner, indices of anxiety, and method of approach to the task. The section labeled *Findings* may begin with a description that is detailed enough for the reader of the report almost to visualize the examinee. For example:

> Silas is a 20-year-old college student with brown, shoulder-length, stringy hair and a full beard. He came to the testing wearing a tie-dyed shirt, cutoff and ragged shorts, and sandals. He sat slouched in his chair for most of the test session, tended to speak only when spoken to, and spoke in a slow, lethargic manner.

Included in this section is mention of any extraneous variables that might in some way have affected the test results. Was testing in a school interrupted by any event such as a fire drill, an earth tremor, or some other disturbance? Did loud or atypical noise in or out of the test site affect the testtaker's concentration? Did the hospitalized patient receive any visitors just before an evaluation, and could such a visit have affected the findings? Answers to these types of questions may prove invaluable in interpreting assessment data.

The *Findings* section of the report is where all the background material, behavioral observations, and test data are integrated to provide an answer to the referral question. Whether or not the examiner makes reference to the actual test data is a matter of personal preference. Thus, for example, one examiner might simply state, "There is evidence of neurological deficit in this record" and stop there. Another examiner might document exactly why this was being asserted:

> There is evidence of neurological deficit, as indicated by the rotation and perseveration errors in the Bender-Gestalt–2 record. Further, on the TAT, this examinee failed to grasp the situation as a whole and simply enumerated single details. Additionally, this examinee had difficulty abstracting—still another index of neurological deficit—as evidenced by the unusually low score on the WISC-IV Similarities subtest.

Ideally, the *Findings* section should lead logically into the *Recommendations* section.

## Recommendations

On the basis of the psychological assessment, with particular attention to factors such as the personal aspects and deficiencies of the examinee, recommendations addressed to ameliorating the presenting problem are given. The recommendation may be for psychotherapy, a consultation with a neurologist, placement in a special class, short-term family therapy addressed to a specific problem—whatever the examiner believes is required to ameliorate the situation is spelled out here.

## Summary

The *Summary* section includes in "short form" a statement concerning the reason for referral, the findings, and the recommendation. This section is usually only a paragraph or two, and it should provide a concise statement of who the examinee is, why the examinee was referred for testing, what was found, and what needs to be done.

"personality description after the manner of P. T. Barnum."[3] Meehl suggested that the term *Barnum effect* be used "to stigmatize those pseudo-successful clinical procedures in which personality descriptions from tests are made to fit the patient largely or wholly by virtue of their triviality." Cognizance of this effect and the factors that may heighten or diminish it is necessary if psychological assessors are to avoid making interpretations in the manner of P. T. Barnum.

## Clinical versus Mechanical Prediction

Should clinicians review test results and related assessment data and then draw conclusions, make recommendations, and take actions that are based on their own education, training, and clinical experience? Alternatively, should clinicians review test results and related assessment data and then draw conclusions, make recommendations, and take actions on the basis of known statistical probabilities, much like an actuary or statistician whose occupation is to calculate risks? A debate regarding the respective merits of what has become known as *clinical versus actuarial prediction* or *clinical versus actuarial assessment* began to simmer more than a half-century ago with the publication of a monograph on the subject by Paul Meehl (1954; see also Dawes et al., 1989; Garb, 1994; Holt, 1970; Marchese, 1992).[4]

---

3. Meehl credited D. G. Patterson with having first used the term *Barnum effect*. The same phenomenon has also been characterized as the *Aunt Fanny effect*. Tallent (1958) originated this term when he deplored the generality and vagueness that plagued too many psychology reports. For example, of the finding that an assessee had "unconscious hostile urges," Tallent wrote, "so has my Aunt Fanny!"

4. Although this debate has traditionally been couched in terms of clinical assessment (or prediction) as compared to statistical or actuarial assessment (or prediction), a parallel debate could pit other applied areas of assessment (including educational, personnel, or organizational assessment, for example) against statistically based methods. At the heart of the debate are questions concerning the utility of a rather subjective approach to assessment that is based on one's training and experience as compared to a more objective and statistically sophisticated approach that is strictly based on preset rules for data analysis.

The increasing popularity of computer-assisted psychological assessment (CAPA) and computer-generated test interpretation has resurrected the clinical-versus-actuarial debate. The battleground has shifted to the frontier of new technology and questions about actuarial assessment compared to clinical judgment. Contemporary scholars and practitioners tend not to debate whether clinicians should be using actuary-like methods to make clinical judgments; it is more *au courant* to debate whether clinicians should be using software that uses actuary-like methods to make clinical judgments.

Some clarification and definition of terms may be helpful here. In the context of clinical decision-making, **actuarial assessment** and **actuarial prediction** have been used synonymously to refer to the application of empirically demonstrated statistical rules and probabilities as a determining factor in clinical judgment and actions. As observed by Butcher et al. (2000), *actuarial assessment* is not synonymous with *computerized assessment*. Citing Sines (1966), Butcher et al. (2000, p. 6) noted that "a computer-based test interpretation (CBTI) system is actuarial only if its interpretive output is wholly determined by statistical rules that have been demonstrated empirically to exist between the output and the input data." It is possible for the interpretive output of a CBTI system to be determined by things other than statistical rules. The output may be based, for example, not on any statistical formulas or actuarial calculations but rather on the clinical judgment, opinions, and expertise of the author of the software. *Computerized assessment* in such an instance would amount to a computerized application of clinical opinion—that is, the application of a clinician's (or group of clinicians') judgments, opinions, and expertise to a particular set of data as processed by the computer software.

**Clinical prediction** refers to the application of a clinician's own training and clinical experience as a determining factor in clinical judgment and actions. Clinical prediction relies on clinical judgment, which Grove et al. (2000) characterized as

> the typical procedure long used by applied psychologists and physicians, in which the judge puts data together using informal, subjective methods. Clinicians differ in how they do this: The very nature of the process tends to preclude precise specification. (p. 19)

Grove et al. (2000) proceeded to compare clinical judgment with what they termed **mechanical prediction,** or the application of empirically demonstrated statistical rules and probabilities (as well as computer algorithms) to the computer generation of findings and recommendations. These authors reported the results of a meta-analysis of 136 studies that pitted the accuracy of clinical prediction against mechanical prediction. In some studies, the two approaches to assessment seemed to be about equal in accuracy. On average, however, Grove et al. concluded that the mechanical approach was about 10% more accurate than the clinical approach. The clinical approach fared least well when the predictors included clinical interview data. Perhaps this was so because, unlike computer programs, human clinicians make errors in judgment; for example, by failing to take account of base rates or other statistical mediators of accurate assessment. The researchers also hinted that the cost of mechanical prediction probably was less than the cost of clinical prediction because the mechanical route obviated the necessity for highly paid professionals and team meetings.

Several studies have supported the use of statistical prediction over clinical prediction. One reason is that some of the methods used in the comparison research seem to tip the scales in favor of the statistical approach. As Karon (2000) observed, "clinical data" in many of the studies was not defined in terms of qualitative information elicited by a clinician but rather in terms of MMPI or MMPI-2 scores. Perhaps many clinicians remain reluctant to place too much trust in CAPA products because, as Karon (1981) argued, variables in the study of personality, abnormal behavior, and other areas of psychology are truly infinite. Exactly which variables need to be focused on in a particular situation can be a very individual matter. Combine these variables with the many other possible variables that may be operative in a situation requiring clinical judgment (such as an assessee's English-speaking ability, cooperativeness, and cultural background), and the size of the software database needed for accurate prediction begins to mushroom. As a result, many clinicians remain willing to hazard their own clinical judgment rather than relying on preprogrammed interpretations.

A compromise of sorts between the two extreme positions in this controversy was proposed by Dana and Thomas (2006). Their review of the literature led them to conclude that clinicians are capable of providing information that computers simply cannot capture in the form of frequency tables, but how such clinical information is used becomes a key question. Dana and Thomas (2006) would rely on mechanical prediction for coming up with the optimal use of such clinical information in the form of decision rules.

Ultimately, it is human hands that are responsible for even the most eloquent computerized narratives, and it is in human hands that the responsibility lies for what further action, if any, will be taken. There is no substitute for good clinical judgment, and the optimal combination of actuarial methods and clinical judgment must be identified for all types of clinical decision making—including clinical decision making that must be made as a result of neuropsychological assessments (not coincidentally, the subject of Chapter 15).

> **JUST THINK . . .**
>
> Will clinicians who increasingly rely on computers for test scoring and test interpretation become better or worse clinicians?

## Self-Assessment

Test your understanding of elements of this chapter by seeing if you can explain each of the following terms, expressions, and abbreviations:

abuse
actuarial assessment
actuarial prediction
ADRESSING
ALI standard
anatomically detailed doll
Barnum effect
biopsychosocial assessment
clinical prediction
clinical psychology
cognitive interview
collaborative interview
competence to stand trial
counseling psychology
culturally informed psychological
    assessment
custody evaluation
*DSM-IV-TR*

Durham standard
duty to warn
emotional and behavioral signs of
    abuse and neglect
emotional injury
evolutionary view of mental
    disorder
fatalism
forensic psychological
    assessment
hypnotic interview
insanity
interview
MacAndrew Alcoholism Scale
    (MAC-R)
managed care
mechanical prediction
mental status examination

M'Naghten standard
neglect
orientation
oriented times 3
physical signs of abuse
    and neglect
premorbid functioning
profiling
psychological report
psychopath
reacculturation
self-efficacy
shifting cultural lenses
social support
standard battery
stress interview
test battery
therapeutic contract

# 15

# *Neuropsychological Assessment*

The branch of medicine that focuses on the nervous system and its disorders is **neurology.** The branch of psychology that focuses on the relationship between brain functioning and behavior is **neuropsychology.** Formerly a specialty area within clinical psychology, neuropsychology has evolved into a specialty in its own right, with its own training regimens and certifying bodies. Neuropsychologists study the nervous system as it relates to behavior by using various tools, including *neuropsychological assessment.* **Neuropsychological assessment** may be defined as the evaluation of brain and nervous system functioning as it relates to behavior. Subspecialty areas within neuropsychology include pediatric neuropsychology (Baron, 2004; Yeates et al., 2000), geriatric neuropsychology (Attix & Welsh-Bohmer, 2006), forensic neuropsychology (Larrabee, 2005), and school neuropsychology (Hale & Fiorello, 2004). A subspecialty within the medical specialty of neurology that also focuses on brain–behavior relationships (with more biochemical and less behavioral emphasis) is **behavioral neurology** (Feinberg & Farah, 2003; Rizzo & Eslinger, 2004). There are even subspecialty areas within behavioral neurology. For example, the assessment professional featured in Chapter 7, Dr. Erik Viirre, is a physician who specializes in **neurotology,** a branch of medicine that focuses on problems related to hearing, balance, and facial nerves.

In what follows, we survey some of the tools and procedures used by clinicians in research and to screen for and diagnose neuropsychological disorders. We begin with a brief introduction to brain–behavior relationships. This material is presented to lay a foundation for understanding how test-taking, as well as other behavior, can be evaluated to form hypotheses about levels of brain intactness and functioning.

## The Nervous System and Behavior

The nervous system is composed of various kinds of **neurons** (nerve cells) and can be divided into the **central nervous system** (consisting of the brain and the spinal cord) and the **peripheral nervous system** (consisting of the neurons that convey messages to and from the rest of the body). Viewed from the top, the large, rounded portion of the brain (called the cerebrum) can be divided into two sections, or hemispheres.

Some brain–behavior correlates are summarized in Table 15–1. Each of the two cerebral hemispheres receives sensory information from the opposite side of the body

**Table 15–1**
**Some Brain–Behavior Characteristics for Selected Nervous System Sites**

| Site | Characteristic |
|---|---|
| Temporal lobes | These lobes contain auditory reception areas as well as certain areas for the processing of visual information. Damage to a temporal lobe may affect sound discrimination, recognition, and comprehension; music appreciation; voice recognition; and auditory or visual memory storage. |
| Occipital lobes | These lobes contain visual reception areas. Damage to an occipital lobe could result in blindness to all or part of the visual field or deficits in object recognition, visual scanning, visual integration of symbols into wholes, and recall of visual imagery. |
| Parietal lobes | These lobes contain reception areas for the sense of touch and for the sense of bodily position. Damage to a parietal lobe may result in deficits in the sense of touch, disorganization, and distorted self-perception. |
| Frontal lobes | These lobes are integrally involved in ordering information and sorting out stimuli. Concentration and attention, abstract-thinking ability, concept-formation ability, foresight, problem-solving ability, and speech, as well as gross and fine motor ability, may be affected by damage to the frontal lobes. |
| Thalamus | The thalamus is a kind of communications relay station for all sensory information transmitted to the cerebral cortex. Damage to the thalamus may result in altered states of arousal, memory defects, speech deficits, apathy, and disorientation. |
| Hypothalamus | The hypothalamus is involved in the regulation of bodily functions such as eating, drinking, body temperature, sexual behavior, and emotion. It is sensitive to changes in environment that call for a "fight or flight" response from the organism. Damage to it may elicit a variety of symptoms ranging from uncontrolled eating or drinking to mild alterations of mood states. |
| Cerebellum | Together with the pons (another brain site in the area of the brain referred to as the hindbrain), the cerebellum is involved in the regulation of balance, breathing, and posture, among other functions. Damage to the cerebellum may manifest as problems in fine motor control and coordination. |
| Reticular formation | In the core of the brain stem, the reticular formation contains fibers en route to and from the cortex. Because stimulation to this area can cause a sleeping organism to awaken and an awake organism to become even more alert, it is sometimes referred to as the reticular activating system. Damage to this area can cause the organism to sleep for long periods of time. |
| Limbic system | Composed of the amygdala, the cingulate cortex, the hippocampus, and the septal areas of the brain, the limbic system is integral to the expression of emotions. Damage to this area may profoundly affect emotional behavior. |
| Spinal cord | Many reflexes necessary for survival (such as withdrawing from a hot surface) are carried out at the level of the spinal cord. In addition to its role in reflex activity, the spinal cord is integral to the coordination of motor movements. Spinal cord injuries may result in various degrees of paralysis or other motor difficulties. |

and also controls motor responses on the opposite side of the body—a phenomenon termed **contralateral control.** It is due to the brain's contralateral control of the body that an injury to the right side of the brain may result in sensory or motor defects on the left side of the body. The meeting ground of the two hemispheres is the corpus callosum, although one hemisphere—most frequently the left one—is dominant. It is because the left hemisphere is most frequently dominant that most people are right-handed. The dominant hemisphere leads in such activities as reading, writing, arithmetic, and speech. The nondominant hemisphere leads in tasks involving spatial and textural recognition as well as art and music appreciation. In the normal, neurologically intact individual, one hemisphere complements the other.

**JUST THINK . . .**

We take for granted everyday activities such as walking, but imagine the complex mechanics of that simple act with reference to the phenomenon of contralateral control.

## Neurological Damage and the Concept of Organicity

Modern-day researchers exploring the link between the brain and the body use a number of varied tools and procedures in their work. Beyond the usual tools of psychological assessment (tests, case studies, etc.), investigators employ high-technology imaging equipment, experimentation involving the electrical or chemical stimulation of various human and animal brain sites, experimentation involving surgical alteration of the brains of animal subjects, laboratory testing and field observation of head-trauma victims, and autopsies of normal and abnormal human and animal subjects. Through these varied means, researchers have learned much about healthy and pathological neurological functioning.

**Neurological damage** may take the form of a lesion in the brain or any other site within the central or peripheral nervous system. A **lesion** is a pathological alteration of tissue, such as that which could result from injury or infection. Neurological lesions may be physical or chemical in nature, and they are characterized as *focal* (relatively circumscribed at one site) or *diffuse* (scattered at various sites). Because different sites of the brain control various functions, focal and diffuse lesions at different sites will manifest themselves in varying behavioral deficits. A partial listing of the technical names for the many varieties of sensory and motor deficits is presented in Table 15–2.

It is possible for a focal lesion to have diffuse ramifications with regard to behavioral deficits. Stated another way, a circumscribed lesion in one area of the brain may affect many different kinds of behaviors, even variables such as mood, personality, and tolerance to fatigue. It is possible for a diffuse lesion to affect one or more areas of functioning so severely that it masquerades as a focal lesion. With an awareness of these possibilities, neuropsychologists sometimes "work backward" as they try to determine from outward behavior where neurological lesions, if any, may be.

**JUST THINK . . .**

A patient complains of problems maintaining balance. At what site in the brain might a neuropsychologist "work backward" from this complaint and identify a problem? *Hint:* You may wish to "work backward" yourself and refer back to Table 15–1.

Neurological assessment may also play a critical role in determining the extent of behavioral impairment that has occurred or can be expected to occur as the result of a neurological disorder or injury. Such diagnostic information is useful not only in designing remediation programs but also in evaluating the consequences of drug treatments, physical training, and other therapy.

The terms *brain damage, neurological damage,* and *organicity* have unfortunately been used interchangeably in much of the psychological literature. The term *neurological damage* is the most inclusive because it covers not only damage to the brain but also damage to the spinal cord and to all the components of the peripheral nervous system. The term **brain damage** is a general reference to any physical or

**Table 15–2**
**Technical Names for Various Kinds of Sensory and Motor Deficits**

| Name | Description of Deficit |
| --- | --- |
| acalculia | Inability to perform arithmetic calculations |
| acopia | Inability to copy geometric designs |
| agnosia | Deficit in recognizing sensory stimuli (for example, *auditory agnosia* is difficulty in recognizing auditory stimuli) |
| agraphia | Deficit in writing ability |
| akinesia | Deficit in motor movements |
| alexia | Inability to read |
| amnesia | Loss of memory |
| amusia | Deficit in ability to produce or appreciate music |
| anomia | Deficit associated with finding words to name things |
| anopia | Deficit in sight |
| anosmia | Deficit in sense of smell |
| aphasia | Deficit in communication due to impaired speech or writing ability |
| apraxia | Voluntary movement disorder in the absence of paralysis |
| ataxia | Deficit in motor ability and muscular coordination |

functional impairment in the central nervous system that results in sensory, motor, cognitive, emotional, or related deficit. The use of the term *organicity* derives from the post–World War I research of the German neurologist Kurt Goldstein. Studies of brain-injured soldiers led Goldstein to conclude that the factors differentiating organically impaired from normal individuals included the loss of abstraction ability, deficits in reasoning ability, and inflexibility in problem-solving tasks. Accordingly, Goldstein (1927, 1939, 1963) and his colleagues developed psychological tests that tapped these factors and were designed to help in the diagnosis of *organic brain syndrome,* or **organicity** for short. Although Goldstein's test is now out of print, it remains useful in illustrating some of the types of tasks still used today to screen for neurological deficit (Figure 15–1).

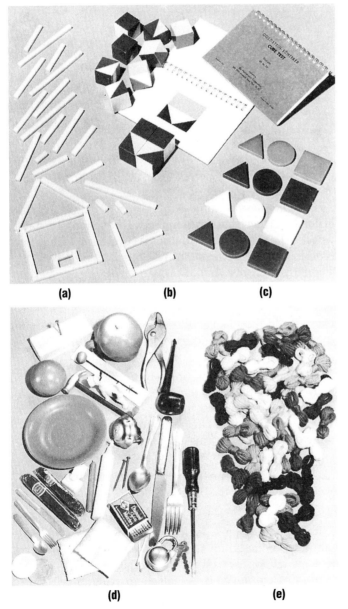

(a)          (b)          (c)

(d)                  (e)

**Figure 15–1**
**The Goldstein-Scheerer Tests of Abstract and Concrete Thinking***

**(a)** *The Stick Test is a measure of recent memory. The subject's task is to use sticks to reproduce designs from memory.* **(b)** *The Cube Test challenges the subject to replicate with blocks a design printed in a booklet. This subtest was the predecessor of the Block Design task on Wechsler intelligence tests. It is used as a measure of nonverbal abstraction ability.* **(c)** *The Color-Form Sorting Test contains twelve objects, including four triangles, four circles, and four squares (each piece in one of four colors). The objects are presented in a random order, and the subject is instructed to sort in terms of which belong together. Once they are sorted, the subject is next asked to sort the objects a different way. The subject's flexibility in shifting from one sorting principle to another is noted.* **(d)** *The Object Sorting Test consists of 89 objects that the subject is required to group. Concrete thinking and organic impairment may be inferred if the subject sorts, for example, by color instead of function.* **(e)** *The Color Sorting Test employs several woolen skeins of varying colors. The task here is to sort the skeins according to a sample sketch displayed by the examiner.*

*The Goldstein-Scheerer Tests of Abstract and Concrete Thinking are now out of print.

In the tradition of Goldstein and his associates, two German psychologists, Heinz Werner and Alfred Strauss, examined brain–behavior correlates in brain-injured children with mental retardation (Werner & Strauss, 1941; Strauss & Lehtinen, 1947). Like their predecessors who had worked with brain-injured adults, these investigators attempted to delineate characteristics common to *all* brain-injured people, including children. Although their work led to a better understanding of the behavioral consequences of brain injury in children, it also led to the presumption that all organically impaired children, regardless of the specific nature or site of their impairment, shared a similar pattern of cognitive, behavioral, sensory, and motor deficits. The unitary concept of organicity that emerged from this work in the 1940s prevailed through much of the 1950s. But by then, researchers such as Birch and Diller (1959) were already beginning to question what they termed the "naïvete of the concept of 'organicity'":

> It is abundantly clear that "brain damage" and "organicity" are terms which though overlapping are not identities and serve to designate interdependent events. "Brain-damage" refers to the fact of an anatomical destruction, whereas "organicity" represents one of the varieties of functional consequences which may attend such destruction. (p. 195)

In fact, the view that organicity and brain damage are nonunitary is supported by a number of observations.

- Persons who have identical lesions in the brain may exhibit markedly different symptoms.

- Many interacting factors—such as the patient's premorbid functioning, the site and diffuseness of the lesion, the cause of the lesion, and its rate of spread—may make one organically impaired individual appear clinically quite dissimilar from another.

- Considerable similarity may exist in the symptoms exhibited by persons who have entirely different types of lesions. Further, these different types of lesions may arise from a variety of causes, such as trauma with or without loss of consciousness, infection, nutritional deficiencies, tumor, stroke, neuronal degeneration, toxins, insufficient cardiac output, and a variety of metabolic disturbances.

- Many conditions that are not due to brain damage produce symptoms that mimic those produced by brain damage. For example, an individual who is psychotic, depressed, or simply fatigued may produce data on an examination for organic brain damage that are characteristically diagnostic of neuropsychological impairment.

- Factors other than brain damage (such as psychosis, depression, and fatigue) influence the responses of brain-damaged persons. Some types of responses are consequences (rather than correlates) of the brain damage. For example, if brain-injured children as a group tend to be described as more aggressive than normals, this may reflect more on the way such children have been treated by parents, teachers, and peers than on the effect of any lesions.

- Persons who are in fact brain-damaged are sometimes able to compensate for their deficits to such an extent that some functions are actually taken over by other, more intact parts of the brain.

**JUST THINK . . .**

Can you think of any other diagnostic labels that are routinely used as though they were unitary but that are really nonunitary?

With this brief introduction to neuropsychology as background, let's look at the neuropsychological examination, including some possible reasons for referral for an evaluation, as well as some of the tools of assessment that may be employed during such an evaluation.

# The Neuropsychological Evaluation

## *When a Neuropsychological Evaluation Is Indicated*

Have you ever had a thorough eye examination by an ophthalmologist (a physician who specializes in disorders of the eye and vision)? How did that compare to the eye examination you received in your general practitioner's office? In all probability, the examination conducted by the specialist was more thorough and quite different in terms of the tools used and the methods employed. The examination in your general practitioner's office may have been relatively superficial, and probably did not take all that long. The examination by the specialist was more complex, and probably took a bit of time. We might characterize the examination of the general practitioner as one designed to screen for problems, whereas the specialist's examination was clearly more diagnostic in nature, and better equipped to understand the precise location of any abnormality, as well as any disease process. In fact, any problems discovered by the general practitioner during a routine screening will surely result in a referral to a specialist for further evaluation.

There is something of a parallel to be drawn with regard to the everyday evaluations of neuropsychological functioning conducted by psychologists who are not specialists in the area, as compared to the evaluations conducted by neuropsychologists. Clinical and counseling psychologists who conduct everyday assessments for a variety of reasons, and school psychologists who conduct everyday assessments with education-related objectives, as well as other mental health professionals who engage in assessment, may all include some sort of neuropsychological evaluation as a component of what they do. However, most typically, what these nonspecialists are trying to do is screen for the presence of a possible neuropsychological problem, rather than definitively diagnose such a problem. If they identify a problem that they believe is neurological in nature, whether through their own examination or through test or case history data, a referral to a specialist ensues.

In some cases, a patient is referred to a psychologist (who is not a neuropsychologist) for screening for suspected neurological problems. In such a case, a battery of tests will typically be administered. This battery at a minimum will consist of an intelligence test, a personality test, and a perceptual-motor/memory test.[1] If suspicious neurological signs are discovered in the course of the evaluation, the patient will be referred for further and more-detailed evaluation. Suspicious signs and symptoms may be documented in case history or test data, or may present themselves in behavior emitted during an interview or test session. Signs of neurological deficit may take the form of troubling episodes (such as a hand tremor or other involuntary movement) that only seem to only occur at home, at work, or some other venue In addition to the presence of signs or symptoms of neurological impairment, the occurrence of various events (such as a concussion sustained as a result of trauma to the head) or the existence of some known pathology (such as any disease known to adversely affect cognition) may prompt a referral for evaluation by a specialist. Table 15–3 lists a sampling of conditions that may prompt such referrals.

---

1. We have listed here what we believe to be the minimum amount of testing for an adequate neuropsychological screening. It is, however, not uncommon for clinicians to administer only a perceptual-motor/memory test, a practice that has been strongly discouraged (Bigler & Ehrenfurth, 1981; Kahn & Taft, 1983).

**Table 15–3**
**Some Conditions that May Prompt Referral for Neuropsychological Evaluation**

| Condition | Possible Reason for Referral |
|---|---|
| Brain injury resulting from stroke, traumatic brain injury (TBI), concussion, or infection | Differential diagnosis of brain injury and disease from psychiatric disorders such as depression. Assessment of current functioning compared to premorbid functioning. Evaluation of treatment progress. |
| Epilepsy, hydrocephaly, or other known neurological conditions | Assessment of change in functioning. For example, neuropsychological testing may evaluate the effectiveness of drug therapies and possible side effects. |
| Acquired immune deficiency syndrome (AIDS) | Assessment of cognitive deterioration associated with the disorder and monitoring of changes in cognitive functioning. |
| Alzheimer's disease and other forms of dementia | Diagnosis and impact of memory loss. Evaluation of drug therapies. |
| Problems with attention and learning | Diagnosis of ADHD, specific learning disorder, or possible psychological problems that may impair learning. Neuropsychological evaluation often leads to an intervention plan to improve functioning. |
| Any significant changes from usual sensory, motor, or cognitive functioning | Determine whether the observed deficit is a **functional deficit** (that is, a deficit that is psychological or without a known physical or structural cause) or an **organic deficit** (that is, a deficit known to have a structural or physical origin). |

The signs signaling that a more thorough neuropsychological or neurological workup by a specialist (such as a neuropsychologist or a neurologist) is advisable are characterized as being "hard" or "soft" depending upon the certainty with which the phenomenon has been known to be related with documented neurological damage. A **hard sign** may be defined as an indicator of definite neurological deficit. Abnormal reflex performance is an example of a hard sign. Cranial nerve damage as indicated by neuroimaging is another example of a hard sign. A **soft sign** is an indicator that is merely suggestive of neurological deficit. One example of a soft sign is an apparent inability to accurately copy a stimulus figure when attempting to draw it. Scores on a test that has verbal and nonverbal components where a significant discrepancy exists between the testtaker's verbal and nonverbal performance is another soft sign. Other soft signs of neurological deficit may take the form of relatively minor sensory or motor deficits.

Although psychologists, neuropsychologists, and other clinicians who are not physicians may refer patients to neurologists for further evaluation, it is also true that neurologists may refer their neurology patients to neuropsychologists for further evaluation. A patient may be referred for an in-depth neuropsychological evaluation, for complaints such as headaches or memory loss—this after the neurologist has done a preliminary examination and could find no medical basis for the complaint. In such cases, the hope would be that the tools of neuropsychology could be applied to shed additional light on the medical mystery. A neuropsychologist may be called upon to help more precisely assess the degree of a neurological patient's impairment in functioning. A patient placed on a particular treatment regimen by a neurologist might be referred to a neuropsychologist to monitor subtle cognitive changes that result as a consequence of that treatment.

## General Elements of a Neuropsychological Evaluation

The objective of the typical neuropsychological evaluation is "to draw inferences about the structural and functional characteristics of a person's brain by evaluating an individual's behavior in defined stimulus-response situations" (Benton, 1994, p. 1). Exactly how the neuropsychological examination is conducted will vary as a function of a number of factors such as the nature of the referral question, the capabilities of the patient, the availability and nature of records regarding the patient, and practical considerations (such as the time available to conduct the examination). The examination of a patient typically begins with a thorough examination of available, relevant records. Case history data—including medical records, educational records, family reports, employer reports, and prior neuropsychological evaluation records—are all useful to the neuropsychologist in planning the examination.

Preparation for a neuropsychological examination entails making sure that the appropriate tools of assessment will be employed. Neuropsychologists assess persons exhibiting a wide range of physical and psychological disabilities. Some, for example, have known visual or auditory deficits, concentration and attention problems, speech and language difficulties, and so forth. Allowance must be made for such deficits, and a way must be found to administer the appropriate tests so that meaningful results can be obtained. In some cases, neuropsychologists will administer preliminary visual, auditory, memory, perceptual, and problem-solving or cognitive processing tasks, to ensure that patients are appropriate candidates for more extensive and specialized evaluation in these areas. Sometimes during the course of such a preliminary evaluation, a deficit is discovered that in itself may change the plan for the rest of the evaluation. An olfactory (sense of smell) deficit, for example, may be symptomatic of a great variety of neurological and nonneurological problems as diverse as Alzheimer's disease (Serby et al., 1991), Parkinson's disease (Serby et al., 1985), and AIDS (Brody et al., 1991). The discovery of such a deficit by means of a test such as the University of Pennsylvania Smell Identification Test (UPSIT; Doty et al., 1984) might be a stimulus for altering the evaluation plan so as to rule out these other disease processes.

> **JUST THINK . . .**
>
> You are a neuropsychologist evaluating a patient whom you suspect has an olfactory deficit. You do not own a copy of the UPSIT. *Improvise!* Describe what you would do.

Common to all thorough neuropsychological examinations are a history taking, a mental status examination, and the administration of tests and procedures designed to reveal problems of neuropsychological functioning. Throughout the examination, the neuropsychologist's knowledge of neuroanatomy, neurochemistry, and neurophysiology are essential for optimal interpretation of the data. In addition to guiding decisions concerning what to test for and how to test for it, such knowledge will also come into play with respect to the decisions concerning *when* to test. Thus, for example, it would be atypical for a neuropsychologist to psychologically test a stroke victim immediately after the stroke has occurred. Because some recovery of function could be expected to spontaneously occur in the weeks and months following the stroke, testing the patient immediately after the stroke would yield an erroneous picture of the extent of the damage.

Increasingly, neuropsychologists must also have a knowledge of the possible effects of various prescription medications taken by their assessees because such medication can actually cause certain neurobehavioral

> **JUST THINK . . .**
>
> What types of behavior caused by a drug or prescription medication could present as a neurological problem?

deficits. For example, certain antipsychotic drugs can cause Parkinsonian-like symptoms such as tremors in the hand. It is also the case that various prescription medications may temporarily mask some of the testtaker's neurobehavioral deficits.

Many of the tools of neuropsychological assessment are tools with which most psychological assessors are quite familiar: the test, the case study, and the interview.

**JUST THINK . . .**

Describe a finding from an intelligence test administration that might prompt an assessor to refer the assessee for a thorough neuropsychological evaluation.

Some tools, such as sophisticated imaging equipment, are modern marvels of technology with which many readers of this book may be unfamiliar. For our purposes, we will focus primarily on the tools of the more familiar variety—although we will briefly overview some of those modern marvels later in this chapter. Two tools "of the more familiar variety" are history taking and evaluation of case history data. So let's begin there.

**History taking, the case history, and case studies** Neuropsychologists pay careful attention to patients' histories as told to them by the patients themselves and as revealed in patients' records. Neuropsychologists also study findings from similar cases in order to better understand their assessees. The typical neuropsychological examination begins with a careful history taking, with special attention paid to certain areas:

- The medical history of the patient.
- The medical history of the patient's immediate family and other relatives. A sample question here might be "Have you or any of your relatives experienced dizziness, fainting, blackouts, or spasms?"
- The presence or absence of certain **developmental milestones,** a particularly critical part of the history-taking process when examining young children. A list of some of these milestones appears in Table 15–4.
- Psychosocial history, including level of academic achievement and estimated level of intelligence; an estimated level of adjustment at home and at work or school; observations regarding personality (for example, "Is this individual hypochondriacal?"), thought processes, and motivation ("Is this person willing and able to respond accurately to these questions?").
- The character, severity, and progress of any history of complaints involving disturbances in sight, hearing, smell, touch, taste, or balance; disturbances in muscle tone, muscle strength, and muscle movement; disturbances in autonomic functions such as breathing, eliminating, and body temperature control; disturbances in speech; disturbances in thought and memory; pain (particularly headache and facial pain); and various types of thought disturbances.

A careful history is critical to the accuracy of the assessment. Consider, for example, a patient who exhibits flat affect, is listless, and doesn't seem to know what day it is or what time it is. Such an individual might be suffering from something neurological in

**JUST THINK . . .**

What else might you like to know about this listless patient with flat affect who doesn't know what day it is or what time it is?

origin (such as a dementia). However, a functional disorder (such as severe depression) might be the problem's true cause. A good history taking will shed light on whether the observed behavior is the result of a genuine dementia or a product of what is referred to as a *pseudodementia* (a condition that presents *as if* it were dementia but is not). Raising a number of history-related

**Table 15–4**
**Some Developmental Milestones**

| Age | Development |
|---|---|
| 16 weeks | Gets excited, laughs aloud. Smiles spontaneously in response to people. Anticipates eating at sight of food. Sits propped up for 10 to 15 minutes. |
| 28 weeks | Smiles and vocalizes to a mirror and pats at mirror image. Many vowel sounds. Sits unsupported for brief period and then leans on hands. Takes solids well. When lying on back, places feet to mouth. Grasps objects and transfers objects from hand to hand. When held standing, supports most of own weight. |
| 12 months | Walks with only one hand held. Says "mamma" and "dada" and perhaps two other words. Gives a toy in response to a request or gesture. When being dressed, will cooperate. Plays "peek-a-boo" games. |
| 18 months | Has a vocabulary of some 10 words. Walks well, seldom falls, can run stiffly. Looks at pictures in a book. Feeds self, although spills. Can pull a toy or hug a doll. Can seat self in a small or adult chair. Scribbles spontaneously with a crayon or pencil. |
| 24 months | Walks up and down stairs alone. Runs well, no falling. Can build a tower of six or seven blocks. Uses personal pronouns ("I" and "you") and speaks a three-word sentence. Identifies simple pictures by name and calls self by name. Verbalizes needs fairly consistently. May be dry at night. Can pull on a simple garment. |
| 36 months | Alternates feet when climbing stairs and jumps from bottom stair. Rides a tricycle. Can copy a circle and imitate a cross with a crayon or pencil. Comprehends and answers questions. Feeds self with little spilling. May know and repeat a few simple rhymes. |
| 48 months | Can dry and wash hands, brushes teeth. Laces shoes, dresses and undresses with supervision. Can play cooperatively with other children. Can draw figure of a person with at least two clear body parts. |
| 60 months | Knows and names colors, counts to 10. Skips on both feet. Can print a few letters, can draw identifiable pictures. |

Source: Gesell and Amatruda (1947).

questions may prove helpful when evaluating such a patient. For example: How long has the patient been in this condition, and what emotional or neurological trauma may have precipitated it? Does this patient have a personal or family history of depression or other psychiatric disturbance? What factors appear to be operating to maintain the patient in this state?

The history-taking interview can help shed light on questions of the organic or functional origin of an observed problem and whether the problem is *progressive* (likely to spread or worsen) or *nonprogressive*. Data from a history-taking interview may also lead the interviewer to suspect that the presenting problem has more to do with malingering than with neuropsychological deficit.

Beyond the history-taking interview, knowledge of an assessee's history is also developed through existing records. Case history files are valuable resources for all psychological assessors, but they are particularly valuable in neuropsychological assessment. In many instances, the referral question concerns the degree of damage that has been sustained relative to a patient's pre-existing condition. The assessor must determine the level of the patient's functioning and neuropsychological intactness prior to any trauma, disease, or other disabling factors. In making such a determination of premorbid functioning, the assessor may rely on a wide variety of case history data, from archival records to videotapes made with the family video camera.

Supplementing a history-taking interview and historical records in the form of case history data, published case studies on people who have suffered the same or a similar type of neuropsychological deficit may be a source of useful insights. Case study material can provide leads regarding areas of evaluation to explore in depth and can also suggest the course a particular disease or deficit will follow and how observed strengths or weaknesses may change over time. Case study material can also be valuable in formulating plans for therapeutic intervention.

**The Interview** A variety of structured interviews and rating forms are available as aids to the neuropsychological screening and evaluation process. Neuropsychological screening devices point the way to further areas of inquiry with more extensive evaluation methods. Such devices can be used economically with members of varied populations who may be at risk for neuropsychological impairment, such as psychiatric patients, the elderly, and alcoholics. Some of these measures, such as the Short Portable Mental Status Questionnaire, are completed by an assessor; others, such as the Neuropsychological Impairment Scale, are self-report instruments.

The Mini-Mental State Exam (MMSE; Folstein et al., 1975) has more than a quarter-century of history as a clinical and research tool used to screen for cognitive impairment. Factor-analytic research suggests that this test primarily measures concentration, language, orientation, memory, and attention (Baños & Franklin, 2003; Jones & Gallo, 2000). In 2010 the second edition of the Mini-Mental State Exam (MMSE-2) was published. This reference work was also published in a brief version (for use in situations with time constraints), as well as an expanded version (designed to be more sensitive to detecting mild cognitive impairment). Another structured interview is the 7 Minute Screen, developed to help identify patients with symptoms characteristic of Alzheimer's disease (Solomon et al., 1998; Ijuin et al., 2008). Tasks on this test tap orientation, verbal fluency, and various aspects of memory. Both the Mini-Mental State Examination and the 7 Minute Screen have value in identifying individuals with previously undetected cognitive impairment (Lawrence et al., 2000), although neither of these screening instruments should be used for the purpose of diagnosis. A useful supplement to a structured interview for screening purposes is the neuropsychological mental status examination.

**The neuropsychological mental status examination** An outline for a general mental status examination was presented in Chapter 14. The neuropsychological mental status examination overlaps the general examination with respect to questions concerning the assessee's consciousness, emotional state, thought content and clarity, memory, sensory perception, performance of action, language, speech, handwriting, and handedness. The mental status examination administered for the express purpose of evaluating neuropsychological functioning may delve more extensively into specific areas of interest.

Throughout the mental status examination, as well as other aspects of the evaluation (including testing and history taking), the clinician observes and takes note of aspects of the assessee's behavior relevant to neuropsychological functioning. For example, the clinician notes the presence of involuntary movements (such as facial tics), locomotion difficulties, and other sensory and motor problems. The clinician may note, for example, that one corner of the mouth is slower to curl than the other when the patient smiles—a finding suggestive of damage to the seventh (facial) cranial nerve. Knowledge of brain–behavior relationships comes in handy in all phases of the evaluation, including the physical examination.

## The Physical Examination

Most neuropsychologists perform some kind of physical examination on patients, but the extent of this examination varies widely as a function of the expertise, competence, and confidence of the examiner. Some neuropsychologists have had extensive training in performing physical examinations under the tutelage of neurologists in teaching hospitals. Such psychologists feel confident in performing many of the same **noninvasive procedures** (procedures that do not involve any intrusion into the examinee's body) that neurologists perform as part of their neurological examination. In the course of the following discussion, we list some of these noninvasive procedures. We precede this discussion with the caveat that it is the physician and not the neuropsychologist who is always the final arbiter of medical questions.

In addition to making observations about the examinee's appearance, the examiner may also physically examine the scalp and skull for any unusual enlargements or depressions. Muscles may be inspected for their tone (soft? rigid?), strength (weak or tired?), and size relative to other muscles. With respect to the last point, the examiner might find, for example, that a patient's right biceps is much larger than his left biceps. Such a finding could indicate muscular dystrophy in the left arm. But it also could reflect the fact that the patient has been working as a shoemaker for the past 40 years—a job that involves constantly hammering nails, thus building up the muscle in his right arm. This patient's case presentation underscores the importance of placing physical findings in historical context, as well as the value of clinical knowledge and experience when it comes to making inferences from observed phenomena.

> **JUST THINK . . .**
>
> Do you agree that neuropsychologists should engage in noninvasive physical examinations? Or do you believe that neuropsychologists should avoid physically examining patients and leave that part of the evaluation completely to physicians?

The clinician conducting a neuropsychological examination may test for simple reflexes. **Reflexes** are involuntary motor responses to stimuli. Many reflexes have survival value for infants but then disappear as the child grows older. One such reflex is the mastication (chewing) reflex. Stroking the tongue or lips will elicit chewing behavior in the normal infant; however, chewing elicited in the older child or adult indicates neurological deficit. In addition to testing for the presence or absence of various reflexes, the examiner might examine muscle coordination by using measures such as those listed in Table 15–5.

The physical examination aspect of the neuropsychological examination is designed to assess not only the functioning of the brain but also aspects of the functioning of the nerves, muscles, and other organs and systems. Some procedures used to shed light on the adequacy and functioning of some of the 12 cranial nerves are summarized in Table 15–6.

## Neuropsychological Tests

A wide variety of tests are used by neuropsychologists as well as others who are charged with finding answers to neuropsychology-related referral questions. Researchers may employ neuropsychological tests to gauge change in mental status or other variables as a result of the administration of medication or the onset of a disease or disorder. Forensic evaluators may employ tests to gain insight into the effect of neuropsychological factors on issues such as criminal responsibility or competency to stand trial.

In what follows, we present only a sample of the many types of tests used in neuropsychological applications. More-detailed presentations are available in a number of sources (for example, Lezak, 2012; Morgan & Ricker, 2007; Rabin et al., 2005; Strauss et al., 2006). Current neuropsychology articles can provide another rich source of information on neuropsychological testing and assessment, as can lectures and presentations by speakers with a background in neuropsychology. Speaking of the latter, one neuropsychologist you can learn from is Dr. Jeanne Ryan—and you don't even have to attend a symposium! Read what she had to say in this chapter's *Meet an Assessment Professional* feature.

## Table 15–5
## Sample Tests Used to Evaluate Muscle Coordination

### Walking-running-skipping

If the examiner has not had a chance to watch the patient walk for any distance, he or she may ask the patient to do so as part of the examination. We tend to take walking for granted, but neurologically speaking it is a highly complex activity that involves proper integration of many varied components of the nervous system. Sometimes abnormalities in gait may be due to nonneurological causes; if, for example, a severe case of bunions is suspected as the cause of the difficulty, the examiner may ask the patient to remove his or her shoes and socks so that the feet may be physically inspected. Highly trained examiners are additionally sensitive to subtle abnormalities in, for example, arm movements while the patient walks, runs, or skips.

### Standing still (technically, the Romberg test)

The patient is asked to stand still with feet together, head erect, and eyes open. Whether patients have their arms extended straight out or at their sides and whether or not they are wearing shoes or other clothing will be a matter of the examiner's preference. Patients are next instructed to close their eyes. The critical variable is the amount of sway exhibited by the patient once the eyes are closed. Because normal persons may sway somewhat with their eyes closed, experience and training are required to determine when the amount of sway is indicative of pathology.

### Nose-finger-nose

The patient's task is to touch her nose with the tip of her index finger, then touch the examiner's finger, and then touch her own nose again. The sequence is repeated many times with each hand. This test, as well as many similar ones (such as the toe-finger test, the finger-nose test, the heel-knee test), is designed to assess, among other things, cerebellar functioning.

### Finger wiggle

The examiner models finger wiggling (that is, playing an imaginary piano or typing), and then the patient is asked to wiggle his own fingers. Typically, the nondominant hand cannot be wiggled as quickly as the dominant hand, but it takes a trained eye to pick up a significant difference in rate. The experienced examiner will also look for abnormalities in the precision of the movements and the rhythm of the movements, "mirror movements" (uncontrolled similar movements in the other hand when instructed to wiggle only one), and other abnormal involuntary movements. Like the nose-finger test, finger wiggling supplies information concerning the quality of involuntary movement and muscular coordination. A related task involves tongue wiggling.

## Table 15–6
## Sample Tests Used by Neurologists to Assess the Intactness of Some of the 12 Cranial Nerves

| Cranial Nerve | Test |
| --- | --- |
| I (olfactory nerve) | Closing one nostril with a finger, the examiner places some odoriferous substance under the nostril being tested and asks whether the smell is perceived. Subjects who perceive it are next asked to identify it. Failure to perceive an odor when one is presented may indicate lesions of the olfactory nerve, a brain tumor, or other medical conditions. Of course, failure may be due to other factors, such as oppositional tendencies on the part of the patient or intranasal disease, and such factors must be ruled out as causal. |
| II (optic nerve) | Assessment of the intactness of the second cranial nerve is a highly complicated procedure, for this is a sensory nerve with functions related to visual acuity and peripheral vision. A Snellen eye chart is one of the tools used by the physician in assessing optic nerve function. If the subject at a distance of 20 feet from the chart is able to read the small numbers or letters in the line labeled "20," then the subject is said to have 20/20 vision in the eye being tested. This is only a standard. Although many persons can read only the larger print at higher numbers on the chart (that is, a person who reads the letters on line "40" of the chart would be said to have a distance vision of 20/40), some persons have better than 20/20 vision. An individual who could read the line labeled "15" on the Snellen eye chart would be said to have 20/15 vision. |
| V (trigeminal nerve) | The trigeminal nerve supplies sensory information from the face, and it supplies motor information to and from the muscles involved in chewing. Information regarding the functioning of this nerve is examined by the use of tests for facial pain (pinpricks are made by the physician), facial sensitivity to different temperatures, and other sensations. Another part of the examination entails having the subject clamp his or her jaw shut. The physician will then feel and inspect the facial muscles for weakness and other abnormalities. |
| VIII (acoustic nerve) | The acoustic nerve has functions related to the sense of hearing and the sense of balance. Hearing is formally assessed with an audiometer. More frequently, the routine assessment of hearing involves the use of a "dollar watch." Provided the examination room is quiet, an individual with normal hearing should be able to hear a dollar watch ticking at a distance of about 40 inches from each ear (30 inches if the room is not very quiet). Other quick tests of hearing involve placing a vibrating tuning fork on various portions of the skull. Individuals who complain of dizziness, vertigo, disturbances in balance, and so forth may have their vestibular system examined by means of specific tests. |

## Meet Dr. Jeanne P. Ryan

One area in which the need for regular and frequent neuropsychological assessment has been recognized is in sport related concussions. As has been highlighted in the media, athletes with histories of concussion as might occur in the NFL and the NHL have been found to have cognitive problems associated with encephalopathy caused by repeated blows to the head over an extended period of time. This concern is now being directed toward our youth, the amateur athletes in middle school, high school and college. New York State has been very progressive in this regard; every athlete in the public school system is required to have a form of baseline neuropsychological assessment, which can then be compared to the athlete's performance on the same instrument following concussion. Follow-up post-concussion neuropsychological screening provides evidence based information to make return to play decisions or to determine if a more comprehensive evaluation is needed.

Neuropsychological assessment instruments are very effective tools for understanding neurocognitive functioning, but the tests are only as good as the psychologist who uses them. Learning to administer neuropsychological tests is not difficult. Merging test interpretation with multiple sources of information to understand the presenting problem and to develop effective interventions is the challenge. Having a sound understanding of the brain–behavior relationship, knowledge of the strengths and limitations of each test, and an ability to integrate aspects of the individual's inherent features and the environmental contributions are essential.

**Jeanne P. Ryan, Ph.D., Professor of Psychology at State University of New York (SUNY) at Plattsburgh, and Clinical Director, SUNY–Plattsburgh Neuropsychology Clinic and Psychoeducational Services**

Knowing how to translate the information into meaningful recommendations is imperative. Communicating the assessment information to the person and the family in understandable terms is necessary so that changes can be made to promote quality of life and well being.

*Read more of what Dr. Ryan had to say—her complete essay—at www.mhhe.cohentesting8.*

## Tests of General Intellectual Ability

Tests of intellectual ability, particularly Wechsler tests, occupy a prominent position among the diagnostic tools available to the neuropsychologist. The varied nature of the tasks on the Wechsler scales and the wide variety of responses required make these tests potentially very useful tools for neuropsychological screening. For example, a clue to the existence of a deficit might be brought to light by difficulties in concentration during one of the subtests. Because certain patterns of test response indicate particular deficits, the examiner looks beyond performance on individual tests to a study of the pattern of test scores, a process termed **pattern analysis.** Thus, for example, extremely poor performance on the Block Design and other performance subtests might be telling in a record that contains relatively high scores on all the verbal subtests. In combination with a known pattern of other data, the poor Block Design performance could indicate damage in the right hemisphere.

A number of researchers intent on developing a definitive sign of brain damage have devised various ratios and quotients based on patterns of subtest scores. David Wechsler himself referred to one such pattern, called a **deterioration quotient** or DQ (also referred to by some as a *deterioration index*). However, neither Wechsler's DQ nor any other WAIS-based index has performed satisfactorily enough to be deemed a valid, stand-alone measure of neuropsychological impairment.

We have already noted the need to administer standardized tests in strict conformance with the instructions in the test manual. Yet testtaker limitations mean that such "by-the-book" test administrations are not always possible or desirable when testing members of the neurologically impaired population. Because of various problems or potential problems (such as the shortened attention span of some neurologically impaired individuals), the experienced examiner may need to modify the test administration to accommodate the testtaker and still yield clinically useful information. The examiner administering a Wechsler scale may deviate from the prescribed order of test administration when testing an individual who becomes fatigued quickly. In such cases, the more taxing subtests will be administered early in the exam. In the interest of shortening the total test administration time, trained examiners might omit certain subtests that they suspect will fail to provide any information beyond that already obtained. Let us reiterate that such deviations in the administration of standardized tests such as the Wechsler scales can be made—and meaningfully interpreted—by trained and experienced neuropsychologists. For the rest of us, it's by the book!

**JUST THINK . . .**

Why should deviations from standardized test instructions be made very judiciously, if at all?

### Tests to Measure the Ability to Abstract

One symptom commonly associated with neuropsychological deficit, regardless of the site or exact cause of the problem, is inability or lessened ability to think abstractly. One traditional measure of verbal abstraction ability has been the Wechsler Similarities subtest, isolated from the age-appropriate version of the Wechsler intelligence scale. The task in this subtest is to identify how two objects (for instance, a ball and an orange) are alike. Another type of task used to assess ability to think abstractly is proverb interpretation. For example, interpret the following proverb:

A stitch in time saves nine.

If your interpretation of this proverb conveyed the idea that haste makes waste, then you have evinced an ability to think abstractly. By contrast, some people with neurological deficits might have interpreted that proverb more concretely (that is, with less abstraction). Here is an example of a concrete interpretation: When sewing, take one stitch at a time—it'll save you from having to do it over nine times. This type of response might (or might not, depending on other factors) betray a deficit in abstraction ability. The Proverbs Test, an instrument specifically designed to test abstraction and related ability, contains a number of proverbs along with standardized administration instructions and normative data. In one form of this test, the subject is instructed to write an explanation of the proverb. In another form of the test, this one multiple-choice, each proverb is followed by four choices, three of which are either common misinterpretations or concrete responses.

Nonverbal tests of abstraction include any of the various tests that require the respondent to sort objects in some logical way. Common to most of these sorting tests are instructions such as "Group together all the ones that belong together" and follow-up questions—for example, "Why did you group those objects together?" Representative of such tests are the Object Sorting Test (refer back to Figure 15–1) and the Color-Form Sorting Test (also known as Weigl's Test), which require testtakers to sort objects of different shapes and colors. Another way that sorting tasks are administered is by grouping a few of the stimulus objects together and requiring the testtaker (a) to explain why those objects go together or (b) to select the object that does not belong with the rest.

The Wisconsin Card Sorting Test-64 Card Version (WCST-64; Kongs et al., 2000) requires the testtaker to sort a pack of 64 cards that contain different geometric figures printed in different colors. The cards are to be sorted according to matching rules that must be inferred and that shift as the test progresses. Successful performance on this test requires several abilities associated with frontal lobe functioning, including concentration, planning, organization, cognitive flexibility in shifting set, working memory, and inhibition of impulsive responding. The test may be useful in screening for neurological impairment with or without suspected injury of the frontal lobe. Caution is suggested when using this or similar tests, as some evidence suggests that the test may erroneously indicate neurological impairment when in reality the testtaker has schizophrenia or a mood disorder (Heinrichs, 1990). It is therefore important for clinicians to rule out alternative explanations for a test performance that indicates neurological deficit.

## Tests of Executive Function

Sorting tests measure one element of **executive function,** which may be defined as organizing, planning, cognitive flexibility, and inhibition of impulses and related activities associated with the frontal and prefrontal lobes of the brain. One test used to measure executive function is the Tower of Hanoi (Figure 15–2), a puzzle that made its first appearance in Paris in 1883 (Rohl, 1993). It is set up by stacking the rings on one of the pegs, beginning with the largest-diameter ring, with no succeeding ring resting on a smaller one. Probably because the appearance of these stacked rings is reminiscent of a pagoda, the puzzle was christened *La Tour de Hanoi*. The Tower of Hanoi, either in solid form for manipulation by hand or adapted for computerized administration in graphic form, has been used by many researchers to measure various aspects of executive function (Aman et al., 1998; Arnett et al., 1997; Butters et al., 1985; Byrnes & Spitz, 1977; Glosser & Goodglass, 1990; Goel & Grafman, 1995; Goldberg et al., 1990; Grafman et al., 1992; Janssen et al., 2010; Leon-Carrion et al., 1991; Mazzocco et al., 1992; Miller & Ozonoff, 2000; Minsky et al., 1985; Schmand et al., 1992; Spitz et al., 1985).

Performance on mazes is another type of task used to measure executive function. As early as the 1930s, psychologist Stanley D. Porteus became enamored with the potential for psychological assessment of the seemingly simple task of identifying the correct path in a maze and then tracing a line to the end point of that maze. This type of task was originally introduced to yield a quantitative estimate of "prudence, forethought, mental alertness, and power of sustained attention" (Porteus, 1942). Porteus urged colleagues to use mazes for varied research purposes ranging from the

**Figure 15–2**
**The Tower of Hanoi**

*This version of the Tower of Hanoi puzzle comes with three pegs and eight rings. The puzzle begins with all of the rings on one of the pegs ordered from the bottom up in decreasing size. To solve the puzzle, all of the rings must be transferred to another peg following three rules: (1) only one ring may be moved at a time; (2) the ring is moved from one peg to another; and (3) no ring may ever be placed on a smaller one.*

exploration of cultural differences (Porteus, 1933) to the study of social inadequacy (Porteus, 1955) to the study of personality traits by means of qualitative analysis of a testtaker's performance (Porteus, 1942). Today, maze tasks like those in the Porteus Maze Test (Figure 15–3) are used primarily as measures of executive function (Daigneault et al., 1992; Krikorian & Bartok, 1998; Mack & Patterson, 1995). Although useful in measuring such functioning in adults, its utility for that purpose in children has been questioned. Shum et al. (2000) observed no adverse impact on Porteus maze performance of children with traumatic brain injury.

**JUST THINK . . .**

How might qualitative analysis of performance on a maze task be telling with regard to the testtaker's personality?

A test used to quickly screen for certain executive functions is the **clock-drawing test (CDT).** As its name implies, the task in this test is for the patient to draw the face of a clock, usually with the hands of the clock indicating a particular time (such as "ten minutes after eleven"). As used clinically, there are many variations of this test—not only in the time that the clock should indicate but also in the setup of the task (some clinicians begin the test with a pre-drawn circle) and in the scoring of the patient's production (there are more than a dozen scoring systems). Observed abnormalities in the patient's drawing may be reflective of cognitive dysfunction resulting from dementia or other neurological or psychiatric conditions. Poor performance on the CDT has also been associated with visual memory deficits (Takahashi et al., 2008), mild cognitive impairment (Babins et al., 2008), and losses in function that ostensibly result with aging (Bozikas et al., 2008; Hubbard et al., 2008). Parks et al. (2010) examined performance on the clock drawing task in elderly individuals with and without Alzheimer's disease, while observing each group's brain functioning by means of special imaging equipment. It was found that performance on the clock drawing was correlated with a specific pattern of brain activity in the healthy participants that was different from the brain activity of those with Alzheimer's disease.

Representative items for four other types of tasks that may be used in neuropsychological assessment are illustrated in Figure 15–4. Part (a) illustrates a **trail-making item.** The task is to connect the circles in a logical way. This type of task is thought to tap many abilities, including visuo-perceptual skills, working memory, and

**Figure 15-3**
**"Where do we go from here, Charly?"**

*A Porteus maze–like task is being illustrated by the woman in the white coat to actor Cliff Robertson as "Charly" in the now-classic film of the same name.*

the ability to switch between tasks (Sanchez-Cubillo et al., 2009). The Trail Making Tests in the Halstead-Reitan Neuropsychological Battery (a fixed battery to be discussed shortly) are among the most widely used measures of brain damage (Salthouse et al., 2000; Thompson et al., 1999) and have been employed in a variety of studies (Bassett, 1999; Beckham et al., 1998; Compton et al., 2000; King et al., 2000; Nathan et al., 2001; Ruffolo et al., 2000; Sherrill-Pattison et al., 2000; Wecker et al., 2000). In a longitudinal study that followed elderly individuals over the course of 6 years, initial performance on the Trail Making Test was able to predict impairments in mobility and even mortality (Vazzana et al., 2010).

Illustration (b) in Figure 15–4 is an example of a **field-of-search item.** Shown a sample or target stimulus (usually some sort of shape or design), the testtaker must scan a field of various stimuli to match the sample. This kind of item is usually timed. People with right hemisphere lesions may exhibit deficits in visual scanning ability, and a test of field-of-search ability can be of value in discovering such deficits. Field-of-search ability has strong adaptive value and can have life-or-death consequences for predator and prey. Research in field of search has found many applications. For example, it helps us to better understand some everyday activities such as driving (Crundall et al., 1998; Duchek et al., 1998; Guerrier et al., 1999; Recarte & Nunes, 2000; Zwahlen et al., 1998) as well as more specialized activities such as piloting aircraft (Seagull & Gopher, 1997) and monitoring air traffic (Remington et al., 2000).

Illustration (c) is an example of a simple line drawing reminiscent of the type of item that appears in instruments such as the Boston Naming Test. The testtaker's task on the Boston (as it is often abbreviated) is **confrontation naming;** that is, naming each stimulus

**Figure 15–4**
**Sample Items Used in**
**Neuropsychological Assessment**

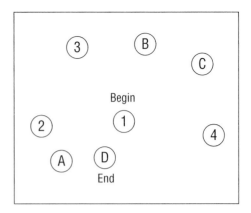

*(a) The Trail Making Test*
The testtaker's task is to connect the dots
in a logical fashion.

*(b) The Field of Search*
*After being shown a sample stimulus,*
*the testtaker's task is to locate a match as*
*quickly as possible.*

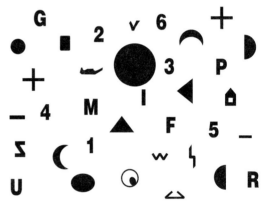

*(c) An Identification Task*
*A task that involves what is known as*
*confrontation naming.*

*(d) A Picture Absurdity*
*The testtaker answers questions such*
*as "What's wrong or silly about this*
*picture?"*

presented. This seemingly simple task entails three component operations: a perceptual component (perceiving the visual features of the stimulus), a semantic component (accessing the underlying conceptual representation or core meaning of whatever is pictured), and a lexical component (accessing and expressing the appropriate name). Difficulty with the naming task could therefore be due to deficits in any or all of these components. Persons who are neurologically compromised as a result of Alzheimer's disease or other dementia typically experience difficulty with naming tasks.

**JUST THINK . . .**

Picture absurdity items have traditionally been found on tests of intelligence or neuropsychological tests. Describe your own, original, picture absurdity item that you believe could have value in assessing personality.

Illustration (d) in Figure 15–4 is what is called a **picture absurdity item.** The pictorial equivalent of a verbal absurdity item, the task here is to identify what is wrong or silly about the picture. It is similar to the picture absurdity items on the Stanford-Binet intelligence test. As with Wechsler-type Comprehension items, this type of item can provide insight into the testtaker's social comprehension and reasoning abilities.

## Tests of Perceptual, Motor, and Perceptual-Motor Function

The term **perceptual test** is a general reference to any of many instruments and procedures used to evaluate varied aspects of sensory functioning, including aspects of sight, hearing, smell, touch, taste, and balance. Similarly, **motor test** is a general reference to any of many instruments and procedures used to evaluate varied aspects of one's ability and mobility, including the ability to move limbs, eyes, or other parts of the body. The term **perceptual-motor test** is a general reference to any of many instruments and procedures used to evaluate the integration or coordination of perceptual and motor abilities. For example, putting together a jigsaw puzzle taps perceptual-motor ability—more specifically, hand–eye coordination. Thousands of tests have been designed to measure various aspects of perceptual, motor, and perceptual-motor functioning. Some of them you may have heard of long before you decided to take a course in assessment. For example, does *Ishihara* sound familiar? The Ishihara (1964) test is used to screen for color blindness. More specialized—and less well-known—instruments are available if rare forms of color perception deficit are suspected.

Among the tests available for measuring deficit in auditory functioning is the Wepman Auditory Discrimination Test. This brief, easy-to-administer test requires that the examiner read a list of 40 pairs of monosyllabic meaningful words (such as *muss/much*) pronounced with lips covered (not muffled, please) by either a screen or a hand. The examinee's task is to determine whether the two words are the same or different. It's quite a straightforward test—provided the examiner isn't suffering from a speech defect, has no heavy accent, and doesn't mutter. The standardization sample for the test represented a broad range within the population, but there is little information available about the test's reliability or validity. The test manual also fails to outline standardized administration conditions, which are particularly critical for this test given the nature of the stimuli (Pannbacker & Middleton, 1992).

A test designed to assess gross and fine motor skills is the Bruininks-Oseretsky Test of Motor Proficiency. Designed for use with children aged 4½ to 14½, this instrument includes subtests that assess running speed and agility, balance, strength, response speed, and dexterity. On a less serious note, the test's box cover could be used as an informal screening device for reading ability by asking colleagues to pronounce the test's name correctly. A test designed to measure manual dexterity is the Purdue Pegboard Test. Originally developed in the late 1940s as an aid in employee selection, the object is to insert pegs into holes using first one hand, then the other hand, and then both hands. Each of these three segments of the test has a time limit of 30 seconds, and the score is equal to the number of pegs correctly placed. Normative data are available, and it is noteworthy that in a population without brain injury, women generally perform slightly better on this task than men do. With brain-injured subjects, this test may help answer questions regarding the lateralization of a lesion.

Perhaps one of the most widely used neuropsychological instruments is the **Bender Visual-Motor Gestalt Test,** usually referred to simply as the Bender-Gestalt or even just "the Bender." As originally conceived by Lauretta Bender (Figure 15–5), the test consisted of nine cards, on each of which was printed one design. The designs had been used by psychologist Max Wertheimer (1923) in his study of the perception of *gestalten* (German for "configurational wholes"). Bender (1938) believed these designs could be used to assess perceptual maturation and neurological impairment. Testtakers were shown each of the cards in turn and instructed "Copy it as best you can." Although there was no time limit, unusually long or short test times were considered to be of diagnostic significance. Average administration time for all nine designs was about five minutes—a fact which also contributed to its wide appeal among test users.

Bender (1938, 1970) intended the test to be scored by means of clinical judgment. It was published with few scoring guidelines and no normative information. Still, a number of quantitative scoring systems for this appealingly simple test soon became

**Figure 15–5**
**Lauretta Bender (1896–1987)**

*Bender (1970) reflected that the objective in her visual-motor test was not to get a perfect reproduction of the test figures but "a record of perceptual motor experience—a living experience unique and never twice the same, even with the same individual" (p. 30).*

available for adult (Brannigan & Brunner, 2002; Hutt, 1985; Pascal & Suttell, 1951; Reichenberg & Raphael, 1992) and child (Koppitz, 1963, 1975; Reichenberg & Raphael, 1992) protocols. A sampling of scoring terminology common to many of these systems is presented in Figure 15–6. Soon, a number of modifications to the administration procedure were proposed. One such modification was the addition of a recall phase. After all nine designs had been copied, a blank piece of paper was placed before the testtaker with the instructions "Now please draw all of the designs you can remember." Gobetz (1953) proposed the recall procedure as a means of testing a hypothesis about differential performance on the Bender as a function of personality. He hypothesized that, owing to the pressure of the unexpected second test, subjects diagnosed as neurotic would be able to recall fewer figures on the recall portion of the test than would normal subjects. The recall procedure gained widespread usage—not as a means of providing

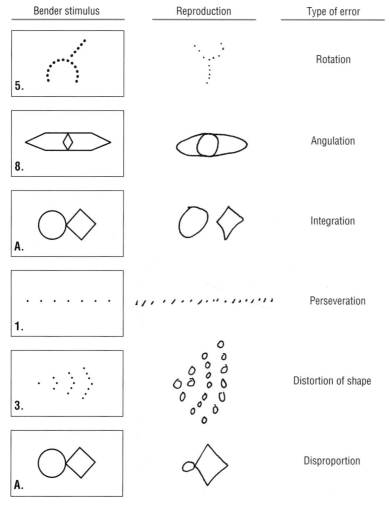

**Figure 15–6**
**Sample Errors on the Bender-Gestalt**

*These types of errors may suggest organic impairment. Not all the illustrated errors are signs of organic impairment at all ages.*

**JUST THINK . . .**

Test authors, Lauretta Bender among them, may intend their instrument to be scored and interpreted only on the basis of clinical judgment. But users of tests demand otherwise. Why?

personality-related data but rather as a means of providing additional neuropsychological data.

Max Hutt (1985) believed that perceptual-motoric behavior offered a sample of behavior not readily tapped by verbal tests. He believed that the copied Bender designs were capable of revealing developmental conflicts in individuals that they themselves might not be aware of. Similar views have been expressed by others advocating the use of the Bender as a projective instrument (Raphael & Golden, 1997; Raphael et al., 2002).

The Bender Visual-Motor Gestalt Test, Second Edition (Bender-Gestalt II; Brannigan & Decker, 2003) added seven new items, extending the range of ability assessed by its predecessor. Four of the items are used exclusively with testtakers from ages 4 years to 7 years 11 months, and three of the new items are used exclusively with testtakers from ages 8 years to 85 or older. A recall phase was built into the test, as were two supplementary tests called the Motor Test and the Perception Test. The supplementary tests were designed to detect deficits in performance or motor skills that would adversely affect performance. The task in the Motor Test is to draw a line between dots without touching borders, and the task in the Perception Test is to circle or point to a design that best matches a stimulus design. The test is conducted by administration of a Copy phase (copying designs), a Recall phase (re-creating the designs drawn from memory), the Motor Test, and then the Perception Test. The Copy and Recall phases are timed. Specific guidelines for scoring are provided throughout. For example, during the Copy phase, resemblance between the design on the stimulus card and the assessee's responses are scored as follows:

0 = None—random drawing, scribbling, lack of design

1 = Slight—vague resemblance

2 = Some—moderate resemblance

3 = Strong—close resemblance, accurate reproduction

4 = Nearly perfect

The Bender-Gestalt-II was standardized on 4,000 individuals from ages 4 to 85+ matched to the 2000 U.S. Census. Included were members of special populations: individuals with mental retardation, learning disorders, attention-deficit hyperactivity disorder, autism, Alzheimer's disease, and the gifted. Numerous studies attesting to the reliability and the validity of the test are presented in the test manual. The types of reliability studies reported on were of the test-retest, internal consistency, and inter-rater variety. The validity studies were interpreted as supporting the view that the test measures what it purports to measure. The test authors concluded that the test

> measures a single underlying construct that is sensitive to maturation and/or development, and scores from the Copy and Recall phases are highly influenced and sensitive to clinical conditions. This dimensionality provides added utility to the test. (Brannigan & Decker, 2003, p. 67)

Visual-motor ability has long been thought to develop through childhood and then remain relatively steady through the lifespan. Using Bender-Gestalt II standardization sample data, one researcher provided suggestive evidence that runs counter to such a sequence of events. Based on his reanalysis of the data, Decker (2008) concluded that visual-motor ability proceeds through adolescence, steadily decreases in adulthood, and then rapidly declines through later age ranges. Whether or not Decker's conclusions are confirmed by others remains to be seen.

## Tests of Verbal Functioning

Verbal fluency and fluency in writing are sometimes affected by injury to the brain, and there are tests to assess the extent of the deficit in such skills. In the Controlled Word Association Test (formerly the Verbal Associative Fluency Test), the examiner says a letter of the alphabet and then it is the subject's task to say as many words as he or she can think of that begin with that letter. Each of three trials employs three different letters as a stimulus and lasts one minute; the testtaker's final score on the test reflects the total number of correct words produced, weighted by factors such as the gender, age, and education of the testtaker. Controlled Word Association Test scores are related in the predicted direction to the ability of dementia patients to complete tasks of daily living, such as using the telephone or writing a check (Loewenstein et al., 1992). And although people with dementia tend to do poorly on the test as compared with controls, the differences observed have not been significant enough to justify using the test as an indicator of dementia (Nelson et al., 1993).

Not to be confused with *aphagia,* **aphasia** refers to a loss of ability to express oneself or to understand spoken or written language because of some neurological deficit.[2] A number of tests have been developed to measure aspects of aphasia. For example, the Reitan-Indiana Aphasia Screening Test (AST), available in both a child and an adult form, contains a variety of tasks such as naming common objects, following verbal instructions, and writing familiar words. Factor analysis has suggested that these tasks load on two factors: language abilities and coordination involved in writing words or drawing objects (Williams & Shane, 1986). Both forms of the test were designed to be screening devices that can be administered in 15 minutes or less. Used alone as a screening tool (Reitan, 1984a, 1984b; Reitan & Wolfson, 1992) or in combination with other tests (Tramontana & Boyd, 1986), the AST may be of value in distinguishing testtakers who have brain damage from those who do not. For testtakers of Hispanic descent, a more culturally relevant instrument might be the Multilingual Aphasia Examination. Rey et al. (1999) found the published norms to be comparable to their own data using a sample of Hispanic testtakers. They also discussed specific problems encountered in neuropsychological research with Hispanics and suggested guidelines and directions for future research.

## Tests of Memory

Memory is a complex, multifaceted cognitive function that has defied simple explanation. To appreciate just how complex it is, consider the following:

> Humans possess an estimated 1 trillion neurons, plus 70 trillion synaptic connections between them. . . . A single neuron may have as many as 10,000 synapses, but during the process of memory formation perhaps only 12 synapses will be strengthened while another 100 will be weakened. The sum of those changes, multiplied neuron by neuron, creates a weighted circuit that amounts to memory. (Hall, 1998, p. 30)

Different models of memory compete for recognition in the scientific community, and no one model has garnered universal acceptance. For our purposes, a sample model is presented in Figure 15–7—along with the caveat that this relatively simple

---

2. **Aphagia** is a condition in which the ability to eat is lost or diminished.

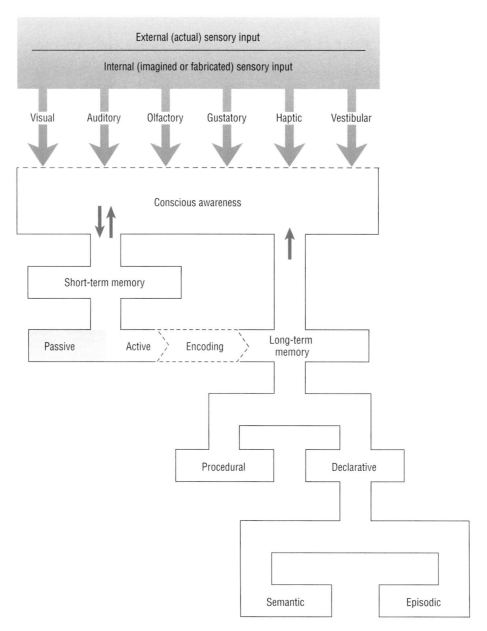

**Figure 15–7**
**A Model of Memory**

*According to our model, memory results from information processing by the nervous system of external (actual) sensory input, such as sights, sounds, smells, and tastes. Your stored vision of a loved one's face, the song you will never forget, and the smell of freshly mowed grass are examples of memories formed from actual sensory input. Memory of a sort may also result from what one produces internally, in the absence of actual sensation. What one imagines, dreams, and misperceives are all examples of this latter sort of memory. Of course, dominance of imagined or fabricated sorts of memories can become a matter of clinical significance. The line between the sensory input channel and conscious awareness is broken to indicate that not all sensory input automatically makes it into conscious awareness; factors such as attention and concentration play a role in determining which stimuli actually make it into conscious awareness.*

model, which was pieced together from various sources, is incomplete at best and *not* universally accepted. Moreover, the model contains elements that are still very much a matter of debate among contemporary researchers.

Contrary to the popular image of memory as a storehouse of sorts, memory is an active process that is presumed to entail both short-term and long-term components (Atkinson & Shiffrin, 1968). Incoming information is processed in short-term memory, where it is temporarily stored for as little as seconds or as long as a minute or two. Short-term memory has also been characterized by some researchers as virtually synonymous with *working memory* (Daneman & Carpenter, 1980; Newell, 1973). The more traditional view of short-term memory is as a passive buffer in which information is either transferred to long-term memory or dissipated (that is, forgotten). Our model allows for both passive and active components of short-term memory, with encoding of long-term memory made from the active, "working" component of short-term memory.

Note in our model the two-way path between short-term memory and conscious awareness. Stimuli from conscious awareness can be fed into short-term memory, and short-term memory can feed stimuli back into conscious awareness. The path to long-term memory is illustrated by a broken line—indicating that not all information in short-term memory is encoded in long-term memory.

With regard to long-term memory, researchers have distinguished between *procedural* and *declarative* memory. **Procedural memory** is memory for things like driving a car, making entries on a keyboard, or riding a bicycle. Most of us can draw on procedural memory with little effort and concentration. **Declarative memory** refers to memory of factual material—such as the differences between procedural and declarative memory. We have compartmentalized the procedural and declarative components of long-term memory for illustrative purposes.

Also illustrated as compartmentalized are what are widely believed to be two components of declarative memory: semantic and episodic memory. **Semantic memory** is, strictly speaking, memory for facts. **Episodic memory** is memory for facts in a particular context or situation. An example of episodic or context-dependent memory might be the recollection of a classmate's name while in class but not at a chance meeting during a social event. Being asked to repeat digits in the context of a memory test is another example of episodic memory because it is linked so intimately to the (testing) context.

**JUST THINK . . .**

Visualize some remembered image or event. Now, referring to our model of memory, outline how that memory may have been established.

As indicated by the one-way path from long-term memory to consciousness, information stored in long-term memory is available for retrieval. Whether information so retrieved can be restored directly to long-term memory or must instead be processed again through short-term memory is a matter of debate. Also somewhat controversial (and not illustrated in our model) is the concept of *implicit memory*. There is research to suggest that memory exists both within conscious awareness and external to conscious control (Greenwald & Banaji, 1995; Richardson-Klavehn & Bjork, 1988; Roediger, 1990; Roediger & McDermott, 1993; Schacter, 1987). The latter variety of memory, which is accessible only by indirect measures and not by conscious recollection, has been referred to as "unconscious memory" or, more recently, **implicit memory.** Support for such proposed divisions of memory can be found in laboratory research and also in the clinical observation of persons with amnesia who exhibit profound compartmentalizations of accessible and nonaccessible memories.

A widely used test of memory (and more) is the California Verbal Learning Test–II (CVLT-II; Dellis et al., 2000). The task is to repeat a list of words that are read by the examiner. A series of trials are administered. The test yields recall and recognition

**JUST THINK . . .**

What is the relationship, if any, between an *implicit motive* (see Chapter 13) and an *implicit memory?*

scores as well as information related to learning rate, error types, and encoding strategies. Items administered in a forced-choice format may be useful in the detection of malingering. Norms are provided for testtakers from ages 16 to 89, and there is a short form available for use with testtakers for whom fatigue or related factors must be taken into consideration. Also available is an alternate form of the test for retesting purposes. A child form of the test has also been published.

The fourth edition of the Wechsler Memory Scale (WMS-IV), published in 2009, is the most recent revision of a brand of memory tests that was preceded by the WMS-III, the WMS-R, and the WMS. Designed for use with testtakers from ages 16 to 90, the materials and tasks in the WMS-IV, much like those in the WAIS-IV, have been revised to be more amenable for use with older testtakers. The WMS provides index scores for Auditory Memory, Visual Memory, Visual Working Memory, Immediate Memory, and Delayed Memory. There is some evidence that the WMS-IV may be a more useful measure of auditory and visual memory than the WMS-III under certain circumstances (Hoelzleet et al., 2011).

**JUST THINK . . .**

What methods might you use to evaluate the psychometric soundness of a test of memory? *Note:* You may wish to check your response against the procedures described in the manual of the WMS-IV.

Two other approaches to memory testing are illustrated in Figure 15–8. In an approach devised by Milner (1971), tactile nonsense (nonrepresentational) figures are employed to measure immediate tactile (or haptic) memory. Another tactile memory test involves an adaptation of the administration of the Seguin-Goddard Formboard. Halstead (1947a) suggested that the formboard could be used to assess tactile memory if examinees were blindfolded during the test and a recall trial added.

A computerized test battery developed by Thomas Crook and described by Hostetler (1987) uses a number of real-world tasks (such as telephone calling and name–face association). The battery has been employed as an outcome measure in studies of the efficacy of various drugs in the treatment of Alzheimer's disease. In terms of the diagnosis of that disease, one group of researchers has compiled a test battery which it claims is superior to diagnostic methods currently in use (Chapman et al., 2010). This brings us to the subject of . . .

**JUST THINK . . .**

What are some real-world tasks that you would recommend be included on Crook's memory test?

### Neuropsychological Test Batteries

On the basis of the mental status examination, the physical examination, and the case history data, the neuropsychologist typically administers a battery of tests for further clinical study. Trained neuropsychologists may administer a prepackaged **fixed battery** of tests, or they may modify a fixed battery for the case at hand. They may choose to administer a **flexible battery,** consisting of an assortment of instruments hand-picked for some purpose relevant to the unique aspects of the patient and the presenting problem.

The clinician who administers a flexible battery has not only the responsibility of selecting the tests to be used but also the burden of integrating all the findings from each of the individual tests—no simple task because each test may have been normed on different populations. Another problem inherent in the use of a flexible battery is that the tests administered frequently overlap with respect to some of the functions tested,

**Figure 15–8**
**Two Tools Used in the Measurement of Tactile Memory**

*At left, four pieces of wire bent into "nonsense figures" can be used in a tactile test of immediate memory. Examinees are instructed to feel one of the figures with their right or left hand (or with both hands) and then to locate a matching figure. Shown at right is one form of the Seguin-Goddard Formboard. Blindfolded examinees are instructed to fit each of the 10 wooden blocks into the appropriate space in the formboard with each hand separately and then with both hands. Afterward, the examinee may be asked to draw the formboard from memory. All responses are timed and scored for accuracy.*

and the result is some waste in testing and scoring time. Regardless of these and other drawbacks, the preference of most highly trained neuropsychologists traditionally has been to tailor a battery of tests to the specific demands of a particular testing situation (Bauer, 2000; Sweet et al., 2002). Of course, all of that may change as a result of judicial action (see this chapter's *Close-Up*).

Fixed neuropsychological test batteries are designed to comprehensively sample the patient's neuropsychological functioning. The fixed battery is appealing to clinicians, especially clinicians who are relatively new to neuropsychological assessment, because it tends to be less demanding in many ways. Whereas a great deal of expertise and skill is required to fashion a flexible battery that will adequately answer the referral question, a prepackaged battery represents an alternative that is not tailor-made but is comprehensive. Several tests sampling various areas are included in the battery, and each is supplied with clear scoring methods. One major drawback of the prepackaged tests, however, is that the specific disability of the patient may greatly—and adversely—influence performance on the test. Thus, for example, an individual with a visual impairment may perform poorly on many of the tasks that require visual skills.

Perhaps the most widely used fixed neuropsychological test battery is the **Halstead-Reitan Neuropsychological Battery.** Ward C. Halstead (1908–1969) was an

# Fixed versus Flexible Neuropsychological Test Batteries and the Law

Do courts have any preferences regarding the specific tests administered by assessors who function as expert witnesses in litigation? With reference to neuropsychological assessment, does it matter if the assessor administered a fixed or a flexible battery? The ruling of a federal court in *Chapple v. Ganger* is enlightening with regard to such questions. In the *Chapple* case, the court applied the *Daubert* standard with regard to the admission of scientific evidence.

## The *Chapple* Case

*Chapple* originated with an automobile accident in which a 10-year-old boy sustained closed head injuries. The plaintiff claimed that these injuries impaired brain functioning and were permanent, whereas the defendant denied this claim. Three neuropsychological examinations of the boy were undertaken by three different assessors at three different times. The first was conducted by a clinical psychologist who administered a flexible battery of tests, including the Aphasia Screening Test, the Benton Visual Retention Test, the Knox Cube, the Rey Complex Figure Test, the Seashore Rhythm Test, the Trails Test, and the Wisconsin Card Sorting Test. In addition, the flexible battery included other tests such as Draw a Bicycle, Draw a Clock, Draw a Family, Draw a Person, Category Test, Incomplete Sentences, Lateral Dominance Test, Manual Finger Tapping Test, and the Peabody Picture Vocabulary Test as well as subtests of the Woodcock-Johnson, the WISC-R, and the WRAT-R.

The second neuropsychological examination, about a year later, also involved a flexible battery, administered this time by a neuropsychologist. The tests used were Trails, Sentence Imitation, Word Sequencing and Oral Direction (subtests of the Detroit Test of Learning Aptitude), Taylor Complex Figure Test, Hooper Visual Organization Test, Attention Capacity (a subtest of the Auditory Verbal Learning Test), Sound and Visual Symbol Recall Test, Paragraph Copy Test, Kaufman Brief Intelligence Test, the Individual Achievement Test, and the Wechsler Reading Comprehension and Listening Comprehension Test.

The third neuropsychological examination, commissioned by the defendant and conducted by neuropsychologist Ralph Reitan, involved administration of most subtests of the Halstead-Reitan Neuropsychological Test Battery for Older Children. In the two earlier examinations, the findings referred to some degree of brain trauma as a result of the accident, which in turn left the child with a degree of permanent impairment. By contrast, as a result of the third examination, Reitan reported that the child scored in the normal range on most of the tests in his fixed battery. Reitan did allow, however, for the possibility of mild impairment attributable to some minor brain dysfunction. Reitan's opinions were based on the child's test performance and on evaluation of case records. The other two psychologists also reviewed the child's records and historical data in coming to their conclusions.

Invoking the *Daubert* standard, the court ruled in favor of the defendant, finding no evidence to support permanent organic brain damage. Reed (1996) observed that the court gave more weight to the results of the fixed than to the flexible batteries, citing the lack of medical and scientific evidence to support conclusions made from the flexible batteries. The court wrote: "The focus is on the methodology of the experts, and not the conclusions which they generate." In *Chapple,* then, testimony regarding the administration of a fixed battery was accepted by the court as medical evidence, whereas testimony regarding the administration of flexible batteries was not.

## The Implications of *Daubert* and *Chapple*

On its face, the implications of *Daubert* seem vague and open to multiple interpretations (Black et al., 1994; Faigman, 1995; Larvie, 1994). However, there may be a lesson to be learned from the 1994 *Chapple* case, at least with regard to the admissibility of evidence obtained as the result of fixed versus flexible neuropsychological batteries. Although administration of flexible batteries is generally accepted in the professional community, a court may look more favorably on conclusions reached as the result of a fixed, standardized battery. The *Chapple* court's decision also suggested that it might accept as evidence results from individual standardized tests if those test results were used to supplement the findings from a fixed neuropsychological test battery. The fallout from *Chapple* remains with us today, and debates regarding the value of fixed versus flexible batteries—at least from a legal perspective—continue as well (Bigler, 2007; Hom, 2008; Russell, 2007).

experimental psychologist whose interest in the study of brain–behavior correlates led him to establish a laboratory for that purpose at the University of Chicago in 1935. His was the first laboratory of its kind in the world. During the course of 35 years of research, Halstead studied more than 1,100 brain-damaged persons. From his observations, Halstead (1947a, 1947b) derived a series of 27 tests designed to assess the presence or absence of organic brain damage—the Halstead Neurological Test Battery. A student of Halstead's, Ralph M. Reitan, later elaborated on his mentor's findings. In 1955, Reitan published two papers that dealt with the differential intellectual effects of various brain lesion sites (Reitan, 1955a, 1955b). Fourteen years and much research later, Reitan (1969) privately published a book entitled *Manual for Administration of Neuropsychological Test Batteries for Adults and Children*—the forerunner of the Halstead-Reitan Neuropsychological Test Battery (H-R; see also Reitan & Wolfson, 1993).

Administration of the H-R requires a highly trained examiner conversant with the procedures for administering the various subtests (Table 15–7). Even with such an examiner, the test generally requires a full workday to complete. Subtest scores are interpreted not only with respect to what they mean by themselves but also in terms of their relation to scores on other subtests. Appropriate interpretation of the findings requires the eye of a trained neuropsychologist, though H-R computer interpretation software—no substitute for clinical judgment but an aid to it—is available. Scoring yields a number referred to as the Halstead Impairment Index, and an index of .5 (the cutoff point) or above is indicative of a neuropsychological problem. Data on more than 10,000 patients in the standardization sample were used to establish that cutoff point. Normative information has also been published with respect to special populations. Cultural factors must also be considered when administering this battery (Evans et al., 2000).

Conducting test-retest reliability studies on the H-R is a prohibitive endeavor, given how long it takes to administer and other factors (such as practice effects and effects of memory). Still, the test is generally viewed as reliable. A large body of literature attests to the validity of the instrument in differentiating brain-damaged subjects from subjects without brain damage and for assisting in making judgments relative to the severity of a deficit and its possible site (Reitan, 1994a, 1994b; Reitan & Wolfson, 2000). The battery has also been used to identify behavioral deficits associated with particular neurological lesions (Guilmette & Faust, 1991; Guilmette et al., 1990; Heaton et al., 2001).

> **JUST THINK . . .**
>
> Just for a moment, don the role of a neuropsychologist who spends the better part of many workdays administering a single neuropsychological test battery to a single assessee. What do you like best about your job? What do you like least about your job?

Another fixed neuropsychological battery is the Luria-Nebraska Neuropsychological Battery (LNNB). The writings of the Russian neuropsychologist Aleksandr Luria served as the inspiration for a group of standardized tests (Christensen, 1975) that were subsequently revised (Golden et al., 1980; Golden et al., 1985) and became known as the LNNB. In its various published forms, the LNNB contains clinical scales designed to assess cognitive processes and functions. Analysis of scores on these scales may lead to judgments as to whether neuropsychological impairment exists, and if so, which area of the brain is affected. The LNNB takes about a third of the time it takes to administer the Halstead-Reitan battery. Still, judging by the use of these tests, the Halstead-Reitan remains the battery of choice for experienced neuropsychological assessors. A neuropsychological test battery for children, also derived in part on the basis of

> **JUST THINK . . .**
>
> The Cognitive Behavioral Driver's Inventory is a neuropsychological battery specially designed to help determine whether an assessee should be driving a motor vehicle. What is another specialized neuropsychological battery that needs to be developed?

**Table 15–7**
**Subtests of the Halstead-Reitan Battery**

### Category

This is a measure of abstracting ability in which stimulus figures of varying size, shape, number, intensity, color, and location are flashed on an opaque screen. Subjects must determine what principle ties the stimulus figures together (such as color) and indicate their answer among four choices by pressing the appropriate key on a simple keyboard. If the response is correct, a bell rings; if incorrect, a buzzer sounds. The test primarily taps frontal lobe functioning of the brain.

### Tactual performance

Blindfolded examinees complete the Seguin-Goddard Formboard (see Figure 14–8) with their dominant and nondominant hands and then with both hands. Time taken to complete each of the tasks is recorded. The formboard is then removed, the blindfold is taken off, and the examinee is given a pencil and paper and asked to draw the formboard from memory. Two scores are computed from the drawing: the memory score, which includes the number of shapes reproduced with a fair amount of accuracy, and the localization score, which is the total number of blocks drawn in the proper relationship to the other blocks and the board. Interpretation of the data includes consideration of the total time to complete this task, the number of figures drawn from memory, and the number of blocks drawn in the proper relationship to the other blocks.

### Rhythm

First published as a subtest of the Seashore Test of Musical Talent and subsequently included as a subtest in Halstead's (1947a) original battery, the subject's task here is to discriminate between like and unlike pairs of musical beats. Difficulty with this task has been associated with right temporal brain damage (Milner, 1971).

### Speech sounds perception

This test consists of 60 nonsense words administered by means of an audiotape adjusted to the examinee's preferred volume. The task is to discriminate a spoken syllable, selecting from four alternatives presented on a printed form. Performance on this subtest is related to left hemisphere functioning.

### Finger-tapping

Originally called the "finger oscillation test," this test of manual dexterity measures the tapping speed of the index finger of each hand on a tapping key. The number of taps from each hand is counted by an automatic counter over five consecutive, 10-second trials with a brief rest period between trials. The total score on this subtest represents the average of the five trials for each hand. A typical, normal score is approximately 50 taps per 10-second period for the dominant hand and 45 taps for the nondominant hand (a 10% faster rate is expected for the dominant hand). Cortical lesions may differentially affect finger-tapping rate of the two hands.

### Time sense

The examinee watches the hand of a clock sweep across the clock and then has the task of reproducing that movement from sight. This test taps visual motor skills as well as ability to estimate time span.

### Other tests

Also included in the battery is the Trail Making Test (see Figure 15–4), in which the examinee's task is to correctly connect numbered and lettered circles. A strength-of-grip test is also included; strength of grip may be measured informally by a handshake grasp and more scientifically by a dynamometer (in Chapter 3, Figure 3–1).

To determine which eye is the preferred or dominant eye, the Miles ABC Test of Ocular Dominance is administered. Also recommended is the administration of a Wechsler intelligence test, the MMPI (useful in this context for shedding light on questions concerning the possible functional origin of abnormal behavior), and an aphasia screening test adapted from the work of Halstead and Wepman (1959).

Various other sensorimotor tests may also be included. A test called the critical flicker fusion test was once part of this battery but has been discontinued by most examiners. If you have ever been in a disco and watched the action of the strobe light, you can appreciate what is meant by a light that flickers. In the flicker fusion test, an apparatus that emits a flickering light at varying speeds is turned on, and the examinee is instructed to adjust the rate of the flicker until the light appears to be steady or fused.

Luria's work, is the NEPSY (Korkman et al., 1997), the inspiration for which was detailed by its senior author (Korkman, 1999).

Many published and unpublished neuropsychological test batteries are designed to probe deeply into one area of neuropsychological functioning instead of surveying for possible behavioral deficit in a variety of areas. Test batteries exist that focus on visual, sensory, memory, and communication problems. The Neurosensory Center Comprehensive Examination of Aphasia (NCCEA) is a battery of tests that focuses on communication deficit. The Montreal Neurological Institute Battery is particularly useful to trained neuropsychologists in locating specific kinds of lesions. The Southern California Sensory Integration Tests make up a battery designed to assess sensory-integrative and motor functioning in children 4 to 9 years of age.

A neuropsychological battery called the Severe Impairment Battery (SIB; Saxton et al., 1990) is designed for use with severely impaired assessees who might otherwise perform at or near the floor of existing tests. The battery is divided into six subscales: Attention, Orientation, Language, Memory, Visuoperception, and Construction. Another specialized battery is the Cognitive Behavioral Driver's Inventory, which was specifically designed to assist in determining whether individuals with brain damage are capable of driving a motor vehicle (Lambert & Engum, 1992).

## Other Tools of Neuropsychological Assessment

Neuropsychologists must be prepared to evaluate persons who are vision-impaired or blind, hearing-impaired or deaf, or suffering from other disabilities. Providing accommodations for such patients while conducting a meaningful assessment can be challenging (Hill-Briggs et al., 2007). As with other evaluations involving accommodation for a disability, due consideration must be given to selection of instruments and to any deviance from standardized test administration and interpretation guidelines. There always seem to be new tools of evaluation in development for possible use with members of special populations. So, for example, Miller et al. (2007) described the development of a test of nonverbal reasoning that utilizes a three-dimensional matrix. Designed for use with the visually impaired and the blind, the test measures nonverbal reasoning primarily through the haptic sense (sense of touch). Marinus et al. (2004) described the development of a short scale designed to evaluate motor function in patients with Parkinson's disease. Clinicians must be keen observers of things like a patient's mobility, and Zebehazy et al. (2005) discussed the use of digital video to assess those observational skills.

Perhaps the greatest advances in the field of neuropsychological assessment have come in the form of high technology and the mutually beneficial relationship that has developed between psychologists and medical personnel. Using relatively new technology, investigators have been exploring the genetic bases of various phenomena related to normal and abnormal neuropsychological functioning, including everyday information processing and decision making (Benedetti et al., 2008; Marcotte & Grant, 2009), attention deficit hyperactivity disorder (Crosbie et al., 2008), and Alzheimer's disease (Borroni et al., 2007). Beyond the level of the gene, more "everyday" miracles in research, diagnosis, and treatment have been brought about through advances in brain imaging technology. One instrument which has shown itself to be very useful in neuropsychological practice and research is the *f*MRI (the functional MRI, usually abbreviated with a lower case, italicized *f*, and the capital letters MRI). "MRI" stands for an imaging procedure called magnetic resonance imaging. The MRI apparatus that many people have some familiarity with (see Figure 3 in this chapter's *Everyday Psychometrics*) is used to create images of structures within the body. The *f***MRI** apparatus creates real-time moving images of internal functioning, and is particularly useful in identifying which parts of the brain are active at various times and during various tasks. Countless thousands of *f*MRI studies have been done on sundry topics since this technology first came in to being in 1992 (Blamire, 2011). In recent years, it

# Medical Diagnostic Aids
## and Neuropsychological Assessment

Data from neuropsychological assessment, combined with data derived from various medical procedures, can in some cases yield a thorough understanding of a neurological problem. For example, certain behavioral indices evident in neuropsychological testing may result in a recommendation to further explore a particular brain site. The suspicion may be confirmed by a diagnostic procedure that yields cross-sectional pictures of the site and clearly reveals the presence of lesions.

The trained neuropsychologist has a working familiarity with the array of medical procedures that may be brought to bear on neuropsychological problems. Here, we take a closer look at a sample of these procedures. Let's begin with a brief description of the medical procedure and apparatus that is perhaps most familiar to us all, whether from experience in a dentist's chair or elsewhere: the X-ray.

To the radiologist, the X-ray photograph's varying shades convey information about the corresponding density of the tissue through which the X-rays have been passed. With front, side, back, and other X-ray views of the brain and the spinal column, the diagnosis of tumors, lesions, infections, and other abnormalities can frequently be made. There are many different types of such neuroradiologic procedures, which range from a simple X-ray of the skull to more complicated procedures. In one procedure, called a **cerebral angiogram,** a tracer element is injected into the bloodstream before the cerebral area is X-rayed.

Perhaps you have also heard or read about another imaging procedure, the **CAT (computerized axial tomography) scan,** also known as a "CT" scan (Figure 1). The CAT scan is superior to traditional X-rays because the structures in the brain may be represented in a systematic series of three-dimensional views, a feature that is extremely important in assessing conditions such as spinal anomalies. The **PET (positron emission tomography) scan** is a tool of nuclear medicine particularly useful in diagnosing biochemical lesions in the brain. Conceptually related to the PET scan is **SPECT (single photon emission computed tomography),** a technology that records the course of a radioactive tracer fluid (iodine) and produces exceptionally clear photographs of organs and tissues (Figure 2).

The term *radioisotope scan* or simply **brain scan** describes a procedure that also involves the introduction of radioactive material into the brain through an injection. The cranial surface is then scanned with a special camera

**Figure 1**
*The CT scan is useful in pinpointing the location of tumors, cysts, degenerated tissue, or other abnormalities, and its use may eliminate the need for exploratory surgery or painful diagnostic procedures used in brain or spinal studies.*

to track the flow of the material. Alterations in blood supply to the brain are noted, including alterations that may be associated with disease such as tumors.

The **electroencephalograph (EEG)** is a machine that measures the electrical activity of the brain by means of electrodes pasted to the scalp. EEG activity will vary as a function of age, level of arousal (awake, drowsy, asleep), and other factors in addition to varying as a function of brain abnormalities. Electroencephalography is a safe, painless, and noninvasive procedure that can be of significant value in diagnosing and treating seizure and other disorders.

Information about nerve damage and related abnormalities may be obtained by electrically stimulating nerves and then noting movement (or lack of movement) in corresponding muscle tissue. The **electromyograph (EMG)** is a machine that records electrical activity of muscles by means of an electrode inserted directly into the muscle. Abnormalities found in the EMG can be used with other clinical and historical data as an aid in making a final diagnosis. The **echoencephalograph** is a machine that transforms electric energy into sound (sonic) energy. The sonic energy ("echoes") transversing the tissue area under study is then converted back into electric energy and displayed as a printout. This printout is used as an adjunct to other procedures in helping the diagnostician to determine

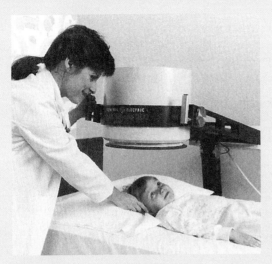

**Figure 2**

*SPECT technology has shown promise in evaluating conditions such as cerebral vascular disease, Alzheimer's disease, and seizure disorders.*

**Figure 3**

*This magnetic resonance system utilizes a magnetic field and radio waves to create detailed images of the body. These and related imaging techniques may be employed not only in the study of neuropsychological functioning but also in the study of abnormal behavior; see, for example, Kellner et al.'s (1991) study of obsessive-compulsive disorder.*

the nature and location of certain types of lesions in the brain. Radio waves in combination with a magnetic field can also be used to create detailed anatomical images, as illustrated in Figure 3.

Laboratory analysis of bodily fluids such as blood and urine can provide clues about neurological problems and also about nonneurological problems masquerading as neurological problems. Examining cerebrospinal fluid for blood and other abnormalities can yield key diagnostic insights. A sample of the fluid is obtained by means of a medical procedure termed a **lumbar puncture,** or spinal

tap. In this procedure, a special needle is inserted into the widest spinal interspace after a local anesthetic has been applied. In addition to providing information concerning the chemical normality of the fluid, the test allows the diagnostician to gauge the normality of the intracranial pressure.

Working together, neuropsychologists and medical professionals can help improve the quality of life of many people with neurological problems.

would seem that research using *f*MRI technology knows no bounds; it is limited only by the imagination (and research budgets) of the researchers. One small sampling of the range of topics explored would include when the brain is prepared to learn (Yoo et al., 2012), how traumatic brain injury impacts the brain network that mediates memory (Kasahara et al., 2011), how neural processing of faces changes over time (Lee et al., 2011), how depression moderates reward anticipation (Olino et al., 2011), how behavior therapy for substance abuse affects neural networks (DeVito et al., 2011), and how one's favorite song activates brain circuitry (Montag et al., 2011).

The tools of neuropsychological assessment, much like many other measuring instruments used by psychologists, can help improve the quality of life of the people who are assessed with them. In the following (final) chapter, we survey how tools of assessment are working to improve, among other things, the quality of *business* life.

# Self-Assessment

Test your understanding of elements of this chapter by seeing if you can explain each of the following terms, expressions, and abbreviations:

aphagia
aphasia
behavioral neurology
Bender Visual-Motor
    Gestalt Test
brain damage
brain scan
CAT (computerized axial
    tomography) scan
central nervous system
cerebral angiogram
clock-drawing test (CDT)
confrontation naming
contralateral control
declarative memory
deterioration quotient
developmental milestone
echoencephalograph
electroencephalograph (EEG)
electromyograph (EMG)

episodic memory
executive function
field-of-search item
fixed battery
flexible battery
fMRI
functional deficit
Halstead-Reitan
    Neuropsychological Battery
hard sign
implicit memory
lesion
lumbar puncture
motor test
neurological damage
neurology
neuron
neuropsychological assessment
neuropsychological mental status
    examination

neuropsychology
neurotology
noninvasive procedure
organic deficit
organicity
pattern analysis
perceptual-motor test
perceptual test
peripheral nervous system
PET (positron emission
    tomography) scan
picture absurdity item
procedural memory
reflex
semantic memory
soft sign
SPECT (single photon
    emission computed
    tomography)
trail-making item

# CHAPTER 16

# *Assessment, Careers, and Business*

*What do you want to be when you grow up?*

It seems just yesterday that we were asked that question . . . For some readers, it really *was* just yesterday.

Questions and concerns about career choice typically occupy the thoughts of people contemplating a transition from student to member of the workforce (Collins, 1998; Murphy et al., 2006). Of course, such questions and concerns are by no means limited to people *entering* the world of work. At any given time, there are millions of people already established in careers who are contemplating career changes.

Professionals involved in career counseling use tools of assessment to help their clients identify the variety of work they might succeed at and would hopefully enjoy doing. In this chapter we survey some of the types of instruments that are used to assist in career choice and career transition. Later in the chapter we'll sample some of the many measures used by businesses, organizations and the military to serve their various objectives.

> **JUST THINK . . .**
>
> How do you think most people decide on their careers? What factors entered (or will enter) into your own career decision?

## Career Choice and Career Transition

A whole world of tests is available to help in various phases of career choice. There are tests, for example, to survey interests, aptitudes, skills, or special talents. There are tests to measure attitudes toward work, confidence in one's skills, assumptions about careers, perceptions regarding career barriers, even dysfunctional career thoughts.

Historically, one variable considered closely related to occupational fulfillment and success is personal interests. It stands to reason that what intrigues, engages, and engrosses would be good to work at. In fact, an individual's interests may be sufficiently solidified by age 15 that they can be useful in career planning (Care, 1996). Further, evidence suggests that these interests will be fairly stable over time (Savickas & Spokane, 1999).

*Measures of Interest*

Assuming that interest in one's work promotes better performance, greater productivity, and greater job satisfaction, both employers and prospective employees should have much to gain from methods that can help individuals identify their interests and jobs tailored to those interests. Using such methods, individuals can discover, for example, whether their interests lie in commanding a starship while "seeking new worlds and exploring new civilizations" or something more along the lines of cosmetic dentistry (Figure 16–1). We may formally define an **interest measure** in the context of vocational assessment and pre-employment counseling as an instrument designed to evaluate testtakers' likes, dislikes, leisure activities, curiosities, and involvements in various pursuits for the purpose of comparison with groups of members of various occupations and professions.

Employers can use information about their employees' interest patterns to formulate job descriptions and attract new personnel. For example, a company could design an employment campaign emphasizing job security if job security were found to be the chief interest of the successful workers currently holding similar jobs. Although there are many instruments designed to measure interests, our discussion focuses on the one with the longest history of continuous use, the Strong Interest Inventory (SII).

**JUST THINK . . .**

Visualize an employer's "want ad" that begins "Wanted: Employees interested in _____." Fill in the blank with a listing of your top three interests. Next, list the possible positions for which this employer might be advertising.

**The Strong Interest Inventory**    One of the first measures of interest was published in 1907 by psychologist G. Stanley Hall. His questionnaire was designed to assess children's interest in various recreational pursuits. It was not until the early 1920s that Edward K. Strong Jr., inspired by a seminar he attended on the measurement of interest, began a program of systematic investigation in this area. His efforts culminated in a 420-item test he called the Strong Vocational Interest Blank (SVIB).

Originally designed for use with men only, the SVIB was published with a test manual by Stanford University Press in 1928 and then revised in 1938. In 1935, a 410-item SVIB for women was published along with a test manual. The women's SVIB was revised in 1946. The men's and women's SVIBs were again revised in the mid-1960s. Amid concern about sex-specific forms of the test in the late 1960s and early 1970s (McArthur, 1992), a merged form was published in 1974. Developed under the direction of David P. Campbell, the merged form was called the Strong-Campbell Interest Inventory (SCII). The test was revised in 1985, 1994, and again in 2004. This latest version, referred to as the Strong Interest Inventory, Revised Edition (SII; Strong et al., 2004), added new items to reflect contemporary career interests such as those related to computer hardware, software, and programming.

**JUST THINK . . .**

Are people interested in things they do well? Or do people develop abilities in areas that interest them?

Strong's recipe for test construction was empirical and straightforward: (1) Select hundreds of items that could conceivably distinguish the interests of a person by that person's occupation; (2) administer this rough cut of the test to several hundred people selected as representative of certain occupations or professions; (3) sort out which items seemed of interest to persons by occupational group and discard items with no discriminative ability; and (4) construct a final version of the test that would yield scores describing how an examinee's pattern of interest corresponded to those of people actually employed in various occupations and professions. With such a test, college students majoring in psychology, for example, could see how closely their interests paralleled those of working psychologists. Presumably, if an individual's interests

**Figure 16–1**
**It's Not Just a Job, It's an Adventure!**

*Had Orin Scrivello, D.D.S. (played by Steve Martin) in the comedy* Little Shop of Horrors *taken an interest survey, the results might have been quite bizarre. As a child, young Orin's interests leaned toward bashing the heads of pussycats, shooting puppies with a BB gun, and poisoning guppies. He was able to put what his mother described as his "natural tendencies" to use in gainful employment: He became a dentist.*

closely match psychologists' (in contrast to the interests of, say, tow-truck operators), that individual would probably enjoy the work of a psychologist.

Test items probe personal preferences in a variety of areas such as occupations, school subjects, and activities. Respondents answer each of these questions on a five-point continuum that ranges from "strongly like" to "strongly dislike." Nine items in a "Your Characteristics" section contain items like "win friends easily"; respondents select an answer on a five-point continuum that ranges from "strongly like me" to "strongly unlike me." Each protocol is computer scored and interpreted, yielding information on the testtaker's personal style, basic interests, and other data useful in determining how similar or dissimilar the respondent's interests are to those of people holding a variety of jobs

**Other interest inventories** In addition to the SII, many other interest inventories are now in widespread use. You may recall one such inventory from Chapter 12 called The Self-Directed Search (SDS). The SDS explores interests within the context of Holland's (1997) theory of vocational personality types and work environments. According to this theory, vocational choice is an expression of one of six personality types: Realistic, Investigative, Artistic, Social, Enterprising, or Conventional. These personality types are variously referred to simply as the "Big 6" or by the acronym "RIASEC."

> **JUST THINK . . .**
>
> Why might differential item functioning by gender be expected in interest measures?

Another interest inventory is the Minnesota Vocational Interest Inventory. Empirically keyed, this instrument was expressly designed to compare respondents' interest patterns with those of persons employed in a variety of nonprofessional occupations (such as stock clerks, painters, printers, and truck drivers). Other measures of interest have been designed for use with people who have one or another deficit or disability. For example, interest inventories for testtakers who do not read well will typically employ drawings and other visual media as stimuli (Elksnin & Elksnin, 1993). Brief descriptions of a sampling of various measures of interest are presented in Table 16–1.[1]

**Table 16–1**
**Some Measures of Interest**

| Test | Description |
| --- | --- |
| Campbell Interest and Skill Survey | Developed by David Campbell, who revised the Strong Interest Inventory, this instrument focuses on occupations that require four or more years of postsecondary education. In addition to assessing interests, it is designed to provide an estimate of the individual's confidence in performing various occupational activities. |
| Career Interest Inventory | Designed for use with students in grades 7 through 12 as well as adults, this test introduces testtakers to the world of occupational and educational alternatives. In addition to career-related interests, the test taps interest in school subjects and school-related activities. |
| Guidance Information System (GIS 3.0) | Available only on disk or CD-ROM, this combination assessment instrument and information retrieval system contains a number of components ranging from information on colleges to information on the types of jobs college majors in different areas tend to get. The interest assessment component of the system is called the Career Decision-Making System. After probing the assessee's interests, interest scores are calculated, and the system provides lists of suggested careers and occupations to explore. |
| Jackson Vocational Interest Survey | This is a forced-choice measure of interests as they relate to 26 work roles (what one does at work) and 8 work styles (the type of work environment preferred, usually related to one's personal values). Designed for use with high-school and college students, the test yields scores on 10 Holland-like themes, as well as validity-related indices. The development of this test has been described in detail by Jackson (1977; Jackson & Williams, 1975). |
| Kuder Occupational Interest Survey (KOIS) | This classic interest-measuring instrument is an outgrowth of the Kuder Preference Survey, which was originally published in 1939. Each item presents testtakers with three choices of activity, and their task is to select their most and least preferred choices. Scores are reported in terms of magnitude of interest in various occupational categories. The test has been criticized for its lack of predictive validity, an assertion that has been addressed by the test's author and his colleagues (Kuder et al. 1998; Zytowski, 1996). |
| Reading-Free Vocational Interest Inventory (R-FVII) | Designed for use with people 10 years of age and older with learning disabilities, mental retardation, or other special needs, this test measures vocational likes and dislikes using pictures of people at work in different occupations. For each item, respondents select one of three drawings depicting the preferred job task. The protocol yields scores on 11 occupational categories that represent types of occupations at which members of special populations might be employed. |
| Self-Directed Search-Form R | Developed by John L. Holland, this is a self-administered, self-scored, and self-interpreted interest inventory appropriate for use by individuals 12 years of age and older. Form-R (1994) contains updated norms. Testtakers complete a booklet in which they are asked questions about various interest-related areas, including activities, aspirations, and competencies. |

1. We parenthetically note a semantic distinction between *interest* and *passion*. According to Vallerand et al. (2003), passion comes in two varieties: *obsessive passion* and *harmonious passion*. Both types derive from internal pressure to engage in activity one likes. However, whereas harmonious passion promotes healthy adaptation, obsessive passion derails it. According to these researchers, obsessive passion leads to rigid persistence, which in turn produces negative affect.

How well do interest measures predict the kind of work in which individuals will be successful and happy? In one study, interest and aptitude measures were found to correlate in a range of about .40 to .72 (Lam et al., 1993). In another study examining the accuracy with which interest and aptitude tests predict future job performance and satisfaction, Bizot and Goldman (1993) identified people who had been tested in high school with measures of vocational interest and aptitude. Eight years later, these individuals reported on their satisfaction with their jobs, even permitting the researchers to contact their employers for information about the quality of their work. The researchers found that when a good match existed between a subject's aptitude in high school and the level of his or her current job, performance was likely to be evaluated positively by the employer. When a poor match existed, a poor performance rating was more likely. The extent to which employees were themselves satisfied with their jobs was not related to aptitudes as measured in high school. As for predictive validity, the interest tests administered in high school predicted neither job performance nor job satisfaction eight years later. The results of this and related studies (for example, Jagger et al., 1992) sound a caution to counselors regarding overreliance on interest inventories. Concern has also been expressed about differential item functioning in interest tests (particularly the Strong) as a function of gender (Einarsdóttir & Rounds, 2009). Of course, it has also been well established that, generally speaking, men and women tend to have different interests (Su et al., 2009). Some research suggests that the predictive efficiency of interest measures may be enhanced if they are used in combination with other measures such as measures of confidence and self-efficacy (Chartrand et al., 2002; Rottinghaus et al., 2003), personality (Larson & Borgen, 2002; Staggs et al., 2003), or a portfolio project (Larkin et al., 2002).

## Measures of Ability and Aptitude

As we saw in Chapter 12, achievement, ability, and aptitude tests all measure prior learning to some degree, although they differ in the uses to which the test data will be put. Beyond that, aptitude tests may tap a greater amount of informal learning than achievement tests. Achievement tests may be more limited and focused than aptitude tests.

Ability and aptitude measures vary widely in topics covered, specificity of coverage, and other variables. The Wonderlic Personnel Test measures mental ability in a general sense. This brief (12-minute) test includes items that assess spatial skill, abstract thought, and mathematical skill. The test may be useful in screening individuals for jobs that require both fluid and crystallized intellectual abilities (Bell et al., 2002).

The Bennet Mechanical Comprehension Test is a widely used paper-and-pencil measure of a testtaker's ability to understand the relationship between physical forces and various tools (for example, pulleys and gears) as well as other common objects (carts, steps, and seesaws). Other mechanical tests, such as the Hand-Tool Dexterity Test, blur the lines among aptitude, achievement, and performance tests by requiring the testtaker actually to take apart, reassemble, or otherwise manipulate materials, usually in a prescribed sequence and within a time limit. If a job consists mainly of securing tiny transistors into the inner workings of an electronic appliance or game, then the employer's focus of interest might well be on prospective employee's perceptual-motor abilities, finger dexterity, and related variables. In such an instance, the O'Connor Tweezer Dexterity Test might be the instrument of choice (Figure 16–2). This test requires the examinee to insert brass pins into a metal plate using a pair of tweezers.

**JUST THINK . . .**

What types of "real-world" tasks might be on a new aptitude test designed to select candidates for admission to a graduate program in psychological testing and assessment?

**Figure 16–2**
**The O'Connor Tweezer Dexterity Test**

*This test is especially useful in evaluating a testtaker's fine motor skills and dexterity. One of the pioneers of the hair transplant industry, cosmetic surgeon Dominic A. Brandy, extolled the benefits of this test when he described its use as a screening tool for hiring surgical hair restoration assistants (Brandy, 1995).*

A number of other tests are designed to measure specific aptitudes for a wide variety of occupational fields. For the professions, there are many psychometrically sophisticated assessment programs for screening or selecting applicants by means of aptitude tests. (An extensive list of these tests was presented in Chapter 12.) For a while, one of the most widely used aptitude tests was the General Aptitude Test Battery (GATB). A description of that test, as well as the controversy surrounding it, follows.

**The General Aptitude Test Battery** The U.S. Employment Service (USES) developed the General Aptitude Test Battery (GATB) and first put it into use in 1947 after extensive research. The GATB (pronounced like "Gatsby" without the *s*) is available for use by state employment services as well as other agencies and organizations, such as school districts and nonprofit organizations, that have obtained official permission from the government to administer it. The GATB is a tool used to identify aptitudes for occupations, and it is a test just about anyone of working age can take. The test is administered regularly at local state offices (referred to by names such as the Job Service, Employment Security Commission, and Labor Security Commission) to people who want the agency to help find them a job. It may also be administered to people who are unemployed and have been referred by a state office of unemployment or to employees of a company that has requested such aptitude assessment.

If you are curious about your own aptitude for work in fields as diverse as psychology, education, and plumbing, you may want to visit your local state employment office and sample the GATB yourself. Be prepared to sit for an examination that will take about three hours if you take the entire test. The GATB consists of 12 timed tests that measure nine aptitudes, which in turn can be divided into three composite aptitudes. About half the time will be spent on psychomotor tasks and the other half on paper-and-pencil tasks. In some instances, depending on factors such as the reason for the assessment, only selected tests of the battery will be administered. The version of the test used to selectively measure aptitudes for a specific line of work is referred to as a Special Aptitude Test Battery, or SATB. SATB data may also be isolated for study from other test data when the entire test is taken.

The GATB has evolved from a test with multiple cutoffs to one that employs regression and *validity generalization* for making recommendations based on test results. The rationale and process by which the GATB has made this evolution has been described by John E. Hunter (1980, 1986), Frank Schmidt, and their associates (Hunter & Hunter, 1984; Hunter & Schmidt, 1983; Hunter et al., 1982). Validity generalization is the subject of this chapter's *Close-Up.*

In the past, recommendations with respect to aptitude for a particular job had been made on the basis of GATB validity studies bearing on specific jobs. For example, if there existed 500 job descriptions covering 500 jobs for which scores on the GATB were to be applied, there would be 500 individual validation studies with the GATB—one validation study for each individual job, typically with a relatively small sample size (many of these single studies containing only 76 subjects on average). Further, there were no validation studies for the other 12,000-plus jobs in the American economy (according to the *Dictionary of Occupational Titles* published by the U.S. Department of Labor, 1991).

Using meta-analysis to cumulate results across a number of validation studies and to correct statistically for errors such as sampling error, Hunter demonstrated that all the jobs could be categorized within five families of jobs, based on the *worker function codes* of the then-current edition of the *Dictionary of Occupational Titles.* The five families of jobs were (1) Setting Up, (2) Feeding and Off-Bearing, (3) Synthesizing and Coordinating, (4) Analyzing, Compiling, and Computing, and (5) Copying and Comparing. Regression equations for each of the families were then developed. Using these equations, Hunter found that recommendations for individual testtakers could be generalized to various jobs.

In the late 1980s the GATB became a center of controversy when it became public knowledge that the test had been race-normed. As described earlier in this book (Chapter 4), *race norming* refers to the process of adjusting scores to show an individual testtaker's standing within his or her own racial group. With the race-normed GATB, high scorers who were categorized within certain groups according to race were recommended for employment. For example, among people being considered for a skilled job, a GATB raw score of 300 was "translated into percentile scores of 79, 62, and 38, respectively, for Blacks, Hispanics, and others" (Gottfredson, 1994, p. 966). Only percentile scores, not raw scores, were reported to employers.

> JUST THINK . . .
>
> What are the pros and cons of race-norming an aptitude test?

In an attempt to address the ensuing controversy, the U.S. Department of Labor asked the National Academy of Sciences (NAS) to conduct a study. The NAS issued a report (Hartigan & Wigdor, 1989) that was generally supportive of race norming. The NAS noted that the GATB appeared to suffer from slope bias such that the test correlated more highly with criterion measures for White samples (.19) than for Black samples (.12). Intercept bias was also present, with the result that the performance of Blacks would be more favorably predicted relative to the performance of Whites if the same regression line were used for both groups. The NAS found race norming to be a reasonable method of correcting for the bias of the test.

The NAS report also addressed more general issues concerning the utility of the GATB as a predictor of job performance. Using a database of 755 studies, the NAS noted that the GATB correlated approximately .22 with criteria such as supervisory ratings.

# Validity Generalization and the GATB

**C**an a test validated for use in personnel selection for one occupation also be valid for use in personnel selection for another occupation? Must the validation of a test used in personnel selection be situation-specific? Stated more generally, can validity evidence for a test meaningfully be applied to situations other than those in which the evidence was obtained? These are the types of questions raised when validity generalization is discussed.

As applied to employment-related decision making on the basis of test scores achieved on the General Aptitude Test Battery (GATB), *validity generalization* means that the same test-score data may be predictive of aptitude for all jobs. The implication is that if a test is validated for a few jobs selected from a much larger cluster of jobs, each requiring similar skills at approximately the same level of complexity, then the test is valid for all jobs in that cluster. For example, if a validation study conclusively indicated that GATB scores are predictive of aptitude for (and ultimately proficiency in) the occupation of assembler in an aircraft assembly plant, then it may not be necessary to conduct an entirely new validation study before applying such data to the occupation of assembler in a shipbuilding plant; if the type and level of skill required in the two occupations can be shown to be sufficiently similar, then it may be that the same or similar procedures used to select aircraft assemblers can profitably be used to select shipbuilders.

Validity generalization (VG) as applied to personnel selection using the GATB makes unnecessary the burden of conducting a separate validation study with the test for every one of the more than 12,000 jobs in the American economy. The application of VG to GATB scores also enables GATB users to supply employers with more precise information about testtakers. To understand why this is so, let's begin by consulting the pie chart in Figure 1.

Note that the inner circle of the chart lists the 12 tests in the General Aptitude Test Battery and the next ring of the circle lists eight aptitudes derived from the 12 tests. Not illustrated here is a ninth aptitude, General Learning Ability, which is derived from scores on the Vocabulary, Arithmetic Reasoning, and Three-Dimensional Space tests. Here is a brief description of each of the eight aptitudes measured by the GATB.

- *Verbal Aptitude* (V): Understanding the meaning of words and their relationships and using words effectively are two of the abilities tapped here. V is measured by Test 4.

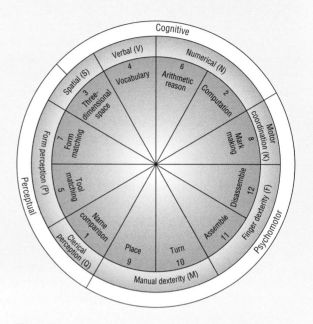

**Figure 1**
**Aptitudes Measured by the General Aptitude Test Battery**

- *Numerical Aptitude* (N): N is measured by tasks requiring the quick performance of arithmetic operations. It is measured by Tests 2 and 6.

- *Spatial Aptitude* (S): The ability to visualize and mentally manipulate geometric forms is tapped here. S is measured by Test 3.

- *Form Perception* (P): Attention to detail, including the ability to discriminate slight differences in shapes, shading, lengths, and widths—as well as the ability to perceive pertinent detail—is measured. P is measured by Tests 5 and 7.

- *Clerical Perception* (Q): Attention to detail in written or tabular material, as well as the ability to proofread words and numbers and to avoid perceptual errors in arithmetic computation, is tapped here. Q is measured by Test 1.

- *Motor Coordination* (K): This test taps the ability to quickly make precise movements that require eye–hand coordination. K is measured by Test 8.

- *Finger Dexterity* (F): This test taps the ability to quickly manipulate small objects with the fingers. F is measured by Tests 11 and 12.

- *Manual Dexterity* (M): The ability to work with one's hands in placing and turning motions is measured here. M is measured by Tests 9 and 10.

In the outermost ring of the diagram, note that the three composite aptitudes can be derived from the nine specific aptitudes: a Cognitive composite, a Perceptual composite, and a Psychomotor composite. The nine aptitudes that compose the three composite aptitudes are summarized in the following table.

| The Nine GATB Aptitudes | | The Three Composite Scores |
|---|---|---|
| G | General Learning Ability (also referred to as *intelligence*) | Cognitive |
| V | Verbal Aptitude | |
| N | Numerical Aptitude | |
| S | Spatial Aptitude | |
| P | Form Perception | Perceptual |
| Q | Clerical Perception | |
| K | Motor Coordination | |
| F | Finger Dexterity | Psychomotor |
| M | Manual Dexterity | |

Traditionally—before the advent of VG—testtakers who sat for the GATB might subsequently receive counseling about their performance in each of the nine aptitude areas. Further, they might have been informed (1) how their own pattern of GATB scores compared with patterns of aptitude (referred to as Occupational Aptitude Patterns, or OAPs) deemed necessary for proficiency in various occupations, and (2) how they performed with respect to any of the 467 constellations of a Special Aptitude Test Battery (SATB) that could potentially be extracted from a GATB protocol. VG provides additional information useful in advising prospective employers and counseling prospective employees, including more precise data on a testtaker's performance with respect to OAPs as well as scores (usually expressed in percentiles) with respect to the five job families.

Research (Hunter, 1982) has indicated that the three composite aptitudes can be used to validly predict job proficiency for all jobs in the U.S. economy. All jobs may be categorized according to five job families, and the aptitude required for each of these families can be described with respect to various contributions of the three composite GATB scores. For example, Job Family 1 (Setup Jobs) is 59% Cognitive, 30% Perceptual, and 11% Psychomotor. GATB scoring is done by computer, as is weighting of scores to determine suitability for employment in each of the five job families.

Proponents of VG as applied to use with the GATB list the following advantages.

1. *The decreased emphasis on multiple cutoffs as a selection strategy has advantages for both prospective employers and prospective employees.* In a multiple cutoff selection model, a prospective employee would have to achieve certain minimum GATB scores in each of the aptitudes deemed critical for proficiency in a given occupation; failure to meet the minimal cutting score in these aptitudes would mean elimination from the candidate pool for that occupation. Using VG, a potential benefit for the prospective employee is that the requirement of a minimum cutting score on any specific aptitude is eliminated. For employers, VG encourages the use of a top-down hiring policy, one in which the best-qualified people (as measured by the GATB) are offered jobs first.

2. *Research has suggested that the relationship between aptitude test scores and job performance is linear (Waldman & Avolio, 1989), a relationship that is statistically better suited to VG than to the multiple cutoff selection model.* The nature of the relationship between scores on a valid test of aptitude and ratings of job performance is illustrated in Figure 2. Given that such a relationship exists, Hunter (1980, 1982) noted that, from a technical standpoint, linear data are better suited to analysis using a VG model than using a model with multiple cutoffs.

3. *More precise information can be reported to employers regarding a testtaker's relative standing in the continuum of aptitude test scores.* Consider in this context Figure 3, and let's suppose that an established and validated cutoff score for selection in a particular occupation using this hypothetical test of aptitude is 155. Examinee X and Examinee Y both meet the cutoff requirement, but Examinee Y is probably better qualified for the job—we say "probably" because there may be exceptions to this general rule, depending on variables such as the specific job's actual demands. Although the score for Examinee X falls below the median score for all testtakers, the score for Examinee Y lies at the high end of the distribution of scores. All other factors being equal, which individual would you prefer to hire if you owned the company? Using a simple cutoff procedure, no distinction with respect to aptitude score would have been made between Examinee X and Examinee Y, provided both scores met the cutoff criterion.

4. *VG better assists employers in their efforts to hire qualified employees.* Studies such as one conducted at the Philip Morris Company suggest that a significant increase in the rate of training success can be expected for employees hired using a selection procedure that uses VG as compared with employees hired by other means (Warmke, 1984).

Is VG the answer to all personnel selection problems? Certainly not. VG is simply one rationale for justifiably avoiding the time and expense of conducting a separate

*(continued)*

## Validity Generalization
and the GATB *(continued)*

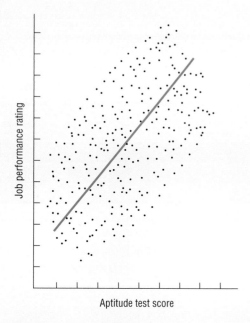

**Figure 2**
**The Linear Relationship between Aptitude Test Scores
and Job Performance Ratings**

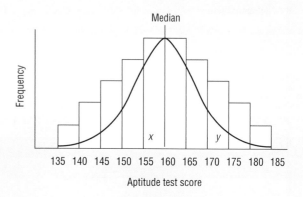

**Figure 3**
**Results of a Hypothetical Aptitude Test**

validation study for every single test with every
possible group of testtakers under every possible set
of circumstances—and usually with too few subjects to
achieve meaningful findings. Note, however, that with the
convenience of VG come many concerns about the efficacy
of the procedures employed. And although we have devoted
a fair amount of time to acquainting you with this important
concept in the personnel selection literature, it is equally
important for you to be aware that a number of technical
issues with respect to VG are currently being debated in the
professional literature.

You will recall that, in the development of VG as applied
to personnel selection, Hunter and his colleagues used a
process called meta-analysis to cumulate findings across a
number of studies. One important aspect of this work involved
statistically correcting for the small sample sizes that occurred
in the studies analyzed. The types of procedures used in such
a process, and the types of interpretations that legitimately
can be made as a result, have been the subject of a number of
critical analyses of VG. The amount of unexplained variance
that remains even after statistical corrections for differences

in sample size (Cascio, 1987), the unknown influence of a
potential restriction-of-range problem with respect to subject
self-selection (Cronbach, 1984), objections about using
employer ratings as a criterion (Burke, 1984), and the fact that
alternative models may explain variation in validity coefficients
as well as the cross-situational consistency model (James
et al., 1986) are some of the technical issues that have been
raised with respect to the use of VG (see also Zedeck &
Cascio, 1984). With specific reference to VG as applied to use
with the GATB, one might inquire further: What problems arise
when more than 12,000 occupations are grouped into five job
families? Is it really meaningful to place an occupation such
as truck driver in the same job family as secretary?

Clearly, much remains to be learned about how VG can
most effectively be brought to bear on problems related to
personnel testing. Difficult questions—some psychometric,
others that relate more to societal values—will have to be
addressed. A detailed critique of VG, beginning with its logic
and ending with its application, can be found in Murphy (2003).

Compounding the task of fairly evaluating VG is a litany
of variables that are neither psychometric in nature nor
directly related to values. Included here are such variables as
the strength of the economy, the size of the available labor
pool, the experience of the available labor pool, the general
desirability of specific jobs, and the salaries offered for
various kinds of work. Whether one looks favorably or not
at the government's experimentation with VG in personnel
selection, it seems reasonable to assume that there is much
to be learned in the process, and the field of personnel
selection may ultimately profit from the experience.

Others had estimated the test's validity to be .20 (Vevea et al., 1993) and .21 (Waldman & Avolio, 1989). These relatively small coefficients were viewed by the NAS as modest but acceptable. To understand why they were considered acceptable, recall from Chapter 6 that criterion validity is limited by the reliability of the measures. Although the GATB had adequate test-retest reliability (around .81), the likely poor reliability of supervisory ratings might very well have depressed the GATB's validity coefficient. Such depression of a validity coefficient could be expected to occur for any test designed to predict job performance that is validated against supervisors' ratings (Hartigan & Wigdor, 1989). Of course, even predictors with modest criterion validity can improve personnel selection decisions. Thus, despite the low criterion validity coefficients, the GATB was widely viewed as a valid means of selecting employees.

The NAS recommendation to continue the practice of race norming the test may have done more to fan the flames of controversy than to quell them. In July 1990, the Department of Labor proposed a two-year suspension in the use of the GATB, during which time the efficacy of the test and its scoring procedures would be further researched. The legality of the practice of race norming had also become a heated topic of debate by that time (Baydoun & Neuman, 1992; Delahunty, 1988). The question of whether race norming of the GATB should continue became moot after Congress passed the Civil Rights Act of 1991, a law that made the practice of race norming illegal.

Today the GATB is still in use by the U.S. Employment Service. Reports to employers are no longer race-normed; the raw scores of people from all racial groups are now converted to interpretable standard scores using the same norms. Still, concerns linger regarding the equity of the test's scoring and cut-score practice as they affect various racial groups (Gardner & Deadrick, 2008). In addition to its potential applied value, the GATB remains a valuable resource for researchers in areas as diverse as rehabilitation counseling (Reid et al., 2007), theory validation (Farrell & McDaniel, 2001), and theory extension (Rashkovky, 2006).

The quest for viable predictors of occupational success has led researchers beyond the study of interests and aptitudes. One area that has been explored quite extensively could be summed up in one word: *personality.*

> **JUST THINK . . .**
>
> Will a person who is outgoing and highly creative find happiness in a career as a data entry technician at a rebate fulfillment center? If not, what type of career is the "best fit" for this type of person? What makes you think so?

## Measures of Personality

Just thinking about the questions raised in our *Just Think* compels one to consider the role of personality in career choice. When researchers consider such questions, they may seek answers in a study that includes the administration of a personality test. Let's mention at the outset that the use of personality measures in employment settings is a topic that has generated a fair amount of debate in the scholarly literature. Concern has been expressed about attempts by employees, or prospective employees (that is, job applicants) to "fake good" on such tests (Birkeland et al., 2006). Such attempts may introduce unanticipated error into the process (Arthur et al., 2001; Mueller-Hanson et al., 2003) and negatively influence selection decisions (Rosse et al., 1998). On the other side of the coin is the view that personality measures are not necessarily fakable (Hogan et al., 2007; Pace & Borman, 2006) and that the collected data is still viable even when attempts at faking occur (Hough, 1998; Ones et al., 1996). Proponents of the use of personality tests in the workplace argue that they have, in some respects, greater utility than cognitive ability tests (Hogan & Roberts, 2001).

Although there are many personality tests, some will be more appropriate for the task at hand than others. For example, the MMPI-2-RF, widely used in clinical settings, may have limited application in the context of career counseling. Other personality tests, such as the Guilford-Zimmerman Temperament Survey and the Edwards Personal Preference Schedule, may be preferred because the measurements they yield tend to be better related to the specific variables under study. Today, two of the most widely used personality tests in the workplace are the NEO PI-R (previously described in Chapter 12 and discussed at length on the companion website to this text) and the Myers-Briggs Type Indicator (MBTI). Following a brief discussion of studies that approach career- and occupation-related questions at the level of the *trait,* we discuss the MBTI and consider such questions at the level of personality *type.*

**Measuring personality traits**   Personality assessment in the context of employment-related research or counseling might begin with the administration of a test designed to measure Costa and McCrae's (1992b) Big Five, Tellegen's (1985) Big Three**,** Holland's Big Six, or some other (Big, Little, or Medium) number of traits or types according to a particular conceptualization of personality.[2] The researcher will then analyze the personality test data in terms of how they compare with other job- or career-related variables.

Most of the research cited above employed Costa and McCrae's (1992b) NEO PI-R. In fact, this test probably is the most widely used today. There are, however, more specialized types of instruments that also fall under the general heading of personality test. For example, we may speak of an **integrity test,** specifically designed to predict employee theft, honesty, adherence to established procedures, and/or potential for violence. Such narrowly defined personality tests used in the context of employment-related research and practice have been characterized as *criterion-focused occupational personality scales,* abbreviated as "COPS" (Ones & Viswesvaran, 2001).

Integrity tests may be used to screen new employees as well as to keep honest those already hired. The use of such tests has increased dramatically with the passage of legislation prohibiting the use of polygraphs (lie detectors) in most employment settings. The trend is away from lengthy paper-and-pencil questionnaires toward measures that can be electronically administered quickly and efficiently. One such measure is the Applicant Potential Inventory (API), which can be administered by computer (online or offline), telephone, or fax. Jones et al. (2002) described the development of this test as well as research designed to explore its psychometric soundness.

Sackett et al. (1989) dichotomized integrity tests into *overt integrity tests* (which may straightforwardly ask the examinee questions like "Do you always tell the truth?") and *personality-based measures,* which resemble in many ways objective personality inventories. Items on the latter type of test may be far more subtle than on the former. The lack of face validity in such personality-based measures may work to the advantage of the test user in terms of obtaining integrity test responses that well, "have integrity." After all, how many people that are motivated to get a job would admit to lying, cheating, and stealing? Responses to items on the personality-based measures are likely to be interpreted with reference to the responses of groups of people known to have or lack integrity (as defined by the particular test).

Whether integrity tests measure what they purport to measure is debatable. Reviews of the validity of such measures have ranged from mixed (American Psychological Association, 1991; Sackett & Harris, 1984; Sackett et al., 1989)

---

2. Holland (1999) made clear that, for him, interest inventories *are* personality inventories. For this reason, it is appropriate to mention Holland's work in discussing interest or personality assessment as an aid to career counseling.

to positive (DePaulo, 1994; Honts, 1994; Sackett, 1994; Saxe, 1994). Perhaps the fairest conclusion from this literature is that when the test has been professionally developed, it stands an excellent chance of meeting acceptable standards of validity. *Model Guidelines for Preemployment Integrity Testing Programs,* a document developed by the Association of Personnel Test Publishers (APTP, 1990), addresses many of the issues surrounding integrity tests, including issues relating to test development, administration, scoring, interpretation, confidentiality, public statements regarding the tests, and test-marketing practices. Specific guidelines in these areas are provided, and the responsibilities of test users and publishers are discussed (see Jones et al., 1990, for an overview).

Beyond issues regarding the validity of integrity tests lie broader questions about various aspects of the use of such tests (Camara & Schneider, 1994). For example, is privacy invaded when a prospective employee is asked to sit for such a test? Can such tests be used to support discrimination practices? Should such tests be used alone or in combination with other measurement procedures as a basis for granting or denying employment? It is interesting that White (1984) suggested that preemployment honesty testing may induce negative work-related attitudes. Having to undergo such a test may be interpreted by prospective employees as evidence of high levels of employee theft—paradoxically resulting in a new and higher norm of stealing by employees.

**Measuring personality types**   How could anyone have foreseen in 1915 that the prospect of having Clarence Myers as a son-in-law would eventually lead Katharine Cook Briggs (see Figure 16–3) down a path that would culminate in the creation of an enduring measure of personality type?

**Figure 16–3**
**A Mother-Daughter Team of Test Developers**

*Katharine Cook Briggs (left) and Isabel Briggs Myers (right) created the Myers-Briggs Type Indicator. Katharine developed an interest in individual differences in 1915 upon being introduced to her future son-in-law, Clarence Myers. For Katharine, Clarence seemed different in fundamental ways from other members of the Briggs family. Owing in part to her desire to better understand these differences, Katharine created a category of psychological types. Years later, Isabel would put her mother's ideas to the test—literally.*

Isabel Briggs Myers and her mother, Katharine Cook Briggs—two women with no formal training in psychology or assessment—were inspired by the writings of Carl Jung (1923) and his ideas about different psychological types. In part, that inspiration was instrumental in the creation of the MBTI (Myers & Briggs, 1943/1962), a test used to classify assessees by psychological type and to shed light on "basic differences in the ways human beings take in information and make decisions" (McCaulley, 2000, p. 117).

From a psychometric perspective, the test has earned mixed reviews. A meta-analysis of published studies did indicate that the test and its scales tended to be internally consistent and stable over time, although some variations were observed (Capraro & Capraro, 2002). Still, many assessment professionals have expressed serious concerns about the MBTI on psychometric and related grounds (Arnau et al., 2003; Girelli & Stake, 1993; Harvey & Murry, 1994; Lorr, 1991; Martin & Bartol, 1986; Pittenger, 1993; Vacha-Haase & Thompson, 2002; Zumbo & Taylor, 1993). Regardless of such criticism, the test remains very popular, especially among counselors and organizational consultants. References to this widely used test in the literature are many, and its applications are likewise wide-ranging. It has been used, for example, to derive profiles of groups as diverse as substance abusers (Cianci, 2008), software engineers (Capretz, 2003) and players of *Dungeons and Dragons* (Wilson, 2008). It has been used to study celebrity worship (McCarley & Escoto, 2003), the personality of college athletes (Reiter et al., 2007), academic performance (DiRienzo et al., 2010), and applicants for admission to a college orthopedics-based honors program (Harstine, 2008). A more detailed description of the MBTI can be found in many published articles (see, for example, Furnham et al., 2003; McCaulley & Moody, 2008; Myers & Carskadon, 2002).

**The relationship between personality and work performance** Most people probably believe that there is a relationship between personality and work performance. However, establishing such a relationship through scholarly research is no easy matter. In fact, owing largely to the methodological obstacles in conducting such research, many researchers have failed to discover a relationship (Barrick et al., 2001). One issue in this kind of research relates to how *work performance* is defined. There is no single metric that can be used for all occupations. For some occupations, such as sales, an objective measure such as "the dollar value of new revenue generated over the course of a calendar year" can be defined. For other occupations, the measure used might not be as objective. For example, the measure relied on might be supervisor ratings—a measure that to varying degrees is idiosyncratic, subjective, and subject to the biases of the supervisors doing the rating.

In addition to issues concerning work performance, there are issues regarding which aspect of personality to measure; different aspects of personality have presumably greater relevance for different occupations. However, studying work performance with regard to Big Five traits has led to some useful findings. Barrick et al. (2001) conducted a **second-order meta-analysis** (a meta-analysis that summarizes other meta-analyses) and determined that in general, high *Conscientiousness* scores were correlated with good work performance, and high *Neuroticism* scores were correlated with poor work performance, *Extraversion* was also positively correlated with good work performance—but why? In follow-up research, Barrick et al. (2002) found that extraverted individuals were more motivated to achieve status, which in turn, predicted higher work performance ratings. Clearly, the relationship between personality and work performance is not straightforward; some personality traits seem helpful with regard to some, but not all types of jobs. Research in the area has increasingly looked at the complex interplay between personality and other variables affecting work performance, such as the perceived work environment (Kacmar et al., 2009; Westerman & Simmons, 2007) and the overall culture of the company (Anderson et al., 2008).

**JUST THINK . . .**

From the perspective of an employer, might there be a "downside" to seeking one specific *type* of employee for a particular position?

Another intriguing question raised by researchers is: "Does the emotional disposition of children have anything to do with how satisfied they are with their jobs as adults?" If you think the question itself is somewhat surprising, hold on to your hats when we tell you that the answer to the question (a resounding *yes*) is even more surprising. Using data from three separate longitudinal studies, Staw et al. (1986) found that dispositional data obtained in infancy predicted job-related attitudes over a time span of some 50 years. Although the interpretation of the data in this study has been questioned, it generally has received support from other researchers (Arvey et al., 1989; House et al., 1996; Judge et al., 1999, 2002; Motowidlo, 1996). It may be that one's temperament mediates emotionally significant events, including those at work, which in turn influence one's level of job satisfaction (Weiss & Cropanzano, 1996).

The findings cited here—and, more generally, the use of personality tests in any employment-related context—have their critics (see, for example, Ghiselli, 1973; Hollenbeck & Whitener, 1988; Kinslinger, 1966; Schmitt et al., 1984). Still, most researchers would probably concede that valuable job- and career-related information can be developed through the study of the assessment of personality (Fontanna, 2000; Ones et al., 2007; see also Judge & Hurst, 2008; Maurer et al., 2008).

## Other Measures

Numerous other tools of assessment may be used in career planning and pre-employment contexts, even though not specifically designed for that purpose. For example, the Checklist of Adaptive Living Skills (CALS; Morreau & Bruininks, 1991) surveys the life skills needed to make a successful transition from school to work. Organized into four broad domains (Personal Living Skills, Home Living Skills, Community Living Skills, and Employment Skills), this test evaluates 794 life skills. The checklist is designed for use with assessees of any age. According to the manual, the individual completing the checklist must have had the opportunity to observe the assessee for at least three months in natural settings. Assessees are judged to be *independent* with regard to a specific skill if they perform the task with good quality at least 75% of the time when needed and without reminder. This criterion-based instrument may be particularly useful in career and preemployment counseling with members of special populations.

Researchers are interested in the role of culture in various aspects of assessment for employment (Blustein & Ellis, 2000; Hofstede, 1998; Leong & Hartung, 2000; Ponterotto et al., 2000; Rotundo & Sackett, 1999; Ryan et al., 2000; Sandoval et al., 1998; Subich, 1996). According to Meyers (1994), the fact that a new job can sometimes result in a kind of "culture shock" prompted the creation of an instrument called the Cross-Cultural Adaptability Inventory (CCAI; Kelley & Meyers, 1992). The CCAI is a self-administered and self-scored instrument designed to provide information on the testtaker's ability to adapt to other cultures. Testtakers respond to 50 items written in a six-point Likert format. The test yields information about one's readiness to adapt to new situations, tolerate ambiguity, maintain one's personal identity in new surroundings, and interact with people from other cultures. The report is organized into information with regard to four factors thought to be relevant to cross-cultural adaptability: Emotional Resilience, Flexibility/Openness, Perceptual Acuity, and Personal Autonomy. The test may hold value in evaluating readiness to take a job or to be relocated overseas. One study showed that the Emotional Resilience and Personal Autonomy scales were positively related to number of international assignments (Nguyen et al., 2010).

Perhaps one of the most important instruments of assessment relevant to a career decision can be a questionnaire devised by assessees themselves, one that is *not* designed for administration to a prospective employee. Rather, it is written by the assessee and designed for administration to a person established in the career the assessee is contemplating. Laker (2002) proposed that students contemplating a career choice think of more than one career they would like to enter. Students should next identify resource persons already in those careers who can address the students' beliefs and assumptions about the nature of work life in that career. Such resource people can be identified by informal means such as "asking around" as well as more formally by the use of a reference work such as the *Encyclopedia of Associations* (Hunt, 2005). Find the association to which the desired resource person belongs, and then contact that association for help in identifying someone local who is willing to assist. In preparation for the meeting, students list their beliefs and assumptions about the career and then translate that list into questions, such as those presented in Table 16–2.

**Table 16–2**
**Sample Questions Derived from Students' Beliefs and Assumptions**

- What background, both educational and professional, is needed to enter this field?
- Briefly describe your career path and the steps you took to get here.
- What do you do on a typical day?
- In what industries and companies would such careers and jobs exist, or what industries and companies would be best for this career?
- What are the sources of stress in your job?
- If you could, what would you change about your job?
- How does one get started or break into this career or job?
- What kind of lifestyle does such a career or job provide or allow?
- What are the compensation range and benefits for this career or job?
- How often are you required to travel, and for what reasons do you travel?
- Would this type of career or job typically require relocation?
- Do you enjoy your work?
- What advancement opportunities are there for individuals in this field?
- Do you find your job or career satisfying and challenging?
- What special skills are required for a position like yours?
- What is the average number of hours worked in a typical work week?
- What types of skills are necessary to be successful in ?
- What should I do or where should I go to acquire these needed skills?
- What is the most challenging aspect of your job?
- What is the most satisfying aspect of your job? What is the least satisfying aspect of your job?
- How would this career impact one's family?
- How important are grades?
- How is your performance evaluated?
- How does your career affect your life outside of work? Spouse? Social? Spiritual?
- What is the job market like in this particular professional area? What do you think it will be like 5–10 years from now?
- What recommendations would you make to me? What would you do if you were me?
- If you were me, who else would you suggest that I talk to? Why would you suggest that person? May I use your name in contacting that person?
- Describe your typical work week.

Source: Laker (2002).

All the tools of assessment we have discussed so far have application not only in career entry but also in career transition. One test specifically designed for use with people contemplating a career change is the Career Transitions Inventory (CTI; Heppner et al., 1994). The purpose of this test is to assess psychological resources during the process of career transition. For the purposes of the test, *career transition* was operationally defined as *task change* (a shift to other types of tasks but essentially the same job), *position change* (a shift in jobs with the same employer), or *occupation change* (a shift in duties and work settings). The test authors presented evidence for the test's reliability as well as evidence they described as "promising" for the construct validity of this instrument.

Career transition is one variety of what could be referred to as an *exit strategy* for a person in a particular career or business. Another type of exit strategy is retirement. The decision to retire is momentous and multifaceted—and one that has also been explored by means of instruments of assessment. A retirement decision should not be made on the basis of a single criterion such as global satisfaction or financial security (Parnes & Less, 1985). To persons considering retirement, counselors may offer assistance in the form of probing interviews and by administering various measures that assess life satisfaction, goal-directedness, leisure satisfaction, and interpersonal support. More specifically, the Goal Instability Scale (Robbins & Patton, 1985), the Life Satisfaction Index A (Neugarten et al., 1961), the Leisure Satisfaction Scale (Beard & Ragheb, 1980), and the Interpersonal Support Evaluations List (Cohen et al., 1985) are some of the instruments that may provide valuable data. Floyd et al. (1992) developed the Retirement Satisfaction Inventory to help assess adjustment to retirement. Of course, Big Five personality traits may also have predictive value when it comes to satisfaction with retirement. In one study, *Extraversion* and *Emotional stability* were found to be positively related to retirement satisfaction (Löckenhoff et al., 2009).

Tests and other tools of assessment may be used by businesses and other organizations to assist in staffing and other personnel-related decisions. Let's now see how.

> **JUST THINK . . .**
>
> How might data from personality tests be useful in counseling an individual who is contemplating retirement?

## Screening, Selection, Classification, and Placement

In the context of employment, **screening** refers to a relatively superficial process of evaluation based on certain minimal standards, criteria, or requirements. For example, a municipal fire department may screen on the basis of certain minimal requirements for height, weight, physical health, physical strength, and cognitive ability before admitting candidates to a training program for firefighters. The government may use a group-administered test of intelligence to screen out people unsuited for military service or to identify intellectually gifted recruits for special assignments.

**Selection** refers to a process whereby each person evaluated for a position will be either accepted or rejected for that position. By contrast, **classification** does not imply acceptance or rejection but rather a rating, categorization, or "pigeonholing" with respect to two or more criteria. The military, for example, classifies personnel with respect to security clearance on the basis of variables such as rank, personal history of political activity, and known associations. As a result of such evaluations, one individual might be granted access to documents labeled *Secret* whereas another individual might be granted access to documents labeled *Top Secret*.

Like classification, *placement* need not carry any implication of acceptance or rejection. **Placement** is a disposition, transfer, or assignment to a group or category that may be made on the basis of one criterion. If, for example, you took a college-level course while still in high school, the score you earned on the advanced placement test in that subject area may have been the sole criterion used to place you in an appropriate section of that college course upon your acceptance to college.

Businesses, academic institutions, the military, and other organizations regularly screen, select, classify, or place individuals. A wide array of tests can be used as aids to decision making. Measures of ability, aptitude, interest, and personality may all be of value, depending on the demands of the particular decision. In the high-profile world of professional sports, where selection errors can be extremely costly, psychological tests may be used to help assess whether a draft choice will live up to his potential (Gardner, 2001) and to measure sundry other aspects of athletic competition (Allen, 2008; Bougard et al., 2008; Brotherhood, 2008; Donohue et al., 2007; Fox, 2008; Gee et al., 2010; Gordon, 2008; Stoeber et al., 2008; Webbe, 2008). Of course, for more everyday types of employment decision making—and especially at the pre-employment stage—some of the most common tools of assessment include the letter of application and the résumé, the job application form, the letter of recommendation, and the interview.

## The Résumé and the Letter of Application

There is no single, standard résumé; they can be "as unique as the individuals they represent" (Cohen, 1994, p. 394). Typically, information related to one's work objectives, qualifications, education, and experience is included on a résumé. A companion cover letter to a résumé, called a letter of application, lets a job applicant demonstrate motivation, businesslike writing skills, and his or her unique personality.

Of course, neither a résumé nor a letter of application is likely to be the sole vehicle through which employment is secured. Both of these documents are usually stepping-stones to personal interviews or other types of evaluations. On the other hand, the employer, the personnel psychologist, or some other individual reading the applicant's résumé and cover letter may use these documents as a basis for *rejecting* an application. The cover letter and the résumé may be analyzed for details such as quality of written communication, perceived sincerity, and appropriateness of the applicant's objectives, education, motivation, and prior experience. From the perspective of the evaluator, much the same is true of another common tool of assessment in employment settings, the application form.

## The Application Form

Application forms may be thought of as biographical sketches that supply employers with information pertinent to the acceptability of job candidates. In addition to demographic information (such as name and address), details about educational background, military service, and previous work experience may be requested. Application forms may contain a section devoted to contact information in which applicants list, for example, home phone, cell phone, e-mail address, and a website (if applicable). Some classic questions relevant to a traditional application form are presented in Table 16–3. The guiding philosophy is that each item in the form be relevant either to consideration for employment or for contacting the applicant. From the perspective of the employer, the application form is a useful tool for quick screening.

**Table 16–3**
**Checklist for an Application Form Item**

1. Is the item necessary for identifying the applicant?

2. Is it necessary for screening out those who are ineligible under the company's basic hiring policies?

3. Does it help to decide whether the candidate is qualified?

4. Is it based on analysis of the job or jobs for which applicants will be selected?

5. Has it been pretested on the company's employees and found to correlate with success?

6. Will the information be used? How?

7. Is the application form the proper place to ask for it?

8. To what extent will answers duplicate information to be obtained at another step in the selection procedure—for example, through interviews, tests, or medical examinations?

9. Is the information needed for selection at all, or should it be obtained at induction or even later?

10. Is it probable that the applicants' replies will be reliable?

11. Does the question violate any applicable federal or state legislation?

Source: Ahern (1949).

## Letters of Recommendation

Another tool useful in the preliminary screening of applicants is the letter of recommendation (Arvey, 1979; Glueck, 1978). Such letters may be a unique source of detailed information about the applicant's past performance, the quality of the applicant's relationships with peers, and so forth. Of course, such letters are not without their drawbacks. It is no secret that applicants solicit letters from those they believe will say only positive things about them. Another possible drawback to letters of recommendation is the variance in the observational and writing skills of the letter writers.

In research that employed application files for admission to graduate school in psychology, it was found that the same applicant might variously be described as "analytically oriented, reserved, and highly motivated" or "free-spirited, imaginative, and outgoing," depending on the letter writer's perspective. As the authors of that study pointed out, "Although favorable recommendations may be intended in both cases, the details of and bases for such recommendations are varied" (Baxter et al., 1981, p. 300). Efforts to minimize the drawbacks inherent in the open-ended letter of recommendation have sometimes taken the form of "questionnaires of recommendation" wherein former employers, professors, and other letter writers respond to structured questions concerning the applicant's prior performance. Some questionnaires employ a forced-choice format designed to force respondents to make negative as well as positive statements about the applicant.

> **JUST THINK . . .**
>
> Put yourself in the position of an employer. Now discuss how much "weight" you assign letters of recommendation relative to test data and other information about the applicant. Explain the basis of your "weightings."

Although originally written to provide a prospective employer with an opinion about an applicant, some letters of reference now serve the function of an archival record—one that provides a glimpse of an unfortunate chapter of American history and the prevailing prejudices of an era. Winston (1996, 1998) documented how letters of reference written by prominent psychologists in the United States for Jewish psychology students and psychologists from the 1920s through the 1950s followed a common practice of identifying the job candidates as Jews. The letters went on to disclose whether or not, in the letter-writer's opinion, the candidate evidenced the "objectionable traits" thought to characterize Jews. These letters support a compelling argument that, although American history tends to treat anti-Semitism as a problem from which European immigrants fled, negative stereotypes associated with being Jewish were very much a part of the cultural landscape in the United States.

## Interviews

Interviews, whether individual or group in nature, provide an occasion for the face-to-face exchange of information. Like other interviews, the employment interview may fall anywhere on a continuum from highly structured, with uniform questions being asked to all, to highly unstructured, with the questions left largely to the interviewer's discretion. As with all interviews, the interviewer's biases and prejudices may creep into the evaluation and influence the outcome. The order of interviewing might also affect outcomes by reason of contrast effects. For example, an average applicant may appear better or less qualified depending on whether the preceding candidate was particularly poor or outstanding. Factors that may affect the outcome of an employment interview, according to Schmitt (1976), include the backgrounds, attitudes, motivations, perceptions, expectations, knowledge about the job, and interview behavior of both the interviewer and the interviewee. Situational factors, such as the nature of the job market, may also affect the outcome of the interview.

## Portfolio Assessment

In the context of industrial/organizational assessment, portfolio assessment entails an evaluation of an individual's work sample for the purpose of making some screening, selection, classification, or placement decision. A video journalist applying for a position at a new television station may present a portfolio of video clips, including rehearsal footage and outtakes. An art director for a magazine may present a portfolio of art to a prospective employer, including rough drafts and notes about how to solve a particular design-related problem. In portfolio assessment, the assessor may have the opportunity (1) to evaluate many work samples created by the assessee, (2) to obtain some understanding of the assessee's work-related thought processes and habits through an analysis of the materials from rough draft to finished form, and (3) to question the assessee further regarding various aspects of his or her work-related thinking and habits. The result may be a more complete picture of the prospective employee at work in the new setting than might otherwise be available.

> **JUST THINK . . .**
>
> What are some things that a portfolio *fails* to tell an employer about a prospective employee?

## Performance Tests

As its name implies, a performance test requires assessees to demonstrate certain skills or abilities under a specified set of circumstances. The typical objective of such an exercise is to obtain a *job-related performance sample.* For example, a word-processing test as a prerequisite for employment as a word processor provides a prospective employer with a job-related performance sample.

Boundaries between performance, achievement, and aptitude tests are often blurred, especially when the work sample entails taking a standardized test of skill or ability. For example, the Seashore Bennett Stenographic Proficiency Test is a standardized measure of stenographic competence. The test materials include a recording in which a voice dictates a series of letters and manuscripts that the assessee must transcribe in shorthand and then type. The recorded directions provide a uniform clarity of voice and rate of dictation. The test protocol may well be viewed as an achievement test, an aptitude test, or a performance sample, depending upon the context of its use.

An instrument designed to measure clerical aptitude and skills is the Minnesota Clerical Test (MCT). The MCT comprises two subtests, Number Comparison and Name Comparison. Each subtest contains 200 items, with each item consisting of either a pair of names or a pair of numbers (depending upon the subtest) to be compared. For each item, the assessee's task is to check whether the two names (or numbers) in the pair are the same or different.

**JUST THINK . . .**

In general, what types of performance assessments lend themselves more to a virtual reality context than to "real-life" reality?

A score is obtained simply by subtracting the number of incorrect responses from the number of correct ones. Because speed and accuracy in clerical work are important to so many employers, this deceptively simple test has been used for decades as an effective screening tool in the workplace. It can be administered and scored quickly and easily, and the pattern of errors or omissions on this timed test may suggest whether the testtaker values speed over accuracy or vice versa.

The kind of special equipment necessary for performance tests varies widely. For a simulation involving a manufacturing problem, for example, all that may be necessary are Tinkertoy parts (Figure 16–4). During World War II, the assessment staff of the Office of Strategic Services (OSS) was charged with selecting personnel to serve as American secret agents, saboteurs, propaganda experts, and other such job titles for assignments overseas. In addition to interviews, personality tests, and other paper-and-pencil tests, the OSS administered situational performance tests. Today, Israeli and other military forces use similar methods.

A commonly used performance test in the assessment of business leadership ability is the **leaderless group technique.** Communication skills, problem-solving ability, the ability to cope with stress, and other skills can also be assessed economically by a group exercise in which the participants' task is to work together in the solution of some problem or the achievement of some goal. As group members interact, the assessors make judgments with respect to questions such as "Who is the leader?" and "What role do other members play in this group?" The answers to such questions will no doubt figure into decisions concerning the individual assessee's future position in the organization.

Another performance test frequently used to assess managerial ability, organizational skills, and leadership potential is the **in-basket technique.** This technique simulates the way a manager or an executive deals with an in-basket filled with mail, memos, announcements, and various other notices and directives. Assessees are instructed that they have only a limited amount of time, usually two or three hours, to deal with all the items in the basket (more commonly a manila envelope). Through posttest interviews and an examination of the way the assessee handled the materials, assessors can make judgments concerning variables such as organizing and planning, problem solving, decision making, creativity, leadership, and written communication skills.

**Testing and assessment for aviators and astronauts**   Almost from the time that aviation became a reality, a need has existed to research physical and psychological factors in aviation. One of the earliest of such studies was conducted by the British physician Henry Graeme Anderson. Anderson enlisted in the military at the outbreak of World War I and wound up being stationed at the British flying school in Vendome, France,

**Figure 16–4**
**Games Psychologists Play**

*Psychologists have long recognized the value of gamelike situations in the process of evaluating prospective personnel. A task referred to as the "Manufacturing Problem" was used as part of the AT&T Management Progress Study conducted in 1957. The assessee's task here is to collaborate with others in buying parts and manufacturing a "product."*

where he held the post of flight surgeon. Although not required to do so, he earned a pilot's license himself. He later would write among the first detailed accounts regarding fitness of recruits to fly, how flying conditions could be improved, and how aerial accidents could be prevented (Anderson, 1919).

As military and commercial aviation matured, psychological testing and assessment would typically be undertaken by the powers that be to evaluate the extent to which prospective pilots and other flight personnel (1) had the ability, skills, and aptitude deemed necessary to perform duties; (2) exhibited personality traits deemed desirable for the specific mission (including, for instance, the ability to function effectively as a team member); and (3) were deemed to be free of psychopathology and pressing distractions that would detract from optimal performance. Specially created performance testing would become the norm for persons who sought the responsibility of piloting aircraft (Retzlaff & Gilbertini, 1988) as well as related employment—including, for example, the job of air traffic controller (Ackerman & Kanfer, 1993).

The dawn of the space age in the 1950s brought with it a new set of demands in terms of personnel selection, particularly with regard to the selection of astronauts. New skills, aptitudes, and tolerances would be required for "crews [who] leave the earth in a fragile vehicle to face a hostile and unforgiving environment" (Helmreich, 1983, p. 445)—one in which weightlessness, isolation, and the absence of an escape option were only the tip of the iceberg in terms of powerful challenges to be met and overcome.

The National Aeronautics and Space Administration (NASA) was formed in 1958. In preparation for a manned mission as part of Project Mercury, NASA administered not only batteries of performance tests to evaluate the physical capabilities of prospective astronauts but also batteries of psychological tests. Psychological tests administered included the MMPI, the Rorschach, the TAT, and the WAIS. In general, NASA was looking for candidates who exhibited promise in terms of operational capabilities (in terms of cognitive and psychomotor functioning), motivation, social abilities, and stress tolerance.

Initially, the selection of astronauts and mission specialists were made from the ranks of male military test pilots. Subsequently, however, the composition of crews became more diverse in many respects; women and people from ethnic minorities were brought on board, and the crews became more multinational in nature. As Helmreich et al. (1979) cautioned, a psychological consideration of the social dynamics of such missions would be critical to their success. Others, such as former NASA psychiatrist Patricia Santy, have been critical of the way that the agency uses—or underutilizes, as the case may be—input from psychologists and psychiatrists. In her book on the subject, *Choosing the Right Stuff: The Psychological Selection of Astronauts and Cosmonauts,* Santy (1994) argued that the culture in the space agency would be well advised to give more weight than it traditionally has to expert psychological and psychiatric opinion. Such arguments rise to the fore when NASA personnel make headlines for the wrong reasons (see Figure 16–5).

By the way, video game enthusiasts may be happy to learn that their experiences with *Flight Simulator* and more sophisticated aviation-related software might be put to good use should they ever pursue a career in aviation. Almost since such software has been available, the industry has taken note of it and employed computer simulations in evaluations (Kennedy et al., 1982). This unique variety of performance assessment permits assessors to evaluate assessees' response to a standardized set of tasks and to monitor precisely the time of response within a safe environment.

**Figure 16–5**
**A High-Profile Employment Screening Failure?**

*On February 5, 2007, astronaut Lisa Nowak was arrested in a bizarre stalking incident. This prompted NASA to conduct an internal review of its extensive program of psychological evaluations for flight personnel.*

**The assessment center** A widely used tool in selection, classification, and placement is the **assessment center.** Although it sounds as if it might be a place, the term actually denotes an organizationally standardized procedure for evaluation involving multiple assessment techniques such as paper-and-pencil tests and situational performance tests. The assessment center concept had its origins in the writings of Henry Murray and his associates (1938). Assessment center activities were pioneered by military organizations both in the United States and abroad (Thornton & Byham, 1982).

In 1956, the first application of the idea in an industrial setting occurred with the initiation of the Management Progress Study (MPS) at American Telephone and Telegraph (Bray, 1964). MPS was to be a longitudinal study that would follow the lives of more than 400 telephone company management and non-management personnel. Participants attended a 3-day assessment center in which they were interviewed for two hours. They then took a number of paper-and-pencil tests designed to shed light on cognitive abilities and personality (for example, the School and College Ability Test and the Edwards Personal Preference Schedule) and participated in individual and group situational exercises (such as the in-basket test and a leaderless group). Additionally, projective tests such as the Thematic Apperception Test and the Sentence Completion Test were administered. All the data on each of the assessees were integrated at a meeting of the assessors, where judgments on a number of dimensions were made. The dimensions, grouped by area, are listed in Table 16–4.

The use of the assessment center method has mushroomed, with many more business organizations relying on it annually for selection, classification, placement, promotion, career training, and early identification of leadership potential. The method has been subject to numerous studies concerning its validity, and the consensus is that the method has much to recommend it (Cohen et al., 1977; Gaugler et al., 1987; Hunter & Hunter, 1984; McEvoy & Beatty, 1989; Schmitt et al., 1984).

## Physical Tests

A lifeguard who is visually impaired is seriously compromised in his or her ability to perform the job. A wine taster with damaged taste buds is of little value to a vintner. An aircraft pilot who has lost the use of an arm . . . the point is clear: Physical requirements of a job must be taken into consideration when screening, selecting, classifying, and placing applicants. Depending on the job's specific requirements, a number of physical subtests may be used. Thus, for example, for a job in which a number of components of vision are critical, a test of visual acuity might be administered along with tests of visual efficiency, stereopsis (distance/depth perception), and color blindness. In its most general sense, a **physical test** may be defined as measurement that entails evaluation of one's somatic health and intactness, and observable sensory and motor abilities.

General physical fitness is required in many jobs, such as police work, where successful candidates might one day have to chase a fleeing suspect on foot or defend themselves against a suspect resisting arrest. The tests used in assessing such fitness might include a complete physical examination, tests of physical strength, and a performance test that meets some determined criterion with respect to running speed and agility. Tasks like vaulting some object, stepping through tires, and going through a window frame could be included to simulate running on difficult terrain.

In some instances, an employer's setting certain physical requirements for employment are so reasonable and so necessary that they would readily be upheld by any court if challenged. Other physical requirements for employment, however, may

**Table 16–4**
**Original Management Progress Study Dimensions**

| Area | Dimension |
|---|---|
| Administrative skills | Organizing and planning—How effectively can this person organize work, and how well does he or she plan ahead?<br>Decision making—How ready is this person to make decisions, and how good are the decisions made?<br>Creativity—How likely is this person to solve a management problem in a novel way? |
| Interpersonal skills | Leadership skills—How effectively can this person lead a group to accomplish a task without arousing hostility?<br>Oral communication skills—How well would this person present an oral report to a small conference group on a subject he or she knew well?<br>Behavior flexibility—How readily can this person, when motivated, modify his or her behavior to reach a goal? How able is this person to change roles or style of behavior to accomplish objectives?<br>Personal impact—How forceful and likable an early impression does this person make?<br>Social objectivity—How free is this person from prejudices against racial, ethnic, socioeconomic, educational, and other social groups?<br>Perceptions of threshold social cues—How readily does this person perceive minimal cues in the behavior of others? |
| Cognitive skills | General mental ability—How able is this person in the functions measured by tests of intelligence, scholastic aptitude, and learning ability?<br>Range of interests—To what extent is this person interested in a variety of fields of activity such as science, politics, sports, music, art?<br>Written communication skill—How well would this person compose a communicative and formally correct memorandum on a subject he or she knew well? How well written are memos and reports likely to be? |
| Stability of performance | Tolerance of uncertainty—To what extent will this person's work performance stand up under uncertain or unstructured conditions?<br>Resistance to stress—To what extent will this person's work performance stand up in the face of personal stress? |
| Work motivation | Primacy of work—To what extent does this person find satisfactions from work more important than satisfactions in other areas of life?<br>Inner work standards—To what extent will this person want to do a good job, even if a less good one is acceptable to the boss and others?<br>Energy—How continuously can this person sustain a high level of work activity?<br>Self-objectivity—How realistic a view does this person have of his or her own assets and liabilities, and how much insight into his or her own motives? |
| Career orientation | Need for advancement—To what extent does this person need to be promoted significantly earlier than his or her peers? To what extent are further promotions needed for career satisfaction?<br>Need for security—How strongly does this person want a secure job?<br>Ability to delay gratification—To what extent will this person be willing to wait patiently for advancement if confident advancement will come?<br>Realism of expectations—To what extent do this person's expectations about his or her work life with the company conform to what is likely to be true?<br>Bell System value orientation—To what extent has this person incorporated Bell System values such as service, friendliness, justice of company position on earnings, rates, wages? |
| Dependency | Need for superior approval—To what extent does this person need warmth and nurturant support from immediate supervisors?<br>Need for peer approval—To what extent does this person need warmth and acceptance from peers and subordinates?<br>Goal flexibility—To what extent is this person likely to reorient his or her life toward a different goal? |

Source: Bray (1982).

fall into a gray area. In general, the law favors physical standards that are both nondiscriminatory and job related.

Also included under the heading of physical tests are tests of sensory intactness or impairment, including tests to measure color blindness, visual acuity, visual depth perception, and auditory acuity. These types of tests are routinely employed in industrial settings in which the ability to perceive color or the possession of reasonably

**JUST THINK . . .**

"A police officer must meet certain minimum height requirements." Your thoughts?

good eyesight or hearing is essential to the job. Additionally, physical techniques have been applied in the assessment of integrity and honesty, as is the case with the polygraph and drug testing.

**Drug testing**  Beyond concerns about traditional physical, emotional, and cognitive job requirements lies great concern about employee drug use. Personnel and human resource managers are increasingly seeking assurance that the people they hire and the staff they currently employ do not and will not use illegal drugs. The dollar amounts vary by source, but estimates of corporate losses in the workplace that are directly or indirectly due to employee drug or alcohol use run into the tens of billions of dollars. Revenue may be lost because of injury to people or animals, damage to products and the environment, or employee absenteeism, tardiness, or sick leave. And no dollar amount can be attached to the tragic loss of life that may result from a drug- or alcohol-related mishap.

In the context of the workplace, a **drug test** may be defined as an evaluation undertaken to determine the presence, if any, of alcohol or other psychotropic substances, by means of laboratory analysis of blood, urine, hair, or other biological specimens. Testing for drug use is a growing practice in corporate America, with nearly half of all major companies conducting drug testing in some form. Applicants for employment may be tested during the selection process, and current employees may be tested as a condition of maintaining employment. Random drug testing (that is, testing that occurs with no advance warning) is increasingly common in private companies and organizations, although it has been in use for years in government agencies and in the military.

Methods of drug testing vary. One method, the Immunoassay Test, employs the subject's urine to determine the presence or absence of drugs in the body by identifying the metabolized by-products of the drug (metabolites). Although widely used in workplace settings, the test can be criticized for its inability to specify the precise amount of the drug that was taken, when it was taken, and which of several possible drugs in a particular category was taken. Further, there is no way to estimate the degree of impairment that occurred in response to the drug. The Gas Chromatography/ Mass Spectrometry (GCMS) Test also examines metabolites in urine to determine the presence or absence of drugs, but it can more accurately specify which drug was used. GCMS technology cannot, however, pinpoint the time at which the drug was taken or the degree of impairment that occurred as a consequence.

**JUST THINK . . .**

Generally speaking, is random drug testing in the workplace a good thing?

Many employees object to drug testing as a condition of employment and have argued that such testing violates their constitutional rights to privacy and freedom from unreasonable search and seizure. In the course of legal proceedings, a question that emerges frequently is the validity of drug testing. The consequences of **false positives** (an individual tests positively for drug use when in reality there has been no drug use) and **false negatives** (an individual tests negatively for drug use when in reality there has been drug use) in such cases can be momentous. A false positive may result in, among other things, the loss of one's livelihood. A false negative may result in an impaired person working in a position of responsibility and placing others at risk.

Modern laboratory techniques tend to be relatively accurate in detecting telltale metabolites. Error rates are well under 2%. However, laboratory techniques may not always be used correctly. By one estimate, fully 93% of laboratories that do drug testing failed to meet standards designed to reduce human error (Comer, 1993). Error may also occur in the interpretation of results. Metabolites may be identified accurately, but whether they originated in the abuse of some illicit drug or from over-the-counter medication cannot always be determined. To help prevent such confusion, administrators of the urine test typically ask the subject to compile a list of any medications currently being taken. However, not all subjects are willing or able to remember all medications they may have taken. Further, some employees are reluctant to report some prescription medications they may have taken to treat conditions to which any possible social stigma may be attached, such as depression or epilepsy. Additionally, some foods may also produce metabolites that mimic the metabolites of some illegal drugs. For example, metabolites of opiates will be detected following the subject's ingestion of (perfectly legal) poppy seeds (West & Ackerman, 1993).

Another question related to the validity of drug tests concerns the degree to which drugs identified through testing actually affect job performance. Some drugs leave the body very slowly. For example, a person may test positive for marijuana use up to a month after the last exposure to it. Thus, the residue of the drug remains long after any discernible impairment from having taken the drug. By contrast, cocaine leaves the body in only three days. It is possible for a habitual cocaine user to be off the drug for three days, be highly impaired as a result of cocaine withdrawal, yet still test negative for drug use. Thus, neither a positive nor a negative finding with regard to a drug test necessarily means that behavior has or has not been impaired by drug use (Comer, 1993).

An alternative to drug testing involves using performance tests to directly examine impairment. For example, sophisticated video game–style tests of coordination, judgment, and reaction time are available to compare current performance with baseline performance as established on earlier tests. The advantages of these performance tests over drug testing include a more direct assessment of impairment, fewer ethical concerns regarding invasion of privacy, and immediate information about impairment. The latter advantage is particularly vital in preventing potentially impaired individuals from hurting themselves or others.

## Cognitive Ability, Productivity, and Motivation Measures

Beyond their use in pre-employment counseling and in the screening, selection, classification, and placement of personnel, tools of assessment are used to accomplish various goals in the workplace. Let's briefly survey some of these varied uses of assessment tools with reference to measures of cognitive ability, productivity, and motivation.

### *Measures of Cognitive Ability*

Selection decisions regarding personnel, as well as other types of selection decisions such as those regarding professional licensure or acceptance for academic training, are often based (at least in part) on performance on tests that tap acquired knowledge as well as various cognitive skills and abilities. In general, cognitive-based tests are popular tools of selection because they have been shown to be valid predictors of future performance (Schmidt & Hunter, 1998). However, along with that impressive track record come a number of potential considerations with regard to diversity issues.

**Personnel selection and diversity issues**   The continued use of tests that tap primarily cognitive abilities and skills for screening, selection, classification, and placement has become controversial. This controversy stems from a well-documented body of evidence that points to consistent group differences on cognitive ability tests. For example, Asians tend to score higher on average than Whites on mathematical and quantitative ability measures, while Whites score higher than Asians on measures of comprehension and verbal ability. On average, Whites also tend to score higher on cognitive ability tests than Blacks and Hispanics. Given that the test scores may differ by as much as 1 standard deviation (Sackett et al., 2001), such differences may have great impact on who gets what job or who is admitted to an institution of higher learning. Average differences between groups on tests of cognitive ability may contribute to limiting diversity.

It is in society's interest to promote diversity in employment settings, in the professions, and in access to education and training. Toward that end, diversity has, in the past, been encouraged by various means. One approach involved using test cut scores established on the basis of group membership. However, there has been a general trend away from efforts that lead to preferential treatment of any group in terms of test scores. This trend is evident in legislation, court actions, and public referenda. For example, the Civil Rights Act of 1991 made it illegal for employers to adjust test scores as a function of group membership. In 1996, Proposition 209 was passed in California, prohibiting the use of group membership as a basis for any selection decision in that state. In that same year, a federal court ruled that race was not a relevant criterion in selecting university applicants (*Hopwood v. State of Texas*, 1996). In the state of Washington, voters approved legislation that banned the use of race as a criterion in college admissions, contracting, and hiring (Verhovek & Ayres, 1998).

**JUST THINK . . .**

In what general ways can society best address these extra-test issues?

How may diversity in the workplace and other settings be achieved while still using tests known to be good predictors of performance and while not building into the selection criteria a preference for any group? Although no single answer to this complex question is likely to satisfy all concerned, there are jobs waiting to be filled and seats waiting to be occupied at educational and training institutions; some strategy for balancing the various interests must be found. One proposal is for developers and users of cognitive tests in the workplace to place greater emphasis on computer-administered evaluations that minimize verbal content and the demand for verbal skills and abilities (Sackett et al., 2001). These researchers further recommended greater reliance on relevant job or life experience as selection criteria. However, Sackett et al. (2001) cautioned that "subgroup differences are not simply artifacts of paper-and-pencil technologies" (p. 316), and it is incumbent upon society at large to effectively address such extra-test issues.

## Productivity

**Productivity** may be defined simply as output or value yielded relative to work effort made. The term is used here in its broadest sense and is equally applicable to workers who make products and to workers who provide services. If a business endeavor is to succeed, monitoring output with the ultimate goal of maximizing output is essential. Measures of productivity help to define not only where a business is but also what it needs to do to get where it wants to be. A manufacturer of television sets, for example, might find that the people who manufacture the housing are working at optimal efficiency but the people responsible for installing the screens in the cabinets are working at one-half the expected efficiency. A productivity evaluation can help identify the factors responsible for the sagging performance of the screen installers.

Using techniques such as supervisor ratings, interviews with employees, and undercover employees planted in the workshop, management might determine what—or, in particular, who—is responsible for the unsatisfactory performance. Perhaps the most common method of evaluating worker productivity or performance is through the use of rating and ranking procedures by superiors in the organization.

One type of ranking procedure used when large numbers of employees are assessed is the **forced distribution technique.** This procedure involves distributing a predetermined number or percentage of assessees into various categories that describe performance (such as *unsatisfactory, poor, fair, average, good, superior*). Another index of on-the-job performance is number of absences within a given period. It typically reflects more poorly on an employee to be absent on, say, 20 separate occasions than on 20 consecutive days as the result of illness.

The **critical incidents technique** (Flanagan & Burns, 1955) involves the supervisor recording positive and negative employee behaviors. The supervisor catalogues the notations according to various categories (for example, *dependability* or *initiative*) for ready reference when an evaluation needs to be made. Some evidence suggests that a "honeymoon" period of about three months occurs when a new worker starts a job and that supervisory ratings will more truly reflect the worker's performance once that period has passed.

**JUST THINK . . .**

What might be the long-range consequences of using evaluation techniques that rely on the use of "undercover employees" in a manufacturing setting?

Peer ratings or evaluations by other workers at the same level have proved to be a valuable method of identifying talent among employees. Although peers have a tendency to rate their counterparts higher than these people would be rated by superiors, the information obtained from the ratings and rankings of peers can be highly predictive of future performance. For example, one study involved 117 inexperienced life insurance agents who attended a three-week training class. At the conclusion of the course, the budding insurance agents were asked to list the three best people in their class with respect to each of 12 situations. From these data, a composite score was obtained for each of the 117 agents. After one year, these peer ratings and three other variables were correlated with job tenure (number of weeks on the job) and with production (n-umber of dollars' worth of insurance sold). As can be seen from Table 16–5, peer ratings had the highest validity in all of the categories. By contrast, a near-zero correlation was obtained between final course grade and all categories.

Is there a downside to peer ratings? Most definitely. Even when peer ratings are carried out anonymously, a person being rated may feel as if some suspected peer rated him or her too low. The reaction of that individual in turn may be to rate the suspected peer extremely low in retaliation. Also, peers do not always have a basis for judging the criteria that the rating scale asks them to judge. But that typically does not stop a rater in the workplace from rating a peer. Instead of rating the peer on the criteria listed on the questionnaire, the rater might use a private "What has this person done for me lately?" criterion to respond to the rating scale.

**JUST THINK . . .**

Suppose your instructor initiated a peer rating system as the sole determinant of your grade in your measurement class. Would such a system be better than the one in place?

**Table 16–5**
**Peer Ratings and Performance of Life Insurance Salespeople**

|  | Job Tenure | | Production | |
|---|---|---|---|---|
|  | 6 months | 1 year | 6 months | 1 year |
| Peer rating | .18* | .29† | .29† | .30† |
| Age | .18* | .24† | .06 | .09 |
| Starting salary | .01 | .03 | .13 | .26† |
| Final course grade | .02 | .06 | −.02 | .02 |

Source: Mayfield (1972).

*$p = .05$ (one-tailed test)

†$p = .01$ (one-tailed test)

In many organizations, people work in teams. In an organizational or workplace context, a **team** may be defined as two or more people who interact interdependently toward a common and valued goal and who have each been assigned specific roles or functions to perform. For a sales team, the division of labor may simply reflect division of sales territories. In the creation of complicated software, the division of labor may involve the assignment of tasks that are too complicated for any one individual. The operation of a cruise ship or military vessel requires a trained team because of the multitude of things that must be done if the ship is to sail. To achieve greater productivity, organizations ask questions such as "What does the team know?" and "How does the collective knowledge of the team differ qualitatively from the individual knowledge and expertise of each of the team members?" These and related questions have been explored with various approaches to the measurement of team knowledge (see, for example, Cannon-Bowers et al., 1998; Cooke et al., 2000; Salas et al., 1998).

## Motivation

Why do some people skip lunch, work overtime, and take home work nightly whereas others strive to do as little as possible and live a life of leisure at work? At a practical level, light may be shed on such questions by using assessment instruments that tap the values of the assessee. Dealing with a population of unskilled personnel may require specially devised techniques. Champagne (1969) responded to the challenge of knowing little about what might attract rural, unskilled people to work by devising a motivational questionnaire. As illustrated by the three items in Figure 16–6, the questionnaire used a paired comparison (forced-choice) format that required the subject to make choices about 12 factors used by companies to entice employment applications: fair pay, steady job, vacations and holidays with pay, job extras such as pensions and sick benefits, a fair boss, interesting work, good working conditions, chance for promotion, a job close to home, working with friends and neighbors, nice people to work with, and praise for good work.

The job-seeking factor found to be most important in Champagne's sample of 349 male and female, rural, unskilled subjects was *steady job.* The least important factor was found to be *working with friends and neighbors. Praise for good work* was a close runner-up for least important. In interpreting the findings, Champagne cautioned that "the factors reported here relate to the job-seeking behavior of the unskilled and are not measures of how to retain and motivate the unskilled once employed . . .What prompts a person to accept a job is not necessarily the same as what prompts a person to retain a job or do well in it" (p. 268).

On a theoretical level, an abundance of theories seek to delineate the specific needs, attitudes, social influences, and other factors that might account for differences in motivation. For example, Vroom (1964) proposed an expectancy theory of motivation, which essentially holds that employees expend energy in ways designed to achieve the outcome they want; the greater the expectancy that an action will achieve a certain outcome, the more energy will be expended to achieve that outcome. Maslow (1943, 1970) constructed a theoretical hierarchy of human needs (Figure 16–7) and proposed that, after one category of need is met, people seek to satisfy the next category of need.

Employers who subscribe to Maslow's theory would seek to identify (1) the need level required of the employee by the job and (2) the current need level of the prospective employee. Alderfer (1972) proposed an alternative need theory of motivation that was not hierarchical. Whereas Maslow saw the satisfaction of one need as a prerequisite to

Vacations and holidays with pay . . .   OR   . . . Job extras such as pensions, sick benefits, etc.

A job close to home . . .   OR   . . . A fair boss

Working with friends and neighbors . . .   OR   . . . chance for a promotion

**Figure 16–6**
**Studying Values with the Unskilled**

*Champagne (1969) used test items such as those pictured here in a recruitment study with a rural, unskilled population.*

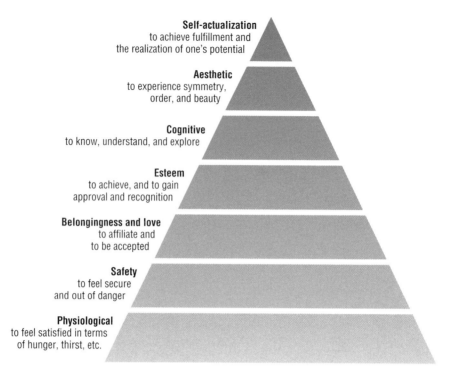

**Figure 16–7**
**Maslow's Hierarchy of Needs (adapted from Maslow, 1970)**

satisfaction of the next need in the hierarchy, Alderfer proposed that once a need is satisfied, the organism may strive to satisfy it to an even greater degree. The Alderfer theory also suggests that frustrating one need might channel energy into satisfying a need at another level.

**JUST THINK . . .**

What motivates you to do what you do? How could that motivation best be measured?

In a widely cited program that undertook to define the characteristics of achievement motivation, McClelland (1961) used as his measure stories written under special instructions about TAT and TAT-like pictures. McClelland described the individual with a high need for achievement as one who prefers a task that is neither too simple nor extremely difficult—something with moderate, not extreme, risks. A situation with little or no risk will not lead to feelings of accomplishment if the individual succeeds. On the other hand, an extremely high-risk situation may not lead to feelings of accomplishment owing to the high probability of failure. Persons with a high need for achievement enjoy taking responsibility for their actions because they desire the credit and recognition for their accomplishments. Such individuals also desire information about their performance so they can constantly improve their output. Other researchers have used TAT-like pictures and their own specially devised scoring systems to study related areas of human motivation such as the fear of failure (Birney et al., 1969; Cohen & Houston, 1975; Cohen & Parker, 1974; Cohen & Teevan, 1974, 1975; Cohen et al., 1975) and the fear of success (Horner, 1973).

Motivation may be conceptualized as stemming from incentives that are either primarily internal or primarily external in origin. Another way of stating this is to speak of *intrinsic motivation* and *extrinsic motivation.* In **intrinsic motivation,** the primary driving force stems from things such as the individual's involvement in work or satisfaction with work products. In **extrinsic motivation,** the primary driving force stems from rewards, such as salary and bonuses, or from constraints, such as job loss.

A scale designed to assess aspects of intrinsic and extrinsic motivation is the Work Preference Inventory (WPI; Amabile et al., 1994). The WPI contains 30 items rated on a four-point scale based on how much the testtaker believes the item to be self-descriptive. Factor analysis indicates that the test does appear to tap two distinct factors: intrinsic and extrinsic motivation. Each of these two factors may be divided into two subfactors. The intrinsic motivation factor may be divided into subfactors that concern the challenge of work tasks and the enjoyment of work. The extrinsic motivation factor may be divided into subfactors that concern compensation for work and external influences, such as recognition of one's work by others. The WPI has been shown to be internally consistent and to correlate in the predicted direction with personality, behavioral and other questionnaire measures of motivation (Amabile et al., 1994; Bipp, 2010).

In some instances, it seems as if the motivation to perform a particular job becomes markedly reduced compared to previous levels. Such is the case with a phenomenon referred to as *burnout*.

**Burnout and its measurement** *Burnout* is an occupational health problem associated with cumulative occupational stress (Shirom, 2003). **Burnout** has been defined as "a psychological syndrome of emotional exhaustion, depersonalization, and reduced personal accomplishment that can occur among individuals who work with other people in some capacity" (Maslach et al., 1997, p. 192). In this definition, *emotional exhaustion* refers to an inability to give of oneself emotionally to others, and *depersonalization* refers to distancing from other people and even developing cynical attitudes toward them. The potential consequences of burnout range from deterioration in service provided to absenteeism and job turnover. The potential effects of burnout on a worker suffering from it range from insomnia to alcohol and drug use. Burnout has been shown to be predictive of the frequency and duration of sick leave (Schaufeli et al., 2009).

The most widely used measure of burnout is the Maslach Burnout Inventory (MBI), Third Edition (Maslach et al., 1996). Developed by Christina Maslach and her colleagues, this test contains 22 items divided into three subscales: Emotional Exhaustion (nine items), Depersonalization (five items), and Personal Accomplishment (eight items). Testtakers respond on a scale ranging from 0 (*never*) to 6 (*every day*) to items like this one from the Exhaustion scale: *Working all day is really a strain for me.* The MBI manual contains data relevant to the psychometric soundness of the tests. Included is a discussion of discriminant validity in which burnout is conceptually distinguished from similar concepts such as depression and job dissatisfaction.

Using instruments such as the MBI, researchers have found that some occupations are characterized by higher levels of burnout than others. For example, personnel in nursing (Happell et al., 2003) and related fields, including staff in residential homes caring for the elderly (Evers et al., 2002) and children (Decker et al., 2002), seem subject to high levels of stress and burnout. Exactly why is not known. In one study of burnout among student support

> **JUST THINK . . .**
>
> Why might it be critically important for some employers to know if their employees are burning out? Besides a test, how else might burnout be gauged?

services personnel, it was found that low levels of job satisfaction led to high levels of the "emotional exhaustion" component of burnout (Brewer & Clippard, 2002). Burnout is a phenomenon that is being actively studied in diverse occupations throughout the world (see, for example, Ahola et al., 2008; Bellingrath et al., 2008; D'Amato & Zijlstra, 2008; Fahrenkopf et al., 2008; Griffin et al., 2010; Ilhan et al., 2008; Krasner et al., 2009; Narumoto et al., 2008; Ranta & Sud, 2008; Schaufeli et al., 2008; Shanafelt et al., 2010).

# Job Satisfaction, Organizational Commitment, and Organizational Culture

An **attitude** may be defined formally as a presumably learned disposition to react in some characteristic manner to a particular stimulus. The stimulus may be an object, a group, an institution—virtually anything. Later in this chapter, we discuss how attitudes toward goods and services are measured. More immediately, however, we focus on workplace-related attitudes. Although attitudes do not necessarily predict behavior (Tittle & Hill, 1967; Wicker, 1969), there has been great interest in measuring the attitudes of employers and employees toward each other and toward numerous variables in the workplace. In what follows, we take a brief look at employee attitudes toward their companies in terms of job satisfaction and organizational commitment. Subsequently, we will briefly explore the attitudes that companies convey toward their employees as reflected by the workplace culture.

## Job Satisfaction

Compared with dissatisfied workers, satisfied workers in the workplace are believed to be more productive (Petty et al., 1984), more consistent in work output (Locke, 1976), less likely to complain (Burke, 1970; Locke, 1976), and less likely to be absent from work or to be replaced (Herzberg et al., 1957; Vroom, 1964). Although these assumptions are somewhat controversial (Iaffaldano & Muchinsky, 1985) and should probably be considered on a case-by-case basis, employers, employees, researchers, and consultants have maintained a long-standing interest in the measurement of job satisfaction. Traditionally, **job satisfaction** has been defined as "a pleasurable or positive emotional state resulting from the appraisal of one's job or job experiences" (Locke, 1976, p. 300).

One diagnostic measure of job satisfaction (or, in this case, dissatisfaction) involves video-recording an employee at work and then playing back the video for the employee. The employee clicks on virtual controls to indicate when an unsatisfactory situation arises, and a window of questions automatically opens. According to data from studies of manual workers, analysis of the responses can be useful in creating a more satisfactory work environment (Johansson & Forsman, 2001).

Other measures of job satisfaction may focus on other elements of the job, including cognitive evaluations of the work (Organ & Near, 1985) and the work schedule (Baltes et al., 1999; Barnett & Gareis, 2000), perceived sources of stress (Brown & Peterson, 1993; Vagg & Spielberger, 1998), various aspects of well-being (Daniels, 2000), and mismatches between an employee's cultural background and the prevailing organizational culture (Aycan et al., 2000; Early et al., 1999; Parkes et al., 2001). Measures of job satisfaction have become quite popular in recent years—this according to our corporation-based guest in this chapter, Dr. Chris Gee. As you read the excerpted portion of his *Meet an Assessment Professional* essay here, keep in mind the potential rewards of developing an instrument that complements "the next major trend in business assessments."

In addition to job satisfaction, other job-related constructs that have attracted the attention of theorists and assessment professionals include job involvement, work centrality, organizational socialization, and organizational commitment (Caught et al., 2000; Nystedt et al., 1999; Paullay et al., 1994; Taormina & Bauer, 2000). Let's briefly take a closer look at the latter construct.

## Meet Dr. Chris Gee

As someone who spent 11 years doing research at a university, and now finds himself in the corporate world, I believe I have a fairly unique perspective on the use of assessment tools. As a student, I believe I only ever saw assessments as information gathering tools to answer particular research questions. The results of the research I was doing oftentimes remained in the theoretical and methodological realms, very infrequently having actual applied value. In my current position, I believe I have a new found understanding of the applied value that particular assessment tools can have, and the tangible impact that they can make. My suggestion to students would be to try and make this perspective shift earlier, as there is a great deal of money to be made in identifying ways in which assessment products can have a tangible impact in the corporate world. Recently, assessments aimed at measuring employee engagement and

**Chris Gee, Ph.D., Director of Research Services, Self Management Group (SMG)**

satisfaction, along with constructs like integrity and trust have become extremely popular. The person who identifies the next major trend in business assessments is due to make millions.

*Read more of what Dr. Gee had to say—his complete essay—at www.mhhe.com/cohentesting8.*

## Organizational Commitment

Organizational commitment has been defined as "the strength of an individual's identification with and involvement in a particular organization" (Porter et al., 1974, p. 604). This "strength" has been conceptualized and measured in ways that emphasize both its attitudinal and behavioral components (Mathieu & Zajac, 1990). In general, **organizational commitment** refers to a person's feelings of loyalty to, identification with, and involvement in an organization. Presumed correlates of high and low organizational commitment as observed by Randall (1987) are summarized in Table 16–6. The most widely used measure of this construct is the Organizational Commitment Questionnaire (OCQ; Porter et al., 1974), a 15-item Likert scale wherein respondents express their commitment-related attitudes toward an organization. Despite its widespread use, questions have been raised regarding its construct validity (Bozeman & Perrewe, 2001).

As you might expect, the measurement of attitude extends far beyond the workplace. For example, politicians seeking reelection may monitor the attitudes of their constituencies on various issues. We will revisit the subject of attitude measurement in somewhat greater detail when we survey measurement in the area of consumer psychology. However, before leaving the world of work and organizations, let's look at the measurement of organizational culture.

## Organizational Culture

*Organizational culture*—or corporate culture, as it is known when applied to a company or corporation—has been defined in many ways. For our purposes, we will follow

**Table 16–6**

**Consequences of Organizational Commitment Level for Individual Employees and the Organization**

| | **Level of Organizational Commitment** | | |
| --- | --- | --- | --- |
| | **Low** | **Moderate** | **High** |
| The Individual Employee | Potentially positive consequences for opportunity for expression of originality and innovation, but an overall negative effect on career advancement opportunities | Enhanced feeling of belongingness and security, along with doubts about the opportunity for advancement | Greater opportunity for advancement and compensation for efforts, along with less opportunity for personal growth and potential for stress in family relationships |
| The Organization | Absenteeism, tardiness, workforce turnover, and poor quality of work | As compared with low commitment, less absenteeism, tardiness, turnover, and better quality of work, as well as increased level of job satisfaction | Potential for high productivity, but sometimes accompanied by lack of critical/ethical review of employee behavior and by reduced organizational flexibility |

Cohen (2001) in defining **organizational culture** as the totality of socially transmitted behavior patterns characteristic of a particular organization or company, including: the structure of the organization and the roles within it; the leadership style; the prevailing values, norms, sanctions, and support mechanisms; and the past traditions and folklore, methods of enculturation, and characteristic ways of interacting with people and institutions outside of the culture (such as customers, suppliers, the competition, government agencies, and the general public).

Much like different social groups at different times throughout history, organizations and corporations have developed distinctive cultures. They have distinctive ceremonies, rights, and privileges—formal as well as informal—tied to success and advancement in addition to various types of sanctions tied to failure (Trice & Beyer, 1984). Organizational cultures have observable artifacts, which may be in the form of an annual report or a video of the office Christmas party. Organizational cultures also typically have sets of core values or beliefs that guide the actions of the organization as well as the direction in which it moves.

Just as the term *culture* is traditionally applied to a group of people who share a particular way of life, the term *organizational culture* applies to a *way of work*. An organizational culture provides a way of coping with internal and external challenges and demands. And just as conflicts between ways of thinking and doing things can cause conflicts between groups of people, so conflicts between organizational cultures may develop. Such conflicts are perhaps most evident when a company with one type of corporate culture acquires or merges with a company that has a very different corporate culture (Brannen & Salk, 2000; Veiga et al., 2000). Any effort to remedy such a clash in corporate cultures must be preceded by sober study and understanding of the cultures involved.

Perhaps because the concept of organizational culture is so multifaceted, obtaining a measure of it is no simple feat. To appreciate just how complex is the task of describing an organizational culture, consider how you would describe any other type of culture—American culture, NASCAR culture, or antiquing culture.

As a qualitative research consultant to many companies, the senior author of this textbook was presented with the challenge of assessing several organizational cultures. Because no satisfactory measure existed for conducting such an assessment, he created an instrument to do so; that instrument is the subject of this chapter's *Everyday Psychometrics*.

**JUST THINK . . .**

Describe in detail a particular culture you know well. What difficulties do you encounter in trying to capture this culture in a description?

# Assessment of Corporate and Organizational Culture

Corporations and other organizations have shown growing interest in self-examination and self-improvement. The Discussion of Organizational Culture (DOC; Cohen, 2001) was devised to assist in those efforts. This interview and discussion guide, designed for administration by a trained interviewer or focus group moderator, is divided into 10 discussion topics. The questions under each discussion topic explore various aspects of organizational culture. Beginning with "First Impressions" and proceeding through other topics that tap content related to the physical space, prevailing values, and other areas, the objective is to develop a sense of what is unique about the culture at a particular company or organization. Diagnostic insights useful in determining where and how the corporate or organizational culture may be improved can be derived from such data. Space limitations preclude the publication of all 10 parts of this comprehensive discussion guide. However, a sense of the types of questions raised for discussion can be gleaned from just the first few parts, reprinted here.

**Discussion of Organizational Culture**

I.   *First Impressions*
   1. What does it mean to be an employee of this corporation? (*Note:* Substitute terminology as appropriate throughout. For example, this question might be rephrased as "What does it mean to be a volunteer at this organization?" or "What does it mean to be an 'IBMer'?")
   2. a. How is working here the same as working anyplace else?
      b. How is working here different from working anyplace else?
      c. What makes working here special?
   3. a. How does working here make you feel part of a team?
      b. How does working here let you shine as an individual?
   4. a. What is obvious about this company to any visitor who has ever taken a tour of it?
      b. What is obvious about this company only to you?
   5. In general, how would you describe the compatibility of personnel at this company and the jobs they are assigned to do?
      a. How much role ambiguity exists in job descriptions?
      b. If such role ambiguity exists, how do you and others deal with it?

II.  *The Physical Space*
   1. In general terms, describe the physical space of this company.
   2. Comment specifically on the physical space with reference to:
      a. the grounds
      b. parking spaces
      c. the general "feel" of the exteriors and interiors
      d. the offices
      e. the dining areas
      f. the restrooms
      g. the storage facilities
      h. other aspects of the physical space
   3. a. Overall, what works about the physical space?
      b. What does not work about it, and how can it be improved?
   4. What does the way that space is laid out here tell you about this company?

III. *Corporate Structure and Roles*
   1. Describe the administrative structure of this company, including a brief description of who reports to whom.
      a. What works about this structure?
      b. What does not work about this structure?
      c. What is unique about this structure?
      d. What does this structure tell you about this company?
   2. Describe the roles associated with key job titles in the organizational structure.
      a. Is there ambiguity in roles, or do employees have a clear idea of their function in the company?
      b. Are there any roles within the company that seem antiquated or unnecessary?
      c. Do any roles need to be created within the company? Strengthened? Better defined?
      d. Describe your own role in the company and how you fit into the "grand scheme" of things.
      e. How might your role be improved for your own personal benefit?
      f. How might your role be improved for the benefit of the company?
   3. What can one tell about this company by analyzing
      a. its annual reports
      b. its company records
      c. the type of information that it makes public
      d. the type of information it maintains as private
      e. the products or services it provides
      f. the way it provides those products or services
      g. the corporate vision as articulated by senior management

# Other Tools of Assessment for Business Applications

Psychometric expertise is applied in a wide range of industrial, organizational, and business-related settings. For example, experimental and engineering psychologists use a variety of assessment tools in their ergonomic (work-related) and human factors research as they help develop the plans for everything from household items (Hsu & Peng, 1993) to components for automobiles (Chira-Chavala & Yoo, 1994) and aircraft (Begault, 1993). These researchers may use custom-designed measurement instruments, standardized tests, or both in their efforts to better understand human response to specific equipment or instrumentation in a particular work environment.

Another business-related area in which tests and other tools of assessment are used extensively is consumer psychology.

## Consumer Psychology

**Consumer psychology** is that branch of social psychology that deals primarily with the development, advertising, and marketing of products and services. As is true of almost all other specialty areas in psychology, some consumer psychologists work exclusively in academia, some work in applied settings, and many do both (Tybout & Artz, 1994). In both applied and research studies, consumer psychologists can be found working closely with professionals in fields such as marketing and advertising to help answer questions such as the following:

- Does a market exist for this new product?
- Does a market exist for this new use of an existing product?
- Exactly who—with respect to age, sex, race, social class, and other demographic variables—constitutes the market for this product?
- How can the targeted consumer population be made aware of this product in a cost-effective way?
- How can the targeted consumer population be persuaded to purchase this product in the most cost-effective way?
- What is the best way to package this product?[3]

One area of interest shared by the consumer psychologist and psychologists in other specialty areas is the measurement of attitudes. For the consumer psychologist, however, the attitude of interest is usually one that concerns a particular product or concept.

## The Measurement of Attitudes

Attitudes formed about products, services, or brand names are a frequent focus of interest in consumer attitude research. Attitude is typically measured by self-report, using tests and questionnaires. A limitation of this approach is that people differ in their ability to be introspective and in their level of self-awareness. People also differ in the extent to which they are willing to be candid about their attitudes. In some instances, the use of an attitude measure may, in essence, create an attitude where none existed before. In such studies, the attitude measured may be viewed as an artifact of the measurement procedure (Sandelands & Larson, 1985).

---

3. Questions concerning packaging and how to make a product stand out on the shelf have been referred to as issues of *shelf esteem* by consumer psychologists with a sense of humor.

Questionnaires and other self-report instruments designed to measure consumer attitudes are developed in ways similar to those previously described for psychological tests in general (see Chapter 8). A more detailed description of the preparation of measures of attitude can be found in the now-classic work *The Measurement of Attitude* (Thurstone & Chave, 1929). A monograph entitled "A Technique for the Measurement of Attitudes" (Likert, 1932) provided researchers with a simple procedure for constructing an instrument that would measure attitudes. Essentially, this procedure consists of listing statements (either favorable or unfavorable) that reflect a particular attitude. These statements are then administered to a group of respondents whose responses are analyzed to identify the most discriminating statements (that is, items that best discriminate people at different points on the hypothetical continuum), which are then included in the final scale. Each statement included in the final scale is accompanied by a five-point continuum of alternative responses. Such a scale may range, for example, from *strongly agree* to *strongly disagree*. Scoring is accomplished by assigning numerical weights of 1 through 5 to each category such that 5 represents the most favorable response and 1 reflects the least favorable response.

Measures of attitude found in the psychological literature run the gamut from instruments devised solely for research and testing of academic theoretical formulations to scales with wide-ranging, real-world applications. In the latter context, we might find sophisticated industrial/organizational measures designed to gauge workers' attitudes toward their work or scales designed to measure the general public's attitudes toward some politician or issue. For example, the Self-Help Agency Satisfaction Scale, which is designed to gauge self-help agency clients' satisfaction with aspects of the support they receive (Segal et al., 2000), is representative of scales designed to measure consumer satisfaction with a product or service. Attitude scales with applied utility may also be found in the educational psychology literature. Consider in this context measures such as the Study Attitudes and Methods Survey (a scale designed to assess study habits) and the Minnesota Teacher Attitude Survey (a scale designed to assess student–teacher relations).

To help answer questions such as those listed in the previous section, consumer psychologists may rely on a variety of methods used individually or in combination. These methods include surveys, "motivation research" (as it is referred to by marketing professionals), and behavioral observation. We discuss these methods following a brief introduction to a relative newcomer on the attitude measurement scene: implicit attitude measurement.

**Measuring implicit attitudes** Louis Thurstone's article entitled "Attitudes Can Be Measured" caused a bit of a stir when it was first published in 1928. This was so because the idea of actually measuring an attitude—or describing an attitude by a "single numerical index," to use Thurstone's words—was still quite novel. In some ways, a counterpart to that twentieth-century article is one from the twenty-first century entitled "Implicit Attitudes Can Be Measured" (Banaji, 2001). Although the author of the latter article freely admitted that its content was hardly as original as Thurstone's, it is nonetheless thought-provoking. So, what is meant by an *implicit attitude*?

An **implicit attitude** is a nonconscious, automatic association in memory that produces a disposition to react in some characteristic manner to a particular stimulus. Stated informally, implicit attitudes may be characterized as "gut-level" reactions.

> **JUST THINK . . .**
>
> You were previously introduced to an *implicit motive* (Chapter 13) and an *implicit memory* (Chapter 15). What is the relationship, if any, between implicit motives, memories, and attitudes?

Attempts to measure implicit attitudes have taken many forms, and a number of physiological measures have been tried (Amodio et al., 2006; Phelps et al., 2000; Vanman et al., 1997). But perhaps the measure most enthusiastically embraced by the research community has been the Implicit Attitude Test (IAT), a computerized sorting task by which implicit attitudes are gauged with reference to the testtaker's reaction times. Simply stated, the test is based on the premise that subjects will find it easier—and take less time to make categorizations—when they perceive the stimuli presented to them as being strongly associated (see Greenwald et al., 1998, and Nosek et al., 2007, for more-detailed explanations). So, for example, the speed with which one reacts to the word *psychology* when it is paired with *pleasant* or *unpleasant* would be (according to the IAT rationale) an indication of one's nonconscious and automatic association to "psychology."

Using the IAT or similar protocols, implicit attitudes toward a wide range of stimuli have been measured. For example, implicit attitudes have been studied in relation to racial prejudices (Greenwald et al., 1998; Greenwald & Nosek, 2001), suicidal ideation (Nock & Banaji, 2007), fear of spiders (Teachman, 2007), voting behavior (Friese et al., 2007), self-esteem and self-concept (Greenwald & Farnham, 2000), psychiatric medication (Rüsch et al., 2009), food groups (Barnes-Holmes et al., 2010), and Barack Obama (Nevid & McClelland, 2010). Evidence for the validity of the methodology for conducting implicit attitude research is seen in many "known groups" studies that have yielded findings in the predicted direction. So, for example, using implicit attitude protocols, it has been found that entomologists show more favorable attitudes toward bugs than nonentomologists (Citrin & Greenwald, 1998). Smokers motivated to smoke show more favorable responses to smoking cues than nonsmokers (Payne et al., 2007). Implicit attitude measurement has been demonstrated to have intriguing potential for applications in the area of consumer psychology and consumer preferences. For more information, interested readers are referred to the October (2010) special issue of *Psychology & Marketing* which was wholly devoted to the topic (Nevid, 2010).

Although the prospect of bypassing conscious controls in the measurement of attitude seems to have great appeal to the research community, many questions remain about this approach. For example, Gawronski and Bodenhausen (2007) raised questions about (a) the theory, if any, underlying implicit attitude measurement, (b) the physiological correlates of the measures, and (c) whether or not the measures truly provide access to mental processes that are not conscious. As the body of literature on the measurement of implicit attitudes continues to grow, so will the depth with which such questions are addressed.

## Surveys

In consumer psychology, a **survey** is a fixed list of questions administered to a selected sample of persons for the purpose of learning about consumers' attitudes, beliefs, opinions, and/or behavior with regard to the targeted products, services, or advertising. There are many different ways to conduct a survey, and these various methods all have specific pros and cons in terms of study design and data interpretation (Johnson et al., 2000; Lavrakas, 1998; Massey, 2000; Schwartz et al., 1998; Visser et al., 2000). One specialized type of survey, the **poll,** is much like an instrument to record votes and usually contains questions that can be answered with a simple *yes–no* or *for–against* response. Politicians, news organizations, and special interest organizations may retain researchers who conduct polls (pollsters) to gauge public opinion about controversial issues.

Surveys and polls may be conducted by means of face-to-face, online, and telephone interviews, as well as by mail. The personal interaction of the face-to-face interview helps ensure that questions are understood and that adequate clarification of queries is provided. Another advantage of this survey method is the ability to present interviewees with stimuli (such as products) that they can hold in their hands and evaluate. However, the face-to-face approach may also introduce bias into the study, as some respondents act to manage favorable impressions or seek to provide responses they believe the interviewer would like to hear. The face-to-face approach may not be the best when the topic discussed is particularly sensitive or when responses may be embarrassing or otherwise place the respondent in a bad light (Midanik et al., 2001). The face-to-face approach is also labor intensive and therefore can be quite costly when it comes to selecting, training, and employing interviewers.

Surveying by face-to-face interview is a common method of survey research, and it can be conducted almost anywhere—on a commuter bus or ferry, at a ball game, or near an election polling station. A common site for face-to-face survey research on consumer products is the shopping mall. *Mall intercept studies,* as they are called, can be conducted by interviewers with clipboards who approach shoppers. The shopper may be asked to participate in a survey by answering some questions right then and there or may be led to a booth or room where a more extended interview takes place. Another face-to-face survey method, this one more popular with political pollsters, is the door-to-door approach. Here an entire neighborhood may be polled by knocking on the doors of individual households and soliciting responses to the questionnaire.

Online, telephone, and mail surveys do not necessarily require personal contact between the researcher and respondent and in many instances may reduce the biases associated with personal interaction. Further, survey methods conducted in the absence of face-to-face interaction tend to be more cost-effective owing to automation of process components, the need for fewer personnel and less training, and the possibility of executing the entire study from a central location. The online survey holds great potential because of its easy access and feedback potential (Kaye & Johnson, 1999), and it can be particularly useful for learning about various aspects of online behavior, such as purchasing (Li et al., 1999) and teamwork (Levesque et al., 2001), as well as self-improvement (Mueller et al., 2000) and deviant online behavior (Greenfield, 1999; Houston et al., 2001; Young et al., 1999). Other researchers have shown that online survey methods may be particularly useful for learning about behaviors known to negatively impact on one's personal health, such as smoking (Ramo et al., 2011). Of course, unsolicited online surveys are viewed by many as unwanted e-mail or spam, and such perceptions may result not only in low response rates but also in a sense that one's privacy has been violated (Cho & LaRose, 1999). Researchers may also feel a certain degree of doubt regarding whether or not respondents actually are who they say they are. In this regard, there is no substitute for a face-to-face interview complete with identity verification.

The telephone survey offers a number of advantages, but it does suffer from some limitations. Generally, the amount of information that can be obtained by telephone is less than what can be obtained by personal interview or mail. It is not possible to show respondents visual stimuli over the phone. In addition, bias may be introduced if telephone directories are used for identifying respondents.

**JUST THINK . . .**

Have you ever participated in a consumer survey of any kind? Whether or not you have, what are your recommendations for improving the process and the quality of the data obtained?

**JUST THINK . . .**

Why might online survey methods be particularly useful for learning about behaviors known to negatively impact on health, such as smoking?

As many as 40% of all telephones in some cities are not listed. Since the institution of a national "do not call" list in 2003, most telephone solicitations cannot be made by random dialing. The primary disadvantage of phone surveys is that they are viewed by many as an unwelcome annoyance and an invasion of privacy.

A mail survey may be the most appropriate survey method when the survey questionnaire is particularly long and will require some time to complete. In general, mail surveys tend to be relatively low in cost because they do not require the services of a trained interviewer and can provide large amounts of information. They are also well suited for obtaining information about which respondents may be sensitive or shy in a face-to-face or even a telephone interview. They are ideal for posing questions that require the use of records or consultation with others (such as family members) for an answer. Note also that much of what we say about mail surveys also applies to electronic mail surveys or surveys conducted by means of fax machines.

The major disadvantages of mail questionnaires are (1) the possibility of no response at all from the intended recipient of the survey (for whatever reason—the survey was never delivered or was thrown out as junk mail as soon as it arrived); (2) the possibility of response from someone (perhaps a family member) who was not the intended recipient of the survey; and (3) the possibility of a late—and hence useless for tabulation purposes—response. If large numbers of people fail to respond to a mail questionnaire, then it is impossible to determine whether those individuals who did respond are representative of those who did not. People may not respond to a mail questionnaire for many different reasons, and various techniques ranging from incentives to follow-up mailings have been suggested for dealing with various types of nonresponse (Furse & Stewart, 1984).

It is possible to combine the various survey methods to obtain the advantages of each. For example, the survey researcher might mail a lengthy questionnaire to potential respondents and then obtain responses by telephone. Alternatively, those individuals not returning their responses by mail might be contacted by telephone or in person.

Many commercial research firms maintain a list of a large number of people or families who have agreed to respond to questionnaires that are sent to them. The people who make up this list are referred to as a **consumer panel.** In return for their participation, panel members may receive incentives such as cash and free samples of all the products about which they are asked to respond. One special type of panel is called a **diary panel.** Respondents on such a panel must keep detailed records of their behavior. For example, they may be required to keep a record of products they purchased, coupons they used, or radio stations they listened to while in the car. There are also specialized panels that serve to monitor segments of the market, political attitudes, or other variables.

Survey research may employ a wide variety of item types. One approach to item construction, particularly popular for surveys administered in writing, is referred to as the **semantic differential technique** (Osgood et al., 1957). Originally developed as a clinical tool for defining the meaning of concepts and relating concepts to one another in a "semantic space," the technique entails graphically placing a pair of bipolar adjectives (such as *good–bad* or *strong–weak*) on a seven-point scale such as this one:

GOOD _____ / _____ / _____ / _____ / _____ / _____ / _____ BAD

Respondents are instructed to place a mark on this continuum that corresponds to their judgment or rating. In research involving certain consumer applications, the bipolar adjectives may be replaced by descriptive expressions that are more consistent with the research objectives. For example, in rating a new cola-flavored soft drink, the phrase *just another cola* might be at one end of the rating continuum and *a very special beverage* might be at the other.

As with any research, care must be exercised in interpreting the results of a survey. Both the quantity and the quality of the data may vary from survey to survey. Response rates may differ, questions may be asked in different forms, and data collection procedures may vary from one survey to another (Henry, 1984). Ultimately, the utility of any conclusions rests on the integrity of the data and the analytic procedures used.

Occasions arise when research questions cannot be answered through a survey or a poll. Consumers may simply lack the insight to be accurate informants. As an example, consider the hypothetical case of Ralph, who smokes a hypothetical brand of cigarettes we will call "Cowboy." When asked why he chose to smoke Cowboy brand cigarettes, Ralph might reply "taste." In reality, however, Ralph may have begun smoking Cowboy because the advertising for this brand appealed to Ralph's image of himself as an independent, macho type—even though Ralph is employed as a clerk at a bridal boutique and bears little resemblance to the Cowboy image portrayed in the advertising.

Consumers may also be unwilling or reluctant to respond to some survey or poll questions. Suppose, for example, that the manufacturers of Cowboy cigarettes wished to know where on the product's packaging the Surgeon General's warning could be placed so that it would be *least* likely to be read. How many consumers would be willing to entertain such a question? Indeed, what would even posing such a question do for the public image of the product? It can be seen that if this hypothetical company were interested in obtaining an answer to such a question, it would have to do so through other means, such as motivation research.

> **JUST THINK . . .**
>
> What is another type of question to which consumers may be unwilling or reluctant to respond in a survey or a poll? What means could a consumer psychologist use to obtain an answer to this type of question?

## Motivation Research Methods

*Motivation research* in consumer psychology and marketing is so named because it typically involves analyzing motives for consumer behavior and attitudes. **Motivation research methods** include individual interviews and focus groups. These two qualitative research methods are used to examine, in depth, the reactions of consumers who are representative of the group of people who use a particular product or service. Unlike quantitative research, which typically involves large numbers of subjects and elaborate statistical analyses, qualitative research typically involves few respondents and little or no statistical analysis. The emphasis in the latter type of research is not on quantity (of subjects or of data) but on the qualities of whatever is under study. Qualitative research often provides the data from which to develop hypotheses that may then be tested with larger numbers of consumers. Qualitative research also has diagnostic value. The best way to obtain highly detailed information about what a consumer likes and dislikes about a product, a store, or an advertisement is to use qualitative research.

A **focus group** is a group interview led by a trained, independent moderator who, ideally, has a knowledge of group discussion facilitation techniques and group dynamics.[4] As their name implies, *focus groups* are designed to *focus* group discussion on

---

4. Focus group moderators vary greatly in training and experience. Ideally, a focus group moderator is independent enough to discuss dispassionately the topics with some distance and perspective. Contrary to this caveat, some advertising agencies maintain an in-house focus group moderator staff to test the advertising produced by the agency. Critics of this practice have likened it to assigning wolves to guard the henhouse.

something, such as a particular commercial, a concept for a new product, or packaging for a new product. Focus groups usually consist of 6 to 12 participants who may have been recruited off the floor of a shopping mall or selected in advance to meet some preset qualifications for participation. The usual objective here is for the members of the group to represent in some way the population of targeted consumers for the product or service. Thus, for example, only beer drinkers (defined, for example, as males who drink at least two six-packs per week and females who drink at least one six-pack per week) might be solicited for participation in a focus group designed to explore attributes of a new brand of beer—including such variables as its taste, its packaging, and its advertising. Another attribute of beer not known to most consumers is what is referred to in the industry as its *bar call*, a reference to the ease with which one could order the brew in a bar. Because of the high costs associated with introducing a new product and advertising a new or established product, professionally conducted focus groups, complete with a representative sampling of the targeted consumer population, are a valuable tool in market research.

Depending on the requirements of the moderator's client (an advertiser, a manufacturer, etc.), the group discussion can be relatively structured (with a number of points to be covered) or relatively unstructured (with few points to be covered exhaustively). After establishing a rapport with the group, the moderator may, for example, show some advertising or a product to the group and then pose a general question (such as "What did you think of the beer commercial?") to be followed up by more specific kinds of questions (such as "Were the people in that commercial the kind of people you would like to have a beer with?"). The responses of the group members may build on those of other group members, and the result of the free-flowing discussion may be new information, new perspectives, or some previously overlooked problems with the advertising or product.

Focus groups typically last from one to two hours and are usually conducted in rooms (either conference rooms or living rooms) equipped with one-way mirrors (from which the client's staff may observe the proceedings) and audio or video equipment so that a record of the group session will be preserved. Aside from being an active listener and an individual who is careful not to suggest answers to questions or draw conclusions for the respondents, the moderator's duties include (1) following a discussion guide (usually created by the moderator in consultation with the client) and keeping the discussion on the topic; (2) drawing out silent group members so that everyone is heard from; (3) limiting the response time of group members who might dominate the group discussion; and (4) writing a report that not only provides a summary of the group discussion but also offers psychological or marketing insights to the client.

Technology may be employed in focus groups so that second-by-second reaction to stimulus materials such as commercials can be monitored. Cohen described the advantages (1985) and limitations (1987) of a technique whereby respondents watching television commercials pressed a calculator-like keypad to indicate how positive or negative they were feeling on a moment-to-moment basis while watching television. The response could then be visually displayed as a graph and played back for the respondent, who could be asked about the reasons for the spontaneous response.

Focus groups are widely employed in consumer research to

- generate hypotheses that can be further tested quantitatively
- generate information for designing or modifying consumer questionnaires
- provide general background information about a product category
- provide impressions of new product concepts for which little information is available

- obtain new ideas about older products
- generate ideas for product development or names for existing products
- interpret the results of previously obtained quantitative results

In general, the focus group is a highly useful technique for exploratory research, a technique that can be a valuable springboard to more comprehensive quantitative studies. Because so few respondents are typically involved in such groups, the findings from them cannot automatically be thought of as representative of the larger population. Still, many a client (including advertising agency creative staff) has received inspiration from the words spoken by ordinary consumers on the other side of a one-way mirror. Most major commercial test publishers, by the way, employ focus groups with test users to learn more about various aspects of market receptivity to their new test (or new edition of a test).

Focus groups provide a forum for open-ended probing of thoughts, which ideally stimulates dialogue and discussion among the participants. Although the open-ended nature of the experience is a strength, the lack of any systematic framework for exploring human motivation is not. No two focus group moderators charged with answering the same questions may approach their task in quite the same way. Addressing this issue, Cohen (1999b) proposed a *dimensional* approach to qualitative research. This approach attempts to apply the overlapping psychological modalities or dimensions found so important by clinician Arnold Lazarus (1973, 1989) in his multimodal diagnostic and therapeutic efforts to nonclinical objectives in qualitative research. Specifically, **dimensional qualitative research** is an approach to qualitative research that seeks to ensure a study is comprehensive and systematic from a psychological perspective by guiding the study design and proposed questions for discussion on the basis of "BASIC ID" dimensions. BASIC ID is an acronym for the key dimensions in Lazarus's approach to diagnosis and intervention. The letters stand for *behavior, affect, sensation, imagery, cognition, interpersonal relations,* and *drugs.* Cohen's adaptation of Lazarus's work adds an eighth dimension, a sociocultural one, thus adding an *s* to the acronym and changing it to its plural form (BASIC IDS). Reflecting on this approach, Cohen wrote,

> JUST THINK . . .
>
> For what type of research questions would a focus group probably not be advisable?

> The dimensions of the BASIC IDS can provide a uniform yet systematic framework for exploration and intervention, yet be flexible enough to allow for the implementation of new techniques and innovation. Anchored in logic, it is an approach that is accessible by nonpsychologists who seek to become more knowledgeable in the ways that psychology can be applied in marketing contexts. . . . Regardless of the specific framework adopted by a researcher, it seems high time to acknowledge that we are all feeling, sensing, behaving, imagining, thinking, socially relating, and biochemical beings who are products of our culture. Once this acknowledgment is made, and once we strive to routinely and systematically account for such variables in marketing research, we can begin to appreciate the added value psychologists bring to qualitative research with consumers in a marketing context. (1999b, p. 365)

In October 2011, the scholarly journal *Psychology & Marketing* devoted a special issue to the subject of dimensional qualitative research. In his guest editorial introducing the articles in that special issue, Haseeb Shabbir (2011) made clear that dimensional qualitative research had applications beyond consumer psychology. He noted that "the application of DQR is by no means limited to marketing or psychology . . . it is worth emphasizing that DQR can be useful in providing a psychologically sophisticated guide to qualitative research in almost any discipline" (p. 977).

**Behavioral observation**   Why did sales of the pain relievers aspirin, Bufferin, Anacin, and Excedrin rise sharply in October 1982? Was this rise in sales due to the effectiveness of advertising campaigns for these products? No. The sales rose sharply in 1982 when it was learned that seven people had died from ingesting Tylenol capsules laced with cyanide. As Tylenol, the pain reliever with the largest share of the market, was withdrawn from the shelves of stores nationwide, there was a corresponding rise in the sale of alternative preparations. A similar phenomenon occurred in 1986.

Just think what would have happened had market researchers based their judgments concerning the effectiveness of an ad campaign for an over-the-counter pain reliever solely on sales figures during the period of the Tylenol scare. No doubt the data easily could have led to a misinterpretation of what actually occurred. How might market researchers add a quality control component to their research methods? One way is by using multiple methods, such as behavioral observation in addition to survey methods.

**JUST THINK . . .**

From your own informal experience, what other types of purchases are probably guided more by input from children than from adults? How could consumer psychologists best test your beliefs regarding this purchase decision?

It is not unusual for market researchers to station behavioral observers in stores to monitor what really prompts a consumer to buy this or that product at the point of choice. Such an observer at a store selling pain relievers in October 1982 might have observed, for example, a conversation with the clerk about the best alternative to Tylenol. Behavioral observers in a supermarket who studied the purchasing habits of people buying breakfast cereal concluded that children accompanying the purchaser requested or demanded a specific brand of cereal (Atkin, 1978). Hence, it would be wise for breakfast cereal manufacturers to gear their advertising to children, not the adult consumer.

**Other methods**   A number of other methods and tools may be brought to bear on marketing and advertising questions. Consumer psychologists sometimes employ projective tests—existing as well as custom designed—as an aid in answering the questions raised by their clients. Special instrumentation, including tachistoscopes and electroencephalographs, have also been used in efforts to uncover consumer motivation. Special computer programs may be used to derive brand names for new products. Thus, for example, when Honda wished to position a new line of its cars as "advanced precision automobiles," a company specializing in the naming of new products conducted a computer search of over 6,900 English-language morphemes to locate word roots that mean or imply "advanced precision." The applicable morphemes were then computer combined in ways that the phonetic rules of English would allow. From the resulting list, the best word (that is, one that has visibility among other printed words, one that will be recognizable as a brand name, and so forth) was then selected. In this case, that word was *Acura* (Brewer, 1987).

Literature reviews are another method available to consumer psychologists. A literature review might suggest, for example, that certain sounds or imagery in a particular brand tend to be more popular with consumers than other sounds or imagery (Figure 16–8). Schloss (1981) observed that the sound of the letter *K* was represented better than six times more often than would be expected by chance in the 200 top brand-name products (such as Sanka, Quaker, Nabisco—and, we might add, Acura). Schloss went on to speculate about the ability of the sounds of words to elicit emotional reactions as opposed to rational ones.

And speaking of eliciting reactions, it is we, Ron Cohen, Mark Swerdlik, and Eddy Sturman, who must now pause to *just think* and wonder: What reaction will be elicited

**Figure 16–8**
**What's in a Name?**

*"What's in a name? A rose by any other name would smell as sweet." Sentiments such as this may be touching to read and beautiful to behold when spoken by talented actors on Broadway. However, they wouldn't have taken William Shakespeare very far on Madison Avenue. The name given to a product is an important part of what is referred to as the "marketing mix": the way a product is positioned, marketed, and promoted in the marketplace. The ad shown, reproduced from a 1927 magazine, touts the benefits of a toothbrush with the name Pro-phy-lac-tic. The creator of this brand name no doubt wished to position this toothbrush as being particularly useful in preventing disease. However, the word* prophylactic *(defined as "protective") became more identified in the public's mind with condoms, a fact that could not have helped the longevity of this brand of toothbrush in the marketplace. Today, researchers use a variety of methods, including word association, to create brand names.*

from you as the realization sets in that you have come to the end of our textbook? Your reaction could range from *extreme sorrow* (you wish there were more pages to turn) to *unbridled ecstasy* (party time!). Whatever, we want you to know that we consider it an honor and a privilege to have helped introduce you to the world of measurement in psychology and education. You have our best wishes for success in your academic and professional development. And who knows? Maybe it will be you and your work that we will present to students in a future edition of *Psychological Testing and Assessment: An Introduction to Tests and Measurement.*

## Self-Assessment

Test your understanding of elements of this chapter by seeing if you can explain each of the following terms, expressions, and abbreviations:

| | | |
|---|---|---|
| assessment center | focus group | organizational culture |
| attitude | forced distribution technique | physical test |
| burnout | GATB | placement |
| classification | implicit attitude | poll |
| consumer panel | in-basket technique | productivity |
| consumer psychology | integrity test | screening |
| critical incidents technique | interest measure | second-order meta-analysis |
| diary panel | intrinsic motivation | selection |
| dimensional qualitative research | job satisfaction | semantic differential technique |
| drug test | leaderless group technique | SII |
| extrinsic motivation | MBTI | survey |
| false negative | motivation research methods | team |
| false positive | organizational commitment | |

Abel, G. G., Rouleau, J., & Cunningham-Rathner, J. (1986). Sexually aggressive behavior. In W. J. Curran, A. L. McGarry, & S. Shah (Eds.), *Forensic psychiatry and psychology: Perspectives and standards for interdisciplinary practice* (pp. 289–314). Philadelphia: Davis.

Abeles, N., & Barlev, A. (1999). End of life decisions and assisted suicide. *Professional Psychology: Research and Practice, 30,* 229–234.

Abidin, R. R. (1990). *Parenting stress index* (3rd ed.). Odessa, FL: Psychological Assessment Resources.

Abrams, D. B., Binkoff, J. A., Zwick, W. R., et al. (1991). Alcohol abusers' and social drinkers' responses to alcohol-relevant and general situations. *Journal of Studies on Alcohol, 52,* 409–414.

Abrams, S. (1977). *A polygraph handbook for attorneys.* Lexington, MA: Heath.

Achenbach, T. M. (1978). *Child Behavior Profile.* Bethesda, MD: Laboratory of Developmental Psychology, National Institutes of Mental Health.

Achenbach, T. M. (1981). A junior MMPI? *Journal of Personality Assessment, 45,* 332–333.

Achenbach, T. M. (1993). Implications of multiaxial empirically based assessment for behavior therapy with children. *Behavior Therapy, 24,* 91–116.

Achenbach, T. M., McConaughy, S. H., & Howell, C. T. (1987). Child/adolescent behavioral and emotional problems: Implications of cross-informant correlations for situational specificity. *Psychological Bulletin, 101,* 213–232.

Ackerman, M. J. (1995). *Clinician's guide to child custody evaluations.* New York: Wiley-Interscience.

Ackerman, P. L., & Heggestad, E. D. (1997). Intelligence, personality, and interests: Evidence for overlapping traits. *Psychological Bulletin, 121,* 219–245.

Ackerman, P. L., & Kanfer, R. (1993). Integrating laboratory and field study for improving selection: Development of a battery for predicting air traffic controller success. *Journal of Applied Psychology, 78,* 413–432.

Acklin, M. W. (1995). Avoiding Rorschach dichotomies: Integrating Rorschach interpretation. *Journal of Personality Assessment, 64,* 235–238.

Acklin, M. W. (1996). Personality assessment and managed care. *Journal of Personality Assessment, 66,* 194–201.

Acklin, M. W. (1997). Swimming with sharks. *Journal of Personality Assessment, 69,* 448–451.

Adams, D. K., & Horn, J. L. (1965). Nonoverlapping keys for the MMPI scales. *Journal of Consulting Psychology, 29,* 284.

Adams, K. M. (1984). Luria left in the lurch: Unfulfilled promises are not valid tests. *Journal of Clinical Neuropsychology, 6,* 455–458.

Adams, K. M. (2000). Practical and ethical issues pertaining to test revisions. *Psychological Assessment, 12,* 281–286.

Adams-Tucker, C. (1982). Proximate effects of sexual abuse in childhood: A report on 28 children. *American Journal of Psychiatry, 139,* 1252–1256.

Addeo, R. R., Greene, A. F., & Geisser, M. E. (1994). Construct validity of the Robson Self-Esteem Questionnaire in a sample of college students. *Educational and Psychological Measurement, 54,* 439–446.

Adelman, S. A., Fletcher, K. E., Bahnassi, A., & Munetz, M. R. (1991). The Scale for Treatment Integration of the Dually Diagnosed (STIDD): An instrument for assessing intervention strategies in the pharmacotherapy of mentally ill substance abusers. *Drug and Alcohol Dependence, 27,* 35–42.

Adler, A. (1927/1965). *Understanding human nature.* Greenwich, CT: Fawcett.

Adler, A. (1933/1964). *Social interest: A challenge to mankind.* New York: Capricorn.

Adler, T. (1990). Does the "new" MMPI beat the "classic"? *APA Monitor, 20*(4), 18–19.

Ahern, E. (1949). *Handbook of personnel forms and records.* New York: American Management Association.

Ahola, K., Kivimäki, M., Honkonen, T., et al. (2008). Occupational burnout and medically certified sickness absence: A population-based study of Finnish employees. *Journal of Psychosomatic Research, 64*(2), 185–193.

Aiello, J. R., & Douthitt, E. A. (2001). Social facilitation from Triplett to electronic performance monitoring. *Group Dynamics, 5,* 163–180.

Aikman, K. G., Belter, R. W., & Finch, A. J. (1992). Human figure drawings: Validity in assessing intellectual level and academic achievement. *Journal of Clinical Psychology, 48,* 114–120.

Airasian, P. W., Madaus, G. F., & Pedulla, J. J. (1979). *Minimal competency testing.* Englewood Cliffs, NJ: Educational Technology Publications.

Akamatsu, C. T. (1993–1994). The view from within and without: Conducting research on deaf Asian-Americans. *Journal of the American Deafness and Rehabilitation Association, 27,* 12–16.

Alderfer, C. (1972). *Existence, relatedness and growth: Human needs in organizational settings.* New York: Free Press.

Alderson, J. C., Krahnke, K. J., & Stansfield, C. W. (1987). *Reviews of English language proficiency tests.* Washington, DC: TESOL.

Alessandri, S. M., Bendersky, M., & Lewis, M. (1998). Cognitive functioning in 8- to 18-month-old drug-exposed infants. *Developmental Psychology, 34,* 565–573.

Alexander, R. C., Surrell, J. A., & Cohle, S. D. (1987). Microwave oven burns in children: An unusual manifestation of child abuse. *Pediatrics, 79,* 255–260.

Alison, L., & Barrett, E. (2004). The interpretation and utilization of offender profiles: A critical review of "traditional" approaches to profiling. In J. R. Adler (Ed.), *Forensic psychology: Concepts, debates and practice* (pp. 58–77). Devon, England: Willan.

Alison, L., West, A., & Goodwill, A. (2004). The academic and the practitioner: Pragmatists' views of offender profiling. *Psychology, Public Policy, and Law, 10,* 71–101.

Allen, J. (2002). Assessment training for practice in American Indian and Alaska native settings. *Journal of Personality Assessment, 79,* 216–225.

Allen, M. J., & Yen, W. M. (1979). *Introduction to measurement theory.* Monterey, CA: Brooks/Cole.

Allen, N. J., & Meyer, J. P. (1990). The measurement and antecedents of affective, continuance, and normative commitment to the organization. *Journal of Occupational Psychology, 63,* 1–18.

Allen, R., Wasserman, G. A., & Seidman, S. (1990). Children with congenital anomalies: The preschool period. *Journal of Pediatric Psychology, 15,* 327–345.

Allen, S. R. (2008). Predicting performance in sport using a portable cognitive assessment device. *Dissertation Abstracts International. Section A. Humanities and Social Sciences, 68*(9-A), 3724.

Allen, T. E. (1994). *Who are the deaf and hard-of-hearing students leaving high school and entering postsecondary education?* (pp. 1–16). U.S. Office of Special Education and Rehabilitative Services: Pelavin Research Institute.

Allport, G. W. (1937). *Personality: A psychological interpretation.* New York: Holt.

Allport, G. W., & Odbert, H. S. (1936). Trait-names: A psycho-lexical study. *Psychological Monographs, 47* (Whole No. 211).

Allport, G. W., Vernon, P. E., & Lindzey, G. (1951). *Study of values* (rev. ed.). Boston: Houghton Mifflin.

Allred, L. J., & Harris, W. G. (1984). *The nonequivalence of computerized and conventional administrations of the Adjective Checklist.* Unpublished manuscript, Johns Hopkins University, Baltimore.

Alpher, V. S., & Blanton, R. L. (1985). The accuracy of lie detection: Why lie tests based on the polygraph should not be admitted into evidence today. *Law & Psychology Review, 9,* 67–75.

Alterman, A. I., McDermott, P. A., Cook, T. G., et al. (2000). Generalizability of the clinical dimensions of the Addiction Severity Index to nonopioid-dependent patients. *Psychology of Addictive Behaviors, 14,* 287–294.

Amabile, T. M., Hill, K. G., Hennessey, B. A., & Tighe, E. M. (1994). The Work Preference Inventory: Assessing intrinsic and extrinsic motivational orientations. *Journal of Personality and Social Psychology, 66,* 950–967.

Amada, G. (1996). You can't please all of the people all of the time: Normative institutional resistances to college psychological services. *Journal of College Student Psychotherapy, 10,* 45–63.

Aman, C. J., Roberts, R. J., & Pennington, B. F. (1998). A neuropsychological examination of the underlying deficit in attention deficit hyperactivity disorder: Frontal lobe versus right parietal lobe theories. *Developmental Psychology, 34,* 956–969.

Ambrosini, P. J., Metz, C., Bianchi, M. D., Rabinovich, H., & Undie, A. (1991). Concurrent validity and psychometric properties of the Beck Depression Inventory in outpatient adolescents. *Journal of the American Academy of Child and Adolescent Psychiatry, 30,* 51–57.

American Association on Mental Retardation. (1992). *Mental retardation: Definition, classification, and systems of supports* (9th ed.). Washington, DC: Author.

American Board of Forensic Odontology, Inc. (1986). Guidelines for analysis of bite marks in forensic investigation. *Journal of the American Dental Association, 12,* 383–386.

American Educational Research Association, Committee on Test Standards, and National Council on Measurements Used in Education. (1955). *Technical recommendations for achievement tests.* Washington, DC: American Educational Research Association.

American Educational Research Association, American Psychological Association, & National Council on Measurement in Education. (1999). *Standards for educational and psychological testing.* Washington, DC: Author.

American Law Institute. (1956). *Model penal code.* Tentative Draft Number 4.

American Psychiatric Association. (1968). *Diagnostic and statistical manual of mental disorders* (2nd ed.). Washington, DC: Author.

American Psychiatric Association. (1980). *Diagnostic and statistical manual of mental disorders* (3rd ed.). Washington, DC: Author.

American Psychiatric Association. (1987). *Diagnostic and statistical manual of mental disorders* (3rd ed., rev.). Washington, DC: Author.

American Psychiatric Association. (1994). *Diagnostic and statistical manual of mental disorders* (4th ed.). Washington, DC: Author.

American Psychiatric Association. (2000). *Diagnostic and statistical manual of mental disorders* (4th ed.; text rev.). Washington, DC: Author.

American Psychiatric Association. (2001). *Diagnostic and statistical manual of mental disorders* (4th ed.; text rev.). [CD-ROM (Windows)]. Washington, DC: Author.

American Psychological Association. (1950). Ethical standards for the distribution of psychological tests and diagnostic aids. *American Psychologist, 5,* 620–626.

American Psychological Association. (1953). *Ethical standards of psychologists.* Washington, DC: Author.

American Psychological Association. (1954). *Technical recommendations for psychological tests and diagnostic techniques.* Washington, DC: Author.

American Psychological Association, American Educational Research Association, & National Council on Measurement in Education. (1966). *Standards for educational and psychological tests and manual.* Washington, DC: Author.

American Psychological Association. (1967). *Casebook on ethical standards of psychologists.* Washington, DC: Author.

American Psychological Association, American Educational Research Association, & National Council on Measurement in Education. (1974). *Standards for educational and psychological tests.* Washington, DC: Author.

American Psychological Association. (1981). Ethical principles of psychologists. *American Psychologist, 36,* 633–638.

American Psychological Association. (1985). *Standards for educational and psychological testing.* Washington, DC: Author.

American Psychological Association. (1987). *Casebook on ethical principles of psychologists.* Washington, DC: Author.

American Psychological Association. (1991). *Questionnaires used in the prediction of trustworthiness in pre-employment selection decisions: An APA Task Force report.* Washington, DC: Author.

American Psychological Association. (1992). Ethical principles of psychologists and code of conduct. *American Psychologist, 47,* 1597–1611.

American Psychological Association. (1993, January). Call for book proposals for test instruments. *APA Monitor, 24,* 12.

American Psychological Association, Committee on Professional Practice and Standards. (1994a). Guidelines for child custody evaluations in divorce proceedings. *American Psychologist, 49,* 677–680.

American Psychological Association. (1994b). C. H. Lawshe. *American Psychologist, 49,* 549–551.

American Psychological Association. (1996a). *Affirmative action: Who benefits?* Washington, DC: Author.

American Psychological Association. (1996b). *Standards for psychological tests.* Washington, DC: Author.

American Psychological Association. (2002). Ethical principles of psychologists and code of conduct. *American Psychologist, 57,* 1060–1073.

American Psychological Association. (2003). Guidelines on multicultural education, training, research, practice, organizational change for psychologists. *American Psychologist, 58,* 377–402.

Ames, S. L., & Stacy, A. W. (1998). Implicit cognition in the prediction of substance use among drug offenders. *Psychology of Addictive Behaviors, 12,* 272–281.

Amodio, D. M., Devine, P. G., & Harmon-Jones, E. (2006). Stereotyping and evaluation in implicit race bias: Evidence for independent constructs and unique effects on behavior. *Journal of Personality and Social Psychology,* *91*(4), 652–661.

Amrine, M. (Ed.). (1965). Special issue. *American Psychologist,* *20,* 857–991.

Anderson, C., Spataro, S. E., & Flynn, F. J. (2008). Personality and organizational culture as determinants of influence. *Journal of Applied Psychology, 93*(3), 702–710.

Anderson, D. (2007). A reciprocal determinism analysis of the relationship between naturalistic media usage and the development of creative-thinking skills among college students. *Dissertation Abstracts International Section A: Humanities and Social Sciences, 67*(7-A), 2007, 2459.

Anderson, G., & Grace, C. (1991). The Black deaf adolescent: A diverse and underserved population. *Volta Review, 93,* 73–86.

Anderson, H. G. (1919). *The medical and surgical aspects of aviation.* London: Oxford Medical.

Anderson, J. W. (1990). The life of Henry A. Murray: 1893–1988. In A. I. Rabin, R. A. Zucker, R. A. Emmons, & S. Frank (Eds.), *Studying persons and lives* (pp. 304–333). New York: Springer.

Anderson, W. P. (1995). Ethnic and cross-cultural differences on the MMPI-2. In J. C. Duckworth & W. P. Anderson (Eds.), *MMPI and MMPI-2: Interpretation manual for counselors and clinicians* (4th ed.; pp. 439–460). Bristol, PA: Accelerated Development.

Andresen, E. M., Malmgren, J. A., Carter, W. B., & Patrick, D. L. (1994). Screening for depression in well older adults: Evaluation of a short form of the CES-D. *American Journal of Preventive Medicine, 10*(2), 77–84.

Andrew, G., Hartwell, S. W., Hutt, M. L., & Walton, R. E. (1953). *The Michigan Picture Test.* Chicago: Science Research Associates.

Andronikof, A. (2005). Science and soul: Use and misuse of computerized interpretation. *Rorschachiana, 27*(1), 1–3.

Angie, A. D., Davis, J. L., Allen, M.T., et al. (2011). Studying ideological groups online: Identification and assessment of risk factors for violence. *Journal of Applied Social Psychology, 41,* 627–657.

Angoff, W. H. (1962). Scales with nonmeaningful origins and units of measurement. *Educational and Psychological Measurement, 22,* 27–34.

Angoff, W. H. (1964). Technical problems of obtaining equivalent scores on tests. *Educational and Psychological Measurement, 1,* 11–13.

Angoff, W. H. (1966). Can useful general-purpose equivalency tables be prepared for different college admissions tests? In A. Anastasi (Ed.), *Testing problems in perspective* (pp. 251–264). Washington, DC: American Council on Education.

Angoff, W. H. (1971). Scales, norms, and equivalent scores. In R. L. Thorndike (Ed.), *Educational measurement* (2nd ed., pp. 508–560). Washington, DC: American Council on Education.

Appelbaum, P., & Grisso, T. (1995a). The MacArthur Treatment Competence Study: I. Mental illness and competence to consent to treatment. *Law and Human Behavior, 19,* 105–126.

Appelbaum, P., & Grisso, T. (1995b). The MacArthur Treatment Competence Study: III. Abilities of patients to consent to psychiatric and medical treatments. *Law and Human Behavior, 19,* 149–174.

Appelbaum, P. S., & Roth, L. H. (1982). Competency to consent to research: A psychiatric overview. *Archives of General Psychiatry, 39,* 951–958.

Arbisi, P. A., Ben-Porath, Y. S., & McNulty, J. (2002). A comparison of MMPI-2 validity in African American and Caucasian psychiatric inpatients. *Psychological Assessment, 14,* 3–15.

Ariel, A., Van der Linden, W. J., & Veldkamp, B. P. (2006). A strategy for optimizing item-pool management. *Journal of Educational Measurement, 43*(2), 85–96.

Arnau, R. C., Green, B. A., Rosen, D. H., et al. (2003). Are Jungian preferences really categorical? *Personality & Individual Differences, 34,* 233–251.

Arnett, P. A., Rao, S. M., Grafman, J., et al. (1997). Executive functions in multiple sclerosis: An analysis of temporal ordering, semantic encoding, and planning abilities. *Neuropsychology, 11,* 535–544.

Arnold, D. S., O'Leary, S. G., Wolff, L. S., & Acker, M. M. (1993). The Parenting Scale: A measure of dysfunctional parenting in discipline situations. *Psychological Assessment, 5,* 137–144.

Aronow, E., & Reznikoff, M. (1976). *Rorschach content interpretation.* Orlando, FL: Grune & Stratton.

Aronow, E., & Reznikoff, M. (1983). *A Rorschach introduction: Content and perceptual approaches.* Orlando, FL: Grune & Stratton.

Aronow, E., Reznikoff, M., & Moreland, K. L. (1995). The Rorschach: Projective technique or psychometric test? *Journal of Personality Assessment, 64,* 213–228.

Aros, S., Mills, J. L., Torres, C., et al. (2006). Prospective identification of pregnant women drinking four or more standard drinks (= 48 g) of alcohol per day. *Substance Use & Misuse, 41*(2), 183–197.

Arthur, T. E., Reeves, I., Morgan, O., et al. (2005). Developing a cultural competence assessment tool for people in recovery from racial, ethnic and cultural backgrounds: The journey, challenges and lessons learned. *Psychiatric Rehabilitation Journal, 28*(3), 243–250.

Arthur, W., Jr., Woehr, D. J., & Graziano, W. G. (2001). Personality testing in employment settings: Problems and issues in the application of typical selection practice. *Personnel Review, 30,* 657–676.

Arvey, R. D. (1979). *Fairness in selecting employees.* Reading, MA: Addison-Wesley.

Arvey, R. D., Bouchard, T. J., Segal, N. L., & Abraham, L. M. (1989). Job satisfaction: Environmental and genetic components. *Journal of Applied Psychology, 74,* 187–192.

Asch, S. E. (1951). Effects of group pressure upon the modification and distortion of judgment. In H. Guetzkow (Ed.), *Groups, leadership, and men.* Pittsburgh, PA: Carnegie.

Asch, S. E. (1955). Opinions and social pressure. *Scientific American, 193,* 33–35.

Asch, S. E. (1957a). Studies of independence and conformity: A minority of one against a unanimous majority. *Psychological Monographs, 70* (9, Whole No. 416).

Asch, S. E. (1957b). An experimental investigation of group influence. In Walter Reed Army Institute of Research (Ed.), *Symposium on preventive and social psychiatry.* Washington, DC: U.S. Government Printing Office.

Association of Personnel Test Publishers (APTP). (1990). Model guidelines for preemployment integrity testing programs. Washington, DC: APTP.

*ASVAB 18/19 Counselor Manual: The ASVAB career exploration program.* (1995). Washington, DC: U.S. Department of Defense.

Atkin, C. K. (1978). Observation of parent–child interaction in supermarket decision making. *Journal of Marketing, 42,* 41–45.

Atkins v. Virginia, 122 S. Ct. 2242 (2002).

Atkinson, J. W. (1981). Studying personality in the context of an advanced motivational psychology. *American Psychologist, 36,* 117–128.

Atkinson, R. C., & Shiffrin, R. M. (1968). A proposed system and its control processes. In K. W. Spence & J. T. Spence (Eds.), *The psychology of learning and motivation: Advances in research and theory* (Vol. 2; pp. 82–90). Oxford: Oxford University Press.

Attix, D. K, & Welsh-Bohmer, K. A. (Eds.). (2006). *Geriatric neuropsychology: Assessment and intervention.* New York: Guilford Press.

Ausburn, L. J., & Ausburn, F. B. (1978). Cognitive styles: Some information and implications for instructional design. *Educational Communications & Technology Journal, 26,* 337–354.

Aycan, Z., Kanungo, R. N., Mendonca, M., et al. (2000). Impact of culture on human resource management practices: A 10-country comparison. *Applied Psychology: An International Review, 49,* 192–221.

Ayres, R. R., & Cooley, E. J. (1986). Sequential versus simultaneous processing on the K-ABC: Validity in predicting learning success. *Journal of Psychoeducational Assessment, 4,* 211–220.

Babins, L., Slater, M.-E., Whitehead, V., & Chertkow, H. (2008). Can an 18-point clock-drawing scoring system predict dementia in elderly individuals with mild cognitive impairment? *Journal of Clinical and Experimental Neuropsychology, 30*(2), 1–14.

Bagasra, A. (2010). *Development and testing of an acculturation scale for Muslim Americans.* Paper presented at the 119th annual convention of the American Psychological Association, Washington, DC.

Bain, S.K. & Gray, R. (2008). Test reviews: Kaufman Assessment Battery for Children, Second Edition. *Journal of Psychoeducational Assessment, 26*(1), 92–101.

Baker, E. L., O'Neill, H. F., & Linn, R. L. (1993). Policy and validity prospects for performance-based assessment. *American Psychologist, 48,* 1210–1218.

Baldridge, D. C., & Veiga, J. F. (2006). The impact of anticipated social consequences on recurring disability. *Journal of Management, 32*(1), 158–179.

Baldwin, A. L., Kalhorn, J., & Breese, F. H. (1945). Patterns of parent behavior. *Psychological Monographs, 58* (Whole No. 268).

Baldwin, J. A. (1984). African self-consciousness and the mental health of African-Americans. *Journal of Black Studies, 15,* 177–194.

Baldwin, J. A., & Bell, Y. R. (1985). The African Self-Consciousness Scale: An Africentric personality questionnaire. *Western Journal of Black Studies, 9*(2), 65–68.

Ball, J. D., Archer, R. P., Gordon, R. A., & French, J. (1991). Rorschach depression indices with children and adolescents: Concurrent validity findings. *Journal of Personality Assessment, 57,* 465–476.

Ball, T. S., & Bernardoni, L. C. (1953). The application of an auditory apperception test to clinical diagnosis. *Journal of Clinical Psychology, 9,* 54–58.

Baltes, B. B., Briggs, T. E., Huff, J. W., et al. (1999). Flexible and compressed workweek schedules: A meta-analysis of their effects on work-related criteria. *Journal of Applied Psychology, 84,* 496–513.

Banaji, M. R. (2001). Implicit attitudes can be measured. In H. L. Roediger III, J. S. Nairne, I. Neath, & A. M. Surprenant (Eds.), *The nature of remembering: Essays in honor of Robert G. Crowder. Science conference series* (pp. 117–150). Washington, DC: American Psychological Association.

Bank, A. L., MacNeill, S. E., & Lichtenberg, P. A. (2000). Cross validation of the MacNeill-Lichtenberg Decision Tree triaging mental health problems in geriatric rehabilitation patients. *Rehabilitation Psychology, 45,* 193–204.

Baños, J. H., & Franklin, L. M. (2003). Factor structure of the Mini-Mental State Examination in adult psychiatric inpatients. *Psychological Assessment, 14,* 397–400.

Barak, A., & Cohen, L. (2002). Empirical examination of an online version of the Self-Directed Search. *Journal of Career Assessment, 10,* 387–400.

Barden, R. C., Ford, M. E., Jensen, A. G., Rogers-Salyer, M., & Salyer, K. E. (1989). Effects of craniofacial deformity in infancy on the quality of mother-infant interactions. *Child Development, 60,* 819–824.

Bardis, P. D. (1975). The Borromean family. *Social Science, 50,* 144–158.

Bardos, A. N. (1993). Human figure drawings: Abusing the abused. *School Psychology Quarterly, 8,* 177–181.

Barends, A., Westen, D., Leigh, J., Silbert, D., & Byers, S. (1990). Assessing affect-tone of relationship paradigms from TAT and interview data. *Psychological Assessment, 2,* 329–332.

Barker, R. (1963). On the nature of the environment. *Journal of Social Issues, 19,* 17–38.

Barko, N. (1993, August). What's your child's emotional IQ? *Working Mother, 16,* 33–35.

Barnes-Holmes, D., Murtagh, L., Barnes-Holmes, Y., & Stewart, I. (2010). Using the implicit association test and the implicit relational assessment procedure to measure attitudes toward meat and vegetables in vegetarians and meat-eaters. *Psychological Record, 60*(2), Article 6.

Barnett, L. A., Far, J. M., Mauss, A. L., & Miller, J. A. (1996). Changing perceptions of peer norms as a drinking reduction program for college students. *Journal of Alcohol & Drug Education, 41*(2), 39–62.

Barnett, R. C., & Gareis, K. C. (2000). Reduced hours, job-role quality, and life satisfaction among married women physicians with children. *Psychology of Women Quarterly, 24,* 358–364.

Baron, I. S. (2004). *Neuropsychological evaluation of the child.* New York: Oxford University Press.

Baron, J., & Norman, M. F. (1992). SATs, achievement tests, and high-school class rank as predictors of college performance. *Educational and Psychological Measurement, 52,* 1047–1055.

Barrick, M. R., Mount, M. K., & Judge, T. A. (2001). Personality and performance at the beginning of the new millennium: What do we know and where do we go next? *International Journal of Selection and Assessment, 9,* 9–30.

Barrick, M. R., Stewart, G. L., & Piotrowski, M. (2002). Personality and job performance: Test of the mediating effects of motivation among sales representatives. *Journal of Applied Psychology, 87,* 43–51.

Barry, D. T. (2001). Development of a new scale for measuring acculturation: The East Asian Acculturation Measure (EAAM). *Journal of Immigrant Health, 3*(4), 193–197.

Bartholomew, D. (1996a). "Metaphor taken as math: Indeterminacy in the factor analysis model": Comment. *Multivariate Behavioral Research, 31,* 551–554.

Bartholomew, D. (1996b). Response to Dr. Maraun's first reply to discussion of his paper. *Multivariate Behavioral Research, 31,* 631–636.

Barton, K. A., Blanchard, E. B., & Veazy, C. (1999). Self-monitoring as an assessment strategy in behavioral medicine. *Psychological Assessment, 11,* 490–497.

Bartram, D., Beaumont, J. G., Cornford, T., & Dann, P. L. (1987). Recommendations for the design of software for computer based assessment: Summary statement. *Bulletin of the British Psychological Society, 40,* 86–87.

Bartram, D., & Hambleton, R. K. (Eds.). (2006). *Computer-based testing and the Internet: Issues and advances.* New York: Wiley.

Bass, B. M. (1956). Development of a structured disguised personality test. *Journal of Applied Psychology, 40,* 393–397.

Bass, B. M. (1957). Validity studies of proverbs personality test. *Journal of Applied Psychology, 41,* 158–160.

Bass, B. M. (1958). Famous Sayings Test: General manual. *Psychological Reports, 4,* Monograph No. 6.

Bassett, S. S. (1999). Attention: Neuropsychological predictor of competency in Alzheimer's disease. *Journal of Geriatric Psychiatry and Neurology, 12,* 200–205.

Batson, D. C. (1975). Attribution as a mediator of bias in helping. *Journal of Personality and Social Psychology, 32,* 455–466.

Bauer, R. M. (2000). The flexible battery approach to neuropsychological assessment. In R. D. Vanderploeg (Ed.), *Clinician's guide to neuropsychological assessment* (pp. 419–448). Mahwah, NJ: Erlbaum.

Baughman, E. E., & Dahlstrom, W. B. (1968). *Negro and white children: A psychological study in the rural South.* New York: Academic Press.

Bauman, M. K. (1974). Blind and partially sighted. In M. V. Wisland (Ed.), *Psychoeducational diagnosis of exceptional children* (pp. 159–189). Springfield, IL: Charles C Thomas.

Bauman, M. K., & Kropf, C. A. (1979). Psychological tests used with blind and visually handicapped persons. *School Psychology Digest, 8,* 257–270.

Baumeister, A. A., & Muma, J. R. (1975). On defining mental retardation. *Journal of Special Education, 9,* 293–306.

Baumeister, R. F. (1990). Suicide as escape from self. *Psychological Review, 97,* 90–113.

Baumrind, D. (1993). The average expectable environment is not good enough: A response to Scarr. *Child Development, 64,* 1299–1317.

Bautista, D. R. (2004). *Da kine scale: Construction and validation of the Hawaii Local Acculturation Scale.* Unpublished doctoral dissertation, Washington State University.

Bavolek, S. J. (1984). *Handbook for the Adult-Adolescent Parenting Inventory.* Eau Claire, WI: Family Development Associates.

Baxter, J. C., Brock, B., Hill, P. C., & Rozelle, R. M. (1981). Letters of recommendation: A question of value. *Journal of Applied Psychology, 66,* 296–301.

Baydoun, R. B., & Neuman, G. A. (1992). The future of the General Aptitude Test Battery (GATB) for use in public and private testing. *Journal of Business and Psychology, 7,* 81–91.

Bayley, N. (1955). On the growth of intelligence. *American Psychologist, 10,* 805–818.

Bayley, N. (1959). Value and limitations of infant testing. *Children, 5,* 129–133.

Bayley, N. (1969). *Bayley Scales of Infant Development: Birth to Two Years.* New York: Psychological Corporation.

Bayley, N. (1993). *Bayley Scales of Infant Development (2nd Edition) Manual.* San Antonio: Psychological Corporation.

Beard, J. G., & Ragheb, M. G. (1980). Measuring leisure satisfaction. *Journal of Leisure Research, 12,* 20–33.

Beatty, P. C., & Willis, G. B. (2007). Research synthesis: The practice of cognitive interviewing. *Public Opinion Quarterly, 71*(2), 287–311.

Beavers, R. (1985). *Manual of Beavers-Timberlawn Family Evaluation Scale and Family Style Evaluation.* Dallas, TX: Southwest Family Institute.

Beck, A. T., Brown, G., & Steer, R. A. (1989). Prediction of eventual suicide in psychiatric inpatients by clinical ratings of hopelessness. *Journal of Consulting and Clinical Psychology, 57,* 309–310.

Beck, A. T., Rush, A. J., Shaw, B. F., & Emery, G. (1979). *Cognitive therapy for depression.* New York: Guilford.

Beck, A. T., & Steer, R. A. (1993). *Beck Depression Inventory manual.* San Antonio: Psychological Corporation.

Beck, A. T., Steer, R. A., & Brown, G. K. (1996). *Manual for the Beck Depression Inventory* (2nd ed.). San Antonio: Psychological Corporation.

Beck, A. T., & Stein, D. (1961). *Development of a self-concept test.* Unpublished manuscript, University of Pennsylvania School of Medicine, Center for Cognitive Therapy, Philadelphia.

Beck, A. T., Ward, C. H., Mendelson, M., Mock, J., & Erbaugh, J. (1961). An inventory for measuring depression. *Archives of General Psychiatry, 4,* 561–571.

Beck, S. J. (1944). *Rorschach's test: Vol. 1. Basic processes.* New York: Grune & Stratton.

Beck, S. J. (1945). *Rorschach's test: Vol. 2. A variety of personality pictures.* New York: Grune & Stratton.

Beck, S. J. (1952). *Rorschach's test: Vol. 3. Advances in interpretation.* New York: Grune & Stratton.

Beck, S. J. (1960). *The Rorschach experiment.* New York: Grune & Stratton.

Becker, H. A., Needleman, H. L., & Kotelchuck, M. (1978). Child abuse and dentistry: Orificial trauma and its recognition by dentists. *Journal of the American Dental Association, 97*(1), 24–28.

Becker, K. A. (2003). *History of the Stanford-Binet intelligence scales: Content and psychometrics.* (Stanford-Binet Intelligence Scales, Fifth Edition, Assessment Service Bulletin No. 1). Itasca, IL: Riverside.

Beckham, J. C., Crawford, A. L., & Feldman, M. E. (1998). Trail Making Test performance in Vietnam combat veterans with and without posttraumatic stress disorder. *Journal of Traumatic Stress, 11,* 811–819.

Beckmann, J. F. (2006). Superiority: Always and everywhere? On some misconceptions in the validation of dynamic testing. *Educational and Child Psychology, 23*(3), 35–49.

Beebe, S. A., Casey, R., & Pinto-Martin, J. (1993). Association of reported infant crying and maternal parenting stress. *Clinical Pediatrics, 32,* 15–19.

Begault, D. R. (1993). Head-up auditory displays for traffic collision avoidance advisories: A preliminary investigation. *Human Factors, 35,* 707–717.

Beier, E. G., & Sternberg, D. P. (1977). Marital communication. *Journal of Communication, 27,* 92–100.

Beier, M. E., & Ackerman, P. L. (2003). Determinants of health knowledge: An investigation of age, gender, abilities, personality, and interests. *Journal of Personality & Social Psychology, 84,* 439–447.

Bell, N. L., Matthews, T. D., Lassiter, K. S., & Leverett, J. P. (2002). Validity of the Wonderlic Personnel Test as a measure of fluid or crystallized intelligence: Implications for career assessment. *North American Journal of Psychology, 4,* 113–120.

Bellack, A. S., & Hersen, M. (Eds.). (1988). *Behavioral assessment: A practical guide* (3rd ed.). Elmsford, NY: Pergamon.

Bellack, A. S., Morrison, R. L., Mueser, K. T., Wade, J. H., & Sayers, S. L. (1990). Role play for assessing the social competence of psychiatric patients. *Psychological Assessment, 2,* 248–255.

Bellak, L. (1971). *The TAT and CAT in clinical use* (2nd ed.). New York: Grune & Stratton.

Bellak, L., & Bellak, S. (1965). *The CAT-H—A human modification.* Larchmont, NY: C.P.S.

Bellak, L., & Bellak, S. S. (1973). *Senior Apperception Technique.* New York: C.P.S.

Bellak, L., & Bellak, S. S. (1973). Manual for the Senior Apperception Technique (revised 1985). New York: C. P. S.

Bellingrath, S., Weigl, T., & Kudielka, B. M. (2008). Cortisol dysregulation in school teachers in relation to burnout, vital exhaustion, and effort-reward-imbalance. *Biological Psychology, 78*(1), 104–113.

Bellini, S., Akullian, J., & Hopf, A. (2007). Increasing social engagement in young children with autism spectrum disorders using video self-monitoring. *School Psychology Review, 36*(1), 80–90.

Benbow, C. P., & Stanley, J. C. (1996). Inequity in equity: How "equity" can lead to inequity for high-potential students. *Psychology, Public Policy, and Law, 2*, 249–292.

Bender, L. (1938). A visual-motor gestalt test and its clinical use. *American Orthopsychiatric Association Research Monographs,* No. 3.

Bender, L. (1970). The visual-motor gestalt test in the diagnosis of learning disabilities. *Journal of Special Education, 4*, 29–39.

Benedetti, F., Radaelli, D., Bernasconi, A., et al. (2008). Clock genes beyond the clock: CLOCK genotype biases neural correlates of moral valence decision in depressed patients. *Genes, Brain and Behavior, 7*, 20–25.

Benedict, R. H., Schretlen, D., & Bobholz, J. H. (1992). Concurrent validity of three WAIS-R short forms in psychiatric inpatients. *Psychological Assessment, 4*, 322–328.

Benjamin, G. A. H., & Gollan, J. K. (2003*). Family evaluation in custody litigation: Reducing risks of ethical infractions and malpractice.* Washington, DC: APA Books.

Bennett, F., Hughes, A., & Hughes, H. (1979). Assessment techniques for deaf-blind children. *Exceptional Children, 45*, 287–288.

Ben-Porath, Y. S. (1990). Cross-cultural assessment of personality: The case for replicatory factor analysis. In J. N. Butcher & C. D. Spielberger (Eds.), *Advances in personality assessment* (Vol. 8; pp. 1–26). Hillsdale, NJ: Erlbaum.

Ben-Porath, Y. S., Greve, K. W., Bianchini, K. J., & Kaufmann, P. M. (2009). The MMPI-2 Symptom Validity Scale (FBS) Is an Empirically Validated Measure of Overreporting in Personal Injury Litigants and Claimants: Reply to Butcher et al. (2008). *Psychological Injury and Law, 2*(1), 62–85.

Ben-Porath, Y., & Tellegen, A. (2008). *The MMPI-2-RF.* Minneapolis: University of Minnesota Press.

Ben-Porath, Y. S., Tellegen, A., Arbisi, P. A., et al. (2007). *Introducing the MMPI-2-RF.* Presentation handout distributed at the 115th Annual Convention of the American Psychological Association, San Francisco.

Ben-Porath, Y. S., & Waller, N. G. (1992). Five big issues in clinical personality assessment: A rejoinder to Costa and McCrae. *Psychological Assessment, 4*, 23–25.

Benton, A. L. (1994). Neuropsychological assessment. *Annual Review of Psychology, 45*, 1–25.

Berk, R. A. (Ed.). (1982). *Handbook of methods for detecting test bias.* Baltimore: Johns Hopkins University.

Berkowitz, L., & Frodi, A. (1979). Reactions to a child's mistakes as affected by her/his looks and speech. *Social Psychology Quarterly, 42*, 420–425.

Bernardin, H. J. (1978). Effects of rater training on leniency and halo errors in student ratings of instructors. *Journal of Applied Psychology, 63*, 301–308.

Bernhardt, G. R., Cole, D. J., & Ryan, C. W. (1993). Improving career decision making with adults: Use of portfolios. *Journal of Employment Counseling, 30,* 67–72.

Bernstein, L. (1956). The examiner as an inhibiting factor in clinical testing. *Journal of Consulting Psychology, 20,* 287–290.

Berry, D. S., & Hansen, J. S. (1996). Positive affect, negative affect, and social interaction. *Journal of Personality and Social Psychology, 71,* 796–809.

Bersoff, D. N., DeMatteo, D., & Foster, E. E. (2012). Assessment and testing. In S.J. Knapp, M.C. Gottlieb, M.M. Handelsman, & L. D. VandeCreek (Eds.), *APA handbook of ethics in psychology Vol. 2: Practice, teaching, and research* (pp. 45–74). Washington, DC: American Psychological Association.

Besetsny, L. K., Ree, M. J., & Earles, J. A. (1993). Special test for computer programmers? Not needed: The predictive efficiency of the Electronic Data Processing Test for a sample of Air Force recruits. *Educational and Psychological Measurement, 53,* 507–511.

Bhatia, M. S., Verma, S. K., & Murty, O.P. (2006). Suicide notes: Psychological and clinical profile. *International Journal of Psychiatry in Medicine, 36*(2), 163–170.

Bias control. (1992). Stanford Special Report, Number 9. San Antonio: Psychological Corporation/Harcourt Brace Jovanovich.

Bienvenu, M. J., Sr. (1978). *A counselor's guide to accompany a Marital Communication Inventory.* Saluda, NC: Family Life.

Bigler, E. D. (2007). A motion to exclude and the 'fixed' versus 'flexible' battery in 'forensic' neuropsychology: Challenges to the practice of clinical neuropsychology. *Archives of Clinical Neuropsychology, 22,* 45–51.

Bigler, E. D., & Ehrenfurth, J. W. (1981). The continued inappropriate singular use of the Bender Visual Motor Gestalt Test. *Professional Psychology, 12,* 562–569.

Billmire, M. G., & Myers, P. A. (1985). Serious head injury in infants: Accident or abuse? *Pediatrics, 75,* 341–342.

Binet, A., & Henri, V. (1895a). La mémoire des mots. *L'Année Psychologique, 1,* 1–23.

Binet, A., & Henri, V. (1895b). La mémoire des phrases. *L'Année Psychologique, 1,* 24–59.

Binet, A., & Henri, V. (1895c). La psychologie individuelle. *L'Année Psychologique, 2,* 411–465.

Binet, A., & Simon, T. (1905). Méthodes nouvelles pour le diagnostic du niveau intellectuel des anormaux. *L'Année Psychologique, 11,* 191–244.

Binet, A., & Simon, T. (1908). La developpement de l'intelligence chez les enfants [The development of intelligence in children] (E. S. Kite, Trans.). In J. J. Jenkins & D. G. Paterson (reprint Eds.), *Studies in individual differences: The search for intelligence* (pp. 90–96). New York: Appleton-Century-Crofts. (Reprinted in 1961.)

Bipp, T. (2010). What do people want from their jobs? The Big Five, core self-evaluations, and work motivation. *International Journal of Selection and Assessment, 18,* 28–39.

Birch, H. G., & Diller, L. (1959). Rorschach signs of "organicity": A physiological basis for perceptual disturbances. *Journal of Projective Techniques, 23,* 184–197.

Birkeland, S. A., Manson, T. M., Kisamore, J. L., Brannick, M. T., & Smith, M. A. (2006). A meta-analytic investigation of job applicant faking on personality measures. *International Journal of Selection and Assessment, 14*(4), 317–335.

Birney, R. C., Burdick, H., & Teevan, R. C. (1969). *Fear of failure.* New York: Van Nostrand Reinhold.

Birren, J. E. (1968). Increments and decrements in the intellectual status of the aged. *Psychiatric Research Reports, 23,* 207–214.

Birren, J. E., & Schaie, K. W. (1985). *Handbook of psychology of aging* (2nd ed.). New York: Van Nostrand Reinhold.

Bizot, E. B., & Goldman, S. H. (1993). Prediction of satisfactoriness and satisfaction: An 8-year follow up. Special issue: The theory of work adjustment. *Journal of Vocational Behavior, 43,* 19–29.

Black, B., Ayala, F., & Saffran-Brinks, C. (1994). Science and the law in the wake of *Daubert:* A new search for scientific knowledge. *Texas Law Review, 72,* 715–802.

Black, H. (1963). *They shall not pass.* New York: Morrow.

Black, H. C. (1979). *Black's law dictionary* (rev. ed.). St. Paul, MN: West.

Black, M., Schuler, M., & Nair, P. (1993). Prenatal drug exposure: Neurodevelopment outcome and parenting environment. *Journal of Pediatric Psychology, 18,* 605–620.

Blalock, S. J., Devellis, B. M., Holt, K., & Hahn, P. M. (1993). Coping with rheumatoid arthritis: Is one problem the same as another? *Health Education Quarterly, 20,* 119–132.

Blamire, A. M. (2011). The Yale experience in first advancing fMRI. *NeuroImage,* October 18, 2011.

Blanck, P. D., & Berven, H. M. (1999). Evidence of disability after *Daubert. Psychology, Public Policy, and Law, 5,* 16–40.

Blazhenkova, O., & Kozhevnikov, M. (2010). Visual-object ability: A new dimension of non-verbal intelligence. *Cognition, 117*(3), 276–301.

Bloom, A. S., Allard, A. M., Zelko, F. A. J., Brill, W. J., Topinka, C. W., & Pfohl, W. (1988). Differential validity of the K-ABC for lower functioning preschool children versus those of higher ability. *American Journal of Mental Retardation, 93*(3), 273–277.

Blum, G. S. (1950). *The Blacky pictures: A technique for the exploration of personality dynamics.* New York: Psychological Corporation.

Blum, M. L., & Naylor, J. C. (1968). *Industrial psychology: Its theoretical and social foundations* (rev. ed.). New York: Harper & Row.

Blumenthal, S. J., & Kupfer, D. J. (Eds.). (1990). *Suicide over the life cycle: Risk factors, assessment, and treatment of suicidal patients.* Washington, DC: American Psychiatric Press.

Blustein, D. L., & Ellis, M. V. (2000). The cultural context of career assessment. *Journal of Career Assessment, 8,* 379–390.

Board of Professional Affairs, Committee on Professional Practice & Standards, Practice Directorate, American Psychological Association. (1999). Guidelines for psychological evaluations in child protection matters. *American Psychologist, 54,* 586–593.

Boccaccini, M. T., & Brodsky, S. L. (1999). Diagnostic test usage by forensic psychologists in emotional injury cases. *Professional Psychology: Research and Practice, 30,* 253–259.

Bock, R. D., & Jones, L. V. (1968). *The measurement and prediction of judgment and choice.* San Francisco: Holden-Day.

Boer, D. P., Starkey, N. J., & Hodgetts, A. M. (2008). The California Psychological Inventory: 434- and 260-item editions. In G. J. Boyle, G. Matthews, & D. H. Saklofske (Eds.), *The Sage handbook of personality theory and assessment, Vol 2: Personality measurement and testing* (pp. 97–112). Thousand Oaks, CA: Sage.

Bogacki, D. F., & Weiss, K. J. (2007). Termination of parental rights: Focus on defendants. *Journal of Psychiatry & Law, 35*(1), 25–45.

Bombadier, C., & Tugwell, P. (1987). Methodological considerations in functional assessment. *Journal of Rheumatology, 14,* 6–10.

Bond, G. G., Aiken, L. S., & Somerville, S. C. (1992). The health belief model and adolescents with insulin-dependent diabetes mellitus. *Health Psychology, 11,* 190–198.

Bond, M. H., & Forgas, J. P. (1984). Linking person perception to behavior intention across cultures: The role of cultural collectivism. *Journal of Cross-Cultural Psychology, 1,* 185–216.

Bond, R., & Smith, P. B. (1996). Culture and conformity. A meta-analysis of studies using Asch's line judgment task. *Psychological Bulletin, 119,* 111–137.

Boone, D. E. (1991). Item-reduction vs. subtest-reduction short forms on the WAIS-R with psychiatric inpatients. *Journal of Clinical Psychology, 47,* 271–276.

Booth, A., & Edwards, J. (1983). Measuring marital instability. *Journal of Marriage and the Family, 45,* 387–393.

Bordnick, P. S., Traylor, A., Copp, H. L., et al. (2008). Assessing reactivity to virtual reality alcohol based cues. *Addictive Behaviors, 33*(6), 743–756.

Boring, E. G. (1923, June 6). Intelligence as the tests test it. *New Republic,* pp. 35–37.

Boring, E. G. (1950). *A history of experimental psychology* (rev. ed.). New York: Appleton-Century-Crofts.

Borkenau, P., & Liebler, A. (1992). Trait inferences: Sources of validity at zero acquaintance. *Journal of Personality and Social Psychology, 62,* 645–657.

Bornstein, P. H., Hamilton, S. B., & Bornstein, M. T. (1986). Self-monitoring procedures. In A. R. Ciminero, C. S. Calhoun, & H. E. Adams (Eds.), *Handbook of behavioral assessment* (pp. 176–222). New York: Wiley.

Bornstein, R. F. (1998). Interpersonal dependency and physical illness: A meta-analytic review of retrospective and prospective studies. *Journal of Research in Personality, 32,* 480–497.

Bornstein, R. F. (1999). Criterion validity of objective and projective dependency tests: A meta-analytic assessment of behavioral prediction. *Psychological Assessment, 11,* 48–57.

Bornstein, R. F., & Masling, J. M. (Eds.). (2005). *Scoring the Rorschach: Seven validated systems.* Mahwah, NJ: Erlbaum.

Bornstein, R. F., Rossner, S. C., Hill, E. L., & Stepanian, M. L. (1994). Face validity and fakability of objective and projective measures of dependency. *Journal of Personality Assessment, 63,* 363–386.

Borroni, B., Brambati, S.M., Agosti, C., et al. (2007). Evidence of white matter changes on diffusion tensor imaging in frontotemporal dementia. *Archives of Neurology, 64,* 246–251.

Borsbroom, D. (2005). *Measuring the mind: Conceptual issues in contemporary psychometrics.* New York: Cambridge University Press.

Boudreau, J. W. (1988). *Utility analysis for decisions in human resource management* (CAHRS Working Paper No. 88-21). Ithaca, NY: Cornell University, School of Industrial and Labor Relations, Center for Advanced Human Resource Studies.

Bougard, C., Moussay, S., & Davenne, D. (2008). An assessment of the relevance of laboratory and motorcycling tests for investigating time of day and sleep deprivation influences on motorcycling performance. *Accident Analysis & Prevention, 40*(2), 635–643.

Boyle, J. P. (1987). Intelligence, reasoning, and language proficiency. *Modern Language Journal, 71,* 277–288.

Bozeman, D. P., & Perrewe, P. L. (2001). The effect of item content overlap on Organizational Commitment Questionnaire–turnover cognitions relationships. *Journal of Applied Psychology, 86,* 161–173.

Bozikas, V. P., Giazkoulidou, A., Hatzigeorgiadou, M., et al. (2008). Do age and education contribute to performance on the clock drawing test? Normative data for the Greek population. *Journal of Clinical and Experimental Neuropsychology, 30*(2), 1–5.

Bracken, B. A. (1985). A critical review of the Kaufman Assessment Battery for Children (K-ABC). *School Psychology Review, 14,* 21–36.

Bracken, B. A., & Barona, A. (1991). State of the art procedures for translating, validating, and using psychoeducational tests in cross-cultural assessment. *School Psychology International, 12,* 119–132.

Braden, J. P. (1985). *Deafness, deprivation, and IQ.* New York: Plenum.

Braden, J. P. (1990). Do deaf persons have a characteristic psychometric profile on the Wechsler Performance Scales? *Journal of Psychoeducational Assessment, 8,* 518–526.

Braden, J. P. (1992). Intellectual assessment of deaf and hard-of-hearing people: A quantitative and qualitative research synthesis. *School Psychology Review, 21,* 82–84.

Braden, J. P., & Ouzts, S. M. (2007) Review of the Kaufman Assessment Battery for Children, Second Edition. In K. F. Geisinger, R. A. Sipes, J. F. Carlson, & B. S. Plake (Eds.), *The 17th Mental Measurements Yearbook* (pp. 517–520). Lincoln: Buros Institute of Mental Measurements, University of Nebraska.

Bradley, J., & Miller, A. (2010). Widening participation in higher education: Constructions of "going to university." *Educational Psychology in Practice, 26*(4), 401–413.

Bradley, J. P., Nicol, A. A., Charbonneau, D., & Meyer, J. P. (2002). Personality correlates of leadership development in Canadian Forces officer candidates. *Canadian Journal of Behavioural Science, 34,* 92–103.

Bradley-Johnson, S. (1994). *Psychoeducational assessment of students who are visually impaired or blind: Infancy through high school.* Austin: PRO-ED.

Bradley-Johnson, S., & Harris, S. (1990). Best practices in working with students with a visual loss. In A. Thomas & J. Grimes (Eds.), *Best practices in school psychology II* (pp. 871–885). Washington, DC: National Association of School Psychologists.

Brady, N. C., & Halle, J. W. (1997). Functional analysis of communicative behaviors. *Focus on Autism and Other Developmental Disabilities, 12*(2), 95–104.

Braginsky, B. M., Braginsky, D. D., & Ring, K. (1969). *Methods of madness.* New York: Holt, Rinehart & Winston.

Bram, A. D. (2010). The relevance of the Rorschach and patient-examiner relationship in treatment planning and outcome assessment. *Journal of Personality Assessment, 92,* 91–115.

Bram, A. D., & Peebles, M. J. (in preparation). *Person- and treatment-focused psychological testing: A psychodynamic approach.* Washington, DC: APA Books.

Brandt, J., & Rogerson, M. (2011). Preliminary findings from an Internet-based risk assessment. *Alzheimer's & Dementia, 7*(4), e94–100.

Brandy, D. A. (1995). The O'Connor Tweezer Dexterity Test as a screening tool for hiring surgical hair restoration assistants. *American Journal of Cosmetic Surgery, 12*(4), 313–316.

Brannen, M. Y., & Salk, J. E. (2000). Partnering across borders: Negotiating organizational culture in a German-Japanese joint venture. *Human Relations, 53,* 451–487.

Brannigan, G. G., & Brunner, N. A. (2002). *Guide to the qualitative scoring system for the modified version of the Bender-Gestalt test.* Springfield, IL: Charles C Thomas.

Brannigan, G. G., & Decker, S. L. (2003). *Bender Visual-Motor Gestalt Test Second Edition, Examiner's Manual.* Itasca, IL: Riverside.

Brassard, M., et al. (Eds.). (1986). *The psychological maltreatment of children and youth.* Elmsford, NY: Pergamon.

Brauer, B. (1993). Adequacy of a translation of the MMPI into American Sign Language for use with deaf individuals: Linguistic equivalency issues. *Rehabilitation Psychology, 38,* 247–259.

Bray, D. W. (1964). The management progress study. *American Psychologist, 19,* 419–429.

Bray, D. W. (1982). The assessment center and the study of lives. *American Psychologist, 37,* 180–189.

Bresolin, M. J., Jr. (1984). A comparative study of computer administration of the Minnesota Multiphasic Personality Inventory in an inpatient psychiatric setting. *Dissertation Abstracts International, 46,* 295B. (University Microfilms No. 85–06, 377).

Brewer, E. W., & Clippard, L. F. (2002). Burnout and job satisfaction among student support services personnel. *Human Resource Development Quarterly, 13,* 169–186.

Brewer, S. (1987, January 11). A perfect package, yes, but how 'bout the name? *Journal-News* (Rockland County, NY), pp. H-1, H-18.

Bricklin, B. (1984). *The Bricklin Perceptual Scales: Child-Perception-of-Parents-Series.* Furlong, PA: Village.

Bricklin, B., & Halbert, M. H. (2004). Can child custody data be generated scientifically? Part 1. *American Journal of Family Therapy, 32*(2), 119–138.

Bringle, R., Roach, S., Andler, C., & Evenbeck, S. (1979). Measuring the intensity of jealous reactions. *Catalogue of Selected Documents in Psychology, 9,* 23–24.

Brittain, H. L. (1907). A study in imagination. *Pedagogical Seminary, 14,* 137–207.

Brody, D., Serby, M., Etienne, N., & Kalkstein, D. C. (1991). Olfactory identification deficits in HIV infection. *American Journal of Psychiatry, 148,* 248–250.

Brody, M. L., Walsh, B. T., & Devlin, M. J. (1994). Binge eating disorder: Reliability and validity of a new diagnostic category. *Journal of Consulting and Clinical Psychology, 62,* 381–386.

Brody, N. (1972). *Personality: Research and theory.* New York: Academic Press.

Brodzinsky, D. M. (1993). On the use and misuse of psychological testing in child custody evaluations. *Professional Psychology: Research and Practice, 24,* 213–219.

Brogden, H. E. (1946). On the interpretation of the correlation coefficient as a measure of predictive efficiency. *Journal of Educational Psychology, 37,* 65–76.

Brogden, H. E. (1949). When tests pay off. *Personnel Psychology, 2,* 171–183.

Brotemarkle, R. A. (1947). Clinical psychology, 1896–1946. *Journal of Consulting and Clinical Psychology, 11,* 1–4.

"Brother Against Brother," (1997, December 7). CBS, *60 Minutes,* reported by Ed Bradley.

Brotherhood, J. R. (2008). Heat stress and strain in exercise and sport. *Journal of Science and Medicine in Sport, 11*(1), 6–19.

Brown, B. (2007). The utility of standardized tests. *Science, 316*(5832), 1694–1695.

Brown, D. C. (1994). Subgroup norming: Legitimate testing practice or reverse discrimination. *American Psychologist, 49,* 927–928.

Brown, G., Nicassio, P. W., & Wallston, K. A. (1989). Pain coping strategies and depression in rheumatoid arthritis. *Journal of Consulting and Clinical Psychology, 57,* 652–657.

Brown, J. M. (1984). Imagery coping strategies in the treatment of migraine. *Pain, 18,* 157–167.

Brown, R. D. (1972). The relationship of parental perceptions of university life and their characterizations of their college sons and daughters. *Educational and Psychological Measurement, 32,* 365–375.

Brown, R. T., Reynolds, C. R., & Whitaker, J. S. (1999). Bias in mental testing since *Bias in Mental Testing. School Psychology Quarterly, 14,* 208–238.

Brown, S. P., & Peterson, R. A. (1993). Antecedents and consequences of salesperson job satisfaction: Meta-analysis and assessment of causal effects. *Journal of Marketing Research, 30,* 63–77.

Bruce, J. M., Bruce, A. S., & Arnett, P. A. (2010). Response variability is associated with self-reported cognitive fatigue in multiple sclerosis. *Neuropsychology, 24*(1), 77–83.

Bryer, J. B., Martines, K. A., & Dignan, M. A. (1990). Millon Clinical Multiaxial Inventory Alcohol Abuse and Drug Abuse scales and the identification of substance-abuse patients. *Psychological Assessment, 2,* 438–441.

Bucholz, K. K., Cadoret, R., Cloninger, C. R., & Dinwiddie, S. H. (1994). A new, semi-structured psychiatric interview for use in genetic linkage studies: A report on the reliability of the SSAGA. *Journal of Studies on Alcohol, 55,* 149–158.

Buck, J. N. (1948). The H-T-P technique: A qualitative and quantitative scoring manual. *Journal of Clinical Psychology, 4,* 317–396.

Buck, J. N. (1950). *Administration and interpretation of the H-T-P test: Proceedings of the H-T-P workshop at Veterans*

*Administration Hospital, Richmond, Virginia.* Beverly Hills, CA: Western Psychological Services.

Buckner, F., & Firestone, M. (2000). "Where the public peril begins": 25 years after *Tarasoff. Journal of Legal Medicine, 21,* 187–222.

Bucofsky, D. (1971). Any learning skills taught in the high school? *Journal of Reading, 15*(3), 195–198.

Budoff, M. (1967). Learning potential among institutionalized young adult retardates. *American Journal of Mental Deficiency, 72,* 404–411.

Budoff, M. (1987). Measures of assessing learning potential. In C. S. Lidz (Ed.), *Dynamic assessment* (pp. 173–195). New York: Guilford Press.

Bukatman, B. A., Foy, J. L., & De Grazia, E. (1971). What is competency to stand trial? *American Journal of Psychiatry, 127,* 1225–1229.

Bumann, B. (2010). The Future of Neuroimaging in Witness Testimony. *Virtual Mentor: American Medical Association Journal of Ethics, 12,* 873–878.

Burger, J. M., Horita, M., Kinoshita, L., et al. (1997). Effects of time on the norm of reciprocity. *Basic and Applied Social Psychology, 19,* 91–100.

Burgess, A. W., McCausland, M. P., & Wolbert, W. A. (1981, February). Children's drawings as indicators of sexual trauma. *Perspectives in Psychiatric Care, 19,* 50–58.

Burisch, M. (1984). Approaches to personality inventory construction: A comparison of merits. *American Psychologist, 39,* 214–227.

Burke, M. J. (1984). Validity generalization: A review and critique of the correlation model. *Personnel Psychology, 37,* 93–115.

Burke, R. J. (1970). Occupational and life strains, satisfactions, and mental health. *Journal of Business Administration, 1,* 35–41.

Burns, A., Jacoby, R., & Levy, R. (1991). Progression of cognitive impairment in Alzheimer's disease. *Journal of the American Geriatrics Society, 39,* 39–45.

Burns, E. (1998). *Test accommodations for students with disabilities.* Springfield, IL: Charles C Thomas.

Burns, R. C., & Kaufman, S. H. (1970). *Kinetic Family Drawings (K-F-D): An introduction to understanding through kinetic drawings.* New York: Brunner/Mazel.

Burns, R. C., & Kaufman, S. H. (1972). *Actions, styles, and symbols in Kinetic Family Drawings (K-F-D).* New York: Brunner/Mazel.

Buros, O. K. (1938). *The 1938 mental measurements yearbook.* New Brunswick, NJ: Rutgers University Press.

Buros, O. K. (1968). The story behind the mental measurements yearbooks. *Measurement and Evaluation in Guidance, 1*(2), 86–95.

Burwen, L. S., & Campbell, D. T. (1957). The generality of attitudes toward authority and nonauthority figures. *Journal of Abnormal and Social Psychology, 54,* 24–31.

Bushard, P., & Howard, D. A. (Eds.). (1994). *Resource guide for custody evaluators: A handbook for parenting evaluations.* Madison, WI: Association for Family and Conciliation Courts.

Bushman, B. J., & Cantor, J. (2003). Media ratings for violence and sex: Implications for policymakers and parents. *American Psychologist, 58,* 130–141.

Bushman, B. J., & Wells, G. L. (1998). Trait aggressiveness and hockey penalties: Predicting hot tempers on the ice. *Journal of Applied Psychology, 83,* 969–974.

Butcher, J. N. (1987). The use of computers in psychological assessment: An overview of practices and issues. In J. N. Butcher (Ed.), *Computerized psychological assessment: A practitioner's guide* (pp. 3–14). New York: Basic Books.

Butcher, J. N. (1990). *MMPI-2 in psychological treatment.* New York: Oxford University Press.

Butcher, J. N. (1994). Psychological assessment by computer: Potential gains and problems to avoid. *Psychiatric Annals, 24,* 20–24.

Butcher, J. N. (2000). Revising psychological tests: Lessons learned from the revision of the MMPI. *Psychological Assessment, 12,* 263–271.

Butcher, J. N. (2003). Discontinuities, side steps, and finding a proper place: An autobiographical account. *Journal of Personality Assessment, 80,* 223–236.

Butcher, J. N., Gass C. S., Cumella, E., Kally, Z., & Williams, C. (2008). Potential for Bias in MMPI-2 Assessments Using the Fake Bad Scale (FBS). *Psychological Injury and Law, 1*(3), 191–209.

Butcher, J. N., & Han, K. (1995). Development of an MMPI-2 scale to assess the presentation of self in a superlative manner: The *S* Scale. In J. N. Butcher & C. D. Spielberger (Eds.), *Advances in personality assessment* (Vol. 10; pp. 25–50). Hillsdale, NJ: Erlbaum.

Butcher, J. N., Perry, J. N., & Atlis, M. M. (2000). Validity and utility of computer-based test interpretation. *Psychological Assessment, 12,* 6–18.

Butcher, J. N., Williams, C. L., Graham, J. R., et al. (1992). *Minnesota Multiphasic Personality Inventory-Adolescent (MMPI-A): Manual for administration, scoring, and interpretation.* Minneapolis: University of Minnesota Press.

Butters, N., Wolfe, J., Martone, M., et al. (1985). Memory disorders associated with Huntington's disease: Verbal recall, verbal recognition and procedural memory. *Neuropsychologia, 23,* 729–743.

Büttner, G., & Hasselhorn, M. (2011). Learning disabilities: Debates on definitions, causes, subtypes, and responses. *International Journal of Disability, Development and Education, 58*(1), 75–87.

Byrne, D. (1974). *An introduction to personality* (2nd ed.). Englewood Cliffs, NJ: Prentice-Hall.

Byrne, G.J., & Bradley, F. (2007). Culture's influence on leadership efficiency: How personal and national cultures affect leadership style. *Journal of Business Research, 60*(2), 168–175.

Byrnes, M. M., & Spitz, H. H. (1977). Performance of retarded adolescents and non-retarded children on the Tower of Hanoi problem. *American Journal of Mental Deficiency, 81,* 561–569.

Cai, C.-H., & Shen, H.-Y. (2007). Self-concept reflected by Rorschach test in private and public college students. *Chinese Mental Health Journal, 21*(8), 539–543.

Cain, L. F., Levine, S., & Elsey, F. F. (1963). *Cain-Levine Social Competency Scale.* Palo Alto, CA: Consulting Psychologists Press.

Calhoon, M. B., Fuchs, L. S., & Hamlett, C. L. (2000). Effects of computer-based test accommodations on mathematics performance assessments for secondary students with learning disabilities. *Learning Disability Quarterly, 23,* 271–282.

Callahan, C. A., Hojat, M., Veloski, J., Erdmann, J. B., & Gonnella, J. S. (2011). The predictive validity of three versions of the MCAT in relation to performance in medical school, residency, and licensing examinations: A longitudinal study of 36 classes of Jefferson Medical College. *Academic Medicine, 85,* 980–987.

Callahan, J. (1994). The ethics of assisted suicide. *Health and Social Work, 19,* 237–244.

Callero, P. L. (1992). The meaning of self-in-role: A modified measure of role-identity. *Social Forces, 71,* 485–501.

Camara, W. J., & Schneider, D. L. (1994). Integrity tests: Facts and unresolved issues. *American Psychologist, 49,* 112–119.

Camilli, G., & Shepard, L. A. (1985). A computer program to aid the detection of biased test items. *Educational & Psychological Measurement, 45,* 595–600.

Campbell, D. P. (1971). *Handbook for the Strong Vocational Interest Blank.* Palo Alto, CA: Stanford University Press.

Campbell, D. P. (1972). The practical problems of revising an established psychological test. In J. N. Butcher (Ed.), *Objective personality assessment: Changing perspectives* (pp. 117–130). New York: Academic Press.

Campbell, D. T., & Fiske, D. W. (1959). Convergent and discriminant validation by the multitrait-multimethod matrix. *Psychological Bulletin, 56,* 81–105.

Campbell, W. H., & Rohrbaugh, R. M. (2006). *The biopsychosocial formulation manual: A guide for mental health professionals.* New York: Taylor & Francis.

Campos, L. P. (1989). Adverse impact, unfairness, and bias in the psychological screening of Hispanic peace officers. *Hispanic Journal of Behavioral Sciences, 11,* 122–135.

Canivez, G. L. (2008). Orthogonal higher-order factor structure of the Stanford-Binet Intelligence Scales for children and adolescents. *School Psychology Quarterly, 23,* 533–541.

Canivez, G. L., Konold, T. R., Collins, J. M., & Wilson, G. (2009). Construct validity of the Wechsler Abbreviated Scale of Intelligence and Wide Range Intelligence Test. *School Psychology Quarterly, 24,* 252–265.

Cannon-Bowers, J. A., Salas, E., Blickensderfer, E., & Bowers, C. A. (1998). The impact of cross-training and workload on team functioning: A replication and extension of initial findings. *Human Factors, 40,* 92–101.

Caplan, L. J., & Schooler, C. (2003). The roles of fatalism, self-confidence, and intellectual resources in the disablement process in older adults. *Psychology and Aging, 18,* 551–561.

Capraro, R. M., & Capraro, M. M. (2002). Myers-Briggs Type Indicator score reliability across studies: A meta-analytic reliability generalization study. *Educational & Psychological Measurement, 62,* 590–602.

Capretz, L. F. (2003). Personality types in software engineering. *International Journal of Human-Computer Studies, 58,* 207–214.

Care, E. (1996). The structure of interests related to college course destinations. *Journal of Career Assessment, 4,* 77–89.

Carey, M. P., Faulstich, M. E., Gresham, F. M., Ruggerio, L., & Enyart, P. (1987). Children's Depression Inventory: Construct and discriminant validity across clinical and non-referred (control) populations. *Journal of Consulting and Clinical Psychology, 55,* 755–761.

Carey, N. B. (1994). Computer predictors of mechanical job performance: Marine Corps findings. *Military Psychology, 6,* 1–30.

Carmichael, L. (1927). A further study of the development of behavior in vertebrates experimentally removed from the influence of external stimulation. *Psychological Review, 34,* 34–47.

Carnevale, J. J., Inbar, Y., & Lerner, J. S. (2011). Individual differences in need for cognition and decision-making competence among leaders. *Personality and Individual Differences, 51,* 274–278.

Carpenter, W. T., Gold, M. J., Lahti, A. C., et al. (2000). Decisional capacity for informed consent in schizophrenia research. *Archives of General Psychiatry, 57,* 533–538.

Carroll, J. B. (1985, May). Domains of cognitive ability. Symposium: Current theories and findings on cognitive abilities. Los Angeles: AAAS.

Carroll, J. B. (1993). *Human cognitive abilities: A survey of factor-analytic studies.* Cambridge: Cambridge University Press.

Carroll, J. B. (1997). The three-stratum theory of cognitive abilities. In D. P. Flanagan et al. (Eds.), *Contemporary intellectual assessment: Theories, tests, and issues* (pp. 122–130). New York: Guilford.

Carroll, K. M. (1998). *A cognitive-behavioral approach: Treating cocaine addiction.* NIH Publication No. 98-4308. Rockville, MD: National Institute on Drug Abuse.

Carroll, K. M., Nich, C., Frankforter, T. L., & Bisighini, R. M. (1999). Do patients change in the ways we intend? Assessing acquisition of coping skills among cocaine-dependent patients. *Psychological Assessment, 11,* 77–85.

Carstairs, J., & Myors, B. (2009). Internet testing: A natural experiment reveals test score inflation on a high-stakes, unproctored cognitive test. *Computers in Human Behavior, 25,* 738–742.

Carter, B. L., & Tiffany, S. T. (1999). Meta-analysis of cue reactivity in addiction research. *Addiction, 94,* 327–340.

Caruso, J. C. (2000). Reliability generalization of the NEO personality scales. *Educational and Psychological Measurement, 60,* 236–254.

Carver, R. P. (1968/1969). Designing an aural aptitude test for Negroes: An experiment that failed. *College Board Review, 70,* 10–14.

Carver, R. P. (1969). Use of a recently developed listening comprehension test to investigate the effect of disadvantagement upon verbal proficiency. *American Educational Research Journal, 6,* 263–270.

Cascio, W. F. (1987). *Applied psychology in personnel management* (3rd ed.). Englewood Cliffs, NJ: Prentice-Hall.

Cascio, W. F. (1994, Winter). Executive and managerial assessment: Value for the money? *Consulting Psychology Journal, 8,* 42–48.

Cascio, W. F. (2000). *Costing human resources: The financial impact of behavior in organizations* (4th ed). Boston: Kent.

Cascio, W. F., Outtz, J., Zedeck, S., & Goldstein, I. L. (1991). Statistical implications of six methods of test score use in personnel selection. *Personnel Psychology, 4,* 233–264.

Cascio, W. F., Outtz, J., Zedeck, S., & Goldstein, I. L. (1995). Statistical implications of six methods of test score use in personnel selection. *Human Performance, 8*(3), 133–164. (Reprinted article)

Cascio, W. F., & Ramos, R. A. (1986). Development and application of a new method for assessing job performance in behavioral/economic terms. *Journal of Applied Psychology, 71,* 20–28.

Cash, T. F., Melnyk, S. E., & Hrabosky, J. I. (2004). The assessment of body image investment: An extensive revision of the Appearance Schemas Inventory. *International Journal of Eating Disorders, 35*(3), 305–316.

Caspi, A., Begg, D., Dickson, N., et al. (1997). Personality differences predict health-risk behaviors in young adulthood: Evidence from a longitudinal study. *Journal of Personality and Social Psychology, 73,* 1052–1063.

Caspi, A., Elder, G., & Bem, D. J. (1987). Moving against the world: Life-course patterns of explosive children. *Developmental Psychology, 23,* 308–313.

Cassel, R. N. (1958). *The leadership q-sort test: A test of leadership values.* Murfreesboro, TN: Psychometric Affiliates.

Castro, V. S. (2003). *Acculturation and psychological adaptation.* Westport, CT: Praeger.

Catalano, R., Novaco, R., & McConnell, W. (1997). A model of the net effect of job loss on violence. *Journal of Personality and Social Psychology, 72,* 1440–1447.

Cates, J. A., & Lapham, R. F. (1991). Personality assessment of the prelingual, profoundly deaf child or adolescent. *Journal of Personality Assessment, 56,* 118–129.

Cattell, H. E. P. (1996). The original big five: A historical perspective. *European Review of Applied Psychology, 46,* 5–14.

Cattell, J. M. (1887). Experiments on the association of ideas. *Mind, 12,* 68–74.

Cattell, J. M., & Bryant, S. (1889). Mental association investigated by experiment. *Mind, 14*, 230–250.

Cattell, P. (1940). *Cattell Infant Intelligence Scale.* New York: Psychological Corporation.

Cattell, R. B. (1940). A culture free intelligence test, Part I. *Journal of Educational Psychology, 31*, 161–179.

Cattell, R. B. (1941). Some theoretical issues in adult intelligence testing. *Psychological Bulletin, 38*, 592.

Cattell, R. B. (1946). *The description and measurement of personality.* New York: Harcourt, Brace & World.

Cattell, R. B. (1947). Confirmation and clarification of the primary personality factors. *Psychometrika, 12*, 197–220.

Cattell, R. B. (1948a). The primary personality factors in the realm of objective tests. *Journal of Personality, 16*, 459–487.

Cattell, R. B. (1948b). The primary personality factors in women compared with those in men. *British Journal of Psychology, Statistical Section, 1*, 114–130.

Cattell, R. B. (1950). *Personality: A systematic theoretical and factual study.* New York: McGraw-Hill.

Cattell, R. B. (1957). *Personality and motivation, structure and measurement.* Yonkers: World Book.

Cattell, R. B. (1965). *The scientific analysis of personality.* Baltimore: Penguin.

Cattell, R. B. (1971). *Abilities: Their structure, growth, and action.* Boston: Houghton Mifflin.

Cattell, R. B., Cattell, A. K. S., & Cattell, H. E. P. (1993). *16 PF, Fifth Edition.* Champaign, IL: Institute for Personality and Ability Testing.

Cattell, R. B., & Horn, J. L. (1978). A check on the theory of fluid and crystallized intelligence with description of new subtest design. *Journal of Educational Measurement, 15*, 139–164.

Cattell, R. B., & Krug, S. E. (1986). The number of factors in the 16 PF: A review of the evidence with special emphasis on methodological problems. *Educational and Psychological Measurement, 46*, 509–522.

Caught, K., Shadur, M. A., & Rodwell, J. J. (2000). The measurement artifact in the Organizational Commitment Questionnaire. *Psychological Reports, 87*, 777–788.

Ceci, S. J., Ross, D. F., & Toglia, M. P. (1987). Suggestibility of children's memory: Psycholegal implications. *Journal of Experimental Psychology, 116*, 38–49.

Celis, W., III. (1994, December 16). Computer admissions test found to be ripe for abuse. *New York Times*, pp. A1, A32.

Cerney, M. S. (1984). One last response to the Rorschach test: A second chance to reveal oneself. *Journal of Personality Assessment, 48*, 338–344.

Chamorro-Premuzic, T., & Furnham, A. (2006). Intellectual competence and the intelligent personality: A third way in differential psychology. *Review of General Psychology, 10*(3), 251–267.

Champagne, J. E. (1969). Job recruitment of the unskilled. *Personnel Journal, 48*, 259–268.

Chan, D. W. (2007). Gender differences in spatial ability: Relationship to spatial experience among Chinese gifted students in Hong Kong. *Roeper Review, 29*(4), 277–282.

Chan, K.-Y., Drasgow, F., & Sawin, L. L. (1999). What is the shelf life of a test? The effect of time on the psychometrics of a cognitive ability test battery. *Journal of Applied Psychology, 84*, 610–619.

Chan, S. S., Lyness, J. M., & Conwell, Y. (2007). Do cerebrovascular risk factors confer risk for suicide in later life? A case control study. *American Journal of Geriatric Psychiatry, 15*(6), 541–544.

Chance, N. A. (1965). Acculturation, self-identification, and personality adjustment. *American Anthropologist, 67*, 372–393.

Chaney, E. F., O'Leary, M. R., & Marlatt, G. A. (1978). Skill training with problem drinkers. *Journal of Consulting and Clinical Psychology, 46*, 1092–1104.

Chang, L., Connelly, B. S., & Geeza, A. A. (2011). Separating method factors and higher order traits of the big five: A meta-analytic multitrait-multimethod approach. *Journal of Personality and Social Psychology*, October 3, 2011, advance online publication with no pagination specified. doi: 10.1037/a))2555.

Chang, S.-R., Plake, B. S., Kramer, G. A. & Lien, S-M. (2011). Development and application of detection indices for measuring guessing behaviors and test-taking effort in computerized adaptive testing. *Educational and Psychological Measurement, 71*(3), 437–459.

Chantler, L., Pelco, L., & Mertin, P. (1993). The psychological evaluation of child sexual abuse using the Louisville Behavior Checklist and human figure drawing. *Child Abuse and Neglect, 17*, 271–279.

Chaplin, W. F., John, O. P., & Goldberg, L. R. (1988). Conceptions of state and traits: Dimensional attributes with ideals as prototypes. *Journal of Personality and Social Psychology, 54*, 541–557.

Chapman, J. C. (1921). *Trade tests.* New York: Holt.

Chapman, L., & Chapman, J. (1967). Genesis of popular but erroneous psychodiagnostic observations. *Journal of Abnormal Psychology, 72*, 193–204.

Chapman, R. M., Mapstone, M., Porsteinsson, A. P., et al. (2010). Diagnosis of Alzheimer's disease using neuropsychological testing improved by multivariate analyses. *Journal of Clinical and Experimental Neuropsychology, 32*(8), 793–808.

Chappin, S. R., & Brook, J. S. (2001). The influence of generational status and psychosocial variables on marijuana use among Black and Puerto Rican adolescents. *Hispanic Journal of Behavioral Sciences, 23*, 22–36.

Chartrand, J. M., Borgen, F. H., Betz, N. E., & Donnay, D. (2002). Using the Strong Interest Inventory and the Skills Confidence Inventory to explain career goals. *Journal of Career Assessment, 10*, 169–189.

Chase, D. (2005). Underlying factor structures of the Stanford-Binet Intelligence Scales–Fifth Edition. Ph.D. diss., Drexel University, idea.library.drexel.edu/bitstream/1860/863/1/Chase Danielle.pdf.

Chase, J. (1986). Application of assessment techniques to the totally blind. In P. Lazarus & S. Storchart (Eds.), *Psycho-educational evaluation of children and adolescents with low incidence handicaps.* New York: Grune & Stratton.

Chase, S., & Schlink, F. J. (1927). *Your money's worth: A study in the waste of the consumer's dollar.* New York: Macmillan.

Chawarski, M. C., Fiellin, D. A., O'Connor, P. G., et al. (2007). Utility of sweat patch testing for drug use monitoring in outpatient treatment for opiate dependence. *Journal of Substance Abuse Treatment, 33*(4), 411–415.

Chen, Y., Nettles, M. E., & Chen, S.-W. (2009). Rethinking dependent personality disorder: Comparing different human relatedness in cultural contexts. *Journal of Nervous and Mental Disease, 197*, 793–800.

Chess, S., & Thomas, A. (1973). Temperament in the normal infant. In J. C. Westman (Ed.), *Individual differences in children.* New York: Wiley.

Cheung, F. M., & Lau, B. (1982). Situational variations of help-seeking behavior among Chinese patients. *Comprehensive Psychiatry, 23*, 252–262.

Chin, J. L. (2003). Multicultural competencies in managed health care. In D. B. Pope-David, H. L. K. Coleman, W. M. Liu, & R. L. Toporek (Eds.), *Handbook of multicultural competencies: In counseling & psychology* (pp. 347–364). Thousand Oaks, CA: Sage.

Chinman, M. J., Allende, M., Weingarten, R., et al. (1999). On the road to collaborative treatment planning: Consumer and provider perspectives. *Journal of Behavioral Health Services & Research, 26*, 211–218.

Chinoy, E. (1967). *Society: An introduction to sociology.* New York: Random House.

Chira-Chavala, T., & Yoo, S. M. (1994). Potential safety benefits on intelligence cruise control systems. *Accident Analysis & Prevention, 26,* 135–146.

Cho, H., & LaRose, R. (1999). Privacy issues in Internet surveys. *Social Science Computer Review, 17,* 421–434.

Christensen, A. L. (1975). *Luria's neuropsychological investigation.* New York: Spectrum.

Christensen, K. M., & Delgado, G. L. (1993). *Multicultural issues in deafness.* White Plains, NY: Longman.

Christiansen, A. J., Weibe, J. S., Smith, T. W., & Turner, C. W. (1994). Predictors of survival among hemodialysis patients: Effects of perceived family support. *Health Psychology, 13,* 521–525.

Church, A. T., & Burke, P. J. (1994). Exploratory and confirmatory tests of the Big Five and Tellegen's three- and four-dimensional models. *Journal of Personality and Social Psychology, 66,* 93–114.

Cianci, H. R. (2008). The Myers-Briggs Type Indicator and self-efficacy in substance abuse treatment planning. *Dissertation Abstracts International: Section B. Sciences and Engineering, 68*(10-B), 6955.

Cicchetti, D., & Carlson, V. (Eds.). (1989). *Child maltreatment: Theory and research on the causes and consequences of child abuse and neglect.* New York: Cambridge University Press.

Citrin, L. B., & Greenwald, A. G. (1998, April). *Measuring implicit cognition: Psychologists' and entomologists' attitudes toward insects.* Paper presented at the annual meeting of the Midwestern Psychological Association, Chicago.

Cizek, G. J. (2003). Review of the Woodcock-Johnson III. In B. S. Plake, J. C. Impara, & R. A. Spies (Eds.), *The fifteenth mental measurements yearbook.* Lincoln: Buros Institute of Mental Measurements, University of Nebraska.

Cizek, G. J., & Bunch, M. B. (2007). *Standard setting: A guide to establishing and evaluating performance standards on tests.* Thousand Oaks, CA: Sage.

Clarizio, H. F. (1989). *Assessment and treatment of depression in children and adolescents.* Brandon, VT: Clinical Psychological Publishing.

Clark, B. (1979). *Growing up gifted.* Columbus, OH: Merrill.

Clark, B. (1988). *Growing up gifted* (3rd ed.). Columbus, OH: Merrill.

Clark, L. A. (1999). Introduction to the special section on the concept of disorder. *Journal of Abnormal Psychology, 108,* 371–373.

Cleckley, H. (1976). *The mask of sanity* (5th ed.). St. Louis: Mosby.

Clements, C. B. (1999). Psychology, attitude shifts, and prison growth. *American Psychologist, 54,* 785–786.

Clift, R. J., Rajlic, G., & Gretton, H. M. (2009). Discriminative and predictive validity of the penile plethysmograph in adolescent sex offenders. *Sexual Abuse: Journal of Research and Treatment, 21*(3), 335–362.

Cloninger, C. R., Przybeck, T. R., & Svrakis, D. M. (1991). The Tridimensional Personality Questionnaire: U.S. normative data. *Psychological Reports, 69,* 1047–1057.

Coalson, D. L., & Raiford, S. E. (2008). *WAIS-IV: Technical and interpretive manual.* San Antonio: NCS Pearson.

*Code of Fair Testing Practices in Education.* (2004). Washington, DC: Joint Committee on Testing Practices.

Coggins, M. H., Pynchon, M. R., & Dvoskin, J. A. (1998). Integrating research and practice in federal law enforcement: Secret Service applications of behavioral science expertise to protect the president. *Behavioral Sciences and the Law, 16,* 51–70.

Cohen, B. M., Moses, J. L., & Byham, W. C. (1977). *The validity of assessment centers: A literature review* (rev. ed.; monograph no. 2). Pittsburgh: Development Dimensions.

Cohen, F., & Lazarus, R. S. (1973). Active coping processes, coping dispositions, and recovery from surgery. *Psychosomatic Medicine, 35,* 375–389.

Cohen, J. (1952a). A factor-analytically based rationale for the Wechsler-Bellevue. *Journal of Consulting Psychology, 16,* 272–277.

Cohen, J. (1952b). Factors underlying Wechsler-Bellevue performance of three neuropsychiatric groups. *Journal of Abnormal and School Psychology, 47,* 359–364.

Cohen, J. (1957a). A factor-analytically based rationale for the Wechsler Adult Intelligence Scale. *Journal of Consulting Psychology, 21,* 451–457.

Cohen, J. (1957b). The factorial structure of the WAIS between early adulthood and old age. *Journal of Consulting Psychology, 21,* 283–290.

Cohen, J., Marecek, J., & Gillham, J. (2006). Is three a crowd? Clients, clinicians, and managed care. *American Journal of Orthopsychiatry, 76*(2), 251–259.

Cohen, O., Fischgrund, J., & Redding, R. (1990). Deaf children from ethnic, linguistic, and racial minority backgrounds: An overview. *American Annals of the Deaf, 135,* 67–73.

Cohen, R. J. (1977). Socially reinforced obsessing: A reply. *Journal of Consulting and Clinical Psychology, 45,* 1166–1171.

Cohen, R. J. (1979). *Malpractice: A guide for mental health professionals.* New York: Free Press.

Cohen, R. J. (1985). Computer-enhanced qualitative research. *Journal of Advertising Research, 25*(3), 48–52.

Cohen, R. J. (1987). Overview of emerging evaluative and diagnostic methods technologies. In *Proceedings of the fourth annual Advertising Research Foundation workshop: Broadening the horizons of copy research.* New York: Advertising Research Foundation.

Cohen, R. J. (1994). *Psychology & adjustment: Values, culture, and change.* Boston: Allyn & Bacon.

Cohen, R. J. (1999a). *Exercises in psychological testing and assessment.* Mountain View, CA: Mayfield.

Cohen, R. J. (1999b). What qualitative research can be. *Psychology & Marketing, 16,* 351–368.

Cohen, R. J. (2001). *Discussion of Organizational Culture (DOC).* Jamaica, NY: Author.

Cohen, R. J. (2005). *Exercises in psychological testing and assessment.* San Francisco: McGraw-Hill.

Cohen, R. J., Becker, R. E., & Teevan, R. C. (1975). Perceived somatic reaction to stress and hostile press. *Psychological Reports, 37,* 676–678.

Cohen, R. J., & Houston, D. R. (1975). Fear of failure and rigidity in problem solving. *Perceptual and Motor Skills, 40,* 930.

Cohen, R. J., Montague, P., Nathanson, L. S., & Swerdlik, M. E. (1988). *Psychological testing: An introduction to tests and measurement.* Mountain View, CA: Mayfield.

Cohen, R. J., & Parker, C. (1974). Fear of failure and death. *Psychological Reports, 34,* 54.

Cohen, R. J., & Smith, F. J. (1976). Socially reinforced obsessing: Etiology of a disorder in a Christian Scientist. *Journal of Consulting and Clinical Psychology, 44,* 142–144.

Cohen, R. J., & Teevan, R. C. (1974). Fear of failure and impression management: An exploratory study. *Psychological Reports, 35,* 1332.

Cohen, R. J., & Teevan, R. C. (1975). Philosophies of human nature and hostile press. *Psychological Reports, 37,* 460–462.

Cohen, S., Nermelstein, R., Karmack, T., & Hoberman, H. (1985). Measuring the functional components of social support. In I. G. Sarason & B. Sarason (Eds.),

*Social support: Theory, research, and practice* (pp. 73–94). Dordrecht, Netherlands: Martinus Nijhoff.

Cole, S. T., & Hunter, M. (1971). Pattern analysis of WISC scores achieved by culturally disadvantaged children. *Psychological Reports, 20,* 191–194.

Coleman, M. R., & Johnsen, S. K. (2011). RtI online resources. In M. R. Coleman & S. K. Johnsen (Eds.), *RtI for gifted students: A CEC-TAG educational resource* (pp. 129–134). Waco, TX: Prufrock Press.

Collier, C. (2011). *Seven steps to separating difference from disability.* Thousand Oaks, CA: Corwin Press.

Collins, J. K., Jupp, J. J., Maberly, G. F., et al. (1987). An exploratory study of the intellectual functioning of neurological and myxoedematous cretins in China. *Australia & New Zealand Journal of Developmental Disabilities, 13,* 13–20.

Collins, L. M. (1996). Is reliability obsolete? A commentary on "Are simple gain scores obsolete?" *Applied Psychological Measurement, 20,* 289–292.

Collins, M. (1998, Spring). Great expectations: What students have to say about the process and practice of launching a career. *Journal of Career Planning and Placement,* 41–47.

Colom, R., Flores-Mendoza, C., & Abad, F. J. (2007). Generational changes on the Draw-A-Man Test: A comparison of Brazilian Urban and Rural Children Tested in 1930, 2002, and 2004. *Journal of Biosocial Science, 39,* 79–89.

Comer, D. R. (1993). Workplace drug testing reconsidered. *Journal of Managerial Issues, 5,* 517–531.

Commons, M. (1985, April). How novelty produces continuity in cognitive development within a domain and accounts for unequal development across domains. Toronto: SRCD.

Compton, D. M., Bachman, L. D., Brand, D., & Avet, T. L. (2000). Age-associated changes in cognitive function in highly educated adults: Emerging myths and realities. *International Journal of Geriatric Psychiatry, 15,* 75–85.

Cone, J. D. (1977). The relevance of reliability and validity for behavioral assessment. *Behavior Therapy, 8,* 411–426.

Cone, J. D. (1981). Psychometric considerations. In M. Hersen & A. S. Bellack (Eds.), *Behavioral assessment: A practical handbook* (2nd ed.). New York: Pergamon.

Cone, J. D. (1986). Idiographic, nomothetic, and related perspectives in behavioral assessment. In R. O. Nelson & S. C. Hayes (Eds.), *Conceptual foundations of behavioral assessment.* New York: Guilford.

Cone, J. D. (1987). Behavioral assessment: Some things old, some things new, some things borrowed? *Behavioral Assessment, 9,* 1–4.

Cone, J. D. (1999). Introduction to the special section on self-monitoring: A major assessment method in clinical psychology. *Psychological Assessment, 11,* 411–414.

Conger, A. J. (1985). Kappa reliabilities for continuing behaviors and events. *Educational and Psychological Measurement, 45,* 861–868.

Connolly, A. J. (2007). *KeyMath 3 Diagnostic Assessment.* San Antonio: Pearson Assessments.

Connolly, J. (1976). Life events before myocardial infarction. *Journal of Human Stress, 3,* 3–17.

Constantinou, M., Ashendorf, L., & McCaffrey, R. J. (2005). Effects of a third party observer during neuropsychological assessment: When the observer is a video camera. *Journal of Forensic Neuropsychology, 4*(2), 39–47.

Conte, J. M., & Gintoft, J. N. (2005). Polychronicity, big five personality dimensions, and sales performance. *Human Performance, 18*(4), 427–444.

Conte, J. M., & Jacobs, R. R. (2003). Validity evidence linking polychronicity and Big Five personality dimensions to absence, lateness, and supervisory performance ratings. *Human Performance, 16,* 107–129.

Conti, R. P. (2007). The concealment of psychopathology on the Rorschach in criminal forensic investigations. *Dissertation Abstracts International: Section B. Sciences and Engineering, 68* (6-B), 4125.

Cooke, N. J., Salas, E., Cannon-Bowers, J. A., & Stout, R. J. (2000). Measuring team knowledge. *Human Factors, 42,* 151–173.

Cooper, A. (1981). A basic TAT set for adolescent males. *Journal of Clinical Psychology, 37*(2), 411–414.

Copas, J. B., & Tarling, R. (1986). Some methodological issues in making predictions. In A. Blumstein et al. (Eds.), *Criminal careers and "career criminals"* (pp. 291–313). Washington, DC: National Academy.

Copersino, M., Meade, C., Bigelow, G., & Brooner, R. (2010). Measurement of self-reported HIV risk behaviors in injection drug users: Comparison of standard versus timeline follow-back administration procedures. *Journal of Substance Abuse Treatment, 38,* 60–65.

Corish, C. D., Richard, B., & Brown, S. (1989). Missed medication doses in rheumatoid arthritis patients: Intentional and unintentional reasons. *Arthritis Care and Research, 2,* 3–9.

Cornell, D. G. (1985). External validation of the Personality Inventory for Children—Comment on Lachar, Gdowski, and Snyder. *Journal of Consulting and Clinical Psychology, 53,* 273–274.

Cortes, D. E., Deren, S., Andia, J., Colon, H., Robles, R., & Kang, S. (2003). The use of the Puerto Rican biculturality scale with Puerto Rican drug users in New York and Puerto Rico. *Journal of Psychoactive Drugs, 35,* 197–207.

Cortina, J. M. (1993). What is coefficient alpha? An examination of theory and applications. *Journal of Applied Psychology, 78,* 98–104.

Corwyn, R. F., & Benda, B. B. (2000). Religiosity and church attendance: The effects on use of "hard drugs" controlling for sociodemographic and theoretical factors. *International Journal for the Psychology of Religion, 10,* 241–258.

Costa, P. T., Jr., & McCrae, R. R. (1985). *The NEO Personality Inventory manual.* Odessa, FL: Psychological Assessment Resources.

Costa, P. T., Jr., & McCrae, R. R. (1986). Major contributions to personality psychology. In S. Modgil & C. Modgil (Eds.), *Hans Eysenck: Consensus and controversy* (pp. 63–72, 86, 87). Barcombe Lewes, Sussex, England: Falmer.

Costa, P. T., Jr., & McCrae, R. R. (1987). On the need for longitudinal evidence and multiple measures in behavior-genetics studies of adult personality. *Behavioral and Brain Sciences, 10,* 22–23.

Costa, P. T., Jr., & McCrae, R. R. (1992a). Four ways five factors are basic. *Personality and Individual Differences, 13,* 653–665.

Costa, P. T., Jr., & McCrae, R. R. (1992b). Reply to Eysenck. *Personality and Individual Differences, 13,* 861–865.

Costa, P. T., Jr., & McCrae, R. R. (1992c). *Revised NEO Personality Inventory (NEO-PI-R) and NEO Five-Factor Inventory (NEO-FFI) professional manual.* Odessa, FL: Psychological Assessment Resources.

Costa, P. T., Jr., & McCrae, R. R. (1997). Stability and change in personality assessment: The Revised NEO Personality Inventory in the year 2000. *Journal of Personality Assessment, 68,* 86–94.

Cote, J. A., McCullough, J., & Reilly, M. (1985). Effects of unexpected situations on behavior-intention differences: A garbology analysis. *Journal of Consumer Research, 12,* 188–194.

Cotton, P. (1992). Women's health initiative leads way as research begins to fill gender gaps. *Journal of the American Medical Association, 267*(4), 469–470, 473.

Coupe, J. J. (2006). A clinical approach to deductive behavioral profiling. *Dissertation Abstracts International: Section B. Sciences and Engineering, 66*(9-B), 5081.

Cox, J. (2006). Review of profiling violent crimes: An investigative tool. *Journal of Investigative Psychology and Offender Profiling, 3*(2), 134–137.

Coyne, I., & Bartram, D. (2006). Design and development of the ITC guidelines on computer-based and internet-delivered testing. *International Journal of Testing, 6*(2), 133–142.

Coyne, J. C. (1976). The place of informed consent in ethical dilemmas. *Journal of Consulting and Clinical Psychology, 44,* 1015–1017.

Cramer, P. (1991). *The development of defense mechanisms: Theory, research, and assessment.* New York: Springer-Verlag.

Cramer, P. (1996). *Storytelling, narrative, and the Thematic Apperception Test.* New York: Guilford.

Crèvecoeur, M. G. St. J. de (1951). What is an American letter? In H. S. Commager (Ed.), *Living ideas in America.* New York: Harper. (Originally published in *Letters from an American farmer,* 1762.)

Crick, N. R. (1997). Engagement in gender normative versus nonnormative forms of aggression: Links to social-psychological adjustment. *Developmental Psychology, 33,* 610–617.

Crick, N. R., Bigbee, M. A., & Howes, C. (1996). Gender differences in children's normative beliefs about aggression: How do I hurt thee? Let me count the ways. *Child Development, 67,* 1003–1014.

Crocker, L., Llabre, M., & Miller, M. D. (1988). The generalizability of content validity ratings. *Journal of Educational Measurement, 25,* 287–299.

Cronbach, L. J. (1949). Statistical methods applied to Rorschach scores: A review. *Psychological Bulletin, 46,* 393–429.

Cronbach, L. J. (1951). Coefficient alpha and the internal structure of tests. *Psychometrika, 16,* 297–334.

Cronbach, L. J. (1970). *Essentials of psychological testing* (3rd ed.). New York: Harper & Row.

Cronbach, L. J. (1975). Five decades of public controversy over mental testing. *American Psychologist, 30,* 1–13.

Cronbach, L. J. (1984). *Essentials of psychological testing* (4th ed.). New York: Harper & Row.

Cronbach, L. J., & Gleser, G. C. (1957). *Psychological tests and personnel decisions.* Champaign, IL: University of Illinois.

Cronbach, L. J., & Gleser, G. C. (1965). *Psychological tests and personnel decisions* (2nd ed.). Urbana: University of Illinois.

Cronbach, L. J., Gleser, G. C., Nanda, H., & Rajaratnam, N. (1972). *The dependability of behavioral measurement: Theory of generalizability for scores and profiles.* New York: Wiley.

Crosbie, J., Pérusse, D., Barr, C. L., & Schachar, R. J. (2008). Validating psychiatric endophenotypes: Inhibitory control and attention deficit hyperactivity disorder. *Neuroscience and Biobehavioral Reviews, 32,* 40–55.

Crosby, F. J., Iyer, A., Clayton, S., & Downing, R. A. (2003). Affirmative action: Psychological data and the policy debates. *American Psychologist, 58,* 93–115.

Cross, T. L., Coleman, L. J., & Stewart, R. A. (1993). The social cognition of gifted adolescents: An exploration of the stigma of the giftedness paradigm. *Roeper Review, 16,* 37–40.

Cross, T. L., Coleman, L. J., & Terhaar-Yonkers, M. (1991). The social cognition of gifted adolescents in schools: Managing the stigma of giftedness. *Journal for the Education of the Gifted, 15,* 44–55.

Crowne, D. P., & Marlowe, D. (1964). *The approval motive: Studies in evaluative dependence.* New York: Wiley.

Crundall, D. E., Underwood, G., & Chapman, P. R. (1998). How much do drivers see? The effects of demand on visual search strategies in novice and experienced drivers. In G. Underwood (Ed.), *Eye guidance in reading and scene perception* (pp. 395–417). Oxford, England: Elsevier.

Cuéllar, I., Arnold, B., & Maldonado, R. (1995). Acculturation Rating Scale for Mexican Americans–II: A revision of the original ARSMA scale. *Hispanic Journal of Behavioral Sciences, 17*(3), 275–304.

Cuéllar, I., Harris, I. C., & Jasso, R. (1980). An acculturation scale for Mexican American normal and clinical populations. *Hispanic Journal of Behavioral Science, 2,* 199–217.

Cundick, B. P. (1976). Measures of intelligence on Southwest Indian students. *Journal of Social Psychology, 81,* 151–156.

Cunningham, M. R. (1988). What do you do when you're happy or blue? Mood, expectancies, and behavioral interests. *Motivation and Emotion, 12,* 309–331.

Cureton, E. E. (1957). The upper and lower twenty-seven percent rule. *Psychometrika, 22,* 293–296.

Cushman, P., & Guilford, P. (2000). Will managed care change our way of being? *American Psychologist, 55,* 985–996.

Dahlstrom, W. G. (1995). Pigeons, people, and pigeon holes. *Journal of Personality Assessment, 64,* 2–20.

Dahlstrom, W. G., & Dahlstrom, L. E. (Eds.). (1980). *Basic readings on the MMPI: A new selection on personality measurement.* Minneapolis: University of Minnesota.

Dahlstrom, W. G., & Welsh, G. S. (1960). *An MMPI handbook: A guide to use in clinical practice and research.* Minneapolis: University of Minnesota.

Dahlstrom, W. G., Welsh, G. S., & Dahlstrom, L. E. (1972). *An MMPI handbook: Vol. 1. Clinical interpretation.* Minneapolis: University of Minnesota.

Daigneault, S., Braun, C. M. J., & Whitaker, H. A. (1992). Early effects of normal aging on perseverative and non-perseverative prefrontal measures. *Developmental Neuropsychology, 8,* 99–114.

Daley, C. E., & Onwuegbuzie, A. J. (2011). Race and intelligence. In Sternberg, R. J., & Kaufman, S. B. (Eds.), *The Cambridge Handbook of Intelligence* (pp. 293–307). New York: Cambridge University Press.

D'Amato, A., & Zijlstra, F. R. H. (2008). Psychological climate and individual factors as antecedents of work outcomes. *European Journal of Work and Organizational Psychology, 7*(1), 33–54.

Dana, J., & Thomas, R. (2006). In defense of clinical judgment . . . and mechanical prediction. *Journal of Behavioral Decision Making, 19*(5), 413–428.

Dana, R. H. (1982). *A human science model for personality assessment with projective techniques.* Springfield, IL: Charles C Thomas.

Dana, R. H. (1995). Culturally competent MMPI assessment of Hispanic populations. *Hispanic Journal of Behavioral Sciences, 17,* 305–319.

Dana, R. H. (1998). Problems with managed mental health care for multicultural populations. *Psychological Reports, 83*(1), 283–294.

Dana, R. H., Aguilar-Kitibutr, A., Diaz-Vivar, N., & Vetter, H. (2002). A teaching model for multicultural assessment: Psychological report contents and cultural competence. *Journal of Personality, 79,* 207–215.

Dana, R. H., & Whatley, P. R. (1991). When does a difference make a difference? MMPI scores and African-Americans. *Journal of Clinical Psychology, 47,* 400–406.

Daneman, M., & Carpenter, P. A. (1980). Individual differences in working memory and reading. *Journal of Verbal Learning and Verbal Behavior, 19,* 450–466.

Danford, G. S., & Steinfeld, E. (1999). Measuring the influences of physical environments on the behaviors of people with impairments. In E. Steinfeld & G. S. Danford (Eds.), *Enabling environments: Measuring the impact of environment on disability and rehabilitation* (pp. 111–137). New York: Kluwer Academic/Plenum.

Daniels, K. (2000). Measures of five aspects of affective well-being at work. *Human Relations, 53,* 275–294.

Darwin, C. (1859). *On the origin of species by means of natural selection.* London: Murray.

Das, J. P. (1972). Patterns of cognitive ability in nonretarded and retarded children. *American Journal of Mental Deficiency, 77,* 6–12.

Das, J. P., Kirby, J., & Jarman, R. F. (1975). Simultaneous and successive synthesis: An alternative model for cognitive abilities. *Psychological Bulletin, 82,* 87–103.

Dattilio, F. M. (2006). Equivocal death psychological autopsies in cases of criminal homicide. *American Journal of Forensic Psychology, 24*(1) 5–22.

Daubert v. Merrell Dow Pharmaceuticals, 113 S. Ct. 2786 (1993).

Davids, A., & Murray, H. A. (1955). Preliminary appraisal of an auditory projective technique for studying personality and cognition. *American Journal of Orthopsychiatry, 25,* 543–554.

Davidson, H. A. (1949). Malingered psychosis. *Bulletin of the Menninger Clinic, 13,* 157–163.

Davidson, T. N., Bowden, L., & Tholen, D. (1979). Social support as a moderator of burn rehabilitation. *Archives of Physical Medicine and Rehabilitation, 60,* 556.

Davies, M., Stankov, L., & Roberts, R. D. (1998). Emotional intelligence: In search of an elusive construct. *Journal of Personality and Social Psychology, 75,* 989–1015.

Davies, P. L., & Gavin, W. J. (1994). Comparison of individual and group/consultation treatment methods for preschool children with developmental delays. *American Journal of Occupational Therapy, 48,* 155–161.

Davis, G. A. (1989). Testing for creative potential. *Contemporary Educational Psychology, 14,* 257–274.

Davis, J. M., & Broitman, J. (2011). *Nonverbal learning disabilities in children: Bridging the gap between science and practice.* New York: Springer Science and Business Media.

Davison, G. C., Vogel, R. S., & Coffman, S. G. (1997). Think-aloud approaches to cognitive assessment and the articulated thoughts in simulated situations paradigm. *Journal of Consulting and Clinical Psychology, 65,* 950–958.

Dawes, R. M., Faust, D., & Meehl, P. E. (1989, March 31). Clinical versus actuarial judgment. *Science, 243,* 1668–1674.

Day, D. V., & Silverman, S. B. (1989). Personality and job performance: Evidence of incremental validity. *Personnel Psychology, 42,* 25–36.

Dazzi, C., & Pedrabissi, L. (2009). Graphology and personality: An empirical study on validity of handwriting analysis. *Psychological Reports, 105*(3, Pt. 2), 1255–1268.

Deary, I. J., Irwing, P., Der, G., & Bates, T. (2007). Brother-sister differences in the *g* factor in intelligence: Analysis of full, opposite-sex siblings from the NLSY1979. *Intelligence, 35*(5), 451–456.

Deary, I. J., Johnson, W., & Houlihan, L. M. (2009). Genetic foundations of human intelligence. *Human genetics, 126*(1), 215–232.

De Champlain, A. F. (2010). A primer on classical test theory and item response theory for assessments in medical education. *Medical Education, 44*(1), 109–117.

Decker, J. T., Bailey, T. L., & Westergaard, N. (2002). Burnout among childcare workers. *Residential Treatment for Children & Youth, 19*(4), 61–77.

Decker, S. L. (2008). Measuring growth and decline in visual-motor processes with the Bender-Gestalt, Second Edition. *Journal of Psychoeducational Assessment, 26*(1), 3–15.

De Corte, W., & Lievens, F. (2005). The risk of adverse impact in selections based on a test with known effect size. *Educational and Psychological Measurement, 65*(5), 643–664.

Delahunty, R. J. (1988). Perspectives on within-group scoring. *Journal of Vocational Behavior, 33,* 463–477.

Del Giudice, M. J. (2010a). What might this be? Rediscovering the Rorschach as a tool for personnel selection in organizations. *Journal of Personality Assessment, 92*(1), 78–89.

Del Giudice, M. J. (2010b). Reply to comment on "What might this be? Rediscovering the Rorschach as a tool for personnel selection in organizations" (Del Giudice, 2010). *Journal of Personality Assessment, 92*(6), 613–615.

Dellis, D. C., Kramer, J. H., Kaplan, E., & Ober, B. A. (2000). *The California Verbal Learning Test–II.* Lutz, FL: PAR.

Deloria, D. J. (1985). Review of the Miller Assessment for Preschoolers. In J. V. Mitchell, Jr. (Ed.), *The ninth mental measurements yearbook.* Lincoln: Buros Institute of Mental Measurements, University of Nebraska.

DeMars, C. E., & Wise, S. L. (2010). Can differential rapid-guessing behavior lead to differential item functioning. *International Journal of Testing, 10*(3), 207–229.

DeMulder, E. K., Denham, S., Schmidt, M., & Mitchell, J. (2000). Q-sort assessment of attachment security during the preschool years: Links from home to school. *Developmental Psychology, 36,* 274–282.

Dennis, W., & Dennis, M. G. (1940). The effect of cradling practice upon the onset of walking in Hopi children. *Journal of Genetic Psychology, 56,* 77–86.

Denton, W. H. (2007). Relational diagnosis: An essential component of biopsychosocial assessment for DSM-V. *American Journal of Psychiatry, 164,* 1146–1147.

Department of Health, Education, and Welfare. (1977a). Nondiscrimination on basis of handicap: Implementation of Section 504 of the Rehabilitation Act of 1973. *Federal Register, 42*(86), 22676–22702.

Department of Health, Education, and Welfare. (1977b). Education of Handicapped Children: Implementation of Part B of the Education of the Handicapped Act. *Federal Register, 42*(163), 42474–42518.

DePaulo, B. M. (1994). Spotting lies: Can humans learn to do better? *Current Directions in Psychological Science, 3,* 83–86.

Derue, D. S., Nahrgang, J. D., Wellman, N., & Humphrey, S. E. (2011). Trait and behavioral theories of leadership: An integration and meta-analytic test of their relative validity. *Personnel Psychology, 64,* 7–52.

Desrochers, M. N., Hile, M. G., & Williams-Mosely, T. L. (1997). Survey of functional assessment procedures used with individuals who display mental retardation and severe problem behaviors. *American Journal on Mental Retardation, 101,* 535–546.

DeVito, E. E., Worhunsky, P. D., Carroll, K. M., et al. (2011). A preliminary study of the neural effects of behavioral therapy for substance use disorders. *Drug and Alcohol Dependence, 122* (3), 228–235.

Devlin, B., Daniels, M., & Roeder, K. (1997). The heritability of IQ. *Nature, 388,* 468–471.

Diamond, B. L. (1980). Inherent problems in the use of pretrial hypnosis on a prospective witness. *California Law Review, 68,* 313–349.

Dickson, C. R. (1975). Role of assessment in behavior therapy. In P. McReynolds (Ed.), *Advances in psychological assessment* (Vol. 3). San Francisco: Jossey-Bass.

Diebold, M. H., Curtis, W. S., & DuBose, R. F. (1978). Developmental scales versus observational measures for deaf-blind children. *Exceptional Children, 44,* 275–278.

Dietz, P. E., Matthews, D. B., Van Duyne, C., et al. (1991). Threatening and otherwise inappropriate letters to Hollywood celebrities. *Journal of Forensic Sciences, 36,* 185–209.

Dimock, P. H., & Cormier, P. (1991). The effects of format differences and computer experience on performance and anxiety on a computer-administered test. *Measurement and Evaluation in Counseling and Development, 24,* 119–126.

Dion, K. K. (1979). Physical attractiveness and evaluation of children's transgressions. *Journal of Personality and Social Psychology, 24,* 207–213.

Dipboye, R. L. (1992). *Selection interviews: Process perspectives.* Cincinnati: South-Western Publishing.

DiRienzo, C., Das, J., Synn, W., Kitts, J., & McGrath, K. (2010). The relationship between MBTI and academic performance: A study across academic disciplines. *Journal of Psychological Type, 70*(5), 53–66.

DiStefano, C. & Dombrowski, S. C. (2006). Investigating the theoretical structure of the Stanford-Binet, Fifth Edition. *Journal of Psychoeducational Assessment, 24,* 123–136.

Diven, K. (1937). Certain determinants in the conditioning of anxiety reactions. *Journal of Psychology, 3,* 291–308.

Dixon, M., Wang, S., Calvin, J., et al. (2002). The panel interview: A review of empirical research and guidelines for practice. *Public Personnel Management, 31,* 397–428.

Dohrenwend, B. P., & Shrout, P. E. (1985). Hassles in the conceptualization and measurement of life stresses variables. *American Psychologist, 40,* 780–785.

Dohrenwend, B. P., Shrout, P. E., Egri, G., & Mendelsohn, F. S. (1980). Non-specific psychological distress and other dimensions of psychopathology. *Archives of General Psychiatry, 37,* 1229–1236.

Doll, E. A. (1917). A brief Binet-Simon scale. *Psychological Clinic, 11,* 197–211, 254–261.

Doll, E. A. (1953). *Measurement of social competence: A manual for the Vineland Social Maturity Scale.* Circle Pines, MN: American Guidance Service.

Dollinger, S. J. (2011). "Standardized minds" or individuality? Admissions tests and creativity revisited. *Psychology of Aesthetics, Creativity, and the Arts, 5*(4), 329–341.

Dolnick, E. (1993). Deafness as culture. *Atlantic, 272*(3), 37–53.

Donahue, E. M., Robins, R. W., Roberts, B. W., & John, O. P. (1993). The divided self: Concurrent and longitudinal effects of psychological adjustment and social roles on self-concept differentiation. *Journal of Personality and Social Psychology, 64,* 834–846.

Donald, A. (2001). The Wal-Marting of American psychiatry: An ethnography of psychiatric practice in the late 20th century. *Culture, Medicine, and Psychiatry, 25*(4), 427–439.

Donders, J. (1992). Validity of the Kaufman Assessment Battery for Children when employed with children with traumatic brain injury. *Journal of Clinical Psychology, 48,* 225–230.

Donohue, B., Silver, N. C., Dickens, Y., et al. (2007). Development and initial psychometric evaluation of the Sport Interference Checklist. *Behavior Modification, 31*(6), 937–957.

Dosajh, N. L. (1996). Projective techniques with particular reference to inkblot tests. *Journal of Projective Psychology and Mental Health, 3,* 59–68.

Doty, R. L., Shaman, P., & Dann, M. (1984). Development of the University of Pennsylvania Smell Identification Test: A standard microencapsulated test of olfactory dysfunction. *Physiological Behavior, 32,* 489–502.

Dougherty, T. M., & Haith, M. M. (1997). Infant expectations and reaction time as predictors of childhood speed of processing and IQ. *Developmental Psychology, 33,* 146–155.

Douglas, C. (1993). *Translate this darkness: The life of Christiana Morgan.* New York: Simon & Schuster.

Draguns, J. G. (1984). Assessing mental health and disorder across cultures. In P. Pedersen, N. Sartorius, & A. J. Marsella (Eds.), *Mental health services: The cross-cultural context* (pp. 31–57). Beverly Hills, CA: Sage.

Drasgow, F., & Olson-Buchanan, J. B. (Eds.). (1999). *Innovations in computerized assessment.* Mahwah, NJ: Erlbaum.

Dreger, R. M., & Miller, K. S. (1960). Comparative studies of Negroes and Whites in the U.S. *Psychological Bulletin, 51,* 361–402.

Drinkwater, M. J. (1976). Psychological evaluation of visually handicapped children. *Massachusetts School Psychologists Association Newsletter, 6.*

Drotar, D., Olness, K., & Wiznitzer, M., et al. (1999). Neuro-developmental outcomes of Ugandan infants with HIV infection: An application of growth curve analysis. *Health Psychology, 18,* 114–121.

DuBois, P. H. (1966). A test-dominated society: China 1115 B.C.E.–1905 A.D In A. Anastasi (Ed.), *Testing problems in perspective* (pp. 29–36). Washington, DC: American Council on Education.

DuBois, P. H. (1970). *A history of psychological testing.* Boston: Allyn & Bacon.

Ducharme, F., Levesque, L., Gendron, M., & Legault, A. (2001). Development process and qualitative evaluation of a program to promote the mental health of family caregivers. *Clinical Nursing Research, 10,* 182–201.

Duchek, J. M., Hunt, L., Ball, K., et al. (1998). Attention and driving performance in Alzheimer's disease. *Journal of Gerontology: Series B: Psychological Science & Social Sciences, 53B*(2), 130–141.

Duclos, C. W. (1999). Factors associated with alcohol, drug, and mental health service utilization among a sample of American Indian adolescent detainees. *Dissertation Abstracts International, Section B: The Sciences & Engineering, 40*(4-B), 1524.

Dudycha, G. J. (1936). An objective study of punctuality in relation to personality and achievement. *Archives of Psychology, 204,* 1–319.

Duff, K., & Fisher, J. M. (2005). Ethical dilemmas with third party observers. *Journal of Forensic Neuropsychology, 4*(2), 65–82.

Dugdale, R. (1877). *The Jukes: A study in crime, pauperism, disease, and heredity.* New York: Putnam.

Dumont, R., & Willis, J. (2001). Use of the Tellegen & Briggs formula to determine the Dumont–Willis indexes (DWI–I & DWI–II) for the WISC–IV. http://alpha.fdu.edu/psychology/.

Duncker, K. (1945). On problem solving. *Psychological Monographs, 5,* 1–13.

Dunham, R. B., Grube, J. A., & Castaneda, M. B. (1994). Organizational commitment: The utility of an integrative definition. *Journal of Applied Psychology, 79,* 370–380.

Dunn, L. B., Lindamer, L. A., Palmer, B. W., et al. (2002). Improving understanding of research consent in middle-aged and elderly patients with psychotic disorders. *American Journal of Geriatric Psychology, 10,* 142–150.

Dunn, L. M., & Dunn, L. M. (1997). *Examiner's manual for the PPVT-III, Peabody Picture Vocabulary Test, Third Edition.* Circle Pines, MN: American Guidance Service.

Duvall, E. D. (2011). No secrets to conceal: Dynamic assessment and a state mandated, standardized 3rd grade reading test for children with learning disabilities. *Dissertation Abstracts International Section A: Humanities and Social Sciences.* 2011, p. 2401.

Dwairy, M. (2004). Dynamic approach to learning disability assessment: DLD test. *Dyslexia: An International Journal of Research and Practice, 10*(1), 1–23.

Dwyer, C. A. (1996). Cut scores and testing: Statistics, judgment, truth, and error. *Psychological Assessment, 8,* 360–362.

Dykes, L. (1986). The whiplash shaken infant syndrome: What has been learned? *Child Abuse and Neglect, 10,* 211.

Dywan, J., & Bowers, K. (1983). The use of hypnosis to enhance recall. *Science, 22,* 184–185.

Earles, J. A., & Ree, M. J. (1992). The predictive validity of the ASVAB for training grades. *Educational and Psychological Measurement, 52,* 721–725.

Early, P. C., Gibson, C. B., & Chen, C. C. (1999). "How did I do?" versus "How did we do?": Cultural contrasts of performance feedback use and self-efficacy. *Journal of Cross-Cultural Psychology, 30,* 594–619.

Eccles, J. S. (1987). Gender roles and women's achievement-related decisions. *Psychology of Women Quarterly, 11,* 135–171.

Edwards, A. L. (1953). *Edwards Personal Preference Schedule.* New York: Psychological Corporation.

Edwards, A. L. (1957a). *The social desirability variable in personality assessment and research.* New York: Dryden.

Edwards, A. L. (1957b). *Techniques of attitude scale construction.* New York: Appleton-Century-Crofts.

Edwards, A. L. (1966). Relationship between probability of endorsement and social desirability scale value for a set of 2,824 personality statements. *Journal of Applied Psychology, 50,* 238–239.

Edwards, A. L., & Walsh, J. A. (1964). Response sets in standard and experimental personality scales. *American Education Research Journal, 1,* 52–60.

Edwards, C. P., & Kumru, A. (1999). Culturally sensitive assessment. *Child and Adolescent Psychiatric Clinics of North America, 8,* 409–424.

Eichler, R. M. (1951). A comparison of the Rorschach and Behn-Rorschach inkblot tests. *Journal of Consulting Psychology, 15,* 185–189.

Einarsdóttir, S., & Rounds, J. (2009). Gender bias and construct validity in vocational interest measurement: Differential item functioning in the Strong Interest Inventory. *Journal of Vocational Behavior, 74*(3), 295–307.

Eisenberg, N., Guthrie, I. K., Cumberland, A., et al. (2002). Prosocial development in early adulthood: A longitudinal study. *Journal of Personality & Social Psychology, 82,* 993–1006.

Eisman, E. J., Dies, R. R., Finn, S. E., et al. (2000). Problems and limitations in using psychological assessment in the contemporary health care delivery system. *Professional Psychology: Research and Practice, 31,* 131–140.

Elder, G. H., Van Nguyen, T., & Caspi, A. (1985). Linking family hardship to children's lives. *Child Development, 56,* 361–375.

Eldredge, N. (1993). Culturally affirmative counseling with American Indians who are deaf. *Journal of the American Deafness and Rehabilitation Association, 26,* 1–18.

Elksnin, L. K., & Elksnin, N. (1993). A review of picture interest inventories: Implications for vocational assessment of students with disabilities. *Journal of Psychoeducational Assessment, 11,* 323–336.

Ellerstein, N. S. (Ed.). (1981). *Child abuse and neglect: A medical reference.* New York: Wiley.

Elliot, H., Glass, L., & Evans, J. (Eds.). (1987). *Mental health assessment of deaf clients: A practical manual.* Boston: Little, Brown.

Elliott, A. N., O'Donohue, W. T., & Nickerson, M. A. (1993). The use of sexually anatomically detailed dolls in the assessment of sexual abuse. *Clinical Psychology Review, 13,* 207–221.

Elliott, C. D. (1990a). *The Differential Ability Scales.* San Antonio: Psychological Corporation.

Elliott, C. D. (1990b). *Technical handbook: The Differential Ability Scales.* San Antonio: Psychological Corporation.

Elliott, R. (2011). Utilising evidence-based leadership theories in coaching for leadership development: Towards a comprehensive integrating conceptual framework. *International Coaching Psychology Review, 6,* 46–70.

Elliott, S. N. (1988). Acceptability of behavioral treatments in educational settings. In J. C. Witt, S. N. Elliott, & F. M. Greshma (Eds.), *The handbook of behavior therapy education* (pp. 121–150). New York: Plenum.

Elliott, S. N., Katochwill, T. R., & McKevitt, B. C. (2001). Experimental analysis of the effects of testing accommodations on the scores of students with and without disabilities. *Journal of School Psychology, 39,* 3–24.

Elliott, T. R., & Carroll, M. N. (1997). *Issues in psychological assessment for rehabilitation services.* Paper presented at the annual convention of the American Psychological Association, August, Chicago.

Embretson, S. E. (1996). The new rules of measurement. *Psychological Assessment, 8,* 341–349.

Endicott, J., & Spitzer, R. L. (1978). A diagnostic interview: The Schedule for Affective Disorders and Schizophrenia. *Archives of General Psychiatry, 35,* 837–844.

Engin, A., Wallbrown, F., & Brown, D. (1976). The dimensions of reading attitude for children in the intermediate grades. *Psychology in the Schools, 13*(3), 309–316.

Epstein, J. L., & McPartland, J. M. (1978). *The Quality of School Life Scale administration and technical manual.* Boston: Houghton Mifflin.

Epstein, N., Baldwin, L., & Bishop, S. (1983). The McMaster Family Assessment Device. *Journal of Marital and Family Therapy, 9,* 171–180.

Erdberg, P., & Weiner, I. B. (2007). John E. Exner Jr. (1928–2006). *American Psychologist, 62*(1), 54.

Erdelyi, M. H. (1974). A new look at the new look: Perceptual defense and vigilance. *Psychological Review, 81,* 1–25.

Erman, A. (1971). *Life in ancient Egypt.* New York: Dover.

Espinosa, M. P., & Gardeazabal, J. (2010). Optimal correction for guessing in multiple-choice tests. *Journal of Mathematical Psychology, 54*(5), 415–425.

Etkind, A. M. (1994). More on L. S. Vygotsky: Forgotten texts and undiscovered contexts. *Journal of Russian & East European Psychology, 32*(6), 6–34.

Evan, W. M., & Miller, J. R. (1969). Differential effects of response bias of computer vs. conventional administration of a social science questionnaire. *Behavioral Science, 14,* 216–227.

Evans, J. D., et al. (2000). Cross-cultural applications of the Halstead-Reitan batteries. In E. Fletcher-Janzen et al. (Eds.), *Handbook of cross-cultural neuropsychology* (pp. 287–303). New York: Kluwer Academic/Plenum.

Evans, M. (1978). Unbiased assessment of locally low incidence handicapped children. In *IRRC practitioners talk to practitioners.* Springfield, IL: Illinois Regional Resource Center.

Evers, W., Tomic, W., & Brouwers, A. (2002). Aggressive behavior and burnout among staff of homes for the elderly. *International Journal of Mental Health Nursing, 11,* 2–9.

Ewing, C. P., and McCann, J.T. (2006). *Minds on trial: Great cases in law and psychology.* New York: Oxford University Press.

Exner, J. E., Jr. (1962). A comparison of human figure drawings of psychoneurotics, character disturbances, normals, and subjects experiencing experimentally induced fears. *Journal of Projective Techniques, 26,* 292–317.

Exner, J. E., Jr. (1969). *The Rorschach systems.* New York: Grune & Stratton.

Exner, J. E., Jr. (1974). *The Rorschach: A comprehensive system.* New York: Wiley.

Exner, J. E., Jr. (1978). *The Rorschach: A comprehensive system: Vol. 2. Current research and advanced interpretations.* New York: Wiley-Interscience.

Exner, J. E., Jr. (1983). Rorschach assessment. In I. B. Weiner (Ed.), *Methods in clinical psychology* (2nd ed.). New York: Wiley.

Exner, J. E., Jr. (1986). *The Rorschach: A comprehensive system: Vol. 1. Basic foundations* (2nd ed.). New York: Wiley.

Exner, J. E., Jr. (1989). Searching for projection in the Rorschach. *Journal of Personality Assessment, 53,* 520–536.

Exner, J. E., Jr. (1990). *Workbook for the comprehensive system* (3rd ed.). Asheville, NC: Rorschach Workshops.

Exner, J. E., Jr. (1991). *The Rorschach: A comprehensive system: Vol. 2. Interpretation* (2nd ed.). New York: Wiley.

Exner, J. E., Jr. (1993). *The Rorschach: A comprehensive system: Vol. 1. Basic foundations* (3rd ed.). New York: Wiley.

Exner, J. E., Jr. (1993). *The Rorschach: A comprehensive system: Vol. 2. Interpretations.* New York: Wiley.

Exner, J. E., Jr. (1997). Critical bits and the Rorschach response process. *Journal of Personality Assessment, 67,* 464–477.

Exner, J. E., Jr. (2003). *The Rorschach: A Comprehensive system: Vol. 1. Basic foundations* (4th ed.). Hoboken, NJ: Wiley.

Exner, J. E., Jr. (2007). A new U.S. adult nonpatient sample. *Journal of Personality Assessment, 89* (Suppl. 1), S154–S158.

Exner, J. E., Jr., & Weiner, I. B. (1982). *The Rorschach: A comprehensive system: Vol. 3. Assessment of children and adolescents.* New York: Wiley.

Exner, J. E., Jr., & Weiner, I. B. (1995). *The Rorschach: A comprehensive system: Vol. 3. Assessment of children and adolescents* (2nd ed.). New York: Wiley.

Eyde, L. D., Kowal, D. M., & Fishburne, F. J., Jr. (1990). The validity of computer-based test interpretations of the MMPI. In S. Wise & T. B. Gutkin (Eds.), *The computer as adjunct to the decision-making process.* Lincoln: Buros Institute of Mental Measurements, University of Nebraska.

Eyde, L. D., Moreland, K. L., Robertson, G. J., Primoff, E. S., & Most, R. B. (1988). Test user qualifications: A data-based approach to promoting good test use. In *Issues in Scientific Psychology: Report of the Test User Qualifications Working Group of the Joint Committee on Testing Practices.* Washington, DC: American Psychological Association.

Eyman, J. R., & Eyman, S. K. (1990). Suicide risk and assessment instruments. In P. Cimbolic & D. A. Jobes (Eds.), *Youth suicide: Issues, assessment, and intervention* (pp. 9–32). Springfield, IL: Charles C Thomas.

Eysenck, H. J. (1961). The effects of psychotherapy. In H. J. Eysenck (Ed.), *Handbook of abnormal psychology: An experimental approach* (pp. 697–725). New York: Basic Books.

Eysenck, H. J. (1967). Intelligence assessment: A theoretical and experimental approach. *British Journal of Educational Psychology, 37,* 81–98.

Eysenck, H. J. (1985). Can personality study ever be scientific? *Journal of Social Behavior and Personality, 1,* 3–19.

Eysenck, H. J. (1991). Dimensions of personality: 16, 5, or 3?—Criteria for a taxonomic paradigm. *Personality and Individual Differences, 12,* 773–790.

Fahrenkopf, A. M., Sectish, T. C., Barger, L. K., et al. (2008). Rates of medication errors among depressed and burnt out residents: Prospective cohort study. *British Medical Journal, 336,* 488.

Fahs, R. L. (2004). Response bias on the Rorschach: Identifying impression management and self-deception positivity. *Dissertation Abstracts International: Section B. Sciences and Engineering, 65* (5-B), 2621.

Faigman, D. L. (1995). The evidentiary status of social science under *Daubert:* Is it "scientific," "technical," or "other" knowledge? *Psychology, Public Policy, and Law, 1,* 960–979.

Faller, K. C. (1988). *Child sexual abuse.* New York: Columbia University.

Farrell, A. D. (1986). The microcomputer as a tool for behavioral assessment. *Behavior Therapist, 1,* 16–17.

Farrell, J. N., & McDaniel, M. A. (2001). The stability of validity coefficients over time: Ackerman's (1988) model and the General Aptitude Test Battery. *Journal of Applied Psychology, 86,* 60–79.

Farrell, S. F. (1998). Alcohol dependence and the price of alcoholic *beverages. Dissertation Abstracts International: Section B: The Sciences and Engineering, 59*(4-B), 1606.

Farrenkopf, T., & Bryan, J. (1999). Psychological consultation under Oregon's 1994 Death With Dignity Act: Ethics and procedures. *Professional Psychology: Research and Practice, 30,* 245–249.

Faust, D. S., & Ziskin, J. (1988a). The expert witness in psychology and psychiatry. *Science, 241,* 31–35.

Faust, D. S., & Ziskin, J. (1988b). Response to Fowler and Matarrazo. *Science, 242,* 1143–1144.

*Federal Rules of Evidence.* (1975). Eagan, MN: West Group.

Feinberg, T. E., & Farah, M. J. (Eds.). (2003). *Behavioral neurology and neuropsychology* (2nd ed.). New York: McGraw-Hill.

Feinstein, A. R., Josephy, B. R., & Wells, C. K. (1986). Scientific and clinical problems in indexes of functional disability. *Annals of Internal Medicine, 105,* 413–520.

Feiz, P., Emamipour, S., Rostami, R., & Sadeghi, V. (2010). The relationships between Wechsler Intelligence Scale for Children (WISC- R) with the Cognitive Assessment System (CAS). *Procedia—Social and Behavioral Sciences, 5,* 1726–1730.

Feldman, L. B., & Rivas-Vazquez, R. (2003). Assessment and treatment of social anxiety disorder. *Professional Psychology: Research and Practice, 34,* 396–405.

Fenn, D. S., & Ganzini, L. (1999). Attitudes of Oregon psychologists toward physician-assisted suicide and the Oregon Death With Dignity Act. *Professional Psychology: Research and Practice, 30,* 235–244.

Ferguson, R. L., & Novick, M. R. (1973). Implementation of a Bayesian system for decision analysis in a program of individually prescribed instruction. *ACT Research Report,* No. 60.

Feuerstein, R. (1977). Mediated learning experience: A theoretical basis for cognitive modifiability. In P. Mittler (Ed.), *Research to Practice in Mental Retardation.* Baltimore: University Park Press.

Feuerstein, R. (1981). Mediated learning experience in the acquisition of kinesics. In B. L. Hoffer & R. N. St. Clair (Eds.), *Development kinesics: The emerging paradigm.* Baltimore: University Park Press.

Feuerstein, R., Rand, Y., & Hoffman, M. B. (1979). *The dynamic assessment of retarded performers: The Learning Potential Assessment Device.* Baltimore: University Park Press.

Field, T. M., & Vega-Lahr, N. (1984). Early interactions between infants with cranio-facial anomalies and their mothers. *Infant Behavior and Development, 7,* 527–530.

Filsinger, E. (1983). A machine-aided marital observation technique: The Dyadic Interaction Scoring Code. *Journal of Marriage and the Family, 2,* 623–632.

*Finding information about psychological tests.* (1995). Washington, DC: American Psychological Association, Science Directorate.

Finello, K. M. (2011). Collaboration in the assessment and diagnosis of preschoolers: Challenges and opportunities. *Psychology in the Schools, 48,* 442–453.

Finkelhor, D., & Dziuba-Leatherman, J. (1994). Victimization of children. *American Psychologist, 49,* 173–183.

Finkelstein, R., & Bastounis, M. (2010). The effect of the deliberation process and jurors' prior legal knowledge on the sentence: the role of psychological expertise and crime scene photo. *Behavioral Sciences & the Law, 28*(3), 426–441.

Finn, S. E. (1996). *Using the MMPI-2 as a therapeutic intervention.* Minneapolis: University of Minnesota Press.

Finn, S. E. (2003). Therapeutic assessment of a man with "ADD." *Journal of Personality Assessment, 80,* 115–129.

Finn, S. E. (2011a). Therapeutic assessment on the front lines: Comment on articles from Westcoast Children's Clinic. *Journal of Personality Assessment, 93*(1), 23–25.

Finn, S. E. (2011b). Use of the Adult Attachment Projective Picture System (AAP) in the middle of a long-term psychotherapy. *Journal of Personality Assessment, 93*(5), 427–433.

Finn, S. E., & Martin, H. (1997). Therapeutic assessment with the MMPI-2 in managed health care. In J. N. Butcher (Ed.), *Objective psychological assessment in managed health care: A practitioner's guide* (pp. 131–152). New York: Oxford University Press.

Finn, S. E., & Tonsager, M. E. (2002). How therapeutic assessment became humanistic. *Humanistic Psychologist, 30*(1–2), 10–22.

Finucane, M. L., & Gullion, C. M. (2010). Developing a tool for measuring the decision-making competence of older adults. *Psychology and Aging, 25,* 271–288.

Fischer, C. T. (1978). Collaborative psychological assessment. In C. T. Fischer & S. L. Brodsky (Eds.), *Client participation in human services: The Prometheus principle* (pp. 41–61). New Brunswick, NJ: Transaction.

Fischer, C. T. (1994). *Individualizing psychological assessment.* Hillsdale, NJ: Erlbaum.

Fischer, C. T. (2004). In what sense is collaborative psychological assessment collaborative? Some distinctions. *SPA Exchange, 16*(1), 14–15.

Fischer, C. T. (2006). Qualitative psychological research and individualized/collaborative psychological assessment: Implications of their similarities for promoting a life-world orientation. *Humanistic Psychologist, 34*(4), 347–356.

Fischer, H. (1999). Exemptions from child abuse reporting. *American Psychologist, 54,* 145.

Fisher, R. P., & Geiselman, R. E. (1992). *Memory-enhancing techniques for investigative interviewing.* Springfield, IL: Charles C Thomas.

Fisher, R. P., Geiselman, R. E., & Amador, M. (1989). Field test of the cognitive interview: Enhancing the recollection of actual victims and witnesses of crime. *Journal of Applied Psychology, 74,* 722–727.

Fisher, R. P., Geiselman, R. E., Raymond, D. S., et al. (1987). Enhancing enhanced eyewitness memory: Refining the cognitive interview. *Journal of Police Science & Administration, 15,* 291–297.

Fiske, D. W. (1967). The subjects react to tests. *American Psychologist, 22,* 287–296.

Fitts, W. H. (1965). *Manual for the Tennessee Self-Concept Scale.* Nashville: Counselor Recordings and Tests.

Fitzgibbons, D. J., & Shearn, C. R. (1972). Concepts of schizophrenia among mental health professionals: A factor-analytic study. *Journal of Consulting and Clinical Psychology, 38,* 288–295.

Flanagan, D. P. (2001). *Comparative features of the* WJ III Tests of Cognitive Abilities (Woodcock-Johnson III. Assessment Service Bulletin No. 1). Itasca, IL: Riverside.

Flanagan, D. P., & McGrew, K. S. (1997). A cross-battery approach to assessing and interpreting cognitive abilities: Narrowing the gap between practice and cognitive science. In D. P. Flanagan, J. L. Genshaft, & P. L. Harrison (Eds.), *Contemporary intellectual assessment: Theories, tests, and issues* (pp. 314–325). New York: Guilford.

Flanagan, J. C. (1938). Review of *Measuring Intelligence* by Terman and Merrill. *Harvard Educational Review, 8,* 130–133.

Flanagan, J. C., & Burns, R. K. (1955). The employee business record: A new appraisal and development tool. *Harvard Business Review, 33*(5), 99–102.

Fletcher, J. M., Lyon, G. R., Barnes, M., et al. (2002). Classification of learning disabilities: An evidence-based evaluation. In R. Bradley, L. Danielson, and D. P. Hallahan (Eds.), *Identification of learning disabilities: Research and practice.* Mahwah, NJ: Erlbaum.

Fletcher, J. M., Stuebing, K. K., & Hughes, L. C. (2010). IQ scores should be corrected for the Flynn Effect in high-stakes decisions. *Journal of Psychoeducational Assessment, 28,* 469–473.

Flett, G. L., & Hewitt, P. L. (2002). *Perfectionism: Theory, research and treatment.* Washington: American Psychological.

Flowers, J. H. (1982). Some simple Apple II software for the collection and analysis of observational data. *Behavior Research Methods and Instrumentation, 14,* 241–249.

Floyd, F. J., Haynes, S. N., Doll, E. R., et al. (1992). Assessing retirement satisfaction and perceptions of retirement experiences. *Psychology and Aging, 7,* 609–621.

Floyd, F. J., & Widaman, K. F. (1995). Factor analysis in the development and refinement of clinical assessment instruments. *Psychological Assessment, 7,* 286–299.

Floyd, R. G., Evans, J. J., & McGrew, K. S. (2003). Relations between measures of Cattell-Horn-Carroll (CHC) cognitive abilities and mathematics achievement across the school-age years. *Psychology in the Schools, 40,* 155–171.

Flynn, J. R. (1984). The mean IQ of Americans: Massive gains 1932 to 1978. *Psychological Bulletin, 95,* 29–51.

Flynn, J. R. (1988). Massive IQ gains in 14 nations: What IQ tests really measure. *Psychological Bulletin, 101,* 171–191.

Flynn, J. R. (1991). *Asian-Americans: Achievement beyond IQ.* Hillsdale, NJ: Erlbaum.

Flynn, J. R. (2000). The hidden history of IQ and special education: Can the problems be solved? *Psychology, Public Policy, and Law, 6,* 191–198.

Flynn, J. R. (2007). *What is intelligence? Beyond the Flynn effect.* New York: Cambridge University Press.

Flynn, J. R. (2009). Requiem for nutrition as the cause of IQ gains: Raven's gains in Britain, 1938–2008. *Economics and Human Biology, 7,* 18–27.

Foerster, L. M., & Little Soldier, D. (1974). Open education and native American values. *Educational Leadership, 32,* 41–45.

Folstein, M. F., Folstein, S. E., & McHugh, P. R. (1975). "Mini-Mental State": A practical method for grading the cognitive state of patients for the clinician. *Journal of Psychiatric Research, 12,* 189–198.

Fontana, V. J., Donovan, D., & Wong, R. J. (1963, December 8). The maltreatment syndrome in children. *New England Journal of Medicine, 269,* 1389–1394.

Fontanna, D. (2000). *Personality in the workplace.* Lewiston, NY: Macmillan.

Forbes, P. A., Happee, R., van der Helm, F., & Schouten, A. C. (2011). EMG feedback tasks reduce reflexive stiffness during force and position perturbations. *Experimental Brain Research, 213*(1), 49–61.

Forer, B. R. (1949). The fallacy of personal validation: A classroom demonstration of gullibility. *Journal of Abnormal and Social Psychology, 44,* 118–123.

Forrest, D. W. (1974). *Francis Galton: The life and works of a Victorian genius.* New York: Taplinger.

Forth, A. E., Hart, S. D., & Hare, R. D. (1990). Assessment of psychopathy in male young offenders. *Psychological Assessment, 2,* 342–344.

Fortune, S., Stewart, A., Yadav, V., & Hawton, K. (2007). Suicide in adolescents: Using life charts to understand the suicidal process. *Journal of Affective Disorders, 100*(1–3), 199–210.

Foster, S. L., Laverty-Finch, C., Gizzo, D. P., & Osantowski, J. (1999). Practical issues in self-observation. *Psychological Assessment, 11*, 426–438.

Foster, T. (2011). Adverse life events proximal to adult suicide: A synthesis of findings from psychological studies. *Archives of Suicide Research, 15*, 1–15.

Fouad, N. A. (2002). Cross-cultural differences in vocational interests: Between-group differences on the Strong Interest Inventory. *Journal of Counseling Psychology, 49*, 282–289.

Fouad, N. A., & Dancer, L. S. (1992). Cross-cultural structure of interests: Mexico and the United States. *Journal of Vocational Behavior, 40*, 129–143.

Fowler, D. R., Finkelstein, A., & Penk, W. (1986). *Measuring treatment responses by computer interview.* Paper presented at the 94th annual meeting of the American Psychological Association, Washington, DC.

Fowler, K. A., & Westen, D. (2011). Subtyping male perpetrators of intimate partner violence. *Journal of Interpersonal Violence, 26*(4), 607–639.

Fox, B. (2008). A new direction in athletic imagery interventions: The relationship between imagery direction, anxiety, and motor performance. *Dissertation Abstracts International: Section A. Humanities and Social Sciences, 68*(7-A), 2873.

Fox, R. K., White, C. S., & Kidd, J. K. (2011). Program portfolios: Documenting teachers' growth in reflection-based inquiry. *Teachers and Teaching: Theory and Practice, 17*(1), 149–167.

Fox, S. J. (2011). A correlational analysis between handwriting characteristics and personality type by the Myers-Briggs Type Indicator. *Dissertation Abstracts International: Section B: The Sciences and Engineering,* p. 7773.

Franco, J. N. (1983). An acculturation scale for Mexican-American children. *Journal of General Psychology, 108*, 175–181.

Frank, E., & Brandstaetter, V. (2002). Approach versus avoidance: Different types of commitment in intimate relationships. *Journal of Personality & Social Psychology, 82*, 208–221.

Frank, J. D. (1974). Psychotherapy: The restoration of morale. *American Journal of Psychiatry, 131*, 271–274.

Frank, L. K. (1939). Projective methods for the study of personality. *Journal of Psychology, 8*, 389–413.

Frank, M. G., Ekman, P., & Friesen, W. V. (1993). Behavioral markers and recognizability of the smile of enjoyment. *Journal of Personality and Social Psychology, 64*, 83–93.

Frederickson, B. L. (1998). What good are positive emotions? *Review of General Psychology, 2*, 300–319.

Fredman, N., & Sherman, R. (1987). *Handbook of measurements for marriage & family therapy.* New York: Brunner/Mazel.

Freeman, S. T. (1989). Cultural and linguistic bias in mental health evaluations of deaf people. *Rehabilitation Psychology, 34*, 51–63.

French, C. C., & Beaumont, J. G. (1991). The Differential Aptitude Test (Language Usage and Spelling): A clinical study of a computerized form. *Current Psychology: Research and Reviews, 10*, 31–48.

French, D. J., Gauthier, J. G., Roberge, C., et al. (1997). Self-efficacy in the thermal biofeedback treatment of migraine sufferers. *Behavior Therapy, 28*, 109–125.

French, J. L. (Ed.). (1964). *Educating the gifted.* New York: Holt, Rinehart & Winston.

Freud, S. (1913/1959). Further recommendations in the technique of psychoanalysis. In E. Jones (Ed.) and J. Riviere (Trans.), *Collected papers* (Vol. 2). New York: Basic Books.

Freund, K. (1963). A laboratory method for diagnosing predominance of homosexual and heterosexual erotic interest in the male. *Behavior Research and Therapy, 1*, 85–93.

Freund, K., Sedlacek, E., & Knob, K. (1965). A simple transducer for mechanical plethysmography of the male genital. *Journal of Experimental Analysis of Behavior, 8*, 169–170.

Friedman, M., & Rosenman, R. H. (1974). *Type A behavior and your heart.* New York: Knopf.

Friedrich, W. N., Fisher, J. L., Dittner, C. A., et al. (2001). Child Sexual Behavior Inventory: Normative, psychiatric, and sexual abuse comparisons. *Child Maltreatment: Journal of the American Professional Society on the Abuse of Children, 6*, 37–49.

Friedrich, W. N., Urquiza, A. J., & Beike, R. (1986). Behavioral problems in sexually abused young children. *Journal of Pediatric Psychiatry, 11*, 47–57.

Friel-Patti, S., & Finitzo, T. (1990). Language learning in a prospective study of otitis media with effusion in the first two years of life. *Journal of Speech and Hearing Research, 33*, 188–194.

Friese, M., Bluemke, M., & Wänke, M. (2007). Predicting voting behavior with implicit attitude measures: The 2002 German parliamentary election. *Experimental Psychology, 54*(4), 247–255.

Frijda, N. H., & Mesquita, B. (1994). The social roles and functions of emotions. In S. Kitayama & H. R. Markus (Eds.), *Emotion and Culture: Empirical studies of mutual influence* (pp. 51–87). Washington, DC: American Psychological Association.

Frolik, L. A. (1999). Science, common sense, and the determination of mental capacity. *Psychology, Public Policy, and Law, 5*, 41–58.

Frumkin, R. M. (1997). Significant neglected sociocultural and physical factors affecting intelligence. *American Psychologist, 52*, 76–77.

Frye v. United States, 293 Fed. 1013 (D.C. Cir. 1923).

Fuchs, D., & Fuchs, L.S. (2006). Introduction to responsiveness-to-intervention: What, why, and how valid is it? *Reading Research Quarterly, 41*, 92–99.

Fuchs, L. S., Compton, D. L., Fuchs, D., et al. (2011). Two-stage screening for math problem-solving difficulty using dynamic assessment of algebraic learning. *Journal of Learning Disabilities, 44*(4), 372–380.

Fuchs, L. S., Fuchs, D., Eaton, S. B., et al. (2000). Using objective data sources to enhance teacher judgments about test accommodations. *Exceptional Children, 67*, 67–81.

Fullan, M., & Loubser, J. (1972). Education and adaptive capacity. *Sociology of Education, 45*, 271–287.

Fullard, W., McDevitt, S. C., & Carey, W. B. (1984). Assessing temperament in one- to three-year-old children. *Journal of Pediatric Psychology, 9*, 205–217.

Furnham, A., Crump, J., & Chamorro-Premuzic, T. (2007). Managerial level, personality and intelligence. *Journal of Managerial Psychology, 8*, 805–818.

Furnham, A., Moutafi, J., & Crump, J. (2003). The relationship between the revised NEO-Personality Inventory and the Myers-Briggs Type Indicator. *Social Behavior & Personality, 31*, 577–584.

Furnham, A., Petrides, K. V., Jackson, C. J., & Cotter, T. (2002). Do personality factors predict job satisfaction? *Personality & Individual Differences, 33*, 1325–1342.

Furse, D. H., & Stewart, D. W. (1984). Manipulating dissonance to improve mail survey response. *Psychology & Marketing, 1*, 71–84.

Gacono, C. B., et al. (Eds.). (2008). *The handbook of forensic Rorschach assessment.* New York: Routledge/Taylor & Francis.

Gagne, J. R., Van Hulle, C. A., Aksan, N., et al. (2011). Deriving childhood temperament measures from emotion-eliciting behavioral episodes: Scale construction and initial validation. *Psychological Assessment, 23*(2), 337–353.

Gaither, G. A., & Sellbom, M. (2003). The Sexual Sensation Seeking Scale: Reliability and validity within a heterosexual college student sample. *Journal of Personality Assessment, 81,* 157–167.

Gallagher, J. J. (1966). *Research summary on gifted child education.* Springfield, IL: State Department of Public Instruction.

Gallo, J. J., & Bogner, H. R. (2006). The context of geriatric care. In J. J. Gallo, H. R. Bogner, T. Fulmer, & G. J. Paveza (Eds.), *The handbook of geriatric assessment* (4th ed., pp. 3–13). Sudbury, MA: Jones & Bartlett.

Gallo, J. J., & Wittink, M. N. (2006). Cognitive assessment. In J. J. Gallo, H. R. Bogner, T. Fulmer, & G. J. Paveza (Eds.), *The handbook of geriatric assessment* (4th ed., pp. 105–151). Sudbury, MA: Jones & Bartlett.

Galton, F. (1869). *Hereditary genius.* London: Macmillan. (Republished in 1892)

Galton, F. (1874). *English men of science.* New York: Appleton.

Galton, F. (1879). Psychometric experiments. *Brain, 2,* 149–162.

Galton, F. (1883). *Inquiries into human faculty and its development.* London: Macmillan.

Gammon, J. A. (1981). Ophthalmic manifestations of child abuse. In N. S. Ellerstein (Ed.), *Child abuse and neglect: A medical reference* (pp. 121–139). New York: Wiley.

Ganellen, R. J. (1996). Comparing the diagnostic efficiency of the MMPI, MCMI-II, and Rorschach: A review. *Journal of Personality Assessment, 67,* 219–243.

Ganellen, R. J. (2007). Assessing normal and abnormal personality functioning. *Journal of Personality Assessment, 89*(1), 30–40.

Ganellen R. J. (2008). Rorschach assessment of malingering and defensive response sets. In C. Gacono & B. Evans (Eds.), *The handbook of forensic Rorschach assessment.* Hillsdale: Routledge

Gann, M. K., & Davison, G. C. (1997). *Cognitive assessment of reactance using the articulated thoughts in simulated situations paradigm.* Unpublished manuscript, University of Southern California, Los Angeles.

Garb, H. N. (1994). Toward a second generation of statistical prediction rules in psychodiagnosis and personality assessment. *Computers in Human Behavior, 11,* 313–324.

Garb, H. N. (2000a). Introduction to the special section on the use of computers for making judgments and decisions. *Psychological Assessment, 12,* 3–5.

Garb, H. N. (2000b). Computers will become increasingly important for psychological assessment: Not that there's anything wrong with that! *Psychological Assessment, 12,* 31–39.

Garcia, M., & Lega, L. I. (1979). Development of a Cuban Ethnic Identity Questionnaire. *Hispanic Journal of Behavioral Sciences, 1,* 247–261.

Gardner, D., & Deadrick, D. L. (2008). Underprediction of performance for U.S. minorities using cognitive ability measures. *Equal Opportunities International, 27*(5), 455–464.

Gardner, F. L. (2001). Applied sport psychology in professional sports: The team psychologist. *Professional Psychology: Research and Practice, 32,* 34–39.

Gardner, H. (1983). *Frames of mind: The theory of multiple intelligences.* New York: Basic Books.

Gardner, H. (1994). Multiple intelligences theory. In R. J. Sternberg (Ed.), *Encyclopedia of human intelligence* (pp. 740–742). New York: Macmillan.

Gardner, R. A. (1971). *The boys' and girls' book about divorce.* New York: Bantam.

Gardner, R. A. (1982). *Family evaluation in child custody litigation.* Cresskill, NJ: Creative Therapeutics.

Gardner, W., Lidz, C. W., Mulvey, E. P., & Shaw, E. C. (1996). Clinical versus actuarial prediction of violence in patients with mental illnesses. *Journal of Consulting and Clinical Psychology, 64,* 602–609.

Garfield, S. L., & Eron, L. D. (1948). Interpreting mood and activity in TAT stories. *Journal of Abnormal and Social Psychology, 43,* 338–345.

Garnier, L. M., Arria, A. M., Caldeira, K. M., et al. (2009). Nonmedical prescription analgesic use and concurrent alcohol consumption among college students. *American Journal of Drug and Alcohol Abuse, 35,* 334–338.

Garred, M., & Gilmore, L. (2009). To WPPSI or to Binet, that is the question: A comparison of the WPPSI-III and SB5 with typically developing preschoolers. *Australian Journal of Guidance & Counselling, 19*(2), 104–115.

Garrett, H. E., & Schneck, M. R. (1933). *Psychological tests, methods and results.* New York: Harper.

Garrett, M. T. & Pichette, E. F. (2000). Red as an apple: Native American acculturation and counseling with or without reservation. *Journal of Counseling and Development, 78,* 3–13.

Gaski, J. F., & Sagarin, J. (2011). Detrimental effects of daylight-saving times on SAT scores. *Journal of Neuroscience, Psychology, and Economics, 4*(1), 44–53.

Gasquoine, P. G. (2010). Comparison of public/private health care insurance parameters for independent psychological practice. *Professional Psychology: Research and Practice, 41*(4), 319–324.

Gaugler, B. B., Rosenthal, D. B., Thornton, G. C., III, & Bentson, C. (1987). Meta-analysis of assessment center validity. *Journal of Applied Psychology, 72,* 493–511.

Gavett, B. E., Lynch, J. K., & McCaffrey, R. J. (2005). Third party observers: The effect size is greater than you might think. *Journal of Forensic Neuropsychology, 4*(2), 49–64.

Gavett, B. E., & McCaffrey, R. J. (2007). The influence of an adaptation period in reducing the third party observer effect during a neuropsychological evaluation. *Archives of Clinical Neuropsychology, 22,* 699–710.

Gavzer, B. (1990, May 27). Should you tell all? *Parade Magazine,* pp. 4–7.

Gawda, B. (2008). A graphical analysis of handwriting of prisoners diagnosed with antisocial personality. *Perceptual and Motor Skills, 107*(3), 862–872.

Gawronski, B., & Bodenhausen, G. V. (2007). What do we know about implicit attitude measures and what do we have to learn? In B. Wittenbrink & N. Schwarz (Eds.), *Implicit measures of attitudes* (pp. 265–286). New York: Guilford Press.

Gee, C. J., Marshall, J. C., & King, J. F. (2010). Should coaches use personality assessments in the talent identification process? A 15 year predictive study on professional hockey players. *International Journal of Coaching Science, 4,* 25–34.

Geisenger, K. F., & McCormick, C. M. (2010). Adopting cut scores: Post-standard-setting panel considerations for decision makers. *Educational Measurement: Issues and Practice, 29,* 38–44.

General Electric Co. v. Joiner, 118 S. Ct. 512 (1997).

George, C., & West, M. (2011). The Adult Attachment Projective Picture System: Integrating attachment into clinical assessment. *Journal of Personality Assessment, 93*(5), 407–416.

Gerety, M.B., Mulrow, C.D., Tuley, M.R., et al. (1993). Development and validation of a physical performance instrument for the functionally impaired elderly: The Physical Disability Index (PDI). *Journal of Gerontology, 48,* M33–M38.

Gerhart, M., Karslo, V., & Griffith, J. D. (2010, May). *Categorization of last statements of Texas inmates on death row.* Poster session presented at Association for Psychological Science (APS) annual meeting, Boston.

Gerry, M. H. (1973). Cultural myopia: The need for a corrective lens. *Journal of School Psychology, 11,* 307–315.

Gesell, A. (1945). *The embryology of behavior: The beginnings of the human mind.* New York: Harper.

Gesell, A. (1954). The ontogenesis of infant behavior. In L. Carmichael (Ed.), *Manual of child psychology.* New York: Wiley.

Gesell, A., & Amatruda, C. S. (1947). *Development diagnosis: Normal and abnormal child development* (2nd ed.). New York: Harper & Row.

Gesell, A., et al. (1940). *The first five years of life.* New York: Harper.

Gesell, A., & Thompson, H. (1929). Learning and growth in identical twin infants. *Genetic Psychology Monographs, 6,* 1–124.

Ghiselli, E. E. (1973). The variety of aptitude tests in personnel selection. *Personnel Psychology, 26,* 461–477.

Ghiselli, E. E., & Barthol, R. P. (1953). The validity of personality inventories in the selection of employees. *Journal of Applied Psychology, 38,* 18–20.

Ghiselli, E. E., Campbell, J. P., & Zedeck, S. (1981). *Measurement theory for the behavioral sciences.* San Francisco: Freeman.

Gibbins, S. (1988, April). *Use of the K-ABC and WISC-R with deaf children.* Paper presented at the Annual Meeting of the National Association of School Psychologists, Chicago.

Gibbins, S. (1989). The provision of school psychological assessment services for the hearing impaired: A national survey. *Volta Review, 91,* 95–103.

Gilbert, P., & Allan, S. (1998). The role of defeat and entrapment (arrested flight) in depression: An exploration of an evolutionary view. *Psychological Medicine, 28,* 585–598.

Gilch-Pesantez, J. R. (2001). Test-retest reliability and construct validity: The Bricklin Perceptual Scales. *Dissertation Abstracts International: Section B: The Sciences and Engineering, 61* (9-B), 4982.

Gill, C. J., Kewman, D. G., & Brannon, R. W. (2003). Transforming psychological practice and society: Policies that reflect the new paradigm. *American Psychologist, 58,* 305–312.

Gill, J. S., Donaghy, M., Guise, J., & Warner, P. (2007). Descriptors and accounts of alcohol consumption: Methodological issues piloted with female undergraduate drinkers in Scotland. *Health Education Research, 22*(1), 27–36.

Gim Chung, R. H., Kim, B. S. K., & Abreu, J. M. (2004). Asian American Multidimensional Acculturation Scale: Development, factor analysis, reliability, and validity. *Cultural Diversity and Ethnic Minority Psychology, 10*(1), 66–80.

Giner, L., Carballo, J. J., Guija, J. A., et al. (2007). Psychological autopsy studies: The role of alcohol use in adolescent and young adult suicides. *International Journal of Adolescent Medicine and Health, 19*(1), 99–113.

Girelli, S. A., & Stake, J. E. (1993). Bipolarity in Jungian type theory and the Myers-Briggs Type Indicator. *Journal of Personality Assessment, 60,* 290–301.

Gittell, J. H. (2008). Relationships and resilience: Care provider responses to pressures from managed care. *Journal of Applied Behavioral Science, 44*(1), 25–47.

Glaser, R., & Nitko, A. J. (1971). Measurement in learning and instruction. In R. L. Thorndike (Ed.), *Educational measurement* (2nd ed.). Washington, DC: American Council on Education.

Glassbrenner, J. (1998). Continuity across contexts: Prison, women's counseling center, and home. In L. Handler (Chair), *Conducting assessments in clients' homes: Contexts, surprises, dilemmas, opportunities.* Symposium presented at the Society for Personality Assessment 1998 Midwinter Meeting, February 20.

Glazer, W. M., Kramer, R., Montgomery, J. S., & Myers, L. (1991). Use of medical necessity scales in concurrent review of psychiatric inpatient care. *Hospital and Community Psychiatry, 42,* 1199–1200.

Glosser, G., & Goodglass, H. (1990). Disorders in executive control functions among aphasic and other brain-damaged patients. *Journal of Clinical and Experimental Neuropsychology, 12,* 485–501.

Gluck, M. R. (1955). The relationship between hostility in the TAT and behavioral hostility. *Journal of Projective Techniques, 19,* 21–26.

Glueck, W. F. (1978). *Personnel: A diagnostic approach.* Dallas: Business Publications.

Gobetz, W. A. (1953). Quantification, standardization, and validation of the Bender-Gestalt test on normal and neurotic adults. *Psychological Monographs, 67,* No. 6.

Goddard, H. H. (1908). The Binet and Simon tests of intellectual capacity. *Training School, 5,* 3–9.

Goddard, H. H. (1910). A measuring scale of intelligence. *Training School, 6,* 146–155.

Goddard, H. H. (1912). *The Kallikak family.* New York: Macmillan.

Goddard, H. H. (1913). The Binet tests in relation to immigration. *Journal of Psycho-Asthenics, 18,* 105–107.

Goddard, H. H. (1916). *Feeblemindedness.* New York: Macmillan.

Goddard, H. H. (1917). Mental tests and the immigrant. *Journal of Delinquency, 2,* 243–277.

Goddard, H. H. (1947). A suggested definition of intelligence. *Training School Bulletin, 43,* 185–193.

Goel, V., & Grafman, J. (1995). Are the frontal lobes implicated in "planning" functions? Interpreting data from the Tower of Hanoi. *Neuropsychologia, 33,* 623–642.

Goffman, E. (1963). *Behavior in public places.* Glencoe, IL: Free Press.

Gokhale, D. V., & Kullback, S. (1978). *The information in contingency tables.* New York: Marcel Dekker.

Gold, D. P., Andres, D., Etezadi, J., et al. (1995). Structural equation model of intellectual change and continuity and predictors of intelligence in older men. *Psychology & Aging, 10,* 294–303.

Goldberg, L. R. (1993). The structure of phenotypic personality traits. *American Psychologist, 48,* 26–34.

Goldberg, T. E., Gold, J. M., Greenberg, R., et al. (1993). Contrasts between patients with affective disorders and patients with schizophrenia on a neuropsychological test battery. *American Journal of Psychiatry, 150,* 1355–1362.

Goldberg, T. E., Saint-Cyr, J. A., & Weinberger, D. R. (1990). Assessment of procedural learning and problem solving in schizophrenic patients by Tower of Hanoi type tasks. *Journal of Neuropsychiatry, 2,* 165–173.

Golden, C. J., Hammeke, T. A., & Purisch, A. D. (1980). *The Luria-Nebraska Neuropsychological Battery: Manual.* Los Angeles: Western Psychological Services.

Golden, C. J., Purisch, A. D., & Hammeke, T. A. (1985). *Luria-Nebraska Neuropsychological Battery: Forms I and II, manual.* Los Angeles: Western Psychological Services.

Goldfried, M. R., & Davison, G. C. (1976). *Clinical behavior therapy.* New York: Holt, Rinehart & Winston.

Goldfried, M. R., Stricker, G., & Winer, I. B. (1971). *Rorschach handbook of clinical and research applications.* Englewood Cliffs, NJ: Prentice-Hall.

Golding, S. L. (1975). Flies in the ointment: Methodological problems in the analysis of the percentage of variance due to persons and situations. *Psychological Bulletin, 82,* 278–288.

Golding, S. L., Roesch, R., & Schreiber, J. (1984). Assessment and conceptualization of competency to stand trial. Preliminary data on the interdisciplinary fitness interview. *Law and Human Behavior, 8*(3–4), 321–334.

Goldman, B. A., & Mitchell, D. F. (Eds.) (1997). *Directory of unpublished experimental mental measures* (Vol. 7). Dubuque, IA: W. C. Brown.

Goldman, B. A., & Mitchell, D. F. (2007). *Directory of unpublished experimental mental measures* (Vol. 9). Washington, DC: APA Books.

Goldstein, K. (1927). Die lokalisation in her grosshin rinde. In *Handb. norm. pathol. psychologie.* Berlin: J. Springer.

Goldstein, K. (1939). *The organism.* New York: American Book.

Goldstein, K. (1963a). The modifications of behavior consequent to cerebral lesions. *Psychiatric Quarterly, 10,* 586–610.

Goldstein, K. (1963b). *The organism.* Boston: Beacon Press.

Goldstein, S. (2011). Learning disabilities in childhood. In S. Goldsteein, J. A. Naglieri, & M. DeVries (Eds.), *Learning and attention disorders in adolescence and adulthood: Assessment and treatment* (2nd ed., pp. 31–58). Hoboken, NJ: Wiley.

Goldstein, T. R., Bridge, J. A., & Brent, D. A. (2008). Sleep disturbance preceding completed suicide in adolescents. *Journal of Consulting and Clinical Psychology, 76*(1), 84–91.

Gomez, R., & Hazeldine, P. (1996). Social information processing in mild mentally retarded children. *Research in Developmental Disabilities, 17,* 217–227.

Good, R. H., Chowdhri, S., Katz, L., Vollman, M., & Creek, R. (1989, March). *Effect of matching instruction and simultaneous/sequential processing strength.* Paper presented at the Annual Meeting of the National Association of School Psychologists, Boston.

Good, R. H., & Lane, S. (1988). *Confirmatory factor analysis of the K-ABC and WISC-R: Hierarchical models.* Paper presented at the Annual Meeting of the American Psychological Association, Atlanta.

Good, R. H., Vollmer, M., Creek, R. J., & Katz, L. (1993). Treatment utility of the Kaufman Assessment Battery for Children: Effects of matching instruction and student processing strength. *School Psychology Review, 22,* 8–26.

Goodman, G. S., & Reed, R. S. (1986). Age differences in eyewitness testimony. *Law and Human Behavior, 10,* 317–332.

Goodman-Delahunty, J. (2000). Psychological impairment under the Americans with Disabilities Act: Legal guidelines. *Professional Psychology: Research and Practice, 31,* 197–205.

Goodman-Delahunty, J., & Foote, W. E. (1995). Compensation for pain, suffering and other psychological injuries: The impact of *Daubert* on employment discrimination claims. *Behavioral Sciences and the Law, 13,* 183–206.

Gopaul-McNicol, S. (1993). *Working with West Indian families.* New York: Guilford.

Gordon, R. A. (2008). Attributional style and athlete performance: Strategic optimism and defensive pessimism. *Psychology of Sport and Exercise, 9*(3), 336–350.

Gosling, S. D., Kwan, V. S., & John, O. P. (2003). A dog's got personality: A cross-species comparative approach to personality judgments in dogs and humans. *Journal of Personality and Social Psychology, 85*(6), 1161–1169.

Gosling, S. D., Rentfrow, P. J., & Swann, W.B., Jr. (2003). A very brief measure of the Big-Five personality domains. *Journal of Research in Personality, 37*(6), 504–528.

Gottfredson, G. D. (2009). John L. Holland (1919–2008). *American Psychologist, 64*(6), 561.

Gottfredson, L. S. (1988). Reconsidering fairness: A matter of social and ethical priorities. *Journal of Vocational Behavior, 33,* 293–319.

Gottfredson, L. S. (1994). The science and politics of race-norming. *American Psychologist, 49,* 955–963.

Gottfredson, L. S. (2000). Skills gaps, not tests, make racial proportionality impossible. *Psychology, Public Policy, and Law, 6,* 129–143.

Gottfried, A. W. (Ed.). (1984). *Home environment and early cognitive development: Longitudinal research.* New York: Academic Press.

Gottfried, A. W., Gottfried, A. E., Bathurst, K., & Guerin, D. W. (1994). *Gifted IQ: Early developmental aspects.* New York: Plenum.

Gough, H. G. (1960). The Adjective Check List as a personality assessment research technique. *Psychological Reports, 6,* 107–122.

Gough, H. G. (1962). Clinical versus statistical prediction in psychology. In L. Postman (Ed.), *Psychology in the making: Histories of selected research problems* (pp. 526–584). New York: Knopf.

Gough, H. G., & Heilbrun, A. B., Jr. (1980). *The Adjective Checklist manual (Revised).* Palo Alto, CA: Consulting Psychologists Press.

Gould, J. W. (2006). *Conducting scientifically crafted child custody evaluations* (2nd ed.). Sarasota, FL: Professional Resource Press/ Professional Resource Exchange.

Grafman, J., Litvan, I., Massaquoi, S., & Stewart, M. (1992). Cognitive planning deficit in patients with cerebellar atrophy. *Neurology, 42,* 1493–1496.

Graham, J. R. (1990). *MMPI-2: Assessing personality and psychopathology.* New York: Oxford University Press.

Granger, C. V., & Gresham, G. E. (Eds.). (1984). *Functional assessment in rehabilitation medicine.* Baltimore: Williams & Wilkins.

Greaud, V. A., & Green, B. F. (1986). Equivalence of conventional and computer presentation of speed tests. *Applied Psychological Measurement, 10,* 23–34.

Green, A. (1986). True and false allegations of sexual abuse in child custody disputes. *Journal of the American Academy of Child Psychology, 25,* 449–456.

Green, B. F. (1984). *Computer-based ability testing.* Paper delivered at the 91st annual meeting of the American Psychological Association, Toronto.

Green, S. B. (2003). A coefficient alpha for test-retest data. *Psychological Methods, 8,* 88–101.

Greene, R. L. (1987). Ethnicity and MMPI performance: A review. *Journal of Consulting and Clinical Psychology, 55,* 497–512.

Greene, R. L. (2000). *The MMPI-2: An interpretive manual* (2nd ed.). Needham Heights, MA: Allyn & Bacon.

Greenfield, D. N. (1999). Psychological characteristics of compulsive Internet use: A preliminary analysis. *Cyber-Psychology & Behavior, 2,* 403–412.

Greenlaw, P. S., & Jensen, S. S. (1996). Race-norming and the Civil Rights Act of 1991. *Public Personnel Management, 25,* 13–24.

Greenspan, S. (1997). Dead manual walking? Why the AAMR definition needs redoing. *Education & Training in Mental Retardation & Developmental Disabilities, 32,* 179–190.

Greenspoon, J. (1955). The reinforcing effect of two spoken sounds on the frequency of two responses. *American Journal of Psychology, 68,* 409–416.

Greenspoon, J., & Gersten, C. D. (1967). A new look at psychological testing: Psychological testing from the standpoint of a behaviorist. *American Psychologist, 22,* 848–853.

Greenwald, A. G., & Banaji, M. R. (1995). Implicit social cognition: Attitudes, self-esteem, and stereotypes. *Psychological Review, 102,* 4–27.

Greenwald, A. G., & Farnham S. D. (2000). Using the Implicit Association Test to measure self-esteem and self-concept. *Journal of Personality and Social Psychology, 79,* 1022–1038.

Greenwald, A. G., McGhee, D. E., & Schwartz, J. L. K. (1998). Measuring individual differences in implicit cognition: The implicit association test. *Journal of Personality and Social Psychology, 74,* 1464–1480.

Greenwald, A. G., & Nosek, B. A. (2001). Health of the Implicit Association Test at age 3. *Zeitschrift für Experimentelle Psychologie, 48*(2), 85–93.

Gregg, P. A. (1998). The effect of impression management on correlations between Rorschach and MMPI-2 variables. *Dissertation Abstracts International: Section B. Sciences and Engineering, 58*(9-B), 5185.

Gregory, N. (2005). Offender profiling: A review of the literature. *British Journal of Forensic Practice, 7*(3), 29–34.

Gresham, F. M. (1989). Review of the Parenting Stress Index. In J. C. Conoley & J. J. Kramer (Eds.), *The tenth mental measurements yearbook.* Lincoln: Buros Institute of Mental Measurements, University of Nebraska.

Gresham, F. M., MacMillan, D. L., & Siperstein, G. N. (1995). Critical analysis of the 1992 AAMR definition: Implications for school psychology. *School Psychology Quarterly, 10*(1), 1–19.

Grey, R. J., & Kipnis, D. (1976). Untangling the performance appraisal dilemma: The influence of perceived organizational context on evaluative processes. *Journal of Applied Psychology, 61,* 329–335.

Griffin, M. L., Hogan, N. L., Lambert, E. G., Tucker-Gail, K. A., & Baker, D. N. (2010). Job involvement, job stress, job satisfaction, and organizational commitment and the burnout of correctional staff. *Criminal Justice and Behavior, 37,* 239–255.

Grisso, T. (1986). *Evaluating competencies: Forensic assessments and instruments.* New York: Plenum.

Grisso T., & Appelbaum, P. S. (1995). MacArthur Treatment Competence Study. *Journal of American Psychiatric Nurses Association, 1,* 125–127.

Grisso, T., & Appelbaum, P. S. (1998). *Assessing competence to consent to treatment: A guide for physicians and other health professionals.* New York: Oxford University Press.

Grisso, T., Appelbaum, P. S., & Hill-Fotouhi, C. (1997). The MacCAT-T: A clinical tool to assess patients' capacities to make treatment decisions. *Psychiatric Services, 48,* 1415–1419.

Groeger, J. A., & Chapman, P. R. (1997). Normative influences on decisions to offend. *Applied Psychology: An International Review, 46,* 265–285.

Groenveld, M., & Jan, J. E. (1992). Intelligence profiles of low vision and blind children. *Journal of Visual Impairment and Blindness, 86,* 68–71.

Grossman, I., Mednitsky, S., Dennis, B., & Scharff, L. (1993). Validation of an "amazingly" short form of the WAIS-R for a clinically depressed sample. *Journal of Psychoeducational Assessment, 11,* 173–181.

Grove, W. M., & Barden, R. C. (1999). Protecting the integrity of the legal system: The admissibility of testimony from mental health experts under *Daubert/Kumho* analyses. *Psychology, Public Policy, and Law, 5,* 224–242.

Grove, W. M., Zald, D. H., Lebow, B. S., et al. (2000). Clinical versus mechanical prediction: A meta-analysis. *Psychological Assessment, 12,* 19–30.

Grutter v. Bollinger, 539 U.S. 306 (2003).

Guastello, S. J., & Rieke, M. L. (1990). The Barnum Effect and the validity of computer-based test interpretations: The Human Resource Development Report. *Psychological Assessment, 2,* 186–190.

Guerrier, J. H., Manivannan, P., & Nair, S. N. (1999). The role of working memory, field dependence, visual search, and reaction time in the left turn performance of older female drivers. *Applied Ergonomics, 30,* 109–119.

Guidubaldi, J., & Duckworth, J. (2001). Divorce and children's cognitive ability. In E. L. Grigorenko & R. J. Sternberg (Eds.), *Family environment and intellectual functioning: A life-span perspective* (pp. 97–118). Mahwah, NJ: Erlbaum.

Guilford, J. P. (1954). A factor analytic study across the domains of reasoning, creativity, and evaluation. I. Hypothesis and description of tests. *Reports from the psychology laboratory.* Los Angeles: University of Southern California.

Guilford, J. P. (1959). *Personality.* New York: McGraw-Hill.

Guilford, J. P. (1967). *The nature of human intelligence.* New York: McGraw-Hill.

Guilford, J. P., et al. (1974). *Structure-of-Intellect Abilities.* Orange, CA: Sheridan Psychological Services.

Guilmette, T. J., & Faust, D. (1991). Characteristics of neuropsychologists who prefer the Halstead-Reitan Battery or the Luria-Nebraska Neuropsychological Battery. *Professional Psychology: Research and Practice, 22*(1), 80–83.

Guilmette, T. J., Faust, D., Hart, K., & Arkes, H. R. (1990). A national survey of psychologists who offer neuropsychological services. *Archives of Clinical Neuropsychology, 5,* 373–392.

Guion, R. M. (1980). On trinitarian doctrines of validity. *Professional Psychology, 11,* 385–398.

Gulliksen, H., & Messick, S. (Eds.). (1960). *Psychological scaling: Theory and applications.* New York: Wiley.

Gustafson, S., Fälth, L., Svensson, I., et al. (2011). Effects of three interventions on the reading skills of children with reading disabilities in grade 2. *Journal of Learning Disabilities, 44*(2), 123–135.

Guttman, L. (1947). The Cornell technique for scale and intensity analysis. *Educational and Psychological Measurement, 7,* 247–280.

Guttman, L. A. (1944a). A basis for scaling qualitative data. *American Sociological Review, 9,* 139–150.

Guttman, L. A. (1944b). A basis for scaling qualitative data. *American Sociological Review, 9,* 179–190.

Haaga, D. A., Davison, G. C., McDermut, W., Hillis, S. L., & Twomey, H. B. (1993). "State of mind" analysis of the articulated thoughts of ex-smokers. *Cognitive Therapy and Research, 17,* 427–439.

Hadaway, N., & Marek-Schroer, M. F. (1992). Multidimensional assessment of the gifted minority student. *Roeper Review, 15,* 73–77.

Haensly, P. A., & Torrance, E. P. (1990). Assessment of creativity in children and adolescents. In C. R. Reynolds & R. W. Kamphaus (Eds.), *Handbook of psychological and educational assessment of children: Intelligence & achievement* (pp. 697–722). New York: Guilford.

Hafemeister, T. L. (2001, February). Ninth Circuit rejects immunity from liability for mental health evaluations. *Monitor on Psychology, 32.*

Hagan, L. D., Drogin, E. Y., & Guilmette, T. J. (2010). Science rather than advocacy when reporting IQ scores. *Professional Psychology: Research and Practice, 41*(5), 420–423.

Haidt, J., Rosenberg, E., & Horn, H. (2003). Differentiating differences: Moral diversity is not like other kinds. *Journal of Applied Social Psychology, 33,* 1–36.

Haier, R. J. (1993). Cerebral glucose metabolism and intelligence. In P. A. Vernon (Ed.), *Biological approaches to the study of human intelligence* (pp. 317–332). Norwood, NJ: Ablex.

Haines, M., & Spear, S. F. (1996). Changing the perception of the norm: A strategy to decrease binge drinking among college students. *Journal of American College Health, 45*(3), 134–140.

Hale, J. B., & Fiorello, C. A. (2004). *School neuropsychology: A practitioner's handbook.* New York: Guilford Press.

Haley, K., & Lee, M. (Eds.). (1998). *The Oregon Death With Dignity Act: A guidebook for health care providers.* Portland: Oregon Health Sciences University, Center for Ethics in Health Care.

Hall, C. I. J. (1997). Cultural malpractice: The growing obsolescence of psychology with the changing U.S. population. *American Psychologist, 52,* 642–651.

Hall, C. S., & Lindzey, G. (1970). *Theories of personality.* New York: Wiley.

Hall, J. A., & Rosenthal, R. (1995). Interpreting and evaluating meta-analysis. *Evaluation and the Health Professions, 18,* 393–407.

Hall, S. S. (1998, February 15). Our memories, our selves. *New York Times Magazine,* pp. 26–33, 49, 56–57.

Halleck, S. L. (1976). Discussion of "Socially Reinforced Obsessing." *Journal of Consulting and Clinical Psychology, 44,* 146–147.

Halpern, A. S., & Fuhrer, M. J. (Eds.). (1984). *Functional assessment in rehabilitation.* Baltimore: Paul H. Brookes.

Halpern, D. F. (1997). Sex differences in intelligence: Implications for education. *American Psychologist, 52,* 1901–1102.

Halpern, D. F. (2000). Validity, fairness, and group differences: Tough questions for selection testing. *Psychology, Public Policy, & Law, 6,* 56–62.

Halpern, F. (1958). Child case study. In E. F. Hammer (Ed.), *The clinical application of projective drawings* (pp. 113–129). Springfield, IL: Charles C Thomas.

Halstead, W. C. (1947a). *Brain and intelligence.* Chicago: University of Chicago.

Halstead, W. C. (1947b). *Brain and intelligence: A quantitative study of the frontal lobes.* Chicago: University of Chicago.

Halstead, W. C., & Wepman, J. M. (1959). The Halstead-Wepman Aphasia Screening Test. *Journal of Speech and Hearing Disorders, 14,* 9–15.

Hambleton, R. K., & Jones, R. W. (1993). Comparison of classical test theory and item response theory and their applications to test development. *Educational Measurement: Issues and Practice, 12*(3), 38–47.

Hambleton, R. K., & Jurgensen, C. (1990). Criterion-referenced assessment of school achievement. In C. R. Reynolds & R. W. Kamphaus (Eds.), *Handbook of psychological and educational assessment of children: Intelligence & achievement* (pp. 456–476). New York: Guilford.

Hambleton, R. K., & Novick, M. R. (1973). Toward and integration of theory and method for criterion-referenced tests. *Journal of Educational Measurement, 15,* 277–290.

Hambleton, R. K., & Swaminathan, H. (1984). *Item response theory: Principles and applications.* Boston: Springer.

Hambleton, S. E., & Swaminathan, H. (1985). *Item response theory: Principles and applications.* Boston: Kluwer Nijoff.

Hambrick, D. Z., Rench, T. A., Poposki, E. M., et al. (2011). The relationship between the ASVAB and multitasking in navy sailors: A process-specific approach. *Military Psychology, 23*(4), 365–380.

Hamera, E., & Brown, C. E. (2000). Developing a context-based performance measure for persons with schizophrenia: The test of grocery shopping skills. *American Journal of Occupational Therapy, 54,* 20–25.

Hammer, E. F. (1958). *The clinical application of projective drawings.* Springfield, IL: Charles C Thomas.

Hammer, E. F. (1981). Projective drawings. In A. I. Rabin (Ed.), *Assessment with projective techniques: A concise introduction* (pp. 151–185). New York: Springer.

Hammitt, J. K. (1990). Risk perceptions and food choice: An exploratory analysis of organic—versus conventional—produce buyers. *Risk Analysis, 10,* 367–374.

Handel, R. W., Ben-Porath, Y. S., Tellegen, A., & Archer, R. P. (2010). Psychometric functioning of the MMPI-2-RF, VRIN-r, and TRIN-r scales with varying degrees of randomness, acquiescence, and counter-acquiescence. *Psychological Assessment, 22,* 87–95.

Handler, L. (1996). John Exner and the book that started it all: A review of *The Rorschach Systems. Journal of Personality Assessment, 66,* 441–471.

Handler, L. (2001). Assessment of men: Personality assessment goes to war by the Office of Strategic Services Assessment Staff. *Journal of Personality Assessment, 76,* 558–578.

Haney, W. (1981). Validity, vaudeville, and values: A short history of social concerns over standardized testing. *American Psychologist, 36,* 1021–1034.

Haney, W., & Madaus, G. F. (1978). Making sense of the competency testing movement. *Harvard Educational Review, 48,* 462–484.

Hansen, J. C. (1987). Cross-cultural research on vocational interests. *Measurement and Evaluation in Counseling and Development, 19,* 163–176.

Hansen, K. K., Prince, J. S., & Nixon, G. W. (2008). Oblique chest views as a routine part of skeletal surveys performed for possible physical abuse: Is this practice worthwhile? *Child Abuse & Neglect, 32*(1), 155–159.

Hansen, N. D. (2002). Teaching cultural sensitivity in psychological assessment: A modular approach used in a distance education program. *Journal of Personality, 79,* 200–206.

Hansen, N. D., Pepitone-Arreola-Rockwell, F., & Greene, A. F. (2000). Multicultural competence: Criteria and case examples. *Professional Psychology: Research and Practice, 31,* 652–660.

Happell, B., Pinikahana, J., & Martin, T. (2003). Stress and burnout in forensic psychiatric nursing. *Stress & Health, 19,* 63–68.

Haque, S., & Guyer, M. (2010). Neuroimaging studies in diminished-capacity defense. *Journal of the American Academy of Psychiatry and the Law, 38*(4), 605–607.

Hare, R. D. (1980). A research scale for the assessment of psychopathy in criminal populations. *Personality and Individual Differences, 1,* 111–119.

Hare, R. D. (1985). *The Psychopathy Checklist.* Unpublished manuscript. University of British Columbia, Vancouver.

Hare, R. D., Harpur, A. R., Hakstian, A. R., Forth, A. E., Hart, S. D., & Newman, J. P. (1990). The Revised Psychopathy Checklist: Reliability and factor structure. *Psychological Assessment, 2,* 338–341.

Harker, L., & Keltner, D. (2001). Expressions of positive emotion in women's college yearbook pictures and their relationship to personality and life outcomes across adulthood. *Journal of Personality and Social Psychology, 80,* 112–124.

Harmon, L. W., Hansen, J. C., Borgen, F. H., & Hammer, A. L. (1994). *Strong Interest Inventory: Applications and technical guide.* Palo Alto, CA: Consulting Psychologists Press.

Harris, D. (1963). *Children's drawings as measures of intellectual maturity.* New York: Harcourt Brace Jovanovich.

Harris, G. T., Rice, M. E., & Cormier, C. A. (1989). Violent recidivism among psychopaths and non-psychopaths treated in a therapeutic community. *Penetanguishene Mental Health Centre Research Report VI* (No. 181). Penetanguishene, Ontario, Canada: Penetanguishene Mental Health Centre.

Harris, P. M. (1994). Client management classification and prediction of probation outcome. *Crime and Delinquency, 40,* 154–174.

Harris, S. L., Delmolino, L., & Glasberg, B. A. (1996). Psychological and behavioral assessment in mental retardation. *Child & Adolescent Psychiatric Clinics of North America, 5,* 797–808.

Harrison, P., & Oakland, T. (2000). *Adaptive Behavior Assessment System.* San Antonio: Psychological Corporation.

Harrison, P. L. (1990). *AGS Early Screening Profiles.* Circle Pines, MN: American Guidance Service.

Harstine, M. A. (2008). Understanding the relationship between the diligence inventory–higher education edition and the Myers-Briggs Type Indicator in the admission of college students to an orthopaedics-based honors program. *Dissertation Abstracts International. Section A. Humanities and Social Sciences, 68* (8-A), 3307.

Hartston, H. (2008). The state of psychotherapy in the United States. *Journal of Psychotherapy Integration, 18*(1), 87–102.

Hart, B., & Risley, T. R. (1992). American parenting of language-learning children: Persisting differences in family-child interactions observed in natural home environments. *Developmental Psychology, 28,* 1096–1105.

Hart, R. R., & Goldstein, M. A. (1985). Computer-assisted psychological assessment. *Computers in Human Services, 1,* 69–75.

Hart, S. D., Kropp, P. R., & Hare, R. D. (1988). Performance of male psychopaths following conditional release from prison. *Journal of Consulting and Clinical Psychology, 56,* 227–232.

Hart, V. (1992). Review of the Infant Mullen Scales of Early Development. In J. J. Kramer & J. C. Conoley (Eds.), *The eleventh mental measurements yearbook.* Lincoln: Buros Institute of Mental Measurements, University of Nebraska.

Hartigan, J. A., & Wigdor, A. K. (1989). *Fairness in employment testing: Validity generalization, minority issues, and the General Aptitude Test Battery.* Washington, DC: National Academy.

Hartman, D. E. (1986a). Artificial intelligence or artificial psychologist? Conceptual issues in clinical microcomputer use. *Professional Psychology: Research and Practice, 17,* 528–534.

Hartman, D. E. (1986b). On the use of clinical psychology software: Practical, legal, and ethical concerns. *Professional Psychology: Research and Practice, 17,* 462–465.

Hartmann, D. P., Roper, B. L., & Bradford, D. C. (1979). Some relationships between behavioral and traditional assessment. *Journal of Behavioral Assessment, 1,* 3–21.

Hartmann, E., Sunde, T., Kristensen, W., & Martinussen, M. (2003). Psychological measures as predictors of military training performance. *Journal of Personality Assessment, 80,* 87–98.

Hartshorne, H., & May, M. A. (1928). *Studies in the nature of character. Vol. 1: Studies in deceit.* New York: Macmillan.

Harvey, R. J., & Hammer, A. L. (1999). Item response theory. *Counseling Psychologist, 27,* 353–383.

Harvey, R. J., & Murry, W. D. (1994). Scoring the Myers-Briggs Type Indicator: Empirical comparison of preference score versus latent-trait methods. *Journal of Personality Assessment, 62,* 116–129.

Hassler, M., & Gupta, D. (1993). Functional brain organization, handedness, and immune vulnerability in musicians and nonmusicians. *Neuropsychologia, 31,* 655–660.

Hathaway, S. R., & McKinley, J. C. (1940). A multiphasic personality schedule (Minnesota): 1. Construction of the schedule. *Journal of Psychology, 10,* 249–254.

Hathaway, S. R., & McKinley, J. C. (1942). A multiphasic personality schedule (Minnesota): III. The measurement of symptomatic depression. *Journal of Psychology, 14,* 73–84.

Hathaway, S. R., & McKinley, J. C. (1943). *The Minnesota Multiphasic Personality Inventory* (rev. ed.). Minneapolis: University of Minnesota.

Hathaway, S. R., & McKinley, J. C. (1951). *The MMPI manual.* New York: Psychological Corporation.

Haworth, C. M. A., Wright, M. J., Luciano, M., et al. (2010). The heritability of general cognitive ability increases linearly from childhood to young adulthood. *Molecular Psychiatry, 15,* 1112–1120

Hayden, D. C., Frulong, M. J., & Linnemeyer, S. (1988). A comparison of the Kaufman Assessment Battery for Children and the Stanford-Binet IV for the assessment of gifted children. *Psychology in the Schools, 25,* 239–243.

Hayes, S. C. (1999). Comparison of the Kaufman Brief Intelligence Test and the Matrix Analogies Test-Short Form in an adolescent forensic population. *Psychological Assessment, 11,* 108–110.

Haynes, R. B., Taylor, D. W., & Sackett, D. L. (Eds.). (1979). *Compliance in health care.* Baltimore: Johns Hopkins University.

Haynes, S. N. (2001a). Clinical applications of analogue behavioral observation: Dimensions of psychometric evaluation. *Psychological Assessment, 13,* 73–85.

Haynes, S. N. (2001b). Introduction to the special section on clinical applications of analogue behavioral observation. *Psychological Assessment, 13,* 3–4.

Haynes, S. N., Follingstad, D. R., & Sullivan, J. (1979). Assessment of marital satisfaction and interaction. *Journal of Consulting and Clinical Psychology, 47,* 789–791.

Haynes, S. N., Jensen, B. J., Wise, E., & Sherman, D. (1981). The marital intake interview: A multimethod criterion validity assessment. *Journal of Consulting and Clinical Psychology, 49,* 379–387.

Haynes, S. N., & Kaholokula, J. K. (2008). Behavioral assessment. In M. Hersen & A. M. Gross (Eds.), *Handbook of clinical psychology: Vol. 1. Adults* (pp. 495–522). Hoboken, NJ: Wiley.

Haynes, S. N., Richard, D. R., & Kubany, E. S. (1995). Content validity in psychological assessment: A functional approach to concepts and methods. *Psychological Assessment, 7,* 238–247.

Hays, P. A. (1996). Culturally responsive assessment with diverse older clients. *Professional Psychology: Research and Practice, 27,* 188–193.

Hays, J. R., Reas, D. L., and Shaw, J. B. (2002). Concurrent validity of the Wechsler Abbreviated Scale of Intelligence and the Kaufman Brief Intelligence Test among psychiatric inpatients. *Psychological Reports, 90*(2), 355–59.

Hays, P. A., & Iwamasa, G. Y. (Eds.). (2006). *Culturally responsive cognitive-behavioral therapy: Assessment, practice, and supervision.* Washington, DC: American Psychological Association.

Haywood, H., & Lidz, C. S. (2007). *Dynamic assessment in practice: Clinical and educational applications.* New York: Cambridge University Press.

Hazlett, R. L., Falkin, S., Lawhorn, W., Friedman, E., & Haynes, S. N. (1997). Cardiovascular reactivity to a naturally occurring stressor: Development and psychometric evaluation of psychophysiological assessment procedure. *Journal of Behavioral Medicine, 20,* 551–571.

He, W. (2011). Optimal item pool design for a highly constrained computerized adaptive test. *Dissertation Abstracts International, 72* (1-A), 167.

Heaton, R. K., Temkin, N., Dikmen, S., et al. (2001). Detecting change: A comparison of three neuropsychological methods, using normal and clinical samples. *Archives of Clinical Neuropsychology, 16,* 75–91.

Hedges, C. (1997, November 25). In Bosnia's schools, 3 ways never to learn from history. *New York Times,* pp. A1, A4.

Heinrichs, R. W. (1990). Variables associated with Wisconsin Card Sorting Test performance in neuropsychiatric patients referred for assessment. *Neuropsychiatry, Neuropsychology, and Behavioral Neurology, 3,* 107–112.

Heinze, M. C., & Grisso, T. (1996). Review of instruments assessing parenting competencies used in child custody evaluations. *Behavioral Sciences and the Law, 14,* 293–313.

Helfer, R. E., & Kempe, R. S. (Eds.). (1988). *The battered child* (4th ed.). Chicago: University of Chicago Press.

Heller, T. S., Hawgood, J. L., & De Leo, D. (2007). Correlates of suicide in building industry workers. *Archives of Suicide Research, 11*(1), 105–117.

Helmes, E., & Reddon, J. R. (1993). A perspective on developments in assessing psychopathology: A critical review of the MMPI and MMPI-2. *Psychological Bulletin, 113,* 453–471.

Helmreich, R. L. (1983). Applying psychology in outer space: Unfilled promises revisited. *American Psychologist, 38*(4), 445–450.

Helmreich, R. L., Wilhelm, J. A., Tamer, T. A., et al. (1979, January). A critical review of the life sciences project management at Ames Research Center for the Spacelab Mission Development Test III (NASA Technical Paper 1364).

Helson, R. (1967). Personality characteristics and developmental history of creative college women. *Genetic Psychology Monographs, 76,* 205–256.

Helson, R., Mitchell, V., & Moane, G. (1984). Personality and patterns of adherence and nonadherence to the social clock. *Journal of Personality and Social Psychology, 46,* 1079–1096.

Henk, W. A. (1993). New directions in reading assessment. *Reading and Writing Quarterly: Overcoming Learning Difficulties, 9,* 103–120.

Henley, N. M., & LaFrance, M. (1984). Gender as culture: Difference in dominance in nonverbal behavior. In A. Wolfgang (Ed.), *Nonverbal behavior: Perspectives, applications, intercultural insights* (pp. 351–371). Lewiston, NY: Hogrefe & Huber.

Henriques, G., Keffer, S., Abrahamson, C., et al. (2011). Exploring the effectiveness of a computer-based heart rate variability biofeedback program in reducing anxiety in college students. *Applied Psychophysiology and Biofeedback, 36*(2), 101–112.

Henry, E. M., & Rotter, J. B. (1956). Situational influences on Rorschach responses. *Journal of Consulting Psychology, 20,* 457–462.

Henry, J. D. (1984). Syndicated public opinion polls: Some thoughts for consideration. *Journal of Advertising Research, 24,* I-5–I-8.

Henry, W. E. (1956). *The analysis of fantasy.* New York: Wiley.

Henson, R. K. (2001). Understanding internal consistency reliability estimates: A conceptual primer on coefficient alpha. *Measurement and Evaluation in Counseling and Development, 34,* 177–189.

Heppner, M. J. (1998). The Career Transitions Inventory: Measuring internal resources in adulthood. *Journal of Career Assessment, 6,* 135–145.

Heppner, M. J., Multon, K. D., & Johnston, J. A. (1994). Assessing psychological resources during career change: Development of the Career Transitions Inventory. *Journal of Vocational Behavior, 44,* 55–74.

Herbranson, W. T., & Schroeder, J. (2010). Are birds smarter than mathematicians? Pigeons (Columba livia) perform optimally on a version of the Monty Hall Dilemma. *Journal of Comparative Psychology, 124*(1), 1–13.

Herlihy, B. (1977). Watch out, IQ myth: Here comes another debunker. *Phi Delta Kappan, 59,* 298.

Hermann, C., Blanchard, E. B., & Flor, H. (1997). Biofeedback treatment for pediatric migraine: Prediction of treatment outcome. *Journal of Consulting and Clinical Psychology, 65,* 611–616.

Hernandez, B., Keys, C., & Balcazar, F. (2003). The Americans wth Disabilities Act Knowledge Survey: Strong psychometrics and weak knowledge. *Rehabilitation Psychology, 48,* 93–99.

Herrnstein, R., & Murray, C. (1994). *The bell curve.* New York: Free Press.

Herzberg, F., Mausner, B., Peterson, R. O., & Capwell, D. F. (1957). Job attitudes: Review of research and opinion. *Journal of Applied Psychology, 63,* 596–601.

Hess, E. H. (1965). Attitude and pupil size. *Scientific American, 212,* 46–54.

Hetherington, E. M., & Parke, R. D. (1993). *Child psychology: A contemporary viewpoint* (4th ed.). New York: McGraw-Hill.

Heyman, R. E. (2001). Observation of couple conflicts: Clinical assessment applications, stubborn truths, and shaky foundations. *Psychological Assessment, 13,* 5–35.

Hibbard, S. (2003). A critique of Lilienfeld et al.'s (2000) "The scientific status of projective techniques." *Journal of Personality Assessment, 80,* 260–271.

Hibbard, S., Farmer, L., Wells, C., et al. (1994). Validation of Cramer's defense mechanism manual for the TAT. *Journal of Personality Assessment, 63,* 197–210.

Hicks, L. K., Lin, Y., Robertson, D. W., et al. (2001). Understanding the clinical dilemmas that shape medical students' ethical development: Questionnaire survey and focus group study. *British Medical Journal, 322,* 709–710.

Hicks, S. J., & Sales, B. D. (2006). The current models of scientific profiling. In S. J. Hicks & B. D. Sales (Eds.), *Criminal profiling: Developing an effective science and practice* (pp. 71–85). Washington, DC: American Psychological Association.

Higgins, P. C. (1983). *Outsiders in a hearing world.* Beverly Hills, CA: Sage.

Hill, J. S., Pace, T. M., & Robbins, R. R. (2010). Decolonizing personality assessment and honoring indigenous voices: A critical examination of the MMPI-2. *Cultural Diversity and Ethnic Minority Psychology, 16*(1), 16–25.

Hill, K. A. (1985). Hartsoeker's homonculus: A corrective note. *Journal of the History of the Behavioral Sciences, 21*(2), 178–179.

Hill-Briggs, F., Dial, J. G., Morere, D. A., & Joyce, A. (2007). Neuropsychological assessment of persons with physical disability, visual impairment or blindness, and hearing impairment or deafness. *Archives of Clinical Neuropsychology, 22*(3), 389–404.

Hiller, J. B., Rosenthal, R., Bornstein, R. F., & Brunell-Neuleib, S. (1999). A comparative meta-analysis of Rorschach and MMPI validity. *Psychological Assessment, 11,* 278–296.

Hills, D. A. (1985). Prediction of effectiveness in leaderless group discussions with the Adjective Check List. *Journal of Applied Psychology, 15,* 443–447.

Hines, M., Chiu, L., McAdams, L. A., Bentler, M. P., & Lipcamon, J. (1992). Cognition and the corpus callosum: Verbal fluency, visuospatial ability, language lateralization related to midsagittal surface areas of the corpus callosum. *Behavioral Neuroscience, 106,* 3–14.

Hinrichsen, J. J., & Bradley, L. A. (1974). Situational determinants of personal validation of general personality interpretations: A re-examination. *Journal of Personality Assessment, 38,* 530–534.

Hirsch, J. (1997). Some history of heredity-vs-environment, genetic inferiority at Harvard(?), and *The* (incredible) *bell curve. Genetics, 99,* 207–224.

Hiscox, M. D. (1983). *A balance sheet for educational item banking.* Paper presented at the annual meeting of the National Council for Measurement in Education, Montreal.

Hiscox, M. D., & Brzezinski, E. (1980). *A guide to item banking in education.* Portland, OR: Northwest Regional Educational Laboratory, Assessment and Education Division.

Hishinuma, E. S., Andrade, N. N., Johnson, R. C., et al. (2000). Psychometric properties of the Hawaiian Culture Scale-Adolescent Version. *Psychological Assessment, 12,* 140–157.

Hishinuma, E. S., & Yamakawa, R. (1993). Construct and criterion-related validity of the WISC-III for exceptional students and those who are "at risk." In B. A. Bracken (Ed.), *Monograph series, Advances in psychoeducational assessment: Wechsler Intelligence Scale for Children, Third Edition; Journal of Psychoeducational Assessment* (pp. 94–104). Brandon, VT: Clinical Psychology Publishing.

Hiskey, M. S. (1966). *Hiskey-Nebraska Test of Learning Aptitude.* Lincoln, NE: Union College.

Ho, M. K. (1987). *Family therapy with ethnic minorities.* Newbury Park, CA: Sage.

Hodapp, R. M. (1995). Definitions in mental retardation: Effects on research, practice, and perceptions. *School Psychology Quarterly, 10*(1), 24–28.

Hoelzle, J. B., Nelson, N. W., & Smith, C. A. (2011). Comparison of Wechsler Memory Scale–Fourth Edition (WMS–IV) and Third Edition (WMS–III) dimensional structures: Improved ability to evaluate auditory and visual constructs. *Journal of Clinical and Experimental Neuropsychology, 33*(3), 283–291.

Hofer, P. J., & Green, B. F. (1985). The challenge of competence and creativity in computerized psychological testing. *Journal of Consulting and Clinical Psychology, 53,* 826–838.

Hoffman, B. (1962). *The tyranny of testing.* New York: Crowell-Collier.

Hoffman, K. I., & Lundberg, G. D. (1976). A comparison of computer monitored group tests and paper-and-pencil tests. *Educational and Psychological Measurement, 36,* 791–809.

Hofstede, G. (1998). Attitudes, values, and organizational culture: Disentangling the concepts. *Organization Studies, 19,* 477–493.

Hogan, J., Barrett, P., & Hogan, R. (2007). Personality measurement, faking, and employment selection. *Journal of Applied Psychology, 92,* 1270–1285.

Hogan, R., & Roberts, B. W. (2001). Introduction: Personality and industrial and organizational psychology. In B. W. Roberts & R. Hogan (Eds.). *Personality psychology in the workplace* (pp. 3–16). Washington, DC: American Psychological Association.

Hoge, R. D. (1999). An expanded role for psychological assessments in juvenile justice systems. *Criminal Justice and Behavior, 26,* 251–266.

Hoge, S. K., Bonnie, R. J., Poythress, N., & Monahan, J. (1999). *The MacArthur Competence Assessment Tool— Criminal Adjudication.* Odessa, FL: Psychological Assessment Resources.

Holahan, C., & Sears, R. (1995). *The gifted group in later maturity.* Stanford, CA: Stanford University Press.

Holden, G. W., & Edwards, L. A. (1989). Parental attitudes toward child rearing: Instruments, issues, and implications. *Psychological Bulletin, 106,* 29–58.

Holland, A. (1980). *Communicative abilities in daily living: A test of functional communication for aphasic adults.* Baltimore: University Park Press.

Holland, J. L. (1973). *Making vocational choices.* Englewood Cliffs, NJ: Prentice-Hall.

Holland, J. L. (1985). *Manual for the vocational preference inventory.* Odessa, FL: Psychological Assessment Resources.

Holland, J. L. (1997). *Making vocational choices: A theory of vocational personalities and work environments* (3rd ed.). Odessa, FL: Psychological Assessment Resources.

Holland, J. L. (1999). Why interest inventories are also personality inventories. In M. L. Savickas & A. R. Spokane (Eds.), *Vocational interests: Meaning, measurement, and counseling use* (87–101). Palo Alto, CA: Davies-Black.

Holland, J. L., Powell, A. B., & Fritzsche, B. A. (1994). *The Self-Directed Search (SDS) professional user's guide—1994 edition.* Odessa, FL: Psychological Assessment Resources.

Holland, W. R. (1960). Language barrier as an educational problem of Spanish-speaking children. *Exceptional Children, 27,* 42–47.

Hollander, E. P., & Willis, R. H. (1967). Some current issues in the psychology of conformity and nonconformity. *Psychological Bulletin, 68,* 62–76.

Hollenbeck, J. R., & Whitener, E. M. (1988). Reclaiming personality traits for personal selection: Self-esteem as an illustrative case. *Journal of Management, 14,* 81–91.

Hollingshead, A. B., & Redlich, F. C. (1958). *Social class and mental illness: A community study.* New York: Wiley.

Holmstrom, R. W., Silber, D. E., & Karp, S. A. (1990). Development of the Apperceptive Personality Test. *Journal of Personality Assessment, 54,* 252–264.

Holt, R. R. (1958). Clinical and statistical prediction: A reformulation and some new data. *Journal of Abnormal and Social Psychology, 56,* 1–12.

Holt, R. R. (1970). Yet another look at clinical and statistical prediction: Or, is clinical psychology worthwhile? *American Psychologist, 25,* 337–349.

Holt, R. R. (1971). *Assessing personality.* New York: Harcourt Brace Jovanovich.

Holt, R. R. (1978). *Methods in clinical psychology: Vol. 2. Prediction and research.* New York: Plenum.

Holtzman, W. H. (1993). An unjustified, sweeping indictment by Motta et al. of human figure drawings for assessing psychological functioning. *School Psychology Quarterly, 8,* 189–190.

Holtzman, W. H., Thorpe, J. S., Swartz, J. D., & Herron, E. W. (1961). *Inkblot perception and personality: Holtzman Inkblot Technique.* Austin: University of Texas Press.

Hom, J. (2008). Commentary. Response to Bigler (2007): The sky is not falling. *Archives of Clinical Neuropsychology, 23,* 125–128.

Honaker, L. M. (1988). The equivalency of computerized and conventional MMPI administration: A review. *Clinical Psychology Review, 8,* 561–577.

Honaker, L. M. (1990, August). Recommended guidelines for computer equivalency research (or everything you should know about computer administration but will be disappointed if you ask). In W. J. Camara (Chair), *The state of computer-based testing and interpretation: Consensus or chaos?* Symposium conducted at the Annual Convention of the American Psychological Association, Boston.

Honaker, L. M., & Fowler, R. D. (1990). Computer-assisted psychological assessment. In G. Goldstein & M. Hersen (Eds.), *Handbook of psychological assessment* (2nd ed., pp. 521–546). New York: Pergamon.

Honts, C. R. (1994). Psychophysiological detection of deception. *Current Directions in Psychological Science, 3,* 77–82.

Honzik, M. P. (1967). Environmental correlates of mental growth: Prediction from the family setting at 21 months. *Child Development, 38,* 337–364.

Hopkins, K. D., & Glass, G. V. (1978). *Basic statistics for the behavioral sciences.* Englewood Cliffs, NJ: Prentice-Hall.

Hopwood v. State of Texas, 78 F.3d 932, 948 (5th Cir. 1996).

Horn, J. (1988). Thinking about human abilities. In J. R. Nesselroade & R. B. Cattell (Eds.), *Handbook of multivariate psychology*. New York: Plenum.

Horn, J. (2008). Response to Bigler (2007): The sky is not falling. *Archives of Clinical Neuropsychology, 23*(1), 125–128.

Horn, J. L. (1968). Organization of abilities and the development of intelligence. *Psychological Review, 75*, 242–259.

Horn, J. L. (1985). Remodeling old theories of intelligence: *GF-Gc* theory. In B. B. Wolman (Ed.), *Handbook of intelligence* (pp. 267–300). New York: Wiley.

Horn, J. L. (1988). Thinking about human abilities. In J. R. Nesselroade & R. B. Cattell (Eds.), *Handbook of multivariate psychology* (rev. ed., pp. 645–685). New York: Academic Press.

Horn, J. L. (1989). Cognitive diversity: A framework for learning. In P. L. Ackerman et al. (Eds.), *Learning and individual differences* (pp. 61–116). New York: W. H. Freeman.

Horn, J. L. (1991). Measurement of intellectual capabilities: A review of theory. In K. S. McGrew et al. (Eds.), *Woodcock-Johnson technical manual* (pp. 197–232). Chicago: Riverside.

Horn, J. L. (1994). Theory of fluid and crystallized intelligence. In R. J. Sternberg (Ed.), *Encyclopedia of human intelligence* (pp. 443–451). New York, NY: Macmillan Publishing Co, Inc.

Horn, J. L., & Cattell, R. B. (1966). Refinement and test of the theory of fluid and crystallized intelligence. *Journal of Educational Psychology, 57*, 253–270.

Horn, J. L., & Cattell, R. B. (1967). Age differences in fluid and crystallized intelligence. *Acta Psychologica, 26*, 107–129.

Horn, J. L., & Hofer, S. M. (1992). Major abilities and development in the adult period. In R. J. Sternberg & C. A. Berg (Eds.), *Intellectual development* (pp. 44–99). Boston: Cambridge University Press.

Hornby, R. (1993). *Cultural competence for human service providers*. Rosebud, SD: Sinte Gleska University Press.

Horne, J. (2007). Gender differences in computerized and conventional educational tests. *Journal of Computer Assisted Learning, 23*(1), 47–55.

Horner, M. S. (1973). A psychological barrier to achievement in women: The motive to avoid success. In D. C. McClelland & R. S. Steele (Eds.), *Human motivation* (pp. 222–230). Morristown, NJ: General Learning.

Horowitz, R., & Murphy, L. B. (1938). Projective methods in the psychological study of children. *Journal of Experimental Education, 7*, 133–140.

Horvath, A. O., Del Re, A. C., Flukiger, C., & Symonds, D. (2011). Alliance in individual psychotherapy. *Psychotherapy, 48*, 9–16.

Hostetler, A. J. (1987). Try to remember. *APA Monitor, 18*(5), 18.

Hough, L. M. (1998). The millennium for personality psychology: New horizons or good ole daze. *Applied Psychology: An International Review, 47*, 233–261.

Hough, L. M., Eaton, N. K., Dunnette, M. D., et al. (1990). Criterion related validities of personality constructs and the effect of response distortion on those validities. *Journal of Applied Psychology, 75*, 581–595.

House, R. J., Shane, S. A., & Herold, D. M. (1996). Rumors of the death of dispositional research are vastly exaggerated. *Academy of Management Review, 20*, 203–224.

Houston, T. K., Cooper, L. A., Vu, H., et al. (2001). Screening the public for depression through the Internet. *Psychiatric Services, 52*, 362–367.

Howard, M. N. (1991). The neutral expert: A plausible threat to justice. *Criminal Law Review* 1991:98–105.

Howe Chief, E. (1940). An assimilation study of Indian girls. *Journal of Social Psychology, 11*, 19–30.

Hsu, S.-H., & Peng, Y. (1993). Control/display relationship of the four-burner stove: A re-examination. *Human Factors, 35*, 745–749.

Hu, Y., Geng, F., Tao, L., et al. (2011). Enhanced white matter tracts integrity in children with abacus training. *Human Brain Mapping, 32*(1), 10–21.

Huang, L. V., Bardos, A. N., & D'Amato, R. C. (2010). Identifying students with learning disabilities: Composite profile analysis using the cognitive assessment system. *Journal of Psychoeducational Assessment, 28*(1), 19–30.

Huang, Y.-C., & Shih, H.-C. (2011). The prosocial and moral character of the spiritual leader. *Social Behavior and Personality, 39*(1), 33–40.

Hubbard, E. J., Santini, V., Blankevoort, C. G., et al. (2008). Clock drawing performance in cognitively normal elderly. *Archives of Clinical Neuropsychology, 23*(3), 295–327.

Hudson, W. W. (1982). *The clinical measurement package: A field manual*. Chicago: Dorsey.

Huesmann, L. R., & Guerra, N. G. (1997). Children's normative beliefs about aggression and aggressive behavior. *Journal of Personality and Social Psychology, 72*, 408–419.

Huffcutt, A. I., & Arthur, W., Jr. (1994). Hunter and Hunter (1984) revisited: Interview validity for entry-level jobs. *Journal of Applied Psychology, 79*, 184–190.

Hughes, T. L., Gacono, C. B., & Owen, P. F. (2007). Current status of Rorschach assessment: Implications for the school psychologist. *Psychology in the Schools, 44*(3), 281–291.

Huguet, S., & Philippe, R. A. (2011). A case study of the emotional aspects of the coach-athlete relationship in tennis. *International Journal of Sport Psychology, 42*(1), 24–39.

Hull, C. L. (1922). *Aptitude testing*. Yonkers, NY: World Book.

Hulse, W. G. (1951). The emotionally disturbed child draws his family. *Quarterly Journal of Child Behavior, 3*, 151–174.

Hulse, W. G. (1952). Childhood conflict expressed through family drawings. *Quarterly Journal of Child Behavior, 16*, 152–174.

Humphreys, L. G. (1996). Linear dependence of gain scores on their components imposes constraints on their use and interpretation: Comment on "Are simple gain scores obsolete?" *Applied Psychological Measurement, 20*, 293–294.

Hunsley, J., & Bailey, J. M. (1999). The clinical utility of the Rorschach: Unfulfilled promises and an uncertain future. *Psychological Assessment, 11*, 266–277.

Hunt, J. McV. (1961). *Intelligence and experience*. New York: Ronald.

Hunt, K. N. (2002). *Encyclopedia of associations*. Farmington Hills, MI: Gale Group.

Hunt, K. N. (2005). *Encyclopedia of associations*. Farmington Hills, MI: Gale Group.

Hunter, J. E. (1980). *Validity generalization for 12,000 jobs: An application of synthetic validity and validity generalization to the General Aptitude Test Battery (GATB)*. Washington, DC: U.S. Employment Service, Department of Labor.

Hunter, J. E. (1982). *The dimensionality of the General Aptitude Test Battery and the dominance of general factors over specific factors in the prediction of job performance*. Washington, DC: U.S. Employment Service, Department of Labor.

Hunter, J. E. (1986). Cognitive ability, cognitive aptitudes, job knowledge, and job performance. *Journal of Vocational Behavior, 29*, 340–362.

Hunter, J. E., & Hunter, R. (1984). Validity and utility of alternate predictors of job performance. *Psychological Bulletin, 96*, 72–98.

Hunter, J. E., & Schmidt, F. L. (1976). A critical analysis of the statistical and ethical implications of various definitions of "test bias." *Psychological Bulletin, 83*, 1053–1071.

Hunter, J. E., & Schmidt, F. L. (1981). Fitting people into jobs: The impact of personal selection on normal productivity.

In M. D. Dunnette & E. A. Fleishman (Eds.), *Human performance and productivity: Vol. 1. Human capability assessment*. Hillsdale, NJ: Erlbaum.

Hunter, J. E., & Schmidt, F. L. (1983). Quantifying the effects of psychological interventions on employee job performance and work-force productivity. *American Psychologist, 38*, 473–478.

Hunter, J. E., & Schmidt, F. L. (1990). *Methods of meta-analysis*. Newbury Park, CA: Sage.

Hunter, J. E., Schmidt, F. L., & Jackson, G. B. (1982). *Meta-analysis: Cumulating research findings across studies*. Beverly Hills, CA: Sage.

Hunter, J. E., Schmidt, F. L., & Judiesch, M. K. (1990). Individual differences in output as a function of job complexity. *Journal of Applied Psychology, 75*(1), 28–42.

Hunter, M. S. (1992). The Women's Health Questionnaire: A measure of mid-aged women's perceptions of their emotional and physical health. *Psychology and Health, 7*, 45–54.

Hurlburt, R. T. (1997). Randomly sampling thinking in the natural environment. *Journal of Consulting and Clinical Psychology, 65*, 941–949.

Hurst, N. H. (1997). A narrative analysis of identity change in treated substance abusers. *Dissertation Abstracts International, Section B: The Sciences & Engineering, 58*(4-B), 2124.

Hutt, M. L. (1985). *The Hutt adaptation of the Bender-Gestalt Test* (4th ed.). Orlando, FL: Grune & Stratton.

Hwang, S. W. (2006). Homelessness and harm reduction. *Canadian Medical Association Journal, 174*(1), 50–51.

Iacono, W. G., & Lykken, D. T. (1997). The validity of the lie detector: Two surveys of scientific opinion. *Journal of Applied Psychology, 82*, 425–433.

Iaffaldano, M. T., & Muchinsky, P. M. (1985). Job satisfaction and job performance: A meta-analysis. *Psychological Bulletin, 97*, 251–273.

Ijuin, M., Homma, A., Mimura, M., Kitamura, S., et al. (2008). Validation of the 7-minute screen for the detection of early-stage Alzheimer's disease. *Dementia and Geriatric Cognitive Disorders, 25*(3), 248–255.

Ilhan, M. N., Durukan, E., Taner, E., et al. (2008). Burnout and its correlates among nursing staff: Questionnaire survey. *Journal of Advanced Nursing, 61*(1), 100–106.

Illovsky, M. E. (2003). *Mental health professionals, minorities, and the poor*. New York: Brunner-Routledge.

Ilyin, D. (1976). *The Ilyin oral interview*. Rowley, MA: Newbury House.

Impara, J. C., & Plake, B. S. (Eds.). (1998). *The thirteenth mental measurements yearbook*. Lincoln: Buros Institute of Mental Measurements, University of Nebraska.

Ingham, B., Clarke, L., & James, I. A. (2008). Biopsychosocial case formulation for people with intellectual disabilities and mental health problems: A pilot study of a training workshop for direct care staff. *British Journal of Developmental Disabilities, 54*(106, Pt. 1), 41–54.

Ingram, P. B., Kelso, K. M., & McCord, D. M. (2011). Empirical correlates and expanded interpretation of the MMPI-2-RF Restructured Clinical Scale 3 (Cynicism). *Assessment, 18*, 95–101.

Inman, A. G., Ladany, N., Constantine, M. G., & Morano, C. K. (2001). Development and preliminary validation of the Cultural Values Conflict Scale for South Asian women. *Journal of Counseling Psychology, 48*(1), 17–27.

Innocenti, M. S., Huh, K., & Boyce, G. C. (1992). Families of children with disabilities: Normative data and other considerations on parenting stress. *Topics in Early Childhood Special Education, 12*, 403–427.

Institute for Juvenile Research. (1937). *Child guidance procedures, methods and techniques employed at the Institute for Juvenile Research*. New York: Appleton-Century.

Institute of Medicine. (1984). *Research and training for the Secret Service: Behavioral science and mental health perspectives: A report of the Institute of Medicine* (IOM Publication No. IOM-84-01). Washington, DC: National Academy Press.

International Test Commission. (1993). *Technical standards for translating tests and establishing test score equivalence*. Amherst, MA: Author. (Available from Dr. Ronald Hambleton, School of Education, University of Massachusetts, Amherst, MA 01003).

Ironson, G. H., & Subkoviak, M. J. (1979). A comparison of several methods of assessing item bias. *Journal of Educational Measurement, 16*, 209–225.

Irvine, S. H., & Berry, J. W. (Eds.). (1983). *Human assessment and cultural factors*. New York: Plenum.

Isen, A. M. (1987). Positive affect, cognitive processes, and social behavior. *Advances in Experimental Social Psychology, 20*, 203–253.

Ishihara, S. (1964). *Tests for color blindness* (11th ed.). Tokyo: Kanehara Shuppan.

Ivancevich, J. M. (1983). Contrast effects in performance evaluation and reward practices. *Academy of Management Journal, 26*, 465–476.

Ivanova, M. Y., Achenbach, T. M., Dumenci, L., et al. (2007a). Testing the 8-syndrome structure of the Child Behavior Checklist in 30 societies. *Journal of Clinical Child and Adolescent Psychology, 36*(3), 405–417.

Ivanova, M. Y., Achenbach, T. M., Rescorla, L. A., et al. (2007b). The generalizability of the Youth Self-Report syndrome structure in 23 societies. *Journal of Consulting and Clinical Psychology, 75*(5), 729–738.

Ivnik, R. J., Malec, J. F., Smith, G. E., Tangalos, E. G., Petersen, R. C., Kokmen, E., & Kurland, L. T. (1992). Mayo's older American normative studies: WAIS-R norms for ages 56–97. *Clinical Neuropsychologist, 6*(Suppl.), 1–30.

Ivnik, R. J., Smith, G. E., Malec, J. F., Petersen, R. C., & Tangalos, E. G. (1995). Long-term stability and intercorrelations of cognitive abilities in older persons. *Psychological Assessment, 7*, 155–161.

Jackson, C. L., & LePine, J. A. (2003). Peer responses to a team's weakest link: A test and extension of LePine and Van Dyne's model. *Journal of Applied Psychology, 88*, 459–475.

Jackson, D. E., O'Dell, J. W., & Olson, D. (1982). Acceptance of bogus personality interpretations: Face validity reconsidered. *Journal of Clinical Psychology, 38*, 588–592.

Jackson, D. N. (1964). Desirability judgments as a method of personality assessment. *Educational and Psychological Measurement, 24*, 223–238.

Jackson, D. N. (1977). *Jackson Vocational Interest Survey manual*. Port Huron, MI: Research Psychologists.

Jackson, D. N. (1986). *Computer-based personality testing*. Washington, DC: Scientific Affairs Office, American Psychological Association.

Jackson, D. N., & Messick, S. (1962). Response styles and the assessment of psychopathology. In S. Messick & J. Ross (Eds.), *Measurement in personality and cognition*. New York: Wiley.

Jackson, D. N., & Rushton, J. P. (2006). Males have greater *g*: Sex differences in general mental ability from 100,000 17- to 18-year-olds on the Scholastic Assessment Test. *Intelligence, 34*(5), 479–486.

Jackson, D. N., & Williams, D. R. (1975). Occupational classification in terms of interest patterns. *Journal of Vocational Behavior, 6*, 269–280.

Jackson, J. F. (1993). Human behavioral genetics, Scarr's theory, and her views on interventions: A critical review and commentary on their implications for African American children. *Child Development, 64*, 1318–1332.

Jackson, J. L. (1999). Psychometric considerations in self-monitoring assessment. *Psychological Assessment, 11*, 439–447.

Jackson, S., Pretti-Frontczak, K., Harjusola-Webb, S., Grisham-Brown J., & Romani, J.M. (2009). Response to intervention: implications for early child professionals. *Language, Speech and Hearing Disorders in Schools, 40*, 1–11.

Jacobs, J. (1970). Are we being misled by fifty years of research on our gifted children? *Gifted Child Quarterly, 14*, 120–123.

Jacobsen, M. E. (1999). Arousing the sleeping giant: Giftedness in adult psychotherapy. *Roeper Review, 22*, 36–41.

Jaffee v. Redmond (1996), 518 U.S. 1; 116 S. Ct. (1923).

Jagger, L., Neukrug, E., & McAuliffe, G. (1992). Congruence between personality traits and chosen occupation as a predictor of job satisfaction for people with disabilities. *Rehabilitation Counseling Bulletin, 36*, 53–60.

Jagim, R. D., Wittman, W. D., & Noll, J. O. (1978). Mental health professionals' attitudes towards confidentiality, privilege, and third-party disclosure. *Professional Psychology, 9*, 458–466.

James, L. R., Demaree, R. G., & Mulaik, S. A. (1986). A note on validity generalization procedures. *Journal of Applied Psychology, 71*, 440–450.

James, L. R., Demaree, R. G., & Wolf, G. (1984). Estimating within-group interrater reliability with and without response bias. *Journal of Applied Psychology, 69*, 85–98.

Janis, I. L. (1972). *Victims of groupthink.* Boston: Houghton Mifflin.

Jankowski, K. (1991). On communicating with deaf people. In L. A. Samovar & R. E. Belmont (Eds.), *Intercultural communication: A reader* (6th ed., pp. 142–150). Belmont, CA: Wadsworth.

Janowsky, D. S., Morter, S., & Hong, L. (2002). Relationship of Myers-Briggs Type Indicator personality characteristics to suicidality in affective disorder patients. *Journal of Pediatric Research, 36*, 33–39.

Janssen, J., Kirschner, F., Erkens, G., Kirschner, P.A., & Paas, F. (2010). Making the black box of collaborative learning transparent: Combining process-oriented and cognitive load approaches. *Educational Psychological Review, 22*(2), 139–154.

Jaspers, K. (1923). *General psychopathology* (translated from German). Chicago: University of Chicago Press, 1968.

Jenkins, C. D., Zyzanski, S. J., & Rosenman, R. H. (1979). *Jenkins Activity Survey: Manual.* San Antonio: Psychological Corporation.

Jenkins, S. R. (2008). *A handbook of clinical scoring systems for thematic apperceptive techniques.* New York: Erlbaum.

Jennings, B. (1991). Active euthanasia and forgoing life-sustaining treatment: Can we hold the line? *Journal of Pain, 6*, 312–316.

Jensen, A. R. (1965). A review of the Rorschach. In O. K. Buros (Ed.), *The sixth mental measurements yearbook* (pp. 501–509). Lincoln: Buros Institute of Mental Measurements, University of Nebraska.

Jensen, A. R. (1969). How much can we boost IQ and scholastic achievement? *Harvard Educational Review, 39*, 1–123.

Jensen, A. R. (1980). *Bias in mental testing.* New York: Free Press.

Jensen, A. R. (2000). Testing: The dilemma of group differences. *Psychology, Public Policy, and Law, 6*, 121–127.

Jobes, D. A., Jacoby, A. M., Cimbolic, P., & Hustead, L. A. T. (1997). Assessment and treatment of suicidal clients in a university. *Journal of Consulting Psychology, 44*, 368–377.

Johansson, H. J., & Forsman, M. (2001). Identification and analysis of unsatisfactory psychosocial work situations: A participatory approach employing video-computer interaction. *Applied Ergonomics, 32*, 23–29.

John, O. P., Donahue, E. M., & Kentle, R. L. (1991). *The Big Five Inventory-Versions 4a and 54.* Berkeley: University of California, Berkeley, Institute of Personality and Social Research.

Johnson, D. L., & Johnson, C. A. (1965). Totally discouraged: A depressive syndrome of the Dakota Sioux. *Psychiatric Research Review, 2*, 141–143.

Johnson, E. S. (2000). The effects of accommodation on performance assessments. *Remedial and Special Education, 21*, 261–267.

Johnson, G. S. (1989). Emotional indicators in the human figure drawings of hearing-impaired children: A small sample validation study. *American Annals of the Deaf, 134*, 205–208.

Johnson, J. A., & Ostendorf, F. (1993). Clarification of the five-factor model with the abridged big five dimensional circumplex. *Journal of Personality and Social Psychology, 65*, 563–576.

Johnson, L. C., Beaton, R., Murphy, S., & Pike, K. (2000). Sampling bias and other methodological threats to the validity of health survey research. *International Journal of Stress Management, 7*, 247–267.

Johnson, L. J., Cook, M. J., & Kullman, A. J. (1992). An examination of the concurrent validity of the Battelle Developmental Inventory as compared with the Vineland Adaptive Scales and the Bayley Scales of Infant Development. *Journal of Early Intervention, 16*, 353–359.

Johnson, R. C. (1963). Similarity in IQ of separated identical twins as related to length of time spent in same environment. *Child Development, 34*, 745–749.

Johnson, W., & Bouchard, T. J., Jr. (2005a). Constructive replication of the Visual-Perceptual-Image Rotation (VPR) Model in Thurstone's (1941) battery of 60 tests of mental ability. *Intelligence, 33*, 417–430.

Johnson, W., & Bouchard, T. J., Jr. (2005b). The structure of human intelligence: It's verbal, perceptual, and image rotation (VPR), not fluid and crystallized. *Intelligence, 33*, 393–416.

Johnson, W., Bouchard, T. J., Jr., McGue, M., et al. (2007). Genetic and environmental influences on the Verbal-Perceptual-Image Rotation (VPR) model of the structure of mental abilities in the Minnesota study of twins reared apart. *Intelligence, 35*(6), 542–562.

Johnston, P. (2011). An instructional frame for RtI. *The Reading Teacher, 63*, 602–604.

Johnston, P. H. (2011). Response to intervention in literacy: Problems and possibilities. *Elementary School Journal, 111*(4), 511–534.

Joiner, T. E., Jr., & Schmidt, K. L. (1997). Drawing conclusions—or not—from drawings. *Journal of Personality Assessment, 69*, 476–481.

Joiner, T. E., Jr., Schmidt, K. L., & Barnett, J. (1996). Size, detail, and line heaviness in children's drawings as correlates of emotional distress: (More) negative evidence. *Journal of Personality Assessment, 67*, 127–141.

Joiner, T. E., Jr., & Walker, R. L. (2002). Construct validity of a measure of acculturative stress in African Americans. *Psychological Assessment, 14*, 462–466.

Jolles, J. (1952). *A catalogue for the qualitative interpretation of the H-T-P.* Los Angeles: Western Psychological Services.

Jonason, P. K., Teicher, E. A., & Schmitt, D. P. (2011). The TIPI's Validity Confirmed: Associations with Sociosexuality and Self-Esteem. *Individual Differences Research, 9*(1), 52–60.

Jones, J. W., Arnold, D., & Harris, W. G. (1990). Introduction to the Model Guidelines for Preemployment Integrity Testing. *Journal of Business and Psychology, 4*, 525–532.

Jones, J. W., Brasher, E. E., & Huff, J. W. (2002). Innovations in integrity-based personnel selection: Building a technology-friendly assessment. *International Journal of Selection and Assessment, 10,* 87–97.

Jones, P., & Rodgers, B. (1993). Estimating premorbid IQ in schizophrenia. *British Journal of Psychiatry, 162,* 273–274.

Jones, R. N., & Gallo, J. J. (2000). Dimensions of the Mini-Mental State Examination among community-dwelling older adults. *Psychological Medicine, 30,* 605–618.

Jones, S. E. (2001, February). Ethics Code Draft published for comment. *APA Monitor, 32.*

Jouriles, E.N., Rowe, L. S., McDonald, R., et al. (2011). Assessing women's responses to sexual threat: Validity of a virtual role-play procedure. *Behavior Therapy, 42*(3), 475–484.

Judge, T. A., & Bono, J. E. (2000). Five-factor model of personality and transformational leadership. *Journal of Applied Psychology, 85,* 751–765.

Judge, T. A., Bono, J. E., & Locke, E. A. (2000). Personality and job satisfaction: The mediating role of job characteristics. *Journal of Applied Psychology, 85,* 237–249.

Judge, T. A., Heller, D., & Mount, M. K. (2002). Five-factor model of personality and job satisfaction: A meta-analysis. *Journal of Applied Psychology, 87,* 530–541.

Judge, T. A., Higgins, C. A., Thoresen, C. J., & Barrick, M. R. (1999). The big five personality traits, general mental ability, and career success across the life span. *Personnel Psychology, 52,* 621–652.

Judge, T. A., & Hurst, C. (2008). How the rich (and happy) get richer (and happier): Relationship of core self-evaluations to trajectories in attaining work success. *Journal of Applied Psychology, 93*(4), 849–863.

Judge, T. A., & Ilies, R. (2002). Relationship of personality to performance motivation: A meta-analytic review. *Journal of Applied Psychology, 87,* 797–807.

Jung, C. G. (1910). The association method. *American Journal of Psychology, 21,* 219–269.

Jung, C. G. (1923). *Psychological types.* London: Routledge & Kegan Paul.

Juni, S. (1996). Review of the revised NEO Personality Inventory. In J. C. Conoley & J. C. Impara (Eds.), *The twelfth mental measurements yearbook* (pp. 863–868). Lincoln: Buros Institute of Mental Measurements, University of Nebraska.

Kacmar, K. M., Collins, B. J., Harris, K. J., & Judge, T. A. (2009). Core self-evaluations and job performance: The role of the perceived work environment. *Journal of Applied Psychology, 94*(6), 1572–1580.

Kagan, J. (1956). The measurement of overt aggression from fantasy. *Journal of Abnormal and Social Psychology, 52,* 390–393.

Kahn, M., & Taft, G. (1983). The application of the standard of care doctrine to psychological testing. *Behavioral Sciences and the Law, 1,* 71–84.

Kail, B. L., & DeLaRosa, M. (1998). Challenges to treating the elderly Latino substance abuser: A not so hidden research agenda. *Journal of Gerontological Social Work, 30,* 128–141.

Kaiser, H. F. (1958). A modified stanine scale. *Journal of Experimental Education, 26,* 261.

Kaiser, H. F., & Michael, W. B. (1975). Domain validity and generalizability. *Educational and Psychological Measurement, 35,* 31–35.

Kalat, J. W., & Matlin, M. W. (2000). The GRE Psychology Test: A useful but poorly understood test. *Teaching of Psychology, 27,* 24–27.

Kalshoven, K., Den Hartog, D. N., & De Hoogh, A. H. B. (2011). Ethical Leadership at Work questionnaire (ELW): Development and validation of a multidimensional measure. *Leadership Quarterly, 22,* 51–69.

Kamin, L. J. (1974). *The science and politics of IQ.* New York: Wiley.

Kamiya, J. (1962). *Conditional discrimination of the EEG alpha rhythm in humans.* Paper presented at the annual meeting of the Western Psychological Association, April.

Kamiya, J. (1968). Conscious control of brain waves. *Psychology Today, 1*(11), 56–60.

Kamphaus, R. W., & Pleiss, K. L. (1993). Comment on "The use and abuse of human figure drawings." *School Psychology Quarterly, 8,* 187–188.

Kanaya, T., Scullin, M. H., & Ceci, S. J. (2003). The Flynn effect and U. S. policies: The impact of rising IQ scores on American society via mental retardation diagnoses. *American Psychologist, 58,* 778–790.

Kane, S. T., Walker, J. H., & Schmidt, G. R. (2011). Assessing college-level learning difficulties and "at riskness" for learning disabilities and ADHD: Development and validation of the Learning Difficulties Assessment. *Journal of Learning Disabilities, 44*(6), 533–542.

Kapusta, N. (2011). Development of a suicide risk assessment scale. *European Psychiatry, 26* (Supplement 1), 1621.

Karantonis, A., & Sireci, S. G. (2006). The bookmark standard-setting method: A literature review. *Educational Measurement: Issues and Practice* (Spring), 4–12.

Karlsen, S., Rogers, A., & McCarthy, M. (1998). Social environment and substance misuse: A study of ethnic variations among inner London adolescents. *Ethnicity & Health, 3,* 265–273.

Karon, B. P. (1981). The Thematic Apperception Test (TAT). In A. I. Rabin (Ed.), *Assessment with projective techniques: A concise introduction* (pp. 85–120). New York: Springer.

Karon, B. P. (2000). The clinical interpretation of the Thematic Apperception Test, Rorschach, and other clinical data: A reexamination of statistical versus clinical prediction. *Professional Psychology: Research and Practice, 31,* 230–233.

Karp, S. A., Holmstrom, R. W., & Silber, D. E. (1990). *Apperceptive Personality Test Manual* (Version 2.0). Orland Park, IL: International Diagnostic Systems.

Kasahara, M., Menon, D. K., Salmond, C. H., et al. (2011). Traumatic brain injury alters the functional brain networking mediating working memory. *Brain Injury, 25*(12), 1170–1187.

Katz, R. C., Santman, J., & Lonero, P. (1994). Findings on the Revised Morally Debatable Behaviors Scale. *Journal of Psychology, 128,* 15–21.

Katz, W. F., Curtiss, S., & Tallal, P. (1992). Rapid automatized naming and gesture by normal and language-impaired children. *Brain and Language, 43,* 623–641.

Kaufman, A. S. (1990). *Assessing adolescent and adult intelligence.* Needham Heights, MA: Allyn & Bacon.

Kaufman, A. S. (1993). Joint exploratory factor analysis of the Kaufman Battery for Children and the Kaufman Adolescent and Adult Intelligence Test for 11- and 12-year-olds. *Journal of Clinical Child Psychology, 22,* 355–364.

Kaufman, A. S. (1994a). *Intelligent testing with the WISC-R.* New York: Wiley.

Kaufman, A. S. (1994b). *Intelligent testing with the WISC-III.* New York: Wiley.

Kaufman, A. S., Ishkuma, T., & Kaufman-Packer, J. L. (1991). Amazingly short forms of the WAIS-R. *Journal of Psycho-educational Assessment, 9,* 4–15.

Kaufman, A. S., & Kaufman, N. L. (1983a). *Kaufman Assessment Battery for Children (K-ABC): Administration and scoring manual.* Circle Pines, MN: American Guidance Service.

Kaufman, A. S., & Kaufman, N. L. (1983b). *Kaufman Assessment Battery for Children (K-ABC) interpretative manual.* Circle Pines, MN: American Guidance Service.

Kaufman, A. S., & Kaufman, N. L. (1990). *Kaufman Brief Intelligence Test (K-BIT): Manual*. Circle Pines, MN: American Guidance Service.

Kaufman, A. S., & Kaufman, N. L. (1993). *Kaufman Adolescent and Adult Intelligence Test (KAIT): Manual*. Circle Pines, MN: American Guidance Service.

Kaufman, A. S., Kaufman, N. L., & Goldsmith, B. (1984). *Kaufman Sequential or Simultaneous (K-SOS)*. Circle Pines, MN: American Guidance Service.

Kaufman, A. S., & Lichtenberger, E. O. (1999). *Essentials of WAIS-III assessment*. New York: Wiley.

Kaufman, A. S., & McLean, J. E. (1986). K-ABC/WISC-R factor analysis for a learning-disabled population. *Journal of Learning Disabilities, 19*, 145–153.

Kaufman, A. S., & McLean, J. E. (1987). Joint factor analysis of the K-ABC and WISC-R with normal children. *Journal of School Psychiatry, 25*, 105–118.

Kaufman, A. S., Reynolds, C. R., & McLean, J. E. (1989). Age and WAIS-R intelligence in a national sample of adults in the 20- to 74-year age range: A cross-sectional analysis with educational level controlled. *Intelligence, 13*, 235–253.

Kaufman, J. C. (2010). Using creativity to reduce ethnic bias in college admissions. *Review of General Psychology, 14*(3), 189–203.

Kavale, K. A. (1995). Meta-analysis at 20: Retrospect and prospect. *Evaluation and the Health Professionals, 18*, 349–369.

Kaye, B. K., & Johnson, T. J. (1999). Taming the cyber frontier: Techniques for improving online surveys. *Social Science Computer Review, 17*, 323–337.

Keating, C. F., Mazur, A., Segall, M. H., et al. (1981). Culture and the perception of social dominance from facial expression. *Journal of Personality and Social Psychology, 40*, 615–626.

Kebbell, M. R., & Wagstaff, G. F. (1998). Hypnotic interviewing: The best way to interview eyewitnesses? *Behavioral Sciences & the Law, 16*, 115–129.

Keddy, P., & Erdberg, P. (2010). Changes in the Rorschach and MMPI-2 after electroconvulsive therapy (ECT): A collaborative assessment case study. *Journal of Personality Assessment, 92*(4), 279–295

Keefe, F. J., Smith, S. J., Buffington, A. L. H., Gibson, J., Studts, J. L., & Caldwell, D. S. (2002). Recent advances and future directions in the biopsychosocial assessment and treatment of arthritis. *Journal of Consulting and Clinical Psychology, 70*, 640–655.

Kehoe, J. F., & Tenopyr, M. L. (1994). Adjustment in assessment scores and their usage: A taxonomy and evaluation of methods. *Psychological Assessment, 6*, 291–303.

Keiser, R. E., & Prather, E. N. (1990). What is the TAT? A review of ten years of research. *Journal of Personality Assessment, 55*, 800–803.

Keith, T. Z. (1985). Questioning the K-ABC: What does it measure? *School Psychology Review, 1*, 21–36.

Keith, T. Z., & Kranzler, J. H. (1999). The absence of structural fidelity precludes construct validity: Rejoinder to Naglieri on what the Cognitive Assessment System does and does not measure. *School Psychology Review, 28*, 117–144.

Keith, T. Z., & Novak, C. G. (1987). Joint factor structure of the WISC-R and K-ABC for referred school children. *Journal of Psychoeducational Assessment, 5*(4), 370–386.

Keith, T. Z., Powell, A. L., & Powell, L. R. (2001). Review of Wechsler Abbreviated Scale of Intelligence. In B. S. Plake & J. C. Impara (Eds.), *The fourteenth mental measurements yearbook* (pp. 1329–1331). Lincoln: University of Nebraska Press.

Keith, T. Z., & Witta, L. (1997). Hierarchical and cross-age confirmatory factor analysis of the WISC-III: What does it measure? *School Psychology Quarterly, 12*, 80–107.

Kelley, C., & Meyers, J. (1992). *Cross-Cultural Adaptability Inventory*. Minneapolis: NCS Assessments.

Kelley, S. J. (1985). Drawings: Critical communications for the sexually abused child. *Pediatric Nursing, 11*, 421–426.

Kelley, S. J. (1988). Physical abuse of children: Recognition and reporting. *Journal of Emergency Nursing, 14*(2), 82–90.

Kelley, T. L. (1927). *Interpretation of educational measurements*. Yonkers, NY: World Book.

Kelley, T. L. (1939). The selection of upper and lower groups for the validation of test items. *Journal of Educational Psychology, 30*, 17–24.

Kellner, C. H., Jolley, R. R., Holgate, R. C., et al. (1991). Brain MRI in obsessive-compulsive disorder. *Psychiatric Research, 36*, 45–49.

Kelly, D. H. (1966). Measurement of anxiety by forearm blood flow. *British Journal of Psychiatry, 112*, 789–798.

Kelly, E. J. (1985). The personality of chess players. *Journal of Personality Assessment, 49*, 282–284.

Kempen, J. H., Kritchevsky, M., & Feldman, S. T. (1994). Effect of visual impairment on neuropsychological test performance. *Journal of Clinical and Experimental Neuropsychology, 16*, 223–231.

Kendall, P. C., Williams, L., Pechacek, T. F., Graham, L. E., Shisslak, C., & Herzof, N. (1979). Cognitive-behavioral and patient education interventions in cardiac catheterization procedures: The Palo Alto Medical Psychology Project. *Journal of Consulting and Clinical Psychology, 47*, 48–59.

Kennedy, M. H., & Hiltonsmith, R. W. (1988). Relationships among the K-ABC Nonverbal Scale, the Pictorial Test of Intelligence and the Hiskey-Nebraska Test of Learning Aptitude for speech- and language-disabled preschool children. *Journal of Psychoeducational Assessment, 6*(1), 49–54.

Kennedy, R. S., Bittner, A. C., Harbeson, M., & Jones, M. B. (1982). Television computer games: A "new look" in performance testing. *Aviation, Space and Environmental Medicine, 53*, 49–53.

Kenny, M. C., Alvarez, K., Donahue, B. C., & Winick, C. B. (2008). Overview of behavioral assessment in adults. In M. Hersen & J. Rosqvist (Eds.), *Handbook of psychological assessment: Case conceptualization and treatment: Vol. 1. Adults* (pp. 3–25). Hoboken, NJ: Wiley.

Kent, G. H., & Rosanoff, A. J. (1910). A study of association in insanity. *American Journal of Insanity, 67*, 37–96, 317–390.

Kent, N., & Davis, D. R. (1957). Discipline in the home and intellectual development. *British Journal of Medical Psychology, 30*, 27–33.

Kerlinger, F. N. (1973). *Foundations of behavioral research* (2nd ed.). New York: Holt.

Kern, J. M., Miller, C., & Eggers, J. (1983). Enhancing the validity of role-play tests: A comparison of three role-play methodologies. *Behavior Therapy, 14*, 482–492.

"KeyMath," (2011). Information posted on the KeyMath3-DA by the test's publisher, Pearson Assessments, accessed December 18, 2011, at http://www.pearsonassessments.com/hai/images/pa/products/keymath3_da/km3-da-pub-summary.pdf.

Khan, S. B., Alvi, S. A., Shaukat, N., & Hussain, M. A. (1990). A study of the validity of Holland's theory in a non-Western culture. *Journal of Vocational Behavior, 36*, 132–146.

Kim, B. S. K., Atkinson, D. R., & Yang, P. H. (1999). The Asian Values Scale: Development, factor analysis, validation, and reliability. *Journal of Counseling Psychology, 46*, 342–352.

King, D. A., Conwell, Y., Cox, C., et al. (2000). A neuropsychological comparison of depressed suicide attempters and nonattempters. *Journal of Neuropsychiatry and Clinical Neurosciences, 12*, 64–70.

King, M. A., & Yuille, J. C. (1987). Suggestibility and the child witness. In S. J. Ceci, M. P. Toglia, & D. F. Ross (Eds.), *Children's eyewitness testimony.* New York: Springer-Verlag.

Kinslinger, H. J. (1966). Application of projective techniques in personnel psychology since 1940. *Psychological Bulletin, 66,* 134–149.

Kinston, W., Loader, P., & Miller, L. (1985). *Clinical assessment of family health.* London: Hospital for Sick Children, Family Studies Group.

Kippax, S., Campbell, D., Van de Ven, P., et al. (1998). Cultures of sexual adventurism as markers of HIV seroconversion: A case control study in a cohort of Sydney gay men. *AIDS Care, 10,* 677–688.

Kirby, J., Moore, P., & Shofield, N. (1988). Verbal and visual learning styles. *Contemporary Educational Psychology, 13,* 169–184.

Kirmayer, L. J., & Young, A. (1999). Culture and context in the evolutionary concept of mental disorder. *Journal of Abnormal Psychology, 108,* 446–452.

Kisamore, J. L., & Brannick, M. T. (2008). An illustration of the consequences of meta-analysis model choice. *Organizational Research Methods, 11,* 35–53.

Klanderman, J. W., Perney, J., & Kroeschell, Z. B. (1985). Comparison of the K-ABC and WISC-R for LD children. *Journal of Learning Disabilities, 18,* 524–527.

Klein, D. F. (1999). Harmful dysfunction, disorder, disease, illness, and evolution. *Journal of Abnormal Psychology, 108,* 421–429.

Klein, N., Kotov R., & Bufferd, S. J. (2011). Personality and Depression: Explanatory Models and Review of the Evidence. *Annual Review of Clinical Psychology, 7,* 269–295.

Kleinman, A., & Kleinman, J. (1991). Suffering and its professional transformation: Toward an ethnography of interpersonal experience. *Culture, Psychiatry and Medicine, 15,* 275–301.

Kleinman, A. M., & Lin, T. Y. (1980). Introduction. In A. M. Kleinman & T. Y. Lin (Eds.), *Normal and abnormal behavior in Chinese cultures* (pp. 1–6). Dordrecht, Netherlands: Reidel.

Kleinmuntz, B., & Szucko, J. J. (1984). Lie detection in ancient and modern times: A call for contemporary scientific study. *American Psychologist, 39,* 766–776.

Kline, R. B., & Lachar, D. (1992). Evaluation of age, sex, and race bias in the Personality Inventory for Children (PIC). *Psychological Assessment, 4,* 333–339.

Kline, R. B., Lachar, D., & Boersma, D. C. (1993). Identification of special education needs with the Personality Inventory for Children (PIC): A hierarchical classification model. *Psychological Assessment, 5,* 307–316.

Kline, R. B., Lachar, D., & Gdowski, C. L. (1992). Clinical validity of a Personality Inventory for Children (PIC) profile typology. *Psychological Assessment, 58,* 591–605.

Kline, R. B., Lachar, D., & Sprague, D. J. (1985). The Personality Inventory for Children (PIC): An unbiased predictor of cognitive and academic status. *Journal of Pediatric Psychology, 10,* 461–477.

Kline, R. B., Snyder, J., Guilmette, S., & Castellanos, M. (1993). External validity of the Profile Variability Index for the K-ABC, Stanford-Binet, and WISC-R: Another cul-de-sac. *Journal of Learning Disabilities, 26,* 557–567.

Klinger, E. (1978). Modes of normal conscious flow. In K. S. Pope & J. L. Singer (Eds.), *The stream of consciousness: Scientific investigations into the flow of human experience* (pp. 225–258). New York: Plenum.

Klonoff, E. A., & Landrine, H. (1999). Acculturation and alcohol use among Blacks: The benefits of remaining culturally traditional. *Western Journal of Black Studies, 23,* 211–216.

Klonoff, E. A., & Landrine, H. (2000). Revising and Improving the African American Acculturation Scale. *Journal of Black Psychology, 26*(2), 235–261.

Klopfer, B., Ainsworth, M., Klopfer, W., & Holt, R. R. (1954). *Developments in the Rorschach technique: Vol. 1. Technique and theory.* Yonkers-on-Hudson, NY: World.

Klopfer, B., & Davidson, H. (1962). *The Rorschach technique: An introductory manual.* New York: Harcourt.

Kluckhohn, F. R. (1954). Dominant and variant value orientations. In C. Kluckhohn & H. A. Murray (Eds.), *Personality in nature, society, and culture* (pp. 342–358). New York: Knopf.

Kluckhohn, F. R. (1960). A method for eliciting value orientations. *Anthropological Linguistics, 2*(2), 1–23.

Kluckhohn, F. R., & Strodtbeck, F. L. (1961). *Variations in value orientations.* Homewood, IL: Dorsey.

Knoff, H. M. (1990a). Evaluation of projective drawings. In C. R. Reynolds and T. B. Gutkin (Eds.), *Handbook of school psychology* (2nd ed., pp. 898–946). New York: Wiley.

Knoff, H. M. (1990b). Review of Children's Depression Inventory. In J. J. Kramer & J. C. Conoley (Eds.), *The supplement to the tenth mental measurements yearbook* (pp. 48–50). Lincoln: Buros Institute of Mental Measurements, University of Nebraska.

Knoff, H. M., & Prout, H. T. (1985). *The Kinetic Drawing System: Family and School.* Los Angeles: Western Psychological Services.

Knowles, E. S., & Condon, C. A. (2000). Does the rose still smell as sweet? Item variability across test forms and revisions. *Psychological Assessment, 12,* 245–252.

Kobak, K. A., Reynolds, W. M., & Greist, J. H. (1993). Development and validation of a computer administered version of the Hamilton Anxiety Scale. *Psychological Assessment, 5,* 487–492.

Koenig, K. A., Frey, M. C., & Detterman, D. K. (2008). ACT and general cognitive ability. *Intelligence, 36*(2), 153–160.

Kollins, S. H., Epstein, J. N., & Conners, C. K. (2004). Conners' Rating Scales—Revised. In M. E. Maruish (Ed.). *The use of psychological testing for treatment planning and outcomes assessment: Volume 2: Instruments for children and adolescents* (3rd ed., pp. 215–233). Mahwah, NJ: Erlbaum.

Kolotkin, R. A., & Wielkiewicz, R. M. (1984). Effects of situational demand in the role-play assessment of assertive behavior. *Journal of Behavioral Assessment, 6,* 59–70.

Kongs, S. K., Thompson, L. L., Iverson, G. L., & Heaton, R. K. (2000). *Wisconsin Card Sorting Test-64 Card Version* (WCST-64). Odessa, FL: Psychological Assessment Resources.

Koppitz, E. M. (1963). *The Bender-Gestalt Test for young children.* New York: Grune & Stratton.

Koppitz, E. M. (1975). *The Bender-Gestalt Test for young children* (Vol. 2). New York: Grune & Stratton.

Korchin, S. J., & Schuldberg, D. (1981). The future of clinical assessment. *American Psychologist, 36,* 1147–1158.

Korkman, M. (1999). Applying Luria's diagnostic principles in the neuropsychological assessment of children. *Neuropsychology Review, 9,* 89–105.

Korkman, M., Kirk, U., & Kemp, S. (1997). *NEPSY.* San Antonio: Psychological Corporation.

Korman, A. K. (1988). *The outsiders: Jews and corporate America.* Lexington, MA: Lexington.

Koson, D., Kitchen, C., Kochen, M., & Stodolsky, D. (1970). Psychological testing by computer: Effect on response bias. *Educational and Psychological Measurement, 30*, 803–810.

Kotov, R., Gamez, W., Schmidt, F., & Watson, D. (2010). Linking "big" personality traits to anxiety, depressive, and substance use disorders: A meta-analysis. *Psychological Bulletin, 136*(5), 768–821.

Kottke, J. L., Olson, D. A., & Shultz, K. S. (2010). The devil is in the details: A comment on "What might this be? Rediscovering the Rorschach as a tool for personnel selection in organizations" (Del Giudice, 2010). *Journal of Personality Assessment, 92*(6), 610–612.

Kouzes, J. M., & Posner, B. Z. (2007). *The leadership challenge* (4th ed.). San Francisco: Jossey-Bass.

Kozhevnikov, M., Kosslyn, S., & Shephard, J. (2005). Spatial versus object visualizers: A new characterization of visual cognitive style. *Memory and Cognition, 33*, 710–726.

Kozhevnikov, M., Motes, M. A., & Hegarty, M. (2007). Spatial visualization in physics problem solving. *Cognitive Science, 31*(4), 549–579.

Kraepelin, E. (1892). *Uber die Beeinflussing einfacher psychischer Vorgange durch einige Arzneimittel.* Jena: Fischer.

Kraepelin, E. (1895). Der psychologische versuch in der psychiatrie. *Psychologische Arbeiten, 1*, 1–91.

Kraepelin, E. (1896). Der psychologische versuch in der psychiatrie. *Psychologische Arbeiten, 1*, 1–91.

Kranzler, G., & Moursund, J. (1999). *Statistics for the terrified* (2nd ed.). Upper Saddle River, NJ: Prentice-Hall.

Kranzler, J. H., & Keith, T. Z. (1999). Independent confirmatory factor analysis of the Cognitive Assessment System (CAS): What does the CAS measure? *School Psychology Review, 28*, 117–144.

Kranzler, J. H., Keith, T. Z., & Flanagan, D. P. (2000). Independent examination of the factor structure of the Cognitive Assessment System (CAS): Further evidence challenging the construct validity of the CAS. *Journal of Psychoeducational Assessment, 18*(2), 143–159.

Krasner, M. S., Epstein, R. M., Beckman, H., et al. (2009). Association of an educational program in mindful communication with burnout, empathy, and attitudes among primary care physicians. *Journal of the American Medical Association, 302*(12), 1284–1293.

Krauss, D. A. (2007). Participant. In A. E. Puente (Chair), *Third party observers in psychological and neuropsychological forensic psychological assessment.* Symposium presented at the 115th Annual Convention of the American Psychological Association, San Francisco.

Krauss, D. A., & Sales, B. D. (1999). The problem of "helpfulness" in applying *Daubert* to expert testimony: Child custody determinations in family law as an exemplar. *Psychology, Public Policy, and Law, 5*, 78–99.

Krauss, M. W. (1993). Child-related and parenting stress: Similarities and differences between mothers and fathers of children with disabilities. *American Journal on Mental Retardation, 97*, 393–404.

Kreifelts, B., Ethofer, T., Huberle, E., et al. (2010). Association of trait emotional intelligence and individual fMRI-activation patterns during the perception of social signals from voice and face. *Human Brain Mapping, 31*(7), 979–991.

Kresel, J. J., & Lovejoy, F. H. (1981). Poisonings and child abuse. In N. S. Ellerstein (Ed.), *Child abuse and neglect: A medical reference* (pp. 307–313). New York: Wiley.

Krikorian, R., & Bartok, J. A. (1998). Developmental data for the Porteus Maze Test. *Clinical Neuropsychologist, 12*, 305–310.

Krohn, E. J., & Lamp, R. E. (1989). Concurrent validity of the K-ABC and Stanford-Binet—Fourth Edition for Head Start Children. *Journal of School Psychology, 27*(1), 59–67.

Krohn, E. J., Lamp, R. E., & Phelps, C. G. (1988). Validity of the K-ABC for a black preschool population. *Psychology in the Schools, 25*, 15–21.

Kronholz, J. (1998, February 12). As states end racial preferences, pressure rises to drop SAT to maintain minority enrollment. *Wall Street Journal*, p. A24.

Krueger, R. F., Eaton, N. R., Clark, L. A., et al. (2011). Deriving an empirical structure of personality pathology for DSM-5. *Journal of Personality Disorders, 25*(2), 170–191.

Kubinger, K. D., Holocher-Ertl, S., Reif, M., et al. (2010). On minimizing guessing effects on multiple-choice items. *International Journal of Selection and Assessment, 18*(1), 111–115.

Kubiszyn, T. W., Meyer, G. I., Finn, S. E., et al. (2000). Empirical support for psychological assessment in clinical health care settings. *Professional Psychology: Research and Practice, 31*, 119–130.

Kuder, F., Diamond, E. E., & Zytowski, D. G. (1998). Differentiation as fundamental validity for criterion-group and scaled interest inventories. *Educational and Psychological Measurement, 58*, 38–41.

Kuder, G. F. (1979). *Kuder Occupational Interest Survey, Revised: General manual.* Chicago: Science Research Associates.

Kuder, G. F., & Richardson, M. W. (1937). The theory of the estimation of reliability. *Psychometrika, 2*, 151–160.

Kuhlmann, F. (1912). A revision of the Binet-Simon system for measuring the intelligence of children. *Journal of Psycho-Asthenics Monograph Supplement, 1*(1), 1–41.

Kumho Tire Co. Ltd. v. Carmichael, 119 S. Ct. 1167 (1999).

Kuncel, N. R., & Hezlett, S. A. (2007a). Standardized tests predict graduate students' success. *Science, 315*(5815), 1080–1081.

Kuncel, N. R., & Hezlett, S. A. (2007b). The utility of standardized tests: Response. *Science 316*(5832), 1696–1697.

Kuncel, N. R., Hezlett, S. A., & Ones, D. S. (2001). A comprehensive meta-analysis of the predictive validity of the Graduate Record Examinations: Implications for graduate student selection and performance. *Psychological Bulletin, 127*, 162–181.

Kupfer, D. J., First, M. B., & Regier, D. A. (Eds.) (2002). *A research agenda for DSM-V.* Washington, DC: American Psychiatric Association.

Kurt, A., & Paulhus, D. L. (2008). Moderators of the adaptiveness of self-enhancement: Operationalization, motivational domain, adjustment facet, and evaluator. *Journal of Research in Personality, 42*(4), 839–853.

Lachar, D. (1982). *Personality Inventory for Children (PIC): Revised format manual supplement.* Los Angeles: Western Psychological Services.

Lachar, D., Gdowski, C. L., & Snyder, D. K. (1985). Consistency of maternal report and the Personality Inventory for Children: Always useful and sometimes sufficient—Reply to Cornell. *Journal of Consulting and Clinical Psychology, 53*, 275–276.

Lachar, D., & Gruber, C. P. (2001). *The Personality Inventory for Children, Second Edition (PIC-2).* Los Angeles: Western Psychological Services.

Lachar, D., Kline, R. B., & Boersma, D. C. (1986). The Personality Inventory for Children: Approaches to actuarial interpretation in clinic and school settings. In H. M. Knoff (Ed.), *The psychological assessment of child and adolescent personality* (pp. 273–308). New York: Guilford.

Lachar, D., & Wirt, R. D. (1981). A data-based analysis of the psychometric performance of the Personality Inventory for Children (PIC): An alternative to the Achenbach review. *Journal of Personality Assessment, 45,* 614–616.

Lacks, P. (1999). *Bender-Gestalt screening for brain dysfunction.* New York: Wiley.

LaCombe, J. A., Kline, R. B., Lachar, D., Butkus, M., & Hillman, S. B. (1991). Case history correlates of a Personality Inventory for Children (PIC) profile typology. *Psychological Assessment, 3,* 678–687.

Laidlaw, T. M. (1999). Designer testing: Using subjects' personal vocabulary to produce individualised tests. *Personality and Individual Differences, 27,* 1197–1207.

Laker, D. R. (2002). The career wheel: An exercise for exploring and validating one's career choices. *Journal of Employment Counseling, 39,* 61–72.

Lally, S. J. (2003). What tests are acceptable for use in forensic evaluations? A survey of experts. *Professional Psychology: Research & Practice, 34,* 491–498.

Lam, C. S., Chan, F., Hilburger, J., Heimburger, M., Hill, V., & Kaplan, S. (1993). Canonical relationships between vocational interests and aptitudes. *Vocational Evaluation and Work Adjustment Bulletin, 26,* 155–160.

Lamb, M. E. (Ed.). (1981). *The role of the father in child development* (2nd ed.). New York: Wiley.

Lambert, E. W., & Engum, E. S. (1992). Construct validity of the Cognitive Behavioral Driver's Inventory: Age, diagnosis, and driving ability. *Journal of Cognitive Rehabilitation, 10,* 32–45.

Lambert, N., Nihira, K., & Leland, H. (1993). *AAMR Adaptive Behavior Scale-School-Second Edition: Examiner's manual.* Austin: PRO-ED.

Lamp, R. E., & Krohn, E. J. (1990). Stability of the Stanford-Binet Fourth Edition and K-ABC for young black and white children from low-income families. *Journal of Psychoeducational Assessment, 8,* 139–149.

Lamp, R. E., & Krohn, E. J. (2001). A longitudinal predictive validity investigation of the SB: FE and K-ABC with at-risk children. *Journal of Psychoeducational Assessment, 19,* 334–349.

Landrum, M. S., & Ward, S. B. (1993). Behavioral assessment of gifted learners. *Journal of Behavioral Education, 3,* 211–215.

Landy, F. J. (1986). Stamp collecting versus science. *American Psychologist, 41,* 1183–1192.

Landy, F. J. (2007). The validation of personnel decisions in the twenty-first century: Back to the future. In S. M. McPhail (Ed.), *Alternative validation strategies: Developing new and leveraging existing evidence* (pp. 409–426). Hoboken, NJ: Wiley.

Landy, F. J., & Farr, J. H. (1980). Performance rating. *Psychological Bulletin, 87,* 72–107.

Lane, H. (1992). *The mask of benevolence: Disabling the deaf community.* New York: Vintage.

Lane, J. C. (1992, August). Threat management fills void in police services. *Police Chief,* pp. 27–29, 31.

Lang, P. J., Greenwald, M. K., Bradley, M. M., & Hamm, A. O. (1993). Looking at pictures: Affective, facial, visceral, and behavioral reactions. *Psychophysiology, 30,* 261–273.

Langer, E. J., & Abelson, R. P. (1974). A patient by any other name: Clinician group difference in labeling bias. *Journal of Consulting and Clinical Psychology, 42,* 4–9.

Langlois, J. H., Ritter, J. M., Casey, R. J., & Sawin, D. B. (1995). Infant attractiveness predicts maternal behaviors and attitudes. *Developmental Psychology, 31,* 464–472.

Lanyon, R. I. (1984). Personality assessment. *Annual Review of Psychology, 35,* 667–701.

Lanyon, R. I. (1993a). Assessment of truthfulness in accusations of child molestation. *American Journal of Forensic Psychology, 11,* 29–44.

Lanyon, R. I. (1993b). Development of scales to assess specific deception strategies on the Psychological Screening Inventory. *Psychological Assessment, 5,* 324–329.

Lanyon, R. I., & Thomas, M. L. (2008). Detecting deception in sex offender assessment. In R. Rogers (Ed.), *Clinical assessment of malingering and deception* (3rd ed., pp. 285–300). New York: Guilford Press.

Larkin, J. E., Pines, H. A., & Bechtel, K. M. (2002). Facilitating students' career development in psychology courses: A portfolio project. *Teaching of Psychology, 29,* 207–210.

Larrabee, G. J. (Ed.). (2005). *Forensic neuropsychology: A scientific approach.* New York: Oxford University Press.

Larson, J. C., Mostofsky, S. H., Goldberg, M. C., et al. (2007). Effects of gender and age on motor exam in typically developing children. *Developmental Neuropsychology, 32*(1), 543–562.

Larson, L. M., & Borgen, F. H. (2002). Convergence of vocational interests and personality: Examples in an adolescent gifted sample. *Journal of Vocational Behavior, 60,* 91–112.

Larson, L. M., & Majors, M. S. (1998). Applications of the Coping with Career Indecision instrument with adolescents. *Journal of Career Assessment, 6,* 163–179.

Larson, L. M., Rottinghaus, P. J., & Borgen, F. H. (2002). Meta-analyses of big six interests and big five personality factors. *Journal of Vocational Behavior, 61,* 217–239.

La Rue, A., & Watson, J. (1998). Psychological assessment of older adults. *Professional Psychology: Research and Practice, 29,* 5–14.

Larvie, V. (1994). Evidence—Admissability of scientific evidence in federal courts—The Supreme Court decides Frye is dead and the Federal Rules of Evidence provide the standard, but is there a skeleton in the closet? *Daubert v. Pharmaceuticals,* 113 S. Ct. 2786. *Land & Water Review, 29,* 275–309.

Larzelere, R., & Huston, T. (1980). The Dyadic Trust Scale: Toward understanding interpersonal trust in close relationships. *Journal of Marriage and the Family, 43,* 595–604.

Latimer, E. J. (1991). Ethical decision-making in the care of the dying and its applications to clinical practice. *Journal of Pain and Symptom Management, 6,* 329–336.

Lattimore, R. R., & Borgen, F. H. (1999). Validity of the 1994 Strong Interest Inventory with racial and ethnic groups in the United States. *Journal of Counseling Psychology, 46,* 185–195.

Laurence, J. R., & Perry, C. W. (1988). *Hypnosis, will, and memory.* New York: Guilford.

Lavin, M. (1992). The Hopkins Competency Assessment Test: A brief method for evaluating patients' capacity to give informed consent. *Hospital and Community Psychiatry, 646,* 132–136.

Lavrakas, P. J. (1998). Methods for sampling and interviewing in telephone surveys. In L. Bickman & D. J. Rog (Eds.), *Handbook of applied social research methods* (pp. 429–472). Thousand Oaks, CA: Sage.

Lawlor, J. (1990, September 27). Loopholes found in truth tests. *USA Today,* p. D-1.

Lawrence, B. S. (1996). Organizational age norms: Why is it so hard to know one when you see one? *Gerontologist, 36,* 209–220.

Lawrence, J., Davidoff, D. A., Katt-Lloyd, D., et al. (2000). A pilot program of community-based screening for memory impairment. *Journal of the American Geriatrics Society, 48,* 854–855.

Lawshe, C. H. (1975). A quantitative approach to content validity. *Personnel Psychology, 28,* 563–575.

Lazarus, A. A. (1973). Multimodal behavior therapy: Treating the BASIC ID. *Journal of Nervous and Mental Disease, 156,* 404–411.

Lazarus, A. A. (1989). *The practice of multimodal therapy.* Baltimore: Johns Hopkins University Press.

Lea, E., & Worsley, A. (2001). Influences on meat consumption in Australia. *Appetite, 36,* 127–136.

Leach, M. M., & Oakland, T. (2007). Ethics standards impacting test development and use: A review of 31 ethics codes impacting practices in 35 countries. *International Journal of Testing, 7*(1), 71–88.

Leahy, A. (1932). A study of certain selective factors influencing prediction of the mental status of adopted children or adopted children in nature-nurture research. *Journal of Genetic Psychology, 41,* 294–329.

Leahy, A. M. (1935). Nature-nurture and intelligence. *Genetic Psychology Monographs, 17,* 241–306.

Leahy, M. M., Easton, C. J., & Edwards, L. M. (2010). Compulsory psychiatric testing. *Journal of the American Academy of Psychiatry and the Law, 38*(1), 126–128.

Ledesma, R. D., Sánchez, R., & Díaz-Lázaro, C. M. (2011). Adjective checklist to assess the Big Five personality factors in the Argentine population. *Journal of Personality Assessment, 93*(1), 46–55.

Lee, H.-J., Goudarzi, K., Baldwin, B., et al. (2011). The Combat Experience Log: A web-based system for the in theater assessment of war zone stress. *Journal of Anxiety Disorders, 25,* 794–800.

Lee, M., Bang, S., & Yang, G. (2011). *Apparatus and method for inducing emotions.* Document dated June 7, 2011, U.S. Department of Commerce, U.S. Patent and Trademark Office.

Lee, S. D. (1968). *Social class bias in the diagnosis of mental illness.* Unpublished doctoral dissertation, University of Oklahoma.

Lee, S. E., Simons-Morton, B. G., Klauer, S. E., et al. (2011). Naturalistic assessment of novice teenage crash experience. *Accident Analysis and Prevention, 43*(4), 1472–1479.

Lee, S.-J., & Tedeschi, J. T. (1996). Effects of norms and norm-violations on inhibition and instigation of aggression. *Aggressive Behavior, 22,* 17–25.

Lee, Y., Grady, C. L., Habak, C., et al. (2011). Face processing changes in normal aging revealed by *f*MRI adaptation. *Journal of Cognitive Neuroscience, 23*(11), 3433–3447.

Lees-Haley, P. R., English, L. T., & Glenn, W. J. (1991). A Fake Bad Scale on the MMPI-2 for personal injury claimants. *Psychological Reports, 68,* 203–210.

Leigh, I. W., Corbett, C. A., Gutman, V., & Moore, D. A. (1996). Providing psychological services to deaf individuals: A response to new perceptions of diversity. *Professional Psychology: Research and Practice, 27,* 364–371.

Lemos, G. C., Almeida, L. S., & Colom, R. (2011). Intelligence of adolescents is related to their parents' educational level but not to family income. *Personality and Individual Differences, 50*(7), 1–6.

Leon-Carrion, J., et al. (1991). The computerized Tower of Hanoi: A new form of administration and suggestions for interpretation. *Perceptual and Motor Skills, 73,* 63–66.

Leong, F. T., & Hartung, P. J. (2000). Cross-cultural career assessment: Review and prospects for the new millennium. *Journal of Career Assessment, 8,* 391–401.

Lerdau, M., & Avery, C. (2007). The utility of standardized tests. *Science, 316*(5832), 1694.

Lerner, B. (1980). *Minimum competence, maximum choice: Second chance legislation.* New York: Irvington.

Lerner, B. (1981). The minimum competence testing movement: Social, scientific, and legal implications. *American Psychologist, 36,* 1056–1066.

Lerner, P. M. (1991). *Psychoanalytic theory and the Rorschach.* New York: Analytic.

Lerner, P. M. (1996a). Current perspectives on psychoanalytic Rorschach assessment. *Journal of Personality Assessment, 67,* 450–461.

Lerner, P. M. (1996b). The interpretive process in Rorschach testing. *Journal of Personality Assessment, 67,* 494–500.

Lesser, G. S., Fifer, G., & Clark, D. H. (1965). Mental abilities of children from different social-class and cultural groups. *Monographs of the Society for Research in Child Development, 30* (Serial No. 102).

Lessinger, L. H. (1998). The relationship between cultural identity and MMPI-2 scores of Mexican-American substance abuse patients. *Dissertation Abstracts International, Section B: The Sciences & Engineering, 59*(2-B), 877.

Levack, N. (1991). *Low vision: A resource guide with adaptations for students with visual impairments.* Austin: Texas School for the Blind and Visually Impaired.

Levesque, L. L., Wilson, J. M., & Wholey, D. R. (2001). Cognitive divergence and shared mental models in software development project teams. *Journal of Organizational Behavior, 22,* 135–144.

Levine, E., & Padilla, A. (1980). *Crossing cultures in therapy.* Monterey, CA: Brooks/Cole.

Levy-Shiff, R., Dimitrovsky, L., Shulman, S., & Har-Even, D. (1998). Cognitive appraisals, coping strategies, and support resources as correlates of parenting and infant development. *Developmental Psychology, 34,* 1417–1427.

Lewinsohn, P. M., Rohde, P., & Seeley, J. R. (1996). Adolescent suicidal ideation and attempts: Prevalence, risk factors and clinical implications. *Clinical Psychology: Science and Practice, 3,* 25–46.

Lewis, D. M., Mitzel, H., Green, D. R. (June, 1996). Standard setting: A bookmark approach. In D. R. Green (Chair), *IRT-based standard-setting procedures utilizing behavioral anchoring.* Paper presented at the 1996 Council of Chief State School Officers National Conference on Large Scale Assessment, Phoenix, AZ.

Lewis, D. M., Mitzel, H., Green, D. R. & Patz, R. J. (1999). *The bookmark standard setting procedure.* Monterey, CA: McGraw-Hill.

Lewis-Fernandez, R. (1998). A cultural critique of the DSM-IV dissociative disorders section. *Transcultural Psychiatry, 35,* 387–400.

Lewis-Fernandez, R., & Diaz, N. (2002). The cultural formulation: A method for assessing cultural factors affecting the clinical encounter. *Psychiatric Quarterly, 73,* 271–295.

Lezak, M. D. (2002). Responsive assessment and the freedom to think for ourselves. *Rehabilitation Psychology, 47,* 339–353.

Lezak, M. D., Howieson, D. B., Bigler, E. D., & Tranel, D. (2012). *Neuropsychological Assessment* (5th ed.). New York: Oxford University Press.

Li, H., Kuo, C., & Russel, M. G. (1999). The impact of perceived channel utilities, shopping orientations, and demographics on the consumer's online buying behavior. *Journal of Computer-Mediated Communication, 5*(2).

Li, J. (2003). The core of Confucian learning. *American Psychologist, 58,* 146–147.

Libby, W. (1908). The imagination of adolescents. *American Journal of Psychology, 19,* 249–252.

Lichtenstein, B., & Nansel, T. R. (2000). Women's douching practices and related attitudes: Findings from four focus groups. *Women and Health, 31*, 117–131.

Lichtenstein, D., Dreger, R. M., & Cattell, R. B. (1986). Factor structure and standardization of the Preschool Personality Questionnaire. *Journal of Social Behavior and Personality, 1*, 165–181.

Lidz, C. S. (1987). Historical perspectives. In C. S. Lidz (Ed.), *Dynamic assessment: An interactional approach to evaluating learning potential* (pp. 288–326). New York: Guilford.

Lidz, C. S. (1991). *Practitioner's guide to dynamic assessment.* New York: Guilford.

Lidz, C. S. (1996). Dynamic assessment and the legacy of L. S. Vygotsky. *School Psychology International, 16*, 143–154.

Lidz, C. W., Mulvey, E. P., & Gardner, W. (1993). The accuracy of predictions of violence to others. *Journal of the American Medical Association, 269*, 1007–1011.

Lievens, F., Decaesteker, C., & Christoph, C. P. (2001). Organizational attractiveness for prospective applicants. *Applied Psychology: An International Review, 50*, 30–51.

Lighthouse Research Institute. (1995). *The Lighthouse National Survey on Vision Loss.* New York: Lighthouse.

Likert, R. (1932). A technique for the measurement of attitudes. *Archives of Psychology,* Number 140.

Lilienfeld, S. O., & Marino, L. (1995). Mental disorder as a Roschian concept: A critique of Wakefield's "harmful dysfunction" analysis. *Journal of Abnormal Psychology, 104*, 411–420.

Lilienfeld, S. O., & Marino, L. (1999). Essentialism revisited: Evolutionary theory and the concept of mental disorder. *Journal of Abnormal Psychology, 108*, 400–411.

Lilienfeld, S. O., Wood, J. M., & Garb, H. N. (2000). The scientific status of projective techniques. *Psychological Science in the Public Interest, 1*(2), 27–66.

Lillibridge, J. R., & Williams, K. J. (1992). Another look at personality and managerial potential: Application of the five-factor model. In K. Kelley (Ed.), *Issues, theory, and research in industrial/organizational psychology: Advances in psychology, 82* (pp. 91–115). Oxford, England: North-Holland.

Lim, J., & Butcher, J. N. (1996). Detection of faking on the MMPI-2: Differentiation among faking-bad, denial, and claiming extreme virtue. *Journal of Personality Assessment, 67*, 1–25.

Lim, K. V., Heiby, E., Brislin, R., & Griffin, B. (2002). The development of the Khmer acculturation scale. *International Journal of Intercultural Relations, 26*(6), 653–678.

Lindell, M. K., Brandt, C. J., & Whitney, D. J. (1999). A revised index of interrater agreement for multi-item ratings of a single target. *Applied Psychological Measurement, 23*, 127–135.

Lindgren, B. (1983, August). N or N–1? [Letter to the editor]. *American Statistician,* p. 52.

Lindskog, C. O., & Smith, J. V. (2001). Review of Wechsler Abbreviated Scale of Intelligence. In B. S. Plake & J. C. Impara (Eds.), *The fourteenth mental measurements yearbook* (pp. 1331–1332). Lincoln: University of Nebraska Press.

Lindstrom, E., Wieselgren, I. M., & von Knorring, L. (1994). Interrater reliability of the Structured Clinical Interview for the Positive and Negative Syndrome Scale for schizophrenia. *Acta Psychiatrica Scandinavica, 89*, 192–195.

Linehan, M. M., Goodstein, J. L., Nielsen, S. L., & Chiles, J. A. (1983). Reasons for staying alive when you are thinking of killing yourself: The Reasons for Living Inventory. *Journal of Consulting and Clinical Psychology, 51*, 276–286.

Lippmann, W. (1922, October). The mental age of Americans. *New Republic.*

Lipsitt, P. D., Lelos, D., & McGarry, A. L. (1971). Competency for trial: A screening instrument. *American Journal of Psychiatry, 128*, 105–109.

Lipton, J. P. (1999). The use and acceptance of social science evidence in business litigation after *Daubert. Psychology, Public Policy, and Law, 5*, 59–77.

Lis, A., Mazzeschi, C., Di Riso, D., & Salcuni, S. (2011). Attachment, assessment, and psychological intervention: A case study of anorexia. *Journal of Personality Assessment, 93*(5), 407–416.

Locke, E. A. (1976). The nature and causes of job satisfaction. In M. D. Dunnette (Ed.), *Handbook of industrial and organizational psychology.* Chicago: Rand McNally.

Locke, H. J., & Wallace, K. M. (1959). Short marital adjustment and prediction tests: Their reliability and validity. *Marriage and Family Living, 21*, 251–255.

Löckenhoff, C.E., Terracciano, A., & Costa, P.T., Jr. (2009). Five-factor model personality traits and the retirement transition: Longitudinal and cross-sectional associations. *Psychology and Aging, 24*(3), 722–728.

Loevinger, J., Wessler, R., & Redmore, C. (1970). *Measuring ego development: Vol. 1. Construction and use of a sentence completion test. Vol. 2. Scoring manual for women and girls.* San Francisco: Jossey-Bass.

Loewenstein, D. A., Rubert, M. P., Berkowitz-Zimmer, N., Guterman, A., Morgan, R., & Hayden, S. (1992). Neuropsychological test performance and prediction of functional capacities in dementia. *Behavior, Health, and Aging, 2*, 149–158.

Lofthouse, N., McBurnett, K., Arnold, L. E., & Hurt, E. (2011). Biofeedback and neurofeedback treatment for ADHD. *Psychiatric Annals, 41*(1), 42–48.

Loftin, M. (1997). Critical factors in assessment of students with visual impairments. *RE: view, 28*, 149–159.

Loftus, E. F., & Davies, G. M. (1984). Distortions in the memory of children. *Journal of Social Issues, 40*, 51–67.

Lohman, D. F. (1989). Human intelligence: An introduction to advances in theory and research. *Review of Educational Research, 59*, 333–373.

Loken, E., Radlinski, F., Crespi, V. H., et al. (2004). Online study behavior of 100,000 students preparing for the SAT, ACT, and GRE. *Journal of Educational Computing Research, 30*(3), 255–262.

London, P. (1976). Psychotherapy for religious neuroses? Comments on Cohen and Smith. *Journal of Consulting and Clinical Psychology, 44*, 145–147.

Longabaugh, R. (1980). The systematic observation of behavior in naturalistic settings. In H. C. Triandis & J. W. Berry (Eds.), *Handbook of cross-cultural psychology: Vol. 2. Methodology* (pp. 57–126). Boston: Allyn & Bacon.

López, S. (1988). The empirical basis of ethnocultural and linguistic bias in mental health evaluations of Hispanics. *American Psychologist, 42*, 228–234.

López, S., & Hernandez, P. (1987). When culture is considered in the evaluation and treatment of Hispanic patients. *Psychotherapy, 24*, 120–127.

López, S. R. (1989). Patient variable biases in clinical judgment: A conceptual overview and methodological considerations. *Psychological Bulletin, 106*, 184–203.

López, S. R. (2000). Teaching culturally informed psychological assessment. In R. H. Dana (Ed.), *Handbook of cross-cultural and multicultural personality assessment* (pp. 669–687). Mahwah, NJ: Erlbaum.

López, S. R. (2002). Teaching culturally informed psychological assessment: Conceptual issues and demonstrations. *Journal of Personality, 79*, 226–234.

Lord, F. M. (1980). *Applications of item response theory to practical testing problems.* Hillsdale, NJ: Erlbaum.

Lord, F. M., & Novick, M. R. (1968). *Statistical theories of mental test scores.* Reading, MA: Addison-Wesley.

Lorr, M. (1991). An empirical evaluation of the MBTI typology. *Personality and Individual Differences, 12,* 1141–1145.

Lovejoy, M. C., Weis, R., O'Hare, E., & Rubin, E. (1999). Development and initial validation of the Parent Behavior Inventory. *Psychological Assessment, 11,* 534–545.

Lowitzer, A. C., Utley, C. A., & Baumeister, A. A. (1987). AAMD's 1983 Classification in Mental Retardation as utilized by state mental retardation/developmental disabilities agencies. *Mental Retardation, 25,* 287–291.

Lowman, J. C. (1980). Measurement of family affective structure. *Journal of Personality Assessment, 44,* 130–141.

Loyd, B. H., & Abidin, R. R. (1985). Revision of the Parenting Stress Index. *Journal of Pediatric Psychology, 10,* 169–177.

Lubin, B., Wallis, R. R., & Paine, C. (1971). Patterns of psychological test usage in the United States: 1935–1969. *Professional Psychology, 2,* 70–74.

Luckasson, R., Schalock, R. L., Snell, M. E., & Spitalnik, D. M. (1996). The 1992 AAMR definition and preschool children: Response from the Committee on Terminology and Classification. *Mental Retardation, 34,* 247–253.

Lüdtke, O., Trautwein, U. & Husemann, N. (2009). Goal and personality trait development in a transitional period: Testing principles of personality development. *Personality and Social Psychology Bulletin, 35,* 428–441.

Lukin, M. E., Dowd, E. T., Plake, B. S., & Kraft, R. G. (1985). Comparing computerized versus traditional psychological assessment. *Computers in Human Behavior, 1,* 49–58.

Lumley, V. A., & Miltenberger, R. G. (1997). Sexual abuse prevention for persons with mental retardation. *American Journal on Mental Retardation, 101,* 459–472.

Lumley, V. A., Miltenberger, R. G., Long, E. S., Rapp, J. T., & Roberts, J. A. (1998). Evaluation of a sexual abuse prevention program for adults with mental retardation. *Journal of Applied Behavior Analysis, 31,* 91–101.

Lung, R. J., Miller, S. H., Davis, T. S., & Graham, W. P. (1977). Recognizing burn injuries as abuse. *American Family Physician, 15,* 134–135.

Luria, A. R. (1966a). *Higher cortical functions in man.* New York: Basic Books.

Luria, A. R. (1966b). *Human brain and psychological processes.* New York: Harper & Row.

Luria, A. R. (1970, March). The functional organization of the brain. *Scientific American, 222,* 66–78.

Luria, A. R. (1973). *The working brain: An introduction to neuropsychology.* New York: Basic Books.

Luria, A. R. (1980). *Higher cortical functions in man* (2nd ed.). New York: Basic Books.

Lutey, C., & Copeland, E. P. (1982). Cognitive assessment of the school-age child. In C. R. Reynolds & T. B. Gutkin (Eds.), *The handbook of school psychology.* New York: Wiley.

Lykken, D. T. (1981). *A tremor in the blood: Uses and abuses of the lie detector.* New York: McGraw-Hill.

Lynn, R. (1997). Direct evidence for a genetic basis for black–white differences in IQ. *American Psychologist, 5,* 73–74.

Lynn, R., & Irwing, P. (2004). Sex differences on the progressive matrices: A meta-analysis. *Intelligence, 32,* 481–498.

Lyons, J. A., & Scotti, J. R. (1994). Comparability of two administration formats of the Keane Posttraumatic Stress Disorder Scale. *Psychological Assessment, 6,* 209–211.

MacAndrew, C. (1965). The differentiation of male alcoholic outpatients from nonalcoholic psychiatric outpatients by means of the MMPI. *Quarterly Journal of Studies on Alcohol, 26,* 238–246.

Machover, K. (1949). *Personality projection in the drawing of the human figure: A method of personality investigation.* Springfield, IL: Charles C Thomas.

Mack, J. L., & Patterson, M. B. (1995). Executive dysfunction and Alzheimer's disease: Performance on a test of planning ability—the Porteus Maze Test. *Neuropsychology, 9,* 556–564.

Macmillan, D. L., Gresham, F. M., & Siperstein, G. N. (1995). Heightened concerns over the 1992 AAMR definition: Advocacy versus precision. *American Journal on Mental Retardation, 100,* 87–95.

Macmillan, D. L., & Meyers, C. E. (1980). Larry P.: An education interpretation. *School Psychology Review, 9,* 136–148.

Madden, J. J., Luhan, J. A., Kaplan, L. A., et al. (1952). Non dementing psychoses in older persons. *Journal of the American Medical Association, 150,* 1567–1570.

Maehler, C., & Schuchardt, K. (2009). Working memory functioning in children with learning disabilities: Does intelligence make a difference? *Journal of Intellectual Disability Research, 53*(1), 3–10.

Mael, F. A. (1991). Career constraints of observant Jews. *Career Development Quarterly, 39,* 341–349.

Magnello, M. E., & Spies, C. J. (1984). Francis Galton: Historical antecedents of the correlation calculus. In B. Laver (Chair), *History of mental measurement: Correlation, quantification, and institutionalization.* Paper session presented at the 92nd annual convention of the American Psychological Association, Toronto.

Maher, L. (1996). Hidden in the light: Occupational norms among crack-using street-level sex workers. *Journal of Drug Issues, 26,* 143–173.

Malec, J. F., Ivnik, R. J., & Smith, G. E. (1993). *Neuropsychology and normal aging.* In R. W. Parks, R. F. Zec, & R. S. Wilson (Eds.), *Neuropsychology of Alzheimer's disease and other dementias* (pp. 81–111). New York: Oxford University Press.

Malgady, R. G., Costantino, G., & Rogler, L. H. (1984). Development of a Thematic Apperception Test (TEMAS) for urban Hispanic children. *Journal of Consulting and Clinical Psychology, 52,* 986–996.

Malgady, R. G., Rogler, L. H., & Constantino, G. (1987). Ethnocultural and linguistic bias in mental health evaluations of Hispanics. *American Psychologist, 42,* 228–234.

Maller, S. J. (1997). Deafness and WISC-III item difficulty: Invariance and fit. *Journal of School Psychology, 35,* 299–314.

Maller, S. J., & Braden, J. P. (1993). The construct and criterion-related validity of the WISC-III with deaf adolescents. *Journal of Psychoeducational Assessment, WISC-III Monograph,* 105–113.

Malone, P. S., Brounstein, P. J., van Brock, A., & Shaywitz, S. S. (1991). Components of IQ scores across levels of measured ability. *Journal of Applied Social Psychology, 21,* 15–28.

Maloney, M. P., & Ward, M. P. (1976). *Psychological assessment.* New York: Oxford University Press.

Mannarino, A. P., Cohen, J. A., & Berman, S. R. (1994). The Children's Attributions and Perceptions Scale: A new measure of sexual-abuse related factors. *Journal of Clinical Child Psychology, 23,* 204–211.

Manz, C. C., & Sims, H. P. (1984). Searching for the "unleader": Organizational member views on leading self-managed groups. *Human Relations, 37,* 409–424.

Maraist, C. C., & Russell, M. T. (2002). *16PF Fifth Edition norm supplement.* Champaign, IL: Institute for Personality and Ability Testing.

Maranell, G. M. (1974). *Scaling: A sourcebook for behavioral scientists.* Chicago: Aldine.

Maraun, M. D. (1996a). The claims of factor analysis. *Multivariate Behavioral Research, 31,* 673–689.

Maraun, M. D. (1996b). Meaning and mythology in the factor analysis model. *Multivariate Behavioral Research, 31,* 603–616.

Maraun, M. D. (1996c). Metaphor taken as math: Indeterminacy in the factor analysis model. *Multivariate Behavioral Research, 31,* 517–538.

Marchese, M. C. (1992). Clinical versus actuarial prediction: A review of the literature. *Perceptual and Motor Skills, 75,* 583–594.

Marcotte, T. D., & Grant, I. (2009). Future directions in the assessment of everyday functioning. In T. D. Marcotte and I. Grant. (Eds.) *Neuropsychology of Everyday Functioning* (pp. 457–461). New York: Guilford Press.

Mardell-Czudnowski, C. D., & Goldenberg, D. S. (1983, 1990). *Developmental Indicators for the Assessment of Learning–Revised.* Circle Pines, MN: American Guidance Service.

Mardell-Czudnowski, C. D., & Goldenberg, D. S. (1998). *Developmental Indicators for the Assessment of Learning–3* (DIAL-3). Circle Pines, MN: American Guidance Service.

Marinangeli, M. G., Butti, G., Scinto, A., et al. (2000). Patterns of comorbidity among DSM-III-R personality disorders. *Psychopathology, 33,* 69–74.

Marinus, J., Visser, M., Stiggelbout, A. M., et al. (2004). A short scale for the assessment of motor impairments and disabilities in Parkinson's disease: The SPS/SCOPA. *Journal of Neurology, Neurosurgery, & Psychiatry, 75*(3), 388–395.

Mark, M. M. (1999). Social science evidence in the courtroom: *Daubert* and beyond? *Psychology, Public Policy, and Law, 5,* 175–193.

Markon, K. E., Chmielewski, M., & Miller, C. J. (2011). The reliability and validity of discrete and continuous measures of psychopathology: A quantitative review. *Psychological Bulletin, 137*(5), 856–879.

Marks, I. (1999). Computer aids to mental health care. *Canadian Journal of Psychiatry, 44,* 548–555.

Markus, H., & Kitayama, S. (1991). Culture and the self: Implications for cognition, emotion, and motivation. *Psychological Review, 98,* 224–253.

Marquette, B. W. (1976). *Limitations on the generalizability of adult competency across all situations.* Paper presented at the annual meeting of the Western Psychological Association, Los Angeles.

Marshall, G. N., Schell, T. L., & Miles, J. N. V. (2009). Ethnic differences in posttraumatic distress: Hispanics' symptoms differ in kind and degree. *Journal of Consulting and Clinical Psychology, 77*(6), 1169–1178.

Marson, D. C., McInturff, B., Hawkins, L., Bartolucci, A., & Harrell, L. E. (1997). Consistency of physician judgments of capacity to consent in mild Alzheimer's disease. *American Geriatrics Society, 45,* 453–457.

Martin, D. C., & Bartol, K. M. (1986). Holland's Vocational Preference Inventory and the Myers-Briggs Type Indicator as predictors of vocational choice among Master's of Business Administration. *Journal of Vocational Behavior, 29,* 51–65.

Martin, H., & Finn, S. E. (2010). *Masculinity and femininity in the MMPI-2 and MMPI-A.* Minneapolis: University of Minnesota Press.

Marx, E. (1998). Sibling antagonism transformed during assessment in the home. In L. Handler (Chair), *Conducting assessments in clients' homes: Contexts, surprises, dilemmas, opportunities.* Symposium presented at the Society for Personality Assessment 1998 Midwinter Meeting, February 20.

Maslach, C., Jackson, S. E., & Leiter, M. P. (1996). *The Maslach Burnout Inventory* (3rd ed.). Palo Alto, CA: Consulting Psychologists Press.

Maslach, C., Jackson, S. E., & Leiter, M. P. (1997). The Maslach Burnout Inventory. In C. P. Zalaquett & R. J. Wood (Eds.), *Evaluating stress: A book of resources* (3rd ed., pp. 191–218). Lanham, MD: Scarecrow.

Masling, J. (1960). The influence of situational and interpersonal variables in projective testing. *Psychological Bulletin, 57,* 65–85.

Masling, J. (1965). Differential indoctrination of examiners and Rorschach responses. *Journal of Consulting Psychology, 29,* 198–201.

Masling, J. M. (1997). On the nature and utility of projective tests and objective tests. *Journal of Personality Assessment, 69,* 257–270.

Maslow, A. H. (1943). A theory of motivation. *Psychological Review, 50,* 370–396.

Maslow, A. H. (1970). *Motivation and personality* (2nd ed.). New York: Harper & Row.

Massey, D. S. (2000). When surveys fail: An alternative for data collection. In A. A. Stone et al. (Eds.), *The science of self-report: Implications for research and practice* (pp. 145–160). Mahwah, NJ: Erlbaum.

Massil, H. (1995). Postpartum sexual function: What is the norm? *Sexual and Marital Therapy, 10,* 263–276.

Masuda, M., Matsumoto, G. H., & Meredith, G. M. (1970). Ethnic identity in three generations of Japanese Americans. *Journal of Social Psychology, 81,* 199–207.

Matarazzo, J. D. (1972). *Wechsler's measurement and appraisal of adult intelligence* (5th ed.) Baltimore: Williams & Wilkins.

Matarazzo, J. D. (1990). Psychological assessment versus psychological testing: Validation from Binet to the school, clinic, and courtroom. *American Psychologist, 45,* 999–1017.

Matarazzo, J. D., & Wiens, A. N. (1977). Black Intelligence Test of Cultural Homogeneity and Wechsler Adult Intelligence Scale scores of black and white police applicants. *Journal of Applied Psychology, 62,* 57–63.

Matchett, W. F. (1972). Repeated hallucinatory experiences as part of the mourning process. *Psychiatry, 35,* 185–194.

Mathieu, J. E., & Zajac, D. M. (1990). A review and meta-analysis of the antecedents, correlates, and consequences of organizational commitment. *Psychological Bulletin, 108,* 171–194.

Matson, J. L. (1995). Comments on Gresham, MacMillan, and Siperstein's paper "Critical analysis of the 1992 AAMR definition: Implications for school psychology." *School Psychology Quarterly, 10*(1), 20–23.

Matson, J. L., Smiroldo, B. B., & Hastings, T. L. (1998). Validity of the Autism/Pervasive Developmental Disorder subscale of the Diagnostic Assessment for the Severely Handicapped–II. *Journal of Autism & Developmental Disorders, 28,* 77–81.

Matsumoto, D., & Kudoh, T. (1993). American-Japanese cultural differences in attributions of personality based on smiles. *Journal of Nonverbal Behavior, 17,* 231–243.

Matsumoto, G. M., Meredith, G. M., & Masuda, M. (1970). Ethnic identification: Honolulu and Seattle Japanese-Americans. *Journal of Cross-Cultural Psychology, 1,* 63–76.

Maurer, T. J., & Alexander, R. A. (1991). Contrast effects in behavioral measurement: An investigation of alternative process explanations. *Journal of Applied Psychology, 76,* 3–10.

Maurer, T. J., & Alexander, R. A. (1992). Methods of improving employment test critical scores derived by judging test content: A review and critique. *Personnel Psychology, 45,* 727–762.

Maurer, T. J., Lippstreu, M., & Judge, T. A. (2008). Structural model of employee involvement in skill development activity: The role of individual differences. *Journal of Vocational Behavior, 72*(3), 336–350.

Maurer, T. J., Palmer, J. K., & Ashe, D. K. (1993). Diaries, checklists, evaluations, and contrast effects in measurement of behavior. *Journal of Applied Psychology, 78,* 226–231.

Maxwell-McCaw, D., & Zea, M. C. (2011). The Deaf Acculturation Scale (DAS): Development and validation of a 58-item measure. *Journal of Deaf Studies and Deaf Education, 16*(3), 325–342.

Mayfield, E. C. (1972). Value of peer nominations in predicting life insurance sales performance. *Journal of Applied Psychology, 56,* 319–323.

Mayotte, S. (2010). Online assessment of problem solving skills. *Computers in Human Behavior, 26,* 1253–1258.

Mays, V. M., Cochran, S. D., Hamilton, E., & Miller, N. (1993). Just cover up: Barriers to heterosexual and gay young adults' use of condoms. *Health Values: The Journal of Health Behavior, Education, and Promotion, 17,* 41–47.

Mazzocco, M. M. M., Hagerman, R. J., & Pennington, B. F. (1992). Problem-solving limitations among cytogenetically expressing Fragile X women. *American Journal of Medical Genetics, 43,* 78–86.

McArthur, C. (1992). Rumblings of a distant drum. *Journal of Counseling and Development, 70,* 517–519.

McArthur, D. S., & Roberts, G. E. (1982). *Roberts Apperception Test for Children manual.* Los Angeles: Western Psychological Services.

McBride, B. A. (1989). Stress and fathers' parental competence: Implications for family life and parent educators. *Family Relations, 38,* 385–389.

McCaffrey, R. J. (2005). Some final thoughts and comments regarding the issues of third party observers. *Journal of Forensic Neuropsychology, 4*(2), 83–91.

McCaffrey, R. J. (2007). Participant. In A. E. Puente (Chair), *Third party observers in psychological and neuropsychological forensic psychological assessment.* Symposium presented at the 115th Annual Convention of the American Psychological Association, San Francisco, CA.

McCaffrey, R. J., Lynch, J. K., & Yantz, C. L. (2005). Third party observers: Why all the fuss? *Journal of Forensic Neuropsychology, 4*(2), 1–15.

McCall, W. A. (1922). *How to measure in education.* New York: Macmillan.

McCall, W. A. (1939). *Measurement.* New York: Macmillan.

McCarley, N. G., & Escoto, C. A. (2003). Celebrity worship and psychological type. *North American Journal of Psychology, 5,* 117–120.

McCaulley, M. H. (2000). Myers-Briggs Type Indicator: A bridge between counseling and consulting. *Consulting Psychology Journal: Practice and Research, 52,* 117–132.

McCaulley, M. H. (2002). Autobiography: Mary H. McCaulley. *Journal of Psychological Type, 61,* 51–59.

McCaulley, M. H., & Moody, R. A. (2008). Multicultural applications of the Myers-Briggs Type Indicator. In L. A. Suzuki & J. G. Ponterotto (Eds.), *Handbook of multicultural assessment: Clinical, psychological, and educational applications* (pp. 402–424). San Francisco: Jossey-Bass.

McClelland, D. C. (1951). *Personality.* New York: Holt-Dryden.

McClelland, D. C. (1961). *The achieving society.* Princeton, NJ: Van Nostrand.

McClelland, D. C., Koestner, R., & Weinberger, J. (1989). How do self-attributed and implicit motives differ? *Psychological Review, 96,* 690–702.

McCloskey, G. W. (1989, March). *The K-ABC sequential simultaneous information processing model and classroom intervention: A report—the Dade County Classroom research study.* Paper presented at the Annual Meeting of the National Association of School Psychologists, Boston.

McClure-Butterfield, P. (1990). Issues in child custody evaluation and testimony. In C. R. Reynolds & R. W. Kamphaus (Eds.), *Handbook of psychological and educational assessment of children: Personality, behavior and context* (pp. 576–588). New York: Guilford.

McConkey, K. M., & Sheehan, P. W. (1996). *Hypnosis, memory, and behavior in criminal investigation.* New York: Guilford.

McCool, J. P., Cameron, L. D., & Petrie, K. J. (2001). Adolescent perceptions of smoking imagery in film. *Social Science & Medicine, 52,* 1577–1587.

McCoy, G. F. (1972). *Diagnostic evaluation and educational programming for hearing impaired children.* Springfield: Office of the Illinois Superintendent of Public Instruction.

McCrady, B. S., & Bux, D. A. (1999). Ethical issues of informed consent with substance abusers. *Journal of Consulting and Clinical Psychology, 67,* 186–193.

McCrae, R. R., & Costa, P. T., Jr. (1983). Social desirability and scales: More substance than style. *Journal of Consulting and Clinical Psychology, 51,* 882–888.

McCrae, R. R., Costa, P. T., Jr., Dahlstrom, W. G., Barefoot, J. C., Siegler, I. C., & Williams, R. B., Jr. (1989). A caution on the use of the MMPI K-correction in research on psychosomatic medicine. *Psychosomatic Medicine, 51,* 58–65.

McCrae, R. R., Costa, P. T., Jr., Del Pilar, G. H., Rolland, J.-P., & Parker, W. D. (1998). Cross-cultural assessment of the five-factor model: The Revised NEO Personality Inventory. *Journal of Cross-Cultural Psychology, 29,* 171–188.

McCrae, R. R., Costa, P. T., Jr., Terracciano, A., et al. (2002). Personality trait development from age 12 to age 18: Longitudinal, cross-sectional and cross-cultural analyses. *Journal of Personality & Social Psychology, 83,* 1456–1468.

McCubbin, H., Larsen, A., & Olson, D. (1985a). F-COPES: Family Crisis Oriented Personal Evaluation Scales. In D. H. Olson, H. I. McCubbin, H. L. Barnes, A. S. Larsen, M. Muxen, & M. Wilson (Eds.), *Family inventories* (rev. ed.). St. Paul: Family Social Science, University of Minnesota.

McCubbin, H. I., Patterson, J. M., & Wilson, L. R. (1985b). FILE: Family Inventory of Life Events and Changes. In D. H. Olson, H. I. McCubbin, H. L. Barnes, A. S. Larsen, M. Muxen, & M. Wilson (Eds.), *Family inventories* (rev. ed.). St. Paul: Family Social Science, University of Minnesota.

McCusker, P. J. (1994). Validation of Kaufman, Ishikuma, Kaufman-Packer's Wechsler Adult Intelligence Scale—Revised short forms on a clinical sample. *Psychological Assessment, 6,* 246–248.

McDermott, P. A., Alterman, A. I., Brown, L., et al. (1996). Construct refinement and confirmation for the Addiction Severity Index. *Psychological Assessment, 8,* 182–189.

McDevitt, S. C., & Carey, W. B. (1978). The measurement of temperament in 3- to 7-year-old children. *Journal of Child Psychology & Psychiatry & Allied Disciplines, 19,* 245–253.

McDonald, R. P. (1996a). Consensus emerges: A matter of interpretation. *Multivariate Behavioral Research, 31,* 663–672.

McDonald, R. P. (1996b). Latent traits and the possibility of motion. *Multivariate Behavioral Research, 31,* 593–601.

McDonald, W. J. (1993). Focus group research dynamics and reporting: An examination of research objectives and moderator influences. *Journal of the Academy of Marketing Science, 21,* 161–168.

McDowell, C., & Acklin, M. W. (1996). Standardizing procedures for calculating Rorschach interrater reliability: Conceptual and empirical foundations. *Journal of Personality Assessment, 66,* 308–320.

McDowell, I., & Newell, C. (1987). *Measuring health: A guide to rating scales and questionnaires.* New York: Oxford University Press.

McElrath, K. (1994). A comparison of two methods for examining inmates' self-reported drug use. *International Journal of the Addictions, 29,* 517–524.

McElwain, B. A. (1998). On seeing Beth at home and in a different light. In L. Handler (Chair), *Conducting assessments in clients' homes: Contexts, surprises, dilemmas, opportunities.* Symposium presented at the Society for Personality Assessment 1998 Midwinter Meeting, February 20.

McEvoy, G. M., & Beatty, R. W. (1989). Assessment centers and subordinate appraisals of managers: A seven-year examination of predictive validity. *Personnel Psychology, 42,* 37–52.

McGaghie, W. C. (2002, September 4). Assessing readiness for medical education: Evolution of the Medical College Admission Test. *Journal of the American Medical Association, 288,* p. 1085.

McGirr, A., Renaud, J., Seguin, M., et al. (2007). An examination of DSM-IV depressive symptoms and risk for suicide completion in major depressive disorder: A psychological autopsy study. *Journal of Affective Disorders, 97*(1–3), 203–209.

McGrew, K. S. (1997). Analysis of the major intelligence batteries according to a proposed comprehensive *Gf-Gc* framework. In D. P. Flanagan, J. L. Genshaft, & P. L. Harrison (Eds.), *Contemporary intellectual assessment: Theories, tests, and issues* (pp. 151–180). New York: Guilford.

McGrew, K. S. (2009). Editorial. CHC theory and the human cognitive abilities project. Standing on the shoulders of the giants of psychometric intelligence research, *Intelligence, 37,* 1–10.

McGrew, K. S., & Flanagan, D. P. (1998). *The intelligence test desk reference:* Gf-Gc cross-battery assessment. Boston: Allyn & Bacon.

McGue, M. (1997). The democracy of the genes. *Nature, 388,* 417–418.

McGurk, F. J. (1975). Race differences—twenty years later. *Homo, 26,* 219–239.

McKinley, J. C., & Hathaway, S. R. (1940). A multiphasic schedule (Minnesota): II. A differential study of hypochondriases. *Journal of Psychology, 10,* 255–268.

McKinley, J. C., & Hathaway, S. R. (1944). The MMPI: V. Hysteria, hypomania, and psychopathic deviate. *Journal of Applied Psychology, 28,* 153–174.

McKinney, W. R., & Collins, J. R. (1991). The impact on utility, race, and gender using three standard methods of scoring selection examinations. *Public Personnel Management, 20*(2), 145–169.

McLearen, A. M., Pietz, C. A., & Denney, R. L. (2004). Evaluation of psychological damages. In W. T. O'Donohue & E. R. Levensky (Eds.). *Handbook of forensic psychology* (pp. 267–299). Amsterdam: Elsevier.

McLellan, A. T., Luborsky, L., Woody, G. E., & O'Brien, C. P. (1980). An improved diagnostic evaluation instrument for substance abuse patients: The Addiction Severity Index. *Journal of Nervous and Mental Disease, 168,* 26–33.

McLemore, C. W., & Court, J. H. (1977). Religion and psychotherapy—ethics, civil liberties, and clinical savvy: A critique. *Journal of Consulting and Clinical Psychology, 45,* 1172–1175.

McMillen, C., Howard, M. O., Nower, L., & Chung, S. (2001). Positive by-products of the struggle with chemical dependency. *Journal of Substance Abuse Treatment, 20,* 69–79.

McNemar, Q. (1964). Lost: Our intelligence. Why? *American Psychologist, 19,* 871–882.

McNemar, Q. (1975). On so-called test bias. *American Psychologist, 30,* 848–851.

McReynolds, P. (1987). Lightner Witmer: Little-known founder of clinical psychology. *American Psychologist, 42,* 849–858.

McReynolds, P., & Ludwig, K. (1984). Christian Thomasius and the origin of psychological rating scales. *ISIS, 75,* 546–553.

Mead, M. (1978). *Culture and commitment: The new relationship between the generations in the 1970s* (rev. ed.). New York: Columbia University Press.

Meadow, K. P., Karchmer, M. A., Petersen, L. M., & Rudner, L. (1980). *Meadow-Kendall Social-Emotional Assessment Inventory.* Washington, DC: Gallaudet University.

Meadows, G., Turner, T., Campbell, L., Lewis, S. W., Reveley, M. A., & Murray, R. M. (1991). Assessing schizophrenia in adults with mental retardation: A comparative study. *British Journal of Psychiatry, 158,* 103–105.

Mednick, S. A. (1962). The associative basis of the creative process. *Psychological Review, 69,* 220–232.

Mednick, S. A., Higgins, J., & Kirschenbaum, J. (1975). *Psychology.* New York: Wiley.

Medvec, V. H., Madey, S. F., & Gilovich, T. (1995). When less is more: Counterfactual thinking and satisfaction among Olympic medalists. *Journal of Personality and Social Psychology, 69,* 603–610.

Medvec, V. H., & Savitsky, K. (1997). When doing better means feeling worse: The efforts of categorical cutoff points on counterfactual thinking and satisfaction. *Journal of Personality and Social Psychology, 72,* 1284–1296.

Meehl, P. E. (1945), The dynamics of "structured" personality tests. *Journal of Clinical Psychology, 1,* 296–303.

Meehl, P. E. (1951). *Research results for counselors.* St. Paul, MN: State Department of Education.

Meehl, P. E. (1954). *Clinical versus statistical prediction: A theoretical analysis and a review of the evidence.* Minneapolis: University of Minnesota.

Meehl, P. E. (1956). Wanted: A good cookbook. *American Psychologist, 11,* 263–272.

Meehl, P. E., & Rosen, A. (1955). Antecedent probability and the efficiency of psychometric signs, patterns, or cutting scores. *Psychological Bulletin, 52,* 194–216.

Mehl, M. R., & Pennebaker, J. W. (2003). The sounds of social life: A psychometric analysis of students' daily social environments and natural conversations. *Journal of Personality and Social Psychology, 84,* 857–870.

Melchert, T. P., & Patterson, M. M. (1999). Duty to warn and interventions with HIV-positive clients. *Professional Psychology: Research and Practice, 30,* 180–186.

Melchior, L. A., Huba, G. J., Brown, V. B., & Reback, C. J. (1993). A short depression index for women. *Educational and Psychological Measurement, 53,* 1117–1125.

Melia, R. P., Pledger, C., & Wilson, R. (2003). Disability and rehabilitation research: Opportunities for participation, collaboration, and extramural funding for psychologists. *American Psychologist, 58,* 285–288.

Mellenbergh, G. J. (1994). Generalized linear item response theory. *Psychological Bulletin, 115,* 300–307.

Mello, E. W., & Fisher, R. P. (1996). Enhancing older adult eyewitness memory with the cognitive interview. *Applied Cognitive Psychology, 10,* 403–418.

Melton, G., Petrila, J., Poythress, N. G., & Slobogin, C. (1997). *Psychological evaluations for the courts: A handbook for mental health professionals and lawyers* (2nd ed.). New York: Guilford.

Melton, G. B. (1989). Review of the Child Abuse Protection Inventory, Form VI. In J. C. Conoley & J. J. Kramer (Eds.), *The tenth mental measurements yearbook.* Lincoln: Buros Institute of Mental Measurements, University of Nebraska.

Melton, G. B., & Limber, S. (1989). Psychologists' involvement in cases of child maltreatment. *American Psychologist, 44,* 1225–1233.

Memon, A., Fraser, J., Colwell, K., Odinot, G., & Mastroberardino, S. (2010). Distinguishing truthful from invented accounts using reality monitoring criteria. *Legal and Criminological Psychology, 15*(2), 177–194.

Mendoza, R. H. (1989). An empirical scale to measure type and degree of acculturation in Mexican-American adolescents and adults. *Journal of Cross-Cultural Psychology, 20,* 372–385.

Menninger, K. A. (1953). *The human mind* (3rd ed.). New York: Knopf.

Mercer, J. R. (1976). A system of multicultural pluralistic assessment (SOMPA). In *Proceedings: With bias toward none.* Lexington: Coordinating Office for Regional Resource Centers, University of Kentucky.

Merrens, M. R., & Richards, W. S. (1970). Acceptance of generalized versus "bona fide" personality interpretation. *Psychological Reports, 27,* 691–694.

Mershon, B., & Gorsuch, R. L. (1988). Number of factors in the personality sphere: Does increase in factors increase predictability of real-life criteria? *Journal of Personality and Social Psychology, 55,* 675–680.

Mesmer, E. M., & Duhon, G. J. (2011). Response to intervention: Promoting and evaluating generalization. *Journal of Evidence-Based Practices for Schools, 12*(1), 75–104.

Messer, S. B. (1976). Reflection-impulsivity: A review. *Psychological Bulletin, 83,* 1026–1052.

Messick, S. (1976). *Individuality in learning: Implications of cognitive style and creativity for human development.* San Francisco: Jossey-Bass.

Messick, S. (1995). Validity of psychological assessment. *American Psychologist, 50,* 741–749.

Meyer, G. J., & Archer, R. P. (2001). The hard science of Rorschach research: What do we know and where do we go? *Psychological Assessment, 13,* 486–502.

Meyer, G. J., & Handler, L. (1997). The ability of the Rorschach to predict subsequent outcome: Meta-analysis of the Rorschach Prognostic Rating Scale. *Journal of Personality Assessment, 69,* 1–38.

Meyer, G. J., & Kurtz, J. E. (2006). Advancing personality assessment terminology: Time to retire "objective" and "projective" as personality test descriptors. *Journal of Personality Assessment, 87,* 223–225.

Meyers, J. (1994, January/February). Assessing cross-cultural adaptability with the CCAI. *San Diego Psychological Association Newsletter, 3*(1 & 2).

Micceri, T. (1989). The unicorn, the normal curve and other improbable creatures. *Psychological Bulletin, 105,* 156–166.

Midanik, L. T., Greenfield, T. K., & Rogers, J. D. (2001). Reports of alcohol-related harm: Telephone versus face-to-face interviews. *Journal of Studies on Alcohol, 62,* 74–78.

Migliore, L. A. (2011). Relation between big five personality traits and Hofstede's cultural dimensions: Samples from the USA and India. *Cross Cultural Management, 18*(1), 38–54.

Mikami, A. Y., Szwedo, D. E., Allen, J. P., et al. (2010). Adolescent peer relationships and behavior problems predict young adults' communication on social networking websites. *Developmental Psychology, 46*(1), 46–56.

Miller, I. W., Kabacoff, R. I., Epstein, N. B., & Bishop, D. S. (1994). The development of a clinical rating scale for the McMaster Model of Family Functioning. *Family Process, 33,* 53–69.

Miller, J. C., Skillman, G. D., Benedetto, J. M., et al. (2007). A three-dimensional haptic matrix test of nonverbal reasoning. *Journal of Visual Impairment and Blindness, 101,* 557–570.

Miller, J. N., & Ozonoff, S. (2000). The external validity of Asperger disorder: Lack of evidence from the domain of neuropsychology. *Journal of Abnormal Psychology, 109,* 227–238.

Miller, N. E. (1969). Learning of visceral and glandular responses. *Science, 163,* 434–445.

Milling, L. S., Coursen, E. L., Shores, J. S., & Waszkiewicz, J. A. (2010). The predictive utility of hypnotizability: the change in suggestibility produced by hypnosis. *Journal of Consulting and Clinical Psychology, 78*(1), 126–130.

Millman, J., & Arter, J. A. (1984). Issues in item banking. *Journal of Educational Measurement, 21,* 315–330.

Millon, T., Millon, C., & Davis, R. (1994). *MCMI-III manual: Millon Clinical Multiaxial Inventory-III.* Minneapolis: National Computer Systems.

Mills v. Board of Education of the District of Columbia, 348 F. Supp 866 (D. DC 1972).

Mills, C. J. (2003). Characteristics of effective teachers of gifted students: Teacher background and personality styles of students. *Gifted Child Quarterly, 47,* 272–282.

Milner, B. (1971). Interhemispheric differences in the localization of psychological processes in man. *British Medical Bulletin, 27,* 272–277.

Milner, J. S. (1986). *The Child Abuse Potential Inventory: Manual* (2nd ed.). Webster, NC: Psytec Corporation.

Milner, J. S. (1989a). Additional cross-validation of the Child Abuse Potential Inventory. *Psychological Assessment, 1,* 219–223.

Milner, J. S. (1989b). Applications of the Child Abuse Potential Inventory. *Journal of Clinical Psychology, 45,* 450–454.

Milner, J. S. (1991). Additional issues in child abuse assessment. *American Psychologist, 46,* 82–84.

Milner, J. S., Gold, R. G., & Wimberley, R. C. (1986). Prediction and explanation of child abuse: Cross-validation of the Child Abuse Protection Inventory. *Journal of Consulting and Clinical Psychology, 54,* 865–866.

Minsky, S. K., Spitz, H. H., & Bessellieu, C. L. (1985). Maintenance and transfer of training by mentally retarded young adults on the Tower of Hanoi problem. *American Journal of Mental Deficiency, 90,* 190–197.

Minton, B. A., & Pratt, S. (2006). Gifted and highly gifted students: How do they score on the SB5? *Roeper Review: A Journal on Gifted Education, 28*(4), 232–236.

Minton, H. L. (1988). *Lewis M. Terman: Pioneer in psychological testing.* New York: New York University Press.

Mirka, G. A., Kelaher, D. P., Nay, T., & Lawrence, B. M. (2000). Continuous assessment of back stress (CABS): A new method to quantify low-back stress in jobs with variable biomechanical demands. *Human Factors, 42,* 209–225.

Mischel, W. (1968). *Personality and assessment.* New York: Wiley.

Mischel, W. (1973). Toward a cognitive social learning re-conceptualization of personality. *Psychological Review, 80,* 252–283.

Mischel, W. (1977). On the future of personality measurement. *American Psychologist, 32,* 246–254.

Mischel, W. (1979). On the interface of cognition and personality: Beyond the person-situation debate. *American Psychologist, 34,* 740–754.

Mishra, D., Khalique, A., & Kumar, R. (2010). Rorschach profile of manic patients. *Journal of Projective Psychology & Mental Health, 17*(2), 158–164.

Misiaszek, J., Dooling, J., Gieseke, M., Melman, H., Misiaszek, J. G., & Jorgensen, K. (1985). Diagnostic considerations in deaf patients. *Comprehensive Psychiatry, 26,* 513–521.

Mitchell, J. (1999). *Measurement in psychology: Critical history of a methodological concept.* New York: Cambridge University Press.

Mitchell, J. V., Jr. (Ed.). (1985). *The ninth mental measurements yearbook*. Lincoln: Buros Institute of Mental Measurements, University of Nebraska.

Mitchell, J. V., Jr. (1986). Measurement in the larger context: Critical current issues. *Professional Psychology: Research and Practice, 17*, 544–550.

Mitzel, H. C., Lewis, D. M., Patz, R. J., & Green, D. R. (2000). The bookmark procedure: Cognitive perspectives on standard setting. In G. J. Cizek (Ed.), *Setting performance standards: Concepts, methods, and perspectives*, Mahwah, NJ: Erlbaum.

Moffic, H. S., & Kinzie, J. D. (1996). The history and future of cross-cultural psychiatric services. *Community Mental Health Journal, 32*(6), 581–592.

Moffitt, T. E., Caspi, A., Krueger, R. F., et al. (1997). Do partners agree about abuse in their relationship? A psychometric evaluation of interpartner agreement. *Psychological Assessment, 9*, 47–56.

Mohatt, G. V., Rasmus, S. M., Thomas, L., Allen, J., Hazel, K., & Hensel, C. (2004). "Tied together like a woven hat:" Protective pathways to Alaska native sobriety. *Harm Reduction Journal, 1*(10), 1–12.

Mohatt, N. V., Fok, C. C. T., Burket, R., Henry, D., & Allen, J. (2011). Assessment of awareness of connectedness as a culturally-based protective factor for Alaska Native youth. *Cultural Diversity and Ethnic Minority Psychology, 17*(4), 444–445.

Monahan, J. (1981). *The clinical prediction of violent behavior*. Washington, DC: U.S. Government Printing Office.

Montag, C., Reuter, M., & Axmacher, N. (2011). How one's favorite song activates the reward circuitry of the brain: Personality matters! *Behavioural Brain Research, 225*(2), 511–514.

Montague, M. (1993). Middle school students' mathematical problem solving: An analysis of think-aloud protocols. *Learning Disability Quarterly, 16*, 19–32.

Montgomery, G. T., & Orozco, S. (1985). Mexican Americans' performance on the MMPI as a function of level of acculturation. *Journal of Clinical Psychology, 41*, 203–212.

Moore, M., Schermer, J. A., Paunonen, S. V., & Vernon, P. A. (2010). Genetic and environmental influences on verbal and nonverbal measures of the Big Five. *Personality and Individual Differences, 48*(8), 884–888.

Moore, M. S., & McLaughlin, L. (1992). Assessment of the preschool child with visual impairment. In E. Vasquez Nutall, I. Romero, & J. Kalesnik (Eds.), *Assessing and screening pre-schoolers: Psychological and educational dimensions* (pp. 345–368). Boston: Allyn & Bacon.

Moos, R. H. (1986). *Work Environment Scale* (2nd ed.). Palo Alto, CA: Consulting Psychologists Press.

Moos, R. H., & Moos, B. S. (1981). *Family Environment Scale manual*. Palo Alto, CA: Consulting Psychologists Press.

Moos, R. H., & Moos, B. S. (1994). *Family environment manual: Development, applications, research*. Palo Alto, CA: Consulting Psychologists Press.

Moreland, K. L. (1985). Validation of computer-based test interpretations: Problems and prospects. *Journal of Consulting and Clinical Psychology, 53*, 816–825.

Moreland, K. L. (1986). An introduction to the problem of test user qualifications. In R. B. Most (Chair), *Test purchaser qualifications: Present practice, professional needs, and a proposed system*. Symposium presented at the 94th annual convention of the American Psychological Association, Washington, DC.

Moreland, K. L. (1987). Computerized psychological assessment: What's available. In J. N. Butcher (Ed.), *Computerized psychological assessment: A practitioner's guide* (pp. 26–49). New York: Basic Books.

Moreland, K. L., Eyde, L. D., Robertson, G. J., Primoff, E. S., & Most, R. B. (1995a). Assessment of test user qualifications: A research-based measurement procedure. *American Psychologist, 50*, 14–23.

Moreland, K. L., Reznikoff, M., & Aronow, E. (1995b). Integrating Rorschach interpretation by *carefully* placing *more* of your eggs in the content basket. *Journal of Personality Assessment, 64*, 239–242.

Morgan, C. D. (1938). Thematic Apperception Test. In H. A. Murray (Ed.), *Explorations in personality: A clinical and experimental study of fifty men of college age* (pp. 673–680). New York: Oxford University Press.

Morgan, C. D., & Murray, H. A. (1935). A method for investigating fantasies: The Thematic Apperception Test. *Archives of Neurology and Psychiatry, 34*, 289–306.

Morgan, C. D., & Murray, H. A. (1938). Thematic Apperception Test. In H. A. Murray (Ed.), *Explorations in personality: A clinical and experimental study of fifty men of college age* (pp. 530–545). New York: Oxford University Press.

Morgan, J. E., & Ricker, J. H. (Eds.). (2007). *Textbook of clinical neuropsychology*. New York: Taylor & Francis.

Morgan, K. E., Rothlisberg, B. A., McIntosh, D. E., & Hunt, M. S. (2009). Confirmatory factor analysis of the KABC-II in preschool children. *Psychology in the Schools, 46*, 515–525.

Morgan, W. G. (1995). Origin and history of Thematic Apperception Test images. *Journal of Personality Assessment, 65*, 237–254.

Mori, L. T., & Armendariz, G. M. (2001). Analogue assessment of child behavior problems. *Psychological Assessment, 13*, 36–45.

Morreau, L. E., & Bruininks, R. H. (1991). *Checklist of Adaptive Living Skills*. Itasca, IL: Riverside.

Moses, S. (1991). Major revision of SAT goes into effect in 1994. *APA Monitor, 22*(1), 35.

Mosier, C. I. (1947). A critical examination of the concepts of face validity. *Educational and Psychological Measurement, 7*, 191–206.

Moss, K., Ullman, M., Johnsen, M. C., et al. (1999). Different paths to justice: The ADA, employment, and administrative enforcement by the EEOC and FEPAs. *Behavioral Sciences and the Law, 17*, 29–46.

Mossman, D. (2003). *Daubert*, cognitive malingering, and test accuracy. *Law and Human Behavior, 27*(3), 229–249.

Motowidlo, S. J. (1996). Orientation toward the job and organization. In K. R. Murphy (Ed.), *Individual differences and behavior in organizations* (pp. 20–175). San Francisco: Jossey-Bass.

Motta, R. W., Little, S. G., & Tobin, M. I. (1993a). The use and abuse of human figure drawings. *School Psychology Quarterly, 8*, 162–169.

Motta, R. W., Little, S. G., & Tobin, M. I. (1993b). A picture is worth less than a thousand words: Response to reviewers. *School Psychology Quarterly, 8*, 197–199.

Mueller, C. G. (1949). Numerical transformations in the analysis of experimental data. *Psychological Bulletin, 46*, 198–223.

Mueller, J. H., Jacobsen, D. M., & Schwarzer, R. (2000). What are computers good for? A case study in online research. In M. H. Birnbaum (Ed.), *Psychological experiments on the Internet* (pp. 195–216). San Diego: Academic Press.

Mueller, U., & Mazur, A. (1996). Facial dominance in *homo sapiens* as honest signaling of male quality. *Behavioral Ecology, 8*, 569–579.

Mueller-Hanson, R., Heggestad, E. D., & Thornton, G. C., III. (2003). Faking and selection: Considering the use of personality from select-in and select-out perspectives. *Journal of Applied Psychology, 88*, 348–355.

Mulaik, S. A. (1996a). Factor analysis is not just a model in pure mathematics. *Multivariate Behavioral Research, 31,* 655–661.

Mulaik, S. A. (1996b). On Maraun's deconstructing of factor indeterminacy with constructed factors. *Multivariate Behavioral Research, 31,* 579–592.

Mulvey, E. P., & Lidz, C. W. (1984). Clinical considerations in the prediction of dangerousness in mental patients. *Clinical Psychology Review, 4,* 379–401.

Muñoz, B.; Magliano, J. P., Sheridan, R., & McNamara, D. S. (2006), Typing versus thinking aloud when reading: Implications for computer-based assessment and training tools. *Behavior Research Methods, 38*(2) 211–217

Murguia, A., Zea, M. C., Reisen, C. A., & Peterson, R. A. (2000). The development of the Cultural Health Attributions Questionnaire (CHAQ). *Cultural Diversity and Ethnic Minority Psychology, 6,* 268–283.

Murphy, G. E. (1984). The prediction of suicide: Why is it so difficult? *American Journal of Psychotherapy, 38,* 341–349.

Murphy, K. A., Blustein, D. L., Bohlig, A., & Platt, M. (2006, August). *College to career transition: An exploration of emerging adulthood.* Paper presented at the 114th Annual Convention of the American Psychological Association, New Orleans.

Murphy, K. M. (1986). When your top choice turns you down: The effect of rejected offers on the utility of selection tests. *Psychological Bulletin, 99,* 133–138.

Murphy, K. R. (Ed.). (2003). *Validity generalization: A critical review.* Mahwah, NJ: Erlbaum.

Murphy, L. L., Conoley, J. C., & Impara, J. C. (1994). *Tests in print IV: An index to tests, test reviews, and the literature on specific tests.* Lincoln: Buros Institute of Mental Measurements, University of Nebraska.

Murphy-Berman, V. (1994). A conceptual framework for thinking about risk assessment and case management in child protective service. *Child Abuse and Neglect, 18,* 193–201.

Murray, C. (2007). The magnitude and components of change in the black-white IQ difference from 1920 to 1991: A birth cohort analysis of the Woodcock-Johnson standardizations. *Intelligence, 35*(4), 305–318.

Murray, H. A. (1943). *Thematic Apperception Test manual.* Cambridge, MA: Harvard University.

Murray, H. A., et al. (1938). *Explorations in personality.* Cambridge, MA: Harvard University.

Murray, H. A., & MacKinnon, D. W. (1946). Assessment of OSS personnel. *Journal of Consulting Psychology, 10,* 76–80.

Murstein, B. I. (1961). Assumptions, adaptation level, and projective techniques. *Perceptual and Motor Skills, 12,* 107–125.

Murstein, B. I., & Mathes, S. (1996). Projection on projective techniques = pathology: The problem that is not being addressed. *Journal of Personality Assessment, 66,* 337–349.

Mussen, P. H., & Naylor, H. K. (1954). The relationship between overt and fantasy aggression. *Journal of Abnormal and Social Psychology, 49,* 235–240.

Mussen, P. H., & Scodel, A. (1955). The effects of sexual stimulation under varying conditions on TAT sexual responsiveness. *Journal of Consulting and Clinical Psychology, 19,* 90.

Myers, I. B. (1962). *The Myers-Briggs Type Indicator: Manual.* Palo Alto, CA: Consulting Psychologists Press.

Myers, I. B., & Briggs, K. C. (1943/1962). *The Myers-Briggs Type Indicator.* Palo Alto, CA: Consulting Psychologists Press.

Myers, K. D., & Carskadon, T. G. (2002). Eminent interview: Katharine Downing Myers. *Journal of Psychological Type, 61,* 43–49.

Myerson, A. (1925). *The inheritance of mental disease.* Oxford, England: Williams & Wilkins.

Nagle, R. J., & Bell, N. L. (1993). Validation of Stanford-Binet Intelligence Scale: Fourth Edition Abbreviated Batteries with college students. *Psychology in the Schools, 30,* 227–231.

Naglieri, J. A. (1985a). Normal children's performance on the McCarthy Scales, Kaufman Assessment Battery and Peabody Individual Achievement Test. *Journal of Psychoeducational Assessment, 3,* 123–129.

Naglieri, J. A. (1985b). Use of the WISC-R and K-ABC with learning disabled, borderline mentally retarded, and normal children. *Psychology in the Schools, 22,* 133–141.

Naglieri, J. A. (1989). A cognitive processing theory for the measurement of intelligence. *Educational Psychologist, 24,* 185–206.

Naglieri, J. A. (1990). *Das-Naglieri Cognitive Assessment System.* Paper presented at the conference "Intelligence: Theories and Practice," Memphis, TN.

Naglieri, J. A. (1993). Human figure drawings in perspective. *School Psychology Quarterly, 8,* 170–176.

Naglieri, J. A. (1997). IQ: Knowns and unknowns, hits and misses. *American Psychologist, 52,* 75–76.

Naglieri, J. A., & Anderson, D. F. (1985). Comparison of the WISC-R and K-ABC with gifted students. *Journal of Psychoeducational Assessment, 3,* 175–179.

Naglieri, J. A., & Das, J. P. (1988). Planning-arousal-simultaneous-successive (PASS): A model for assessment. *Journal of School Psychology, 26,* 35–48.

Naglieri, J. A., & Das, J. P. (1997). *Das-Naglieri Cognitive Assessment System: Interpretive handbook.* Itasca, IL: Riverside.

Naglieri, J. A., Drasgow, F., Schmit, M., et al. (2004). Psychological testing on the Internet: New problems, old issues. *American Psychologist, 59,* 150–162.

Nakamura, B. J., Ebesutani, C., Bernstein, A., & Chorpita, B. F. (2009). A psychometric analysis of the Child Behavior Checklist DSM-Oriented Scales. *Journal of Psychopathology and Behavioral Assessment, 31*(3), 178–189.

Narumoto, J., Nakamura, K., Kitabayashi, Y., et al. (2008). Relationships among burnout, coping style, and personality: Study of Japanese professional caregivers for elderly. *Psychiatry and Clinical Neurosciences, 62*(2), 174–176.

Nathan, J., Wilkinson, D., Stammers, S., & Low, L. (2001). The role of tests of frontal executive function in the detection of mild dementia. *International Journal of Geriatric Psychiatry, 16,* 18–26.

National Association of School Psychologists. (2000). *Professional conduct manual* (4th ed.). Washington, DC: Author.

National Center on Response to Intervention. (2011). *Essential components of RtI: A closer look at response to intervention.* Document accessed at National Center on Response to Intervention website at www.rti4success.org/pdf/rtiessentialcomponents_042710.pdf.

National Council on Disability. (1996). *Cognitive impairments and the application of Title I of the Americans with Disabilities Act.* Washington, DC: Author.

National Joint Committee on Learning Disabilities. (1985). *Learning disabilities and the preschool child: A position paper of the National Joint Committee on Learning Disabilities.* Baltimore: Author.

Naylor, J. C., & Shine, L. C. (1965). A table for determining the increase in mean criterion score obtained by using a selection device. *Journal of Industrial Psychology, 3,* 33–42.

Neale, E. L., & Rosale, M. L. (1993). What can art therapists learn from projective drawing techniques for children?

A review of the literature. *The Arts in Psychotherapy, 20,* 37–49.

Neath, J., Bellini, J., & Bolton, B. (1997). Dimensions of the Functional Assessment Inventory for five disability groups. *Rehabilitation Psychology, 42,* 183–207.

Needham, J. (1959). *A history of embryology.* New York: Abelard-Schuman.

Nehring, W. M. (2007). Accommodations for school and work. In C. L. Betz & W. M. Nehring (Eds.), *Promoting health care transitions for adolescents with special health care needs and disabilities* (pp. 97–115). Baltimore: Brookes.

Neisser, U. (1979). The concept of intelligence. *Intelligence, 3,* 217–227.

Neisser, U., Boodoo, G., Bouchard, T. J., Jr., et al. (1996). Intelligence: Knowns and unknowns. *American Psychologist, 51,* 77–101.

Nellis, L., & Gridley, B. E. (1994). Review of the Bayley Scales of Infant Development—Second Edition. *Journal of School Psychology, 32,* 201–209.

Nelson, C. A., Wewerka, S., Thomas, K. M., et al. (2000). Neurocognitive sequelae of infants of diabetic mothers. *Behavioral Neuroscience, 114,* 950–956.

Nelson, D. V., Harper, R. G., Kotik-Harper, D., & Kirby, H. B. (1993). Brief neuropsychologic differentiation of demented versus depressed elderly inpatients. *General Hospital Psychiatry, 15,* 409–416.

Nelson, L. D. (1994). Introduction to the special section on normative assessment. *Psychological Assessment, 4,* 283.

Nelson, R. O., Hay, L. R., & Hay, W. M. (1977). Comment on Cone's "The relevance of reliability and validity for behavior assessment." *Behavior Therapy, 8,* 427–430.

Nester, M. A. (1993). Psychometric testing and reasonable accommodation for persons with disabilities. *Rehabilitation Psychology, 38,* 75–85.

Nettelbeck, T., & Rabbit, P. M. A. (1992). Aging, cognitive performance, and mental speed. *Intelligence, 16,* 189–205.

Neugarten, B., Havighurst, R. J., & Tobin, S. (1961). The measurement of life satisfaction. *Journal of Gerontology, 16,* 134–143.

Nevid, J. S. (2010). Implicit measures of consumer response—The search for the Holy Grail of marketing research: Introduction to the special issue. *Psychology & Marketing, 27*(10), 913–920.

Nevid, J. S., & McClelland, N. (2010). Measurement of implicit and explicit attitudes toward Barack Obama. *Psychology & Marketing, 27*(10), 989–1000.

Newborg, J., Stock, J. R., Wnek, L., et al. (1984). *Battelle Developmental Inventory.* Allen, TX: DLM Teaching Resources.

Newcomb, T. M. (1929). *Consistency of certain extrovert-introvert behavior patterns in 51 problem boys.* New York: Columbia University Bureau of Publications.

Newell, A. (1973). Production systems: Models of control structures. In W. G. Chase (Ed.), *Visual information processing* (pp. 463–526). New York: Academic Press.

Newman, D. A., Kinney, T., & Farr, J. L. (2004). Job performance ratings. In J. C Thomas (Ed.), *Comprehensive handbook of psychological assessment, Volume 4: Industrial and organizational assessment* (pp. 373–389). Hoboken, NJ: Wiley.

Newman, H. H., Freeman, F. N., & Holzinger, K. J. (1937). *Twins.* Chicago: University of Chicago.

Nguyen, H. H., & von Eye, A. (2002). The Acculturation Scale for Vietnamese Adolescents (ASVA): A bidimensional perspective. *International Journal of Behavioral Development, 26*(3), 202–213.

Nguyen, N. T., Biderman, M. D., & McNary, L. D. (2010). A validation study of the cross-cultural adaptability inventory. *International Journal of Training and Development, 14*(2), 112–129.

Nichols, D. S. (2006). The trials of separating bathwater from baby: A review and critique of the MMPI-2 restructured clinical scales. *Journal of Personality Assessment, 87,* 121–138.

Nilsson, J. E., Berkel, L. A., Flores, L. Y., et al. (2003). An 11-year review of *Professional Psychology: Research and Practice:* Content and sample analysis with an emphasis on diversity. *Professional Psychology: Research and Practice, 34,* 611–616.

Nock, M. K., & Banaji, M. R. (2007). Prediction of suicide ideation and attempts among adolescents using a brief performance-based test. *Journal of Consulting and Clinical Psychology, 75*(5), 707–715.

Nordanger, D. (2007). Discourses of loss and bereavement in Tigray, Ethiopia. *Culture, Medicine and Psychiatry, 31*(2), 173–194.

Norton, P. J., & Hope, D. A. (2001). Analogue observational methods in the assessment of social functioning in adults. *Psychological Assessment, 13,* 59–72.

Nosek, B. A., Greenwald, A. G., & Banaji, M. R. (2007). The Implicit Association Test at age 7: Methodological and conceptual review. In J. A. Bargh (Ed.), *Social psychology and the unconscious: The automaticity of higher mental processes. Frontiers of social psychology* (pp. 265–292). New York: Psychology Press.

Notarius, C., & Markman, H. (1981). Couples Interaction Scoring System. In E. Filsinger & R. Lewis (Eds.), *Assessing marriage: New behavioral approaches.* Beverly Hills, CA: Sage.

Notarius, C. I., & Vanzetti, N. A. (1983). The Marital Agendas Protocol. In E. Filsinger (Ed.), *Marriage and family assessment: A sourcebook for family therapy.* Beverly Hills, CA: Sage.

Novick, M. R., & Lewis, C. (1967). Coefficient alpha and the reliability of composite measurements. *Psychometrika, 32,* 1–13.

Nunnally, J. C. (1967). *Psychometric theory.* New York: McGraw-Hill.

Nunnally, J. C. (1978). *Psychometric theory* (2nd ed.). New York: McGraw-Hill.

Nurss, J. R. (1994). *Metropolitan Readiness Tests, Sixth Edition* (MRT6). San Antonio: Pearson Assessments.

Nyborg, H., & Jensen, A. R. (2000). Black–white differences on various psychometric tests: Spearman's hypothesis tested on American armed services veterans. *Personality and Individual Differences, 28,* 593–599.

Nye, C. D., Roberts, B. W. Saucier, G., & Zhou, X. (2008). Testing the measurement equivalence of personality adjective items across cultures. *Journal of Research in Personality, 42*(6), 1524–1536.

Nystedt, L., Sjoeberg, A., & Haegglund, G. (1999). Discriminant validation of measures of organizational commitment, job involvement, and job satisfaction among Swedish army officers. *Scandinavian Journal of Psychology, 40,* 49–55.

Obasi, E. M., & Leong, F. T. L. (2010). Construction and validation of the Measurement of Acculturation Strategies for People of African Descent (MASPAD). *Cultural Diversity and Ethnic Minority Psychology, 16*(4), 526–539.

O'Boyle, M. W., Gill, H. S., Benbow, C. P., & Alexander, J. E. (1994). Concurrent finger-tapping in mathematically gifted males: Evidence for enhanced right hemispheric involvement during linguistic processing. *Cortex, 30,* 519–526.

O'Connor, E. (2001, February). Researchers pinpoint potential cause of autism. *Monitor on Psychology, 32*(2), 13.

Oden, M. H. (1968). The fulfillment of promise: 40-year follow-up of the Terman gifted group. *Genetic Psychology Monographs, 77,* 3–93.

O'Donnell, W. E., DeSoto, C. B., & DeSoto, J. L. (1993). Validity and reliability of the Revised Neuropsychological Impairment Scales (NIS). *Journal of Clinical Psychology, 49,* 372–382.

O'Donnell, W. E., DeSoto, C. B., DeSoto, J. L., & Reynolds, D. M. (1993). *The Neuropsychological Impairment Scale (NIS) manual.* Los Angeles: Western Psychological Services.

O'Hare, T., & Van Tran, T. (1998). Substance abuse among Southeast Asians in the U.S.: Implications for practice and research. *Social Work in Health Care, 26,* 69–80.

Okazaki, S., & Sue, S. (1995). Methodological issues in assessment research with ethnic minorities. *Psychological Assessment, 7,* 367–375.

Okazaki, S., & Sue, S. (2000). Implications of test revisions for assessment with Asian Americans. *Psychological Assessment, 12,* 272–280.

O'Keefe, J. (1993). Disability, discrimination, and the Americans with Disabilities Act. *Consulting Psychology Journal, 45*(2), 3–9.

O'Leary, K. D., & Arias, I. (1988). Assessing agreement of reports of spouse abuse. In G. T. Hotaling, D. Finkelhor, J. T. Kirkpatrick, & M. A. Straus (Eds.), *Family abuse and its consequences* (pp. 218–227). Newbury Park, CA: Sage.

Olino, T. M., McMakin, D. L., Dahl, R. E., et al. (2011). "I won, but I'm not getting my hopes up": Depression moderates the relationship of outcomes and reward anticipation. *Psychiatry Research: Neuroimaging* (November 11).

Olkin, R., & Pledger, C. (2003). Can disability studies and psychology join hands? *American Psychologist, 58,* 296–304.

Olson, D. H., & Barnes, H. L. (1985). Quality of life. In D. H. Olson, H. I. McCubbin, H. L. Barnes, A. S. Larsen, M. Muxen, & M. Wilson (Eds.), *Family inventories* (rev. ed.). St. Paul: Family Social Science, University of Minnesota.

Olson, D. H., Larsen, A. S., & McCubbin, H. I. (1985). Family strengths. In D. H. Olson, H. I. McCubbin, H. L. Barnes, A. S. Larsen, M. Muxen, & M. Wilson (Eds.), *Family inventories* (rev. ed.). St. Paul: Family Social Science, University of Minnesota.

Olweus, D. (1979). Stability of aggressive reaction patterns in males: A review. *Psychological Bulletin, 86,* 852–875.

Ones, D. S., Dilchert, S., Viswesvaran, C., & Judge, T. A. (2007). In support of personality assessment in organizational settings. *Personnel Psychology, 60*(4), 995–1027.

Ones, D. S., & Viswesvaran, C. (2001). Integrity tests and other criterion-focused occupational personality scales (COPS) used in personnel selection. *International Journal of Selection and Assessment, 9,* 31–39.

Ones, D. S., Viswesvaran, C., & Reiss, A. D. (1996). Role of social desirability in personality testing for personnel selection: The red herring. *Journal of Applied Psychology, 81,* 660–670.

Oregon Death With Dignity Act, 2 Ore. Rev. Stat. §§127.800–127.897 (1997).

Organ, D. W., & Near, J. P. (1985). Cognition versus affect in measures of job satisfaction. *International Journal of Psychology, 20,* 241–253.

Orne, M. T. (1979). The use and misuse of hypnosis in court. *International Journal of Clinical and Experimental Hypnosis, 27,* 311–341.

Orr, D. B., & Graham, W. R. (1968). Development of a listening comprehension test to identify educational potential among disadvantaged junior high school students. *American Educational Researcher Journal, 5,* 167–180.

Orr, F. C., DeMatteo, A., Heller, B., Lee, M., & Nguyen, M. (1987). Psychological assessment. In H. Elliott, L. Glass, & J. W. Evans (Eds.), *Mental health assessment of deaf clients* (pp. 93–106). Boston: Little, Brown.

Orr, R. R., Cameron, S. J., Dobson, L. A., & Day, D. M. (1993). Age-related changes in stress experienced by families with a child who has developmental delays. *Mental Retardation, 31,* 171–176.

Osberg, T. M., Haseley, E. N., & Kamas, M. M. (2008). The MMPI-2 Clinical Scales and Restructured Clinical (RC) Scales: Comparative psychometric properties and relative diaganostic efficiency in young adults. *Journal of Personality Assessment, 90*(1), 81–92.

Osgood, C. E., Suci, G. J., & Tannenbaum, P. H. (1957). *The measurement of meaning.* Urbana: University of Illinois Press.

Osipow, S. H., & Reed, R. (1985). Decision-making style and career indecision in college students. *Journal of Vocational Behavior, 27,* 368–373.

OSS Assessment Staff. (1948). *Assessment of men: Selection of personnel for the Office of Strategic Service.* New York: Rinehart.

O'Toole, M. E. (2004). Criminal profiling: The FBI uses criminal investigative analysis to solve crimes. In J. H. Campbell & D. DeNevi (Eds.), *Profilers: Leading investigators take you inside the criminal mind* (pp. 223–228). Amherst, NY: Prometheus Books.

Otto, R. (2007). Participant. In A. E. Puente (Chair), *Third party observers in psychological and neuropsychological forensic psychological assessment.* Symposium presented at the 115th Annual Convention of the American Psychological Association, San Francisco.

Ouellette, S. E. (1988). The use of projective drawing techniques in the personality assessment of prelingually deafened young adults: A pilot study. *American Annals of the Deaf, 133,* 212–217.

Outtz, J. (1994, June). Cited in T. DeAngelis, New tests allow takers to tackle real-life problems. *APA Monitor, 25,* 14.

Owens, C., Lambert, H., Lloyd, K., & Donovan, J. (2008). Tales of biographical disintegration: How parents make sense of their son's suicides. *Sociology of Health & Illness, 30*(2), 237–254.

Ozer, D. J. (1985). Correlation and the coefficient of determination. *Psychological Bulletin, 97,* 307–315.

Ozonoff, S. (1995). Reliability and validity of the Wisconsin Card Sorting Test in studies of autism. *Neuropsychology, 9,* 491–500.

Pace, V. L., & Borman, W. C. (2006). The use of warnings to discourage faking on noncognitive inventories. In R. L. Griffith & M. H. Peterson, *A closer examination of applicant faking behavior* (pp. 281–302). Charlotte, NC: Information Age.

Pack v. K-Mart, 166 F.3d, 1300 (10th Cir. 1999).

Padawer, J. R. (2001, October). Computer-modified Rorschach inkblots: A new method for studying projectives. *Dissertation Abstracts International: Section B: The Sciences and Engineering,* p. 2072.

Padden, C. (1980). The deaf community and the culture of deaf people. In C. Baker & R. Battison (Eds.), *Sign language and the deaf community* (pp. 89–103). Washington, DC: National Association of the Deaf.

Padden, C., & Humphries, T. (1988). *Deaf in America: Voices from a culture.* Cambridge, MA: Harvard University Press.

Padilla, A. M., Wagatsuma, Y., & Lindholm, K. J. (1985). Acculturation and personality as predictors of stress in Japanese and Japanese Americans. *Journal of Social Psychology, 125,* 295–305.

Paivio, A. (1971). *Imagery and verbal processes.* New York: Holt, Rinehart & Winston.

Palacio, C., García, J., Diago, J., et al. (2007). Identification of suicide risk factors in Medellin, Columbia: A case-control study of psychological autopsy in a developing country. *Archives of Suicide Research, 11*(3), 297–308.

Palermo, G. G. (2002). Criminal profiling: The uniqueness of the killer. *International Journal of Offender Therapy and Comparative Criminology, 46*(4), 383–385.

Palmer, B. W., Dunn, L. B., Depp, C. A., Eyler, L. T., & Jeste, D. V. (2007). Decisional capacity to consent to research among patients with bipolar disorder: comparison with schizophrenia patients and healthy subjects. *Journal of Clinical Psychiatry, 68*, 689–696.

Palmore, E. (Ed.). (1970). *Normal aging.* Durham, NC: Duke University Press.

Panell, R. C., & Laabs, G. J. (1979). Construction of a criterion-referenced, diagnostic test for an individualized instruction program. *Journal of Applied Psychology, 64*, 255–261.

Pannbacker, M., & Middleton, G. (1992). Review of Wepman's Auditory Discrimination Test, Second Edition. In J. J. Kramer & J. C. Conoley (Eds.), *The eleventh mental measurements yearbook.* Lincoln: Buros Institute of Mental Measurements, University of Nebraska.

Paolo, A. M., & Ryan, J. J. (1991). Application of WAIS-R short forms to persons 75 years of age and older. *Journal of Psychoeducational Assessment, 9*, 345–352.

PARC v. Pennsylvania, 334 F. Supp. 1257 (E.D. PA 1972).

Parette, H. P., & Brotherson, M. J. (1996). Family participation in assistive technology assessment for young children with mental retardation and developmental disabilities. *Education & Training in Mental Retardation & Developmental Disabilities, 31*, 29–43.

Parke, R. D., Hymel, S., Power, T., & Tinsley, B. (1977, November). Fathers and risk: A hospital-based model of intervention. In D. B. Sawin (Chair), *Symposium on psychosocial risks during infancy.* Austin: University of Texas at Austin.

Parke, R. D., & Sawin, D. B. (1975, April). *Infant characteristics and behavior as elicitors of maternal and paternal responsivity in the newborn period.* Paper presented at the meetings of the Society for Research in Child Development, Denver.

Parker, T., & Abramson, P. R. (1995). The law hath not been dead: Protecting adults with mental retardation from sexual abuse and violation of their sexual freedom. *Mental Retardation, 33*, 257–263.

Parkes, L. P., Bochner, S., & Schneider, S. K. (2001). Person-organisation fit across cultures: An empirical investigation of individualism and collectivism. *Applied Psychology: An International Review, 50*, 81–108.

Parks, R. W., Thiyagesh, S. N., Farrow, T. F. D., Ingram, L., Wilkinson, K., Hunter, M. D., Wilkinson, I. D., et al. (2010). Performance on the clock drawing task correlates with FMRI response to a visuospatial task in Alzheimer's disease. *International Journal of Neuroscience, 120*(5), 335–343.

Parnes, H. S., & Less, L. J. (1985). Introduction and overview. In H. S. Parnes, J. E. Crowley, R. J. Haurin, et al. (Eds.), *Retirement among American men.* Lexington, MA: Lexington Books.

Pascal, G. R., & Suttell, B. J. (1951). *The Bender-Gestalt Test: Quantification and validity for adults.* New York: Grune & Stratton.

Patterson, W. M., Dohn, H. H., Bird, J., & Patterson, G. A. (1983). Evaluation of suicidal patients: The SAD PERSONS scale. *Psychosomatics, 24*, 343–349.

Paul, G. L. (1987). *The time-sample behavioral checklist: Observational assessment instrumentation for service and research.* Champaign, IL: Research Press.

Paul, V., & Jackson, D. W. (1993). *Toward a psychology of deafness.* Boston: Allyn & Bacon.

Paulhus, D. L. (1984). Two-component models of socially desirable responding. *Journal of Personality and Social Psychology, 46*, 598–609.

Paulhus, D. L. (1986). Self-deception and impression management in test responses. In A. Angleitner & J. S. Wiggins (Eds.), *Personality assessment via questionnaire* (pp. 142–165). New York: Springer.

Paulhus, D. L. (1990). Measurement and control of response bias. In J. P. Robinson, P. R. Shaver, & L. Wrightsman (Eds.), *Measures of personality and social-psychological attitudes* (pp. 17–59). San Diego: Academic Press.

Paulhus, D. L., & Holden, R. R. (2010). Measuring self-enhancement: From self-report to concrete behavior. In C. R. Agnew, D. E. Carlston, W. G. Graziano, & J. R. Kelly (Eds.), *Then a miracle occurs: Focusing on behavior in social psychological theory and research* (pp. 227–246). New York: Oxford University Press.

Paulhus, D. L., & Levitt, K. (1987). Desirable response triggered by affect: Automatic egotism? *Journal of Personality and Social Psychology, 52*, 245–259.

Paulhus, D. L., & Reid, D. B. (1991). Enhancement and denial in socially desirable responding. *Journal of Personality and Social Psychology, 60*, 307–317.

Paullay, I. M., Alliger, G. M., & Stone-Romero, E. F. (1994). Construct validation of two instruments designed to measure job involvement and work centrality. *Journal of Applied Psychology, 79*, 224–228.

Paunonen, S. V., Jackson, D. N., & Ashton, M. C. (2004). Nonverbal Personality Questionnaire (NPQ) and Five-Factor Nonverbal Personality Questionnaire (FFM NPQ) manual. London, Canada: Sigma Assessment Systems, Inc.

Payne, B. K., McClernon, F. J., & Dobbins, I. G. (2007). Automatic affective responses to smoking cues. *Experimental and Clinical Psychopharmacology, 15*(4), 400–409.

Pearson, K., & Moul, M. (1925). The problem of alien immigration of Great Britain illustrated by an examination of Russian and Polish Jewish children. *Annals of Eugenics, 1*, 5–127.

Penner-Williams, J., Smith, T. E. C., & Gartin, B. C. (2009). Written language expression: Assessment instruments and teacher tools. *Assessment for Effective Intervention, 34*(3), 162–169.

Pennsylvania Department of Corrections v. Yeskey, 118 F.3d, 168 (1998).

Perez, J. A., Dasi, F., & Lucas, A. (1997). Length overestimation bias as a product of normative pressure arising from anthropocentric vs. geocentric representations of length. *Swiss Journal of Psychology, 56*, 243–255.

Perry, C., & Laurence, J. R. (1990). Hypnosis with a criminal defendant and a crime witness: Two recent related cases. *International Journal of Clinical and Experimental Hypnosis, 38*, 266–282.

Petersen, N. S., & Novick, M. R. (1976). An evaluation of some models for culture-fair selection. *Journal of Educational Measurement, 13*, 3–29.

Peterson, C. A. (1997). *The twelfth mental measurements yearbook: Testing the tests. Journal of Personality Assessment, 68*, 717–719.

Peterson, R. J., Safer, M. A., & Jobes, D. A. (2008). The impact of suicidal rock music lyrics on youth: An investigation of individual differences. *Archives of Suicide Research, 12*, 161–169.

Petrie, K., & Chamberlain, K. (1985). The predictive validity of the Zung Index of Potential Suicide. *Journal of Personality Assessment, 49*, 100–102.

Petscher, Y., Kim, Y.-S., & Foorman, B. R. (2011). The importance of predictive power in early screening assessments: Implications for placement in the response to intervention framework. *Assessment for Effective Intervention, 36*(3), 158–166.

Petty, M. M., McGhee, G. W., & Cavender, J. W. (1984). A meta-analysis of the relationships between individual job satisfaction and individual performance. *Academy of Management Review, 9*, 712–721.

Phelps, E. A., O'Connor, K. J., Cunningham, W. A., et al. (2000). Performance on indirect measures of race evaluation predicts amygdala activation. *Journal of Cognitive Neuroscience, 12*, 729–738.

Phelps, L., & Branyon, B. (1988). Correlations among the Hiskey, K-ABC Nonverbal Scale, Leiter, and WISC-R Performance Scale with public school deaf children. *Journal of Psychoeducational Assessment, 6*, 354–358.

Phillips, B. A. (1996). Bringing culture to the forefront: Formulating diagnostic impressions of deaf and hard-of-hearing people at times of medical crisis. *Professional Psychology: Research and Practice, 27*, 137–144.

Phillips, M. R., Shen, Q., Liu, X., et al. (2007). Assessing depressive symptoms in persons who die of suicide in mainland China. *Journal of Affective Disorders, 98* (1–2), 73–82.

Piaget, J. (1954). *The construction of reality on the child.* New York: Basic Books.

Piaget, J. (1971). *Biology and knowledge.* Chicago: University of Chicago.

Piedmont, R. L., & McCrae, R. R. (1996). *Are validity scales valid in volunteer samples? Evidence from self-reports and observer ratings.* Unpublished manuscript, Loyola College, Maryland.

Piedmont, R. L., McCrae, R. R., Riemann, R., & Angleitner, A. (2000). On the invalidity of validity scales: Evidence from self-reports and observer ratings in volunteer samples. *Journal of Personality and Social Psychology, 78*, 582–593.

Pierson, D. (1974). *The Trojans: Southern California football.* Chicago : H. Regnery Co.

Pilgrim, C., Luo, Q., Urberg, K. A., & Fang, X. (1999). Influence of peers, parents, and individual characteristics on adolescent drug use in two cultures. *Merrill-Palmer Quarterly, 45*, 85–107.

Pintner, R. (1931). *Intelligence testing.* New York: Holt.

Piotrowski, C., & Armstrong, T. (2002). Convergent validity of the KeyPoint pre-employment measure with the MBTI. *Psychology & Education: An Interdisciplinary Journal, 39*, 49–50.

Piotrowski, C., Belter, R. W., & Keller, J. W. (1998). The impact of "managed care" on the practice of psychological testing: Preliminary findings. *Journal of Personality Assessment, 70*, 441–446.

Piotrowski, Z. (1957). *Perceptanalysis.* New York: Macmillan.

Pisani, A. R., Cross, W. F., & Gould, M. S. (2011). The assessment and management of suicide risk: State of workshop education. *Suicide and Life-Threatening Behavior, 41*, 255–276.

Pittenger, D. J. (1993). The utility of the Myers-Briggs Type Indicator. *Review of Educational Research, 63*, 467–488.

Pledger, C. (2003). Discourse on disability and rehabilitation issues: Opportunities for psychology. *American Psychologist, 58*, 279–284.

Plucker, J. A., & Levy, J. J. (2001). The downside of being talented. *American Psychologist, 56*, 75–76.

Podymow, T., Turnbull, J. Coyle, D., et al. (2006). Shelter-based managed alcohol administration to chronically homeless people addicted to alcohol. *Canadian Medical Association Journal, 174*(1), 45–49.

Poehner, M. E. & van Compernolle, R. A. (2011). Frames of interaction in Dynamic Assessment: Developmental diagnoses of second language learning. *Assessment in Education: Principles, Policy & Practice, 18*, 183–198.

Polizzi, D. (1998). Contested space: Assessment in the home and the combative marriage. In L. Handler (Chair), *Conducting assessments in clients' homes: Contexts, surprises, dilemmas, opportunities.* Symposium presented at the Society for Personality Assessment 1998 Midwinter Meeting, February 20.

Pollard, R. Q. (1993). 100 years in psychology and deafness: A centennial retrospective. *Journal of the American Deafness & Rehabilitation Association, 26*, 32–46.

Pomplun, M., & Custer, M. (2005). The construct validity of the Stanford-Binet 5 measures of working memory. *Assessment, 12*, 338–346.

Pomplun, M., & Omar, M. H. (2000). Score comparability of a state mathematics assessment across students with and without reading accommodations. *Journal of Applied Psychology, 85*, 21–29.

Pomplun, M., & Omar, M. H. (2001). Score comparability of a state reading assessment across selected groups of students with disabilities. *Structural Equation Modeling, 8*, 257–274.

Ponterotto, J. G., Rivera, L., & Sueyoshi, L. A. (2000). The Career-in-Culture interview: A semi-structured protocol for the cross-cultural intake interview. *Career Development Quarterly, 49*, 85–96.

Porter, L. W., Steers, R. W., Mowday, R. T., & Boulian, P. V. (1974). Organizational commitment, job satisfaction, and turnover among psychiatric technicians. *Journal of Applied Psychology, 59*, 603–609.

Porteus, S. D. (1933). *The Maze Test and mental differences.* Vineland, NJ: Smith.

Porteus, S. D. (1942). *Qualitative performance in the Maze Test.* San Antonio: Psychological Corporation.

Porteus, S. D. (1955). *The Maze Test: Recent advances.* Palo Alto, CA: Pacific Books.

Posthuma, A., Podrouzek, W., & Crisp, D. (2002). The implications of *Daubert* on neuropsychological evidence in the assessment of remote mild traumatic brain injury. *American Journal of Forensic Psychology, 20*(4), 21–38.

Pouliot, L., & De Leo, D. (2006). Critical issues in psychological autopsy studies. *Suicide and Life-Threatening Behavior, 36*(5), 491–51.

Powell, D. H. (1994). *Profiles in cognitive aging.* Cambridge, MA: Harvard University Press.

Poythress, N.G. (2004). Editorial. "Reasonable medical certainty:" Can we meet *Daubert* standards in insanity cases? *Journal of the American Academy of Psychiatry and the Law, 32*, 228–230.

Poythress, N., Nicholson, R., Otto, R., Edens, J., Bonnie, R., Monahan, J., & Hoge, S. (1999). *The MacArthur Competence Assessment Tool—Criminal Adjudication: Professional manual.* Odessa, FL: Psychological Assessment Resources.

Preston, R. (1961). Improving the item validity of study habits inventories. *Educational and Psychological Measurement, 21*, 129–131.

Price, G., Dunn, R., & Dunn, K. (1982). *Productivity Environmental Survey manual.* Lawrence, KS: Price Systems.

Price, J. (1969). The ritualization of agonistic behaviour as a determinant of variation along the neuroticism/stability dimension of personality. *Proceedings of the Royal Society of Medicine, 62*, 1107–1110.

Price, J. (1972). Genetic and phylogenetic aspects of mood variation. *International Journal of Mental Health, 1*, 124–144.

Prince, R. J., & Guastello, S. J. (1990). The Barnum Effect in a computerized Rorschach interpretation system. *Journal of Psychology: Interdisciplinary and Applied, 124*, 217–222.

Pritchett, R. Kemp, J., Wilson, P., et al. (2011). Quick, simple measures of family relationships for use in clinical practice and research: A systematic review. *Family Practice, 28*, 172–187.

*Procedures for evaluating specific learning disabilities.* (1977). *Federal Register,* December 29, Part III.

Prinzie, P., Onghena, P., & Hellinckx, W. (2007). Reexamining the Parenting Scale. *European Journal of Psychological Assessment, 23*(1), 24–31.

Prout, H. T., & Phillips, P. D. (1974). A clinical note: The kinetic school drawing. *Psychology in the Schools, 11,* 303–396.

Psychological Corporation. (1992a). *Wechsler Individual Achievement Test.* San Antonio: Author.

Psychological Corporation. (1992b). *Wechsler Individual Achievement Test manual.* San Antonio: Author.

Psychological Corporation. (2009). *The Wechsler Individual Achievement Test-III.* San Antonio: Pearson Assessments.

Pullen, L., & Gow, K. (2000). University students elaborate on what young persons "at risk of suicide" need from listeners. *Journal of Applied Health Behaviour, 2,* 32–39.

Putnam, W. H. (1979). Hypnosis and distortions in eyewitness memory. *International Journal of Clinical and Experimental Hypnosis, 27,* 437–448.

*Q and A on balancing the SAT scores.* (1994). New York: College Board.

Qu, C., Zhang, P., Zheng, R., et al. (1992). An examination of the IQs of 319 hearing-impaired students in 5 cities in China. *Chinese Mental Health Journal, 6,* 219–221.

Quay, H. C., & Peterson, C. (1983). *Manual for the Revised Behavior Problem Checklist.* Coral Gables, FL: Authors.

Quay, H. C., & Peterson, D. R. (1967). *Behavior Problem Checklist.* Champaign: University of Illinois Press.

Quill, T. E., Cassel, C. K., & Meier, D. E. (1992). Care of the hopelessly ill: Proposed clinical criteria for physician-assisted suicide. *New England Journal of Medicine, 327,* 1380–1384.

Quinsey, V. L., Chaplin, T. C., & Upfold, D. (1984). Sexual arousal to nonsexual violence and sadomasochistic themes among rapists and nonsex-offenders. *Journal of Consulting and Clinical Psychology, 52,* 651–657.

Rabin, L. A., Barr, W. B., & Burton, L. A. (2005). Assessment practices of clinical neuropsychologists in the United States and Canada: A survey of INS, NAN, and APA Division 40 members. *Archives of Clinical Neuropsychology, 20,* 33–65.

Radzikhovskii, L. A., & Khomskaya, E. D. (1981). A. R. Luria and L. S. Vygotsky: Early years of their collaboration. *Soviet Psychology, 20*(1), 3–21.

Raifman, L. J., & Vernon, M. (1996). Important implications for psychologists of the Americans with Disabilities Act: Case in point, the patient who is deaf. *Professional Psychology: Research and Practice, 27,* 372–377.

Raju, N. S., Drasgow, F., & Slinde, J. A. (1993). An empirical comparison of the area methods, Lord's chi-square test, and the Mantel-Haenszel technique for assessing differential item functioning. *Educational and Psychological Measurement, 53,* 301–314.

Ramirez, M., III. (1984). Assessing and understanding biculturalism-multiculturalism in Mexican-American adults. In J. L. Martinez Jr. & R. H. Mendoza (Eds.), *Chicano psychology* (pp. 77–94). Orlando, FL: Academic Press.

Ramo, D. E., Hall, S. M., & Prochaska, J. J. (2011). Reliability and validity of self-reported smoking in an anonymous online survey with young adults. *Health Psychology, 30*(6), 693–701.

Randall, A., Fairbanks, M. M., & Kennedy, M. L. (1986). Using think-aloud protocols diagnostically with college readers. *Reading Research & Instruction, 25,* 240–253.

Randall, D. M. (1987). Commitment and the organization: The organization man revisited. *Academy of Management Review, 12,* 460–471.

Randolph, C., Mohr, E., & Chase, T. N. (1993). Assessment of intellectual function in dementing disorders: Validity of WAIS-R short forms for patients with Alzheimer's, Huntington's, and Parkinson's disease. *Journal of Clinical and Experimental Neuropsychology, 15,* 743–753.

Ranseen, J. D., & Humphries, L. L. (1992). The intellectual functioning of eating disorder patients. *Journal of the American Academy of Child and Adolescent Psychiatry, 31,* 844–846.

Ranta, R. S., & Sud, A. (2008). Management of stress and burnout of police personnel. *Journal of the Indian Academy of Applied Psychology, 34*(1), 29–39.

Rapaport, D. (1946–1967). Principles underlying nonprojective tests of personality. In M. M. Gill (Ed.), *David Rapaport: Collected papers.* New York: Basic Books.

Rapaport, D., Gill, M. M., & Schafer, R. (1945–1946). *Diagnostic psychological testing* (2 vols.). Chicago: Year Book.

Rapaport, D., Gill, M. M., & Schafer, R. (1968). In R. R. Holt (Ed.), *Diagnostic psychological testing* (rev. ed.). New York: International Universities.

Raphael, A. J., & Golden, C. J. (1997). Prediction of job retention using a brief projective test battery: A preliminary report. *International Journal of Selection and Assessment, 5*(4), 229–232.

Raphael, A. J., Golden, C., & Cassidy-Feltgen, S. (2002). The Bender-Gestalt Test (BGT) in forensic assessment. *Journal of Forensic Psychology Practice, 2*(3), 93–105.

Rappeport, J. R. (1982). Differences between forensic and general psychiatry. *American Journal of Psychiatry, 139,* 331–334.

Rashkovky, B. (2006). Extending the job component validity (JCV) model to include personality predictors. *Dissertation Abstracts International: Section B. Sciences and Engineering, 66*(7-B), 3986.

Ratcliff, J. J., Greenspan, A. I., Goldstein, F. C., et al. (2007). Gender and traumatic brain injury: Do the sexes fare differently? *Brain Injury, 21*(10), 1023–1030.

Raven, J. C. (1976). *Standard Progressive Matrices.* Oxford: Oxford Psychologists.

Raz, S., Glogowski-Kawamoto, B., Yu, A. W., et al. (1998). The effects of perinatal hypoxic risk on developmental outcome in early and middle childhood: A twin study. *Neuropsychology, 12,* 459–467.

Razran, G. (1961). The observable unconscious and the inferable conscious in current Soviet psychophysiology: Introceptive conditioning, semantic conditioning, and the orienting reflex. *Psychological Review, 68,* 81–147.

Recarte, M. A., & Nunes, L. M. (2000). Effects of verbal and spatial-imagery tasks on eye fixations while driving. *Journal of Experimental Psychology: Applied, 6,* 31–43.

Reckase, M. D. (1996). Test construction in the 1990s: Recent approaches every psychologist should know. *Psychological Assessment, 8,* 354–359.

Reckase, M. D. (2004). What if there were a "true standard theory" for standard setting like the "true score theory" for tests? *Measurement: Interdisciplinary Research and Perspecrtives, 2*(2), 114–119.

Redshaw, M., & Martin, C. R. (2009). Validation of a perceptions of care adjective checklist. *Journal of Evaluation in Clinical Practice, 15*(2), 281–288.

Ree, M. J., & Earles, J. A. (1990). *Differential validity of a differential aptitude test* (Report no. 89–59). Texas: Brooks Air Force Base.

Reece, R. N., & Groden, M. A. (1985). Recognition of non-accidental injury. *Pediatric Clinics of North America, 32,* 41–60.

Reed, J. E. (1996). Fixed vs. flexible neuropsychological test batteries under the Daubert standard for the admissibility of scientific evidence. *Behavioral Sciences & the Law, 14,* 315–322.

Reed, T. E. (1997). "The genetic hypothesis": It was not tested but it could have been. *American Psychologist, 52,* 77–78.

Reed, T. E., & Jensen, A. R. (1992). Conduction velocity in a brain nerve pathway of normal adults correlates with intelligence level. *Intelligence, 16,* 259–272.

Reed, T. E., & Jensen, A. R. (1993). Choice reaction time and visual pathway conduction velocity both correlate with intelligence but appear not to correlate with each other: Implications for information processing. *Intelligence, 17,* 191–203.

Reeder, G. D., Maccow, G. C., Shaw, S. R., Swerdlik, M. E., Horton, C. B., & Foster, P. (1997). School psychologists and full-service schools: Partnerships with medical, mental health, and social services. *School Psychology Review, 26,* 603–621.

Reeve, B. B., Hays, R. D., Bjorner, J. B., et al. (2007). Psychometric evaluation and calibration of health-related quality of life item banks: Plans for the Patient-Reported Outcomes Measurement Information System (PROMIS). *Medical Care, 45*(5), S22–S31.

Reeve, C. L., Meyer, R. D., & Bonaccio, S. (2005). *Relations among general and narrow dimensions of intelligence and personality.* Paper presented at 20th Annual Conference of the Society for Industrial and Organizational Psychology, Los Angeles.

Reichenberg, N., & Raphael, A. J. (1992). *Advanced psychodiagnostic interpretation of the Bender-Gestalt Test: Adults and children.* Westport, CT: Praeger.

Reid, C. A., Kolakowsky-Hayner, S. A., Lewis, A. N., & Armstrong, A. J. (2007). Modern psychometric methodology: Applications of item response theory. *Rehabilitation Counseling Bulletin, 50*(3), 177–188.

Reik, T. (1948). *Listening with the third ear.* New York: Farrar, Straus.

Reik, T. (1952). *The secret self.* New York: Grove.

Reimers, T. M., Wacker, D. P., & Koeppel, G. (1987). Acceptability of behavioral treatments: A review of the literature. *School Psychology Review, 16,* 212–227.

Reinehr, R. C. (1969). Therapist and patient perceptions of hospitalized alcoholics. *Journal of Clinical Psychology, 25,* 443–445.

Reise, S. P., & Henson, J. M. (2003). A discussion of modern versus traditional psychometrics as applied to personality assessment scales. *Journal of Personality Assessment, 81,* 93–103.

Reise, S. P., Waller, N. G., & Comrey, A. L. (2000). Factor analysis and scale revision. *Psychological Assessment, 12,* 287–297.

Reiser, M. (1980). *Handbook of investigative hypnosis.* Los Angeles: Lehi.

Reiser, M. (1990). Investigative hypnosis. In D. C. Raskin (Ed.), *Psychological methods in criminal investigation evidence* (pp. 151–190). New York: Springer.

Reitan, R. (1994, July). *Child neuropsychology and learning disabilities.* Advanced Workshop, Los Angeles.

Reitan, R. M. (1955a). An investigation of the validity of Halstead's measures of biological intelligence. *Archives of Neurology and Psychiatry, 73,* 28–35.

Reitan, R. M. (1955b). Certain differential effects of left and right cerebral lesions in human adults. *Journal of Comparative and Physiological Psychology, 48,* 474–477.

Reitan, R. M. (1969). *Manual for administration of neuropsychological test batteries for adults and children.* Indianapolis: Author.

Reitan, R. M. (1984a). *Aphasia and sensory-perceptual disorders in adults.* South Tucson, AZ: Neuropsychology Press.

Reitan, R. M. (1984b). *Aphasia and sensory-perceptual disorders in children.* South Tucson, AZ: Neuropsychology Press.

Reitan, R. M. (1994). Ward Halstead's contributions to neuropsychology and the Halstead-Reitan Neuropsychological Test Battery. *Journal of Clinical Psychology, 50,* 47–70.

Reitan, R. M., & Wolfson, D. (1990). A consideration of the comparability of the WAIS and WAIS-R. *Clinical Neuropsychologist, 4,* 80–85.

Reitan, R. M., & Wolfson, D. (1992). A short screening examination for impaired brain functions in early school-age children. *Clinical Neuropsychologist, 6,* 287–294.

Reitan, R. M., & Wolfson, D. (1993). *The Halstead-Reitan Neuropsychological Test Battery: Theory and clinical interpretation* (2nd ed.). Tucson, AZ: Neuropsychology Press.

Reitan, R. M., & Wolfson, D. (2000). The neuropsychological similarities of mild and more severe head injury. *Archives of Clinical Neuropsychology, 15,* 433–442.

Reiter, M. D., Liput, T., & Nirmal, R. (2007). Personality preferences of college student-athletes. *College Student Journal, 41*(1), 34–36.

Remington, R. W., Johnston, J. C., Ruthruff, E., et al. (2000). Visual search in complex displays: Factors affecting conflict detection by air traffic controllers. *Visual Cognition, 7,* 769–784.

Retzlaff, P. D., & Gibertini, M. (1988). Objective psychological testing of U.S. Air Force officers in pilot training. *Aviation, Space, and Environmental Medicine, 59,* 661–663.

Rey, G. J., Feldman, E., Rivas-Vazquez, R., et al. (1999). Neuropsychological test development and normative data on Hispanics. *Archives of Clinical Neuropsychology, 14,* 593–601.

Reynolds, C. E., & Brown, R. T. (Eds.). (1984). *Perspectives on bias in mental testing.* New York: Plenum.

Reynolds, C. R., Sanchez, S., & Wilson, V. L. (1996). Normative tables for calculating the WISC-III Performance and Full Scale IQs when Symbol Search is substituted for Coding. *Psychological Assessment, 8,* 378–382.

Reynolds, M. R., Keith, T. Z., Fine, J. G., et al. (2007). Confirmatory factor structure of the Kaufman Assessment Battery for Children—Second Edition: Consistency with Cattell-Horn-Carroll theory. *School Psychology Quarterly, 22*(4), 511–539

Reynolds, W. M. (1987). *Suicidal Ideation Questionnaire.* Odessa, FL: Psychological Assessment Resources.

Rezmovic, V. (1977). The effects of computerized experimentation on response variance. *Behavior Research Methods and Instrumentation, 9,* 144–147.

Reznikoff, M., & Tomblen, D. (1956). The use of human figure drawings in the diagnosis of organic pathology. *Journal of Consulting Psychology, 20,* 467–470.

Riaz, I. A. (2006). The effect of managed care on professional psychology. *Dissertation Abstracts International: Section B. Sciences and Engineering, 67*(2-B), 1164.

Rice, M. E., & Harris, G. T. (1995). Violent recidivism: Assessing predictive validity. *Journal of Consulting and Clinical Psychology, 63,* 737–748.

Richardson, M. W., & Kuder, G. F. (1939). The calculation of test reliability based upon the method of rational equivalence. *Journal of Educational Psychology, 30,* 681–687.

Richardson-Klavehn, A., & Bjork, R. A. (1988). Measures of memory. *Annual Review of Psychology, 39,* 475–543.

Richman, J. (1988). The case against rational suicide. *Suicide & Life-Threatening Behavior, 18*, 285–289.

Richters, J. E., & Hinshaw, S. (1999). The abduction of disorder in psychiatry. *Journal of Abnormal Psychology, 108*, 438–445.

Rierdan, J., & Koff, E. (1981). Sexual ambiguity in children's human figure drawings. *Journal of Personality Assessment, 45*, 256–257.

Riethmiller, R. J., & Handler, L. (1997a). The great figure drawing controversy: The integration of research and clinical practice. *Journal of Personality Assessment, 69*, 488–496.

Riethmiller, R. J., & Handler, L. (1997b). Problematic methods and unwarranted conclusions in DAP research: Suggestions for improved research procedures. *Journal of Personality Assessment, 69*, 459–475.

Riggs, D. S., Murphy, C. M., & O'Leary, K. D. (1989). Intentional falsification in reports of interpartner aggression. *Journal of Interpersonal Violence, 4*, 220–232.

Rindermann, H., Flores-Mendoza, C., & Mansur-Alves, M. (2010). Reciprocal effects between fluid and crystallized intelligence and their dependence on parents' socioeconomic status and education. *Learning and Individual Differences, 20*, 544–548.

Ritson, B., & Forest, A. (1970). The simulation of psychosis: A contemporary presentation. *British Journal of Medical Psychology, 43*, 31–37.

Ritzler, B. (1995). Putting your eggs in the content analysis basket: A response to Aronow, Reznikoff and Moreland. *Journal of Personality Assessment, 64*, 229–234.

Ritzler, B. A., Sharkey, K. J., & Chudy, J. F. (1980). A comprehensive projective alternative to the TAT. *Journal of Personality Assessment, 44*, 358–362.

Riverside Publishing. (2001). *Report Writer for the WJ III.* Itasca, IL: Author.

Rizzo, M., & Eslinger, P. J. (Eds.). (2004). *Principles and practice of behavioral neurology and neuropsychology.* Philadelphia: Saunders.

Roach, R. J., Frazier, L. P., & Bowden, S. R. (1981). The Marital Satisfaction Scale: Development of a measure for intervention research. *Journal of Marriage and the Family, 21*, 251–255.

Roback, A. A. (1961). *History of psychology and psychiatry.* New York: Philosophical Library.

Robbins, S. B., & Patton, M. J. (1985). Self-psychology and career development: Construction of the Superiority and Goal Instability Scales. *Journal of Counseling Psychology, 32*, 221–231.

Roberts, B. W., & DelVecchio, W. F. (2000). The rank-order consistency of personality traits from childhood to old age: A quantitative review of longitudinal studies. *Psychological Bulletin, 126*, 3–25.

Roberts, B. W., Robins, R. W., Caspi, A., & Trzesniewski., K. (2003). Personality trait development in adulthood. In J. Mortimer & M. Shanahan (Ed.). *Handbook of the life course* (pp. 579–598). New York: Kluwer Academic.

Roberts, B. W., Walton, K., & Viechtbauer, W. (2006). Personality changes in adulthood: Reply to Costa & McCrae (2006). *Psychological Bulletin, 132*, 29–32.

Roberts, M. W. (2001). Clinic observations of structured parent-child interaction designed to evaluate externalizing disorders. *Psychological Assessment, 13*, 46–58.

Roberts, R. N., & Magrab, P. R. (1991). Psychologists' role in a family-centered approach to practice, training, and research with young children. *American Psychologist, 46*, 144–148.

Robertson, G. J. (1990). A practical model for test development. In C. R. Reynolds & R. W. Kamphaus (Eds.), *Handbook of psychological and educational assessment of children: Intelligence & achievement* (pp. 62–85). New York: Guilford.

Robin, A. L., Koepke, T., & Moye, A. (1990). Multidimensional assessment of parent-adolescent relations. *Psychological Assessment, 2*, 451–459.

Robinson, F. G. (1992). *Love's story untold: The life of Henry A. Murray.* Cambridge, MA: Harvard University.

Robinson, N. M., Zigler, E., & Gallagher, J. J. (2000). Two tails of the normal curve: Similarities and differences in the study of mental retardation and giftedness. *American Psychologist, 55*, 1413–1424.

Rodriguez, O., & Santiviago, M. (1991). Hispanic deaf adolescents: A multicultural minority. *Volta Review, 93*, 89–97.

Roe, A., & Klos, D. (1969). Occupational classification. *Counseling Psychologist, 1*, 84–92.

Roediger, H. L. (1990). Implicit memory: Retention without remembering. *American Psychologist, 45*, 1043–1056.

Roediger, H. L., & McDermott, K. B. (1993). Implicit memory in normal human subjects. In F. Boller & J. Grafman (Eds.), *Handbook of neuropsychology* (Vol. 8, pp. 63–181). Amsterdam: Elsevier.

Roesch, R., Webster, C. D., & Eaves, D. (1984). *The Fitness Interview Test: A method for assessing fitness to stand trial.* Toronto: University of Toronto Centre of Criminology.

Rogers, C. R. (1959). A theory of therapy, personality, and interpersonal relationships, as developed in the client-centered framework In S. Koch (Ed.), *Psychology: A study of a science* (Vol. 3, pp. 184–256). New York: McGraw-Hill.

Rogers, L. S., Knauss, J., & Hammond, K. R. (1951). Predicting continuation in therapy by means of the Rorschach Test. *Journal of Consulting Psychology, 15*, 368–371.

Rogers, R. (1986). *Structured interview of reported symptoms (SIRS).* Unpublished scale. Toronto: Clarke Institute of Psychiatry.

Rogers, R., Bagby, R. M., & Dickens, S. E. (1992). *Structured Interview of Reported Symptoms (SIRS) and professional manual.* Odessa, FL: Psychological Assessment Resources.

Rogers, R., & Cavanaugh, J. L. (1980). Differences in psychological variables between criminally responsible and insane patients: A preliminary study. *American Journal of Forensic Psychiatry, 1*, 29–37.

Rogers, R., & Cavanaugh, J. L. (1981). Rogers Criminal Responsibility Assessment Scales. *Illinois Medical Journal, 160*, 164–169.

Rogers, R., Dolmetsch, R., & Cavanaugh, J. L. (1981). An empirical approach to insanity evaluations. *Journal of Clinical Psychology, 37*, 683–687.

Rogers, R., Jackson, R. L., Sewell, K. W., & Harrison, K. S. (2004). An Examination of the ECST-R as a Screen for Feigned Incompetency to Stand Trial. *Psychological Assessment, 16*(2), 139–145

Rogers, R., Seman, W., & Wasyliw, D. E. (1983). The RCRAS and legal insanity: A cross validation study. *Journal of Clinical Psychology, 39*, 554–559.

Rogers, R., Sewell, K. W., & Gillard, N. D. (2010). *Structured Interview of Reported Symptoms (SIRS) and professional manual.* Lutz, FL: Psychological Assessment Resources, Inc.

Rogers, R., Wasyliw, D. E., & Cavanaugh, J. L. (1984). Evaluating insanity: A study of construct validity. *Law & Human Behavior, 8*, 293–303.

Rogers, R. R., Sewell, K. W., Harrison, K. S., & Jordan, M. J. (2006). The MMPI-2 Restructured Clinical scales: A paradigmatic shift in scale development. *Journal of Personality Assessment, 87*, 139–147.

Rogler, L. H. (2002). Historical generations and psychology: The case of the Great Depression and World War II. *American Psychologist, 57,* 1013–1023.

Rohl, J. S. (1993). The Tower of Hanoi. Supplementary information supplied with *Jarrah Wooden Tower of Hanoi.* Mt. Lawley, Australia: Built-Rite Sales.

Rohner, R. P. (1984). Toward a conception of culture for cross-cultural psychology. *Journal of Cross-Cultural Psychology, 15,* 111–138.

Roid, G. H. (2003a). *Stanford-Binet Intelligence Scales, Fifth Edition.* Itasca, IL: Riverside.

Roid, G. H. (2003b). *Stanford-Binet Intelligence Scales, Fifth Edition, Examiner's manual.* Itasca, IL: Riverside.

Roid, G. H. (2003c). *Stanford-Binet Intelligence Scales, Fifth Edition, Technical manual.* Itasca, IL: Riverside.

Roid, G. H. (2006). Designing ability tests. In S. M. Downing & T. M. Haladyna (Eds.), *Handbook of test development* (pp. 527–542). Mahwah, NJ: Erlbaum.

Roid, G. H., Woodcock, R. W., & McGrew, K. S. (1997). *Factor analysis of the Stanford-Binet L and M forms.* Unpublished paper. Itasca, IL: Riverside.

Rokeach, M. (1973). *The nature of human values.* New York: Free Press.

Romanczyk, R. G. (1986). *Clinical utilization of microcomputer technology.* New York: Pergamon.

Romano, J. (1994, November 7). Do drunken drivers get railroaded? *New York Times,* pp. NNJ1, NNJ19.

Rome, H. P., Mataya, P., Pearson, J. S., Swenson, W., & Brannick, T. L. (1965). Automatic personality assessment. In R. W. Stacey & B. Waxman (Eds.), *Computers in biomedical research* (Vol. 1, pp. 505–524). New York: Academic Press.

Ronan, G. G., Date, A. L., & Weisbrod, M. (1995). Personal problem-solving scoring of the TAT: Sensitivity to training. *Journal of Personality Assessment, 64,* 119–131.

Rorer, L. G. (1965). The great response-style myth. *Psychological Bulletin, 63,* 129–156.

Rorschach, H. (1921/1942). *Psycho-diagnostics: A diagnostic test based on perception* (P. Lemkau & B. Kronenburg, Trans.). Berne: Huber. (First German edition: 1921. Distributed in the United States by Grune & Stratton.)

Rorschach, H., & Oberholzer, E. (1923). The application of the interpretation of form to psychoanalysis. *Journal of Nervous and Mental Diseases, 60,* 225–248, 359–379.

Rosen, A. (1962). Development of MMPI scales based on a reference group of psychiatric patients. *Psychological Monographs 76* (8 Whole No. 527).

Rosen, J. (1998, February 23/March 2). Damage control. *New Yorker, 74,* 64–68.

Rosenberg, E., & DeMaso, D. R. (2008). A doubtful guest: Managed care and mental health. *Child and Adolescent Psychiatric Clinics of North America, 17*(1), 53–66.

Rosenman, R. H., Brand, R. J., Jenkins, C. D., Friedman, M., Straus, R., & Wurm, M. (1975). Coronary heart disease in the Western Collaborative Group Study: Final followup experience of 8½ years. *Journal of the American Medical Association, 233,* 872–877.

Rosenzweig, S. (1945). The picture-association method and its application in a study of reactions to frustration. *Journal of Personality, 14,* 3–23.

Rosenzweig, S. (1978). *The Rosenzweig Picture Frustration (P-F) Study: Basic manual.* St. Louis: Rana House.

Rosse, J. G., Stecher, M. D., Miller, J. L., & Levin, R. A. (1998). The impact of response distortion on preemployment personality testing and hiring decisions. *Journal of Applied Psychology, 83,* 634–644.

Roszkowski, M. J., & Spreat, S. (1981). A comparison of the psychometric and clinical methods of determining level of mental retardation. *Applied Research in Mental Retardation, 2,* 359–366.

Roth, L. H., Meisel, A., & Lidz, C. W. (1977). Tests of competence to consent to treatment. *American Journal of Psychiatry, 134,* 279–284.

Roth, P. L., Bobko, P., & Mabon, H. (2001). Utility analysis: A review and analysis at the turn of the century. In N. Anderson, D. S. Ones, H. K. Sinangil, & C. Viswesvaran (Eds.), *Handbook of industrial, work, and organizational psychology.* Thousand Oaks, CA: Sage.

Rothberg, J. M., & Geer-Williams, C. (1992). A comparison and review of suicide prediction scales. In R. W. Maris et al. (Eds.), *Assessment and prediction of suicide* (pp. 202–217). New York: Guilford.

Rotter, J. B. (1966). Generalized expectancies for internal versus external control of reinforcement. *Psychological Monographs, 80* (Whole Number 609).

Rotter, J. B., Lah, M. I., & Rafferty, J. E. (1992). *Rotter Incomplete Sentences Blank manual.* San Antonio: Psychological Corporation.

Rotter, J. B., & Rafferty, J. E. (1950). *The manual for the Rotter Incomplete Sentences Blank.* New York: Psychological Corporation.

Rottinghaus, P. J., Betz, N. E., & Borgen, F. H. (2003). Validity of parallel measures of vocational interests and confidence. *Journal of Career Assessment, 11,* 355–378.

Rotton, J., & Kelly, I. W. (1985). Much ado about the full moon: A meta-analysis of lunar-lunacy research. *Psychological Bulletin, 97,* 286–306.

Rotundo, M., & Sackett, P. R. (1999). Effect of rater race on conclusions regarding differential prediction in cognitive ability tests. *Journal of Applied Psychology, 84,* 815–822.

Rouse, S. V., Butcher, J. N., & Miller, K. B. (1999). Assessment of substance abuse in psychotherapy clients: The effectiveness of MMPI-2 substance abuse scales. *Psychological Assessment, 11,* 101–107.

Routh, D. K., & King, K. W. (1972). Social class bias in clinical judgment. *Journal of Consulting and Clinical Psychology, 38,* 202–207.

Roy, P. (1962). The measurement of assimilation: The Spokane Indians. *American Journal of Sociology, 67,* 541–551.

Rozeboom, W. W. (1996a). Factor-indeterminacy issues are not linguistic confusions. *Multivariate Behavioral Research, 31,* 637–650.

Rozeboom, W. W. (1996b). What might common factors be? *Multivariate Behavioral Research, 31,* 555–570.

Ruch, G. M. (1925). Minimum essentials in reporting data on standard tests. *Journal of Educational Research, 12,* 349–358.

Ruch, G. M. (1933). Recent developments in statistical procedures. *Review of Educational Research, 3,* 33–40.

Ruch, W. (1993). Exhilaration and humor. In M. Lewis & J. M. Haviland (Eds.), *Handbook of emotions* (pp. 605–616). New York: Guilford.

Ruffolo, L. F., Guilmette, T. J., & Grant, W. W. (2000). Comparison of time and error rates on the Trail Making Test among patients with head injuries, experimental malingerers, patients with suspect effort on testing, and normal controls. *Clinical Neuropsychologist, 14,* 223–230.

Rüsch, N., Todd, A. R., & Bodenhausen, G. V., et al. (2009). Implicit versus explicit attitudes toward psychiatric medication: Implications for insight and treatment adherence. *Schizophrenia Research, 112,* 119–122.

Russell, E. W. (2007). Commentary on "A motion to exclude and the 'fixed' versus 'flexible' battery in 'forensic' neuropsychology." *Archives of Clinical Neuropsychology, 22,* 787–790.

Russell, J. S. (1984). A review of fair employment cases in the field of training. *Personnel Psychology, 37*, 261–276.

Russell, T. L., & Peterson, N. G. (1997). The test plan. In D. L. Whetzel & G. R. Wheaton (Eds.). *Applied measurement methods in industrial psychology* (pp. 115–139). Palo Alto, CA: Davies-Black.

Russo, D. C., Bird, B. L., & Masek, B. J. (1980). Assessment issues in behavioral medicine. *Behavioral Assessment, 2*, 1–18.

Rutherford, A. (2003). B. F. Skinner and the auditory inkblot: The rise and fall of the verbal summator as a projective technique. *History of Psychology, 6*, 362–378.

Ryan, A. M., Sacco, J. M., McFarland, L. A., & Kriska, S. D. (2000). Applicant self-selection: Correlates of withdrawal from a multiple hurdle process. *Journal of Applied Psychology, 85*, 163–169.

Ryan, J. J., Paolo, A. M., & Brungardt, T. M. (1990). Standardization of the Wechsler Adult Intelligence Scale—Revised for persons 75 years and older. *Psychological Assessment, 2*, 404–411.

Ryan, J. J., & Ward, L. C. (1999). Validity, reliability, and standard errors of measurement for two seven-subtest short forms of the Wechsler Adult Intelligence Scale–III. *Psychological Assessment, 11*, 207–211.

Ryan, T., & Xenos, S. (2011). Who uses Facebook? An investigation into the relationship between the Big Five, shyness, narcissism, loneliness, and Facebook usage. *Computers in Human Behavior, 27*(5), 1658–1664.

Sabatelli, R. M. (1984). The Marital Comparison Level Index: A measure for assessing outcomes relative to expectations. *Journal of Marriage and the Family, 46*, 651–662.

Sachs, B. B. (1976). Some views of a deaf Rorschacher on the personality of deaf individuals. *Hearing Rehabilitation Quarterly, 2*, 13–14.

Sackett, P. R. (1994). Integrity testing for personnel selection. *Current Directions in Psychological Science, 3*, 73–76.

Sackett, P. R., Burris, L. R., & Callahan, C. (1989). Integrity testing for personnel selection: An update. *Personnel Psychology, 42*, 491–529.

Sackett, P. R., & Harris, M. M. (1984). Honesty testing for personnel selection: A review and critique. *Personnel Psychology, 37*, 221–245.

Sackett, P. R., Schmitt, N., Ellingson, J. E., & Kabin, M. B. (2001). High-stakes testing in employment, credentialing, and higher education: Prospects in a post-affirmative action world. *American Psychologist, 56*, 302–318.

Sackett, P. R., & Wilk, S. L. (1994). Within-group norming and other forms of score adjustment in preemployment testing. *American Psychologist, 49*, 929–954.

Sacks, E. (1952). Intelligence scores as a function of experimentally established social relationships between child and examiner. *Journal of Abnormal and Social Psychology, 47*, 354–358.

Sacks, O. (1989). *Seeing voices: A journey into the world of the deaf.* Berkeley: University of California.

Salas, E., Cannon-Bowers, J. A., Church-Payne, S., & Smith-Jentsch, K. A. (1998). Teams and teamwork in the military. In C. Cronin (Ed.), *Military psychology: An introduction* (pp. 71–87). Needham Heights, MA: Simon & Schuster.

Saldanha, C. (2005). Daubert and suicide risk of antidepressants in children. *Academy of Psychiatry and the Law, 33*(1), 123–125.

Sale, R. (2006). International guidelines on computer-based and internet-delivered testing: A practitioner's perspective. *International Journal of Testing, 6*(2), 181–188.

Salthouse, T. A. (2009). When does age-related cognitive decline begin? *Neurobiology of Aging, 30*(4), 507–514.

Salthouse, T. A., Toth, J., Daniels, K., et al. (2000). Effects of aging on efficiency of task switching in a variant of the Trail Making Test. *Neuropsychology, 14*, 102–111.

Salvia, J., & Hritcko, T. (1984). The K-ABC and ability training. *Journal of Special Education, 18*, 345–356.

Samuda, R. J. (1982). *Psychological testing of American minorities: Issues and consequences.* New York: Harper & Row.

Sanchez, H. G. (2006). Inmate suicide and the psychological autopsy process. *US Department of Justice Jail Suicide/Mental Health Update, 15*(2).

Sanchez, L. M., & Turner, S. M. (2003). Practicing psychology in the era of managed care. *American Psychologist, 58*, 116–129.

Sanchez-Cubillo, J. A., Perianez, D., Adrovier-Roig, J. M., et al. (2009). Construct validity of the Trail Making Test: Role of task-switching, working memory, inhibition/interference control, and visuomotor abilities. *Journal of the International Neuropsychological Society, 15*, 438–450.

Sánchez-Meca, J. & Marín-Martínez, F. (2010). Meta-analysis in psychological research. *International Journal of Psychological Research, 3*, 151–163.

Sandelands, L. E., & Larson, J. R. (1985). When measurement causes task attitudes: A note from the laboratory. *Journal of Applied Psychology, 70*, 116–121.

Sanders, J. (2010). Applying Daubert Inconsistently?: Proof of individual causation in toxic tort and forensic cases. *75 Brooklyn Law Review, 1367*, 1370–1374.

Sandoval, J. (1995). Review of the Wechsler Intelligence Scale for Children, Third Edition. In J. C. Conoley & J. C. Impara (Eds.), *The twelfth mental measurements yearbook.* Lincoln: Buros Institute of Measurements, University of Nebraska.

Sandoval, J. (2003). Review of the Woodcock-Johnson III. In B. S. Plake, J. C. Impara, & R. A. Spies (Eds.), *The fifteenth mental measurements yearbook.* Lincoln: Buros Institute of Mental Measurements, University of Nebraska.

Sandoval, J., et al. (Eds.). (1998). *Test interpretation and diversity: Achieving equity in assessment.* Washington, DC: American Psychological Association.

Sanfilippo, J., et al. (1986). Identifying the sexually molested preadolescent girl. *Pediatric Annals, 15*, 621–624.

Santelices, M. V., & Wilson, M. (2010). Unfair treatment? The case of Freedle, the SAT, and the standardized approach to differential item functioning. *Harvard Educational Review, 80*(1), 106–133.

Santor, D. A., Zuroff, D. C., Ramsay, J. O., Cervantes, P., & Palacios, J. (1995). Examining scale discriminability in the BDI and CES-D as a function of depressive severity. *Psychological Assessment, 7*, 131–139.

Santy, P. A. (1994). *Choosing the right stuff: The psychological selection of astronauts and cosmonauts.* Westport, CT: Praeger.

Sattler, J. M. (1991). How good are federal judges in detecting differences in item difficulty on intelligence tests for ethnic groups? *Psychological Assessment, 3*, 125–129.

Sattler, J. M. (1992). *Assessment of children: WISC-III and WPPSI-R supplement.* San Diego: Author.

Saunders, E. A. (1991). Rorschach indicators of chronic childhood sexual abuse in female borderline inpatients. *Bulletin of the Menninger Clinic, 55*, 48–65.

Savickas, M. L., Alexander, D. E., Osipow, S. H., & Wolf, F. M. (1985). Measuring specialty indecision among career-decided students. *Journal of Vocational Behavior, 27*, 356–357.

Savickas, M. L., & Spokane, A. R. (Eds.). (1999). *Vocational interests: Meaning, measurement, and counseling use.* Palo Alto, CA: Davies-Black.

Savickas, M. L., Taber, B. J., & Spokane, A. R. (2002). Convergent and discriminant validity of five interest inventories. *Journal of Vocational Behavior, 61*, 139–184.

Saxe, L. (1994). Detection of deception: Polygraph and integrity tests. *Current Directions in Psychological Science, 3,* 69–73.

Saxe, L., & Ben-Shakhar, G. (1999). Admissibility of polygraph tests: The application of scientific standards post-*Daubert. Psychology, Public Policy, and Law, 5,* 203–223.

Saxton, J., McGonigle-Gibson, K. L., Swihart, A. A., Miller, V. J., & Boller, F. (1990). Assessment of the severely impaired patient: Description and validation of a new neuropsychological test battery. *Psychological Assessment, 2,* 298–303.

Sayer, A. G., Willett, J. B., & Perrin, E. C. (1993). Measuring understanding of illness causality in healthy children and in children with chronic illness: A construct validation. *Journal of Applied Developmental Psychology, 14,* 11–36.

Sayette, M. A., Shiffman, S., Tiffany, S. T., et al. (2000). The measurement of drug craving. *Addiction, 93*(Suppl. 2), S189–S210.

Scarr, S. (1992). Developmental theories for the 1990s: Development and individual differences. *Child Development, 63,* 1–19.

Scarr, S. (1993). Biological and cultural diversity: The legacy of Darwin for development. *Child Development, 64,* 1333–1353.

Schacter, D. L. (1987). Implicit memory: History and current status. *Journal of Experimental Psychology: Learning, Memory, and Cognition, 13,* 501–518.

Schaie, K. W. (1978). External validity in the assessment of intellectual development in adulthood. *Journal of Gerontology, 33,* 695–701.

Schaufeli, W. B., Bakker, A. B. & Van Rhenen, W. (2009). How changes in job demands and resources predict burnout, work engagement, and sickness absenteeism. *Journal of Organizational Behavior, 30,* 893–917.

Schaufeli, W. B., Taris, T. W., & van Rhenen, W. (2008). Workaholism, burnout, and work engagement: Three of a kind or three different kinds of employee well-being? *Applied Psychology: An International Review, 57*(2), 173–203.

Scheid, T. L. (1999). Employment of individuals with mental disabilities: Business response to the ADA's challenge. *Behavioral Sciences and the Law, 17,* 73–91.

Schein, J. D., & Delk, M. T., Jr. (1974). *The deaf population in the United States.* Silver Springs, MD: National Association for the Deaf.

Schellings, G., Aarnoutse, C., & van Leeuwe, J. (2006). Third-grader's think aloud protocols: Types of reading activities in reading an expository text. *Learning and Instruction, 16*(6), 549–568

Schildroth, A., Rawlings, B., & Allen, T. (1991). Deaf students in transition: Education and employment issues for deaf adolescents. In O. Cohen & G. Long (Eds.), Selected issues in adolescence and deafness [Special issue]. *Volta Review, 93*(5), 41–53.

Schjelderup-Ebbe, T. (1921). Beiträge zur Biologie und Sozial- und Individualpsychologie bei Gallus domesticus, Greifswald.

Schloss, I. (1981). Chicken and pickles. *Journal of Advertising Research, 21,* 47–49.

Schmand, B., Brand, N., & Kuipers, T. (1992). Procedural learning of cognitive and motor skills in psychotic patients. *Schizophrenia Research, 8,* 157–170.

Schmidt, F. L. (1988). The problem of group differences in ability scores in employment selection. *Journal of Vocational Behavior, 33,* 272–292.

Schmidt, F. L., & Hunter, J. E. (1974). Racial and ethnic bias in psychological tests: Divergent implications of two definitions of test bias. *American Psychologist, 29,* 1–8.

Schmidt, F. L., & Hunter, J. E. (1992). Development of a causal model of processes determining job performance. *Current Directions in Psychological Science, 1,* 89–92.

Schmidt, F. L., & Hunter, J. E. (1998). The validity and utility of selection methods in personnel psychology: Practical and theoretical implications of 85 years of research findings. *Psychological Bulletin, 124,* 262–274.

Schmidt, F. L., Hunter, J. E., McKenzie, R. C., & Muldrow, T. W. (1979). Impact of valid selection procedures on work force productivity. *Journal of Applied Psychology, 64,* 609–626.

Schmidt, F. L., Hunter, J. E., Outerbridge, A. N., & Trattner, M. H. (1986). The economic impact of job selection methods on size, productivity, and payroll costs of the federal work force: An empirically based demonstration. *Personnel Psychology, 32,* 1–29.

Schmitt, N. (1976). Social and situational determinants of interview decisions: Implications for the employment interview. *Personnel Psychology, 29,* 79–101.

Schmitt, N., Gooding, R., Noe, R., & Kirsch, M. (1984). Meta-analysis of validity studies published between 1964 and 1982 and the investigation of study characteristics. *Personnel Psychology, 37,* 407–422.

Schmitter-Edgecombe, M. & Bales, J. W. (2005). Understanding text after severe closed-head injury: Assessing inferences and memory operations with a think-aloud procedure. *Brain and Language, 94*(3), 331–346.

Schneider, B. (1987). The people make the place. *Personnel Psychology, 40,* 437–453.

Schneider, M. F. (1989). *Children's Apperceptive Story-Telling Test.* Austin: PRO-ED.

Schönemann, P. H. (1996a). The psychopathology of factor indeterminacy. *Multivariate Behavioral Research, 31,* 571–577.

Schönemann, P. H. (1996b). Syllogisms of factor indeterminacy. *Multivariate Behavioral Research, 31,* 651–654.

Schoop, L. H., Herrman, T. D., Johnstone, B., Callahan, C. D., & Roudebush, I. S. (2001). Two abbreviated versions of the Wechsler Adult Intelligence Scale–III: Validation among persons with traumatic brain injury. *Rehabilitation Psychology, 46,* 279–287.

Schouten, P. G. W., & Kirkpatrick, L. A. (1993). Questions and concerns about the Miller Assessment for Preschoolers. *Occupational Therapy Journal of Research, 13,* 7–28.

Schuh, A. J. (1978). Contrast effect in the interview. *Bulletin of the Psychonomic Society, 11,* 195–196.

Schuler, M. E., Nair, P., & Harrington, D. (2003). Developmental outcome of drug-exposed children through 30 months: A comparison of Bayley and Bayley-II. *Psychological Assessment, 15,* 435–438.

Schulte, A. A., Gilbertson, E., Kratochwil, T. R. (2000). Educators' perceptions and documentation of testing accommodations for students with disabilities. *Special Services in the Schools, 16,* 35–56.

Schultz, B. M., Dixon, E. B., Lindenberger, J. C., & Ruther, N. J. (1989). *Solomon's sword: A practical guide to conducting child custody evaluations.* San Francisco: Jossey-Bass.

Schwartz, L. A. (1932). Social situation pictures in the psychiatric interview. *American Journal of Orthopsychiatry, 2,* 124–132.

Schwartz, N., Groves, R. M., & Schuman, H. (1998). Survey methods. In D. T. Gilbert et al. (Eds.), *The handbook of social psychology* (4th ed., Vol. 1, pp. 143–179). New York: McGraw-Hill.

Scott, L. H. (1981). Measuring intelligence with the Goodenough-Harris Drawing Test. *Psychological Bulletin, 89,* 483–505.

Seagull, F. J., & Gopher, D. (1997). Training head movement in visual scanning: An embedded approach to the development of piloting skills with helmet-mounted displays. *Journal of Experimental Psychology: Applied, 3,* 163–180.

Searight, H. R., & Searight, B. K. (2009). Working with foreign language interpreters: Recommendations for psychological practice. *Professional Psychology: Research and Practice, 40,* 454–451.

Sears, R. R. (1977). Sources of life satisfaction of the Terman gifted men. *American Psychologist, 32,* 119–281.

Seashore, C. E. (1938). *Psychology of music.* New York: McGraw-Hill.

Sebold, J. (1987). Indicators of child sexual abuse in males. *Social Casework, 68,* 75–80.

Segal, S. P., Redman, D., & Silverman, C. (2000). Measuring clients' satisfaction with self-help agencies. *Psychiatric Services, 51,* 1148–1152.

Seibert, S. E., & Kraimer, M. L. (2001). The five-factor model of personality and career success. *Journal of Vocational Behavior, 58,* 1–21.

Serby, M., Corwin, J., Conrad, P., et al. (1985). Olfactory dysfunction in Alzheimer's disease and Parkinson's disease. *American Journal of Psychiatry, 142,* 781–782.

Serby, M., Larson, P., & Kalkstein, D. (1991). The nature and course of olfactory deficits in Alzheimer's disease. *American Journal of Psychiatry, 148,* 357–360.

Serin, R. C., Peters, R. DeV., & Barbaree, H. E. (1990). Predictors of psychopathy and release outcome in a criminal population. *Psychological Assessment, 2,* 419–422.

Serpell, R. (1979). How specific are perceptual skills? A cross-cultural study of pattern reproduction. *British Journal of Psychology, 70,* 365–380.

Sevig, T. D., Highlen, P. S., & Adams, E. M. (2000). Development and validation of the Self-Identity Inventory (SII): A multicultural identity development instrument. *Cultural Diversity and Ethnic Minority Psychology, 6,* 168–182.

Shabbir, H. (2011). Dimensional qualitative research as a paradygmatic shift in qualitative inquiry: An introduction to the special issue. *Psychology & Marketing, 28*(10), 977–979.

Shah, S. A. (1969). Privileged communications, confidentiality, and privacy: Privileged communications. *Professional Psychology, 1,* 56–59.

Shahim, S. (2007). Psychometric characteristics of the Iranian Acculturation Scale. *Psychological Reports, 101*(1), 55–60.

Shakow, D., & Rosenzweig, S. (1940). The use of the tautophone ("verbal summator") as an auditory apperceptive test for the study of personality. *Character and Personality, 8,* 216–226.

Shanafelt, T. D., Balch, C. M., Bechamps, G. (2010). Burnout and Medical Errors Among American Surgeons. *Annals of Surgery, 251,* 995–1000.

Shapiro, E. S., & Skinner, C. H. (1990). Principles of behavior assessment. In C. R. Reynolds & R. W. Kamphaus (Eds.), *Handbook of psychological and educational assessment of children: Personality, behavior & context* (pp. 343–363). New York: Guilford.

Sharkey, P. T. (2006). Navigating dangerous streets: The sources and consequences of street efficacy. *American Sociological Review, 71*(5), 826–846.

Shavelson, R. J., Webb, N. M., & Rowley, G. L. (1989). Generalizability theory. *American Psychologist, 44,* 922–932.

Shaw, S. R., Swerdlik, M. E., & Laurent, J. (1993). Review of the WISC-III. In B. A. Bracken (Ed.), *Monograph series, Advances in psychoeducational assessment: Wechsler Intelligence Scale for Children, Third Edition: Journal of Psychoeducational Assessment* (pp. 151–159). Brandon, VT: Clinical Psychology Publishing.

Shaywitz, B. A., Shaywitz, S. E., Pugh, K. R., et al. (1995). Sex differences in the functional organization of the brain for language. *Nature, 373,* 607–609.

Shectman, F., & Harty, M. (1986). Treatment implications of object relationships as they unfold during the diagnostic interaction. In M. Kissen (Ed.), *Assessing object relations phenomena* (pp. 279–303). Madison, CT: International Universities Press.

Shedler, J. (2000). The Shedler QPD Panel (Quick PsychDiagnostics Panel): A psychiatric "lab test" for primary care. In M. E. Maruish (Ed.), *Handbook of psychological assessment in primary care settings* (pp. 277–296). Mahwah, NJ: Erlbaum.

Sheehan, P. W., Grigg, L., & McCann, T. (1984). Memory distortion following exposure to false information in hypnosis. *Journal of Abnormal Psychology, 93,* 259–296.

Sheffield, D., Biles, P. L., Orom, H., Maixner, W., & Sheps, D. S. (2000). Race and sex differences in cutaneous pain perception. *Psychosomatic Medicine, 62,* 517–523.

Shell, R. W. (1980). Psychiatric testimony: Science or fortune telling? *Barrister, 7,* 6–12.

Shepard, L. A. (1983). The role of measurement in educational policy: Lessons from the identification of learning disabilities. *Journal of Special Education, 14,* 79–91.

Sheppard, L. D. (2008). Intelligence and speed of information-processing: A review of 50 years of research. *Personality and Individual Differences, 44*(3), 533–549.

Sherley, J. L. (2007). The utility of standardized tests. *Science, 316*(5832), 1695–1696.

Sherrill-Pattison, S., Donders, J., & Thompson, E. (2000). Influence of demographic variables on neuropsychological test performance after traumatic brain injury. *Clinical Neuropsychologist, 14,* 496–503.

Shiffman, S. (2009). How many cigarettes did you smoke? Assessing cigarette consumption by global report, time-line follow-back, and ecological momentary assessment. *Health Psychology, 28,* 519–526.

Shiffman, S., Gwaltney, C. J., Balabanis, M. H., et al. (2002). Immediate antecedents of cigarette smoking: An analysis from ecological momentary assessment. *Journal of Abnormal Psychology, 111,* 531–545.

Shiffman, S., Hufford, M., Hickcox, M., et al. (1997). Remember that? A comparison of real-time versus retrospective recall of smoking lapses. *Journal of Consulting and Clinical Psychology, 65,* 292–300.

Shirom, A. (2003). Job-related burnout: A review. In J. C. Quick & L. E. Tetrick (Eds.), *Handbook of occupational health psychology* (pp. 245–264). Washington, DC: American Psychological Association.

Shneidman, E. S. (1952). Manual for the Make a Picture Story Method. *Projective Techniques Monographs, 2.*

Shneidman, E. S. (1958). Some relationships between thematic and drawing materials. In E. F. Hammer (Ed.), *The clinical applications of projective drawings* (pp. 296–307). Springfield, IL: Charles C Thomas.

Shock, N. W., Greulich, R. C., Andres, R., et al. (1984). *Normal human aging: The Baltimore longitudinal study of aging* (NIH Publication No. 84–2450). Washington, DC: U.S. Government Printing Office.

Shockley, W. (1971). Models, mathematics, and the moral obligation to diagnose the origin of Negro IQ deficits. *Review of Educational Research, 41,* 369–377.

Shriner, J. G. (2000). Legal perspectives on school outcomes assessment for students with disabilities. *Journal of Special Education, 33,* 232–239.

Shrout, P. E., & Yager, T. J. (1989). Reliability and validity of screening scales: Effect of reducing scale length. *Journal of Clinical Epidemiology, 42,* 69–78.

Shuey, A. M. (1966). *The testing of Negro intelligence* (2nd ed.). New York: Social Science.

Shum, D., Short, L., Tunstall, J., et al. (2000). Performance of children with traumatic brain injury on a 4-disk version of the Tower of London and the Porteus Maze. *Brain & Cognition, 44*, 59–62.

Shuman, D. W., & Sales, B. D. (1999). The impact of *Daubert* and its progeny on the admissibility of behavioral and social science evidence. *Psychology, Public Policy, and Law, 5*, 3–15.

Siegler, R. S., & Richards, D. (1980). The development of intelligence. In R. S. Sternberg (Chair), *People's conception of the nature of intelligence.* Symposium presented at the 88th annual convention of the American Psychological Association, Montreal.

Silka, V. R., & Hauser, M. J. (1997). Psychiatric assessment of the person with mental retardation. *Psychiatric Annals, 27*(3), 162–169.

Silverman, W., Miezejeski, C., Ryan, R., Zigman, W., Krinsky-McHale, S., & Urv, T. (2010). Stanford-Binet & WAIS IQ differences and their implications for adults with intellectual disability (aka mental retardation). *Intelligence, 38*(2), 242–248.

Silverstein, A. B. (1990). Short forms of individual intelligence tests. *Psychological Assessment, 2*, 3–11.

Silverstein, M. L., & Nelson, L. D. (2000). Clinical and research implications of revising psychological tests. *Psychological Assessment, 12*, 298–303.

Simms, L. J., Casillas, A., Clark, L. A., et al. (2005). Psychometric evaluation of the restructured clinical scales of the MMPI-2. *Psychological Assessment, 17*, 345–358.

Simpson, R. (1970). Study of the comparability of the WISC and WAIS. *Journal of Consulting and Clinical Psychology, 2*, 156–158.

Simpson, R. L., Griswold, D. E., & Myles, B. S. (1999). Educators' assessment accommodation preferences for students with autism. *Focus on Autism and Other Developmental Disabilities, 14*(4), 212–219, 230.

Sinadinovic, K., Wennberg, P., & Berman, A. H. (2011). Population screening of risky alcohol and drug use via Internet and Interactive Voice response (IVR): A feasibility and psychometric study in a random sample. *Drug and Alcohol Dependence, 114*, 55–60.

Sines, J. O. (1966). Actuarial methods in personality assessment. In B. A. Maher (Ed.), *Progress in experimental personality research* (Vol. 3, pp. 133–193). New York: Academic Press.

Siperstein, G. N., Leffert, J. S., & Wenz-Gross, M. (1997). The quality of friendships between children with and without learning problems. *American Journal on Mental Retardation, 102*, 111–125.

Sivec, H. J., Lynn, S. J., & Garske, J. P. (1994). The effect of somatoform disorders and paranoid psychotic role-related dissimulations as a response set on the MMPI-2. *Assessment, 1*, 69–81.

Skafte, D. (1985). *Child custody evaluations: A practical guide.* Beverly Hills, CA: Sage.

Skaggs, G., Hein, S. F., & Awuor, R. (2007). Setting passing scores on passage-based tests: A comparison of traditional and single-passage bookmark methods. *Applied Measurement in Education, 20*(4), 405–426.

Skinner, B. F. (1979). *The shaping of a behaviorist.* New York: Knopf.

Skinner, H. A., & Allen, B. A. (1983). Does the computer make a difference? Computerized versus face-to-face versus self-report assessment of alcohol, drug, and tobacco use. *Journal of Consulting and Clinical Psychology, 51*, 267–275.

Skinner, H. A., & Pakula, A. (1986). Challenge of computers in psychological assessment. *Professional Psychology: Research and Practice, 17*, 44–50.

Skolnick, J. H. (1961). Scientific theory and scientific evidence: An analysis of lie detection. *Yale Law Journal, 70*, 694–728.

Slakter, M. J., Crehan, K. D., & Koehler, R. A. (1975). Longitudinal studies of risk taking on objective examinations. *Educational and Psychological Measurement, 35*, 97–105.

Slate, J. R., Jones, C. H., Murray, R. A., & Coulter, C. (1993). Evidence that practitioners err in administering and scoring the WAIS-R. *Measurement and Evaluation in Counseling and Development, 25*, 156–161.

Slater, S. B., Vukmanovic, C., Macukanovic, P., et al. (1974). The definition and measurement of disability. *Social Science and Medicine, 8*, 305–308.

Slay, D. K. (1984). A portable Halstead-Reitan Category Test. *Journal of Clinical Psychology, 40*, 1023–1027.

Slobogin, C. (1999). The admissibility of behavioral science information in criminal trials: From primitivism to *Daubert* to Voice. *Psychology, Public Policy, and Law, 5*, 100–119.

Sloman, L., & Gilbert, P. *Subordination and defeat: An evolutionary approach to mood disorders and their therapy.* Mahwah NJ: Erlbaum.

Sloman, L., & Price, J. (1987). Losing behavior (yielding subroutine) and human depression: Proximate and selective mechanisms. *Ethology and Sociobiology, 8*, suppl. 3, 99S–109S.

Smith, D. E. (1986). Training programs for performance appraisal: A review. *Academy of Management Review, 11*, 22–40.

Smith, D. K. (1985). *Test use and perceived competency: A survey of school psychologists.* Unpublished manuscript, University of Wisconsin–River Falls, School Psychology Program.

Smith, D. K., Bolin, J. A., & Stovall, D. R. (1988). K-ABC stability in a preschool sample: A longitudinal study. *Journal of Psychoeducational Assessment, 6*, 396–403.

Smith, D. K., & Knudtson, L. S. (1990). *K-ABC and S-B: FE relationships in an at-risk preschool sample.* Paper presented at the Annual Meeting of the American Psychological Association, Boston.

Smith, D. K., Lasee, M. J., & McCloskey, G. M. (1990). *Test-retest reliability of the AGS Early Screening Profiles.* Paper presented at the Annual Meeting of the National Association of School Psychologists, San Francisco.

Smith, D. K., & Lyon, M. A. (1987). *Children with learning difficulties: Differences in ability patterns as a function of placement.* Paper presented at the Annual Meeting of the American Educational Research Association, Washington, DC. (ERIC Document Reproduction Service No. ED 285 317.)

Smith, D. K., St. Martin, M. E., & Lyon, M. A. (1989). A validity study of the Stanford-Binet Fourth Edition with students with learning disabilities. *Journal of Learning Disabilities, 22*, 260–261.

Smith, G. E., Ivnik, R. J., Malec, J. F., Kokmen, E., Tangalos, E. G., & Kurland, L. T. (1992). Mayo's older Americans normative studies (MOANS): Factor structure of a core battery. *Psychological Assessment, 4*, 382–390.

Smith, G. T., McCarthy, D. M., & Anderson, K. G. (2000). On the sins of short form development. *Psychological Assessment, 12*, 102–111.

Smith, J. D. (1985). *Minds made feeble: The myth and legacy of the Kallikaks.* Austin: Pro–Ed.

Smith, M. (1948). Cautions concerning the use of the Taylor-Russell tables in employee selection. *Journal of Applied Psychology, 32*, 595–600.

Smith, R. E. (1963). Examination by computer. *Behavioral Science, 8*, 76–79.

Smith, R. G., & Iwata, B. A. (1997). Antecedent influences on behavior disorders. *Journal of Applied Behavior Analysis, 30,* 343–375.

Smith, T., Smith, B. L., Bramlett, R. K., & Hicks, N. (2000). WISC-III stability over a three-year period in students with learning disabilities. *Research in the Schools, 7,* 37–41.

Smith, T. C., Matthews, N., Smith, B., & Kennedy, S. (1993). Subtest scatter and Kaufman regroupings on the WISC-R in non-learning-disabled and learning-disabled children. *Psychology in the Schools, 30,* 24–28.

Smith, T. T., Myers-Jennings, C., & Coleman, T. (2000). Assessment of language skills in rural preschool children. *Communication Disorders Quarterly, 21,* 98–113.

Smither, J. W., Reilly, R. R., & Buda, R. (1988). Effect of prior performance information on ratings of present performance: Contrast versus assimilation revisited. *Journal of Applied Psychology, 73,* 487–496.

Smither, R., & Rodriguez-Giegling, M. (1982). Personality, demographics, and acculturation of Vietnamese and Nicaraguan refugees to the United States. *International Journal of Psychology, 17,* 19–25.

Snook, B., Eastwood, J., Gendreau, P., et al. (2007). Taking stock of criminal profiling: A narrative review and meta-analysis. *Criminal Justice and Behavior, 34*(4), 437–452.

Snowden, L. R., & Hines, A. M. (1999). A scale to assess African American acculturation. *Journal of Black Psychology, 25,* 36–47.

Snyder, C. R., Shenkel, R. J., & Lowery, C. R. (1977). Acceptance of personality interpretations: The "Barnum effect" and beyond. *Journal of Consulting and Clinical Psychology, 45,* 104–114.

Snyder, C. R., Shenkel, R. J., & Schmidt, A. (1976). Effect of role perspective and client psychiatric history on locus of problem. *Journal of Consulting and Clinical Psychology, 44,* 467–472.

Snyder, D. K. (1981). *Marital Satisfaction Inventory (MSI) manual.* Los Angeles: Western Psychological Services.

Snyder, D. K. (2000). Computer-assisted judgment: Defining strengths and liabilities. *Psychological Assessment, 12,* 52–60.

Snyder, D. K., Widiger, T. A., & Hoover, D. W. (1990). Methodological considerations in validating computer-based test interpretations: Controlling for response bias. *Psychological Assessment, 2,* 470–477.

Snyder, P., Lawson, S., Thompson, B., Stricklin, S., & Sexton, D. (1993). Evaluating the psychometric integrity of instruments used in early intervention research: The Battelle Developmental Inventory. *Topics in Early Childhood Special Education, 32,* 273–280.

Sobell, L. C., & Sobell, M. B. (1992). Timeline followback: A technique for assessing self-reported alcohol consumption. In R. Z. Litten & J. P. Allen (Eds.), *Measuring alcohol consumption* (pp. 41–71). Totowa, NJ: Humana Press.

Sobell, L. C., & Sobell, M. B. (2000). Alcohol timeline followback (TLFB). In American Psychiatric Association (Ed.), *Handbook of psychiatric measures* (pp. 477–479). Washington, DC: American Psychiatric Association.

Sodowsky, G. R., & Carey, J. C. (1988, July). Relationships between acculturation-related demographics and cultural attitudes of an Asian-Indian immigrant group. *Journal of Multicultural Counseling and Development, 16,* 117–136.

Sokal, M. M. (1991). Psyche Cattell (1893–1989). *American Psychologist, 46,* 72.

Solomon, I. L., & Starr, B. D. (1968). *The School Apperception Method.* New York: Springer.

Solomon, P. R., Hirschoff, A., Kelly, B., et al. (1998). A 7-minute neurocognitive screening battery highly sensitive to Alzheimer's disease. *Archives of Neurology, 55,* 349–355.

Sommers-Flanagan, J., & Sommers-Flanagan, R. (1995). Intake interviewing with suicidal patients: A systematic approach. *Professional Psychology: Research and Practice, 26,* 41–47.

Sontag, L. W., Baker, C. T., & Nelson, V. L. (1958). Personality as a determinant of performance. *American Journal of Orthopsychiatry, 25,* 555–562.

South, S. C., Oltmanns, T. F., Johnson, J., & Turkheimer, E. (2011). Level of agreement between self and spouse in the assessment of personality pathology. *Assessment, 18*(2), 217–226.

Spangler, W. D. (1992). Validity of questionnaire and TAT measures of need for achievement: Two meta-analyses. *Psychological Bulletin, 112,* 140–154.

Spanier, G. (1976). Measuring dyadic adjustment: New scales for assessing the quality of marriage and similar dyads. *Journal of Marriage and the Family, 38,* 15–28.

Spanier, G. B., & Filsinger, E. (1983). The Dyadic Adjustment Scale. In E. Filsinger (Ed.), *Marriage and family assessment.* Beverly Hills, CA: Sage.

Sparrow, S. S., Balla, D. A., & Cicchetti, D. V. (1984a). *Vineland Adaptive Behavior Scales, Interview Edition: Expanded form manual.* Circle Pines, MN: American Guidance Service.

Sparrow, S. S., Balla, D. A., & Cicchetti, D. V. (1984b). *Vineland Adaptive Behavior Scales, Interview Edition: Survey form manual.* Circle Pines, MN: American Guidance Service.

Sparrow, S. S., Balla, D. A., & Cicchetti, D. V. (1985). *Vineland Adaptive Behavior Scales, Classroom Edition manual.* Circle Pines, MN: American Guidance Service.

Spearman, C. (1927). *The abilities of man: Their nature and measurement.* New York: Macmillan.

Spearman, C. E. (1904). "General intelligence" objectively determined and measured. *American Journal of Psychiatry, 15,* 201–293.

Spearman, C. E. (1930–1936). Autobiography. In C. Murchison (Ed.), *A history of psychology in autobiography* (3 vols.). Worcester, MA: Clark University Press.

Speece, D. L., Schatschneider, C., Silverman, R., et al. (2011). Identification of reading problems in first grade within a response-to-intervention framework. *Elementary School Journal, 111*(4), 585–607.

Speth, E. B. (1992). *Test-retest reliabilities of Bricklin Perceptual Scales.* Unpublished doctoral dissertation, Hahneman University Graduate School, Philadelphia.

Spiegel, J. S., Leake, B., Spiegel, T. M., et al. (1988). What are we measuring? An examination of self-reported functional status measures. *Arthritis and Rheumatism, 31,* 721–728.

Spielberger, C. D., et al. (1980). *Test Anxiety Inventory: Preliminary professional manual.* Palo Alto, CA: Consulting Psychologists Press.

Spitz, H. H., Minsky, S. K., & Bessellieu, C. L. (1985). Influence of planning time and first-move strategy on Tower of Hanoi problem-solving performance of mentally retarded young adults and non-retarded children. *American Journal of Mental Deficiency, 90,* 46–56.

Spitzer, R. L. (1999). Harmful dysfunction and the *DSM* definition of mental disorder. *Journal of Abnormal Psychology, 108,* 430–432.

Spivack, G., & Spotts, J. (1966). *Devereux Child Behavior Rating Scale manual.* Devon, PA: Devereux Foundation.

Spivack, G., Spotts, J., & Haimes, P. E. (1967). *Devereux Adolescent Behavior Rating Scale.* Devon, PA: Devereux Foundation.

Spokane, A. R., & Decker, A. R. (1999). Expressed and measured interests. In M. L. Savickas & A. R. Spokane

(Eds.), *Vocational interests: Meaning, measurement, and counseling use* (pp. 211–233). Palo Alto, CA: Davies-Black.

Spranger, E. (1928). *Types of men* (P. J. W. Pigors, Trans.). Halle, Germany: Niemeyer.

Spray, J. A., & Huang, C.-Y. (2000). Obtaining test blueprint weights from job analysis surveys. *Journal of Educational Measurement, 37*(3), 187–201.

Spreen, O., & Benton, A. L. (1965). Comparative studies of some psychological tests for cerebral damage. *Journal of Nervous and Mental Disease, 140*, 323–333.

Spruill, J., & May, J. (1988). The mentally retarded offender: Prevalence rates based on individual versus group intelligence tests. *Criminal Justice and Behavior, 15*, 484–491.

Spruill, J. A. (1993). Secondary assessment: Structuring the transition process. *Learning Disabilities Research & Practice, 8*, 127–132.

Staggs, G. D., Larson, L. M., & Borgen, F. H. (2003). Convergence of specific factors in vocational interests and personality. *Journal of Career Assessment, 11*, 243–261.

Stahl, P. M. (1995). *Conducting child custody evaluations.* Thousand Oaks, CA: Sage.

Stanczak, D. E., Lynch, M. D., McNeil, C. K., & Brown, B. (1998). The Expanded Trail Making Test: Rationale, development, and psychometric properties. *Archives of Clinical Neuropsychology, 13*, 473–487.

Stanley, J. C. (1971). Reliability. In R. L. Thorndike (Ed.), *Educational measurement* (2nd ed.). Washington, DC: American Council on Education.

Starch, D., & Elliot, E. C. (1912). Reliability of grading of high school work in English. *School Review, 20*, 442–457.

Starr, B. D., & Weiner, M. B. (1979). The Projective Assessment of Aging Method (PAAM). New York: Springer.

Staw, B. M., Bell, N. E., & Clausen, J. A. (1986). The dispositional approach to job attitudes: A lifetime longitudinal test. *Administrative Science Quarterly, 31*, 56–77.

Steadman, H. J. (1983). Predicting dangerousness among the mentally ill: Art, magic, and science. *International Journal of Law and Psychiatry, 6*, 381–390.

Stedman, J. M., Hatch, J. P., & Schoenfeld, L. S. (2000). Pre-internship preparation in psychological testing and psychotherapy: What internship directors say they expect. *Professional Psychology: Research and Practice, 31*, 321–326.

Steiger, J. H. (1996a). Coming full circle in the history of factor indeterminacy. *Multivariate Behavioral Research, 31*, 617–630.

Steiger, J. H. (1996b). Dispelling some myths about factor indeterminacy. *Multivariate Behavioral Research, 31*, 539–550.

Steinberg, M., Cicchetti, D., Buchanan, J., & Hall, P. (1993). Clinical assessment of dissociative symptoms and disorders: The Structured Clinical Interview for DSM-IV Dissociative Disorders (SCID-D). *Dissociation: Progress in Dissociative Disorders, 6*, 3–15.

Stephens, J. J. (1992). Assessing ethnic minorities. *SPA Exchange, 2*(1), 4–6.

Stephenson, M. (2000). Development and validation of the Stephenson Multigroup Acculturation Scale (SMAS). *Psychological Assessment, 12*(1), 77–88.

Stephenson, W. (1953). *The study of behavior: Q-technique and its methodology.* Chicago: University of Chicago.

Stern, B. H. (2001). Admissability of neuropsychological testimony after Daubert and Kumho. *NeuroRehabilitation, 16*(2), 93–101.

Sternberg, R. J. (1981). The nature of intelligence. *New York Education Quarterly, 12*(3), 10–17.

Sternberg, R. J. (1982, April). Who's intelligent? *Psychology Today*, pp. 30–33, 35–36, 38–39.

Sternberg, R. J. (1985). *Beyond IQ: A triarchic theory of human intelligence.* Cambridge: Cambridge University Press.

Sternberg, R. J. (1986). Intelligence is mental self-government. In R. J. Sternberg & D. K. Detterman (Eds.), *What is intelligence?* (pp. 141–148). Norwood, NJ: Ablex.

Sternberg, R. J. (1994). PRSVL: An integrative framework for understanding mind in context. In R. J. Sternberg & R. K. Wagner (Eds.), *Mind in context* (pp. 218–232). Cambridge: Cambridge University Press.

Sternberg, R. J. (1997a). Managerial intelligence. *Journal of Management, 23*, 475–493.

Sternberg, R. J. (1997b). *Successful intelligence.* New York: Plume.

Sternberg, R. J., & Berg, C. A. (1986). Quantitative integration: Definitions of intelligence: A comparison of the 1921 and 1986 symposia. In R. J. Sternberg & D. K. Detterman (Eds.), *What is intelligence?* (pp. 155–162). Norwood, NJ: Ablex.

Sternberg, R. J., Conway, B. E., Ketron, J. L., & Bernstein, M. (1981). People's conceptions of intelligence. *Journal of Personality and Social Psychology, 41*, 37–55.

Sternberg, R. J., & Detterman, D. K. (Eds.). (1986). *What is intelligence?* Norwood, NJ: Ablex.

Sternberg, R. J., Grigorenko, E. L., & Kidd, K. K. (2005). Intelligence, race, and genetics. *American Psychologist, 60*, 46–59

Sternberg, R. J., Lautrey, J., & Lubart, T. I. (Eds.). (2003). *Models of intelligence.* Washington, DC: APA Books.

Sternberg, R. J., & Williams, W. M. (1997). Does the Graduate Record Examination predict meaningful success in the graduate training of psychologists? A case study. *American Psychologist, 52*, 630–641.

Stevens, C. D., & Macintosh, G. (2003). Personality and attractiveness of activities within sales jobs. *Journal of Personal Selling & Sales Management, 23*, 23–37.

Stice, E., Fisher, M., & Lowe, M. R. (2004). Are dietary restraint scales valid measures of acute dietary restriction? Unobtrusive observational data suggest not. *Psychological Assessment, 16*, 51–59.

Stillman, R. (1974). *Assessment of deaf-blind children: The Callier-Azusa Scale.* Paper presented at the Intercom '74, Hyannis, MA.

Stinnett, T. A. (1997). "AAMR Adaptive Behavior Scale-School: 2" Test review. *Journal of Psychoeducational Assessment, 15*, 361–372.

Stoeber, J., Stoll, O., Pescheck, E., & Otto, K. (2008). Perfectionism and achievement goals in athletes: Relations with approach and avoidance orientations in mastery and performance goals. *Psychology of Sport and Exercise, 9*(2), 102–121.

Stokes, J., Pogge, D., Sarnicola, J., & McGrath, R. (2009). Correlates of the MMPI—A Psychopathology Five (PSY-5) facet scales in an adolescent inpatient sample. *Journal of Personality Assessment, 91*(1), 48–57.

Stokes, J. B. (1977). Comment on "Socially reinforced obsessing: Etiology of a disorder in a Christian Scientist." *Journal of Consulting and Clinical Psychology, 45*, 1164–1165.

Stone, A. A. (1986). Vermont adopts *Tarasoff:* A real barn-burner. *American Journal of Psychiatry, 143*, 352–355.

Stone, B. J. (1992). Prediction of achievement by Asian-American and White children. *Journal of School Psychology, 30*, 91–99.

Stone, D. R. (1950). A recorded auditory apperception test as a new projective technique. *Journal of Psychology, 29*, 349–353.

Stone, H. K., & Dellis, N. P. (1960). An exploratory investigation into the levels hypothesis. *Journal of Projective Techniques, 24*(3), 333–340.

Stoppard, J. M., & Gruchy, C. D. G. (1993). Gender, context, and expression of positive emotion. *Personality and Social Psychology Bulletin, 19,* 143–150.

Storandt, M. (1994). General principles of assessment of older adults. In M. Storandt & G. R. VandenBos (Eds.), *Neuro-psychological assessment of dementia and depression in older adults: A clinician's guide* (pp. 7–32). Washington, DC: American Psychological Association.

Storholm, E. D., Fisher, D. G., Napper, L. E., et al. (2011). A psychometric analysis of the Compulsive Sexual Behavior Inventory. *Sexual Addiction & Compulsivity, 18*(2), 86–103.

Stout, C. E., Levant, R. F., Reed, G. M., & Murphy, M. J. (2001). Contracts: A primer for psychologists. *Professional Psychology: Research and Practice, 32,* 89–91.

Straus, M. A. (1979). Measuring intrafamily conflict and violence: The Conflict Tactics (CT) Scales. *Journal of Marriage and the Family, 41,* 75–85.

Strauss, A. A., & Lehtinen, L. E. (1947). *Psychopathology and education of the brain injured child.* New York: Grune & Stratton.

Strauss, E., Ottfried, S., & Hunter, M. (2000). Implications of test revisions for research. *Psychological Assessment, 12,* 237–244.

Strauss, E., Sherman, E. M.S., & Spreen, O. (2006). *A compendium of neuropsychological tests: Administration, norms, and commentary* (3rd ed.). New York: Oxford University Press.

Streiner, D. L. (2003a). Being inconsistent about consistency: When coefficient alpha does and doesn't matter. *Journal of Personality Assessment, 80,* 217–222.

Streiner, D. L. (2003b). Starting at the beginning: An introduction to coefficient alpha and internal consistency. *Journal of Personality Assessment, 80,* 99–103.

Streiner, D. L. (2010). Measure for measure: New developments in measurement and item response theory. *The Canadian Journal of Psychiatry / La Revue canadienne de psychiatrie, 55*(3), 180–186.

Stricker, G., & Gold, J. R. (1999). The Rorschach: Toward a nomothetically based, idiographically applicable configurational model. *Psychological Assessment, 11,* 240–250.

Stricker, G., & Healey, B. J. (1990). Projective assessment of object relations: A review of the empirical literature. *Psychological Assessment, 2,* 219–230.

Strober, L. B., & Arnett, P. A. (2009). Assessment of depression in three medically ill, elderly populations: Alzheimer's disease, Parkinson's disease, and stroke. *Clinical Neuropsychologist, 23,* 205–230.

Strong, E. K., Jr., Donnay, D. A. C., Morris, M. L., et al. (2004). *Strong Interest Inventory, Second Edition.* Palo Alto, CA: Consulting Psychologists Press.

Strong, E. K., Jr., Hansen, J. C., & Campbell, D. C. (1985). *Strong Vocational Interest Blank. Revised edition of Form T325, Strong-Campbell Interest Inventory.* Stanford, CA: Stanford University. (Distributed by Consulting Psychologists Press.)

Stroud, L. R., Paster, R. L., Papandonatos, G. D., et al. (2009). Maternal smoking during pregnancy and newborn neurobehavior: Effects at 10 to 27 days. *Journal of Pediatrics, 154,* 10–16.

Sturges, J. W. (1998). Practical use of technology in professional practice. *Professional Psychology: Research and Practice, 29,* 183–188.

Sturman, E. D. (2005). The capacity to consent to treatment and research: A review of standardized assessment tools and potentially impaired populations. *Clinical Psychology Review, 25,* 954–974.

Sturman, E. D. (2011). Involuntary subordination and its relation to personality, mood, and submissive behavior. *Psychological Assessment, 23,* 262–276.

Sturman, E. D., Cribbie, R. A., & Flett, G. L. (2009). The average distance between item values: A novel approach for estimating internal consistency. *Journal of Psychoeducational Assessment, 27,* 409–420.

Sturman, E. D., & Mongrain, M. (2008). Entrapment and perceived status in graduate students experiencing a recurrence of major depression. *Canadian Journal of Behavioural Science, 40,* 185–188.

Su, R., Rounds, J., & Armstrong, P. I. (2009). Men and things, women and people: A meta-analysis of sex differences in interests. *Psychological Bulletin, 135*(6), 859–884.

Subich, L. M. (1996). Addressing diversity in the process of career assessment. In M. L. Savickas & W. B. Walsh (Eds.), *Handbook of career counseling: Theory and practice* (pp. 277–289). Palo Alto, CA: Davies-Black.

Suczek, R. F., & Klopfer, W. G. (1952). Interpretation of the Bender-Gestalt Test: The associative value of the figures. *American Journal of Orthopsychiatry, 22,* 62–75.

Sue, D. W., & Sue, D. (2003). *Counseling the culturally diverse: Theory and practice* (4th ed.). New York: Wiley.

Sugarman, A. (1991). Where's the beef? Putting personality back into personality assessment. *Journal of Personality Assessment, 56,* 130–144.

Suinn, R. M., Rickard-Figueroa, K., Lew, S., & Vigil, S. (1987). The Suinn-Lew Asian Self-Identity Acculturation Scale: An initial report. *Educational and Psychological Measurement, 47,* 401–407.

Sullivan, H. S. (1953). *The interpersonal theory of psychiatry.* New York: Norton.

Sullivan, P. M. (1982). Administration modifications on the WISC-R Performance Scale with different categories of deaf children. *American Annals of the Deaf, 127,* 780–788.

Sullivan, P. M., & Brookhouser, P. E. (Eds.). (1996). *Proceedings of the Fourth Annual Conference on the Habilitation and Rehabilitation of Hearing Impaired Adolescents.* Boys Town, NE: Boys Town.

Sullivan, P. M., & Burley, S. K. (1990). Mental testing of the deaf child. In C. Reynolds & R. Kamphaus (Eds.), *Handbook of psychological and educational assessment of children* (pp. 761–788). New York: Guilford.

Sullivan, P. M., & Montoya, L. A. (1997). Factor analysis of the WISC-III with deaf and hard-of-hearing children. *Psychological Assessment, 9,* 317–321.

Sullivan, P. M., & Schulte, L. E. (1992). Factor analysis of WISC-R with deaf and hard-of-hearing children. *Psychological Assessment, 4,* 537–540.

Sundberg, N. D. (1955). The acceptability of "fake" versus "bona fide" personality test interpretations. *Journal of Abnormal and Social Psychology, 50,* 145–147.

Sundberg, N. D., & Gonzales, L. R. (1981). Cross-cultural and cross-ethnic assessment: Overview and issues. In P. McReynolds (Ed.), *Advances in psychological assessment* (Vol. 5, pp. 460–541). San Francisco: Jossey-Bass.

Sundberg, N. D., & Tyler, L. E. (1962). *Clinical psychology.* New York: Appleton-Century-Crofts.

Super, C. M. (1983). Cultural variation in the meaning and uses of children's "intelligence." In J. B. Deregowski, S. Dziurawiec, & R. C. Annis (Eds.), *Explorations in cross-cultural psychology.* Lisse, Netherlands: Swets & Zeitlinger.

Sutton v. United Airlines, 527 U.S. 471, 119 S. Ct. 213 (1999).

Sutton-Simon, K., & Goldfried, M. R. (1979). Faulty thinking patterns in two types of anxiety. *Cognitive Therapy and Research, 3,* 193–203.

Suzuki, L. A., Ponterotto, J. G., & Meller, P. J. (Eds.). (2000). *Handbook of multicultural assessment* (2nd ed.). San Francisco: Jossey-Bass.

Swallow, R. (1981). Fifty assessment instruments commonly used with blind and partially seeing individuals. *Journal of Visual Impairment and Blindness, 75,* 65–72.

Swanson, H. L. (2011). Learning disabilities: Assessment, identification, and treatment. In M. A. Bray, T. J. Kehle, & P. E. Nathan (Eds.), *The Oxford handbook of school psychology* (pp. 334–350). New York: Oxford University Press.

Swanson, J. L. (1992). The structure of vocational interests for African-American college students. *Journal of Vocational Behavior, 40,* 144–157.

Sweet, J. J., Moberg, P. J., & Tovian, S. M. (1990). Evaluation of Wechsler Adult Intelligence Scale—Revised premorbid IQ formulas in clinical populations. *Psychological Assessment, 2,* 41–44.

Sweet, J. J., Peck, E. A., III, Abramowitz, C., & Etzweiler, S. (2002). National Academy of Neuropsychology/ Division 40 of the American Psychological Association practice survey of clinical neuropsychology in the United States: Part I: Practitioner and practice characteristics, professional activities, and time requirements. *Clinical Neuropsychologist, 16,* 109–127.

Swensen, C. H. (1968). Empirical evaluations of human figure drawings: 1957–1966. *Psychological Bulletin, 70,* 20–44.

Swerdlik, M. E. (1985). Review of Brigance Diagnostic Comprehensive Inventory of Basic Skills. In J. V. Mitchell, Jr. (Ed.), *The ninth mental measurements yearbook* (pp. 214–215). Lincoln: Buros Institute of Mental Measurements, University of Nebraska.

Swerdlik, M. E. (1992). Review of the Otis-Lennon School Ability Test. In J. J. Kramer & J. C. Conoley (Eds.), *The eleventh mental measurements yearbook.* Lincoln: Buros Institute of Mental Measurements, University of Nebraska.

Swerdlik, M. E., & Dornback, F. (1988, April). *An interpretation guide to the fourth edition of the Stanford-Binet Intelligence Scale.* Paper presented at the annual meeting of the National Association of School Psychologists, Chicago.

Sykes, R. C., & Hou, L. (2003). Weighting constructed-response items in IRT-based exams. *Applied Measurement in Education, 16*(4), 257–275.

Sylvester, R. H. (1913). Clinical psychology adversely criticized. *Psychological Clinic, 7,* 182–188.

Symonds, P. M. (1949). *Adolescent fantasy: An investigation of the picture-story method of personality study.* New York: Columbia University.

Takahashi, M., Sato, A., & Nakajima, K. (2008). Poor performance in Clock-Drawing Test associated with memory deficit and reduced bilateral hippocampal and left temporoparietal regional blood flows in Alzheimer's disease patients. *Psychiatry and Clinical Neurosciences, 62*(2), 167–173.

Takeuchi, J., Solomon, F., & Menninger, W. W. (Eds.). (1981). *Behavioral science and the Secret Service: Toward the prevention of assassination.* Washington, DC: National Academy.

Tallent, N. (1958). On individualizing the psychologist's clinical evaluation. *Journal of Clinical Psychology, 114,* 243–244.

Tamkin, A. S., & Kunce, J. T. (1985). A comparison of three neuropsychological tests: The Weigl, Hooper and Benton. *Journal of Clinical Psychology, 41,* 660–664.

Tan, U. (1993). Normal distribution of hand preference and its bimodality. *International Journal of Neuroscience, 68,* 61–65.

Taormina, R. J., & Bauer, T. N. (2000). Organizational socialization in two cultures: Results from the United States and Hong Kong. *International Journal of Organizational Analysis, 8,* 262–289.

Tarasoff v. Regents of the University of California, 17 Cal. 3d 425, 551 P.2d 334, 131 Cal. Rptr. 14 (Cal. 1976).

Tate, D. G., & Pledger, C. (2003). An integrative conceptual framework of disability: New directions for research. *American Psychologist, 58,* 289–295.

Taylor, D. M. (2002). *The quest for identity: From minority groups to Generation Xers.* Westport, CT: Praeger.

Taylor, H. C., & Russell, J. T. (1939). The relationship of validity coefficients to the practical effectiveness of tests in selection. *Journal of Applied Psychology, 23,* 565–578.

Taylor, L. B. (1979). Psychological assessment of neurosurgical patients. In T. Rasmussen & R. Marino (Eds.), *Functional neurosurgery.* New York: Raven.

Taylor, P. J., Gooding, P., Wood A. M., & Tarrier, N. (2011a). The role of defeat and entrapment in depression, anxiety, and suicide. *Psychological Bulletin, 137*(3), 391–420.

Taylor, P. J., Wood, A. M, Gooding, P. A., & Tarrier, N. (2011b). Prospective predictors of suicidality: Defeat and entrapment lead to changes in suicidal ideation over time. *Suicide and Life Threatening Behaviour, 41,* 297–306.

Taylor, R. L. (1980). Use of the AAMD classification system: A review of recent research. *American Journal of Mental Deficiency, 85,* 116–119.

Teachman, B. A. (2007). Evaluating implicit spider fear associations using the Go/No-go Association Task. *Journal of Behavior Therapy and Experimental Psychiatry, 38*(2), 156–167.

Teague, W. (State Superintendent of Education). (1983). *Basic competency education: Reading, language, mathematics specifications for the Alabama High School Graduation Examination* (Bulletin No. 4). Montgomery: Alabama State Department of Education.

Tein, J.-Y., Sandler, I. N., & Zautra, A. J. (2000). Stressful life events, psychological distress, coping, and parenting of divorced mothers: A longitudinal study. *Journal of Family Psychology, 14,* 27–41.

Tellegen, A. (1985). Structures of mood and personality and their relevance to assessing anxiety, with an emphasis on self-report. In A. H. Tuma & J. D. Maser (Eds.), *Anxiety and the anxiety disorders* (pp. 681–706). Hillsdale, NJ: Erlbaum.

Tellegen, A., & Ben-Porath, Y. S. (1992). The new uniform *T* scores for the MMPI-2: Rationale, derivation, and appraisal. *Psychological Assessment, 4,* 145–155.

Tellegen, A., Ben-Porath, Y. S., McNulty, J. L., et al. (2003). *The MMPI-2 Restructured Clinical (RC) scales: Development, validation, and interpretation.* Minneapolis: University of Minnesota Press.

Tellegen, A., Ben-Porath, Y. S., Sellbom, M., et al. (2006). Further evidence on the validity of the MMPI-2 Restructured Clinical (RC) scales: Addressing questions raised by Rogers, Sewell, Harrison, and Jordan and Nichols. *Journal of Personality Assessment, 87*(2), 148–171.

Tenopyr, M. L. (1999). A scientist-practitioner's viewpoint on the admissibility of behavioral and social scientific information. *Psychology, Public Policy, and Law, 5,* 194–202.

Teplin, S. W., et al. (1991). Neurodevelopmental health, and growth status at age 6 years of children with birth weights less than 1001 grams. *Journal of Pediatrics, 118,* 768–777.

Terman, L. M. (1916). *The measurement of intelligence: An explanation of and a complete guide for the use of the Stanford revision and extension of the Binet-Simon Intelligence Scale.* Boston: Houghton Mifflin.

Terman, L. M., et al. (1925). *The mental and physical traits of a thousand gifted children: Vol. 1. Genetic studies of genius.* Stanford, CA: Stanford University.

Terman, L. M., & Miles, C. C. (1936). *Sex and personality: Studies in masculinity and femininity.* New York: McGraw-Hill.

Terzis, V. & Economides, A. A. (2011). The acceptance and use of computer based assessment. *Computers & Education, 56*, 1032–1044.

Tharinger, D. J., Finn, S. E., Wilkinson, A. D., & Schaber, P. (2007). Therapeutic assessment with a child as a family intervention: A clinical and research case study. *Psychology in the Schools, 44*(3), 293–309.

Tharinger, D. J., & Stark, K. (1990). A qualitative versus quantitative approach to evaluating the Draw-A-Person and Kinetic Family Drawing: A study of mood- and anxiety-disorder children. *Psychological Assessment, 2,* 365–375.

Thiry, B. (2009). Exploring the validity of graphology with the Rorschach test. *Rorschachiana, 30*(1), 26–47.

Thomas, A. D., & Dudek, S. Z. (1985). Interpersonal affect in Thematic Apperception Test responses: A scoring system. *Journal of Personality Assessment, 49*, 30–36.

Thomas, M. L., & Locke, D. E. C. (2010). Psychometric properties of the MMPI-2-RF Somatic Complaints (RC1) scale. *Psychological Assessment, 22*, 492–503.

Thomas, T., & Solomon, A. (1989). *The films of 20th Century-Fox.* New York: Citadel Press.

Thompson, A. E. (1986). An object relational theory of affect maturity: Applications to the Thematic Apperception Test. In M. Kissen (Ed.), *Assessing object relations phenomena* (pp. 207–224). Madison, CT: International Universities.

Thompson, C. (1949). The Thompson modification of the Thematic Apperception Test. *Journal of Projective Techniques, 13,* 469–478.

Thompson, J. K., & Smolak, L. (Eds.). (2001). *Body image, eating disorders, and obesity in youth: Assessment, prevention, and treatment.* Washington, DC: APA Books.

Thompson, J. K. & Thompson, C. M. (1986). Body size distortion and self-esteem in asymptomatic, normal weight males and females. *International Journal of Eating Disorders, 5*, 1061–1068.

Thompson, J. M., & Sones, R. (1973). *The Education Apperception Test.* Los Angeles: Western Psychological Services.

Thompson, M. D., Scott, J. G., & Dickson, S. W. (1999). Clinical utility of the Trail Making Test practice time. *Clinical Neuropsychologist, 13*, 450–455.

Thompson, R. J., Gustafson, K. E., Meghdadpour, S., & Harrell, E. S. (1992). The role of biomedical and psychosocial processes in the intellectual and academic functioning of children and adolescents with cystic fibrosis. *Journal of Clinical Psychology, 48,* 3–10.

Thoresen, S., Mehlum, L., Roysamb, E., & Tonnessen, A. (2006). Risk factors for completed suicide in veterans of peacekeeping: Repatriation, negative life events, and marital status. *Archives of Suicide Research, 10*(4), 353–363.

Thorndike, E. L., et al. (1921). Intelligence and its measurement: A symposium. *Journal of Educational Psychology, 12,* 123–147, 195–216.

Thorndike, E. L., Bregman, E. O., Cobb, M. V., Woodward, E., & the staff of the Division of Psychology of the Institute of Educational Research of Teachers College, Columbia University. (1927). *The measurement of intelligence.* New York: Bureau of Publications, Teachers College, Columbia University.

Thorndike, E. L., Lay, W., & Dean, P. R. (1909). The relation of accuracy in sensory discrimination to general intelligence. *American Journal of Psychology, 20,* 364–369.

Thorndike, R. (1985). Reliability. *Journal of Counseling & Development, 63,* 528–530.

Thorndike, R. L. (1949). *Personnel selection.* New York: Wiley.

Thorndike, R. L. (1971). Concepts of cultural fairness. *Journal of Educational Measurement, 8,* 63–70.

Thorndike, R. L., Hagan, E. P., & Sattler, J. P. (1986). *Technical manual for the Stanford-Binet Intelligence Scale, Fourth Edition.* Chicago: Riverside.

Thorndike, R. M. (2007). Review of the Kaufman Assessment Battery for Children, Second Editon. In K. F. Geisinger, R. A. Sipes, J. F. Carlson, & B. S. Plake (Eds.), *The 17th Mental Measurements Yearbook* (pp. 520–522). Lincoln: Buros Institute of Mental Measurements, University of Nebraska.

Thornton, G. C., & Byham, W. C. (1982). *Assessment centers and managerial performance.* New York: Academic Press.

Thrash, T. M., Maruskin, L. A., Cassidy, S. E., Fryer, J. W., et al. (2010). Mediating between the muse and the masses: Inspiration and the actualization of creative ideas. *Journal of Personality and Social Psychology, 98*(3), 469–487.

Thurstone, L. L. (1925). A method of scaling psychological and educational tests. *Journal of Educational Psychology, 16,* 433–451.

Thurstone, L. L. (1927). A law of comparative judgment. *Psychological Review, 34,* 273–286.

Thurstone, L. L. (1929). Theory of attitude measurement. *Psychological Bulletin, 36,* 222–241.

Thurstone, L. L. (1931). *Multiple-factor analysis.* Chicago: University of Chicago Press.

Thurstone, L. L. (1935). *The vectors of mind.* Chicago: University of Chicago Press.

Thurstone, L. L. (1938). Primary mental abilities. *Psychometric Monographs,* No. 1. Chicago: University of Chicago Press.

Thurstone, L. L. (1947). *Multiple factor analysis.* Chicago: University of Chicago.

Thurstone, L. L. (1959). *The measurement of values.* Chicago: University of Chicago.

Thurstone, L. L., & Chave, E. J. (1929). *The measurement of attitude.* Chicago: University of Chicago.

Tillman, M. H. (1973). Intelligence scale for the blind: A review with implications for research. *Journal of School Psychology, 11,* 80–87.

Timbrook, R. E., & Graham, J. R. (1994). Ethnic differences on the MMPI-2? *Psychological Assessment, 6,* 212–217.

Tinsley, H. E. A., & Weiss, D. J. (1975). Interrater reliability and agreement of subjective judgments. *Journal of Counseling Psychology, 22,* 358–376.

Tittle, C. R., & Hill, R. J. (1967). Attitude measurement and prediction of behavior: An evaluation of conditions and measurement techniques. *Sociometry, 30,* 199–213.

Torrance, E. P. (1966). *Torrance Tests of Creative Thinking.* Bensenville, IL: Scholastic Testing Service.

Torrance, E. P. (1987a). *Guidelines for administration and scoring/Comments on using the Torrance Tests of Creative Thinking.* Bensenville, IL: Scholastic Testing Service.

Torrance, E. P. (1987b). *Survey of the uses of the Torrance Tests of Creative Thinking.* Bensenville, IL: Scholastic Testing Service.

Touliatos, J., Perlmutter, B. F., & Strauss, M. A. (1991). *Handbook of family measurements.* Newbury Park, CA: Sage.

Townsend, E. (2007). Suicide terrorists: Are they suicidal? *Suicide and Life-Threatening Behavior, 37*(1), 35–49.

Tracey, T. J. G. (2010). Interest assessment using new technology. *Journal of Career Assessment, 18,* 336–344.

Tramontana, M. G., & Boyd, T. A. (1986). Psychometric screening of neuropsychological abnormality in older children. *International Journal of Clinical Neuropsychology, 8,* 53–59.

Tran, L., Sanchez, T., Arellano, B., & Swanson, H. L. (2011). A meta-analysis of the RTI literature for children at risk for reading disabilities. *Journal of Learning Disabilities, 44*(3), 283–295.

Trautscholdt, M. (1883). Experimentelle unterschungen uber die association der vorstellungen. *Philosophische Studien, 1,* 213–250.

Trent, J. W. (2001). "Who shall say who is a useful person?" Abraham Myerson's opposition to the eugenics movement. *History of Psychiatry, 12*(45, Pt.1), 33–57.

Trice, H. M., & Beyer, J. M. (1984). Studying organizational cultures through rites and ceremonies. *Academy of Management Review, 9,* 653–669.

Trimble, M. R. (Ed.). (1986). *New brain imaging techniques and psychopharmacology.* Oxford: Oxford University Press.

Tropp, L. R., Erkut, S., Garcia Coll, C., Alarcon, O., & Vazquez Garcia, H. A. (1999). Psychological acculturation: development of a new measure for Puerto Ricans on the U.S. mainland. *Educational and Psychological Measurement, 59,* 351–367.

Truant, G. S., O'Reilly, R., & Donaldson, L. (1991). How psychiatrists weigh risk factors when assessing suicide risk. *Suicide and Life-Threatening Behavior, 21,* 106–114.

Tryon, R. C. (1957). Reliability and behavior domain validity: Reformulation and historical critique. *Psychological Bulletin, 54,* 229–249.

Tsai, Y.-F., Viirre, E., Strychacz, C., Chase, B., & Jung T.-P. (2007). Task performance and eye activity: Predicting behavior relating to cognitive workload. *Aviation, Space, and Environmental Medicine, 78* (5, Suppl.), B176–B185.

Tsaousis, I., & Georgiades, S. (2009). Development and psychometric properties of the Greek Personality Adjective Checklist (GPAC). *European Journal of Psychological Assessment, 25*(3), 164–174.

Tuerlinckx, F., De Boeck, P., & Lens, W. (2002). Measuring needs with the Thematic Apperception Test: A psychometric study. *Journal of Personality and Social Psychology, 82,* 448–461.

Tugg v. Towey. (1994, July 19). *National Disability Law Reporter, 5,* 999–1005.

Tulchin, S. H. (1939). The clinical training of psychologists and allied specialists. *Journal of Consulting Psychology, 3,* 105–112.

Tulsky, D., Zhu, J., & Ledbetter, M. F. (Project directors). (1997). *WAIS-III, WMS-III Technical manual.* San Antonio: Psychological Corporation.

Tulsky, D. S., & Ledbetter, M. F. (2000). Updating to the WAIS-III and WMS-III: Considerations for research and clinical practice. *Psychological Assessment, 12,* 253–262.

Turchik, J. A., Karpenko, V., Hammers, D., & McNamara, J. R. (2007). Practical and ethical assessment issues in rural, impoverished, and managed care settings. *Professional Psychology: Research and Practice, 38*(2), 158–168.

Turvey, C. L., Wallace, R. B., & Herzog, R. (1999). A revised CES-D measure of depressive symptoms and a DSM-based measure of Major Depressive Episodes in the elderly. *International Psychogeriatrics, 11,* 139–148.

Tuttle, F. B., & Becker, A. (1980). *Characteristics and identification of gifted and talented students.* Washington, DC: National Education Association.

Tybout, A. M., & Artz, N. (1994). Consumer psychology. *Annual Review of Psychology, 45,* 131–169.

Tyler, L. E. (1961). Research explorations in the realm of choice. *Journal of Counseling Psychology, 8,* 195–202.

Tyler, L. E. (1965). *The psychology of human differences* (3rd ed.). New York: Appleton-Century-Crofts.

Tyler, R. S. (1993). Cochlear implants and the deaf culture. *American Journal of Audiology, 2,* 26–32.

Tyler, R. W. (1978). *The Florida accountability program: An evaluation of its educational soundness and implementation.* Washington, DC: National Education Association.

Tziner, A., & Eden, D. (1985). Effects of crew composition on crew performance: Does the whole equal the sum of its parts? *Journal of Applied Psychology, 70,* 85–93.

Udry, J. R. (1981). Marital alternatives and marital disruption. *Journal of Marriage and the Family, 43,* 889–897.

Ulrich, R. E., Stachnik, T. J., & Stainton, N. R. (1963). Student acceptance of generalized personality interpretations. *Psychological Reports, 13,* 831–834.

Unger, J. B., et al. (2002). The AHIMSA Acculturation Scale: A new measure of acculturation for adolescents in a multicultural society. *Journal of Early Adolescence, 22*(3), 225–251.

University of Minnesota. (1984). *User's guide for the Minnesota Report: Personal Selection System.* Minneapolis: National Computer Systems.

U.S. Department of Education, Office of Special Education and Rehabilitative Services, National Institute on Disability and Rehabilitation Research. (2000). *Long range plan: 1999–2003.* Washington, DC: Author.

U.S. Department of Labor. (1991). *Dictionary of occupational titles* (4th ed., rev.). Washington, DC: Author.

Utley, C. A., Lowitzer, A. C., & Baumeister, A. A. (1987). A comparison of the AAMD's definition, eligibility criteria, and classification schemes with state departments of education guidelines. *Education and Training in Mental Retardation, 22*(1), 35–43.

Vacha-Haase, T., & Thompson, B. (2002). Alternative ways of measuring counselees' Jungian psychological-type preferences. *Journal of Counseling & Development, 80,* 173–179.

Vagg, P. R., & Spielberger, C. D. (1998). Occupational stress: Measuring job pressure and organizational support in the workplace. *Journal of Occupational Health Psychology, 3,* 294–305.

Vale, C. D., & Keller, L. S. (1987). Developing expert computer systems to interpret psychological tests. In J. N. Butcher (Ed.), *Computerized psychological assessment: A practitioner's guide* (pp. 64–83). New York: Basic Books.

Vale, C. D., Keller, L. S., & Bentz, V. J. (1986). Development and validation of a computerized interpretation system for personnel tests. *Personnel Psychology, 39,* 525–542.

Vallerand, R. J., Blanchard, C., Mageau, G. A., et al. (2003). Les passions de l'âme: On obsessive and harmonious passion. *Journal of Personality and Social Psychology, 85,* 756–767.

Van Dam, N. T., & Earleywine, M. (2011). Validation of the Center for Epidemiologic Studies Depression Scale-Revised (CESD-R): Pragmatic depression assessment in the general population. *Psychiatry Research, 186*(1), 128–132.

Vanderhoff, H., Jeglic, E. L., & Donovick, P. J. (2011). Neuropsychological assessment in prisons: Ethical and practical challenges. *Journal of Correctional Health Care, 17,* 51–60.

Vander Kolk, C. J. (1977). Intelligence testing for visually impaired persons. *Journal of Visual Impairment & Blindness, 71,* 158–163.

Van der Linden, W. J., Veldkamp, B. P., & Reese, L. M. (2000). An integer programming approach to item bank design. *Applied Psychological Measurement, 24*(2), 139–150.

Van der Merwe, A. B., & Theron, P. A. (1947). A new method of measuring emotional stability. *Journal of General Psychology, 37,* 109–124.

Vanderwood, M. L., McGrew, K. S., Flanagan, D. P., & Keith, T. Z. (2001). The contribution of general and specific cognitive abilities to reading achievement. *Learning and Individual Differences, 13,* 159–188.

Vanman, E. J., Paul, B. Y., Ito, T. A., & Miller, N. (1997). The modern face of prejudice and structural features that moderate the effect of cooperation on affect. *Journal of Personality and Social Psychology, 73,* 941–959.

van Praag, H. M., Plutchik, R., & Apter, A. (Eds.). (1990). *Violence and suicidality: Perspectives in clinical and psychobiological research* (pp. 37–65). New York: Brunner/Mazel.

Varon, E. J. (1936). Alfred Binet's concept of intelligence. *Psychological Review, 43,* 32–49.

Vaughan-Jensen, J., Adame, C., McLean, L., & Gámez, B. Test review of *Wechsler Individual Achievement Test (3rd ed.). Journal of Psychoeducational Assessment, 29*(3), 286–291.

Vause, T., Yu, C. T., & Martin, G. L. (2007). The Assessment of Basic Learning Abilities test for persons with intellectual disability: A valuable clinical tool. *Journal of Applied Research in Intellectual Disabilities, 20*(5), 483–489.

Vazzana, R., Bandinelli, S., Lauretani, F., et al. (2010). Trail making test predicts physical impairment and mortality in older persons. *Journal of the American Geriatrics Society, 58,* 719–723.

Veiga, J., Lubatkin, M., Calori, R., & Very, P. (2000). Measuring organizational culture clashes: A two-nation post-hoc analysis of a cultural compatibility index. *Human Relations, 53,* 539–557.

Velasquez, R. J., Gonzales, M., Butcher, J. N., et al. (1997). Use of the MMPI-2 with Chicanos: Strategies for counselors. *Journal of Multicultural Counseling and Development, 25,* 107–120.

Velden, M. (1997). The heritability of intelligence: Neither known nor unknown. *American Psychologist, 52,* 72–73.

Vento, A. E., Schifano, F., Corkery, J. M., et al. (2011). Suicide verdicts as opposed to accidental deaths in substance-related fatalities (UK, 2001–2007). *Progress in Neuro-Psychopharmacology & Biological Psychiatry, 35,* 1279–1283.

Verdon, B. (2011). The case of thematic tests adapted to older adults: On the importance of differentiating latent and manifest content in projective tests. *Rorschachiana, 32*(1), 46–71.

Verhovek, S. H., & Ayres, B. D., Jr. (1998, November 4). The 1998 elections: The nation—referendums. *New York Times,* p. B2.

Vernon, M. (1989). Assessment of persons with hearing disabilities. In T. Hunt & C. J. Lindley (Eds.), Testing older adults: A reference guide for geropsychological assessments (pp. 150–162). Austin: PRO-ED.

Vernon, M., & Andrews, J. E., Jr. (1990). *Psychology of deafness: Understanding deaf and hard-of-hearing people.* New York: Longman.

Vernon, M., Blair, R., & Lotz, S. (1979). Psychological evaluation and testing of children who are deaf-blind. *School Psychology Digest, 8,* 291–295.

Vernon, M., & Brown, D. W. (1964). A guide to psychological tests and testing procedures in the evaluation of deaf and hard-of-hearing children. *Journal of Speech and Hearing Disorders, 29,* 414–423.

Vernon, P. A. (1993). *Biological approaches to the study of human intelligence.* Norwood, NJ: Ablex.

Vernon, P. E. (1950). *The structure of human abilities.* New York: Wiley.

Vernon, P. E. (1964). *Personality assessment: A critical survey.* New York: Wiley.

Vevea, J. L., Clements, N. C., & Hedges, L. V. (1993). Assess the effects of selection bias on validity data for the General Aptitude Test Battery. *Journal of Applied Psychology, 78,* 981–987.

Vickers-Douglas, K. S., Patten, C. A., Decker, P. A., et al. (2005). Revision of the Self-Administered Alcoholism Screening Test (SAAST-R): A pilot study. *Substance Use & Misuse, 40*(6), 789–812.

Vig, S., & Jedrysek, E. (1996). Application of the 1992 AAMR definition: Issues for preschool children. *Mental Retardation, 34,* 244–246.

Viglione, D. J. (1999). A review of recent research addressing the utility of the Rorschach. *Psychological Assessment, 11,* 251–265.

Vingoe, F. J. (1995). Beliefs of British law and medical students compared to expert criterion group on forensic hypnosis. *Contemporary Hypnosis, 12,* 173–187.

Vinkhuyzen, A. A. E., van der Sluis, S., de Geus, E. J., Boomsma, D. I., & Posthuma, D. (2010). Genetic influences on "environmental" factors. *Genes, Brain & Behavior, 9*(3), 276–287.

Visser, P. S., Krosnick, J. A., & Lavrakas, P. J. (2000). Survey research. In H. T. Reis & C. M. Judd (Eds.), *Handbook of research methods in social and personality psychology* (pp. 223–252). New York: Cambridge University Press.

Volkmar, F. R., Klin, A., Marans, W., & Cohen, D. J. (1996). The pervasive developmental disorders: Diagnosis and assessment. *Child & Adolescent Psychiatric Clinics of North America, 5,* 963–977.

Vollmann, J., Bauer, A., Danker-Hopfe, H., & Helmchen, H. (2003). Competence of mentally ill patients: a comparative empirical study. *Psychological Medicine, 33,* 1463–1471.

von Knorring, L., & Lindstrom, E. (1992). The Swedish version of the Positive and Negative Syndrome Scale (PANSS) for schizophrenia: Construct validity and interrater reliability. *Acta Psychiatrica Scandinavica, 86,* 463–468.

von Wolff, C. (1732). *Psychologia empirica.*

von Wolff, C. (1734). *Psychologia rationalis.*

Vossekuil, B., & Fein, R. A. (1997). *Final report: Secret Service Exceptional Case Study Project.* Washington, DC: U.S. Secret Service, Intelligence Division.

Vroom, V. H. (1964). *Work and motivation.* New York: Wiley.

Vygotsky, L. S. (1978). *Mind in society: The development of higher psychological processes.* Cambridge, MA: Harvard University Press.

Waddell, D. D. (1980). The Stanford-Binet: An evaluation of the technical data available since the 1972 restandardization. *Journal of School Psychology, 18,* 203–209.

Waehler, C. A. (1997). Drawing bridges between science and practice. *Journal of Personality Assessment, 69,* 482–487.

Wagner, B. M. (1997). Family risk factors for child and adolescent suicidal behavior. *Psychological Bulletin, 121,* 246–298.

Wagner, E. E. (1983). *The Hand Test.* Los Angeles: Western Psychological Services.

Wagner, R. K., & Compton, D. L. (2011). Dynamic assessment and its implications for RTI models. *Journal of Learning Disabilities, 44*(4), 311–312.

Wagstaff, G. F., Wheatcroft, J. M., Caddick, A. M., Kirby, L. J., & Lamont, E. (2011). Enhancing witness memory with techniques derived from hypnotic investigative interviewing: Focused meditation, eye-closure, and context reinstatement. *International Journal of Clinical and Experimental Hypnosis, 59*(2), 146–164.

Wainer, H. (1990). *Computerized adaptive testing: A primer.* Hillsdale, NJ: Erlbaum.

Wakefield, J. C. (1992a). The concept of mental disorder: On the boundary between biological facts and social values. *American Psychologist, 47,* 373–388.

Wakefield, J. C. (1992b). Disorder as harmful dysfunction: A conceptual critique of DSM-III-R's definition of mental disorder. *Psychological Review, 99,* 232–247.

Wald, A. (1947). *Sequential analysis.* New York: Wiley.

Wald, A. (1950). *Statistical decision function.* New York: Wiley.

Waldman, D. A., & Avolio, B. J. (1989). Homogeneity of test validity. *Journal of Applied Psychology, 74,* 371–374.

Wallen, G. R., Feldman, R. H., & Anliker, J. (2002). Measuring acculturation among Central American women with the use of a brief language scale. *Journal of Immigrant Health, 4,* 95–102.

Walker, H. M. (1976). *Walker Problem Behavior Identification Checklist.* Los Angeles: Western Psychological Services.

Walker, L. S., & Greene, J. W. (1991). The Functional Disability Inventory: Measuring a neglected dimension of child health status. *Journal of Pediatric Psychology, 16,* 39–58.

Walkup, J. (2000). Disability, health care, and public policy. *Rehabilitation Psychology, 45,* 409–422.

Wallace, A., & Liljequist, L. (2005). A comparison of the correlational structures and elevation patterns of the MMPI-2 Restructured Clinical (RC) and Clinical scales. *Assessment, 12,* 290–294.

Wallace, I. F., Gravel, J. S., McCarton, C. M., & Ruben, R. J. (1988). Otitis media and language development at 1 year of age. *Journal of Speech and Hearing Disorders, 53,* 245–251.

Wallen, G. R., Feldman, R. H., & Anliker, J. (2002). Measuring acculturation among Central American women with the use of a brief language scale. *Journal of Immigrant Health, 4,* 95–102.

Waller, N. G., & Zavala, J. D. (1993). Evaluating the big five. *Psychological Inquiry, 4,* 131–135.

Wallston, K. A., Wallston, B. S., & DeVellis, R. (1978). Development of the Multidimensional Health Locus of Control (MHLC) Scales. *Health Education Monographs, 6,* 160–170.

Wang, N. (2003). Use of the Rasch IRT model in standard setting: An item-mapping method. *Journal of Educational Measurement, 40*(3), 231–252.

Wang, T.-H. (2011). Implementation of Web-based dynamic assessment in facilitating junior high school students to learn mathematics. *Computers & Education, 56,* 1062–1071.

Wang, Y. J., & Minor, M. S. (2008). Validity, reliability, and applicability of psychophysiological techniques in marketing research. *Psychology & Marketing, 25*(2), *in press.*

Wantz, R. A. (1989). Review of the Parenting Stress Index. In J. C. Conoley & J. J. Kramer (Eds.), *The tenth mental measurements yearbook.* Lincoln: Buros Institute of Mental Measurements, University of Nebraska.

Ward, P. B., McConaghy, N., & Catts, S. V. (1991). Word association and measures of psychosis proneness in university students. *Personality and Individual Differences, 12,* 473–480.

Warfield, J. J., Kondo-Ikemura, K., & Waters, E. (2011). Measuring attachment security in rhesus macaques (Macaca mulatta): Adaptation of the attachment Q-set. *American Journal of Primatology, 73*(2), 109–118.

Waring, E. M., & Reddon, J. (1983). The measurement of intimacy in marriage: The Waring Questionnaire. *Journal of Clinical Psychology, 39,* 53–57.

Warmke, D. L. (1984). *Successful implementation of the "new" GATB in entry-level selection.* Presentation at the American Society for Personnel Administrators Region 4 Conference, October 15, Norfolk, VA.

Watkins, C. E., Jr. (1986). Validity and usefulness of WAIS-R, WISC-R, and WPPSI short forms. *Professional Psychology: Research and Practice, 17,* 36–43.

Watkins, C. E., Jr., Campbell, V. L., Nieberding, R., & Hallmark, R. (1995). Contemporary practice of psychological assessment by clinical psychologists. *Professional Psychology: Research and Practice, 26,* 54–60.

Watkins, E. O. (1976). *Watkins Bender-Gestalt Scoring System.* Novato, CA: Academic Therapy.

Watson, C. G. (1967). Relationship of distortion to DAP diagnostic accuracy among psychologists at three levels of sophistication. *Journal of Consulting Psychology, 31,* 142–146.

Watson, C. G., Felling, J., & Maceacherr, D. G. (1967). Objective draw-a-person scales: An attempted cross-validation. *Journal of Clinical Psychology, 23,* 382–386.

Watson, C. G., Thomas, D., & Anderson, P. E. D. (1992). Do computer-administered Minnesota Multiphasic Personality Inventories underestimate booklet-based scores? *Journal of Clinical Psychology, 48,* 744–748.

Watson, S. M. R., Gable, R. A., & Greenwood, C. R. (2011). Combining ecobehavioral assessment, functional assessment, and response to intervention to promote more effective classroom instruction. *Remedial and Special Education, 32*(4), 334–344.

Weaver, C. B., & Bradley-Johnson, S. (1993). A national survey of school psychological services for deaf and hard-of-hearing students. *American Annals of the Deaf, 138,* 267–274.

Webb, E. J., Campbell, D. T., Schwartz, R. D., & Sechrest, L. (1966). *Unobtrusive measures: Nonreactive research in the social sciences.* Chicago: Rand McNally.

Webb, M. S., Rodriguez-Esquivel, D., Baker, E., Reis, I. M. & Carey, M. P. (2010). Cognitive behavioral therapy to promote smoking cessation among African American smokers: A randomized clinical trial. *Journal of Consulting and Clinical Psychology, 78,* 24–33.

Webbe, F. M (2008). Sports neuropsychology. In A. M. Horton Jr. & D. Wedding (Eds.), *The neuropsychology handbook* (3rd ed.). New York: Springer.

Webster, C. D., Harris, G. T., Rice, M. E., Cormier, C., & Quinsey, V. L. (1994). *The violence prediction scheme.* Toronto: University of Toronto Centre of Criminology.

Webster, L., & Joubert, D. (2011). Use of the Adult Attachment Projective Picture System in an assessment of an adolescent in foster care. *Journal of Personality Assessment, 93*(5), 417–426.

Wechsler, D. (1939). *The measurement of adult intelligence.* Baltimore: Williams & Wilkins.

Wechsler, D. (1944). *The measurement of adult intelligence* (3rd ed.). Baltimore: Williams & Wilkins.

Wechsler, D. (1955). *Manual for the Wechsler Adult Intelligence Scale.* New York: Psychological Corporation.

Wechsler, D. (1958). *The measurement and appraisal of adult intelligence* (4th ed.). Baltimore: Williams & Wilkins.

Wechsler, D. (1967). *Manual for the Wechsler Preschool and Primary Scale of Intelligence.* New York: Psychological Corporation.

Wechsler, D. (1974). *Manual for the Wechsler Intelligence Scale for Children—Revised.* New York: Psychological Corporation.

Wechsler, D. (1975). Intelligence defined and undefined: A relativistic appraisal. *American Psychologist, 30,* 135–139.

Wechsler, D. (1981). *Manual for the Wechsler Adult Intelligence Scale—Revised.* New York: Psychological Corporation.

Wechsler, D. (1991). *Manual for the Wechsler Intelligence Scale for Children—Third Edition.* San Antonio: Psychological Corporation.

Wechsler, D. (1997). *Wechsler Adult Intelligence Scale—Third Edition.* San Antonio: Psychological Corporation.

Wechsler, D. (2002). *Wechsler Preschool and Primary Scale of Intelligence—Third edition (WPPSI-III), Technical and interpretive manual.* San Antonio: Psychological Corporation.

Wechsler, D. (2003). *Wechsler Intelligence Scale for Children—Fourth edition (WISC-IV), Technical and interpretive manual.* San Antonio: Psychological Corporation.

Wecker, N. S., Kramer, J. H., Wisniewski, A., et al. (2000). Age effects on executive ability. *Neuropsychology, 14,* 409–414.

Weed, N. C. (2006). Syndromal complexity, paradigm shifts, and the future of validation research: Comments on Nichols and Rogers, Sewell, Harrison, and Jordan. *Journal of Personality Assessment, 87,* 217–222.

Weed, N. C., Butcher, J. N., McKenna, T., & Ben-Porath, Y. S. (1992). New measures for assessing alcohol and drug abuse with the MMPI-2: The APS and AAS. *Journal of Personality Assessment, 58,* 389–404.

Wehmeyer, M. L., & Smith, J. D. (2006). Leaving the garden: Henry Herbert Goddard's exodus from the Vineland Training School. *Mental Retardation, 44,* 150–155.

Weiner, B. A. (1980). Not guilty by reason of insanity: A sane approach. *Chicago Kent Law Review, 56,* 1057–1085.

Weiner, I. B. (1966). *Psychodiagnosis in schizophrenia.* New York: Wiley.

Weiner, I. B. (1997). Current status of the Rorschach Inkblot Method. *Journal of Personality Assessment, 68,* 5–19.

Weiner, I. B. (2005). Integrative personality assessments with self-report and performance based measures. In S. Strack (Ed.), *Handbook of personology and psychopathology* (pp. 317–331). Hoboken, NJ: Wiley.

Weiner, I. B., & Kuehnle, K. (1998). Projective assessment of children and adolescents. In M. Hersen & A. Bellack (Eds.), *Comprehensive clinical psychology,* Vol. 3. Tarrytown, NY: Elsevier Science.

Weinstock, J., Ledgerwood, D. M., & Petry, N. M. (2007). The association between post-treatment gambling behavior and harm in pathological gamblers. *Psychology of Addictive Behaviors, 21,* 185–193.

Weinstock, J., Whelan, J. P., & Meyers, A. W. (2004). Behavioral assessment of gambling: An application of the Timeline Followback Method. *Psychological Assessment, 16,* 72–80.

Weinstock, J., Whelan, J. P., Meyers, A. W., & McCausland, C. (2007). The performance of two pathological gambling screens in college students. *Assessment, 14,* 399–407.

Weir, R. F. (1992). The morality of physician-assisted suicide. *Law, Medicine and Health Care, 20,* 116–126.

Weiss, A., King, J. E., & Enns, R. M. (2002). Subjective well-being is heritable and genetically correlated with dominance in chimpanzees (*Pan troglodytes*). *Journal of Personality and Social Psychology, 83,* 1141–1149.

Weiss, D. J. (1985). Adaptive testing by computer. *Journal of Consulting and Clinical Psychology, 53,* 774–789.

Weiss, D. J., & Davison, M. L. (1981). Test theory and methods. *Annual Review of Psychology, 32,* 629–658.

Weiss, D. J., & Vale, C. D. (1987). Computerized adaptive testing for measuring abilities and other psychological variables. In J. N. Butcher (Ed.), *Computerized psychological assessment: A practitioner's guide* (pp. 325–343). New York: Basic Books.

Weiss, H. M., & Cropanzano, R. (1996). Affective events theory: A theoretical discussion of the structure, causes, and consequences of affective experiences at work. *Research in Organizational Behavior, 18,* 1–74.

Weiss, L. G., Saklofske, D. H., Prifitera, A., & Holdnack, J. (2006). *WISC-IV Advanced Clinical Interpretation.* San Diego: Elsevier.

Weiss, M. D. (2010). The unique aspects of assessment of ADHD. *Primary Psychiatry, 17,* 21–25.

Weiss, P. A., Weiss, W. U., & Gacono, C. B. (2008). The use of the Rorschach in police psychology: Some preliminary thoughts. In C. B. Gacono et al. (Eds.), *The handbook of forensic assessment* (pp. 527–542). New York: Routledge/Taylor & Francis.

Weiss, R., & Summers, K. (1983). Marital Interaction Coding System III. In E. Filsinger (Ed.), *Marriage and family assessment: A sourcebook of family therapy.* Beverly Hills, CA: Sage.

Weisse, D. E. (1990). Gifted adolescents and suicide. *School Counselor, 37,* 351–358.

Weissman, H. N. (1991). Forensic psychological examination of the child witness in cases of alleged sexual abuse. *American Journal of Orthopsychiatry, 6,* 48–58.

Weizmann-Henelius, G., Kivilinna, E., & Eronen, M. (2009). The utility of Rorschach in forensic psychiatric evaluations: A case study. *Nordic Psychology, 62*(3), 36–49.

Welsh, G. S. (1948). An extension of Hathaway's MMPI profile coding system. *Journal of Consulting Psychology, 12,* 343–344.

Welsh, G. S. (1952). A factor study of the MMPI using scales with the item overlap eliminated. *American Psychologist, 7,* 341.

Welsh, G. S. (1956). Factor dimensions A and R. In G. S. Welsh & W. G. Dahlstrom (Eds.), *Basic readings on the MMPI in psychology and medicine* (pp. 264–281). Minneapolis: University of Minnesota Press.

Welsh, G. S., & Dahlstrom, W. G. (Eds.). (1956). *Basic readings on the MMPI in psychology and medicine.* Minneapolis: University of Minnesota Press.

Welsh, J. R., Kucinkas, S. K., & Curran, L. T. (1990). *Armed Services Vocational Aptitude Battery (ASVAB): Integrative review of validity studies* (Rpt 90-22). San Antonio: Operational Technologies Corp.

Werner, H., & Strauss, A. A. (1941). Pathology of figure-background relation in the child. *Journal of Abnormal and Social Psychology, 36,* 236–248.

Wertheimer, M. (1923). Untersuchungen zur Lehre von der Gestalt. *Psychologische Forschung* [Studies in the theory of Gestalt Psychology. *Psychology for Schools*], *4,* 301–303. Translated by Don Cantor in R. J. Herrnstein & E. G. Boring (1965), *A sourcebook in the history of psychology.* Cambridge, MA: Harvard University Press.

Wesman, A. G. (1968). Intelligent testing. *American Psychologist, 23,* 267–274.

West, L. J., & Ackerman, D. L. (1993). The drug-testing controversy. *Journal of Drug Issues, 23,* 579–595.

Westen, D., Barends, A., Leigh, J., Mendel, M., & Silbert, D. (1988). *Manual for coding dimensions of object relations and social cognition from interview data.* Unpublished manuscript, University of Michigan, Ann Arbor.

Westen, D., Silk, K. R., Lohr, N., & Kerber, K. (1985). *Object relations and social cognition: TAT scoring manual.* Unpublished manuscript, University of Michigan, Ann Arbor.

Westerman, J. W., & Simmons, B. L. (2007). The effects of work environment on the personality-performance relationship: An exploratory study. *Journal of Managerial Issues, 19*(2), 288–305.

Westling, D. L. (1996). What do parents of children with moderate and severe mental disabilities want? *Education and Training in Mental Retardation and Developmental Disabilities, 31,* 86–114.

Wexley, K. N., Yukl, G. A., Kovacs, S. Z., & Sanders, R. E. (1972). Importance of contrast effects in employment interviews. *Journal of Applied Psychology, 56,* 45–48.

White, B. L. (1971). *Human infants: Experience and psychological development.* Englewood Cliffs, NJ: Prentice-Hall.

White, D. M., Clements, C. B., & Fowler, R. D. (1985). A comparison of computer administration with standard administration of the MMPI. *Computers in Human Behavior, 1,* 153–162.

White, J. A., Davison, G. C., Haaga, D. A. F., & White, K. L. (1992). Cognitive bias in the articulated thoughts of depressed and nondepressed psychiatric patients. *Journal of Nervous and Mental Disease, 180,* 77–81.

White, J. M. (1963). *Everyday life in ancient Egypt.* New York: G. P. Putnam's Sons.

White, L. T. (1984). Attitudinal consequences of the preemployment polygraph examination. *Journal of Applied Social Psychology, 14,* 364–374.

White, R. W., Sanford, R. N., Murray, H. A., & Bellak, L. (1941, September). *Morgan-Murray Thematic Apperception Test: Manual of directions* [mimeograph]. Cambridge, MA: Harvard Psychological Clinic.

White, S., Santilli, G., & Quinn, K. (1988). Child evaluator's roles in child sexual abuse assessments. In E. B. Nicholson & J. Bulkley (Eds.), *Sexual abuse allegations in custody and visitation cases: A resource book for judges and court personnel* (pp. 94–105). Washington, DC: American Bar Association.

Whittington, M. K. (1998). The Karp inkblot response questionnaire: An evaluation of social desirability responding. *Dissertation Abstracts International: Section B. Sciences and Engineering, 59*(4-B), 1872.

Whitworth, R. H. (1984). Review of Halstead-Reitan Neuropsychological Battery and allied procedures. In D. J. Keyser & R. C. Sweetland (Eds.), *Test critiques* (Vol. 1, pp. 305–314). Kansas City: Test Corporation of America.

Whitworth, R. H., & Unterbrink, C. (1994). Comparison of MMPI-2 clinical and content scales administered to Hispanic and Anglo-Americans. *Hispanic Journal of Behavioral Sciences, 16,* 255–264.

Wicker, A. W. (1969). Attitudes versus actions: The relationship of verbal and overt behavioral responses to attitude objects. *Journal of Social Issues, 25,* 41–78.

Wickes, T. A., Jr. (1956). Examiner influences in a testing situation. *Journal of Consulting Psychology, 20,* 23–26.

Widiger, T. A. (1993). The DSM-III-R categorical personality disorder diagnoses: A critique and an alternative. *Psychological Inquiry, 4*(2), 75–90.

Widiger, T. A., & Clark, L. A. (2000). Toward DSM-V and the classification of psychopathology. *Psychological Bulletin, 126,* 946–963.

Widiger, T. A., & Samuel, D. B. (2009). Evidence-based assessment of personality disorders. *Personality Disorders: Theory, Research, and Treatment, S*(1), 3–17.

Wienstock, J., Whelan, J. P., & Meyers, A. W. (2004). Behavioral assessment of gambling: An application of the timeline followback method. *Psychological Assessment, 16,* 72–80.

Wigdor, A. K., & Garner, W. R. (1982). *Ability testing: Uses, consequences, and controversies.* Washington, DC: National Academy.

Wiggins, N. (1966). Individual viewpoints of social desirability. *Psychological Bulletin, 66,* 68–77.

Wilcox, R., & Krasnoff, A. (1967). Influence of test-taking attitudes on personality inventory scores. *Journal of Consulting Psychology, 31,* 185–194.

Wilkinson, G. S., & Robertson, G. J. (2006). *Wide Range Achievement Test-4 (WRAT-4).* Lutz, FL: Psychological Assessment Resources.

Willcutt, E. G., Boada, R., Riddle, M. W., et al. (2011). Colorado Learning Difficulties Questionnaire: Validation of a parent-report screening measure. *Psychological Assessment, 23*(3), Sep 2011, 778–791.

Williams, A. D. (2000). Fixed versus flexible batteries. In R. J. McCaffrey et al. (Eds.), *The practice of forensic neuropsychology: Meeting challenges in the courtroom* (pp. 57–70). New York: Plenum.

Williams, C. L. (1986). Mental health assessment of refugees. In C. L. Williams & J. Westermeyer (Eds.), *Refugee mental health in resettlement countries* (pp. 175–188). New York: Hemisphere.

Williams, C. L., & Butcher, J. N. (2011). *A beginner's guide to the MMPI–A.* Washington, DC: American Psychological Association.

Williams, J. M., & Shane, B. (1986). The Reitan-Indiana Aphasia Screening Test: Scoring and factor analysis. *Journal of Clinical Psychology, 42,* 156–160.

Williams, R. (1975). The BITCH-100: A culture-specific test. *Journal of Afro-American Issues, 3,* 103–116.

Williams, R. H., & Zimmerman, D. W. (1996a). Are simple gains obsolete? *Applied Psychological Measurement, 20,* 59–69.

Williams, R. H., & Zimmerman, D. W. (1996b). Are simple gain scores obsolete? Commentary on the commentaries of Collins and Humphreys. *Applied Psychological Measurement, 20,* 295–297.

Williams, S. K., Jr. (1978). The Vocational Card Sort: A tool for vocational exploration. *Vocational Guidance Quarterly, 26,* 237–243.

Williams, T. H., McIntosh, D. E., Dixon, F., Newton, J. H., & Youman, E. (2010). A confirmatory factor analysis of the Stanford–Binet Intelligence Scales, Fifth Edition, with a high-achieving sample. *Psychology in the Schools, 47,* 1071–1083.

Williams, T. Y., Boyd, J. C., Cascardi, M. A., & Poythress, N. (1996). Factor structure and convergent validity of the Aggression Questionnaire in an offender population. *Psychological Assessment, 8,* 398–403.

Wilmer, H. A., & Husni, M. (1951, December). An auditory sound association technique. *Science, 114,* 621–622.

Wilson, D. L. (2008). An exploratory study on the players of "Dungeons and Dragons." *Dissertation Abstracts International: Section B. Sciences and Engineering, 68*(7-B), 4879.

Wilson, G. G., & Vitousek, K. M. (1999). Self-monitoring in the assessment of eating disorders. *Psychological Assessment, 11,* 480–489.

Wilson, J. A. (1951). *The culture of ancient Egypt.* Chicago: University of Chicago Press.

Wilson, P. T., & Spitzer, R. L. (1969). A comparison of three current classification systems for mental retardation. *American Journal of Mental Deficiency, 74,* 428–435.

Wilson, S. L., Thompson, J. A., & Wylie, G. (1982). Automated psychological testing for the severely physically handicapped. *International Journal of Man-Machine Studies, 17,* 291–296.

Winner, E. (1996). *Gifted children: Myths and realities.* New York: Basic Books.

Winner, E. (2000). The origins and ends of giftedness. *American Psychologist, 55,* 159–169.

Winston, A. S. (1996). "As his name indicates": R. S. Woodworth's letters of reference and employment for Jewish psychologists in the 1930s. *Journal of the History of the Behavioral Sciences, 32,* 30–43.

Winston, A. S. (1998). "The defects of his race": E. G. Boring and antisemitism in American psychology, 1923–1953. *History of Psychology, 1,* 27–51.

Wirt, R. D., Lachar, D., Klinedinst, J. K., & Seat, P. D. (1984). *Multidimensional description of child personality: A manual for the Personality Inventory for Children.* (1984 revision by David Lachar.) Los Angeles: Western Psychological Services.

Wish, J., McCombs, K. F., & Edmonson, B. (1980). *Socio-Sexual Knowledge & Attitudes Test.* Chicago: Stoelting.

Witkin, H. A., & Berry, J. W. (1975). Psychological differentiation in cross-cultural perspective. *Journal of Cross-Cultural Psychology, 6,* 4–87.

Witkin, H. A., Dyk, R. B., Faterson, H. F., Goodenough, D. R., & Karp, S. A. (1962). *Psychological differentiation.* New York: Wiley.

Witkin, H. A., & Goodenough, D. R. (1977). Field dependence and interpersonal behavior. *Psychological Bulletin, 84,* 661–689.

Witkin, H. A., & Goodenough, D. R. (1981). *Cognitive styles: Essence and origins* (Psychological Issues Monograph 51). New York: International Universities.

Witkin, H. A., Lewis, H. B., Hertzman, M., Machover, K., Meissner, P. B., & Wapner, S. (1954). *Personality through perception: An experimental and clinical study.* New York: Harper.

Witkin, H. A., Moore, C.A., Goodenough, D. R., & Cox, P. W. (1977). Field-dependent and field-independent cogntive styles and their implications. *Review of Educational Research, 47,* 1–64

Witmer, L. (1907). Clinical psychology. *Psychological Clinic, 1,* 1–9.

Witt, J. C., & Elliott, S. N. (1985). Acceptability of classroom management strategies. In T. R. Kratochwill (Ed.), *Advances in school psychology* (Vol. 4, pp. 251–288). Hillsdale, NJ: Erlbaum.

Witt, P. (2003) Expert opinion: Some observations on observers of psychological testing. *American Psychology Law Society News, 23,* 3.

Witty, P. (1940). Some considerations in the education of gifted children. *Educational Administration and Supervision, 26,* 512–521.

Wixson, K. (2011). A systematic view of RTI research: Introduction to the special issue. *Elementary School Journal, 111*(4), 503–510.

Wober, M. (1974). Towards an understanding of the Kiganda concept of intelligence. In J. W. Berry & P. R. Dasen (Eds.), *Culture and cognition: Readings in cross-cultural psychology* (pp. 261–280). London: Methuen.

Wolfe, M. M., Yang, P. H., Wong, E. C., & Atkinson, D. R. (2001). Design and development of the European American values scale for Asian Americans. *Cultural Diversity and Ethnic Minority Psychology, 7*(3), 274–283.

Wolfner, G., Fause, D., & Dawes, R. M. (1993). The use of anatomically detailed dolls in sexual abuse evaluations: The state of the science. *Applied and Preventive Psychology, 2,* 1–11.

Wolfram, W. A. (1971). Social dialects from a linguistic perspective: Assumptions, current research, and future directions. In R. Shuy (Ed.), *Social dialects and interdisciplinary perspectives.* Washington, DC: Center for Applied Linguistics.

Wolf-Schein, E. G. (1993). Assessing the "untestable" client: ADLO. *Developmental Disabilities Bulletin, 21,* 52–70.

Wolk, R. L., & Wolk, R. B. (1971). *The Gerontological Appreception Test.* New York: Behavioral Publications.

Wollersheim, J. P. (1974). The assessment of suicide potential via interview methods. *Psychotherapy, 11,* 222–225.

Wong-Rieger, D., & Quintana, D. (1987). Comparative acculturation of Southeast Asians and Hispanic immigrants and sojourners. *Journal of Cross-Cultural Psychology, 18,* 145–162.

Woodcock, R. W. (1990). Theoretical foundations of the WJ-R measures of cognitive ability. *Journal of Psychoeducational Assessment, 8,* 231–258.

Woodcock, R. W. (1997). The Woodcock-Johnson Tests of Cognitive Ability–Revised. In D. P. Flanagan, J. L. Genshaft, & P. L. Harrison (Eds.), *Contemporary intellectual assessment: Theories, tests, and issues* (pp. 230–246). New York: Guilford.

Woodcock, R. W. (2011). *The Woodcock Reading Mastery Tests, Third Edition* (WRMT-III). San Antonio: Pearson Assessments

Woodcock, R. W., & Mather, N. (1989a). *WJ-R Tests of Cognitive Ability—Standard and Supplemental Batteries: Examiner's manual.* In R. W. Woodcock & M. B. Johnson, *Woodcock-Johnson Psychoeducational Battery—Revised.* Allen, TX: DLM Teaching Resources.

Woodcock, R. W., & Mather, N. (1989b, 1990). *WJ-R Tests of Achievement: Examiner's manual.* In R. W. Woodcock & M. B. Johnson, *Woodcock-Johnson Psychoeducational Battery–Revised.* Allen, TX: DLM Teaching Resources.

Woodcock, R. W., McGrew, K. S., & Mather, N. (2000). *Woodcock-Johnson III.* Itasca, IL: Riverside.

Woodward, J. (1972). Implications for sociolinguistics research among the deaf. *Sign Language Studies, 1,* 1–7.

Woodworth, M., & Porter, S. (2000). Historical foundations and current applications of criminal profiling in violent crime investigations. *Expert Evidence, 7*(4), 241–264.

Woodworth, R. S. (1917). *Personal Data Sheet.* Chicago: Stoelting.

Worchel, F. F., & Dupree, J. L. (1990). Projective story-telling techniques. In C. R. Reynolds & R. W. Kamphaus (Eds.), *Handbook of psychological and educational assessment of children: Personality, behavior, & context* (pp. 70–88). New York: Guilford.

World Health Organization. (2001). *International classification of functioning, disability, and health.* Geneva, Switzerland: Author.

Worlock, P., et al. (1986). Patterns of fractures in accidental and non-accidental injury in children. *British Medical Journal, 293,* 100–103.

Wright, B. D., & Stone, M. H. (1979). *Best test design: Rasch measurement.* Chicago: Mesa.

Wright, D. B., & Hall, M. (2007). How a "reasonable doubt" instruction affects decisions of guilt. *Basic and Applied Social Psychology, 29*(1), 91–98.

Wu, W., West, S. G., & Hughes, J. N. (2010). Effect of grade retention in first grade on psychosocial outcomes. *Journal of Educational Psychology, 102*(1), 135–152.

Wylonis, L. (1999). Psychiatric disability, employment, and the Americans with Disabilities Act. *Psychiatric Clinics of North America, 22,* 147–158.

Yañez, Y. T., & Fremouw, W. (2004). The application of the *Daubert* standard to parental capacity measures. *American Journal of Forensic Psychology, 22*(3) 5–28.

Yantz, C. L., & McCaffrey, R. J. (2005). Effects of a supervisor's observation on memory test performance of the examinee: Third party observer effect confirmed. *Journal of Forensic Neuropsychology, 4*(2), 27–38.

Yantz, C. L., & McCaffrey, R. J. (2009). Effects of parental presence and child characteristics on children's neuropsychological test performance: Third party observer effect confirmed. *Clinical Neuropsychologist, 23,* 118–132.

Yao, E. L. (1979). The assimilation of contemporary Chinese immigrants. *Journal of Psychology, 101,* 107–113.

Yarnitsky, D., Sprecher, E., Zaslansky, R., & Hemli, J. A. (1995). Heat pain thresholds: Normative data and repeatability. *Pain, 60,* 329–332.

Yeates, K. O., Ris, M. D., & Taylor, H. G. (Eds.). (2000). *Pediatric neuropsychology: Research, theory, and practice.* New York: Guilford Press.

Yell, N. (2008). A taxometric analysis of impression management and self-deception on the MMPI-2 and Rorschach among a criminal forensic population. *Dissertation Abstracts International: Section B. Sciences and Engineering, 68*(7-B), 4853.

Yerkes, R. M. (Ed.). (1921). *Psychological examining in the United States Army: Memoirs of the National Academy of Sciences* (Vol. 15). Washington, DC: Government Printing Office.

Yin, P., & Fan, X. (2000). Assessing the reliability of Beck Depression Inventory scores: Reliability generalization across studies. *Educational and Psychological Measurement, 60,* 201–223.

Yoo, J. J., Hinds, O., Ofen, N., et al. (2012). When the brain is prepared to learn: Enhancing human learning using real-time fMRI. *NeuroImage, 59*(1), 846–852.

Young, K. S. (2011). Clinical assessment of Internet-addicted clients. In K. S. Young & C. N. de Abreu (Eds.), *Internet addiction: A handbook and guide to evaluation and treatment* (pp. 19–34). Hoboken, NJ: Wiley.

Young, K. S., Pistner, M., O'Mara, J., & Buchanan, J. (1999). Cyber disorders: The mental health concern for the new millennium. *CyberPsychology & Behavior, 2,* 475–479.

Younger, J. B. (1991). A model of parenting stress. *Research on Nursing and Health, 14,* 197–204.

Youngjohn, J. R., & Crook, T. H., III. (1993). Stability of everyday memory in age-associated memory impairment: A longitudinal study. *Neuropsychology, 7,* 406–416.

Yussen, S. R., & Kane, P. T. (1980). *Children's conception of intelligence.* Madison report for the project on studies of instructional programming for the individual student, University of Wisconsin, Technical Report #546.

Zapf, P. A., & Roesch, R. (2011). Future directions in the restoration of competency to stand trial. *Current Directions in Psychological Science, 20,* 43–47.

Zea, M. C., Asner-Self, K. K., Birman, D., & Buki, L. P. (2003). The Abbreviated Multidimensional Acculturation Scale: Empirical validation with two Latino/Latina samples. *Cultural Diversity and Ethnic Minority Psychology, 9*(2), 107–126.

Zebehazy, K. T., Zimmerman, G. J., & Fox, L. A. (2005). Use of digital video to assess orientation and mobility observational skills. *Journal of Visual Impairment and Blindness, 99,* 646–658.

Zedeck, S., & Cascio, W. F. (1984). Psychological issues in personnel decisions. *Annual Review of Psychology, 35,* 461–518.

Zedeck, S., Cascio, W. F., Goldstein, I. L., & Outtz, J. (1996). Sliding bands: An alternative to top-down selection. In R. S. Barrett (Ed.), *Fair employment strategies in human resource management* (pp. 222–234). Westport, CT: Quorum Books/Greenwood.

Zelig, M., & Beidleman, W. B. (1981). Investigative hypnosis: A word of caution. *International Journal of Clinical and Experimental Hypnosis, 29,* 401–412.

Zenderland, L. (1998). *Measuring minds: Henry Herbert Goddard and the origins of American intelligence testing.* Cambridge, MA: Cambridge University Press.

Zhang, L.-M., Yu, L.-S., Wang, K.-N., et al. (1997). The psychophysiological assessment method for pilot's professional reliability. *Aviation, Space, & Environmental Medicine, 68,* 368–372.

Zhou, X., Zhu, J., & Weiss, L.G. (2010). Peeking inside the "Black Box" of the Flynn effect: Evidence from three Wechsler instruments. *Journal of Psychoeducational Assessment, 28,* 399–411.

Zickar, M. J., & Broadfoot, A. A. (2009). The partial revival of a dead horse? Comparing classical test theory and item response theory. In C. F. Lance, & R. J. Vandenberg (Eds.), *Statistical and methodological myths and urban legends: Doctrine, verity and fable in the organizational and social sciences* (pp. 37–59). New York: Routledge.

Zieziula, F. R. (Ed.). (1982). *Assessment of hearing-impaired people.* Washington, DC: Gallaudet College.

Zimmerman, I. L., & Woo-Sam, J. M. (1978). Intelligence testing today: Relevance to the school age child. In L. Oettinger (Ed.), *Psychologists and the school age child with MBD/LD.* New York: Grune & Stratton.

Zinchenko, V. P. (2007). Thought and word: The approaches of L. S. Vygotsky and G. G. Shpet. In H. Daniels, M. Cole, & J.V. Wertsch (Eds.), *The Cambridge companion to Vygotsky* (pp. 212–245). New York: Cambridge University Press.

Zink v. State, 278 SW 3d 170–Mo: Supreme Court 2009.

Zirkel, P. A., & Krohn, N. (2008). RtI after IDEA: A summary of state laws. *Teaching Exceptional Children, 40*(3), 71–73.

Zonda, T. (2006). One-hundred cases of suicide in Budapest: A case-controlled psychological autopsy study. *Crisis: The Journal of Crisis Intervention and Suicide Prevention, 27*(3), 125–129.

Zubeidat, I., Sierra, J. C., Salinas, J. M., & Rojas-García, A. (2011). Reliability and validity of the Spanish version of the Minnesota Multiphasic Personality Inventory–Adolescent (MMPI-A). *Journal of Personality Assessment, 93*(1), 26–32.

Zubin, J. (1939, November 20). Letter to B. F. Skinner. (B. F. Skinner Papers, Harvard University Archives, Cambridge, MA).

Zubin, J., Eron, L. D., & Schumer, F. (1965). *An experimental approach to projective techniques.* New York: Wiley.

Zucker, S. (1985). *MSCA/K-ABC with high risk pre-schoolers.* Paper presented at the Annual Meeting of the National Association of School Psychologists, Las Vegas.

Zucker, S., & Copeland, E. P. (1987). *K-ABC/McCarthy Scale performance among three groups of "at-risk" pre-schoolers.* Paper presented at the Annual Meeting of the National Association of School Psychologists, Las Vegas.

Zuckerman, M. (1979). Traits, states, situations, and uncertainty. *Journal of Behavioral Assessment, 1,* 43–54.

Zuckerman, M. (1990). Some dubious premises in research and theory on racial differences. *American Psychologist, 45,* 1297–1303.

Zumbo, B. D., & Taylor, S. V. (1993). The construct validity of the Extraversion subscales of the Myers-Briggs Type Indicator. *Canadian Journal of Behavioural Science, 25,* 590–604.

Zuniga, M. E. (1988). Assessment issues with Chicanas: Practice implications. *Psychotherapy, 25,* 288–293.

Zuroff, D. C., Mongrain, M., & Santor, D. A. (2004). Conceptualizing and measuring personality vulnerability to depression: Comment on Coyne and Whiffen (1995). *Psychological Bulletin, 130*(3), 489–511.

Zwahlen, H. T., Schnell, T., Liu, A., et al. (1998). Driver's visual search behaviour. In A. G. Gale et al. (Eds.), *Vision in vehicles–VI* (pp. 3–40). Oxford, England: Elsevier.

Zweigenhaft, R. L. (1984). *Who gets to the top? Executive suite discrimination in the eighties.* New York: American Jewish Committee Institute of Human Relations.

Zwick, R., & Himelfarb, I. (2011). The effect of high school socioeconomic status on the predictive validity of SAT scores and high school grade-point average. *Journal of Educational Measurement, 48*(2), 101–121.

Zytowski, D. G. (1996). Three decades of interest inventory results: A case study. *Career Development Quarterly, 45,* 141–148.

# Credits

## Text/Line Art

**Chapter 6**—Table 6-1: From C. H. Lawshe, "A Quantitative Approach to Content Validity," Personnel Psychology(1975) 28, 563-575. Reprinted with permission from Personnel Psychology; Fig. 6-4: From the Manual of Differential Aptitude Tests, Fifth Edition, Form C (DAT 5). Copyright © 1990 NCS Pearson, Inc. Reproduced with permission. All rights reserved. "Differential Aptitude Tests" and "DAT" are trademarks, in the US and/or other countries, of Pearson Education, Inc. or its affiliate(s); Table 6-2: From the Manual of Differential Aptitude Tests, Fifth Edition, Form C (DAT 5). Copyright © 1990 NCS Pearson, Inc. Reproduced with permission. All rights reserved. "Differential Aptitude Tests" and "DAT" are trademarks, in the US and/or other countries, of Pearson Education, Inc. or its affiliate(s); Fig. 6-5: From Test Service Bulletin #37, "How Effective Are Your Tests?" Copyright © 1980 NCS Pearson, Inc. Reproduced with permission. All rights reserved.

**Chapter 8**—Close-Up: From J. Millman and J.A. Arter, 1984, "Issues in Item Banking," Journal of Educational Measurement, 21, 315-330; copyright © 1984 by the National Council on Measurement Education. Reprinted with permission; Fig. 8-4: Reprinted by permission of Waveland Press, Inc. from M.J. Allen and W.M. Yen, Introduction to Measurement Theory, First Edition. (Long Grove, IL: Waveland Press, Inc., 1979 [reissued 2002]). All rights reserved; Fig. 8-5: Reprinted by permission of Waveland Press, Inc. from M.J. Allen and W.M. Yen, Introduction to Measurement Theory, First Edition. (Long Grove, IL: Waveland Press, Inc., 1979 [reissued 2002]). All rights reserved; Fig. 8-6: From Measurement Theory for the Behavioral Sciences by Ghiselli, Campbell, and Zedeck. Copyright © 1981 by W.H. Freeman and Company. Used with permission.

**Chapter 10**—Table 10-1: From the Stanford-Binet Intelligence Scales, Fifth Edition, "Assessment Service Bulletin 1: History of the Stanford-Binet Intelligence Scales: Content and Psychometrics," by Kirk A. Becker, © 2003, Austin: PRO-ED. Used with permission.

**Chapter 11**—Table 11-3: From Kaufman Sequential or Simultaneous (K-SOS). Copyright © 1984 NCS Pearson, Inc. Reproduced with permission. All rights reserved.

**Chapter 13**—Table 13-5: From D.B. Hartmann, B.L. Roper, and D.C. Bradford, "Some Relationships between Behavioral and Traditional Assessment," in Journal of Behavioral Assessment, 1, 3-21. © 1979. Reprinted with kind permission from Springer Science+Business Media B.V; Everyday Psychometrics: Text and photo courtesy of Supervised Lifestyles Health, Inc.

**Chapter 14**—Fig. 14-1 (right): Reproduced by permission of Jason Aronson, Inc.

**Chapter 15**—Fig. 15-6: From "Use of the Visual Motor Gestalt Teset in the Diagnosis of Learning Disabilities" by Lauretta Bender, 1970, The Journal of Special Education, 4(1), 29-39. Copyright © 1970 The Journal of Special Education by PRO-ED, Inc. Reproduced with permission of PRO-ED, Inc. in the format Textbook via Copyright Clearance Center.

**Chapter 16**—Table 16-2: From Dennis R. Laker, "The Career Wheel," in Journal of Employment Counseling, June 2002, p. 71. Reproduced with permission of American Counseling Association in the format Textbook via Copyright Clearance Center; Table 16-4: From D.W. Bray, "The Assessment Center and the Study of Lives," American Psychologist, 1982, 37, 180-189, Table 2 p. 184. Copyright © 1982 by the American Psychological Association. Reprinted with permission; Fig. 16-6: From J.E. Champagne, "Job Recruitment of the Unskilled," Personnel Journal, 48, 259-268.

## Photos

**Chapter 1**—P. 5: Courtesy of Stephen Finn; P. 8: Julian Finney/Getty Images; P. 11: Kevin Winter/Tonight Show/Getty Images; P. 12: Time & Life Pictures/Getty Images; P. 13: Brigitte Sporrer/cultura/Corbis; P. 15: Courtesy of Gary A. Mirka, Department of Industrial Engineering, North Carolina State University; P. 20: © 2008 Ronald Jay Cohen. All rights reserved; P. 28 (top to bottom): Tom Stewart/Corbis; © 2001 Ronald Jay Cohen. All rights reserved; David Linton; P. 29 (top to bottom): © 1940 Meier Art Judgment Test, The University of Iowa, Iowa City, IA; Courtesy Sammons Preston Rolyan; Helicorp, Inc.; P. 30: National Archives; P. 32: Jeff Topping/AFP/Getty Images; P. 34: Courtesy of the Buros Center for Testing.

**Chapter 2**—P. 39: The Art Archive at Art Resource, NY; P. 42 left: Archives of the History of American Psychology—The University of Akron Archives; P. 42 right: Courtesy of Hudson Cattell; P. 46: Brown Brothers; P. 48: Archives of the History of American Psychology—The University of Akron Archives; P. 54: Courtesy of Nathaniel V. Mohatt; P. 59: NASA; P. 69: Library of Congress Prints and Photographs Division [LC-USZ62-72266].

**Chapter 3**—P. 82: Courtesy Stoelting Co, Wood Dale, IL; P. 108: University College, London; P. 110: Archives of the History of American Psychology—The University of Akron Archives; P. 116: Courtesy of Benoit Verdon.

**Chapter 4**—P. 119: Brand X Pictures/Jupiterimages; P. 130: Brand X Pictures/PunchStock; P. 142 top: Courtesy of Steve Julius; P. 142 bottom: Courtesy of Howard Atlas.

**Chapter 5**—P. 149: Byron Rollins/AP Images; P. 165: Brand X Pictures; P. 174: Courtesy of Bryce B. Reeve.

Chapter 6—P. 183: Arthur Schatz/Getty Images; P. 185: Courtesy of Adam Shoemaker; P. 186: John Rowley/Getty Images; P. 189 both: Ingram Publishing.

Chapter 7—P. 214: Dynamic Graphics/Jupiterimages; P. 216: Courtesy of Erik Viirre; P. 234: Ethan Miller/Getty Images.

Chapter 8—P. 247: Courtesy of University of North Carolina at Chapel Hill, L.L. Thurstone Psychometric Laboratory; P. 269: Courtesy of Scott Birkeland.

Chapter 9—P. 293: Con Tanasiuk/Design Pics; P. 297: Courtesy of Barbara C Pavlo; P. 298: Reproduced with permission from the author from Well, Assessment and Management of Developmental Changes and Problems in Children, Second Edition, C.V. Mosby, 1981; P. 301: The Granger Collection; P. 304: Bongarts/Getty Images; P. 307: Jon Kopaloff/FilmMagic/Getty Images; P. 310: Chase Jarvis/Getty Images; P. 316: © 2012 Ronald Jay Cohen. All rights reserved. May not be reproduced without permission. Thanks to photo model, Susan R. Cohen.

Chapter 10—P. 327: © 2004 Ronald Jay Cohen. Photo by Angel G. Morales with special thanks to Terence Ramnarine and "les zombies", Ricky Ilermont and Ulrick Pierre; P. 353: Courtesy of Rebecca Anderson; P. 354: Courtesy of Maria Kozhevnikov. May not be reproduced without permission.

Chapter 11—P. 360: Courtesy of Eliane Hack; P. 362: Sovofoto; P. 372: Annie Griffiths Belt/Corbis; P. 375: Courtesy Mark E. Swerdlik.

Chapter 12—P. 396: AFP/Getty Images; P. 397: Johns Hopkins University; P. 400: © 1993 Ronald Jay Cohen; P. 407: Drexel University; P. 408: U.S. Navy photo by MC3 Remus Borisov; UNCLASSIFIED/Cleared for Public release; CDR Robert T. Durand, JTF-GTMO PAO; P. 409: Courtesy of Sublogic Corporation, Champaign, IL; P. 410:

TM and Copyright © 20th Century-Fox Film Corp. All Rights Reserved. Everett Collection; P. 428: Courtesy of Dr. James Butcher.

Chapter 13—P. 443: © Hans Huber Publishers, Bern; P. 447: Courtesy of Rorschach Workshops; P. 450: Courtesy of Harvard University News Office; P. 451: Courtesy Henry A. Murray; P. 460: Bettmann/Corbis; P. 469: Courtesy of Anthony Bram; P. 477: Courtesy of Supervised Lifestyles Health, Inc.; P. 483 top left: Paul Burns/Blend Images/Getty Images; P. 483 top right: Ingram Publishing; P. 483 bottom left: Photo Alto/PunchStock; P. 483 bottom right: The McGraw-Hill Companies, Inc./Joe DeGrandis, photographer; P. 485:© 2001 by Shirley Eberson. All rights reserved. May not be reproduced without permission; P. 486: Paul J. Sutton/Duomo/Corbis.

Chapter 14—P. 503: Courtesy of Joel Goldberg; P. 513: Doug Mills/AFP/Getty Images; P. 520 left: CAT-H Card reproduced by permission of the publisher, CPS. Inc., Larchmont, NY; P. 520 right: Reproduced by permission of Jason Aronson, Inc.

Chapter 15—P. 533: Goldstein-Scheerer Tests of Abstract and Concrete Thinking. © 1945, renewed 1972 by the Psychological Corporation. Reproduced by permission; 543: Courtesy of Jeanne P. Ryan; P. 546: © 2001 Ronald Jay Cohen. All rights reserved; P. 547: Archive Photos/Getty Images; P. 550: Courtesy of Dr. Peter Schilder; P. 557: Courtesy Stoelting Co, Wood Dale, IL; Pp. 562, 563: Courtesy General Electric Medical Systems.

Chapter 16—P. 567: © Warner Bros. Pictures/Everett Collection; P. 570: Courtesy Lafayette Instrument Co.; P. 577 both: Courtesy of the Center for Applications of Psychological Type, Inc.; P. 586: Courtesy of Dr. Douglas Bray; P. 587: Redd Huber-Pool/Getty Images; P. 599: Courtesy of Chris Gee; P. 611: Public domain.

# Name Index

Brogden, H. E., 229
Broitman, J., 359
Brook, J. S., 510
Brotemarkle, R. A., 42
Brotherhood, J. R., 582
Brown, C. E., 13
Brown, D. C., 208
Brown, R. D., 413
Brown, R. T., 204, 205
Brown, S. P., 598
Bruce, J. M., 26
Bruininks, R. H., 579
Brunch, M. B., 141
Brunner, N. A., 551
Bryan, J., 69, 70, 71
Bryant, S., 458
Bucholz, K. K., 500
Buck, J. N., 347, 463, 464
Buckner, F., 75
Bucofsky, D., 392
Budoff, M., 361
Bukatman, B. A., 515
Bumann, B., 66
Burgess, A. W., 523
Burisch, M., 402, 422
Burke, M. J., 574
Burke, P. J., 419
Burke, R. J., 598
Burns, A., 100
Burns, E., 33
Burns, R. C., 464
Burns, R. K., 593
Buros, O. K., 34, 44, 66
Burwen, L. S., 395
Bushman, B. J., 396
Butcher, J. N., 277, 428, 429,
    433, 434, 528
Butters, N., 545
Büttner, G., 359
Bux, D. A., 510
Byham, W. C., 588
Byrne, D., 393
Byrne, G. J., 4
Byrnes, M. M., 545

Cai, C.-H., 466
Calhoon, M. B., 33
Callahan, C. A., 380
Callahan, J., 69
Callero, P. L., 401
Camara, W. J., 577
Camilli, G., 271
Campbell, D. P., 277, 566
Campbell, D. T., 203, 395
Campbell, W. H., 494
Campos, L. P., 405
Canivez, G. L., 326, 342
Cannon-Bowers, J. A., 594
Caplan, L. J., 495
Capraro, M. M., 578
Capraro, R. M., 578
Capretz, L. F., 578
Care, E., 565
Carey, J. C., 436
Carey, N. B., 196
Carey, W. B., 376
Carlson, V., 521

Carmichael, L., 302
Carnevale, J. J., 4
Carpenter, P. A., 555
Carpenter, W. T., 72
Carroll, J. B., 293, 294,
    295, 336
Carroll, K. M., 510
Carskadon, T. G., 578
Carstairs, J., 17
Carstairs, J., 17
Carter, B. L., 509
Caruso, J. C., 158
Carver, R. P., 317n5
Cascio, W. F., 209, 219, 220,
    236, 574
Cash, T. F., 277
Caspi, A., 311, 485
Cassel, R. N., 413
Catalano, R., 512
Cattell, H. E. P., 419
Cattell, J. M., 41, 42, 458
Cattell, P., 315, 375
Cattell, R. B., 42, 293, 294,
    309, 324, 394, 414, 419
Caught, K., 598
Cavanaugh, J. L., 516
Ceci, S. J., 523
Cerney, M. S, 445
Chamberlain, K., 192
Chamorro-Premuzic, T., 310
Champagne, J. E., 594, 595
Chan, D. W., 311
Chan, K.-Y., 349
Chance, N. A., 436
Chaney, E. F., 509
Chang, L., 420
Chang, S.-R., 269
Chantler, L., 523
Chaplin, W. F., 118, 398
Chapman, J., 467
Chapman, J. C., 2
Chapman, R. L., 556
Chapman, L., 467
Chappin, S. R., 510
Chartrand, J. M., 569
Chase, D., 326
Chave, E. J., 244, 603
Chawarski, M. C., 213
Chen, Y., 55
Chess, S., 310
Cheung, F. M., 506
Chin, J. L., 508
Chinoy, E., 312
Chira-Chavala, T., 602
Cho, H., 605
Christensen, A. L., 559
Church, A. T., 419
Cianci, H. R., 578
Cicchetti, D., 521
Citrin, L. B., 604
Cizek, G. J., 141, 388
Clark, B., 308
Clark, L. A., 492
Cleckley, H., 516
Clift, R. J., 482
Clippard, L. F., 597
Cloninger, C. R., 101
Coalson, D. L., 335

Coggins, M. H., 513, 514
Cohen, B. M., 588
Cohen, J., 289, 507, 588
Cohen, R. J., 26, 45, 64,
    501n2, 512, 582, 596,
    600, 601, 608, 609, 610
Cohen, S., 581
Cole, D. J., 389
Cole, S. T., 313
Coleman, M. R., 359
Collier, C., 359
Collins, J. R., 220
Collins, L. M., 150
Collins, M., 565
Colom, R., 309
Comer, D. R., 590, 591
Compton, D. L., 362
Compton, D. M., 547
Condon, C. A., 277
Cone, J. D., 475, 478
Connolly, A. J., 383
Constantinou, M., 20
Conti, R. P., 466
Cooke, N. J., 594
Cooley, E. J., 384
Cooper, A., 451
Copas, J. B., 512
Copersino, M., 474
Cornell, D. G., 403
Cortes, D. E., 436
Cortina, J. M., 158
Corwyn, R. F., 510
Costa, P. T., Jr., 406, 415, 416,
    419, 420, 576
Cote, J. A., 484
Coupe, J. J., 518
Court, J. H., 501n2
Cox, J., 518
Coyne, I., 71
Coyne, J. C., 501n2
Cramer, P., 454
Cronbach, L. J., 154, 157,
    167, 168, 195, 229, 230,
    305n3, 574
Crook, T. H., III., 304, 556
Crosbie, J., 561
Crosby, F. J., 57
Cross, T. L., 308
Crowne, D. P., 203
Crundall, D. E., 547
Cuéllar, I., 436
Cundick, B. P., 312
Cunningham, M. R., 485
Cureton, E. E., 266
Custer, M., 327

Dahlstrom, L. E., 422
Dahlstrom, W. B., 312
Dahlstrom, W. G., 398, 422,
    423, 428
Daigneault, S., 546
Daley, C. E., 312
D'Amato, A., 597
Dana, J., 529
Dana, R. H., 416, 497, 504,
    505, 508
Daneman, M., 555

Danford, G. S., 33
Dangerfield, R., 183, 184
Daniels, K., 598
Das, J. P., 295, 296, 346, 384
Dattilio, F. M., 21
Davenport, C., 49
Davids, A., 461
Davidson, H., 444
Davies, G. M., 523
Davies, P. L., 100
Davis, D. R., 311
Davis, G. A., 308
Davis, J. M., 359
Davison, G. C., 274
Dawes, R. M., 527
Dazzi, C., 410
De Champlain, A. F.,
    173, 281
De Corte, W., 220
De Leo, D., 21
Deadrick, D. L., 436
Deary, I. J., 309, 311
Decker, J. T., 597
Decker, S. L., 552
Decroly, O., 48
Del Giudice, M. J., 448
Delahunty, R. J., 575
DeLaRosa, M., 510
Dellis, D. C., 555
Dellis, N. P., 468
DelVecchio, W. F., 120, 395
DeMars, C. E., 282
DeMaso, D. R., 507
DeMoivre, A., 98
DeMulder, E. K., 413
Dennis, M. G., 302
Dennis, W., 302
Denton, W. H., 494
DePaulo, B. M., 577
Derue, D. S., 4
Detterman, D. K., 286
DeVito, E. E., 563
Devlin, B., 311
Diamond, B. L., 497
Dickson, C. R., 476
Dietz, P. E., 514
Diller, L., 534
Dion, K. K., 373
Dipboye, R. L., 10
DiRienzo, C., 578
DiStefano, C., 326
Diven, K., 467
Dixon, M., 10
Dohrenwend, B. P., 430
Dollinger, S. J., 378
Dombrowski, S. C., 326
Donahue, E. M., 401
Donald, A., 507
Doty, R. L., 537
Dougherty, T. M., 304
Douthitt, E. A., 20
Draguns, J. G., 505
Dreger, R. M., 312
Drogin, E. Y., 309
DuBois, P. H., 38
Duchek, J. M., 547
Duckworth, J., 311

Kebbell, M. R., 496, 497
Keddy, P., 448
Keefe, F. J., 495
Kehoe, J. F., 128
Keiser, R. E., 454
Keith, T. Z., 296, 342, 384
Kelley, C., 579
Kelley, S. J., 521, 523
Kelley, T. L., 66, 266
Kellner, C. H., 563
Kelly, D. H., 482
Kelly, E. J., 397
Keltner, D., 485
Kempe, R. S., 521
Kendall, P. C., 274
Kennedy, R. S., 587
Kenny, M. C., 487
Kent, G. H., 458
Kent, N., 311
Kerlinger, F. N., 82
Kern, J. M., 481
Kim, B. S. K., 436
King, D. A., 547
King, K. W., 467
King, M. A., 523
Kingslinger, H. J., 579
Kinston, W., 519
Kinzie, J. D., 508
Kippax, S., 510
Kirby, J., 354
Kirmayer, L. J., 493
Kisamore, J. L., 115, 575
Kitayama, S., 54, 55
Klauer, S. E., 25
Klein, D. F., 493
Klein, N., 399
Kleinman, A., 505
Kleinman, A. M., 506
Kleinman, J., 505
Kleinmuntz, B., 483
Kline, R. B., 403
Klinger, E., 274
Klonoff, E. A., 436, 510
Klopfer, B., 73, 444
Kluckhohn, F. R., 438
Knoff, H. M., 463, 464
Knowles, E. S., 277
Koenig, K. A., 378
Koff, E., 463n7
Kollins, S. H., 374
Kolotkin, R. A., 481
Kongs, S. K., 545
Koppitz, E. M., 551
Korchin, S. J., 444
Korkman, M., 560
Korman, A. K., 56
Kotov, R., 399
Kottke, J. L., 448
Kouzes, J. M., 4
Kozhevnikov, M., 274, 354
Kraepelin, E., 42, 458
Kranzler, G., 80n5
Kranzler, J. H., 296
Krasner, M. S., 597
Krasnoff, A., 467
Krauss, D. A., 66
Kreifelts, B., 286
Kresel, J. J., 522

Krikorian, R., 546
Krohn, E. J., 304, 384
Krohn, N., 358
Krug, S. E., 419
Kubinger, K. D., 269
Kubiszyn, T. W., 57, 507
Kuder, F., 568
Kuder, G. F., 154, 155
Kudoh, T., 485
Kuehnle, K., 468
Kuhlmann, F., 321
Kullback, S., 80n5
Kuncel, N. R., 379, 380
Kupfer, D. J., 492, 512
Kurt, A., 405
Kurtz, J. E., 468
Kwan, V. S., 399, 400, 420

Laabs, G. J., 141
Lachar, D., 403
LaFrance, M., 485
Laker, D. R., 580
Lally, S. J., 511
Lam, C. S., 569
Lamb, M. E., 518
Lambert, E. W., 561
Lamp, R. E., 304, 384
Landrine, H., 436, 510
Landy, F. J., 182, 206
Lane, H., 513
Lane, S., 384
Lang, P. J., 509
Langer, E. J., 467
Langlois, J. H., 372, 373
Lanyon, R. I., 428, 482
Laplace, M. d., 98
Larkin, J. E., 569
LaRose, R., 605
Larrabee, G. J., 530
Larson, J. C., 311
Larson, J. R., 602
Larson, L. M., 399, 569
Larvie, V., 558
Larzelere, R., 519
Latimer, E. J., 69
Lau, B., 506
Laurence, J. R., 497
Lavin, M., 70
Lavrakas, P. J., 604
Lawrence, J., 540
Lawshe, C. H., 187
Lazarus, A. A., 609
Leach, M. M., 19, 67n5
Leahy, A., 303
Ledbetter, M. F., 277–278
Ledesma, R. D., 413
Lee, H.-J., 483
Lee, M., 70, 563
Lee, S. D., 467
Lee, S. E., 25
Lees-Haley, P. R., 428
Lega, L. I., 436
Lehtinen, L. E., 534
Lemos, G. C., 203
Leon-Carrion, J., 545
Leong, F. T., 579
Leong, F. T. L., 436
LePine, J. A., 399

Lerdau, M., 380
Lerner, B., 366
Lerner, P. M., 444
Lesser, G. S., 312
Lessinger, L. H., 510
Levesque, L. L., 605
Levine, E., 438
Levitt, K., 405
Lewinsohn, P. M., 512
Lewis, C., 157
Lewis, D. M., 238
Lewis-Fernandez, R., 491
Lezak, M. D., 541
Li, H., 605
Libby, W., 449
Lichtenberger, E. O., 328
Lichtenstein, D., 419
Lidz, C. S., 6
Lidz, C. W., 192, 512
Liebler, A., 485
Lievens, F., 220
Likert, R., 247, 248, 603
Lilienfeld, S. O., 465, 493
Liljequist, L., 432
Lim, J., 428
Lim, K. V., 436
Limber, S., 193, 194
Lin, T. Y., 506
Lindell, M. K., 187
Lindgren, B., 96
Lindskog, C. O., 342
Lindstrom, E., 101, 499
Lindzey, G., 393, 394
Linehan, M. M., 512
Lipinski, T., 304
Lipsitt, P. D., 515
Lipton, J. P., 66
Lis, A., 468
Little Soldier, D., 314
Locke, D. E. C., 432
Locke, E. A., 598
Locke, H. J., 202, 519
Löckenhoff, C. E., 581
Loevinger, J., 459
Loewenstein, D. A., 553
Lofthouse, N., 482
Loftus, E. F., 523
Loken, E., 380
London, P., 501n2
Longabaugh, R., 505
López, S., 405, 416
López, S. R., 435, 505, 506
Lord, F. M., 168
Lorr, M., 578
Lovejoy, M. C., 376
Lowman, J. C., 519
Loyd, B. H., 523, 524
Lüdtke, O., 120
Lung, R. J., 522
Luria, A. R., 295, 346, 362, 384, 559
Lykken, D. T., 483
Lynn, R., 303, 311

MacAndrew, C., 509
Machover, K., 463, 464
Mack, J. L., 546
MacKinnon, D. W., 2

Madaus, G. F., 366
Madden, J. J., 24
Maehler, C., 359
Mael, F. A., 56
Magnello, M. E., 108
Malec, J. F., 305
Malgady, R. G., 416
Malone, P. S., 307
Mannarino, A. P., 523
Manson, T. M., 575
Manz, C. C., 481
Maraist, C. C., 419
Maraun, M. D., 204
Marchese, M. C., 487, 527
Marcotte, T. D., 561
Marek-Schroer, M. F., 389
Marinangeli, M. G., 494
Marin-Martinez, F., 115
Marino, L., 493
Marinus, J., 561
Mark, M. M., 65
Markman, H., 478
Markon, K. E., 494
Markus, H., 54, 55
Marlowe, D., 203
Marquette, B. W., 299
Marshall, G. N., 26
Marson, D. C., 72
Martin, C. R., 413
Martin, D. C., 578
Martin, H., 4, 434
Marx, E., 406
Maslach, C., 597
Masling, J. M, 447, 467, 487, 488
Maslow, A. H., 594, 596
Massey, D. S., 604
Masuda, M., 436
Matarazzo, J. D., 300, 317, 511
Matchett, W. F., 507
Mathes, S., 452
Mathieu, J. E., 599
Matsumoto, D., 485
Maurer, T. J., 236, 486, 579
Maxwell-McCaw, D., 436
May, M. A., 395
Mayfield, E. C., 593
Mayotte, S., 17
Mazur, A., 485
Mazzocco, M. M. M., 545
McArthur, C., 566
McArthur, D. S., 455
McCaffrey, R. J., 20
McCall, W. A., 103
McCann, J. T., 66
McCarley, N. G., 578
McCarthy, D. M., 341
McCaulley, M. H., 578
McClelland, D. C., 393, 596
McClelland, N., 604
McCloskey, G. W., 384
McClure-Butterfield, P., 518
McConkey, K. M., 496
McCormick, C. M., 141
McCrady, B. S., 510
McCrae, R. R., 399, 406, 415, 416, 419, 420

McCubbin, H. I., 519
McDaniel, M. A., 575
McDermott, K. B., 555
McDevitt, S. C., 376
McDonald, R. P., 204
McDowell, C., 446, 448
McElrath, K., 501
McElwain, B. A., 406
McEvoy, G. M., 588
McGaghie, W. C., 380
McGirr, A., 21
McGrew, K. S., 294, 295
McGue, M., 287, 311
McGurk, F. J., 313
McKinley, J. C., 423, 424, 426
McKinney, W. R., 220
McLean, J. E., 384
McLearen, A. M., 66
McLemore, C. W., 501n2
McNemar, Q., 57
McReynolds, P., 42
Mead, M., 143
Mednick, S. A., 355
Medvec, V. H., 8
Meehl, P. E., 426, 468, 525, 527
Mehl, M. R., 476
Melchert, T. P., 75
Melchior, L. A., 502
Mellenbergh, G. J., 271
Mello, E. W., 497
Melton, G., 517
Melton, G. B., 193, 194
Memon, A., 497
Menninger, K. A., 393
Mercer, J. R., 312
Merrens, M. R., 525
Merrill, M., 323
Mesmer, E. M., 359
Mesquita, B., 485
Messer, S. B., 354
Messick, S., 182, 353, 406
Meyer, G. J., 448, 468
Meyers, J., 579
Micceri, T., 100
Michael, W. B., 157
Midanik, L. T., 605
Middleton, G., 549
Migliore, L. A., 17
Mikami, A. Y., 25
Miles, C. C., 424
Miller, A., 413
Miller, I. W., 500
Miller, J. C., 561
Miller, J. N., 545
Miller, K. S., 312
Miller, N. E., 482
Milling, L. S., 26
Millman, J., 259
Millon, T., 502
Milner, B., 556, 560
Milner, J. S., 193, 194, 523
Minsky, S. K., 545
Minton, B. A., 338
Minton, H. L., 321
Mirka, G. A., 15
Mischel, W., 395, 471

Mishra, D., 448
Mitchell, D. F., 35
Mitzel, H. C., 238
M'Naghten, D., 515
Moffic, H. S., 508
Moffitt, T. E., 150
Mohatt, G. V., 54
Mohatt, N. V., 53, 54
Monahan, J., 512
Montag, C., 563
Montague, M., 274
Montgomery, G. T., 416
Moody, R. A., 578
Moore, M., 421
Moos, R. H., 376, 519
Moreland, K. L., 444
Morgan, C. D., 45, 450, 461
Morgan, J. E., 541
Morgan, K. E., 386
Morgan, W. G., 450
Mori, L. T., 480
Morreau, L. E., 579
Mosier, C. I., 272
Moss, D., 428n9
Mossman, D., 66
Motowidlo, S. J., 579
Motta, R. W., 347
Moul, M., 303
Moursund, J., 80n5
Muchinsky, P. M., 598
Mueller, C. G., 205
Mueller, J. H., 605
Mueller, U., 485
Mueller-Hanson, R., 575
Mulaik, S. A., 204
Mulvey, E. P., 192
Muñoz, B., 274
Murphy, G. E., 192
Murphy, K. A., 565
Murphy, K. M., 232
Murphy, K. R., 574
Murphy, L. B., 442n1
Murphy-Berman, V., 196
Murray, C., 303, 312, 318
Murray, H. A., 2, 45, 450, 451, 452, 457n4, 460, 461, 588
Murry, W. D., 578
Murstein, B. I., 452, 465, 466
Mussen, P. H., 454, 467
Myers, C., 577
Myers, I. B., 397, 577, 578
Myers, K. D., 578
Myers, P. A., 521
Myerson, A., 49
Myors, B., 17

Nagle, R. J., 342
Naglieri, J. A., 296, 346, 347
Nakamura, B. J., 373
Narumoto, J., 597
Nathan, J., 547
Naylor, H. K., 454
Naylor, J. C., 226–228
Neale, E. L., 462
Near, J. P., 595
Needham, J., 301
Nehring, W. M., 33

Neisser, U., 57, 286, 303, 312, 318
Nelson, D. V., 553
Nelson, L. D., 129, 277
Nelson, R. O., 476
Nettelbeck, T., 305
Neugarten, B., 581
Neuman, G. A., 575
Nevid, J. S., 604
Newcomb, T. M., 395
Newell, A., 555
Newman, D. A., 55
Newman, H. H., 303
Nguyen, H. H., 436
Nguyen, N. T., 580
Nichols, D. S., 432, 433
Nitko, A. J., 141
Nock, M. K., 604
Nordanger, D., 172
Norton, P. J., 480
Nosek, B. A., 604
Notarius, C., 478
Notarius, C. I., 519
Novak, C. G., 384
Novick, M. R., 141, 157, 168, 208, 238
Nowak, L., 587
Nunes, L. M., 547
Nunnally, J. C., 79n4, 247, 261, 325, 406
Nurss, J. R., 376
Nye, C. D., 405
Nystedt, L., 598

Oakland, T., 19, 67n5
Obama, B., 604
Obasi, E. M., 436
Oberholzer, E., 444
O'Boyle, M. W., 307
Odbert, H. S., 119, 414, 419
Oden, M. H., 305
O'Hare, T., 510
Okazaki, S., 277
O'Leary, K. D., 150
Olino, T. M., 563
Olson, D. H., 519
Olweus, D., 512
Omar, M. H., 33
Ones, D. S., 575
Onwuegbuzie, A. J., 312
Organ, D. W., 595
Orne, M. T., 595
Orozco, S., 416
Orr, D. B., 317n5
Orr, R. R., 524
Osberg, T. M., 432
Osgood, C. E., 412, 606
Ostendorf, F., 419
O'Toole, M. E., 518
Ouzts, S. M., 386
Owens, C., 21
Ozer, D. J., 109n8
Ozonoff, S., 277, 545

Pace, V. L., 575
Padawer, J. R., 444
Padilla, A., 438
Padilla, A. M., 436

Paivio, A., 354
Palacio, C., 21
Palmer, B. W., 72
Palmore, E., 305
Panell, R. C., 141
Pannbacker, M., 549
Paolo, A. M., 341
Parke, R. D., 162, 372, 373
Parker, C., 596
Parkes, L. P., 598
Parks, R. W., 546
Parnes, H. S., 581
Pascal, G. R., 551
Pastore, N., 50
Patterson, D. G., 527n3
Patterson, M. B., 546
Patterson, M. M., 75
Patterson, W. M., 512
Patton, M. J., 581
Paulhus, D. L., 405
Paullay, I. M., 598
Paunonen, S. V., 421
Pavlo, B. C., 297, 298
Payne, B. K., 604
Pearson, K., 41, 98, 107, 108, 303
Pedrabissi, L., 410
Peng, Y., 602
Pennebaker, J. W., 476
Penner-Williams, J., 359
Perrewe, P. L., 599
Perry, C., 497
Perry, C. W., 497
Petersen, N. S., 208
Peterson, C. A., 34
Peterson, N. G., 187
Peterson, R. A., 598
Peterson, R. J., 454
Petrie, K., 192
Petscher, Y., 359
Petty, M. M., 598
Phelps, E. A., 604
Philippe, R. A., 26
Phillips, M. R., 21
Phillips, P. D., 464
Piaget, J., 289–291
Pichette, E. F., 436
Piedmont, R. L., 415
Pierson, D., 48
Pilgrim, C., 510
Pintner, R., 43, 44
Pisani, A. R., 512
Pittenger, D. J., 578
Pleiss, K. L., 347
Plucker, J. A., 308
Podymow, T., 131
Poehner, M. E., 6
Polizzi, D., 406
Pomplun, M., 33, 327
Ponterotto, J. G., 579
Porter, L. W., 599
Porter, S., 518
Porteus, S. D., 545, 546
Posner, B. Z., 4
Posthuma, A., 66
Pouliot, L., 21
Powell, D. H., 305
Poythress, N. G., 66, 515

Prather, E. N., 454
Pratt, S., 338
Preston, R., 391
Price, B., 311
Price, G., 519
Price, J., 492, 493
Price, L., 393
Princip, G., 188, 189
Pritchett, R., 376
Prout, H. T., 464
Putnam, W. H., 496

Quill, T. E., 69
Quinsey, V. L., 482
Quintana, D., 436

Ragheb, M. G., 581
Raiford, S. E., 335
Raju, N. S., 272
Ramirez, M., III, 436
Ramo, D. E., 605
Ramos, R. A., 219
Randall, A., 274
Randall, D. M., 599
Randolph, C., 341
Ranta, R. S., 597
Rapaport, D., 332, 446, 458, 504
Raphael, A. J., 551, 552
Rappeport, J. R., 511
Rasch, G., 169
Rashkovsky, B., 575
Razran, G., 467
Recarte, M. A., 547
Reckase, M. D., 236, 274
Reddon, J., 519
Reddon, J. R., 429
Redlich, F. C., 467
Redshaw, M., 413
Ree, M. J., 349
Reece, R. N., 521
Reed, J. E., 558
Reed, R. S., 523
Reed, T. E., 288, 303
Reeder, G. D., 371
Reeve, B. B., 173, 174, 283
Reeve, C. L., 310
Reichenberg, N., 551
Reid, C. A., 575
Reid, D. B., 405
Reik, T., 487, 488
Reinehr, R. C., 413
Reise, S. P., 173, 277
Reiser, M., 496
Reitan, R. M., 277, 553, 558, 559
Reiter, M. D., 578
Remington, R. W., 547
Retzlaff, P. D., 586
Rey, G. J., 553
Reynolds, C. E., 205
Reynolds, M. R., 386
Reynolds, W. M., 512
Riaz, I. A., 507
Rice, M. E., 512
Richards, D., 287
Richards, W. S., 525
Richardson, M. W., 154, 155

Richardson-Klavehn, A., 555
Richman, J., 69
Richters, J. E., 493
Ricker, J. H., 541
Rierdan, J., 463n7
Riethmiller, R. J., 464
Riggs, D. S., 150
Risley, T. R., 311
Ritzler, B., 444
Rizzo, M., 530
Roach, R. J., 200, 201, 202, 203, 519
Robbins, S. B., 581
Roberts, B. W., 120, 395, 575
Roberts, G. E., 455
Roberts, M. W., 480
Robertson, G. J., 131, 363
Robin, A. L., 519
Robinson, N. M., 101
Rodriguez-Giegling, M., 436
Roediger, H. L., 555
Roesch, R., 515
Rogers, C. R., 411
Rogers, R., 496, 515, 516
Rogers, R. R., 432
Rogerson, M., 16
Rogler, L. H., 143
Rohl, J. S., 545
Rohner, R. P., 417
Rohrbaugh, R. M., 494
Roid, G. H., 173, 324, 325, 326, 329
Rokeach, M., 80, 438
Romano, J., 164
Ronan, G. G., 454
Ronseen, J. D., 100
Roosevelt, F., 149
Rorer, L. G., 406
Rorschach, H., 44, 443, 444, 448
Rosale, M. L., 462
Rosanoff, A. J., 458
Rosen, A., 430
Rosen, J., 62, 63
Rosenberg, E., 507
Rosenman, R., 397
Rosenthal, R., 115
Rosenzweig, S., 456, 461
Rosse, J. G., 575
Roth, L. H., 72
Roth, P. L., 218
Rothberg, J. M., 512
Rotter, J. B., 408, 412, 459, 4670
Rottinghaus, P. J., 569
Rotundo, M., 579
Rounds, J., 569
Routh, D. K., 467
Roy, P., 436
Rozeboom, W. W., 204
Ruch, G. M., 66
Ruch, W., 485
Ruffolo, L. F., 547
Rüsch, N., 604
Russell, E. W., 558
Russell, J. S., 206n6
Russell, J. T., 219
Russell, M. T., 419

Russell, T. L., 187
Russo, D. C., 475
Rutherford, A., 461
Ryan, A. M., 579
Ryan, C. W., 389
Ryan, J. J., 305, 335, 341
Ryan, J. P., 543

Sabatelli, R. M., 519
Sackett, P. R., 208, 209, 576, 577, 579, 592
Sagarin, J., 378
Salas, E., 594
Saldanha, C., 66
Sales, B. D., 66, 518
Salk, J. E., 600
Salthouse, T. A., 305, 547
Salvia, J., 384
Samuda, R. J., 313
Samuel, D. B., 405
Sanchez, H. G., 21
Sanchez, L. M., 507
Sanchez-Cubillo, J. A., 547
Sánchez-Meca, J., 115
Sandelands, L. E., 602
Sanders, J., 66
Sandoval, J., 388, 579
Sanfilippo, J., 522
Santelices, M. V., 378
Santor, D. A., 502
Santy, P. A., 587
Sattler, J. M., 204, 289, 347
Saunders, E. A., 446
Savickas, M. L., 565
Savitsky, K., 8
Sawin, D. B., 372
Saxe, L., 66, 577
Saxton, J., 561
Sayette, M. A., 509
Scarr, S., 311
Schacter, D. L., 555
Schaie, K. W., 299, 304
Schaufeli, W. B., 597
Schellings, G., 274
Schjelderup-Ebbe, T., 492
Schloss, I., 610
Schmand, B., 545
Schmidt, F. L., 57, 115, 208, 229, 231, 232, 571, 591
Schmitt, N., 579, 584, 588
Schmitter-Edgecombe, M., 274
Schneck, M. R., 44
Schneider, D. L., 577
Schneider, M. F., 455
Schneider, W. J., 343
Schooler, C., 495
Schoop, L. H., 341
Schroeder, J., 25
Schuchardt, K., 359
Schuh, A. J., 486
Schuldberg, D., 444
Schulte, A. A., 33
Schwartz, L. A., 449
Schwartz, N., 604
Scodel, A., 467
Scott, L. H., 347
Seagull, F. J., 547
Searight, B. K., 51

Searight, H. R., 51
Sears, R., 305
Sears, R. R., 305
Seashore, C. E., 380
Sebold, J., 522
Segal, S. P., 603
Sellbom, M., 401
Serby, M., 517, 537
Serpell, R., 312
Sevig, T. D., 436
Shabbir, H., 609
Shah, S. A., 74
Shahim, S., 436
Shakow, D., 461
Shanafelt, T. D., 597
Shane, B., 553
Shapiro, E. S., 478
Sharkey, P. T., 310
Shavelson, R. J., 167
Shaw, S. R., 289
Shaywitz, B. A., 311
Shearn, C. R., 467
Shectman, F., 469
Sheehan, P. W., 496
Sheffield, D., 304
Shen, H.-Y., 466
Shepard, L. A., 271
Sheppard, L. D., 288
Sherley, J. L., 380
Sherman, R., 486
Sherrill-Pattison, S., 547
Shiffman, S., 474, 479
Shiffrin, R. M., 555
Shine, L. C., 226–228
Shirom, A., 597
Shneidman, E. S., 455, 463
Shock, N. W., 304
Shockley, W., 304
Shoemaker, A., 185
Shriner, J. G., 33
Shrout, P. E., 502
Shuey, A. M., 312
Shum, D., 546
Siegler, R. S., 287
Silverman, W., 335
Silverstein, A. B., 341
Silverstein, M. L., 277
Simmons, B. L., 579
Simms, L. J., 432
Simon, T., 43, 312, 321, 381
Simons-Morton, B. G., 25
Simpson, R., 33
Sims, H. P., 481
Sinadinovic, K., 16
Sines, J. O., 528
Sireci, S. G., 237
Skaggs, G., 238
Skinner, B. F., 460, 461
Skolnick, J. H., 483
Slakter, M. J., 271
Slobogin, C., 66
Sloman, L., 483, 493
Smith, B. L., 305, 376
Smith, D. E., 159
Smith, D. K., 304, 374, 464
Smith, F. J., 501n2
Smith, G. T., 341
Smith, J. D., 50

Weissman, H. N., 523
Weizmann-Henelius, G., 448
Wells, G. L., 396
Welsh, G., 428
Welsh, G. S., 422, 423, 427, 430
Welsh, J. R., 349
Welsh-Bohmer, K. A., 530
Wepman, J. M., 560
Werner, H., 534
Wertheimer, M., 550
Wesman, A. G., 287, 299, 304
West, L. J., 591
West, M., 468
Westen, D., 452
Westerman, J. W., 579
Wexley, K. N., 486
Whatley, P. R., 416
White, B. L., 311
White, J. A., 274
White, J. M., 40
White, L. T., 577
White, R. W., 450
White, S., 523
Whitener, E. M., 579
Whittington, M. K., 466
Whitworth, R. H., 416
Wicker, A. W., 598
Wickes, T. A., Jr., 467
Widaman, K. F., 203
Widiger, T. A., 405, 492, 494
Wielkiewicz, R. M., 481

Wiens, A. N., 317
Wigdor, A. K., 57, 571, 575
Wiggins, N., 425
Wilcox, R., 467
Wilk, S. L., 208, 209
Wilkinson, G. S., 363
Willcutt, E. G., 359
Williams, C. L., 434, 505
Williams, D. R., 568
Williams, J. M., 553
Williams, R., 314, 316
Williams, R. H., 150
Williams, T. H., 326
Williams, T. Y., 512
Willis, G. B., 497
Willis, J., 334
Willis, R. H., 395
Wilmer, H. A., 461
Wilson, D. L., 578
Wilson, G. G., 479
Wilson, J. A., 40
Wilson, M., 378
Winner, E., 306
Winston, A. S., 583
Wirt, R. D., 403
Wise, S. L., 282
Witkin, H. A., 28, 353
Witmer, L., 42, 43
Witt, P., 20
Wittink, M. N., 24
Witty, P., 307
Wixson, K., 359
Wober, M., 312
Wolfe, M. M., 436

Wolff, C. v., 40
Wolff, C. von, 40
Wolfner, G., 523
Wolfram, W. A., 52
Wolfson, D., 277, 553, 559
Wolk, R. B., 455
Wolk, R. L., 455
Wollersheim, J. P., 512
Wong-Rieger, D., 436
Woodcock, R. W., 382, 386
Woodworth, M., 518
Woodworth, R. S., 44, 417, 424
Worchel, F. F., 454
Worlock, P., 522
Wright, D. B., 274
Wu, W., 25
Wundt, W. M., 41

Yager, T. J., 502
Yamakawa, R., 289
Yañes, Y. T., 126
Yantz, C. L., 20
Yao, E. L., 436
Yeates, K. O., 530
Yell, N., 466
Yen, W. M., 169, 264, 265, 266
Yerkes, R. M., 347, 348
Yin, P., 158
Yoo, J. J., 563
Young, A., 493
Young, K. S., 16, 605
Youngjohn, J. R., 304

Yuille, J. C., 523
Yussen, S. R., 287

Zajac, D. M., 599
Zapf, P. A., 515
Zavala, J. D., 419
Zea, M. C., 436
Zebehazy, K. T., 561
Zedeck, S., 220, 574
Zelig, M., 496
Zenderland, L., 49, 50
Zhang, L.-M., 482
Zhou, X., 309
Zickar, M. J., 164, 166, 281
Zijlstra, F. R. H., 597
Zillmer, E. A., 407, 408
Zimmerman, D. W., 150
Zimmerman, I. L., 338, 339
Zinchenko, V. P., 362n
Zink, D., 66
Zirkel, P. A., 358
Ziskin, J., 511
Zonda, T., 21
Zubeidat, I., 434
Zubin, J., 460
Zuckerman, M., 119, 312, 471
Zumbo, B. D., 578
Zuniga, M. E., 438
Zuroff, D. C., 399
Zwahlen, H. T., 547
Zweigenhaft, R. L., 56
Zwick, R., 378
Zytowski, D. G., 568

**alternate forms:** Different versions of the same test or measure; contrast with *parallel forms*, 151

**alternate forms reliability:** An estimate of the extent to which item sampling and other errors have affected scores on two versions of the same test; contrast with *parallel-forms reliability*, 151–152, 161

**alternate item:** A test item to be administered only under certain conditions to replace the administration of an existing item on the test, 323

Alzheimer's disease, 24

American Board of Assessment Psychology (ABAP), 25

American Board of Professional Psychology (ABPP), 25

American Psychological Association (APA), 66, 67

Americans with Disabilities Act of 1990, 60

**analogue behavioral observation:** The observation of a person or persons in an environment designed to increase the assessor's chance of observing targeted behaviors and interactions, 479–480

**analogue behavioral observation,** 479

**analogue study:** Research or behavioral intervention that replicates a variable or variables in ways that are similar to or analogous to the real variables the experimenter wishes to study; for example, a laboratory study designed to research a phobia of snakes in the wild, 479

**anatomically detailed dolls** (ADDs): A human figure in doll form with accurately represented genitalia, typically used to assist in the evaluation of sexually abused children, 523

**anchor protocol:** A test answer sheet developed by a test publisher to check the accuracy of examiners' scoring, 280

ancient Egypt, 39

**Angoff method:** A way to set fixed cut scores that entails averaging the judgments of experts, 236

**APA:** American Psychological Association; in other sources, particularly medical texts, this may refer to the American Psychiatric Association, 66, 67

APA Committee on Psychological Tests and Assessment, 17

APAT. *See* Accounting Program Admission Test (APAT)

APD. *See* average proportional distance (APD)

**Apgar number:** American Psychological Association; in other sources, particularly

medical texts, this may refer to the American Psychiatric Association, 372

**aphagia:** A condition in which the ability to eat is lost or diminished, 553n2

**aphasia:** A loss of ability to express oneself or to understand spoken or written language due to a neurological deficit, 553

API. *See* Applicant Potential Inventory (API)

**apperceive:** To perceive in terms of past perceptions (from this verb, the noun apperception is derived), 451

Apperceptive Personality Test (APT), 457

Applicant Potential Inventory (API), 576

application forms, 582–583

application letter, 582

APS. *See* Addiction Potential Scale (APS)

APT. *See* Apperceptive Personality Test (APT)

**aptitude tests:** A test that usually focuses more on informal as opposed to formal learning experiences and is designed to measure both learning and inborn potential for the purpose of making predictions about the testtaker's future performance; also referred to as a *prognostic test* and, especially with young children, a *readiness test*, 369–381

career choice/career transition, 569–575

elementary school level, 376–377

GRE, 379–380

MAT, 380

preschool level, 370–376

secondary school level, 377–378

**arithmetic mean:** Also referred to simply as the *mean*, a measure of central tendency derived by calculating an average of all scores in a distribution, 89

Armed Forces Qualification Test (AFQT), 349

Armed Services Vocational Aptitude Battery (ASVAB), 348–349, 350–351

**Army Alpha test:** An intelligence and ability test developed by military psychologists for use in World War I to screen literate recruits; contrast with *Army Beta test*, 347–348

**Army Beta test:** A nonverbal intelligence and ability test developed by military psychologists for use in World War I to screen illiterate and foreign-born recruits; contrast with *Army Alpha test*, 347–348

Army General Classification Test (AGCT), 348

articles, 34–35

ASI. *See* Addiction Severity Index (ASI)

assessment

assessor's role, 4

behavioral observation, 12–13

case history data, 11–12

clinical. *See* clinical assessment

collaborative, 4

computers as tools, 14–17

conducting, 27–33

culture, and, 45–58

defined, 12

dynamic, 4–6

educational. *See* educational assessment

interview, 9–10

legal/ethical considerations, 58–76

life-or-death, 69–70

neuropsychological. *See* neuropsychological assessment

personality. *See* personality assessment

portfolio, 10

process of, 4–6

psychological testing, contrasted, 3

public policy, and, 57–58

reference sources, 33–36

role-play tests, 14

self-assessment, 36

settings, 22–27

society at large, 21–22

state licensing laws, 68

test, 6–9

test developers, 18–19

test user, 19

testtaker, 19–21

therapeutic, 4

tools of, 6–18

**assessment center:** An organizationally standardized procedure for evaluation involving multiple assessment techniques, 588

assessor, 2, 4

**assimilation:** In Piagetian theory, one of two basic mental operations through which humans learn, this one involving the active organization of new information into what is already perceived, known, and thought; contrast with *accommodation*, 290

assumption of monotonicity, 170–171

astronauts, testing, 585–587

**at risk:** Defined in different ways by different school districts, but in general a reference to functioning that is deficient and possibly in need of intervention, 374

**at-risk infant or toddler:** According to IDEA, a child under 3 years of age who would be in danger of experiencing a substantial developmental delay if early intervention services were not provided, 374

**brain damage:** Any physical or functional impairment in the central nervous system that results in sensory, motor, cognitive, emotional, or related deficits, 532

**brain scan:** More formally referred to as a *radioisotope scan,* a procedure in neurology used to detect tumors and other possible abnormalities that entails the introduction of radioactive material into the brain for the purpose of tracking its flow, 562

branched testing, 326

breathalyzer test, 165

Bricklin Perceptual Scales (BPS), 126–127

broad-band instruments, 478

**Brogden-Cronbach-Gleser formula:** A formula used to calculate the dollar amount of a utility gain resulting from the use of a particular selection instrument under specified conditions, 229

Bruininks-Oseretsky Test of Motor Proficiency, 549

**burnout:** A psychological syndrome of emotional exhaustion, depersonalization, and reduced personal accomplishment, 597

business applications, 602–612
  attitudes, measurement of, 602–604
  consumer psychology, 602
  motivation research methods, 607–612
  surveys, 604–607

business settings, 24

BYI-II. *See* Beck Youth Inventories–Second Edition (BYI-II)

California
  Proposition 209, 62–63

California Psychological Inventory (CPI 434), 407

California Test of Mental Maturity, 351

California Verbal Learning Test–II (CVLT-II), 555

CALS. *See* Checklist of Adaptive Living Skills (CALS)

Campbell Interest and Skill Survey, 568

Cannot Say scale, 425

CAP. *See* Child Abuse Potential Inventory (CAP)

**CAPA:** An acronym that stands for computer assisted psychological assessment, 15, 68–71

Career Interest Inventory, 568

career opportunities
  ability/aptitude measures, 569–575
  burnout, 597
  business applications, 602–612. *See also* business applications
  career choice/career transition, 565–581
  cognitive ability measures, 591–592
  interest measure, 566–569

job satisfaction, 598
motivation, 594–597
organizational commitment, 599
organizational culture, 599–601
personality measures, 575–579
productivity, 592–594
screening/selection/classification/placement, 581–591

Career Transitions Inventory (CTI), 581

**case history:** Also referred to as a *case study,* this is a report or illustrative account concerning a person or an event that was compiled on the basis of case history data, 538–539

**case history data:** Records, transcripts, and other accounts in any media that preserve archival information, official and informal accounts, and other data and items relevant to an assessee, 11–12, 501

**case study:** Also referred to as a *case history,* this is a report or illustrative account concerning a person or an event that was compiled on the basis of case history data, 12, 538–539

CAT. *See* **computerized adaptive testing (CAT)**

**CAT:** An acronym that stands for a neurological scanning technology called computerized axial tomography, 562

categorical cutoff, 8

**categorical scaling:** A system of scaling in which stimuli are placed into one of two or more alternative categories that differ quantitatively with respect to some continuum, 249

category response curve. *See* **item characteristic curve (ICC)**

category scoring. *See* **class scoring**

Cattell Infant Intelligence Scale (CIIS), 42

Cattell-Horn-Carroll (CHC) model. *See* **CHC model**

CBA. *See* **curriculum-based assessment (CBA)**

CBCL. *See* Achenbach Child Behavior Checklist (CBCL)

CBM. *See* **curriculum-based measurement (CBM)**

CCAI. *See* Cross-Cultural Adaptability Inventory (CCAI)

CDT. *See* **clock-drawing test (CDT)**

ceiling, 327

**ceiling effect:** Diminished utility of a tool of assessment in distinguishing testtakers at the high end of the ability, trait, or other attribute being measured, 259, 307

**ceiling level:** A stage in a test achieved by a testtaker as a result of meeting some preset criterion to discontinue testing-for example, responding incorrectly to two

consecutive items on an ability test that contains increasingly difficult items may establish a presumed "ceiling" on the testtaker's ability; contrast with *basal level* and *testing the limits,* 328

Center for Epidemiological Studies Depression scale (CES-D), 502

**central nervous system:** All of the neurons or nerve cells in the brain and the spinal cord; contrast with the *peripheral nervous system,* 530

**central processing:** Computerized scoring, interpretation, or other conversion of raw test data that is physically transported from the same or other test sites; contrast with *teleprocessing* and *local processing,* 14

**central tendency error:** A type of rating error wherein the rater exhibits a general reluctance to issue ratings at either the positive or negative extreme and so all or most ratings cluster in the middle of the rating continuum, 205

**cerebral angiogram:** A diagnostic procedure in neurology that entails the injection of a tracer element into the bloodstream prior to taking X-rays of the cerebral area, 562

CES-D. *See* Center for Epidemiological Studies Depression scale (CES-D)

CFA. *See* **confirmatory factor analysis**

*Chapple* case, 558

**CHC model:** An abbreviation for the Cattell-Horn-Carroll model of cognitive abilities, 294–295
  K-ABC/KABC-II, 386
  SB5, and, 325

**checklist:** A questionnaire formatted to allow a person to mark items indicative of information such as the presence or absence of a specified behavior, thought, event, or circumstance, 371–374

Checklist of Adaptive Living Skills (CALS), 579

Chicago Bulls, 142

Child Abuse Potential Inventory (CAP), 193–194, 523, 524

**child abuse:** Nonaccidental infliction or creation of conditions that result in a child's physical injury or emotional impairment, or a sexual offense committed against a child, 521–524

child evaluation, custody proceedings, 519–521

**child neglect:** The failure by an adult responsible for a child to exercise a minimum degree of care in providing the child with food, clothing, shelter, education, medical care, and supervision, 521–524

**competence to stand trial:** Understanding the charges against one and being able to assist in one's own defense, 512–515

completion item, 254

**composite judgment:** An averaging of multiple ratings of judgments for the purpose of minimizing rater error, 486

**comprehensive system:** John Exner's integration of several methods for administering, scoring, and interpreting the Rorschach test, 447

**computer assisted psychological assessment.** *See* **CAPA**

**computerized adaptive testing (CAT):** An interactive, computer-administered testtaking process wherein items presented to the testtaker are based in part on the testtaker's performance on previous items, 15, 255–256

**computerized axial tomography.** *See* **CAT**

computers, as tools, 14–17

conceptual items, 368

**concurrent validity:** A form of criterion-related validity that is an index of the degree to which a test score is related to some criterion measure obtained at the same time (concurrently), 190, 191–192

**confidence interval:** A range or band of test scores that is likely to contain the "true score," 177

**confidentiality:** The ethical obligation of professionals to keep confidential all communications made or entrusted to them in confidence, although professionals may be compelled to disclose such confidential communications under court order or other extraordinary conditions, such as when such communications refer to a third party in imminent danger; contrast with *privacy right*, 74

configural interpretation of scores, 426

**confirmatory factor analysis (CFA):** A class of mathematical procedures employed when a factor structure that has been explicitly hypothesized is tested for its fit with the observed relationships between the variables, 203, 345

**confrontation naming:** Identifying a pictured stimulus in a neuropsychological context, such as in response to administration of items in the Boston Naming Test, 547

Connors Rating Scales–Revised (CRS-R), 371, 373–374

**co-norming:** The test norming process conducted on two or more tests using the same sample of testtakers; when used to validate all of the tests being normed, this process may also be referred to as *co-validation*, 138n4, 278

consent, 72–73

**construct:** An informed, scientific idea developed or generated to describe or explain behavior; some examples of constructs include "intelligence," "personality," "anxiety," and "job satisfaction," 119, 198

**construct validity:** A judgment about the appropriateness of inferences drawn from test scores regarding individual standings on a variable called a construct, 198–204
  changes with age, 200–201
  convergent evidence, 202
  defined, 198
  discriminant evidence, 202–203
  factor analysis, 203–204
  homogeneity, 199–200
  intelligence tests, 306
  method of contrasted groups, 201–202
  pretest-posttest changes, 201

**constructed-response format:** A form of test item requiring the testtaker to construct or create a response, as opposed to simply selecting a response (e.g., items on essay examinations, fill-in-the-blank, and short-answer tests); contrast with *selected-response format*, 252

**consultative report:** A type of interpretive report designed to provide expert and detailed analysis of test data that mimics the work of an expert consultant, 15

**consumer panel:** A sample of respondents, selected by demographic and other criteria, who have contracted with a consumer or marketing research firm to respond on a periodic basis to surveys, questionnaires, and related research instruments regarding various products, services, and/or advertising or other promotional efforts, 606

**consumer psychology:** The branch of social psychology dealing primarily with the development, advertising, and marketing of products and services, 602

content of test, 5

**content sampling:** The variety of the subject matter contained in the items; frequently referred to in the context of the variation between individual test items in a test or between test items in two or more tests and also referred to as *item sampling*, 147

content scales, 425

**content validity:** A judgment regarding how adequately a test (or other tool of measurement) samples behavior representative of the universe of behavior it was designed to sample, 184–189

**content validity ratio (CVR):** A formula, developed by C. H. Lawshe, used to gauge agreement among raters regarding how essential an individual test item is for inclusion in a test, 187–188

content-referenced testing and assessment, 140

continuous scale, 78

**contralateral control:** Phenomenon resulting from the fact that each of the two cerebral hemispheres receives sensory information from the opposite side of the body and also controls motor responses on the opposite side of the body; understanding of this phenomenon is necessary in understanding brain–behavior relationships and in diagnosing neuropsychological deficits, 531

**contrast effect:** A potential source of error in behavioral ratings when a dissimilarity in the observed behaviors (or other things being rated) leads to a more or less favorable rating than would have been made had the dissimilarity not existed, 486

**control group:** (1) In an experiment, the untreated group; (2) in test development by means of empirical criterion keying, a group of randomly selected testtakers who do not necessarily have in common the shared characteristic of the standardization sample, 424

Controlled Word Association Test, 553

convenience sample, 133

**convergent evidence:** With reference to construct validity, data from other measurement instruments designed to measure the same or a similar construct as the test being construct-validated and that all point to the same judgment or conclusion with regard to a test or other tool of measurement; contrast with *discriminant evidence*, 202

**convergent thinking:** A deductive reasoning process that entails recall and consideration of facts as well as a series of logical judgments to narrow down solutions and eventually arrive at one solution; contrast with *divergent thinking*, 355

**convergent validity:** Data indicating that a test measures the same construct as another test purporting to measure the same construct, 202n3

Cooperative Achievement Test, 365

COPS. *See* criterion-focused occupational personality scales

**core subtest:** One of a test's subtests that is routinely administered during any administration of the test; contrast with *supplemental* or *optional subtest*, 332

corporate culture, 599–601

correlation, 106–116
  concept of, 106–107
  graphic representation, 111–114
  meta-analysis, 115
  Pearson *r*, 107–109
  Spearman's rho, 110–111

**correlation:** An expression of the degree and direction of correspondence between two things, when each thing is continuous in nature, 106–116

correlation coefficient, 106

**cost:** As related to test utility, disadvantages, losses, or expenses in both economic and noneconomic terms, 213–215

**counseling psychology:** A branch of psychology that has to do with the prevention, diagnosis, and treatment of abnormal behavior, with emphasis on "everyday" types of concerns and problems such as those related to marriage, family, academics, and career, 489

counseling settings, 23

Couples Interaction Scoring System, 478

**co-validation:** The test validation process conducted on two or more tests using the same sample of testtakers; when used in conjunction with the creation of norms or the revision of existing norms, this process may also be referred to as *co-norming*, 278

cover letter, 582

CPI. *See* Cognitive Proficiency Index (CPI)

CPI 434. *See* California Psychological Inventory (CPI 434)

cranial nerve damage, 536

creativity, 354–355

criminal responsibility, 515–516

**criterion:** The standard against which a test or a test score is evaluated; this standard may take many forms, including a specific behavior or set of behaviors, 139, 190, 421

**criterion contamination:** A state in which a criterion measure is itself based, in whole or in part, on a predictor measure, 190

**criterion group:** A reference group of testtakers who share characteristics and whose responses to test items serve as a

standard by which items will be included or discarded from the final version of a scale; the shared characteristic of the criterion group will vary as a function of the nature and scope of the test being developed, 421–423

criterion-focused occupational personality scales, 576

**criterion-referenced testing and assessment:** Also referred to as *domain-referenced testing and assessment* and *content-referenced testing and assessment*, a method of evaluation and a way of deriving meaning from test scores by evaluating an individual's score with reference to a set standard (or criterion); contrast with *norm-referenced testing and assessment*, 139–141, 163–164, 243

**criterion-related validity:** A judgment regarding how adequately a score or index on a test or other tool of measurement can be used to infer an individual's most probable standing on some measure of interest (the criterion), 190–198
  concurrent validity, 191–192
  criterion, defined, 190
  defined, 190
  expectancy data, 196–198
  incremental validity, 195–196
  predictive validity, 192–198

**critical incidents technique:** In workplace settings, a procedure that entails recording employee behavior evaluated as positive or negative by a supervisor or other rater, 593

**cross-battery assessment:** Evaluation that employs tests from different test batteries and entails interpretation of data from specified tests to provide a comprehensive assessment, 295

Cross-Cultural Adaptability Inventory (CCAI), 579

**cross-validation:** A revalidation on a sample of testtakers other than the testtakers on whom test performance was originally found to be a valid predictor of some criterion, 278

CRS-R. *See* Connors Rating Scales–Revised (CRS-R)

**crystallized intelligence:** In Cattell's two-factor theory of intelligence, acquired skills and knowledge that are highly dependent on formal and informal education; contrast with *fluid intelligence*, 293

CTI. *See* Career Transitions Inventory (CTI)

CTT. *See* **classical test theory (CTT)**

cultural considerations
  assessment, and, 45–48
  evaluation standards, 53–55
  evolving interest in, 46–51

intelligence, and, 311–317

managed care, and, 507–508

nonverbal communication/behavior, 52–53

personality assessment, 435–439

verbal communication, 51–52

**culturally informed psychological assessment:** An approach to evaluation that is keenly perceptive about and responsive to issues of acculturation, values, identity, worldview, language, and other culture-related variables as they may affect the evaluation process or the interpretation of resulting data, 143, 504–508

**culture:** The socially transmitted behavior patterns, beliefs, and products of work of a particular population, community, or group of people, 45

**culture loading:** An index of the magnitude to which a test incorporates the vocabulary, concepts, traditions, knowledge, and feelings associated with a particular culture, 313–316

**culture-fair intelligence test:** A test or assessment process designed to minimize the influence of culture on various aspects of the evaluation procedures, such as the administration instructions, the item content, the responses required of the testtaker, and the interpretations made from the resulting data, 313–316

**culture-free intelligence test:** In psychometrics, the ideal of a test that is devoid of the influence of any particular culture and therefore does not favor people from any culture, 312

culture-specific tests, 47

**cumulative scoring:** A method of scoring whereby points or scores accumulated on individual items or subtests are tallied and then, the higher the total sum, the higher the individual is presumed to be on the ability, trait, or other characteristic being measured; contrast with *class scoring* and *ipsative scoring*, 121

**curriculum-based assessment (CBA):** A general term referring to school-based evaluations that clearly and faithfully reflect what is being taught, 368

**curriculum-based measurement (CBM):** A type of curriculum-based assessment characterized by the use of standardized measurement procedures to derive local norms to be used in the evaluation of student performance on curriculum-based tasks, 368

**curvilinearity:** Usually with regard to graphs or correlation scatterplots, the degree to which the plot or graph is characterized by curvature, 111

**custody evaluation:** A psychological assessment of parents or guardians and their parental capacity and/or of children and their parental needs and preferences—usually undertaken for the purpose of assisting a court in making a decision about awarding custody, 518–521

**cut score:** Also referred to as a *cutoff score*, a reference point (usually numerical) derived as a result of judgment and used to divide a set of data into two or more classifications, with some action to be taken or some inference to be made on the basis of these classifications, 7

  Angoff method, 236
  defined, 233
  fixed, 233
  IRT-based methods, 237–238
  known groups method, 236–237
  multiple cut scores, 233
  norm-referenced, 233
  relative, 233

CVLT-II. *See* California Verbal Learning Test–II (CVLT-II)

CVR. *See* **content validity ratio (CVR)**

DAP test. *See* Draw a Person (DAP) test

DAS. *See* Differential Ability Scales (DAS)

DAT. *See* Dental Admission Test (DAT)

data reduction methods, 418–421

databases, 35

*Daubert v. Merrell Dow Pharmaceuticals,* 64–65, 558

*De Formatione Pulli in Ovo* (Malphigi), 301

"Death with Dignity" legislation, 68–70

*Debra P. v. Turlington,* 61

**decision study:** Conducted at the conclusion of a generalizability study, this research is designed to explore the utility and value of test scores in making decisions, 168

**decision theory:** A body of methods used to quantitatively evaluate selection procedures, diagnostic classifications, therapeutic interventions, or other assessment or intervention-related procedures in terms of how optimal they are (most typically from a cost-benefit perspective), 229–232

**declarative memory:** Memory of factual material; contrast with *procedural memory,* 555

**dementia:** A loss of cognitive functioning (which may affect memory, thinking, reasoning, psychomotor speed, attention, and related abilities, as well as personality) that occurs as the result of damage or loss of brain cells, 24

Dental Admission Test (DAT), 381

**deterioration quotient (DQ):** Also referred to as a *deterioration index,* this is a pattern of subtest scores on a Wechsler test that Wechsler himself viewed as suggestive of neurological deficit, 544

**developmental milestones:** Important event during the course of one's life that may be marked by the acquisition, presence, or growth of certain abilities or skills or by the failure, impairment, or cessation of such abilities or skills, 538, 539

**developmental norms:** Norms derived on the basis of any trait, ability, skill, or other characteristic that is presumed to develop, deteriorate, or otherwise be affected by chronological age, school grade, or stage of life, 137

deviation, 94

**deviation IQ:** A variety of standard score used to report "intelligence quotients" (IQs) with a mean set at 100 and a standard deviation set at 15; on the Stanford-Binet, it is also referred to as a *test composite* and represents an index of intelligence derived from a comparison between the performance of an individual testtaker and the performance of other testtakers of the same age in the test's standardization sample, 323

**diagnosis:** A description or conclusion reached on the basis of evidence and opinion through a process of distinguishing the nature of something and ruling out alternative conclusions, 22

Diagnostic and statistical manual (DSM)
  DSM-II, 500
  DSM-III, 500
  DSM-III-R, 500
  DSM-IV, 491, 500
  DSM-IV-TR, 491–493, 500
  DSM-V, 493–494

*Diagnostic and Statistical Manual of Mental Disorders IV-TR,* 79

**diagnostic information:** In educational contexts, test or other data used to pinpoint a student's difficulties for the purpose of remediating them; contrast with *evaluative information,* 382

*Diagnostic Psychological Testing* (Rapaport), 504

**diagnostic test:** A tool used to make a diagnosis, usually to identify areas of deficit to be targeted for intervention, 22, 382

diagnostic tests, 381–383

**diary panel:** A variety of consumer panel in which respondents have agreed to keep diaries of their thoughts and/or behaviors, 606

**dichotomous test item:** A test item or question that can be answered with only one of two response options, such as *true-false* or *yes-no,* 169

dichotomy, 468–470

*Dictionary of Occupational Titles,* 571

DIF. *See* differential item function (DIF); **differential item functioning (DIF)**

**DIF analysis:** In IRT, a process of group-by-group analysis of item response curves for the purpose of evaluating measurement instrument or item equivalence across different groups of testtakers, 282

**DIF items:** In IRT, test items that respondents from different groups, who are presumably at the same level of the underlying construct being measured, have different probabilities of endorsing as a function of their group membership, 282

Differential Ability Scales (DAS), 346

differential item function (DIF), 174

**differential item functioning (DIF):** In IRT, a phenomenon in which the same test item yields one result for members of one group and a different result for members of another group, presumably as a result of group differences that are not associated with group differences in the construct being measured, 282

**dimensional qualitative research:** An adaptation of Lazarus's multimodal clinical approach for use in qualitative research applications and designed to ensure that the research is comprehensive and systematic from a psychological perspective and is guided by discussion questions based on the seven modalities (or dimensions) named in Lazarus's model, which are summarized by the acronym BASIC ID (behavior, affect, sensation, imagery, cognition, interpersonal relations, and drugs); Cohen's adaptation of Lazarus's work adds an eighth dimension, sociocultural, changing the acronym to BASIC IDS, 609

direct correlation, 106–107

direct estimation, 251

*Directory of Unpublished Experimental Mental Measures,* 35

**disability:** As defined in the Americans with Disabilities Act of 1990, a physical or mental impairment that substantially limits one or more of the major life activities of an individual, 30, 68, 358, 374

discrete scale, 78

**discriminant analysis:** A family of statistical techniques used to shed light on the relationship between certain variables and two or more naturally occurring groups, 238

**discriminant evidence:** With reference to construct validity, data from a test or other measurement instrument showing little relationship between test scores or other variables with which the scores on the test being construct-validated should not theoretically be correlated; contrast with *convergent evidence,* 202–203

**discrimination:** In IRT, the degree to which an item differentiates among people with higher or lower levels of the trait, ability, or whatever it is that is being measured by a test, 169

Discussion of Organizational Culture, 601

**distribution:** In a psychometric context, a set of test scores arrayed for recording or study, 83

**divergent thinking:** A reasoning process characterized by flexibility of thought, originality, and imagination, making several different solutions possible; contrast with *convergent thinking,* 355

diversity issues, personnel selection, 591–592

**domain sampling:** (1) A sample of behaviors from all possible behaviors that could be indicative of a particular construct; (2) a sample of test items from all possible items that could be used to measure a particular construct, 121n1

domain sampling theory, 166

**domain- (content-referenced) testing and assessment.** *See* **criterion-referenced testing and assessment**

DQ. *See* **deterioration quotient (DQ)**

Draw a Person (DAP) test, 463

drawings, 461–464

drug addiction, 509–510

**drug test:** In the workplace, an evaluation undertaken to determine the presence, if any, of alcohol or other psychotropic substances, by means of laboratory analysis of blood, urine, hair, or other biological specimens, 590–591

DSM. *See* Diagnostic and statistical manual (DSM)

**DSM-IV-TR:** Abbreviation for *Diagnostic and Statistical Manual of Mental Disorders, Fourth Edition, Text Revision* (published in May 2000), a slightly modified version of DSM-IV (published in 1994), 491–492, 500

dual-easel format, 375

**Durham standard:** A standard of legal insanity in *Durham v. United States* wherein the defendant was not found culpable for criminal action if his unlawful act was the product of a mental disease or defect; contrast with the *ALI standard* and the *M'Naghten standard,* 516

*Durham v. United States,* 516

*Dusky v. United States,* 512

**duty to warn:** A legally mandated obligation—to advise an endangered third party of their peril—which may override patient privilege; therapists and assessors may have a legal duty to warn when a client expresses intent to hurt a third party in any way, ranging from physical violence to disease transmission, 512

dynamic assessment, 4, 361–363

**dynamic characteristic:** A trait, state, or ability presumed to be ever-changing as a function of situational and cognitive experiences; contrast with *static characteristic,* 162

dynamometer, 82

easel format, 375

Ebers papyrus, 40

**echoencephalograph:** In neurology, a machine that transforms electrical energy into sound energy for the purpose of diagnostic studies of brain lesions and abnormalities, 562

**ecological momentary assessment:** A behavioral diary-keeping methodology that entails the real-time recording, on a handheld computer, of events related to problem behaviors, 474

ECSP. *See* Exceptional Case Study Project (ECSP)

ECST-R. *See* Evaluation of Competency to Stand Trial–Revised (ECST-R)

Education for All Handicapped Children (PL 94-142), 60, 371

educational assessment
  achievement tests, 363–368
  aptitude tests, 369–381
  authentic assessment, 390
  diagnostic tests, 381–383

dynamic assessment, 361–363
  peer appraisal, 390–391
  performance assessment, 388–389
  psychoeducational test batteries, 383–388. *See also* **psychoeducational test batteries**
  role of, 357–363
  RtI model, 358–361
  study habits/interests/attitudes, measuring, 391–392

Educational Resources Information Center (ERIC), 35

educational settings, 22

Educational Testing Service (ETS), 35

Edwards Personal Preference Schedule (EPPS), 260–261

Edwin Smyth Papyrus, 39

EEG. *See* **electroencephalograph (EEG)**

EEOC. *See* Equal Employment Opportunity Commission (EEOC)

**effect size:** A statistic used to express the strength of the relationship or the magnitude of the differences in data; in meta-analysis, this statistic is most typically a correlation coefficient, 115

*18th Annual Mental Measurement Yearbook,* 34

elaboration, 354

**electroencephalograph(EEG):** A machine that records electrical activity of the brain by means of electrodes pasted to the scalp, 562

**electromyograph (EMG):** A machine that records electrical activity of muscles by means of an electrode inserted directly into the muscle, 562

Ellis Island, immigrant testing, 46

EMG. *See* **electromyograph (EMG)**

**emotional injury:** A term sometimes used synonymously with *mental suffering, emotional harm,* and *pain and suffering* to convey psychological damage, 517

**emotional intelligence:** A popularization of aspects of Gardner's theory of multiple intelligences, with emphasis on the notions of interpersonal and intrapersonal intelligence, 293

**empirical criterion keying:** The process of using criterion groups to develop test items, where the scoring or keying of items has been demonstrated empirically to differentiate among groups of testtakers, 421

employment opportunities. *See* career opportunities

*English Men of Science* (Galton), 302

Entrance Examination for Schools of Nursing (RNEE), 381

**episodic memory:** Memory for facts but only within a particular context or situation; contrast with *semantic memory,* 555

EPPS. *See* Edwards Personal Preference Schedule (EPPS)

Equal Employment Opportunity Commission (EEOC), 62

Equal Opportunity Employment Act, 60

**equipercentile method:** A procedure for comparing scores on two or more tests (as in the creation of national anchor norms) that entails calculating percentile norms for each test and then identifying the score on each test that corresponds to the percentile, 138

ERIC. *See* Educational Resources Information Center (ERIC)

**error:** Collectively, all of the factors other than what a test purports to measure that contribute to scores on the test; error is a variable in all testing and assessment, 78–79, 122–123. *See also* reliability

**error of central tendency:** Less than accurate rating or evaluation by a rater or judge due to that rater's general tendency to make ratings at or near the midpoint of the scale; contrast with *generosity error* and *severity error*, 403

**error variance:** In the true score model, the component of variance attributable to random sources irrelevant to the trait or ability the test purports to measure in an observed score or distribution of scores; common sources of error variance include those related to test construction (including item or content sampling), test administration, and test scoring and interpretation, 123, 146

"Essay in Dioptrics" (Hartsoeker), 301

essay item, 255

estimate of inter-item consistency, 152

ethical considerations, 58–76

*Ethical Principles of Psychologists and Code of Conduct*, 73

*Ethical Standards for the Distribution of Psychological Tests and Diagnostic Aids*, 67

**ethics:** A body of principles of right, proper, or good conduct; contrast with *laws*, 58

ETS. *See* Educational Testing Service (ETS)

**eugenics:** The science of improving qualities of a breed through intervention with factors related to heredity, 49

Evaluation of Competency to Stand Trial–Revised (ECST-R), 515

evaluation standards, 53–55

**evaluative information:** Test or other data used to make judgments such as class placement, pass-fail, and admit-reject decisions; contrast with *diagnostic information*, 382

**evolutionary view of mental disorder:** The view that an attribution of mental disorder requires a scientific judgment (from an evolutionary perspective) that there exists a failure of function as well as a value judgment (from the perspective of social values) that the failure is harmful to the individual, 492

**evidence-based practice:** Methods, protocols, techniques, and procedures, used by professionals, that have a basis in clinical and research findings, 115

examiner, 27

examiner-related variables, 148

Exceptional Case Study Project (ECSP), 514

**executive function:** In neuropsychology, organizing, planning, cognitive flexibility, inhibition of impulses, and other activities associated with the frontal and prefrontal lobes of the brain, 545–549

**expectancy chart:** Graphic representation of an expectancy table, 196

**expectancy data:** Information, usually in the form of an expectancy table, illustrating the likelihood that an individual testtaker will score within some interval of scores on a criterion measure, 196–198, 219–229

**expectancy table:** Information presented in tabular form illustrating the likelihood that an individual testtaker will score within some interval of scores on a criterion measure, 196

**expert panel:** In the test development process, a group of people knowledgeable about the subject matter being tested and/or the population for whom the test was designed who can provide input to improve the test's content, fairness, and other related ways, 274–275

exploratory factor analysis, 345

**exploratory factor analysis:** A class of mathematical procedures employed to estimate factors, extract factors, or decide how many factors to retain, 203

**extended scoring report:** A type of scoring report that provides not only a listing of scores but statistical data as well, 14

**extra-test behavior:** Observations made by an examiner regarding what the examinee does and how the examinee reacts during the course of testing (e.g., how the testtaker copes with frustration; how much support the testtaker

seems to require; how anxious, fatigued, cooperative, or distractible the testtaker is) that are indirectly related to the test's specific content but of possible significance to interpretations regarding the testtaker's performance, 329

**extrinsic motivation:** A state in which the primary force driving an individual comes from external sources (such as a salary or bonus) and external constraints (such as job loss); contrast with *intrinsic motivation*, 597

eye contact, 52

**face validity:** A judgment regarding how well a test or other tool of measurement measures what it purports to measure that is based solely on "appearances," such as the content of the test's items, 183–184

**facets:** In generalizability theory, variables of interest in the universe including, for example, the number of items in the test, the amount of training the test scorers have had, and the purpose of the test administration, 167

fact-based items, 368

factor analysis, 343–346

**factor analysis:** A class of mathematical procedures, frequently employed as data reduction methods, designed to identify variables on which people may differ (or factors), 203–204

factor loading, 313, 344

**factor loading:** In factor analysis, a metaphor suggesting that a test (or an individual test item) carries with it or "loads" on a certain amount of one or more abilities that, in turn, have a determining influence on the test score (or on the response to the individual test item), 203

**factor-analytic theories,** 291

**fairness:** As applied to tests, the extent to which a test is used in an impartial, just, and equitable way, 206–210

Faking Bad Scale (FBS), 428

**false negative:** A specific type of *miss* characterized by a tool of assessment indicating that the testtaker does not possess or exhibit a particular trait, ability, behavior, or attribute when in fact, the testtaker does possess or exhibit this trait, ability, behavior, or attribute, 193, 590

**false positive:** An error in measurement characterized by a tool of assessment indicating that the testtaker possesses or exhibits a particular trait, ability, behavior, or attribute when in fact the testtaker does not, 193, 590

Family Education Rights and Privacy Act, 60

family environment, 311

**fatalism:** The belief that what happens in life is largely out of a person's control, 494

FBS. *See* Faking Bad Scale (FBS)

FF-NPQ. *See* Five-Factor Nonverbal Personality Questionnaire (FF-NPQ)

field (context) dependent people, 28

field independent people, 28

**field-of-search item:** A type of test item used in ability and neurodiagnostic tests wherein the testtaker's task is to locate a match to a visually presented stimulus, 547

fifty plus or minus ten scale, 103

**figure drawing test:** A general reference to a type of test in which the testtaker's task is to draw a human figure and/or other figures, and inferences are then made about the testtaker's ability, personality, and/or neurological intactness on the basis of the figure(s) produced, 463

figure drawings, 461–464

first moments of the distribution, 109

FIT. *See* Fitness Interview Test (FIT)

Fitness Interview Test (FIT), 515

Five-Factor Nonverbal Personality Questionnaire (FF-NPQ), 421

**fixed battery:** A prepackaged test battery containing a number of standardized tests to be administered in a prescribed fashion, such as the Halstead-Reitan Neuropsychological Battery; contrast with *flexible battery*, 556

**fixed cut score:** Also known as an *absolute cut score*, a reference point in a distribution of test scores used to divide a set of data into two or more classifications that is typically set with reference to a judgment concerning a minimum level of proficiency required to be included in a particular classification; contrast with *relative cut score*, 233

**fixed reference group scoring system:** A system of scoring wherein the distribution of scores obtained on the test from one group of testtakers (the fixed reference group) is used as the basis for the calculation of test scores for future administrations; the SAT and the GRE are scored this way, 139

flexibility, 354

**flexible battery:** Best associated with neuropsychological assessment, a group of tests hand-picked by the assessor to provide an answer to the referral question; contrast with *fixed battery*, 556

floor, 327

**floor effect:** A phenomenon arising from the diminished utility of a tool of assessment in distinguishing testtakers at the low end of the ability, trait, or other attribute being measured, 256–259

fluency, 354

**fluid intelligence:** In Cattell's two-factor theory of intelligence, nonverbal abilities that are relatively less dependent on culture and formal instruction; contrast with *crystallized intelligence*, 293

**Flynn effect:** "Intelligence inflation"; the fact that intelligence measured using a normed instrument rises each year after the test was normed, usually in the absence of any academic dividend, 306–309

*f*MRI: An imaging device that creates real-time, moving images of internal functioning (particularly useful in identifying which parts of the brain are active at various times and during various tasks), 561–563

**focus group:** Qualitative research conducted with a group of respondents who typically have been screened to qualify for participation in the research, 607

**forced distribution technique:** A procedure entailing the distribution of a predetermined number or percentage of assessees into various categories that describe performance (such as categories ranging from "unsatisfactory" to "superior"), 593

**forced-choice format:** A type of item sometimes used in personality tests wherein each of two or more choices has been predetermined to be equal in social desirability, 412

**forensic psychological assessment:** The theory and application of psychological evaluation and management in a legal context, 510–518

competency to stand trial, 512–515

criminal responsibility, 515–516

dangerousness to oneself/others, 511–512

emotional injury, 517

parole/probation readyness, 516–517

profiling, 517–518

Secret Service, 513–514

**format:** A general reference to the form, plan, structure, arrangement, or layout of test items as well as to

related considerations such as time limits for test administration, 7

**frame of reference:** In the context of item format, aspects of the focus of the item such as the time frame (past, present, or future), 411

**free association:** A technique, most frequently used in psychoanalysis, wherein the subject relates all his or her thoughts as they occur. *Contrast with* **word association,** 458n5

**frequency distribution:** A tabular listing of scores along with the number of times each score occurred, 83–85

**frequency polygon:** A graphic illustration of data wherein numbers indicating frequency are set on the vertical axis, test scores or categories are set on the horizontal axis, and the data are described by a continuous line connecting the points where the test scores or categories meet frequencies, 85, 86

*Frye v. the United States*, 64

FSIQ. *See* Full Scale IQ (FSIQ)

Full Scale IQ (FSIQ), 334

**functional analysis of behavior:** In behavioral assessment, the process of identifying dependent and independent variables, 479

**functional deficit:** In neuropsychology, any sensory, motor, or cognitive impairment that is psychological or without a known physical or structural cause. *Contrast with* **organic deficit,** 536

functional MRI, 561

*g* **factor:** In Spearman's two-factor theory of intelligence, the general factor of intelligence; also, the factor that is measured to greater or lesser degrees by all tests of intelligence; contrast with *s factor* and *group factors*, 292, 303, 311, 344

GAI. *See* General Ability Index (GAI)

Gas Chromatography Mass Spectrometry (GCMS), 590

GATB. *See* General Aptitude Test Battery (GATB)

GCMS. *See* Gas Chromatography Mass Spectrometry (GCMS)

GCR. *See* group conformity rating (GCR)

gender, 311

General Ability Index (GAI), 334

General Aptitude Test Battery (GATB), 570–575

*General Electric Co. v. Joiner*, 65

**generalizability study:** In the context of generalizability theory, research conducted to explore the impact of different facets of the universe on a test score, 167

**implicit attitude:** A nonconscious, automatic association in memory that produces a disposition to react in some characteristic manner to a particular stimulus, 603–604

Implicit Attitude Test (IAT), 604

**implicit memory:** Memory that is outside of conscious control and accessible only by indirect measures, 555

**implicit motive:** A nonconscious influence on behavior, typically acquired on the basis of experience, 454

**impression management:** Attempting to manipulate others' opinions and impressions through the selective exposure of some information, including false information, usually coupled with the suppression of other information; in responding to self-report measures of personality, psychopathology, or achievement, impression management may be synonymous with attempts to "fake good" or "fake bad," 405

**in-basket technique:** A measurement technique used to assess managerial ability and organizational skills that entails a timed simulation of the way a manager or executive deals with an in-basket filled with mail, memos, announcements, and other notices and directives, 585

**incidental sampling:** Also referred to as *convenience sampling,* the process of arbitrarily selecting some people to be part of a sample because they are readily available, not because they are most representative of the population being studied, 133

**incremental validity:** Used in conjunction with *predictive validity,* an index of the explanatory power of additional predictors over and above the predictors already in use, 195–196

indirect estimation, 251

**individualist culture:** A culture in which value is placed on traits such as autonomy, self-reliance, independence, uniqueness, and competitiveness, 54–55

Individuals with Disabilities Education Act (IDEA), 60, 359

**infant or toddler with disability:** According to IDEA, a child under 3 years of age who needs early intervention service because of developmental delays or a diagnosed physical or mental condition that has a high probability of resulting in developmental delay, 374

**inference:** A logical result or a deduction in a reasoning process, 181

**inflation of range:** Also referred to as *inflation of variance,* a reference to a phenomenon associated with reliability estimates wherein the variance of either variable in a correlational analysis is inflated by the sampling procedure used and so the resulting correlation coefficient tends to be higher; contrast with *restriction of range,* 162

**informal evaluation:** A typically nonsystematic, relatively brief, and "off-the-record" assessment leading to the formation of an opinion or attitude, conducted by any person in any way for any reason, in an unofficial context and not subject to the same ethics or standards as evaluation by a professional; contrast with *formal evaluation,* 22, 373

information function, 171

**information-processing theories:** A way of looking at intelligence that focuses on *how* information is processed rather than *what* is processed, 291

information-processing view, 295–296

**informed consent:** Permission to proceed with a (typically) diagnostic, evaluative, or therapeutic service on the basis of knowledge about the service and its risks and potential benefits, 72–73

inheritance, 304

inkblot, 443–449

**inquiry:** A typical element of Rorschach test administration; following the initial presentation of all ten cards, the assessor asks specific questions designed, among other things, to determine what about each card led to the assessee's perceptions, 445

**insanity:** A legal term denoting an inability to tell right from wrong, a lack of control, or a state of other mental incompetence or disorder sufficient to prevent that person from standing trial, being judged guilty, or entering into a contract or other legal relationship, 515

**instrumental values:** Guiding principles in the attainment of some objective—for example, honesty and ambition; contrast with *terminal values,* 438

**integrative assessment:** A multidisciplinary approach to evaluation that assimilates input from relevant sources, 359

**integrative report:** A form of interpretive report of

psychological assessment, usually computer-generated, in which data from behavioral, medical, administrative, and/or other sources are integrated; contrast with *scoring report* and *interpretive report,* 15

**integrity test:** A screening instrument designed to predict who will and will not be an honest employee, 576

intellectual ability tests, 543–544

intelligence

    measurement of, 43–44

**intelligence:** A multifaceted capacity that manifests itself in different ways across the life span but in general includes the abilities and capacities to acquire and apply knowledge, to reason effectively and logically, to exhibit sound judgment, to be perceptive, intuitive, mentally alert, and able to find the right words and thoughts with facility, and to be able to cope with and adjust to new situations and new types of problems

    Binet's views, 288
    CHC model, 294–295
    construct validity of tests, 306
    crystallized, 293
    culture, 311–317
    defined, 285
    factor-analysis theories, 291–295
    family environment, 311
    fluid, 293
    Flynn effect, 306–309
    Galton's views, 287–288
    gender, 311
    information-processing view, 295–296
    lay public views, 286–287
    measuring, 297–301
    nature *vs.* nurture, 301–304
    personality, 309–311
    Piaget's views, 289–291
    stability of, 304–306
    Wechsler's views, 288–289

intelligence inflation, 306

intelligence quotient (IQ). *See* **IQ (intelligence quotient)**

intelligence testing, 320–356. *See also* Stanford-Binet Intelligence Scale; Wechsler intelligence tests

    ASVAB, 350–351
    cognitive style, 353–355
    factor analysis, 343–346
    group administration, tests for, 347–349
    individual administration, tests for, 346–349

**interactionism:** The belief that heredity and environment interact to influence the development of one's mental capacity and abilities, 291

interactionist perspective, 304

**intercept bias:** A reference to the intercept of a regression line exhibited by a test or measurement procedure that systematically underpredicts or overpredicts the performance of members of a group; contrast with *slope bias*, 571

**interest measure:** In the context of vocational assessment and preemployment counseling, an instrument designed to evaluate testtakers' likes, dislikes, leisure activities, curiosities, and involvements in various pursuits for the purpose of comparison with groups of members of various occupations and professions, 566–569

**inter-item consistency:** The consistency or homogeneity of the items of a test, estimated by techniques such as the split-half method, 154

**internal consistency estimate of reliability:** An estimate of the reliability of a test obtained from a measure of inter-item consistency, 152

**internal consistency reliability,** 161

International Guidelines on Computer-Based and Internet-Delivered Testing, 71

**interpersonal intelligence:** In Gardner's theory of multiple intelligences, the ability to understand other people, what motivates them, how they work, and how to work cooperatively with them; contrast with *intrapersonal intelligence*, 292

Interpersonal Support Evaluations List, 581

**interpretive report:** A formal or official computer-generated account of test performance presented in both numeric and narrative form and including an explanation of the findings; the three varieties of interpretive report are descriptive, screening, and consultative; contrast with *scoring report* and *integrative report*, 15

**interquartile range:** An ordinal statistic of variability equal to the difference between the third and first quartile points in a distribution that has been divided into quartiles, 94

interrogation, 2

**inter-scorer reliability:** Also referred to as *inter-rater reliability*, observer reliability, judge reliability, and scorer reliability, an estimate of the degree of agreement or consistency between two or more scorers (or judges or raters or observers), 159, 161

**interval scales:** A system of measurement in which all things measured can be rank-ordered into equal intervals, where every unit on the scale is equal to every other and there is no absolute zero point (which precludes mathematical operations on such data), 81

**interview:** A tool of assessment in which information is gathered through direct, reciprocal communication, 9–10, 495, 540, 584

**intrapersonal intelligence:** In Gardner's theory of multiple intelligences, a capacity to form accurate self-perceptions, to discriminate accurately between emotions, and to be able to draw upon one's emotions as a means of understanding and an effective guide; contrast with *interpersonal intelligence*, 292

**intrinsic motivation:** A state in which the primary force driving an individual comes from within, such as personal satisfaction with one's work; contrast with *extrinsic motivation*, 596

ipsative approach, 415

**ipsative scoring:** An approach to test scoring and interpretation wherein the testtaker's responses and the presumed strength of a measured trait are interpreted relative to the measured strength of other traits for that testtaker; contrast with class scoring and cumulative scoring, 260

**IQ (intelligence quotient):** A widely used, shorthand reference to intelligence that echoes back from days now long gone when a testtaker's mental age as determined by a test was divided by chronological age and multiplied by 100 to determine the "intelligence quotient". *See also* **intelligence**

defined, 323
deviation IQ, 323
Flynn effect, 306–309
nature *vs.* nurture, 303
ratio IQ, 323

IRT. *See* item response theory (IRT)

**item analysis:** A general term to describe various procedures, usually statistical, designed to explore how individual test items work as compared to other items in the test and in the context of the whole test (e.g., to explore the level of difficulty of individual items on an achievement test or the reliability of a personality test); contrast with *qualitative item analysis*, 262–275

defined, 262
guessing, 269–271
item fairness, 271–272
item-characteristic curves, 268
item-difficulty index, 263–264
item-discrimination index, 264–268
item-reliability index, 264
item-validity index, 264
qualitative, 272–275
speed tests, 272

**item bank:** A collection of questions to be used in the construction of tests, 255, 257–259, 282–284

**item branching:** In computerized adaptive testing, the individualized presentation of test items drawn from an item bank based on the testtaker's previous responses, 260

**item characteristic curve (ICC):** A graphic representation of the probabilistic relationship between a person's level on a trait (or ability or other characteristic being measured) and the probability for responding to an item in a predicted way; also known as a *category response curve,* an *item response curve,* or an *item trace line,* 171, 281

**item fairness:** A reference to the degree of bias, if any, in a test item, 271–272. *See also* biased test item

**item format:** A reference to the form, plan, structure, arrangement, or layout of individual test items, including whether the items require testtakers to select a response from existing alternative responses or to construct a response, 252–255

**item pool:** The reservoir or well from which items will or will not be drawn for the final version of the test; the collection of items to be further evaluated for possible selection for use in an item bank, 251

**item response theory (IRT):** Also referred to as *latent-trait theory* or *the latent-trait model,* a system of assumptions about measurement (including the assumption that a trait being measured by a test is unidimensional) and the extent to which each test item measures the trait, 166, 168–173

cutoff scores, setting, 237–238
test revision, 280–284

**item sampling:** Also referred to as *content sampling,* the variety of the subject matter contained in the items; frequently referred to in the

**linear transformation:** In psychometrics, a process of changing a score such that (a) the new score has a direct numerical relationship to the original score and (b) the magnitude of the difference between the new score and other scores on the scale parallels the magnitude of differences between the original score and the other scores on the scales from which it was derived; contrast with *nonlinear transformation,* 104

Listening Comprehension Test, 317n5

*Listening with the Third Ear* (Reik), 487

**litigation:** Law resulting from the court-mediated resolution of legal matters of a civil, criminal, or administrative nature, also referred to as "judge-made law", 63–66

LNNB. *See* Luria-Nebraska Neuropsychological Battery (LNNB)

local independence, 170

**local norms:** Normative information about some limited population, frequently of specific interest to the test user, 134, 138

**local processing:** On-site, computerized scoring, interpretation, or other conversion of raw test data; contrast with *central processing* and *teleprocessing,* 14

**local validation studies:** The process of gathering evidence, relevant to how well a test measures what it purports to measure, for the purpose of evaluating the validity of a test or other measurement tool; typically undertaken in conjunction with a population different from the population for whom the test was originally validated, 182

**locator tests:** A pretest or routing test, usually for determining the most appropriate level of test, 364

**locus of control:** The self-perceived source of what happens to oneself, 408

long-term memory, 555

LPAD. *See* Learning Potential Assessment Device (LPAD)

LSAT. *See* Law School Admissions Test (LSAT)

**lumbar puncture:** A diagnostic procedure typically performed by a neurologist in which spinal fluid is extracted from the spinal column by means of an inserted needle; also referred to as a *spinal tap,* 562

Luria-Nebraska Neuropsychological Battery (LNNB), 559

MacAndrew Alcoholism Scale, 509

MacArthur Competence Assessment Tool-Criminal Adjudication (MacCAT-CA), 515

MacArthur Competence Assessment Tool-Treatment (MacCAT-T), 72

MacCAT-T. *See* MacArthur Competence Assessment Tool-Treatment (MacCAT-T)

MAC-R, 509

**maintained abilities:** In the Cattell-Horn model of intelligence, cognitive abilities that do not decline with age and tend to return to pre-injury levels after brain damage; contrast with *vulnerable abilities,* 293

mall intercept studies, 605

**managed care:** A health care system wherein the products and services provided to patients by a participating network of health care providers are mediated by an administrative agency of the insurer that works to keep costs down by fixing schedules of reimbursement to providers, 507

Management Progress Study (MPS), 586, 588, 589

*Manual for Administration of Neuropsychological Test Batteries for Adults and Children* (Reitan), 559

Marital Interaction Coding System, 478

Marital Satisfaction Scale (MSS), 200–203, 202

Marlowe-Crowne Social Desirability Scale, 202

Maslach Burnout Inventory (MBI), Third Edition, 597

MAST. *See* Michigan Alcohol Screening Test (MAST)

mastery tests, 140

MAT. *See* Miller Analogies Test (MAT)

matching item, 253

MBTI. *See* Myers-Briggs Type Indicator (MBTI)

MCAT. *See* Medical College Admission Test (MCAT)

MCMI-III. *See* Million Clinical Multiaxial Inventory–III (MCMI-III)

MCT. *See* Minnesota Clerical Test (MCT)

MDBS-R. *See* Morally Debatable Behaviors Scale-Revised (MDBS-R)

**mean:** Also called the *arithmetic mean,* a measure of central tendency derived by calculating an average of all scores in a distribution, 89

"Mean IQ of Americans: Massive Gains 1932 to 1978" (Flynn), 306

**measure of central tendency:** One of three statistics indicating the average or middlemost score between the extreme scores in a distribution; the *mean* is a measure

of central tendency and a statistic at the ratio level of measurement, the *median* is a measure of central tendency that takes into account the order of scores and is ordinal in nature, and the *mode* is a measure of central tendency that is nominal in nature, 89

**measurement:** Assigning numbers or symbols to characteristics of people or objects according to rules, 78–79

**measurement error:** Collectively, all of the factors associated with the process of measuring some variable, other than the variable being measured, 146

*Measurement of Attitude, The* (Thurstone/Chave), 603

*Measurement of Intelligence in Infants and Young Children, The* (Cattell), 42

**measures of variability:** A statistic indicating how scores in a distribution are scattered or dispersed; range, standard deviation, and variance are common measures of variability, 92

**mechanical prediction:** The application of computer algorithms together with statistical rules and probabilities to generate findings and recommendations; contrast with *clinical prediction* and *actuarial prediction,* 528

**median:** A measure of central tendency derived by identifying the middlemost score in a distribution, 89–91

Medical College Admission Test (MCAT), 380, 381

memory model, 554

memory tests, 553–556

**mental age:** An index, now seldom used, that refers to the chronological age equivalent of one's performance on a test or subtest; derived by reference to norms indicating the age at which most testtakers can pass or meet some performance criterion with respect to individual or groups of items, 299

mental disorders, 491–501
 biopsychosocial assessment, 494–495
 clinical assessment interview, 495–501
 DSM-IV-TR, 492–493
 DSM-V, 493–494

*Mental Measurement Yearbook* (MMY), 34

**mental status examination:** A specialized interview and observation used to screen for intellectual, emotional, and neurological deficits by touching on areas such as the interviewee's appearance, behavior, memory, affect, mood, judgment, personality, thought content, thought processes, and state of consciousness, 498, 540

mental test, 41

**mesokurtic:** A description of the kurtosis of a distribution that is neither extremely peaked nor flat in its center, 97

**Meta-analysis:** A family of techniques used to statistically combine information across studies to produce single estimates of the statistics being studied, 115

method of contrasted groups. *See* **known groups method**

**method of paired comparisons:** Scaling method whereby one of a pair of stimuli (such as photos) is selected according to a rule (such as "select the one that is more appealing"), 248

**method of predictive yield:** A technique for identifying cut scores based on the number of positions to be filled, 238

Metropolitan Readiness Tests–Sixth edition (MRT6), 376–377

Michigan Alcohol Screening Test (MAST), 509

military testing, 24, 28, 347–349

Miller Analogies Test (MAT), 380

Million Clinical Multiaxial Inventory–III (MCMI-III), 502

*Mills v. Board of Education of District of Columbia*, 63–66

Mini-Mental State Exam (MMSE), 540

**minimum competency testing programs:** Formal evaluation program in basic skills such as reading, writing, and arithmetic designed to aid in educational decision making that ranges from remediation to graduation, 61

Minnesota Clerical Test (MCT), 585

Minnesota Multiphasic Personality Inventory (MMPI), 409, 416, 423–427

clinical scales in, 423, 431–432

criterion groups, 423

MMPI-2, 427–429, 504–505

MMPI-2-RF, 429–433

MMPI-A, 433–434

restructured clinical (RC) scales, 430–432

revisions/progeny in perspective, 434–435

supplementary scales, 425

T scores, 429

Minnesota Teacher Attitude Survey, 603

Minnesota Vocational Interest Inventory, 568

**miss rate:** The proportion of people a test or other measurement procedure fails to identify accurately with respect to the possession or exhibition of a trait, behavior, characteristic, or attribute; a "miss" in this context is an inaccurate classification or prediction; may be subdivided into *false positives* and *false negatives*, 193

*Mitchell v. State*, 61

MMPI. *See* Minnesota Multiphasic Personality Inventory (MMPI)

MMSE. *See* Mini-Mental State Exam (MMSE)

MMY. *See Mental Measurement Yearbook* (MMY)

**M'Naghten standard:** Also known as the "right or wrong" test of insanity, a (since replaced) standard that hinged on whether an individual knew right from wrong at the time of commission of a crime; contrast with the *Durham standard* and the *ALI standard*, 515

**mode:** A measure of central tendency derived by identifying the most frequently occurring score in a distribution, 89, 91–92

*Model Guidelines for Preemployment Integrity Testing Programs,* 577

monotonicity, 170

Morally Debatable Behaviors Scale–Revised (MDBS-R), 246–247

moron, 49

motivation, 594–597

**motivation research methods:** Tools and procedures (e.g., in-depth interviews and focus groups), typically qualitative, associated with consumer research to explore consumer attitudes, behavior, and motivation, 607–612

**motor test:** A general reference to a type of instrument or evaluation procedure used to obtain information about one's ability to move one's limbs, eyes, or other parts of the body (psychomotor ability) as opposed to abilities that are more strictly cognitive, behavioral, or sensory in nature, 549

MRT6. *See* Metropolitan Readiness Tests–Sixth edition (MRT6)

MSS. *See* Marital Satisfaction Scale (MSS)

Multiaxial Empirically Based Assessment system, 404

Multilingual Aphasia Examination, 553

**multiple cut scores:** The use of two or more cut scores with reference to one predictor for the purpose of categorizing testtakers into more than two groups, or the use of a different cut score for each predictor when using multiple predictors for selection, 233

**multiple hurdle:** A multistage decision-making process in which the achievement of a particular cut score on one test is necessary in order to advance to the next stage of evaluation in the selection process, 234

multiple-choice format, 252

**multiple regression:** The analysis of relationships between more than one independent variable and one dependent variable to understand how each independent variable predicts the dependent variable, 235

**multitrait-multimethod matrix:** A method of evaluating construct validity by simultaneously examining both convergent and divergent evidence by means of a table of correlations between traits and methods, 203

Myers-Briggs Type Indicator (MBTI), 397, 576, 578

narrow-band instruments, 478

NASA. *See* National Aeronautics and Space Administration (NASA)

National Aeronautics and Space Administration (NASA), 587

**national anchor norms:** An equivalency table for scores on two nationally standardized tests designed to measure the same thing, 138

National Defense Education Act, 59

**national norms:** Norms derived from a standardization sample that was nationally representative of the population, 137

**naturalistic observation:** Behavioral observation that takes place in a naturally occurring setting (as opposed to a research laboratory) for the purpose of evaluation and information-gathering, 13

nature *vs.* nurture, 301–304

**Naylor-Shine tables:** Statistical tables once widely used to assist in judging the utility of a particular test, 227, 228

NCCEA. *See* Neurosensory Center Comprehensive Examination of Aphasia (NCCEA)

NCLB. *See* No Child Left Behind (NCLB) Act of 2001

**need:** According to personality theorist Henry Murray, determinants of behavior arising from within the individual; contrast with the Murrayan concept of *press*, 452

negative (inverse) correlation, 107

negative skew, 97

negatively skewed distribution, 87

**neglect:** Failure on the part of an adult responsible for the care of another to exercise a minimum degree of care in providing food, clothing, shelter, education, medical care, and supervision; contrast with *abuse*, 521–524

NEO Personality Inventory (NEO-PI), 420

NEO PI-R. *See* Revised NEO Personality Inventory (NEO PI-R)

NEPSY, 560

nervous system, 530–534

neurodevelopment training ball, 29

**neurological damage:** Impairment, injury, harm, or loss of function of any part or process of the central or peripheral nervous systems, 531–534

**neurology:** A branch of medicine that focuses on the nervous system and its disorders; contrast with *neuropsychology*, 530

**neuron:** Nerve cell, 530

**neuropsychological assessment:** The evaluation of brain and nervous system functioning as it relates to behavior, 530–564
  defined, 530
  executive function tests, 545–549
  general intellectual ability tests, 543–545
  medical diagnostic aids, 562–563
  memory tests, 553–556
  nervous system and behavior, 530–534
  neuropsychological evaluation, 535–541
  neuropsychological tests, 541–561
  perceptual/motor/perceptual-motor tests, 549–553
  test batteries, 556–561
  verbal functioning tests, 553

**neuropsychological mental status examination:** A general clinical evaluation designed to sample and check for various possible deficiencies in brain-behavior functioning, 540

**neuropsychology:** A branch of psychology that focuses on the relationship between brain functioning and behavior; contrast with *neurology*, 530

Neurosensory Center Comprehensive Examination of Aphasia (NCCEA), 561

**neurotology:** A branch of medicine that focuses on problems relating to hearing, balance, and facial nerves, 530

No Child Left Behind (NCLB) Act of 2001, 60

**nominal scale:** A system of measurement in which all things measured are classified or categorized based on one or more

distinguishing characteristics and placed into mutually exclusive and exhaustive categories, 79–80

nominating technique, 391

**nominating technique:** A method of peer appraisal in which members of a class, team, work unit, or other type of group are asked to select (or nominate) people in response to a question or statement, 308

**nomothetic approach:** An approach to assessment characterized by efforts to learn how a limited number of personality traits can be applied to all people; contrast with *idiographic approach*, 414

**noninvasive procedures:** A method of evaluation or treatment that does not involve intrusion (by surgical procedure, X-ray, or other means) into the body; for example, in a neuropsychological evaluation, observation of the client walking or skipping, 541

**nonlinear transformation:** In psychometrics, a process of changing a score such that (a) the new score does not necessarily have a direct numerical relationship to the original score and (b) the magnitude of the differences between the new score and the other scores on the scale may not parallel the magnitude of differences between the original score and the other scores on the scales from which the original score was derived; contrast with *linear transformation*, 104

nonverbal communication, 52–53

**norm:** (1) Behavior or performance that is usual, average, normal, standard, expected, or typical; (2) singular form of *norms*, 128

**normal curve:** A bell-shaped, smooth, mathematically defined curve highest at the center and gradually tapered on both sides, approaching but never actually touching the horizontal axis, 85, 87, 98

**normalized standard score scale:** Conceptually, the end product of "stretching" a skewed distribution into the shape of a normal curve, usually through nonlinear transformation, 104–106

**normalizing a distribution:** A statistical correction applied to distributions meeting certain criteria for the purpose of approximating a normal distribution, thus making the data more readily comprehensible or manipulable, 104

normative approach, 414

**normative sample:** Also referred to as a *norm group*, a group of people presumed to be representative of the universe of people who may take a particular test and whose performance data on that test may be used as a reference source or context for evaluating individual test scores, 128, 134–135

**norming:** The process of deriving or creating norms, 128

**norm-referenced cut score.** *See* **relative cut score**

norm-referenced evaluation, 139–141

**norm-referenced testing and assessment:** A method of evaluation and a way of deriving meaning from test scores by evaluating an individual testtaker's score and comparing it to scores of a group of testtakers on the same test; contrast with *criterion-referenced testing and assessment*, 128, 243

**norms:** The test performance data of a group of testtakers, designed as a reference for evaluating, interpreting, or otherwise placing in context individual test scores; also referred to as *normative data*, 128–129, 135–138
  age norms, 136
  grade norms, 136–137
  local norms, 128
  national anchor norms, 137
  national norms, 137
  percentiles, 135
  subgroup norms, 138

OAT. *See* Optometry Admission Test (OAT)

**objective methods of personality assessment,** 440–441

**objective personality test:** Typically a test consisting of short-answer items wherein the assessee's task is to select one response from the two or more provided and all scoring is done according to set procedures involving little if any judgment on the part of the scorer, 440

observer reliability, 159

obsessive passion, 568

O'Connor Tweezer Dexterity Test, 569, 570

ODDA. *See* Oregon's Death with Dignity Act (ODDA)

**odd-even reliability:** An estimate of split-half reliability of a test, obtained by assigning odd-numbered items to one-half of the test and even-numbered items to the other half, 153

Office of Strategic Services (OSS), 2, 348, 409, 481, 585

**performance task or test:** (1) In general, a work sample designed to elicit representative knowledge, skills, and values from a particular domain of study; (2) in employment settings, an instrument or procedure that requires the assessee to demonstrate certain job-related skills or abilities under conditions identical or analogous to conditions on the job, 389, 584–585

**peripheral nervous system:** All of the nerve cells that convey neural messages to and from the body except those nerve cells of the brain and spinal cord; contrast with *central nervous system*, 530

Personal Data Sheet, 44, 417, 424
personal interview stage, 234
personality, 44, 309–311
  measures of, 575–579
**personality:** An individual's unique constellation of psychological traits and states, including aspects of values, interests, attitudes, worldview, acculturation, sense of personal identity, sense of humor, cognitive and behavioral styles, and related characteristics, 394

**personality assessment:** The measurement and evaluation of psychological traits, states, values, interests, attitudes, worldview, acculturation, personal identity, sense of humor, cognitive and behavioral styles, and/or related individual characteristics
  behavioral assessment methods, 470–487. *See also* behavioral assessment methods
  criterion groups, 421–435
  culture, and, 435–439
  data reduction methods, 418–421
  defined, 394
  dichotomy, 461–468
  drawings, 461–468
  how?, 407–417, 475–476
  inkblots, 443–449
  logic/reason, 417–418
  objective methods, 440–441
  personality, and, 393–399
  pictures, as projective stimuli, 449–457
  projective methods, 442–488
  sounds, as projective stimuli, 460–461
  TAT, 450–454
  theory, 418
  traits, 394–396
  what?, 405–406, 473
  when?, 474
  where?, 406–407, 474–475
  who?, 399–405, 472–473
  words, as projective stimuli, 457–460
Personality Inventory for Children (PIC), 403

**personality profile:** A description, graph, or table representing the extent to which a person has demonstrated a particular pattern of traits and states, 398
*Personality Projection in the Drawing of the Human Figure* (Machover), 463
personality states, 398
personality test battery, 503
**personality trait:** Any distinguishable, relatively enduring way in which one individual varies from another, 394–396
Personality Disorder Trait Specified (PDTS) diagnosis, 494
**personality type:** A constellation of traits and states that is similar in pattern to one identified category of personality within a taxonomy of personalities, 396–398
personality-based measures, 576
personnel selection, 591–592
**PET (positron emission tomography) scan:** A tool of nuclear medicine particularly useful in diagnosing biochemical lesions in the brain, 562
**phallometric data:** the record from a study conducted using a penile plethysmograph with a male testtaker that is indicative of penile tumescense in response to stimuli, 482
Pharmacy College Admission Test (PCAT), 381
physical examination, 540–541
**physical test:** A measurement that entails evaluation of one's somatic health and intactness, and observable sensory and motor abilities, 588–591
Piaget's stages of cognitive development, 290
PIC. *See* Personality Inventory for Children (PIC)
**picture absurdity item:** A type of test item that presents the testtaker with the task of identifying what is wrong or silly about a stimulus image, 549
pictures, as projective stimuli, 449–457
Piers-Harris Self-Concept Scale, 401
**pilot work:** Also referred to as *pilot study* and *pilot research*, the preliminary research surrounding the creation of a prototype test; a general objective of pilot work is to determine how best to measure, gauge, assess, or evaluate the targeted construct(s), 243–244
PL 94-142, 60, 371
**placement:** A disposition, transfer, or assignment to a group or category that may be made on the basis of one criterion, 582
**platykurtic:** A description of the kurtosis of a distribution that is relatively flat in its center, 97

**plethysmograph:** An instrument that records changes in the volume of a part of the body arising from variations in blood supply, 482
PMAs. *See* primary mental abilities (PMAs)
**point scale:** A test with items organized into subtests by category of item; contrast with *age scale*, 324
political correctness, 189
**poll:** A type of survey used to record votes, usually containing questions that can be answered with a "yes-no" or "for-against" response, typically used to gauge opinion about issues, 605
**polygraph:** The instrument popularly known as a lie detector, 482
polygrapher, 482–483
**polytomous test item:** A test item or question with three or more alternative responses, where only one alternative is scored correct or scored as being consistent with a targeted trait or other construct, 169
**portfolio:** A work sample; referred to as *portfolio assessment* when used as a tool in an evaluative or diagnostic process, 10, 389
portfolio assessment, 389, 584
positive (direct) correlation, 106–107
positive skew, 97
positively skewed distribution, 87
positron emission tomography scan. *See* **PET scan**
**power test:** A test, usually of achievement or ability, with (1) either no time limit or such a long time limit that all testtakers can attempt all items and (2) some items so difficult that no testtaker can obtain a perfect score; contrast with *speed test*, 163
**predeterminism:** The doctrine that one's abilities are predetermined by genetic inheritance and that no amount of learning or other intervention can enhance what is genetically coded to unfold, 302
predictive validity, 192–198
**predictive validity:** A form of criterion-related validity that is an index of the degree to which a test score predicts some criterion measure, 190
**preformationism:** The doctrine that all living organisms are preformed at birth and that intelligence, much like other preformed "structures," cannot be improved upon by environmental intervention, 301
**premorbid functioning:** The level of psychological and physical performance prior to the

development of a disorder, an illness, or a disability, 490

preschool level aptitude tests, 370–376

**press:** According to personality theorist Henry Murray, determinants of behavior arising from within the environment; contrast with the Murrayan concept of *need*, 452

primary mental abilities (PMAs), 320

**privacy right:** The freedom of people to choose the time, circumstances, and extent to which they wish to share or withhold from others personal beliefs, opinions, and behavior; contrast with *confidentiality*, 74

**privileged information:** Data protected by law from disclosure in a legal proceeding; typically, exceptions to privilege are also noted in law; contrast with *confidential information*, 74

probation/parole readiness, 516–517

**problem-solving model:** As used in the context of RtI, the use of interventions tailored to students' individual needs that are selected by a multidisciplinary team of school professionals. *See also* response to intervention model, 359

**procedural memory:** Memory for how to do certain things or perform certain functions; contrast with *declarative memory*, 555

**process score:** A score on a test designed to help the test user understand the way that the testtaker processes information, 337

**productivity:** Output or value yielded relative to work effort, 592–594

**productivity gain:** A net increase in work output, which in utility analyses may be estimated through the use of a particular test or other evaluative procedure, 229

product-moment coefficient of correlation, 109

product-moment correlation, 109

Proficiency Examination Program (PEP), 367

**profile:** A narrative description, graph, table, or other representation of the extent to which a person has demonstrated certain targeted characteristics as a result of the administration or application of tools of assessment; also (a verb) *to profile*, 398

**profile analysis:** The interpretation of patterns of scores on a test or test battery, frequently used to generate diagnostic hypotheses from intelligence test data, 398n1

**profiler:** An occupation associated with law enforcement; one who creates psychological profiles of crime suspects to help law enforcement personnel capture the profiled suspect, 398n1

**profiling:** Referred to by the FBI as "criminal investigative analysis," a crime-solving process that draws upon psychological and criminological expertise applied to the study of crime-scene evidence, 517–518

**prognostic test:** A tool of assessment used to predict; sometimes synonymous with *aptitude test*, 370

program norms. *See user norms*

**projective hypothesis:** The thesis that an individual supplies structure to unstructured stimuli in a manner consistent with the individual's own unique pattern of conscious and unconscious needs, fears, desires, impulses, conflicts, and ways of perceiving and responding, 442

**projective method:** A technique of personality assessment in which some judgment of the assessee's personality is made on the basis of his or her performance on a task that involves supplying structure to relatively unstructured or incomplete stimuli, 442

projective methods of personality assessment, 442–488

projective test, 44

projective test battery, 503

Proposition 209, 592

**protocol:** (1) The form or sheet on which testtakers' responses are entered; (2) a method or procedure for evaluation or scoring, 27

Proverbs Test, 544

**pseudodementia:** A loss of cognitive functioning that mimics dementia but that is not due to the loss or damage of brain cells, 24, 538

PSI. *See* Parenting Stress Index (PSI)

PsycARTICLES, 35

psychasthenia, 424

PsychCorp, 42n2

**psychoanalysis:** A theory of personality and psychological treatment originally developed by Sigmund Freud, 52

*Psychodiagnostics* (Rorschach), 443

**psychoeducational assessment:** Psychological evaluation in a school or other setting, usually conducted to diagnose, remedy, or measure academic or social progress or to otherwise enrich a student's education, 295

**psychoeducational test battery:** A packaged kit containing tests that measure educational achievement and abilities related to academic success, 383–388

defined, 383

K-ABC/KABC-II, 384–386

WJ III, 386–388

**psychological assessment:** The gathering and integrating of psychological data for psychological evaluation, through the use of tests, interviews, case studies, behavioral observation, and specially designed apparatuses and measurement procedures; contrast with *psychological testing*, 1–4. *See also* assessment; clinical assessment; educational assessment; **neuropsychological assessment; personality assessment;** preschool assessment, 2

psychological assessor, 2, 4

**psychological autopsy:** A reconstruction of a deceased individual's psychological profile on the basis of archival records, artifacts, and interviews with the assessee while living or with people who knew the deceased, 21

Psychological Corporation, 41, 42n2

**psychological report:** An archival document describing findings as a result of psychological testing or assessment, Barnum effect in, 524–529

**psychological test:** A measuring device or procedure designed to measure psychology-related variables, 5, 501–504

psychological test user, 2

**psychological testing:** The measuring of psychology-related variables by means of devices or procedures designed to obtain samples of behavior 229

*Psychological Tests and Personnel Decisions* (Cronbach/Gleser), 229

psychological trait, 118

psychologist-client relationship, 74

psychometric soundness

projective methods of personality assessment, 467

SB5, 325–326

utility, 212–213

WAIS-IV, 335

**psychometric soundness:** The technical quality of a test or other tool of assessment, 9

**psychometrician:** A professional in testing and assessment who typically holds a doctoral degree in psychology or education and specializes in areas such as individual differences, quantitative psychology, or theory of assessment; contrast with *psychometrist*, 9

**psychometrics:** The science of psychological measurement (synonymous with the antiquated term *psychometry*), 9

**psychometrist:** A professional in testing and assessment who typically holds a master's degree in psychology or education and is qualified to administer specific tests; contrast with *psychometrician,* 9

**psychopath:** A diagnosis that describes individuals with few inhibitions who may pursue pleasure or money with callous disregard for the welfare of others, 516

Psychopathy Checklist (PCL), 516

**psychophysiological methods:** Techniques for monitoring physiological changes known to be influenced by psychological factors, such as heart rate and blood pressure, 481–484

**PsycINFO:** An online electronic database, maintained by the American Psychological Association and leased to institutional users, designed to help individuals locate relevant documents from psychology, education, nursing, social work, law, medicine, and other disciplines, 35

PsycLAW, 35

PsycSCAN: Psychopharmacology, 35

Public Law (PL) 94-142, 60, 371

public policy, 57–58

Purdue Pegboard Test, 550

**purposive sampling:** The arbitrary selection of people to be part of a sample because they are thought to be representative of the population being studied, 132

**Q-sort technique:** An assessment technique in which the task is to sort a group of statements, usually in perceived rank order ranging from "most descriptive" to "least descriptive"; the statements, traditionally presented on index cards, may be sorted in ways that reflect various perceptions, such as how respondents *see* themselves or would like to see themselves, 411–413

**qualitative item analysis:** A general term for various nonstatistical procedures designed to explore how individual test items work, both compared to other items in the test and in the context of the whole test; in contrast to statistically based procedures, qualitative methods involve exploration of the issues by verbal means such as interviews and group discussions conducted with testtakers and other relevant parties, 272–275

**qualitative methods:** Techniques of data generation and analysis that rely primarily on mathematical or statistical rather than verbal procedures, 272

quality assurance, test revision, 279

**quality of life:** In psychological assessment, an evaluation of variables such as perceived stress, loneliness, sources of satisfaction, personal values, quality of living conditions, and quality of friendships and other social support, 23

Quality of School Life Scales, 392

**quartile:** One of three dividing points between the four quarters of a distribution, each typically labeled Q1, Q2, or Q3, 93

**quota system:** A selection procedure whereby a fixed number or percentage of applicants with certain characteristics or from certain backgrounds are selected regardless of other factors such as documented ability, 63

**race norming:** The controversial practice of norming on the basis of race or ethnic background, 128

*Raising Children with Love and Limits* (Cattell), 42

**random error:** A source of error in measuring a targeted variable, caused by unpredictable fluctuations and inconsistencies of other variables in the measurement process. Contrast with *systematic error,* 146

**range:** A descriptive statistic of variability derived by calculating the difference between the highest and lowest scores in a distribution, 93

rank-difference correlation coefficient. *See* **Spearman's rho**

rank-order correlation coefficient. *See* **Spearman's rho**

**ranking:** The ordinal ordering of persons, scores, or variables into relative positions or degrees of value, 206

**rank-order correlation coefficient,** 110

**rapport:** A working relationship between examiner and examinee in testing or assessment, 27

Rasch model, 169

RAT. *See* Remote Associates Test (RAT)

**rating:** A numerical or verbal judgment that places a person or attribute along a continuum identified by a scale of numerical or word descriptors called a *rating scale,* 205

**rating error:** A judgment that results from the intentional or

unintentional misuse of a rating scale; two types of rating error are *leniency error* (or *generosity error*) and *severity error,* 205

**rating scale:** A system of ordered numerical or verbal descriptors on which judgments about the presence/absence or magnitude of a particular trait, attitude, emotion, or other variable are indicated by raters, judges, examiners, or (when the rating scale reflects self-report) the assessee, 205, 247, 371

**ratio IQ:** An index of intelligence derived from the ratio of the testtaker's mental age (as calculated from a test) divided by his or her chronological age and multiplied by 100 to eliminate decimals, 323

**ratio scale:** A system of measurement in which all things measured can be rank-ordered, the rank ordering does imply something about exactly how much greater one ranking is than another, equal intervals exist between each number on the scale, and all mathematical operations can be performed meaningfully because a true or absolute zero point exists; few scales in psychology or education are ratio scales, 81–83

**raw score:** A straightforward, unmodified accounting of performance, usually numerical and typically used for evaluation or diagnosis, 83

RC scales. *See* restructured clinical (RC) scales

RCRAS. *See* Rogers Criminal Responsibility Assessment Scale (RCRAS)

reacculturation, 510

**reactivity:** Changes in an assessee's behavior, thinking, or performance that arise in response to being observed, assessed, or evaluated, 479

**readiness test:** A tool of assessment designed to evaluate whether an individual has the requisites to begin a program or perform a task; sometimes synonymous with *aptitude test,* 370

reading tests, 382–383

Reading-Free Vocational Interest Inventory (R-FVII), 568

reasonable boundaries, 181

recommendation letters, 583–584

rectangular distribution, 87

reference sources, 33–36

reference volumes, 34

**reflex:** Involuntary motor response to a stimulus, 541

*Regents of the University of California v. Bakke*, 61

Reitan-Indiana Aphasia Screening Test (AST), 553

**relative cut score:** Also referred to as a *norm-referenced cut score*, a reference point in a distribution of test scores used to divide a set of data into two classifications based on norm-related considerations rather than on the relationship of test scores to a criterion, 233

reliability, 124–125

**reliability:** The extent to which measurements are consistent or repeatable; also, the extent to which measurements differ from occasion to occasion as a function of measurement error
average proportional distance (APD), 157–158
coefficient. *See* reliability coefficient
coefficient alpha, 157
concept of, 145–150
defined, 146
error variance sources, 147–150
individual scores, and, 173–180
inter-scorer reliability, 159
Kuder-Richardson formulas, 155–156
parallel-forms/alternate forms reliability estimates, 151–152
split-half reliability estimates, 152–154
test-retest reliability, 150–151

**reliability coefficient:** General term for an index of reliability or the ratio of true score variance on a test to the total variance 145
breathalyzer test, 165
classical test theory (CTT), 164–166
defined, 145
domain sampling theory, 166–167
generalizability theory, 167–168
item response theory, 168–173
nature of test, 161–164
purpose of, 160–161

Remote Associates Test (RAT), 355

resolver, 280

**response style:** A tendency to respond to a test item or interview question in some characteristic manner regardless of content; for example, an acquiescent response style (a tendency to agree) and a socially desirable response style (a tendency to present oneself in a favorable or socially desirable way), 405–406

**response to intervention model (RtI):** A multilevel prevention framework applied in educational settings that is designed to maximize student achievement through the use of data that identifies students at risk for poor learning outcomes combined with evidence-based intervention and teaching that is

adjusted on the basis of student responsiveness. 358–361. *See also* problem-solving model

response-contingent testing, 326

**restriction of range:** Also referred to as *restriction of variance*, a phenomenon associated with reliability estimates wherein the variance of either variable in a correlational analysis is restricted by the sampling procedure used and so the resulting correlation coefficient tends to be lower; contrast with *inflation of range,* 162

restructured clinical (RC) scales, 430–432

résumé, 582

**return on investment:** A ratio of the economic and/or noneconomic benefits derived from expenditures to initiate or improve a particular testing program, training program, or intervention as compared to all of the costs of the initiative or improvements, 226

Revised NEO Personality Inventory (NEO PI-R), 415, 419–420, 576

Revised Psychopathy Checklist (PCL-R), 517

R-FVII. *See* Reading-Free Vocational Interest Inventory (R-FVII)

right or wrong test, 515

Rogers Criminal Responsibility Assessment Scale (RCRAS), 516

Rokeach Value Survey, 80–81

**role play:** Acting an improvised or partially improvised part in a simulated situation, 14, 481

**role-play test:** An assessment tool wherein assessees are instructed to act as if they were placed in a particular situation, 14

Rorschach Inkblot Test, 8, 443–449

Rosenzweig Picture-Frustration Study, 456

Rotter Incomplete Sentences Blank, 459

**routing test:** A subtest used to direct or route the testtaker to a suitable level of items, 326

RtI model. *See* **response to intervention model (RtI)**

Rule 702, 64

SADS. *See* Schedule for Affective Disorders and Schizophrenia (SADS)

SAI. *See* School Ability Index (SAI)

**sample:** A group of people presumed to be representative of the total population or universe of people being studied or tested, 129

**sampling:** A general reference to the process of developing a sample, 129

SAT, 35, 139

SATB. *See* Special Aptitude Test Battery (SATB)

SB5. *See* Stanford-Binet Intelligence Scale

SB:FE. *See* Stanford-Binet Fourth Edition (SB:FE)

**scale:** (1) A system of ordered numerical or verbal descriptors, usually occurring at fixed intervals, used as a reference standard in measurement; (2) a set of numbers or other symbols whose properties model empirical properties of the objects or traits to which numbers or other symbols are assigned, 78

**scaling:** (1) In test construction, the process of setting rules for assigning numbers in measurement; (2) the process by which a measuring device is designed and calibrated and the way numbers (or other indices that are scale values) are assigned to different amounts of the trait, attribute, or characteristic measured; (3) assigning numbers in accordance with empirical properties of objects or traits, 244–251
categorical, 249
comparative, 249
defined, 244
Guttman scale, 249
Likert scale, 247
MDBS-R, 246–247
methods, 246–251
scale types, 244–246

**scalogram analysis:** An item-analysis procedure and approach to test development that entails a graphic mapping of a testtaker's responses, 250

scatter diagram. *See* **bivariate distribution**

scattergram. *See* **bivariate distribution**

**scatterplot:** Also referred to as a *scatter diagram,* a graphic description of correlation achieved by graphing the coordinate points for the two variables, 111

Schedule for Affective Disorders and Schizophrenia (SADS), 496

**schema:** In Piagetian theory, an action or mental structure that, when applied to the world, leads to knowing or understanding, 289

**schemata:** The plural of *schema*, as in "Infants are born with several simple schemata, including sucking and grasping," 289

Scholastic Aptitude Test (SAT). *See* SAT

School Ability Index (SAI), 352

SCID. *See* Structured Clinical Interview for *DSM-IV* (SCID)

SCII. *See* Strong-Campbell Interest Inventory (SCII)

score. *See* test scores

**score:** A code or summary statement—usually but not necessarily numerical—that reflects an evaluation of the performance on a test, task, interview, or other sample of behavior, 7

scorer reliability, 159

**scoring:** The process of assigning evaluative codes or statements to performance on tests, tasks, interviews, or other behavior samples, 7

**scoring drift:** A discrepancy between the scoring in an anchor protocol and the scoring of another protocol, 280

scoring items, 260

scoring/interpretation procedures, 7

**scoring report:** A formal or official computer-generated account of test performance, usually represented numerically; the two varieties are the *simple scoring report* (containing only a report of the scores) and the *extended scoring report* (containing item statistics); contrast with *interpretive report* and *integrative report,* 14–15

**screening:** A relatively superficial process of evaluation based on certain minimal standards, criteria, or requirements; contrast with *selection, classification,* and *placement,* 581

**screening tool:** (1) An instrument or procedure used to identify a particular trait or constellation of traits at a gross or imprecise level, as opposed to a test of greater precision used for more definitive diagnosis or evaluation; (2) in preschool assessment, an instrument or procedure used as a first step in identifying a child who is "at risk" or not functioning within normal limits; (3) in employment settings, an instrument or procedure used as a gross measure to determine who meets minimum requirements set by the employer, 348

SDMT4. *See* Stanford Diagnostic Mathematics Test, Fourth Edition (SDMT4)

SDS. *See* Self-Directed Search (SDS)

Seashore Bennett Stenographic Proficiency Test, 584

Seashore Measures of Musical Talents, 380

second moments of the distribution, 109

secondary-school level aptitude tests, 377–378

second-order factors, 344

**second-order meta-analysis:** a meta-analysis that summarizes two or more other meta-analyses, 578

Secret Service, 513–514

**selected-response format:** A form of test item requiring testtakers to select a response (e.g., true-false, multiple-choice, and matching items) as opposed to constructing or creating one; contrast with *constructed-response format,* 252

**selection:** A process whereby each person evaluated for a position is either accepted or rejected; contrast with *screening, classification,* and *placement,* 581

**selection ratio:** A numerical value that reflects the relationship between the number of people to be hired and the number of people available to be hired, 219

**self-concept:** One's attitudes, beliefs, opinions, and related thoughts about oneself, 401

**self-concept differentiation:** The degree to which an individual has different self-concepts in different roles, 401

**self-concept measure:** An instrument designed to yield information about how an individual sees him- or herself with regard to selected psychological variables, the data from which are usually interpreted in the context of how others may *see* themselves on the same or similar variables, 401

Self-Directed Search (SDS), 567

Self-Directed Search-Form R, 568

**self-efficacy:** Confidence in one's own ability to accomplish a task, 495

Self-Help Agency Satisfaction Scale, 603

**self-monitoring:** The act of systematically observing and recording aspects of one's own behavior and/or events related to that behavior, 478–479

**self-report:** The process wherein an assessee supplies personal information in forms such as responding to questions, keeping a diary, or reporting on self-monitored thoughts and/or behaviors, 44, 400–402

Self-Report of Personality (SRP), 374

SEM. *See* **standard error of measurement (SEM)**

**semantic differential technique:** An item format characterized by bipolar adjectives separated by a seven-point rating scale on which respondents select one point to indicate their response, 412, 606

**semantic memory:** Memory for facts; contrast with *episodic memory,* 555

**semi-interquartile range:** A measure of variability equal to the interquartile range divided by 2, 94

Sensation-Seeking Scale (SSS), 119

**sensitivity review:** A study of test items, usually during test development, in which items are examined for fairness to all prospective testtakers and for the presence of offensive language, stereotypes, or situations, 274

**sentence completion**: A task in which the assessee is asked to finish an incomplete sentence or phrase, 459

sentence completion format, 413

**sentence completion stem:** All the words that make up the part of a sentence completion item, not including the blank space to be completed by the testtaker, 459

**sentence completion test:** A projective tool of assessment that contains a series of incomplete phrases wherein the task of the assessee is to insert a word or words that will make each of the phrases a complete sentence, 459

sequential processing, 295–296

sequential testing, 326

Sequential Tests of Educational Progress (STEP) battery, 364

7 Minute Screen, 540

Severe Impairment Battery (SIB), 561

**severity error:** Less than accurate rating or error in evaluation due to the rater's tendency to be overly critical; contrast with *generosity error,* 205, 403

shelf-esteem, 602n3

shifting cultural lenses, 505

**short form:** An abbreviated version of a test that has typically been reduced in number of items from the original, usually to reduce the time needed for test administration, scoring, and/or interpretation, 341–342

Short Portable Mental Status Questionnaire, 540

short-answer item, 254

short-term memory, 555

SIB. *See* Severe Impairment Battery (SIB)

simple frequency distribution, 84

**simple scoring report:** A type of scoring report that provides only a listing of scores, 14

**simultaneous processing:** Also called *parallel processing;* based on Luria's writings, a type of information processing whereby information is integrated and synthesized all at once and as a whole; contrast with *successive processing,* 295, 296

single photon emission computed tomography. *See* SPECT

SIRS-2. *See* Structured Interview of Reported Symptoms-2 (SIRS-2)

**situational performance measure:** A procedure that typically involves the performance of a task by the

**stratified-random sampling:** The process of developing a sample based on specific subgroups of a population in which every member has the same chance of being included in the sample, 129

**stress interview:** An interview purposely designed to pressure or stress the interviewee in order to gauge reaction to that stress, 496

stresseraser, 29

Strong Vocational Interest Blank (SVIB), 566

Strong-Campbell Interest Inventory (SCII), 566

Structured Clinical Interview for *DSM-IV* (SCID), 496

**structured interview:** Questions posed from a guide with little if any leeway to deviate from the guide, 410

Structured Interview of Reported Symptoms-2 (SIRS-2), 496

Study Attitudes and Methods Survey, 392, 603

Study Habits Checklist, 391

**subgroup norms:** Norms for any defined group within a larger group, 138

substance abuse, 509–510

**successful intelligence:** A cross-cultural conception of intelligence gauged by the extent to which one effectively adapts, shares, shapes, and selects environments in a way that conforms to both personal and societal standards of success, 296

**successive processing:** Also referred to as *sequential processing*; based on Luria's writings, a type of information processing whereby information is processed in a sequential, bit-by-bit fashion and arranged and rearranged until it is logical; contrast with *simultaneous processing*, 295–296

summation notation, 89

**summative scale:** An index derived from the summing of selected scores on a test or subtest, 247

**supplemental subtest:** Also referred to as an *optional subtest*, one of a test's subtests that may be used either for purposes of providing additional information or in place of a core subtest if, for any reason, the use of a score on a core subtest would be questionable; contrast with *core subtest*, 332

supplementary scales, 425

**survey:** In consumer psychology, a fixed list of questions administered to a selected sample of persons, typically to learn about consumers' attitudes, beliefs, opinions, and/or behavior regarding targeted products, services, or advertising, 604–607

Survey of School Attitudes, 392

Survey of Study Habits and Attitudes (SSHA), 392

SVIB. *See* Strong Vocational Interest Blank (SVIB)

**syndrome:** A set of co-occurring emotional and behavioral problems, 373

**systematic error :** a source of error in measuring a variable that is typically constant and proportionate to what is presumed to be the true value of the variable being measured. Contrast with *random error,* 146

*T* **score:** Named for Thorndike, a standard score calculated using a scale with a mean set at 50 and a standard deviation set at 10; used by developers of the MMPI, 103, 429

**tail:** The area on the normal curve between 2 and 3 standard deviations above the mean, and the area on the normal curve between –2 and –3 standard deviations below the mean; a normal curve has two tails, 101

tailored testing, 326

*Tarasoff v. Regents of the University of California,* 61, 74, 512

TAT. *See* Thematic Apperception Test (TAT)

tautophone, 461

**Taylor-Russell tables:** Statistical tables once extensively used to provide test users with an estimate of the extent to which inclusion of a particular test in the selection system would improve selection decisions, 219, 226–228

**teaching item:** A test item designed to illustrate the task required and assure the examiner that the examinee understands what is required for success on the task, 326

team, 594

*Technical Recommendations for Achievement Tests,* 66

*Technical Recommendations for Psychological Tests and Diagnostic Tests,* 66

telephone surveys, 605

**teleprocessing:** Computerized scoring, interpretation, or other conversion of raw test data sent over telephone lines by modem from a test site to a central location for computer processing; contrast with *central processing* and *local processing,* 14

**temperament:** With reference to personality assessments of infants, the distinguishing manner of the child's observable actions and reactions, 310

Ten Item Personality Inventory (TIPI), 420

Tennessee Self-Concept Scale, 401

**terminal values:** Guiding principles and a mode of behavior that are an endpoint objective; for example, "a comfortable life" and "an exciting life"; contrast with *instrumental values,* 438

**"termites":** Humorous reference to gifted children who participated in Lewis M. Terman's study of intelligence initiated in 1916, 305n3

**test:** A measuring device or procedure, 6. *See also specific tests*

test administration SB5, 326

test administrator, 27, 147–148

test analysis, 240

**test battery:** A selection of tests and assessment procedures typically composed of tests designed to measure different variables but having a common objective; for example, an intelligence test, a personality test, and a neuropsychological test might be used to obtain a general psychological profile of an individual, 155n5, 502–504. *See also specific batteries*

test bias, 204–206

**test blueprint:** A detailed plan of the content, organization, and quantity of the items that a test will contain, 184, 186

test catalogues, 33–34

**test composite:** A test score or index derived from the combination and/or mathematical transformation of one or more test scores, 324

**test conceptualization:** An early stage of the test development process wherein the idea for a particular test or test revision is first conceived, 240, 241–244

test construction, 147, 244–261

    scaling, 244–251

    scoring items, 260–261

    writing items, 251–260. *See also* writing items

**test construction:** A stage in the process of test development that entails writing test items (or rewriting or otherwise revising existing items), as well as formatting items, setting scoring rules, and otherwise designing and building a test, 240

test developers, 18–19

**test development:** An umbrella term for all that goes into the process of creating a test, 240–284

    defined, 240

    item analysis, 262–275. *See also* **item analysis**

    item revision, 275–284

**trait:** Any distinguishable, relatively enduring way in which one individual varies from another; contrast with *state*, 118

**transient error:** A source of error attributable to variations in the testtaker's feelings, moods, or mental state over time, 160

TRIN. *See* True Response Inconsistency (TRIN)

trinitarian model of validity, 182

True Response Inconsistency (TRIN), 427

**true score:** A value that, according to classical test theory, genuinely reflects an individual's ability (or trait) level as measured by a particular test, 164

**true score model.** *See* classical test theory (CTT)

**true score theory:** Also referred to as the *true score model* or *classical test theory*, a system of assumptions about measurement that includes the notion that a test score (and even a response to an individual item) is composed of a relatively stable component that actually is what the test or individual item is designed to measure as well as a random component that is error, 123

**true variance:** In the true score model, the component of variance attributable to true differences in the ability or trait being measured that are inherent in an observed score or distribution of scores, 146

true–false item, 254

truth-in-testing legislation, 61

**two-factor theory of intelligence:** Spearman's theory of general intelligence, which postulates the existence of a general intellectual ability factor (*g*) that is partially tapped by all other mental abilities, 291

Tyler Vocational Classification System, 413

**type:** As in *personality type,* a constellation of traits and states similar in pattern to one identified category of personality within a taxonomy of personalities, 397

**Type A personality:** In Friedman and Rosenman's typology, a personality characterized by competitiveness, haste, restlessness, impatience, feelings of being time-pressured, and strong needs for achievement and dominance, 397

**Type B personality:** In Friedman and Rosenman's typology, a personality characterized by traits (e.g., "mellow" and "laid-back") that are opposite the Type A personality, 397

*Types of Men* (Spranger), 436

unidimensionality assumption, 170

*Uniform Guidelines on Employee Selection Procedures*, 62

**uniform *T* score:** Abbreviated *UT*, a variety of *T* score used in the MMPI-2, 429

**universe:** In generalizability theory, the total context of a particular test situation, including all the factors that lead to an individual testtaker's score, 167

**universe score:** In generalizability theory, a test score corresponding to the particular universe being assessed or evaluated, 167

University of Pennsylvania Smell Identification Test (UPSIT), 537

**unobtrusive measure:** A type of measure that does not necessarily require the presence or cooperation of respondents, often a telling physical trace or record, 484

UPSIT. *See* University of Pennsylvania Smell Identification Test (UPSIT)

**user norms:** Also referred to as *program norms,* descriptive statistics based on a group of testtakers in a given period of time rather than on norms obtained by formal sampling methods, 128

UT score. *See* **uniform T score**

**utility (also test utility):** In the context of psychological testing and assessment, a reference to how useful a test or assessment technique is for a particular purpose, 9, 211–239

decision theory, and, 229–232

defined, 212

factors affecting, 212–218

**utility analysis:** A family of techniques designed to evaluate the costs and benefits of testing and not testing in terms of likely outcomes, 218–235

Brogden-Cronbach-Gleser formula, 229

cut score, 233–238

decision theory, 229–232

defined, 218

expectancy data, 219–229

job applicants pool, 232

job complexity, 232–233

**utility gain:** An estimate of the benefit, monetary or otherwise, of using a particular test or selection method, 229

**validation:** The process of gathering and evaluating validity evidence, 182

**validation study:** Research that entails gathering evidence relevant to how well a test measures what it purports to measure for the

purpose of evaluating the validity of a test or other measurement tool, 182

**validity:** A general term referring to a judgment regarding how well a test or other measurement tool measures what it purports to measure; this judgment has important implications regarding the appropriateness of inferences made and actions taken on the basis of measurements, 125

concept of, 181–189

construct validity, 198–204. *See also* **construct validity**

content validity, 184–189

criterion-related, 190–198. *See also* **criterion-related validity**

defined, 181

face validity, 183–184

incremental, 195–196

test bias, and, 204–206

**validity coefficient:** A correlation coefficient that provides a measure of the relationship between test scores and scores on a criterion measure, 192–195

validity generalization (VG), 572–574

**validity scale:** A subscale of a test designed to assist in judgments regarding how honestly the testtaker responded and whether or not observed responses were products of response style, carelessness, deliberate efforts to deceive, or unintentional misunderstanding, 406

**validity shrinkage:** The decrease in item validities that inevitably occurs after cross-validation, 278

**values:** That which an individual prizes; ideals believed in, 436

**variability:** An indication of how scores in a distribution are scattered or dispersed, 92–96

Variable Response Inconsistency (VRIN), 427

**variance:** A measure of variability equal to the arithmetic mean of the squares of the differences between the scores in a distribution and their mean, 95, 146

VCAT. *See* Veterinary College Admission Test (VCAT)

verbal communication, 51–52

verbal functioning tests, 553

**Verbal, Perceptual, and Image Rotation (VPR) model:** A hierarchical model of the structure of mental abilities, with a *g* factor that contributes to verbal, perceptual, and image rotation abilities in addition to eight more specialized abilities, 303

verbal summator, 461

Veterinary College Admission Test (VCAT), 381

VG. *See* validity generalization (VG)

video, as assessment tool, 17

**visual-object intelligence:** The ability to process information about the visual appearance of objects as well as the object's pictorial properties (such as shape, color and texture), 354

VPR model. *See* **Verbal, Perceptual, and Image Rotation (VPR) model**

VRIN. *See* Variable Response Inconsistency (VRIN)

**vulnerable abilities:** In the Cattell-Horn model of intelligence, cognitive abilities that decline with age and that do not return to pre-injury levels after brain damage; contrast with *maintained abilities*, 293

WAIS. *See* Wechsler Adult Intelligence Scale (WAIS)

Washington University Sentence Completion Test, 459

WASI. *See* Wechsler Abbreviated Scale of Intelligence (WASI)

WCST-64. *See* Wisconsin Card Sorting Test-64 Card Version (WCST-64)

Wechsler Abbreviated Scale of Intelligence (WASI), 342

Wechsler Adult Intelligence Scale (WAIS), 43, 47
    fourth edition, 330–335
    general item types, 331
    psychometric soundness, 335
    standardization/norms, 335
    subtests grouped according to indexes, 334
    test today, 332–334
    test's heritage, 332
    third edition, 332
    WAIS III, 289
    WAIS-IV, 278

Wechsler Full Scale, 307

Wechsler Individual Achievement Test–Third Edition (WIAT-III), 364

Wechsler Intelligence Scale for Children (WISC), 47

Wechsler Intelligence Scale for Children, Fourth Edition (WISC-IV), 279–280, 336–338

Wechsler Intelligence Scale for Children–Revised (WISC-R), 336

Wechsler intelligence tests, 329–330. *See also specific tests*
    at a glance, 340
    short forms, 341–342

Wechsler Memory Scale (WMS-IV), 278, 556

Wechsler Memory Scale–Third Edition (WMS-III), 332

Wechsler Preschool and Primary Scale of Intelligence–Third Edition (WPPSI-III), 338–341

Wechsler-Bellevue Intelligence Scale, 47

Weigl's Test, 545

**Welsh codes:** A shorthand summary of a testtaker's scores on the MMPI clinical and validity scales, 427

Wepman-Auditory Discrimination Test, 549

What I Like to Do Interest Inventory, 392

WIAT-III. *See* Wechsler Individual Achievement Test–Third Edition (WIAT-III)

Wide Range Intelligence Test (WRIT), 342

Wiggins Content Scales, 425

WISC. *See* Wechsler Intelligence Scale for Children (WISC)

WISC-IV. *See* Wechsler Intelligence Scale for Children, Fourth Edition (WISC-IV)

Wisconsin Card Sorting Test-64 Card Version (WCST-64), 545

WISC-R. *See* Wechsler Intelligence Scale for Children–Revised (WISC-R)

WJ III. *See* Woodcock-Johnson III (WJ III)

WMS-IV. *See* Wechsler Memory Scale (WMS-IV)

Wonderlic Personnel Test, 569

Woodcock Reading Mastery Tests–Revised (WRMT-III), 382–383

Woodcock-Johnson III (WJ III), 386–388

Woodworth Psychoneurotic Inventory, 417

**word association:** A type of task that may be used in personality assessment in which an assessee verbalizes the first word that comes to mind in response to a stimulus word. *Contrast with* **free association**, 457, 458n5

**word association test:** A semistructured, individually administered, projective technique of personality assessment that involves the presentation of a list of stimulus words, to each of which an assessee responds verbally or in writing with whatever comes immediately to mind first upon first exposure to the stimulus word, 457, 458

words as projective stimuli, 457–461

work performance, 578

Work Preference Inventory (WPI), 597

working memory, 555

**worldview:** The unique way people interpret and make sense of their perceptions in light of their learning experiences, cultural background, and related variables, 439

WPPSI-III. *See* Wechsler Preschool and Primary Scale of Intelligence–Third Edition (WPPSI-III)

WRIT. *See* Wide Range Intelligence Test (WRIT)

writing items, 251–260
    computerized adaptive testing (CAT), 255–260
    item format, 252–255

WRMT-III. *See* Woodcock Reading Mastery Tests-Revised (WRMT-III)

*z* **score:** A standard score derived by calculating the difference between a particular raw score and the mean and then dividing by the standard deviation; a *z* score expresses a score in terms of the number of standard deviation units that the raw score is below or above the mean of the distribution, 102–103

zero plus minus one scale, 102, 103

*Zink vs. State*, 66

**zone of proximal development:** Lev Vygotsky's concept of the area that exists, in theory, between a testtaker's ability as measured by a formal test and what might be possible as the result of instruction, 361